International Directory of
COMPANY
HISTORIES

International Directory of

COMPANY HISTORIES

VOLUME 10

Editor
Paula Kepos

ST. JAMES PRESS

An International Thomson Publishing Company

I(T)P

NEW YORK • LONDON • BONN • BOSTON • DETROIT • MADRID
MELBOURNE • MEXICO CITY • PARIS • SINGAPORE • TOKYO
TORONTO • WASHINGTON • ALBANY NY • BELMONT CA • CINCINNATI OH

STAFF

Paula Kepos, *Editor*

David Collins, Nicolet V. Elert, Margaret Mazurkiewicz, *Associate Editors*
Janice Jorgensen, *Contributing Editor*

∞™ The paper used in this publication meets the minimum requirements of American National Standard for Information Sciences— Permanence Paper for Printed Library Materials, ANSI Z39.48-1984.

This book is printed on recycled paper that meets Environmental Protection Agency Standards.

Library of Congress Catalog Number: 89-190943

British Library Cataloguing in Publication Data

International directory of company histories. Vol. 10
I. Paula Kepos
338.7409

ISBN 1-55862-325-6

Printed in the United States of America
Published simultaneously in the United Kingdom

The trademark **ITP** is used under license.

Cover photograph of the Boston Stock Exchange courtesy of Deb Finnegan.

10 9 8 7 6 5 4 3 2 1

CONTENTS

Company Histories

PREFACE

International Directory of Company Histories provides detailed information on the development of the world's largest and most influential companies. To date, *Company Histories* has covered more than 2000 companies in ten volumes.

Inclusion Criteria

Most companies chosen for inclusion in *Company Histories* have achieved a minimum of US$200 million in annual sales and are leading influences in their industries or geographical locations. State-owned companies that are important in their industries and that may operate much like public or private companies also are included. Wholly owned subsidiaries are presented if they meet the requirements for inclusion.

St. James Press does not endorse any of the companies or products mentioned in this book. Companies that appear in *Company Histories* were selected without reference to their wishes and have in no way endorsed their entries. The companies were given the opportunity to participate in the compilation of the articles by providing information or reading their entries for factual accuracy, and we are indebted to many of them for their comments and corrections. We also thank them for allowing the use of their logos for identification purposes.

Entry Format

Each entry in this volume begins with a company's legal name, the address of its headquarters, its telephone number and fax number, and a statement of public, private, state, or parent ownership. A company with a legal name in both English and the language of its headquarters country is listed by the English name, with the native-language name in parentheses.

Also provided are the company's earliest incorporation date, the number of employees, and the most recent sales figures available. Sales figures are given in local currencies with equivalents in U.S. dollars. For some private companies, sales figures are estimates. The entry lists the exchanges on which a company's stock is traded, as well as the company's principal Standard Industrial Classification codes. American spelling is used, and the word ''billion'' is used in its American sense of one thousand million.

Sources

The histories were compiled from publicly accessible sources such as general and academic periodicals, books, annual reports, and material supplied by the companies themselves. *Company Histories* is intended for reference use by students, business people, librarians, historians, economists, investors, job candidates, and others who want to learn more about the historical development of the world's most important companies.

Cumulative Indexes

An Index to Companies and Persons provides access to companies and individuals discussed in the text. Beginning with Volume 7, an Index to Industries allows researchers to locate companies by their principal industry.

A.B.	Aktiebolaget (Sweden)
A.G.	Aktiengesellschaft (Germany, Switzerland)
A.S.	Atieselskab (Denmark)
A.S.	Aksjeselskap (Denmark, Norway)
A.Ş.	Anomin Sirket (Turkey)
B.V.	Besloten Vennootschap met beperkte, Aansprakelijkheid (The Netherlands)
Co.	Company (United Kingdom, United States)
Corp.	Corporation (United States)
G.I.E.	Groupement d'Intérêt Economique (France)
GmbH	Gesellschaft mit beschränkter Haftung (Germany)
H.B.	Handelsbolaget (Sweden)
Inc.	Incorporated (United States)
KGaA	Kommanditgesellschaft auf Aktien (Germany)
K.K.	Kabushiki Kaisha (Japan)
LLC	Limited Liability Company (Middle East)
Ltd.	Limited (Canada, Japan, United Kingdom, United States)
N.V.	Naamloze Vennootschap (The Netherlands)
OY	Osakeyhtiöt (Finland)
PLC	Public Limited Company (United Kingdom)
PTY.	Proprietary (Australia, Hong Kong, South Africa)
S.A.	Société Anonyme (Belgium, France, Switzerland)
SpA	Società per Azioni (Italy)

DA	Algerian dinar	Dfl	Netherlands florin
A$	Australian dollar	NZ$	New Zealand dollar
Sch	Austrian schilling	N	Nigerian naira
BFr	Belgian franc	NKr	Norwegian krone
Cr	Brazilian cruzado	RO	Omani rial
C$	Canadian dollar	P	Philippine peso
DKr	Danish krone	Esc	Portuguese escudo
E£	Egyptian pound	SRls	Saudi Arabian riyal
Fmk	Finnish markka	S$	Singapore dollar
FFr	French franc	R	South African rand
DM	German mark	W	South Korean won
HK$	Hong Kong dollar	Pta	Spanish peseta
Rs	Indian rupee	SKr	Swedish krona
Rp	Indonesian rupiah	SFr	Swiss franc
IR£	Irish pound	NT$	Taiwanese dollar
L	Italian lira	B	Thai baht
¥	Japanese yen	£	United Kingdom pound
W	Korean won	$	United States dollar
KD	Kuwaiti dinar	B	Venezuelan bolivar
LuxFr	Luxembourgian franc	K	Zambian kwacha
M$	Malaysian ringgit		

International Directory of
COMPANY HISTORIES

A.H. BELO CORPORATION

A. H. Belo Corporation

P.O. Box 655237
Dallas, Texas 75265-5237
U.S.A.
(214) 977-6600
Fax: (214) 977-6603

Public Company
Incorporated: 1926
Employees: 2,788
Sales: $545.8 million
Stock Exchanges: New York
SICs: 2711 Newspapers; 4833 Television Broadcasting
   Stations

Originating as a small-town publisher of the *Dallas Morning News* and the *Texas Almanac,* A. H. Belo Corporation has become a diversified media company of national significance. The oldest continuously operating business in the state of Texas, Belo owns and operates newspapers and television stations in five U.S. metropolitan areas. The newspapers published by Belo are the *Dallas Morning News* and eight Dallas-Fort Worth community papers. In its broadcasting division, Belo operates its flagship station, WFAA-TV (ABC) in Dallas-Fort Worth; KHOU-TV (CBS) in Houston, Texas; KXTV (CBS) in Sacramento, California; WVEC-TV (ABC) in Hampton-Norfolk, Virginia; and KOTV (CBS) in Tulsa, Oklahoma. The company also operates a program development unit, Belo Productions, Inc., and DFW Printing Company, which prints *USA Today*'s regional edition.

A. H. Belo Corporation traces its roots to the Galveston *Daily News,* which was published by Samuel Bangs with a circulation under 200 in 1842, when Texas was still a republic. In 1857, Willard Richardson, who had replaced Bangs as publisher of the fledgling *Daily News,* created the *Texas Almanac.* Ten thousand copies of the first edition were sold. The *Almanac* became a valuable reference book for Texas farmers, ranchers, and businessmen, as well as a voice for the promotion of immigration. Richardson's editorials advocated the importance of the railroads to the growth of the state of Texas—and to the future of newspaper distribution. By 1865, Richardson had turned the Galveston *Daily News* into the most powerful newspaper in Texas.

Former Confederate Colonel Alfred H. Belo joined the *Daily News,* succeeding Richardson as publisher and becoming majority owner of the company, in 1865. In 1881, Belo incorporated the Galveston *Daily News.* Belo expanded the company by starting a new newspaper in 1885 under the recommendation of George Bannerman Dealey, who Belo had hired as an office boy in 1874. The *Dallas Morning News* published its first edition in what was then the prairie town of Dallas, population 18,000. Using the telegraph to communicate across 315 miles, the Galveston *Daily News* and the *Dallas Morning News* issued the first wire-connected publication with joint issues. *Dallas Morning News* issues were delivered that year on special trains to Fort Worth, Dennison, and Waco to reach a year-end circulation of 5,678 daily and 6,435 Sunday papers. In its early years, the *Dallas Morning News* experienced steady growth in circulation.

Dealey's prominence grew with the paper's, and in 1920 he became president. Dealey became a well-known civic leader and visionary, bringing George Kessler to Dallas to devise a city plan, and urging the *Morning News* to take advantage of the sure potential of the new medium that was sweeping the nation: radio. In 1922, WFAA went on the air as the *Dallas Morning News*'s radio service and the first network radio station in Texas. The early broadcasts took place in the library of the *Morning News* office, with a canvas tent used for soundproofing. By 1930, WFAA would become the first super-power radio station in the South and Southwest, broadcasting at 50,000 watts. Nevertheless, the company maintained a decided emphasis on newspaper publishing and did not become seriously involved in broadcast media until the 1980s.

In 1923, the company sold its interest in the Galveston *Daily News,* focusing its newspaper operations entirely on the *Dallas Morning News.* Dealey acquired a majority interest in the company from Col. Belo's heirs in 1926. With partner John F. Lubben, Dealey incorporated the company, naming it A. H. Belo Corporation in honor of his late employer and mentor. Still linked to the farm-based economy, the *Dallas Morning News* sponsored a ''More Cotton on Fewer Acres'' competition, with participation by over 7,000 farmers. Winners received cash prizes and publication of their farming techniques in a bulletin distributed in the Cotton Belt and overseas in Egypt, India, Brazil, and Mexico.

In 1950, Belo acquired KBTV (later renamed WFAA-TV), and became one of the first television broadcasting companies. Belo moved slowly into the television industry, however, with its primary focus remaining the *Dallas Morning News.* Belo would not buy a second television station until 1968, or a third until 1979. Nevertheless, Belo continued to expand in the 1960s, acquiring News-Texan, Inc., a publisher of seven community newspapers that would later form the Dallas-Fort Worth Suburban Newspapers, Inc.

By 1970, the *Dallas Morning News* had a circulation of 239,367 papers daily and 280,696 papers on Sunday—more than twice the circulation of 1940, and over thirteen times the population of Dallas when Dealey had returned from his scouting mission in 1885. Seeking to further improve its product, the *Morning News* commissioned a study of the interests of Dallas readers in 1978. As a result of the study, the paper increased its coverage of high-interest areas, especially through the development of innovative fashion and entertainment sections. The *Morning News* garnered three Pulitzer Prizes during the 1970s, and its sports coverage was recognized by the Associated Press Sports Editors in its national 10 best sports sections list.

A. H. Belo Corporation became a public company in 1981, with its initial offering of 3.9 million shares on the New York Stock Exchange priced at $11.50 per share. In 1983, Belo shed its publishing-only orientation by making the largest broadcast purchase in national history. For $606 million, Belo acquired KHOU-TV (Houston), KXTV (Sacramento), and WVEC (Norfolk), all of which were licensed to Corinthian Broadcast Corporation from the Dun & Bradstreet Corporation. To comply with Federal Communications Commission rules regarding the purchase, Belo sold Texas station KDFM-TV and Tennessee station WTVC, recouping approximately $105 million. An asset redeployment plan led to the sale of the company's cable system and its four radio stations, and Belo raised additional capital by selling 4.4 million shares of stock.

It appeared that the acquisition might bring trouble to Belo when the biggest of the four television stations, KHOU-TV in Houston, was hurt by a lagging Texas economy. However, Belo's revenues reached $354 million in 1984, with KHOU-TV and the flagship station WFAA contributing two-thirds of the company's total revenues. Though the company's stock had risen 29 percent (to $42.50 per share) between 1981 and 1983, when it made its intention to acquire the Corinthian outlets public, Belo's stock reached a record high of $55 per share in 1985. The next year, after 40 years with Belo, chairman and CEO James Moroney retired, and Robert Decherd took the mantle.

Overproduction of oil and overbuilding of real estate struck a blow to the Texas economy in the mid-1980s. Ward Huey, president of Belo's broadcast division, recognized the danger posed to the earnings of Belo's newly acquired television stations by Texas' lagging economy. Huey instituted cost-cutting measures including layoffs, salary freezes, and the postponement of plans for new transmitter towers and upgraded production equipment. Due to the weak economy in Dallas-Fort Worth and Houston, net earnings continued to decrease in 1986, although both television and newspaper revenues showed increased profits.

Even with financial difficulties, the *Dallas Morning News* took the lead over its local competitor, the *Dallas Times-Herald,* in the 1980s. In 1986, the *Morning News* achieved a new circulation record and won a Pulitzer Prize for a story on housing discrimination that resulted in Senate hearings and national corrective actions. The *Dallas Morning News* circulation grew to 404,812 daily and 618,283 Sunday by 1991.

Belo moved forward in a bold new direction when it formed a partnership in 1989 with Kansas City-based Universal Press Syndicate to create programming based on the UPS roster of comics and columnists. The first Universal Belo project was an animated strip based on the ''Tank MacNamara'' comic, designed for prime-time specials and network sports events. Animation for the strip was created at the California Film Roman studios. The *Dallas Times-Herald* lost all of its Universal columns and cartoons as a result of the new partnership and

brought an antitrust lawsuit against the *Morning News.* The lawsuit and its appeal were unsuccessful, but Belo paid a $1.5 million settlement to its competitor.

The Texas economy began to rebound as the 1980s came to a close, and Belo's television ratings soared. In 1989, Belo syndicated *Mr. Peppermint,* a Dallas children's program it had aired for 25 years. WFAA's *Texas Country Reporter* was sold in 22 Southwestern markets, and WFAA, after several flat years, saw a 16 percent increase in earnings between 1987 and 1989, when earnings reached $73.3 million. During that same period, KHOU-TV increased its revenues by 9 percent to $46 million. By 1990, the formerly troubled KHOU-TV had risen in the ratings from a distant third to number two, giving Belo a number one or two rating for all of its television stations.

Just as the Texas economy improved, a national recession began that dramatically impacted newspaper advertising. Newspapers experienced their worst year in a decade in 1990. While the *Dallas Times-Herald* slashed its advertising rates, Belo CEO Decherd held a firm line with rate cards. The *Dallas Morning News* achieved only slight gains in overall advertising, but boosted its circulation by 4 percent daily and 6 percent Sunday, posting higher increase rates than those experienced by the *Dallas Times-Herald.* By this time, the *Morning News*'s circulation rates doubled those of the *Times-Herald.*

The war between Dallas's two major newspapers ended in 1991. On December 9th, the *Dallas Times-Herald* published its last issue after 112 years. Belo acquired the *Herald*'s assets in a $55 million deal, becoming the only major newspaper publisher in Dallas. Twelve other major newspapers also succumbed to the recession, closing their doors in 1991.

The acquisition of the *Times-Herald* caused Belo to change its financial plan in 1992. With circulation boosted in one year to a half million papers daily (a 26 percent increase) and 800,000 Sunday (a 31 percent increase), the *Morning News* was pushing its production capacity. The newspaper recession showed signs of ending, and circulation figures placed the *Morning News* among the nation's most highly read papers for the first time, making national advertising a strong possibility. While other newspapers experienced slow recovery, the *Morning News* used 30 percent more newsprint in 1992 than it had the previous year, publishing a Sunday paper on December 6th that was so large it delayed deliveries by an hour. Decherd adamantly refused to raise the newsstand price from 25 cents, espousing the philosophy that rampant price increases at other newspapers were too aggressive, cutting into reader retention. To manage its growth, Belo invested $41 million in the expansion of its newspaper production plant in Plano, Texas.

The production facility expansion was completed in 1993, and the suburban newspaper operation in Dallas-Fort Worth was restructured into two separate entities, one printing eight community newspapers and the other functioning as a commercial printer. The *Dallas Morning News* won its fifth Pulitzer Prize in eight years, for sport news photography of the 1992 summer Olympics. Circulation of the *Morning News* held strong at 527,387 daily and 814,404 on Sunday.

Television as well as newspapers were profitable for the company in 1993. Four of Belo's five television stations were rated number one in overall audience delivery, and Belo announced plans to purchase WWL-TV, an affiliate of CBS in New Orleans. Programming activities were placed under the authority of the newly created Belo Productions, Inc. (BPI), an entity that oversees potential pay-as-you-go cable and television programs in conjunction with Universal Belo Productions. In 1993, Belo's stock reached $53 per share and sales were $545 million.

A. H. Belo Corporation's future will undoubtedly contain new technological challenges, signalled by the advent of the information superhighway and its implications for publishing. Belo's history demonstrates careful planning, thoughtful expansion, and a philosophy of "doing a few things well" that has allowed the company to weather changes in the economy. Should the company's future follow the pattern of its past, the next few years are likely to be spent fine-tuning Belo's role in the broadcasting market while continuing—as Belo has for over 150 years—to publish a quality daily newspaper.

Principal Subsidiaries: Dallas Morning News; DFW Suburban Newspapers, Inc.; DFW Printing Company, Inc.; WFAA-TV (ABC) Channel 8 (Dallas-Fort Worth, Texas); KHOU-TV (CBS) Channel 11 (Houston, Texas); KXTV (CBS) Channel 10 (Sacramento, California); WVEC-TV (ABC) Channel 13 (Hampton-Norfolk, Virginia); KOTV (CBS) Channel 6 (Tulsa, Oklahoma); Belo Productions, Inc.

Further Reading:

A. H. Belo Corporation, Commemorating One Hundred and Fifty Years 1842–1992, Dallas: A. H. Belo Corporation, 1992.

"A. H. Belo: Ready to Continue Its Expansion," *Editor & Publisher,* August 17, 1985, p. 13.
"A. H. Belo's Fortune Tied to Texas Economy; Rated Good Longterm Buy," *Television/Radio Age,* July 11, 1988, p. 87.
"Belo's $600 Million Deal Highlights 1983 Broadcast Sales," *Editor & Publisher,* January 7, 1984, p. 46.
Beschloss, Steven, "Leaders of the Pack," *Channels,* August 13, 1990, pp. 26–30.
"*Dallas Times-Herald* Folds," *Editor & Publisher,* December 14, 1991, p. 12.
"Financial Focus: Publicly-Owned Station Groups," *Television/Radio Age,* May 26, 1986, pp. 42–43.
Garneau, George, "A Flat Year Expected for 1992," *Editor & Publisher,* January 4, 1992, pp. 12–13, 42.
——, "Cutting Costs, Boosting Prices," *Editor & Publisher,* January 5, 1991, pp. 12–13, 36–37.
——, "Newspaper Financial Reports," *Editor & Publisher,* September 4, 1993, p. 16.
——, "Small Gains Forecast for Newspapers in '93," *Editor & Publisher,* January 2, 1993, pp. 14–15, 20.
——, "Soft Year Comes to a Close," *Editor & Publisher,* March 2, 1991, p. 12.
P. H., "A. H. Belo Corporation, Making Up for Lost Time," *Financial World,* April 17–30, 1985, p. 23.
R. J. P., "The Benefits of Corporate Marriage," *Financial World,* October 15, 1983, p. 30.
Rosenberg, Jim, "Dallas Puts $41 Million into Expansion," *Editor & Publisher,* May 23, 1992, p. 25.
"Sales, Acquisitions Continue Apace at Station Groups," *Television/Radio Age,* June 8, 1987, pp. 43–44.

—Heidi Feldman

Abbey National PLC

Abbey House
Baker Street
London NW1 6XL
United Kingdom
(071) 612-4000
Fax: (071) 612-4010

Public Company
Incorporated: 1944
Employees: 15,458
Total Assets: £83.80 billion (US$57.0 billion)
Stock Exchanges: London
SICs: 6012 Recognized Banks

One of the top-rated banks in the United Kingdom, Abbey National PLC has a long history. Abbey National grew to become Britain's second largest building society from its nineteenth-century roots as two separate entities: the National Building Society, established in 1849, and the Abbey Road Building Society, founded in 1874. Later Abbey National became the first such society to convert to a public limited company.

Building societies originated as mutual groups, known as "friendly societies," which proliferated during the urbanization trend of the mid-eighteenth century. As towns and cities swelled, a substitute was needed for the social support traditionally offered by the community in rural areas. The first friendly societies were early forms of insurance—self-help organizations whose members paid regular subscriptions and were entitled to financial help from the group's funds when necessary. From this general concept evolved the "building clubs" of the late eighteenth century. These were temporary organizations formed to build houses from money collected from subscribers; they were dissolved once that purpose was accomplished. The first known permanent building society was established in 1845, just four years before the National came into being.

The National's founders (among whom were the social reformers and members of Parliament Richard Cobden and Joseph Hume) had a political rather than a commercial agenda. In an age when voting rights were heavily restricted and tied to land ownership, they sought to increase suffrage by increasing the number of those who owned the freehold on their land and were thus entitled to vote. Essentially, then, the National was a land society, not a building society, and was popularly known as The National Freehold Land Society. It was officially named The National Permanent Mutual Benefit Building Society in order to give the association a legal framework under the Building Societies Act of 1836. The new organization enjoyed tremendous initial success, though not exactly in the way its founders had intended. Relatively few members took electoral advantage of their new status; most were far more interested in the National as a savings and loan institution, and in building on their new land.

Britain in the mid-1800s was economically buoyant and socially progressive. More people were earning more money than ever before, industry was booming, the population was growing, the railroads were revolutionizing travel and communications, and society was becoming ever more urbanized. Yet only a tiny proportion of the population owned their own homes. There was great demand for the National's 30 shares, and within four years the society was the largest of its kind in the country.

Under the 1836 Building Societies Act, societies were not permitted to own land themselves, so the National held its land in the name of trustees until 1856, when it formed the British Land Company for that purpose. With this division of operations, the National moved a step closer to becoming a building—rather than a land—society, a process completed in 1878 when the National and the British Land Company separated.

Unlike the National, the Abbey Road Building Society was formed in recognition of the growing need for home ownership. An outgrowth of a self-help organization, the Abbey Road Baptist Church's benefit society, the association was masterminded by Frank Yerbury, a builder, in order to purchase houses for its 500 members. Led by conservative directors in its early years, the Abbey Road enjoyed modest but steady success.

Building societies suffered a setback toward the end of the nineteenth century. In 1892 the Liberator, one of the National's principal competitors, was forced out of business by a combination of unwise speculation and fraud. In the wake of the scandal, tighter government controls were instituted on building societies, and public confidence was severely shaken.

The Abbey Road, and particularly the National, suffered along with the others. But the societies fortunes improved at the beginning of the twentieth century, when an affluent middle class was growing and demanding suburban housing developments. In the cities, much of the older housing had degenerated into slum areas and needed replacement. However, another crisis in public confidence occurred in 1911, caused by the failure of the Birkbeck. Technically a building society, the Birkbeck operated more as a bank (only 10 percent of its assets were in mortgages), but nonetheless its fall caused panic among building society investors and gave pause to building societies (such as the National) which had harbored thoughts of branching out into banking operations. Indeed, a comment made early in 1912 by the National's chairman tried to allay investors fears: "Now, in the case of the National, we have never done anything, and we never mean to do anything, which remotely or indirectly suggests banking. We never have, and we never will."

World War I curtailed the activities and products of the building societies, and following the war the Liberal government dealt them a further blow by declaring housing for the poor the province of local authorities, giving the building societies their first real taste of how party politics could affect their business. Nonetheless, the interwar years proved on the whole prosperous. In 1923, under a Conservative government, a Housing Act was passed to provide a subsidy to private enterprise for house building. Another great building boom was taking place. Whereas in 1919 fewer than 10 percent of the population owned their own home, by 1938 that figure had grown to 25 percent.

During this period the Abbey Road prospered. Under the leadership of Harold Bellman, who favored bold initiatives and—heretofore unusual in British business—aggressive marketing, the Abbey Road rocketed from sixteenth to second place in the building society hierarchy. In 1921, the Abbey Road had £1 million in assets; by 1925 assets had risen to £3.6 million and by 1929 to £19 million. For the first time the society ventured out of London; branches were opened in Southend, Watford, Reading, and Blackpool. By 1935, the Abbey Road had 110 branch outlets and employed more than 500 people.

Meanwhile the National, though it had slipped from the high position it had enjoyed in its earliest days, continued on a prosperous course, though it could not compare to the spectacular rise of the Abbey Road at that time. In 1929, Bruce Wycherley took over operations, introducing more modern commercial ideas and machinery, improving profits, and opening new branches. By the late 1930s, the society had a dozen U.K. branches.

Business suffered with the outbreak of World War II. Staff shortages were chronic, building materials were lacking, and less building work was being undertaken. As with the Great War, it was a time of stagnation for building societies. Nevertheless, as the end of the war approached, the Abbey Road and the National signaled their intention to continue to expand in the expected postwar boom by announcing, in 1943, their decision to merge. The move became official the following year.

Because the Abbey Road was the second largest building society in the United Kingdom and the National was the sixth, their merger made the new Abbey National a formidable force indeed. But this force was blunted, temporarily, by the postwar Labour government, which embarked on an ambitious program of state-financed building. Almost a million new homes were built and rented by the government.

The building societies still prospered, however, as savings and loan institutions, and by 1951 a Conservative government sympathetic to the building societies' aims had taken power. Party politics continued to ebb and flow, but the 1950s and 1960s were years of expansion for most building societies, and the Abbey National's record was one of steady growth. The demand for privately owned housing was still on the rise (in the 1960s the proportion of owner-occupied houses reached 50 percent), and the Abbey National was firmly ensconced in second place in this favorable market. By the end of 1962, the Abbey National could boast assets of £500 million—as compared with £80 million at the time of the two societies' merger. By 1968, assets had reached £1 billion and the society had

nearly 150 branches. Within a few years the Abbey National's assets had doubled and it was opening a new branch office every other week. New products and services were introduced, including Bounty Bonds, which offered life insurance as well as an increased range of savings and property bonds.

The early 1970s were troubled years financially for the country, with house prices, mortgage rates, and inflation all rising dramatically. On two occasions the government offered loans to the building societies in an effort to keep interest rates down. While economic commentators might argue over whether the building societies were partly to blame for these bleak conditions or whether they were simply victims of the prevailing economic winds, from the societies' point of view their profits and expansion were affected little by adverse conditions. In 1979, the Abbey National had 500 branches across the United Kingdom and assets of £5.8 billion.

Clive Thornton became chief general manager and instituted a number of new initiatives designed to bring Abbey National a higher profile in 1979. An office was opened in Brussels, Belgium (the first overseas office of any building society), the society participated in a loan scheme to renovate housing in inner-city areas, and it introduced various new savings and loans opportunities to attract new customers and offer existing ones more choice. (Thornton even capitalized on the company's address of 221 Baker Street by marketing Sherlock Holmes souvenirs.)

Abbey National's move into areas previously the province of banks was gradual but inexorable. In 1983, it announced its intention to withdraw from its agreement to keep its interest rates in line with those recommended by the Building Societies Association. And under Peter Birch, who succeeded Thornton as chief executive in 1984, the society continued its trend of providing more and varied banking services to its customers. The Abbey National offered improved transaction services, more comprehensive insurance coverage, an increased number of service products—including conveyancing, structural surveys, and financial counseling—, and more credit options. In 1988, interest-bearing checking accounts became available to all customers for the first time and the society established a national real estate agency under the name Cornerstone. The result of all this activity was that Abbey National (still firmly in place as the second largest building society in the United Kingdom, with assets of over £31 billion and more than nine million members) had moved into areas of direct competition with banks.

While the continually evolving legal definition of building societies allowed such diversification, the Abbey National came to believe that it could operate more efficiently and competitively as a public limited company. As a building society, the Abbey National was prevented by law from diversifying into new businesses, restricted in its capacity to raise capital, and limited in its access to wholesale markets. Especially irksome were the restrictions on the provision of unsecured lending; under the conditions laid down by the 1986 Building Societies Act, a society could have only 15 percent of its assets in that category, whereas a bank was free to do as it wished.

Intense interest was sparked by the board's proposal to go public, announced in 1988. The conversion of a building society to a public limited company was unprecedented. With no established procedure to follow, the implementation of the plan took a full year. The Bank of England had to carry out a review to grant a banking license. The Building Societies Commission had to be consulted every step of the way. Teams of lawyers ironed out legal questions and potential difficulties. Most importantly, Abbey National had to inform the public and its members of the ramifications of the proposed change in status. To that end, the society organized a massive media campaign, even including 17 public "roadshows" held at various locations around the country where members could ask questions directly of Abbey National's directors.

An opposition group was formed, called Abbey Members Against Flotation, which tried to stop the conversion, accusing Abbey National of underhanded practices in presenting the matter to its customers. There were questions over the fairness of certain proposals; for example, Abbey National had offered to give each member 100 free shares of the new company, but this did not apply to minors, and in the case of joint accounts, only the first-named was to receive shares (invariably, critics pointed out, the husband in married couples' accounts). Opposition and doubts notwithstanding, when it came to the test, of the 65 percent of members who voted, 90 percent voted to go public. On June 6, 1989 the Building Societies Commission officially confirmed Abbey National's conversion to a public limited company.

The controversy did not end with the vote, however, for the flotation was attended by administrative mismanagement and farcical mishaps. Thousands of letters and share certificates were sent to incorrect addresses, refund checks failed to be sent at all, countless people received the wrong number of shares, and in one bizarre and mysterious incident share certificates were discovered burning in a skip outside one of the mailing houses.

Abbey National's success made people forget the debacle of the changeover. In the years since its flotation, the Abbey National has continued to grow in what it terms its "three mutually reinforcing businesses": U.K. retail banking, life assurance, and treasury operations, the latter a rapid-growth area for Abbey National since its conversion. Although the company had to sell its unprofitable real estate agency, Cornerstone, in 1993, in other areas it continues to prosper.

As the fourth largest bank in the United Kingdom, Abbey National offers a wide range of checking accounts and savings options. It aimed to widen its share of the mortgage market by acquiring, in 1994, the U.K. residential mortgage business of the Canadian Imperial Bank of Commerce, retitled Abbey National Mortgage Finance. In 1993, the company acquired a new subsidiary, Abbey National Life, which, together with the previously acquired Scottish Mutual, enabled Abbey National to provide its customers with wide coverage in life insurance, long-term savings, and pension products. The company is expanding its business in derivatives, having established in 1993 a joint operation with Baring Brothers & Co., Ltd., called Abbey National Baring Derivatives. In addition, the bank has operations in several European countries.

From the early years when the National and the Abbey Road came into being to meet political and social needs, through the growing years of British home ownership, to the Abbey National's pioneering change in status, the history of the company has mirrored modern financial trends. With a solid base of 12 million customers, a net lending figure of £3.2 billion, and an 18.5 percent share of the net mortgage lending market in 1993, it seems likely that the bank will continue to be at the forefront of new developments, as the United Kingdom has, in the words of the company's advertising slogan, "got the Abbey habit."

Principal Subsidiaries: Abbey National Financial Services Ltd.; Abbey National Homes Ltd.; Abbey National Investment Holdings Ltd.; Abbey National Life plc; Abbey National Personal Finance Ltd.; Abbey National Property Services Ltd.; Abbey National Treasury Services plc; Scottish Mutual Assurance plc.

Further Reading:

Ashworth, Herbert, *The Building Society Story,* London: Franey, 1980.
Barnes, Paul, "A Shabbey Habit to Shake Off," *Accountancy,* December, 1989, pp. 25–26.
Bellman, Sir Harold, *Bricks and Mortals: A Study of the Building Society Movement and the Story of the Abbey National Building Society, 1849–1949,* London: Hutchinson, 1949.
Birch, Peter, "Abbey National: A Continuous Process," *Banking World,* December, 1992, pp. 23–24.
Fry, John M., "Abbey National Becomes a Company," *Long Range Planning,* Vol. 23, no. 3, 1990, pp. 49–56.
Price, Seymour J., *Building Societies: Their Origins and History,* London: Franey, 1958.
Reid, Margaret, "Sir Christopher Tugendhat—All-Purpose Top Person," *Banking World,* January, 1992, pp. 16–18.
Ritchie, Berry, *A Key to the Door: The Abbey National Story,* London: Abbey National plc, 1990.

—Robin DuBlanc

ABC Appliance, Inc.

One Silverdome Industrial Park
P.O. Box 436001
Pontiac, Michigan 48343-6001
U.S.A.
(810) 335-4222
Fax: (810) 335-5920

Private Company
Incorporated: 1964
Employees: 1,500
Sales: $340 million
SICs: 5722 Household Appliances; 5731 Radio, TV &
   Electronics Stores; 7622 Radio & TV Repair

ABC Appliance, Inc., a leading retail supplier of radio, television, and consumer electronics, operates establishments under the names ABC Warehouse, Hawthorne Appliance and Electronics, Mickey Shorr Mobile Electronics, and White Automotive. ABC Warehouse, a chain with locations in Michigan, Ohio, and Indiana, sells appliances, personal computers, and other consumer electronics in a ''no frills'' warehouse style setup. Hawthorne Appliance and Electronics, an upscale store, also markets appliances and home electronics. Mickey Shorr Mobile Electronics handles and installs mobile electronics, including automotive audio equipment, security systems, and car phones. White Automotive merchandises custom vehicle accessories.

ABC Appliance, Inc. was founded by Gordon Hartunian in 1964 as a single store. The store's philosophy was based on Hartunian's belief that consumers were more interested in value and service than in merchandising frills. During the company's first twenty years in operation, it experienced slow but steady growth.

The mid-1980s marked a period of increased expansion for ABC. In 1984, the company acquired Mickey Shorr Mobile Electronics. In 1985, ABC opened three new stores in the metropolitan Detroit area. By the year's end, ABC was operating ten ABC Warehouses and five Mickey Shorr outlets.

In a ranking of electronic retailing companies compiled by *Consumer Electronics Monthly,* ABC was listed 23rd in the nation in 1985. Two of the company's principal competitors in its primary market area were also listed as national leaders:

Highland Superstores, headquartered in Plymouth, Michigan was listed 14th; and Fretter Appliance, headquartered in Livonia, Michigan, was listed 21st. The consumer electronics industry, which included items such as audio and video equipment, personal computers, and telephones, generated revenues of approximately $35 billion annually. An industry report published in the *Detroit News* in 1985 predicted continued expansion. Although some categories within the industry already enjoyed high market penetration (such as televisions), industry watchers considered their potential for future growth to be excellent because the items were seen as necessities. Other product categories not viewed as necessities also held the potential for significant growth because the numbers of U.S. households owning them was low.

In 1986, ABC opened six more stores. They included outlets in Lansing, Flint, and Grand Rapids, marking the company's first venture to cities outside the metropolitan Detroit area. Unlike some of its competitors who financed their expansion efforts through public stock offerings, ABC financed its expansion internally. A typical new ABC Warehouse location established during the mid-1980s had 10,000 square feet and cost approximately $1 million. The average Mickey Shorr store was much smaller and cost about $250,000 to open.

By 1988, ABC operated 15 retail appliance stores in Michigan and Ohio and 10 Mickey Shorr retail and installation outlets, all located in Michigan. The company began to focus on advertising to help spur growth. Early ads featured Jim Varney and his ''KnoWhutIMean?'' slogan. ABC's position in the market was further enhanced when the NATM Buying Corporation selected ABC Warehouse as its Detroit affiliate. NATM, a large appliance buying group, had previously been affiliated with Highland Superstores, an ABC competitor.

During the late 1980s, ABC pioneered the sale of cellular telephones. The phones were first sold through Mickey Shorr and White Automotive. Although cellular phones requiring installation remained linked to the company's automotive outlets, an innovation termed the ''bag phone'' enabled ABC Warehouse stores to sell transportable cellular phones. As a result, ABC achieved recognition as the first NATM member to successfully sell cellular phones at retail.

ABC's expansion continued at a steady pace. In 1989, ABC opened a store in Southfield, Michigan, a suburb located north of Detroit. The following year, ABC opened an outlet in Port Huron, Michigan. The Port Huron location, 56 miles from Detroit, represented another move into markets removed from the chain's primary concentration of stores in the metropolitan Detroit area.

By 1990, the chain consisted of 18 ABC Warehouse outlets, 14 Mickey Shorr outlets, and White Automotive. In addition to increasing the number of stores, the company also expanded the number of items sold in its stores. According to one estimate, the mix of major appliances to electronics at the time was about 50/50. To accommodate its growth, ABC purchased a 135,000 square foot building from the city of Pontiac (Michigan) to serve as company headquarters and to provide needed warehouse space. Approximately 15,000 square feet of the building were allocated for the company's offices; the remaining

110,000 was allocated for warehouse needs. Another change in 1990 was the acquisition of Hawthorne Appliance and Electronics. Hawthorne, a single store appliance dealer, gave ABC the ability to market to new home builders and buyers and to develop a built-in appliance merchandizing strategy.

Despite is growth, ABC's sales volume in 1990 was still judged to be behind that of one of its major competitors in the metropolitan Detroit area, Highland Superstores. Sales volumes, however, were thought to be ahead of those achieved by another competitor, Fretter Inc. ABC's expansion came at a time when the market for major appliances was generally considered soft and industry participants were involved in intense competition. According to a report in *HFD,* market conditions had not diminished ABC's margins because the price increases imposed by major manufacturers were being passed on to consumers.

Competition within the industry increased when Sears and Montgomery Wards created the "store-within-a-store" concept. Sears opened "Brand Central" and Montgomery Ward introduced "Electric Avenue." ABC adopted the concept of a store-within-a-store and incorporated the design into its own outlets. The store-within-a-store idea provided a way to present higher-priced and more upscale lines with improved success. By highlighting groupings of products with special features, sales staff members were better able to help customers find desired features and styling aspects than when products were simply placed beside middle-range merchandise.

In 1991, ABC's advertising campaign titled "Programmed for Growth in These Challenging Times" helped the company achieve its objectives during a year marked by recessionary conditions. The company's Mickey Shorr outlets also thrived and gained a reputation as specialists in expert installation. Mickey Shorr's annual sales were estimated at $20 million. The company reported that compact disc players and car security items represented the largest segments of its business. Sales of cellular telephones were also growing. The number of cellular telephones sold in 1992 was up 60 percent over the number sold in 1991.

In 1992, ABC launched a new advertising campaign featuring Sal Richards using the catch phrase "Botta Boom, Botta Bing." The campaign was aimed at educating consumers on the ABC's of buying. An innovative advertising promotion offering customers a 50 percent rebate on purchases between $199 and $5,000 drew some criticism, however. Under the terms of the offer, customers who made a qualifying purchase and filled out a form within 21 days, received a cash-back rebate certificate. On the ten-year anniversary of their purchase, the cash-back certificate could be redeemed for the rebate. Rebates were guaranteed by an insurance arrangement. The promotion drew criticism from competitors who noted that ABC had suspended its lowest-price guarantee. Other critics of the promotion claimed that because the rebate was not adjusted for inflation it was apt to have diminished purchasing power.

By 1992, the ABC Warehouse chain had grown to 22 stores. In 1993, according to an estimate made by Hartunian and reported in *Discount Merchandiser,* "white" goods (home appliances, including items such as refrigerators and washing machines) accounted for about 45 percent of the company sales. The remaining 55 percent of sales were "brown" goods and traffic goods, which included items such as housewares and personal electronics. The average size of an ABC Warehouse store had grown to be about 18,000 square feet. The company continued to focus on its no frills philosophy and remained committed to traditional, staple appliance products. Hartunian told *Discount Merchandiser* that each of the company's stores achieved a local market share of approximately 33 to 34 percent.

Hartunian attributed the company's success to its sales staff, who worked entirely on commission. In a statement published by *Discount Merchandiser* he explained, "Our stores have always been very sales driven, meaning that the people on the sales floor are highly motivated, and consequently we follow their direction, rather than have the administration dictate a number of things." In order to project an image of a more personable, friendly sales staff, the company's 1993 advertising campaign featured the "ABC Employee Choir."

Another change in 1993 was the addition of in-store demonstrations aimed at increasing the sales of home theater systems. Home theater technology enabled consumers to get better sound quality in stereo and television sets. ABC Warehouse promoted the concept based on a building block approach to help overcome price resistance among consumers who wanted the benefits of home theater but who were not willing to spend thousands of dollars for special equipment, new furniture, and room remodeling. ABC put together different packages designed for simple installation. The lowest price system was tagged at $899. To demonstrate the benefits of home theater systems, ABC instituted in-store "The Big Red Button" demonstrations. By pressing a red button, customers could activate a three-minute demonstration of a typical system containing a large-screen television, laser disc player, receivers, and speakers. The presentation explained the process of beginning with a television set and progressing through a series of upgrades to create a home theater.

During 1993 ABC also benefitted from the bankruptcy of a major competitor, Highland Superstores. ABC purchased $60 million of Highland inventory and liquidated it in 45 days. ABC also purchased five former Highland locations. The locations enabled ABC to expand four of its existing stores into larger facilities and to open a new store in Indiana. By 1994, the ABC Warehouse chain consisted of 25 stores.

One of the fastest growing products was the cellular phone. Cellular phones, originally marketed as a business tool, shifted to the consumer market during the early 1990s. Per unit prices fell from an average of $340 in 1992 to $298 in 1993. As the phones became more affordable, sales by consumer retail outlets increased. According to one report there were an estimated 14,163 cellular telephone subscribers at the end of 1993. The number was expected to increase to 17,350 by the end of 1994 and to more than double by the end of 1998. The marketplace also benefitted from an increasing variety in the types of phones available. In early 1994, there were three basic types on the market, portable (pocket-sized phones with small low-power batteries); mobile phones (larger units intended for permanent mounting in cars); and transportable (the same size as a mobile unit but including a battery pack to enable use outside the vehicle). ABC Warehouse sold portable and transportable models in its ABC Warehouse stores. Brands offered included Novatel, Technophone, Motorola, Pulsar, and Mitsubishi DiamondTell. ABC's Mickey Shorr, Hawthorne Electronics and Appliances, and White Automotive also sold cellular phones but carried a different variety of brands and packaged the phones with distinctive service offerings.

The cellular phone market was considered a challenge because of the complexity involved in making a sale. In addition to merely selling the actual phone, steps included selling phone service, programming the phone, activating the phone, and in many cases, installing the phone. Phone sales were often bundled with phone service agreements and merchants received subsidies from service providers. Although this practice permitted merchants to offer phones at low prices, consumers were required to sign service contracts for a specified time period, usually at least a year.

The industry practice of bundling phone sales with phone service agreements gave ABC an advantage over some of its competitors. National companies had to cope with a wide variety of regional service providers offering a multitude of activation incentives. This led to significant price discrepancies between different regions and made cellular phones difficult to advertise on a national basis. ABC, a regional competitor, was able to benefit from a consistent working relationship with one local phone service provider. ABC attributed its success in selling cellular phones to this relationship.

ABC Warehouse also prided itself on making cellular phone purchases simple. A company executive quoted in *HFD* stated, "We wanted to make it no more difficult for consumers to buy a cellphone than to buy a washing machine." In addition, ABC Warehouse worked to provide fast activations. ABC claimed that the activation process took between 11.5 and 14 minutes; in other stores the procedure was reported to take up to a day and a half. ABC was able to provide fast service because of its ability to assign phone numbers and access to instant credit verification services. In addition, ABC Warehouse sold only those telephones which were able to be programmed from the handset at the store.

Hartunian, ABC's founder and owner, planned to continue the company's policy of steady growth. *Discount Merchandiser* reported his strategy included the addition of more stores in areas chosen to maximize the company's distribution channels. ABC also planned to increase its offerings in some departments, especially within the computer arena.

Principal Subsidiaries: ABC Warehouse; Hawthorne Appliance and Electronics; Mickey Shorr Mobile Electronics; White Automotive.

Further Reading:

"ABC Picked," *Detroit News,* February 16, 1988.
Brauer, Molly, "Wall Street Plugs in to Consumer Electronics," *Detroit News,* December 22, 1985.
Courter, Eileen, "Selling the Category in Building Blocks," *HFD,* January 10, 1994.
Hogan, Monica, "Motor City Autosound Dealer Rides High Despite Recession," *Dealerscope Merchandising,* March, 1992.
Jones, David, "ABC Warehouse Expanding: New Quarters, Storage and High-End Products," *HFD,* April 30, 1990.
Roach, Loretta, "Slow and Steady," *Discount Merchandiser,* September, 1993.
Serju, Tricia, "ABC Offers 50-Percent Rebates to Those Who Can Wait 10 Years," *Detroit News,* May 13, 1992.
Silberg, Lurie, "A Hard Cell," *HFD,* March 21, 1994.

—Karen Bellenir

ACCOR

Accor SA

2 Rue de la Mare-Neuve
91021 Évry Cedex
France
(33) 1 60 87 43 20
Fax: (33) 1 60 77 04 58

Public Company
Incorporated: 1983
Employees: 135,000
Sales: FFr82 billion (US$14.04 billion)
Stock Exchanges: Paris
SICs: 7011 Hotels & Motels; 5812 Eating Places; 4724
    Travel Agencies; 7514 Passenger Car Rental

Accor SA, a Paris-based conglomerate comprised of hotels, restaurants, travel agencies, car rental companies, and restaurant voucher firms, has a history of remarkably rapid expansion, having grown 20 percent annually since 1967. By the mid-1990s, Accor was the largest hotel company in Europe and ranked second worldwide after Holiday Inn. The company maintains a strong presence in all sectors of the hotel market from luxury Sofitels to budget Formule 1s; similarly, its restaurant holdings range from wine bars and steakhouses to fast food. The company's success has been attributed to its decentralized management style, imaginative co-chairmen, and timely moves into new market niches ahead of the competition.

In 1967, Gérard Pelisson and Paul Dubrule opened their first Novotel hotel on a roadside near Lille in northern France. Travel was booming in France in the 1960s, and the hotel industry had not yet expanded to meet the demand, as French hotels, in general, were either rural inns or luxury hotels in city centers. Dubrule decided to build American-style highway hotels in the medium price range and collaborated with Pelisson, a former head of market research at IBM-Europe. Through Pelisson's connections, the partners were able to secure a bank loan, and their Novotel company was launched. The company's ensuing success was facilitated largely by its being first to break into the unexploited European market for highway lodging. Each Novotel provided standardized rooms, ample parking facilities, and restaurants featuring local cuisine. Soon Novotels were also established at airports as well as popular vacation sites such as the seaside and mountain areas.

Pelisson and Dubrule developed their expanding company with a philosophy of decentralized management and a unique dual chairmanship. Although to comply with French law the partners took turns holding the official position of chairperson, they made all decisions jointly and generally shared responsibilities, immersing themselves in all aspects of the business. The company's specialty became variety, providing hotel chains to fit every need. In 1973, Sphere SA was created as a holding company for a new chain of two-star, no-frills hotels, called Ibis; the first Ibis was opened the following year. During this time, the company also acquired Courte Paille, a chain of roadside steakhouses, founded in 1961, which reflected many of the same priorities as Novotel: practicality, easy parking, constant quality, and quick service. The purchase of the Mercure hotel chain in 1975 pushed the company into metropolitan areas and the business traveler market, and again, as with Novotel, these hotels varied according to regional demands in style, character, and restaurant offerings. By the end of the 1970s, Novotel had become the premier hotel chain in Europe with 240 establishments in Europe, Africa, South America, and the Far East.

In 1980, Novotel invested in Jacques Borel International, which owned restaurants and luxury Sofitel hotels. Jacques Borel had begun his career with the establishment of one restaurant in 1957, and, by 1975, when he took over Belgium's Sofitel chain, he was Europe's top restauranteur. After losses in the hotel business forced Borel to sell the Sofitel chain to Pelisson and Dubrule in 1982, Novotel and its holdings were incorporated under the name Accor and became one of the top ten hotel operations in the world, an elite group typically dominated by American firms. The merger doubled the partners' holdings and infused new talent into the senior management, as Bernard Westercamp became vice-president and general manager of Accor. Sofitel's luxury services, which were aimed at business and holiday travelers and located in the center of international cities, near airports, and in prestigious tourist areas, introduced Accor to the higher-priced end of the hotel industry.

Accor's initial expansion into the American market, which began in 1979 with the opening of a hotel in Minneapolis, was not as successful as its ventures in Europe, due to a saturated market in the United States and Accor's slow development. The company brought Novotel, Ibis, and Sofitel hotels to the United States, as well as a chain of eateries in California called Seafood Broiler, but all operated at a loss. Nonetheless, Pelisson and Dubrule made American-style service culture fundamental to their business in Europe. After visiting training schools at McDonald's Corp. and Disneyland, they opened Accor Academy at the company headquarters in Évry in 1985. The academy offered seminars in topics ranging from phone etiquette to team-building skills and the exploration of new technologies. Accor spent a reported two percent of its annual payroll on training.

During the mid-1980s, Accor developed investments in the restaurant and travel businesses. The company opened Pizza del Arte, a chain of Italian restaurants, in 1983, installing them in commercial and city centers, and entered into a partnership with the bakery and catering company, Lenôtre, two years later. Accor also entered the travel industry during this time, buying into Africatours, the largest tour operator to Africa, which became the third of its major investments, along with hotels and restaurants. The company expanded to North and South America, Asia, and the South Pacific through the purchases of Americatours, Asietours, and Ted Cook's Islands in the Sun. In an effort to attract weekend clientele in Europe, Accor developed Épisodes, an agency specializing in short trips offering weekend rooms in hotels usually filled by business travelers.

In 1985, Hotec, a subsidiary of Accor, brought forth a completely new idea in the hotel industry with the creation of Formule 1, a one-star budget hotel chain that offered no reception staff, no restaurant, and no private bathrooms. Travelers simply inserted a credit card at the entrance to gain access to the rooms, which were plain yet practical and cost $15 a night. Formule 1 hotels appealed to vacationing young people and families of limited financial resources. Costs were kept to a minimum by the use of pre-fabricated construction and staffs of only two to run each 60-room hotel. Occupancy rates were high, and ten Formule 1s were in operation by early 1987, while another 30 were under construction across Europe.

From 1981 to 1986, Accor's revenues doubled to around $2 billion, with net profits of $32 million. Novotel, with hotels in 31 countries, remained the most profitable of Accor's holdings, while Sofitel faced stiff competition in the luxury hotel market, particularly from American firms. Nevertheless, Accor expanded a far swifter rate than its international rivals. The company was the largest operator in Europe. It led the market in France, West Germany, and the Benelux and was expanding in the medium and economy range in Spain, Italy, and Britain with its $75 million investment budget. The company's European base provided three-quarters of its revenue, with more than half coming from hotels and the rest from restaurants, catering, and lunch tickets.

In 1985, Accor took control of Britain's Luncheon Voucher, the company that invented meal tickets, which companies distributed their employees as a benefit. Accor overhauled the company's communications and management systems and restored its market presence through a new sales drive. By 1987, Accor was the world leader in restaurant vouchers for employees, and was exploring similar voucher programs for child care in the United States and groceries in Latin America.

In 1987, Accor exploited another growing market: homes for the elderly. The company's Hotelia homes provided 24-hour medical and nursing care, as well as more traditional hotel services. Also that year, Accor created the successful Parthénon chain of residential hotels in Brazil. In 1988, the company invested in France Quick, ranked second in the French fast-food market, and launched the Free Time fast-food chain. With several partners, Accor then invested in Cipal-Parc Astérix, a theme park north of Paris, based on a Gallic cartoon character, and expressed interest in becoming involved with catering and lodging for the then-projected EuroDisney amusement park. Accor's rapid growth was not without its setbacks, however, as made an unsuccessful bid for the Hilton International Co. and tried unsuccessfully to merge with Club Méditerranée.

In early 1987, the company underwent a large-scale reorganization in order to help it better cope with its diversification of products and its two decades of growth. The group was restructured according to product, so that each chain would have its own general management. Accor was still committed to decentralization and expected the management of each chain to act autonomously as directors of small- or medium-sized companies. Pelisson and Dubrule maintained a flexible, dynamic structure and were committed to remaining accessible. During this reorganization, the company's business continually improved, with 1989 profits up 30 percent from 1988, on sales of $3.6 billion. Accor enjoyed yearly 12 percent earnings-per-share increases from 1983 to 1989. Steady growth allowed the company to sell equity, including a $340 million issue in January 1990.

Accor made a major move into the U.S. market when it purchased the Dallas-based budget hotel chain Motel 6 in 1990 for $1.3 billion. The deal made Accor the second largest hotel company in the world in terms of rooms, 157,000, and represented an attempt by Pelisson and Dubrule to build an American hotel empire to match their extremely successful operation in Europe, where 85 percent of their hotels were located. Accor paid a hefty price to enter the crowded U.S. market and took on an additional $1 billion debt from the seller Kohlberg Kravis Roberts & Co. However, Pelisson and Dubrule were committed to expanding in America, planning to implement the same cost-cutting measures which had worked so well for Formule 1, including credit card payment and limited maintenance staff. The company used a radio ad campaign and trans-Atlantic marketing to lure Europeans to Motel 6. While Accor agreed not to overhaul the management of Motel 6's parent company, Motel 6 G.P. Inc., it did sell a 60 percent stake of Motel 6 to French institutional investors. In 1991, Accor bought 53 Regal Inns and Affordable Inns from RHC Holding Corp. in order to expand Motel 6 into the preeminent budget hotel company in the world. Motel 6's success in the early 1990s was due in part to Accor's financial backing and ability to pay cash, as well as its decision to purchase company-owned properties outright rather than franchising them.

In 1990, with Société Générale de Belgique, Accor bought a 26.7 percent stake in Wagons-Lits, a Belgian company that dominated the European railroad sleeping car business and was the second-largest hotel chain in continental Europe, owning about 300 hotels in Europe, Thailand, and Indonesia. In 1992, the European Community approved Accor's nearly $1 billion bid for a 69.5 percent controlling interest in Wagons-Lits. At the end of the year, Accor became the world leader in its industry with 2,100 hotels, 6,000 restaurants, and 1,000 travel agencies.

With the privatization of industry in Hungary, Accor entered into a partnership in 1993 to buy 51 percent of the hotel company Pannonia from the Hungarian government. Pannonia owned medium-priced hotels in Hungary, Germany, and Austria and gained exclusive rights to develop under Accor in Bulgaria, Albania, Romania, Slovakia, Hungary, and the former Soviet Union and Yugoslavia, as well as to develop the Mercure chain in Austria. Accor also launched the Coralia label in 1993 to distinguish holiday hotels from business hotels. Around 30 Accor hotels in the Mediterranean and Indian Ocean regions added the Coralia label by 1994 and more were planned in the Caribbean, Central America, and Venezuela.

In the early 1990s, Accor subsidiary Atria was developing economic centers in cities and towns, composed of conference centers, offices, and hotels, particularly Novotels and Mercures, in conjunction with local chambers of commerce. The company also had investments in Thalassa International spas and luxury hotels and casinos in France. Accor began a hotel-rebranding strategy in June 1993 to eliminate the Pullman Hotels International chain, which it had acquired in 1991, while expanding its Sofitel International and Mercure brands. Through renovations, the company transformed 27 Pullman hotels into its four-star Sofitel hotels, while another 25 Pullman hotels became Mercure hotels.

Similarly, Accor continued to expand its restaurant business in the early 1990s, with L'Arche cafeterias, L'Écluse winebars, Boeuf Jardinier steakhouses, Café Route highway cafés, Actair airport restaurants, Terminal train station buffets, and Meda's Grills in Spain. The company increased its partnership in France Quick and began building independent ''villas'' for Pizza del Arte. In 1994, Lenôtre, the bakery and catering chain which Accor had developed in six countries, merged with Rosell, a chain specializing in organization, expansion, and management of catering services, for mutual advantages.

With Wagons-Lits, Accor continued its expansion in restaurants and sleeping compartments aboard trains. In the car-rental business, the company shared control of Europcar Interrent International with Volkswagen in 89 countries in Europe, Africa, and the Middle East. In March 1994, Accor merged with Carlson Companies, a leading travel company, to form a network of 4,000 agencies, in 125 countries, worth $10.8 billion. Such mergers and expansions in the mid-1990s were characteristic of Accor's investment strategy, which it planned to continue throughout the 1990s, remaining committed to moving into new markets before the competition and enlarging its empire of hotels, restaurants, travel agencies, and vouchers, while retaining a decentralized and personal management style that extended all the way up to its two chairpersons, Dubrule and Pelisson.

Principal Subsidiaries: Sofitel; Novotel; Mercure; Ibis; Hotelia; Parthénon (Brazil); Lenôtre (93.06%); Formule 1 (70%); Carlson Wagonlit Travel (50%); Europcar Interrent International (50%); Atria (50%); IBL (39.5%); Holpa (Luxemburg; 36.4%); Parc Astérix (14.92%).

Further Reading:

Bergsman, Steve, ''Accor Gains Ground with U.S. Acquisitions,'' *Hotel & Motel Management,* May 27, 1991, pp. 3, 60–1.
Bond, Helen, ''Motel 6 Eyes More Moves,'' *Hotel & Motel Management,* May 27, 1991, pp. 1, 76.
Bruce, Leigh, ''The Two-Headed Chairmanship that Keeps Accor Soaring,'' *International Management,* January 1987, pp. 26–8.
''Circling the Wagons,'' *The Economist,* January 27, 1990.
Jones, Sandra, ''Accor Launches Rebranding, Proposes Venture with Air France,'' *Hotel & Motel Management,* July 3, 1993, p. 11.
Reier, Sharon, ''Bedroom Eyes,'' *Financial World,* June 9, 1992, pp. 56–8.
Riemer, Blanca, ''This Buy-America Bandwagon Could Hit a Few Potholes,'' *Business Week,* July 30, 1990, p. 21.
Toy, Stewart, ''Accor Goes with the Modified American Plan,'' *Business Week,* October 1, 1990, pp. 78–9.

—Jennifer Kerns

Acuson Corporation

1220 Charleston Road
P.O. Box 7393
Mountain View, California 94039-7393
U.S.A.
(415) 969-9112
Fax: (415) 962-8018

Public Company
Incorporated: 1982
Employees: 1,500
Sales: $295 million
Stock Exchanges: New York
SICs: 3845 Electromedical Apparatus

Acuson Corporation is one of the top manufacturers of ultrasound imaging equipment for medical diagnosis. These systems beam low-power, high-frequency sound waves into the body, and the returning echoes are processed as real-time, moving images of internal organs and blood flows. In 1993, Acuson led the radiology segment of the industry, with a market share estimated at 40 to 50 percent, and was strongly competitive in cardiology, ranking second only to Hewlett-Packard.

Founder Samuel Maslak became interested in ultrasound in the early 1970s, when he was a doctoral student at the Massachusetts Institute of Technology. At that time, his wife was pregnant with their second child, and doctors ordered an examination of the fetus using ultrasound to test for intrauterine growth retardation. His daughter turned out to be fine, but Maslak noted that the existing technology was relatively crude. Moreover, he recognized that ultrasound had the potential to give doctors a tremendous amount of information, noninvasively, about the body. Maslak thus found a subject for his dissertation, as well as the keystone for a $300 million company.

After graduating from MIT, Maslak moved to California to work on ultrasound for Hewlett-Packard. While his achievement in creating and patenting a key subsystem of the company's ultrasound system was recognized, Hewlett-Packard did not want to press ahead with additional improvements. However, Maslak believed that much greater advances could be made, and he left the company in December 1978, continuing to investigate ultrasound technology and the potential market for innovative products. Over the next nine months, he supported

himself through a part-time job as a circuit design consultant, drawing on personal savings and home equity as well.

In September 1979, Maslak formed a general partnership with Robert Younge, a colleague at Hewlett-Packard; another engineer, Amin Hanafy, came on board in 1981. Maslak later asserted that instead of aiming at an immediate market introduction, the three spent much of their time thinking about how they could contribute to the industry's development. During this period, they picked up $100,000 in seed money from entrepreneur Karl Johannsmeier, and, late in 1981, the three partners distributed a business plan among several venture capital firms. While all of the firms expressed interest in the company, the partners decided that, besides Johannsmeier, they would limit their outside investors to the firm of Kleiner, Perkins, Caufield & Byers of Palo Alto. Kleiner, Perkins initially invested $2.5 million, raising another $22 million over the next three years. The partners filed incorporation papers in 1982, and the following year Acuson introduced its first ultrasound machine. Acuson gained listing on the New York Stock Exchange in 1986, raising $21 million in an initial public offering.

Describing industry conditions during this time, *Business Week* observed that "the market is nearly saturated, and sales have started to slip," while one of Acuson's competitors characterized the industry as "very difficult . . . to break into, because the mature companies can quickly match any advances that come along." Nevertheless, the fledgling Acuson increased its sales from $3 million in 1983 to $18 million in 1984, while revenues rose 60 percent or more annually, reaching $169 million by 1988. Moreover, following the usual initial losses for a start-up company during this time, Acuson's pretax margins reached 13 percent in 1985, and from 1986 to 1988 they were a superlative 24 to 26 percent. Acuson managed to overcome the odds through the superiority of their product.

Ultrasound was often the physician's imaging technique of choice, because is was noninvasive, easy to use, and relatively inexpensive. Although good for soft tissue, the ultrasound could not penetrate bone or air-filled tissue, and was therefore not used to examine the brain or lungs, for example. However, in a wide variety of applications ultrasound was the first test that doctors ordered, being both the safest—there was no ionizing radiation or toxic dye—and the cheapest.

Given the strong preference for ultrasound testing, Maslak predicted that hospitals and doctors would be willing to pay more—as much as 30 percent more—for superior equipment that produced a clearer, sharper image. Acuson's first offering, the Acuson 128 ultrasound system, was so-named because it was equipped with 128 separate transmit/receive channels for image formation, which enabled it to produce a better picture than existing machines that had only 64 channels.

The Acuson system could utilize more channels because it was based on a hybrid analog/digital computer. While computer technologies had long been used in ultrasound systems to control ancillary functions, like measurements and calculations, in Acuson's machines the image itself was formed in an ultrasound computer under software control. As in photography, conventional ultrasound technology produced images that had much sharper resolution in the focal center of their fields than elsewhere. In contrast, Acuson systems could electronically focus at each point of the field of view, optimize the lens aperture at each focal point, and substantially filter out stray reflected sound ordinarily captured by conventional units. The result was superior pictures that doctors widely praised. Indeed, in some cases it allowed them to make diagnoses that would have been unlikely using conventional equipment. And Acuson systems proved extremely reliable, with up-time of better than 99.9 percent.

The emphasis on computer technology was also essential to the second key factor in Acuson's success: field upgradeability. Every unit that Acuson sold could be upgraded, at the customer's site, to the level of the most advanced current model, simply by adding new software. Although complete upgradeability would appear to act as a drag on sales of new machines, sales of new units continued to rise in the 1980s, since doctors continued to find new applications in which Acuson's products outperformed those of competitors.

Acuson's string of impressive sales increases reflected its commitment to upgrading its technology. Outlays for product development rose from $2 million in 1983 to $18 million in 1988, representing ten to 12 percent of sales for most of this period. In late 1985, Acuson began to market its Doppler option, which measured the velocity of blood flow in the heart and major arteries. Doppler could instantly alert doctors to constricted blood flow in a vessel, helping them determine the extent of the blockage and the need for further intervention. In September 1987, Acuson shipped its first color Doppler imaging system, an important diagnostic tool for physicians since it allowed them to visualize directly the flow of blood, depicted as a color overlay on the standard black and white ultrasound image.

Early on, Acuson established an international presence, setting up operations in the United Kingdom and Germany. Wholly owned sales and service subsidiaries followed in Sweden and Australia in 1986 and in Canada and France in 1987. The company also began to make significant shipments to China and other Asian markets. By 1989, 18 percent of Acuson's sales, $40 million, came from international operations, up 68 percent from the prior year.

That year, Acuson passed several milestones. Cardiology equipment became its second largest segment, after radiology. Acuson employed over 1,000 people worldwide, and sales surged beyond the $200 million level for the first time, rising 35 percent from the prior-year total to $227 million. Profitability remained stunning, with gross, pretax, and net margins at 62, 27, and 17 percent. Net income rose to $38 million, up 40 percent from the prior year and more than double the $17 million recorded in 1987.

In July 1990, Acuson introduced its 128XP, its first new system mainframe since it entered the ultrasound market in 1983. The new model featured Vector Array, which provided a wider field of view in many ultrasound applications where anatomical access to the organ of interest was limited, such as when imaging near ribs, wounds, sutures, or bandages. The new machine also provided for higher resolution and higher quality images. The company continued to post record results; sales for the year totaled $282 million (up 24 percent) and net earnings

were $48 million (up 26 percent). Strong performance continued in 1991, as sales grew 19 percent and earnings 22 percent. During that year, the company introduced the 128XP Xcelerator, which significantly enhanced the capabilities that the 128XP had introduced.

In 1992, Acuson suffered its first significant reversal. During a period of economic recession worldwide, hospitals became more cost-conscious, and, instead of buying new systems, they were making do with older equipment. Moreover, the ultrasound market had been driven by dramatic technological improvements, and while the company's new products represented significant advances, they were not as revolutionary as those it had introduced in the 1980s. Earnings dropped from $59 million to $37 million on basically flat sales of $343 million. Acuson's decline in net income was also a result of its increased expenses for expanding the field sales organization and for product development. Indeed, while other companies cut research and development when business conditions worsened, Acuson continued to increase product development expenditures, regardless of market conditions; outlays more than doubled to $47 million between 1989 and 1992, representing almost 14 percent of total sales.

Acuson's hopes for a quick turnaround in 1993 were dashed when Bill Clinton assumed the U.S. presidency. Clinton's plans for health care reform caused a great deal of uncertainty in the medical sector, and makers of ultrasound equipment—like those of other medical devices—found that hospitals and clinics were postponing significant new purchases until they had a clearer idea of the possible impacts of new health care plans. In this tough business climate, the company decided to cut its work force by 15 percent and took a $12 million charge for restructuring costs. In addition, continuing recessions in Europe and Japan hurt overseas markets, and international sales fell from $88 million to $78 million, or about 26 percent of total revenue. For the year, worldwide sales at Acuson were down 14 percent to $295 million, while earnings tumbled 89 percent to just $4 million.

Acuson also faced the possibility of new competition in the market. By 1993, large medical equipment makers—General Electric, Siemens A.G. of Germany, and Philips Electronics NV of the Netherlands—had not significantly penetrated the ultrasound sector, each having market shares of less than ten percent. However, these firms were beginning to realize that, with hospitals scrambling to cut costs, relatively inexpensive ultrasonic systems would prove more attractive to hard-pressed administrators than their magnetic resonance imaging (MRI) machines and computed topography (CT) scanners. Moreover, ultrasound had already replaced MRI and CT as the preferred imaging method in some applications and was well positioned to challenge the two competing modes in cardiology and abdominal imaging. Thus, the shift of health care dollars to ultrasound promised bigger markets for the industry's leaders in the future. Although smaller companies like Acuson had proved more flexible and quicker to bring new technologies to market, some large firms considered refocusing their operations to compete in the ultrasound market, representing a palpable threat to Acuson.

Nevertheless, Acuson held an advantage as an established and reputable player in the ultrasound industry. Moreover, the company continued to win praise for its steadfast commitment to product development. Despite the contraction in sales and profits in 1993, the company continued to pour funds into research and development, bolstered by its strong, debt-free balance sheet. In fact, its research and development outlays increased to $58 million—up 22 percent from 1992 levels and representing nearly 20 percent of sales. This expenditure proved worthwhile, as Acuson introduced successful new products, like Acoustic Response Technology, which provided a significant enhancement to image quality. With its commitment to innovation, Acuson appeared well positioned to take advantage of potential upturns in the industry's fortunes.

Further Reading:

Aragon, Lawrence, ''Acuson Probes Human Body for Its Growth,'' *The Business Journal (San Jose),* January 7, 1991, p. 1.

Aragon, Lawrence, ''Ultrasound Equipment Makers Hurt by Hospital Spending Cuts,'' *The Business Journal (San Jose),* August 3, 1992, p. 1.

Barrier, Michael, ''The Ultimate in Ultrasound,'' *Nation's Business,* September 1991, pp. 53–54.

Brammer, Rhonda, ''Ultra-Cheap Ultrasound?'' *Barron's,* June 7, 1993, p. 20.

Cone, Edward, ''Ultrasound, Ultraprofitable,'' *Forbes,* October 31, 1988, pp. 142–44.

Naj, Amal Kumar, ''Big Medical-Equipment Makers Try Ultrasound Market,'' *Wall Street Journal,* November 30, 1993, p. B4.

Seligman, Philip, ''Acuson Corp.,'' *Value Line Investment Survey Ratings & Reports,* June 17, 1994, p. 195.

''Ultrasound Is Probing New Markets,'' *Business Week,* May 2, 1983, pp. 35–37.

—Bob Schneider

ADC Telecommunications, Inc.

4900 West 78th Street
Minneapolis, Minnesota 55435
U.S.A.
(612) 938-8080
Fax: (612) 946-3292

Public Company
Incorporated: 1953
Employees: 2,300
Sales: $366.1 million
Stock Exchanges: NASDAQ
SICs: 3661 Telephone & Telegraph Apparatus; 3669
    Communications Equipment Nec; 3679 Electronic
    Components Nec

ADC Telecommunications, Inc. is a Minneapolis-based supplier of networking products and systems for telecommunications, cable television, broadcast, cellular, and enterprise networks. The company is a diversified niche marketer with a unique amalgam of products that enable it to work closely with industry giants as a collaborator, rather than competitor. A major aspect of the company's operations is sales, with direct sales offices located in the United States, Canada, Europe, the Pacific Basin, Australia, and Central and South America. The company was formed as a result of the merging of Audio Development Company (ADC Incorporated) and Magnetic Controls Company.

Audio Development Company was founded by two Bell Laboratory engineers in 1935 as a telecommunications company, creating custom transformers and amplifiers for the radio broadcast industry. ADC also manufactured audiometers (machines that test children's hearing). In 1941, ADC participated in a pivotal project—the development of a sophisticated audio system for Coffman Union at the University of Minnesota. As part of this enterprise, the company produced jacks, plugs, patch cords, and jackfields, foreshadowing its future involvement in the telephone industry.

As a result of the technological development during the postwar era, Magnetic Controls Company was founded and incorporated in Minnesota in 1953. The company produced high quality custom power supplies and magnetic amplifiers and was involved in military and space exploration programs. Magnetic Controls Company merged with ADC Incorporated in 1961,

bringing magnetics and telecommunications together. While the firm used the umbrella name Magnetic Controls Company, ADC's trade name was retained in telecommunications. In 1961, the company advanced its most significant product innovation, the Bantam jack, an amalgam of miniaturized components which became standard for telephone circuit access and patching. The company launched an ongoing involvement with major space missions in 1962, eventually designing and manufacturing sensors for the *Columbia* space shuttle.

The 1960s and 1970s ushered in technological advancement in all areas of telecommunications and data processing. Public and private computer use increased as products became more affordable, and telecommunications evolved into the computer age, with telephonic digital transmission and the expansion of data communications. As an innovator in these fields, the Magnetic Controls Company grew dramatically. In 1970, Charles Denny was encouraged by shareholders to quit his marketing executive job at Honeywell and take over leadership of the company. Under Denny's leadership, the company's earnings, which stood at $6 million in 1970, compounded at 20 percent a year for the next 20 years.

Magnetic Controls Company pioneered yet another industry standard during the 1970s—the digital signal cross-connect (DSX) product line. DSX products access and cross connect digital telephony circuits. The company also developed specialized test boards for long distance telephone companies, and designed and manufactured power conversion equipment for major data processing manufacturers. In addition to the proliferation of new products that addressed the digitalization of the industry, the company continued to introduce telecommunications hardware, including prewired connectorized jackfields and wired assemblies.

By 1981, Magnetic Controls Company had sales of $61.5 million, and by 1983 sales rose to $76.3 million. Nonetheless, the company was struggling. Although its telecommunications products were profitable, the magnetics division, which manufactured transformers and power supplies for mainframe peripherals, lost $1.2 million in fiscal year 1983. The company cut its losses in 1984, selling its magnetics assets and moving forward as solely a telecommunications company. Writing off the magnetics division as a $3.95 million one-time loss, the company incurred a $2.7 million corporate-wide loss for the final quarter of fiscal year 1984.

Having rid itself of its failing magnetics division and having purchased shares of its own stock, the company repositioned itself in the growth industry of telecommunications by investing in acquisitions and trimming expenses. In 1984, Magnetic Controls Company acquired TMS Systems, Inc., a private Massachusetts company that manufactured telephone call management equipment and software. With TMS functioning as a separate subsidiary, Magnetic Controls now sold the TMS product line, in addition to manufacturing telecommunications components and local and remote-access test systems. Also in 1984, the company began subcontracting assembly work in Mexico, where production costs could be lessened. In addition, a computer-based manufacturing resource planning system was implemented to streamline domestic manufacturing operations, and manufacturing personnel grew by approximately 20 percent.

In 1985, the company purchased Aetna Life & Casualty Company's Fiber Optic Component division in Westborough, Massachusetts. The company's focus was now decidedly on telecommunications, and the corporate name was no longer appropriate. Recalling its heritage, in March 1985, Magnetic Controls Company changed its name to ADC Telecommunications and renamed its new subsidiary ADC Advanced Fiber Optics Corp. Four Magnetic Controls employees who were already working on fiber optics development were relocated to join the new Massachusetts staff.

After the disastrous dip in its sales in 1984, the newly named company emerged victorious in 1985. The company focused its efforts on manufacturing, selling, and servicing two groups of telecommunications products: communications connectors and electronics. Rather than trying to compete with the industry giants in its fields, ADC's product strategy was to manufacture and sell products in diversified industries, finding and occupying niches that were not already filled by larger companies. New orders, backlogs, revenues, and operating income soared to new highs in the first quarter. The increased demand for ADC's products was attributed to an energized telecommunications industry, resulting from technological change and the deregulation in long distance telephone service. GTE, Sprint, MCI, and Allnet entered the $40 billion long distance market as major players and potential new customers for ADC Telecommunications.

ADC's customer base in the early 1980s was a diverse pool of public and private networks, with no single customer representing more than 10 percent of 1984 net sales. Foreign buyers accounted for 8 percent of sales that year. ADC's clientele consisted of public telecommunications networks, telephone operating companies and other common carriers, and private telecommunications networks used by large businesses and government agencies. ADC's customer list included IBM, AT&T, the Bell Operating Companies, MCI, GTE, ITT, Allnet, and Northern Telecom.

In 1988, slightly over half of ADC's business was in public networks. ADC products were divided into five categories: network management and control products, termination products, test products, transmission products, and access products. Access products were the most significant category, accounting for approximately 61 percent of sales. Responding to a demonstrated growth area in new technology, ADC took steps to become more involved in the fiberization process of local loops and local area networks (LANs). The company began working on fiber distribution, fiber termination, and broadwidth limiter technology, as well as a fiber loop converter. New products introduced by ADC in 1988 included EDSX (an electronic digital signal cross-connect product) and Series 3000 tester software. The company's international sales had grown from 8 percent in 1980 to 15 percent in 1988, and ADC sought further foreign growth, with marketing efforts in Europe, the Pacific Rim, Canada, Latin America, and the Middle East.

ADC narrowly avoided a buyout when the Lodestar Group, a New York investment fund specializing in mergers and acquisi-

tions, acquired a 6.4 percent stake in the company in 1989. Shares of ADC were $16.75, making the market value of the company $221 million. Lodestar told ADC President Charles Denny that it intended to implement a takeover unless ADC borrowed $200 million and declared a one-time dividend. Denny was furious, feeling that a debt of that magnitude would preclude any investment in future growth for the company. He refused to comply.

Meanwhile, Denny had been pursuing negotiations regarding a potential acquisition, a much better use of ADC resources, in Denny's opinion. In 1989, ADC acquired Kentrox Industries (a maker of products for high-speed private telecommunications networks) for $31 million and restructured its operations into three areas: telecom, diversified markets, and operations. Lodestar did not make good on its threat, but instead sold its shares at a small profit. Over the next four years, those shares would triple in value.

Beginning the 1990s with a new president—Denny's chosen successor and former AT&T executive Bill Cadogan—, ADC entered the video services delivery market, acquiring American Lightwave Systems, Inc., a leading supplier of fiber-optic video transmission equipment for cable operators. ADC purchased the company for $10.7 million, with an agreement to make payments totaling at least $4 million over the next three and a half years. ADC also acquired Telinq Inc. in 1990 and utilized its newly acquired fiber-optics expertise to develop a local loop system with the goal of providing economical fiber directly to private homes. Fiber products contributed approximately $18 million to ADC's total sales in 1990, having doubled every year since 1987. Cadogan directed the company to expand its fiber division toward a goal of $250 million in sales in 1995. Simultaneously, Cadogan mandated that costs be kept low, and that ADC act as an early follower—rather than a leader—in the developing industry.

In 1991, ADC acquired Fibermux, a maker of high-speed, fiber-optic equipment for local area networks (LANs). The company was purchased for $50 million, with a $40 million loan. Fibermux proved so successful an investment for ADC that the loan was paid off by 1993.

In an effort to increase productivity, ADC joined a number of employers implementing plans using company stock to match employee contributions, whereby a portion of the match was tied to company performance. ADC's Retirement Savings Plus Plan, combining a 401(k) and a non-leveraged ESOP, was implemented in 1991 in an effort to provide an employee incentive to improve company performance, while raising long-term stock value and controlling benefits costs. In June of 1990, 84 percent of ADC's 1,395 employees had elected to participate in the voluntary plan.

In 1992, ADC formed a collaborative development venture with Fulcrum Communications in Birmingham, England, devising a system to carry voice and video signals over fiber-optic cable to businesses and residences in North America in a more cost-effective way than that of existing systems. ADC also created Networx, a new transmission platform that integrates cable management and private networking products, using synchronous optical network and the asynchronous transfer mode

(ATM). The cornerstone of Networx was Sonoplex, a multirate, multimedia system that brings fiber to the customer's work or residence site, while making use of existing copper plant. In 1991, ADC had formed a similar partnership with South Central Bell, Mississippi Educational Television, Northern Telecom, IBM Corp., and Apple Computer to create Fibernet, a network linking students at four high schools in Clarksville, Corinth, West Point, and Philadelphia, Mississippi, with teachers at Mississippi State University, Mississippi University for Women, and Mississippi School for Mathematics and Science to create "electronic classrooms."

ADC's—and its competitors'—marketing strategies were dramatically impacted in 1992 by work force reductions and early retirement programs implemented by large local exchange carriers. Seeking to build a stronger relationship with its customers to secure longevity, ADC adopted strategies including simplifying product lines; providing more detailed support materials; and improving ordering, customer service, quality of products, and maintenance support. Sales in 1992 reached $316 million, with shares priced at $56.75.

ADC had become a leader in a growth field in 1993. With the advent of ATM technology and the scrambling of television, computer, and telephone industries to board the information superhighway, telecommunications was booming and wireless telecommunications had a growth rate of 25 percent. The company's products included fiber-optic video, data, and voice transmission systems, and its clients included phone companies, TV broadcasters, and all major cable TV operators. Its new cellular radio switch was undergoing testing by seven large cellular phone operators. ADC continued to market new products, including an Ethernet converter, a coaxial cable delivery option for its Homeworx broadband access system, and a Sonoplex flexible access platform. ADC's Homeworx system was selected by Rochester Telephone Corp. in May of 1993 for a six-month video-on-demand trial.

ADC became an "early follower" into the asynchronous transfer mode (ATM) market, announcing a multiyear agreement with Loral Data Systems for an ATM switch. The ATM switch would create the capability of handling the massive flows of simultaneous high-speed digital information that the industry projected would be generated during the latter half of the 1990s and the twenty-first century, arising from the blending of the communications, computing, and entertainment industries. The company also landed a coup in March of 1994, when Ameritech chose ADC to supply equipment for its $75–$100 million video system, to be developed over the next five years. This $4.4 billion project would bring 70 channels of analog television and 40 channels of digital video to customers, with unlimited program choices and interactive, customer-controllable programming.

In 1994, Charles Denny announced his retirement as chairman of the board, making way for a new generation of executives to lead the company into a rapidly changing telecommunications industry. Bill Cadogan replaced Denny. During Denny's tenure, the company's revenues had grown from $6 million in 1970 to $366 million in 1993, with a market value approaching a billion dollars. Records set in 1993 included ADC's highest annual

order, revenues, gross profits, operating income, net income, and earnings per share.

As ADC Telecommunications, Inc. moves into a new era of leadership, its strategies include a new focus on cable TV and cellular communications, increased international presence, and increased fiber optics and electronic product offerings in the multimedia market. As always, ADC will be an "early follower" in this emerging market, preparing itself to take advantage of expanded opportunities as the multimedia telecommunications market experiences a sweeping convergence of customers, technologies, and products.

Principal Subsidiaries: ADC Telecom Canada Inc.; ADC Europe NV; ADC Telecommunications U.K. Limited; ADC Telecommunications Australia, Pty. Ltd.; ADC Telecomunicaciones Venezuela, S.A.; ADC de Mexico, S.A. de C.V.; ADC Telecommunications Singapore PTE Limited; American Lightwave Systems, Inc.; Fibermux Corporation; Kentrox Industries, Inc.

Further Reading:

"ADC Acquires an LPL Unit," *Wall Street Journal,* July 5, 1990, p. A5.

"ADC Buys Kentrox, Restructures Both," *Telephone Engineer & Management,* December 1, 1989, pp. 22–24.

"ADC Telecommunications Declares Stock Split," *Wall Street Transcript,* March 31, 1986, p. 81327.

Bernier, Paula, "Rochester Tel Taps ADC for Video Trial," *Telephony,* May 31, 1993, pp. 9–10.

Brammer, Rhonda, "Yes, Virginia, There Are Still Bargains," *Barron's,* September 16, 1991, p. 18.

"Broker Reports," *Wall Street Transcript,* May 6, 1985, p. 11784.

"Corporate Profile," Minneapolis: ADC Telecommunications, Inc., 1993.

"Digest of Earnings Reports," *Wall Street Journal,* December 23, 1982, p. 115.

"Digest of Earnings Reports," *Wall Street Journal,* December 30, 1983, p. 129.

Durgin, Hillary, "Redesigning Stock Plans," *Pensions & Investments,* September 17, 1990, pp. 3, 53.

"Go for the Middle," *Forbes,* April 29, 1991, p. 148.

Green, Connie, "Mississippi Tests Electronic Classrooms," *Atlanta Journal & Constitution,* March 21, 1992, p. A3.

"Investments by Lodestar," *New York Times,* September 26, 1989.

Karpinski, Richard, "ADC Unveils Transparent LAN Gear," *Telephony,* April 12, 1993, pp. 14, 16.

Karr, Albert R., and Christina Duff, "Hiring Levels Remain Low, Belying Late-Spring Optimism for a Rebound," *Wall Street Journal,* August 26, 1991, pp. A2, A7.

Lannon, Larry, "ADC is Eyeing a Strategic Shift," *Telephony,* July 18, 1988, pp. 24–26.

"Magnetic Controls Buys Aetna Unit," *Electronic News,* March 25, 1985, p. 14.

"Magnetic Controls Buys TMS Sys.," *Electronic News,* April 16, 1984, p. 40.

"Magnetic Controls Sees Fall in Fiscal '84 Net on Ongoing Operations," *Wall Street Journal,* March 28, 1984, p. 24.

"Magnetic Controls Shares," *Wall Street Journal,* March 16, 1984, p. 17.

"Magnetic Controls to Change Name," *Electronic News,* May 13, 1985, p. 46.

"Mag. Controls to Exit Power Supplies," *Electronic News,* January 2, 1984, p. 14.

"Newsbreaks," *Laser Focus World,* February 1992, p. 13.

Schramm, Sabine, ''No Stunting Growth Stocks,'' *Pensions & Investments,* December 13, 1993, pp. 19–20.

Slutsker, Gary, '' 'I Still Think They're Idiots,' '' *Forbes,* July 19, 1993, pp. 85–86.

''Supercom Vendors Ready New Products,'' *Telephony,* April 19, 1993, pp. 26–30.

Titch, Steven, ''ADC Unveils Loop Product Strategy,'' *Telephony,* February 24, 1992, pp. 9–10.

Van, Jon, ''Ameritech Awards Deal in Video Plan,'' *Chicago Tribune,* March 31, 1994, sec. 3, pp. 1–2.

Wilson, Carol, ''ADC Launches Fiber-Coax Platform,'' *Telephony,* May 24, 1993, pp. 11–12.

——, ''ADC, Loral Link on ATM,'' *Telephony,* May 24, 1993, pp. 12, 14.

——, ''ADC Plots Course in Local Loop,'' *Telephony,* September 17, 1990, p. 9.

——, ''ADC Unveils Fiber Product,'' *Telephony,* June 21, 1993, pp. 12, 14.

——, ''LECS Confront a Serious People Problem,'' *Telephony,* March 9, 1992, p. 76.

—Heidi Feldman

Adobe Systems Incorporated

1585 Charleston Road
P.O. Box 7900
Mountain View, California 94039-7900
U.S.A.
(415) 961-4400
Fax: (415) 961-3769

Public Company
Incorporated: 1982
Employees: 1,000
Sales: $313.5 million
Stock Exchanges: NASDAQ
SICs: 7371 Computer Programming Services; 7372
   Prepackaged Software

Adobe Systems Incorporated develops and provides support service for computer software products and technologies. Since the founding of the company in the early 1980s, Adobe products have had a profound impact on the fields of communications, publishing, and printing. The company's PostScript page description language became the industry standard for the imaging and printing of electronic documents.

Adobe was founded in 1982 by John Warnock and Charles Geschke, both former employees of Xerox Corp.'s Research Center in Palo Alto, California. At Xerox, Warnock conducted interactive graphics research, while Geschke directed computer science and graphics research as the manager of the company's Imaging Sciences Laboratory. In a 1989 interview with *The San Jose Business Journal,* Warnock recalled that he and Geschke were frustrated at Xerox "because of the difficulty in getting our products out of the research stage." Believing in the profitability of an independent venture, they left Xerox to establish their own business, which they named after a creek that ran by their homes in Los Altos, California.

Shortly after it was launched, Adobe introduced PostScript, a powerful computer language that essentially described to a printer or other output device the appearance of an electronic page, including the placement of characters, lines, or images. The introduction of PostScript proved integral to the desktop publishing revolution. With a personal computer and a laser printer equipped with PostScript, users could produce polished, professional-looking documents with high quality graphics. An article in a 1989 issue of *The Los Angeles Times* stated that

Adobe's PostScript "made desktop publishing possible by enabling laser printers, typesetting equipment and other such devices to produce pages integrating text and graphics." Advertising agencies, in particular, soon found the new technology indispensable.

Realizing the wealth of potential uses for the PostScript language, Adobe marketed and licensed PostScript to manufacturers of computers, printers, imagesetters, and film recorders. In 1985, Apple Computer, Inc., maker of the MacIntosh computer, incorporated PostScript for its LaserWriter printer. Shortly thereafter, Apple invested in a 19 percent stake in Adobe, which had reported revenues of $1.7 million the year before. Adobe's rapid growth led to an increase in staff from 27 in 1985 to 54 by 1986.

Over 5,000 PostScript applications were developed and made available for every operating system and hardware configuration. In 1986, Adobe signed an agreement to supply Texas Instruments Inc. with the software for two of its laser printers, producing the first PostScript-equipped printers made for use with IBM-compatible personal computers. In addition, PostScript soon became available for use with minicomputers and mainframes, and it remained the only page description language available for multiple-computer environments, such as corporate office networks. Independent software vendors marketed products that used PostScript to render images and text onto film, slides, and screens, for less money than traditional typesetting methods incurred. Used by corporations, professional publishers, and the U.S. government, PostScript rapidly became one of the most ubiquitous computer languages worldwide.

To supplement the PostScript language system, Adobe introduced a software technology known as Type 1, which provided digital type fonts that could be printed at any resolution. Vendors soon began developing different Type 1 typefaces, until there were more than 15,000, including Japanese and Cyrillic character sets. By the end of 1986, Adobe reported sales of $16 million and income of $3.6 million. During this time, the company was taken public and began expanding its customer base to include IBM and Digital Equipment Corp.

The strategy of marketing and licensing technology to original equipment manufacturers (OEMs) such as Apple became the cornerstone of Adobe's success. In 1986, Apple accounted for 80 percent of Adobe's sales, while the other 20 percent was comprised of retail sales, an area that Adobe moved into the following year.

In 1987, the company introduced the Adobe Illustrator, a design and illustration software program. Enabling users to create high-quality line drawings, the Illustrator became popular among graphic designers, desktop publishers, and technical illustrators. The company also released the Adobe Type Library, which contained a large selection of type fonts, many of which were original typefaces Adobe had created especially for the electronic medium. The Type Library would eventually become the most widely used collection in the industry.

As graphics became more widely used in business communications, Adobe was poised to offer new technologies. The company's introduction of a new version of the Illustrator, designed for use with Microsoft's Windows program, offered pc users an exciting array of graphics tools and helped pave the way for other PostScript language-based graphics packages. By 1988, many industries and universities had adopted the Illustrator standard. Moreover, the Type Library, with 300 typefaces, had become the world's largest collection of typefaces for personal computers.

Having successfully marketed its technology to both Macintosh and IBM, Adobe tackled a new project—developing the Illustrator and the Type Library for the NeXT computer system. Once this was accomplished, the NeXT computer system became the first to implement a new Adobe technology, Display PostScript. This adaptation of the original PostScript was unique in that it communicated directly with the computer's screen, rather than through the printer. Representing a breakthrough in the long struggle for what computer buffs called "WYSIWIG" (What You See Is What You Get), Display PostScript ensured users that images on the screen would be replicated exactly on paper through the printer. Display PostScript also allowed users to manipulate graphics on the screen; rotating, scaling, and skewing could all be performed to suit the user's needs. IBM and Digital Equipment Corp. soon followed NeXT's lead, licensing Display PostScript for their desktop systems.

In 1988, more than 25 PostScript printers and typesetters were on the market, and 20 computer corporations had signed PostScript licensing agreements with Adobe. The company's revenues for 1988 were an impressive $83.5 million, representing a 112 percent increase over revenues of $39.3 million the year before. Moreover, net income for 1988 increased 137 percent, reaching $21 million. During this time, Apple Computer remained the company's biggest customer, accounting for 33 percent of Adobe's revenues. By the following year, Adobe's staff had increased to 300. As one of the fastest-growing software developers, Adobe sought to maintain its position in the industry and foil any potential competitors. Toward this end, Adobe kept its typeface strategies confidential, while continuing to expand into new areas.

At the 1989 MacWorld Exposition in San Francisco, Adobe introduced two new applications. Adobe Streamline software permitted users to reproduce hard-copy graphics on-screen, converting bitmapped images into high quality, PostScript artwork. The second product, Collectors Edition II, could be used to set patterns. Adobe eventually adapted these technologies for IBM and IBM-compatible computers that used the Windows program.

Next on Adobe's agenda was international expansion. The company signed an agreement with Canon Inc. of Japan, under which Canon had full licensing rights to Adobe PostScript. The world's leading manufacturer of laser printers, Canon could bring the PostScript technology to international and multinational customers. To enhance its Type Library, Adobe signed agreements that permitted several companies to develop downloadable typefaces based on Adobe's proprietary technology.

Adobe ended the 1980s on a high note; revenues in 1989 were more than $121 million, and net income reached $33.7 million. That year, the company introduced Adobe Type Manager. This program used Adobe's outline fonts to generate scalable charac-

ters on screen, giving users greater flexibility and better WYSIWYG. The Type Manager also represented an expansion of the Adobe Type Library to 420 typefaces.

Also during this time, Adobe announced that it had acquired all rights to a software program called PhotoShop, an image editing application. PhotoShop, designed especially for artists and desktop publishers, was slated for market in conjunction with the Apple Macintosh. Designed to work with type, line art, and other images, PhotoShop provided users with a complete toolbox for editing, creating, and manipulating images. Other unique PhotoShop features included color correction, retouching, and color separation capabilities.

By the end of the decade, the incredible boom in the computer business was showing signs of subsiding. In a 1989 *Los Angeles Times* interview, Adobe's president, John Warnock, suggested that "if you think you have a formula for success, you'd better figure out how to change it from year to year." Coming up with fresh formulas to ensure continued success was Adobe's focus as the company entered the 1990s. One of its strategies involved developing software that could operate platform-independent, allowing documents to be worked on and sent over many different computers and networks. In other words, Adobe envisioned a world in which a document could be produced on an IBM pc, for example, and sent directly to a MacIntosh.

On the way to realizing that goal, Adobe continued to set the pace for technological developments in the industry. In 1990, Adobe received what was believed to be the first copyright registration for a typeface program. The ITC Garamond font program was registered with the U.S. Copyright Office, a move that suggested that typeface programs could be considered creative works of authorship.

By this time, the Adobe Type Library had burgeoned from the original 12 type families to 134. The downloadable typefaces were available for both IBM and Macintosh personal computers. The Type Manager, Adobe's scalable-font technology, was made available for IBM pcs, as well as UNIX, DOS, and OS/2 systems. Adobe launched PostScript Level 2, which enhanced the PostScript language with new features, such as improved forms handling, color support, and pattern manipulation, making PostScript a more practical and convenient language. One important feature of Level 2 was its use of data compression to reduced transmission times and save disk space by reducing the size of PostScript files on disk. Level 2 also boasted new screening and halftoning technology, better memory, and better printer support features, allowing users to specify color choices and receive those colors in their output.

Late in 1990, Adobe acquired BluePoint Technologies, a leading creator of chips for rendering type. Adobe also signed a new agreement with Apple Computer to work jointly on developing new products using Adobe's PostScript software and Apple's printer technology. Moreover, Adobe announced the creation of Adobe Illustrator for the NeXT system, providing NeXT users with the same powerful design and illustration tool used by owners of MacIntosh and IBM pcs.

Adobe's revenues continued to soar. In 1990, the company hit a new record of $168.7 million in revenues, with net income of $40 million. The following year, Adobe announced that it was developing a new type technology, multiple master typefaces, which would allow users to control the weight, width, visual scale, and style of a single typeface to produce endless variations.

Furthering its strategy of providing numerous licensing agreements throughout the early 1990s, Adobe signed contracts with Lotus Development Corp., Eastman Kodak, Tektronix, Inc., and others. In addition to its updated version of PhotoShop, Adobe was also responsible for another breakthrough in printing technology with the development of the Adobe Type 1 Coprocessor. The new device could render text 25 times faster than the fastest existing printers.

The company celebrated another year of record earnings in 1991. Revenues increased 36 percent to $229.7 million, and income shot up 29 percent to $51.6 million. Founders Charles Geschke and John Warnock received the *MacUser* magazine's John J. Anderson Distinguished Service Award, for "enduring achievement in the Macintosh industry."

Adobe's efforts to create a universal standard for viewing complex documents continued in 1992. That year, the company marked its tenth anniversary and branched out into new ventures. With Hayden, a division of Prentice Hall Computer Publishing, Adobe signed an agreement to create Adobe Press, a joint publishing venture for developing books about graphic arts, Adobe computer applications, and advanced technologies.

During this time, competition in the industry intensified, and Adobe sought new ways to maintain its lead in the industry. Adobe Carousel was the company's first foray into electronic transmission of newspapers, magazines, and other print media. Carousel would allow such materials to be displayed on screen complete with pictures, color, and multiple typefaces.

In June 1992, Adobe President and CEO Charles Geschke was kidnapped. Although he was eventually returned safely and began granting interviews two months after the incident, he refused to discuss details of the abduction. In an interview with *The San Jose Business Journal,* Geschke discussed Adobe's plans for the future. Maintaining that the company was beginning "a long journey down a digital highway," Geschke revealed that its primary mission was to make text, pictures, video, and perhaps sound computer-readable. Toward that end, Adobe acquired OCR Systems, an optical character recognition company that turned scanned documents in to manipulable text.

With the introduction of Adobe Premiere 3.0 for Macintosh in 1993, Adobe entered the fields of video and multimedia. The software enabled users to perform desktop video editing formerly achieved only with expensive equipment. Adobe Premiere featured nonlinear editing, graphics, and special effects.

In 1993, Adobe realized its goal of enabling incompatible computer systems to communicate. Adobe Acrobat software was designed to turn computers into information distributors that would allow Mac users to view a document in its original form, with formatting and graphics intact, even if the document had been created on an IBM. Analysts hailed Acrobat as a tool that could facilitate electronic distribution of everything from interoffice memos to training manuals to magazines. Adobe's revenues for the year rose to $313.4 million, up from $265.9 million in 1992, and net income was reported at $57 million. As the company set its course for the remainder of the decade, further forays into multimedia seemed likely and potentially profitable.

Further Reading:

Collins, LaVon, "Adobe and IBM Sign Joint Marketing Agreement," *Business Wire,* November 16, 1988.

Downing, David, "Adobe Sets New Direction in Digital Type," *Business Wire,* March 5, 1991.

Goldman, James S., "Will Steve Jobs Buy Apple's Former Stake in Adobe Systems?" *The Business Journal—San Jose,* July 10, 1989, p. 1.

Groves, Martha, "Adobe: Redesigning the Future," *Los Angeles Times,* April 30, 1989, p. 9.

Hansen, Brenda, "Adobe Announces Adobe Illustrator for the IBM Personal Computer," *Business Wire,* September 14, 1988.

Leone, Genevieve, "High-Flying Adobe Succeeds in Holding Off Clone Products," *The Business Journal—San Jose,* January 23, 1989, p. 4.

Privett, Cyndi, "Adobe Supplies Software for New Laser Printers," *The Business Journal—San Jose,* May 26, 1986, p. 15.

Prosser, Linda, "Adobe Previews PostScript Level 2," *Business Wire,* June 4, 1990.

Rensbarger, Fran, "Have Desk, Will Publish," *Washington Business Journal,* March 9, 1987, p. 9.

Weber, Jonathan, "Adobe Software Could Start New Era in Computer Communication," *Los Angeles Times,* June 15, 1993, p. 1.

Weisman, Jonathan, "Adobe's Hopes Riding on Carousel," *The Business Journal—San Jose,* August 24, 1992, p. 1.

Young, Margaret, "Adobe Expands Retail Role with Two Distribution Pacts," *The Business Journal—San Jose,* October 19, 1987, p. 11.

—Marinell James

The AES Corporation

1001 N. 19th St.
Arlington, Virginia 22209
U.S.A.
(703) 522-1315
Fax: (703) 528-4510

Public Company
Incorporated: 1981 as Applied Engineering Services, Inc.
Employees: 1,435
Sales: $520 million
Stock Exchanges: NASDAQ
SICs: 4911 Electric Services

One of the largest and fastest growing independent power producers in the United States, The AES Corporation is a builder, owner, and operator of power plants around the world. In the early 1990s AES operated seven power plants in the United States, was conducting activities in 17 foreign nations, and was rapidly expanding into China, India, and several other thriving power markets.

A relatively young company, AES was formed after federal legislation enacted in the late 1970s opened the door to privatized power generating facilities. The industry-renowned Public Utilities Regulation Policies Act (PURPA), passed by Congress in 1978, was originally intended to reduce U.S. utilities' reliance on oil. However, it actually prompted a healthy market for nonutility power generators (NUGs) like AES.

Between the 1930s and the late 1970s, production, transmission, and distribution of electric power was relegated exclusively to vertically integrated, monopolistic utilities. The industry operated under the guidelines of the Public Utility Holding Company Act (PUHCA) of 1935, which essentially barred independents from participating in the generation (and distribution) of power. When the oil crises of the late 1970s arose, however, PURPA was passed as a means of encouraging smaller companies to create and sell alternative (non-oil generated) forms of power to the utilities. In many cases, utilities were required by federal law to purchase power from these new "qualifying facilities," or NUGs.

Two members of the Nixon administration's Federal Energy Administration were Roger Sant and Dennis Bakke. In the years leading up to the passage of PURPA, Sant, who also lectured at

Stanford University's business school, was in charge of energy conservation and the environment, while Bakke, a recent graduate of Harvard's business school, served as Sant's deputy. Following the passage of PURPA, Bakke and Sant teamed up in 1981 to form a consulting firm, Applied Engineering Services, Inc., that advised utilities on low-cost energy planning.

Through their consulting experiences, the two entrepreneurs quickly realized that a much more lucrative niche existed for companies that could generate high-volume, low-cost power for sale to utilities and large power consumers. By drawing on America's vast and stable coal reserves, an efficient independent could undercut large power producers and reap significant returns. Also, in addition to federal mandates abetting the independents, private coal-fired plants would not be subject to the binding state rate regulations that fettered established utilities.

Under PURPA, AES's facilities would have to meet at least one of two specified conditions: they would have to generate less than 80 megawatts of power, a small amount in comparison to some large utility generators; or, each facility would be required to sell both steam and power, a process referred to as cogeneration. By developing large-scale cogeneration plants, Sant and Bakke determined that they could undercut the competition and still capture sizable profits, despite being susceptible to federal price controls.

AES started its power plant building operation in December of 1983. Unable to finance the construction of an entire power generating facility, the company utilized an arrangement similar to that used by real estate developers. It had only limited ownership (and liability) in the project and garnered funding from outside investors. AES also borrowed against long-term contracts to supply utilities with power. Besides its ownership share, AES received compensation for developing and managing the project.

The company's first cogeneration facility, Deepwater, began selling power in June of 1986. Located in Houston, Deepwater was a petroleum coke-fired power plant capable of generating 140 megawatts of power. AES sold Deepwater's electricity to Houston Lighting and Power, the city's state-regulated utility, and an adjacent petrochemical refinery bought the residual steam to help power its operations. Although AES retained a relatively meager ownership interest in the plant, Deepwater provided valuable experience for Sant, the company's CEO, and Bakke, who served as president and chief operating officer.

Even before Deepwater was in operation, AES initiated two other major projects. Begun in September of 1985, the Beaver Valley gas-fired cogeneration facility near Pittsburgh began selling its power in July of 1987. AES was able to sell the electricity from the 120-megawatt plant to West Penn Power, and the steam byproduct was consumed by nearby Arco Chemical. The company's Placerita plant, located in Newhall, California, was also a 120-megawatt plant, but it was powered by natural gas. Started in 1986 and finished in August of 1988, Placerita sold its electricity to Southern California Edison.

By 1989 AES had three facilities up and running, had started construction on two more, and was working to secure financing for several other projects. Furthermore, in the five years that the company had been involved in developing cogeneration facilities, it had boosted its annual revenues to $99 million and swelled its assets to a whopping $861 million. While net income reached only $4 million, future profit expectations were extremely positive—in fact, net income bounded to $16 million in 1990 and $43 million in 1991.

AES' success at attracting funding and customers for its cogeneration projects reflected the overall success of post-PURPA NUGs that were springing up around the nation during the early to mid-1980s. On average, NUGs were generating between 15 and 17 percent returns on invested capital, versus only ten to 12 percent returns for traditional state regulated utilities. As a result, the independent power producers flourished. By the mid-1980s, in fact, the NUGs were building more power generation capacity than the entire U.S. utility industry, and while AES benefitted from generally positive industry trends, the company also outperformed its competitors during the 1980s.

Sant and Bakke attributed much of the company's stellar growth to its unique management structure and style. To the amusement and dismay of some analysts, AES employees held four "shared values": integrity, fairness, fun, and social responsibility. At one point, the Securities and Exchange Commission wanted to identify the values as an investment risk factor. As stated in the company's prospectus, "AES desires that people employed by the company and those people with whom the company interacts have fun in their work. [The company's] goal has been to create and maintain an environment where each person can flourish in the use of his or her gifts and skills and thereby enjoy the time spent at AES."

While some observers snickered at AES's management philosophy, workers took it seriously and the company seemed to be profiting from its unorthodox approach. AES empowered its workers to make most of the day-to-day decisions at its plants, and it organized its labor force into small teams that cooperated to accomplish specific tasks. Its plants had no shift or maintenance supervisors, no personnel department, and almost no middle-level managers or administrators. Workers were hired only after completing a five-step interviewing process that stressed attitudes and values, rather than technical ability. Finally, incentive-based compensation was an integral element of the AES employment creed. "In this organization you don't give orders and have them filter down. It's the opposite of that," explained Dave McMillen, plant manager for AES, in *The Washington Post*. "In this culture, a manager gets his fun from seeing other people succeed."

Sticking with its management style and strategy of growth through development of new cogeneration facilities, AES brought two new plants on line in the early 1990s. Its coal-fired Thames plant in Montville, Connecticut, opened in March of 1990 and began providing a full 180 megawatts of power to Connecticut Light & Power, while selling steam to Stone Container Corp. Not quite a year later, AES opened one of the largest cogeneration facilities in North America, the Shady Point plant in Poteau, Oklahoma. Another coal-fired enterprise, the plant generated an enormous 320 megawatts of power for sale to Oklahoma G&E.

AES had experienced an overall high level of success with its plants—assets had grown to almost $1.4 billion by 1991, sales

had reached $334 million, and total power capacity was at 860 megawatts. However, Sant and Bakke as well as many other independent power industry executives began to question the future viability of the U.S. cogeneration market. In addition to frustrating regulatory requirements that obstructed success in the industry, AES and its competitors were under increasing pressure from government and special interest groups to reduce pollution.

Although AES pointed out that its environmental record was almost beyond reproach, critics of its plants argued that coal-fired generation facilities were a detriment to the environment. The company encountered heated opposition—mostly from local residents—to proposed cogeneration projects in several states, which resulted in substantial losses. In Maine, AES lost $5 million when it had to abandon plans for a facility near the Penobscot River; environmentalists complained that the plant would ruin the river bank. Also, community opposition caused the company to walk away from a plant in Florida that was partially completed.

Given their admirable record of public service and sensitivity to the environment, Sant and Bakke were frustrated by allegations of environmental negligence. Sant, for example, sat on the boards of four environmental organizations in the early 1990s, including the World Wildlife Fund and the Environmental Defense Fund. The company gave the Nature Conservancy a donation sufficient to purchase a rain forest in Paraguay that was large enough to offset the emissions from its Deepwater plant. In 1989 AES also funded a program in Guatemala to plant 52 million trees by the year 2000 in order to offset emissions from its Connecticut plant. "The company really does seem to have a corporate culture that values the environment," a lobbyist for Environmental Action commented in *The Washington Post*.

In addition to environmental problems, AES experienced setbacks in some of its operations during the early 1990s. The company's Houston facility, for example, was near bankruptcy in 1991, unable to meet payments on its loans; AES was stung by falling natural gas prices, which were used to determine the contract price that the utility had to pay for the power it got from the plant. Worse yet, in 1992 AES revealed that employees at its Oklahoma plant had falsified environmental reports given to the Environmental Protection Agency (EPA). Shareholders filed embarrassing class action suits related to that and a similar incident in Florida. "It's as if 11 years of near-perfection are being forgotten because of two unfortunate incidents in a very short period of time," lamented Sant in *The Washington Post*.

Despite these problems, however, AES continued to realize steady and rapid growth during the early 1990s. In 1992 the company opened its sixth U.S. facility—a 180-megawatt, coal-fired plant in Oahu, Hawaii—and that year earnings jumped 31 percent to $56 million from sales of $401 million. Likewise, the company's asset base increased to more than $1.5 billion. Furthermore, AES was beginning to augment its efforts in the increasingly treacherous U.S. market with aggressive expansion overseas. In fact, in June of 1992 AES opened a huge 520-megawatt coal/gas cogeneration facility and a 240-megawatt coal-fired plant, both of which were located in Northern Ireland.

The company also began constructing a massive 660-megawatt gas-fired generator in the United Kingdom.

However, the three European plants were just minor experiments compared to the ambitious international agenda being formulated by AES management going into the mid-1990s. For instance, AES planned to take control of a giant 650-megawatt coal/gas/oil generation facility in Buenos Aires, Argentina, in 1993. By that time the company had also raised over $1 billion to build at least three more plants in Great Britain that would deliver 1,500 megawatts. Most importantly, Sant and Bakke had big plans for China and India, which they believed would require three times as much new generating capacity as the United States by 2003.

AES was backing its Asian projections with action in 1993. A separately traded subsidiary, AES China Generating Co. Ltd., was created to concentrate solely on developing Chinese projects. AES also was actively pursuing a range of new projects in both China and Pakistan. Likewise, new projects were in the works in Italy, Peru, Singapore, Latin America, and former Eastern Bloc countries. AES expected to garner returns as much as two times greater than those available domestically, partially to compensate for increased risk related to investing overseas. ''We're probably spending 90 percent of our development capacity outside the United States,'' Sant estimated in *Forbes*.

Despite the company's heavy emphasis on overseas markets in the mid-1990s, AES was also banking on strong domestic growth through the turn of the century. Government estimates indicated that about 120,000 additional megawatts of capacity would be required by the U.S. power generation industry by the end of the 1990s, while 30,000 megawatts of existing capacity would need to be replaced. Furthermore, proposed changes to PUHCA that would favor independent cogenerators could substantially boost the share of the new capacity supplied by companies like AES.

Meanwhile, AES continued to boost earnings and assets in the mid-1990s. Sales jumped to $519 million in 1993 as profits climbed to $71 million, an impressive 27 percent gain. Total company assets reached $1.7 billion. In addition, at least one respected analyst predicted the company's earnings would grow at a ten to 15 percent clip through 1995, and at a rate of 15 to 20 percent through the end of the decade. Although unexpected environmental legislation or global political instability, among other factors, could significantly diminish these projections, AES management remained optimistic.

Principal Subsidiaries: AES Barbers Point, Inc.; AES Beaver Valley, Inc.; AES Deepwater, Inc.; AES China Generating Co. Ltd.; AES Electric, Ltd. (United Kingdom); AES Shady Point, Inc.; AES Thames, Inc.

Further Reading:

Abrahms, Doug, ''AES Corp. Plans Public Stock Offering,'' *Washington Business Journal,* May 20, 1991, Sec. 1, p. 3.

The AES Corporation, Arlington, VA: AES Corp., 1993.

Crittenden, Ann, ''Generating Competition; Electric Utilities Face a Host of New Rivals,'' *Barron's,* February 3, 1992, pp. 14–15.

Cropper, Carol M., ''A Four-Letter Dirty Word,'' *Forbes,* January 17, 1994, p. 83.

Egan, John, ''Power Plays; Power Generators AES and Destec are Growing Fast, But Some Doubters Remain,'' *Financial World,* February 4, 1992, pp. 28–29.

Hamilton, Martha, ''AES Forms Subsidiary, Declares Stock Split,'' *The Washington Post,* December 18, 1993.

Hinden, Stan, ''Power Plant Firm's Stock Sale Could Generate Big Profits,'' *The Washington Post,* June 24, 1991, Sec. E, p. 33.

Kripalani, Manjeet, ''Electric Utilities,'' *Forbes,* January 3, 1994, pp. 134–136.

——, ''Speculative Utilities,'' *Forbes,* October 26, 1992, p. 234.

Prakash, Snigda, ''Independent Power Producer Gets Contract to Supply Utility,'' *The Washington Post,* February 3, 1992, Sec. 2, p. 7.

Southerland, Daniel, ''AES Sees Powerful Opportunity Overseas,'' *The Washington Post,* June 7, 1993, Sec. E, p. 1.

Tessier, Marie, ''Power Plant Builder Tries to Reenergize Environmental Image,'' *The Washington Post,* July 6, 1992, Sec. E, p. 1.

—Dave Mote

AFLAC Inc.

1932 Wynnton Road
Columbus, Georgia 31999
U.S.A.
(404) 323-3431
Fax: (404) 323-1448

Public Company
Incorporated: 1973
Employees: 3,618
Assets: $11.9 billion
Stock Exchanges: New York Pacific Tokyo
SICs: 6321 Accident & Health Insurance; 4833 Television
   Broadcasting Stations; 6719 Holding Companies, Not
   Elsewhere Classified

Established in April of 1973 as the holding company for a specialized insurance subsidiary, AFLAC now operates more than 25 insurance and broadcasting units throughout the world. The company's chief operating units in Columbus, Georgia, and Japan have developed a number of unique marketing techniques to sell a product that they introduced more than 30 years ago: supplementary cancer expense insurance. The company has been one of the fastest-growing companies in the health insurance industry. AFLAC was founded in 1955 with about $300,000 in capital. The company now has assets in excess of $11 billion.

In 1955 a young lawyer named John B. Amos returned to his hometown of Columbus, Georgia, and with his two brothers, Bill and Paul, and father Shelby founded the American Family Life Assurance Company of Columbus, Georgia. After struggling for three years selling life, health, and accident insurance door-to-door in Georgia and Alabama, Amos decided that AFLAC would do better if it could find a specific market niche. In 1958 he developed a cancer insurance policy based on the polio policies of previous decades, and AFLAC's 150 licensed agents sold 5,810 cancer care policies in the first year.

AFLAC's cancer-care policy was intended to cover the expenses not covered by comprehensive health insurance. John Amos's research reckoned that most comprehensive policies covered only about 70 percent of the costs of cancer treatment. The early policies were designed to cover up to 50 percent of the average cost of cancer treatment, with the extra coverage to help protect against such expenses as travel and loss of income. The

increase of cancer incidence and the high cost of its treatment made the policies popular. By the end of 1959, AFLAC was writing $900,000 in premiums and had begun to operate in Florida.

The company continually looked for new ways to market its policies. In 1964 it began making presentations to groups rather than to individuals and developed the ''cluster-selling'' technique, which was very successful. Agents first approached a company or organization for permission to make a presentation to its employees or members. The agent made a group sales pitch with the implicit endorsement of the company. This method allowed agents to reach more prospects at a given time, and the cooperation of the organization was a selling point. In addition, many companies implemented a payroll deduction plan for the premiums, reducing AFLAC's processing costs. Cluster-selling boosted the company's premiums to $7 million by 1967.

Cluster-selling proved a very effective way to sell cancer insurance. AFLAC built up an aggressive, well-paid sales force that would typically sell to 5 percent of a group's members immediately. The salesman would return later and usually sign up the rest. Years later John Amos explained the technique's success: ''Sooner or later, there's going to be a cancer in the group. If he's insured, he's satisfied, and the word gets around to the rest of them. And if he's not insured, he's sorry, and we get the rest of them.''

During the late 1960s AFLAC greatly increased the number of states in which it did business. An agreement with the Globe Life Insurance Company of Chicago, which was licensed to sell insurance throughout the country, resulted in AFLAC's policies being sold nationwide; Globe sold the policies and AFLAC reinsured them, so that when AFLAC wanted to be licensed itself, it could show state insurance commissioners that its policies were already available in their state and that the company was already making good on claims. Between 1969 and 1971 AFLAC increased the number of states in which it operated from 11 to 42.

In 1973 the American Family Corporation was formed as a holding company for AFLAC. A year later the company's headquarters moved from a modest collection of houses into the new 18-story American Family Center. In June 1974, American Family's shares were listed on the New York Stock Exchange.

During the 1970s a number of companies, seeing AFLAC's success, introduced cancer policies of their own. By the end of the decade there were about 300 insurers selling cancer coverage. AFLAC, however, handily controlled the market, having sold about 60 percent of all cancer policies. The company, in fact, claimed to be the world's fastest-growing insurance company. Between 1972 and 1977 annual premium income rose 294 percent to $205 million, while earnings jumped to $25 million—a 181 percent increase.

Much of AFLAC's success in the mid-1970s was the result of its entry into the rapidly expanding Japanese market. When Chairman John Amos visited Japan in 1970, he was convinced that it would be an excellent market for his cancer-care policies. The Japanese industry, however, was well entrenched, and foreign companies found it virtually impossible to get licensing.

Amos was not deterred and quickly formulated a plan to gain acceptance for his company's product in Japan.

When AFLAC was licensed by Japan's Ministry of Finance to sell insurance in 1974, it was only the second U.S. company to be allowed to do so in more than two decades. Part of AFLAC's success came from the fact that it offered a product that was not yet available from Japanese insurers, at a time when cancer awareness was expanding. Another factor was AFLAC's decision to employ retired workers as its agents, a move that impressed both former co-workers—potential policyholders—and the Ministry of Finance. Also, Amos's choice of company officers was truly inspired: it included many luminaries of the Japanese insurance industry. Furthermore, these executives enlisted the support of the medical community even before AFLAC applied for its license.

Once AFLAC received permission to sell its product, it further moved to insure its own success by signing up large Japanese industrial and financial groups as agents, a variation on the cluster-selling theme. AFLAC paid commissions to the companies, which made the presentations themselves. Huge conglomerates like the Mitsui and Mitsubishi groups and the Dai-Ichi Kangyo and Sanwa banks tapped thousands of their own employees before having to search for customers. The plan was an unprecedented success. Japanese consumers had the money to buy coverage, meticulously paid their premiums, and had a very high rate of policy renewal. By 1987 the Japanese market accounted for two-thirds of AFLAC's total revenues, and 70 percent of aftertax earnings.

Just as AFLAC's cancer insurance began taking off in Japan, the cancer insurance industry came under close scrutiny from a number of consumer groups in the United States. Two congressional committees investigated the product. The major complaints were that cancer insurance had limited value because it did not cover the entire cost of the disease and that the companies selling it, including AFLAC, used hard-sell tactics that exploited fear of cancer, particularly in elderly people.

John Amos was characteristically aggressive in defense of his company and its product. In 1979 AFLAC sued the American Broadcasting Company for alleged damages that resulted from a segment on insurance fraud on the network's *World News Tonight* program. A similar lawsuit was filed against *Changing Times* magazine several months later.

In June of 1980 John Amos appeared before the Senate Subcommittee on Antitrust and Monopoly. A Senate aide described the scene to *Barron's* (July 28, 1980): ''Amos sat with an attorney on each side of him and four corporate vice presidents behind. There were public relations people handing out press kits by the door. They brought their own easels to display a bunch of charts. The hearing room was packed with sales agents and satisfied policyholders from every state. There were four senators there—Hatch, Laxalt, Leahy, and Thurmond—to introduce their satisfied constituents. There was applause and cheers from the audience at every statement Amos made, and groans every time [Senator] Metzenbaum spoke.''

The Metzenbaum committee's report, a study from the Federal Trade Commission, another from the Massachusetts Department of Insurance, and several independent reports all suggested that cancer insurance was not a good buy because it covered only about a third of the actual costs of the disease, left a policyholder uncovered if struck by any other disease, and had a high premium relative to benefits.

AFLAC pointed out that in spite of all the controversy millions of informed customers wanted the coverage and continued to buy it. On the subject of fear being used to make sales, John Amos commented, ''All insurance is sold on fear.'' By the time the controversy began to die down in 1982, Missouri, New York, New Jersey, and Connecticut had all placed restrictions on the sale of dread-disease policies.

AFLAC had, meanwhile been building a chain of television and radio stations in the southern United States. In 1978, as the company passed the $1 billion mark in assets, AFLAC acquired WYEA-TV in Columbus, Georgia, and an NBC affiliate in Huntsville, Alabama. In 1979 two CBS affiliates were acquired, in Cape Girardeau, Missouri, and Savannah, Georgia. A year later the Black Hawk Broadcasting Group, which consisted of two Iowa NBC affiliates, was purchased for $34.2 million.

Throughout the 1980s AFLAC continued to deal in media-oriented companies. In 1981 the group sold WYEA-TV to remain flexible within FCC regulations at a gain of about $1 million. Communicorp, an advertising and print media subsidiary, was also formed that year. In 1982 the cable franchises acquired in the Black Hawk Broadcasting deal were sold to CBS for a profit. In 1984 the Howard Printing Company was purchased for 56,952 shares and merged into Communicorp. Several more television stations were acquired in the latter half of the decade: WITN-TV in Washington-New Bern, North Carolina, for $25 million, in 1985; a Baton Rouge, Louisiana, CBS station for $59 million, in 1988; and an ABC station in Columbus, Georgia, in 1989, for $45 million. By the end of the 1980s, the broadcasting group was contributing about 5 percent of AFLAC's total revenues.

In 1983 several executive changes took place at AFLAC. Paul Amos, John Amos's brother, was moved up from president—a position he had held since his brother Bill's retirement in 1978—to vice chairman. Sal Diaz-Verson became president of the holding company, and Daniel P. Amos was elected president of AFLAC. Daniel Amos, John Amos's nephew, became deputy CEO in 1988, in preparation for his eventual promotion to CEO.

AFLAC's business in Japan became more significant throughout the 1980s. By 1986 AFLAC Japan's policies increased to 5.4 million, compared to 731,000 a decade earlier. In 1981 cancer became the leading cause of death in Japan, and while cancer insurance was criticized in the United States, it was welcomed by the Japanese, whose general health insurance picture was very different. Health insurance was written under the country's nationalized medicine program, and certain diseases were not covered. A co-payment of at least 10 percent was also a standard feature. Supplemental dread-disease policies, therefore, became extremely popular, particularly with cancer, where many costs are non-medical. Cancer insurance was widely accepted, and AFLAC Japan controlled 88 percent of the market by 1988.

While AFLAC's success in Japan has been stunning, there are certain pitfalls. Japanese regulations prevent the repatriation of Japanese earnings to the United States. The company earns 70 percent of its revenues in Japan and cannot invest that money outside the country. Also, with such a large percentage of its income earned in yen, fluctuation in the value of the foreign currency is a threat to AFLAC's bottom line.

While the overwhelming majority of AFLAC's revenues have been, and continue to be, generated by cancer insurance, the company has introduced a number of other products over the years. In 1970 intensive-care coverage was introduced. Supplemental senility policies were introduced in Japan in 1984, providing coverage for Alzheimer's disease and three other forms of senility. In 1985 a universal life insurance policy was introduced, followed by a Medicare supplemental policy a year later. In 1988 two new lines were introduced: accident insurance and advance life insurance, which allowed a policyholder to receive 25 percent of death benefits upon diagnosis of heart attack, internal cancer, or stroke, leaving 75 percent for beneficiaries. In 1990 AFLAC launched Super Cancer, a new upgraded policy for Japanese customers. Super Cancer offered a higher daily benefit than did the previously available product, as well as an additional lump sum payment for first occurrences. The policy also covered outpatient services.

AFLAC's earnings grew from $117 million on $2.7 billion in revenue in 1990 to $149 million on revenues of $3.3 billion in 1991. By that time, the company's share of the Japanese market for cancer insurance had grown to 90 percent, with 9.9 million policies covering 25 million people (one fifth of Japan's population) in force. On the first day of 1992, holding company American Family Corporation changed its name officially to AFLAC Inc. The company turned in record performances again that year, as total revenue reached the $4 billion mark for the first time. In May of 1992 AFLAC introduced a new product called Super Care, designed to meet the long-term needs of Japan's rapidly growing elderly population. Super Care was AFLAC's first non-cancer product offered in Japan. Among Super Care's benefits were nursing home coverage and a death benefit. Meanwhile, AFLAC's market share for supplemental cancer policies in Japan continued to creep up steadily, reaching 94 percent in 1992. During that year, 88 percent of AFLAC's new cancer policy sales in Japan were made through corporate-sponsored payroll deduction plans.

In spite of the popularity of cancer policies in Japan, cancer policies accounted for less than a third of the new AFLAC policies sold in the United States in 1992. The balance of U.S. sales came from supplemental health care protection other than for cancer. One new market that AFLAC began attempting to tap in the United States around this time was HMO members. As employers stared asking workers to contribute as much as 30 percent of the cost of their HMO membership, AFLAC began approaching HMOs about offering AFLAC's supplemental policies to their subscribers.

Preliminary figures for 1993 showed another big gain in company revenue, as much as 25 percent from the previous year. Toward the end of the year, AFLAC initiated a joint marketing agreement with CIGNA Corporation. Under the agreement, the two companies would cooperate in the development of group long-term disability products, which would then be marketed under the AFLAC name.

During the late 1980s founder John Amos himself suffered from cancer. Amos died in 1990 and was succeeded as chairman by his brother, Paul Amos. Paul Amos's son, Daniel P. Amos, acquired the duties of CEO and chief operating officer of AFLAC. John Amos had built a huge financial corporation out of a small market niche. With assets of over $11 billion, the company's future looks secure, despite the deregulation of the Japanese insurance industry scheduled for 1995.

Principal Subsidiaries: American Family Life Assurance Company of Columbus; AFLAC Japan; AFLAC International, Inc.; American Family Broadcast Group, Inc.; Communicorp, Inc.

Further Reading:

"American Family: Big Profits from Cancer Insurance," *Dun's Review,* March 1978.

Englade, Kenneth F., "The First American Family of Japan," *Across the Board,* March 1987.

Hardman, Adrienne, "American Sumo," *Financial World,* August 3, 1993, pp. 42–43.

Lohr, Steve, "Under the Wing of Japan Inc., A Fledgling Enterprise Soared," *New York Times,* January 15, 1992, p. A1.

McMennamin, Breeze, " 'A Heck of A Sales Force,' " *Forbes,* March 1, 1977.

Montgomery, Leland, "AFLAC: Good Book, Bad Chapter," *Financial World,* October 13, 1992, p. 16.

—updated by Robert R. Jacobson

Air Products and Chemicals, Inc.

7201 Hamilton Boulevard
P.O. Box 538
Allentown, Pennsylvania 18105-1501
U.S.A.
(610) 481-4911
Fax: (610) 481-6642

Public Company
Incorporated: 1940 as Industrial Gas Equipment Co.
Employees: 14,075
Sales: $3.33 billion
Stock Exchanges: New York Pacific
SICs: 2813 Industrial Gases; 2821 Plastics Materials and
   Resins; 2865 Cyclic Crudes and Intermediates; 2869
   Industrial Organic Chemicals, Nec.; 2891 Adhesives and
   Sealants; 3443 Fabricated Plate Work (Boiler Shops)

Air Products and Chemicals, Inc. is the world's third largest producer of industrial, specialty, and medical gases such as oxygen, nitrogen, argon, and hydrogen. Industrial gases contribute over half of the company's sales and nearly three-fourths of its profits. The company's chemicals and intermediates segment, which comprises about one-third of sales, claims U.S. leadership in polyurethanes, polymers, performance, and industrial segments. Air Products is also a fully-integrated supplier of industrial and specialty gases, equipment, and technical services to the electronics industry; the company dominated this market, with over one-fourth of the electronics industry's sales in the early 1990s. In the late 1980s and early 1990s, Air Products diversified into environmental energy systems, including waste-to-energy projects, tire recycling, and flue-gas desulfurization. Geographic expansion into Europe and the Pacific Rim has also opened new opportunities to the firm. The creation, development, and growth of Air Products has been characterized by innovation. As former company president Dexter F. Baker noted in *Research Management* magazine in 1986, the company found success through the employment of four fundamental criteria: "finding a market that is not being well-satisfied, creating a superior technical solution, commercializing the solution, and acting as an investor in one's own new creative solution."

Air Products founder Leonard Parker Pool began his career as a teenager selling oxygen to industrial customers, and, by the age of 30, he was district manager for Compressed Industrial Gases.

In 1938, when Pool began his work, the oxygen market was dominated by such large companies as Linde A.G. and the Air Reduction Company, which avoided price wars and did not intrude in each other's sales territory. Oxygen was inexpensive to distill, and the raw material from which it is distilled, air, is free, so the chief costs involved shipping oxygen in heavy containers. Pool's idea was to distill oxygen in the customer's plant; however, the cost of this plan would have been prohibitive unless a cheap oxygen generator could be designed.

Pool, the son of a boiler-maker, had only a high school education, so, to design the generator he needed, he hired a young engineer by the name of Frank Pavlis to work with him. Pool's and Pavlis's design was revolutionary because it used a compressor lubricated with liquid oxygen and graphite. At that time, competitor compressors were lubricated with water due to the fear that the compressed oxygen, in contact with a lubricating oil, would ignite when exposed to the smallest spark. When oxygen was compressed using water, several steps were required to then remove the water from the oxygen. The new generator, however, could skip these steps and, as a result, it was less expensive to build, install, and maintain.

By 1940, Pool and Pavlis had a functioning generator. Pool quit his job, sold his insurance policy, and borrowed all the money that his wife—a schoolteacher—had saved. With this capital, he founded Air Products Inc. and opened shop in a former mortuary. In these last years of the Great Depression, the American business climate was dismal, and Pool had a great deal of difficulty selling his generators.

With the onset of World War II, however, Air Products began to thrive, manufacturing mobile oxygen generators for the armed services and heavy industry. When the war ended, Air Products lost many of its clients and was forced to aggressively pursue new accounts. Although Air Products could provide oxygen at a cost 25 percent lower than its competitors, customers were slow to take advantage of the new system, which was offered through five- to ten-year leasing agreements, under which Air Products would maintain the generator and teach employees how to operate it. While customers found the idea appealing, many were locked into long-term contracts with a company that shipped oxygen to their plants.

In desperation, Pool traveled to Pittsburgh and used a sales technique called "door-stepping" to win a major contract with Weirton Steel. This sales technique involved staying at the customer's plant until the contract was signed. Pool said years later, "God, we just *lived* at Weirton Steel when we learned they were interested in our proposition." Indeed, Weirton was practically Air Product's only customer at that time.

In need of funds to construct a new plant, Air Products sent out a prospectus to potential investors. Pool acknowledged the company's inexperience, stating that Air Products "has no background in prewar civil business," and that in competing "by a new method of distribution in a well-established field against experienced competitors who have much greater resources" Air Products expected "to operate at a loss following the completion of its government contracts." The company's boldness and candor apparently impressed investors, and the necessary $300,000 was raised. Soon, Air Products had installed generators at several chemical companies and had built a huge generator for Weirton Steel, a generator 100 times larger than any that had been built before.

Pool attributed a large part of his company's success to his "tiger pack," a group of aggressive young engineers serving as sales staff at Air Products. Pool maintained a close watch over operations, and, although he became known for his sense of humor and his commitment to his employees, he was also capable of dealing out a tongue-lashing to anyone who mislead a customer or lost a sale.

In the mid-1950s, Air Products profited from the launching of the first Soviet Sputnik, which American scientists surmised was powered by liquid hydrogen. When the U.S. defense department wanted liquid hydrogen, Air Products was asked to supply it. As a security precaution, new Air Products Company plants were provided with such code names as "Baby-Bear" and "Project Rover"; one large plant was disguised as the "Apix Fertilizer Company."

In addition to the production of liquid hydrogen, Air Products also branched out into new areas of chemistry like fluorine chemistry and cryogenics (the science of ultra-low temperatures). The company's oxygen business also continued to grow. The company no longer leased generators but built multi-million dollar operations near major customers, including Ford Motor Co. and U.S. Steel, selling any excess capacity to smaller customers.

Throughout the 1960s, Air Products thrived; sales rose 400 percent, while earnings rose 500 percent. The expansion into merchant gas (gas sold in tanks) proved profitable for the company, although Air Products was a latecomer to the field. Air Products used its late entrance into the field to its advantage by conceding the saturated markets to its well established rivals, Linde and Air Reduction Co., seeking out smaller, more receptive markets instead. In fact, as Air Products saw its fortunes growing, competitors like Linde experienced decreased profits.

During this time, oxygen-fired furnaces became a popular alternative to the hearth-style furnaces used in the steel-making industry, increasing oxygen consumption considerably. Nitrogen, another Air Products specialty, was also in demand as a refrigerant. Air Products also began selling the implements necessary to handling gases, such as welding tools, anesthesia equipment and cryogenic systems. Gases and gas-related equipment accounted for approximately three-fourths of Air Product's profits during the 1960s; the remainder came from chemicals and engineering services.

The diversification of Air Products into chemicals began in 1962 with the company's purchase of Houdry Chemicals and, later, Air Company, a specialty chemical company. When the Air Company was purchased by Air Products, it was losing money. To achieve a turnaround, Air Products took Air Company's acetylic chemicals and made them into specialty chemicals which fetched a higher price; the plant became profitable almost immediately. In 1969, Air Products purchased Escambia Chemicals, paying a cash price well below its market value. Escambia's attraction lay in a product called DABCO, regarded as the best catalyst for making urethane foam.

Due to the energy crisis and a recession, the 1970s was a difficult period for many chemical companies. While Air Products could not sustain the phenomenal growth it experienced in the 1960s, its annual sales and profits increased at least nine percent and sometimes as high as 20 percent. During this time, the company held a strong position in industrial gases both in the United States and abroad, as its gases were used by virtually every major industry. The chemical division performed erratically, however, and, during the recession, its engineering services division, which designed pipelines and plants, yielded disappointing results. Nevertheless, Air Products' industrial gases kept the company afloat.

The energy crisis had both positive and negative effects on Air Products. The industrial gases division, which consumed a large amount of electricity, was sensitive to rising utility rates. However, as the price of organic fuels rose, oxygen became a more popular fuel. The increased production costs of petro-chemicals and plastics were offset by higher demand for cryogenic equipment and gases to liquify natural gas. Like many other successful chemical companies, Air Products was thus able to benefit from the high energy prices in some cases.

During this time, the OPEC oil embargo convinced company management to invest in synthetic fuels. In 1980, Air Products, Wheelbraton Fry Inc., the state of Kentucky, and the U.S. Department of Energy formed a joint venture to produce a high energy, low pollution fuel from coal. Air Products invested $45 million in the project, while the bulk of the money, $748 million, came from the federal government. As none of the various synthetic fuel projects were successful, Air Products' only consolation was the high levels of oxygen consumed in the unsuccessful venture. Still, Air Products remained interested in energy development. In 1985, the company bought a methane recovery plant and accelerated development of a plant that converted garbage to steam and electricity.

Despite the disappointment of the synfuel project, Air Products sales grew an average of 20 percent per year throughout the 1970s. A 12-year, $281 million contract to supply liquid hydrogen for the space shuttle bolstered earnings as did the discovery of expanded uses for industrial gases. For instance, the food industry increased its use of hydrogen for hydrogenating vegetable oils, and flash-freezing, a process which required nitrogen, became an increasingly more popular technique.

In the 1970s and the early 1980s, Air Products, like other highly successful chemical companies of the same size, became concerned with having a product that could be used by a myriad of industries, in order to avoid overdependance on staple products linked to cyclical industries. Toward this end, Air Products focused on marketing oxygen and industrial gases to a wide variety of clients, so that dramatic downturns in an industry—such as steel manufacturing—would not be fatal to the company.

Also during this time, Air Products established a reputation for hiring highly competent, professional engineers, chemists, and business staff. Rather than assuming responsibility for such hirings, company president Edward Donley delegated the job to the vice-presidents and line managers, whom, according to Donley, were better judges of an applicant's potential than a professional recruiter. The applicants hired by Air Products sometimes spent up to three years working in different departments of their choice, in order to decide where their skills would be best employed. Air Products also believed the exposure of engineers and chemists to management positions would prove vital to future success.

Air Products also demonstrated a commitment to the health and safety of its workers. In the 1970s, when three employees died from PVC induced cancer, Air Products periodically tested 492 other workers at two plants for possible exposure, and steps were taken to minimize health risks. In the late 1980s and early 1990s, the company developed ''Responsible Care'' objectives to promote safety, environmentalism, and health at its facilities. At the same time, however, the company initiated a legal challenge to industry regulations, claiming that many were unfeasible to implement.

In 1986, Air Products embarked on a ten-year strategic plan that added a third core business, environment-energy, and focused on globalization of the firm. Between 1986 and 1993, the company invested $1 billion in European facilities as part of its strategy to replace older, less efficient plants, add new production capacity, and create new products. Significant investments in Asia resulted in the construction of seven industrial gas plants by 1992. The company also gained access to significant markets by buying mid-size competitors and entering into joint ventures.

By 1990, investments of $1.2 billion in the environmental-energy systems segment had expanded that division to include: a refuse-fired cogeneration facility; the American REF-FUEL joint venture with Browning-Ferris for building waste-to-energy facilities; a joint venture with Mitsubishi Heavy Industries to market flue gas desulfurization systems; and a methane gas reclamation business for landfills. Air Products' tire recycling program, which was undertaken in 1988, came to fruition in the early 1990s, as the rubber recovered from scrap tires promised to reduce the environmental and health hazards presented by scrap tires and offered cost savings for the production of rubberized asphalt, shoe soles, carpet underlay, and other products. Although Air Products faced well-established competition in the environmental arena, the rapid expansion of that market promised significant returns.

During this time, Air Products' earnings per share increased about 20 percent per year, double the rate of Standard & Poor's industrial index. In 1992, Harold A. Wagner, who had been a key proponent of the strategic plan, replaced Dexter Baker as chairperson and chief executive officer, and Air Products launched a two-year program to consolidate and restructure its $1.1 billion chemical business. The reorganization streamlined the chemicals segment from four to three divisions, realigned its management, and reduced its work force by seven to ten percent, or 1,000 to 1,400 jobs. In 1993, Air Products achieved record cash flows, sold record volumes of industrial gases and chemicals, and ranked as the third largest supplier of industrial gases in the world. The company planned to continue expanding its global investment programs throughout the 1990s.

Principal Subsidiaries: Air Products International Corp.; Air Products Manufacturing Corp.; Air Products REF-FUEL Holdings Corp.; Air Products REF-FUEL of Essex County, Inc.; Air Products REF-FUEL of Hempstead, Inc.; APCI (U.K.), Inc.; GSF Energy Inc.; Permea, Inc.; Prodair Corp.; Stearns-Catalytic Corp.; Air Products S.A. (France); Air Products Management S.A. (Belgium); Air Products Gases Industriais Ltda. (Brazil); Air Products Canada; Air Products Japan Inc.; Prodair S.A.; Air Products Nederland B.V.; Air Products plc (United Kingdom); Air Products (GB) Ltd.; Air Products (U.K.) Ltd.; Air Products (B.R) Ltd.; Anchor Chemical Group plc; Air Products GmbH (Germany).

Further Reading:

Butrica, Andrew J., *Out of Thin Air: A History of Air Products and Chemicals, Inc., 1940–1990,* New York: Praeger, 1990.
Storck, William J., ''Air Products on Course in Ambitious Strategic Plan,'' *Chemical & Engineering News,* October 5, 1992, pp. 44–46.
Swaim, Will, ''Air to the Throne,'' *World Trade,* February 1993, pp. 66–68.

—updated by April Dougal Gasbarre

Aldus Corporation

41 First Avenue South
Seattle, Washington 98104-2871
U.S.A.
(206) 622-5500
Fax: (206) 343-4225

Public Company
Incorporated: 1984
Employees: 1007
Sales: $174.1 million
Stock Exchanges: New York
SICs: 7372 Prepackaged Software

Aldus Corporation revolutionized the use of personal computers when it introduced its PageMaker program in 1985, virtually creating the desktop publishing industry. Although the company has not been able to match the inventiveness of its original program, it is a major American producer of desktop publishing and graphics software, selling a dozen different computer programs in 19 languages in 50 different countries. Since the mid-1980s, the company has grown steadily, but has continued to rely heavily on its flagship program into the 1990s.

Aldus was founded in late February 1984 by Paul Brainerd. Brainerd had earned a graduate degree in journalism at the University of Minnesota before taking a job in production at the *Minneapolis Star and Tribune.* In 1980 he joined Atex, a company that sold computer-assisted publishing equipment to the newspaper industry. In 1983, this company was purchased by Eastman Kodak, which decided to close the plant in Redmond, Washington, where Brainerd was working. Rather than transfer to another location, Brainerd and five other Atex engineers decided to stay in the Pacific Northwest and start up their own company.

After selling his Atex stock, Brainerd used the $100,000 he had earned to found the new enterprise. He and his partners decided to name their company Aldus, after Aldus Manutius, a fifteenth-century Venetian pioneer in publishing. Manutius had standardized the rules of punctuation and also invented italic type. He went on to found the first modern publishing house, the Aldine Press.

The founders of Aldus set out to produce a computer software program that would allow its users to "paste up" text and graphics together on a screen, creating a product that closely resembled a page made in the conventional fashion, with cutting and pasting. When a page was completed, it would then be printed out all at once on a computer laser printer. They aimed for a process that would be relatively easy to use and far less expensive than conventional printing processes. Brainerd called this innovation "desktop publishing." This advance was made possible by the graphic capabilities of the newly introduced Macintosh computer, marketed by Apple Computer Inc., so Brainerd and his partners designed their program explicitly for use on the Macintosh.

After 16 months of work, Aldus released PageMaker in July of 1985. With this software program, users could create professional-quality newspapers, newsletters, brochures, pamphlets, and other graphic products. Retailing for $495, PageMaker opened up a whole new field of possibilities for use of the personal computer (PC). The program's popularity soon began to drive sales of the Macintosh computer.

The interdependency of Aldus and Apple products spurred the companies' close cooperation. Aldus helped Apple to market its hardware to customers who wanted desktop publishing capabilities. In return, Apple featured Aldus's software in much of its advertising, and also helped the fledgling company distribute its program.

In October 1985, Aldus released an international version of PageMaker; half a year later, it began to market an upgraded version of the program, PageMaker 1.2. Demand for its unique software had grown rapidly, and Aldus anticipated sales of $10 million for 1986. Aldus took steps to expand its software offerings beyond the market made up by Macintosh owners to reach the vast majority of computer users who relied on IBM-compatible PCs. In October 1986, Aldus announced an agreement with two other companies to create a desktop publishing package. The Hewlett-Packard Company agreed to supply its Vectra computers and its LaserJet printers, and the Microsoft Corporation contributed its Windows operating system and its Microsoft Word word processing program. Together, the three companies agreed to spend about $2 million promoting the new system.

In January 1987, these efforts bore fruit when Aldus introduced its IBM-compatible PageMaker software for use with Windows operating systems. IBM later endorsed PageMaker as part of its own desktop publishing program. In addition, in December 1986 Aldus had finalized an agreement with computer maker Wang Laboratories to distribute Aldus software. Three months later, it also linked up with the Digital Equipment company to sell Aldus programs for use on Digital's VAX computers.

After successfully making the PageMaker program accessible to all kinds of computers, Aldus decided to offer its program to computer users outside the United States. In January 1987, Aldus joined with a partner to form Aldus Scotland, Ltd., of which it owned 30 percent. The purpose of this venture was to market Aldus products throughout the United Kingdom and Europe. Nine months later, Aldus took one step toward further expansion when it converted Aldus Scotland, Ltd. to Aldus Europe, Ltd. Based in Craigcrook Castle, a sixteenth-century turreted stronghold outside Edinburgh, Scotland, Aldus had established itself as Europe's leading producer of desktop publishing software by the spring of 1988. Controlling nearly half of the British, French, and German markets for these products, PageMaker was the world's fourth most popular software program.

By March 31, 1987, annual sales of PageMaker had risen to $18.4 million, an increase of more than 100 percent over the preceding 12 months. In light of this dramatic expansion, Aldus offered shares in the company to the public for the first time in June 1987. Although the company had initially presented its stock at $14 to $16 a share, interest among investors proved so strong that the price was raised to $20. Enthusiasm for Aldus's prospects was so high that this price had nearly doubled by the end of the first day of trading. Overall, more than 2.2 million shares were sold, reflecting confidence in Aldus's strong position in the desktop publishing market. As the leader in that field, Aldus had sold more than 60,000 PageMaker programs for Macintosh.

Despite the popularity of the PageMaker, Aldus's status as a single-product company caused some concern among investors. The company needed to move beyond PageMaker to other products and functions in order to continue its rapid growth and remain profitable. In November 1987, Aldus took its first step towards diversifying its product offerings when it bought the distribution rights to FreeHand, a drawing program which produced high-quality graphics. In addition, Aldus introduced SnapShot, an instant electronic photography software package for use on personal computers.

By the end of the year, sales of the company's products had reached $39.5 million, and profits had tripled to $7.2 million. A third of those revenues had come from overseas sales, primarily in Europe, Australia, and New Zealand—areas where English language capabilities were strong and Macintosh computers were available. Aldus hoped to increase its international sales to 40 percent of its gross by adding products customized for foreign markets, such as a Japanese language version of Page-Maker.

Even though new products were introduced, the company relied heavily on sales of PageMaker. In January 1988, sales of the PageMaker program topped 200,000, with 90,000 copies of the program shipped in the preceding year. That spring, Aldus introduced updated versions of PageMaker for use on the Macintosh and on IBM-compatible PCs. With this advance, Aldus maintained its dominant grip on the desktop publishing market.

In October 1988, in an effort to protect their copyrights and to fight international software piracy, Aldus joined with four other computer software marketers to form the Business Software Association. One month later, Aldus introduced another product that would be vulnerable to such abuses, Aldus Persuasion, to be used on the Macintosh. This program, which the company bought the marketing and development rights to, marked Aldus's first departure from the desktop publishing field. Persuasion was designed as presentation software, to combine text and graphics in slides, transparencies for use on an overhead projector, and printed handouts for use during business meetings.

Despite efforts to diversify its offerings, Aldus's growth slowed as PageMaker encountered more and more competition. Not only had other companies had a chance to catch up to Aldus's innovations but the structure of the industry had also shifted. On the low end of the market, ordinary word processing programs had become powerful enough to incorporate more and more of the desktop publishing features that had originally been offered only through PageMaker. At the opposite end, other companies were offering packages popular with publishers and other corporate clients. Aldus's days of steady expansion on the strength of one program's popularity were over.

Aldus reacted sluggishly to the new industry challenges. The company was slow to bring new products to market, and much-needed updates of its old programs were delayed. To compound the company's problems, two key members of Aldus's management team, a marketing executive and the software designer who had originally created PageMaker, quit the company in May 1989 because they were unhappy with the overly aggressive and interfering management style of company founder Brainerd. Recognizing the problems in the company, Brainerd brought in a new management team and removed himself from day-to-day control of the company, taking on the task of developing new ideas for software, instead.

In an effort to freshen its product offerings, Aldus introduced a color version of PageMaker for the Macintosh and a long-awaited Japanese version. PageMaker for IBM machines in Japan followed. In September 1989, Aldus shipped a Page-Maker program for use with the new IBM operating system, OS/2. In addition, the company instituted a restructured customer service program.

Despite these steps, however, Aldus's earnings seemed to have reached a plateau, as unsold inventories of its products accumulated and sales slowed. Overall, gross revenues rose only 11 percent in 1989, and earnings were up only six percent, to $15.4 million. After years of much faster growth, these disappointing results caused the price of Aldus's stock to drop.

In an effort to branch out beyond its core desktop publishing field and speed company growth, Aldus purchased Silicon Beach Software, a privately held computer program producer, in 1990 for $25.5 million worth of stock. This company's offerings included SuperPaint, a drawing program, Personal Press, an inexpensive desktop publishing product, and Digital Darkroom, which allowed users to retouch photos. These products allowed Aldus to tap into the market of novice computer users, who were unfamiliar with more high-powered graphics programs.

In addition to this acquisition, Aldus made further progress in its push into international markets. The company introduced an updated version of its PageMaker program in Japanese. In May 1990, the company introduced a long-awaited upgrade of its American PageMaker program, which Aldus hoped would enable it to hold onto its 70 percent market share of desktop publishing software for the Macintosh. Nevertheless, Aldus's executives indicated that they hoped to have this program contribute no more than half of the company's revenues in the coming years, as other products gained popularity. Chief among these other products was Persuasion, the company's presentation software, which had attained the number two spot in its market, behind a Microsoft program.

Aldus continued its campaign to win market share overseas in July 1990, when it introduced PageMaker versions in Chinese and Russian. In addition, the company brought a number of products obtained with its Silicon Beach acquisition to market, further diversifying its software offerings. By the end of the year, these efforts had led to an increase in sales of 37 percent, bringing revenues to $135 million. Sixty-six percent of these sales were contributed by PageMaker, which then retailed for $795 and could be used in 17 languages.

Aldus continued to expand its product line beyond PageMaker in 1991, as the company purchased the marketing rights to a number of programs, among them PhotoStyler, PressWise, and PageAhead. The company also continued to release updated versions of its old programs. To support these new product releases, Aldus renewed its advertising campaign in various publications.

Sales of Aldus's old standbys, products such as Persuasion and PageMaker, were given a boost in 1991 when an updated version of the operating system for IBM-compatible computers, Windows 3.0, stimulated demand for new versions of programs to run on it. To further tap into this market, Aldus announced an aggressive trade-in marketing push, in which a customer who turned in one of the company's competitors' programs would get an updated version of Persuasion for Windows 3.0 for only $99, a deeply discounted price.

Despite domestic efforts, Aldus did not experience dramatic growth in 1992. To strengthened its position and spur growth, Aldus focused on its international prospects. It began by purchasing 80 percent of its joint venture in Japan, Aldus Kabushiki Kaisha, for $7 million. In an effort to make further international sales possible, Aldus joined with the other members of the Business Software Alliance to test Mexican copyright laws, suing companies which had pirated its programs. This move was intended to make it possible for U.S. companies to increase their sales of software in Mexico, a potentially lucrative market, without risking large losses to counterfeiters.

Shortly after this legal action was taken, Aldus found itself involved in another type of legal dispute, when two shareholders claimed that executives at the company had sold high-priced shares in Aldus on the basis of inside information. This complaint was brought as a result of the company's continued poor returns, which had caused its stock price to drop. In July 1992, this trend took a more ominous turn when Aldus reported its first quarterly loss. One month later, the company announced that it would trim its staff by 13 percent—100 employees—as a cost-cutting measure. The company attributed the need for this restructuring to continued economic and competitive pressures in the industry as a whole, as the software industry went through a period of slowing sales.

Although Aldus was admired for its ability to produce software to be used on both IBM and Macintosh operating systems, the company's new introductions never matched the popularity of PageMaker. This pattern continued throughout 1992, as Aldus released updated versions of its old programs and brought out new products acquired from other sources. Among the new introductions were Fetch, a multimedia software tool which allowed images to be retrieved for manipulation, and Intelli-Draw, a sophisticated drawing program.

In further efforts to boost sales, Aldus announced the creation of a Consumer Division to market its software to individual users outside a corporate setting. This indicated a shifting focus to low-cost, high-value consumer software. In addition, Aldus tried to upgrade its relationships with mail-order software distributors and retail superstores to increase the number of outlets for its products. Further marketing changes included the introduction of new product packaging. Nevertheless, sales responded only slightly, as the company suffered intense competition from two other software developers, Quark and Frame Technology. Aldus ended 1992 with revenues of $174.1 million, a small upturn from the previous year.

In January 1993, Aldus released PageMaker 5.0. The company hoped that this major upgrade would enhance sales. As Aldus moved into the mid-1990s, the company had a solid record of stability and growth behind it, provided largely by its perennially popular PageMaker program. Although its future did not appear to include the kind of spectacular early advances which the company had once enjoyed, Aldus was well situated to meet the challenges of the changing environment in specialized software.

Principal Subsidiaries: Aldus Europe Limited (U.K.); Aldus Software G.M.B.H. (Germany); Aldus France S.A.R.L.; Silicon Beach Software, Inc.; Aldus Kabushiki Kaisha (Japan); Aldus Canada, Inc.; Aldus Software Pty. Ltd. (Australia).

Further Reading:

Buell, Barbara, "For Aldus, Being No. 1 Isn't Enough Anymore," *Business Week,* June 11, 1990.
Davies, John, "Tiny Aldus Hits Software Bonanza," *Journal of Commerce,* March 23, 1988.
Wiegner, Kathleen K., "Visual Persuasion," *Forbes,* September 16, 1991.

—Elizabeth Rourke

Alexander & Alexander Services Inc.

1211 Avenue of the Americas
New York, New York 10036
U.S.A.
(212) 840-8500
Fax: (212) 444-4697

Public Company
Incorporated: 1922 as Alexander & Alexander, Inc.
Employees: 14,500
Sales: $1.34 billion
Stock Exchanges: New York
SICs: 6411 Insurance Agents, Brokers & Service; 8742
   Management Consulting Services; 6719 Holding
   Companies Nec

Alexander & Alexander Services Inc. (A&A) is the second largest insurance brokerage company, and the largest retail insurance broker, in the world. Through a network of subsidiaries and affiliates, A&A acts as intermediary between clients (usually corporations) and insurance underwriters, receiving a commission based on the premium paid by the client. A&A also offers a variety of risk management consulting services, including loss control and cost studies. Through its Alexander Howden Intermediaries subsidiary, A&A specializes in insurance packages for events and institutions with large, complex risk situations. Another A&A unit, Alexander Howden Reinsurance Brokers Limited, is one of the leading reinsurance brokering companies operating in the London and international markets. In addition, through its Alexander Consulting Group, Inc. (ACG), A&A is engaged in the human resources consulting business, designing employee benefit packages and providing retirement program planning and actuarial services for over 20,000 clients. A truly global organization, A&A operates over 300 offices located in over 80 countries.

Alexander & Alexander was founded as a partnership, late in the nineteenth century, for providing companies with insurance policies. By 1910, the company's client list included Wagons-Lits, the Paris based operator of train coaches, including those of the renowned Orient Express. In 1922, the company began providing services for the Sun Company, which had recently opened its first gas station. After a couple decades of healthy growth, the company was incorporated in Maryland in 1922. A&A's modest but steady growth lead to the expansion of its

operations in Canada in the 1940s. The company's personnel management consulting business was also growing strong by the 1950s, and, in 1958, specialty chemical and health care product manufacturer W.R. Grace & Co. came on board as a consulting client.

A&A grew into an international giant in the insurance industry during the 1960s. In 1966, having earned $742,000 on revenue of $13.6 million, the company embarked on an acquisition spree. Over the next five years, A&A acquired 42 insurance brokerages and agencies, one actuarial consulting firm, and a risk analysis and consulting firm. By 1969, the company's revenues were up to $34.5 million, and net income had nearly tripled to over $2 million. A&A's expansion was part of an industry-wide trend that saw the total number of insurance brokerage houses drop dramatically as the larger outfits overtook smaller ones and went public. A&A's initial offering came in April 1969, with its stock opening at $26 a share. By the end of the decade, A&A was operating 23 offices in the United States, five in Canada, and one in Paris. Insurance brokering was generating about three-fourths of the company's revenue. A&A was also operating two subsidiaries: Alexander & Alexander Securities Dealers, Inc. and Benefacts, Inc., which provided employees of client companies information about their group coverage.

A&A's rapid expansion continued into the 1970s, as the company launched a major offensive in the battle to become the first international insurance supermarket. In 1971, the company established a network of eight subsidiaries across Europe. The eight companies, each joint ventures with established European brokerages, included Alexander-Berkeow Mendes (Netherlands), Alexander-Havag (Germany), Alexander-Menage & Jowa (Belgium), Alexander-Bouly (France), Alexander-Pratolongo (Italy), Alexander-Coyle Hamilton (Ireland), Alexander-Sedgwick Services, Ltd. (England), and Alexander-Gonzales (Spain).

In 1973, Alexander & Alexander Services Inc. was created as a holding company for A&A Inc. and its various subsidiaries. By that time, A&A had over 2,000 employees, and its headquarters had been moved from Baltimore to New York. That year, eight new firms with a combined $3.7 million in annual revenue were merged into the company, bringing the total number acquired since 1969 to 69 (65 of them insurance brokerage and agency operations). More acquisitions came the following year. Utica Mutual Assoc.; Lewis M. Gabbe & Co.; and Barton, Curle & McLaren, Inc. were all purchased during 1974. 1975's buying binge included Shand, Morahan & Co., an insurance underwriting management firm; Houston's ECCO General Agency, Inc.; and Great Northeast Agency, Inc., based in Long Island, New York.

By the middle of the 1970s, management at A&A felt it necessary to began searching for a British partner. Meanwhile, the company continued to grow domestically through acquisitions. In 1976, A&A acquired Eastern Brokerage Co. in a stock deal. Herman C. Wolff Co., Inc., one of the oldest agencies in Indianapolis, was also merged into the company that year. 1978 was a huge year for acquisitions, which included Anchor Agency, Inc.; Property Tax Services, Inc.; American Risk Management, Inc.; John B. Meyer; Francis S. Carnes, Inc.; May & Son Brokerage Corp.; Boland Insurance Agency, Inc.; and at least eight other firms. By the end of the decade, A&A was leading the industry in return on equity, at over 30 percent. The precision with which the company chose its acquisition targets was regarded as remarkable.

A&A's first choice for a major merger in England was the highly regarded Sedgwick Group, Lloyd's of London's largest broker. Two and a half years were spent exploring merger possibilities between the two companies. Despite these efforts, the idea was abandoned in July 1981. In the United States, however, the company maintained the pace of its expansion. R.B. Jones Corp. was acquired for stock in 1979, and other companies were added in 1980.

The failure to pull off the Sedgwick merger left A&A was anxious to find an alternative partner and make up for lost time. However, a period of industry weakness, ill-timed decisions, and bad luck ensued for A&A. In January 1982, A&A purchased Alexander Howden Group in a $300 million takeover deal. A&A had discussed merging with Howden—Lloyd's fourth largest broker and largest underwriter—twice in the past, and the two companies had already entered into a joint underwriting venture in Bermuda. To A&A chairperson and chief executive John Bogardus, Jr., Howden seemed the logical second choice for a merger. Unfortunately for Bogardus and A&A, however, the deal was laced with apparent fraud, saddling A&A with devastating losses that would take years to overcome.

Shortly after the purchase of Howden, some $50 million in Howden assets turned up missing, allegedly embezzled. Some of the assets seemed to have been diverted to corporations based in Panama and Liechtenstein. A&A's initial plan was to simply write off the loss as goodwill over 40 years. However, the Securities and Exchange Commission (SEC) deemed that accounting tactic unacceptable, and the company was forced to take a $40 million charge against profits for 1982, resulting in a net loss of $14.4 million for the year. The deal and subsequent $40 million write-off led to a slew of lawsuits. Moreover, underwriting losses from underreserved Howden units totaled another $185 million. In 1983, still reeling from the Howden affair, A&A eliminated 355 jobs and asked one-fourth of its 7,000 remaining employees to take sizable pay cuts. Bogardus himself, as well as president and chief operating officer Tinsley Irvin, took cuts in salary. Another problem was the blow taken by the company's reputation. New clients suddenly became scarce, and several important employees jumped ship. Finally, the company's problems were exacerbated by a generally soft insurance market that saw steep drops in premiums. For 1984, A&A showed a $47 million net loss.

Although preoccupied by the crisis, A&A did not let up in its expansion drive. In November 1982, the company restructured its 88 U.S. offices into three new regional operating groups as part of a more aggressive sales strategy. That year, A&A acquired Clifton & Co. of San Francisco; Banque Du Rhone et de LaTamise, S.A., a Swiss company (later sold); and a minority interest in Industries—Asserkuranz G.m.b.H. & Co. A Boston-based insurance company, OBrion, Russell & Co., was acquired in 1983, and, over the next two years, the company acquired Summit Consulting Inc. of Lakeland, Florida, specialists in workers' compensation self-insurance programs; Long

Island's American Coverage Inc.; and Reed Stenhouse Companies Ltd., a Canadian retail brokerage.

By 1985 steps were being taken to reverse A&A's desperate situation. Most of the cases from the Howden fiasco had been resolved by 1986, and, the following year, Irvin became chief executive of A&A. In his first year as CEO, Irvin accelerated the company's retreat from the highly volatile underwriting business, divesting Sphere Drake Insurance Group P.L.C. and Shand Morahan & Co., the last of its major underwriting affiliates. He chose instead to concentrate on the company's core brokerage business and its drive for more of an international presence. At the same time, Irvin sought to create a greater sense of unity among the company's ranks of operating units, a collection of entities resulting from more than 500 acquisitions over the years. Events of 1987 included the opening of offices in Canada, the United Kingdom, and Australia for A&A's Anistics division, its main risk-management consulting branch. The company's employee benefits group also crossed the Atlantic during that year. For 1987, A&A reported revenue of $1.1 billion.

The direct costs of the Howden acquisition were all paid off by the end of the decade. Nevertheless, a soft insurance market kept revenues flat during this time, reaching only $1.25 billion in 1989. Of that total, 62 percent was generated by the company's retail brokerage operations, 8.5 percent by reinsurance brokerage, and 9.3 percent by the Alexander Consulting Group. About 38 percent of revenue came from outside the United States. The Reed Stenhouse unit was particularly active in carrying out A&A's international expansion.

In 1991, A&A posted a net loss of $12.6 million, its first year in the red since 1985. The loss was largely due to a one-time $75 million charge covering the costs of restructuring the company's brokerage operations, including closing some offices and consolidating others. That year, the company was awarded a $350 million insurance brokerage contract by the government of Kuwait to find marine and war-risk insurance for $500 million worth of cargo to be shipped from all over the world as part of an international relief effort.

Unexpected challenges developed for A&A in the 1990s. The company was forced to set aside reserves to cover an open ended liability for claims against Sphere Drake Insurance Group, once a Howden unit. New legal entanglements seemed to crop up at every turn. In autumn 1993, A&A announced that it had been overstating the revenue of ACG, its consulting operation that had been generating about 16 percent of its earnings. A few days after the announcement, ACG chief executive Angelo D'Alessandro died, having been in a coma for six weeks after falling from an elevated rail system in Mexico City during a business trip. A&A was also stung by the surprise resignation of Ron Forrest, chairperson and CEO of A&A Inc., the company's U.S. retail brokerage operation.

In January 1994, Irvin resigned as the board's chairperson and was succeeded by board member Robert Boni. Irvin temporarily retained his position as CEO while an international search was launched for a replacement. On June 7, 1994, A&A named Frank G. Zarb as chairman, CEO, and president. Zarb had been vice chairman and group chief executive of Travelers Inc.

A&A also received a $200 million capital infusion from American International Group, Inc. AIG agreed to invest this sum in a new issue of Series B convertible preferred stock with an eight percent annual dividend. A&A would use a portion of the proceeds of this investment to strengthen its core businesses and finance reinsurance to further insulate the company and its subsidiaries from exposures relating to discontinued underwriting units, primarily those related to the Sphere Drake Insurance Group. Almost immediately, Zarb announced that reinsurance had been arranged.

During A&A's period of crises, other insurance brokers, particularly Marsh & McLennan, gained a competitive edge. Nevertheless, A&A has managed to overcome many of its difficulties, without help from the insurance market in general, which has remained extremely weak for the better part of a decade. When the insurance industry finally manages to right itself, analysts' suggest, A&A may have the opportunity to produce the kind of results it had shown before 1982, when the Howden scandal made it the perpetrator of what may be one of the worst takeover deals in history.

Principal Subsidiaries: Alexander & Alexander Inc.; Alexander Insurance Managers Limited; Alexis Inc.; Anistics; Alexander Howden Holdings plc; Alexander Howden Reinsurance Brokers Limited; Alexander Reinsurance Intermediaries, Inc.; Alexander Consulting Group Inc.

Further Reading:

"A&A Inc. Merges Eight New Firms," *Journal of Commerce,* February 20, 1973, p. 7.

"A&A Merges with Wolff," *Journal of Commerce,* May 10, 1976, p. 2.

Aarstein, Barbara, "Alexander & Alexander Inc. Restructures 88 US Offices," *Journal of Commerce,* November 15, 1982, p. 11A.

"Alexander Chairman Steps Down," *New York Times,* January 18, 1994, p. D3.

Andresky, Jill, "Follow the Leader," *Forbes,* June 29, 1987, pp. 40–41.

Berg, Eric N., "Insurance Broker Still Suffering from Scandal," *New York Times,* June 22, 1983, p. D1.

Bray, Edward C., "The Security I Like Best," *Commercial and Financial Chronicle,* March 26, 1970, p. 2.

Brenner, Lynn, "The $300 Million Misunderstanding," *Institutional Investor,* February 1983, pp. 179–89.

Freudmann, Aviva, "Kuwait Awards Insurance Broker Massive Contract," *Journal of Commerce,* March 14, 1991, p. 1.

Greene, Richard, "Men of Goodwill, Disagreeing," *Forbes,* December 6, 1982, p. 168.

Greenwald, Judy, "Alexander & Alexander Services Inc.," *Business Insurance,* June 18, 1990, pp. 21–24; June 29, 1992, p. 21–23.

"Insurance Brokers: Going Public," *Financial World,* August 18, 1971, pp. 9–10.

Jaffe, Thomas, "Problems, Problems," *Forbes,* May 16, 1988, p. 154.

Roberts, Sally, "A&A Vows to Rebound from Woes," *Business Insurance,* November 8, 1993, p. 1.

Robinson, Jeffrey, "Foxes and Hounds: Which Is Which at Lloyd's?" *Barron's,* October 11, 1982, p. 15.

Rosenberg, Hilary, "Turnaround Time at A&A?" *Institutional Investor,* February 1988, pp. 161–64.

Steinmetz, Greg, "Insurance Broker Could Use a Policy Against Problems," *Wall Street Journal,* November 5, 1993, p. B4.

Steinmetz, Greg, "Shift at Alexander & Alexander Leads to New Chairman," *Wall Street Journal,* January 18, 1994, p. B7.

—Robert R. Jacobson

Alexander & Baldwin, Inc.

822 Bishop St.
P.O. Box 3440
Honolulu, Hawaii 96801-3440
U.S.A.
(808) 525-6611
Fax: (808) 525-6652

Public Company
Incorporated: 1900 as Alexander & Baldwin, Ltd.
Employees: 3,709
Sales: $979.5 million
Stock Exchanges: NASDAQ
SICs: 4423 Deep Sea Domestic Transportation of Freight;
   2061 Raw Cane Sugar; 7359 Equipment Rental & Leasing
   Nec; 6552 Subdividers & Developers Nec

Alexander & Baldwin, Inc., one of the original "Big Five" Hawaiian companies, is a diversified corporation with operations in ocean transportation, container leasing, food products, and property development and management. Ocean transportation, overseen by Matson Navigation Company, Inc., a wholly owned subsidiary, accounts for about 56 percent of the company's revenue. Through Matson, Alexander & Baldwin (A&B) is the leading carrier of containerized cargo and automobiles between Hawaii and the U.S. Pacific Coast and is the ninth largest lessor of marine shipping containers in the world. Matson's fleet provides services to several other Pacific islands as well. Another six percent of A&B's revenue is generated by its container leasing operation, conducted through Matson Leasing Company, Inc., a wholly owned subsidiary of Matson Navigation. A&B conducts its food products business through another wholly owned subsidiary, A&B-Hawaii, Inc. (ABHI), whose California and Hawaiian Sugar Company is the largest producer of raw sugar in Hawaii; ABHI also is the largest coffee grower in the United States. Food products contributed about 31 percent of A&B's revenue in 1993. A&B's fourth major business segment, property development and management, is also conducted by ABHI. In 1994, the company owned about 94,000 acres of land in Hawaii, the majority of it on the island of Maui. Property development and management provided about seven percent of the company's 1993 revenue.

Although A&B was not incorporated until 1900, the company was founded 30 years earlier by the two men whose names it bears, Samuel T. Alexander and Henry P. Baldwin, both sons of missionaries living in Hawaii. Longtime friends, the two men began working together in the mid-1860s, when Alexander hired the younger Baldwin as his assistant in managing a sugar plantation in Waihee on the island of Maui. In 1869, the pair purchased 12 acres of land in central Maui, and, the following year, with an additional 559 acres, they established their own plantation, which marketed sugar on the mainland through such exporting firms as Castle & Cooke. Alexander and Baldwin became in-laws that year when Baldwin married Emily Alexander, his partner's sister.

By 1876, the volume of sugar cane growing on the plantation had increased so much that the readily available supply of water could not support it. To address this problem, Alexander devised a sophisticated irrigation plan that involved the construction of a gigantic ditch through rain forest terrain. The resulting Hamakua ditch, 17 miles long and capable of carrying 60 million gallons of water a day from the waters of East Maui, was completed in 1878 and served as the model for many other such irrigation projects throughout Hawaii.

The partnership of Alexander and Baldwin was incorporated in 1883 under the name Paia Plantation. That year, Alexander resigned as manager of the neighboring Haiku Sugar Company, a position he had held since before the opening of Paia, and moved to California, leaving Baldwin to manage both plantations. Over the next few years, Paia acquired controlling interest in Haiku, as the partners continued to acquire land and expand their sugar production.

In 1894, A&B launched its own sugar agency, based in San Francisco. The agency was headed by Alexander's son, Wallace, and Joseph P. Cooke, son of Castle & Cooke co-founder Amos S. Cooke. In its first year of operation, the Alexander & Baldwin agency turned a profit of $2,670. By 1899, A&B was serving as agent for a formidable collection of companies, including the Paia and Haiku plantations, the Hawaiian Sugar Company, and the Hawaiian Commercial & Sugar Company (HC&S) and its subsidiary, Kahului Railroad Company.

By 1900, the company had outgrown its partnership structure, and a new corporation, Alexander & Baldwin, Ltd., was formed. The company's headquarters were in Honolulu, a branch office was maintained in San Francisco, and Baldwin served as president. That year, the corporation reported its first annual profit, of $150,000. A&B went into the insurance business the following year, establishing a division overseen by Alexander's son-in-law, John Waterhouse. By 1920, the division was acting as agent for several established insurance companies, including Home Insurance Company, German Alliance Insurance Association, and the Commonwealth Insurance Company, all based in New York. The insurance division thrived for several decades before it was sold off in 1967.

Another new entity, the Maui Agricultural Company (MA Co.), was founded in 1903, in order to offset the effects of the Organic Act, which limited the amount of land a new corporation could hold to 1,000 acres. In response, A&B formed five companies with less than 1,000 acres each. These five companies were then combined with the Paia and Haiku plantations to form MA Co. In MA Co. and HC&S, A&B now controlled the operations of two of Maui's most important plantations.

Samuel Alexander died in 1904. In 1906, Henry Baldwin was succeeded as manager of HC&S by his son Frank, and when Henry died five years later, Frank became HC&S president, a position he would retain until his death in 1960. Both MA Co. and HC&S prospered during the first part of the twentieth century. In 1908, the two companies jointly formed the East Maui Irrigation Company (EMI) to manage the extensive system of irrigation ditches that was in development. In 1917, MA Co. built a distillery for producing alcohol from molasses, the first such facility in the United States. HC&S completed several other major projects during this time, including the construction of the new Waihee ditch and the modernization of its power plant and other equipment. Another plantation, Kihei, was merged into HC&S during this period as well.

A&B's cargo shipping business was developed to complement its sugar operations. In 1909, the company became a minority shareholder in Matson Navigation Company, which had been handling most of A&B's shipping between Hawaii and San Francisco for years. A&B continued to increase its investment in Matson, and the company eventually became a wholly owned subsidiary of A&B in 1969.

Wallace Alexander served as CEO of A&B from 1918 to 1930. During this time, the company began marketing pineapples, EMI completed construction of the Wailoa ditch, its final major ditch project, and A&B's headquarters building in Honolulu was completed. The following year, John Waterhouse succeeded Wallace Alexander as company president.

The 1930s were a period of technological advancement in A&B's sugar operations. In 1932, the company completed construction on the Alexander Dam, one of the largest hydraulic fill earth dams in the world. The Alexander Dam, located at the company's McBryde plantation, cost over $360,000 to build and was the site of a 1930 mud slide that killed several people. Both HC&S and MA Co. switched from steam plows to tractors around this time, and HC&S began mechanical harvesting on a large scale in 1937.

A&B sold its Hawaiian Sugar Company plantation in 1941. Although this plantation remained productive and profitable, it was situated on leased land, and A&B was unable to negotiate favorable lease terms or a purchase agreement. In 1945, Waterhouse was replaced as president of A&B by J. Platt Cooke, who served for a year before turning over the office to Frank Baldwin. In 1948, the HC&S and MA Co. plantations merged, creating one large plantation operating under the HC&S name. The two plantations produced over 100,000 tons of sugar during the first year of the merger. Soon thereafter, the plantation began to phase out its railroad distribution system in favor of trucking.

At the end of the 1940s, A&B began to move into property development, forming Kahului Development Co., Ltd. as a subsidiary of HC&S. In response to the complaints of plantation employees regarding the inadequate housing available to them, Kahului Development built a new residential community, which was opened in 1950 and became known as Dream City.

This development gradually evolved into the city of Kahului, Maui's most populous community.

A&B operated several general stores on plantations and railroad sites. In 1950, its stores and equipment manufacturing concerns, as well as the lumberyard and mill operations of the Kahului Railroad Company, were organized under the A&B Commercial Company. The following year, A&B opened the first A&B Super Market, as well as the Kahului Store, Maui's first complete department store.

The company made several technological strides in its sugar operations during the 1950s. In 1951, HC&S's two factories combined to produce a record 151,000 tons of sugar. Several improvements in machinery for weed control and harvesting were introduced during this time, and, in 1957, HC&S put the world's largest bagasse (cane residue) burning boiler into operation at its Paia sugar factory.

Up until the 1960s, A&B had remained essentially a sales agent that held substantial interest in the companies it represented. Its income came from agency fees and dividends on the stock it owned in its client companies. However, this began to change as A&B started turning many of its clients into subsidiaries. Much of this shift took place under C.C. Cadagan, who was named president of A&B in 1960, becoming the first chief executive from outside the founding families. In 1962, HC&S was merged into A&B, becoming a division of the company. HC&S's three subsidiaries, Kahului Railroad Company (KRR), East Maui Irrigation Company, and Kahului Development Company all became subsidiaries of A&B. A&B Commercial Company, which ran the HC&S plantation stores, was made a division. At the same time, the last word of the company's name was changed from Ltd. to Inc.

Using funds it had received from the liquidation of Honolulu Oil Corporation, a company in which it had initially invested in 1911, A&B acquired a 94 percent controlling interest in Matson Navigation Company in 1964. The following year, the company eliminated what remained of KRR's unprofitable railroad operations, and that subsidiary was later renamed Kahului Trucking & Storage, Inc. By the end of the decade, the company had terminated its pineapple business and had increased its holding in Matson to 100 percent. The McBryde and Kahuke plantations had become wholly owned subsidiaries as well.

The 1970s were a frustrating period of stalled expansion plans for A&B. In 1970, Allen Wilcox was named CEO, replacing Stanley Powell, Cadagan's successor four years before. Under Wilcox, A&B abandoned its plans to expand its Far East shipping operations, choosing instead to concentrate on its business closer to home, such as developing some of its Maui land for resort use. Another change in leadership took place in 1972, when Lawrence Pricher was named CEO. Under Pricher, the company launched another expansion push, which included investments in oil refiner Pacific Resources, Inc. and Teakwood Holdings Ltd. (a Hong Kong furniture company), the purchase of Rogers Brothers Co., (an Idaho potato business), and the formation of a consulting firm called A&B Agribusiness Corporation. None of these ventures proved particularly fruitful, and, at the same time, some earlier investments that also proved unprofitable were sold off, including Edward R. Bacon Company and Acme Fast Freight, Inc. With the price of sugar falling, and profits at Matson unimpressive, A&B's net income remained sluggish through the mid-1970s.

Yet another change in command took place in 1978, when Gilbert Cox left Amfac Inc., Hawaii's biggest sugar producer, to assume the presidency of A&B. Cox's strategy for growth involved selling off most of Pricher's small acquisitions, such as the potato company, and using the money for a major acquisition. In 1979, an agreement was reached under which A&B would acquire the 80 percent of Pacific Resources it did not already own. However, this deal fell through following opposition from a group of stockholders led by well-known investor Harry Weinberg.

The rapid succession of new presidents at A&B finally slowed in 1980 with the arrival of Robert Pfeiffer, formerly the CEO at Matson. An upward swing in sugar prices helped boost the company's profits that year, and, by 1983, sugar accounted for 21 percent of A&B's $395 million in sales. As the company again considered diversification, Harry Weinberg, Hawaii's largest individual landowner, increased his holding in A&B to 25 percent. In 1984, Weinberg forced a proxy battle for control of the company, arguing that A&B's land holdings were worth far more than its books indicated and that property development should be the company's top priority. Unlike most of his boardroom conflicts with large Hawaiian companies, however, this one ended with Weinberg and his associates forced off the A&B board of directors.

In January 1987, A&B got rid of its merchandising division, selling A&B Commercial Company to Monarch Building Supply, Inc., a Honolulu-based company. By this time, A&B had revenues of $655 million, the bulk of which was generated by Matson, which controlled about 75 percent of the container cargo shipping market between Hawaii and the West Coast. Between 1983 and 1987, profits more than doubled to $120 million, and about three-fourths of that total came from Matson. In the late 1980s, A&B sold off its remaining shares of Pacific Resources to Australia's Broken Hill Proprietary Company and began preparing to grow coffee through a joint venture between its McBryde subsidiary and Hills Brothers. A&B recorded net income of $199 million on revenue of $846 million in 1989. Two years later Pfeiffer passed the reins of the company to John C. Couch, who became president and CEO. Couch had served A&B for 15 years, initially with Matson Navigation Company.

A&B's revenues stagnated and net income slumped during the first part of the 1990s. With sales hovering around the $750 million mark from 1990 to 1992, company earnings dipped to under $19 million in 1992, the lowest level in over a decade. That figure included a $15.8 million charge to cover losses from Hurricane Iniki, which devastated Kauai in 1992. Nevertheless, A&B mounted a successful comeback the following year. The company reported major increases in both profit and revenue, up to $67 million and $979 million, respectively. Moreover, in June 1993, A&B's purchase of the 72 percent of California and Hawaiian Sugar Company that it did not already own helped bolster revenues and profits. As the global economy improved during the first half of 1994, A&B expected to see gains in its shipping and container leasing operations, as well as increased profits from real estate leasing. A&B was the last of Hawaii's Big Five companies to remain independent and based on the islands; its durability over more than a century of operation has proven that a mainland address is not a prerequisite for long-term success.

Principal Subsidiaries: A&B-Hawaii, Inc.; A&B Development Company; A&B Properties, Inc.; California and Hawaiian Sugar Company; East Maui Irrigation Company, Ltd.; Kahului Trucking & Storage, Inc.; Kauai Commercial Company, Inc.; Kukui'ula Development Company, Inc.; McBryde Sugar Company, Ltd.; South Shore Community Services, Inc.; South Shore Resources, Inc.; WDCI, Inc.; Matson Navigation Company, Inc.; Matson Intermodal System, Inc.; Matson Leasing Company, Inc.; Matson Services Company, Inc.; Matson Terminals, Inc.

Further Reading:

"Alexander & Baldwin: Cutting Sugar's Role with Big Acquisitions," *Business Week,* February 12, 1979, pp. 88–91.

"Alexander & Baldwin: Will It Put Its Money Where Its Mouth Is?" *Business Week,* March 19, 1984, pp. 92–93.

Beauchamp, Marc, "Hunkering Down Is No Strategy," *Forbes,* October 31, 1988, pp. 54–62.

"Can Alexander & Baldwin Do It Again?" *Financial World,* May 15, 1981, pp. 27–28.

Christensen, Kathryn, "After Years of Turmoil, a Hawaii Sugar Firm Returns to Stability," *Wall Street Journal,* August 20, 1981 p. 1.

Cieply, Michael, "East of Eden," *Forbes,* January 31, 1983, pp. 34–36.

Davies, John, "Coffee Replaces Sugar in Some Hawaiian Fields," *Journal of Commerce,* July 9, 1990, p. 1A.

Garcia, Art, "Spotlight on Alexander & Baldwin," *Journal of Commerce,* April 7, 1980, p. 3.

"An Hawaiian Company Invests Its Sugar Profits," *Business Week,* April 14, 1975, pp. 80–81.

Smith, Christopher, and Cynthia Green, "A Seasoned Raider Loses His Touch," *Business Week,* May 13, 1985, p. 31.

"A Sweet Stock from the Islands," *Fortune,* November 25, 1985, pp. 161–68.

Wastler, Allen R., "Accounting Changes, Iniki Fallout Depress Alexander & Baldwin Profit," *Journal of Commerce,* February 3, 1993, p. 1B.

Zipser, Andy, "When Its Ship Comes In," *Barron's,* pp. 28–29.

—Robert R. Jacobson

Alleghany Corporation

Park Avenue Plaza
New York, New York 10055
U.S.A.
(212) 752-1356
Fax: (212) 759-8149

Public Company
Incorporated: 1929
Employees: 10,100
Assets: $4.86 billion
Stock Exchanges: New York
SICs: 6361 Title Insurance; 6036 Savings Institutions Except
    Federal; 1499 Miscellaneous Nonmetallic Minerals; 5072
    Hardware

Alleghany Corporation is a large company involved through its
subsidiaries in several different industries. Through Chicago
Title & Trust Co. (CT&T), acquired by Alleghany in 1985, the
company sells and writes title insurance and provides other
related services. CT&T and its subsidiaries Chicago Title Insurance Co. and Security Union Title Insurance Co. make up the
largest title insurance combine in the world, with 200 offices
and 3,800 agents in 49 states, Puerto Rico, the Virgin Islands,
and Canada. CT&T also provides financial services such as
asset management to Chicago area clients. Alleghany's other
major financial institution is Sacramento Savings & Loan, a
thrift operating over 40 branches in north central California.
Alleghany is also involved in the industrial minerals business
through Celite Corporation, which it purchased from Manville
Corporation in 1991. Celite is probably the world's leading
producer of diatomite, a silica-based mineral. The company also
mines and processes perlite (a volcanic mineral) and produces
calcium and magnesium silicate products. Another Alleghany
division is Heads and Threads, which imports and distributes
metal fasteners. About 40 percent of Alleghany's stock is controlled by the Kirby family heirs to the fortune of Woolworth
co-founder Fred Morgan Kirby.

Alleghany was founded in 1929 by the well-known and eccentric Van Sweringen brothers of Cleveland as a holding company
for their railroad investments. When Alleghany slid into receivership in 1934, control of the company passed to J. P. Morgan
and others. Shares of the company floated around among a few
different parties for the next few years, eventually landing in the
hands of George Ball, of Ball Jar fame. Wheeler-dealer Robert
R. Young bought the stock from Ball in 1937. Most of the
money Young used to acquire controlling interest in Alleghany
was put up by Allan P. Kirby, Fred's son. Young became
chairman of Alleghany, while Kirby remained behind the
scenes as his silent partner. The centerpiece of the extensive but
struggling Alleghany empire was its 2 million plus shares of the
Chesapeake and Ohio Railroad.

Young spent his first few years at Alleghany whittling down the
company's massive debt and untangling its gnarled finances. A
legal victory against Ball provided much of the desperately
needed cash for the task, and eventually Alleghany's books
were in order. Under Young, the Chesapeake & Ohio (C&O)
underwent something of a facelift. Equipment was modernized
and many new conveniences were introduced in its passenger
service. In 1945 Young decided to go after another railroad, the
New York Central. That year he purchased 225,400 shares of
the Central for $4.2 million. Two years later more shares were
acquired. Initially, Interstate Commerce Commission (ICC)
regulations prevented Alleghany from taking control of additional railroads. Several years of maneuvering followed, including the sale of most of Alleghany's C&O stock to associates.
Young finally managed to wrest control of the New York
Central away from its bank-dominated board of directors in a
hotly contested proxy battle in 1954.

Meanwhile, Alleghany was transforming itself from strictly a
railroad force into a financial force as well. In 1949 the company purchased controlling interest in Investors Diversified
Services, Inc. (IDS), the worlds largest mutual fund group. At
the same time Young was purging the Alleghany portfolio of
dozens of unwanted holdings. From 66 different securities in
1947, the company pared its collection down to less than ten a
decade later. By 1957 Alleghany's investments consisted primarily of a ''big four'': the New York Central, now the company's main railroad project; IDS, in which Alleghany still
maintained a strong position although actual control had been
sold to Texan Clint Murchison, a longtime Young accomplice;
the Missouri Pacific Railroad, a holdover from the Van
Sweringen empire that had lingered in bankruptcy for decades;
and Webb & Knapp, a real estate firm.

In 1958 Young committed suicide. Business had taken a severe
turn for the worse, and some speculated that Young was depressed over the possibility of his company's collapse. Whether
Alleghany's condition was on Young's mind was never determined for sure. Consequently, the publicity-shy Kirby was
forced out of the shadows. He took over as chairman, president,
and undisputed leader of Alleghany. The contrast between the
two men could not have been more stark. While Young was a
flamboyant operator, fond of speaking out in the press about
almost anything, Kirby relished his role as silent partner. His
style of doing business did not require much in the way of
public exposure.

Under Kirby's guidance, Alleghany's fortunes reversed again,
and by the end of the 1950s the company had returned to health.
Kirby, unlike Young, was willing to delegate day-to-day operations to others, and the companies in the Alleghany fold responded positively to this new leadership approach. IDS started
performing particularly well. With nearly $3 billion under man-

agement, IDS reported net income of $12.7 million in 1958, earning $1.4 million in dividends for Alleghany. It was quite possibly already the world's largest investment management company by that time.

In 1959 Kirby faced his first challenge for control of Alleghany. That year, Boston real estate speculator Abraham Sonnabend began picking up Alleghany stock in large chunks. He also managed to gain the support of Alleghany Vice-President David Wallace, a close friend of Young's. Kirby responded by firing Wallace, which alienated Young's widow, also a major stockholder. Kirby emerged from the skirmish with his control of the company intact, but it was the first sign that his grip on Alleghany was vulnerable.

In his next proxy fight, Kirby was not as successful. In 1961 he lost control of Alleghany to the Murchison brothers, Clint Jr. and John, the sons of Young's former ally. At the heart of the struggle was a philosophical clash. The Murchisons were free-wheeling businessmen in the Texas tradition, while Kirby conducted his affairs with an extreme degree of caution. The brothers managed to convince many shareholders that Kirby's conservatism was holding the company back, eventually gaining enough support to oust him from power. This proved to be a short-lived victory, however. With 35 percent of Alleghany still in hand, Kirby was able to block all of the Murchisons' attempts to overhaul the company. By 1962 they were ready to give up. John Murchison resigned as president of Alleghany and was replaced by Minneapolis businessman Bertin Gamble, to whom the brothers sold much of their Alleghany stock at a loss. Gamble had sold his controlling interest in IDS to Alleghany 13 years earlier, just before its stock began to skyrocket.

Like his associates the Murchisons, Gamble was also unable to work with Kirby, and in 1963 controlling interest in Alleghany was sold back to Kirby and his allies. Kirby now owned 43 percent of Alleghany's common stock, and another 16 percent belonged to his associated and friends. Kirby returned to the position of chairman, and longtime associate Charles Ireland was named company president. Control of the company has remained firmly in the hands of the Kirby family ever since.

In 1965 Fred Kirby II, Allan's son, was elected chairman of the IDS executive committee. Fred continued serving as executive vice-president of Alleghany, a position he had held since his father's return to power two years earlier. The company sold most of its shares of the New York Central in 1966, marking the end of its railroad-controlling era. In 1967 Alleghany won another legal battle, preventing a reorganization plan from taking place at Missouri Pacific that would have severely diluted Alleghany's holdings in that company. Later that year, the elder Kirby suffered a major stroke. Fred II and his brother, Allan Jr., were named guardians for their father, by then generally acknowledged to be one of the richest men in America, and Fred took over as chairman of Alleghany.

After years as Alleghany's principal legal tactician, Ireland left the company in 1968 to take a job at International Telephone and Telegraph Corporation, on whose board he had sat as Alleghany's representative since 1965. In 1970 Alleghany acquired Jones Motor Co., a motor carrier of modest size. This was done primarily in order to avoid being reclassified as a personal holding company by the Internal Revenue Service. Jones never performed as hoped, and it was sold off in 1982.

Despite its legal classification, by 1974 Alleghany was for all practical purposes the family holding company of the Kirby family, who now held nearly half of the company's stock. That year Alleghany took a major step in its attempt to transform itself into more of an asset management company. First, the legal wrangling over reorganization of the Missouri Pacific finally ended for good, with Alleghany trading in its shares for $42 million in cash and $7.2 million more in new common stock. Alleghany then purchased MSL Industries, a metals fabricating company, using cash from the Missouri Pacific deal. Alleghany's other involvements around this time included its 44 percent interest in IDS; a $15.5 million investment in Court House Square, a real estate development in Denver; and its holdings in Missouri Pacific, TI Corporation, USM, Pittston Company, and United Corp.

Further cautious attempts to diversify peppered the remainder of the 1970s, with as many assets shed as added. Alleghany's last batch of Missouri Pacific shares was sold to Mississippi River Corporation in 1975. The following year, the company sold its Court House Square Square property for cash and acquired Allied Structural Steel Company. In 1979 Alleghany paid $198 million for the 45 percent of IDS it did not already own. By 1981 95 percent of Alleghany's income was coming from the investment business. IDS had $6 billion worth of mutual funds under management and $11 billion of life insurance (hawked by the same 3,400-person sales team) in force. In September of that year, the company sold off the IDS Center building in Minneapolis to a Canadian development company for about $200 million, producing a huge capital gain. Another investment management company, New York's Gray, Seifert and Co., was acquired in 1983.

Alleghany undertook a major and more rapid shift in strategy in the mid-1980s. In January 1984 the company consummated a blockbuster deal initiated the previous summer in which IDS was sold to American Express Company for $800 million in cash and securities. When Consolidated Rail Corporation (Conrail) went up for sale, Kirby put in a bid to go back into the rail business using the proceeds for the IDS transaction. Instead, the government took Conrail public, and Alleghany's focus turned toward the title insurance business. Toward the end of 1984, Alleghany Financial Corporation was formed as a wholly owned subsidiary for acquiring insurance and other financial oriented concerns. Its most important acquisition in that area came in 1985, with the purchase of Chicago Title and Trust Co. from Lincoln National Corporation for $60 million in cash and a six-year $68 million note. Two more insurance moves followed in the next two years. In 1986 the company acquired Shelby Insurance Co. for $40 million. SAFECO Title Insurance Co., later renamed Security Union Title Insurance Co., was purchased by the Chicago Title subsidiary the following year. The acquisitions of Chicago Title and Security Union made Alleghany the nation's leading title insurance outfit, while Shelby gave the company entry into the property and casualty insurance arena.

Meanwhile, Alleghany shareholders approved a plan for liquidating the company in December of 1986. Under the terms of the plan, most of the company's nonfinancial holdings would be disposed of, and the surviving Alleghany Financial subsidiary would be renamed Alleghany Corporation. Shareholders would receive $41 cash and a share of new Alleghany Corporation stock for each old Alleghany share. One of the first things to go was most of the company's substantial holding in American Express, acquired in the IDS deal. Among Alleghany's other 1987 deals was the June acquisition of the steel and nonresidential construction business of Cyclops Corporation from Dixons Group plc of London. These businesses were then immediately spun off to Alleghany stockholders as a new public company, Cyclops Industries Inc.

Alleghany initiated a new round of acquisitions beginning in about 1989. That year the company acquired Sacramento Savings & Loan Association and two associated companies for $150 million in cash. By the end of 1992, Sacramento Savings had total assets of $2.8 billion, and deposits of $2.6 billion. In March of 1991 Chicago Title acquired Ticor Title Insurance Co., a California operation that expanded Alleghany's reach in that business. Later that year Alleghany purchased Celite Corporation, Manville Corporation's filtration and industrial minerals business, for $144 million. Shelby Insurance Company, Alleghany's property, casualty, life, and annuity subsidiary, was sold to The Associated Group for cash at the end of 1991. For 1991 Alleghany had net income of $64 million on $1.42 billion in revenue.

Fred Kirby II stepped down as chief executive officer of Alleghany in 1992 at the age of 72. He retained his position as chairman of the board, as well as an active voice in company affairs. Kirby's hand-picked replacement as CEO was John Burns Jr., who had been with the company since 1968 and served as president since 1977. Burns was the first CEO at Alleghany from outside the Kirby family since 1957. During the last few years, Alleghany has increased its participation in both the insurance and minerals industries. In November of 1992 the company acquired Harborlite Corporation, a producer of the volcanic material perlite. Underwriters Reinsurance Co. was purchased in 1993.

Like his father, Fred Kirby II is about as secretive about business as the head of a public corporation can be. The Institutional Voting Research Service in Belmont, Massachusetts once called Alleghany "the most heavily insulated company we have ever analyzed." The company is historically mistrustful of the press and not at all eager for publicity. In spite of these characteristics, Alleghany and the Kirby family cannot seem to avoid the spotlight of controversy. Bitter disagreements between Fred Kirby II and his siblings threaten the kind of unity that gives family owned businesses the advantage of long-term planning. Several family members resent Kirby's autocratic control of the company and question the legitimacy of that control. The success or failure of the Kirby family to smooth out its differences will play an important role in future developments at Alleghany.

Principal Subsidiaries: Alleghany Financial Corporation; Chicago Title & Trust Co.; Heads & Threads; Sacramento Savings & Loan Association; Ticor Title Insurance Co.; World Minerals; Celite Corporation; Allied Structural Steel Company; Cyclops Industries, Inc.; MSL Industries; Pittston Company; Harborlite Corporation; Underwriters Reinsurance Co.

Further Reading:

"Allan Kirby Cleared on Murchison Fraud Charge," *New York Times,* January 14, 1965, p. 49.

"Alleghany Completes Purchase of Investors Diversified Services," *Wall Street Journal,* May 11, 1979, p. 39.

"Biding His Time on Rails," *Business Week,* January 21, 1950, pp. 27–28.

Blumstein, Michael, "The Power behind the Alleghany Deal," *New York Times,* July 17, 1983, p. F6.

"The Corporate Marine," *Time,* January 5, 1968, p. 71.

Cowan, Alison Leigh, "Kirby Keeps Control over Foundation," *New York Times,* June 6, 1991, p. D4.

——, "Promise into Peril: The Kirby Fight," *New York Times,* June 10, 1990, p. F1.

Elliott, J. Richard, Jr., "Switch for Alleghany?," *Barron's,* February 4, 1957, p. 3.

"Fred M. Kirby Succeeds Father as Alleghany Corp. Chairman," *New York Times,* September 15, 1967, p. 69.

"Hands Untied," *Forbes,* August 15, 1964, pp. 16–17.

"Kirby's Luck," *Forbes,* February 1, 1959, p. 29.

"Kirby vs. Sonnabend," *Forbes,* December 1, 1959, pp. 15–16.

"New Man at Alleghany," *Time,* December 21, 1962, p. 68.

"$930 Buys $1,250," *Business Week,* April 19, 1941, pp. 67–68.

"Practicing What Papa Preached," *Forbes,* March 1, 1974, pp. 60–61.

Rudnitsky, Howard, "Polishing the Family Jewels," *Forbes,* December 7, 1981, pp. 77–78.

Tannenbaum, Jeffrey A., "Alleghany Chief Kirby Transfers Post to J. Burns," *Wall Street Journal,* June 18, 1992, p. B3.

"Texas on Wall Street," *Time,* June 16, 1961, pp. 80–84.

"Tired of Railroading?," *Business Week,* November 23, 1946, pp. 80–86.

"Winner By a Knockout," *Time,* July 12, 1963, p. 88.

"Young's Empire: The Seeds He Sowed Bear Fruit," *Business Week,* February 14, 1959, pp. 108–116.

—Robert R. Jacobson

Allergan, Inc.

2525 Dupont Drive
P.O. Box 19534
Irvine, California 92715
U.S.A.
(714) 752-4500
Fax: (714) 955-6987

Public Company
Incorporated: 1948
Employees: 4,749
Sales: $858.9 million
Stock Exchanges: New York
SICs: 3851 Opthalmic Goods; 2834 Pharmaceutical
  Preparations; 3841 Surgical and Medical Instruments; 3842
  Surgical Appliances and Supplies

Allergan, Inc. is a global provider of specialty therapeutic products, primarily in eye and skin care. Acknowledged as a world leader in eye care, Allergan also develops, manufactures, and markets new products for skin care and neuromuscular disorders.

In 1950, Gavin S. Herbert, Sr. started a small opthalmic business in a laboratory above one of his Los Angeles drugstores. Stanley Bly, who had only a bachelor's degree in chemistry, created the business's first product, an antihistamine eye drop named Allergan. Under the company name Allergan, Bly developed additional products, including a cortisone eye drop, Cortefrin. The small business was assisted by the salesmanship of Herbert's son, Gavin Herbert, Jr., a 19-year-old student at the University of Southern California.

In 1953, Bly's sudden death almost caused the company to close. Sales at that time were approximately $25,000, and many of Bly's product formulas were undocumented. A young associate professor at the University of Southern California's School of Pharmacy, John Biles, reformulated Allergan's products and saved the company from failure. The next year, Allergan continued to struggle when Gavin Herbert, Jr. was drafted into the navy during the Korean War, and Herbert, Sr. was involved in an automobile accident and was hospitalized for several months. Herbert, Jr. kept the company alive by commuting from his station in San Diego to Los Angeles on weekends. In 1957, Gavin Herbert, Jr. was discharged, and Allergan sales had reached $100,000.

In the late 1950s, Allergan moved out of the upstairs laboratory into a 6,000-square-foot space in a converted Los Angeles theater. With the assistance of Jack Browning, an ad agency executive and former employee of SmithKline, Allergan also launched its first marketing plan. A key element of that plan was the advent of Allergan's first national product, Prednefrin, a corticosteroid. By 1960, Allergan was a million dollar company and the company moved its operations to a 30,000-square-foot plant in Santa Ana, California.

Allergan continued to grow in the 1960s, with an increased focus on in-licensing products such as Herplex. Herplex, introduced by Allergan in 1965, was the first antiviral approved by the FDA for use in the United States, and the second drug of any type to be approved after the emergence of new FDA rules requiring that manufacturers prove the efficacy of all new drugs. The new FDA rules provided Allergan with a competitive advantage over larger companies, who were less adaptable. Dean McCann, who later became the company's senior vice-president of legal affairs, began advising Allergan in compliance with the FDA rules as early as 1957.

In 1960, hard contact lenses first became available. Allergan demonstrated its propensity to take advantage of new technology when it entered the contact lens market that year. Liquifilm, a wetting solution for hard contact lenses, became an important vehicle for Allergan's opthalmic products.

Allergan began to develop a global outlook in 1964, when it created its first foreign distributorships in Puerto Rico and Iraq. In 1965, Allergan established its first foreign subsidiary in Canada. The company's only competition abroad was Alcon, and Allergan's growth in the international market and the success of its hard contact lens care products combined to bring sales growth of 20 to 25 percent during the 1960s.

Allergan had achieved $10 million in sales by 1970, and was preparing to become a public company. To take the company public, a long-term plan for managing growth was developed. Toward the realization of that plan, Allergan purchased 24 acres from the Irvine Ranch Company and, in 1968, built its Von Karman production facility on that site. In 1971, Allergan went public, erecting its first office building in Irvine, California.

By the mid-1970s, the company had become a major opthalmic producer, meeting a growing demand for soft contact lens products. Soft contact lenses had become available in 1970, and Allergan became a contractual supplier of soft contact lens solutions to industry giant Bausch & Laumb. Allergan's two lens products were Hydrocare (introduced in 1974) and its enzymatic cleaner. The company's international business flourished due to the success of Allergan's soft contact lens cleaner, which had become the focus of Allergan's European sales since it required no regulatory approval. Allergan established its first manufacturing sites outside the United States in the 1970s, in Puerto Rico and Ireland. The company's operations realized growth of 30 percent in net profits between 1970 and 1975, with total sales reaching $33 million in the latter year.

This period of growth was bolstered by a thriving U.S. opthalmic market, estimated at a value of $90 million at the manufacturer's level in 1975. Business that year rose by 18 percent (an average increase would be 10-12 percent), due to price increases and an exacerbated allergy season. In 1975, Allergan held approximately 30 percent of the hard contact lens market, and increased its considerable share of prescription opthalmics by 27 percent.

In 1977, Allergan was reincorporated in Delaware. In 1978, Gavin Herbert, Sr., Allergan's co-founder and chairman, died. Gavin Herbert, Jr. succeeded his father, adding chairman to his titles of president and chief executive officer. Growth continued in the latter half of the 1970s, with revenue rising from $46.4 million in 1978 to $62.6 million in 1979.

SmithKline Beckman Corporation purchased Allergan for $236 million, and Allergan became a wholly owned subsidiary in 1980. That year, Allergan approached $100 million in sales, a 20 percent increase for the decade. For Allergan, the association with a larger pharmaceutical company was a way to combat its dependence on in-licensing and development. As a subsidiary of SmithKline, Allergan was able to create new products through its first research program. For SmithKline, the purchase of Allergan was the first step in its implementation of a new strategy. In 1970, large profits generated by Thorazine had become a double-edged sword when the patent expired, due to SmithKline's shortsighted lack of investment in research and its failure to develop new ventures. Ten years later, SmithKline's president and CEO Henry Wendt recognized that the company was again becoming dependent on a single product, the anti-ulcer drug Tagamet, with a patent that would expire in 1993.

The purchase of Allergan was Wendt's first step forward in a new strategy to link diagnostic and therapeutic products. In addition, the purchase was to be a catalyst for new partnerships resulting in lucrative research and innovation. Accordingly, SmithKline put Allergan scientists to work, seeking applications of the research knowledge that produced Tagamet to cures for eye or skin diseases.

The potential market for soft contact lenses was enormous. In 1984, according to *Industry Week,* 120 million Americans suffered from a vision problem, but only 12 percent wore soft contact lenses. Two additional factors made soft contacts a lucrative product: a shorter life span (soft lens wearers replaced lenses every 15 months or so), and the advent of tinted lenses, over 20 percent of whose wearers had no vision problems. Finally, the availability and increased affordability of soft contact lenses for astigmatic wearers caused the traditional 10 percent increase in new wearers to jump to 20 percent between 1982 and 1984, according to *Industry Week.*

In 1984, SmithKline strengthened its investment in Allergan—which then held 20 percent of the contact lens solutions market—when it acquired International Hydron, the number two maker of soft contact lenses (behind the industry giant Bausch & Laumb, which held 40 percent of the lens and solutions business). International Hydron became part of Allergan in 1987. At the time of SmithKline's purchase, the contact lens market was reshuffling; some twenty companies had folded in the 1970s, but the remaining thirty businesses were struggling to maintain their positions behind Bausch & Laumb and to take advantage of the unprecedented market potential of soft contacts. Billion-dollar companies such as Nestle and John-

son & Johnson began eyeing the market as its potential became apparent.

By 1987, the $500 million contact lens care market was growing at about 20 to 25 percent annually, and Allergan and its competitors were locked in fierce competition. Allergan stepped forward with an innovative new product, Ultrazyme Enzymatic Cleaner, the first weekly enzymatic cleaner that could be used during disinfection. This product was responsive to an increased focus on better lens care, as studies began to demonstrate that unsanitary lenses led to eye problems. Between 1980 and 1989, Allergan's sales increased from $100 million to $800 million.

Allergan employed two strategies to manage this rapid growth: updating its information systems and restructuring its human relations departments. Michael Garrison, who sold computers for General Electric prior to becoming Allergan's director of information management, developed innovative information strategies for Allergan in the late 1980s. These computer-based systems included an in-house voice mail system that linked ophthalmologists directly to Allergan; a million dollar campaign to provide laptop computers for all 300 U.S. sales representatives to increase territory management; and the donation of computers and communication software to doctors' offices, which made briefs written to support products being considered for Federal Drug Administration approval instantly available for downloading by Allergan researchers.

William C. Shepherd, who would become president of Allergan's U.S. operations and later CEO, envisioned a strengthened human resources structure that would enable the company to manage and increase its sales and promote itself as the world's leading eye care company. Supporting 20 percent annual growth and rapid expansion, Allergan restructured its human resources department, utilizing both centralized and decentralized models. Shepherd hired Rick Hilles, who later became Allergan's senior vice-president of human resources, to create and implement this new structure. Hilles divided the company into six strategic operating areas (SOAs) and separated the responsibilities of the human resources department into two separate areas. A decentralized area focused on specific market segments and goals, while a centralized structure provided technological benefits, information flow, research and development, marketing, manufacturing, and overall management. The restructuring was publicly lauded when Allergan received the 1991 Optimas Award.

Allergan again became a public company in 1989, when Smith-Kline merged with Beecham Corporation, spinning off distribution of Allergan to shareholders. The transition period posed problems for Allergan, which had high costs, inefficient manufacturing systems, gaps in new product development, and large debt. The eye care market was no longer growing at the dramatic pace of the 1980s. Sales had moved away from traditional contact lenses, as disposable lenses and fashion glasses—neither of which were sold by Allergan—took the industry lead. With ophthalmologists spending less, Allergan's diagnostic equipment business was also experiencing little profit.

Allergan's business strategy had become unmanageable because it forced the company to compete over too broad a range of business sectors: from pharmaceuticals to consumer products to diagnostic eye-care instruments. In 1990, Allergan was close to a billion dollar company, but its stock had fallen from $25 a share (at the time of its spinoff) to $15 a share. Investment analysts began to advise investors that Allergan was prime for a takeover, pointing to Nestle's Alcon Laboratories as a potential purchaser.

Allergan changed its business strategy to reflect market needs in the early 1990s. Under the leadership of president and CEO William Shepherd, Allergan reshaped its operations with a three-prong strategy: making more money available for research and development, containing costs, and implementing quality. Between 1989 and 1991, Allergan reduced employment by 10 percent, consolidated some manufacturing operations, reduced its debt, and improved its cash flow, resulting in the elevation of its price on the stock market. In addition, in 1991 the company's board of directors approved a plan to realign Allergan into market-focus business groups with a regional structure giving the company a global focus on the Americas, Europe, Pan-Asia, and Japan.

With a new focus on specialty pharmaceuticals, Allergan began to emerge as a developer of therapeutic products. In 1991, Allergan acquired Oculinum, Inc., and gained an advantage as the only firm marketing Type A botulinum toxin, a product of the bacterium that causes botulism which had been shown to be safe and effective in treating neuromuscular disorders. Botox, the market name for the substance manufactured by Oculinum, Inc., generated $5 million in sales during its first year. Also in 1991, Allergan researcher David Woodward patented a composition that can be used in treating glaucoma. At that time, most glaucoma treatments inhibited the formation of fluids. The new Allergan composition, a derivative of protoglandin (a fat molecule produced in the eye), helps the eye drain, relieving fluid pressure.

A product generating less excitement was Allergan's first one-bottle contact lens disinfecting solution, UltraCare Disinfectant/ Neutralizer. Allergan was late to enter the one-step market, and its solution was considered inferior to its competitors by analysts, according to the *New York Times*. In 1992, Allergan sold its North and South American contact lens business, and in 1993 the company sold its remaining contact lens business.

In 1993, Allergan became involved in a proxy battle, as a result of new rules adopted that year by the Securities and Exchange Commission. The State of Wisconsin Investment Board in Madison rallied support from other institutions to put Allergan's ''poison pill'' shareholders' rights plan to a vote by the holders. Allergan's management position was that shareholder control of the plan would render the board impotent in case of a sudden takeover. However, Allergan's shareholders passed what became one of the first successful shareholder solicitations by a slight majority (52 percent) at the April 1993 annual meeting.

The 1990s restructuring improved Allergan's growth, with sales increasing from $762 million in 1991 to $858 million in 1993. In an interview with *Fortune* magazine, Samuel Isaly, manager of the Medical Research Investment Fund, indicated that investment in Allergan, ''one of the world leaders in ophthalmologi-

cal pharmaceuticals,'' is an excellent value, with earnings and stock projected to rise at 15 percent a year.

As Allergan prepared to enter the twenty-first century, it focussed on new products. Research projects in the mid-1990s included a topical retinoid tarazotene for acne and psoriasis; a new multifocal interocular lens (IOL) that will allow cataract patients to see well over a range of distances; a joint venture for the anti-cancer usage of Retinoic acid with Ligand Pharmaceutical; the development of topical opthalmic uses for cyclosporine A (with Sandoz Pharmaceuticals Corporation in Japan); and collaborative projects with several academic institutions.

As the U.S. healthcare system is reviewed in the 1990s, Allergan must adjust to new regulations and industry challenges. The Safe Medical Devices Act of 1990 increased reporting requirements of adverse events associated with medical devices, and the Prescription Drug Law Fee Act of 1992 required payment of substantial fees to the FDA for new drug applications. Other regulatory measures are pending. In addition, the total cost of providing health care services is under governmental review, and there is serious pressure to lower the cost of health care. Allergan anticipates that products such as IOLs and pharmaceutical products may be targeted for price reductions. Because these products accounted for some 60 percent of Allergan's 1993 sales, such a reduction would seriously impact Allergan's profits.

Even though the changes in the healthcare industry may change the profitability of Allergan dramatically, Allergan has proven its ability to adapt to industry changes. In 1994, the company that began in a small laboratory above a drugstore was a world leader in eye care, with sales approaching $1 billion. Allergan's ability to restructure itself to meet the needs of an ever-changing market should keep the company profitable into the future.

Principal Subsidiaries: Allergan S.A.I.C. y F. (Argentina); Laboratorios Oftalmologicos Argentinos S.A.I.C.I.F.; Allergan Australia Pty. Ltd.; Allergan Holdings Pty. Ltd. (Australia); Allergan Warenvertriebsgesellschaft MbH (Austria); Allergan NV/SA, (Belgium); Allergan-Lok Produtos Farmaceuticos Ltda. (Brazil); Allergan Inc. (Canada); Allergan Laboratorios Limitada (Chile); Allergan de Colombia S.A.; Allergan ApS (Denmark); Allergan France S.A.; Allergan Sophia S.A. (France); Pharm-Allergan GmbH (Germany); Allergan Optical GmbH (Germany); Allergan Asia Limited (Hong Kong); Allergan Botox Limited (Ireland); Allergan Ireland (Sales) Limited; Allergan S.p.a. (Italy); Allergan K.K. (Japan); Allergan Hydron K.K. (Japan); Allergan Afrasia Limited (Malta); Allergan S.A. de C.V. (Mexico); Laboratoires Allergan Dulcis S.A.M. (Monaco); Pharmac, S.A.M. (Monaco); Allgergan B.V. (Netherlands); Allergan New Zealand Limited (New Zealand); Allergan A/S (Norway); Allergan Pakistan (Private) Limited; Allergan Inter America S.A. (Panama); Allergan Pharmaceuticals (Ireland) Ltd., Inc.; Allergan Singapore Pte., Ltd.; Allergan South Africa (Pty.), Ltd.; Allergan Pharmaceuticals (Pty.) Ltd. (South Africa); Allergan S.A.E. (Spain); Corlens S.A. (Spain); Allergan Norden AB (Sweden); Allergan AG (Switzerland); Allergan Optik Mamulleri Ve Ticaret Limited Sirketi (Turkey); Allergan Limited (United Kingdom); Allergan Holdings Limited (United Kingdom); Allergan Farnborough Limited (United Kingdom); Allertgan Research Centre Ltd. (United Kingdom);

Allergan America; Allergan Medical Optics; Herbert Laboratories; Allergan Caribe, Inc.; Allergan Optical Inc.; Allergan Puerto Rico, Inc.; Allergan Retinoid Corporation; Allergan International Limited (U.S. Virgin Islands); Allergan de Venezuela, S.A.

Further Reading:

"Allergan Inc.," *Wall Street Journal,* December 7, 1993, p. B4.
"Allergan Pharmaceuticals," *Wall Street Transcript,* March 22, 1976, p. 1.
"Allergan Shareholders Pass Proposal Forcing Vote on Poison Pill," *Wall Street Journal,* April 28, 1993, p. A6.
Chen, Ingfei, "Toxin to the Rescue," *Science News,* January 19, 1991, pp. 42–43.
Chernoff, Joel, and Patricia Limbacher, "3 Companies in Proxy Battles," *Pensions and Investments,* April 19, 1993, pp. 1, 34.
"Companies Seek to Test Cancer Drug on People," *Journal of Commerce,* December 1, 1993, p. 5A.
"Composition May Help in Treating Glaucoma," *New York Times,* May 11, 1991.
"Drugs and Biotech: New Hope for the Dead?," *Fortune,* November 29, 1993, p. 32.
Filipowski, Diane, "Allergan's Structuring for Success," *Personnel Journal,* March 1991, pp. 56–57.
Lev, Michael, "Allergan Gains from a Reduction," *New York Times,* December 5, 1991, p. C8.
Marcial, Gene G., "Allergan: Seeing Past the Myopia," *Business Week,* February 5, 1990, p. 78.
McCusker, Tom, "Using Technology to Listen Better," *Datamation,* January 15, 1988, pp. 38–42.
"1991 Optimas Awards," *Personnel Journal,* January, 1991, p. 53.
"SmithKline Beckman Unit to Acquire French Company," *Wall Street Journal,* February 2, 1984, p. 11E.
"SmithKline Plans to Buy Allergan for $259 Million," *Wall Street Journal,* December 7, 1979, p. 14.
"SmithKline: Reducing its Dependence on Drugs," *Business Week,* November 14, 1983, pp. 211–212.
"Takeover Defenses, One Step Backward in the Proxy Arena," *Mergers & Acquisitions,* September/October, 1993, pp. 11–12.
"Tale of a Topnotch Team," *Insight Magazine,* Irvine: Allergan Inc., March 1994.
Verespej, Michael, "Eye-to-eye Combat," *Industry Week,* October 15, 1984, pp. 30–32.
——, "Nowhere to No. 2," *Industry Week,* October 1, 1984, pp. 87–88.
Winters, Patricia, "Lens-care Battle in Sight," *Advertising Age,* October 19, 1987, p. 12.

—Heidi Feldman

Allstate®

The Allstate Corporation

Allstate Plaza
Northbrook, Illinois 60062
U.S.A.
(708) 402-5000
Fax: (708) 402-0045

Public Subsidiary of Sears, Roebuck and Co.
Incorporated: 1931 as Allstate Insurance Company
Employees: 47,900
Sales: $20.95 billion
Stock Exchanges: New York Chicago
SICs: 6331 Fire, Marine & Casualty Insurance; 6311 Life
   Insurance; 6719 Holding Companies, Nec

The Allstate Corporation is the holding company for Allstate Insurance Company, the second largest property and casualty insurance company by premiums in the United States. Allstate controls about 12 percent of the U.S. home and auto insurance market, second only to State Farm Insurance Companies. In addition, Allstate Life Insurance Company offers life, annuity and pension products, its Business Insurance offers select coverages for small and medium-sized businesses, and its PMI Mortgage Insurance Company is one of the nation's largest private mortgage guaranty insurers.

Allstate's 20 million customers are served by 14,600 agents through over 9,300 locations in the United States and Canada. Personal property and casualty policies account for about three-fourths of Allstate's revenue. Life Operations account for fourteen percent of company revenue. In June 1993, Sears, Roebuck and Co. offered nearly 20 percent of Allstate's stock to the public in the largest initial public stock offering in U.S. history, making Allstate the nation's largest publicly held personal property and casualty insurance company.

The idea for Allstate came during a bridge game on a commuter train in 1930, when insurance broker Carl L. Odell proposed to his neighbor, Sears, Roebuck and Co. president and CEO Robert E. Wood, the idea of selling auto insurance by direct mail. Odell suggested that selling insurance by mail could sharply reduce costs by eliminating commissions paid to salesmen. The idea appealed to Wood, and he passed the proposal on to the Sears board of directors, whose members were also intrigued by the concept. Allstate Insurance Company, named after an automobile tire marketed by Sears, went into business in April 1931,

offering auto insurance by direct mail and through the Sears catalog. Lessing J. Rosenwald was Allstate's first chairman of the board, and Odell was named vice-president and secretary.

The company's early success proved Odell and Wood correct with regard to cost cutting. Selling primarily through the regular Sears catalog, Allstate took in $118,323 in premiums on 4,217 policies in 1931, with a staff of 20 employees based at Sears headquarters in Chicago. Although the company showed underwriting losses in its first two years of operation, by 1933 it earned a profit of $93,000 from 22,000 active policies. That year, the first sale made by an Allstate agent was completed from a Sears booth at the Chicago World's Fair.

In 1934, Allstate opened its first permanent sales office in a Chicago Sears store, marking the beginning of a transition from direct mail to agents as its principal avenue of sales. The use of Sears stores enabled the company to keep a lid on costs even with the added expense of agents' commissions. Allstate's growth through the remainder of the Depression was slow but steady. By 1936, the company's premium volume had reached $1.8 million. Revenue from premiums more than tripled by 1941, reaching $6.8 million from over 189,000 policies in force. In 1943, James Barker was named chairman of Allstate's board.

The United States' participation in World War II slowed Allstate's growth somewhat, since automobile production and usage were curtailed. New legislation, however, helped pave the way for a period of explosive growth that the company would experience after the war's end. In 1941, when only about a quarter of U.S. drivers had auto liability insurance, a law was passed in New York firmly establishing the financial responsibility of drivers for damage or injuries resulting from auto mishaps. New York's law inspired a flurry of legislation in other states, and by the mid-1950s nearly every state had some sort of financial responsibility law on its books.

During the ten year period after World War II, Allstate grew at a phenomenal pace, nearly doubling its size every two years. There were 327,000 Allstate policyholders paying premiums totaling over $12 million in 1945, and by 1955 Allstate's sales had risen to $252 million, with more than 3.6 million policies in force.

Growth was facilitated by a change in the company's structure that was implemented in 1947. That year, Allstate decentralized its operations, adopting a three-tiered structure. Research and policy development were conducted at Allstate's home office. Zone offices were created to interpret company directives, and in turn oversee the regional offices, where the programs were put into effect. Some regions were further organized into district service offices and local sales/service centers. The restructuring extended to the first foreign offices, as well. Allstate became an international company in 1953 when its first Canadian office opened. Along with the restructuring, the 1947 introduction of the Illustrator Policy, which simplified the language of policies and added pictures to enhance customers' understanding of their coverage, facilitated growth.

During the 1950s, Allstate became more than an auto insurer. Throughout the decade, Allstate expanded its services to include the entire spectrum of insurance. Personal liability insurance was introduced in 1952. In 1954, Allstate began offering residential fire insurance. Commercial fire, personal theft, and homeowners insurance were all added in 1957. Through a subsidiary, Allstate Life Insurance Company, life insurance became part of the company's package in 1957 as well. In 1958, personal health and commercial liability insurance were added to the Allstate line. By the end of the decade, boat owners, group life, and group health insurance were all being offered. A new entity, Allstate Enterprises, Inc., was created in 1960 as an umbrella for a whole batch of non-insurance businesses to come. Among the activities eventually conducted under the Allstate Enterprises banner were a motor club and a number of finance operations, including vehicle financing, mortgage banking, and mutual fund management.

Allstate's now well-known slogan, "You're in Good Hands With Allstate," first appeared in 1950 after its creation by the company's general sales manager, Davis W. Ellis. By the end of the decade it was used in the company's first network television advertising campaign, which featured actor Ed Reimers.

Allstate's growth throughout the 1950s paved the way for continued growth over the next few decades. Not only did the company increase its sales volume but it increased its offerings and its operating space. In 1963, the Allstate Life Insurance subsidiary passed the $1 billion mark in insurance in force, after only six years of operation. By that time, over 5,000 agents were selling Allstate life, automobile, home, and business insurance. Two new subsidiaries, Allstate Insurance Company of Canada and Allstate Life Insurance Company of Canada, were formed the following year. In 1966, the Judson B. Branch Research Center (later renamed the Allstate Research and Planning Center) was opened in Menlo Park, California. The company's home office was moved to a new 723,000-square-foot complex in the Chicago suburb of Northbrook, Illinois a year later. Meanwhile, Allstate continued to make additional types of insurance available to its customers throughout the decade, including worker's compensation insurance in 1964, surety bonds in 1966, ocean marine coverage in 1967, and a business package policy in 1969.

By 1970, there were 6,500 Allstate Insurance agents. That year, Allstate unveiled a mutual fund. In 1972 Allstate entered the mortgage banking business by acquiring National First Corporation. The following year, the company purchased PMI Mortgage Insurance Company, marking its initial entry into that field. Around the same time, Allstate insurance became available through independent agents in rural areas not covered by agents working directly for the company. For 1973, Allstate generated earnings of $203 million, nearly 30 percent of parent company Sears's total.

The 1970s also saw Allstate increase its presence abroad dramatically. In 1975, the company entered the Japanese market through a joint venture (Seibu Allstate Life Insurance Company, Ltd.) and purchased Lippmann & Moens, a group of Dutch insurance operations. The remainder of the decade also included the formation of Tech-Cor, Inc., an auto-body research and reclamation firm, in 1976; the establishment of a Commercial Insurance Division (later called Allstate Business Insurance) to oversee the company's commercial operations in 1978; and the formation of a new wholly owned subsidiary, Northbrook Property and Casualty Insurance Company, in

1978. Allstate Reinsurance Co. Limited, a London Subsidiary of Allstate International, was incorporated in 1978. Two new policies, the Basic Homeowners Policy and the Healthy American Plan (life insurance) were introduced in 1978 and 1979, respectively.

Allstate was the sixth largest insurance group in the United States by 1980. At that time, the company was operating four zone offices, 31 regional offices, 219 claim-service offices, 687 automobile damage inspection stations, and 2,720 sales/service centers. For 1980, the company reported $450 million in net income on revenue of $6.2 billion, as well as assets of $10.5 billion and 40,000 employees. In 1981, two Dean Witter Reynolds insurance companies, Surety Life Insurance Company and Lincoln Benefit Life Company, became part of the Allstate Life Insurance group. Allstate, Dean Witter, and Coldwell Banker joined forces the following year to form the Sears Financial Network, first appearing in eight Sears stores and later expanding to many other locations.

Donald F. Craib, Jr. was named chairman of the board at Allstate in 1982. Under Craib, a major reorganization of Allstate's corporate structure was initiated. The "New Perspective," as it was called, entailed the elimination of zone offices, as well as other streamlining and decentralizing moves. A new, more flexible life insurance plan, the Universal Life policy, was also unveiled that year. By the end of 1983, Allstate's claim staff consisted of 12,500 employees, the largest force in the industry.

In 1985, Allstate rolled out its Neighborhood Office Agent (NOA) program. In its first year, the NOA program placed 1,582 agents in 944 locations. The following year, the company launched an extensive $30 million advertising campaign that included nine new television commercials and the creation of a new tag line: "Leave It to the Good Hands People." The campaign, which extended to print and radio as well, emphasized family protection. For 1986, the company reported income of over $750 million on revenue of $12.64 billion.

A number of business insurance developments took place at Allstate in 1987. First, the company's Commercial Insurance Division and Reinsurance operation were combined under the Business Insurance umbrella. In addition, two new programs were launched in that area. The "Topflight" program created special ties between the company's Northbrook subsidiary and certain independent agents. The STAR-PAK program offered a new business package policy that provided special services such as the delivery of price quotes within five hours. Allstate also launched the Allstate Advantage Program, a three-tiered rating system for auto insurance, in 1987. A new board chairman and chief executive officer, Wayne E. Hedien, was named in 1989.

Throughout the 1980s, the company had grown at a rate that could not be supported by its profits. It had roughly doubled its premiums during the decade, but in doing so it had burdened itself with a large number of high-risk policyholders. This growth had increased the company's costs both in terms of claims payouts and regular operating expenses. Meanwhile, the company also had to contend with customer backlash against insurance rates, including an ongoing court battle in California involving the 1988 passage of Proposition 103, which called for a rollback on premium rates. Allstate's income shrank from $946 million in 1987 to $701 million in 1990. Resolving Proposition 103 issues put some major concerns behind the company.

After a solid year in 1991, Allstate suffered losses from Hurricane Andrew in 1992 that obscured an otherwise outstanding year for the company. This natural disaster led to a net loss of $825 million for the year. Subsequently, an insurance crisis developed in Florida. The legislature was unable to enact a solution the following spring, and Allstate announced a plan to nonrenew some 300,000 Florida property customers living in high hurricane risk areas. A state-mandated moratorium on nonrenewals was imposed until November 15, 1993. On November 9, 1993, the Florida Legislature approved a catastrophe fund bill designed to protect insurance consumers and the insurance industry from the financial devastation caused by severe hurricanes. The bill enabled Allstate to renew about 97 percent of its Florida property customers in 1994.

In June 1993, 20 percent of Allstate was offered to the public. The offering was an extraordinary success, generating $2.4 billion in capital. That sum was the largest ever raised in an initial public offering in the United States. The separation of Allstate from Sears was part of Sears's new focus on its traditional business of merchandising. With newly found financial strength from the successful public offering, Allstate posted impressive numbers for 1993: a record net income of $1.3 billion on revenue of $20.9 billion.

Principal Subsidiaries: Allstate Insurance Company; Allstate Automobile and Fire Insurance Co., Ltd. (Japan, 50%); Allstate Life Insurance Company; Allstate Indemnity Compnay; All-state Life Insurance Company of New York; Allstate Reinsurance Co., Ltd.; Glenbrook Life Insurance Company; Glenbrook Life and Annuity Company; Lincoln Benefit Life Company; Northbrook Life Company; Northbrook Property and Casualty Company; Northbrook National Insurance Company; PMI Mortgage Insurance Company; Surety Life Insurance Company; Saison Life Insurance Co., Ltd. (Japan, 50%); Samshin Allstate Life Insurance Co., Ltd. (Korea, 50%); Tech-Cor, Inc.

Further Reading:

Allstate Corporation, *This is Allstate,* Northbrook, IL: Allstate Corporation.

"Allstate Insurance: Playing the Field from Now On," *Business Week,* July 11, 1959, pp. 76–88.

Boe, Archie R., *Allstate: The Story of the Good Hands Company,* New York: Newcomen Society, 1981.

Cole, Robert J., "Allstate Chief Heads an Investment Army," *New York Times,* May 3, 1970, p. F3.

Durgin, Hillary, "A New Hand Dealt to 1990s Allstate," *Crain's Chicago Business,* December 20, 1993, p. 1.

——, "Allstate IPO Scores Big," *Crain's Chicago Business,* June 7, 1993, p. 38.

Elsner, David M., " 'Good Hands People' Play Tough, Propelling Allstate's Profits Up," *Wall Street Journal,* October 4, 1974, p. 1.

Levin, Gary, "Allstate's Ads Hand It to 'Family'," *Advertising Age,* January 20, 1986, p. 1.

"Something New in Stock for Sears Shoppers," *Business Week,* April 25, 1970, pp. 120–22.

Steinmetz, Greg, "Allstate Stock Sale Raises $2.12 Billion, Largest Initial Offering for a U.S. Firm," *Wall Street Journal,* June 3, 1993, p. A3.

—Robert R. Jacobson

istration, and finances, and his first task was to find an architect to design the building that would become the company's head-quarters.

Although the company was small, it pursued its mission diligently, filing a patent application for a transdermal system invented by Zaffaroni in 1969. The transdermal system was innovative because it would allow medicines to be absorbed through the skin for a controlled, continuous dosage. While waiting for FDA approval, ALZA became a public company, as Syntex distributed its shares. In 1974, Ocusert Pilo-20/40, used in the treatment of glaucoma, became the first ALZA product to gain FDA approval.

In 1977, Ciba-Geigy Corp., a pharmaceutical giant, acquired a controlling interest in ALZA. This was the beginning a difficult five-year period for ALZA and its stockholders, who began losing money. Despite economic challenges, however, the company continued to improve upon its drug delivery systems, and in August 1981, the FDA approved ALZA's first transdermal product, the Transderm Scop for treatment of motion sickness. Two months later, Transderm-Nitro won FDA approval for use in the treatment of angina. Both transdermal treatments were administered via small patches that resembled adhesive bandages. Once the patches were applied, a steady dosage of the drugs they contained permeated the skin and entered the bloodstream at a regulated rate.

The benefits of transdermal drug therapy were numerous. In addition to providing consistent drug levels in the bloodstream, the transdermal system offered improved absorption. Unlike the medication in orally-ingested pills—which was often destroyed or neutralized in the stomach, intestine, or liver before reaching the bloodstream—transdermal delivery allowed more of the medication to be absorbed, making lower dosages possible. The transdermal system can also reduce the incidence of side effects.

ALZA was nearly bankrupt when it split from Ciba-Geigy in 1982 and began working with other large players in the pharmaceutical industry. The company had its first profitable year in 1983 and was listed on the American Stock Exchange. The following year, ALZA purchased land in Vacaville, California, to build a 117,000 square-foot commercial manufacturing facility. The Vacaville facility became the center for the manufacture of several transdermal and oral products.

ALZA flourished during the late 1980s. Transderm-Nitro became the first ALZA product to hit $100 million in annual sales, and company revenues had reached $71 million by 1987, when Gerstel was named CEO and co-chairman. The following year, the company opened new facilities in Mountain View, California, to accommodate its growing research and development team. In 1989, the FDA approved ALZA's Procardia XL tablets, and Pfizer Inc. began to market the drug for treatment of angina and hypertension under a royalty license from ALZA.

Procardia XL reflected ALZA's contribution to osmotic technology, which controlled the release rate of medication in capsule or tablet form. This technology, known as OROS, involved the osmotic design of the capsule's core and membrane, which contained both the drug and osmotic agent. When a patient swallowed an OROS tablet, water would be drawn

ALZA Corporation

950 Page Mill Road
P.O. Box 10950
Palo Alto, California 94303-0802
U.S.A.
(415) 494-5000
Fax: (415) 494-5151

Public Company
Incorporated: 1968
Employees: 1,100
Sales: $234 million
Stock Exchanges: New York
SICs: 8731 Commercial Physical Research; 2834 Pharmaceutical Preparations; 5122 Drugs, Drug Proprietaries, and Druggists's Sundries

As one of the world's leading producers of drug delivery systems, ALZA Corporation develops and manufactures a variety of systems that make administration of medication more efficient and effective. A pioneer in the field of transdermal therapy, ALZA developed the Nicoderm patch marketed by Marion Merrell Dow as an aid to help smokers kick the habit. Other well-known products developed by ALZA include Procardia XL for both angina and hypertension and Duragesic for the management of cancer pain.

ALZA was founded in 1968 by Alejandro Zaffaroni, a co-founder of the major pharmaceutical company Syntex Corporation, based in Palo Alto, California. ALZA was to be unique in that its research and development activities would be directed not toward creating new drugs, but rather toward developing better delivery systems for existing medications. Specifically, the company's mission was to improve on the long-standing methods of injections and pills taken orally by introducing products and systems that would help to stabilize the amount of drug in a patient's bloodstream.

The fledgling company leased land in Stanford's Research Park for its first facility, and Martin Gerstel, who had recently graduated from Stanford's business school, became the company's second employee after Zaffaroni. In a 1989 interview for San Jose's *Business Journal,* Gerstel recalled that when he asked Zaffaroni about a title, the founder replied "that I could be anything I wanted except president. He wanted that title." So Gerstel became the vice-president in charge of planning, admin-

from the membrane to saturate the drug, which would then be released in liquid form drop by drop through laser-drilled holes in the tablet. This permitted a gradual release of the drug and led to reduced side effects and predictable levels of the drug in the bloodstream.

ALZA's Acutrim—an appetite suppressant marketed over-the-counter by Ciba Consumer Pharmaceuticals—also utilized the OROS osmotic technology. In late 1989, ALZA filed a new drug application with the FDA for a nasal decongestant tablet that would use the OROS controlled-release technology. The product, designed for sufferers of colds and allergies, was a once-a-day tablet that continuously delivered pseudoephedrine for 24 hours. Called Efidac/24, the cold medication is sold over the counter and is used to relieve nasal congestion from colds, hay fever, and sinusitis.

By 1990, ALZA had about 40 products in development and 650 employees, more than half of whom comprised the research and development team. In January of that year, ALZA announced the development of an osmotic syringe pump for subcutaneous or intravenous delivery of medications. A wearable, disposable system, the pump consisted of two reservoirs—one for water and one for the drug being administered—and an osmotic tablet compartment. The tablet facilitated the workings of the syringe pump, so that a mixture of water and drug could be introduced into the patient's bloodstream. Unlike traditional intravenous devices, the osmotic syringe pump did not rely on gravity and permitted the patient to move about freely.

During this time, ALZA entered into several joint agreements intended to bolster its development of new technologies. A partnership with Procter & Gamble Co., focusing on the development, manufacture, and marketing of treatments for periodontal disease, resulted in the July 1994 U.S. introduction of Actisite Periodontal Fiber, which delivers the antibiotic tetracycline directly to the affected site. Another joint effort, with Pfizer Inc., led to the development of Glucotrol XL, Pfizer's oral hypoglycemic medicine for non-insulin-dependent diabetics. With Pfizer, ALZA developed a once-daily form of the drug—cleared for marketing by the FDA—incorporating ALZA's OROS controlled-release technology.

Moreover, ALZA established a new company called Bio-Electro Systems Inc. This company, formed independent of ALZA in order to minimize risk to shareholders, explored the concept of electro transport, in which electrical currents propel drugs into the skin. Bio-Electro's mission also included the development of Alzamer, erodible polymers that could be filled with a drug and then injected or inserted into the body.

In 1990, the FDA approved ALZA's Duragesic transdermal system, designed to deliver fentanyl for the relief of chronic pain in cancer patients. Revenues for that year reached $109.4 million, up from $92.7 million in 1989. The considerable increase, due mainly to royalties from the sale of Procardia XL, was nothing new for ALZA; since the early 1980s, the company had enjoyed annual revenue growth of 48 percent and yearly profits growth of 220 percent. Analysts noted that ALZA had no real competition, since no other company concentrated exclusively on the development of a broad range of drug delivery systems covering various technologies.

In 1991, to consolidate its stake in electrotransport systems, the company announced that it would acquire Bio-Electro Systems as well as Medtronic Inc.'s electrotransport business unit. ALZA stock was trading at $80 a share in late 1991, double the price it garnered the year before. There were 11 ALZA products on the market, and a dozen more awaited FDA approval.

During the final months of 1991, ALZA and Marion Merrel Dow faced a patent lawsuit that threatened the introduction of Nicoderm, the first transdermal nicotine delivery system. Although the FDA approved Nicoderm in November, sales of the breakthrough technology were suspended by court order for one month, when an Irish pharmaceutical company, Elan Corp. plc, claimed that ALZA's nicotine patch infringed on one of its patents. Elan's American marketing partner, American Cyanamid joined in the lawsuit, but by mid-1992 the suit was withdrawn, and the parties reached an out-of-court settlement with no financial impact to those involved. Nicotine patch sales were quick to take off, and the products immediately became popular among the thousands of people trying to stop smoking. However, due to the companies' inability to supply enough product to meet the extraordinary demand, sales dropped and stayed below original launch levels.

ALZA recovered its stride, and the company's stock began trading on the New York Stock Exchange in the summer of 1992. By the end of the year, Procardia XL became the first ALZA-developed product to hit $1 billion in annual sales. Moreover, Efidac/24, a nasal decongestant utilizing OROS technology, received FDA approval. Other ALZA innovations during this time included the development of MOTS (Mucosal Oral Therapeutic System) nystatin, a controlled-release lozenge designed to deliver nystatin for the treatment of oral candidiasis in AIDS patients.

In 1992, ALZA announced the development of two new systems based on its proprietary osmotic technology. One system, Chronset, was designed to deliver proteins and peptides orally. The second system was a veterinary implant called VITS. ALZA also continued its research into electrotransport, developing prototypes of small, reusable devices that delivered drug through the skin. The mild electrical currents emitted by the system propelled controlled, consistent drug dosages into the bloodstream and allowed the patient direct control.

ALZA finished 1992 with $250.5 million in revenues and net income of $72.2 million. More than 50 new products were in development, including an oral form of an anti-epileptic drug, Dilantin. In addition, the company was working with G.D. Searle & Co. to develop a new hypertensive therapy based on the OROS system. The new therapy, Calan OROS, was designed to release medication early in the morning, when dangers from high blood pressure are greatest.

The company celebrated its 25th anniversary in 1993. Fifty-seven patents were granted worldwide, and the company announced the development of its unique Human Implantable Therapeutic Systems (HITS). This new system was designed for long-term, subcutaneous delivery of drugs to patients suffering from such chronic diseases as Alzheimer's, hepatitis, and prostatic cancer. That year, the company also formed Therapeutic Discovery Corp. in order to develop new human pharmaceutical products that would combine ALZA's proprietary drug delivery systems with various drug compounds. Despite these promising developments, ALZA's net income for 1993 was reported at $45.6 million, a decrease attributed to a one-time manufacturing charge.

ALZA's Testoderm system was introduced early in 1994. This transdermal system was designed to deliver testosterone for hormone replacement therapy in hypogonadal males. The company continued its aggressive research into electrotransport systems during this time and signed agreements with companies in the United States, Europe, and Japan to collaborate on research for several other technologies. Another area for expansion involved treatment for diseases of the central nervous system. ALZA entered into collaboration with Warner-Lambert to create controlled-release oral delivery systems of Dilantin, an anticonvulsant, and Cognex, a drug used for treating Alzheimer's disease.

Principal Subsidiaries: ALZA Development Corporation.

Further Reading:

Alexander, Kera, "ALZA Corp. and Bio-Electro Systems Announce Approval of Merger," *Business Wire,* February 6, 1992.

Barry, David, and James S. Goldman, "ALZA Opens Throttle on Expansion," *The Business Journal - San Jose,* May 6, 1991, p. 1.

Burdett, Bonnie J., "ALZA, American Cyanamid, Elan and Marion Merrell Dow Conclude Agreements and Reach Out of Court Settlement," *Business Wire,* May 28, 1992.

Burdett, Bonnie J., "ALZA Corp. Announces the Development of Two New Therapeutic Systems Based on the Company's Osmotic Technology," *Business Wire,* June 23, 1992.

Burdett, Bonnie J., "ALZA Develops Osmotic Syringe Pump for Controlled Administration of Compounds for Intravenous, Subcutaneous Drug Delivery," *Business Wire,* January 8, 1990.

Burdett, Bonnie J., "CEO of ALZA Corp. Announces Development and Clinical Results of ALZA-Developed Product," *Business Wire,* February 6, 1992.

Burdett, Bonnie J., Laura Mills, and F. Robert Kniffen, "ALZA and Janssen Pharmaceutical Announce FDA Approval for Marketing of Fentanyl Transdermal System," *Business Wire,* August 7, 1990.

Gengo, Lorraine, "Martin Gerstel: Modesty Masks Highly Praised, Innovative Leader," *The Business Journal - San Jose,* January 9, 1989, p. 10.

Goldman, James S., "ALZA Buys Back a Firm, Agrees on Marketing Pact," *The Business Journal - San Jose,* November 18, 1991, p. 2.

Goldman, James S., "ALZA's Key Product is Target of Patent Dispute," *The Business Journal - San Jose,* December 2, 1991, p. 2.

Mills, Laura, "ALZA and Procter and Gamble Sign Agreement," *Business Wire,* February 15, 1990.

Mills, Laura, "ALZA Corp. and Ciba-Geigy Announce Marketing Agreement," *Business Wire,* October 18, 1988.

Mills, Laura, "ALZA Corp. Announce Appointment of Gary L. Neil to Head Therapeutic Discovery Corp.," *Business Wire,* April 1, 1993.

Sloan, Allan, "Miracle Drug for Earnings: ALZA Shooting Fish in a Barrel with Merrill Lynch's Arrow," *Newsday,* April 11, 1993, p. 68.

—Marinell James

America Online, Inc.

8619 Westwood Center Drive
Vienna, Virginia 22182
U.S.A.
(703) 448-8700

Public Company
Incorporated: 1985 as Quantum Computer Services, Inc.
Employees: 124
Sales: $40 million
Stock Exchanges: New York
SICs: 7375 Information Retrieval Services

America Online, Inc. is the fastest-growing provider of information services that are delivered to customers' personal computers (PCs) over phone lines. The America Online service includes a wide variety of electronic mail facilities, bulletin boards, conferences and classes, as well as software, games, and publications. America Online's trademark has been easy-to-use, visually oriented services which make the on-line environment accessible and not intimidating to ordinary customers.

America Online got its start in the mid-1980s as an adjunct offering for owners of one type of personal computer and expanded by branching out to other brands. In the 1990s, America Online's offerings were restructured and updated for more current operating systems, and, after the institution of an aggressive marketing drive, the company's customer base skyrocketed. Profitable from the start as a niche-based product, America Online later expanded through agreements with a wide variety of computer manufacturers and media companies, considerably broadening its offerings and its reach.

America Online was founded by Stephen M. Case, a marketer who worked in the consumer division of PepsiCo Inc. In 1982, Case became intrigued by the possibilities of interacting with other personal computer owners through electronic telecommunications. At the time, there were small networks available for use, including the sharing of news and other data, but they were extremely difficult and cumbersome to use, and, as a consequence, were mainly employed by computer buffs or other specialists in the field. Case reasoned that the demand for on-line computer communication would be much greater if it was easier for people to use.

In 1985, Case got an opportunity to put some of his ideas into practice when he formed Quantum Computer Services, Inc., in partnership with Commodore International, Ltd., a leading manufacturer of personal computers, and Control Video. Using $2 million in venture capital, Case created an exclusive on-line service for owners of Commodore computers. The deal worked well for both partners. Commodore had an added selling point for its products, and Quantum had a ready-made pool of customers for its service. Named "Q-Link," the service consisted of a few rudimentary bulletin boards, to which users gained access from their personal computers via a telephone modem.

Within two years, the Q-Link concept had proven its merit. Quantum's revenues had reached $9 million by 1987, and the company had started to turn a profit. With the Commodore Q-Link service as a model, Quantum then branched out to offer programs to owners of computers made by other companies. First, the company set up an alliance with the Tandy Corporation, which manufactured IBM-compatible computers. In November 1988, on-line services for owners of IBM-compatible PCs were introduced. Later, Quantum also began offering services to owners of Apple computers. This service began in September 1989, after a dispute with Apple about whether its name would include the designation "Apple." As personal computers became cheaper and more plentiful, and new, more powerful software and modems were developed, Quantum's subscriber base grew quickly and the company boomed.

In October, 1989, Quantum introduced a new nationwide network for computer owners under the name "America Online." Two years later, the company changed its name to that of its main offering. At the same time, the company began to reorganize its operations, consolidating the services it offered to owners of different computers and focusing its efforts on the IBM-compatible and Macintosh market.

In addition, America Online undertook an ambitious marketing campaign to increase the number of its subscribers. Each customer who signed up for the America Online service was charged $7.95 a month for the first two hours spent on the network, and then ten cents a minute after that. In mid-1991, the company expanded its pool of possible subscribers when it introduced services for IBM-compatible computers using DOS operating systems.

As part of its push to expand its subscriber base, America Online devised a number of creative ways to attract new users. In keeping with a policy of growth through strategic alliances, America Online entered into a joint venture with the Tribune Company, the owner of the *Chicago Tribune,* in an effort to ease its move into the Midwestern market. America Online created a news and information service designed especially for Chicago by making use of materials from the local daily paper. The product was a success, as thousands of Chicago residents began logging on to the service to exchange opinions on local politics, team sports, and other issues. In addition, America Online gained additional capitalization from the deal, as the Tribune Company bought a 9.5 percent stake in the company for $5 million.

In another such arrangement, America Online teamed up with a group called SeniorNet, an organization formed to encourage senior citizens to use computers. With its 5,000 members, SeniorNet provided a new source of customers for America Online, which paid the group a premium for every new member who signed on. In return, America Online offered specialized programming to attract seniors, instituting special news and bulletin services covering topics of interest to them, such as health care.

Case described America Online's strategy as being focused on exploiting niches, such as those formed by the senior citizens group. Rather than trying to enroll the general population, as some larger network services did, America Online has turned a profit catering to smaller special groups. "We see ourselves as a series of specialized magazines catering to specific interests," he told *Business Week* in 1992.

In May 1992, America Online capitalized on its history of solid growth when it sold stock to the public for the first time. The company's offering was greeted with enthusiasm, and its stock price rose sharply. At the end of June 1992, America Online reported its fifth annual profit in its last six years of operation. The company's revenues had reached $26.6 million, yielding profits of $3.5 million, a stark contrast to the persistent red ink generated by its larger competitors in the on-line services field. Continued growth and profitability appeared likely, as America Online's subscriber base grew rapidly, increasing by nearly 50 percent every 12 months.

At the end of 1992, America Online announced another important strategic alliance when Apple Computer Inc. signed a licensing and development agreement with America Online to use its technology in Apple's own future information services. The company was to earn $15 million from the agreement over five years. In addition, Apple contracted to pay for America Online's conversion of its technology for use on Apple machines. The two companies announced that they intended to improve the America Online technology and develop it into an industry-wide standard for on-line information services. This joint venture lent weight and authority to America Online's efforts to expand its market share beyond the ten percent it then held.

In January 1993, America Online expanded its offerings further, introducing an on-line service designed especially for the Windows operating system. As users of IBM-compatible computers moved in droves to the new, easier operating system, America Online saw an opportunity to convert them to its own graphically-based on-line environment. The America Online Windows service featured the company's trademark high-quality graphics and ease of access, and quickly became the most popular new product America Online had ever marketed.

America Online formed another corporate alliance when it reached an agreement with the Sprint Corporation, a long distance telephone company, in April 1993. In return for discounts on the telephone usage that America Online needed to send its service out to users, America Online gave Sprint a large package of stock options.

By the spring of 1993, America Online's success had attracted the interest of another innovator in the computer industry, Paul G. Allen, a cofounder of the Microsoft Corporation. When Allen's stock holdings in the company began to approach 25 percent of America Online's outstanding shares, the company's board of directors moved to prevent him from threatening America Online's independence by adopting a secret shareholders' rights plan that would go into effect if any one party's holdings in the company topped one quarter. In response, Allen filed documents with the Securities and Exchange Commission indicating his interest in acquiring America Online. He also stated that he might seek a seat on the company's board of directors and reported that he had refused to sign a statement proposed by America Online promising that he would not involve himself any further in the company's affairs.

Case and other America Online executives were concerned that any one overwhelming alliance would limit America Online's ability to maneuver and negotiate with other companies. "We've built this company by establishing strategic alliances with a wide range of companies, and we believe it's the best strategy for the company to remain independent," he told the *Wall Street Journal*. On May 11, 1993, Allen met with America Online executives and proposed that America Online and his other high tech ventures work together to develop software for use in multimedia formats. This overture was initially rebuffed by America Online. Ultimately, Allen withdrew from his attempt to increase his involvement in America Online, as the two parties worked out an agreement to collaborate on some future endeavors.

The fruits of another America Online alliance were unveiled in June 1993, when Casio, Inc. and the Tandy Corporation, two computer manufacturers, introduced the "Zoomer," the first in a new generation of products called personal digital assistants. This device incorporated software developed by America Online to offer electronic communications, such as fax, electronic mail, and access to other on-line services. The company believed that devices of this sort would open the interactive services market to a much broader segment of the population. Consequently, it agreed to work with Apple on its hand-held Newton product and with Sharp on its Personal Digital Assistant.

By the end of June 1993, America Online's annual revenues had topped $40 million, an increase of 50 percent over the previous year. In addition, the company's subscriber base had grown to exceed 300,000, also an increase of two-thirds. Not surprisingly, these gains made America Online the country's fastest growing commercial on-line services company. By September, America Online's consumer base had grown even more, as an additional 50,000 customers logged on, pushing subscriber growth to 80 percent.

As America Online's subscriber base grew exponentially, the company began to move away from its early emphasis on niche marketing—the strategy which had provided its initial growth and profitability—toward a stress on a broader array of services which would appeal to its new, broader selection of customers. As part of this effort, the company took a number of steps. It announced that it would offer access to the Internet, a consortium of smaller governmental and academic computer networks that was run as a cooperative. In this way, America Online hoped to tap into the popularity of the Internet, which had a reputation as the fastest-growing on-line service, with over 10 million users in more than 50 different countries. Internet was known as a difficult on-line environment to master, but America Online hoped to simplify its use by offering its customers access to the network through its own software.

In addition to its Internet venture, America Online also embarked upon a series of alliances with media companies. The service added features from the Knight-Ridder newspaper chain, *Time, Omni,* the *Atlantic,* and the *New Republic,* among other magazines, and from the cable network CNN. America Online also joined a branch of the Disney entertainment conglomerate called Disney Adventures.

Along with its expanded offerings, America Online instituted an aggressive marketing program to insure that its subscriber base would continue to grow at a healthy rate. The company started selling membership kits at bookstores and computer supply stores, and also began to have starter disks bound into selected computer trade magazines. In addition, America Online continued to pre-install its software in many computers, making it particularly easy for new computer buyers to join the on-line community. Manufacturers incorporating America Online software into their products included IBM, Apple, Compaq, AST, Tandy, NEC, and Compudyne. Finally, in an effort to make its service appear more economical, America Online revised its pricing structure, lowering some costs. Although this move would have a negative impact on the company's revenues, America Online believed that this would be offset by the fact that more people would sign up, and those who were already signed up would keep paying for the service longer.

By October 1993, America Online's campaign to increase its subscriber base and enhance its market share had pushed its number of users past 400,000, as its blistering pace of growth continued. The size of the company's customer core had more than doubled in the last twelve months. This was followed in the same month by a report that quarterly revenues had also doubled for a year before. In addition, the company's web of media linkages became more complex, as it brought on-line National Public Radio, the San Jose *Mercury News,* and a number of publications produced by Matra Hachette, the world's largest magazine company. In November 1993, America Online sponsored an "interactive event" with Christian evangelist Billy Graham. At a pre-arranged time, America Online users could send messages to Graham through their computer and receive general or, possibly, personal messages in return.

At the start of December 1993, America Online took another step to maintain its position on the cutting edge of information technology when it announced that it would join with three other companies to take part in a trial in California in which America Online's interactive service would be delivered to customers through a cable network, instead of through a telephone line hooked up to a modem. Cable delivery paved the way for fuller integration of video and sound into the multime-

dia mix of text and graphics already provided through personal computer-based services. In this way, America Online hoped to position itself to survive and thrive in a changing information services market and mitigate the danger that advances in technology would leave its offerings behind, or that huge information, communications, and computing behemoths, such as AT&T and Microsoft, would move into a revolutionized marketplace and squeeze smaller competitors such as America Online out of business. To this end, the company also announced plans to work with General Instrument, a manufacturer of cable television equipment, to develop services for interactive television.

In addition to these futuristic plans, America Online continued to strengthen its position by adding subscribers, whose number had passed the half-a-million mark by the end of 1993, and by adding media partners, including Rodale Press, a health and fitness magazine publisher, a re-invented on-line *Saturday Review,* and the *New York Times.* In the area of hardware alliances, America Online added Dell and US Robotics to the list of manufacturers which incorporated America Online products into their own.

By the end of January 1994, America Online's subscriber base had topped 600,000 members, and quarterly revenues had grown by 130 percent, as the company's customer base continued to skyrocket. "The unprecedented demand for America Online has caught us by surprise," Case announced in a company press release. "Our focus now is on expanding our infrastructure." As part of that process, America Online cemented its second agreement with a major television network when it added NBC Online to its offerings. In addition, at the end of January 1994, the company announced a further use of the network's interactive capabilities when it joined with Shopper's Express to provide a grocery and pharmacy ordering and home delivery service.

As America Online moved into the mid-1990s, the company appeared to be ideally situated to prosper in the ever-accelerating field of interactive information networks and services. Although the rapid pace of technological development and the uncertain nature of the future market made the survival of any participant in the industry far from certain, America Online, with its easy-to-use product and policy of forming strategic alliances, appeared more than capable of continuing its success.

Further Reading:

Eng, Paul M., "America Online Is Hooked Up for Growth," *Business Week,* June 21, 1993.

Miller, Michael W., "Tycoon Is Tapping into On-Line Service," *Wall Street Journal,* May 24, 1993.

Schwartz, Evan I., "For America Online, Nothing Is as Nice as a Niche," *Business Week,* September 14, 1992.

—Elizabeth Rourke

American Express Company

American Express Tower
World Financial Center
New York, New York 10285
U.S.A.
(212) 640-2000
Fax: (212) 619-9743

Public Company
Incorporated: 1965
Employees: 100,188
Operating Revenues: $14.17 billion
Stock Exchanges: New York Boston Chicago Pacific London
    Zurich Geneva Basel Düsseldorf Frankfurt Paris
    Amsterdam Toronto Tokyo Brussels
SICs: 6211 Security Brokers and Dealers; 6221 Commodity
    Contracts Brokers, Dealers; 6141 Personal Credit
    Institutions; 6153 Short-term Business Credit; 6020
    Commercial Banks; 6311 Life Insurance; 6082 Foreign
    Trade and International Banks

The American Express Company, a multibillion dollar holding company whose subsidiaries provide travel and financial services worldwide, traces its roots to a New York express business founded by Henry Wells in 1841. From the safe transport of valuables it grew naturally into money orders and traveler's checks; from there its travel service operations, including its credit card, also grew naturally. In the 1980s, American Express expanded into financial planning through Investors Diversified Services, Inc. (IDS) to merger and acquisition advice from Shearson Lehman Hutton. Faced with intensifying competition and poor public relations in the early 1990s, American Express divested itself from many of the businesses it had acquired in the previous decade. Throughout its history, American Express has enjoyed a reputation for innovation, profitability, and integrity.

Henry Wells began his career as an expressman as an agent for William Harnden, who had founded the first express company in the United States in 1839. Express companies were in the business of transporting money and other valuables safely. Wells was an ambitious man who repeatedly proposed expanding the business westward—to Buffalo, New York, the Midwest, and the far West. When Harnden refused to leave the East Coast, Wells struck out on his own, organizing Wells & Co. in 1841.

At first Wells and his associate, Crawford Livingston, served only New York City and Buffalo, then an arduous route by five rickety shortline railroads and wagon or stagecoach for the last 65 miles into or out of Buffalo. A few years later, Wells and William G. Fargo launched an express service from Buffalo to major midwestern cities. Although appreciated by the midwestern business community, the new express service simply did not pay. In 1846, Wells decided to retrench and focus his energies on the growing routes serving New York City, Buffalo, Boston, and Albany, leaving the express business west of Buffalo to Fargo's company, Livingston, Fargo and Co.

In 1849 John Butterfield, a wealthy and experienced transportation mogul, entered the express business with Butterfield, Wasson & Co., a direct competitor to Wells & Company on New York state routes. Later that year, Butterfield proposed that he, Fargo, and Wells eliminate their wasteful competition by joining forces. On March 18, 1850, the three companies consolidated to form the American Express Company, a joint-stock company with initial capital of $150,000. Wells was elected the new company's first president; Fargo became vice-president.

Under Wells's leadership American Express was immediately and unexpectedly profitable, expanding rapidly and acquiring small competitors in the Midwest, negotiating contracts with the first railroads, and running packet boats on the Illinois Canal to connect Ohio, Illinois, and Iowa with steamship lines on the Illinois River. In 1851, American Express reached an amicable agreement with its major rival, Adams and Co. (reorganized as Adams Express Co. in 1854). American Express was to expand north and west of New York while Adams was free to grow south and east. This agreement was kept and renewed over the next 70 years, buying American Express time to establish its business solidly.

Despite their agreement with Adams and Co., Wells and Fargo still distrusted their rival and feared the company would gain a monopoly in the California gold fields. When Wells proposed his old dream of a transcontinental express service to the American Express board of directors, they rejected his idea. But in 1852 Wells and Fargo got the board's blessing to launch an independent venture, Wells Fargo & Company, to provide express and banking services in California.

In 1854, trouble developed with the New York, Lake Erie & Western Railroad (American Express's link to the Midwest) when Daniel Drew, the railroad's owner, became outraged that American Express had picked off the Erie's most profitable freight business by shipping light, high-rate freight on the Erie under its express contract. Drew was determined to award the express rights to others. In response, American Express created an affiliate and presented it as a bona fide competitor. American Express loaned the funds to start a new company to Danforth Barney, then president of Wells Fargo. Barney's new company, United States Express Co., then acquired the Erie express rights from Drew and split the lucrative midwestern business with American Express.

American Express's first decade saw two other noteworthy accomplishments. In 1857, American Express launched the Overland Mail Co. as a joint venture with Wells Fargo, Adams Express Co., and United States Express Co. The Overland Mail

Co. (later controlled by Wells Fargo) won the first transcontinental mail contract from the United States Postal Service, which led to its involvement with the *Pony Express*. Also, James C. Fargo, William's younger brother, proposed the establishment of a fast, bulk freight express service for merchants. Merchants Dispatch, created in 1858, proved immediately successful.

The Civil War was enormously profitable for American Express, as it was for the express industry generally. American Express shipped supplies to army depots, took election ballots to soldiers, and delivered parcels to parts of the Confederacy taken by Union forces. During this period, American Express distributed huge dividends to its shareholders.

After the war, the express industry attracted the attention of financial raiders. The first raid, by National Bankers Express Co. in 1866, was thwarted at relatively low cost. American Express quickly reached an agreement with Adams Express and United States Express to neutralize the threat by giving National Bankers Express shares of the established companies and a seat on the American Express board of directors.

The second raid had much more serious consequences. Late in 1866, a group of New York merchants established Merchants Union Express Co., to both get into the express business and destroy the three largest express lines—Adams, American, and United States. Merchants Union first hired away the older companies' experienced agents and then invaded their territories. American Express suffered such losses in 1867 that for the first and only time in its history it failed to pay a dividend. On December 21, 1868, the four express companies reached a peace agreement, dividing the express and fast-freight business and pooling and distributing net earnings. American Express got the worst of the deal; Merchants Union acquired rights on railways that had been its bread-and-butter lines (the Hudson River and New York Central railroads) and lost its supremacy in the express business. In 1868, American Express was forced to merge with Merchants Union to form the American Merchants Union Express Company (shortened in 1873 back to the American Express Company). Also in 1868 Wells retired and was replaced as president by William G. Fargo.

Fargo's tenure saw the beginning of two trends that would later prove significant. First, Fargo's brother, James, expanded Merchants Dispatch operations to Europe. Soon Merchants Dispatch was transporting more than half the first-class tonnage from New York City to over a dozen European cities, making international operations a lucrative sideline for American Express. Second, high express rates set after the Panic of 1873 created public demand for a government operated parcel post. In 1874, the U.S. Postal Service began to deliver packages at a new, low rate. The following year, Congress set the parcel rate at a half-cent per ounce, far below cost. This cut deeply into express company profits. Express industry lobbying and the post office's substantial operating loss soon persuaded Congress to raise rates to a more reasonable level, but the precedent for governmental involvement in the express business had been established.

William Fargo's death in 1881 and James's succession to the presidency began a new era for American Express. Although

James Fargo was often described as autocratic, aloof, and old-fashioned, he was also remarkably innovative. During his term of office, American Express first diversified into the financial services industry with the introduction of two instruments—the American Express Money Order in 1882 and the American Express Travelers Cheque in 1891.

The post office first introduced the postal money order in 1864. This immediately threatened the express industry because it reduced the demand by banks and merchants for the transport of money and other valuables. The postal money order, however, had a serious flaw: its face value could be altered without detection. Although American Express directors had discussed introducing a money order since the end of the Civil War, it took James Fargo to galvanize the company into action. At his direction Marcellus Berry, an American Express employee, designed a safer money order. American Express's money order was an immediate hit; it could be used to settle charges on express shipments, was more readily available than the postal money order, and was simpler, cheaper, and easier to negotiate. Not only did the money order provide a new source of revenue (over 250,000 were issued the first year), but for the first time American Express had a credit balance (or "float"—funds from instruments that had been paid for but were not yet cashed) that could be safely invested to bring in additional income.

The traveler's check filled a similar financial niche. Before 1891, tourists and business travelers could transfer funds from the United States to Europe only via a letter of credit, a time-consuming and cumbersome method: only specified correspondents of the issuing United States bank could negotiate letters of credit, and then only during banking hours and after an appreciable delay. Fargo, annoyed by his own experience with the procedure, again directed Marcellus Berry to find a solution. The American Express Travelers Cheque was a marked improvement over the letter of credit in several respects: its simple signature and countersignature provision made the instrument very secure; it could easily be converted into foreign currency at any American Express freight office; and, if lost or stolen, American Express would refund the owner's money. The value and convenience of the traveler's check was recognized at once, and its popularity again provided American Express with additional revenues and float.

After the traveler's check was introduced in 1891, travelers began making American Express freight offices their informal headquarters—places to convert funds, to seek information about hotels and travel arrangements, and simply to congregate. American Express officers saw the opportunities offered by the travel industry and urged diversification in that direction. James Fargo, however, was absolutely opposed to the idea. He allowed American Express agents to offer travel information purely as a service to customers, but drew the line there. American Express's official entry into the travel industry, which became one of its best-known and most lucrative businesses, was delayed until after Fargo's retirement in 1914.

After the turn of the century, the express industry came under attack from a number of quarters. The railroads had steadily eroded express profits by raising their rates from 40 percent of gross receipts to more than 55 percent by 1910. Also in 1910, long-overdue government regulation of the express industry began with passage of the Mann-Elkins Act, which made express companies common carriers subject to the scrutiny of the Interstate Commerce Commission (ICC). In 1912, New York express company drivers and their helpers went on strike for higher wages and fewer working hours (they were underpaid and overworked, even in an era of low pay and long hours), exciting highly unfavorable press and public reaction. In 1913, the U.S. Post Office again expanded parcel delivery services at reduced rates, while the ICC set express rates that the industry feared were prohibitively low.

When George C. Taylor, a longtime American Express employee, was elected the company's fourth president after Fargo's retirement in 1914, the end of the laissez-faire express industry was in sight. Taylor's first actions, to expand foreign remittance operations and to officially inaugurate travel services by opening a travel department in 1915, saved the company when its domestic express division was nationalized in 1918 and became part of the American Railway Express Co. as a wartime measure. Another of Taylor's accomplishments was to establish the American Express Co. This wholly owned subsidiary was created in 1919 primarily to expand international banking operations (which had been conducted sporadically through foreign remittance offices since 1904). Although American Express was slow to gain a foothold in Europe, its international banking operations flourished in Asia during the 1920s and 1930s, especially in Hong Kong and Shanghai.

In the late 1920s, American Express again changed hands. The express industry was targeted for takeovers during this period because most express companies had been organized prior to antitrust legislation, raising the possibility of their exemption from antitrust regulations. American Express was especially attractive because its net income had more than doubled in the six years ending in 1928. In 1927 Albert H. Wiggin, chairman of the Chase National Bank, started buying American Express stock through dummies. By July, Wiggin had acquired two seats on the board and 42 percent of the stock, at a bargain price. In 1929, Chase Securities Corp., an affiliate of Chase National Bank, acquired control of American Express in a stock exchange and Wiggin was elected first chairman of the American Express board.

In May of 1930 Chase National merged with the giant Equitable Trust Co. to become the largest bank in the world. John D. Rockefeller supplanted Wiggin as largest shareholder and Winthrop W. Aldrich, Rockefeller's brother-in-law, became chairman of both the Chase Securities and the American Express boards.

This was a difficult time for American Express management, headed by Frederick P. Small (who became president on Taylor's death in 1923). Not only were the directors preoccupied with their power struggles, but the financial climate was steadily worsening. Then the Great Depression hit. Between 1930 and 1932, roughly a third of all American banks failed. In early 1933, President Franklin D. Roosevelt announced a national bank holiday to allow banks to recover from the panic. The bank holiday brought commerce to a virtual standstill. During this period American Express, since it was not a bank and thus not required to close, enjoyed a tremendous advantage: it remained open and redeemed traveler's checks, providing the only finan-

cial services available to individuals and merchants while the nation's assets were frozen. The traveler's check business ultimately allowed American Express to remain profitable throughout the Depression and World War II.

In 1944 Ralph T. Reed replaced Small as president. Under Reed's management, the late 1940s and the 1950s were a period of expansion, primarily in the booming travel industry. Within seven years the number of American Express offices increased by 400 percent and international operations surpassed their prewar level.

When Diners Club introduced the first credit card in the mid-1950s, American Express executives proposed investigating this new line of business. Reed, who thought the company should improve existing business and feared a credit card would threaten its traveler's check business, opposed the proposal. In 1958, Reed reversed himself and the American Express travel-and-entertainment card (the American Express green card) was introduced virtually overnight. The company had 250,000 to 300,000 applications for cards on hand the day the card went on the market, and 500,000 cardmembers within three months. Introduction of the green card began an era of unprecedented growth: earnings rose from $8.4 million in 1959 to $85 million in 1970.

A new era of management began when Howard L. Clark was elected president and CEO on April 26, 1960. Clark transformed American Express from a renowned but fairly small company to a corporate giant with diverse interests. Clark's goal was to establish a balanced earnings base dependent on multiple sources and thus more resistant to economic fluctuations. His strategy was to expand American Express's business within its areas of expertise—travel and financial services.

But before Clark could put his plan in operation, the company had to be streamlined and modernized. Management had long been centralized and the chain of command obscure. Clark gave each division room to innovate and made each directly responsible for its own performance. Also, the company had no uniform identity. The now famous "blue box" logo was developed at Clark's direction and adopted by all the divisions.

Next, the company's accounting system had to be overhauled, since the system then in place was obsolete and unable to handle the high volume of charge card transactions. Moreover, the travel division (the glue that held the various divisions together and gave the company its identity) had to improve its profitability. By the time the jet airline industry made an impact on commercial travel, American Express was ready.

Also, the charge card had yet to show a profit, in large part because American Express had no experience dealing directly with merchants and consumers or with credit controls. Clark brought in George Waters, formerly of IBM and the Colonial Stores supermarket chain, to put the charge card division on a sounder footing. Waters used two simple strategies: first, he raised the card fee and merchant discount; next, he persuaded merchants to think of American Express as their marketing partner by dedicating .05 percent of gross sales to retail advertising. By the end of 1962 more than 900,000 cards had been issued, and by the end of 1963 the card division had shown a profit.

Finally, marginal operations had to be divested. Ridding the company of one subsidiary, American Express Field Warehousing Co., proved to be a nightmare. When the field warehousing division was sold to Lawrence Warehouse Co. in 1963, Clark withheld the two most profitable accounts, Allied Crude Vegetable Oil Refining Co. and Freezer House (both owned by Anthony ''Tino'' De Angelis), pending an investigation of other field warehousing opportunities. Late that year, Clark decided to sell the two accounts to Lawrence Warehouse. An independent audit conducted prior to closing revealed that about 800 million tons of vegetable oil was missing. Holders of some $150 million in security interests and notes (some forged by De Angelis) were understandably upset. The American Express board realized the company's reputation was at stake and quickly issued a statement to the effect that American Express assumed moral responsibility for the losses caused by its subsidiary. American Express's assurances did little to appease those defrauded. The ''salad oil swindle,'' as it was dubbed by the press, involved American Express in complex and protracted litigation that was settled in 1965 (although a final case lingered until 1970) at a cost to American Express of $60 million, excluding attorneys' fees.

With the salad oil episode behind it and reorganization of the divisions completed, the late 1960s and early 1970s were good years for American Express. Consolidated net income grew steadily, and Clark concentrated on expanding the company's financial services. In 1966, American Express acquired W. H. Morton & Co., an investment banking house with an excellent reputation for underwriting municipal and government bonds. And in 1968, American Express made the most important purchase yet in its diversification strategy: the Fireman's Fund Insurance Company, one of the largest property and casualty insurers in the nation.

Even the international monetary crisis of 1971, culminating in the devaluation of the dollar and the suspension of almost all dollar transactions, did not phase American Express. The company honored its traveler's checks at the exchange rate posted before trading was suspended and its card continued to be accepted internationally. American Express extended emergency funds to thousands of tourists caught short abroad, and its international banking subsidiary advised corporate clients on how to protect their foreign assets and import-export payments during the crisis.

During the late 1970s, however, American Express seemed to lose its direction, and its integrity and soundness were challenged on many fronts. In 1975, the *Washington Post* suggested that American Express was successful only because it was not regulated as banks and other financial institutions were. When Visa and MasterCard started competing in the traveler's check market, Citicorp, a major issuer of bank credit cards, took out a full-page advertisement accusing American Express of false and deceptive advertising of its traveler's checks. American Express also received unfavorable publicity when four acquisition attempts in a row failed.

The last of these attempts, a bid for the McGraw-Hill Publishing Co. in 1979, produced the worst repercussions. Roger Morley (who had replaced James D. Robinson III to become American Express's tenth president when Clark resigned in 1977 and

Robinson became chairman and CEO) was a member of the McGraw-Hill board at the time. After American Express bid for the publisher, McGraw-Hill sued the company and Morley, accusing them of breach of trust and corporate immorality.

But in 1981 American Express made the big acquisition it had been looking for when it bought Shearson Loeb Rhoades Inc., one of the nation's leading brokerage houses, which became an independently operated subsidiary. Shearson in short order acquired Robinson-Humphrey, an Atlanta-based brokerage firm; Foster & Marshall, a well-respected securities firm; and Balcor, Inc., the largest real estate syndicator in the United States.

In 1982, American Express was reorganized under a holding company called American Express Corp.; its travel services became a wholly owned subsidiary, American Express Travel Related Services.

Sanford I. Weill, formerly of Shearson Loeb Rhoades Inc., was elected the twelfth president of American Express in early 1983. Under Weill, American Express continued to expand. That same year, American Express acquired Ayco Corp., a financial counseling firm, and in 1984 it bought Allegheny Corporation's principal subsidiary, the financial planning company Investors Diversified Services, Inc. (IDS). Also in 1984, Shearson acquired Lehman Bros. Kuhn Loeb, one of the most respected Wall Street brokerage firms, to form Shearson Lehman Brothers Holdings Inc.

In 1985 American Express announced that it would spin off Fireman's Fund Insurance Company, the property and casualty insurer it had purchased in 1968. Stiff competition in the insurance industry during the early 1980s had led to price wars, and the subsidiary's profits had been declining since 1983. In addition, in 1983 and 1984, American Express had to spend $430 million strengthening Fireman's reserves. The first public offering of Fireman's Fund stock was made in October, 1985; by December, 1987, American Express retained only 31 percent of the company. In 1988 its holding was reduced to 20 percent and American Express formally exited the insurance business.

Also in 1985 the American Express International Banking Corp., established in 1919 to help American Express expand internationally, became simply American Express Bank, Ltd. In the mid-1990s, American Express was a thoroughly international company; its bank, with a presence in more than 40 countries, completed the range of financial services the company offered, focusing on private banking for wealthy individuals.

1987 was a dramatic—and difficult—year at most financial companies, and American Express was no exception. The stock market crash in October shook Shearson Lehman, and fears about Third World debt forced American Express Bank to add nearly $1 billion to its loan-loss reserves. But American Express's core business, Travel Related Services continued to prosper. That year it introduced its Optima Card, American Express's first credit card (regular American Express cards are charge cards; the balance must be paid in full each month). By late 1989, Optima had garnered some 2.5 million members.

In the 1980s, as competition in the card industry intensified, American Express pursued both an increased customer and increased merchant base. At the beginning of the decade, American Express had 10 million cardmembers who had roughly 400,000 places to use their cards. By the end of the decade those numbers had grown to 33 million cardholders around the world whose cards were accepted at 2.7 million places. But sheer size was not the objective: American Express emphatically positions its services as "premium"—its card costs much more than credit cards, like Visa and MasterCard, offered by banks, and it charges merchants a higher percentage of the bills charged to the card than its competitors do. These higher fees to merchants are warranted, the company tells them, by the business its generally high-income cardmembers generate; the higher card dues buy better services. Nevertheless, American Express has run into heavy competition, especially abroad, where its greatest hopes for expansion lie.

At the beginning of 1988, Shearson made another dramatic acquisition when it bought E. F. Hutton and became Shearson Lehman Hutton. Such growth in so short a time added up to a second year of decreased earnings—a 5 percent drop on top of 1987's 70 percent drop. At the end of 1989 Shearson was still struggling to cut costs and raise profits. American Express announced plans, in December of 1989, to pump an additional $900 million into its ailing subsidiary. The recapitalization included $350 million of American Express's own money. The rest was to come from notes.

American Express toppled from its perch as the preeminent charge card due to a number of serious problems in the early 1990s. The flagship charge card suffered fading customer loyalty, intense competition from lower-priced bank cards, and loss of service establishments accepting the card because of high fees to the merchants. Some observers blamed advertising for a public relations fiasco that damaged the company's image. But the company's 1991 revelation that its Optima revolving credit card—which analysts and investors had previously regarded as one of American Express's biggest successes—lost $300 million in write-offs, also eroded its credibility. At the same time, the Travel Related Services unit was battered by competition from no-fee bank cards and debit cards. As a recession deepened, merchants dropped the high-fee American Express card in droves. Profits dropped from $1.16 billion in 1989 to $461 million in 1992.

In 1993, Harvey Golub advanced to American Express's chief executive office upon the resignation of Robinson, who had served in that capacity since 1977. He instituted several recovery strategies at the firm, including retrenchment to core businesses, new product launches, cost-cutting, and brand-building.

Part of American Express's recovery strategy involved aggressive brand promotion, launching what were derisively called "guerrilla" or "ambush" marketing campaigns. In response to a Visa advertising campaign tied to the 1988 Olympic Games, American Express engaged in a campaign in which it ran television and space ads featuring those cities where the Olympics were held, trying to affiliate itself with the games without directly sponsoring them. American Express also launched a legal battle with Visa, claiming that the rival's "But they don't take American Express" commercials implied broader exclusivity than existed. Visa retorted that its ad claims were valid, and that American Express was simply using legal maneuvers,

public relations, and newspaper ads to blunt its advertising effectiveness. Early in 1994, Gary Levin, of *Advertising Age,* declared that "neither is entirely blameless, and both are unlikely to surrender." In 1994, American Express's promotional efforts were extended internationally, with a global advertising campaign targeting Italy, Germany, Japan, and the United Kingdom. The company planned to take sixty new ads to thirty countries around the world.

American Express's new products included Cheques for Two, introduced in 1992; a Senior Member card featuring special services and benefits; and a corporate purchasing card. American Express hoped to capture a significant share of the prospective $300 billion market segment, only 1 percent of which had been put on plastic by 1994. In 1993, American Express won the federal government's travel and transportation payment system contract—the largest corporate card account in the world. Some industry analysts interpreted the introduction of these new products as a sign of "renewed vigor" at American Express.

Golub aimed to cut $1 billion in costs by 1995, and planned to use those savings to finance the rate cutting necessary to attract the nearly 200,000 new merchant locations he expected to sign up. He also made several divestments that brought funds to the company and helped refocus on core businesses. Early in 1993, American Express sold its Shearson brokerage operations to Primerica Corp.'s Smith Barney, Inc. for $859 million in cash and about $275 million in Primerica stock. American Express netted $1.1 billion on the 1993 sale of 32 million shares of First Data Corp. to the public. And in January of 1994, American Express announced that it would contribute over $1 billion to Lehman Brothers, then spin the subsidiary off to shareholders. The capital injection enabled Lehman Brothers to sustain an "A" credit rating as an independent venture.

Credit Card Management magazine named American Express its "1993 Turnaround of the Year," praising Golub's recovery plan. That year, American Express's worldwide charge volume increased 5.5 percent to $117.5 billion, discount revenues from merchants increased 3.2 percent and merchant locations grew 4.5 percent. American Express's net income made a dramatic comeback as well, tripling from $461 million to $1.48 billion.

Principal Subsidiaries: American Express Travel Related Services; Investors Diversified Services, Inc.; IDS Financial Corp.; Leo Aircraft Leasing Ltd.; Broadgate International Fund Management Co.; American Express Bank, Ltd.; American Express Bank S.A. (France); AMEX Gestion S.A.; American Express Bank International; American Express Leasing Ltd. (UK); AMEX Asia Ltd.; American Express Middle East Development Company S.A.L.; AMEX Nominees Private Ltd.; American Express Nominee Ltd.; Argentamax S.A.; AMEX do Brasil Emprindimentos e Participacoes Ltd.; INAF, Inc.; AMEX Capital Investments Ltd. (UK); AMEXNET Ltd.; A.E.B. plc (UK); AMEX Nominees Pte Ltd. (S); A.E.B. Asset Management A.G.; AMEX Bank Nominee Hong Kong Ltd.; American Express Ltd. (Poland); Sociedad Gestinver de Fundos de Pensiones; Far East Leasing Ltd.; Geneva Nominees Ltd.; J.O.S. Leasing; American Express Bank S.A.; Acuma Financial Products Ltd.; Ainwick Corp.; Alair Holdings Inc.; American Express Asset Management Holdings, Inc.; American Express

Cable Franchise, Inc.; American Express Corp.; American Express Receivables Financing Corp.; Amexco Risk Financing Holding Co.; Brighton Corp.; National Express Co., Inc.; Rexport, Inc.; Ava Co.; Umpawaug I Corp.; Umpawaug II Corp.; Umpawaug III Corp.; Umpawaug IV Corp.; WGT Leasing Corp.

Further Reading:

Burrough, Bryan, *Vendetta: American Express and the Smearing of Edmond Safra,* New York: HarperCollins, 1992.
Carrington, Tim, *The Year They Sold Wall Street,* Boston: Houghton Mifflin, 1985.
Friedman, Jon, *House of Cards: Inside the Troubled Empire of American Express,* New York: Putnam, 1992.
Grossman, Peter Z., *American Express: The Unofficial History of the People Who Built the Great Financial Empire,* New York: Crown, 1987.
Hatch, Alden, *American Express: A Century of Service,* Garden City, New York: Doubleday, 1950.
Promises to Pay, New York: American Express Company, 1977.
Reed, Ralph Thomas, *American Express: Its Origin and Growth,* New York: Newcomen Society in North America, 1952.

—updated by April Dougal Gasbarre

American General Corporation

2929 Allen Parkway
Houston, Texas 77019
U.S.A.
(713) 522-1111
Fax: (713) 831-1980

Public Company
Incorporated: 1926 as American General Insurance Company
Employees: 11,600
Total Assets: $43.98 billion
Stock Exchanges: New York Pacific London Zürich Basel
    Geneva Lausanne
SICs: 6311 Life Insurance; 6371 Pension, Health, and
    Welfare Funds; 6141 Personal Credit Institutions

American General Corporation (AG) is one of the nation's largest insurance and financial services organizations, consisting of three business segments—retirement annuities, consumer finance, and life insurance. The life insurance division includes American General Life and Accident; focusing on the door-to-door sale and service of traditional life insurance products in the home, this division accounted for about 44 percent of the corporation's operating earnings in 1993. American General Finance and its subsidiaries—which together comprised about 31 percent of the corporations 1993 operating earnings—offer a wide range of consumer loans and other credit-related products and services through a national network of 1,200 branch offices. AG's retirement annuity segment is represented by The Variable Annuity Life Insurance Company (VALIC), which specializes in providing tax-deferred retirement plans for teachers and other employees of not-for-profit organizations and contributed about 25 percent of the company's operating earnings in 1993. Beginning in the 1980s, American General developed a reputation for buying other insurance companies—a practice unprecedented in the industry—and assimilating them profitably. This strategy of growth through acquisition became a corporate hallmark, and AG's assets quadrupled during the 1980s.

The history of AG may be traced to Gus Sessions Wortham, a native of Houston, Texas, who established the John L. Wortham & Son Agency insurance firm with his father early in the twentieth century. Gus was managing the agency when his father died in 1924, and, the following year, he formed his own business after the Commission of Appeals of Texas ruled that single insurance companies could combine lines of business, allowing multi-line underwriting of both fire and casualty insurance. With the backing of several business associates and the John L. Wortham & Son Agency, Gus formed one of the nation's first multi-line insurance companies on May 8, 1926: the American General Insurance Company. Operations began on June 7, 1926.

With the help of Wortham's experience and business instincts, AG earned an underwriting profit in its first year of operation. The company paid its first dividend on common stock during its third year, shortly before the stock market crash of 1929. Despite the effects of the Great Depression and numerous economic downturns in the ensuing decades, dividends were paid every year, without reduction or interruption, into the 1990s.

AG, like the city of Houston in general, saw tremendous growth through the 1930s. The company's capital and surplus topped the $1 million mark by 1936; three years later, the company was licensed to operate in nine states, including Texas, and had assets of nearly $2.2 million. In 1939, AG established its first subsidiary, The American General Investment Corporation, which was the company's first foray beyond fire and casualty insurance. The American General Investment Corporation eventually expanded its original offerings—financing for automobiles and real estate projects—to become a main link in the company's mortgage and real estate business segment. In 1945, AG made its first acquisition, implementing the growth strategy for which it would later become unique in the industry. The acquired company, Seaboard Life Insurance Company, was a successful Houston-based life and health insurer that predated AG by one year.

In 1953, AG hired Benjamin N. Woodson away from the National Association of Life Underwriters, where he was managing director. At AG, Woodson focused on expansion into the national market, using his extensive business contacts to find and acquire other companies. The company's emphasis during the 1960s was on expanding its life and health insurance segment. Toward that end, AG purchased life insurance companies in Nebraska, Hawaii, Oklahoma, Pennsylvania, and Houston, as well as a fire and casualty company in Marshall, Texas.

A milestone was reached in 1964 when AG purchased the Maryland Casualty Company, a Baltimore-based property and liability company dating to 1898. Through this acquisition, long a goal of Gus Wortham, AG doubled its size and became a major property and casualty insurer in all 50 United States as well as in Canada. Moreover, construction of a new 24-story AG headquarters building was begun one mile west of downtown Houston, on the banks of Buffalo Bayou. The corporation moved in 1965, and this location would include 36 acres and five office buildings by 1990.

The New York life insurance market became AG's next territory, with the acquisition of Patriot Life Insurance Company in 1966. The following year, the Variable Annuity Life Insurance Company (VALIC) attracted AG's interest. VALIC was noted for innovations in sales of tax-deferred annuities to the employees of nonprofit organizations. AG acquired majority stock in VALIC by 1975, and VALIC eventually became a wholly owned subsidiary. At the end of 1968, AG surpassed $1 billion in assets when it acquired a 65-year-old regional insurer, the Life and Casualty Insurance Company of Tennessee. That year, AG bought one-third of California-Western States Life Insurance Company (Cal-West), increasing its share to 63 percent over the next few years. Cal-West was a large but struggling company, and a new, dynamic 38-year-old president and CEO was striving to achieve a turnaround in the company's fortunes.

AG showed increasing interest in the man who was engineering Cal-West's rebound: Harold Swanson Hook. Hook had been raised on his family's dairy farm outside of Kansas City, Missouri, and, upon graduating from the University of Missouri, he was hired as an assistant to the president of National Fidelity of Kansas. Within five years, the 31-year-old Hook made industry history as the youngest insurance company president in the nation. Hook later served as president of U.S. Life Insurance in New York, and he became known for his successful development of management programs. His success in bringing Cal-West back to profitability drew notice from AG, and he was hired by AG in 1975 as president, overseeing the network of acquisitions made by Woodson. Hook became chairman and CEO when Woodson retired in 1978.

Emphasizing the importance of size to a company's success in the insurance industry, Hook focused on acquisition as the most efficient policy in a growth strategy. As he told *Business Week* in 1983, "our competitive advantage is our ability to acquire, integrate and control complex operations." To this end, Hook applied his theories of management in a system taught to more than 80 percent of AG's employees, usually by graduates of Hook's Main Event Management Corporation in Sacramento, California. Hook contended that this implementation of a uniform philosophy and language accounted for AG's remarkable record with regard to acquisition, assimilation, and management. The company successfully integrated more than 20 companies during the 1980s, and the company's name was changed to American General Corporation to reflect its wider concerns.

Between 1982 and 1984, the corporation doubled in size, launching what it called "the most aggressive acquisition program" in insurance industry history. In 1982, under this program, AG made the largest single life insurance company acquisition in history, with the purchase of NLT Corporation. NLT was the parent company of the National Life and Accident Insurance Company of Nashville, Tennessee. When AG failed to receive approval from the state of Tennessee to purchase the ten percent stock maximum, AG offered a stock swap. However, NLT refused and, in turn, made a bid for AG. AG rejected the bid and filed suit to stop the takeover proceeding, announcing what was dubbed the "godfather offer" in that it was difficult to refuse: a $46 per share merger proposal. This $1.5 billion, two-step merger was completed in late 1982. In response to initial concerns over the new company's debt load, Hook shaved NLT staff by one-third and divested overlapping and irrelevant subsidiaries, increasing cash flow more than $50 million. NLT was reportedly 70 percent absorbed within six months of the purchase.

That year, AG also acquired Credithrift Financial of Indiana, entering into the consumer credit business, which was later bolstered by the addition of General Finance Corporation. Another important acquisition during this time included the insurance properties of Gulf United Corporation, purchased for $1.2 billion.

In 1988, AG's consumer finance operations were doubled by the acquisition of the consumer finance division of Manufacturers Hanover. In order to rid the firm of its most cyclical units and concentrate on the faster-growing operations, AG shed its property-liability insurance business, as well as its group life and health insurance operations. On May 26, 1989, AG sold its property liability segment to Zurich Insurance Company—a multi-line, Swiss-based insurer—for $740 million. An agreement for the sale of AG's group insurance operations to Associated Insurance Companies for total consideration of up to $195 million, including $175 million in cash, was announced on September 21, 1989.

AG was the subject of a takeover bid in April 1990, when the Torchmark Corporation offered $6.3 billion to acquire AG. The bid was withdrawn within days, after receiving a chilly reception, and Torchmark then undertook a proxy battle to win five seats on AG's 15-member board. Once again, AG rebuffed Torchmark, but its slim 60 percent victory persuaded the American General board to take action. At the May 2, 1990 annual meeting, Hook announced that AG was putting itself up for sale, and that he expected the company to fetch more than $7 billion. The board's decision to put AG on the block was made, according to Hook, because "we recognized that . . . we were in play. We wanted to be in control of the process." Hook also noted that if an acceptable offer was not received in several months, the company was prepared to dismantle and sell its subsidiaries.

AG's stock soared during the proxy battle, but by the time Hook took the corporation off the auction block late in 1990, its price had plummeted to a six-year low. Hook agreed to sell portions of the company in September but rejected Torchmark's $3.6 billion bid for the home-service (door-to-door) life insurance as too low. During this time, Hook kept AG's options open, while continuing to streamline operations and expand through acquisitions. Divesting its real estate segment, AG acquired New Jersey Life Insurance Co.'s 28,000 policies worth $3 billion in 1993. Another aspect of American General's retrenchment involved a long-term stock buyback: from 1987 through 1992, the company invested over $1.5 billion to repurchase about 29 percent of its outstanding shares.

After having its home service insurance operations up for sale for nearly three years, AG announced its decision to remain in that segment of the business and expand those operations through acquisitions. AG consolidated this division in Nashville, Tennessee, reducing workforce by over 25 percent, automating many processes, and overhauling the organizational structure, which had been in place since the subsidiary was founded.

In the mid-1990s, AG referred to itself as "a company for all years," a designation based, in part, on its consistent stockholder returns and overall financial stability. In 1993, the company's ratings for both debt-paying and claims-paying ability were among the strongest in the industry. The company provided financial services to over six million households in all 50 United States, Puerto Rico, the Virgin Islands, and Canada. Moreover, AG lead its principal markets, ranking as the largest provider of voluntary savings plans to employees in public education; one of the largest consumer finance branch office networks, serving over two million customers; and selling more life insurance policies than any other shareholder-owned life insurance organization in the United States.

Principal Subsidiaries: AGC Life Insurance Co.; The Variable Annuity Life Insurance Co.; American General Finance, Inc.; American General Investment Corp.; Financial Life Assurance Co. of Canada; Knickerbocker Corp.; Lincoln American Corp.

Further Reading:

American General Corporation: History 1926–1986, Houston: American General Corporation, 1986.
Byrne, Harlan S., ''American General,'' *Barron's,* December 21, 1992, pp. 39–40.
Ivey, Mark, ''Harold Hook: A Hunter Who Feels Hunted,'' *Business Week,* April 22, 1991, pp. 92, 94.

—Carol I. Keeley
updated by April Dougal Gasbarre

American Home Products

Five Giralda Farms
Madison, New Jersey 07940-0074
U.S.A.
(212) 986-1000

Public Company
Incorporated: 1926
Employees: 51,399
Sales: $7.87 billion
Stock Exchanges: New York
SICs: 2834 Pharmaceutical Preparations; 2830 Drugs; 2844
    Toilet Preparations; 2096 Potato Chips and Similar
    Snacks; 2098 Macaroni and Spaghetti; 2099 Food
    Preparations, Nec; 3841 Surgical and Medical Instruments

American Home Products, one of the largest health care concerns in the United States and a conglomerate that includes food and household-product divisions, has been referred to as "Anonymous Home Products" or the "withdrawn corporate giant." Though the company markets such popular products as Black Flag insecticides, Easy-Off oven cleaner, Woolite, and Chef Boyardee, as well as the familiar pharmaceuticals Anacin, Advil, Dristan, Robitussin, and Dimetapp, the corporate name has never appeared on its products' labels. Public relations was considered such a low priority that until recently switchboard operators answered the phone with the company phone number instead of the company name. And although executives at American Home Products had made few efforts to influence Wall Street analysts until recently, the company's forty plus consecutive years of increased sales and earnings make AHP shares a very popular investment.

American Home Products' unusual combination of anonymity and financial success stems from its history of competent management, product diversification through acquisition, and close-fisted expenditures on virtually everything except advertising. AHP has been able to strike a balance between the aggressive advertising of its consumer package goods and maintaining a reputable name within the medical community, which is often reluctant to accept the idea of ethical drugs supported by the pressure of advertising.

AHP's strict management policy allows for a minimal margin of error. If a product does not show promise before money is spent on promotion, it is dropped. If a division does not increase sales and earnings by 10 percent annually, a division president could be out of a job. Until recently, AHP found little reason to invest in research, preferring to wait for competitors to release innovative products, and then launching its own improved line. Or it would simply buy the competitor.

Expenditures are so closely monitored at AHP that in 1983 employees at the Whitehall division paid $20 each to attend their own Christmas party. A journalist from *Business Week,* researching a rumor in 1970 that then AHP chairman and president William F. LaPorte had reduced the size of the toilet paper in the executive washrooms to save money, discovered that, in fact, the paper was 9/16-inch narrower than regulation size. As late as 1980, LaPorte was personally approving any expenditures of more than $500, including anything from the purchase of a typewriter to a secretarial pay raise.

American Home Products' knack for acquiring little-known products and companies at a reduced price and turning them into money-makers dates back to AHP's earliest years. In 1926, a group of executives associated with Sterling Products Inc. and Household Products Inc. consolidated several independent nostrum makers into a holding company. Its subsidiaries sold such medicinal products as Hill's Cascara Quinine, St. Jacob's Oil, Wyeth's Sage and Sulphur, Kolynos dental cream, and Old English No Rubbing Floor Polish.

W. H. Kirn was named chairman of the new company in 1930 and served until 1935, when Alvin G. Brush, a salesman of Dr. Lyon's toothpaste, took over as president and chief executive officer, a position he held for the next 30 years. Brush's penchant for expansion through acquisition, while maintaining a sizable amount of cash in reserve, set the pattern for AHP's operating style. In his first eight years as president, Brush acquired 34 food and drug companies for a total of $25.6 million in cash and stock. One of AHP's earliest prizes was the acquisition of a sunburn oil in 1935 that the company transformed into Preparation H, which became one of the world's best selling hemorrhoid treatments.

Other purchases included the 3-in-One Oil Company and Affiliated Products Inc., which made cosmetics and toiletries under such names as Outdoor Girl, Kissproof, and Neet. In 1938, AHP acquired Eff Laboratories, a manufacturer of commercial vitamin products, and S.M.A. Corporation, a producer of infant foods and vitamins. In 1939, the Black Flag Company came under the AHP umbrella, followed in 1943 by the G. Washington Coffee Refining Company, a manufacturer of grocery specialties. In 1946, another grocery-specialties firm, Chef-Boy-Ar-Dee Quality Foods Inc., came aboard.

AHP's marketing genius transformed its newly acquired products into household words. Preparation H is a good example. By 1981, Preparation H had captured 64 percent of the hemorrhoid-treatment market, and its success was attributable exclusively to the company's aggressive advertising. In 1968, AHP spent more than $2 million on radio spots and $6 million on television advertising for Preparation H. These amounts may seem exorbitant for a single product; the figures become even more impressive when one realizes that the radio code standards only readmitted the controversial advertisements for hemorrhoidal medications in 1965 and that the National Association of

Broadcasters continued to debate approval for television. AHP advocated a broadened scope of code approval even as it appropriated more funds for advertising on noncode television stations.

The struggle for an expanded consumer audience was fought not only over advertising codes for personal products; AHP's aggressive marketing style also brought investigations of the company's advertising copy. In 1967, the Federal Trade Commission (FTC) ordered AHP and three other companies to refrain from making false claims with regard to the therapeutic value of their hemorrhoid treatments. Citing the advertisements' unsubstantiated claims, the FTC prohibited any future misrepresentation.

Company executives were not intimidated by the FTC ruling. AHP, deeming the commission's findings "capricious" and "arbitrary," asked for a review before a federal appeals court. The company continued to run advertisements in more than 1,100 newspapers, 700 radio stations, and 100 television stations. In response, the FTC temporarily enjoined AHP from continuing to run the advertisements. The court finally upheld most of the commission's findings, and the advertising copy for Preparation H had to be permanently modified.

Throughout this controversy AHP executives remained characteristically unavailable for comment. This combination of persistent product promotion (at the risk of damaging company reputation) and a united but anonymous executive front came to the fore in the promotion of another AHP product. In 1930, the company had purchased the rights to manufacture a little-known painkiller called Anacin, previously promoted through samples to dentists. AHP's Anacin grew in popularity and became the nation's leading over-the-counter analgesic. As with Preparation H, it took aggressive marketing to propel Anacin into this position.

By 1971, AHP had spent more money on the promotion of Anacin than had any other analgesic manufacturer on a comparable product. Total costs for radio advertising reached $1.5 million, and for television advertising surpassed $25 million. In 1972, the FTC charged that AHP and two other analgesic manufacturers were promoting their products through misleading and unsubstantiated claims. Because no reliable scientific evidence existed as to the superiority of one brand over another, or the ability of analgesics to relieve nervous tension, the FTC disputed therapeutic claims and advertisements that did not identify generic ingredients such as aspirin and caffeine.

AHP and the other manufacturers refused to negotiate consent agreements, and so the FTC issued formal complaints and ordered hearings before an FTC administrative judge. The case was finally settled in 1981 and permanent limits were placed on misleading claims in Anacin advertisements. In 1982, a federal appeals court upheld the FTC ruling after AHP attempted to have it overturned.

During the hearings on aspirin advertisements, Johnson & Johnson's Tylenol made its market appearance. To maintain their market share, AHP and other aspirin manufacturers launched a campaign to promote aspirin's anti-inflammatory action. After several suits and countersuits between AHP and Johnson & Johnson, a federal court judge in 1978 ordered the

discontinuance of the advertising of Anacin's anti-inflammatory property as a claim of superiority over Tylenol.

Competition in the pain-reliever market was intensified by the introduction of ibuprofen. The drug is a non-steroidal anti-inflammatory agent that is as effective as aspirin and aspirin substitutes, but without the side effect of digestive-tract irritation. AHP marketed its ibuprofen under the name Advil. Industry analysts suggested that ibuprofen could capture as much as 30 percent of the pain-reliever market.

The pattern of controversy and investigation established in the marketing for Preparation H and Anacin continued with several other AHP products. Easy-Off oven cleaner, Black Flag insecticide, Easy-On starch, and Aero Wax were all involved in an FTC investigation into deceptive advertising. Yet, for all of the controversy, no one can dispute AHP's success in capturing markets and acquiring products that have become household staples.

AHP's advertising budget for 1985 was estimated at more than $412 million. Despite or perhaps because of this great expenditure, AHP is notorious among advertising agencies as a demanding and uncompromising client. Paying the lowest possible commission rates, the company will, nonetheless, demand the best price for prime-time spots on television and expect promotion to be effective on strict budgets. In 1967, Ted Bates & Company, the fifth largest advertising agency in the world at that time, resigned AHP's $20 million account because of "differences in business policy." This was not the first time an AHP account had been abandoned by an agency. Grey Advertising Inc. and J. Walter Thompson similarly dropped the demanding company's account. The Bates agency was replaced with an in-house agency called the John F. Murray Company. At the time of the replacement, industry-owned agencies were rare.

By 1983, AHP grudgingly began to change its attitude toward promotion. The company hired world-renowned photographer Richard Avedon and actress Catherine Deneuve to promote its line of Youth Garde cosmetics. But despite this willingness to "upscale" its advertising, AHP was voted as one of the ten worst clients of 1983 by *Adweek*.

The success of AHP's proprietary goods has overshadowed the company's position as a leading manufacturer of ethical drugs. In 1932, AHP acquired Wyeth Chemical Company (now Wyeth Laboratories), a pharmaceutical manufacturer with a long history, under unusual circumstances. Wyeth was run by family descendants until the death of Stuart Wyeth, a bachelor. He bequeathed the laboratory to Harvard, his alma mater, and the university in turn sold the company to AHP at a generous price. In the early 1940s, AHP also acquired two other pharmaceutical laboratories, Ives and Ayerst.

AHP's prescription drugs and medical supplies accounted for 47 percent of sales and 62 percent of profits in 1983. Among the ethical drugs AHP produces are Ovral, a low-dosage oral contraceptive, and Inderal, a drug that reduces blood pressure and slows the heartbeat. Inderal was introduced in 1968, and by 1983 supplied more than half of the U.S. market for beta-blocker drugs. The company was also busy developing new pharmaceuticals: AHP filed 21 new drug applications with the Food and Drug Administration in 1985 alone.

In 1981, company president John W. Culligan was promoted to chairman and chief executive officer. LaPorte, who had been chairman since 1965, continued as chairman of the executive committee. Culligan, 64 years old at the time of the promotion, had been with the company since 1937. John R. Stafford, a lawyer recruited from Hoffmann-LaRoche in 1970 as general counsel, was named company president on December 1, 1986. Some observers predicted that AHP's management changes would herald a modernization of LaPorte's highly centralized style of management and financial control, which contradicted contemporary theories of corporate management.

Nevertheless, this anachronistic approach has guaranteed shareholders a handsome return on investment. In 1982, *Fortune* magazine's directory of the 500 largest U.S. industrial corporations ranked American Home Products 76th in sales and 24th in profits. The company had no long-term debt, and it paid out 60 percent of earnings in dividends. Despite a chronically low stock price in the late 1980s and early 1990s, AHP saw higher earnings and increased dividends every year from 1951 to 1993.

In 1983, AHP spent $425 million to buy the Sherwood Medical Group. A manufacturer of medical supplies, Sherwood placed AHP in a competitive position to capture the lion's share of the growing medical-device market. That subsidiary was supplemented with the 1992 acquisition of Symbiosis Corp., a developer and manufacturer of disposable instruments for minimally-invasive laparoscopic and endoscopic surgery.

Under Stafford's guidance in the late 1980s and early 1990s, American Home Products worked to transform itself into a health care company through acquisitions and divestments. In 1989, the firm divested its Boyle-Midway division and purchased A. H. Robins Co., an over-the-counter drug manufacturer that complimented the Whitehall laboratories subsidiary. In response to criticism of its low research and development expenditures, AHP spent a record 11 percent of sales on R&D in 1990. The firm invested in Genetics Institute, Inc., a biotechnology firm specializing in blood cell regulation, bone repair, and immune system modulation, in 1992.

AHP's marketing of infant formula came under intense scrutiny and criticism in the late 1980s and early 1990s. Prior to 1988, infant formula was marketed strictly as a pharmaceutical product. Given historical product loyalty, formula makers offered their products free to pediatricians and hospitals in the hopes that the first formula a mother used would be the one she continued to purchase. According to a 1990 *Business Week* article, many doctors began to allege that hospitals promoted infant formula over breast-feeding—despite the inherent advantages of breast feeding—because of the money and services received from manufacturers. And when the federal govern-

ment directed the states to purchase all their formula from one manufacturer to garner lower prices, formula manufacturers were forced to compete directly for Women, Infants and Children (WIC) contracts, which constituted about 35 percent of state formula purchases. In June of 1993, *Advertising Age* reported that the Federal Trade Commission had charged the top three formula marketers—divisions of Abbott Laboratories, Bristol-Myers Squibb Co., and American Home Products Corp.—with price fixing in government nutrition programs.

Although food products received less attention in the 1990s, American Home Products did augment its Chef Boyardee line with the 1992 purchase of Ro*Tel, the leading brand of canned tomatoes and green chilies in the Mexican food category. In 1993, the company added M. Polaner Inc., a jam maker, to the food products segment.

By 1993, over 60 percent of American Home Products' global revenues came from pharmaceuticals. Uncertainty due to the Clinton Administration's proposed overhaul of the American health care system suppressed the company's stock price, but with one-third of revenue derived from proprietary drugs and specialty foods, AHP was considered a relatively safe investment. The company's sales and profits increased steadily from 1988 to 1992, from $6.4 billion to $7.87 billion and $.995 billion to $1.46 billion, respectively.

Principal Subsidiaries: AH Investments Ltd.; A.H. Robins Co., Inc.; A.H. Robins Intnl. Co.; AHP Subsidiary Holding Corp.; AHP Subsidiary Corp.; American Home Food Products Inc.; American Home Foods Inc.; Ayerst Laboratories Inc.; Ayerst-Wyeth Pharmaceuticals Inc.; Corometrics Medical Systems Inc.; Genetics Institute Inc.; Quinton Instrument Co.; Sherwood Medical Co.; Symbiosis Corp.; Vermont Whey Co.; Viobon Corp.; Wyeth-Ayerst Intl. Inc.; Wyeth-Ayerst Ltd.; American Drug Corp.; American Home Investments Ltd.; Ayerst Intl S.A.; Ayerst Organics Ltd.; Ayerst McKenna & Harrison Inc.; Brenner-Efeka Pharma GmbH; Home Products Italiana SpA; Laboratorios Wyeth Whitehall Ltda; Much Pharma A.G.; Sherwood Medical Industries Ltd.; Sherwood Medical Industries of Ireland Ltd.; Whitehall-Robins Canada Inc.; Wyeth Ltd. Ireland; Wyeth Corp.; John Wyeth & Brother Ltd.; Wyeth Ltd. Canada; Wyeth-Pharma GmbH; Wyeth Pharmaceuticals Pty ltd.; Wyeth S.A. de C.V.; Wyeth SpA; Wyeth-Suaco Laboratories Inc.; Sherwood Medical S.A.; Whitehall Laboratories Inc.; Whitehall Laboratories Ltd.; Wyeth Laboratories Inc.; Wyeth Nutritionals Inc.

Further Reading:
Levin, Gary, "Time for Bottle: Infant Formula Ads May Spurt," *Advertising Age,* June 7, 1993, pp. 3, 42.
Siler, Julia Flynn, "The Furor over Formula Is Coming to a Boil," *Business Week,* April 9, 1990, pp. 52–53.

—updated by April Dougal Gasbarre

American Premier Underwriters, Inc.

1 East Fourth Street
Cincinnati, Ohio 45202-3717
U.S.A.
(513) 579-6600
Fax: (513) 579-0108

Public Company
Incorporated: 1846 as Pennsylvania Central Railroad
  Company
Employees: 5,400
Sales: $1.8 billion
Stock Exchanges: Boston Midwest New York Pittsburgh
  Pacific
SICs: 6331 Fire, Marine and Casualty Insurance

Although property and casualty insurance company American Premier Underwriters, Inc. adopted its current focus over the past few years, the company has a history of over 150 years that reflects the development of the national transportation and commerce industries. In the nineteenth century, the company gained renown as the Pennsylvania Central Railroad Company. Developing into a highly diversified conglomerate, the company was known as The Penn Central Corporation from 1978 through March 1994, when it dropped its well known rail-related name in favor of a title that more accurately described its business activities in the 1990s—property and casualty insurance.

The Pennsylvania Railroad Company and the New York Central Railroad, which merged in 1968 to form the Penn Central Transportation Company, were the two largest railroads in the United States and traced their histories to the early 1800s. The Pennsylvania Railroad, or ''Pennsy,'' as it became known, had first linked the Atlantic seaboard with the tributaries of the Mississippi River system in the 1850s. During this time, Pennsy grew so powerful that it called itself ''the Standard Railroad of the World.''

The Pennsylvania Railroad Company was incorporated by the Commonwealth of Pennsylvania in 1846 with a capitalization of $10 million. Formed by a group of Philadelphia businessmen and politicians who hoped to link the City of Brotherly Love to the bustling commerce of the West, the railroad paid a dividend in 1848, the first of an uninterrupted series that lasted until the Pennsylvania Railroad was absorbed into Penn Central in 1968.

Pennsy's principal investors were primarily involved in industries that would benefit from the railroad, and none devoted their full attention to the Pennsy. The company's first president, Samuel Vaughn Merrick, had no specialized knowledge of railroads, and he soon hired J. Edgar Thomson, a chief engineer with 20 years of railroad experience, who was known as one of the nation's leading railroad experts. Thomson soon proved so valuable and knowledgeable that he could virtually run the railroad without his superiors. Merrick resigned in 1849, and after continued conflicts with new president William Patterson, Thomson led a successful coup in 1852 that culminated in his election as chairperson and president. That year, the Pennsy completed its initial 30-mile line from Harrisburg to Pittsburgh.

Thomson quickly set out to realize his ambitious plans for the Pennsy. After legislation was passed permitting the purchase of interests in other railroads, Thomson acquired stakes in four small, struggling lines in Ohio and Indiana. In 1857, he completed three years of negotiations to purchase Pennsylvania's Main Line railroad for $7.5 million in bonds, making the Pennsy the state's premier rail system. During his 20-year tenure at the Pennsylvania Railroad, Thomson increased the railroad's trackage from 350 to over 1,000 miles and its gross revenues from $2 million to over $22 million annually. By the onset of the Civil War, the Pennsylvania Railroad had expanded from Pittsburgh through Fort Wayne and on to Chicago, with access to virtually all of southern Ohio, Indiana, and Illinois.

In 1872, Thomson created The Pennsylvania Company, a holding company organized to manage the system, which by this time extended along the East Coast from Jersey City to Washington, D.C., went as far west as St. Louis, and featured northern destinations in New York and Mackinac City in Michigan's upper peninsula. That year, the respected railroader died at the age of 66 and was replaced by a close ally, Thomas Scott, formerly senior vice-president of the Pennsy. Scott managed the railroad during an eight-year period during which stockholder concerns about overextension prevented further expansion westward.

During this time, the Pennsy's future partner, New York Central, was also gaining prominence. New York Central was created from the 1853 consolidation of ten separate short lines under the direction of merchant-financier-manufacturer Erastus Corning. Unlike the Pennsy, however, the New York Central had a rocky start; Corning regarded the railroad as an extension of his own businesses, and his self-interest stunted the railroad's early development.

The New York Central began to realize greater success after the presidency was assumed by Cornelius Vanderbilt in 1867. Known as the Commodore, Vanderbilt was an esteemed speculator and one of the wealthiest men in the United States. Using his own railroad holdings to close off the New York Central's vital link to New York City, Vanderbilt forced the Central's stock prices down. He then took advantage of the low stock price, purchasing 87 percent of the stock and capturing the presidency. After Vanderbilt's death in 1877, son William Vanderbilt assumed the presidency, overseeing expansion in the form of several important acquisitions, including that of the Nickel Plate Railroad in 1882. During this period, financier J.P. Morgan earned a seat on the board of New York Central and soon became a key figure in American railroading. William Vanderbilt resigned in 1883 and selected James Rutter as his successor. When Rutter died suddenly two years later, a younger Cornelius Vanderbilt assumed the presidency. Chauncey M. Depew, a lawyer and lobbyist, replaced Vanderbilt in 1899 and served until his death in 1928.

Neither the New York Central nor the Pennsy expanded its routes substantially in the early years of the twentieth century, in spite of the unremitting shift of economic power from the East Coast to the West and South. Due to government regulation and mutual agreement, the two railroads had largely curtailed their previously cutthroat competition. At this time, the New York Central had almost twice as much trackage as the Pennsy, while the latter moved more freight and people. New York Central controlled almost every important anthracite coal carrier in the region, and the Pennsy dominated bituminous coal commerce.

The Pennsy reached the apex of its power during the presidency of Alexander Johnston Cassatt (brother of painter Mary Cassatt), who succeeded Frank Thomson after his death in 1899. Trained as an architectural engineer, Cassatt concentrated on enhancing the railroad's capacity for transporting people and goods. Within seven years, he invested almost $500 million in improvements and additions, including the quadrupling of the trackage between New York City and Altoona, Pennsylvania. Cassatt's greatest accomplishment, however, was extending the railway directly into Manhattan. Before 1910, New York bound passengers ended their rail trip on the Pennsy at Jersey City, where they transferred to ferries for the trip across the Hudson River to New York City. In 1900, the Pennsy purchased control of the Long Island Railroad and undertook construction of an underground railway from New Jersey under the Hudson River to a terminal in New York City and under the East River to Long Island. Construction of this costly, complicated project commenced in 1904, and the first trains arrived in New York's Pennsylvania Station in 1910.

From the 1860s until World War I, the rail industry held a virtual monopoly on ground transport, and the Pennsy and New York Central dominated transportation in the East, where industry was central and freight and passenger traffic was greatest. To link Chicago and New York, both railroads built luxurious, first-class lines, the opulence of which symbolized their dominance in the industry.

However, for most American railroads the advent World War I meant high labor and maintenance costs and artificially low rates, which forced them to borrow to maintain lines and order new rolling stock. During the global conflict, the federal government assumed control of all railroads in the country to coordinate them for the war effort. These events precipitated a shake out in the rail industry after the government relinquished control.

Moreover, beginning in the 1920s, the establishment of highways and the trucking industry began to challenge the railroads' monopoly on inland transportation. Despite technological advancements in electric and diesel locomotion, rail transportation had several disadvantages in competition with trucking. For example, railroads were forced to maintain large, expensive freight yards in all major cities, and were less flexible than the trucking industry. To offset its losses, the Pennsy began to purchase passenger bus companies in the late 1920s, taking an equity position in the Motor Transit Corporation (which became the Greyhound Corporation and adding 8,000 route miles to the eastern bus line. The railroad also made its services more versatile through the acquisition of several trucking companies during this time.

The diversion of traffic from rail to road accelerated in the 1930s. Although gasoline and rubber shortages during World War II temporarily reversed this trend, the use of trucks and buses continued to increase in the post-war era. Nevertheless, in the 1950s the Pennsylvania Railroad was America's largest transportation business, as its more than 10,000 miles of tracks linked New York City, Chicago, and St. Louis, three of the nation's largest commercial centers. In 1956, *Fortune* magazine noted that the railroad's assets totaled over $3 billion, significantly more than the second largest transportation company, the New York Central, whose assets topped $2.5 billion. Only three of *Fortune's* 500 largest industrial corporations reported more assets than the Pennsy.

Nevertheless, the financial security of the Pennsy and New York Central during this time began to weaken. Robert Young, a leader of the Chesapeake and Ohio Railroad, had begun amassing shares in the New York Central in preparation for a takeover in 1946 and was rebuffed two years later by the Interstate Commerce Commission (ICC), which was wary of railroad monopoly. In 1954, Young made a second, more blatant overture: after garnering 15 percent of the New York Central's equity, he launched a dramatic proxy fight with then-chairperson William White. White and Young launched campaigns—complete with slogans, buttons, and public appearances—for control of the railroad, and Young won the contest by more than a million proxies.

The new, relatively inexperienced chairperson brought in Alfred Perlman as president to help modernize and automate operations and develop the company's freight transport system. Upon accepting the position, Perlman found that the New York Central was close to bankruptcy, having invested $264 million in its passenger services from 1946 to 1957 and losing $500 million in the process. Perlman immediately undertook cost-cutting measures, firing 25,000 employees between 1954 and 1957, selling $9 million in real estate in 1955 alone, and investing as little as possible in passenger services. Despite Perlman's efforts, however, stock declined to its 1946 price of $15.

The Pennsy was also struggling. Although its freight business was profitable—it brought in a record $787 million in 1953—its passenger service faced several challenges. The strong demand for rush-hour rail service into large cities forced the Pennsy to maintain large pools of equipment and a substantial labor force to service a limited number of passengers between

6:00 and 9:30 a.m. and 4:30 and 7:00 p.m. Led by chairperson James Symes, the Pennsy tried to achieve economies by trimming its less profitable lines as much as the ICC would allow. Still, operating revenues declined from over $1 billion in 1953 to $844 million in 1958, and dividends were slashed from $1.25 per share in 1947 to $.25 in 1958.

Leading railroaders petitioned Washington for help, claiming that the taxes they paid supported competitive forms of transportation such as state and federal highway systems, waterways, airlines and airports, and public bus and truck terminals. The Transportation Act of 1958 offered government loans to struggling railroads, but by this time, rail leaders had arrived at their own solution, and cautious merger talks began.

During this time, Symes and Robert Young initiated merger negotiations between the Pennsylvania and New York Central railroads, but several factors and factions stood in the way of the merger. The ICC, the U.S. Justice Department, congressional anti-monopolists, executives of other eastern railroads, and the trucking interests all contested the alliance. Merger talks continued for over a decade, often hindered further by poor relations between New York Central's Perlman (who entered the negotiations after Young's suicide) and Symes and his 1963 successor, Stuart Saunders, of the Pennsy.

In the meantime—using the nearly 100-year-old Pennsylvania Company as an investment vehicle—Saunders began to diversify the Pennsylvania Railroad. During his first two years as company chairperson, he spent over $200 million developing or purchasing real estate (including part of Madison Square Garden), coal and salt mines, the Buckeye Pipe Line Company (the eighth-largest processor of crude oil in the United States), and amusement parks. He also recouped $65 million on the 1965 sale of most of the Long Island Railroad to New York's Metropolitan Commuter Transportation Authority.

The ICC approved the merger of the New York Central and Pennsylvania railroads in March 1965. The U.S. Supreme Court finally ruled in its favor early in 1968, and the alliance was formalized in February of that year. The Pennsy clearly dominated from the onset: Saunders assumed the chair, Perlman became vice-chairperson, and the company's first annual report traced the company's history to 1846, the date of the Pennsy's charter.

The company that emerged from this amalgamation, Penn Central Transportation, operated one-third of America's passenger trains and three-fourths of all long-haul services, totaling over 20,000 route miles in 16 states, two Canadian provinces, and the District of Columbia. However, the company's new stature also brought problems. A staff of 94,000 consumed 59 percent of the company's revenues, and Penn Central racked up a $49 million deficit in 1969 and lost $83.4 million in the first quarter of 1970 alone. Facing long-term loan payments of nearly $200 million that would soon be due, Saunders sought the help of the Nixon Administration. When Congress declined to honor loan assurances offered by the Department of Defense, Penn Central's board of directors fired Saunders, Perlman, and other top officials in June 1970. Later that month, Penn Central filed for reorganization under Section 77 of the Bankruptcy Act, which enabled continued operations rather than liquidation of the

corporation. Penn Central was followed into bankruptcy by six other northeastern railroads.

Realizing the importance of a massive rail system to many industries and travelers, the government worked to bolster Penn Central. In the hopes that eliminating passenger operations would help revive the railroads, the government developed the National Railroad Passenger Corporation (Amtrak) in 1971 to take over operation of the nation's passenger trains. Still, all seven northeastern railroads would hobble through a recession, a destructive hurricane, and finally the oil crisis, until April 1976, when a new federally funded entity, the Consolidated Rail Corporation (Conrail) was created to assume their rail operations.

During this time, Penn Central's board brought in a veteran railroader, William H. Moore, as president in September 1970. Moore first tackled lingering rivalries between Pennsy and Central employees, replacing old logos with a symbol for the new corporation, but, like his predecessors, he found deeper problems. After nursing Penn Central through four of its toughest years, Moore was unceremoniously replaced by trustee Jervis Langdon, Jr.

Penn Central began a new life with the assets accumulated primarily by Stewart Saunders, including the gas pipeline company, coal leases, valuable real estate and air rights over such parcels as New York City's Grand Central Terminal. Then, in January 1981, the company received cash of $2.1 billion in compensation for its rail properties from the U.S. government and tax loss carry forwards of $2.2 billion. Penn Central used this cash to make several acquisitions, including Marathon Manufacturing, which made oil rigs; G.K. Technologies, an electronics company; Buckeye Gas Products, which dealt in propane gas; and Sprague Electric, a manufacturer of capacitors. Many of these acquisitions proved to be unprofitable. By 1982, American Financial Corp.'s Carl Lindner amassed enough stock in Penn Central to be elected to the company's board, and in 1983, he became chairman.

In the mid-1980s, the company began narrowing its focus by selling certain of its operating assets, primarily Buckeye Pipe-Line and Buckeye Gas. By the spring of 1987, Lindner had assumed the additional role of chief executive officer, and Penn Central accelerated the sales of most of its earlier acquisitions, increasing its available cash to $1.1 billion and reducing its debt to five percent of capital.

In 1989, the company acquired its first insurance operation, Republic Indemnity Co. of America, a large writer of worker's compensation insurance in California. In 1990, three non-standard auto insurance companies were acquired.

In the early 1990s, Lindner continued to refine Penn Central's focus to profitable insurance businesses. General Cable Corp. was formed to control Penn Central's primary manufacturing businesses and then was spun off to shareholders in 1992. Later that year, the company put its defense and industrial products units, including Vitro Corp. (a provider of systems and software engineering for the military) up for sale. Nine non-insurance business units and major assets were sold over an 18-month period beginning in 1992, providing about $330 million in sales proceeds. Penn Central's 1993 revenues totaled $1.76 billion, a

$338.4 million increase over the previous year. The divestitures of non-insurance businesses were virtually completed by the end of 1993, and culminated in the March 1994 name change to American Premier Underwriters, Inc. Upon announcing the name change, Carl Lindner III—who joined his father at the company as president and chief operating officer—remarked that the new name reflected the company's sole focus on property and casuality insurance and that he hoped to expand American Premier Underwriters' automobile insurance businesses through both internal growth and acquisition.

Principal Subsidiaries: Republic Indemnity Company of America; Atlanta Casualty Company; Infinity Insurance Company; Windsor Insurance Company; Leader National Insurance Co.; Apparatus Division; Penn Central Real Estate Group.

Further Reading:

Hartley, Scott, *Conrail Volume 1: 1976–1982,* Piscataway, New Jersey: Railpace Company, Inc., 1990.

Mitchell, Russell, "With Lindner in Charge, Penn Central Is on the Prowl," *Business Week,* April 20, 1987, pp. 80–1.

Rudnitsky, Howard, "Gearing Down," *Forbes,* December 1, 1986, pp. 176, 178.

Salsbury, Stephen, *No Way to Run a Railroad: The Untold Story of the Penn Central Crisis,* New York: McGraw-Hill Book Company, 1982.

Sobel, Robert, *The Fallen Colossus,* New York: Weybright and Talley, 1977.

Stern, Marilyn, "Glory Days," *Across the Board,* October 1991, p. 41.

—April Dougal Gasbarre

AMERICAN
RE-INSURANCE COMPANY

American Re Corporation

555 College Rd. E.
Princeton, New Jersey 08543-5241
U.S.A.
(609) 243-4200
Fax: (609) 243-4257

Public Company
Incorporated: 1992
Employees: 1,200
Sales: $1.44 billion
Stock Exchanges: New York
SICs: 6331 Fire, Marine and Casualty Insurance; 6719
   Holding Companies Nec

American Re Corporation, through its subsidiaries, is a leading international property and casualty reinsurer. It was the third largest U.S. reinsurer going into the mid-1990s, operated main offices in Chile and Great Britain, and provided reinsurance and consulting services on every populated continent in the world. A holding company formed by Kohlberg, Kravis, Roberts & Co., American Re Corporation's principal subsidiary is American Re-Insurance Company (American Re). American Re and four other American companies provide more than 50 percent of all reinsurance in the United States.

Reinsurance companies, while operating in relative obscurity compared to insurance establishments, play a key role in insurance markets. They provide stability by insuring the insurers. A company that primarily insures homes in California, for example, would likely be bankrupted by a major earthquake. By purchasing reinsurance, the company can protect itself from such catastrophes.

The property/casualty insurance industry, which American Re serves, was largely a corollary of the Great Fire of London (1666), after which fire insurance was established. In the United States, it was not until early in the 20th century that the hazards of wind, water, damage, personal accident, and explosion were added to established lines of fire insurance. Major British companies, such as Lloyd's of London, provided most reinsurance for American insurers during the early- and mid-1900s.

The American Re-Insurance Company, the first U.S.-owned reinsurer, was founded on March 15, 1917 in Huntington, Pennsylvania. Seven families in that coal mining region formed the

enterprise as a vehicle to provide a workers' compensation program for local miners. Because of a dire need by mining families for protection from risks associated with dangerous mining occupations, the company grew quickly. In 1921 the company moved its headquarters to Philadelphia, allowing it to better serve its geographically expanding business. Likewise, the organization transferred its headquarters to New York City in 1933, using the temporary title New York Re-Insurance Company.

American Re continued to expand during the 1930s and 1940s, as property and casualty insurance increased in popularity. During that period, insurance companies were regulated solely by state governments. Therefore, insurance practices varied by region. In 1944, however, the federal government, in *United States v Southeastern Underwriters Association*, made the insurance industry subject to Congressional powers. Growth was particularly brisk after 1948, when states began allowing insurers to write multiple lines of insurance rather than limiting them to just one segment of the market. These changes, combined with strong demand for all types of insurance by burgeoning U.S. corporations, generated an influx of reinsurance activity.

American Re broadened its scope in the 1950s by acquiring American Reserve Insurance Company, of New York. In 1963, moreover, it purchased Inter-Ocean Reinsurance Company, of Cedar Rapids, Iowa. The company continued to boost its assets and services throughout the mid-1900s by focusing on customer service, cultivating long-term client relationships, diversifying its products and services, and emphasizing a conservative approach to investing its assets and reserves. Besides its acquisition activities and straight-forward management style, the company broadened its operations through international expansion beginning in the 1950s.

A fundamental goal of the company's overall business strategy during the mid-1900s (and into the late 1900s) was a reduction of the effect of underwriting cycles on its financial performance—the insurance industry, in general, is heavily impacted by inevitable downturns in new insurance underwriting activity. By diversifying globally and across markets, and by securing long term relationships with healthy clients, American Re was able to weather industry downturns with few financial problems compared to many other reinsurance industry participants. Going into the 1990s, for example, American Re continued to serve clients enlisted shortly after it was founded.

Aetna Life and Casualty Insurance Company, of Hartford, Connecticut, purchased American Re in 1969 in an effort to diversify its holdings. Under Aetna's ownership, American Re continued to attract new clients, boost its reserves, and expand geographically. Indeed, during the 1970s and 1980s the company opened offices across North America—in San Francisco, Kansas City, Chicago, Dallas, Atlanta, Montreal, Minneapolis, and several other cities. It also initiated operations in Mexico City; Bermuda; Bogota, Columbia; Santiago, Chile; Tokyo; Singapore; Melbourne and Sydney, Australia; London; Brussels; Vienna; and Cairo, Egypt.

Although Aetna paid only $340 million for the reinsurer, its new subsidiary proved, over time, to be a major boon to its bottom line. By the early 1980s, in fact, American Re was underwriting about $400 million in reinsurance premiums annually, despite a cyclical industry recess that lingered through 1984. And during the mid-1980s, a cyclical upswing propelled American Re-Insurance's underwriting revenues to more than $1 billion by 1987, providing a healthy addition to Aetna's aggregate earnings during that period.

Relatively healthy reinsurance underwriting activity, combined with relaxed regulatory oversight of insurance industry investment practices, induced several new companies to enter both the reinsurance and insurance industries during the mid-1980s. Despite unspectacular profits from insurance underwriting activity during that period, many insurance companies were able to generate fat profits by placing their assets in lucrative, yet risky, investment vehicles, such as real estate and junk bonds. Reinsurers benefitted.

In the late 1980s, however, the insurance industry suffered from numerous setbacks. Sloppy management and investment practices caught up with many insurers in the late 1980s, as interest rates and investment returns plummeted during the U.S. economic recession. Worse yet, record losses from catastrophes jolted property/casualty insurers in 1989, 1991, and 1992. Hurricane Hugo, the San Francisco earthquake, the Oakland fires, and hurricanes Andrew and Niki stressed insurance industry reserves with billions of dollars in damage. As property/casualty insurers filed record claims, many reinsurers suffered a significant depletion of their reserves.

Despite general industry turmoil, American Re profited from the conservative investment and management approach that it had practiced throughout most of the century. As the number of establishments competing in the U.S. reinsurance industry plummeted from about 130 in the mid-1980s to approximately 60 by 1992, American Re managed to increase its underwriting revenues, boost its reserves, and increase its annual operating income. For example, American Re-Insurance's combined ratio (a standard industry statistic reflective of financial stability) was the best (lowest) in the reinsurance industry in the early 1990s, and had remained significantly below the industry average throughout the 1980s.

American Re-Insurance's stability became increasingly important to the Aetna organization during the U.S. recession. In 1989, for example, the subsidiary contributed $128 million of Aetna's total $676 million in earnings. As Aetna's insurance company investments plummeted in value during the early 1990s, moreover, this ratio ballooned. In 1991, in fact, Aetna's earnings had slipped to $505 million, of which $133 million, or 26 percent, came from American Re Company. Despite its reliance on the reinsurer, Aetna decided to sell the operation in 1992 in an effort to generate much-needed cash to shore up its lagging insurance divisions.

Kohlberg Kravis Roberts & Co. (KKR), in the largest leveraged buyout in history of the U.S. insurance industry, purchased American Re Company in 1992 for $1.43 billion. KKR formed a new entity, American Re Corporation, to act as a holding company for American Re-Insurance Company (American Re) and related subsidiaries. While KKR was taking ownership of the company, it planned to leave direct control of American Re in the hands of existing management. "We'll be a stand alone, separate company and will be totally unrelated to other KKR companies," said Edward Jobe, American Re CEO since 1987, in the June 24, 1992 issue of *Business for Central New Jersey*.

American Re's management strategy following the KKR takeover entailed a four-pronged approach complementary of the organization's legacy of stability and conservatism: Client focus, financial strength, global reach, and commitment to innovation. Client focus was achieved by taking a specialist, or "Whole Account Concept," approach to service and by seeking long-term relationships. Every American Re client gets a multi-disciplined team of specialists to brainstorm needs and opportunities. "We then respond with customized products and specialized services," explained Jobe in the July 5, 1993 issue of *National Underwriter*. The company augments its client focus with direct underwriting, long practiced by American Re. By underwriting reinsurance directly, rather than through independent brokers, the company believes it is able to establish better relationships and attract a more stable client base in comparison to most of its competitors.

American Re's second management guideline, financial strength, was accomplished through an ongoing emphasis on exceptional cash reserves to back its potential liabilities; high asset quality, which is the result of cautious investments and a conservative asset mix; and a lack of dependence on underwriting cycles. Indeed, in 1993 American Re retained its distinction as having the lowest combined ratio in the industry. In addition, it maintained one of the three largest surpluses in the nation, 94 percent of which was invested in cash and bonds.

Global reach, American Re's third corporate focus, was extended during the early 1990s by providing specialized services to overseas clients and by promoting a reputation for stability. The latter earmark was particularly pivotal in attracting overseas business. "Every client in the world has access to all of our corporate resources," Jobe told *National Underwriter*, "including our multi-disciplined client teams ... which partially accounts for the substantial growth in international premium writings we've been experiencing. [We have] an international network of direct relationships." American Re operated ten overseas branches on five continents going into 1994, in addition to its 17 U.S. offices.

American Re was exhibiting its commitment to innovation, its fourth corporate tenant, in the early 1990s through automation, managing environmental risks, and rethinking its catastrophic risk policies. It established computer links among its international offices during the 1980s and early 1990s, for example, allowing the company to efficiently integrate global accounting and currency efforts. The company had also implemented the use of advanced risk analysis software to help it accurately predict damage from natural catastrophes. And the company had taken a leading role in the management of environmental risks, such as pollution and indoor air quality—an increasingly important sector of the industry in the 1990s.

In addition to its four-pronged management strategy, the company continued to achieve stability through market diversification following the KKR acquisition. The company began decreasing its reliance on conventional underwriting and investment revenues in the early 1990s, instead seeking profits from related fee services. By 1993, in fact, American Re Corp.'s new subsidiaries were contributing a significant portion of earnings growth. Am-Re Services, Inc., for example, was established to provide clients with various reinsurance-related services. Likewise, Am-Re Brokers, Inc., provided client access to worldwide reinsurance resources. Similarly, the Becher + Carlson (B + C) subsidiary specialized in risk management consulting and brokerage for commercial and public entities. Finally, Am-Re Managers, Inc. provided a variety of underwriting and consulting services to non-insurance businesses.

KKR's acquisition of American Re began to pay off in 1993. Company assets grew from $5.89 billion in 1992 to more than $6.23 billion in 1993, a 5.5 percent increase. And total revenue climbed from $1.1 billion in 1992 to an impressive $1.4 billion in 1993, resulting in net 1993 earnings of $75 million. Although company growth slightly lagged some industry statistical averages for larger reinsurers, those figures failed to reflect American Re's stability and growth potential. For instance, the company's international division boosted its gross premiums 39 percent in 1993, to $279 million. Furthermore, American Re's debt was significantly reduced and its combined ratio improved a healthy three percentage points.

Going into the mid-1990s, American Re Corp. expected to continue to benefit most from overseas expansion and growth in fee services. The decline of competing European reinsurers, particularly Lloyd's of London, boded well for international gains. Furthermore, American Re was striving to establish itself in many fast-growth developing markets, such as Russia, China, and Eastern Europe. B + C, for example, secured a consulting contract in 1993 with one of Russia's largest companies, which was also one of the world's largest truck manufacturers. It also forecasted steady growth in several high-profile niche markets, such as environmental risk management and advanced catastrophe analysis. Another area of expansion in the mid-1990s was

expected to be "treaty" business, whereby blocks of coverage are sold to clients.

"The new ownership will create an environment that will make it easier for us to work," said Paul H. Inderbitzin, executive vice president of American Re, in the September 16, 1992 issue of *Business Central New Jersey*. "We will be aggressive in alternative markets ... there are no barriers for the future growth of our activities."

Principal Subsidiaries: Am-Re Brokers, Inc.; Am-Re Managers, Inc.; Am-Re Services, Inc.; The Becher + Carlson Companies.

Further Reading:

"Am Re Posts Improved 1993 Results," *National Underwriter*, February 14, 1994.
Darian, Ryan, "100 Largest Groups See Slowdown in Growth," *Best's Review Property/Casualty*, January 1994.
Geet, Carolyn T., "Insurance," *Forbes*, January 3, 1994.
Howard, Lisa S., "U.S. Cat Losses Not Expected, Says Am Re CEO," *National Underwriter Property/Casualty*, October 18, 1993.
Jennings, John, "Am Re, Independent Again, Shifts Market Focus," *National Underwriter*, July 5, 1993.
"Paul Inderbitzin on How That Big American Re and KKR Deal is Coming Along," *Business for Central New Jersey*, September 16, 1992.
Peltz, Michael, "KKR Market-Times its Move Into Reinsurance," *Institutional Investor*, January 1993.
"Reinsurer Finds New Technologies," *Environmental Manager*, April 1993.
Snyder, John H., "Reinsurance - 1992," *Best's Review Property/Casualty*, November 1993.
Taber, George, "KKR Takes Over American RE in a $1.4 Billion Deal," *Business for Central New Jersey*, June 24, 1992.

—Dave Mote

Amgen, Inc.

Amgen Center
1840 Dehavilland Drive
Thousand Oaks, California 91320-1789
U.S.A.
(805) 499-5725
Fax: (805) 499-9315

Public Company
Incorporated: 1980
Employees: 1,700
Sales: $645.3 million
Stock Exchanges: NASDAQ
SICs: 2834 Pharmaceutical Preparations

Amgen, Inc. stands out in the biotechnology industry as one of the only businesses to transform itself from a drug-development company into a pharmaceutical manufacturer while maintaining steady sales. The largest independent biotechnology company in the United States by 1993, Amgen became a billion-dollar company after five initial years in the red. This transformation was due mostly to two gene-spliced drugs. Amgen continues to develop human bio-pharmaceutical products using proprietary recombinant DNA technology.

Amgen was formed in 1980 by a group of scientists and venture capitalists. The company's impressive scientific advisory board included several members of the National Academy of Sciences. Amgen's first chairman and CEO was George B. Rathmann, a former vice president for research and development in the diagnostics division of Abbott Laboratories.

With a $19 million private-equity placement from venture capital firms and two major corporations (including Abbott Laboratories), Amgen began operations in 1981. Its Thousand Oaks, California, location assured proximity to thriving research centers at three nearby universities, including UCLA and the California Institute of Technology. Through public stock offerings in 1983, 1986, and 1987, the company raised the capital needed to pursue its research. In its first five years, Amgen recorded losses. In 1986 it showed a humble profit, but 96 percent of its revenues that year came not from products but from interest income and research partnerships with major drug companies.

By 1986 Amgen had five genetically engineered drugs undergoing human testing, the final step before filing for Food and Drug Administration (FDA) approval. The most promising of these drugs was erythropoietin, or EPO, a hormone that promotes red blood cell production. EPO is usually produced by the kidneys to prevent anemia by inducing cells in the bone marrow to produce red blood cells. The drug was targeted for people with kidney disease who are dependent on dialysis, a process that lowers the kidneys' natural production of EPO. The product proved to be a marvel of genetic engineering: a synthetic form of a natural hormone that stimulates production of red blood cells. In January of 1987 an article in the *New England Journal of Medicine* increased excitement over EPO by detailing positive results of a study involving 25 kidney-dialysis patients.

Because the total worldwide market for patients with kidney failure is about $350 million a year, the market for EPO would seem to have a ceiling. In addition, since there were fewer than 200,000 kidney-dialysis patients in the United States at the time, Amgen's EPO was accorded "orphan drug" status by the FDA. "Orphan drug" status conferred an exclusive seven-year marketing rights privilege to the first company to develop a drug that benefits fewer than 200,000 people. Its purpose was to create an incentive for researchers to develop drugs that seemed not to promise much profit. But EPO was not just a drug for those suffering kidney failure; many argued that its applications for all causes of anemia were unlimited. Anemia was a common side effect of certain treatments for cancer, arthritis, and AIDS. The drug could also be used to reduce the need for blood transfusions during surgery.

With those uses in mind, in 1985 Amgen sold Johnson & Johnson the right to market EPO for treatment of anemia in the United States and for all uses in Europe. The previous year, Amgen had formed a joint venture with Kirin Brewery Company, Ltd of Japan, capitalized at $24 million, with Kirin gaining the right to manufacture and market EPO in Japan. Amgen, with the rights to the U.S. dialysis market firmly in its pocket, stood to benefit first as this was the first area of use under review by the FDA.

In the biotechnology industry of the 1980s, five to ten years and an average of more than $150 million were needed to develop a product. Products needed to be tested extensively, put through stiff regulatory approval, manufactured, and marketed before an idea began to repay its investors. In the early 1980s, capital to fund new products to promising new companies like Genentech, Cetus, Genetics Institute, and Amgen was plentiful. Nine years later, however, few of the companies that started off as gene-splicers were still in business, and many of the smaller companies had merged with larger competitors to stay alive.

The primary method by which biotech companies raised the cash they needed to develop promising drugs was to make deals to swap potential profits and technology. Amgen was unusual both in its attractive agreements with large companies and in its luck. It retained the right to manufacture and sell its EPO to dialysis patients in the United States and began building an EPO manufacturing facility near its headquarters even before the company was granted its first patent for its recombinant human erythropoietin, which it named Epogen. Two days after receiving the patent in October of 1987, Amgen filed with the FDA.

While awaiting approval, Amgen continued to develop other drugs, including a vaccine against hepatitis B, three products to stimulate the body's disease-fighting system (interleukin 2), and two kinds of interferon (antiviral substances). In 1985 Amgen became the first company to genetically engineer a substance called granulocyte colony-stimulating factor (G-CFS). As part of the family of substances that compel cells in the bone marrow to produce disease-fighting white blood cells, researchers were hopeful it would help fight bacterial infections and certain types of cancer, as well as offset the effects of radiation and chemotherapy. G-CFS was undergoing testing on cancer patients in chemotherapy in 1987.

Meanwhile, Amgen was about a year ahead of its closest rivals in the race to market EPO. However, one of Amgen's competitors, Genetics Institute (GI), had also received a patent on EPO, and the two companies sued each other for infringement. Amgen's patent covered rights to genetically engineered EPO, while GI's patent covered rights to natural, highly purified EPO. Although EPO is a hormone that occurs naturally, it can be manufactured through recombinant DNA technology in quantities that are commercially viable. The first company to isolate and patent the human gene responsible for making EPO, as well as the first to reproduce the drug in large quantities, was Amgen. It reproduced the drug by transplanting the isolated gene into the ovarian cells of hamsters. GI, on the other hand, was the first to isolate a purified strain of the protein. GI's patent was for the compound itself. The battle became acrimonious due to the high stakes: GI had licensed its patents to Chugai Pharmaceutical Company. The Japanese firm planned to market EPO in the United States through Upjohn Company. Amgen asked the International Trade Commission (ITC) to block imports of Chugai's EPO while the patent war continued. An ITC judge declined to do so in January of 1989.

While Amgen was awaiting the FDA's green light, Johnson & Johnson's Ortho Pharmaceutical Corporation slapped Amgen with a lawsuit. Ortho sought an injunction to delay marketing of EPO until a dispute over terms of their joint venture was settled. The issue was what Ortho claimed would be ''spillover sales.'' It could take another year or so before approval was granted for non-dialysis use, but because physicians often prescribe drugs outside their approved uses, it seemed likely that EPO would be used to treat many different forms of anemia before Ortho was able to claim the profits. At the same time, several U.S. senators were trying to change the orphan drug law and claimed that EPO should not qualify for exclusivity because it had huge money-making potential. The law in general, senators claimed, allowed manufacturers to reap large monopoly profits. Before its prize child even came on the market, Amgen was being fired upon on all sides by those convinced of EPO's potential.

These legal tangles caused further delay in FDA approval of the drug, which allowed competitors to pull ahead in their efforts to market the drug. The delay in approval also meant financial losses for Amgen. The company was poised to begin immediate shipments to patients with end-stage renal, or kidney, disease. These patients often require blood dialysis several times a week, and frequent blood transfusions on top of that to keep red blood cell counts at healthy levels. The company determined that EPO's annual tab for dialysis patients would run $6,000. Medi-

care would pick up the bill for dialysis patients, most of whom are hit by the huge cost of dialysis itself.

In March of 1989 a federal judge ruled that Ortho and Amgen must submit a joint application for FDA approval of EPO. Other aspects of that legal battle continued: The feud between Amgen and GI over patent rights suggested that cross-licensing might be a solution. Meanwhile, GI was nearing the finish line in its own labs. Intensifying the race was the orphan drug award, a seven-year monopoly on sales to the winner.

On June 1, 1989, the FDA approved Amgen's EPO for treatment of anemia in kidney-dialysis patients. The next day Amgen shipped its first batch to UCLA Medical Center. By the end of June, it had sold nearly $17 million worth of the drug. After nine years in business, Amgen was finally selling its first product. While legal wrangles continued, Amgen had the market to itself. GI's version of EPO was still awaiting FDA approval. Around this time, CEO Rathmann passed his title to longtime CFO Gordon M. Binder, the author of Amgen's deal with Kirin Brewery.

In 1990 the U.S. House of Representatives cleared a measure amending the orphan drug law, but EPO was exempt due to furious lobbying by both GI and Amgen. A federal magistrate ruled that Amgen was infringing on GI's patent, and vice versa; a ruling which accorded no clear victory but seemed again to aim at a cross-licensing agreement. Encouraged, GI stepped up its attack on Amgen by asking a federal court to freeze the company's profits on EPO sales and sought an injunction to stop Amgen from producing the drug. The court's decision held that both companies had valid patents and that each was guilty of infringing on the other's patent. The decision allowed Chugai to use Amgen's patented genetic coding to produce the drug in Japan, then import and sell it without infringing any patents. Meanwhile, Amgen was ringing up profits. Product sales went from $2.8 million in 1989 to roughly $140 million in 1990.

In March of 1990 a federal judge ordered Amgen and GI to exchange royalty-free cross-licenses on EPO. The judge ruled that GI's product, called Marogen, was also covered by the orphan drug status. The ruling was considered a significant setback for Amgen. In June of 1990, an official from the Department of Health and Human Services told a house subcommittee that dialysis centers across the country were earning a more than 40 percent profit on administered EPO. Amgen's pricing of the drug also came under scrutiny. The company had accrued up $190 million in sales in EPO's first year on the market.

Meanwhile, expectations were great for Amgen's new drug, Neupogen. This G-CSF (granulocyte colony stimulating factor) was a protein that stimulated white blood cell production and was being tested to combat chronic white blood cell deficiencies in cancer patients undergoing chemotherapy. In the process of chemotherapy, not only are cancerous cells destroyed, but so are healthy white blood cells. Since white blood cells are the primary component of the body's immune system, damaging them increases a patient's risk of incurring a potentially fatal infection.

Amgen retained much greater marketing rights for Neupogen than for Epogen. Amgen received the first U.S. patent on recombinant G-CSF in 1989 and FDA approval for Neupogen was issued in February of 1991. In clinical studies G-CSF performed resoundingly well. The hope was that the drug's use would extend beyond chemotherapy patients to include others who would benefit from increased immunization. Since G-CSF was not considered an orphan drug, many other biotechnology companies were racing to bring their own version of the product to market. The speculation was that Neupogen could launch Amgen into the arena of international drug companies. The initial market for Neupogen was calculated to be twice that of Epogen, with Amgen retaining full domestic marketing rights to the drug. Kirin Brewery had exclusive license for sales of G-CSF in Japan, Korea, and Taiwan.

In March of 1991 Amgen received more good news: A federal court of appeals issued the final verdict in Amgen's ongoing struggle with Genetics Institute over EPO, and the decision favored Amgen. GI was blocked from selling its version of the anti-anemia drug. The judge ruled that GI had failed to demonstrate just how it made the purified form of EPO from human urine—the factor by which GI's product differed from Amgen's. It was a severe setback for GI, which had been battling the patent dispute for two years in hopes of bringing its product to market. Thus, Amgen was given a legal monopoly over domestic EPO sales.

Amgen had shipped about $53 million of Neupogen by May of 1991, and in the process the company became known as a biotechnology leader. Amgen was cautious, however, to avoid the fate that rocked Genentech in 1988 when its genetically engineered heart attack drug, TPA, failed to live up to the fanfare preceding its release. That incident caused Genentech's stock to plunge, knocking it off balance. Genentech eventually sold a majority of its stock to Hoffmann-La Roche, Co.

The few outstanding lawsuits over EPO began to reach settlements. In 1991 Amgen was ordered to pay Johnson & Johnson's subsidiary, Ortho Pharmaceuticals Corporation, $164 million in damages for violation of their 1985 EPO marketing agreement. Ortho's rights to market the drug for all therapeutic uses other than dialysis were sabotaged by the fact they did not bring their brand to market at the same time as Amgen's Epogen brand. Epogen was ultimately sold and used for purposes under Ortho's jurisdiction during the 19 months it took for Ortho to bring its product to the market. The judge ruled that Amgen frustrated Johnson & Johnson's attempts to win regulatory approval for its EPO brand.

Conversely, in 1992 Johnson & Johnson was ordered to pay Amgen $90 million for failing to comply with another aspect of the same 1985 agreement. According to the contract, Johnson & Johnson was to develop both a hepatitis B vaccine and interleukin 2, and Amgen was to receive royalties from those products. Johnson & Johnson failed to meet those obligations. The net result of the two-part case was that Amgen would pay Johnson & Johnson around $85 million.

Thus, Amgen became the only biotech company to near the status of independent global pharmaceutical company. Looking back over the other firms that had begun with the same goal, most had folded or entered alliances with more established pharmaceutical giants in order to survive. In fall of 1992, Amgen tapped Kevin W. Sharer to fill the long-vacant post of president and COO. At the time, Sharer was president of the telephone giant MCI Communications Corporation. In 1993 Amgen announced an expansion of its research and development investment to nearly double what its 1992 expenditure had been. New research focused on blood-cell growth factors, soft-tissue growth factors, and neurobiology, inflammation, and nucleic acid therapeutics. The company was also exploring growth factors to help heal burns, surgical wounds, bone damage, and other injuries. In addition, Amgen has applied recombinant technology to produce a vaccine for the potential prevention of hepatitis B and has pursued other products with immunologic possibilities against certain cancers and infectious diseases.

Amgen closed 1992 as a billion-dollar company. As of early 1993, Neupogen still had no competition in the market, and its growth potential remained considerable. Conversely, Epogen use among dialysis patients had reached its ceiling. Amgen entered into a multi-year collaboration with Regeneron Pharmaceuticals Inc. in 1990 to develop and commercialize two neurotrophic substances which were still in development by the end of 1993.

Principal Subsidiaries: Amgen Australia Pty Ltd.; Amgen N.V.; Amgen Canada Inc.; Amgen Greater China Ltd.; Amgen GmbH (Germany); Amgen S.A. (France); Amgen S.p.A. (Italy); Amgen K.K. (Japan); Amgen B.V. (Netherlands); Amgen-Biofarmaceutica (Portugal); Amgen S.A. (Spain); Amgen (Europe) AG (Switzerland); Kirin-Amgen, Inc. (Switzerland); Amgen Limited (U.K.); Amgen Sales Corporation (West Indies).

Further Reading:

"Amgen Inc.," *Wall Street Journal,* January 13, 1993, p. B4.

"Amgen Patent Claim on Drug for Anemia Is Rejected by Court," *Wall Street Journal,* May 1, 1990, p. A8.

"Amgen Wins Ruling in Its Patent Dispute," *Wall Street Journal,* April 18, 1990, p. A12.

Andrews, Edmund, "Rival Seeking to Freeze Amgen Profits on Drug," *New York Times,* January 31, 1990, p. D5; "Drug Ruling Is a Setback for Amgen," *New York Times,* March 15, 1990, pp. D1, D8.

Armstrong, Larry, "Churning Out Earnings as the Economy Starts to Slow," *Business Week,* July 31, 1989, p. 30; "Two Rising Stars," *Business Week,* April 3, 1992.

"Blood Money," *Economist,* April 20, 1991, pp. 86–87.

"Ex-Official of Amgen Sues Others, Charging Insider Stock Trading," *Wall Street Journal,* May 15, 1991, p. A5.

Flynn, Julie, "The Hormone That's Making Amgen Grow," *Business Week,* March 16, 1987, pp 96–97.

Giltenan, Edward, "Bioprofits," *Forbes,* January 7, 1991, pp. 10–11.

Hamilton, Joan, "Amgen is Hot—And Bothered," *Business Week,* January 23, 1989, pp. 40–41; "A Drug That Could Replace Transfusions—If It Ever Reaches The Market," *Business Week,* March 27, 1989, pp 60–61; "The Gene Jockeys are Finally Seeing Some Green," *Business Week,* July 2, 1990, p. 77.

"Looking for the Biotech Blockbusters," *Fortune,* July 7, 1986, pp. 109–110.

Marcial, Gene, "Biotech Fans Love Amgen's One-Two Punch," *Business Week,* August 13, 1990, p. 104.

Noah, Timothy, "U.S. Aide Urges Cut in Payments on Amgen Drug," *Wall Street Journal,* June 15, 1990, p. B4; "House Panel Clears Measure Amending Orphan Drug Law," *Wall Street Journal,* June 22, 1990, p. B4.

Palmer, Jay, "Trader," *Barron's,* March 11, 1991, p. 71.

Petruno, Tom, "Amgen: Getting the Worst of Both Worlds," *Los Angeles Times,* February 1, 1993, p. D1.

Pollack, Andrew, "Focus of Attention in Biotechnology," *New York Times,* May 24, 1991, p. D6.

Quickel, Stephen, "Say, Can You Spare a Biobuck?," *Business Month,* November 1989, pp. 91–92.

Rundle, Rhonda, "FDA Approves Amgen Cancer Drug, but Rivals Loom," *Wall Street Journal,* February 22, 1991, p. B1; "Amgen Wins Biotech Drug Patent Battle," *Wall Street Journal,* March 7, 1991, p. A3; "Amgen Posts a More Than Fivefold Rise in Net Income for its Fourth Quarter," *Wall Street Journal,* May 2, 1991, p. A4; "Amgen Told to Pay $154 Million to Johnson & Johnson Subsidiary, *Wall Street Journal,* July 2, 1991, p. B4; "Amgen Inc. is Expected to be Awarded $90 Million from Johnson & Johnson," *Wall Street Journal,* September 10, 1992, p. B8; "Amgen Picks MCI's Sharer as President, Tapping Talent Outside the Industry," *Wall Street Journal,* October 19, 1992, p. B5.

Savitz, Eric, "Fulfilling Their Promise," *Barron's,* September 25, 1989.

Serwer, Andrew, "Biotech Stocks are Poised to Pay Off in the 1990s," *Fortune,* March 12, 1990, pp 25–28.

Stavro, Barry, "Amgen Stock Soars as FDA Approves Antibacterial Drug, *Los Angeles Times,* February 22, 1991, pp. D1–D2; "Investors Tracking Insiders' Stock Sales for Clues on Amgen," *Los Angeles Times,* March 26, 1991, p. D1.

Stipp, David, "Genetics Institute, Japanese Firm Seek Injuction Against Amgen in Patent Case," *Wall Street Journal,* January 31, 1990, p. B2.

Sugawara, Sandra, "Going-It-Alone Gives Way to Partnerships in Biotech," *Washington Post,* August 25, 1992, pp. C1, C4.

Teitelman, Robert, "Amgen: Biotech's Next Big Attraction?," *Financial World,* January 26, 1988, pp. 12–13.

"Uncorking the Genes," *Barron's,* May 5, 1986.

Welling, Kathryn, "The Conversion of Paul," *Barron's,* September 7, 1987.

Wyatt, Edward, "What Price Promise?," *Barron's,* April 10, 1989.

Yoder, Stephen, "Trade Associations for Biotechnology Becomes Unspliced," *Wall Street Journal,* March 28, 1990, p. B8.

—Carol I. Keeley

Petroleum Corporation

Anadarko Petroleum Corporation

17001 Northchase Drive
P.O. Box 1330
Houston, Texas 77251-1330
U.S.A.
(713) 875-1101
Fax: (713) 874-3282

Public Company
Incorporated: 1959 as Anadarko Production Company
Employees: 1,020
Sales: $476 million
Stock Exchanges: New York
SICs: 1311 Crude Petroleum & Natural Gas; 1381 Drilling
  Oil & Gas Wells

Anadarko Petroleum Company is a major independent oil and natural gas exploration and production company. The largest share of Anadarko's natural gas reserves are located in Kansas' Hugoton gas basin, the largest natural gas field in the United States. Among the other places the company drills onshore are the Arkoma and Golden Trend Basins of Arkansas and Oklahoma, the Permian Basin of West Texas, and the Rocky Mountain regions of Nevada, Wyoming, and southern Alberta, Canada. Anadarko is also engaged in offshore exploration in the Gulf of Mexico. In the early 1990s, the company stepped up its overseas operations, with its most important exploration taking place in Algeria. Owning interest in 17 gas gathering systems and 20 gas processing plants in the mid-continent area, the company produced 7.9 million barrels of oil, 161.9 billion cubic feet of natural gas, and 2.7 million barrels of natural gas liquids in 1993. Its proved reserves consisted of 1.88 trillion cubic feet of natural gas and 78.5 million barrels of crude oil, condensate, and natural gas liquids.

Anadarko was created in 1959 as a wholly owned subsidiary of Panhandle Eastern Pipe Line Company. At that time, Federal Power Commission (FPC) rules placed lower price limits on gas produced from properties owned by pipeline companies than on gas produced from independently owned properties. Panhandle owned a substantial amount of gas-producing property, located primarily in the Anadarko Basin, a gas-rich region covering parts of the Texas and Oklahoma panhandles and southwestern Kansas. Since regulations prevented Panhandle from charging the market price for the gas it produced, the company sought

ways to skirt these price ceilings. Efforts in the courtroom failed, leaving the creation of a wholly owned subsidiary for gas exploration and production as the only option. Anadarko Production Company was officially incorporated in June 1959, with Panhandle owning all of its stock. Headquarters for the new company were established in Liberal, Kansas; Frederick Robinson was named chairperson, and Robert Harkins became company president.

Since properties developed by Anadarko were not subject to FPC pipeline pricing regulations, all of Panhandle's undeveloped properties were transferred to its new subsidiary. Although its gas properties that were already developed remained under FPC jurisdiction, Panhandle's oil producing properties were not subject to the same pricing rules. Therefore, they were transferred to Anadarko as well. By the end of 1959, Anadarko had drilled 17 wells in the Anadarko Basin, 14 of which were development wells, all of which producers. One of the three exploratory wells was also a producer. Before its first full year of operation had ended, Anadarko had spent $2.5 million on exploration and had purchased 27 Texas panhandle producing gas wells.

Anadarko signed its first major long-term contract in 1960, a 20-year agreement with Pioneer Natural Gas Company to provide gas from the Red Cave formation in the Texas panhandle to several communities in the area. The following year, the company built an 84-mile pipeline in Kansas. The pipeline carried gas from the Spivey Grabs Field in Kingman and Harper counties to the Skelly Oil Refinery in El Dorado. Anadarko continued to grow quickly over the next few years, mainly by exploiting its rich properties on its home turf, the Anadarko basin. Between 1962 and 1964, the company doubled its sales of natural gas, from 27 billion cubic feet to 53 billion. Its oil sales doubled over the same period, from 911,000 to 1.8 million barrels.

By the mid-1960s, Anadarko's future growth clearly depended on expansion outside the Anadarko Basin. Toward this end, in August 1965, the company purchased Ambassador Oil Corporation of Ft. Worth, Texas, for $12 million. In purchasing Ambassador, Anadarko acquired assets that included undeveloped leases and proven oil and gas reserves totaling about 600,000 acres, located in 19 states and Canada. Most of Ambassador's personnel were retained, and because of its more central location, Ambassador's Ft. Worth offices were designated as Anadarko's new headquarters. While this transfer was taking place, Anadarko president Harkins died, and Richard O'Shields was named to replace him.

In 1968, O'Shields was promoted to executive vice-president of parent Panhandle Eastern, and R.C. Dixon succeeded him as Anadarko's top officer. Although the bulk of its operations were still taking place in the Anadarko Basin, the company was quite active in other places, particularly Alberta, Canada, where it was participating in seven oil wells near the Bantry West Field. This Alberta development program also included the acquisition of producing properties with 1.4 million barrels of estimated reserves. By 1969, 12 percent of parent company Panhandle's net income was being generated by Anadarko.

Anadarko's involvement in offshore exploration began in 1970. That year, the company acquired a one-eighth working interest in drilling rights to nine property blocks in the Gulf of Mexico. In 1971, Robert Stephens succeeded Dixon as Anadarko's president, and under Stephens, the company placed increasing emphasis on offshore operations, developing its own methods for collecting and analyzing geological and geophysical information used to evaluate potential offshore drilling leases. Of the Gulf of Mexico properties in which Anadarko had working interests, 24 blocks showed oil or gas in exploratory drilling between 1971 and 1976, and ten of them proved commercially productive.

In 1972, Panhandle created Pan Eastern Exploration Company, a new wholly owned subsidiary. All of Panhandle's remaining producing properties were transferred to Pan Eastern, which was to be operated by Anadarko. Pan Eastern spent $29 million on leases and drilling in its first year of existence and produced 116 billion cubic feet of gas from its Anadarko Basin reserves. Pan Eastern became part of Anadarko in 1981 and was eventually renamed APX Corporation in 1987. Anadarko's headquarters were moved from Ft. Worth to Houston in 1974. Two years later, when Stephens left the company, his replacement was Robert Allison, Jr., a petroleum engineer whom Stephens had brought on board as vice-president of operations.

Anadarko closed its second decade of operation by breaking the $100 million revenue barrier for the first time in 1978. By 1979, the company was contributing about 30 percent of Panhandle's net income. Around that time, Anadarko sought to expand its activities in the Gulf of Mexico, as higher gas prices resulting from the passage of the Gas Policy Act of 1978 created a major boom in gas exploration. Anadarko joined this boom by entering a farm-in arrangement with Amoco Corporation, in which Anadarko was to operate a project until a discovery was made. After the discovery, Amoco would have the option of re-entering the project as a half-interest partner. Located on Matagorda Island, the block (Matagorda 623) became a producer in early 1980. The group, consisting of Anadarko, Amoco, and Champlin Petroleum Company (to whom Anadarko had sold 25 percent of its deal with Amoco), then bid on a neighboring block that geophysical testing had shown to be promising. In 1982, the first well at Matagorda 622 was completed, and the block was found to have huge gas reserves. The Matagorda 622/623 blocks taken together represented a huge find for Anadarko, and the discovery sparked new interest in the Gulf of Mexico among many wildcat drillers.

During this time, the company's onshore projects continued to operate successfully as well. A producing natural gas and oil-like condensate discovery well, 100 percent owned and operated by Anadarko, was completed in San Patricio County, Texas, in 1982. By the mid-1980s, Anadarko was clearly the most important subsidiary of Panhandle, accounting for 37 percent of Panhandle's 1984 profit while contributing only 11 percent of its revenue. Panhandle management recognized that the price of its stock was not reflecting the true value of the company, given the impressive results being turned in by Anadarko. As a result, management decided to spin Anadarko off to Panhandle's stockholders, in order to discourage potential takeover attempts. Anadarko Petroleum Corporation was created in 1985, and all of Anadarko Production Company's oil and gas assets were handed over to the new company.

However, one major obstacle prevented the spinoff from taking place immediately. In 1975, Panhandle had entered a 20-year contract with Sonatrach, Algeria's national energy company, to import liquified natural gas from that country during the gas shortages of that period. By the time Algeria began shipping the gas in 1982, however, conditions in the United States had changed, and there was no longer a market for the wildly overpriced Algerian gas. Panhandle suspended deliveries, leading to an international squabble between the two companies, during which Panhandle could not spin off any assets, including Anadarko. In 1986, when Panhandle received word that a takeover attempt by a Texas investment group was imminent, attention to the Sonatrach negotiations was heightened and the dispute was settled, with Sonatrach receiving six million shares of Panhandle stock and $300 million in cash. Anadarko then became an independent company, taking APX Corporation, Anadarko Petroleum of Canada, and other exploration and production subsidiaries with it.

Although the spinoff was essentially a friendly one, it was not entirely without conflict. Late in 1986, Anadarko sued its former parent over contracts the company felt were unfair. Under the terms of the contracts, Anadarko sold gas to Panhandle at below-market prices, an agreement made when Anadarko's board was still dominated by Panhandle officials. The Federal Energy Regulatory Commission eventually freed Anadarko from those agreements. For 1986, its first year as an independent company, Anadarko had net income of $10.1 million on revenue of $205.7 million.

By 1987, Anadarko had natural gas reserves of 1.7 trillion cubic feet, of which only 200 to 250 million cubic feet per day were being produced. In order to make better use of its reserves, in February of that year, the company launched a program of infill drilling at its Hugoton Field property in southwestern Kansas. Infill drilling involved the addition of a second well at an existing unit capable of tapping deeper gas reserves. Infill gas could be sold at a higher price than gas produced by the original well at a site. By early 1989, the company had drilled 146 infill wells. In addition to beefing up its exploration activities, Anadarko grew through acquisition during its first few years on its own. Among its purchases were certain oil producing properties in western Texas from Parker & Parsley Developments Partners, a regional energy company. By 1989, the company's revenue had grown to $361 million.

Ground was broken in Houston in 1991 for Anadarko Towers, the company's new headquarters building and the first major commercial office building started in that city in over five years. Anadarko's revenue slipped to $336.6 million in 1991, but rebounded slightly to $375 million the following year. However, the company's earnings dropped further, sinking to $27 million, half that reported in 1990. In early 1993, Anadarko became the first foreign-owned company to discover oil in Algeria. The company had initially entered that country in 1989, the first year it was opened to foreign investment. Along with two European partners in the venture, Anadarko maintained drilling rights to a 5.1 million-acre area in the Sahara Desert. Anadarko's interest in the venture was 50 percent.

Sonatrach, Algeria's national oil and gas enterprise, in turn retained over ten percent ownership of Anadarko's common stock.

Later in 1993, Anadarko teamed up with Amoco and Phillips Petroleum in discovering a huge shallow-water oil field in the Gulf of Mexico. The field, called Mahogany, was thought to hold at least 100 million barrels of oil, 37.5 percent of which was owned by Anadarko. For fiscal 1993, Anadarko reported record-high net income of $117 million on revenue of $476 million. For the twelfth consecutive year, the company more than matched its production volumes of oil and gas with new proved reserves. Anadarko increased its exploration activities in the Gulf in early 1994. In April, the company paid $98 million for 26 different Gulf properties in a Minerals Management Service lease sale, hoping to repeat the success of Mahogany. Like Mahogany, the properties were nearly all "sub-salt plays," or potential finds located under salt formations. Anadarko also announced further oil discoveries in the deserts of Algeria, and development of those properties was accelerated.

In the short period since its spinoff from Panhandle Eastern, Anadarko's rate of success at wildcat drilling was remarkable. Its wealth of natural gas reserves in the Hugoton basin also gave the company a great deal of control over its production, a huge advantage in an industry susceptible to market fluctuations. Anadarko was expected to become an even larger force among independent energy companies, if its discoveries of oil and gas in the Gulf of Mexico and Algeria continued into the late 1990s.

Principal Subsidiaries: Anadarko Algeria Corporation; Anadarko Petroleum of Canada Ltd.; Anadarko Marketing Co.; Anadarko Trading Co.; Anadarko Gathering Company.

Further Reading:

Burrough, Bryan, "Panhandle Eastern Considering Spinoff or Sale of Unit as Anti-Takeover Move," *Wall Street Journal,* August 19, 1985, p. 5.

Byrne, Harlan S., "Anadarko Petroleum," *Barron's,* December 18, 1989, p. 56.

Frazier, Steve, "Anadarko Sues Panhandle Eastern Over Gas Contracts," *Wall Street Journal,* November 25, 1986, p. 18.

Ivanovich, David, "Anadarko Pays $98 Million for Gulf of Mexico Blocks," *Journal of Commerce,* April 4, 1994, p. 5B.

Ivanovich, David, "Oil Discovery Is a First For Anadarko in Algeria," *Journal of Commerce,* February 22, 1993, p. 6B.

Mack, Toni, "Elephants, Anyone?" *Forbes,* April 11, 1994, p. 71.

Mack, Toni, "Of Sharks and Albatrosses," *Forbes,* September 23, 1985, pp. 114–15.

Marcial, Gene G., "A Slick Play in Energy," *Business Week,* December 27, 1993, p. 88.

Stuart, Lettice, "New Office Tower Project Is Houston's First in 5 Years," *New York Times,* February 20, 1991, p. D20.

"Thirty Years of History," Houston: Anadarko Petroleum Corporation, 1989.

Thomas, Paulette, "Anadarko to Post Third-Quarter Profit, Faces Choices on Drilling, Acquisitions," *Wall Street Journal,* September 8, 1987, p. 16.

—Robert R. Jacobson

Analog Devices, Inc.

One Technology Way
P.O. Box 9106
Norwood, Massachusetts 02062-9106
U.S.A.
(617) 329-4700
Fax: (617) 326-8703

Public Company
Incorporated: 1965
Employees: 5,400
Sales: $666 million
Stock Exchanges: New York
SICs: 3674 Semiconductors & Related Devices

Analog Devices, Inc. is one of the world's leading producers of precision performance electronic components, including linear, mixed-signal, and digital integrated circuits, which are used to help convert sensory data into a digital format that can be understood by computers. Analog's integrated circuits are used in laboratory test equipment, medical devices that sense information such as heartbeats, systems for controlling airplane cabin pressure, and controls on oil wells and military weapons. The company has also moved increasingly into the computer, communications, automotive, and consumer industries. Analog has helped develop integrated circuits for processing voice commands into personal computers and has introduced new digital signal processors that integrate voice, audio, fax/modem, and speech recognition functions for computer circuit boards. Analog's products are also used in laptop and notebook computers, as well as in advanced telecommunications systems, including the U.S. cellular phone network. The company's signal processing technology resulted in the development of a pocket-sized pager, which, when used with a satellite system, allows owners to receive messages anywhere in the world. Other cutting edge technologies include signal processors for electronic cameras, color scanners, digital copiers, and a unique crash sensor used to control automobile airbags. With nearly half of its sales in North America, 30 percent in Europe, and 16 percent in Japan, the company maintains manufacturing facilities in Massachusetts, California, and North Carolina, as well as Ireland, Japan, the Philippines, and Taiwan.

Analog Devices was founded in 1965 by Ray Stata and Matthew Lorber. Upon graduating from the engineering pro-

gram at the Massachusetts Institute of Technology, Stata was hired by Hewlett-Packard in Cambridge, Massachusetts, where he shared an apartment with his former classmate Lorber, who was also an engineer. The two soon decided to go into business together, and, working out of the basement of their apartment building, they produced devices to test gyroscopes, calling their company Solid State Instruments. Although Stata and Lorber regarded their business as a failure, they were able to sell the company to Kollmorgen Corp. for $100,000 in stock. With this stock, they were then able to secure bank loans to launch their second company, Analog Devices. Now more familiar with the electronics market, Stata and Lorber selected a new product to manufacture: operational amplifiers—circuits that strengthened and clarified electrical signals. It was a niche market, without significant competition, and the new company immediately made money. By 1968, sales had reached $5.7 million, and, one year later, Analog Devices went public.

Lorber and Stata had difficulty adapting to the daily administrative duties involved in running a growing company. When the company went public, Lorber sold half of his stock and moved on to other ventures. While Stata remained, he preferred to concentrate on developing and marketing new products, so he hired an outsider to take the job of president. After a year, Stata, the company's largest stockholder, found that he had to make the major financial and organizational decisions whether he wanted to or not, and he let his hired president go. In spite of his reluctance, Stata proved himself an adept manager, and several shrewd choices he made early in his career led the company through years of uninterrupted growth.

Stata worked hard to nurture entrepreneurial talent within his company, and he also acquired small companies with interesting product lines. In 1969, Analog Devices bought Pastoriza Research, a firm that had developed highly specialized integrated circuits that converted analog signals to digital. Analog signals included nonelectrical measurements such as temperature or pressure, and the converter changed these signals into a digital form that could be read by a computer. Stata speculated correctly that computers would become widely used in industry for controlling machinery, and Pastoriza's specialized product would become a growing necessity. Analog Devices also began funding a manufacturer of semiconductors in 1969. Semiconductors—silicon chips that could perform the analog to digital conversion previously handled by bulkier components such as transistors—were a relatively new thing, and Stata took a gamble that the industry would grow. Using his stock in Analog Devices as collateral, he raised $2 million in capital, which he offered to three young engineers to start a semiconductor firm named Nova Devices. Two years later, Analog acquired Nova under a predetermined buy-out plan, and the company became Analog's semiconductor division. This became Analog's fastest-growing area, and, by 1982, semiconductors accounted for half the company's income.

Sales rose an average of 25 percent a year at Analog, and the company continued to invest heavily in new product lines. Between eight and nine percent of sales were reinvested in research and development, and the company carried a debt of over $3 million. In spite of the high cost, funding new ventures was the key to Analog's growth. In 1973, the company began backing Micro-Sensors, Inc., a small company that made sensors for measuring textile yarns during production. The company continued to work independently on improving the product, and Analog took over marketing and sales operations, a relationship typical of the way Analog moved into new product areas.

Beginning in the late 1960s, Analog Devices established sales subsidiaries in Germany and France, and, in 1976, the company moved more substantially into the European market. Accepting 40 percent financial backing from the Irish government, Analog built its first manufacturing plant abroad, in Limerick, Ireland. The new facility made metal oxide semiconductor integrated circuits, which were first developed by Analog engineers in Santa Clara, California, and had become the company's single largest capital investment. The product line was quickly expanded to include multiple chip integrated circuits.

Financing new start-up ventures and building new facilities proved a strain on the company's resources, and, in 1977, Analog sought investment capital. That year, Standard Oil of Indiana bought a 15 percent interest in Analog Devices in exchange for nearly $5 million in cash. Paying 50 percent over the market rate for Analog's stock, Standard Oil regarded the deal as an investment in Analog's growing semiconductor division. Analog doubled the size of its semiconductor plant in Wilmington, Massachusetts, and added a second facility to its new factory in Ireland. Then, in 1980, Standard Oil and Analog entered into a second agreement, establishing a joint venture called Analog Devices Enterprises. The five-year plan called for the oil company to capitalize start-up companies that Analog chose, as a means to acquiring new technologies. Between 1980 and 1983, Analog invested in 11 different high-tech companies, bringing Analog new products in such areas as digital signal processing circuits, image processing systems, and telecommunications instruments.

By 1982, Analog Devices, Inc. had sales of $156 million, shipping over 200 products to over 15,000 customers in the United States, Europe, and Japan. The company's product line was diverse, and though it served large companies, including Hewlett-Packard and Digital Equipment Corp., no single company accounted for more than two percent of sales. Analog Devices' products were used by wineries, aluminum smelting plants, medical diagnostic labs, and a growing variety of industries that used computers for inspection or control. Although sales at times were somewhat impeded by the effect of the strong dollar on the European market and by industry-wide slowdowns, Analog Devices' performance in the first half of the 1980s was generally strong. The company was at the forefront of several high-tech areas and became a recognized leader in converters that could continuously change signals from analog to digital and back. The company also pioneered a highly regarded computer-based system called MACSYM that measured and controlled physical processes. Analog expanded its manufacturing capacity abroad in the early 1980s, building assembly plants in Japan and the Philippines.

Stata had taken his company through a series of five-year plans, carefully projecting growth and moving into strategic areas of new technology, and, in 1982, he predicted that Analog Devices would be a billion-dollar company within eight years. However, by the mid-1980s, profits at Analog began to decline. The joint venture company Analog Devices Enterprises was terminated in September 1985, and, the following year, Standard Oil of Indiana (which had become Amoco Corp.) sold its stock in Analog in order to concentrate on its core oil business. Moreover, military budget cutbacks led to reduced sales of established product lines.

Forced to spend a substantial share of its resources on developing new technologies, which did not immediately translate into new products, Analog Devices saw its stock price decline in the late 1980s. By 1990, the share price stood where it had ten years earlier, and the company posted its first loss. The company had not reached its $1 billion goal—sales were about $485 million in 1990—and it was too large to compete with the smaller high-tech firms that were overtaking niche markets.

Plans were made to turn the company around. In 1990, the company bought Precision Monolithics, Inc., a specialty circuit manufacturer, giving Analog new manufacturing technology and significantly expanding sales. Stata also undertook several organizational changes in order to streamline the company, combining several divisions into a single Industrial Electronics Division. Industrial automation, automatic test equipment, motion controls, and industrial controls, all of which were previously developed in facilities across the United States and the United Kingdom, came under one roof at corporate headquarters in Norwood, Massachusetts. European operations were also combined under a single European headquarters in Germany. In late 1990, the company cut about 600 jobs, bringing the workforce down by more than ten percent.

Perhaps the most significant shift in the company's direction involved a new product that was slow to reach the market. Since the late 1980s, the company spent more than one-third of its research and development funds on a new technology: digital signal processing—an exciting process that allowed a single chip to perform functions that previously required a circuit board. With a variety of applications in markets that were new to Analog, the chips could be used to process voice signals into digital signals for use in telephone technology and in personal computing. Analog also entered an alliance with Hewlett-Packard in 1992 to develop mixed-signal semiconductors, which could combine analog and digital processing on a single chip.

The company poured money into research, and, by late 1991, it reported promising results. Its mixed-signal technology had allowed Analog to build a minute sensor that was used to trigger an automobile airbag in case of a collision. While the standard system used multiple sensors and extensive wiring, with an installation cost of $400 to $600, Analog's single sensor sold for only $5, bringing the total cost of an airbag system to around $100. Perfected in 1991, the sensor was first deployed in 1994 Saab automobiles, and an American car manufacturer was expected to follow in 1995. Analog had not made products for the automotive market before, but its first effort seemed extremely promising, and the company soon brought out other sensors and converters that could be used in a variety of consumer products. Analog introduced a low-cost, accurate, and stable temperature controller in 1993 that could be used in residential thermostats. During this time, Sony Corporation became an Analog customer, using a new high-speed analog to digital converter in its digital camcorder.

In 1992, Analog's digital signal processing chips debuted in the personal computing market in Asia, and by the following year many major personal computer and component manufacturers, including Compaq and Microsoft, signed deals to use the new technology. The chips could be used to manipulate real-world sounds and images, making them important to many new computer software applications. Moreover, the chips could be programmed to enable a computer to read material back to the user, or to allow people to give instructions to their computers over the telephone. Texas Instruments, AT&T, and Motorola also sold digital signal processing technology—representing larger sales than Analog's 1992 figure of $60 million—but only Analog priced its chips low enough to appeal to the personal computing industry, and the company expected sales to boom in the coming years. Analog also had a strong market presence in consumer audio and telecommunications, as its digital signal processing chips could be used in compact disc players and cellular phone handsets. With the success of its newest wave of products, Analog Devices' sales swelled, its stock recovered from its early 1990s low, and revenues from digital signal processing were expected to more than double by the end of the decade. After losing some its earlier customers, the company skillfully used its resources to develop new products for growing markets, and by the mid-1990s, Analog Devices seemed clearly on the rise again.

Principal Subsidiaries: Analog Devices Limited (United Kingdom); Analog Devices, GmbH (Germany); Analog Devices S.A. (France); Analog Devices K.K. (Japan); Analog Devices APS (Denmark); Analog Devices S.A. (Switzerland); Analog Devices Nederland, B.V. (Netherlands); Analog Devices International, Inc.; Analog Devices Israel, Ltd.; Analog Devices A.B. (Sweden); Analog Devices SRL (Italy); Analog Devices HDLSGESMBH M.B.H. (Austria); Analog Devices Korea, Ltd.; Analog Devices, B.V. (Netherlands); Analog Devices Finance N.V. (Netherlands Antilles); Memory Devices Finance Bermuda, Ltd.; Analog Devices Holdings, B.V. (Netherlands); Analog Devices Research & Development Ltd. (Ireland); Analog Devices Inc. (Philippines); Analog Devices Marketing Limited (Great Britain); Analog Devices Foreign Sales Corporation, B.V. (Netherlands); Analog Devices Domestic International Sales Corporation; Memory Devices, Limited (Great Britain); Analog Devices Asian Sales, Inc.; Analog Devices Taiwan, Ltd.

Further Reading:

"A Micromachine that Cuts Air-Bag Costs," *Business Week,* November 4, 1991, p. 105.

"Analog Devices Expects to Post 45% Net Gain," *Wall Street Journal,* December 1, 1972, p. 22.

"Analog Devices in Hewlett Tie," *New York Times,* January 28, 1992, p. D4.

"Analog Net Off 89%; Firm Cutting 600 Jobs," *Electronic News,* August 26, 1991, p. 16.

Andrews, Walter, "IBM, Analog Devices SiGe Deal Spurs GaAs Attack," *Electronic News,* December 13, 1993, p. 52.

Burrows, Peter, "Analog Devices Guns to be the Intel of DSP," *Electronic Business,* March, 1993, pp. 101–04.

"Current Corporate Reports: Analog Devices," *Barron's,* February 24, 1986, p. 51; March 20, 1989, p. 78; March 27, 1989, p. 47; May 8, 1989, p. 70; November 19, 1990, p. 62.

Grund, Howard, "Analog Terminates Nu, Gerber," *Electronic News,* January 21, 1991, p. 23.

Helzner, Jerry, "Straw Hats in December?" *Barron's,* December 30, 1991, p. 16.

"How Analog Devices Nurtures New Ventures," *Business Week,* October 18, 1976, pp. 84–86.

Leibowitz, David S., "Friendless Stocks," *Financial World,* February 5, 1991, p. 94.

Leibowitz, David, S., "What to Buy After the Fall," *Financial World,* March 3, 1992, p. 78.

Levy, Robert, "The Humanist at Analog Devices," *Dun's Business Month,* March 1982, pp. 56–57.

Main, Jeremy, "A Chipmaker Who Beats the Business Cycle," *Fortune,* December 23, 1985, pp. 114–20.

Mayet, Helene, "Analog Devices: Bet on the Book-to-Bill," *Financial World,* September 14, 1993, p. 16.

Rosenberg, Ron, "Standard Oil of Ind. Acquires 15% Interest in Analog Div.," *Electronic News,* May 30, 1977, p. 14.

"Stata Strategy is $49 Million in 5 Steps," *Electronics,* March 1, 1973, p. 14–15.

"Will Lightning Strike Twice?" *Financial World,* February 1, 1982, pp. 27–28.

—A. Woodward

THE ANALYTIC SCIENCES CORPORATION

Analytic Sciences Corporation

55 Walkers Brook Drive
Reading, Massachusetts 01867
U.S.A.
(617) 942-2000
Fax: (617) 942-7100

Subsidiary of Primark Corp.
Incorporated: 1966
Employees: 2,200
Sales: $296 million
SICs: 7373 Computer Integrated Systems Design; 7372
   Prepackaged Software; 7389 Business Services, Nec; 8711
   Engineering Services

The Analytic Sciences Corporation (TASC) is a leading provider of applied information technology services. The company is primarily a government contractor, providing services to the Department of Defense and the national security apparatus. Founded in the 1960s, TASC grew steadily throughout its early years, then expanded dramatically during the military build-up of the 1980s. With the downsizing of the military due to relaxed Cold War tensions in the early 1990s, however, the company worked to diversify its business into the industrial and commercial sectors.

TASC got its start in June, 1966, when Arthur Gelb and Harry B. Silverman, both engineers, got together with two other engineers to found the business. The company set up offices along the Route 128 technology corridor outside Boston and set out to solve technical problems through applied information technology. TASC's primary client became the U.S. government.

For the first 16 years of its operation, TASC worked on contracts from the Department of Defense and other federal agencies. In connection with this work, TASC set up a Washington-area office, located in Arlington, Virginia, in 1976. About half of TASC's government work was in connection with so-called "black" or top secret programs. Among the projects the company contributed to were guidance systems for the Trident nuclear submarine, design of the space shuttle, and other analysis and engineering projects. On the basis of this work, TASC's revenue and profits increased steadily each year.

In 1980, with the election of Ronald Reagan and the dramatic increase in the nation's defense budget, TASC's operations and revenues began to grow at a rapid rate. By 1983, the company's revenues were nearing $40 million a year, and TASC had grown to include more than 500 employees. At this time, TASC made its first acquisition, which allowed the company to diversify its operations somewhat beyond its core defense contracting business. In 1983, the company purchased the WSI Corporation, a weather satellite operator based in nearby Billerica, Massachusetts. WSI maintained the world's largest weather database and was best known for providing the enhanced satellite images and radar used on television newscasts.

WSI drew its raw information from geostationary and polar-orbiting satellites, as well as other sensors based in the air, on the ground, and in the ocean. In addition, WSI interpreted this data through advanced mathematical formulas and computer programs and then communicated it to clients in the aviation, agriculture, and utility industries, as well as to media weathermen.

On the basis of WSI's returns, and its own booming defense business, TASC's revenues and earnings continued to grow in the mid-1980s. By 1986, revenues had more than quadrupled from their 1980, pre-Reagan levels to exceed $80 million, and earnings had reached $3 million. TASC's roster of employees had also grown to 800.

Among the TASC products marketed for civilian use at this time were the Cobol Renewal Series, created by TASC's Commercial Information Systems Division. In February, 1986, this Division introduced its latest version of Trailblazer, a product designed to help systems analysts design computer programs in the Cobol language more efficiently. Designed for use on IBM computers, Trailblazer was expected to reduce test times by up to 75 percent. TASC set the price of this product at $50,000.

Three months later, another programming tool, called Fastbol, was released as part of this series. Fastbol was designed to speed up analysis by programmers. The product worked by integrating two maintenance steps—analysis and change. Used as an editor, Fastbol featured five commands: Logic Flow, How-Set, How-Used, Comments, and History. In this way, programmers could move about easily within a computer's code of instructions and also leave records of what they had done for future programmers to consult. This tool was priced at $25,000.

By 1987, TASC's revenues had topped the $100 million mark. The bulk of this revenue was derived from the company's consulting business with the federal government, which was run in part out of two offices in the Washington, D.C. area. Company operations near the capitol had been split between the Virginia cities of McLean and Rosslyn. In July, 1987, TASC broke ground for a new office building in another Virginia suburb, Reston. The company planned to move about 600 employees from McLean to the new facility.

By the end of the 1980s, TASC revenues had topped $200 million a year, nearly doubling from 1987 levels in just three years. In May, 1991, the company's annual revenues reached $228 million. With the collapse of the Eastern Bloc in 1989 and the arrival of greater fiscal austerity in the 1990s, however, it became clear that the U.S. defense budget would undergo steep cuts. This posed a problem for TASC, since 90 percent of the company's revenues, by 1991, were derived from government contracts. Half of those contracts concerned top secret national security projects, and the other half were for non-classified Defense Department work. Only TASC's weather satellite subsidiary contributed any non-defense related revenues. TASC's large reliance on military funding, which had fueled its rapid growth, could not continue indefinitely. Accordingly, the company began to re-position itself to seek new clients outside the military.

With its strengths in software development, information technologies, and systems engineering, TASC began to re-tool for the new era. The company's systems management group, based in Virginia, began to hire new employees in the industrial resources field in 1991. Called senior technical analysts, these executives were assigned to increase company business in non-defense related government agencies, as well as in the private sector.

In the midst of this effort to shift its focus, TASC's founders sold the company to the Primark Corporation in July, 1991 for $165 million. At the time of its sale, TASC operations had expanded to include 1,800 people working at 13 locations around the United States, as well as in the company's Boston and Washington bases. TASC offered expertise in communications, image processing, massively parallel processing, networking, artificial intelligence, atmospheric sciences, and other fields. In addition to its traditional strength in national security operations, Primark hoped to exploit the company's expertise for greater commercial uses.

In purchasing TASC, Primark was taking an important step in its effort to re-position itself as an information services provider. The company had spun off its primary business, the Michigan Consolidated Gas Company, in 1988, and with the funds from this sale had sought to enter the applied information technology field. Although it had bought and sold several companies in the previous three years, with its purchase of TASC Primark made its first serious foray into this field, and TASC became by far the largest component of the company. "This will give us an excellent position in the applied information technology field," Primark chairman Joseph E. Kasputys told the *Washington Post* at the time of the sale. "TASC is an excellent company with commercial sector applications in image processing, networking and communications technology."

Primark also hoped to benefit from shared expertise between TASC and its other major unit, Wellmark, Inc. This company processed medical claims, and Primark expected that TASC's experience in networking and graphics display could help Wellmark grow. Indeed, Primark envisioned TASC as a "technology engine" that would support the efforts of all of the company's units.

For TASC, the influx of cash from its sale meant that money would be available to help fund the company's transition from military contractor to commercial consultant. "This merger will give us capital for our growth to expand our commercial venture operations," company founder Gelb told the *Washington Post*. "We are ready to become a diversified ownership company." Primark also guaranteed that its purchase of the company would not result in the lay-off of any of TASC's employees.

By early August, 1991, the purchase of TASC had been completed for a final price of $166.6 million. With this acquisition, Primark reported sharply higher revenues for the quarter ending that month, when TASC contributed $121 million of the company's $148 million total. This pattern held true for the year as a whole—as Primark reported a profit by February, 1992.

In August, 1992, Primark made another acquisition, which it planned to integrate with TASC. The company purchased Datastream International, which provided computerized historical financial information, in hopes that its products would be complemented by TASC's information technology expertise. Then in October, 1992, TASC moved to further diversify its activities into the commercial sector, when it announced a joint marketing program with the MCI Communications Corporation to offer business customers TASC's document and imaging products and services. By the end of 1992, TASC's corporate parent was reporting sales which had doubled and revenues which had multiplied by eight. These gains were attributed to TASC and its fellow subsidiary Datastream.

TASC made further headway in marketing its products to commercial customers in July, 1993, when the company's Image Systems Integration Division won a contract in excess of $1 million to provide document imaging services to T. Rowe Price, a Baltimore-based mutual fund company. Under the contract, TASC used its TASC-Flow graphical workflow tool, and its PictureCom compression software, to automate the company's processing and transfer agent functions. This was done by converting paper into electronic images, and then using routing software to send these images to 160 different information processors. In addition, the new system would link up more than 300 telephone operators to the data flow.

One month later, TASC won another large civilian job that made use of this technology when the North Carolina Employment Security Commission awarded the company a $2.5 million contract to develop an image-based application for collection of unemployment taxes. TASC planned to create and install a document imaging system that would employ TASC-Flow and PictureCom image compression technology to automate the Commission's operations. Other customers for this proprietary technology included a major credit card processor, a mortgage banking operation, an overnight delivery company, and other firms in the utilities, healthcare, and real estate industries.

Also in August, 1993, TASC moved to expand its WSI subsidiary by buying two weather information companies. TASC acquired two British firms, The Weather Department, Ltd., (TWD) and The Computer Department, Ltd., (TCD). TWD provided weather predicting services to broadcasting and cable television clients in the United Kingdom, Ireland, Scandinavia, and Portugal. TCD provided computer programs to interpret raw weather data. With the technology of WSI, these two companies were able to expand their offerings to European clients. "The acquisitions are a natural expansion to TASC's U.S. operations and provide us with a strong foothold in the rapidly growing European weather market, Primark's Kasputys told the *PR Newswire* in August, 1993.

In October, 1993, TASC made further headway in its diversification program when it was named a contractor in a large U.S.

Department of Energy program to improve automotive efficiency. In addition, the company won three major contracts from the U.S. Department of Transportation. By the end of the year, TASC was also able to report that its national security business had expanded, despite government cutbacks and increased competition. Although the company lost $14 million worth of work when the Strategic Defense Initiative was severely pruned by Congress, TASC still increased its defense-related work by 15 percent, or $6 million. With this gain, the company's defense-related returns grew to 89 percent. TASC finished 1993 with revenues of $296 million.

TASC attributed its continuing defense-related output to its concentration on basic research and development and information technology—areas which were less affected by government cutbacks. In addition, national security operations began to shift toward surveillance, tactical intelligence, smart weapons, systems upgrades, and simulation, all of which related to TASC's applied information technology expertise.

In February, 1994, TASC won another government contract, this one related to its optical devices. Joining with two other firms, TASC embarked on a three-year attempt to develop and integrate a next-generation, all-optical network, in which data would be transferred from one point to another without being broken down into electronic data and then reconstituted. The company's Vision Computing Division took on this task for the Advanced Research Projects Agency, an arm of the Department of Defense. In addition, TASC continued its work with the National Institute of Standards and Technology.

In April, 1994, Primark announced the appointment of John Holt, formerly of the A.C. Nielsen Co., as its new president. In the years ahead, TASC hopes to move forward by relying on its strength in national security, its growing market in civilian government agencies, and continued efforts to enhance its commercial opportunities. With a strong record of profitable operation behind it, the company appeared well-situated to thrive in the coming years.

Principal Subsidiaries: WSI Corporation

Further Reading:

Babcock, Pamela, "Analytic Sciences Breaks Ground for Offices," *Washington Post*, August 17, 1987.
Glater, Jonathan, "Analytic Sciences Accepts Offer from Primark of $165 million," *Boston Globe*, July 10, 1991.
Goldberg, Eddy, "TASC Hurls Fastbol at Maintenance Time, Automates Analysis," *Computerworld*, May 12, 1986.
Levine, Stephen, "Primark Corp. Purchases Information Services Firm," *Washington Post*, July 9, 1991.
Wilson, David L., "Washington's Movers and Shakers: New Vistas," *The National Journal*, March 9, 1991.

—Elizabeth Rourke

Anchor Bancorp, Inc.

1420 Broadway
Hewlett, New York 11557
U.S.A.
(516) 596-3900
Fax: (516) 295-1292

Public Company
Incorporated: 1868 as the Bay Ridge Savings Bank
Employees: 1,500
Sales: $88.1 million
Stock Exchanges: New York
SICs: 6712 Bank Holding Companies; 6035 Federal Savings
   Institutions

Anchor Bancorp, Inc., and its wholly owned subsidiary, Anchor Savings Bank F.S.B., are among the largest publicly owned savings and loan institutions in the United States. The bank focuses its activities on the New York metropolitan area, with additional operations in Florida. After 100 years of uneventful activity in Brooklyn, Anchor began to expand through acquisitions in the late 1960s and 1970s. In the 1980s, Anchor's size exploded, as it moved rapidly into areas outside its core operations. By the late 1980s, however, as the savings and loan industry was thrown into a deep crisis, Anchor found itself badly overextended and undercapitalized. In the 1990s, Anchor worked steadily to move back from the brink of disaster to a position of greater financial health.

Anchor was founded in 1868 as the Bay Ridge Savings Bank. Located in the Bay Ridge section of Brooklyn, the bank served many sailors and their families who had settled in the neighborhood around the bank. On its first day of operation, four customers made deposits. By 1926, the Bay Ridge Savings Bank had grown large enough to become the first institution of its kind in New York to open a branch office. This second location was established in Boro Park, Brooklyn. Forty years later, in 1966, a third office was opened in the suburbs of Long Island, reflecting the shift in the bank's population of customers from urban Brooklyn to more rural areas. With three locations, the bank boasted assets of $330 million.

In 1968, poised to begin a more dramatic expansion, the Bay Ridge Savings Bank changed its name to the Anchor Savings Bank. This change was intended to reflect the fact that the bank's role had expanded beyond the boundaries of its original neighborhood, as it operated a total of five offices. The bank's new name was taken from a motif present in the stained glass windows that decorated its main branch building. Many small anchors made up a nautical design in the windows, reflecting the profession of many of the bank's customers, and thus the Anchor Savings Bank was born.

In the fall of 1969, a year after changing its name, Anchor merged with another Brooklyn-based savings bank, the Bushwick Savings Bank, which had been chartered by the state of New York in the same year that the Bay Ridge Savings Bank was born. Together, the two banks had a total of nine offices, five in Brooklyn, one in Manhattan, one on Staten Island, and two in Nassau County, on Long Island. Within five years, three more branch locations had been added, and the company's assets had topped $1 billion.

In 1977, Anchor merged with another bank, the North New York Savings Bank. This institution served customers in the Bronx and in Westchester and Rockland counties, making a good geographical match for Anchor and expanding its coverage of the New York metropolitan area. With the addition of the assets of the North New York Savings Bank, Anchor now boasted 20 offices, with assets of $1.6 billion.

On the last day of 1980, Anchor became the first mutual savings bank in New York, and the second in the nation, to be awarded a federal charter, making it a federal savings bank (F.S.B.). With its new charter, Anchor was able to offer its customers a wider range of services than before, including a broader range of loans and corporate checking accounts.

One year later, Anchor continued its pattern of growth through acquisition of other banks when it merged with the Guardian Federal Savings and Loan Association, based on Long Island, and with the New York and Suburban Savings and Loan Association. This move added eleven more branch offices to the bank's total in the New York area.

Anchor made its first move outside New York when it purchased Mortgage Resources, Inc., which was based in Atlanta, Georgia. This company became a wholly owned subsidiary of the bank, called Anchor Mortgage Resources, Inc., which offered mortgage services to customers located primarily in the southeastern United States.

In early 1982, Anchor expanded its New York operations beyond New York City for the first time, when the First Federal Savings and Loan Association of Hamburg, based in upstate New York, became a part of the company. Later that year, Anchor also merged with the Niagara First Savings and Loan Association. With this move, the bank gained eight more branch offices in Erie and Niagara Counties, in western New York state, and further expanded the scope of its activities across its home state.

In October of 1982, Anchor continued its rapid expansion through a string of acquisitions when it purchased the Dime Banking and Loan Association of Rochester, New York. This bank had 14 separate locations, which were converted to Anchor branches. In November, Anchor solidified its operations in western New York when it opened a new location in Buffalo. By this time, the company boasted a total of 56 bank offices.

In late 1982, Anchor's financial strength, and its operations in Georgia, were tapped by the Federal Home Loan Bank Board, when it chose to merge the ailing Peachtree Federal Savings and Loan Association of Atlanta and the First Federal Savings and Loan Association of Crisp County, Georgia, into Anchor. With this move, Anchor became an interstate bank. The company's Georgia operations expanded further in March of 1983, when it purchased the Standard Federal Savings and Loan Association, with branches in Dooly and Wilcox counties in Georgia. This moved brought the company's number of branches in the Atlanta area to 20. Three months later, Anchor added the property of the Tri-City Federal Savings and Loan Association. This added three more locations to the family of Anchor operations in Georgia.

Expansion also took place during this time in Anchor's northern holdings. In June of 1983, the company returned to its roots when it opened a new office in Bay Ridge, Brooklyn. Two months later, Anchor made another move in the metropolitan area when it purchased the Suburban Savings and Loan Association, which ran 27 offices in New Jersey. With the purchase of Suburban, Anchor became the first bank in the New York metropolitan area to have branches on both sides of the Hudson River, allowing people who lived in New Jersey and commuted to New York to work to take care of banking both at home or at work. Anchor converted Suburban to a wholly owned subsidiary of the company, and changed its name to Anchor Savings Bank FSB New Jersey. With this move, Anchor became the country's second largest federally chartered savings bank.

As part of its purchase of Suburban, Anchor also attained ownership of the Suburban Coastal Corporation, located in Wayne, New Jersey. This company, which provided mortgage servicing for loans that totaled more than $6 billion, became known as Anchor Mortgage Services, Inc., following its change in ownership. This subsidiary operated 21 loan servicing offices in 10 states, including Texas and California, increasing the geographical scope of Anchor's holdings further.

At the end of September of 1983, Anchor acquired another bank in the New York area, when it merged with the Heritage Federal Savings and Loan Association of Huntington, New York. This move gave Anchor a total of 19 offices on Long Island.

In 1984, Anchor opened an additional office in both New York and Georgia, adding branches in Rego Park, its first outlet in the borough of Queens, and also one in Marietta, Georgia. In August, Anchor purchased United Federal Savings and Loan of Waycross, Georgia. With this move, the company's number of branch offices grew to 111.

The mid-1980s saw a continuation of Anchor's steady growth through acquisition of other banks. In October of 1985, the company bought the First Federal Savings Bank of Brunswick, based in southern Georgia. With this purchase, Anchor's assets topped $7 billion, and its number of branch offices reached 115. The bulk of the company's offices, 58, were located in New York state, but it also had 31 in Georgia and 26 in New Jersey.

At the end of 1985, Anchor expanded its operations to include another state when it purchased the Sun Federal Savings and Loan Association of Tallahassee, Florida. This bank had 18 branch offices, located throughout the Florida peninsula.

In the following year, Anchor moved outside the financial services industry for the first time, when it acquired an equipment leasing company that became Anchor Financial Corporation. Based in Fairfield, Connecticut, this company rented specialized equipment to the graphic arts, paper, and transportation industries. Its operations were based in the northeast, in Illinois, and in California. Anchor hoped that this company would be able to attract customers from among the bank's business clients.

By the end of 1986, Anchor had solid banking operations in place in four of the fastest growing markets in the United States: New York, New Jersey, Georgia, and Florida. In addition, the company owned two mortgage servicing enterprises and three insurance agencies: Standard of Georgia Insurance Agency, Inc.; ASB Agency, Inc.; and ASB/NJ Agency, Inc. After a decade and a half of aggressive expansion through acquisition, Anchor had become the 17th largest thrift institution in the United States, with deposits exceeding $6 billion. In just five years, between 1981 and 1986, the company had taken over 13 savings and loan associations, most of which were in financial difficulty at the time that they were purchased.

Having attained this impressive size, Anchor converted from a mutual savings and loan association into a publicly held company on April 1, 1987. This was done through an offering of stock to people who held accounts at the bank's various branches. After a series of community meetings, shares in the bank were sold in a six week subscription period.

In the following year, Anchor increased its holdings in the mortgage industry, purchasing the Residential Funding Corporation for $61 million. This company specialized in very large, or "jumbo" mortgage loans. This move was part of an overall attempt by Anchor to sharpen its focus on the residential mortgage lending field, in which it saw high potential for profit.

At the same time, however, Anchor also began to streamline its activities in other areas and implement a cost-containment program, as its financial position weakened alarmingly. The company withdrew from its participation in the indirect market for automobile loans and drastically de-emphasized its commercial loan operations, firing all its employees in this area. These moves were designed to offset the squeeze on Anchor's profits caused by high interest rates on deposits. Overall, Anchor fired more than 12 percent of its workforce. In addition, the company shut down seven mortgage offices, sold eight banking branches in southern Georgia, and consolidated three locations in Northern Florida.

Anchor's financial condition worsened in 1989, as the entire savings and loan industry suffered a crisis and shakeout in which many banks failed. In March of 1989, the Hamilton Holding Company, which had signed a letter of intent to purchase Anchor, withdrew from its agreement to do so, citing uncertainty about pending federal legislation designed to redress the mess in the thrift industry. In early August of 1989, the Financial Institution Reform, Recovery, and Enforcement Act went into effect, changing the climate of business for Anchor and the nation's other savings and loan associations. By redefining assets, this bill left Anchor undercapitalized by $329 million. In order to comply with this regulation, the company was forced to begin a major effort to raise capital to avoid being closed by the federal government. To do so, and also to eliminate less profitable operations that were dragging down results, Anchor began to sell off many of its assets.

As part of this process, Anchor decided to withdraw completely from its activities in Georgia and Florida. In August of 1989, the bank sold nine of its bank branches in northern Florida to the Citizen's Federal Savings Bank. In addition, the company put its leasing subsidiary on the block and closed additional mortgage operations. Further staff cuts bought the number of employees let go to nearly 1,000.

In an effort to rebuild its declining market share, in September of 1989, Anchor shifted its promotional slogan, for the first time since its name change 22 years earlier, from ''Your Anchor Bankers . . . Understand'' to ''We're Your Anchor Bankers . . . Here For You.'' Nevertheless, the company's difficulties continued, and at the end of 1989, Anchor reported a loss of $23.1 million. It appeared extremely likely that Anchor would join the long list of other American thrift institutions which had failed.

In the first year of the 1990s, in dire straits, Anchor continued its efforts to overcome the problems brought about as a result of its rapid expansion and diversification in the previous decade. In early March, the company sold its Residential Funding Corporation unit to the GMAC Mortgage Corporation, a subsidiary of General Motors. In April of 1990, Anchor announced that it would take a $175 million loss in order to shed assets, including 68 more bank branches. In July, the company continued its process of divestment by selling off 19 bank branches in Georgia. In addition, Anchor closed 15 mortgage offices outside the New York area, shut down a construction loan operation in Georgia, and sold its credit card business. The point of these changes was to allow the bank to focus exclusively on its core area, the New York City metropolitan region, and its core business: gathering deposits and lending those funds to people who wished to buy houses.

After losing nearly $150 million in 1990, Anchor made progress toward profitability in the following year, posting profits of $65 million, almost all of which resulted from the sale of assets. The company was steadily accruing the capital required by law and solidifying its operations in its basic business areas, despite the difficulties caused by a real estate slump throughout the Northeast.

In March of 1991, after an arduous process, Anchor formed a holding company, Anchor Bancorp, Inc., so that it could restructure its stock offerings to increase its capitalization. Although Anchor's effort to move out of the Georgia market had been completed, its program to shed its Florida assets had stalled. Because so many savings and loans had failed or been taken over by the government, the market was saturated with thrift branch offices, and Anchor was unable to demand a reasonable price for its Florida property and deposits. As a result of its inability to raise capital by selling branch offices, the company turned instead to sales of its mortgage operations.

By June of 1992, these efforts had shown fruit, as Anchor was released from close regulatory supervision of its efforts to rebuild capital. The company finally appeared to be out of the woods after the crisis of the late 1980s. Its profitability improved throughout 1992, attaining a level of $50.9 million, with only $7 million of that contributed by asset sales. This progress came despite an unexpected blow to one of Anchor's key operations, as historically low-interest rates caused many people to refinance their houses, paying off their old high-interest mortgages, which were valuable revenue raisers for Anchor, and taking out new, much cheaper loans. To keep pace with this trend, Anchor retooled its advertising program, moving from an emphasis on gathering deposits to a focus on making loans.

In 1993, as the thrift business as a whole began to recover, Anchor was able to complete its original plan to sell off some of its more far-flung branches. The company shed 14 outlets in western New York state, along with two locations in southern New Jersey, and another two in Florida. Plans were completed to transfer six more branches in northern Florida, leaving Anchor with only a token presence in southern Florida, an area to which many New Yorkers retired.

With its newly solidified capital position, Anchor began to cautiously expand the scope of its activities. The company aimed to move from banking in which the bulk of revenues were generated by fees for various basic transactions, to banking based on long-term, more complex relationships with its customers, shifting from a traditional savings and loan, to a full-service consumer bank. To that end, Anchor instituted a limited commercial mortgage lending program to make loans for the purchase of multifamily houses and small commercial properties. In addition, the company sought to increase its market share of its traditional constituency, middle and lower-middle income people, by adding more minority customers. By the end of June of 1993, Anchor's profits over a yearlong period had reached $52 million.

As it moved into the mid-1990s, Anchor was able to look forward to the future with cautious optimism. Although it had survived the worst of its financial crisis and was able to anticipate future expansion within its core market area, Anchor remained chastened and somewhat limited financially by its close brush with disaster. Nevertheless, it appeared likely that the institution which first opened its doors in the mid-19th century would still be operating at the dawn of the 21st century.

Principal Subsidiaries: Anchor Mortgage Resources, Inc.; Anchor Savings Bank F.S.B.; Anchor Savings Bank F.S.B. New Jersey; Anchor Mortgage Services, Inc.

Further Reading:

''Large Write-Down Is Set; Firm May Sell 68 Branches,'' *Wall Street Journal,* April 20, 1990.

—Elizabeth Rourke

Andersen Corporation

100 Fourth Avenue North
Bayport, Minnesota 55003-1096
U.S.A.
(612) 439-5150
Fax: (612) 430-7364

Private Company
Incorporated: 1903 as Andersen Lumber Company
Employees: 3,700
SICs: 2431 Millwork; 3089 Plastics Products, Nec

Andersen Corporation is the world's largest wood window manufacturer and is believed to control roughly 15 percent of the domestic market. The 90-year-old company manufactures a wide variety of window styles, available in over 1,100 different sizes, at a single 63-acre plant in Bayport, Minnesota, alongside the St. Croix river. Although the majority of the company is owned by Andersen family members, some 27 percent of the stock is held by the employees of the company. Employee turnover is practically nonexistent at the company, which from the beginning has emphasized employee satisfaction as a top priority. Andersen relies on a nationwide network of dealers, particularly lumberyards and building supply stores, to sell its products. The dealers receive Andersen products from nearly 120 wholesale distributors.

The company was founded in 1903 by Danish immigrant Hans Jacob Andersen, on the other side of the St. Croix River, in Hudson, Wisconsin. Andersen had years of experience as a lumber dealer and manufacturer; during the 1880s, he acquired his own sawmill in St. Cloud, Minnesota. Later on, he managed a mill in Hudson, bringing with him some of his best St. Cloud employees. According to a company retrospective, when the Hudson owners asked that the workers be let go during the off-season, "Hans refused to be disloyal to these men and resigned on the spot. He then launched his own retail lumber yard and hired the men to work for him," assisted by his sons, Fred and Herbert.

The lumber yard was ideally situated to take advantage of the large stretches of white pine in the St. Croix river valley; another yard, in Afton, Minnesota, also began operations in 1904. Within a year of incorporation, the Andersen Lumber Company became more than just a lumber business when Hans and his sons hit upon the idea of manufacturing standardized

wood window frames out of the raw pine to which they had ready access. Suppliers and builders, the Andersens believed, would realize the wisdom of accepting standard window measurements.

The venture revolutionized the window industry, for as yet there was no dependable, mass-produced window frame on the market. A success from the start, the Andersen frame business brought in $74,000 in sales during its first year. In 1905, the company signed its first distributor and adopted a "two-bundle" method of packaging its horizontal and vertical frame pieces. Three years later, the Andersens sold their two lumber yards in order to concentrate on the window frame business; the family would reenter the lumber business in 1916 and considerably expanding its holdings before again selling off its yards beginning in the 1930s. By 1912, the company required more space, and a site was found on the other side of the St. Croix; a new plant was completed within a year and began operations with 59 employees. Sales more than doubled during the company's first decade. With Hans Andersen's death in 1914, Fred was elected president, and Herbert became vice-president, secretary-treasurer, and factory manager. That year, the company provided employees with a generous profit-sharing plan—the third oldest in the nation.

In 1921, Herbert died at the age of 36. But, as Kenneth D. Ruble noted in *The Magic Circle,* Fred Andersen "proved to be a 'Jack of all trades' and master of every one—business manager, inventor, salesman, purchasing agent, civic leader, accountant, mechanic, manpower recruiter, teacher and above all one who loves and believes in his fellow man." Fred fully implemented the business vision of cooperation and achievement contemplated by his father, whose first English words—"all together boys"—were learned on the job and never forgotten.

The new Andersen president established an enduring corporate philosophy, which he called the Magic Circle. Consisting of eight links, the circle included: 1) highly trained and motivated employees; 2) sound management; 3) ongoing research; 4) a strong sales organization; 5) a distributor-dealer network based on repeat business and good will; 6) builders and architects interested in quality products; 7) consumers interested in paying for the best materials; and 8) "the premise that in better homes and buildings on the one hand—and in a higher standard of living on the other—there is benefit to all members of the Magic Circle, from maker to user."

In 1928, the company surpassed the one million mark in the number of frames produced. The following year, the company changed its name to the Andersen Frame Corporation, symbolizing its ascendancy to the top of the high-end window manufacturing industry. The following decade was characterized by several innovations, beginning with the production of a Master Frame, complete with locked sill joint, in 1930. Two years later, an employee named Earl Swanson (who would become the company's first non-family president in 1960, when Fred Andersen retired) designed and introduced the casement ("crank-out") window, which was the first complete Andersen window unit and the first factory-made window, as the responsibility for securing the frames to window glass previously resided with the builder or retailer. Two years later, the company introduced its first basement window. In 1937, a final name change was in order to signal the company's evolution from frame-maker to full-fledged window manufacturer.

The Andersen Corporation opened the 1940s auspiciously, with the unveiling of a new concept in window design, the gliding window. Also during this time, consumer advertising, beginning with the Home Planner's Scrap Book in 1943, became increasingly important to the company. Growth during the 1950s was fueled by the Flexivent awning window, which featured welded insulating glass and helped eliminate the need for conventional storm windows. The invention was so popular that it doubled Andersen's market share within two years, and, by 1963, ten million Flexivent windows had been shipped. The 1960s saw the introduction of the gliding door and the Perma-Shield system. Featuring a low-maintenance vinyl cladding designed to protect wood frames from exposure to the elements, Perma-Shield was, according to the company, "perhaps the most monumental innovation by Andersen," one which "became the standard of the industry."

In 1978, a year after the dedication of a new research and development facility, the window maker celebrated its 75th anniversary. Sales totaled $280 million, 75 percent directly traceable to Perma-Shield products. Through the 1980s and into the 1990s, Andersen dedicated itself to remaining "the most popular window name in America" and maintaining its loyalty to its now greatly expanded Bayport plant and workforce. As the vast resources of raw material in the Upper Midwest had been depleted, Andersen began importing its pine primarily from the Pacific Northwest. However, through Andersen's pioneering efforts, the Upper Midwest remained the basin in which the leading U.S. window manufacturers (including such Andersen competitors as Marvin Windows of Warroad, Minnesota, and Pella Corp. of Pella, Iowa), as well as several smaller window businesses, were located.

In 1988, Kate Fitzgerald reported for *Advertising Age* that Andersen was facing especially stiff competition from both Pella and Peachtree Doors and that the battle was fueling increased ad spending. By that time, Andersen and Pella had moved into patio door manufacturing to complement their window specialties, while Peachtree remained a recognized leader in entry doors. Between 1984 and 1994, Andersen tripled its revenues through the addition of more customized and environmentally state-of-the-art products, claiming that it outsold its closest three competitors combined. In July 1993, Marianne Wilson reported in *Chain Store Age Executive* on the construc-

tion of a prototype Wal-Mart store in Lawrence, Kansas: "The store has a sophisticated skylight system that allows 40% more daylight into the building than conventional skylights. Developed by the Andersen Corp., it features nine skylights fashioned with an 'eyebrow' design that captures early morning and late evening sun." Andersen's unique, specially designed prototype units featured solar-optic films that dispersed sunlight evenly, resulting in energy savings of up to 50 percent annually.

In 1994, the *Wall Street Journal*'s Joe Pine reported on Andersen's Window of Knowledge, a "multimedia kiosk" available to retailers, enabling them to specially design their own window combinations. Implementation of the software program translated into a reduction in order errors, an increase in production efficiency, and average sales increases of 20 percent for well-trained retailers who regularly used the system. Clearly, the Magic Circle concept continued to thrive at Andersen. "Many experts have referred to Andersen as 'the Cadillac of the window industry,' " wrote Ruble, "but a host of employees and retirees insist the reverse is true—that Cadillac is the Andersen of the automobile business." In fact, the company's 3,700 employees—many from families in which employment at Andersen is a tradition—prided themselves on efficiency and innovation and were handsomely rewarded for their contributions.

Further Reading:

Cannon, Carl M., "Golden Shackles," *Business Month,* September 1988, pp. 56–63.
Cook, William J., "Four Better Mousetraps (Andersen Windows)," *U.S. News & World Report,* August 24, 1992, pp. 53–54.
Fitzgerald, Kate, "Ad Storm Hits Window/Door Field," *Advertising Age,* October 24, 1988, p. 12.
Gelbach, Deborah L., "Andersen Corporation," *From This Land: A History of Minnesota's Empires, Enterprises, and Entrepreneurs,* Chatsworth, CA: Windsor Publications, 1988.
Neal, Mollie, "Andersen Takes Great 'Panes' to Build Relationships," *Direct Marketing,* April 1993, pp. 28–30, 68.
Pine, Joe, "Customers Don't Want Choice," *Wall Street Journal,* April 18, 1994, p. A14.
Ruble, Kenneth D., *The Magic Circle: A Story of the Men and Women Who Made Andersen the Most Respected Name in Windows,* Bayport, Minnesota: Andersen Corporation, 1978.
Wilson, Marianne, "Wal-Mart Makes a Green Statement," *Chain Store Age Executive,* July 1993, pp. 23–26.
"Windows of Opportunity," *Corporate Report Minnesota,* January 1983, pp. 24–25.

—Jay P. Pederson

Andrew Corporation

10500 W. 153rd Street
Orland Park, Illinois 60642
U.S.A.
(708) 349-3300
Fax: (708) 349-5943

Public Company
Incorporated: 1947
Employees: 2,924
Sales: $430 million
Stock Exchanges: NASDAQ
SICs: 3679 Electronic Components Nec; 3357 Nonferrous
   Wiredrawing & Insulating

Andrew Corporation is an international supplier of communications systems equipment and services. Long known as the world's leading supplier of parabolic microwave antennas, Andrew also presides over large portions of the international markets for satellite dishes, cellular phone system equipment, and coaxial cable. The company operates in three main areas of business. Its commercial division provides antenna systems and coaxial cable for telecommunication. A government division manufactures specialized antenna and radar systems for detection and surveillance for use by the U.S. government and its allies. Andrew Corporation's Network division manufactures products which allow computers to link networks worldwide.

Andrew's sophisticated technology is employed in various forms throughout the world. For example, Andrew developed a steam-resistant fiber optic cable which is the only type approved for use in New York City's steam ducts. The company also built a substantial business providing cellular communication in tunnels, where cellular users had traditionally had problems. Andrew worked on communications for the new English Channel tunnel and received contracts to install distributed communications systems in the subways of Vienna, Warsaw, and Sofia, Bulgaria. Andrew also developed earth station antennas which were powerful enough to transmit signals to a satellite from remote locations, yet were small enough to be carried in a suitcase.

The company was founded in 1937, when 34-year-old engineer Victor J. Andrew began to manufacture equipment for the directional antennas used by AM radio broadcasters. Andrew received a Ph.D. from the University of Chicago in 1932, and then worked at the Army Signal Corps Laboratories in Fort Monmouth, New Jersey, and at Westinghouse in Chicopee Falls, Massachusetts. But Dr. Andrew soon returned to Chicago to go into business for himself. He rented a bungalow on the city's southwest side and installed a modest array of tools and equipment. His first sales were for custom designed phasing, tuning, and transmission line equipment for AM radio, though Andrew also offered his services as an engineering consultant to broadcast antenna users. Andrew had intended to make consulting the major part of his business, but World War II brought with it a ban on new broadcast station construction, and so he had little consulting work to do. Andrew concentrated instead on manufacturing, developing a number of new products, and achieving significant sales of phasing and tuning equipment and of coaxial cables and rigid coaxial lines.

A strong demand for broadcast products spurred the company's initial growth, and the company moved to new quarters in the same Chicago neighborhood several times in its first ten years. During World War II, Andrew received large orders from the military for coaxial cables and later for dry air pumps which the Air Force used to pressurize airborne radar pods. After the war, Andrew continued its ties to the military, supplying coaxial transmission line which was used to monitor nuclear blast testing both above and below ground. In 1947, the company was incorporated as Andrew Corporation, with Victor Andrew installed as board chairman and CEO, and his wife Aileen named president. That same year, Andrew bought 430 acres of undeveloped land in the Chicago suburb of Orland Park. The clear land was necessary for outdoor testing of antennas, and eventually the company built its manufacturing and management facilities there as well.

Andrew Corporation began marketing microwave antennas for both civilian and military communications in 1949, and Cold War demand for Andrew's products during the 1950s kept the company busy. Andrew made switching devices, waveguides and high powered coaxial lines that were used in military radar systems. Its HELIAX continuous, semi-flexible coaxial cable came on the market in 1953 and became an important part of company growth. Coaxial cable, including HELIAX and RADIAX slotted coaxial cable, continued to make up the bulk of the company's business in the early 1990s.

As demand for Andrew's products grew, the company opened new offices in the United States and abroad. The company incorporated a branch, Andrew California Corporation in 1951, in order to take advantage of the growing west coast electronics industry. And two years later, the firm opened a Canadian affiliate because Andrew had had substantial export sales to Canada. The Whitby, Ontario affiliate immediately did well for itself. The Whitby affiliate was involved in other British Commonwealth markets and opened up new opportunities for Andrew abroad.

Andrew Corporation had been actively scouting European markets since 1958, and in 1966 the company was offered a large microwave antenna system contract in England, with the proviso that a portion of the equipment had to be manufactured in Australia. Due to the clause, Andrew entered both the British and Australian markets at once, founding Andrew Antennas Proprietary Limited in Australia and Andrew Antenna Systems

Limited in the United Kingdom the same year. The Australian division took on a contract for the installation of microwave equipment along a 1,500 mile route from Adelaide to Perth. The company experienced many initial difficulties caused by the long distance between the U.S. design team and the Australian affiliate. But despite many costly set-backs, the project was completed satisfactorily, and the Australian branch eventually became one of Andrew's most successful foreign operations.

In the early 1970s, Andrew's market began to change from government and military contracts to private sector applications. In the United States, companies were allowed to compete with AT&T in long distance communication beginning in 1972, and these so-called Other Common Carriers (OCCs) utilized microwave antennas for their telephone service. Andrew was an acknowledged world leader in microwave technology, and its business grew appreciably as the OCCs such as MCI and SPRINT undertook large scale construction projects. Andrew's growth in the microwave antenna business was at times as much as 25 percent a year between 1972 and 1984. The company held around 60 percent of the world market share in microwave antenna systems, with higher percentages in its top markets in the United States, Canada, and Australia.

The company had unparalleled technical expertise and had been in the market longer than any of its competitors, and in the early 1980s Andrew's dominance was unchallenged. Sales in 1980 reached $89 million, with two-thirds coming from domestic markets. That year Andrew began a public company, though the Andrew family retained a substantial portion of the stock.

When the U.S. Justice Department broke up AT&T in 1982, Andrew grew even more rapidly. AT&T itself was one of the company's top customers, and with the breakup it and the OCCs demanded more and more Andrew microwave transmission technology. The company experienced record sales, peaking in the fourth quarter of 1984. But sales declined abruptly in 1985 when fiber optics began to supersede microwave technology in some areas. Fiber optic cables were found to transmit voice and data faster than microwave systems and with less distortion. Andrew management had had some signs that this might happen, but had anticipated more time to get ready for the new technology.

Floyd English, who became president of Andrew in 1982, had worried for years that the company was too narrowly focused. As soon as Andrew's sales began to slacken, English took measures to shift the company into other markets. The company began acquiring smaller firms that would help Andrew open new markets. Andrew was particularly interested in cellular telephone technology and in re-entering government work with intelligence gathering communications systems. Andrew bought Scientific Communications, Inc. and Kintec Corp. in 1986, both small military communications manufacturers. With these acquisitions, Andrew was able to get domestic army and navy and international contracts for antenna receivers and optical tracking equipment, and by 1987 sales in the company's government products division had climbed by 88 percent.

Though sales had increased, earnings did not, and the defense electronics business experienced difficulty because of cost over-runs and technical problems. Andrew's government division operated at a $3.9 million loss in 1988. In 1991, DRAGON FIX radio transmission interceptors manufactured by Andrew were utilized in the Persian Gulf War, yet the government division still did not turn a profit.

In the late 1980s, the company predicted that corporations would continue to need enhanced communications between distant computer work stations, and Andrew planned on becoming a major player in the computer networking market. Andrew bought two companies involved in computer linking technology, Scott Communications, Inc. and Local Data, Inc., in 1987. In 1990, it spent $15 million on a similar company, Emerald Technology, Inc. These acquisitions formed the core of what became a major business area for Andrew. By 1993, computer interconnect technology made up about 15 percent of Andrew's total sales.

Andrew also expanded its mobile communications business rapidly. Andrew developed an innovative slotted coaxial cable called RADIAX that eliminated problems with cellular phone use in tunnels, subways, and buildings. The company won a contract to wire the new English Channel rail tunnel with a new distributed communications system utilizing the company's RADIAX cable, and subsequently worked on many subway projects, particularly in Europe and Russia. Andrew entered joint ventures in Russia to build fiber optic communication systems in subway systems in Moscow and St. Petersburg and then created another joint venture to build and operate a 400 mile fiber optic network between Moscow and St. Petersburg. The Andrew network gave callers from these metropolitan areas clearer signals and access to international communications links. This was especially important to Western companies operating in Russia, who had not had effective communication with home offices. In 1994, Andrew worked on in-building communication systems for the new Denver International Airport and in one of the world's largest office buildings, the USAA building in San Antonio, Texas.

By 1992, Andrew had completely recovered from the decline in its U.S. microwave telecommunications business. Sales that year were a record $442 million, with almost half coming from overseas (an area that had been just 10 percent of profits in 1990). Earnings were also strong, and the company's stock performed well. The computer networking business area turned only a modest profit, but 1992 was the first year the government business area was profitable. While this area had lost $1.9 million in 1991, the next year profits were $5.6 million on sales of $66 million.

Though the U.S. cellular market showed signs of maturing, Andrew had hopes for continued growth abroad. Andrew had been a major supplier to a consortium led by its long-time customers AT&T and GTE, and their Argentina contract was worth an estimated $35 million. Andrew also took on a $5.6 million job for subway communications in Hong Kong in 1994, and had many new orders in Eastern Europe. In addition, Andrew's involvement in Russia promised substantial growth opportunity because the country averaged 10 phones per one hundred inhabitants.

Andrew has grown in diverse directions throughout its history. Andrew's early years were devoted primarily to military applications of broadcast technology, whereas the 1970s and early 1980s saw a narrow concentration on microwave antennas for U.S. long distance telephone carriers. After this market declined in 1985, Andrew recovered relatively quickly by investing in new markets and technologies. Andrew's worldwide market presence leaves the company poised to take advantage of developing needs in many countries. With a global customer base that is stable or growing, Andrew seems well positioned to continue expanding its core business lines.

Principal Subsidiaries: Andrew Data Corp.; Antennes Andrew S.A.R.L. (France); Andrew S.R.L. (Italy); Andrew Kommunikationssysteme AG (Switzerland); Andrew Corp. Mexico S.A. de C.V.; Andrew VSAT Systems, Inc.; Andrew Ltd. (United Kingdom); Andrew Canada, Inc.; Andrew Australia; Andrew Corp. (Japan); Andrew Systems Inc.; Andrew SciComm GmbH (Germany); Andrew NPG, Ltd. (United Kingdom); Andrew KMW Systems Corp.; Andrew Kintec Inc.; UCI/Unified Communications, Inc. (80%); Andrew SciComm Inc.; Andrew AG (Switzerland); Andrew International (Russia); Andrew SciComm Inc. (Saudi Arabia); Andrew Espana, S.A. (Spain).

Further Reading:

"Andrew Corp.: High-tech Products, Global Ambitions," *Barron's,* March 29, 1993, pp. 42–44.

"Andrew Corporation Investors Brief," *Wall Street Transcript,* September 12, 1988, p. 90888.

"Andrew Corporation Presentation," *Wall Street Transcript,* April 19, 1982, p. 65412.

Autry, Ret, "Companies to Watch: Andrew," *Fortune,* June 17, 1991, p. 70.

Berss, Marcia, "Crossed Signals?" *Forbes,* December 21, 1992, p. 344.

Cleaver, Joanne, "Antennas Fading Out, Andrew Corp. Eyes Its Also-ran Markets," *Crain's Chicago Business,* February 14, 1985, p. 3.

Cox, Russell, *Andrew 1937–1987: A Half Century in Communications,* Orland Park, IL: Andrew Corp., 1987.

Ditlev-Simonsen, Cecilie, "Technology and Tradition: Andrew Corp. Hews to Traditions," *Chicago Tribune,* June 29, 1987, sec. 4, p. 1

Goodman, JoEllen, "Ailing Andrew Spurns Recapitalization Plan," *Crain's Chicago Business,* August 18, 1986, p. 55.

——, "Andrew Takes Aim at Military Market with Acquisition," *Crain's Chicago Business,* December 1, 1986, p. 3.

Gorak, David A., "Earthbound Microwave Unit a Drag on Andrew's Growth," *Crain's Chicago Business,* February 16, 1987, p. 24.

——, "Andrew Set to Dial Up Sales in Non-Telephone-Related Biz," *Crain's Chicago Business,* February 17, 1986, p. 20.

Murphy, H. Lee, "Adaptable Manufacturer Andrew Undaunted by Defense Cutbacks," *Crain's Chicago Business,* March 5, 1990, p. 30.

——, "Andrew Catches a Wave as Earnings, Stock Swell," *Crain's Chicago Business,* December 21, 1992, p. 4.

——, "Andrew Sets Sights Overseas for Growth," *Crain's Chicago Business,* February 14, 1994, p. 52.

——, "Andrew's Military Campaign Becoming Obstacle Course," *Crain's Chicago Business,* February 27, 1989, p. 58.

——, "Ex-Military Topsider Adds Macho to Andrew Offensive," *Crain's Chicago Business,* February 22, 1988, p. 49.

Young, David, "Wiring Russia: Andrew Installing Fiber-Optics System," *Chicago Tribune,* December 18, 1992, sec. 3, pp. 1–3.

—A. Woodward

Anheuser-Busch Companies, Inc.

One Busch Plaza
St. Louis, Missouri 63118
U.S.A.
(314) 577-2000
Fax: (314) 577-4013

Public Company
Incorporated: 1979
Employees: 43,345
Sales: $13.19 billion
Stock Exchanges: New York London Frankfurt Tokyo Paris
   Zurich Geneva Basle Boston Midwest Cincinnati Pacific
   Philadelphia
SICs: 2082 Malt Beverages; 3411 Metal Cans; 2079 Edible
   Fats and Oils, Nec.; 2068 Salted and Roasted Nuts and
   Seeds; 7996 Amusement Parks; 6719 Holding Companies,
   Nec.

The Anheuser-Busch Companies, Inc. is a diversified corporation with subsidiaries that oversee operations of the world's largest brewer and U.S. industry leader since 1957; America's second-largest producer of fresh-baked goods; and one of the largest theme park operations in the country. The company's 19 brands of malted beverages—including flagships Budweiser, Michelob, and Busch—dominated the U.S. market, with 1993 sales volume comprising over 44 percent of the total brewing industry, including imports. The company operated breweries in five foreign countries and exported Budweiser to over 60 others. Efforts to integrate vertically over the decades have brought Anheuser-Busch into several related industries, including refrigerated transportation, metal container production and recycling, labeling, farming of raw materials, and marketing communications. The company's other businesses include production of snack foods and baked goods, operation of a chain of ten theme parks, real estate holdings, and ownership of the St. Louis National Baseball Club, Inc.

Anheuser-Busch has been overseen by a member of its founding family since 1852, when Eberhard Anheuser, a prosperous soap manufacturer in St. Louis, bought a failing brewery from Bavarian immigrant George Schneider. The brewery's cool underground caverns near the Mississippi River were conducive to good brewing, and Anheuser was determined to turn the business around, but he lacked experience in the industry. He therefore hired his son-in-law, Adolphus Busch, a recent German immigrant schooled in the art of brewing, as his general manager. Together, Anheuser and Busch approached the enterprise with an aggressive business strategy and knowledge in quality brewing, two factors that have informed Anheuser-Busch's history ever since.

According to a popular company legend, Adolphus Busch obtained the recipe for his beer during a visit to a German monastery. There, monks provided him with a recipe and some of their brewer's yeast, the secret of their excellent beer. That recipe became the basis of Anheuser-Busch beers, and the original strain of yeast, allegedly preserved for years in Adolphus' ice-cream freezer, remained in use in the 1990s. Although fictitious, the story highlighted two important philosophies at Anheuser-Busch: only the finest "European" ingredients were to be used and the basic recipe would remain essentially unchanged.

In 1853, Anheuser and Busch increased the rejuvenated brewery's capacity from 3,000 to 8,000 barrels per year and began to expand their sales effort into Texas and Louisiana, as well as their home state of Missouri. The beverage became increasingly popular, as cowboys reportedly deserted their beloved red-eye whiskey for the light Bohemian beer, which became known as Budweiser in 1891, when the company purchased the rights to the name from the Bohemian brewer of "Budweis."

Budweiser's formula was enhanced by innovations in the brewing industry, particularly as pasteurization allowed for longer preservation periods. Moreover, newly invented refrigerated railroad cars permitted the transport of beer across state borders, and the bottling of beer allowed for easier distribution throughout the country. Regional brewers lost their advantage to large breweries such as Anheuser-Busch, which had found the means to supply beer to every state in the union. Despite the growth of its market, however, Anheuser-Busch still referred to itself as a "regional brewery"—an institution that understood the distinct needs and tastes of local people.

Anheuser gave over the day-to-day operations to Busch in the 1870s. The company continued to prosper, and its work force increased. During his tenure, Busch initiated the concept of considering employees members of a family: cared for and nurtured by the company and expected to remain loyal to the company for a lifetime. Anheuser-Busch considered this unique relation between employer and employee, intimate and cooperative, vital in producing an outstanding product.

In the 1890s, Pabst, a competitor, was the best-selling beer in the United States. However, Busch and his "family" thwarted the competition with the introduction of Michelob in 1896. Forceful and frequent advertising promoted Budweiser and Michelob as the most popular beers in the country, and this goal was realized in 1901, when Anheuser-Busch was the leading brewery in the country.

Busch died in 1913, and his son, August A. Busch, Sr., took over; the younger Busch soon focused on diversifying the company's interests. Toward this end, Busch patented the first diesel engine, which was installed in the brewery to increase production. With the onset of World War I, Busch founded a subsidiary to produce the engines for Navy submarines. In addition, the Anheuser-Busch family purchased sufficient war bonds to finance two bombers—each named ''Miss Budweiser.''

After the war, in November 1918, President Wilson signed the bill that instituted Prohibition. During this hiatus, Anheuser-Busch diversified into related fields. Malt syrup was canned and sold to people who required malt for their homemade brews. A refrigeration car company was established to transport perishables. Bevo, a soft drink made from ingredients similar to those in beer, was a great success for three years; it later failed when Prohibition laws concerning the use of yeast forced the company to change ingredients. Nevertheless, Anheuser-Busch began a trend toward diversification that would thereafter characterize the history of the company.

When Prohibition ended, the company experienced an unforeseen problem: people had become used to the sweet taste of the soft drinks and homemade brews that were available during Prohibition and were not willing to return to the more bitter commercial beer. In response, many brewers changed their formulas to achieve a sweeter taste. However, Anheuser-Busch refused to alter the formula for best-selling Budweiser, a decision endorsed by Dr. Robert Gall, the company's post-Prohibition brewmaster. Instead, the company initiated a major advertising campaign, challenging consumers to a ''five day test.'' Busch predicted that after five days of drinking Budweiser the consumer would not drink a sweet beer again. The advertising campaign was successful and established a trend for future consumer appeals.

During World War II, the company, led by Adolphus Busch III, again made substantial contributions to the war effort. Anheuser-Busch supplied the military with ammunition hoists, which were in production at a new company subsidiary. Moreover, the distribution of Budweiser beer was withdrawn from the Pacific Coast in order to supply the government with additional freight cars for war essentials, and spent grain was sold to financially troubled war-time farmers for poultry and livestock food. These patriotic actions elevated sales and advanced Anheuser-Busch's image as a patriotic company.

Between 1935 and 1950, the demand for Anheuser-Busch beer consistently exceeded the supply. In 1941, three million barrels of beer were produced, a figure that doubled by 1950. After the death of Adolphus Busch III in 1946, the company temporarily relinquished its lead in the industry. But with the succession of his brother, August ''Gussie'' Busch, Jr., the company became the nation's top brewer once again.

August Busch, Jr. continued the practice of aggressive advertising established by his brother and father, which had involved the distribution of pocket knives and gold pieces; advertisements featuring reproductions of patriotic art such as ''Custer's Last Stand''; and the 1933 introduction of the famous Clydesdale horses, which remained popular in the 1990s. Under August Busch, Anheuser-Busch became the first brewery to sponsor a radio network. Positive consumer response prompted William Bien, the vice-president of marketing, to design a legendary advertising campaign: ''pick-a-pair-of-six-packs.'' The campaign cost $2.5 million for two months, but was the most successful promotion in the history of the beer industry.

Despite its successful promotions, Anheuser-Busch entered a close competition at the beginning of the 1950s with Carling beer. During this time, a holiday was declared in Newark, New Jersey, in honor of the opening of a new Anheuser-Busch factory in that city. However, the new facility and new equipment necessitated a price hike, and Carling profited when its economical beer attracted customers put off by Anheuser-Busch's higher prices. In response, Busch introduced a new, low-priced lager beer and also pursued aggressive advertising promotions. In 1953, Anheuser-Busch bought the St. Louis Cardinals baseball team, targeting sports fans as a new category of consumers. Ultimately, the company was successful in rebuffing Carling's challenge.

Another brewery soon attempted to displace Anheuser-Busch from its number one market ranking. Decreasing the price of its beer in the 1960s, the Schlitz brewery hoped to force Anheuser-Busch into a price war. August Busch, Jr. remained confident that consumers would recognize Anheuser-Busch beer as superior in quality. However, public opinion was never tested, as Schlitz committed several marketing and advertising mistakes, and Anheuser-Busch retained its ranking.

During this time, August Busch III began his career at his father's company. After attending college for two years in Arizona and undergoing instruction in the art of brewing at a school in Chicago, Busch III started in an entry level position at the company. In 1979, he took over as CEO, vowing to uphold Adolphus Busch's philosophy that natural ingredients be used to distinguish the company's fine brewing from the lower quality brewing of other beers.

The Miller Brewing Company challenged this philosophy during the 1970s and 1980s. Miller introduced a light, low calorie beer in 1974, which became the best selling beer for a few months. Although Anheuser-Busch soon edged back into the top ranking, it remained closely followed by the Miller brewery. In response to Miller's challenge, Anheuser-Busch introduced two light beers in 1977, Natural Light and Michelob Light, and the popular Budweiser Light was introduced soon thereafter.

Under Busch III, the company developed a unique strategy for dealing with competition that included introducing new brands, increasing the advertising budget, and expanding its breweries. Moreover, Busch III refocused the company's marketing practices to target more specific groups of consumers. He hired a team of 100 college graduates to promote the sale of Anheuser-Busch beers on college campuses. He also oversaw the development of new advertisements designed to appeal to the working class. In the process, the company's marketing budget quadrupled, and sales increased.

Busch III also adopted a ''management control system'' that increased the efficiency of the company, redefining it as a modern corporation rather than a small family business. The new management system emphasized planning, teamwork, and communications, controls that, ironically, were intended to promote Anheuser-Busch's image as a regional brewery producing different beers to satisfy individual tastes. Anheuser-Busch continued to rank first in the brewing industry into the 1980s. By 1980, sales had reached 50 million barrels, increasing to 86.8 million barrels by 1992. While competition with Miller remained intense, the Budweiser brand outsold its next four competitors combined.

Anheuser-Busch initially espoused an acquisition policy of purchasing companies that would enhance its brewing operations, including malt plants in Wisconsin and Minnesota, beer can factories in Florida and Ohio, and yeast plants in Missouri, New Jersey, California, and Florida. The St. Louis Refrigerator Car Company inspected and maintained the 880 refrigerated railroad cars used to transport the company's beer across the country. Manufacturers Railway shipped Anheuser-Busch beer after it has been manufactured at the brewery with help from the malt and yeast subsidiaries.

Other subsidiaries, however, were soon established that were not directly related to the beer industry. Campbell-Taggart, Inc., the second largest bakery in the United States, was acquired in 1982, associating Anheuser-Busch's name with the food industry. In the 1980s, 6.7 percent of Anheuser-Busch's operating income was spent on food products. Another acquisition, Eagle Snacks, Inc., nationally distributed food products to bars, taverns, and convenience stores. Despite intense competition from Frito-Lay and Planters Peanuts, Eagle Snacks enhanced Anheuser-Busch's beer business by targeting consumers likely to purchase beer to complement their food products.

Anheuser-Busch also developed and acquired theme parks, forming the Busch Entertainment Corporation in 1979. The first "Busch Gardens" had opened 20 years earlier in Tampa, Florida, featured a 300-acre park boasting one of the world's largest collections of wildlife under private ownership. Another tourist attraction, "The Old Country," in Williamsburg, Virginia, was modeled after villages in seventeenth-century Europe. Anheuser-Busch also acquired the eight-park Sea World chain of mostly aquatic theme parks in 1989 for $1.3 billion. Although these entertainment parks were not particularly profitable, they helped expose Anheuser-Busch's name to a new target group—a younger generation and their parents—and enhanced the company's reputation for contributing to the public welfare. Anheuser-Busch's ownership of the St. Louis Cardinals served a similar function.

Anheuser-Busch also devoted considerable energy to nurturing its foreign market. The corporation formed Anheuser-Busch International, Inc. in 1981 to expand its presence in the global beer market through joint ventures, licensing agreements, and equity investments in foreign brewers. The corporation's timing in this venture proved fortuitous: the fall of trade barriers and conversion of formerly communist and socialist governments to free enterprise systems opened a wealth of opportunity for Anheuser-Busch. By 1993, the company's beers were offered in 21 European countries and ranked as the second most popular lager beer in the Republic of Ireland and the United Kingdom. Budweiser was introduced to Japan in 1981 and stood as that country's leading import by the early 1990s due to successful promotion to the young adult market. With a nine percent market share worldwide, Anheuser-Busch had the largest export volume of any American brewer in 1993, accounting for over 45 percent of U.S. beer exports.

During the early 1990s, Anheuser-Busch was compelled to face the declining—and more discerning—use of alcoholic beverages among Americans. The company had introduced LA, the first low alcohol beer, in 1984, but this product didn't prove widely successful. However, LA was replaced by O'Doul's in 1990, which soon became the nation's most popular non-alcohol brew. Moreover, as Americans' tastes grew more refined and microbreweries made unprecedented inroads into the modern beer industry, Anheuser-Busch sought to enhance the appeal of its brew. The company introduced eight new beers between 1984 and 1991, and, by 1993, Anheuser-Busch offered nineteen beer brands, three of which were imports. Anheuser-Busch's Bud Dry and Ice Draft from Budweiser appealed to such premium-beer drinkers. New brand introductions did not seem to detract from Budweiser's brand power; the new variations captured 17 percent of the market, while Bud only lost half a share point.

The challenges facing Anheuser-Busch in the early 1990s included an aging population, increasing state and federal excise taxes, a static beer market in the United States, and increased price competition. Acknowledging heightened competition and adverse economic conditions, the company adopted a Profitability Enhancement Program in September 1993, taking a one-time, pre-tax restructuring charge of $565 million, reducing the salaried work force by ten percent, and implementing productivity measures to ensure future success.

Principal Subsidiaries: Anheuser-Busch, Inc.; Busch Entertainment Corporation; Manufacturers Railway Company; St. Louis Refrigerator Car Company; St. Louis National Baseball Club, Inc.; Busch Properties, Inc.; Metal Container Corporation; Anheuser-Busch Recycling Corporation; International Label Company; Anheuser-Busch International, Inc.; Busch Media Group; Busch Creative Services Corporation; Busch Agricultural Resources, Inc.; Civic Center Corporation; Eagle Snacks, Inc.; Campbell Taggart, Inc.

Further Reading:

Baron, Stanley Wade, *Brewed in America: A History of Beer and Ale in the U.S.* New York: Arno Press, 1972.
Delaney, Lawrence, Jr., "Beer Brawl," *World Trade,* March 1993, pp. 34–40.
The History of Anheuser-Busch Companies—A Fact Sheet, St. Louis: The Anheuser-Busch Companies, Inc., 1992.
Krebs, Roland, *Making Friends Is Our Business: 100 Years of Anheuser-Busch,* St. Louis: Cuneo Press, 1953.
Lubove, Seth. "Unfinished Business," *Forbes,* December 10, 1990, pp. 170, 172.

—updated by April Dougal Gasbarre

Apache Corp.

2000 Post Oak
Houston, Texas 77056-4400
U.S.A.
(713) 296-6000
Fax: (713) 296-6480

Public Company
Incorporated: 1954
Employees: 1,200
Sales: $470 million
Stock Exchanges: New York
SICs: 1311 Crude Petroleum and Natural Gas; 1382 Oil and
    Gas Exploration Services

Apache Corp. is one of the largest and fastest growing crude
petroleum and natural gas producers in the United States. Headquartered in Texas, Apache is active in 18 states and Australia,
China, Egypt, and Indonesia.

CEO Raymond Plank, more than any other individual, is
credited with creating and building Apache Corp. Plank's first
foray into the business world occurred at age nine, in 1931,
when he started making and selling cider from his family's
Minnesota orchard. "It drove my mother crazy," mused Plank
in the January 3, 1994 issue of *Forbes*, "But I was a gleaner."
Indeed, his unceasing entrepreneurial penchant has been his
earmark throughout most of his life.

Plank served as a bomber pilot during World War II before
completing his education at Yale University in 1946. He and
fellow alum and roommate W. Brooks Field, who was also a
World War II veteran and Minneapolis native, headed back to
their hometown with grandiose dreams of starting a business.
They planned to begin publishing a magazine for midwestern
readers that would be patterned after then-popular *Time* or *The
Atlantic Monthly*. It was this loosely formed plan that would
lead to the creation of one of the nation's most prosperous
independent oil companies.

After returning to Minnesota in their $400 army surplus jeep,
Fields and Plank found that the printing house they had counted
on to help finance and print their publication had just been
purchased by a new owner. They quickly decided to start an
accounting and tax assistance service, instead. Despite an abso-
lute dearth of experience in their newly chosen profession,
Plank and Fields opened Northwest Business Service in down-

town Minneapolis. The partners' surplus jeep became the company car, and their first employee carried her own typewriter to
work. After a rough start, Plank and Fields were able to pay themselves a meager monthly salary of $20. Of this early venture,
Plank recalls, "Failure back then was never a thought."

Fields soon left the company to enter the grain brokerage
business. Replacing him was Plank's childhood friend Charles
Arnao, Jr. and Truman E. Anderson, a young and successful
insurance salesman. Although its accounting and bookkeeping
business continued to prosper in the early 1950s, the team
formed a partnership called APA (for Anderson, Plank, and
Arnao), a subsidiary meant to investigate new ventures.
Through APA the partners discovered a lucrative, though risky,
niche in investing in oil and gas exploration. Excited by the
possibilities offered by the emerging industry, Plank and his
friends decided to concentrate solely on oil and gas operations.

The three partners founded Apache Oil Corp. in 1954 to arrange
and participate in investments related to oil and gas exploration.
Three original principles continued to guide the company
throughout most of the 20th century. First, rather than investing
through a (potentially corrupt) third-party promoter, as was the
common practice in Minneapolis, Apache would ensure that the
drillers worked directly for the investors. Second, Apache
would ensure that a professional staff managed the drilling and
financial operations of each venture. Finally, Apache would
spread its investors' resources over several drilling ventures,
thus reducing their risk of losing all or most of their money from
a single failed endeavor.

Apache Oil Corp. finished its first producing oil well in 1955 in
Cushing, Oklahoma. Although the well only churned out a
paltry seven barrels per day, Apache's second attempt resulted
in a well that generated more than 30 barrels an hour. Plank and
friends, who were sweating it out in a ramshackle Minneapolis
office, were relieved by the success—up to that point, the
venture had been on very shaky ground. As a result of a few
successful drilling ventures, the company was able to report a
net profit of $12,535 in 1955 from sales of $190,000.

After surviving its first year—the company was even able to
replace its card table and chairs with some real office furniture—Apache basked in a string of successes. The company
generated revenues of $630,000 in 1956, wowing its investors
with solid returns. And by 1959 the enterprise had expanded
into 23 states and two Canadian provinces. Its base of shareholders quickly grew from 1,000 in 1959 to more than 4,000 by
the early 1960s. Furthermore, the company formed a second
investment subsidiary, First Apache Realty Program (later
named Apache Realty Corp.). It was formed as a limited partnership to invest in commercial real estate. Apache's first
project was a 50-store shopping plaza in Minneapolis.

Apache's entrance into real estate was largely the result of
Anderson's efforts. Anderson and Plank—Arnao left the company to form his own business—both agreed that increasing
government regulation of the oil and gas exploration industry
threatened to virtually extinguish their company. More diversification was needed in ventures such as telephone companies
and steel. However, Plank didn't share Anderson's enthusiasm
for emphasizing real estate investments. An escalating rift between the co-founders climaxed in 1963. Anderson, in a star-

tling move, called a board meeting and asked its members to fire Plank because he was showing signs of "overwork." At the same meeting, the board accepted Anderson's resignation and transferred all management responsibilities to Plank.

With Plank solely in charge after ten years of operation, Apache posted 1964 sales of $9.2 million, net income of $661,000, and $9.3 million in new drilling capital from its investors. Confirming its commitment to continued growth through risk and innovation, Apache issued a corporate objective on its tenth anniversary. Authored by Plank, it included these words: "the capacity of the individual is infinite. Limitations are largely of habit, convention, acceptance of things as they are, fear, or lack of self confidence."

Although other limitations, namely government price caps and regulation, battered its competitors, Apache remained profitable during the 1960s as the number of oil industry participants plummeted from 30,000 to 13,000. Besides its diversification into other businesses and its acquisition of several struggling competitors, Apache benefitted from one of its most successful oil finds. In 1967, Apache drilled a well in the tiny town of Recluse, Wyoming, which immediately began delivering 50 barrels per hour. After drilling 11 more wells nearby, Apache was getting 2,800 barrels of oil each day from its Recluse operations. Analysts credited Apache's skilled management team with allowing the company to successfully exploit a sudden strike of that magnitude.

Despite this fortuitous discovery, Apache continued to diversify through acquisition during the late 1960s and early 1970s in an effort to minimize the effects of oil industry woes. By 1970, in fact, the company had established a network of 24 subsidiary firms ranging from engineering and electronics companies to farming and water supply operations. It continued to expand its holdings during the 1970s, evolving into a large conglomerate. Important contributors to Apache's success during that period included Jaye Dyer, John Black, John D. Hansen, Roland E. Menk, and John A. Kocur. In addition, Plank invited his old roommate Fields to join the company's board in 1973—Fields and Plank had remained good friends throughout the years. "Who can turn down an invitation like that," said Fields.

Recognizing a trend toward higher oil prices, which would hurt its non-oil and non-gas producing subsidiaries, Apache began formulating plans during the mid-1970s to sell many of its diversified holdings. In 1977 the company established a timetable for the sale of most of Apache's remaining subsidiaries, a move that would also increase funding for oil and gas development. Although Apache had received much criticism for its widespread diversification, company management credited its external investments with helping the company survive the 1960s and early 1970s.

Apache lost a large portion of its oil and gas operations in 1977 when it sold its Apexco subsidiary. Apexco had been created to handle Apache Corp.'s energy endeavors. But Apache re-emphasized its expertise in the gas and oil business in the late 1970s, and by the early 1980s had again established itself as a major player in the industry. Even by 1978 Apache was recognized as one of the leading deep drilling companies in the United States. Almost as though it was signalling an end to Apache's oil and gas adversity, the era of the late 1970s and early 1980s was punctuated by the largest blowout (oil well explosion) in the history of the petroleum industry. An Apache well in Texas erupted in a blaze that took 16 months and $42 million to extinguish.

After achieving notable success with its oil and gas ventures in the late 1970s, Apache formed the Apache Petroleum Company (APC) in 1981. APC, the first publicly traded limited partnership to appear on the board of the New York Stock Exchange, was created as an innovative investment vehicle that would take advantage of favorable tax laws. As industry drilling activity vaulted to post-1950s highs in the early 1980s, APC attracted nearly 60,000 limited partners and Apache sales leapt to $221 million by 1984. Plank ranked the creation of APC as the most significant development in the company's history. Indeed, APC spawned an entirely new industry of publicly traded master limited partnerships (MLPs).

Apache realized record income levels during the early and mid-1980s; net income fluctuated around $22 million during the early 1980s before slipping to a still-healthy $9.4 million in 1985. In 1986, however, the oil and gas industries spiraled into a down cycle. After declining slowly throughout the early 1980s, prices, particularly for oil, plummeted in 1986 as the market became glutted. The downturn was magnified for Apache by the Tax Reform Act of 1986 (TRA), which Congress passed. The TRA effectively eliminated the tax advantages associated with limited partnerships, crushing one of the most lucrative sides of Apache's business. The company recorded its first full-year loss, of $10.9 million, in 1986.

Undaunted by analyst's predictions of doom for Apache and its industry peers, Plank and his management team immediately began plotting a strategy for the future. In 1986, in fact, the company went out on a limb by investing a large portion of its available resources in new oil and gas reserves, which were selling at record low prices. And, demonstrating his ability to adapt to change, Plank pioneered a complete reorganization of the company in 1987 and 1988. Surprising analysts, Plank changed the entire focus of the company from an organizer of limited partnerships and investment vehicles to a conventional exploration and production company relying on internal cash flow to fund operations.

Evidencing the significance of the change was the movement of company headquarters from Minneapolis to Denver, and a significant reduction of the Apache Corp. work force. Distressed by both Apache's rapid transition out of its core business and its negative earnings—in 1987 Apache posted a $71 million net loss—investors registered their concerns on Wall Street. The company's stock price declined in 1988 as Apache continued to buy up new reserves, increase its debt burden, and restructure. "Given what was happening in our industry, that wasn't surprising," said Plank in the October 16, 1989 issue of the *Denver Business Journal*. "We were changing our whole basis of doing business, so it's understandable that the market got a little pessimistic."

Plank's arrival on the Denver business scene underscored the aggressive, no-holds-barred management style that had made Apache so successful in the past. Plank was irritated by both a lack of an intelligible U.S. energy policy and government intervention in the oil and gas industry, and he had been prodding his

Denver peers to get organized and take action since 1985, when he invested in locally owned drilling operations. Not surprisingly, he clashed with many of the local industry elites. "Frankly, they're entitled to their opinion, and I don't happen to care what it is," stated Plank in the May 1989 issue of *Corporate Minnesota Report.* "I was getting pretty tough on the independent sector of our industry, and I have no regrets whatever. They sat there and watched their butts melt and themselves go broke."

Just as it had weathered the industry fallout of the 1960s, Apache began to emerge from its predicament in 1988, when it posted a positive net income of $9 million. Furthermore, after increasing its exploration and development expenditures to $45 million in 1988, it planned to more than double that figure to $92 million in 1989. Apache was conducting its oil and gas reserve acquisition and development program with the help of industry veteran Mick Merelli, who joined the Apache team in 1987 as president and chief operating officer. Apache's new strategy allowed it to discredit its detractors as sales shot up 74 percent in 1989, to $247 million, and net income lurched to $22.1 million. In 1990, moreover, sales and income reached a record $273 million and $40.3 million.

Despite his company's remarkable recovery and restored reputation, the 68-year-old Plank had no intention of slowing down going into the 1990s. Adhering to its strategy of growth through acquisition and development of oil and gas reserves, Apache doubled its reserves between 1990 and 1993 to more than 225 million barrels. A majority of this increase resulted from, perhaps, the most significant investment in the company's 37-year history. In 1991, Apache purchased oil and gas properties, which included 111 million barrels of reserves, from Amoco for $545 million. "Shortly afterward, a cow leaned against one of the plugged wells and knocked out the plug," jested Plank in the January 3, 1994 issue of *Forbes.* "When crude flowed out, Apache put the well back into production and drilled more wells around it."

Apache complemented its Amoco deal with an additional $350 million in acquisitions during 1992 and 1993. And, as prices for oil stabilized and those for natural gas began a slow recovery, Apache continued to boost its production. Total output rose steadily from 17 million barrels of oil equivalent (MMboe), a measure that also applies to gas production, in 1989 to 31 MMboe in 1993. As a result, Apache's revenues grew from $247 million to $467 during the same period, reflecting a jump of 90 percent. Net income hovered in the $35 million to $45 million range throughout the early 1990s. Importantly, despite its intense acquisition efforts, Apache had succeeded in reducing its ratio of debt-to-equity from 53 percent in 1991 to a healthier 37 percent in 1993.

Augmenting rapid domestic expansion during the early 1990s were Apache operations overseas. Although they represented a negligible share of company receipts, foreign drilling ventures were becoming an increasingly important component of Apache's growth strategy. Western Australia represented the core of its international operations. However, in 1994 Apache agreed to purchase a one-third interest in an exploratory off-

shore venture in eastern China. Also in 1994, the company planned to drill two exploratory wells in different regions of Indonesia, and one well south of Cairo, Egypt. Domestic revenues were garnered primarily from drilling operations in the Southwest, particularly in the Gulf of Mexico. But the company was active in Nevada and several northwestern states, as well.

Apache's quick response to falling prices and the TRA of 1986 allowed it to get a jump on its competitors and establish itself as a shrewd industry contender. Although total sales lagged behind those of the huge leaders, such as Phillips Petroleum and Atlantic Richfield, Apache lead its peers going into the mid-1990s in categories such as sales growth, five-year earnings per share, and debt as a percentage of equity. Furthermore, Apache's concentration on acquisition and development of natural gas reserves during the late 1980s and early 1990s boded well for its future success.

In addition to its business exploits during the early 1990s, Apache Corp.—guided by Plank's affection for outdoor sports—was notable for its environmental awareness. This was reflected in efforts to restrict development of 20,000 acres of foothill grazing lands in Wyoming. In 1992 and 1993, moreover, Apache's Australian division received the West Australian "Environmental Excellence" award for conducting drilling and pipeline rehabilitation operations with minimal disruption to sensitive wildlife habitats. "The degree to which we're defiling this planet, it's a greater threat than nuclear annihilation," Plank observed in the May 1989 issue of *Corporate Report Minnesota.*

Going into the mid-1990s, Plank continued to play a dominant role in Apache's operations. And his philosophy of risk-taking and innovation still permeated the company's management. As stated in Apache's 1993 annual report, "Apache's operating objectives have their roots in the company's corporate culture: to achieve consistent, profitable growth in production, reserves, and cash flow through a mixture of moderate-risk drilling, field operations, and acquisitions." Apache's large reserve base and proven knack for adapting to change bestowed credibility on these goals.

Principal Subsidiaries: Hadson Energy Limited (Australia).

Further Reading:

Byrne, Harlan S., "Apache," *Barron's,* September 20, 1993.
David, Gregory E., "Apache Corp.: Bargain Basement Buyer," *Financial World,* July 20, 1993.
Even, Beth, "Whatever Happened to Ray Plank?" *Corporate Report Minnesota,* May 1989.
Journey Into Risk Country: The First Thirty Years of Apache Corporation, Minneapolis: Apache Corp., 1985.
Mack, Toni, "Energy," *Forbes,* January 3, 1994.
Percefull, Gary, "Denver Independent Most Active Driller in Oklahoma," *Tulsa World,* August 27, 1989.
Rudnitsky, Howard, "Hedging," *Forbes,* September 28, 1992.
Sample, James D., "Apache Investors Like What They See in Revamped Company," *Denver Business Journal,* October 16, 1989.
"U.S. Drilling: Industry Needs to Think Positive," *World Oil,* February 1994.

—Dave Mote

Applied Bioscience International, Inc.

4350 North Fairfax Drive
Arlington, Virginia 22203
U.S.A.
(703) 516-2490
Fax: (703) 516-2494

Public Company
Incorporated: 1986
Employees: 2,200
Sales: $181 million
Stock Exchanges: New York
SICs: 8734 Testing Labs; 8731 Commercial Physical
   Research

Applied Bioscience International, Inc. (APBI) is a leading provider of consulting services and contract research in the environmental and life sciences. When the company began, it concentrated exclusively on biological safety testing of pharmaceuticals, foods, and chemicals. However, through a rapid series of acquisitions, APBI broadened its business to include a complete array of testing services for drugs and chemicals in the environment and in human subjects.

APBI got its start in 1986, when the company was created from two subsidiaries of IMS International, Inc. IMS had operations around the world that provided research services to the pharmaceutical, personal care, and chemical industries. In September of 1986, IMS incorporated APBI as a wholly owned subsidiary, which was comprised of Bio/Dynamics, Inc. and Life Science Research, Inc.; the two companies that previously had made up the Life Sciences Division of IMS Bio/Dynamics had been providing toxicological testing services at facilities in East Millstone, New Jersey, since 1961, while Life Science Research, Ltd., had conducted similar activities at its labs in Suffolk, England, beginning in 1972. On March 26, 1987, IMS divested itself of APBI, selling three million shares of stock in the company in the over-the-counter market. By April 2, the company's initial public offering had been oversubscribed and closed.

As a part of the fledgling contract research industry, APBI was hired to advise other companies on the development of products from the point of discovery to the point of sale. APBI's opera-tions involved the testing of pharmaceutical, food, and chemical substances to make sure that they were not harmful in any way. The company specialized in drugs and chemicals, which were tested on animal subjects in special laboratories.

APBI's goal was to capitalize on the growing number of environmental and safety regulations imposed on companies bringing products to market. In addition to an ever-more-complex welter of regulations to navigate, controversy surrounding the use of animal testing made the option of contracting out for testing attractive to many companies. APBI took care of the complicated business of complying with regulations, and it also took the heat for using animals as test subjects in the process. To protect its customers from controversy, the company adopted the policy of not revealing the names of its clients.

At the end of its first year in business, APBI had 750 full-time employees and more than 360,000 square feet of office and laboratory space. Headquartered in New Jersey, the company was constructing another 62,000 square feet of space. After reporting a 35 percent increase in third quarter revenues as well as a 50 percent rise in earnings, APBI finished the year with $33 million in revenues on $2.8 million in sales, both up about a third from the previous year. These results garnered the company the honor of being named the 47th fastest growing small company in the United States by *Business Week* magazine in May of 1988.

That same month APBI announced that it had been selected to take part in the formation of a testing laboratory to be founded by the State of Victoria, in Australia. With APBI's management and technical advice, the state hoped to foster growth in biotechnology by using the laboratory to perform safety evaluations of foods, drugs, and chemicals. This was followed by the further expansion of its British operations, achieved with the purchase of Cambridge Applied Nutrition Toxicology and Biosciences Ltd. (CANTAB) in March of 1989. CANTAB and APBI's English unit had long been affiliated, and the acquisition was part of the company's strategic program of growth. It represented APBI's first move into the lucrative market for outside clinical services, which consisted of Phase I clinical trials for drugs, involving the use of healthy human volunteers. In addition, the company performed nutritional tests and other types of studies.

In the spring of 1989, controversy over APBI's use of animal subjects resulted in a brief dip in the company's stock price, as public pressure caused several cosmetics companies to debate an end to the use of animal lab subjects. Analysts questioned whether investors would ultimately wish to be associated with the controversial practice.

Later that year, in September, APBI announced a second acquisition, as the company continued its program to extend its services to include other aspects of the development process for pharmaceutical and agricultural chemicals. The Valdosta, Georgia-based Landis International, Inc., which APBI acquired for stock, managed testing programs for pesticides and other agricultural chemicals to determine their impact on plants and the environment as a whole. APBI's two acquisitions, CANTAB and Landis, together cost about $4 million.

With more than 170 corporate clients, Landis specialized in satisfying the testing requirements of the Environmental Protection Agency (EPA) and other regulatory bodies. In addition to research facilities in Georgia, Landis also conducted tests in California and Washington. In addition, the company operated a year-round testing facility in the Central American nation of Belize, allowing the company to conduct tests even during the winter months. These activities netted $2.4 million in revenues for 1989. In the wake of its Landis purchase, APBI merged two of its British operations, CANTAB and the Clinical Technology Centre (International) Ltd., a longtime subsidiary of Life Science Research, into a third entity, Clinical Science Research Ltd., in an effort to market their human subject testing services more efficiently.

By the beginning of 1990 APBI had racked up a strong record of double-digit growth in earnings and revenues. A large part of the company's growth came from its rapidly expanding overseas business. The company found 26 percent of its business in North America, 37 percent in Europe, and an equal amount in Japan. Because APBI had no facilities in the Far East, Japanese customers were required to send their materials to the United States or Britain for testing. Overall, APBI held nine percent of the worldwide market for biological safety testing.

In an effort to expand that market share further, APBI announced in January of 1990 that it would merge with the ENVIRON International Corporation. This privately held company, based in Arlington, Virginia, provided risk assessment and environmental risk management services. With field offices in New Jersey and California, ENVIRON provided a wide variety of services relating to human exposure to environmental toxins, including expert counsel and technical assistance in chemical risk assessment, toxicology, environmental liability assessments, remedial investigations, and litigation and regulatory advice. The company brought fiscal 1989 earnings of $1.17 million to the merger, which was completed in September of 1990.

By October of that year, APBI was reporting quarterly revenues up 30.3 percent to $25.3 million. The company reported a loss, however, because of the costs of the merger with ENVIRON, principally the write-off of rental fees on the company's corporate headquarters.

A month later APBI called off arrangements for yet another acquisition, when its plans for the $10 million purchase of the drug-testing laboratories of a Baltimore-based competitor, PharmaKinetics Laboratories, Inc., were cancelled. This move came in the wake of a scandal involving PharmaKinetics, in which the company had implicated its largest client in an illegal drug-switching scam, only to become the target of an investigation itself. Rather than get involved with the tainted operations, APBI withdrew from the tentative agreement at the end of 1990. Despite this setback, APBI announced its intention to press ahead with its plans for expansion, both internally and through acquisitions.

By 1991, APBI's efforts to expand and diversity its activities had begun to show significant fruit. Biological testing, which accounted for 100 percent of the company's revenues in 1988, had come to make up less than 40 percent of APBI's returns just three years later. Instead, one-third of the company's operations had to do with environmental testing and consulting, while 28 percent comprised clinical drug development research.

APBI diversified its operations further in September of 1991, when the company purchased the commercial laboratory business of the Environmental Testing and Certification Corporation (ETC), a wholly owned subsidiary of the OHM Corporation. This company operated three commercial laboratories that served the environmental services industry, performing sophisticated analyses of contamination in soil, water, and other environmental samples. With the purchase of ETC, APBI made another move towards becoming a complete chemical risk assessment company. As the owner of ETC, APBI would now be able to perform in-house many testing functions that it had previously been forced to subcontract out. ETC's facilities were located in Edison, New Jersey; Baton Rouge, Louisiana; and Santa Rosa, California. Together, these operations contributed $18 million in revenues in 1990.

Although the company felt that its operations were more complete with the addition of ETC, APBI still needed additional facilities. After searching throughout the contract testing industry for more than a year, the company announced in February of 1992 that it would merge with Pharmaco Dynamics Research, Inc., a company based in Austin, Texas, which conducted toxicology testing on humans in clinical trials. With the addition of Pharmaco, APBI became a fully unified provider of the complete range of services necessary to bring a product to market. APBI was now able to take an environmental or pharmaceutical substance from the animal testing stage, to human clinical trials, to final approval before the Food and Drug Administration. By joining with Pharmaco, which had an unusually high annual compound growth rate of 60 percent, APBI hoped to position itself as one of the two main players in the contract research and development field.

In addition, APBI hoped that its merger with the Texas firm would help it to bring some much-needed managerial expertise to its operations. During its period of rapid growth, the company had failed to install controls on its operations to unify its subsidiaries or create a strong marketing effort. As a result, much duplication of effort took place between the different units of APBI, and a lack of communication within the company meant that customers often received repeated sales calls.

After the merger with Pharmaco, APBI took steps to integrate its company organization and streamline administration, thereby reducing operating costs. Relying on the marketing management and information systems that Pharmaco had previously perfected, APBI moved to implement them throughout its entire organization. The company restructured its operations, dividing its subsidiaries and services into two groups: the Life Sciences Group, and the Environmental Sciences Group. In this way, APBI hoped to shift from a decentralized holding company to a better-integrated organization with central management. Due to the cost of the corporate restructuring, APBI reported a net loss for the first quarter of 1992. However, with this new framework in place, APBI hoped in the future to seek out aggressively and effectively a greater share of its market.

In June of 1992 APBI resumed its series of acquisitions when its subsidiary ETC purchased National Express Laboratories, Inc. (NATEX). This company ran three commercial laboratories in the South and on the West Coast, all of which took part in the U.S. Environmental Protection Agency Contract Laboratory Program. This meant that NATEX had contracts with the state environmental quality agencies in the areas that it served, and they were able to produce high level, litigation-quality data. The company's president was assigned by APBI to lead both the NATEX and ETC operations in the wake of the purchase.

The following month APBI's Pharmaco subsidiary opened one of the world's largest overnight medical research facilities, with 198 beds, in Austin, Texas. This enhanced the company's ability to provide Phase I testing of new drugs. In this process, healthy human volunteers were given doses of a substance, and then blood or urine samples were collected at timed intervals to test the level of the drug remaining in the body. With the addition of the Austin facility, Pharmaco reported that its workload was at an all time high. This contrasted with the operations of other APBI units, as the overall economic downturn of the early 1990s caused a weakening in demand for consulting services and for animal testing services in the United Kingdom.

Indeed, despite Pharmaco's strong showing, APBI reported a quarterly loss in December of 1992, as a result of the costs associated with its merger of Pharmaco and its overall restructuring of the Life Sciences Group, which included Pharmaco, Bio/Dynamics, and Life Science Research. For the year as a whole, the company showed slower than expected earnings. In addition to general economic conditions, which caused a large drop in corporate environmental expenditures, APBI cited increased expenditures in marketing and sales as a factor in its low returns.

Despite these disappointing results, APBI made a further acquisition in January of 1993, with the purchase of Ensys Environmental Products, Inc. Ensys marketed on-site test kits to detect the presence of such hazardous chemicals as PCBs and petroleum products in the environment. Its operations were added to those of APBI's ETC unit.

Later that month, APBI further restructured its holdings when it combined its Life Sciences operations into a new company to be called Pharmaco-LSR. The new company comprised 14 facilities in locations around the world, including the United States, England, France, Germany, Belgium, and Sweden. Pharmaco-

LSR hoped to provide complete, global product development to a wide variety of clients in a cost-effective manner. At the time of this shift, APBI also moved its headquarters from New Jersey to Arlington, Virginia.

By April of 1993 APBI was once again reporting lower than expected revenues. In response, the company launched a global advertising campaign, and undertook aggressive cost-cutting measures. Contributing to APBI's drop in earnings were losses from its ETC analytical environmental testing unit. In mid-1994 APBI announced that this unit would be spun off to join two other environmental labs in forming a new company that would operate under the name of one of the partners, PACE, Inc. APBI would retain ownership of PACE, Inc., which constituted 23 labs.

APBI had anticipated significant consolidation in the environmental laboratory business, which had an excess of capacity and resulted in cut-throat competition. In addition, the company saw the market for contract lab services, an industry pioneered by APBI, mature and grow more competitive. Although the company's rapid growth through acquisition and the growing pains it experienced due to restructuring and integration had caused its profitability to slow, overall APBI appeared able to maintain its leading position in these fields well into the late 1990s.

Principal Subsidiaries: APBI Environmental Sciences Group, Inc.; Pharmaco-LSR International, Inc.

Further Reading:

"APBI Merger With Pharmaco Creates Synergy," *Portfolio Letter,* February 17, 1992.

Collins, Beverly, "Restructuring Hits APBI Earnings," *Washington Times,* December 23, 1992.

"Environmental Health Company Merges With Research Firm," *Washington Business Journal,* September 17, 1990.

Lang, Steven, "Consolidation Reshaping U.S. Lab Market as Two Deals Create New Giants," *Hazardous Waste Business,* May 18, 1984.

"Merger With English Firm Will Allow Research Pooling," *Washington Business Journal,* May 21, 1990.

Southerland, Dan, "Applied Bioscience Merges Three Affiliates," *Washington Post,* January 19, 1993.

"Testing Firm Hurt by Bolar Scandal," *Baltimore Sun,* December 19, 1990.

—Elizabeth Rourke

Applied Materials, Inc.

P.O. Box 58039
Santa Clara, California 95052
U.S.A.
(408) 727-5555
Fax: (408) 748-9943

Public Company
Incorporated: 1967
Employees: 4,739
Sales: $1.08 billion
Stock Exchanges: NASDAQ
SICs: 3559 Special Industry Machinery

Applied Materials, Inc. is the leading manufacturer of wafer fabrication systems and services to the worldwide semiconductor industry. Applied Materials is also the first company within the industry to surpass $1 billion in sales of semiconductor equipment. With 44 sales and service offices in 13 countries and with manufacturing centers in the United States, Europe, Japan, and Israel, the company is poised to take advantage of forecasts which project that the $60 billion semiconductor equipment market in 1993 will grow to more than $110 billion by the beginning of the twenty-first century.

Applied Materials was founded in 1967 to manufacture chemical vapor deposition systems for semiconductor wafer fabrication. The semiconductor industry itself, however, which makes the microcircuitry used in all electronics products, dates back to the invention of the first transistor during the early 1950s by scientists working at Bell Telephone Laboratories. With the advent of the transistor, it was possible to make electronic circuitry smaller and this, in turn, led to the manufacture of products which were lighter weight, more compact, and more energy efficient. During the late 1950s, semiconductor chip makers who initially both designed and built their own production equipment began to contract with vendors that supplied the equipment used to make their miniaturized devices. This trend helped to develop the semiconductor equipment industry. In the modern world, semiconductor manufacturing technology has revolutionized the industrialized nations, providing the basis for all electronic products ranging from advanced fighter aircraft instrumentation to consumer goods such as radios and digital clocks. Indeed, it is not an overstatement to say that economies and national cultures have been dramatically affected by the semiconductor industry.

Within this historical context, Applied Materials' place in the development of the semiconductor manufacturing industry is unique. From 1967 to 1973, company revenues grew at a pace of more than 40 percent annually, and its total market share of the semiconductor equipment industry reached 6.5 percent. With such rapid market expansion and such enviable financial success, in 1972 the company decided to go public. In 1974, management decided to acquire Galamar Industries, a manufacturer of silicon wafers. During the mid 1970s, however, a severe recession had a very negative effect on the entire semiconductor industry. Applied Materials was hit especially hard, suffering a 45 percent drop in sales in 1975. Despite the drop in sales, management pursued prospects for growth, entering into a joint venture with Fairchild Camera and Instrument Corporation to construct a silicon production site in the same year.

Persistent financial problems related to non-semiconductor areas throughout 1976 and 1977 necessitated both organizational and management changes. James C. Morgan, formerly a partner in a private venture capital firm and with extensive experience in management at Textron's high-technology divisions, became president and chief executive officer. Morgan immediately shut down the unprofitable Galamar Industries, sold its share in the silicon manufacturing center, and concentrated on improving its area of expertise in the semiconductor industry. In 1978, Applied Materials reported an increase in sales of approximately 17 percent. And in 1979, sales grew by a phenomenal 51 percent over the previous year.

Applied Materials, under the guidance of Morgan, continued its expansion strategy and acquired the ion implantation division of British-based Lintott Engineering, Ltd. in 1979. The company also formed Applied Materials Japan, Inc., a joint venture created to increase the company's share of the growing Japanese semiconductor equipment market. Sales reached $69.3 million in 1980, but by 1982 the company was once again hit hard by a worldwide recession in the semiconductor industry. At the end of that year, Applied Materials reported a loss of $9.4 million on total sales of $88.2 million.

The company's commitment to research and development, however, helped it weather the recession much better than many other vendors. The introduction of the AME 8100 Series Plasma Etch Systems revolutionized the dry etching of semiconductors. The quick market acceptance of this product and an agreement reached with the General Electric Venture Capital Corporation (GEVENCO) supplying a $20 million investment helped the company ride out the remainder of the recession. By 1983, the company was financially healthy once again; sales broke the $100 million mark. With 30 percent of its total sales originating from Japan, management steered a course to increase participation in the Japanese semiconductor market and started construction of a technology facility which would not only include a state-of-the-art research and development laboratory but also incorporate the most advanced technology for processing semiconductor wafers.

In 1984, increased demand for semiconductors pushed worldwide sales up a record 45 percent to approximately $26 billion, and Applied Materials benefitted from this strong upturn to report sales of $168.4 million, a 60 percent surge over 1983. Yet in 1985, the cyclical nature of the semiconductor industry was again apparent when worldwide sales decreased by almost 20 percent. This downturn led to the worst recession ever for the semiconductor equipment industry and, as the recession deepened in 1986, many of the company's major customers began to reduce their equipment budgets. As a result, revenues continued to decline although Applied Materials was still performing better than most other companies in the semiconductor equipment market.

A large part of Applied Materials' success during the recession was due to the development of leading-edge technology. In 1986, the company introduced the Precision Etch 8300A, featuring major improvements in contamination control and higher than previous levels of automation. In 1987, the company introduced the Precision 5000 CVD, a new system which meets the industry need for significant improvements in the low-temperature deposition of dielectric materials. Orders for this new technology helped Applied Materials improve its financial position, as did a public stock offering which brought in an additional $54.7 million. In the same year, James W. Bagley, Applied Materials senior vice-president of operations since 1981, with over 15 years of previous experience in engineering and project management at Texas Instruments, was appointed president and chief operating officer. Morgan, after serving 12 years as president, remained chief executive officer and chairman of the company's board of directors.

The combination of Applied Materials' commitment to new product introduction and a renewed demand in the worldwide semiconductor equipment market made 1988 a record year for the company. Net sales of $362.8 million more than doubled the previous year's sales figures. By continuing to introduce new products and by improving the technology and applications in its existing product lines, revenues jumped to $501.8 million in 1989. With the previous addition of a service center in Beijing, China, and a regional office in Seoul, Korea, during the mid-1980s, in 1989 the company continued to build upon its presence in the Pacific Rim with the construction of new facilities in Japan. After 10 years, over 40 percent of the company's revenues were coming from the Asia/Pacific market.

New product development was the cornerstone of management's strategy for improving the company's market position in the early 1990s. In 1990, the company introduced the Endura 5500 PVD in order to enter a new market, physical vapor deposition. In 1991, the firm announced its intention to enter the market for Thin Film Transistor Liquid Crystal Display manufacturing equipment. Shipments for systems which manufacture these flat panel displays started in 1993. In 1992, Applied Materials was beginning to reap the benefits of its strategy for product introduction and its expansion in Japan and the Pacific Rim. Total revenues were reported at $751.4 million, backlog orders at $254 million, and net income at $39.5 million. The geographical distribution of sales broke down as follows: 40 percent in the United States, 30 percent in Japan, 18 percent in Europe, and 12 percent in the Pacific Rim.

In 1993, Applied Materials entered into an agreement with Komatsu, Ltd., a Japanese firm, to form a new company named Applied Komatsu Technology, Inc. The company was created in order to develop, manufacture, and market systems that are employed in producing Flat Panel Displays. Operating with facilities in both the United States and Japan, it was agreed upon that company headquarters were to be established in Japan. In October 1993, the company announced its first product, the AKT 1600 PECVD, for chemical vapor deposition of thin films employed in manufacturing Thin Film Transistor structures in Flat Panel Displays. The development of this technology has broad applications ranging from desktop and laptop computers to any electronic products that use high quality, color displays.

The strategy of Applied Materials in establishing partnerships like the one with Komatsu has been extremely profitable for the firm. Joint ventures increase the company's market share in Japan because the new operation functions like a Japanese firm and relies on Japanese employees to provide the manufacturing base, marketing skills, and sales techniques required to do business in that country. In addition, the intimate relationships created with valued Japanese customers help sell Applied Materials' products when the customer decides to open a plant in the U.S. or somewhere overseas. The success of this strategy is the reason why nearly one-third of all Applied Materials sales involve Japanese semiconductor customers.

Not only will Applied Materials continue to focus on establishing long-term relationships with users of semiconductor equipment, but it also intends to take advantage of foreseeable trends in manufacturing technology. For example, as the semiconductor industry produces more and more circuits with smaller geometries, particulate contamination in what is called the "cleanroom" will become a major concern requiring contaminant-free manufacturing environments. One solution to this problem of particulate contamination is the trend toward through-the-wall equipment design, where manufacturing equipment is completely encased in an airtight shell (a "cleanroom" environment) with only one access port which connects the equipment to the wafer fabrication facility. Applied Materials is developing new and highly reliable equipment for semiconductor customers to use within this "cleanroom" manufacturing environment.

In 1993, Applied Materials reached one of its long-term goals: it became the first company within the semiconductor equipment industry to hit the $1 billion mark in revenues. Total sales in 1993 amounted to $1.08 billion. One critical element in the company's financial success is the 13 percent of total revenue, or $140.2 million in fiscal 1993, invested in research and development. The commitment of a significant portion of its revenue to developing new technology has provided stability and helped the company weather the cyclical periods of growth and recession in the semiconductor industry. A continued emphasis on developing new technology, along with a strategy of creating close working partnerships with customers by means of a global presence, makes Applied Materials the company to watch in the semiconductor manufacturing industry.

Further Reading:

Pitta, Julia, "The Realist," *Forbes,* May 13, 1991, pp. 116–117.
Cohen, Charles, "Applied Materials Combines the Best of East and West," *Electronic Business,* May 6, 1991, pp. 52–54.

—Thomas Derdak

ARCO Chemical Company ✦

ARCO Chemical Company

3801 West Chester Pike
Newtown Square, Pennsylvania 19073-2387
U.S.A.
(610) 359-2000
Fax: (610) 359-2479

Public Subsidiary of Atlantic Richfield Company
Incorporated: 1987
Employees: 4,000
Sales: $3.1 billion
Stock Exchanges: New York
SICs: 2819 Industrial Inorganic Chemicals Nec

The ARCO Chemical Company manufactures intermediate chemicals used in a broad range of consumer and industrial products. Major chemicals include propylene oxide, used in a variety of plastics, foams, and paints; tertiary butyl alcohol, used in the production of oxygenated fuels that are blended with gasoline to reduce emissions and improve octane; and styrene, used in the production of insulation, foam cups, and engineering resins.

By the middle 1990s, ARCO was a worldwide company with chemical plants in the U.S., the Netherlands, France, Belgium, Taiwan, Indonesia, China, and Japan. International sales accounted for about half the company's revenues of $3.1 billion in 1993. Company headquarters were in Newtown Square, Pennsylvania.

ARCO Chemical originated in 1966 as a division of the Atlantic Richfield Company, one of the largest and oldest oil companies in the United States. Atlantic Richfield was founded in 1865 as the Atlantic Refining Company, and established the first refinery in the United States in Philadelphia, Pennsylvania that same year. Atlantic Refining was swallowed by the Standard Oil Company in 1874, but reemerged as an independent company in 1911, when the Standard Oil Trust was broken up by the U.S. Supreme Court under the Sherman Antitrust Act.

The Rio Grande Oil Company, which would become the Richfield Oil Company, was founded in 1915 at El Paso, Texas. The company grew rapidly, in part by supplying the U.S. Army during its pursuit of Pancho Villa after the Mexican guerrilla's raid on Columbus, New Mexico in 1916. However, the company fell on hard times during the Great Depression, and was forced to merge with several other companies in 1936 in the California-based Richfield Oil Co.

In 1957, Richfield, which had become a major producer of high-octane aviation fuel during World War II, became the first company to strike oil in Alaska, and eventually acquired leases on 2.5 million acres of federal land. However, by the mid-1960s, Richfield still was producing only 50 percent of its own crude for refining, and in 1966, the company merged with Atlantic Refining to form Atlantic Richfield. Two years later when the largest oil field in the Western Hemisphere was discovered at Prudhoe Bay, Alaska, the newly formed Atlantic Richfield was the largest federal leaseholder in the state.

At the time of the merger, Atlantic Richfield formed ARCO Chemical as a wholly owned subsidiary with the goal of developing a petrochemical business to complement its oil refineries. Robert D. Bent, former vice president of manufacturing for Atlantic Refining, was named president of ARCO Chemical, and would serve in that capacity until his retirement in 1977.

Initially, ARCO Chemical produced a modest line of waxes, ammonia, aromatics, and detergents. Then, in 1967, Atlantic Richfield and Halcon International formed the Oxirane Chemical Company, an engineering design and consulting company that also engaged in research and development. In 1969, Oxirane moved into manufacturing and built a $30 million plant at Bayport, Texas to produce propylene oxide, an intermediate chemical used in a broad range of consumer products, including production of urethane foam. The demand for propylene oxide grew rapidly—by the late 1970s, Oxirane was a $1 billion company in annual sales. In 1980, Atlantic Richfield purchased Halcon's share of Oxirane for $270 million and the assumption of $380 million in debt. Oxirane became part of ARCO Chemical, which became the world's leading producer of propylene oxide.

In 1969, the Department of Justice dropped its opposition to a merger between Atlantic Richfield and the Sinclair Oil & Refining Company. Richfield Oil had actually acquired Sinclair almost 30 years earlier, but continued to operate the company as a separate entity while the Department of Justice contested the merger as a violation of antitrust laws.

After the merger was finally allowed, Atlantic Richfield melded Sinclair Petrochemicals, Inc., a wholly owned subsidiary of Sinclair Oil, with ARCO Chemical. Among the assets ARCO Chemical acquired in the deal were intermediate chemical facilities on the former Lyondell Country Club property at Channelview, Texas. ARCO Chemical also launched a $1 billion expansion, which included opening petrochemical plants in Rotterdam, the Netherlands, and Ciba, Japan.

In 1979, ARCO Chemical built the world's first chemical plant designed specifically to produce methyl tertiary butyl ether (MTBE), an additive used to replace lead and enhance the octane of oxygenated fuels. In 1994, the Channelview plant was the largest MTBE facility in the world, and ARCO Chemical supplied MTBE to most of the major gasoline manufacturers in the United States.

Atlantic Richfield spun off part of ARCO Chemical in 1985 to create the Lyondell Petrochemical Corporation, another wholly owned subsidiary. Lyondell focused on developing commercial uses for olefins, a class of hydrocarbons that includes propylene, ethelyne, and butylenes, which had been a drain on ARCO Chemical's earnings. Lyondell grew dramatically in the late 1980s, and in 1989, Atlantic Richfield decided to sell 50 percent of the company in a public offering that brought in $1.4 billion.

Two years earlier, Atlantic Richfield, believing that ARCO Chemical could not reach its potential for growth as a wholly owned subsidiary, had also sold 17 percent of the company in a public offering that netted $591 million. All assets and liabilities of the ARCO Chemical division were transferred to the ARCO Chemical Company, which was officially incorporated in October 1987, with Atlantic Richfield retaining 83 percent of the stock. Earlier that year, ARCO Chemical had also acquired a chemical plant in Belgium. The following year, the company acquired majority interest in the Chiunglong Petrochemical Company in Taiwan and opened a chemical plant in Fos-sur-Mer, France.

In July 1990, an explosion at ARCO Chemical's petrochemical plant in Channelview, Texas, on the Houston Ship Channel, killed 17 workers and injured five others. An investigation by the Occupational Safety and Health Administration (OSHA) indicated that the nighttime explosion occurred when flammable vapors built up inside an empty 900,000 gallon tank used to hold chemicals and wastewater for treatment. The tank was being repaired and the vapors apparently were ignited by a spark from equipment being used by maintenance workers. Eleven of those killed were maintenance workers.

OSHA cited ARCO Chemical with 347 "willful" safety violations—one for each worker at the site—for failing to protect employees against the hazards of an explosive atmosphere and using improper electrical devices in a hazardous area. OSHA also cited the company for 16 "serious" violations, including providing inadequate employee training on handling hazardous wastes, failing to adequately maintain fire-fighting equipment, and failing to develop an emergency's response plan in conjunction with local, state, or federal agencies. The plant was shut down after the explosion and was not fully back in operation until January 1991—six months later.

In 1991, ARCO Chemical agreed to pay a record fine of $3.48 million. At the time, the company said it did "not agree with all of the OSHA citations, but ... feels its interests are better served by focusing on improving work place safety" than challenging the charges.

Harold A. Sorgenti, who had become president of ARCO Chemical in 1979, took early retirement in 1991, a move many industry analysts ascribed to the Channelview explosion. He was succeeded by Alan R. Hirsig, who had been president of ARCO Chemical Europe. In 1992, Hirsig told the *Philadelphia Business Journal*, "[The explosion] was a shock to the com-

pany. [We] had always prided ourselves on our technological expertise, which we certainly had. But we had expanded so rapidly in the middle to late 80s that I think the Channelview tragedy really made us stand back and say, 'We need to slow down our expansion, our building of new plants.'"

Hirsig instituted a quality control program. He also announced that ARCO Chemical would begin placing greater emphasis on foreign opportunities, especially in Europe, where governments were expected to implement air-quality standards that would create expanded markets for the company's gasoline additives.

However, despite the strong prospects for growth, ARCO Chemical failed to earn its dividend in 1993 for the third straight year. With a net income of $214 million on sales of $3.2 billion, the company earned $2.23 per common share while paying out a dividend of $2.50. In the annual report for 1993, Hirsig and Lodwrick M. Cook, chairman of the board, blamed lower gasoline prices in the United States for driving down the price of MTBE, one of the company's leading products. ARCO Chemical also took a $56 million charge in 1993 to divest itself of a poorly performing joint venture in Korea.

In 1993, the company introduced ethyl tertiary butyl ether (ETBE), a gasoline additive made from corn-based ethanol. ARCO Chemical expects ETBE to be a key ingredient in reformulated gasolines when stricter U.S. automobile emission standards go into effect in 1995. MTBE has been used primarily to reduce carbon monoxide during cold weather. The new standards will require the use of reformulated gasolines year-round in high-pollution urban areas.

The 1993 annual report quotes marketing manager Alex Blagojevic: "We now have the ability to serve as a regular, large volume supplier of ETBE nearly two years before the (reformulated gasoline) requirement. This strongly differentiates us from the competition. With these two products (MTBE and ETBE), we also can provide customers with excellent options for both winter and summer air quality programs."

Principal Subsidiaries: ARCO Chemical Americas Company, Newtown Square, Pennsylvania; ARCO Chemical Europe, Inc. (England); ARCO Chemical Asia Pacific, Ltd. (Hong Kong).

Further Reading:

"1966–1991: 25 Years of Excellence," ARCO Chemical Company, Newtown Square, PA, 1991.
"ARCO Paying Record Safety Fine," *Business Insurance*, January 7, 1991.
Roberts, William L., "Arco Chemical CEO Hirsig: New Initiatives or the Future," *Philadelphia Business Journal*, June 29, 1992.
Suro, Roberto, "Explosion Kills 17 at Petrochemical Plant in Texas," *The New York Times*, July 7, 1990.

—Dean Boyer

ᎡᏒᏒᎧᏯ

Arrow Electronics, Inc.

25 Hub Drive
Melville, New York 11727
U.S.A.
(516) 391-1300
Fax: (516) 391-1401

Public Company
Incorporated: 1935 as Arrow Radio
Employees: 4,600
Sales: $2.56 billion
Stock Exchanges: New York
SICs: 5065 Electronic Parts & Equipment NEC

With operations in North America, Europe, and the Pacific Rim, Arrow Electronics, Inc., based in Melville, New York, is the largest distributor of electronic components in the world. Sales, which reached $2.56 billion in 1993, were expected to exceed $3 billion in 1994, as the company continued a strategy of growth built on acquisitions, consolidations, and economies of scale begun in the late 1970s.

Arrow Electronics was founded in 1935 as Arrow Radio, a retail outlet in New York City selling used radio equipment. However, Arrow's emergence as a major distributor of electronic components dates from 1968, when the company was purchased by three recent graduates of the Harvard School of Business.

By the mid-1960s, Arrow was selling a variety of home entertainment products and also had moved into electronic parts distribution. In 1968, B. Duke Glenn, Jr., Roger E. Green, and John C. Waddell, then working for an investment banking firm in New York, recognized the potential for growth in electronic parts distribution, and bought the company for $1 million in borrowed capital. They also purchased a company that reclaimed lead from old car batteries.

Using cash from the profitable lead reclamation business, the new owners began expanding Arrow's inventory of electronic parts, which allowed them to service their customers better. They also sacrificed profits, through aggressive pricing, in order to build volume. By 1971, Arrow had become the tenth largest electronic parts distributor in the United States, although still far behind Avnet, Inc., the leading electronic parts distributor.

During the 1970s, Arrow continued its climb up the ranks of the largest distributors of electronic parts in the United States—to number nine in 1972, number five in 1976, and number four in 1977—primarily through internal growth. In 1974, Arrow also became the first distributor of electronic parts to introduce an on-line computerized inventory system to speed up delivery. Then in 1979, Arrow acquired West Coast-based Cramer Electronics, then the country's second largest distributor of electronic parts, with $150 million in annual sales. Although the acquisition, financed with junk bonds, left Arrow heavily in debt, it more than doubled the company's revenues. Its chief rival, Avnet, was still three times as big, but for the first time, Arrow could claim a national presence. Arrow was listed on the New York Stock Exchange in 1979.

With the takeover of Cramer Electronics, Arrow appeared to have fulfilled the vision of its 1969 annual report, which had predicted: "Significant opportunities exist for us in the electronics distribution business owing mainly to the fragmented competitive environment. . . . It appears likely that the future will belong increasingly to those few substantial distribution companies with the financial resources, the professional managements, and the modern control systems necessary to participate fully in the industry's current consolidation phase." Arrow would close 1980 with $350 million in sales.

But in December of 1980, a blistering fire raced through the conference center of a hotel in Harrison, New York, killing 13 senior executives from Arrow, who had gathered for the company's annual budget meetings. Among the dead were Glenn, then chairman of the company; Green, then an executive vice-president, and all the department heads from the electronics distribution division. Only Waddell, then an executive vice-president, who had stayed behind at company headquarters to answer questions about a two-for-one stock split announced earlier that day, survived from the senior management team.

In a remarkable display of courage, Lynn Glenn, the widow of the company's chief executive, addressed employees at company headquarters the day after the fire. "I don't know your faces," she said, "but I'd know your names, because Duke always talked about you. The company will go on. It won't be sold. You'll be getting calls from competitors, but don't be spooked. Keep the faith." According to *Fortune,* she then "fled into an adjoining office and burst into tears." Despite her resolve, Arrow's stock fell 19 percent on the first day of trading after the fire, and fell another 14 percent before the month was out.

Waddell, who was named acting chief executive officer, embarked on what *Fortune* described as "a one-man campaign to assure security analysts, money managers, and journalists that the company was stable and recovery was underway." However, although sales held steady and none of the remaining managers were lured away to the competition, Arrow's stock continued to fall. That spring, the electronics industry was plunged into a recession, further crippling Arrow's recovery. By the time Arrow's stock bottomed out early in 1982, it had lost 60 percent of its value.

Meanwhile, Waddell also was trying to rebuild Arrow's senior management team. One of his first decisions was to go outside the company to recruit senior executives, rather than promote from within. That included finding someone to become chief executive officer. ''If I'd had my druthers,'' Waddell later told *Fortune*, ''I would have said to the board, there's only one person who can be CEO of this company for the time being, because nobody understands this child the way Waddell understands it.''

However, the board did not the same opinion of Waddell, whom *Fortune* described as ''slender and elegant . . . a figure from a bygone era, an apparition out of F. Scott Fitzgerald or The Thin Man,'' and in July of 1981, Arrow lured Alfred J. Stein away from Motorola to be president and chief executive officer. Waddell remained as chairman. ''Stein was clearly the biggest management coup in the history of distribution,'' Waddell told *Fortune* three years later. ''You should have seen the congratulatory letters and telegrams.''

Unfortunately, Stein, who also had worked at Texas Instruments, did not mesh well at Arrow. Rob Klatell, then company attorney, later told *Fortune* that with Stein's background in manufacturing, he ''kept looking for a facility to manage, and all he had were these crazy salesmen running around.'' The board fired Stein early in 1982, and named Waddell to the position he felt he deserved. Six months later, Waddell recruited Stephen Kaufman, a former partner with McKinsey & Co., to be president of Arrow's electronics division.

In 1982, sales held steady at about $550 million and Arrow lost $1.19 a share. But in 1983, with the recession in the electronics industry over, sales reached $1.4 billion and Arrow earned 85 cents per share. In 1984, *Fortune* declared that ''Kaufman's arrival marks the moment at which Arrow's cruelly unconventional problem came to an end.''

In 1983, with Arrow celebrating its financial and emotional recovery, Waddell told *Forbes*: ''Our strategic exercise for a decade has been to get position. It cost us a lot of time, money and aggravation. [After the fire] the overwhelming reality in my life was that I had a job to do. Now it's time to turn our attention to cashing in on a ten year investment.''

The company made a major move in 1985 when Arrow purchased a 40 percent interest in Spoerle Electronic, which was already the largest distributor of electronic components in Germany. As *Forbes* later reported, Kaufman, who spent several years in Europe as a consultant with McKinsey & Co., was ''a confirmed internationalist. At the time, no other American electronics distributor had invested consistently in the fragmented European market, but Kaufman was convinced that Europe's internal trade barriers would fall and that Arrow could score big.'' Since then, Arrow has increased its share in Spoerle to 70 percent, and has acquired 14 more European companies to become the largest electronics distributor in Europe.

However, Arrow first had to struggle through another downturn in the electronics industry, which struck about the same time the company unveiled the first fully automated robotic warehouse for electronics parts distribution in Brookhaven, New York. Annual sales fell by 30 percent and Arrow lost $45 million

between 1985 and 1988. Waddell relinquished the role of CEO to Kaufman in 1986, although he remained chairman.

Arrow resumed its growth strategy in 1988 by acquiring Kierulff Electronics, then the fourth largest electronics distributor in the United States, for $125 million. *Financial World* noted, ''Although economies of scale in electronics distribution are notoriously hard to come by, the . . . purchase complements Arrow's network nicely—and gives Arrow the $1 billion heft it has been looking for.'' Arrow shut down all four Kierulff warehouses and, as *Forbes* reported, ''As if by a miracle, within a year Arrow's bottom line went from a $16 million operating loss in 1987 to operating profits of $10 million.'' To reduce its debt, Arrow also sold its lead reclamation business in 1988.

In 1991, Arrow acquired Lex Electronics, formerly Schweber Electronics and the third largest distributor in the United States, and Almac Electronics Corporation, from their British-based parent Lex Service, Plc. The company also acquired a 50 percent interest in Silverstar Ltd. S.p.A., the largest electronics distributor in Italy. A year later, Arrow purchased Lex Service's distribution businesses in France and the United Kingdom. Arrow affiliate Spoerle acquired Lex Electronics in Germany.

In 1993, Arrow became the first electronics distributor to claim a global reach when it acquired Components Agents Ltd., the largest multinational Pacific Rim distributor with operations in Hong Kong, Singapore, Malaysia, China, and South Korea. The same year, Arrow purchased the distribution division of Zeus Components, Inc., a distributor of high-reliability electronic components for the U.S. military; CCI Electronique, a French distributor; and majority interest in Amitron S.A. and the ATD Group, electronics distributors in Spain and Portugal.

Arrow moved into Scandinavia in 1994 by acquiring Field Oy, a Finnish company, and the TH:s Group, the leading distributor in Norway. The company also acquired Exatec A/S, one of the largest electronics distributors in Denmark, and increased its stake in Silverstar to a majority share. Kaufman also became chairman of the company in 1994, with Waddell retaining the title of vice-chairman.

Although Avnet remained the largest electronics distributor in the United States, it was late entering the European market and Arrow was easily the global leader with 125,000 original equipment manufacturers and commercial customers around the world. The company also maintained more than $500 million in inventory from more than 200 leading manufacturers.

In its annual report for 1993, Arrow noted, ''In the global markets served by Arrow, electronics distribution is now nearly a $25 billion business, with growth prospects greater today than at any time in the past.'' The annual report goes on to predict, ''As we embark on a second quarter-century of strategic leadership, Arrow will remain the company that others follow into the new world of electronics distribution.''

Principal Subsidiaries: Cramer Electronics; Spoerle Electronic; Arrow Electronique S.A.; Components Agents Ltd.; Silverstar Ltd., S.p.A.; Arrow-Field Oy; TH:s Electronik AB; Amitron-Arrow S.A.; ATD Electronica S.A.; Arrow Electronics Ltd.; Almac Electronics Corporation; Zeus Components, Inc.

Further Reading:

Alster, Norm, "I Am a Growth Guy," *Forbes,* February 15, 1993, p. 118.
Bernstein, James, "Unrivaled Rivals," *Newsday,* June 13, 1994, p. C1.
Magnet, Myron, "Arrow Electronics Struggles Back," *Fortune,* April 30, 1984, p. 77.
McGough, Robert, "Phoenix," *Forbes,* June 6, 1983, p. 82.
Rayner, Bruce C. P., "Arrow's Kaufman: Planning a Profitable Path," *Electronic Business,* May 1, 1987, p. 47.

—Dean Boyer

Arthur Andersen & Company, Société Coopérative

18, quai General-Guisan
1211 Geneva 3
Switzerland
41 22 214 444
Fax: 41 22 214 418

Private Company
Incorporated: 1989
Employees: 66,478
Operating Revenues: $6.02 billion
SICs: 8721 Accounting, Auditing & Bookkeeping Services;
  8742 Management Consulting Services

Arthur Andersen & Company, Société Coopérative, is a Swiss-based entity created to manage and coordinate the worldwide operations of Arthur Anderson and Company and Andersen Consulting, two divisions of Arthur Anderson, the largest accounting and consulting firm in the United States and the third largest in the world after Ernst & Young and KPMG. The two units were created in 1989; Arthur Anderson and Co. provides auditing and tax services as well as specialty business and corporate services, while Andersen Consulting is the world's largest provider of management consulting services in technology, systems integration, and application software products.

The founder and guiding force behind the early years of the accounting firm was Arthur Edward Andersen. Born in Plano, Illinois, in 1885, Andersen was the son of a Norwegian couple who had immigrated to the United States four years earlier. At a young age, Andersen displayed a propensity for mathematics. Upon graduating from high school, he worked in the office of the comptroller at Allis-Chalmers Company in Chicago, while attending classes at the University of Illinois. In 1908, he received a degree as a certified public accountant from the university and at 23 years old became the youngest CPA in Illinois.

From 1907 to 1911, Andersen served as senior accountant for Price Waterhouse in Chicago. Following a one-year term as comptroller for the Uihlein business interests in Milwaukee, primarily Schlitz Brewing Company, Andersen was appointed chairperson of Northwestern University's accounting depart-

ment. Soon thereafter, however, in 1913, Andersen decided to establish his own accounting firm. At the age of 28, he founded the public accounting firm of Andersen, DeLany & Company in Chicago.

Andersen's small company began to grow rapidly, as demand for auditing and accounting services increased dramatically following Congress's establishment of federal income tax and the Federal Reserve in 1913. One of Arthur Andersen's first clients was Schlitz Brewing, and the company's client list soon expanded to include International Telephone & Telegraph, Colgate-Palmolive, Parker Pen, and Briggs & Stratton. However, the company's primary business consisted of numerous utility companies throughout the Midwest, including Cincinnati Gas & Electric Company, Detroit Natural Gas Company, Milwaukee Gas Light Company, and Kansas City Power & Light Company. Into the 1920s, work for utility companies comprised about 50 percent of Andersen's total revenues, and the company became known as a "utility firm," a dubious distinction in accounting circles. In 1917, Andersen was awarded the degree of B.B.A. from Northwestern University, and, the following year, when DeLany left the partnership, his firm became known as Arthur Andersen & Company.

Licensed as accountants and auditors in many states across the country, the company grew rapidly during the 1920s. The firm opened six offices nationwide, the most important of which were located in New York (1921), Kansas City (1923), and Los Angeles (1926). Serving as auditor for many large industrial corporations, Arthur Andersen also began providing financial and industrial investigation services during this time. In 1927, company representatives testified as expert witnesses in the Ford Motor Company tax case. However, the company's most important investigation, a milestone in the history of Arthur Andersen & Company, involved Samuel Insull's financial empire.

Samuel Insull emigrated from England to the United States in 1892. Hired as a secretary by Thomas Edison, Insull would soon prove to be an adept entrepreneur. During this time, the use of Edison's incandescent lights was provided only to licensed utility companies, which became known as "Edison Companies." As many of Chicago's utilities approached bankruptcy early in the twentieth century, Edison sought someone to organize them and keep them solvent. Insull volunteered for the job and immediately began to acquire and manage his own utility companies. In a few years, Insull had built an empire of utility companies, including the first utility to construct a generator with a capacity more than 12,000 kilowatts. In 1907, Insull created Commonwealth Edison, which was formed by the merger of two Insull holdings, Commonwealth Electric and Chicago Edison.

By the early 1930s, Insull's utilities, many of which had suffered during the Great Depression, represented a complicated network of holdings nearly $40 million in debt and badly in need of reorganization. When the Chicago banking community—on which Insull had always relied exclusively—was unable to provide the required cash, Insull was forced to turn to the East Coast banks for help. The East Coast banks refused to extend financial assistance, but, rather than forcing Insull into bankruptcy, they chose Arthur Andersen to act as their representative and manage the reorganization and refinancing of Insull's business holdings.

In 1932, the firm was placed in charge of supervising all the Insull utility companies' income and expenditures and was also involved in the subsequent financial reorganization of all the Edison companies within Insull's empire. To Arthur Andersen's credit, none of the utility companies went bankrupt; the firm maintained a firm control on all the assets during the period of refinancing. Moreover, Arthur Andersen not only increased its gross revenues by 20 percent through the Insull account but also garnered a reputation for honesty and independence that heightened its stature in the business community across the country. Thereafter, the company had no difficulty attracting large corporate clients. The incident also gave rise to the company's self-proclaimed role as watchdog of the accounting industry's methods and procedures.

Andersen not only provided direction for his company and personally approved of all the firm's clients, but he remained involved in nearly every aspect and detail of company business. Until the day he died, he paid himself 50 percent of the firm's profits, while the other 50 percent was distributed among the rest of the partners. As he grew older, and as the company grew increasingly successful, Andersen became less tolerant of those within the firm who disagreed with him or began to eclipse his leadership, and he tended to fire or drive out those with whom he wasn't compatible. Nevertheless, he had an uncanny sense of hiring particularly talented accountants, and many of the individuals hired during the 1920s and 1930s would play prominent roles in the company's development years later.

Under the watchful eye of its founder, Arthur Andersen and Company brought in many new accounts during the 1930s, including Montgomery Ward, one of the most sought-after clients during the decade. By 1928, the company employed approximately 400 people, and, by 1940, that figure had increased to 700. To provide greater accessibility to its clients, the firm opened new offices in Boston and Houston (1937) and in Atlanta and Minneapolis (1940).

During World War II Andersen himself reached the pinnacle of his success. His numerous writings on accounting—including "Duties and Responsibilities of the Comptroller" and "Present Day Problems Affecting the Presentation and Interpretation of Financial Statements"—prompted a growing admiration and respect for him in financial, industrial, and academic circles. Andersen served as president of the board of Trustees at Northwestern University and as a faculty member in accounting at the school. In recognition of his contribution to the field of accounting, and also for his devotion to preserving Norwegian history, he was awarded honorary degrees by Luther College, St. Olaf College, and Northwestern.

During this time, Andersen began grooming his associate, Leonard Spacek, for the company's leadership position. Spacek joined the company in 1928 and was named a partner in 1940, becoming one of Andersen's closest and most trusted confidants. Upon Andersen's death in January 1947, Spacek took over the company, remaining committed to the regimented management style of the founder. During Spacek's tenure, the

firm grew from a regional operation located in Chicago with satellite offices across the United States into an international organization with one-stop, total service offices located around the world. Most importantly, however, Spacek began to focus on Andersen's idea that the company serve the public role of industry policeman.

Until the 1950s, the accounting profession was generally regarded as a club, with its own principles, methods, and procedures that had developed over the years without any standardization. Spacek began a campaign to improve accounting methods and practice by emphasizing the importance of implementing uniform accounting principles that would ensure "fairness." Spacek argued that accounting principles should be fair to the consumer, to labor, to the investor, to management, and to the public. Spacek hoped that his concept of fairness would serve as a foundation for accounting principles that the whole profession would ultimately find acceptable.

Most business historians agree that Spacek did the profession a service by initiating the standardization movement within the industry and by bringing public attention to the fact that existing auditing practices varied according to each company. Yet like Andersen before him, Spacek drew considerable criticism from the profession. Unable to change the prevailing attitudes of those within the industry, Spacek focused on his own company, creating Andersen University, with its Center for Professional Education. A training center located in St. Charles, Illinois, the university provided company employees with the opportunity to attend courses in a variety of accounting subjects.

By the time Spacek retired from the company in 1973, Arthur Andersen & Company had opened 18 new offices in the United States and over 25 offices in countries throughout the world. With a staff of over 12,000 and an increase of revenues from $6.5 million to over $51 million during the period from 1947 to 1973, Andersen had grown into one of the world's preeminent accounting firms. The company also featured a profitable consulting service, helping large corporations install and use their first computer systems in the 1950s and branching out into production control, cost accounting, and operations research in the 1960s. Moreover, with audit and accounting revenues reaching a plateau due to the maturity of the industry, the company's consulting services began to represent an increasing share of Andersen's income. In the 1970s, Arthur Andersen became involved in a host of consulting activities, including systems integration services, strategic services, developing software application products, and providing a variety of additional technological services.

Under the aggressive leadership of Spacek's successor, Harvey Kapnick, the consulting services developed rapidly, and by 1979, its fees represented over 20 percent of Andersen's total revenues. Anticipating the importance of the burgeoning market for consulting services, Kapnick proposed to split the company into two separate firms, one to oversee auditing and another to focus on consulting as a comprehensive service business. When he presented this proposal to the company's partners, however, he met with protest. The auditors summarily rejected Kapnick's strategy, demanding proprietary control over all aspects of the company's managerial and financial affairs.

Kapnick resigned in October 1979 and was replaced by Duane Kullberg, who had joined the company in 1954 as an auditor. Reassuring the auditors that he would not take any action to split the company along operational lines, Kullberg nevertheless gave more operating control to the consulting side of the business, where employees were becoming increasingly irritated with the centralized control of the auditors. Kullberg's strategy seemed to work; internal discord subsided and both the auditing partners and the consulting principals (who were not called partners until later) devoted themselves to their respective businesses.

However, other problems arose for Arthur Andersen. In the mid-1980s, the company was the subject of several lawsuits filed by creditors and shareholders of bankrupt companies the firm had audited. These companies—including DeLorean Motors Company, Financial Corporation of American (American Savings & Loan), Drysdale Government Securities, and others—claimed that Arthur Andersen had failed to realize the extent of their financial struggles, and, moreover, had failed to inform the public of their findings. In 1984, Arthur Andersen was forced to pay settlements amounting to $65 million within a two-month period.

Nevertheless, Arthur Andersen's business continued to thrive, particularly in the field of consulting services. By 1988, 40 percent of the company's total revenues were generated from consulting fees, making Arthur Andersen the largest consulting firm in the world. During this time, conflict between the auditors and the consultants flared up again, centering on discrepancies in the pay scale and disagreement over the control of consulting operations. Specifically, consultants questioned why they should earn less than auditors, when typical auditing projects brought in $4 million in fees in 1988, and consulting jobs garnered as much as $25 million. Furthermore, consultants took issue with the company's practice of allowing accounting partners to manage the consulting business.

Tensions continued to increase; when the firm's disgruntled consulting partners resigned, management filed lawsuits and infiltrated meetings held by the consultants. Finally, in an effort to end the chaos, Kullberg agreed to restructure the company. Under Kullberg's plan, Arthur Andersen was divided into two entities, an auditing and tax firm known as Arthur Andersen & Company and a consulting firm dubbed Andersen Consulting. Each of these firms then became separate financial entities under the Swiss-based Arthur Andersen Societe Cooperative, the ruling body of the company's worldwide organization,

which would coordinate the activities of the entire firm's operations. In addition, the traditional management hierarchy, in which consultants reported to auditors, was altered, allowing consultants to report to managers in their field all the way up through the level of consulting partner.

In 1989, Lawrence A. Weinbach replaced Kullberg as chief executive officer. A graduate of the Wharton Business School, Weinbach had joined Arthur Andersen and became a partner after nine years. Known for his diplomacy, Weinbach helped smooth over the harsh feelings among auditing and consulting partners, encouraging everyone to concentrate on increasing business. Under his leadership, Arthur Andersen's revenues skyrocketed. Between 1988 and 1992, Andersen's revenues increased from just under $3 billion to almost $5.6 billion, an increase of nearly 50 percent brought on mostly by the company's burgeoning consulting activities. During these years, revenue from Andersen Consulting grew by 89 percent while revenue from Arthur Andersen & Company's accounting and tax services grew by 38 percent. Clearly, Weinbach recognized the importance of the company's position as the largest management consultant firm in the world.

In the early 1990s, Arthur Andersen was beset with lawsuits from creditors of thrifts that had collapsed during the 1980s. Furthermore, in 1992, the company was sued by the government's watchdog Resolution Trust Corporation for negligence in its auditing of the failed Ben Franklin Savings & Trust. Nevertheless, the company weathered these difficulties, renewing its commitment to high-quality, irreproachable auditing services and focusing on improving and developing both its auditing and consulting services. In 1993, total revenues surpassed the $6 billion mark, primarily due to an increase in management consulting fees.

As it approached the turn of the century, the company's future seemed to depend on the success of the measures taken by Kullberg and Weinbach to settle the rift between auditors and consultants, as well as the company's ability to overcome accusations of negligence made earlier in the decade. However, most analysts regarded Arthur Andersen's position as the world's preeminent auditing and consulting firm secure.

Further Reading:

Spacek, Leonard, *The Growth of Arthur Andersen and Company, 1928–1973: An Oral History,* New York: Garland, 1989.
Stevens, Mark, *The Big Six,* Simon & Schuster: New York, 1991.

—Thomas Derdak

Autodesk, Inc.

2320 Marinship Way
Sausalito, California 94965
U.S.A.
(415) 332-2344
Fax: (415) 331-8093

Public Company
Incorporated: 1982
Employees: 1,565
Sales: $353.2 million
Stock Exchanges: NASDAQ
SICS: 7372 Prepackaged Software

Autodesk, Inc. is the largest design automation software company in the world, with a variety of software products available in more than 85 countries and in 18 languages. Autodesk has holdings in Switzerland, Austria, Spain, Germany, England, Japan, Australia, and the Czech Republic. Its headquarters are located in Sausalito, California, a few miles north of San Francisco.

Autodesk was founded in 1982 by computer programmer and entrepreneur John Walker, whom *PC Week* columnist Jesse Berst described as "the most brilliant and the most bizarre person I've ever met." Walker acquired the software for a computer-aided design program known as AutoCAD from inventor Michael Riddle, in exchange for $10 million in royalties. The following year, his new company, Autodesk, introduced the AutoCAD program to the public. As the market for personal computers and software escalated, Autodesk experienced rapid success. During this time, Autodesk established a unique policy of eschewing conventional management personnel, experienced in business strategies and financial planning, in favor of a management team consisting of computer programmers like Walker.

In 1985, Walker took Autodesk public, and, the following year, he left his position in the company's management in order to pursue his interest in programming. As a result, Walker developed an AutoCAD supplement designed specifically for the construction industry. The supplement, marketed through Autodesk, allowed engineers to generate price quotes and construction schedules from information available in their designs. By this time, 40,000 AutoCAD packages had been shipped for sale.

In the summer of 1987, Autodesk initiated a second issuing of stock, offering 2.5 million shares at $24.00 per share. The capital generated from this offering enabled the company to eliminate some of its debts. In 1988, Autodesk had assets of over $100 million in cash and securities, while revenues increased 40 percent over the previous year. By 1989, Autodesk was enjoying a 60 percent share of the market for personal computer automated design software, with sales worth $117 million.

By the early 1990s, growth at Autodesk, and the company's dependence on AutoCAD, necessitated a restructuring of the company's operations. Five separate support units were created, each overseeing one of the company's five main product lines, all of which were designed for use with AutoCAD. Moreover, the company purchased a 20 percent equity interest in Ithaca Software, producer of the Hoops Graphics System. Hoops Graphics proved valuable when integrated with AutoCAD, resulting in a more user-friendly product, and Autodesk would acquire Ithaca Software in its entirety in August 1993.

In April 1992, Carol A. Bartz was named CEO of Autodesk. Bartz, who had a bachelor's degree in computer science from the University of Wisconsin and had served as a vice-president at Sun Microsystems, became one of only two women to head a major U.S. company in the high technology industry. In addition to her duties at Autodesk, Bartz was a boardmember of Cadence Design Systems, Inc. and Airtouch Communications, Inc., a company owned by Pacific Telesis.

Upon her appointment at Autodesk, Bartz developed three primary goals for the company: building Autodesk into a $1 billion company by 1999, decreasing the company's reliance on AutoCAD as the primary source of revenue, and moving the company into computer-aided manufacturing in addition to design. Bartz also reorganized the company, imposing a more traditional management structure, building a new executive team, and working with software engineers to further tailor AutoCAD to the needs of the public.

In order to sharpen its focus on design automation, Autodesk divested its interests in AMIX, an electronic shopping network, and Xanadu, a database software company, while acquiring Micro Engineering Solutions, a firm concerned with computer modeling software. In 1993, Autodesk purchased the net assets of Woodbourne, Inc., an acquisition which brought Woodbourne's solid-modeling technology to Autodesk.

That year, a lien was placed on $5 million of Autodesk's fourth quarter profits, as a result of a class action suit filed by stockholders. The plaintiffs had purchased stock in the company between May 6, 1991 and January 30, 1992, and, when Autodesk experienced a 35 percent drop in earnings in the second quarter of 1992, they filed the lawsuit. Although Autodesk maintained that the suit was without merit, the company paid a settlement in an attempt to curb litigation costs. In fiscal 1994, Autodesk expended over $70 million for the repurchase of common stock in order to avoid dilution caused by employee stock plans.

John Walker officially severed his ties with Autodesk in 1994, in favor of engineering special projects in Switzerland. By that time, Autodesk had shipped one million software packages worldwide, and AutoCAD remained the primary source of company revenue. Sales of AutoCAD and AutoCAD updates accounted for 85 percent of Autodesk's revenues in 1994, while net revenues reached $405.6 million, with foreign sales accounting for 58 percent of those revenues.

Nevertheless, Autodesk had developed several other product lines, including: Generic CADD; AutoCAD LT, a CAD program compatible with Windows; AutoSketch, a two-dimensional drafting program available with either DOS or Windows compatibility; AutoCAD Designer, a program enabling the user to perform solid-model drafting; Advanced Modeling Extension 2.1, another solid-modeling program, which interfaced with AutoCAD; Generic CADD 6.1, a design and drafting program compatible with AutoCAD files; and AutoCAD Data Extension, a program allowing the user to work with multiple drawings concurrently. The company also developed AutoSurf, a program based on AutoCAD Release 12, for two-and three-dimensional design; Autodesk Manufacturingexpert, another program incorporating AutoCAD Release 12; Aemulus and Aemulusmf, allowing interchange between AutoCAD and CADAM files; AutoCAD IGES Translator 5.1, a CAD translation program; Home Series, a program for use in home design drafting; 3D Studio, a program with a variety of modeling and animation applications; and Autovision, a program interactive with AutoCAD Release 12 which enabled users to produce photorealistic still renderings. A pioneer in the exploration of the potential of virtual reality, Autodesk also offered Animator Pro, 3-D Studio, and a Cyperspace Developer Kit.

Autodesk's products had applications in a wide variety of fields, including architecture, engineering, construction, geographic information systems, mechanical design, and videography. Among Autodesk's major clients were Chevron, Kohler, Sony Pictures, and Japan's Nippon Telegraph and Telephone Corporation. Chevron used a combined package of AutoCAD Release 12, ADE software, and an Autodesk Geological Information System program to monitor its assets and leases on land and offshore; Kohler used AutoCAD, AutoSurf, and AutoMill to design plumbing fixtures such as bathtubs, toilets, and sinks; and Sony Pictures employed 3D Studio in plotting camera angles prior to actual filming. In addition, Autodesk earned a $550 million contract to provide CAD 2 to the Naval Facilities Engineering Command.

Autodesk continued to cooperate with other software purveyors, forming alliances in which the companies involved produced programs while maintaining their autonomy. In 1993, Autodesk developed a means of using AutoCAD Release 12 on an IBM OS/2 2.0 operating system, and, the following year, Autodesk announced a cooperative venture with Xaos Tools, Inc., intended to produce image-processing software compatible with Autodesk's 3D Studio Release 3. Autodesk also announced the release of AutoSketch 2 for Microsoft's Windows. Other joint ventures included an agreement with Microsoft to develop Microsoft-compatible CAD programs for integration into Microsoft Office; the formation of a consulting agreement with UGC Consulting, a firm knowledgeable about the Geological Information Systems market; and an agreement with Silicon Graphics to jointly develop and release a program integrating a rendering feature of Autodesk's 3D Studio Release 3 into a Silicon Graphics program as well as to develop a Silicon Graphics-compatible edition of Autodesk's AutoVision.

In 1994, Autodesk operated approximately 750 Training Centers worldwide for the purpose of educating users in the applications of AutoCAD and other Autodesk software. Autodesk depended upon a network of dealers, distributors, and direct sales to disseminate its products, and devised a system of cooperation with third party software developers. This system, called AutoCAD Development system, or ADS, was devised in 1990 and was structured to encourage independent software developers to create add-on programs for Autodesk products and new applications for Autodesk's technologies. Over 2,000 independent developers worked to create specialized applications using Autodesk programs in 1994.

In the mid-1990s, Autodesk owned no real property; all facilities for management, product development, marketing, and production activities throughout the United States, Europe, and Asia were leased, including the facilities in Neufchatel, Switzerland, opened in 1993 at an expense of $1.4 million, in order to concentrate Autodesk's European production. Although Autodesk owned most of the equipment used in its business, the company's intellectual property and its network of programming and business talent were regarded as its chief assets.

Autodesk, like many other software companies, was challenged by the effects of software piracy in the early 1990s. In order to combat this practice, Autodesk joined forces with other high technology firms to form several regional organizations, including the Canadian Alliance Against Software Theft (CAAST) and the Business Software Alliance (BSA). The company has prevailed in litigation to protect its copyrights, including a 1994 suit against Cadisys Corporation, the result of which was a $100,000 settlement in Autodesk's favor on May 23, 1994.

As technology in the computer software industry changed, Autodesk remained flexible and willing to explore new technological and business possibilities, hoping to maintain its rank among the leading software companies. Autodesk's expansion into multimedia appeared to be keeping pace with, and even anticipating, market needs for innovations in these fields.

Principal Subsidiaries: Autodesk Retail Products, Inc.; Micro Engineering Solutions, Inc.

Further Reading:

''Autodesk: A Success Story,'' *Information Week,* July 23, 1990.

''Autodesk, Inc.,'' *Datamation,* June 12, 1993.

''Autodesk's Lucky Strike,'' *PC World,* December 1987.

Berst, Jesse, ''A Grown-Up Autodesk Faces the Cross-Roads,'' *PC Week,* January 17, 1994.

Clancy, Heather, ''Developing New Directions: Bartz Expected to Draft Plan for Resurgence at Autodesk,'' *Computer Reseller News,* April 27, 1992, p. 2.

Coale, Kristi, ''Leave Your Titles at the Door,'' *InfoWorld,* June 11, 1990, p. 55.

Dubashi, Jagannath, ''Autodesk: A Savvy Stock Player, Too,'' *Financial World,* February 23, 1988, p. 17.

Fisher, Lawrence M., ''Imposing a Hierarchy on a Gaggle of Techies,'' *New York Times,* November 29, 1992, p. F4.

Ould, Andrew, ''Autodesk Reorganizes into 5 Business Units,'' *PC Week,* July 8, 1991, p. 13.

"Quiet Winds of Change," *Computer-Aided Engineering,* May 1990, p. 8.

Rohrbough, Linda, "Autodesk to Pay $5 Million to Shareholders," *Newsbytes,* December 11, 1992.

——, "Sun Executive Carol Bartz Joins Autodesk as CEO," *Newsbytes,* April 15, 1992.

Zachary, G. Pascal, "Tech Shop: 'Theocracy of Hackers' Rules Autodesk Inc., a Strangely Run Firm," *Wall Street Journal,* May 28, 1992, p. A1(W)

—Susan Taylor-Babcock

B·A·A

BAA plc

130 Wilton Road
London SW1V 1LQ
United Kingdom
(071) 834-9449
Fax: (071) 932-6699

Public Company
Incorporated: 1987
Employees: 8,417
Sales: £2.85 billion
Stock Exchanges: London
SICs: 6711 Holding Companies; 4582 Airports & Airfields;
6799 Investors, Nec; 6552 Real Estate—Subdividers and
Developers

Celebrated by Margaret Thatcher as "a continuing British success story," BAA plc is a holding company for the world's largest organization of airports. BAA's seven airports—Heathrow, Gatwick, Stansted, Glasgow, Edinburgh, Aberdeen, and Southampton—service 73 percent of the passenger traffic and 84 percent of air cargo transportation in the United Kingdom. Originating as a government-owned enterprise known as the British Airports Authority, BAA became a private company in 1987 and has achieved a position of preeminence in airport development in the United Kingdom and around the world.

Great Britain's commercial airline industry began in 1919, when the Department of Civil Aviation was established as a division of the government's Air Ministry. When foreign competition nearly forced most British airlines out of business in 1921, the government provided temporary financial relief, and two years later, the Civil Air Transport Subsidies Committee was established to investigate long-term solutions to the airlines' economic struggles. The result was the 1924 formation of the government-owned and operated Imperial Airways, the first in a long line of British airlines under state ownership.

While World War II brought a halt to commercial aviation, wartime aeronautical developments left the industry poised for advancement when hostilities ceased. Under the postwar Labour government, the expanding industry consisted of three state-run airways corporations: British Overseas Airways Corporation (serving the Commonwealth, North America, and the Far East), British European Airways (covering domestic and short European flights), and British South American Airways.

Air traffic control facilities and the airports under development at this time were also run by the state.

Expansion in the industry was inevitable and remarkably swift during the 1950s, as air travel became a popular means of transportation. Faced with increasing numbers of passengers and technological developments in commercial aircraft, British airports strove to provide efficient, smoothly running, and attractive facilities that would lure the business of the country's most successful airlines.

As the boom in air transport continued into the 1960s, the burden of maintaining a network of state-of-the-art airports proved too complex and cumbersome a task for the government, and British airports began losing money. In 1965, the British government passed the Airports Authority Bill, which created a single statutory body to own and oversee operations of the country's airports while remaining answerable to Parliament. The following year, the new British Airports Authority officially took control of Heathrow, Gatwick, Stansted, and Prestwick. Under the direction of chairperson Peter Masefield, the British Airports Authority transformed the industry from a bureaucratic operation, similar to that of a public utility, into a profitable semi-independent business.

During the 1970s and early 1980s, airport profits rose dramatically, and a program of expansion and refurbishment was undertaken. In fact, the industry's increasing success prompted the Conservative government to consider the Authority a prime candidate for a privatization program it was planning for some of the country's industries. Towards this end, the Airports Act of 1986 permitted the creation of a new company, BAA plc, a public holding company for airports. The ensuing advertising campaign for BAA stock was designed to appeal to a wide variety of investors. In one publicity stunt, the company hired people to dress up as Harry Heathrow—a teddy bear character created especially for the promotion—and carry placards around airport terminals advertising BAA's initial stock offering price of 245 pence per share. With nearly two and a half million applications, the stock was oversubscribed ten times and the flotation—on July 16, 1987—was a resounding success. BAA fared well since its public offering. From 1987 to 1993, passenger numbers increased by 42 percent, BAA's share price more than tripled, and profits increased by 130 percent.

Among BAA's established operations during this time, none rivalled the rapid growth and success of London's premier airport, Heathrow. Originally envisioned as a ring of city airports, the "London Airport—Heath Row" was planned during the war and opened in 1946. At that time, tents served as Heathrow's terminals, while its offices were set up in vans. Eventually a more substantial terminal, the North Side Terminal, was established and remained in use through the 1950s, when it was replaced by the Europa terminal, later known as Terminal 2. The Heathrow Oceanic terminal (which became Terminal 3) opened in 1961, followed by two more terminals in 1968 and 1986.

By the 1990s, Heathrow was the world's busiest international airport. During this time, BAA proposed construction of a third runway at Heathrow. While airlines welcomed the idea of expanded facilities, local residents and environmental groups, including the Federation of Heathrow Anti-Noise Groups, were strongly opposed to the plan, which would have involved the demolition of some 3,500 homes in surrounding villages. In the face of such protests, BAA withdrew the proposal in May 1994. Similarly, BAA's plan to build a fifth terminal at Heathrow met with opposition. The terminal, expected to increase Heathrow's annual passenger capacity from 50 million in the early 1990s to 80 million by 2013, was criticized as involving further noise pollution and traffic jams in the area. However, BAA argued that new aircraft technology, including the development of larger aircraft, would allow more passengers without necessitating more planes and increased noise levels.

While some remained skeptical of BAA's promises, the company maintained that it was simply planning to ensure that London's airports remained adequately equipped to keep up with increasing demand. With 30 percent of Heathrow's business consisting of connecting flights, rather than final destinations, BAA faced the potential threat of competition in this sector from airports in Amsterdam, Brussels, Paris, and Frankfurt, which were poised to accommodate customers. Public inquiry into the feasibility of BAA's fifth terminal was set to begin at the end of 1994 and would likely continue for years; construction was not expected to be completed before the twenty-first century if at all. Nevertheless, BAA continued to expand services at Heathrow. Construction of a new flight connection center was expected to be completed in 1995, and, in an agreement with British Rail, the company was developing a Heathrow Express rail link to Paddington Station, due to open in 1997.

The second largest BAA airport servicing the London area was Gatwick, located 27 miles south of the city. During the late 1940s and early 1950s, Gatwick was known primarily as an airport for charter flights or as an alternative in the event of bad weather at Heathrow. Major reconstruction completed in 1956, however, helped Gatwick develop into a popular international flight destination. Plans to purchase more land and add a second runway to Gatwick stalled in 1979, when the British Airports Authority agreed with the West Sussex County Council that it would not pursue expansion for 40 years.

When Stansted Airport, established in the London area in the 1940s, was designated for expansion in 1967, strong local opposition forced the Authority to relocate Stansted off the Essex coast, in Maplin Sands. In the early 1970s, plans for expansion at this site were also abandoned, when the oil crises and economic recession prompted predictions of declines passenger volume. By the late 1970s, however, increasing air traffic was inevitable, and the expansion of Stansted seemed imminent, particularly since competition from nearby foreign airports, particularly in Amsterdam, had intensified.

Again, the Authority found itself embroiled in a lengthy public debate of the issue. In addition to environmentalist objections to the expansion, several airlines, including British Airways, protested the move, preferring their existing arrangements at Heathrow and Gatwick. Moreover, another interest group, the North of England Regional Consortium, representing northern regional airports and local authorities, lobbied to fill the growing market by developing provincial facilities rather than expanding Stansted. In 1985, a compromise was reached under

which Stansted would undergo development in phases monitored by Parliament.

Despite its ambitious $400 million redevelopment program, which garnered numerous awards for architecture, environmental sensitivity, and marketing, Stansted did not meet expectations for increased capacity and profits. In fact, in 1993, American Airlines withdrew its services from Stansted, and the airport reported heavy losses. During this time, Stansted's direct competitor, Luton, claimed that BAA was unfairly subsidizing Stansted from profits derived from Heathrow, creating artificially low prices in an effort to attract customers.

In addition to its London airports, BAA also acquired facilities in Scotland, including airports at Prestwick, Edinburgh, Glasgow, and Aberdeen, during the 1960s and 1970s. Until 1990, Prestwick was the only Scottish airport allowed to accommodate transatlantic flights. Then, under the government's new "open skies" policy, several airlines began gravitating toward the more popular sites of Glasgow and Edinburgh, boosting profits at these airports and prompting BAA to sell the relatively unprofitable Prestwick airport. Although BAA's Scottish airports service significantly fewer passengers than its London airports, the growth rate for Scotland's air travel industry surpassed that of London in 1993. Thus, BAA expected its Scottish airports to play an increasingly more prominent role in U.K. commercial aviation.

While a healthy percentage of BAA's profits reflected fees levied on the airlines that used its airports, the bulk of BAA's profits during the early 1990s were generated from an auxiliary enterprise: retail sales. Attracting many large retailers and caterers, BAA established vast shopping complexes at its airports, which featured outlets for Harrods, Yves St. Laurent, Burberry's, The Body Shop, Cartier, McDonald's, Burger King, and several others. Retail profits were also bolstered by companies providing car rental and parking lot operations.

Unlike most commercial operations, BAA's retail sales were largely unaffected by the economic recession of the early 1990s. In fact, while retail chains across the nation suffered losses, their airport branches reported healthy profits. Analysts suggested two reasons for this surprising statistic: many shoppers at airport stores were from foreign countries largely unaffected by the recession, and air travelers on the whole were likely to have more disposable income than the average consumer. To offset expected retail losses beginning in 1999, when Europeans will no longer be able to purchase duty-free goods, BAA increased retail space in its London airports by 50 percent between 1992 and 1994 and planned to double this area again by 1996. Restaurant operations at the airports were also expanded and diversified. The phenomenal success of BAA's airport shopping facilities prompted its mid-1990s joint venture with the U.S.-based McArthur Glen Realty to develop and operate outlet malls in the United Kingdom and Europe, where manufacturers will sell direct to the public.

An acknowledged expert in the industry, BAA increasingly put its experience to use in a variety of consultancy roles. In 1992, the company won a contract from the Greater Pittsburgh International Airport to develop and operate that airport's shops and restaurants. Moreover, as a designer of modern facilities known for their efficiency as well as their aesthetic merit, BAA secured several consulting contracts throughout the United Kingdom, Australia, Japan, Mexico, Hungary, St. Lucia, and the Bahamas, and played a prominent role in the planning of new airports in Hong Kong and Kuala Lumpur. Forecasting, engineering, computing, and market research are among the other skills that BAA offered its clients.

In response to increasing public concern for the environment, BAA created an Environment Department to address issues surrounding the airline industry's role in noise pollution, air quality, water quality, and wildlife preservation. The company published a policy statement, affirming its commitment to environmental conservation, and began the annual publication of a report on its performance in these areas. In the mid-1990s, BAA explored options to acquire equity stakes in airports around the world. Despite the strength of its retail and consultancy operations, BAA's commitment to this core business was evidenced by its plans to continue refurbishing and upgrading its airport facilities, as it strives to realize its avowed goal of becoming "the most successful airport company in the world."

Principal Subsidiaries: Aberdeen Airport Ltd.; Airports UK (Southampton) Ltd.; BAA Pittsburgh Inc.; Edinburgh Airport Ltd.; Gatwick Airport Ltd.; Glasgow Airport Ltd.; Heathrow Airport Ltd.; Lynton Holdings Ltd.; Lynton MHA Ltd.; Lynton Properties Ltd.; Stansted Airport Ltd.

Further Reading:

"Blue Skies Ahead for BAA," *Investors Chronicle,* March 12, 1993.

Davies, Peter, "Letter to the Editor," *The Times,* May 19, 1994, p. 17.

Donne, Michael, *Above Us the Skies: The Story of BAA,* London: BAA plc, 1991.

"Duty Free Heads for the Stratosphere," *Evening Standard,* March 1, 1994.

Elliott, Harvey, "BAA Abandons Third Runway for Heathrow," *The Times,* May 16, 1994, pp. 1–2.

Kay, William, "Ground Control Charts Way for Airport Boss" (interview with Sir John Egan), *Independent on Sunday,* November 21, 1993.

King, John, and Geoffrey Tait, *Golden Gatwick: 50 Years of Aviation,* London: The Royal Aeronautical Society Gatwick Branch and the British Airports Authority, 1980.

"Luton Accuses BAA of Predatory Airport Pricing," *Financial Times,* June 5, 1993.

Masefield, Sir Peter, "Letter to the Editor," *The Times,* May 19, 1994, p. 17.

"Nowhere to Land," *Economist,* August 14, 1993.

"Protests Greet Heathrow Scheme for Fifth Terminal," *Independent,* February 18, 1993.

"Special Report on Airports UK: Can the Plane Take the Strain?" *Evening Standard,* March 14, 1994.

"Special Report on Airports UK: Shops Strike it Rich," *Evening Standard,* March 14, 1994.

"Special Report on Airports UK: Why We Must Have Terminal Five," *Evening Standard,* March 14, 1994.

"The Terminal?" *Evening Standard,* June 21, 1993.

—Robin DuBlanc

Babbage's, Inc.

10741 King William Drive
Dallas, Texas 75220
U.S.A.
(214) 401-9000
Fax: (214) 401-9002

Public Company
Incorporated: 1983
Employees: 2,400
Sales: $233.4 million
Stock Exchanges: NASDAQ
SICs: 5734 Computer & Software Stores

Babbage's, Inc. is one of the largest consumer specialty software retailers in the United States, operating a chain of more than 300 stores, virtually all of which are located in regional shopping centers. Specializing in programs for home entertainment, productivity, and educational use, Babbage's outlets sell software in cartridge, floppy disk, and CD-Rom formats, supporting more than a dozen major personal computer and video game system platforms. Babbage's product line consists of over 1,400 items, which generally sell for below manufacturers' list prices. Major brands of video game systems, game software, and other entertainment software for personal computers represent about two-thirds of the company's sales. The company also sells computer accessories and supplies.

Babbage's, named for Charles Babbage, the nineteenth-century British mathematician generally credited with inventing the first major forerunner of a computer, traces its roots to two Harvard Business School classmates, James B. McCurry and Gary M. Kusin. At Harvard during the mid-1970s, McCurry and Kusin discussed going into business together but went in separate directions after graduation; McCurry became a consultant for Bain & Company's San Francisco office, while Kusin became a Dallas-based general merchandise manager for the Sanger-Harris division of Federated Department Stores. In 1982, McCurry approached Kusin with a business proposal to establish a chain of software stores that would capitalize on the burgeoning computer and home video game industries. His idea was based on the expectation that increasing consumer interest in computer equipment and games would make the specialty store the ideal marketing outlet. Kusin, who had been watching such specialty stores gradually take over department store business,

liked the idea, and, at the end of the year, both men quit their jobs and began seeking startup financing for a software business.

McCurry's and Kusin's business plan met with little interest among venture capitalists until February 1983, when businessman Ross Perot—who knew Kusin's family in Texarkana—offered to provide a $3 million credit line in exchange for one-third ownership in the company. Perot also advised the entrepreneurs to shelve their plan for immediately opening 20 stores in favor of establishing one outlet, which they would manage themselves until they knew the business inside and out. McCurry and Kusin took Perot's money and advice, and, on Memorial Day 1983, they opened the first Babbage's store in a Dallas regional mall. McCurry, the company's chairperson, managed the company's finances, while Kusin, the company's president, acquired software products from local distributors. Both partners took turns opening and closing the store and seeing to other administrative details.

During this time, McCurry and Kusin tested their business strategy, which involved four key provisions: a constantly updated mix of products, a competitive pricing system, a flexible store design with sections devoted to various computer and entertainment system platforms and software categories, and an enthusiastic, noncommissioned sales staff that would not intimidate customers with technical jargon. Two months after opening the first Babbage's store, McCurry and Kusin met their sales projections and hired their first full-time employee, Mary Evans, who later became vice-president of stores. Between Labor Day and Thanksgiving of 1983, Evans helped open and manage four more Dallas-area stores.

Babbage's set a precedent of selling entertainment software for the most popular computer and video game systems; at the time, the dominant home video game system was the Atari 2600, which featured four-color graphics. Eventually Atari was superseded by Nintendo and Sega of America systems, and Babbage's redirected its product line accordingly.

In 1984, Babbage's first full year of operations, the company lost $560,000 on sales of $3 million. Two years later, it broke even after generating nearly $10 million in revenues from an expanded chain of 23 stores, financed through the private sales of company stock. In 1987, Babbage's added another 35 stores and began selling software for the then-dominant eight-bit Nintendo Entertainment System with 16-color graphics. For fiscal 1987, the company earned $1.16 million on sales of $29 million.

In July 1988, Babbage's took its software specialty store concept public, offering 30 percent of the company's equity for $20 million, or $13 a share. Following the public offering, Perot tendered his stake in the company, and Babbage's continued accelerating its expansion drive with the proceeds of stock sales, opening 50 new stores that year to give the company 108 retail outlets. This expansion resulted in rising sales; in 1988, Babbage's annual revenues doubled to $58 million, while earnings shot up 136 percent to $2.7 million.

In 1989, Babbage's began losing business due to severe allocations of video games. Struck by a string of losses in the first three quarters of the year, the company responded by reducing prices on leading computer software titles and adding new cartridge-based video games to its line. Moreover, in the fall, Babbage's helped introduce the new 16-bit, 64-color Sega Genesis entertainment system, which quickly changed the landscape of the video game industry. Because of its superior capabilities, Sega Genesis generated a renewed interest in home video game systems. Rising sales of entertainment systems and software contributed to a strong 1989 holiday sales season for Babbage's, as the company managed a $2.3 million profit on annual sales that increased 62 percent to $95 million.

Fifty-three new store openings in 1989 (bringing the company's total to 160) and a barrage of new, low profit margin products pushed the company's earnings and its stock's trading value down. By early 1990, Babbage's stock, which had debuted at $13, had plummeted to less than $5. Babbage's responded to its financial troubles by scaling back the company's expansion program—opening only 19 stores in 1990—and focusing on cost-control measures and improved inventory turnover. Moreover, a new computerized point-of-sale inventory system was established, tracking sales and inventory after each business day and automatically generating orders for shipment from the company's Dallas warehouse the following morning. Powered by a surge in video game systems and software—including Sega's 16-bit Genesis and Nintendo's hand-held Gameboy player—the company's revenues rose 39 percent to $132.8 million in 1990 as earnings increased to $4.1 million.

Opal P. Ferraro, who joined Baggage's in 1986 as controller, was named chief financial officer in 1991, and, two years later, Ferraro joined McCurry and Kusin as the only other company officer on Babbage's board of directors. With the company in improved financial shape, Babbage's boosted its number of stores from 178 to 204, and reported 1991 earnings of $5.58 million on sales of $168.3 million.

In 1992, Babbage's added more than 40 new stores and began selling a CD-ROM peripheral attachment for the Sega 16-bit system that allowed interaction with digitized video footage. Sparked by a price war in the computer industry, sales of IBM-compatible software and 16-bit video systems and software rose substantially, and the company's stock value increased accordingly, climbing to more than $24 per share. The company's earnings also increased 21 percent to $6.78 million, and sales jumped 24 percent to $209.1 million.

In the fall of 1993, Babbage's began selling Panasonic's 32-bit game system, which operated through compact discs. This new technology threatened to render the 16-bit systems obsolete, and Babbage's experienced rapid declines in its sales of video game systems and software during the Christmas season, with the average Babbage's store posting five percent lower sales than a year earlier. Realizing that the market for 16-bit technology had

matured, Babbage's slashed prices on hundreds of video game titles early the following year, in an effort to unload its inventory of the increasingly dated software.

In 1993, Babbage's opened 56 new stores. However, the company generated only a 12 percent increase in sales, and, for the first time since 1989, increased revenues did not translate into higher earnings for the company. Earnings fell 36 percent to $4.3 million that year, as entertainment software continued to comprise about two-thirds of Babbage's business. Education and productivity software, along with computer supplies and accessories, cumulatively accounted for the remaining third.

Babbage's entered 1994 with a 300-store chain and plans to open between 30 and 40 more stores that year. As a result of holiday season price reductions, Babbage's stores had substantially reduced their inventory. However, the company was in a stronger financial position, as it had no long-term debt and maintained a cash surplus of $10.5 million. Babbage's entered the mid-1990s facing increasing competition from other software specialty stores, mass merchandisers, computers centers and superstores, electronics stores, toy stores, and mail order outlets, many of which were larger operations and had greater resources at their disposal. Nevertheless, Babbage's remained confident that its broad product selection, competitive prices, and customer service would continue to draw customers into its stores.

The company expected a continued decline in sales of video game systems and software in the near term, until the next generation of entertainment systems and programs were introduced. Those planned introductions included the late 1994 release of a 32-bit Sega system and Nintendo's promised debut of a 64-bit system, expected in 1995. Babbage's expected entertainment software to continue to comprise the fastest growing part of its business, and that developments in multimedia systems utilizing the CD-ROM format would bolster sales. While the market for interactive software was still evolving in 1994, Babbage's believed the potential for growth in that market was substantial and hoped that as such software moved closer to what is known as "virtual reality," more adults would be drawn into the market for entertainment software. Babbage's also appeared well positioned to benefit from the anticipated expansion of the market for home computer software stemming from trends in personal computing, including price wars among computer manufacturers and the rise in the number of households owning computers or upgrading their systems.

Further Reading:

Poole, Claire, "Learn to Walk before You Try to Run," *Forbes,* December 21, 1992, pp. 96–98.

—Roger W. Rouland

BAKER & MᶜKENZIE

Baker & McKenzie

One Prudential Plaza, Suite 3900
130 East Randolph Drive
Chicago, Illinois 60601
U.S.A.
(312) 861-8000
Fax: (312) 861-8823

Private Company
Incorporated: 1949
Employees: 4,843
Sales: $503.5 million
SICs: 8111 Legal Services

Baker & McKenzie is the world's largest law firm, with 49 offices in 31 countries. The firm has long held the lead in number of lawyers, employing nearly 1,700, including over 500 partners; but in 1992, it became the largest in terms of revenue as well, passing the New York-based Skadden, Arps, Slate, Meagher & Flom for the first time. Baker & McKenzie's practice covers every major field of law, both domestically and internationally.

Several characteristics set this company apart from the other so-called "megafirms." The firm's philosophy stresses the importance of understanding the culture and customs of the areas in which it operates as well the laws. Thus Baker & McKenzie tends to staff its overseas offices with local lawyers, rather than sending American lawyers abroad. In addition, about 75 percent of the revenue generated by a foreign office remains in that country, a much higher share than most firms allow. Because of these practices, many competitors have criticized Baker & McKenzie as a franchise operation akin to a fast food chain. Its "McLaw" approach has confounded the critics, however, by producing results unmatched by any of the other megafirms in recent years.

Although Baker & McKenzie was created in 1949, its roots can be traced to founder Russell Baker's initial law practice, established shortly after his 1925 graduation from the University of Chicago Law School. Baker, who had traveled to Chicago from his native New Mexico by hopping freight trains, began his legal career while still in law school. Working for the Chicago Motor Club, Baker was allowed to try minor traffic cases for Club members before a Justice of the Peace. After graduation, Baker set up a practice with Dana Simpson, a friend and University of Chicago classmate. The firm, Simpson & Baker, specialized in providing services for Chicago's growing Mexican-American community.

Baker's early experience working with Mexican lawyers sparked his interest in international law. Recognizing Chicago's important and expanding role in international trade, Baker conceived the idea of establishing a law firm that would be truly international in scope. After handling the worldwide legal matters for Abbott Laboratories in 1934, Baker built a reputation as an expert in international law. By that time, Simpson had left the practice, and Baker was a partner in Hubbard, Baker & Rice. He was engaged by Abbott to handle its worldwide legal matters, including contract negotiations, acquisitions, and patent and trademark litigation. Working for Abbott, Baker had the opportunity to travel throughout Latin America and Europe, and his notion of creating an international law firm became more concrete.

Since his current partners were not as interested in developing an international practice, Baker began to search for a new partnership. In 1949, he teamed up with John McKenzie, a trial lawyer he had met in a taxi a few years earlier, to form Baker & McKenzie. The firm also included Dwight Hightower and Andrew Brainerd. Since McKenzie had already established a reputation as a skilled litigator, Baker was free to travel in search of international contacts while McKenzie handled the firm's domestic matters.

Baker & McKenzie's list of clients grew impressively in the early 1950s. The list included such major companies as Eli Lilly, G. D. Searle, Wrigley, and Honeywell. As the firm's domestic client list grew so did its international list. In 1955, a Venezuelan lawyer contacted Baker to explore the possibility of setting up a joint venture to handle U.S. business interests in Caracas, prompting the establishment of Baker & McKenzie's first foreign office. By the end of the 1950s, the firm had established six other foreign offices, and its staff of lawyers had grown from 4 to 30. In 1957, offices were opened in Washington, Brussels, and Amsterdam. Zurich, New York, and Sao Paolo were added over the next two years. International expansion continued throughout the 1960s.

Throughout this period of incredibly rapid international development, the firm hired lawyers trained locally to man the new offices. Once recruited, a lawyer usually spent time working out of the firm's home base in Chicago, learning the finer points of its operations, before being reassigned to the company office in his or her native country. Lawyers working out of these foreign offices were treated as equal partners in the firm, not as affiliates or minor leaguers. They had as much say in firm decisions as their American counterparts, and as much opportunity to share in the firms profits. Because the lawyers were trained where they worked, the foreign offices were capable of taking on work from local clients as well as from international concerns.

Throughout its history Baker & McKenzie has tried to make timely moves into areas where the flow of new business activity is about to create a greater need for available legal services. Thus much of Baker & McKenzie's expansion during the 1970s focused on the Far East. A Hong Kong office was established in 1974, and among others, offices were opened in Bangkok and

Taipei three years later. By 1978 Baker & McKenzie had 26 offices in 20 countries.

In nearly every case, Baker & McKenzie would start up its foreign offices from scratch, sending attorneys abroad to open an outpost, or recruiting local lawyers and bringing them to Chicago for a few years of orientation before returning them home to set up shop. The office opened in 1979 in Bogotá, Colombia, was a rare exception. It was created through a merger with an 11-lawyer Bogotá firm already in existence.

Founder Russell Baker died on the last day of the firm's annual partnership meeting in 1979. Under chairman Wulf Doser, from the company's Frankfurt office, Baker & McKenzie entered a consolidation phase. During this period, in which the Tokyo office was reorganized and the young Minneapolis office was closed, the firm's approach became more businesslike, something of a contrast from Baker's "lawyer's manage thyselves" philosophy.

Doser was succeeded as chairman in 1981 by Thomas Bridgman, a litigator from the firm's Chicago home base. When Bridgman's three-year term expired in 1983, Robert Cox was elected to a five-year term as chairman, and the role of that position in the firm was expanded. Unlike his immediate predecessors, Cox gave up his regular law practice to concentrate on managing the firm full time. By 1985, Baker & McKenzie's lawyer count was at 752 and growing. The firm was operating 30 offices in 22 countries. Its annual revenue was in excess of $125 million, second highest among law firms to Skadden, Arps.

The second half of the 1980s was an extremely prolific period in Baker & McKenzie's spread across the globe. It opened offices along the U.S.-Mexican border in 1986 to take advantage of the industrial boom taking place there. And Baker & McKenzie was one of the first American law firms to anticipate the opening of Eastern European markets, as offices were opened in Budapest (1987), Moscow (1989), and Berlin (1990). Like many other law firms, Baker & McKenzie also launched a full-scale assault on California during the late 1980s, expecting a huge rush of investment there by companies from Japan and elsewhere in Asia. The firm opened offices in Palo Alto, Los Angeles, and San Diego. This California expansion included the assimilation of MacDonald, Halsted, and Laybourne, a 68-partner firm with offices in Los Angeles and San Diego. Western Europe was not ignored either, and an office was established in Barcelona in 1988. In 1989 Baker & McKenzie attorneys opened associated offices in Seoul, Korea and Jakarta, Indonesia.

The firm's revenue and lawyer rolls were growing as quickly as its geographical range. Between 1987 and 1990, annual revenue doubled, from $196 million to $404 million. Baker & McKenzie cracked the 1,000-lawyer mark in 1988 (1,179), and it took only two more years to pass 1,500. By 1990, the company was operating a total of 49 offices on 6 continents. In addition to the company growth, prestige came to the offices as well, when David Ruder, the recently retired chairman of the Securities and Exchange Commission, joined the firm's domestic corporate and securities practice.

Baker & McKenzie has not escaped controversy. Three controversies brought unwanted publicity to Baker & McKenzie. In 1991, Ingrid Beall, who had become the firm's first woman partner in 1961, filed a discrimination suit against the firm. The suit revolved around Ms. Beall's claim that she was systematically deprived of the opportunity to advance within the firm on the basis of her age and gender. In a second well-publicized episode, the firm dropped the Church of Scientology as a client, turning its back on $2 million of revenue in the process. Some observers hinted that the move may have resulted from pressure applied to the firm by Eli Lilly, one of its oldest and best customers. The Church of Scientology has been a vocal critic of the antidepressant drug Prozac, which is manufactured by Lilly. And at the end of 1993, Baker & McKenzie was ordered by the New York State Division of Human Rights to pay $500,000 in compensatory damages and back pay to the estate of Geoffrey Bowers. In one of the earliest AIDS discrimination cases in the United States, Bowers had argued that his firing by the company in 1986 was due to his illness rather than his performance, as was claimed by the firm. The decision was contested by Baker & McKenzie.

Many of the firm's foreign offices were generating a substantial share of their own business by 1992. At the company's Latin American outposts, as much as 35 percent of the client base was not U.S.-based. The Paris office's clientele was 40 percent French, and a significant portion of the remainder was Japanese or German, as well as American. For 1992, Baker & McKenzie reported revenue of $503.5 million, moving the firm past Skadden, Arps into first place among law firms. The company's foreign offices accounted for 60 percent of that revenue, a figure far higher than that of most other top international firms.

As the 1990s continue, the competition among international law firms appears to be intensifying. Additional competition is expected to come from large accounting firms, such as Arthur Andersen, which are interested in diversifying into legal services by forging alliances with established law firms in foreign countries. Baker & McKenzie is preparing itself for the increased competition under the guidance of the chairman of the executive committee John McGuigan, an Australian, who joined Baker & McKenzie in 1973 and had served most recently as managing partner at the firm's Hong Kong office. In 1993, new offices were established in Prague and Beijing, reflecting the firm's ongoing emphasis on Asia and Eastern Europe.

For much of its history, Baker & McKenzie has been derided by its competitors for its approach to global expansion. Critics have been quick to argue that it is a loose alliance of local law firms rather than a unified international entity. By employing lawyers in their native regions, however, Baker & McKenzie has succeeded in developing relationships with major companies in those areas more quickly than might otherwise be possible. Throughout the growing markets of Asia and Eastern Europe, many of these critics are reluctantly admitting that the firm they have called "McLaw" has positioned itself remarkably well.

Further Reading:

Abramowitz, Michael, "One Woman v. Her Law Firm," *Washington Post,* October 14, 1991, p. D1.
Baker & McKenzie, Chicago: Baker & McKenzie, 1988.
Baker, Russell, *History of Baker & McKenzie,* Chicago: Baker & McKenzie, 1978.

Baker, Wallace R., *What Is Baker & McKenzie?* Chicago: Baker & McKenzie, 1991.

"Cover Profile: Baker & McKenzie's John McGuigan," *Asia Today,* February 1994, pp. 5–6.

Elstrom, Peter J. W., "Law Firm Gets a Plum as Ruder Joins Practice," *Crain's Chicago Business,* February 26, 1990, p. 47.

Feder, Barnaby J., "The Unorthodox Behemoth of Law Firms," *New York Times,* March 14, 1993, sec. 3, p. 1.

"Firm Drops L.A. Office," *Wall Street Journal,* October 18, 1993, p. B8.

Gill, Donna, "Baker's Unique Niche," *Chicago Lawyer,* January 1992, p. 1.

Goldberg, Stephanie, "Law Firm Blankets Globe," *Crain's Chicago Business,* October 26, 1992, p. 17.

Lyons, James, "Baker & McKenzie: The Belittled Giant," *American Lawyer,* October 1985, pp. 115–22.

"McLaw Acquitted," *Economist,* July 3, 1993, pp. 61–2.

Navarro, Mireya, "Vindicating a Lawyer with AIDS, Years too Late," *New York Times,* January 21, 1994, p. B18.

"On the Way to Becoming the Dominant Provider of Legal Services," *Frankfurter Allgemeine Zeitung,* October 15, 1993.

Rice, Robert, "Going Global," *Financial Times,* May 18, 1993.

Stevens, Mark, *Power of Attorney: The Rise of the Giant Law Firms,* New York: McGraw-Hill, 1986.

—Robert R. Jacobson

Ball Corporation

Ball Corporation

345 South High Street
Muncie, Indiana 47305-0407
U.S.A.
(317) 747-6100
Fax: (317) 747-6850

Public Company
Incorporated: 1922
Employees: 14,400
Sales: $2.18 billion
Stock Exchanges: New York
SICs: 3411 Metal Cans; 3221 Glass Containers; 5099
  Durable Goods, Nec; 3085 Plastic Bottles; 3081
  Unsupported Plastics Film and Sheet; 3812 Search and
  Navigation Equipment; 3679 Electronic Components, Nec

Although the Ball Corporation is best known for its distinctive home canning jars, that business was just one segment of the diversified company in the 1990s. Glass packaging constituted only 29 percent of Ball's annual sales by that time, while metal packaging—including aluminum beverage containers, and food and aerosol cans—brought in about 60 percent of yearly revenues. The firm ranks as one of America's top beverage-can manufacturers. Ball's emphasis on quality has helped it compete well in the highly competitive can market: by 1994, the company was the third largest supplier to the combined U.S.-Canadian food can market. The remaining eleven percent of the corporation's annual income came from aerospace and communications subsidiaries. Ball has secured numerous U.S. Defense Department contracts and participates in the Space Shuttle Program of the National Aeronautics and Space Administration (NASA).

Ever since the five Ball brothers discovered that John Mason's patent on canning jars had expired in the late 1800s, the Ball Corporation has been making the preferred canning equipment in America. Five generations of Americans have preserved everything from pickle relish and apricots to cherry jam and tomatoes in the well known jars, whose design has gone virtually unchanged for over 100 years. Though Ball finally went public in 1972, 60 percent of the company's stock is still owned by the family.

The Ball Corporation began in 1880 when the Ball brothers went into the business of making tin-jacketed glass containers

for kerosene lamps. From this type of operation it was an easy shift to the manufacture of canning jars and lids. Moreover, it was wise business strategy: Thomas Edison's recent invention of the incandescent light bulb had antiquated the kerosene lamp. The glass jar, on the other hand, had a great future.

Until the end of World War II, Ball was primarily a jar and bottle manufacturer with few other interests. In the late 1940s, however, a problem had to be confronted—nearly 70 percent of the company's glass production facilities were in need of modernization. Ball had either to diversify and grow in order to underwrite necessary modernization costs or liquidate the company. The family decided to diversify the company because a 1947 antitrust ruling prohibited Ball from purchasing more glass subsidiaries. Under president Edmund F. Ball, they made a number of key acquisitions outside the glass container field. Before the company ventured too far afield, Ball hired a New York management consulting team to help establish a long-range program. In the words of Edmund Ball's successor, John Fisher, "We wanted to plan for growth, not just hope for it."

The significant changes at Ball, those which have molded the company's future, took place in the late 1950s and early 1960s. The launching of Sputnik by the Soviets in 1958 ushered in the Space Age and created many new opportunities in the field of aerospace. Ball decided to take advantage of the situation. "We got into the space field because it was the beginning of the biggest scientific effort in our nation's history," said Fisher. "We knew it could be profitable for us, and that we could get commercial 'fall-out' from it."

The Ball management proved itself correct on both counts. A substantial portion of the company's business presently comes from the sale of computer components, pointing controls for NASA satellites, electronic data display devices, and many related items such as Sound-Guard, a preservative for phonograph records that is a derivative of a lubricant developed for spacecraft. The company also built the cameras for the Viking I and II spacecraft that were used to determine the landing site on Mars; the Space Shuttle tether system, which allows small payloads to trail up to 65 miles away from the parent ship; and the telescope on the Infrared Astronomical Satellite launched in 1983 that has helped scientists to determine more precisely the size of the Milky Way galaxy. Ball procured $180 million in defense contracts alone by 1987. Chief Executive Officer Richard Ringoen hoped the company's "strong position in infrared and ultraviolet instrumentation [would] continue to allow it to compete favorably with larger aerospace firms like General Dynamics."

Ironically, Ball had entered the high-tech market almost by mistake. In the 1950s, the company hired a small engineering firm in Boulder, Colorado, to develop a device that would more accurately weigh glass batch materials. The original device was never developed, but Ball was impressed enough by the technical skill of the small operation to purchase it. From this small start Ball invested heavily in research and development and made this sector a vital part of the company's overall business.

The 1960s were years of unparalleled growth in the container industry, especially in the consumer beverage area. Americans began drinking more beer and soft drinks than ever before, and innovations such as the pop-top can and the non-returnable bottle helped container companies to make large profits. While not being a large-volume can manufacturer on the order of American Can or Continental, Ball has nonetheless been extremely successful in this competitive market. Cans soon made up two-thirds of the company's packaging sales, supplanting jars and bottles as the company's primary container product.

Ball's success in this area can be traced back to 1968 when the firm made an early switch to two-piece cans. The two-piece can, which is lighter, less expensive, and faster to make, is now used to package 70 percent of all soft drinks and 94 percent of all beer. Since Ball was already in the container industry, it was able to win manufacturing contracts from such important customers as PepsiCo, Inc., The Coca-Cola Co., and Anheuser-Busch Co. In fact, Anheuser-Busch and Ball constructed a $32 million plant in New England that manufactures two-piece aluminum cans for the brewer on an exclusive basis. While Ball controlled less than one percent of the total can market in the 1980s, it had seven to eight percent of the two-piece can market.

Ball's diversification efforts during the 1950s and 1960s were bold in concept but fairly modest in scope. The man responsible for creating the widely diversified company that the Ball Corporation would become, John W. Fisher, was chosen president and chief executive officer in 1971. Fisher directed Ball into such fields as petroleum engineering equipment, photo-engraving, and plastics, and established the company as a leading manufacturer of computer components and high-tech hardware for defense and space.

Fisher, the last company president to be a member of the Ball family (his wife was the daughter of one of the five founding Ball brothers), resisted the traditionalists within his firm and pushed Ball into new markets all over the world. In 1972, Fisher acquired a Singapore-based petroleum equipment company that built and sold production gear and provided engineering expertise to oil firms in the Pacific. This purchase gave Ball subsidiary operations in Singapore, Malaysia, Indonesia, Panama, and Japan. The following year the Ball-Bartoe Aircraft Corporation was established in Boulder, Colorado. It was involved in the development of an experimental STOL (short take-off and landing) military jet in the 1980s.

The company then acquired agricultural systems and prefabricated housing. Fisher established a Ball Corporation division in Boulder devoted solely to the production and sale of "turnkey" irrigation packages for agricultural development in arid but arable areas of Libya and other nations in the Middle East. Ball also designed a modular home that could be erected on-site in a little more than six hours. In desert nations where building materials are scarce and therefore expensive, Ball has succeeded in selling a large number of these "kit" houses. Then, in 1974, Fisher acquired a small California computer company. This concern was expanded into Ball Computer Products Division based in Sunnyvale, California, in the heart of Silicon Valley.

Following Ball's success in the foreign petroleum engineering equipment business, Fisher established similar operations in the United States. However, stiff competition, higher technological standards, and prohibitive start-up costs thwarted this venture

from the start. Fisher wasted no time in selling it in 1976 for 40 cents per share. In the mid 1970s, Ball also developed and introduced Freshware food containers. Made of plastic with tight-fitting lids, these were designed to compete with Tupperware. The product was never actually marketed and Ball had to write it off as a loss, phasing out the project in a matter of months. But these were relatively small setbacks. Fisher's management strategy was long-term and he was willing to bear the burden of brief, small-scale problems. The two large obstacles he never surmounted, however, were the company's image and the stock market's ambivalent opinion of it. Despite its interesting acquisitions, the American public still associated Ball almost exclusively with its glass jars.

Ball Corporation went public in 1972 for two reasons. The company management wanted to establish accurately the market value of the Ball family holdings, and they intended to raise equity money to finance the company's diversification efforts. But despite its impressive history, Ball's stock price did not significantly increase. Fisher's efforts to give Ball a more technological image, his trips across the United States to speak with investors, and his dedication to growth did not change the minds of many people. The executive could not understand why a profitable company would not be an attractive stock purchase. He remarked, "We live in a world where products must be packaged, in good times or bad. This is all a bit mystifying to me."

When Fisher retired in 1981 he was replaced by Richard Ringoen. Ringoen concentrated on two areas, technology and packaging. Many of the other sectors, while being neither divested not disregarded, had been left to operate on their own. From 1988 to 1992, Ball's annual sales increased dramatically, from $86 million to $2.177 billion, on the force of acquisitions. But net income only increased slightly, from $50.5 million to $69.1 million during the same period.

In the late 1980s, Ball began to focus on international packaging markets where growth far outpaced that of the United States. In 1986, Ball entered into a joint venture with Guangzhou M. C. Packaging in China. By 1993, that business ranked as one of that country's most successful foreign joint ventures, and Ball had established five beverage can manufacturing plants in China, one in Taiwan, and one in Hong Kong.

Ringoen served Ball for a decade, and was succeeded by Delmont A. Davis in 1991. Davis led Ball's early 1990s consolidation and rationalization. In 1992, the company acquired Kerr Group Inc.'s commercial glass assets for $68.4 million, which helped boost Ball's share of that market. Heekin Can, Inc., one of the Midwest's largest food can manufacturers, was purchased in 1993 through a tax-free exchange of stock. The integration of Heekin and Ball's existing Canadian can operations made Ball the third largest supplier to the combined U.S.-Canadian food can market. At the same time, Ball spun off its Alltrista Corporation subsidiary, which was comprised of Ball's consumer products, zinc products, metal decorating and services, industrial systems, and plastics businesses, to shareholders.

Ball's aerospace business also faced challenges in the late 1980s and early 1990s, as the end of the Cold War and the shifting governmental priorities that resulted helped reduce the federal defense budget and intensify competition for contracts. Still, in 1993, Ball was proud to have played a major role in the well-publicized repair of the Hubble Space Telescope. The Ball-built COSTAR optics system helped correct the telescope's notoriously blurry vision.

The net result of these reorganizational activities was that Ball's sales more than doubled from $1.12 billion in 1990 to $2.44 billion in 1993, while the corporation's staff was reduced by over ten percent. Ball was compelled to take a $95 million pretax restructuring provision, half of which was used for plant shutdowns and consolidations. Although CEO Davis rightly called Ball's $65.1 million loss for the year "simply not acceptable," he also expressed confidence that the company's "unparalleled restructuring" would bring new opportunities for profitability in the last half of the decade.

Principal Subsidiaries: Ball Brothers AG (Germany); Ball-Canada Holdings Inc.; Ball Efratom Elektronik GmbH (Germany); Ball Efratom Corporation Ltd.; Ball Foreign Sales Corp.; Ball Holdings Corp.; Ball-Incon Glass Packaging Corp.; Ball Metal Container Corp.; Ball Packaging Products Canada, Inc.; Ball Systems Technology Ltd.; Ball Technology Licensing Corp.; Ball Technology Services Corp.; CCD, Inc.; Heekin Can, Inc.; Madera Glass Co.; Muncie & Western Railroad Co.; Verac, Inc.

Further Reading:

Birmingham, Frederic Alexander, *Ball Corporation: The First Century,* Indianapolis: Curtis Publishing Co.

—updated by April Dougal Gasbarre

Banc One Corporation

100 East Broad Street
Columbus, Ohio 43271-0251
U.S.A.
(614) 248-5944
Fax: (614) 248-5220

Public Company
Incorporated: 1968 as First Banc Group of Ohio, Inc.
Employees: 45,300
Total Assets: $7.22 billion
Stock Exchanges: Boston Midwest New York Pittsburgh
    Pacific
SICs: 6712 Bank Holding Companies; 6021 National
    Commercial Banks; 6022 State Commercial Banks; 6162
    Mortgage Bankers & Loan Correspondents; 7389 Business
    Services, Nec; 6099 Functions Related to Depository
    Banking, Nec; 6091 Nondeposit Trust Facilities

Banc One Corporation ranks among the most esteemed, profitable, and fastest-growing banking organizations in the United
States. In the early 1990s, *Euromoney* featured Banc One on its
list of Best Banks in the World, *Institutional Investor* named it
America's Best Bank, and analyst Joseph A. Stieven told *Bank
Management* magazine that the corporation was "the best bank
in the country regarding acquisitions." The corporation's phenomenal growth was facilitated by its formation of over 100
"Uncommon Partnerships"—Banc One's euphemism for
mergers—beginning in the late 1960s. The basic principles of
the Uncommon Partnership remain affiliate autonomy, centralized support, market diversity and balance, and emphasis on
high margin products. In 1993, Banc One had affiliate banking
organizations in the American Midwest, South, and West, providing a variety of financial services, including: data processing, venture capital, investment and merchant banking, trust,
brokerage, investment management, equipment leasing, mortgage banking, consumer finance, and insurance. Banc One has
been led by three successive generations of John McCoys—
John Hall, John Gardner, and John Bonnet—each distinguished
by his mother's maiden name and all three of whom had served
on the Federal Reserve advisory board.

While the corporation was created in 1968 as First Banc Group
of Ohio, Inc., a holding company of The City National Bank &
Trust Company of Columbus, the organization's origins may be

traced to the Great Depression and the McCoy family. John H.
McCoy began his career in banking when he left the eighth
grade to work in a bank in Marietta, Ohio. By 1930, he was
successful in the field and began serving on the Ohio state bank
advisory board, soon thereafter becoming the Ohio representative to President Herbert Hoover's Reconstruction Finance
Corp. (RFC). In 1935, the RFC appointed McCoy president of
Columbus' City National Bank & Trust (CNB).

CNB, formed from the consolidation of two small Columbus
banks, had an infamous anniversary: October 29, 1929, Black
Friday. The bank had struggled through the Depression, surviving only with the help of the RFC, and when John H. McCoy
took control, the two banks were still operating semi-autono-
mously. During this time, two families dominated banking in
the state capitol; the Huntingtons, with their namesake Huntington National Bank, and the Wolfes, who owned Ohio National Bank and several major media outlets. While the Huntingtons controlled the lucrative trust business, Ohio National,
by far the biggest bank in town, had the majority of the commercial lending.

Moreover, during this time Ohio state regulations prohibited
banks from expanding across county lines, limiting growth
possibilities and creating interdependence among banks in most
of Ohio's 88 predominantly rural counties. When large transactions were required, smaller banks established affiliations with
bigger banks like Huntington National in Columbus or Fifth
Third in Cincinnati, which in turn established ties to money
center banks in New York or Chicago. These cooperative banking relationships in Ohio formed a "pyramid" in which small
banks were, out of necessity, dependent on larger ones. As a
result, there was little competition among local banks, and none
at all among banks in different counties.

John H. McCoy made a fortuitous decision when he opted to
focus CNB's operations on retail banking, a field virtually
untapped by his primary Columbus competitors. John H. was an
impressive figure and established an enduring corporate culture
at CNB. He is said to have worked so hard that he fainted
several times at CNB, and, despite enduring four heart attacks
between 1943 and his death in 1958, the patriarch never quit the
bank. He established strictures against drinking coffee in the
office and alcohol at lunch, and he earned the nickname "five
percent McCoy" due to his insistence on charging customers
five percent interest on loans, when most bankers were charging
much less. John H. maintained that the valuable added services
CNB offered its customers were worth these higher rates. Mc-
Coy's progeny carried on that legacy: net interest margins still
ranked among the highest in the business in 1992. Moreover,
CNB's corporate culture came to reflect John H.'s often para-
doxical principles: autonomy, control, individuality, and uniformity; over the years, CNB entered many new ventures, as long
as the stakes were low and the potential fallout from failure was
limited.

In 1937, John G. McCoy finished his studies at Stanford and
joined his father at the bank. One of the keys to CNB's local
success during this time was its transformation of branch banks
from smaller replicas of cold, imposing bank buildings to
friendlier neighborhood centers. During World War II, John G.
served in the Navy and a younger McCoy, Chuck, ran the bank

when a heart attack briefly put John H. out of commission. John G. returned to find that Columbus in general, and his father's bank, in particular, were enjoying a boom in retail. Moreover, Chuck had introduced several innovations at the branches, including carpeting, modern lighting, community rooms with kitchens for local meetings, and continuous counters to replace the traditional teller cages. In the postwar period, CNB built the first drive-in branch bank; a few other banks were providing window service, but CNB built a specially designed, freestanding, drive-in bank.

When John H. McCoy suffered a fifth heart attack and died in November 1958, CNB was still ranked third among the banks in Columbus. John G., an operations specialist, was quickly named president, and, one year later, he was asked to take over as chairperson. The 46-year-old countered the board's offer with demands of his own, including the creation of a research fund consisting of three percent of the bank's profits. The board agreed, and John G. went to work. The research fund provided financial support for the technological innovations CNB would pioneer in the years to come, including a computer center for check-reading and other data processing functions.

By the late 1950s, the increasingly profitable CNB was gaining on local competitors Huntington and Ohio National, and John G. brought on an innovative advertiser, John Fisher, to promote new retail products like checking accounts. Over the course of his 30-year career at CNB, John Fisher combined marketing and computing intuition to revolutionize CNB and the banking industry as a whole. Moreover, Fisher, a former disc jockey, cultivated a unique image for the bank when he hired comedienne Phyllis Diller as CNB's spokesperson in 1962. Board members worried that Diller would not convey the dignified image typically cultivated by banking institutions, and they voiced their concerns to John G. at subsequent board meetings. As Fisher told *Institutional Investor* in 1991, the CEO defended his visionary marketing director to the board by saying, "Gentlemen, it's very simple: You can have either dignity or dividends. I vote for dividends."

While Fisher's outlandish campaign gave CNB a higher profile among competitors as well as customers, his unconventional ideas were not limited to advertising. At his and McCoy's instigation, CNB became the first bank outside of California to market Bankamericard (which later became Visa) in 1966, beginning a very profitable credit card processing sideline. Handling all the data processing duties associated with the credit card, CNB helped to make Bankamericard the first nationally accepted credit card. This innovation not only poured revenue and credibility into CNB but helped transform Americans' buying and spending habits, ushering in the "age of plastic." In 1968, CNB helped issue more than one million credit cards through 50 banks. Two years later, on Columbus Day, Fisher activated the country's first automated teller machine (ATM). Fisher also led unprecedented, and ultimately failed, efforts into videotex-based home banking, with which customers could view their accounts and pay their bills using their television screens.

During this time, John G. devised a plan to sidestep state banking regulations prohibiting interstate mergers and acquire other Ohio banks in the process. He decided to develop a

holding company—a corporate body that, technically, was not a bank and thus could lawfully expand across county and state lines. The holding company, formed in October 1967, was called First Banc; its unusual spelling was the result of Ohio laws forbidding holding companies from calling themselves "banks." John G. first approached the directors of Farmers Savings & Trust, a county-seat bank in Mansfield, Ohio. The directors of Farmers Savings, nearing retirement and looking to sell the company, agreed to the merger proposition, becoming CNB's first acquisition through a stock swap.

Strict guidelines for acquisition soon developed. Proposed acquisitions were required to have assets amounting to no more than one-third of those of the buyer, a policy that ensured manageable deals and allowed the buyer to survive a bad acquisition. In addition, acquisitions were forbidden from diluting earnings, even during the first year of the merger. First Banc usually avoided such turnaround situations by focusing on acquiring banks that were strongest in its own retail and small business markets, which would generate economies of scale in areas such as processing. Under First Banc's merger policy, salaries, hiring and firing, staff allocation, and even the pricing of products and services remained the responsibility of the affiliate bank, which maintained its own president, board of directors, and business plan.

First Banc soon proved especially proficient at consolidating management information systems. Each new affiliate was required to submit detailed monthly reports, which were then compiled on First Banc's powerful computer system for comparative purposes. The surveys induced competition among the branches and provided an incentive to match the best. Virtually all new affiliates met the challenge and improved their return on assets and profitability after merging with First Banc.

From 1968 to 1978, First Banc acquired at least 15 Ohio banks, raising its profits to over $25 million annually, and formed First Banc Group Financial Services Corporation to offer personal property leasing and mortgage servicing. The company's growth was also fueled by the liberalization of Ohio banking laws during this time, which were amended to allow statewide branching and mergers between banks located in any county. The holding company's name was changed to Banc One in 1979, and by 1980 the corporation was one of only seven banking organizations among the 100 largest in the United States to have recorded ten consecutive years of increases in both earnings and dividends. In 1981, *Time* magazine called Banc One "perhaps the most advanced financial institution in the United States."

The corporation's assets passed the $5 billion mark in 1982, as barriers to interstate branching continued to deteriorate. Federal and state banking regulations changed dramatically in September 1985, enabling Banc One to enter its first agreement with a banking organization outside of Ohio. Purdue National Corporation in Lafayette, Indiana, became the first out-of-state bank to affiliate itself with Banc One. After a relative lull in acquisitions from 1983 to 1986, Banc One's merger activity picked up. In 1987, for example, the company purchased the $4.4 billion American Fletcher of Indianapolis, and the next year it acquired $4.3 billion Marine Corp. of Milwaukee. Banc One took advantage of nationwide reciprocal banking soon after it was legitimized in Ohio in 1988. By the end of the following year, the corporation had added affiliates in Kentucky, Michigan, and Wisconsin. Nevertheless, the corporation focused on regional operations until the early 1990s, when it began to extend its presence west and south as virtually every barrier to interstate banking was removed.

John B. McCoy, son of John G., also entered the banking business. Like his father, John B. graduated from Stanford. After three years in the U.S. Air Force, he took a position at Citicorp in New York, where he stayed for less than a year before returning home to Columbus in 1970. The younger McCoy worked his way through six different sections of the bank—including the credit card division, which he built into one of the nation's largest—and, in 1984, he was named CEO of the corporation. John B.'s efforts to keep Banc One focused on consumer banking allowed the corporation to avoid the real estate loans, Third World debt, and leveraged-buyout problems that troubled many banks during the 1980s. The bank lent more to consumers than to businesses and rarely offered loans at all to large companies. From 1984 to 1990, John B. engineered 54 acquisitions, thereby tripling Banc One's assets to $27 billion. These acquisitions helped Banc One to thrive during an early 1990s recession.

Banc One continued to refine the branch banking experience in the 1980s by decreasing its number of tellers, adding new drive-in lanes and ATMs, giving the platform officers separate offices, adding travel agencies and a discount securities broker, and leasing space to insurance agents and real estate brokers. The corporation also introduced such innovative concepts as Sunday hours in Ohio, "weekly specials," and credit card tie-ins with groups such as the American Association of Retired Persons and airline frequent flyer programs.

However, by the beginning of the 1990s, Banc One's five-state Midwestern market, in which the population had remained stagnant for years, was becoming saturated. In order to maintain the corporation's customary 15 percent annual profit growth, John B. decided on a course of expansion. Focusing on Texas, the nation's third-largest bank state with $175 billion in deposits in 1990, McCoy found a retail void in the banking market that could be filled by his bank's successful formula. First, he agreed to the government-assisted purchase of 20 failed Texas banks, known as MCorp, for $500 million, which brought Banc One's assets to approximately $36 billion. Just two days after taking control of those former MCorp banks, he bought Dallas-based Bright Banc Savings Association and its 48 branches for $45 million from the Resolution Trust Corporation, making Banc One the country's 16th-largest bank, with $37 billion in assets. MCorp was Banc One's first turnaround situation, and observers wondered whether the corporation was up to the challenge, especially given the competitive banking environment in Texas. Led by John B., the corporation achieved that

and more, acquiring banks in Colorado, Arizona, California, Utah, West Virginia, Kentucky, and Oklahoma in 1992 and 1993.

For fiscal 1993, Banc One earned a return on assets of 1.53 percent, marking the first time in history that an American banking institution with over $50 billion in assets crossed the 1.5 percent mark. The company sustained its annual earnings per share increase, becoming one of only 14 nationally traded U.S. companies to do so in 25 years. *American Banker* named John B. McCoy "Banker of the Year" for 1993.

In the mid-1990s, analysts' primary fear was that Banc One would encounter a crisis of rising expectations. Mark Lynch, an analyst at Shearson Lehman Brothers, pointed out that the corporation would have to keep up the somewhat hectic acquisitions pace just to satisfy the market's expectation of growing earnings per share. Moreover, others questioned Banc One's ability to maintain the "friendly hometown bank" atmosphere that brought it to prominence in the first place, as its operations expanded increasingly further from its Midwestern roots. Nevertheless, many analysts displayed confidence in Banc One; Richard Fredericks of Montgomery Securities, for example, predicted that Banc One will become America's first nationwide bank.

Principal Subsidiaries: Banc One Ohio Corp.; Bank One Lexington N.A.; Premier Acquisition Corp.; Banc One Colorado Corp.; Banc One Illinois Corp.; Banc One Interim Corp.; Banc One Indiana Corp.; Banc One Alpha Corp.; Bank One West Virginia Corp.; Sterling Assurance Co.; Banc One Diversified Services Corp.; Banc One Investor Services Group; Banc One Capital Corporation; Banc One Community Development Corporation; Banc One Funds Management Company; Banc One Management and Consulting Corporation; Banc One Services Corporation.

Further Reading:

"Banc One: Costly Hedging," *The Economist,* December 25, 1993, pp. 100–01.

"Banc One: Mightier than Its Parts," *The Economist,* December 19, 1992, p. 76.

Phillips, Stephen, "Just Your Friendly Hometown Banker—With a Megabank," *Business Week,* April 9, 1990, pp. 64–6.

Rifkin, Glenn, "He Changed the Rules in Banking," *Computerworld,* April 25, 1988, pp. 1, 84–5.

Svare, J. Christopher, "Acquiring for Growth and Profit: The Banc One Experience," *Bank Management,* November 1990, pp. 18–24.

Taylor, John H., "A Tale of Two Strategies," *Forbes,* August 31, 1992, pp. 40–1.

Teitelman, Robert, "The Magnificent McCoys: Running America's Best Bank," *Institutional Investor,* July 1991, pp. 47–56.

—April Dougal Gasbarre

Barnes & Noble, Inc.

Barnes & Noble
Booksellers   Since 1873
Inc.

122 Fifth Ave.
New York, New York 10011
U.S.A.
(212) 633-3300
Fax: (212) 807-6033

Public Company
Incorporated: 1894 as C. M. Barnes Company
Employees: 15,000
Sales: $1.08 billion
Stock Exchanges: New York
SICs: 5942 Book Stores; 5961 Catalog and Mail Order
   Houses; 6719 Holding Companies Nec

Barnes & Noble, Inc. operates the largest chain of book superstores in the United States. The company revolutionized
book selling by introducing giant, supermarket-style stores with
deeply discounted books in the 1970s, and by 1994 it operated
more than 200 such superstores across the country. Barnes &
Noble is also the second largest operator of mall bookstores,
running the well-known B. Dalton chain, and Scribner's and
Doubleday Book Shops. Barnes & Noble is a leading supplier
of books through mail-order catalogs as well. The company
sells discounted publishers' remainders and imported books
through its catalog, as well as books under its own ''Barnes &
Noble Books'' imprint.

The Barnes family's history in the book business started in
1873, when Charles Montgomery Barnes went into the second-
hand book business in Wheaton, Illinois. Barnes soon moved to
Chicago, selling new and used books. By 1894, Barnes' firm,
reorganized as C. M. Barnes Company, dealt exclusively in
school books. In 1902, C. M. Barnes' son, William R. Barnes,
became president of the firm, and he continued the business in
partnership with several other men. The younger Barnes sold
his interest in his father's company in 1917, when he moved to
New York. In New York, he acquired an interest in the educational bookstore Noble & Noble, which was soon renamed
Barnes & Noble. Though Mr. Noble withdrew from the business in 1929, the name Barnes & Noble stuck.

The company's early business was wholesaling, selling mainly
to schools, colleges, libraries, and dealers. Barnes & Noble
entered the retail textbook trade somewhat reluctantly. A report
in *College Store* magazine recounted that single book customers

were tolerated, but that the store's counters and display shelves
functioned as barricades against their encroachment. Eventually
the store took a building on Fifth Avenue that included a small
retail space. The public then ''launched a campaign of book
buying that soon banished all doubt as to the need for a general
retail textbook house in New York.'' Barnes & Noble opened a
large retail store on Fifth Avenue and 18th Street, and this
became the company's flagship. The quarters were enlarged and
remodeled in 1941, and the store set the standard for college
bookstores.

Barnes & Noble served the students of hundreds of New York
City schools and colleges, and the store had to operate at top
efficiency to accommodate the rush for textbooks at the beginning of each semester. In 1941, the store instituted a ''book-a-
teria'' service that was soon picked up by other college bookstores. A clerk handed the customer a sales slip as he entered the
store. Purchases were recorded on the slip by one clerk, money
taken by another, and wrapping and bagging done by another.
Barnes & Noble installed a telephone service that was quite
advanced for the time, with five lines manned by specially
trained staff. The New York store was also a pioneer in the use
of ''Music by Muzak,'' with the piped-in music interrupted at
twelve-minute intervals by announcements and advertising.
Staff during the textbook rush season sometimes numbered over
300, and the store boasted a stock of 2 million books.

The successful retail division continued alongside Barnes &
Noble's original business of wholesaling to schools and libraries. The company also ran an import and an export division,
an out-of-print book service, and published several series of
non-fiction books, including the *College Outline Series* of
study guides. In 1944, Barnes & Noble began putting out
children's educational books after it took over the publishing
firm Hinds, Hayden & Eldredge. The company also opened
branches in Brooklyn and Chicago, and operated an outlet for
used books and publishers' remainders called the Economy
Book Store.

Barnes & Noble operated on a grand scale from the 1940s
onward. Its wholesale textbook division bought used books
from around 200 campus bookstores all across the East and
Midwest. The flagship retail store earned a place in the *Guinness Book of World Records* in 1972 as ''the World's Largest
Bookstore,'' and Barnes & Noble also claimed this store did
the largest dollar volume of any retail bookstore in the
country.

But Barnes & Noble began to grow in more ways when it came
under the sway of a new young owner, Leonard Riggio. Riggio
began his stellar career in the book business at age eighteen,
when he was a poorly paid clerk at the New York University
bookstore. Riggio initially studied engineering at night at the
university, and in some sense he was unprepared for working
with books. He recalled being embarrassed by a customer who
asked for a copy of *Moby Dick*—Riggio had never heard of it.
Nevertheless, he caught on to book selling like no one else. In
1965, when he was only 24, Riggio borrowed $5,000 to open his
own college bookstore, the Waverly Book Exchange. Though
his store was only one-eighth the size of the official NYU
bookstore, he soon rivalled his old employer's sales. He offered
exceptional service to his student customers, airlifting text-

books to the store if necessary. The success of the Waverly Book Exchange allowed Riggio to buy or open ten more college book stores over the next several years.

When Leonard Riggio set his sights on Barnes & Noble, the venerable bookstore was in a slump. President John Barnes, grandson of the founder, had died in 1969, and the retail and wholesale divisions of the company were purchased by a conglomerate called Amtel, which made toys, tools, and various other products. Business declined under the new management, and Amtel decided to sell. In 1971, Leonard Riggio purchased Barnes & Noble from Amtel for $750,000. He quickly changed the names of his ten other bookstores to Barnes & Noble, and revitalized the old Fifth Avenue store.

The new owner made Barnes & Noble an educational bookstore with a broader focus that included all kinds of how-to and non-fiction books. Riggio believed that more people read books for information than for entertainment, and he changed the set-up of the flagship store to give customers easier access to books they might want. He organized the stock into new, more specific categories, for example dividing the traditional category of philosophy into yoga and mysticism. Other sections of special interest books included cooking, Judaica, handyman books, study aids, and dictionaries. Riggio also opened a special children's section in the Fifth Avenue store, which, like the adult sections, emphasized educational books.

Under Leonard Riggio's management, Barnes & Noble expanded to include stores in New York, New Jersey, and Pennsylvania. By 1976, the company leased and operated 21 campus bookstores, and the combined retail and wholesale divisions brought in $32 million in sales. His early success led Riggio to gamble on a new kind of bookstore—the book supermarket. Across the street from the old Fifth Avenue Barnes & Noble, Riggio opened a giant sales annex that sprawled over three buildings. All books at the annex were discounted between 40 and 90 percent, even new books and best-sellers. Shoppers spent hours piling bargains into shopping carts, as Riggio explained to *Publishers Weekly* that he had "set the customer free in an unintimidating atmosphere to roam over a vast space." The prairie-like annex included fiction, textbooks, children's books, reference books, art books, and gift books. Corners were devoted to books on special topics ranging from Latin America to transportation, and huge black and yellow signs directing customers to different categories could be read from 176 feet away. Riggio claimed that most of Barnes & Noble's customers did not intend to read the books they bought, and the casual, warehouse atmosphere of the sales annex was geared to the everyday shopper, not the scholar or bibliophile. It was a marketing technique that worked brilliantly.

Barnes & Noble's thriving sales encouraged the company to grow and innovate. In 1979, Barnes & Noble acquired a chain of retail stores called Bookmasters, and then bought up Marboro Books, Inc., a remainder company with discount retail outlets. Barnes & Noble operated a chain of Supermart Books which serviced drug store and supermarket book departments, and ran the Missouri Book Co., selling used college textbooks. Barnes & Noble also more than tripled its college store leases in the mid-1980s, increasing from 40 in 1983 to 142 in 1986.

Total sales grew to about $225 million in 1985, and the next year Barnes & Noble made a major acquisition. For a price estimated at around $300 million, Barnes & Noble bought B. Dalton Bookseller, a bookstore chain with 798 outlets, from Dayton Hudson Corporation. B. Dalton was the second-biggest chain bookstore, behind Waldenbooks, and its sales were estimated at $538 million in 1985. The acquisition put Barnes & Noble in the second place spot, and the company continued to acquire chains. In March of 1990, Barnes & Noble purchased an upscale chain of 40 bookstores, Doubleday Book Shops, for an estimated $20 million. A few months later, the company became sole owner of a Texas and Florida chain of discount bookstores called Bookstop.

Barnes & Noble had used the name BDB Corp. for the holding company that owned Barnes & Noble, Inc., B. Dalton, and its other businesses. Leonard Riggio was the majority owner, and had a financial partner in a Dutch conglomerate called Vendex. The name of the holding company changed back to Barnes & Noble, Inc. in 1991, and the company re-acquired rights to publish under the Barnes & Noble name. These rights had been sold after John Barnes died in 1969.

Barnes & Noble, Inc. had grown enormously in the 1980s through acquisitions. The company embarked on a new growth strategy in the 1990s, opening new "superstores" at a breath-taking pace. The superstores differed somewhat from the earlier Fifth Avenue "book supermarket" Barnes & Noble sales annex. The superstores were large, carrying as many as 150,000 titles, or six times the size of a typical mall bookstore, but they had amenities such as coffee bars and children's play areas, and were designed to be pleasant public spaces where people would browse, read, and mingle. Wide aisles and scattered chairs and benches encouraged customers to linger, and local managers had the autonomy to arrange poetry readings and puppet shows. The discounted (usually by ten to 40 percent) superstore stock was vast, yet the space was as posh and inviting as that of many independent bookstores. Barnes & Noble operated 23 superstores in 1989. Three years later there were 105, and the company intended to open 100 more each year through 1994. On one day in August 1992, Barnes & Noble opened five superstores, and two months later opened three more.

The superstores cost more than $1 million a piece to build, outfit, and stock, and Barnes & Noble lost money by opening so many so quickly. Though sales for 1991 were more than $892 million, Barnes & Noble, Inc. posted a loss of close to $8 million that year. But overall sales continued to rise, and the superstores contributed some impressive revenues. Eighty percent of new superstores contributed to company profits in their first year of operation. A Barnes & Noble superstore on the Upper West Side in Manhattan was expected to bring in $12 million in sales its first year, but it proved so popular with New Yorkers that it actually brought in between $16 and $18 million. The average superstore brought in a much more modest $3.5 million. The superstores generated on the average twice the sales of mall bookstores, and in 1992, superstore sales rose by 114 percent.

Other booksellers complained about Barnes & Noble's rapid growth, believing that the market could not hold so many bookstores. But Leonard Riggio went on the record repeatedly to dispel claims that his growing chain was predatory. The amount Americans spent on books rose a hefty 12.5 percent in 1992, and Riggio believed the market would continue to grow. But the expansion of Barnes & Noble prompted competitive chains to build more stores too. Waldenbooks made planned to more than double the size of its mall stores, from 3,000 square feet to 6,000 to 8,000 square feet. Borders Inc., a chain of superstores owned by Kmart, planned to open two new stores a month in 1993.

With its growth so enormous and debt so high, Barnes & Noble, Inc. decided to raise cash by selling its stock to the public. An initial stock offering in 1992 was postponed because of adverse market conditions. Wall Street analysts had been skeptical of the company's ability to sustain its profits, but a year after the first offering was withdrawn, superstore sales had continued to climb. These sales accounted for almost half the company's total revenue, up from 26 percent in 1992, and the company seemed more solid. Barnes & Noble stock began trading on the New York Stock Exchange on September 28, 1993, and demand was so high that brokers were unable to purchase as much as they wanted. The stock had been expected to sell for around $17 a share: it closed at $29.25 its first day. Leonard Riggio retained about a third of Barnes & Noble, Inc., and another third was controlled by his Dutch partner Vendex.

For the fiscal year ending in January 1994, Barnes & Noble reported an 87 percent gain in revenue at its superstores. The textbook area of the company continued to be quite profitable too, and the company ran almost 300 college bookstores across the country. Children's books also sold very well, and Riggio made plans to expand the square footage of the Barnes & Noble Jr. stores that were a part of the superstores. The growth of the Barnes & Noble chain under Leonard Riggio had been spectacular.

In spite of critics' fears that the company's rapid expansion would saturate the book market or set off vicious wars for market share, Barnes & Noble seemed able to keep abreast of what the public wanted in a book store, and supply just what was needed. The discount sales annex had been a radical step, eliminating the high-brow atmosphere long associated with bookstores. The superstores managed to combine the savings and huge selection of the discount store with an environment tailored equally well to book lovers, socializers, and bargain hunters. In many ways Barnes & Noble set the standard for its competitors from the early textbook store to the present day, by innovating in areas such as store design and marketing of software, and by its pioneering efforts such as providing books for children with disabilities, and offering a literary award to first-time novelists. Barnes & Noble faces increasing competition from independent booksellers and other chains, as these

seek to duplicate what Barnes & Noble has done, but the company is used to setting the pace and will undoubtedly find creative solutions to new problems that lie ahead.

Principal Subsidiaries: Barnes & Noble Superstores, Inc.; B. Dalton Bookseller, Inc.; Doubleday Book Shops, Inc.

Further Reading:

''Barnes & Noble, Educational Bookstore, Celebrates 75 Years of Service,'' *Publishers Weekly,* February 12, 1949, pp. 901–904.

''Barnes & Noble Encouraged by Software Sales,'' *Publishers Weekly,* October 26, 1984, p. 69.

Barnes & Noble, Inc. Company Reports, New York: Barnes & Noble, Inc., 1993–94.

''Barnes & Noble Remodels Its Quarters for Efficiency,'' *Publishers Weekly,* December 6, 1941, pp. 2090–2093.

''Barnes & Noble Stock Soars,'' *Publishers Weekly,* October 4, 1993, p. 14.

''Barnes & Noble to Buy Doubleday Book Shops,'' *Publishers Weekly,* March 2, 1990, p. 8.

''Barnes & Noble's Revitalization Program,'' *Publishers Weekly,* September 28, 1970, pp. 69–70.

''BDB Corp. Becomes Barnes & Noble Inc. and Plans to Expand,'' *Wall Street Journal,* January 9, 1991, p. B5.

Berreby, David, ''The Growing Battle of the Big Bookstores,'' *New York Times,* November 8, 1992, sec. 3, p. 5.

Bhargava, Sunita Wadekar, ''Espresso, Sandwiches, and a Sea of Books,'' *Business Week,* July 26, 1993, p. 56.

Cox, Meg, ''Barnes & Noble Boss Has Big Growth Plans that Booksellers Fear,'' *Wall Street Journal,* September 11, 1992, p. A1.

——, ''Barnes & Noble Cancels Proposal to Offer Stock,'' *Wall Street Journal,* September 30, 1992, p. A4.

Freilicher, Lila, ''Barnes & Noble Success Spawns New Mall Stores,'' *Publishers Weekly,* August 5, 1974, pp. 43–44.

——, ''Barnes & Noble: The Book Supermarket—Of Course, Of Course,'' *Publishers Weekly,* January 19, 1976, pp. 71–73.

''Literary Supermarket,'' *Forbes,* May 15, 1976, p. 49.

''Marboro Sells Part of Assets to Barnes & Noble,'' *Publishers Weekly,* October 29, 1979, p. 28.

McDowell, Edwin, ''Book Chain Refinances, Easing Debt,'' *New York Times,* November 18, 1992, p. D4.

Milliot, Jim, ''Barnes & Noble Reports Strong Superstore Sales—Up 114% in '93,'' *Publishers Weekly,* April 26, 1993, p. 17.

——, ''Superstores Success Spurs New Try at B & N Offering,'' *Publishers Weekly,* September 13, 1993, p. 12.

Mutter, John, ''Crown Sells Interest in Bookstop to BDB for $8.3 Million,'' *Publishers Weekly,* June 1, 1990, p. 15.

Strom, Stephanie, ''Barnes & Noble Goes Public: Vol. 2,'' *New York Times,* September 3, 1993, p. D1.

Symons, Allene, ''Barnes & Noble to Buy B. Dalton: Will Become Largest Chain,'' *Publishers Weekly,* December 12, 1986, p. 17.

Tangora, Joanne, ''Major Chains Set New Software Strategies,'' *Publishers Weekly,* August 24, 1984, pp. 38–39.

—A. Woodward

Battelle

. . . Putting Technology To Work

Battelle Memorial Institute, Inc.

505 King Ave.
Columbus, Ohio 43201-2681
U.S.A.
(614) 424-6424
Fax: (614) 424-3889

Private Nonprofit Company
Incorporated: 1925
Employees: 8,796
Sales: $854 million
SICs: 8731 Commercial Physical and Biological Research;
   8733 Noncommercial Research Organizations

Battelle Memorial Institute, Inc. ranks among the world's oldest and largest independent research and development organizations. With 48 locations worldwide, the firm identifies, evaluates, refines, and applies new and existing technologies for government and private clients in a wide variety of disciplines, including: manufacturing, health sciences, computer technology, space travel, and environmental research. Battelle Memorial Institute has been instrumental in the development of such diverse products and processes as: xerography, no-melt chocolate, plastic six-pack straps, liquid correction fluid, cruise control for automobiles, and the universal product code (UPC) system. Battelle's Scientific Advances, Inc. subsidiary capitalizes venture businesses, including the institute's other subsidiaries: Geosafe Corporation, Information Dimensions, Inc., and Survey Research Associates. During 1992, Battelle had 5,688 projects for over 1,650 clients in progress. Due to an increasingly competitive research and development environment, the company began marketing its processes and products more aggressively in the early 1990s.

Battelle Memorial Institute was created through the beneficence of Gordon Battelle, the only son of a steel magnate in Columbus, Ohio. After attending Yale University, Battelle returned to Columbus to work in the steel mills run by his father, Colonel John Gordon Battelle. Seeking to cultivate his own business interests, however, the younger Battelle traveled to Joplin, Missouri, in the 1910s, where he invested in mining and smelting operations.

During the course of his investment research, he became interested in the work of former university professor W. George Waring, who was then developing a process for recovering usable chemicals from mining waste. Battelle financed a small laboratory for Professor Waring's research that facilitated the formulation of a commercially viable process. The experience piqued Battelle's interest in applied science, and he spent a year visiting laboratories across the United States and developing an innovative plan to make research facilities more accessible to industry by promoting cooperation between science and industry.

In 1920, Gordon Battelle drew up a will mandating the creation of the Battelle Memorial Institute. Three years later, he died unexpectedly at the age of 40 after complications from a routine appendectomy. Battelle had willed almost half of his estate to the creation of the Institute, and when his mother, Annie Norton Battelle, died two years later, she left the balance of the family fortune to the Institute, bringing the total endowment to $3.5 million.

Battelle's will stipulated that the Institute would focus on "education in connection with and the encouragement of creative and research work and the making of discoveries and inventions in connection with the metallurgy of coal, iron, steel, zinc and their allied industries." The Battelle Memorial Institute was incorporated as a nonprofit corporation in 1925, and construction of its headquarters commenced on a ten-acre site on King Avenue adjacent to The Ohio State University. As a nonprofit organization, the Institute generated revenues designated for reinvestment in research and donation to charitable pursuits. The Institute's first laboratory opened in October 1929 with a staff of about 30. Despite economic constraints necessitated by the onset of the Great Depression, research expenditures during the first year amounted to $71,000.

The Institute's first director was Dr. Horace W. Gillett, known to his peers as "The Dean of American Metallurgy." In accordance with the will and Dr. Gillett's expertise, the Institute's early focus was on metallurgy, the science of extracting metals from their ores, purifying them, and creating useful products from them. Although the Institute would eventually diversify into a wide variety of disciplines, metallurgy and materials technology would remain a strong suit throughout its existence. The first sponsored project was the preparation of *The Alloys of Iron Research Monograph Series,* a multi-volume reference work on metallurgy. This classic publication marked the beginning of the Institute's ongoing contribution to technical literature; by the late 1980s, the Institute was credited with over 9,000 professional publications.

Research in the 1930s investigated the properties of cast iron, the uses of pulverized coal, and the durability of nickel, copper, and steel. A particularly interesting study that commenced in 1933 sought an antimagnetic, rustproof alloy for watch springs. The material that resulted from this research was later patented and called "the most outstanding development in watch manufacture in 200 years." Like many of Battelle's products and processes, the alloy proved useful in a variety of applications, including the development of a mechanical valve for the human heart.

More interested in research than administrative duties, Dr. Gillett resigned his directorship in 1934 and was replaced by Clyde E. Williams. Williams took a proactive approach to

Battelle's work: since industrialists of the period were reluctant to elicit the Institute's services, he resolved to make them more readily available. Throughout the decade, Williams also began to broaden Battelle's scope beyond materials technology to include chemistry, physics, engineering, and economics.

The onset of World War II prompted research on both the composition and propulsion of rockets and missiles. Moreover, in 1943, Battelle technologists began studying the fabrication of the virtually unknown metal uranium in conjunction with the Manhattan Project. The Institute eventually became one of the country's leading nuclear research centers. Its research on nuclear propulsion led to the development of the nuclear submarine Nautilus in 1948. In the early 1950s, Battelle purchased a large tract of land near Columbus and erected the world's first privately owned nuclear research center, which included a research reactor, critical assembly facility, and hot cells.

During this time, Battelle also became involved in perhaps its best known technological achievement, xerography. After submitting his idea for "electrophotographic dry copying" to at least 20 companies, inventor Chester Carson approached the Institute in 1944. Through a subsidiary, Battelle Development Corporation, the Institute penned an agreement to help Carson refine the invention. Battelle and Carson invested over five years and hundreds of thousands of dollars in the development of this technology, which was based on static electricity.

During this time, Battelle initiated a long-term relationship with the struggling Haloid Company. Haloid agreed to assume sponsorship of Battelle's ongoing xerography research in exchange for the opportunity to commercialize the process. In the early 1960s, Battelle traded its hundreds of xerography patents to the cash-poor Haloid Company—which subsequently became the Xerox Corporation—for equity in the corporation. Xerox's success was phenomenal, and the company's increasingly valuable stock dramatically boosted Battelle's financial assets. By the early 1970s, the market value of the Institute's investment portfolio exceeded $225 million.

The financial windfall enabled Battelle—under the direction of Dr. B. D. Thomas from the late 1950s through the 1960s—to expand the scope of its research into such diverse areas as oceanography, health care, ecology, pollution control, and urban planning, as well as to establish laboratories in Germany and Switzerland. The Battelle Institute Program was launched during this time to fund fellowships for staff members and academicians interested in conducting private research. The program began with a 1966 budget of about $1.5 million, which grew into a $5 million annual endowment by the early 1970s.

The Institute also achieved many breakthroughs that affected food preparation, fashion, and currency. In 1963, Battelle research developed the Stabilized Acid Process, which reduced production time for such dairy products as sour cream and buttermilk from hours to minutes. The following year, the Institute's researchers automated the manufacture of shoulder pads for jackets, thereby shortening production time from two minutes to 18 seconds. In 1965, Battelle conducted a study for the U.S. Treasury Department that resulted in the development of coins made of a copper/nickel "sandwich," a money-saving solution that remained in use through the 1990s.

Battelle's profitability and diversification was challenged by the Internal Revenue Service and the Ohio Attorney General in the 1960s and early 1970s. The IRS called into question the taxability of Battelle's activities in 1961, eventually settling for payment of $47 million in taxes and the relinquishment of the Institute's tax-free status. In March 1969, the Ohio Attorney General called for a reexamination of Gordon Battelle's will, advocating reforms in the scope of the Institute's activities and the distribution of revenue to other philanthropic institutions. The series of lawsuits that ensued were settled in 1975 with the formulation of a modern interpretation of Gordon Battelle's will and the Institute's distribution of $80 million to other charitable enterprises. The Institute donated at least $1 million annually to charities thereafter. These two decisions mandated the divestiture of most of Battelle's investment portfolio, which resulted in the rapid and severe cutback in Battelle's research, development, and educational programs.

In 1981, governmental and corporate cutbacks resulting from a national economic recession raised the level of competition among research and development firms. Battelle found itself contending not only with such traditional rivals as Arthur D. Little and SRI International, but also universities—where overhead was often only about half as high. A concurrent rise in research and development costs due to the quickening pace of technological obsolescence increased financial pressures.

During this time, the Institute brought on Ron Paul, a former physicist for General Electric, as chief executive. Paul put his experience in industry to work, focusing first on making the company more profitable by garnering lucrative government contracts. Battelle had already been selected by the U.S. Department of Energy (DOE) to manage a major program on commercial nuclear waste isolation in 1978. Paul helped solidify this relationship by erecting a fully equipped hazardous materials laboratory near its Columbus headquarters.

Battelle also operated the DOE's Pacific Northwest Laboratories (PNL), which specialized in applied physics; earth, environmental, molecular, materials, chemical, and life sciences; and waste, engineering, and reactor technology. Scientists at PNL realized many major accomplishments, including a robotic mannequin with human physiological traits (perspiration, for example), which was used to test space suits, fire fighting gear, and other garments designed for hostile environments. Another PNL breakthrough, a thermochemical environmental energy system, designed for food processing plants, converted waste materials like potato peelings into methane gas, which could be recycled to fuel boilers. Battelle Memorial Institute's $1.9 billion contract with the DOE to run the PNL was renewed in 1992.

The Seattle Research Center, an advanced study facility for Battelle-sponsored workshops and conferences, was also operated out of Battelle's Northwest operations. The Human Affairs Research Center (HARC) there analyzed social problems relating to technology. Work in these fields greatly expanded Battelle's client base. For example, *Cosmopolitan* magazine hired Battelle to undertake an in-depth study of demographic shifts from the 1940s through the 1990s, noting in particular the way such changes have affected the lifestyles, attitudes, and consumer habits of American women.

HARC made headlines in 1993, when it released the findings of its controversial survey of sexual behavior in the United States. The study refuted previous estimates that ten percent of American men were homosexual, instead reporting that gays comprised between two and four percent of the population. These findings were contested by activists in the homosexual community, who brought the accuracy of the survey into question, fearing it would lead to further political and social marginalization of gay people.

Under CEO Paul, Battelle formed a venture-investing operation, Scientific Advances, Inc., to commercialize its own inventions through subsidiaries. Information Dimensions, Inc. (IDI), formed in 1986, developed a computer-integrated design system for small manufacturers that was named one of *Business Week* magazine's "24 Outstanding Achievements" for that year. Another software package created by IDI brought computer-aided design capabilities to genetic engineering.

Paul retired in 1987 and was replaced by Douglas Olesen, who guided Battelle through a restructuring that resulted in the creation of specific business groups targeted at such growth markets as health, transportation, manufacturing systems, environment, and national security. The reorganization was aimed at streamlining management and more effectively marketing and advertising Battelle's services.

Battelle's Geosafe Corporation subsidiary was formed in 1988 to commercialize a hazardous waste disposal process perfected at PNL. The vitrification process used high temperatures to melt radioactive and hazardous chemical wastes into a glass-like solid said to immobilize the dangerous materials for a million years.

Battelle also became an authority on forming strategic alliances with a variety of partners. Joint ventures helped reduce lead time to get new products to market, cut development costs, diversified its technological resources, and opened new markets to the Institute. In the 1990s, joint ventures with the Gas Research Institute, Vorwerk, and the Alternative Fuels Coalition resulted in the development of high-efficiency gas appliances and the creation of fleets of electric, propane, methane, and methanol powered vehicles. Cooperative efforts with the DOE, auto and airplane manufacturers, universities, and aluminum manufacturers underway in the early 1990s focused on creating "superplastic metals" that would dramatically reduce vehicle weight, and, in turn, reduce fuel consumption and emissions.

Battelle has originated over 2,000 U.S. patents and has received several awards and citations for its innovations. In 1992, Battelle staff members patented 63 inventions, and the firm garnered *R&D Magazine*'s R&D 100 Awards for a new type of radiation detector, an oil spill outline monitor, a chemical process to clean up PCBs, and a process for producing advanced ceramic powders. Battelle focused not only on developing innovative products and processes, but also on producing tangible value from those advances. Its success in that arena was indicated by an 11 percent revenue increase to $854 million between 1991 and 1992.

Principal Subsidiaries: Geosafe Corporation; Information Dimensions, Inc.; Scientific Advances, Inc.; Survey Research Associates.

Further Reading:

Gibson, W. David, "Holy Alliances!" *Sales & Marketing Management,* July 1993, pp. 84–7.

Hick, Virginia Baldwin, "Gays Assail Study, but Rue Political Implications," *St. Louis Post-Dispatch,* April 16, 1993, p. C1.

Louis, J. C., "R & D's Big Three: Tales from the Leading Edge," *Management Review,* August 1986, pp. 35–40.

Science Serving Human Needs: A History of Battelle Memorial Institute, Columbus, Ohio: Battelle Memorial Institute, 1978.

Siwolop, Sana, "Physician, Heal Thyself," *Financial World,* June 13, 1989, pp. 77–80.

—April Dougal Gasbarre

Baxter International Inc.

One Baxter Parkway
Deerfield, Illinois 60015-4633
U.S.A.
(708) 948-2000
Fax: (708) 948-2887

Public Company
Incorporated: 1931
Employees: 60,400
Sales: $8.88 billion
Stock Exchanges: New York
SICs: 2834 Pharmaceutical Preparations; 3841 Surgical and
Medical Instruments; 5122 Drugs, Proprietaries and
Sundries; 5047 Medical and Hospital Equipment; 3845
Electromedical Equipment; 3842 Surgical Appliances and
Supplies; 2830 Drugs

Baxter International Inc. is the world's largest manufacturer and
distributor of hospital supplies and a leading provider of medical specialty products. Serving over 5,000 hospitals, Baxter
operates in two primary industry segments: medical specialties
and medical/laboratory products and distribution. The company's major products and services include dialysis systems,
cardiovascular devices, laboratory and surgical equipment, and
intravenous and diagnostic systems. Over the course of its history, Baxter has introduced several medical innovations, including: blood banks; the first commercial kidney dialysis system;
and continuous ambulatory peritoneal dialysis (CAPD), a self-
administered alternative to hemodialysis in a hospital. In the
early 1990s, Baxter held an overwhelming 75 percent of the
worldwide market for CAPD.

In 1931, two Iowa physicians, Dr. Ralph Falk and Dr. Donald
Baxter, launched the Don Baxter Intravenous Products Company to distribute intravenous solutions commercially to hospitals in the Midwest. During this time, only large research
centers and university hospitals had the facilities to produce
intravenous solutions, which were of variable quality and limited in quantity. Falk and Baxter planned to overcome these
problems by manufacturing large, closely controlled supplies of
solutions and packing them in evacuated containers. In 1933,
the company opened a plant in Glenview, a Chicago suburb.
The staff of six employees produced Baxter's complete line of
five solutions and packaged them in glass containers; the Amer-

ican Hospital Supply Corporation, also based in Chicago, distributed the Baxter products.

In 1935, Falk bought his partner's interest in the company; soon
thereafter, he established a research and development division
and built a second manufacturing facility, in Canada. In 1939,
the company introduced the Transfuso-Vac blood collection
system, a sterile vacuum-type collection and storage unit for
blood. Prior methods allowed blood to be stored for only a few
hours, but the Transfuso-Vac provided storage of up to 21 days,
giving rise to the practice of blood banking. In 1941, Baxter
introduced the Plasma-Vac container, which enabled the medical community to separate plasma from whole blood and store
the plasma for later use.

During World War II, Baxter provided blood collection products and intravenous solutions to the U.S. armed forces. The
company opened several temporary facilities in order to meet
the military's increasing demand, and after the war these operations were consolidated in the Glenview plant. Late in the
1940s, the company moved into a new office and production
facility in the Chicago suburb of Morton Grove; that facility
would continue to house research and materials management
operations into the 1990s.

During the 1940s, Willem Kolff, a Dutch physician, was applying dialysis procedures to treatment of kidney failure, and
Baxter began making commercial use of his methods in the
United States. In 1948, Baxter's product line was expanded to
include Fenwal Laboratories' new unbreakable plastic container for blood storage, the precursor to the Viaflex plastic IV
bag, a product that would serve as a basis for the development
of a plastic delivery system for dialysis solutions. Baxter
formed a pharmaceutical specialties division under the name
Travenol Laboratories in 1949. This division was responsible
for developing and marketing chemical compounds and medical
equipment.

The company expanded considerably during the 1950s, opening
a facility in Cleveland, Mississippi, which would later produce
intravenous and irrigating solutions, needles, dialysis solutions,
respiratory therapy products, and many disposable devices used
in medical treatment. In addition, Baxter made several important acquisitions during the decade, including Hyland Laboratories of Los Angeles in 1952, as well as Flint, Eaton and Company and Fenwal Laboratories of Boston in 1959. That year, the
company also established its international division, which later
was divided into two separate divisions, Travenol Europe and
the Americas-Pacific Division, both of which established manufacturing facilities in 17 countries and distributed products in
more than 100 countries.

One of the most important company developments of the 1950s
was the appointment of William B. Graham as Baxter's president and chief executive officer. Named to these posts in 1953,
Graham was responsible for the decision to support Dr. Kolff's
research effort on the production of artificial kidneys. In 1956,
Baxter introduced the first commercially-built kidney dialysis
system, representing the company's first move into a field in
which it would become known as an innovator.

Baxter shares began trading on the New York Stock Exchange
in 1961. The company's steady growth during subsequent years

prompted shareholders to vote in favor of several two-for-one stock splits. In 1963, Baxter ended its 30-year-old distribution contract with American Hospital Supply and thereafter developed its own sales force. The company also built two Arkansas facilities during this time and acquired Disposable Hospital Products as well as Dayton Flexible Products Company and Cyclo Chemical Corporation. Moreover, Baxter's international operations were making extensive inroads into European markets, especially through the development of its wholly owned subsidiaries.

Several important technological innovations occurred at Baxter during the 1960s and 1970s. The first disposable total bypass oxygenator for open-heart surgery was introduced in 1962, and, in 1968, Baxter marketed the Hemofil antihemophilic factor, which was six times as powerful as any similar product offered at that time. The company also developed the Autoplex anti-inhibitor coagulant, another important innovation in the treatment of hemophilia. In 1979, Baxter offered continuous ambulatory peritoneal dialysis as an alternative to hemodialysis for kidney failure. CAPD proved popular as it could be performed at home by the patient, was less costly than hospital treatment, provided more uniform results, and allowed increased patient mobility.

Baxter's sales totaled $242 million in 1972, securing the company a spot on the *Fortune 500* list. By 1978, sales had quadrupled to $1 billion, and the company could boast an earnings growth rate of 21 percent for the preceding 24 continuous years. During this time, Baxter built a new plant in North Carolina and a new corporate headquarters in Deerfield, Illinois. In a series of acquisitions, the company bought American Instrument Company and Surgitool in 1970, Vicra Sterile Products in 1974, and Clinical Assays in 1976. That year, Baxter shareholders voted to adopt the name Baxter Travenol for the parent company, with Travenol Laboratories as the major domestic operating subsidiary. In 1980, Vernon R. Loucks, Jr. replaced William Graham as president and chief executive officer; he would become chairperson seven years later.

During the 1980s, industry analysts predicted a continued strong demand for intravenous solutions and equipment, kidney dialysis equipment, and various blood-derived products, all market areas that Baxter dominated. The company's earnings per share rose steadily, from $1.86 in 1980 to $2.64 in 1982, and further rises were expected. Expansion into foreign markets, development of "mini-bags" of pre-mixed drugs, and domination of the CAPD market were all factors favoring the company's continued growth.

Nevertheless, Loucks and other leaders at Baxter believed that the company's continued growth depended on its exploitation of new markets for health care products and services. Under Loucks' guidance, Baxter acquired Medcom Inc., a medical education and information company, in 1982 and subsequently purchased two computer software firms specializing in health management applications. In late 1983, the company formed a partnership with Genentech Inc. to develop, manufacture, and market products in the human diagnostics field.

Loucks also initiated a comprehensive cost-cutting program intended to make Baxter the lowest-cost supplier of medical products and services. Toward that end, Baxter's research and development focused on such cost-cutting products as premixed drugs, rather than the sophisticated, expensive items it had emphasized. Moreover, the new research and development programs, many of which were joint ventures, sought to adapt traditionally expensive products for less costly use in the home.

In 1982, when the federal government announced reductions in the fees it would pay Medicare and Medicaid patients undergoing kidney dialysis treatment, industry observers predicted that Baxter would take the lead in home dialysis methods. Baxter's sales of home dialysis products had risen 40 percent since 1978, when the company introduced CAPD, and the company had also developed a device called an ultraviolet germicidal chamber to reduce the risk of infection from tactile contamination. Although the company seemed well-positioned to gain market share, several factors instead contributed to a poor performance.

At the end of 1983, due to a special charge of $116.1 million after taxes, consolidations involving the closing of three manufacturing facilities, and asset revaluations, Baxter announced that its earnings for the following year were likely to be below the average of previous years; in fact, net sales for 1984 decreased 2.3 percent, net income dropped a precipitous 86.7 percent, and the average price for Baxter common stock declined 29 percent. Moreover, several market trends worked against Baxter. In response to pressure from government and private insurance companies, hospitals sought to control their costs, and demand for Baxter's traditional hospital-oriented products declined sharply. Although the company had anticipated these events and had shifted its research into growth areas, it was unable to offset the slackened demand from hospitals and the resulting competitive pricing in the industry. The high investment in research and development of products for Baxter's new non-hospital products and services had not yet begun to pay off.

One of Baxter's most significant adjustments to changes in the medical industry was its development of a "package deal" of products and services for hospitals. The plan combined the company's traditional products—intravenous supplies, blood therapy products, and hemodialysis and urological goods— with consulting services to help its hospitals reduce costs. Through the plan, Baxter hoped to establish contacts with hospitals engaged in setting up home health care systems. However, to make a profit in home health care, a company had to be able to rely on a large patient pool, particularly because many patients were short-term, and Baxter did not have access to such a pool.

Moreover, Baxter had to bear the expense of maintaining extensive production facilities for the manufacture of its products, particularly intravenous solutions and equipment, while domestic demand for such products decreased. Although demand remained strong in international markets, conducting business in foreign territory proved problematic at times. For example, in 1985, when labor strikes in the Philippines caused turmoil at Baxter's intravenous operation, the company was forced to close its operations there, a withdrawal that cost Baxter its $10 million investment in the facility. Furthermore, in the late 1980s, perceived and real risks of contracting Acquired Immune

Deficiency Syndrome (AIDS) from blood transfusions depressed the demand for blood therapy products. Although a reliable blood screening test was developed relatively quickly, analysts predicted that a return to earlier levels of use of blood therapy products was unlikely in the near future.

In 1985, Baxter acquired its early partner, American Hospital Supply Company, for $51 per share in cash and securities, through a hostile takeover. Although earnings were diluted by the merger, investors remained confident in the future of the company. Stock rose 35 percent as assimilation of American progressed. With its new name, Baxter International, and new emphasis on high profit products, including diagnostic equipment and computer software for hospitals, the Baxter-American merger promised increased competition in a crowded market.

Two years later, Baxter acquired Caremark Inc., an alternative site health care business that provided products and services for use outside of hospitals. The purchase doubled Baxter's holdings in that segment, which soon became its fastest-growing business. However, Baxter's traditional hospital customers soon began to resent the threat Caremark posed to their own home health care programs. Moreover, in 1991 a criminal investigation of Caremark for alleged Medicare kickbacks was initiated. Baxter decided to spin Caremark off to shareholders in 1992.

Rumors that the Baxter-American merger had resulted in difficulties between the divergent corporate cultures seemed to be confirmed in ensuing years, as the firm entered a state of frequent restructuring. Early in 1990, the company announced the largest restructuring in its history, involving the closing of 21 plants, divesting marginal businesses, and laying off about ten percent of the work force. The 1990 retrenchment focused largely on Baxter's hospital supply businesses, and the revamp two years later eliminated its alternative site health care business.

During this time, Baxter lost several lucrative contracts, having gained a reputation as a high-cost, high-priced distributor whose practices tended to anger and frustrate hospital purchasing managers. According to an October 1993 *Health Industry Today* article, Baxter's contract with Premier Health Alliance Inc., which represented $32 million in 1992 sales, was not renewed in 1993. Furthermore, the Veterans Administration proposed to exclude Baxter from bidding on and being awarded contracts for the next year, following allegations by the VA that Baxter knowingly misled and provided false information to the government agency's officials. In a conciliatory measure, Baxter accelerated programs to revamp its sales structure and lines of authority as well as slash executive pay.

In spite of the firm's efforts to improve its reputation, damaging information continued to emerge. In March 1993, Loucks admitted that Baxter had violated laws against aiding the Arab League's boycott of Israel when it sold its Travenol Laboratories Ltd. operations in Israel and entered into a joint venture with the Syrian army. Asserting that such illegal actions were inadvertent, the corporation nevertheless plead guilty to federal charges and agreed to pay $6.5 million in fines. Also that year, Baxter was implicated in a lawsuit brought by hemophiliacs infected by HIV-tainted clotting agents, and took a $700 million charge for divesting some divisions and reorganizing its diagnostics subsidiary. At year's end, President James Tobin quit, and Baxter's stock plunged to a four-year low. Moreover, Baxter's proposed merger with third-ranking Stuart Medical Inc. was terminated, and Stuart quickly engaged another suitor, Owens & Minor Inc. Their combined operations promised to threaten Baxter's top position in medical/surgical supply, as the new company would follow Baxter by only about $300 million in annual revenues.

Loucks's 1993 letter to shareholders acknowledged that the company's "earnings and stock price [had] not performed well," and announced 1993 losses of $268 million. Nevertheless, sales at Baxter had increased every year from 1988 through 1993, with net sales increasing over $400 million from 1992 to 1993. Loucks vowed to "achieve the potential that exists for Baxter International" by emphasizing service, international growth, and technological innovation through its new "Network 2000," a $400 million plan to expand, consolidate, and modernize facilities and operations.

Principal Subsidiaries: Baxter Diagnostics Inc.; Baxter Export Corporation; Baxter Vascular Systems; Bentley; Biotech Group; Clinical Alternate Site; Clintec Nutrition Company; Dietary Products; Edwards Critical Care; Edwards CVS; Hospital Supply; Hospitex; Interventional Cardiology; I.V. Systems; Novacor; Renal; Scientific Products; Scientific Products Industrial and Life Sciences; Surgical Group; Valuelink Business Center.

Further Reading:

"Baxter, Losing Business Opportunities, Responds with Corporate Restructuring," *Health Industry Today,* September 13, 1993, p. 2.
Berss, Marcia, "2 + 2 = 3," *Forbes,* February 28, 1994, pp. 82–83.
Braly, Damon, "Owens & Minor Knocking on Baxter's Back Door with Stuart Medical Buy," *Health Industry Today,* February 1994, pp. 1, 12.
Cody, Thomas G., *Strategy of a Megamerger: An Insider's Account of the Travenol-American Hospital Supply Combination,* New York: Quorum Books, 1990.
Wagner, Mary, "Baxter Admits Mistake in Boycott Case," *Modern Healthcare,* March 29, 1993, p. 4.

—updated by April Dougal Gasbarre

Bear Stearns Companies, Inc.

245 Park Avenue
New York, New York 10167
U.S.A.
(212) 272-2000
Fax: (212) 272-8239

Public Company
Incorporated: 1985
Employees: 6,300
Operating Revenues: $2.8 billion
Stock Exchanges: New York
SICs: 6211 Security Brokers and Dealers

Bear Stearns Companies, Inc., the holding company that owns Bear, Stearns & Company, Inc., was created on October 29, 1985 as the successor to Bear Stearns & Company and Subsidiaries, a partnership organized in 1957. The partnership, in turn, was the successor to a company founded in 1923 by Joseph Bear, Robert Stearns, and Harold Mayer as an equity trading house. Bear Stearns today is a full service brokerage and investment banking firm.

Throughout its history, Bear Stearns has been characterized as aggressive and opportunistic, willing to forego long-range planning in favor of immediate profits, and willing to take risks where others would not. This approach has certainly paid off for the company: Bear Stearns has not had an unprofitable year since its founding in 1923.

The original company was founded with $500,000 in capital in response to the thriving investment climate of the early 1920s. World War I, with its heavy demand for capital, had encouraged the public to enter the securities markets in mass, and the young Bear Stearns prospered in the frenzied optimism of those markets. The company began trading in government securities, and it is still one of the leading traders in this area.

Trading fell off sharply, of course, when the New York stock market crashed in 1929. Though Bear Stearns suffered setbacks, it had accumulated enough capital to survive quite well: during this crisis it not only avoided any employee layoffs but continued to pay bonuses. As the country struggled out of the Depression, Bear Stearns entered into the bond market to promote President Franklin Roosevelt's call for renewed development of the nation's infrastructure through the New Deal.

During the period following Roosevelt's reform measures, the nation's banking system had accumulated a large amount of cash, since demand for loans was very low. At the same time, bonds were very cheap. Bear Stearns made its first substantial profits by selling large volumes of these bonds to cash rich banks around the country.

By 1933 the firm had grown from its original seven employees to 75, had opened is first regional office in Chicago (after buying out the Chicago-based firm of Stein, Brennan), and had accumulated a capital base of $800,000. That year Salim L. "Cy" Lewis, a former runner for Salomon Brothers, was hired to direct Bear Stearns's new institutional bond trading department. Lewis, who became a partner in 1938, a managing partner in the 1950s, and then chairman, built Bear Stearns into the large, influential firm it is today. An almost legendary character, Lewis's outspokenness and drive were what gave Bear Stearns the style that makes it stand out on Wall Street to this day.

In 1935, Congress passed the Securities & Exhange Commission's (SEC) Public Utilities Holding Company Act, which precipitated a breakup of utility holding companies. As new securities were being issued for the formerly private companies, Bear Stearns positioned itself to take advantage of the opportunity, trading aggressively at what Lewis later called "the most ridiculous prices you ever saw in your life."

Revolutions in the freight and transportation industries beginning in the 1940s offered other opportunities. As auto transportation became more efficient and civil aviation more feasible, the once booming rail industry began to decline. Bear Stearns was quick to see an opportunity, and as most of the nation's railroads went into bankruptcy, Bear Stearns became one of the biggest arbitrators of mergers and acquisitions between railroad companies.

In 1948 Bear Stearns opened an international department, although it was not until 1955 that the firm opened its first international office, in Amsterdam. As its international business prospered, the company opened other foreign offices, in Geneva, Paris, London, Hong Kong, and Tokyo.

In the 1950s, Lewis was one of the originators of block trading, which by the 1960s was the bread and butter of most of Wall Street. Bear Stearns, like other companies, profited nicely from this trading until May 1, 1975, when the SEC's Security Act amendments, which eliminated fixed brokerage commissions, went into effect.

Bear Stearns began expanding its retail business operations in the late 1960s, once again ahead of the trend. It opened an office in San Francisco in 1965, and between 1969 and 1973 opened offices in Los Angeles, Dallas, Atlanta, and Boston. The company was very successful at attracting and managing accounts for wealthy individuals. These accounts also laid the foundation for the company's successful margin operations. In margin trading, brokerage houses loan their clients' securities to short sellers, who match the fund with their own capital and use the entire amount to finance trade, paying interest on the amount loaned. Bear Stearns currently manages about 300,000 margin accounts.

In 1975, when New York City was near bankruptcy, Bear Stearns proved again that it was a risk taker by investing $10 million in the city's securities. Though it came close to losing millions of dollars, the firm eventually profited greatly from the gamble.

In May of 1978, Alan "Ace" Greenberg became chairman of Bear Stearns, following the death of Cy Lewis. Greenberg had joined the firm as a clerk in 1949. He moved up rapidly within the company; by 1953, at age 25, he was running the risk arbitrage desk and by 1957 he was trading for the firm. By the time he became chairman, Greenberg had earned a reputation as one of the most aggressive traders on Wall Street. Like his predecessor, Greenberg shunned long-range planning in favor of immediate returns. It soon became apparent that Greenberg's abilities equaled and perhaps surpassed those of his predecessor. From the time he took over as chairman until Bear Stearns went public in 1985, the firm's total capital went from $46 million to $517 million; in 1989, it was $1.4 billion.

Bear Stearns's willingness to take risks has pushed it into the forefront of corporate takeover activity. The firm has been described as a "breeding ground" for corporate takeover attempts, and as masterful at disguising takeover maneuvers. In some instances, however, Bear Stearns's aggressiveness has earned it an unsavory reputation. The firm has been known to wage proxy battles against its own clients, as it did in 1982 against Global Natural Resources after deciding that Global's management had undervalued its assets and could realize greater profits. In 1986, Bear Stearns developed an option agreement that essentially allowed clients to buy stock under Bear Stearns's name, a tactic that facilitates corporate takeover attempts. The Justice Department and the SEC put an end to such tactics by filing suits against several of Bear Stearns' clients for "parking" stock (all of them settled).

In October of 1985, Greenberg and the firm's executive committee announced that Bear Stearns would make a public stock offering in an effort to increase the company's ability to raise capital to finance larger trades. Part of the strategy included the formation of a holding company named Bear Stearns Companies, Inc. Shortly after the initial 20 percent offering, Bear Stearns reorganized from a brokerage house into a full-service investment firm with divisions in investment banking, institutional equities, fixed income securities, individual investor services, and mortgage-related products.

The company was hit hard by the 1987 Wall Street crash, and numerous positions at Bear Stearns were eliminated. This streamlining, however, actually helped the company when the economy fired up once again and revenues from its investment banking division and its brokerage commissions began to substantially increase. By 1991, Bear Stearns had become the top equity underwriter in Latin America. By 1992, the company had successfully included capital industry, biotechnology, and machinery stocks in its ever-expanding analysis of the corporate sector.

In 1992, Bear Stearns had the best year in its history when earnings doubled to over $295 million. During the same year, the company managed more than $13 billion in new issues of stock, otherwise known as initial public offerings (IPOs), for a variety of American and foreign corporations. The company also has become a leader in clearing trades for other brokers and brokerages, and boasts one of the best ratios in the industry of analysts to brokers.

Much of Bear Stearns's success has been realized through short-term profit making ventures. Although the company has been successful in its initial attempts to build an identity as a major investment banking firm, it will have to attract larger corporate clients who seek long-term financial planning and commitment. Given its historical focus on short-term profits, some industry analysts question the company's ability to succeed in context of the longer term horizons required in investment banking. So far, however, Bear Stearns's profits and capital continue to grow.

Principal Subsidiaries: Bear Stearns & Company, Inc.; Custodial Trust Co.; Bear Stearns Mortgage Capital Corp.; Bear Stearns Fiduciary Services, Inc.; Bear Stearns International, Ltd.; Bear Stearns S.A.; Bear Stearns, Ltd. (Japan); Bear Stearns Securities Corp.; Correspondent Clearing; Bear Stearns Home Loans Ltd.

Further Reading:
"The New Bull Market in Brokerage Stocks," *Fortune,* July 15, 1991.

—Tony Jeffris
updated by Thomas Derdak

BEN&JERRY'S®

Ben & Jerry's Homemade, Inc.

P.O. Box 240
Waterbury, Vermont 05676
U.S.A.
(802) 244-6957
Fax: (802) 244-5944

Public Company
Incorporated: 1978
Employees: 446
Sales: $132 million
Stock Exchanges: New York
SICs: 2024 Ice Cream & Frozen Desserts; 6794 Patent
   Owners & Lessors; 5812 Eating Places

Ben & Jerry's Homemade, Inc. produces super premium ice cream, frozen yogurt, and ice cream novelties in rich and original flavors. The company sells its unique offerings in grocery stores, restaurants, and franchised ice cream shops, and it holds about one-third of the market for its products. Started by two friends who never intended to become big businessmen, Ben & Jerry's is distinguished by a corporate philosophy that stresses social action and liberal ideals in addition to profit making, and is known for innovative and creative marketing devices that express this unorthodox spirit.

Ben & Jerry's was founded in May 1978, when Ben Cohen and Jerry Greenfield opened an ice cream shop in Burlington, Vermont. Cohen had been teaching crafts, and Greenfield had been working as a lab technician when the two decided that ''we wanted to do something that would be more fun,'' as Greenfield later told *People* magazine. In addition, the two wanted to live in a small college town. In 1977, they moved to Burlington, Vermont, and completed a five dollar correspondence course in ice cream making from Pennsylvania State University. With $12,000 in start-up money, a third of which they borrowed, the two renovated an old gas station on a corner in downtown Burlington and opened Ben & Jerry's Homemade.

The first Ben & Jerry's store sold 12 flavors, made with an old fashioned rock salt ice cream maker and locally produced milk and cream. Initially, ice cream production ran into some glitches. ''I once made a batch of rum raisin that stretched and bounced,'' Greenfield told *People*. With time, however, the pair's rich, idiosyncratic, chunky offerings such as Dastardly Mash and Heath Bar Crunch gained a loyal following. In the

summer of 1978, Ben & Jerry inaugurated the first of the many creative marketing ploys that would help drive the growth of their company when they held a free summer movie festival, projecting films onto a blank wall of their building.

By 1980, Ben & Jerry had begun selling their ice cream to a number of restaurants in the Burlington area. Ben delivered the products to customers in an old Volkswagen squareback station wagon. On his delivery route, he passed many small grocery and convenience stores and decided that they would be a perfect outlet for their products. In 1980, the pair rented space in an old spool and bobbin factory in Burlington and began packaging their ice cream in pint-size cartons with pictures of themselves on the package. ''The image we wanted was grass roots,'' Cohen later told *People*.

The popularity of Ben & Jerry's products brought the company growth, despite the laissez-faire attitude of its two proprietors. At one point, the two were forced to close the doors of their store for a day to devote themselves to sorting out paperwork. In 1981, Ben & Jerry's expanded its pint-packing operations to more spacious quarters behind a car dealership. Shortly thereafter, the company opened its second retail outlet, a franchise on Route 7 in Shelburne, Vermont.

Despite its exclusively local operations, Ben & Jerry's first gained national attention in 1981 when *Time* magazine hailed its products as ''the best ice cream in the world'' in a cover story on ice cream. In the following year, Ben & Jerry's began to expand its distribution beyond the state of Vermont. First, an out-of-state store opened, selling Ben & Jerry's products in Portland, Maine. Then, the company began to sell its pints in the Boston area, distributing their goods to stores through independent channels. At the same time, Ben & Jerry's continued its policy of promoting itself through unique and whimsical activities. In 1983, for instance, the company took part in the construction of the world's largest ice cream sundae in St. Albans, Vermont.

With its continuing expansion, Ben & Jerry's developed a need for tighter financial controls on its operations, and the company's founders brought in a local nightclub owner with business experience to be chief operating officer. As sales grew sharply, Cohen and Greenfield slowly came to realize that their small-scale endeavor had exceeded their expectations. They were not entirely happy about this unexpected success. ''When Jerry and I realized we were no longer ice cream men, but businessmen, our first reaction was to sell,'' Cohen told *People* magazine. ''We were afraid that business exploits its workers and the community.''

Ultimately, Cohen and Greenfield did decide to keep the company, but they vowed not to allow the growth of their enterprise to overwhelm their ideas of how a business could be a force for positive change in a community. ''We decided to adapt [the company] so we could feel proud to say we were the businessmen of Ben & Jerry's,'' Cohen concluded. Among the stipulations they made to ensure that their company would be different from other parts of corporate America was a salary cap, limiting the best-paid people in the company to wages just five times higher than those of the lowest-paid employees. As Ben &

Jerry's grew, this unusual limitation would complicate the company's high-level staffing.

To finance further growth, Greenfield and Cohen decided to raise capital to expand by selling stock to the public. However, in an effort to maintain a sense of local accountability in the company, they limited the stock offering to residents of Vermont, utilizing a little-known clause of the state law governing stocks and brokering. With the proceeds from this sale of stock, the company began construction of a new plant and corporate headquarters in Waterbury, Vermont, about half an hour away from Burlington.

As Ben & Jerry's products continued to garner attention, its prime competitor in the premium ice cream market, Häagen-Dazs, took steps to protect its own share of the market. In 1984, Pillsbury, Häagen-Dazs' corporate parent, threatened to withhold its products from distributors who also sold Ben & Jerry's ice cream. Ben & Jerry's retaliated by filing suit against Pillsbury, and also by launching a publicity campaign with the slogan ''What's the Doughboy Afraid Of?'' Pillsbury took steps to restrict distribution again in 1987, when it threatened to stop selling its ice cream to retailers who also sold Ben & Jerry's products. In both cases, legal action brought the restrictive practices to an end. By the end of 1984, sales of Ben & Jerry's products had exceeded $4 million, a figure more than twice as large as the previous year's revenues.

In 1985, Ben & Jerry's expanded distribution of its products dramatically, starting up sales of its pints in New York, New Jersey, Pennsylvania, Virginia, Washington, D.C., Georgia, Florida, and Minnesota. To supply these new markets, the company completed work on its modern manufacturing plant. Among the new offerings that year was New York Super Fudge Chunk, created at the suggestion of a customer from New York City. Throughout 1985, sales of Ben & Jerry's products continued at a break-neck pace. By the end of the year, revenues had reached $9 million, an increase of 143 percent from 1984. As part of their program to remain true to their ideals, Cohen and Greenfield established the Ben & Jerry's Foundation to fund community oriented projects. In addition to the Foundation's initial capitalization, the two pledged 7.5 percent of the company's annual pre-tax profits to the charity.

In 1986, facing demand for its products that its one Vermont plant was unable to meet, Ben & Jerry's contracted with Dreyer's Grand Ice Cream, an ice cream company located in the Midwest, to manufacture Ben & Jerry's ice cream in its plants and distribute its products in most markets outside the Northeast. In addition, the company introduced its newest pint flavor, Coffee Heath Bar Crunch.

To promote this and other flavors, as well as the corporate identity, Ben & Jerry's began conducting tours of its Waterbury, Vermont, plant in 1986. In addition, the company launched its ''Cowmobile,'' an altered mobile home that Cohen and Greenfield set out to drive across the country, distributing free scoops of ice cream as they went. Four months into the trip, the Cowmobile burned to the ground outside Cleveland without causing any injuries, bringing the planned expedition to a premature end. These efforts had pushed company sales to $20

million by the end of 1986, as Ben & Jerry's continued to post a remarkable rate of growth.

Cohen and Greenfield's original plan for a cross country trip was brought to fruition in 1987, when ''Cow II'' made its maiden voyage, dispensing free scoops of ice cream along the way. After the October 1987 stock market crash, Cow II appeared on Wall Street to hand out scoops of ''That's Life'' and ''Economic Crunch'' ice cream to financial industry workers. Along with these highly topical creations, Ben & Jerry's introduced pints of ''Cherry Garcia,'' named for the long-time lead guitarist of the rock group Grateful Dead. In addition, the company began to market its first ice cream novelty, the Brownie Bar. This product consisted of a square of French Vanilla ice cream, sandwiched between two brownies.

At their manufacturing plant in Vermont, Ben & Jerry's also took steps to keep the company in compliance with its ideal of being a unique enterprise. To reduce its impact on the environment, Ben & Jerry's began using its ice cream waste to feed pigs being raised on a farm in Stowe, Vermont. In addition, to keep plant employees happy, the company instituted a variety of gestures, including Elvis day and Halloween costume celebrations, to break the monotony of life in a factory. By the end of 1987, company revenues had increased again, to reach $32 million.

In 1988, Ben & Jerry's opened its first outlets outside the United States when ice cream shops began operating in Montreal, Quebec and in St. Maarten in the Caribbean. By the end of the year, more than 80 ''scoop shops'' were flying the Ben & Jerry's banner across 18 different states. At this time, the company decided to hold back on further franchising to make sure that product quality and service in its existing stores met its standards.

Also in 1988, Ben & Jerry's responded to continuing growth in demand for the company's products by opening its second manufacturing facility in Springfield, Vermont. This plant was used to make ice cream novelties, including the ''Peace Pop,'' a chocolate covered ice cream bar on a stick. The name of this product referred to ''One Percent for Peace,'' a nonprofit group founded in part by Cohen and Greenfield that was dedicated to redirecting national resources towards peace.

To aid in running their own company, Cohen and Greenfield with their employees formulated a three-part statement of mission that was designed to sum up the company's unique corporate philosophy. Relying on a theory of ''linked prosperity,'' the mission statement asserted that Ben & Jerry's had a product mission, a social mission, and an economic mission. The company hoped to use this credo to enhance the lives of individuals and communities through its actions. As part of its philosophy of linked prosperity, Ben & Jerry's introduced several new flavors of ice cream that incorporated ingredients from special sources. Rainforest Crunch, marketed in 1989, used nuts produced by rain forest trees. Chocolate Fudge Brownie, brought out in February 1990, used brownies made at a bakery in New York where formerly unemployed and homeless people worked.

Beginning in the late 1980s, Ben & Jerry's joined the trend toward producing low-fat ice cream and yogurt. Ben & Jerry's

Light, introduced in 1989, had reduced levels of fat and choles-terol compared to the regular Ben & Jerry's ice cream, but no less fat than other "regular" products then on the market. "It was sort of an oxymoron," the company's chief financial officer admitted to the *Wall Street Journal*. Sales of the products never exceeded about $9 million, and in December 1991 the line was declared a mistake and phased out.

Ben & Jerry's frozen yogurt proved far more successful. Boast-ing a butterfat content between one and five percent—as op-posed to the 17 percent butterfat levels in the regular ice cream—Ben & Jerry's yogurt was selling in 13 cities around the United States in 1992. Within five months, yogurt sales were accounting for 15 to 18 percent of the company's revenues, and by the end of the year, it had become the leader in the super premium yogurt market. In addition, Ben & Jerry's introduced a pint version of one of its most popular scoop shop offerings, chocolate chip cookie dough. The company had spent five years finding a way to get the chunks of dough into pints of ice cream without having them stick together and gum up the packaging machines. The product was an immediate hit, and soon became the company's best-selling flavor. Finally, the company began to market its ice cream novelties, Peace Pops and Brownie Bars, in "multi-paks" in supermarkets.

In response to continuing demand for its new products, Ben & Jerry's moved to increase its output in Vermont. The company added a pint production line at its Springfield plant, and also borrowed space at the St. Alban's Cooperative Creamery to open another temporary production facility. To increase its capacity over the long term, Ben & Jerry's broke ground on a third ice cream factory in St. Alban's in late 1992. Financed through an additional stock offering, this plant was scheduled to be functional in 1994. In addition, the company completed a new distribution center in Bellows Falls, Vermont. Ben & Jerry's also renewed its co-packing agreement with Dreyer's Grand Ice Cream, Inc., its Midwestern partner. By the end of 1992, Ben & Jerry' sales overall had reached $132 million, up from $77 million in 1989.

Further from home, Ben & Jerry's opened two ice cream shops in the Russian cities of Petrozavodsk and Kondopoga. With two Russian partners, the company had spent three years navigating the Soviet bureaucracy and finding supplies for the venture, which Cohen and Greenfield hoped would promote friendship between Russians and Americans. After lining up reliable sources of cream and importing equipment, the company was able to open a combination ice cream plant and parlor, which was blessed by a Russian Orthodox priest on its first day.

As Ben & Jerry's moved into the mid 1990s, it could look back on a streak of extraordinary growth. From one small shop in downtown Burlington, Vermont, it had grown to include a chain of nearly 100 franchised shops, and a line of products sold in stores across the country. Company leaders were aware that it was unlikely that this rate of expansion could continue forever, since Ben & Jerry's growth had come in a mature and stable market. With its idiosyncratic corporate culture, and its strong track record of introducing innovative flavors that drove ever-stronger sales, however, it appeared that Ben & Jerry's was well positioned to continue its success.

Further Reading:

Alexander, Suzanne, "Life's Just a Bowl of Cherry Garcia for Ben & Jerry's," *Wall Street Journal,* July, 1992.
Hubbard, Kim, "For New Age Ice Cream Moguls Ben and Jerry, Making 'Cherry Garcia' and 'Chunky Monkey' Is a Labor of Love," *People,* September 10, 1990.

—Elizabeth Rourke

UNITED COLORS OF BENETTON.

Benetton Group S.p.A.

Via Villa Minelli 1
31050 Ponzano Veneto (VE)
Italy
(39) 1422-4491

Public Company
Incorporated: 1965 as Maglificio di Ponzano Veneto dei
   Fratelli Benetton
Employees: 5,715
Sales: L1362 billion
Stock Exchanges: Milan Rome Turin Venice New York
   Frankfurt Madrid Toronto London
SICs: 2321 Men's and Boy's Shirts; 2329 Men's and Boy's
   Clothing; 2331 Women's and Misses' Blouses and Shirts;
   2339 Women's and Misses' Outerwear

Colorful clothing and innovative, sometimes controversial, ad campaigns distinguish Benetton Group S.p.A., the world's largest consumer of virgin wool and designer and manufacturer of distinctive casual apparel for men, women, and children. Headquartered in Treviso, in northeast Italy, Benetton markets wool, cotton, and denim products under the United Colors of Benetton trademark through more than 80 regional independent sales agents, who coordinate more than 7,000 independently licensed stores in about 120 countries. Benetton also operates manufacturing joint ventures with local partners in developing countries and licenses its trademarks worldwide for toys, shoes, linens, watches, cosmetics, eye glass frames, as well as other fashion accessories to enhance brand recognition in tentative markets. Benetton maintains a competitive advantage with flexible, vertically integrated, state-of-the-art production, warehousing, telecommunications, and distribution operations that are integrated across national boundaries, allowing Benetton to efficiently produce large quantities of merchandise at moderate prices.

Luciano and Giuliana Benetton, the founders of the Benetton Group, came from humble origins. The Benetton family grew up poor; their father, who owned a car and bicycle rental business, died while they were children. But Giuliana Benetton developed a skill that would make her family rich. At age five, she fell in love with knitting. In her early teens, Giuliana worked during the day in a tiny knitting business, producing scratchy, somber-colored woolen sweaters. At night, she used a borrowed knitting machine to make her own brightly colored designs. Her brother Luciano, who was then 20 and had worked as a men's clothing salesman in Treviso, realized his 17-year-old sister's talent. The two siblings sold their bicycle and accordion and scraped together enough cash to buy their first second-hand knitting machine in 1955. Then Luciano sold a small collection of Giuliana's knitted creations to local Veneto area stores. The enthusiastic reception of her designs gave the company a solid start.

In the early 1960s, the "Brothers of the Rainbow" invested about two thousand dollars to buy another second-hand hosiery knitting machine, which Luciano converted to make sweaters and jersey materials, and to build a small factory in Ponzano, a few miles from Treviso. Then in 1965, the Benetton company was formed as a partnership, called Maglificio di Ponzano Veneto dei Fratelli Benetton, with Luciano as chairman, his brother Gilberto in charge of administration, their younger brother Carlo running production, and Giuliana as chief designer.

To compete in the casual clothing market, which is marked by its competitive and volatile nature, the small company's designs needed to be creative but so did its management. The company flourished by making "industrial fashion," fashionable apparel made and sold through flexible, cost-effective retailing and production systems.

To attract attention to their sweaters, Luciano decided to sell directly to the consumer through specialized knitwear shops rather than to retail outlets which sold competing products. This decision formed the basis for the Benetton retail outlets, which sell the Benetton line exclusively; the first such store was opened in 1968 in Belluno in the Italian Alps. The following year, the company opened its first shop in Paris. Luciano thought that it would be a challenge to bring Italian fashion to the sophisticated Paris market, but if Benetton was successful there, Benetton could make it anywhere.

Production at the company was also unique. In 1972 Luciano introduced a time and money saving production technique. By dyeing assembled garments made of unbleached wool rather than batches of yarn before knitting, manufacturing time was trimmed and Benetton could produce garments upon demand, which minimized the need to maintain an extensive inventory.

To produce many sweaters at reduced cost and financial risk, Benetton took advantage of an old Italian cottage industry. Benetton farmed out labor-intensive production—knitting and sewing—to small, family-owned companies (many owned in whole, or part, by Benetton management) throughout northeast Italy. Employing advanced technology, these companies allowed Benetton to manufacture in response to increased market demand both domestically and abroad with reduced financial risk. About 80 percent of production was farmed out to 450 subcontractors who employed about 20,000 workers in the Veneto region. The remaining 20 percent of value-added, capital-intensive production—quality control and cutting and dyeing—was performed in house. By 1983 Benetton payments for contract work equalled nearly six times the labor expense for work performed in its factories, according to the Harvard School of Business.

Benetton's early success is attributable as much to Luciano's genius, as to the Italian and local business climate, however. According to journalist Dante Ferrari of the Italian business daily *Il Sole-24 Ore*, Benetton's management style evolved from the heritage of the Veneto region, which offered a strong artisan tradition, an abundance of labor created from shrinking agricultural production, and hydraulic energy provided by many rivers and springs. During the years 1971 to 1981, despite weak governments and rampant inflation, highly productive, technologically advanced small-to-medium businesses in Italy outpaced those of the other European Community (EC) partners. By 1977 Italy had become the largest producer of knitted overwear in Europe, producing 60 percent of all EC output.

In 1978 Benetton became a limited liability company. Sales, which included T-shirts and denim jeans, reached $78 million, 98 percent of which came from the domestic market. With 1,000 stores in Italy alone, Benetton realized that the home market was saturated, and launched a major export campaign. Benetton targeted the rest of Europe and made plans to enter U.S. and Japanese markets. In 1979 the first store was opened in North America. By 1981, Benetton, operating under the name Invep S.p.A., had become the world leader in the field of knitwear, generating three times the sales volume of the next largest manufacturer. By 1982, with 1,900 shops in Europe (1,165 of which were in Italy), Benetton was opening shops in Europe at the rate of one each working day. To handle its expansion, Benetton invested in distribution and marketing operations, building a $30 million dollar computerized state-of-the-art warehouse, which made it possible for a staff of seven to handle more than 30,000 incoming and outgoing boxes in a 16-hour work day in 1983.

Having grown to a mature multinational company, Benetton needed expert managerial direction. Aldo Palmieri, from the Bank of Italy, became Benetton's first managing director in 1982, and brought the company into an era of wide expansion, globalizing its capital base. Although Luciano Benetton was not initially receptive, leading Palmieri to leave in 1990, the company eventually adopted Palmieri's vision after he had been rehired in 1992.

In 1984, 55 percent of Benetton's $303 million in sales revenues were generated from foreign turnover, outperforming domestic sales for the first time. The United States became Benetton's fastest growing market by early 1985, boosting sales by 35 percent. Retail operations were also opened in Eastern Europe—Budapest in March and Prague in September—marking the opening of the first shop by a Western manufacturer since 1948. Following a corporate reorganization in December 1985, the company was renamed Benetton Group S.p.A. It was now one of the world's largest garment producers, with four factories in Italy and one each in France, Spain, Scotland, and North Carolina, and an annual production growth rate of about 30 percent.

In July 1986, Benetton made its first public offering on the Milan and Venice stock exchanges, and the listing was subsequently extended to the Rome and Turin exchanges. Through an innovative corporate finance deal, Benetton sold 20 percent of its equity on the London and Frankfurt capital markets, raising about $500 million, of which some $100 million was earmarked for research and development over the next three years.

In early 1987, Palmieri approached the international capital market, focusing on the U.S. market, and also began to finance acquisitions and joint ventures. In March, he raised an international syndicated loan with Citibank and authorized Morgan Guaranty Trust to place in behalf of Benetton Group S.p.A. eight to nine million American Depository Receipts—worth about $150 million—on the New York Stock Exchange. This was the first time that an Italian company had attempted to float stock directly on Wall Street. In addition, Benetton formed Benetton U.S.A. Corporation, listed on the Toronto, Madrid, Tokyo, and Frankfurt exchanges, and made private placements in Europe and Japan. These moves were aimed not only at eliminating short-term debt but also at broadening the shareholder base between Italian and international investors, expanding corporate awareness as Benetton attempted to expand in North America and the Far East, and instilling the discipline required by the U.S. Securities and Stock Exchange into its corporate culture.

Because financial services were poor in Italy, Benetton began lending to its suppliers. By 1986 this informal business grew to $400 million in leasing and factoring. Bencom S.p.A. was incorporated as a subsidiary in 1987 to undertake leasing activities, and a financial services company was formed. Like the retail line, financial services were structured with the Benetton management philosophy—independent entrepreneurs selling and receiving commissions. The financial services evolved to include insurance products and personal and corporate financial services. Other nonretail interests included stakes in Italy's largest department-store chains, banks, hotels, and real estate. Unfortunately, these ventures required heavy capital investments and took away concentration of management time from the retail sector. Nevertheless, Benetton's retail line was expanded.

Palmieri pushed Benetton to extend the retail product line and introduce a nonretail line, to shift to global manufacturing, and to find local partners able to penetrate difficult or emerging markets in the developing world. The company introduced a new watch and cosmetic line, incorporated Benetton Japan K.K. to penetrate the Japanese and potential Far East market, and signed licensing agreements to produce clothing in the Middle East and Far East through Benetton International N.V. Benetton Group sales rose to $2.5 billion in 1987, an increase of about 15 percent over 1986 figures. At that time, there were about 5,000 shops in 70 countries; the EC accounted for 68 percent of sales, North America for 20 percent, and the Far East for two percent.

In 1988, after years of double-digit profit growth, Benetton's attempts to diversify faltered with consolidated net income flat at about $99.5 million and stock at about half its initial offering price. Sales stalled in Italy. In the United States, which accounted for about 15 percent of total sales, revenue fell 20 percent. The slowdown was due to a weak dollar, rising apparel prices, saturated markets, the rising cost of Italian labor, and shifting tastes, especially in the United States.

Moreover, in late 1988, several Benetton store owners filed suit in the United States against Benetton's agents, alleging unfair trade practices and also complaining about the disorganization of U.S. operations and the Benetton Group's practice of clustering stores, which was intended to promote competition among store owners. Benetton countersued two former store owners for alleged defamation. Conceding that these problems were brought about by rapid expansion (250 shops in 1983 to 758 shops in 1988) in North America, Benetton brought in former McKinsey & Co. consultant Federico Minoli to head Benetton U.S.A. Corporation as an autonomous entity and to improve relations with store owners.

Although Benetton spent three years expanding into financial services, reaching the $300 million mark, in 1988 it sold its merchant banking interests and refocused on its retail line. Benetton acquired interests in four apparel-related manufacturing companies: Calzaturificio di Varese S.p.A., a shoe manufacturer and distributor; Galli Filati S.p.A., a producer of woolen yarn; and Columbia S.p.A. and Altana Uno S.p.A., both licensed to produce and market under the Benetton trademark. To integrate group logistics, Benetton also acquired Azimut S.p.A., Benair S.p.A., and Benlog S.p.A. To enhance global production and marketing, Benetton built a factory in Argentina to add to facilities built the year before in Brazil; acquired, incorporated, or sold marketing companies in various countries; opened stores in Warsaw, Moscow, and Cairo; listed on the New York and Toronto stock exchanges; planned to expand Benetton Cosmetics, which had operated in North America and Europe for the last three years, into the Japanese and South American markets; and entered into a joint venture with the Japanese trading company Marubeni, creating Benetton Shoes Corporation, to sell shoes in the United States and Canada. Negotiations were also made with Toyobo on joint plans to enter both the Japanese and Brazilian markets, and with Seibu-Saison to convert its license to a production and marketing joint venture.

These developments were representative of Benetton's strategy to first use licensees to gain wide exposure in new markets and then to convert the license into production and marketing joint ventures. Accordingly, growth was also accelerated by granting licenses to producers in noncompeting industries. The Home Colors trademark was developed by acquiring an interest in Eliolona S.p.A., which was to produce linens under license agreements in Brazil and Israel and to sell them in European markets. A new joint venture called United Optical was formed between H. J. Heinz and the Italian manufacturer Anser to produce spectacles. Furthermore, W.I.D.E. Corporation was incorporated in the U.S. as a joint venture with Avendero S.p.A. to manage international forwarding and customs clearance operations.

By 1989 exports rose to 65.5 percent of total annual sales. To finance this expansion, Benetton aimed to attract investors in the United States, Canada, Japan, and Europe by making a capital issue of 24 million shares. In that year, Benetton's holding company, Edizione Holding, reinvested its funds from the sale of financial services by buying Nordica, a ski-equipment firm, for $150 million and soon acquired several other retail sports lines. Moreover, the trademark United Colors of Benetton was adopted. In the meantime, the Federal Trade Commission conducted a preliminary investigation to determine whether Benetton had violated federal statutes by failing to file as a franchisor but dropped the inquiry after Benetton asserted

that contracts are negotiated by independent sales agents and that store owners pay no fees or royalties, even though they are required to follow stringent merchandising rules.

In the late 1980s, Benetton gained additional competitive advantage by implementing global networking to connect sales and production. A point-of-sale computerized program, which linked the shops to headquarters, was designed to handle order management, cost accounting, production control, and distribution support. Thus, agents began booking 80 percent of each seasonal order six months in advance; the remaining orders were placed midseason and relayed to headquarters by computer. The point-of-sale program was replaced by late 1989, and Benetton's decentralized operations were linked by a global electronic data interchange network, which also included freight forwarding and customs applications.

Although sales grew by 24 percent in 1990, Benetton lost $6.6 million in the United States that year, and another $10 million in 1991, a loss of 28 percent since 1987. Thus, in 1991 Benetton started to consolidate its stores in the United States as well as Europe, replacing the clusters of smaller stores with the megastore concept, which carried the full Benetton line. In addition, Benetton turned its marketing and sales efforts once again to developing markets in the Near and Far East and to Eastern Europe, and halved its dividend to have more funds for expansion and acquisition. In December, Benetton signed a joint manufacturing agreement with Alexanian in Egypt in light of plans to open 30 stores in that country, and in 1992, 12 stores were opened in Poland. A joint venture agreement was signed for manufacturing facilities in Armenia, which was to produce apparel for the Soviet market under the United Colors of Benetton trademark; however, future expansion plans came to a halt owing to lagging productivity at this plant.

To beat the worldwide recession and increase market share, in 1992 Benetton developed strategies to achieve the following goals: to improve operating margins, reducing prices by about 15 percent, increasing production volume, improving product mix, and taking advantage of the devaluation of the lira; to improve operating efficiency, reducing number of styles of its collection from 4000 to 2600, and acquiring and integrating the operations of four key former subcontractors; and to improve cash flows, refinancing short- and medium-term debt. The mix of items was improved by introducing sophisticated classic professional apparel through shops dedicated to these higher margin product lines—*And* for dress shirts, Di Varese for shoes, and Benetton Uomo and Benetton Donna for mature men and women—and by continuing to expand into the sporting good market. By mid 1992, Benetton bought the remaining interest in Galli Filati and consolidated interests in four suppliers of woolen and cotton materials; now about 68 percent of the cost of production was represented by charges from subcontractors, compared with 87 percent in 1991. As a result, 1992 group sales rose ten percent.

By early 1993, Benetton had continued to close stores in the United States and, for production and marketing reasons, ceased operations at the Rocky Mountain plant in North Carolina. A technologically advanced factory opened at Castrette, Italy, which was designed to expand manufacturing capacity to 20 million pieces per year with about 15 people, using sophisticated robotic technology. Goods were now exported in greater numbers from Italy, where Benetton benefitted from the abolition of wage indexation system and the devaluation of the lira following its withdrawal from the exchange rate mechanism of the European Monetary System. At this point, Benetton had 32 factories, of which 27 were in Italy, and license agreements in 13 countries. In addition, Benetton decided to expand in developing countries, forming a joint venture with a major Indian manufacturer to produce linens and stationery, opening its 7,047th store, in Cuba, and transforming Benetton Mexico from a sales subsidiary to a manufacturing operation for the North American market. These developments, particularly the continued effort to rationalize production, resulted in Benetton's stock reaching a five-year high. Consolidated revenues increased in 1993 by about ten percent compared with the previous year, and net income rose 39 percent since 1990.

Benetton's global advertising campaign succeeded in generating a mix of praise and criticism and, ultimately, a fair amount of free publicity since about 1989. The ads, which were initially product-oriented campaigns on themes of multinational and multiracial harmony, eventually focused on institutional-oriented campaigns that featured documentaries on AIDS, sexuality, the environment, interracial relationships, and the war in Bosnia-Herzegovina. Although many of the ads became the subject of controversy and were withdrawn or banned throughout the world, the United Colors of Benetton ad campaign, which hinged on racial diversity, won Benetton's art director Oliviero Toscani the UNESCO Grand Prix award.

Despite the ad controversy, Benetton managed to maintain a sterling corporate image during Italian government kickback investigations conducted during 1993 that involved more than 5,000 of the country's political and business elite. In fact, Luciano had gotten involved in national politics as part of a movement to overthrow the old system, and in 1992 was elected to the Italian Senate as a member of the Republican party. In 1994, however, Luciano retreated from politics, believing that the Italian government had met its objective, to pursue his talent for minding the family business.

In early 1994, Palmieri diversified Benetton by planning substantial acquisitions of either well-known brands or companies in the developing world. One such expansion was a joint venture agreement signed with Timex and Junghans Uhren to produce watches and alarm clocks. In addition, Palmieri

planned to double turnover by 1996. To fund these ambitious plans, he placed 11 million shares in foreign markets. This issue was expected to raise the float from 20 to 30 percent, with the remaining stock controlled by the Benetton family.

Benetton has successfully grown from a home-based business to a multinational conglomerate. With Luciano Benetton's global vision and natural intelligence and creativity combined with the company's increased pricing competitiveness, creativity of design, and strong financial base, Benetton is poised to attain continued growth in both mature and developing markets.

Principal Subsidiaries: Benfin S.p.A.; Bencom S.p.A.; Galli Filati S.p.A.; Fabrica S.p.A.; Benetton Fashion S.p.A.; Benlong S.p.A.; Benetton Services Ltd. (United Kingdom); Benetton U.S.A. Corp.; Benetton Capital Investments N.V. (Netherlands); Benetton Holdings N.V. (Netherlands); Benetton International N.V. (Netherlands).

Further Reading:

Benetton, Luciano, with Andrea Lee, *Io e i miei fratelli: La storia del nostro successo,* Milan: Sperling and Kupfer Editori, 1990.

Camuffo, Arnaldo, and Giovanni Costa, ''Strategic Human Resource Management—Italian Style,'' *Sloan Management Review,* winter 1993, pp. 59–67.

Cento Bull, Anna, and Paul Corner, *From Peasant to Entrepreneur: The Survival of the Family Economy in Italy,* Oxford: Berg Publishers Limited, 1993.

Dapiran, Peter, ''Benetton—Global Logistics in Action,'' *International Journal of Physical Distribution and Logistics Management,* volume 22, number 6, 1992, pp. 7–11.

Harvard Business School, ''Benetton S.p.A.: Industrial Fashion'' (case study), Boston: HBS Services, 1987.

''How Benetton Has Streamlined and Branched Out Worldwide in Casual Clothing Market: Case Studies from Academia,'' *International Management,* May 1985, pp. 79–82.

Ketelhohn, Werner, *European Management Journal,* ''An Interview with Aldo Palmieri of Benetton: The Early Growth Years,'' September 1993, pp. 321–331; ''An Interview with Aldo Palmieri of Benetton: The Return as CEO,'' December 1993, pp. 481–84.

Lee, Andrea, ''Profiles,'' *New Yorker,* November 1986, pp. 53–74.

Pepper, Curtis Bill, ''Fast Forward,'' *Business Month,* February 1989, pp. 25–30.

Stillit, Daniel, ''Benetton: Italy's Smart Operator,'' *Corporate Finance,* June 1993, pp. 30–39.

—Marina L. Rota

Betz Laboratories, Inc.

4636 Somerton Road
Trevose, Pennsylvania 19053-6783
U.S.A.
(215) 355-3300
Fax: (215) 953-2484

Public Company
Incorporated: February 21, 1957
Employees: 4,115
Sales: $684.87 million
Stock Index: NASDAQ New York
SICs: 2899 Chemical Preparations, Nec; 3533 Oil and Gas
   Field Machinery; 3589 Service Industry Machinery, Nec;
   3625 Relays and Industrial Controls; 7389 Business
   Services, Nec

Betz Laboratories, Inc. is a specialty chemical products manufacturer with emphasis on the engineered chemical treatment of water and wastewater in industrial and commercial applications. In the early 1990s, the company had 13 U.S. plants and eight overseas locations.

The inauspicious beginnings of a father and son partnership in 1925 gave little indication of Betz Laboratories' major participation in the future development of the water treatment industry. William H. Betz and L. Drew Betz founded their modest business in Philadelphia, Pennsylvania to produce a water purification compound. Nearly seven decades later Betz Laboratories, its international sales alone exceeding $153.5 million, reaped the benefits of a growing movement in favor of pollution control. With the enactment of the 1971 Clean Water Act and increased government incentives to place the burden of regulation on the industries themselves, the company's customer base grew to include the accounts of major oil refineries and steel mills. However, developments in these industries—reflecting problems of overcapacity in petrochemicals and a drastic reduction in domestic steel production—placed Betz's future expansion at a turning point. Although much of its traditional customer base has been significantly diminished, Betz management proved to be considerably adept at conforming to a changing market.

Betz's first product, K-Gel, a colloidal substance used in the purification of boiler water, remained on the manufacturer's list for fifty years. After just one year of sales, this product made the

company approximately $30,000. Despite the difficulties of the Depression, Betz fared well in the 1930s. With sales surpassing $100,000 the company announced the addition of Collogel to its product line. This chemical compound dispersed sodium alginate in domestic water systems. Two years later a third product line, named Adjunct for its use in connection with K-Gel, entered the market. Although the company experienced two years of decreased sales, by 1936 a consulting service had been started that would eventually grow large enough to warrant a separate division.

As the company expanded into new areas, its older operations benefitted from a more integrated production. A new processing plant on the coast of Maine exploited natural resources available in the ocean floor. Using algin and alginic acid extracted from ocean kelp, this plant successfully processed ingredients later used in the production of K-Gel. Although initially successful, the plant was subsequently sold when a 1945 hurricane destroyed the kelp beds. Interestingly, at this point in Betz' history, the company's services, now widely recognized as a reputable leader, were solicited in order to fulfill an unusual request. To ensure the comfort of their unprecedented visit to the White House in 1939, George VI and Elizabeth, the reigning monarchs of the United Kingdom, were given tea brewed with synthetic London water. Betz was given the honor of synthesizing and bottling this water.

In 1940, John Drew Betz, the son and grandson of the company founders, officially joined the partnership. The young executive's tenure at Betz began while still in high school; the boy worked as a sample bottle washer in the summer of 1932. Eight years later the company embraced its third generation of family management, enabling this newest partner to participate in the manufacturing of Betz's first patented product. Remosil, a chemical compound of magnesium oxide used in the treatment of water containing silica, received U.S. patent approval in January of 1943.

By the end of the decade Betz entered its first foreign market through a Canadian partnership. During this period of time research was also underway to combat pitting and tuberculation in industrial cooling water systems. This research ultimately produced a line of patented products under the name Dianodic, and due to their innovative uses established Betz's position as an industry leader. One such product, a zinc-Dianodic, so effectively protected systems against corrosion that it remained a preferred product for years. In addition to these achievements sales surpassed, for the first time, the $2 million mark.

Water treatment chemicals were not the sole representatives of Betz's product line. In entering the paper processing industry the company developed biocides and other products useful to the manufacture of paper. In 1957 the original partnership established over 30 years earlier was transformed into a corporation and renamed Betz Laboratories, Inc. Two years later, while serving as chairman of the board, William H. Betz died. L. Drew Betz then stepped up to the position of chairman and John Drew assumed the title of president. The company issued its first common stock in 1965 signaling the transition from private to public ownership.

After observing the inauguration of Betz de Mexico, L. Drew Betz retired as chairman of the board of directors on the same day he turned 71. However, his list of achievements continued to grow until his death in 1971. The company's board of directors conferred upon him the position of chairman emeritus, and several years later the Drexel Institute of Technology awarded him an honorary doctorate in engineering. Following L. Drew's retirement, John Drew assumed the title of chairman and a young executive by the name of John J. Maguire, who was not a family member, was promoted to executive vice-president. Only two years later Maguire assumed the position of company president, signifying the end of the founding family's traditional tenure in this position.

Under the new president's leadership, industry observers watched the company consolidate its newly initiated European operations (including a joint venture with the British B.T.I. Chemicals Limited and a marketing office established in Belgium) into Betz International, Inc. This wholly owned subsidiary held the responsibility of guiding Betz's entrance into the international market. By 1972 Betz International successfully established operations in Central and South America, the Caribbean, Africa, the Middle East, and parts of Asia. In addition, an office was established in Austria for the purpose of penetrating communist bloc countries in Eastern Europe, and an office was established in Taiwan to arrange for Betz products to enter the market of the Republic of China.

The company's consulting business, operating under an independent division, similarly experienced a period of expansion during the later 1960s and early 1970s. First acquiring Albright & Friel, a consulting firm with over 75 years of experience, and then purchasing Fridy-Gauker & Fridy, a planning and architectural company, Betz's consulting services grew to achieve industry prominence. So important did this aspect of Betz's operations become that it was consolidated in 1971 into Betz Environmental Engineers, and later cited as a catalyst in the company's ability to secure customers. While Betz's product line consisted in commonplace bulk chemicals, its marketing of the uses and benefits of these products tallied the figures of the company's success.

By 1975 consolidated sales surpassed $100 million as compounded annual earnings growth reached 20 percent. The company's success was due not only to increased foreign operations and expanding services but also to a highly favorable economic and political climate. The enactment of the 1971 Clean Air Act, as well as the summit accord reached between U.S. President R. Nixon and Soviet Premier L. Brezhnev to cooperate on environmental protection issues, created an constructive environment for the pollution control industry. With estimates high for domestic expenditures needed to protect national resources, the government searched for ways to defray costs. These attempts included tax relief incentives for industry to regulate itself, tax-exempt pollution control bonds, and federal legislation. In addition, the high price of oil served to bolster Betz's profit margins. Scale deposits on boilers increased fuel bills; Betz's products removed scale deposits and therefore decreased the cost for maintenance.

While Betz continued to control an impressive 18 percent market share during 1984, fluctuations in the economy reflected a changing market configuration. The company, on the whole, operates independently from the drastic effects of economic cycles; no matter how much industry suffers through a recession, few companies would forgo the cost of basic maintenance. Yet fundamental changes in the economy demanded a realignment of Betz's customer base. 75 percent of the U.S. market for water treatment chemicals can be attributed to under 12 companies. The reason for this market dominance was due to the fact that these customers represented four heavy industries, including oil refineries, petrochemical plants, and steel and paper mills. Yet production overcapacity in both the petrochemical and paper industries as well as the virtual disappearance of many domestic steel companies and oil refineries found Betz searching for new customers.

Much of John F. McCaughan's tenure as Betz's chief executive officer focused on this issue of securing new markets. Despite the difficulties surrounding Betz's four major industry customers, McCaughan pointed to the company's success in consolidating business in the "middle" market, such as the auto and textile industries. Similarly, Betz executives emphasized the fact of dropping levels of water tables as an incentive for future growth. Since water represents a finite resource, some industries find themselves searching for alternative coolants, including the use of treated sewage water. Furthermore, an innovative new product called Dianodic II, an organic water treatment compound, entered the marketplace in a company effort to conform with the Environmental Protection Agency's policy on discontinuing the use of allegedly toxic chemicals contained in some water treatment compounds.

So successful was McCaughan's careful management of this period of market transition that he was honored by the *Wall Street Transcript* in 1986 with the bronze award for best chief executive in specialty chemicals. Citing his "conservative, carefully calculated course," the award commended McCaughan for the company's market strategy in a time of heavy industry consolidation, avoiding long-term debt, and capitalizing on growing demands for customized water treatment systems.

McCaughan's company achieved another important industry standard in 1992, when all 12 of its U.S. plants earned the International Standards Organization's (ISO) 9002 certification in only eight months. ISO sanction usually took 24 months. It was hoped that conforming to these primarily European criteria would boost Betz's international business, which had grown from $6 million in annual revenues to over $160 million. (Many overseas operations had previously been certified.) The company invested over $750,000 to bring its operations up to standard, but industry observers emphasized that certification sanctioned the company's quality claims, thereby opening new opportunities to the company. For example, Senior Vice-President B. C. Moore told *Business Week* in 1993 that two U.S. companies had placed sizable orders specifying that their water treatment systems be manufactured by an ISO-9000 certified plant. Annual savings of $100,000 in manufacturing costs were icing on Betz's cake.

Betz is proud that its products and processes not only help customers conform to internal and external water treatment standards, but also save them money. In 1992, the company's documented total annual return to customers on their investment in Betz treatment programs exceeded the firm's 1991 sales. In December of 1992, Betz was listed on the New York Stock Exchange. It was hoped that this exposure would bring the company increased liquidity and visibility.

In 1993, Betz marked an unfortunate milestone when, for the first time since the company went public in 1965, sales and pretax earnings decreased, from $706.97 million to $684.87 million and $82.05 million to $65.52 million, respectively. Company executives blamed a $16.2 million pretax restructuring charge for the deficiency. The charge reflected personnel reductions, facilities consolidation, divestment of unproductive assets, and the cost of reorganizing global marketing efforts. A key aspect of the reorganization was the decentralization of the company's largest operating segment, Betz Industrial. The subsidiary was split into four separate technology divisions: refining and chemicals; pulp and paper; power industry; and manufacturing industries.

Betz also cited "sluggish growth in the industrial sector of the economy, particularly the chemical, refining, and paper industries, our major customers," for its first decline, and raised its dividend regardless. John F. McCaughan resigned the chief executive office at the end of 1993 in favor of accepting the chairmanship. William R. Cook, who had joined Betz in 1972, added the responsibilities of CEO to his role as president.

In spite of Betz' slide, the outlook for companies in the water treatment business remained positive. According to Rick Mullin, writing for *Chemical Week* magazine, the proliferation of water treatment regulations, combined with the sheer volume of water used in the United States, would expand the $3 billion domestic market by six to eight percent during the mid-1990s. As the second largest player in its industry, Betz Laboratories' positioning as an environmental "guidance counselor" to industry promised to help it recover from its sales and earnings lapse.

Principal Subsidiaries: Betz International, Inc.; Betz Entec, Inc.; Betz Process Chemicals, Inc.; Betz Europe, Inc. (Belgium); Betz PaperChem, Inc.; Betz, Inc. (Canada); Betz Energy Chemicals, Inc.; Betz Industrial; Betz Limited (UK); Betz MetChem Division; Betz G.m.b.H. (Germany); Betz N.V. (Belgium); Betz Sud S.p.A. (Italy); Betz Pty., Ltd. (Australia); Betz Pte., Ltd. (Singapore); Betz Bes.m.b.H. (Austria); Betz Industries S.A. (France); Finn Betz Oy (Finland); Betz Korea, Ltd.; Betz Kemi AB (Sweden); Betz de Venezuela, C.A.; Betz Environmental Engineers; Betz de Mexico.

Further Reading:

Kiesche, Elizabeth S., "Water Treatment: Measuring Up to the Challenges," *Chemical Week,* May 15, 1991, pp. 24–32.
Mullin, Rick, "Above the Fray in Environmental Management," *Chemical Week,* May 12, 1993, pp. 37–40.

—updated by April Dougal Gasbarre

Biomet, Inc.

P.O. Box 587
Warsaw, Indiana 46581
U.S.A.
(219) 267-6639
Fax: (219) 267-8137

Public Company
Incorporated: 1981
Employees: 750
Sales: $340 million
Stock Exchanges: NASDAQ
SICs: 3842 Orthopedic, Prosthetic, and Surgical Appliances
    & Supplies

Biomet, Inc. is one of the largest and fastest growing U.S. manufacturers of orthopedic medical devices and supplies. Biomet and its subsidiaries design, develop, manufacture, and market products used primarily by orthopedic specialists in surgical and non-surgical therapy, including reconstructive implants and artificial joints, electrical bone growth stimulators, and operating room supplies.

Located in Warsaw, Indiana, Biomet is part of a seemingly average midwestern community with a population of less than 30,000. What makes Warsaw unique, however, is its reputation as a high-tech hotbed of orthopedic equipment industry innovation. Recognized as the birthplace of the business—industry leaders Depuy Inc. and Zimmer Inc. started operations there in 1885 and 1926, respectively—the north Indiana town is home to three of the four largest orthopedic supplies companies in the world. It is from this pool of long-standing talent that Biomet emerged.

Dane A. Miller, Jerry Ferguson, Ray Haroff, and Niles Noblitt were all employed in Warsaw's diverse orthopedic equipment industry in the mid-1970s. While working for different companies, they became acquainted with each other through their business dealings. As early as 1975 the four had shared their dissatisfaction with what they viewed as a stifling corporate culture within the industry, but it was not until the late 1970s that they decided to do something about it.

Ranging in age from only 26 to 31, the four entrepreneurs quit their jobs in 1978 to start Biomet. The group pooled $130,000 of its own money, received a $500,000 loan from the Small

Business Administration, and secured a $100,000 line of credit from a local bank. By taking suggestions from surgeons and emphasizing short product development cycles, they believed they could improve upon artificial joint implant designs offered by the companies they abandoned. Their diverse experience in marketing, engineering, and finance could be parlayed into a formidable force in the orthopedic implants industry. Notably, Miller, who would become Biomet's CEO, brought a PhD in biochemical engineering to the table.

With good reason, critics of the new venture wondered about the timing of the start-up. Shortly before the friends left their safe corporate jobs, amendments to the federal Food and Cosmetics Act placed squelching legislation on the artificial implants industry. Indeed, many industry participants believed that new safety regulations and product liability hazards had made the implant business too risky. "People laughed at us for starting up a new company after the new device legislation went into effect," Miller recalled in *Indiana Business.* "[Getting the company started] was traumatic. In retrospect, it was a lot more traumatic than it seemed at the time."

Despite hardship, Biomet was able to find a role in the marketplace as a developer and marketer of orthopedic products, contracting with independent manufacturing shops to make its implants. In its first year of operation the company developed a breakthrough titanium "total hip replacement" implant, the first of which was implanted in Miller's grandmother. Total hip replacement devices and the use of titanium both became industry standards by the late 1980s. Although Biomet had only $17,000 in sales during its first year of operation and lost a total of $63,000, by 1980 the struggling enterprise was turning a meager profit.

Unfortunately, Miller and his three partners realized that they were essentially training the manufacturing shop operators to build and sell Biomet-inspired products to their competitors. Unable to locate financing for their own manufacturing program to overcome this dilemma, the Biomet founders considered selling the fledgling business. However, the company was saved by two brothers from Kalamazoo, Michigan, who provided $500,000 in venture capital in return for one-third ownership of the business. Thus the Biomet team found itself in the manufacturing business.

Biomet's second major product innovation occurred in 1980, when it introduced the metal-backed acetabular cup. It was a device used in total joint replacement that increased the longevity of implant-to-bone stem attachments. "That was one example of how we took an opportunity, responded to it quickly, and then took it to the market," Miller related in *Indiana Business.* The company broke new ground again in 1983 with its development of a high-tech knee implant system that allowed a surgeon to align ligaments precisely, ensuring that the joint worked properly. The invention was held up for several years, however, because of technical problems and FDA approval.

Breakthroughs like the acetabular cup and titanium hip replacements were central to the momentum Biomet was gaining during the early 1980s. Likewise, aggressive marketing and innovative delivery systems placed the company on the forefront of customer service and cost-containment. Contradicting their detractors, the Biomet management team slowly boosted annual company revenues and profits. By 1984 annual sales had grown to $10.6 million and earnings topped a healthy $1.6 million.

Aside from innovations in product development, marketing, and operations, Biomet founders attributed much of their success to a unique corporate culture that bred creativity and achievement. The company was founded on a premise of risk-taking and teamwork, and maintains a very loose structure. Biomet has developed only one organizational chart during its history, and that was created only to please a potential lender. "We try to avoid a lot of structure. . . . Whoever is there to make a decision makes it," CEO Miller stated in *Indiana Business.*

In addition to its unorthodox organization, the company prospers by shattering many business school myths that Miller believes are a hindrance to other corporations. While many organizations rely on detailed planning to reach their goals, for example, Biomet spends about one percent of its time planning and the rest of the time implementing and monitoring results. "Too much planning sometimes keeps a company from responding to a world that is changing around it," Miller explained in the *Elkhart (Indiana) Truth.* Another myth, according to Miller, is that a company should set a goal and not let anything interfere with the accomplishment of that mission. "One thing you have to let get in the way from time to time is reality," he said.

Also a part of Biomet's management strategies is intimate worker involvement in, and employee reliance on, the company's performance. All employees are stockholders, either through stock options or by way of a benefit plan. And half of senior management's compensation is directly dependent on Biomet's financial performance. Miller sets the example for his employees by accepting a comparatively conservative compensation package. In fact, Miller was cited in *Business Week* during 1992 for giving shareholders more for their money than any other CEO surveyed—he received only $712,000 between 1989 and 1991 while shareholders garnered huge returns. In the *Indianapolis Business Journal,* Miller declared "I'd have to admit that if my board came to me and said, 'We're cutting your salary to zero,' I'm having enough fun that I'd come into work anyway."

Indeed, if Miller's job satisfaction was any reflection of the company's performance during the mid- to late 1980s, he was a very happy man. After posting its $1.6 million profit in 1984, Biomet entered a sustained period of steady, rapid growth that soon earned the company international recognition within the industry. In 1985 Biomet acquired Orthopedic Equipment Co., a local manufacturer, for $8.4 million, boosting its revenues for that year more than 300 percent. Sales continued to swell through 1988, when the company purchased New Jersey-based Electronic-Biology Inc. (EBI), which develops and produces devices that stimulate bone growth. As a result of this important acquisition, Biomet's 1989 revenues leapt to $136 million, of which one-third was contributed by EBI.

Even by the mid-1980s, Biomet's success had earned the company a lofty position in the hierarchy of Warsaw's orthopedic supplies business. Biomet was still dwarfed by Zimmer and

Depuy, but its rapid growth and unique products garnered the company third place in the local industry, making Biomet a competitive force that could not be ignored. All three major producers credited the local community with supplying a high-quality, hard-working supply of labor that helped to ensure their success. The region also provided an excellent location for distribution and offered fantastic land prices, cost-of-living advantages, and a high quality of life.

While grateful to the community, by the late 1980s Biomet had already begun to branch out from its native turf. Not only was the company seeking domestic growth, but Biomet management was fully committed to an international expansion effort that was expected to carry the corporation into the 21st century. In fact, Biomet had been chasing international business even before becoming incorporated in 1981. By the early 1990s, international sales represented about 25 percent of the company's revenues and comprised more than 30 percent of its annual growth.

The success of Biomet's important international business reflected the drive and initiative of Chuck Niemier, senior vice president of international operations. Niemier was a 24-year-old accountant at an outside audit firm when he was introduced to Miller and the small Biomet team. "I think because of my hairline, he thought I was older," recalled Niemier in *Indiana Business.* Miller liked Niemier, and was able to lure him to Biomet with an offer of $26,000 per year and a chance to own some Biomet shares.

Niemier played an early role in developing Biomet's international expansion, which entailed delivering cutting-edge implant products to overseas buyers. During the 1980s and early 1990s, the company expanded into Europe, South America, Japan, the Middle East, the Soviet Union, and other regions. In those countries where Biomet maintained manufacturing facilities, including Germany and England, a direct sales force was established; in other countries it worked through dealer organizations. Niemier benefitted from Biomet's flat organizational structure and decentralized decision-making process. The Berlin Wall had barely fallen, for example, before Biomet acquired what became a successful German orthopedics firm.

Not all of Biomet's international deals played out so nicely, however. When the company received a multi-million-dollar order for trauma products from Iraq in the early 1990s, for instance, Biomet managers were excited. Several months later, though, Iraq invaded Kuwait, providing insight into Iraq's giant order and ending Biomet's dealings with the aggressor nation. Likewise, Biomet invested in several ventures in the Soviet Union during the early 1990s, only to have that market dry up as a result of inner political turmoil. Regardless of minor setbacks, international growth remained a priority for the company going into the mid-1990s. Biomet was operating in about 100 countries by 1992.

Augmenting rising international sales in the late 1980s and early 1990s were continued product and manufacturing innovations that kept Biomet on the leading edge of the industry. In 1989, for example, Biomet technicians began utilizing computer-aided-design (CAD) systems to create three-dimensional images of diseased and damaged joints. When integrated into the production process, the CAD systems allowed Biomet to customize artificial joints for individual patients. The company also became involved in advanced research projects related to bone-growth protein, flexible carbon-fiber implants, and the use of naturally occurring soft tissue to lubricate artificial joints.

By the early 1990s, Biomet's stellar rise had earned the company a reputation on Wall Street as a solid growth stock. In 1992, for example, *USA Today* listed Biomet as one of "the hot stocks to watch in the 1990s." Although the 30 percent growth rate in the company's stock price enjoyed by shareholders during the late 1980s and early 1990s had subsided by 1993, it continued to outperform many of its competitors and was considered a good, long-term purchase by a number of analysts.

Furthermore, Biomet's profit growth continued unabated in the early 1990s and was even accelerating going into the mid-1990s. Sales jumped 22 percent in 1993 to $335 million, and net income ballooned to $64 million. These figures represented five-year compound annual revenue growth of 28 percent in the reconstructive device segment (56 percent of Biomet sales) and 17 percent in the EBI division (25 percent of sales); the remaining revenue was generated from the sale of miscellaneous supplies.

But aside from sales and stock statistics, Miller and the Biomet managed team looked to another, less tangible measure of their company's success—its victories in helping people to lead better lives. "I believe as we look back 10 years, the evolution of orthopedics has led to the rehabilitation of America," Miller explained in *Indiana Business.* "Ten years ago, if you were incapacitated with a bad knee or hip, you were in bed for the rest of your life. . . . In the last ten years, the tools and products have been developed to allow . . . patients to live a normal life."

Going into the mid-1990s, Miller and Noblitt were the only Biomet founders left at the company (Ferguson opened a classic car dealership, and Haroff bought a golf course). They and other company leaders had ambitious plans for the future, including development of new high-tech products, aggressive global growth, and diversification into new technologies and markets. In the meantime Biomet's entrepreneurial atmosphere and quick-response management structure would be retained, owing to the success of such technological breakthroughs as the Maxim, a cutting-edge knee implant introduced in 1993, which was expected to significantly boost profits from the fast-growing knee replacement market. In a nutshell, Biomet intended to cling to its reputation as a customer-oriented supplier of leading edge, low-cost, high-performance orthopedic devices.

Despite Biomet's past successes and management's rosy outlook, several impediments to the company's success loomed on the horizon. Chief among them was the impending federal health care reform plan, which could mean many of the products sold by Biomet might become subject to the buying decisions of government regulators. Under the plan proposed by the Clinton administration in 1994, companies like Biomet would have to seek federal approval of new innovations because the government would choose those technologies that could be purchased by health care providers. The effects of reform proposals (as well as increasingly torpid Food and Drug Administration product approvals) were already having a negative impact on Biomet in the early 1990s, as funding for new research and development waned.

On the other hand, demographics boded well for the future success of Biomet and its Warsaw contemporaries. Indeed, the Census Bureau estimated that the number of Americans aged 55 to 74 would leap 42 percent between 1989 and 2010, resulting in massive market growth for Biomet's products. The 75-and-older group will grow even faster. Furthermore, new long-lasting implants will allow surgeons to use Biomet offerings in increasingly younger patients, and for a range of new applications. Overseas demand, moreover, should outstrip domestic growth by a potentially wide margin.

Principal Subsidiaries: EBI Medical Systems.

Further Reading:

Andrews, Greg, "Cha-Ching! CEO's Salaries Outpace Earnings at Hoosier Firms," *Indianapolis Business Journal,* May 4, 1992, Sec. 1, p. 1.

"Biomet: Wall Street Likes What It Sees," *Indiana Business,* April 1985, Sec. 1, p. 55.

Howey, Brian, "Biomet: Bringing R&D to Market," *Indiana Business,* May 1988, Sec. 1, p. 72.

Kaelble, Steve, "International Business Person of the Year," *Indiana Business,* October 1992, Sec. 1, p. 1.

Kurowski, Jeff, "Indiana Business's Industrialist of the Year: Dane Miller, CEO, Biomet," *Indiana Business,* December 1989, Sec. 1, p. 1.

Miller, Jim, "Biomet Founder Recalls Years Filled With 'Sheer Excitement'," *Elkhart Truth,* October 29, 1992, Sec. Bus.

Panzica, Lisa, "Getting a Knee Up on the Competition," *Tribune Business Weekly,* September 22, 1993, Sec. 1, p. 14.

Sasso, Greg, "Biomet Announces Record Second Quarter and First Half Results," *Business Wire,* December 10, 1992.

Shankle, Greta, "FDA proposes Stiffening Regulation of the Medical Device Industry," *Indianapolis Business Journal,* January 10, 1994, Sec. 1, p. 11A.

Welles, Ed, ed., "Stock Pick; Biomet, Inc.," *Common Stocks, Common Sense,* December 1993, pp. 3–4.

—Dave Mote

BlueCross BlueShield Association

An Association of Independent
Blue Cross and Blue Shield Plans

Blue Cross and Blue Shield Association

676 North St. Clair Street
Chicago, Illinois 60611
U.S.A.
(312) 440-6000
Fax: (312) 440-6609

Private Company
Incorporated: 1982
Employees: 700
Operating Revenues: $134 million
SICs: 6794 Patent Owners and Lessors; 6324 Hospital and
    Medical Service Plans

The Blue Cross and Blue Shield Association is a nationwide
organization that coordinates 70 independent health care plans
which operate under the Blue Cross and Blue Shield banner.
The association owns the Blue Cross and Blue Shield names
and trademarks, and licenses them to its members. All Blue
Cross and Blue Shield plans (often referred to collectively as the
"Blues") are run autonomously, but must meet standards laid
out by the association. Taken together, the Blues are the largest
health insurers in the United States, covering about 25 percent
of the nation's population. Sixty-eight million Americans are
currently enrolled in Blue Cross and Blue Shield plans. Licensees also operate in Canada, Jamaica, and the United Kingdom. The Blues serve an additional 34 million individuals
through their role as contractors for Medicare processing.

Eighty-seven percent of the Blue Cross and Blue Shield network's subscribers belong to group insurance plans, while the
rest are enrolled as individuals. Five and a half million Blues
customers in 42 states participate in Health Maintenance Organizations (HMOs). Another 15.5 million customers receive their
health care through Preferred Provider Organizations (PPOs), in
which members may choose any physician or hospital, but
receive greater benefits for choosing from among those "preferred" by the plan. In 1992, the plans collectively processed
over a half billion claims, paying out $63 billion in benefits.
Nearly another half billion Medicare bills were processed by the
Blues as well.

Dr. Justin Ford Kimball, a Baylor University administrator, is
generally recognized as the originator of Blue Cross. Kimball

noticed that among the university hospital's unpaid bills were
those of a disproportionate number of local school teachers. In
1929, he addressed this problem by organizing a plan in which
teachers could be covered for a three-week hospital stay in a
semi-private room by prepaying as little as 50 cents a month.
The first group health plan was off the ground when 1,250
Dallas-area teachers enrolled at once.

Other groups of Dallas employees joined the program, and it
began to attract attention across the United States. Similar plans
sprang up in Iowa and Illinois. Like the Dallas prototype, those
plans involved only one hospital. In the early 1930s, plans were
created that offered customers a choice of different hospitals in
their communities. California, New Jersey, and New York were
among the first locations for programs of that type. The Blue
Cross name and symbol were developed in 1934 by E. A. van
Steenwyk, a pioneer of St. Paul, Minnesota's group health plan.
By 1935, there were 15 Blue Cross plans in 11 states. The
following year, the American Hospital Association (AHA) created the Committee on Hospital Services to oversee the growing
batch of Blue Cross organizations nationwide. The Committee's early leader was C. Rufus Rorem, who had been involved
with the AHA for several years. By 1938, there were 38 Blue
Cross plans in the United States, with a total enrollment of
1.4 million. In comparison, only about 100,000 people were
covered for hospitalization by private insurance companies
at that time.

Meanwhile, a similar movement had begun for covering the
costs of physicians' services. In the Pacific Northwest, a few
lumber and mining companies had begun making arrangements
to pay doctors a monthly fee for providing their employees with
health care services. The first of these plans appeared in
Tacoma, Washington, in 1917. The first modern Blue Shield
plan was established in 1939 in California. Modeled on the
earlier programs, the California Plan enabled its customers to
receive physician services for $1.70 a month. Only those with
income under $3,000 a year were eligible for the program. The
medical societies of other states began to develop similar programs, and in 1946 the first handful of such plans banded into a
national group called the Associated Medical Care Plans, overseen by the American Medical Association (AMA). This group
informally adopted the Blue Shield as its symbol two years
later, and it eventually became known as the Blue Shield Association.

Between 1940 and 1945, the number of Blue Cross plans
operating nationwide grew from 56 to 80, and enrollment increased from 6 million to 19 million. Blue Shield's enrollment
was approximately 3 million. This growth was largely due to
the wartime emphasis on fringe benefits as a way to increase
wages without boosting salaries. In 1946, Rorem resigned as
executive director of the AHA commission overseeing Blue
Cross plans, and was replaced by Richard M. Jones, whom
Rorem had hired as head of public relations. The organization's
name was then changed to the Blue Cross Commission.

In 1948, Blue Cross and Blue Shield agreed to merge. The move
was blocked by the AMA, however, on the grounds that such
cooperation between hospitals and physicians could lead to
actions in restraint of trade. Nevertheless, the Blues began
working together around that time on public policy issues, while

remaining independent, competing entities. To facilitate their continued growth, both Blues set up nonprofit agencies to coordinate the activities of their member plans. The Blue Cross Commission established Health Services, Inc. (HSI), a stock insurance company, to coordinate national enrollment in Blue Cross plans and to act as an underwriter to make up for differences in benefits between member plans when national contracts made it necessary. The Blue Cross Association was created as a holding company for HSI stock, which was actually owned by the plans themselves. Blue Shield set up a similar structure, establishing Medical Indemnity of America (MIA) as its counterpart to HSI.

Although the Blues continued to grow in the 1950s, they began to face stiff competition for the first time from commercial insurance companies. In 1945, Blue Cross controlled 61 percent of the national market for hospital insurance. By 1951, private commercial hospital insurance customers outnumbered Blue Cross members for the first time, 40 million to 37.4 million. The emergence of major medical policies, in which the customer shares the risk by paying a ''deductible'' sum before any benefits kick in, posed a strong challenge to the Blues in the 1950s. As major medical coverage bloomed, primarily through labor contracts, the Blues attempt to counter by offering coverage for longer hospital stays and broadening the range of medical conditions for which it would pay the costs.

Enrollment in the 77 Blue Cross plans was up to 51 million in 1955. The following year the Blue Cross Association (BCA) was given an additional role. Previously a paper corporation set up to meet the legal necessities of stockholding, the BCA now became the primary vehicle for cultivating new national enrollment contracts. The Blue Cross Commission (BCC), under new leader Basil C. MacLean, continued to serve as the coordinating agency and trade association for member plans. In 1960, most of the functions previously carried out by the BCC were shifted to the BCA, and the BCA became the sole organization for the national coordination of Blue Cross plans. Its president was James Stuart, originally an officer of the Cincinnati Blue Cross plan.

Nearly 56 million people, or one-third of the U.S. population, were members of a Blue Cross plan in 1960. Walter J. McNerney took over as head of the BCA in 1961. The Blues continued to lose ground to private insurers through the 1960s, although they retained their strongholds in major urban centers. Their dominance in those areas was mainly due to their ability to strike national deals with large employers, including all of the major automakers. By 1963, 46 percent of all Americans with hospital insurance had some Blue Cross coverage. In metropolitan areas, however, Blue Cross continued to insure over half the population.

Later in the decade, Blue Cross and Blue Shield benefitted from the establishment of Medicare. With the passage of the Medicare Act in 1965, Blue Cross was assigned the task of implementing the federal program to provide medical assistance for the elderly. Many states began operating their Medicaid programs through Blue Cross as well. These federal health care programs helped enable the Blues to maintain their dominant position in the area of hospital insurance despite the entry of numerous major insurance companies into the field. By 1969,

35 percent of the civilian population of the United States under age 65 (70.6 million people) was enrolled in Blue Cross. About half the $10 billion in premiums Blue Cross was collecting by 1970 came from government agencies.

By the early 1970s, Blue Cross and Blue Shield began to feel the effects of health care costs spiraling out of control. The Blues attempted to meet this challenge with a combination of rate hikes and cost control measures such as utilization reviews of hospital admissions. The public did not react well to these actions, and many customers became suspicious of the close relationship between Blue Cross and the AHA. A feeling persisted among policyholders that this affiliation meant that decisions at Blue Cross were inevitably being driven by the interests of the hospitals rather than those of Blue Cross customers, who had come to rely on the Blues as the insurers of last resort. Partly as a reaction to these concerns, the BCA's official ties with the AHA were severed in 1972, and ownership of the Blue Cross name and symbol were transferred to the BCA.

As the 1970s continued, the financial situation worsened for the Blues. By 1975, the entire Blue Cross system had reserves of only $1.2 billion, far short of its needs. That year, Blue Cross plans ran at a collective deficit of $455 million. The nation's 70 Blue Shield plans were not faring much better, recording a $291 million shortfall for 1975. Meanwhile, medical costs continued to skyrocket, and Blue Cross was feeling pressures from both sides of the issue. Government regulators, which had usually passed Blue Cross rate increase proposals with little or no resistance in the past, became stingier in response to public outcry. At the same time, some hospitals, faced with accelerating inflation coupled with increased competition from overbuilding, began clamoring for the elimination of special discounts Blue Cross had always been able to negotiate.

Blue Cross' response to the steep escalation in the cost of health care was to look for ways to shorten hospital stays. By 1975, 27 plans across the United States were sponsoring HMOs, which emphasize preventive care with the goal of minimizing the need for hospitalization. Pre-admission testing programs, which encourage subscribers to have routine testing done on an outpatient basis well in advance of scheduled in-patient treatment or surgery, was also being offered as a benefit by 56 plans. Sameday surgery, home care, and other outpatient services were incorporated into a number of plans scattered across the country.

Entering the 1980s, the Blues continued to be plagued by soaring health care costs, which tripled between 1967 and 1981. Frustrated by the failure of most plans to heed his urging to modernize their operations, McNerney resigned as president of the BCA in November 1981, and was succeeded by Bernard Tresnowski. In 1982, Blue Cross and Blue Shield finally completed their long-awaited merger, and although the two types of plans were still run separately in some areas, both were coordinated by the same organization, the Blue Cross and Blue Shield Association based in Chicago. The number of Blue Cross and Blue Shield plans numbered 97 in 1983. That year, the association announced the formation of a 21-state network of 38 HMOs. The HMO network was designed to make the Blues attractive to large companies with employees located across the nation.

The Blues continued to falter financially through the remainder of the 1980s. Between 1980 and 1988, the system lost about 10 million customers and the number of plans declined. The 75 member plans in operation in 1987 and 1988 ran a combined deficit of $3 billion for those two years. Competition from commercial insurance companies, independent HMOs, and other health care sources dragged the Blues' market share down to 31 percent. At the same time, some member plans found it necessary to operate more like commercial insurance companies. The community rating system, in which rates are determined according to collective rather than individual statistics (a guiding principle of the Blues from the start), was even abandoned by a few plans. Some plans began to compete with each other through subsidiary operations outside their home states.

The beginning of the 1990s brought more bad news for the Blues. In late 1990, Blue Cross/Blue Shield of West Virginia became insolvent, the first financial collapse in the history of the Blues, when $53 million in medical bills went unpaid. Several other plans were discovered to be on shaky financial ground. Early in 1991, it was revealed that executives of some member plans were receiving the kinds of salaries and perks normally associated with more profit-driven businesses, including sports skyboxes, lavish golf outings, and flights on the Concorde. Allegations of widespread mismanagement throughout the system prompted a Senate investigation of Blue Cross and Blue Shield operations. The Senate panel, chaired by Georgia Senator Sam Nunn, turned up evidence of reckless spending at several of the plans.

By late 1992, several plans required financial bailouts by neighboring association members. For example, Blue Cross and Blue Shield of Virginia was called upon to rescue the floundering Group Hospitalization and Medical Services (parent company to Blue Cross and Blue Shield of the National Capital Area) when it lost 50 percent of its reserves to bad investments. This sort of marriage by necessity shrank the number of Blue Cross and Blue Shield plans nationwide to 72 by the end of 1992. The Blues' market share continued to erode as well, slipping to an all-time low of about 30 percent, as the system's credibility deteriorated in the aftermath of the Senate hearings.

In spite of the litany of problems, every member plan managed to operate profitably in 1992, and the system reported an aggregate gain of $1.9 billion. Searching for ways to offset the public relations beating it was taking, the association announced a new set of financial standards to which member plans would be held in early 1993. As part of the new policy, plans were required to participate in state guaranty funds or other similar programs which protect consumers in the event of bankruptcy.

In March 1993, the Blues and IBM announced a joint project to expand the system's electronic claims processing capability. The development of the new network would also allow Blue Cross and Blue Shield to process the claims of other insurers for a fee. Bad press for the Blues continued to flow freely, however. Overspending, misrepresentation of losses, and other improprieties were uncovered in 1993 at the system's largest member, Empire Blue Cross of New York. Plans in Washington, D.C. and Ohio were under the scrutiny of government agencies as well.

By the mid 1990s, the Blue Cross and Blue Shield Association stood at a crossroads. In spite of the huge difficulties of recent years, many of them self-imposed, the Blues still control a huge share of the health insurance market. Most of the association's member plans are in reasonably sound financial shape, and a functioning nationwide infrastructure is still in place and going strong for the most part. With health care in the United States on the brink of dramatic changes, the destiny of the Blues will be determined largely by what role, if any, it ends up with in the American health care scheme to be concocted over the next few years.

Further Reading:

"Adding Insult to Injury," *Forbes,* March 1, 1977, pp. 33–4.

"Aid for Blue Cross in Nixon's Plan," *Business Week,* February 27, 1971, pp. 94–96.

Anderson, Odin W., *Blue Cross Since 1929: Accountability and the Public Trust,* Cambridge, MA: Ballinger Publishing Company, 1975.

"Blue Cross-Blue Shield Binds Health Agencies into 21-State Network," *Wall Street Journal,* December 9, 1983, p. 20.

Blue Cross and Blue Shield Fact Book, Chicago: Blue Cross and Blue Shield Association, 1993.

"Blue Cross Plans Support Programs to Reduce Need for Hospitalization," *Journal of Commerce,* April 21, 1975, p. 2A.

"Blues Awash in Controversy; Salary Probe Tarnishes Image," *Journal of Commerce,* March 16, 1991, p. 5A.

Borzo, Greg, "Blues Begin Processing Other Carriers' Claims," *American Medical News,* April 26, 1993, p. 33.

Freudenheim, Milt, "Fiscally Battered Blue Cross Fights to Remain Top Insurer," *New York Times,* April 2, 1989, p. 24.

Garland, Susan B., "A Black Eye for the Blues?" *Business Week,* July 20, 1992, p. 33.

"A Health Insurer that Needs a Cure," *Business Week,* May 10, 1982, pp. 158–164.

Kenkel, Paul J., "The Blues at a Crossroads," *Modern Healthcare,* December 14, 1992, pp. 33–40.

Law, Sylvia A., *Blue Cross: What Went Wrong?,* New Haven: Yale University Press, 1974.

Millenson, Michael L., "US 'Blues' Association Tightening Standards," *Journal of Commerce,* February 11, 1993, p. 8A.

Perham, John C., "Battle of Policies," *Barron's,* October 29, 1956, p. 3.

Siegel, Max H., "Blue Shield, Blue Cross Reach Accord on Merger," *New York Times,* March 12, 1974, p. 1.

Simon, Ruth, "What Cracks in the Blue Cross System Can Mean for You," *Money,* May 1991, pp. 27–28.

Steinmetz, Greg, "Parent of Blue Cross, Blue Shield Unveils Reforms," *Wall Street Journal,* February 16, 1993 p. A4.

Weissenstein, Eric, "Report for Senate Subcommittee Questions Financial Stability, Practices of Blues Plans," *Modern Healthcare,* July 6, 1992, p. 3.

Winslow, Ron, "IBM, Blue Cross Join in Plan to Boost Electronic Handling of Medical Claims," *Wall Street Journal,* March 12, 1993, p. B6.

—Robert R. Jacobson

The Boeing Company

7755 East Marginal Way South
Seattle, Washington 98108
U.S.A.
(206) 655-2121

Public Company
Incorporated: July 19, 1934 as Boeing Airplane Company
Employees: 98,700
Sales: $16.34 billion
Stock Exchanges: New York Amsterdam Brussels London
    Zurich Geneva Basel Tokyo Boston Cincinnati Midwest
    Philadelphia
SICs: 3721 Aircraft; 3760 Guided Missiles, Space Vehicles,
    Parts; 3663 Radio and TV Communications Equipment;
    3724 Aircraft Engines and Engine Parts; 3728 Aircraft
    Parts and Equipment, Nec

The Boeing Company was one of America's most successful corporations and ranked as the country's number one exporter in the early 1990s. The corporation had the highest sales volume of any aerospace firm in the United States and was the world's leading manufacturer of commercial jet aircraft. Boeing has been characterized as one of the world's best managed companies, having made difficult but vital decisions in the face of intensifying global competition, the worst downturn in the history of the airline industry, and substantial defense and space cutbacks in the United States.

Founder William Boeing was raised in Michigan, where his father operated a lucrative forestry business. While he was in San Diego, California, in 1910, Boeing met a French stunt pilot named Louis Paulhan who was performing at the International Air Meet. When Paulhan took Boeing for an airplane ride, it marked the beginning of Boeing's fascination with aviation.

After two years of study at Yale's Sheffield School of Science, Boeing returned to Michigan to work for his father. He was sent first to Wisconsin and later to the state of Washington to acquire more timber properties for the family business. In Seattle he met a Navy engineer named Conrad Westerveldt who shared his fascination for aviation. A barnstormer named Terah Maroney gave the two men a ride over Puget Sound in his seaplane. Later Boeing went to Los Angeles to purchase his own seaplane, thinking it would be useful for fishing trips. The man who sold him the plane and taught him how to fly was Glenn Martin, who later founded Martin Marietta.

While in Seattle, Boeing and Westerveldt made a hobby of building their own seaplanes on the backwaters of Puget Sound. It became more than a hobby when a mechanic named Herb Munter and a number of other carpenters and craftsmen became involved. In May of 1916, Boeing flew the first "B&W" seaplane. The next month he incorporated his company as the Pacific Aero Products Company. The company's first customer was the government of New Zealand, which employed the plane for mail delivery and pilot training.

Boeing and his partners anticipated government interest in their company when the United States became involved in World War I. They discovered their hunch was correct when the company was asked to train flight instructors for the army. After the war, Boeing sold a number of airplanes to Edward Hubbard, whose Hubbard Air Transport is regarded as the world's first airline. The company shuttled mail between Seattle and the transpacific mailboat which called at Victoria, British Columbia. Later, when the post office invited bids for various airmail routes, Hubbard tried to convince Boeing to apply for the Chicago to San Francisco contract. Boeing mentioned the idea to his wife, who thought the opportunity looked promising. In the prospect, he and Hubbard created a new airline named the Boeing Air Transport Company. They submitted a bid and were awarded the contract.

To meet the demands of their new business Boeing and his engineers developed an extremely versatile and popular airplane called the Model 40. Fitted with a Pratt & Whitney air-cooled Wasp engine, it could carry 1000 pounds of mail and a complete flight crew, and still have room enough for freight or passengers. The Kelly Airmail Act of 1925 opened the way for private airmail delivery on a much wider scale. As a result, a number of airline companies formed with the intention of procuring the stable and lucrative airmail contracts. One of these companies was Vernon Gorst's Pacific Air Transport, which won various routes along the Pacific Coast. Boeing purchased this company and then ordered a young employee named William Patterson to purchase its outstanding stock. Boeing also purchased Varney Airlines, which began operation in 1925 and won almost every mail contract it applied for until it became over-extended and had financial difficulties.

With the addition of National Air Transport, Boeing's airline holdings formed the original United Air Lines. In 1928 all these companies were organized under a holding company called the Boeing Aircraft and Transportation Company. In 1929 a larger holding company was formed, the United Aircraft and Transportation Company. Included in this group were the "United" airlines and Stout Airlines; Pratt & Whitney (engines); Boeing, Sikorsky, Northrop, and Stearman (manufacturers); and Standard Steel Prop and Hamilton Aero Manufacturing (propellers). Boeing was made chairman of the company and Fred Rentschler of Pratt & Whitney was named president.

Boeing and Rentschler became extremely wealthy in this reorganization by exchanging stock with the holding company in a method similar to J. P. Morgan's controversial capital manipulation. They multiplied their original investments by a factor of as much as 200,000 times. It was, however, entirely legal at the time. In 1933 the government conducted an investigation of fraud and other illegal practices in the airline industry. Boeing was called upon to testify and explain his windfall profits before a Senate investigating committee. Under examination he admitted to making $12 million in stock flotations.

Boeing was so infuriated with the investigation that he retired from the company (at age 52) and sold all his aviation stocks. Upon Boeing's departure the company's production manager, Phil Johnson, was named the new president. But Boeing was not forgotten by the aircraft industry. In 1934 William Boeing was recognized for his emphasis on innovation and experimentation in aeronautical research and development. He was awarded the Daniel Guggenheim medal, ''for successful pioneering and achievement in aircraft manufacturing and air transport.''

In 1934 a government investigation of collusion in the airmail business led to a suspension of all contracts awarded. As a result, the U.S. Congress declared that airline companies and manufacturers could not be part of the same business concern. This led to the break up of the three aeronautic conglomerates: Boeing's United, the Aviation Corporation of the Americas, and North American Aviation. All of the Boeing company's aeronautic properties east of the Mississippi became part of a new company, United Aircraft, operated by Fred Rentschler. The western properties, principally the Boeing Airplane Company, remained in Seattle exclusively manufacturing airframes. Pat Patterson was put in charge of the commercial air carriers which retained the name of United Air Lines and based its operations at Chicago's Old Orchard (later O'Hare) airport.

In the years leading up to World War II the Boeing company led the way in developing single-wing airplanes. They were constructed completely of metal to make them stronger and faster; more efficient aerodynamic designs were emphasized; retractable landing gear and better wings were developed, along with multiple ''power plant'' technology; finally, directional radios were installed which enabled better navigation and night flying. Boeing had established itself as the leading manufacturer of airplanes.

When the United States launched its wartime militarization program, Boeing was called upon to produce hundreds of its B-17 ''Flying Fortresses'' for the Army. During the war the B-17 became an indispensable instrument for the U.S. Air Corps. In June of 1944, when production was at its peak, Boeing's Seattle facility turned out 16 of these airplanes every 24 hours. By this time the company was also producing an improved bomber called the B-29 ''Super Fortress.'' It was this airplane that dropped the atomic bombs on Hiroshima and Nagasaki in August of 1945.

Boeing's president, Phil Johnson, died unexpectedly during the war. He was replaced with the company's chief lawyer, William M. Allen, on the last day of the war. Under Allen's leadership, Boeing produced a number of new bombers, including the B-47, B-50, and the B-52. Boeing's B-307 Stratoliner, a B-17 converted for transporting passengers, was succeeded by the B-377 Stratocruiser in 1952. The Stratocruiser was a very popular double-deck transport, most widely used by Northwest Ori-

ent. It was also Boeing's only airplane built for the commercial airline market since before the war.

In the spring of 1953 Bill Allen convinced the secretary of the U.S. Air Force, Harold Talbot, to allow Boeing the use of the government-owned B-52 construction facilities for the development of a new civilian/military jet. Boeing invested $16 million in the project, which was intended to put the company ahead of the Douglas Aircraft Company. Douglas had dominated the commercial airplane market for years with its popular propeller-driven DC series.

This new jet, the B-707, first flew on May 15, 1954. American Airlines, a loyal Douglas customer, was the first to order the new jet. Their defection so alarmed Douglas that the company accelerated development of its nearly identical DC-8 passenger jetliner. The government later took delivery of Boeing's military version of the jet, the KC-135 tanker, alternately known as the ''missing 717.''

Boeing, which changed its name to The Boeing Company in 1961, enjoyed a large degree of success and profitability with the 707. The company devoted its resources to the development of a number of other passenger jet models, including the 720 (a modified 707) and the 727, which was introduced in 1964. The 727 was Boeing's response to a successful French model called the Caravelle. The Caravelle's engines were located in the rear of the fuselage, uncluttering the wings and reducing cabin noise. Boeing adopted this design for its three-engine 727, which carried 143 passengers. Douglas, eager not to be left out, introduced a similar two-engine model called the DC-9 in 1965.

During this time the company also recognized a demand for a smaller 100-passenger jetliner for shorter routes. As a result, Boeing developed the 737 model. The 737 seemed to run counter to the general trend at Boeing of building larger, more technologically advanced jetliners, but it did have a place in the market and made a profit.

Boeing's next engineering accomplishment was the creation of a very large passenger transport designated the 747. This new jetliner was capable of carrying twice as many passengers as any other airplane. Its huge dimensions and powerful four-engine configuration made it the first of a new class of ''jumbo jets,'' later joined by McDonnell Douglas's DC-10 and Lockheed's 1011 Tri-Star.

The 747 program required such a large investment that it nearly forced the company into bankruptcy. One hundred and sixty orders were placed for the jetliner by the time it was delivered in 1969, but no more were placed until 1972. During this period, Boeing was also developing the 2707, a supersonic transport better known as the ''SST.'' Progress on this aircraft was slow and costly. Despite the support of Senator Henry Jackson, the U.S. Congress voted not to fund further development of the SST. Shortly thereafter Boeing abandoned the project altogether.

In 1969 a new chief executive was appointed to head the organization. An engineer named Thornton Wilson took charge of Boeing in a way reminiscent of his predecessor, Bill Allen, 25 years before. Faced with an impending disaster, Wilson's response was to pare the workforce down from 105,000 to

38,000. The layoffs at Boeing had a profound effect on the local economy, as unemployment in Seattle rose to 14 percent.

Wilson's strict austerity measures paid off quickly. Soon Boeing's jets were rolling off the tarmac and employees were called back to work. After the company's initial recovery, it received a deluge of commercial airplane orders and military contracts. Boeing started development of two new passenger jet models intended to take the company into the twenty-first century.

These new jetliner models, the 757 and the wide-body 767, became available in the early 1980s. Utilizing advanced technology and improved engines, these jetliners were Boeing's response to McDonnell Douglas's MD series and the European Airbus consortium's 300 series. The current customer in the commercial jetliner market is more concerned with labor costs than fuel efficiency, owing to consistently cheaper oil. However, Boeing's newest entries are doubly efficient, requiring smaller crews as well as less fuel. Besides the 757 and 767, Boeing offered an updated 737 for the shorter-range rural "puddle-jumper" market and modified 747s capable of greater range and passenger capacity.

During this period of prosperity with commercial jetliners, Boeing made several attempts to diversify its business. Not all of them were successful. In the 1970s Boeing entered the metrorail business, manufacturing mass transit systems for Boston, San Francisco, and Morgantown, West Virginia. The systems were modern, computerized, and efficient. They were also prone to frequent breakdowns. After fulfilling its obligation to rectify the systems (at great cost), Boeing decided to discontinue its ground transport business.

Most of Boeing's business in the early 1990s came through four principal divisions: civilian aircraft manufactured and sold by the Boeing Commercial Airplane Company; helicopters for the armed services produced by the Boeing Vertol Company, acquired in 1960; strategic and tactical missiles and space products produced by Boeing Aerospace; and bombers, tankers, and high-technology surveillance aircraft built by the Boeing Military Airplane Company.

Boeing's military business has been more stable than its commercial airlines business. That stability did not, however, ensure the company against debilitating losses in its civilian business during the 747 crisis or during the period after "deregulation" in America when demand for new jetliners declined. Despite steady revenue from government contracts, Boeing's military divisions have remained viable and competitive in winning contracts, and in designing, developing, and producing a wide variety of state-of-the-art military hardware.

Boeing's major contributions to the military include the KC-135 tanker and the versatile mainstay of the United States Air Force, the B-52 bomber. The company builds E-3 Airborne Warning and Control System aircraft (AWACs) for the Air Force, the North Atlantic Treaty Organization, and Saudi Arabia. In addition, Boeing builds the E-4 command post and the E-6 submarine communications aircraft. Under a consortium led by Northrop, it is developing a new bomber intended to replace the aging B-52, designated the B-1B. Boeing's other (top secret) project is a role in the development of the F-19

Stealth bomber. Boeing's Vertol facilities, located in Philadelphia, produce CH-46 and CH-47 (Chinook) helicopters.

In the aerospace division, Boeing won a $4 billion defense department contract in 1980 to manufacture the air-launched cruise missile. It builds the MX intercontinental ballistic missile and the Roland air defense missile. The company also provides modernization services for existing Minuteman ICBMs. Boeing's aerospace business includes the production of inertial upper stage boosters for satellites delivered into orbit by Titan rockets or the Space Shuttle. But the dismantling of the USSR in the late 1980s, which ushered in substantial defense budget cuts, promised to limit the growth of this business segment.

Boeing established an "Advanced Products Group" in the latter years of the decade to oversee the company's more futuristic aircraft and keep it at the technological vanguard. Boeing's three-engine 777, originally scheduled to be introduced with the 757 and 767, attracted little interest and was temporarily shelved. The development of the fuel-efficient, 150-passenger 7J7 was also delayed when declining fuel costs and rising research and development expenses reduced demand. Perhaps their most radically designed project was the 907 flying wing. Equipped with eight jet engines, this airplane could carry 1000 passengers, twice the capacity of a 747. Looking something like a boomerang, it was scheduled for service sometime in the 21st century. If this project is successful, it could allow Boeing to change the future of aviation once again.

Frank Shrontz advanced to Boeing's chief executive office in 1986, at the start of the world's largest aircraft order binge in history, and led the manufacturer from sales of $16.3 billion in 1986 to $29.31 billion in 1991. Although Boeing remained profitable, its earnings declined steadily in the mid 1980s and its stock dropped twenty points in October 1987. Boeing jets were involved in four fatal air accidents from December 1988 to March 1989, and the company missed its first delivery deadline in two decades when the 747-400 experienced production delays. These internal problems were exacerbated by increased competition from Airbus, which was heavily subsidized by a consortium of European companies and governments.

Nevertheless, in 1990, Boeing chalked up record sales and net profits of $27.6 billion and $1.4 billion, respectively, and ended the year with a $97 billion backlog. But after its experiences of the 1980s, and due to CEO Shrontz's vigilance, Boeing began to institute retrenchment moves. Although the manufacturer experienced three years of rising sales and earnings from 1989 to 1992, prospects for the company's—and the industry's—future, were not bright. Worldwide orders of all aircraft declined from 1,662 in 1989 to 439 in 1991, and cancellations from the besieged airlines diminished expected delivery figures even more. The commercial airline industry's downturn started in 1990, heralding brutal price wars and canceled aircraft orders. By the fall of 1992, Boeing's stock suffered on Wall Street, selling for about $35 per share, down from a high of nearly $62 in 1990.

Shrontz moved to reduce Boeing's cost structure by 20 to 30 percent by 1997, even though his firm was the world's lowest-cost aircraft producer. Production cuts soon led to layoffs. Boeing's workforce declined each year from 1989 to 1993, for a total of 40,000 jobs lost. Early in 1994, Shrontz announced that about 30,000 jobs—one-fourth of the company's remaining workforce—would be eliminated over the course of the year. Sales for 1993 declined to $25.44 billion from 1992's $30.18 billion, and net earnings slid from $1.55 billion to $1.24 billion. Despite Boeing's cost cutting measures, industry analysts worried that the commercial airplane industry had entered a period of vast, irrevocable change, wherein airlines' continuously mounting debt would prevent them from purchasing Boeing planes, no matter how inexpensive they were.

Principal Subsidiaries: Aileron Inc.; Aldford Ltd.; Andsell Ltd.; Aldford-1 Corp.; Aldsell-1 Corp.; Argosystems Inc.; A.S.I. Electronics; Astro, Ltd.; Boeing Technology International, Inc.; Boeing of Canada, Ltd.; Boeing International Corp.; Boeing Financial Corp.; Boeing Equipment Holding Company; Boeing Leasing Co.; Boeing International Sales Corp.; BCS Richland, Inc.; Boecon Corp.; Boeing Aerospace Operations Inc.; Boeing Canada Technology Ltd.; Boeing China Inc.; Boeing Commercial Space Development Co.; Boeing Defense & Space-Corinth Co.; Boeing Defense & Space-Irving Co.; Boeing Domestic Sales Corp.; Boeing Computer Support Services, Inc.; Boeing Agri-Industrial Co.; BE&C Engineers, Inc.; Boeing Georgia, Inc.; Boeing Operations International, Inc.; Boeing Middle East, Ltd.; Astro-II, Inc.; Boeing Sales Corp.; Boeing Investment Co., Inc.; Boeing Mississippi, Inc.; Boeing Nevada Inc.; Boeing Sales Corp. Ltd.; Energy Enterprises Inc.; Longacres Park Inc.; Montana Aviation Research Co.; Rainier Aircraft Leasing Inc.; 767ER Inc.; Boeing Offset Co., Inc.; Boeing Petroleum Services, Inc.

Further Reading:

Bauer, Eugene E., *Boeing in Peace and War,* Taba Publishing, 1991.
Bilstein, Roger E., *Flight in America, 1900–1983: From the Wrights to the Astronauts,* Baltimore: Johns Hopkins University Press, 1984.
Bowers, Peter M., *Boeing Aircraft Since 1916,* Naval Institute Press, 1989.
Ingells, Douglas J., *747: The Story of The Boeing Super Jet,* Fallbrook, CA: Aero Publishers, 1970.
Kuter, Lawrence S., *The Great Gamble: The Boeing 747,* University of Alabama Press, 1973.
Mansfield, Harold, *Billion Dollar Battle: The Story Behind the ''Impossible'' 727 Project,* edited by James Gilbert, Ayer, 1965.
——, *Vision: A Saga of the Sky,* Ayer, 1965.
Redding, Robert, and Bill Yenne, *Boeing: Planemaker to the World,* London: Arms and Armour Press, 1983.
Serling, Robert J., *Legend & Legacy: The Story of Boeing and Its People,* St. Martin, 1992.

—updated by April Dougal Gasbarre

THE **BOMBAY** COMPANY, INC.

The Bombay Company, Inc.

550 Bailey Avenue
Suite 700
Fort Worth, Texas 76107
U.S.A.
(817) 347-8200
Fax: (817) 332-7066

Public Company
Incorporated: 1987 as Bombay Company
Employees: 2,900
Sales: $231 million
Stock Exchanges: New York
SICs: 5712 Furniture Stores

The Bombay Company, Inc., is a retailer of small pieces of ready-to-assemble furniture and home accessories, which operates nearly 450 stores in malls across North America. The company runs two chains: its signature store, which sells traditional, dark stained English-styled wooden furniture, and Alex & Ivy, a much smaller chain of stores with a country theme. Founded as a mail-order outfit, the Bombay Company exploited the fact that its affordable furniture pieces came packed in flat boxes to introduce impulse buying and mall-oriented shopping to the furniture business.

The Bombay Company got its start in 1975 as a mail-order business based in New Orleans. The company sold mahogany stained reproductions of small 18th and 19th century English furniture pieces, such as plant stands, night stands, and butler's tables, which were manufactured in the Far East. After running advertisements in upscale magazines such as the *New Yorker,* the Bombay Company shipped its goods to customers in flat boxes, for assembly. Usually, all the customer had to do was screw the legs on. Entrepreneur Brad Harper, who founded the company with a partner, named the enterprise "Bombay Company" in an effort to conjure up the glory of the British Empire at its height. However, most people missed the reference.

By the end of the 1970s, the Bombay Company was racking up annual sales of about $1.5 million, offering 12 different items of accent furniture through ads in magazines. Overall, however, the company was losing money. The quality of the products it sold was uneven, as its distant Asian manufacturers proved unreliable. Also, the Bombay Company's growth was also severely limited by its reliance on mail order.

In 1979, the Bombay Company signed an agreement with Canadian entrepreneur Robert E. M. Nourse to begin selling its products in Canada. For rights to the Canadian market, Nourse paid one dollar, plus a four percent royalty on sales. Since Canadian mail-order opportunities were extremely limited, Nourse set out to convert the Bombay Company into a successful retail property.

In April of 1980, Nourse's first Bombay Company store opened in Toronto's Eaton Centre mall. Nourse had concluded that the Bombay Company was able to offer customers three things that made location in a mall advantageous: value, fashion, and instant accessibility. Value was provided by the fact that the company's products, manufactured in Taiwan and other East Asian countries, were not high-priced.

Fashion, the hook to lure customers out of the mall and into the Bombay Company store, was provided by an elaborate store design. Under the watchful eye of a designer, the company's 2,000-square-foot space was transformed into a replica of England's Fountain Court, located at Henry VIII's palace, Hampton Court. In order to pay for this renovation, and other start-up expenses, Nourse invested $125,000 of his own money, and borrowed an equal amount from a bank.

To justify this expense, and the high rent of a mall space, the Bombay Company needed to attract impulse buyers. Since Bombay Company products came boxed flat, a large number of them could be kept in stock without taking up an excess amount of space for storage. Because of this, customers could take home their purchases right after deciding to buy them. In this way, the Bombay Company introduced an element of immediate gratification to the furniture market, in contrast to a traditional furniture store, where customers ordered items, and then waited six to twelve weeks for delivery. In the Bombay Company store, 35 styles of furniture were available to be carried out of the store at the time of purchase. With these elements of a successful retail operation in place, the Bombay Company store in the Eaton Centre mall was an immediate success.

Three months after the opening of the Toronto Bombay Company store, in July of 1980, Harper sold 80 percent of the U.S. operations of the Bombay Company to a Fort Worth-based holding company called Tandy Brands, Inc., for $26,000 plus assumption of the company's debts. The Bombay Company's new corporate parent was a miniconglomerate, spun off from the Tandy computer corporation in 1975. Five months later, in July of 1981, Tandy Corporation acquired the remaining 20 percent of the Bombay Company.

After a year of successful operation of the Eaton Centre Bombay Company outlet, Nourse was looking for additional financing to buy further inventory and expand his store. Since the general financial climate for borrowing money at that time was highly forbidding, he felt that he had no choice but to sell out to Tandy. In August of 1981, Tandy also bought out Nourse's Canadian operation. "I had mixed feelings about [Tandy] buying me out," Nourse later told *Inc.* magazine. "If capital had been available at a reasonable cost, I never would have sold. But at the time it was the only way to grow the company."

Under the terms of the sale, Nourse retained control of the Canadian operations of the Bombay Company. With the influx of money from Tandy, he was able to build 13 stores by 1983, all of which proved profitable.

South of the Canadian border, however, the situation looked very different. Tandy had built 36 Bombay Company stores since taking over the company, and the business was hemorrhaging money, having racked up $3 million in losses in just three years. By the end of 1983, the situation had become desperate. In an effort to revive its American operation, Tandy's chief executive officer moved to merge the company's successful Canadian operations into its money losing American operations, and put Nourse in charge of both.

Nourse took control of the consolidated Bombay Company operations at the start of 1984. His strategy for renovating the company's ailing American operations was to implement the profitable store model which he had developed in Canada in the Bombay Company's American locations. To do so, however, it was necessary to close a number of unprofitable American stores in weak locations. Within three months of Nourse's arrival, nine of the company's 36 stores had been shut down. "We saw our concept as selling home decor in malls and other high-traffic locations," Nourse later told *HFD—The Weekly Home Furnishings Magazine,* an industry journal. "A number of the stores were in bad locations; that first year we closed more stores than we opened."

In addition to pruning unprofitable stores, the Bombay Company revamped its product line, under the direction of Nourse's wife, Alexandra "Aagje" Nourse, an advertising executive who had taken responsibility for the company's design operations. Under her direction, the company shifted away from masculine, military style furniture, that looked like it might have been used in a British military campaign of the previous century, toward more feminine and traditional Chippendale, Hepplewhite, and Queen Anne styles. In addition, the company began to market more home accessories, such as mirrors and lamps, and also started to offer printed fabrics for decorating. To keep customers interested, a constant flow of new products was moved through the store, and seven different catalogues a year alerted customers to the presence of new items.

In 1984, the Bombay Company began to open additional stores, relying on the other subsidiaries of Tandy Brands for financing. At the end of the fiscal year, the company posted a loss of $3 million, but by the middle of 1985, the Bombay Company was back in the black, turning a profit of $500,000. With these gains, the Bombay Company began to step up its plans for expansion. Its first targets for growth were areas of the United States where traditional furniture was best accepted: the mid-Atlantic states, the Southeast, the Midwest, and the Pacific Northwest. By 1986, the company was operating stores in 75 different locations, and earnings had hit $2 million. In 1987, the number of Bombay Company stores reached 114.

In 1988 and 1989, the Bombay Company moved its expansion into the Sunbelt for the first time, opening stores in Los Angeles and South Florida, with exterior architecture carefully calibrated to blend with other surrounding structures. "We have to be careful," Nourse told *HFD* in 1989. "We always wondered about the Sunbelt. But our Southern California stores and our store in Palm Beach are going gangbusters."

By April of 1989, the Bombay Company had opened 190 mall stores, and the company's revenues had reached $79 million, up from $55 million the year before. The company had introduced a line of products with neoclassical styling, to complement its other Georgian and Victorian offerings. In September of 1989, the Bombay Company opened a flagship East Coast store on Madison Avenue in Manhattan, which soon began turning in record sales.

While the Bombay Company was steadily growing, its corporate parent, Tandy, was gradually streamlining its operations, shedding other properties and companies that were smaller and less profitable than the Bombay Company. In 1984, it closed two chains of retail stores, Western World and Ryon's, and two years later, Tandy sold its Tex Tan Western Leather division for about $3 million. In March of 1987, the company sold its Grate Home and Fireplace Company for $1.6 million. By the end of the decade, it had effectively centered its operations on the Bombay Company. Accordingly, on November 9, 1990, the company changed its name to The Bombay Company, Inc., and two months later, it completed the final transfer of its other accessories operations to its shareholders.

In the midst of this consolidation and concentration on the home furnishings market, the Bombay Company also moved to expand its franchise in this area. In the fall of 1990, the company opened three new concept test stores in Southern California. Called Alex & Ivy, these outlets offered the same type of merchandise as Bombay Company stores, but with a more relaxed, country theme. Nourse characterized Alex & Ivy merchandise in a 1990 *HFD* article as "more casual, yet traditional stylings. They will include European country, Italian Renaissance, French country and some traditional Swedish country . . . lots of painted finishes . . . a little more whimsical than Bombay."

The stores were opened in areas where the Bombay Company did not already have retail outlets. A second test of another three stores was planned for locations right next door to Bombay Company stores, to measure how much their success would come at the expense of their older retail sibling. Both store chains were planned to take advantage of the same structure for manufacturing and distribution, and to appeal to the same demographic group of customers: well-educated women, with higher than average incomes.

"We constantly had comments from Bombay customers who said, 'I love your stores, but it isn't exactly our kind of furnishings,' " Aagje Nourse told *HFD* in 1994. "We . . . had hopes we could do something that was the other side of Bombay's lifestyle." Each Alex & Ivy store was slated to look exactly like all the others, arranged according to elaborate plans from the company headquarters, and the merchandise mix was set at half furniture, half accessories, such as quilts, pillows, lamps, and wall art.

Despite the recession of the early 1990s, which flattened the Bombay Company's earnings somewhat, the company continued to post strong growth in sales. By mid-1990, sales had reached $112 million, and earnings were at $12.3 million. By the middle of 1991, 43 more stores had been opened, nudging revenues up by a quarter to $140 million, but earnings had remained flat.

By the start of 1992, the Bombay Company's steady stream of new products had started to produce stores that were cramped with merchandise. In an effort to alleviate this problem, and to shake up the company's entrenched retail formula, the company opened a superstore in lower Manhattan as an experiment. The new store had about 3,500 square feet of space, instead of the usual 1,700. When this concept showed promise, the Bombay Company converted two more stores to the new, larger format.

In February of 1993, the Bombay Company decided to convert almost all of its retail outlets to superstores. "I believe a business, and certainly a retail business that changes so quickly, has to keep reinventing itself or it will whither and die," Nourse told *Inc.*, in explaining the chain's decision to leave its original store concept behind.

By the end of 1993, the Bombay Company had opened 100 superstores, and plans were on the board to add 50 more each year. In November of that year, the company marked the opening of its 400th store. In its Alex & Ivy operation, the Bombay Company had opened 26 stores, in California, Texas, Connecticut, Delaware, Georgia, Maryland, New Hampshire, New York, and New Jersey. Revenues from these combined operations reached $232 million, and earnings were at $16 million.

This pattern of strong growth continued in 1994, after the Bombay Company reported a strong holiday sales season at the end of the previous year. With these results, the company decided to expand its program to double the size of its stores in its fledgling Alex & Ivy chain as well. Tests of the "international country" concept had demonstrated that it appealed to a different set of customers within the company's basic demographic target, and that sales lost in the Bombay Company stores to Alex & Ivy outlets equaled only five percent of business.

In January of 1994, the company began to install a new merchandising computer system, to speed up customer transactions and upgrade inventory controls. In addition, the company laid plans to open a fourth distribution center in Altanta to provide goods to its newly enlarged stores. This facility joined three other distribution sites located in Texas, Pennsylvania, and Canada.

One month later, the Bombay Company announced that it would also take part in another distribution scheme, when it announced that it would participate in a television shopping network called "Catalog 1," to be produced as a joint venture of Time Warner Entertainment TV and Spiegel Inc. Despite exceptionally poor weather across the United States during the first months of 1994, the Bombay Company continued to post strong financial returns and to open new stores at a brisk pace. With a well-tested retail formula, and a second retail concept providing ample room for expansion, it appeared that the Bombay Company was well-positioned to continue its dramatic growth throughout the 1990s.

Principal Subsidiaries: The Bombay Furniture Company of Canada; Alex & Ivy.

Further Reading:

Chakravarty, Subrata N., "Queen Anne at the Mall," *Forbes,* June 24, 1991.
Finegan, Jay, "Survival of the Smartest," *Inc.,* December, 1993.
Gilbert, Les, "Bombay Company Sets Alex & Ivy Test," *HFD—The Weekly Home Furnishings Magazine,* February 19, 1990.
——, "Three Fundamentals Fuel Bombay Company," *HFD—The Weekly Home Furnishings Magazine,* February 26, 1990.
Jones, John A., "Bombay Company's Furniture Sales Still Growing Strongly," *Investor's Business Daily,* February 7, 1994.
Santorelli, Dina, "Country Road, Take Me Home," *HFD—The Weekly Home Furnishings Magazine,* March 21, 1994.
Seymour, Liz, "Bombay Company Breaks with Convention," *HFD—The Weekly Home Furnishings Magazine,* April 17, 1989.
Spence, Rick, "Local Boy Makes Good Down South," *Profit,* spring, 1994.

—Elizabeth Rourke

Thereafter, Bond sought to acquire and build cash-generating businesses in order to provide a steady source of revenue even during economic downturns. In this way, Bond would be able to back up his borrowings with an operation that had either a strong cash flow or valuable assets, which could be used as collateral. In line with this strategy, Bond moved strongly into the brewing industry. In 1983 Bond moved from being merely a wealthy man to being an Australian national hero, winning the America's Cup in the *Australia II;* Bond was the first non-American ever to win the prestigious yachting race.

After this triumph, Bond's high-stakes dealings in international finance began in earnest, as he expanded his holdings beyond Australia. In 1983 Bond's holdings were worth about $450 million. By 1985, they had nearly doubled, to $810 million. In that year, Bond increased his holdings in the brewing industry when he bought Castlemaine Tooheys, a beer company based in Brisbane. With this acquisition, Bond took control of more than 40 percent of the Australian beer market.

In 1986 Bond moved into the American beer market, buying Pittsburgh Brewing, which made Iron City beer, for $30 million in 1986. The following year he borrowed money to buy Australia's Channel Nine television network, the majority of Chile's national phone company, and the fourth-largest American brewer, the G. Heilman Brewing Company, based in LaCrosse, Wisconsin. Founded in the nineteenth century, Heilman had been a local operation until 1959, when it began to buy up other regional brewers. By 1980 the company had purchased 13 other beer producers.

With the Heilman purchase, the first signs of trouble in the Bond empire began to surface. Intent on solidifying his position in the highly competitive American beer market, Bond paid $1.26 billion for the Wisconsin company, which was three times higher than some estimates of the company's worth. Heilman's revenues had been flat for three years at the time of the purchase, and its strategy of growth through acquisition had come to an end when it had run out of plausible targets for purchase. Bond acquired the company at the height of the stock market inflation of 1987, just before the crash that took place in October of that year. Nonetheless, convinced that Heilman's network of distributors could help to introduce his Australian beers to the United States, Bond poured money into marketing and advertising for Heilman.

After the stock market crash, which ruined some other Australian entrepreneurs, Bond stepped up his acquisitions. In an auction at Sotheby's in New York, he paid $72 million for a painting of irises by Vincent Van Gogh. By the end of the year, his empire was focused in four major areas: real estate, media, natural resources and energy, and brewing. Other ventures included Australia's first private university.

In April 1988, Bond raised $350 million by selling off his American bakery division. With these funds, the company continued on its international buying spree. In May he bought Australia's Bell Group from fellow financier Robert Holmes á Court for $685 million. In June 1988 the Bond Corporation released figures showing a 70 percent rise in after-tax earnings, to $224 million, and operating revenues of $1.4 billion, up 100 percent from the year before.

Bond Corporation Holdings Limited

Level 5
214 St. George's Terrace
Perth, Western Australia 6000
Australia
61-9-321-6588
Fax: 61-9-321-6585

Public Company
Incorporated: 1969 as West Australian Land Holdings
SICs: 6719 Holding Company, Nec

Bond Corporation Holdings, Limited, was an international conglomerate with operations in four primary fields: real estate, brewing, media, and natural resources. In addition, the company owned a wide and ever-changing variety of other properties. The company's founder, Australian entrepreneur Alan Bond, became famous in the 1980s as a high-stakes international financier, buying and selling properties worth millions by cleverly manipulating debt. In the wake of the 1987 stock market crash, however, Bond's juggling act became far more complicated, and his company collapsed into bankruptcy in the early 1990s.

Bond Holdings got its start in the 1950s when Alan Bond dropped out of high school. In 1957, after a stint as an apprentice sign painter, he took out a loan to start his own property development business. Within two years, Bond, at the age of 21, had become a millionaire.

In that year, 1959, Bond formed the Progress Development Organisation, which gradually acquired interests in 14 other companies, primarily property holders. In 1969 Bond incorporated his various holdings as West Australia Land Holdings, Limited, with headquarters in Perth. West Australia's properties expanded to include more real estate, as well as television and radio stations.

In 1974 Bond changed the name of his company to Bond Corporation Holdings. In the following year, risky borrowing to finance acquisitions brought Bond to the brink of financial ruin, when an effort to buy an iron-ore extraction company in Western Australia in the midst of an unexpected economic downturn nearly bankrupted him. Disaster was averted when Australia's ANZ Bank allowed him sufficient time to restructure his $73 million debt.

At the same time, Bond Corporation Holdings also reported $5.7 billion in debts, and the source of the company's strong financial returns provided additional cause for concern. In theory, Bond's brewing, liquor, and hotel operations provided the cash to fuel the rest of the company. In reality, however, only 37 percent of the company's revenues in 1988 came from these subsidiaries. Nearly 56 percent came from property, international, and corporate divisions, which produced one-time profits from real estate sales, sales of ownership in other companies, and foreign currency exchanges.

Problems in Bond's American brewing operations were symptomatic of those plaguing the company as a whole. Heilman's sales dropped significantly after Bond increased the price of the company's products, in an effort to pump up revenues to pay off debt, and tried to market Heilman beers to young urban professionals rather than the blue-collar consumers that made up the company's traditional customer base. The company's former customers were alienated, and the projected new customers did not materialize. In an eight-month period ending in June 1988, Heilman lost $75.6 million. Heilman's losses continued in the following year, mounting to $126.7 million, as the company's share of the American beer market fell to 6.8 percent.

Despite these worrisome signs, Bond's buying continued. In October 1988, the company paid $220 million for the St. Moritz Hotel in New York. Ignoring warnings that his debts, which had suddenly reached $7 billion, were attaining dangerous levels, Bond spent the fall of 1988 amassing shares of three British firms, including the British Satellite Broadcasting company, Allied-Lyons PLC, a major beer and liquor producer, and Lonrho PLC, a mining, agriculture, newspaper, and hotel conglomerate with annual revenues of $5.6 billion. Bond paid $610 million for shares of Allied-Lyons, and $590 million for a 20.4 percent stake in Lonrho. Lonrho's principal owner counterattacked by issuing a 93-page analysis of the Bond holdings, labeling them ''technically insolvent.'' Although Bond denied these charges, they caused an already jittery investment community to become more wary. The price of the company's stock slid on markets in Australia, Europe, and the United States.

In an attempt to counter this lack of confidence on the part of investors, Bond spent $116 million to buy back shares of Bond Corporation International, Limited, a Hong Kong-based subsidiary of his company. In Australia, he sold $1.64 billion worth of major properties, including real estate in downtown Sydney, a 14.9 percent stake in the Standard Chartered Bank of Britain, and a 5.5 percent stake in Australia's largest company, the Broken Hill Proprietary Company. His sales of assets were hampered by the fact that observers predicted disaster for the company, prompting buyers to hold out for a lower price.

In addition to these troubles, Bond was forced to defend himself against charges that he had abused his status as a broadcaster and had no right to own 14 Australian radio and television licenses. Other government investigations questioned the accuracy of the Bond Corporation's 1988 financial reporting, looking for stock violations, and government tax accountants scrutinized the company's elaborate tax shelters. By the start of 1989, Bond's sprawling empire was coming apart at the seams. Estimates of the company's debt ran as high as A$10 billion.

By May 1989, Bond had decided to unload his Lonrho holdings, worth $610 million, but no buyers appeared to purchase the stock. The company was more successful in selling off a prime piece of Hong Kong real estate, the 46-story Bond Centre office tower, which brought $284 million.

In November 1989, however, one of Bond's primary subsidiaries, which included his brewing properties, reported a debt of A$7.5 billion, and losses for the previous year of A$928.7 million, the worst in Australian history. In the annual report, the company's auditors concluded by expressing ''substantial doubt'' that the company ''could continue as a going concern.'' One other major subsidiary and the Bond holding company itself failed to submit annual reports on time. In response, the Australian Stock Exchange suspended trading in the company's stocks.

By this time, Bond's interest payments on his debt had reached almost $1 billion a year. Bond outlined a complicated plan to reduce the company's debt to $2.2 billion in the next nine months by selling remaining assets and rearranging his stock holdings.

In December 1989, a group of banks led by the Australia National Bank, Limited, convinced an Australian court that Bond's brewing subsidiary had violated the conditions of a loan agreement, and the company was put into receivership. In February 1990 the brewer emerged from receivership, but the banks returned to court to have it put back in receivership one month later.

In June the holding company missed a debt payment of $2.8 billion. The following month Bond agreed to step down as head of Bond Corporation Holdings, Limited, in a move to appease the company's many creditors. The company's valuable Australian brewing properties were sold to Bell Resources, an independently managed affiliate of Bond, but the struggling Heilman was retained.

By February 1991, the Bond companies had reduced their debt to $3.1 billion. Nevertheless, the company missed a $340 million payment to Australian Consolidated Investments, Limited, formerly Bell Resources. Rather than shutting Bond down, however, the company, which was also partially owned by Bond, agreed to a debt-for-equity swap that allowed Bond to stay afloat.

In June 1991 Bond Corporation Holdings reported that its revenues had dropped 96 percent over the past year, and that it had lost $512.7 million over the previous nine months. The explanation for these losses was that the company had devalued many of its investments and had divested itself of 97 percent of the Heilman brewery, which had filed for bankruptcy protection in January 1991.

In mid-1991 Bond Holdings finally declared bankruptcy, and the company began an effort to sell off all of its remaining assets, under the administration of the Ferrier Hodgson accounting group. The company sold its Australian brewing companies, Swan, Castlemaine, and Toohey, its energy holdings in petroleum, minerals, and coal, and its interest in the Chilean phone company. In December 1991 the company sold the last of its breweries, Pittsburgh Brewing, which was purchased by U.S.

investor Michael Carlow. One month earlier, Heilman, now independent, had emerged from bankruptcy.

Although the once-mighty Bond empire had been almost completely dismantled by the start of 1992, the effects of its collapse lingered on. Former employees of the Bond company were charged with "major breaches of the law" by the Australian Securities Commission in 1992. In April of that year, Alan Bond was declared personally bankrupt, after failing to pay $194 million to a Hong Kong bank to which he had personally guaranteed a loan to a nickel mining project. In addition, Bond was involved in investigations into business-government relations in West Australia state, and possible violations of the Australian Securities Code.

At the end of May, Bond was convicted of fraud in connection with the 1988 bail-out of a bank that had failed after the 1987 stock market crash. Bond had convinced a friend to invest $6 million to save the bank, without revealing that Bond's company was receiving a $12 million fee for the deal. When the bank finally collapsed, $200 million, including all of the friend's investment, was lost. Bond was sentenced to two-and-a-half years in prison.

In August 1992, however, Bond was released from jail on bond after an appeals court ordered a retrial. This was not the end of Bond's legal difficulties, however. Two years later, he was again charged with fraud in connection with the sale of a painting by Edouard Manet. In May 1994, a doctor testified that Bond was too ill to withstand trial, having suffered brain damage during open heart surgery in February 1993.

Further Reading:

"Alan Bond Is Declared Bankrupt in Australia," *New York Times,* April 15, 1992.

Alexander, Paul, "Rise and Fall of a Tycoon," *Glasgow Herald,* May 30, 1992.

Hutcheon, Stephen, "Suddenly, Alan Bond Is Losing His Gilt Edge," *Business Week,* May 29, 1989.

Rose, Michael, "Sailing Close to the Wind," *Maclean's,* December 4, 1989.

Wieffering, Eric J., "A Tapped-out Buyout," *Corporate Report Minnesota,* May, 1990.

Yang, Dori Jones, "Alan Bond's Buying Spree," *Business Week,* November 14, 1988.

—Elizabeth Rourke

BOOZ·ALLEN & HAMILTON

Booz Allen & Hamilton Inc.

8283 Greensboro Drive
McLean, Virginia 22102
U.S.A.
(703) 902-5000
Fax: (703) 902-3333

Private Company
Incorporated: 1962
Employees: 5,600
Sales: $814 million
SICs: 8742 Management Consulting Services; 8748 Business
    Consulting Services

Booz Allen & Hamilton Inc., a pioneer in the development of
the consulting industry, is recognized as an international management and technology consulting firm offering business strategy, operations, technology, and systems consulting services
through more than 50 offices worldwide. Involved in such areas
as environmental services, computer systems, space research,
transportation, weapons technology, human resources, telecommunications systems, health care, and management, the firm has
two major businesses: the Worldwide Commercial Business
provides management consulting services to major corporations, and the Worldwide Technology Business provides technology consulting and systems development services primarily
to government clients, but also to some commercial clients.

Booz Allen & Hamilton traces its roots to Edwin G. Booz. A
student at Chicago's Northwestern University in the early
1900s, Booz received a bachelor's degree in economics and a
master's degree in psychology, upon completion of his thesis
"Mental Tests for Vocational Fitness." In 1914, Booz established a small consulting firm in Chicago, and, two years later,
he and two partners formed the Business Research and Development Company, which conducted studies and performed in-
vestigational work for commercial and trade organizations. This
service, which Booz labeled as the first of its kind in the
Midwest, soon attracted such clients as Goodyear Tire & Rubber Company, Chicago's Union Stockyards and Transit Company, and the Canadian & Pacific Railroad.

During World War I, Booz was drafted as a private but moved
quickly through the ranks by performing personnel work and
helping the Army reorganize its bureaus' business methods.
Booz left the service in March 1919 as a major in the Inspector

General's Office and returned to Chicago to start a new firm,
Edwin G. Booz, Business Engineering Service. One of Booz's
first clients after the war was Sewell Avery of the State Bank &
Trust Company of Evanston, Illinois, who helped Booz get a
loan for his new venture. In return, Booz conducted a bank
survey for Avery.

During the early 1920s, Booz's client list grew to include Harris
Trust and Savings Bank in Chicago, the Walgreen Company,
and Booz's alma mater, Northwestern University. In 1924,
Booz changed the name of his firm to Business Surveys, to more
accurately reflect his firm's focus: business surveys and subsequent analysis and recommendations. Unlike other early "effi-
ciency-engineering" consulting firms, Booz adopted a person-
nel-oriented, applied-psychology approach that included
interviewing employees as part of the process of studying the
organizational structures of companies.

In 1925, Booz hired his first permanent, full-time assistant,
George Fry, another Northwestern alumnus. That year, Business Surveys began working for U.S. Gypsum Company (then
under the direction of Sewell Avery), which remained a staple
client throughout the decade. Other Business Surveys clients
during the latter half of the 1920s included the *Chicago Tribune,* Hart Schaffner & Marx, The Chicago Association of
Commerce, Eversharp, Inc., Stock Yards National Bank, and
Chicago Daily News publisher Walter Strong, who agreed on
Booz's recommendation to build a newspaper office across the
river from the Civic Opera House.

In 1929, Booz moved his own office into the new Chicago Daily
News Building and hired a third consultant, James L. Allen,
who had just graduated from Northwestern. By 1931, Avery
was back on Business Surveys' client list, this time as chairperson of Montgomery Ward, which was losing sales to the new
retail operations of Sears, Roebuck and Company. Booz took an
office just down the hall from Avery, where he worked full-time
and pioneered the "multi-vector" executive appraisal method,
which used cross-checking independent criteria in evaluating
and hiring managers.

By 1936, Booz had helped push Montgomery Ward back in the
black. Informing the company that Avery had been its central
problem, Booz resigned from the assignment and returned to his
firm's office, where Allen had recently resigned and Booz Surveys itself was in need of organization. By February of that
year, Booz had persuaded Allen to return and had hired another
consultant, Carl Hamilton. The firm then became a partnership
and adopted a new name: Booz, Fry, Allen & Hamilton. The
following year, the firm moved into the new Field Building in
Chicago, where it would remain for the next 44 years before
relocating its headquarters to New York City and taking more
modern space for its Chicago operations.

By the late 1930s, the firm's marketing brochure was promising
"independence that enables us to say plainly from the outside
what cannot always be said safely from within." The firm was
also providing executive recruiting services for its clients,
which during the late 1930s included the Chicago Title and
Trust Company, the University of Chicago, General Mills, and
the *Washington Post.* During this period, Booz personally conducted the first-ever study of a nationwide institution, the Amer-

ican National Red Cross, which propelled the firm into institutional consulting.

Booz, Fry, Allen & Hamilton entered the 1940s with a significant midwestern client base and a newly established New York branch office. In 1940, the firm expanded into military consulting, when U.S. Navy Secretary Frank Knox, former publisher of the *Chicago Daily News,* hired the company to assess the Navy's preparedness for a major war and to evaluate the Navy's shipyards, telephone systems, and intelligence operations.

After the United States entered the war, the firm continued to work for the Navy, as well as for the Army and the War Production Board. By 1942, a growing percentage of the firm's billings came from government and military assignments. The firm's increasing interest in work for the government, which Fry denounced as the wrong market for a consulting service, led to friction with Booz and in the midst of the feud a frustrated Allen again left the firm. Fry resigned from the partnership in December 1942 to start his own consulting business, and Allen returned early the following year to a renamed partnership—Booz Allen & Hamilton, where he was asked to help mold the firm's organizational structure and chair a newly established executive committee.

By war's end, Booz Allen had nearly 400 clients throughout the country being served by offices in Chicago, New York, and a new Los Angeles location. In 1946, Hamilton died, and, the following year, Booz retired, leaving Allen as chairperson of the firm's governing board. The firm's early postwar work included assignments for S.C. Johnson (known as Johnson Wax) and Radio Corporation of America (RCA), whose chairperson, General David Sarnoff, initially hired Booz Allen to do an organizational survey of RCA. During the late 1940s, Booz Allen also worked for RCA's subsidiary, National Broadcasting Company (NBC), conducting studies of NBC's radio/record division and the young television industry.

Booz Allen's work for the federal government and its military organizations continued in peacetime, and, in 1947, the firm received an Air Force contract to conduct the government's original production management study on guided missiles. Between 1949 and 1955, Booz Allen landed nearly two dozen of these so-called Wright Field assignments, which included a study of Air Force contractors' missile production capabilities.

Booz Allen entered the 1950s as one of only a few management consultant firms in the United States. During the early 1950s, the firm continued to build on its traditional midwestern manufacturing client base, which grew to include Maytag, Parker Pen, Johnson Wax, and Cessna, a small-airplane manufacturer. In 1951, Edwin G. Booz died, leaving behind a pioneering company on the verge of international expansion and diversification.

In 1953, Booz Allen landed its first international contract, an assignment to study and help reorganize land-ownership records for the newly established Philippine government. About the same time, the firm began helping reorganize the government of Egypt's customs operations and a government-owned Egyptian textile manufacturer. By the mid-1950s, Booz Allen had created an international subsidiary and moved into Italy to conduct studies of a nationalized steel company and state-owned oil company.

In 1955, a group of key Booz Allen partners formed Booz Allen Applied Research, Inc. (BAARINC) as a separate corporate entity. Utilizing the Wright Field studies on missile production as a foundation, BAARINC was designed to launch the firm's diversification into the intelligence arena and was formed around a Booz Allen team of guided missile specialists. BAARINC was soon hired by the federal government to help determine where the Soviet Union was manufacturing missiles and to compile a so-called Red Book, which outlined technical problems Soviets experienced in developing weaponry. During the late 1950s, Booz Allen also worked with the National Aeronautics and Space Administration (NASA)—helping to determine the best way to reach the moon—and served on a Navy task force which developed PERT, or the Program Evaluation and Review Technique designed to improve the planning and production of the Polaris submarine missile.

By the close of the decade, Booz Allen was, in the words of a 1959 *Time* article, "the world's largest, most prestigious management consultant firm," having served three-fourths of the country's largest businesses, two-thirds of the federal government's departments, and most types of nonprofit institutions during its first 46 years. During the 1950s, the firm's number of partners grew from 12 to 60, while its total professional staff increased to more than 500, one-third of which were specialists.

In 1962, in order to establish profit sharing and retirement plans for its partners, Booz Allen became a private corporation, and the partnership that had governed the firm legally was dissolved (although the term "partner" continued to be used). That year, James Allen became the new corporations's chairperson and passed the reigns of active leadership to Charlie Bowen, who was named president. Between 1962 and 1964, BAARINC acquired two subsidiaries, Designers for Industry (renamed Design & Development) and Foster D. Snell Laboratory. Shortly thereafter, BAARINC also became a Booz Allen subsidiary, bringing to the firm a client list that included IBM, Abbott Labs, United Airlines, and the U.S. Department of the Interior.

During this time, Booz Allen's nonfederal government work included a study on the efficiency of the Nassau County, Louisiana, government and a study of the Chicago public school system. In the corporate arena, Booz Allen helped Johnson Wax expand in Europe, aided Deere & Company in a restructuring, and orchestrated the merger of Rockwell Standard and North American Aviation, resulting in formation of North American Rockwell Corp.

Overseas expansion continued as well, with Booz Allen deployed to evaluate a variety of European industries, including British heavy industry and consumer goods manufacturers and West German and Scandinavian steel producers. Booz Allen was also engaged in a series of assignments for the World Bank to help the governments of Brazil, Argentina, and Venezuela develop steel industries. Moreover, Booz Allen was hired by the Algerian government to help it develop an integrated oil operation which could operate in the world marketplace; similar assignments soon followed in Iran, Abu Dhabi, and Saudi Arabia.

During the Vietnam War, Booz Allen conducted studies for Secretary of Defense Robert McNamara, including a series of feasibility studies involving the so-called Supersonic Transport plane. Booz Allen also provided the U.S. military with assessments of communications equipment during the firm's first "field work" assignment, in which consultants accompanied military patrols in gathering information on the use of American communications equipment by Vietnamese allies.

By 1969, Booz Allen—the largest consulting firm in the United States—had more than 15 major or project offices on five continents, generating annual revenues of $55 million and earnings of $3.5 million. Having experienced explosive growth during the decade, Booz Allen considered going public, launching a brief debate regarding the ethics of public ownership of a business that stressed confidentiality.

The following year, James Allen retired, Bowen was named chairperson and chief executive, and James W. Taylor became president. In January 1970, the firm went public, following the lead of Arthur D. Little, Inc., which had initiated public ownership of large consulting firms a year earlier. The Booz Allen public offering was designed to help the company diversify by giving the firm the ability to acquire specialized companies through stock swaps. Between 1969 and 1972, Booz Allen purchased several small specialty consulting firms. These acquisitions included firms involved in transportation, household chemicals, airport management, real estate, market research, and television advertising testing. The market research, airport, and chemicals operations were later spun off. In 1972, the firm also established a Japanese subsidiary.

During the early 1970s, BAARINC was hired by NASA to assess the ability of a $100 million satellite to orbit the earth for one year. BAARINC predicted the satellite would fail within four days, which it did, building BAARINC's reputation in space systems work and leading to a subsequent assignment to test a redesigned satellite, which met Booz Allen specifications and stayed in orbit for 18 months.

During this time, Booz Allen's government assignments leveled off and then declined, as did commercial work during this "energy crisis" period when consultants became a discretionary budget item for many companies. As a result, Booz Allen's profit margins suffered, and its stock prices slid, as government billings were cut in half and profits from Europe became nearly nonexistent.

In 1973, with the firm in decline, Taylor was asked to resign and Bowen named James Farley as Taylor's successor. Farley formed a cabinet of advisors comprised of unit business heads, and then expanded that team concept with the establishment of a larger operating council, which included the firm's principal managers. The company then made its officers owners, allowing each officer to buy a certain percent of Booz Allen stock. The firm also stepped up its push into international markets—via such avenues as a new Italian subsidiary—and increased its diversification into specialized markets.

In 1976, after four years of gradually buying back its stock, Booz Allen again became a private company in a final buyout that paid outside shareholders $7.75 a share, considerably less than the $24 per share price Booz Allen's stock debuted at earlier in the decade. Farley was named chairperson and chief executive, and John L. Lesher became president. The retirement of Bowen that year marked the close of a quick turnaround for Booz Allen, which saw its billings rise from $54 million in 1972 to $100 million by the end of 1976.

During the mid and late 1970s, Booz Allen conducted studies of the telecommunications market and the Bell telephone system for AT&T and was engaged in a seven-year assignment for the city of Wichita, Kansas, to help establish a prototype municipal computer information system, which brought the firm national recognition. Booz Allen's expanded work in communications electronics and commercial telecommunications led the firm into new, specialized markets, including communications security, strategic and national command and control systems, and intelligence systems. One result of this increasing technological diversification was a contract to work on the Tri-Service Tactical Communications Program, which involved the coordination of U.S. Army, Navy, and Air Force communications.

In 1978, BAARINC changed its name to Public Management & Technology Center (later becoming known simply as the Technology Center) and refocused its office automation, manufacturing technology, and space systems services, leading to work on the commercialization of space stations. PMTC diversified into new markets—including nuclear survivability, electronic systems engineering, avionics, and software verification and validations—and began offering clients cost containment and flexible pricing options. Key contracts for PMTC during the late 1970s included Navy assignments to help develop the Trident missile and help rebuild Saudi Arabia's navy.

During this time, Booz Allen also helped Chrysler Corporation in its historic turnaround by devising a plan to secure federal loan guarantees for the automaker and then by serving as a troubleshooter after the federal bailout, monitoring the company's performance for the federal loan guarantee board. Booz Allen also helped orchestrate Hong Kong and Shanghai Banking Corporation's acquisition of Marine Midland after providing HSBC with a comprehensive study of the American banking network.

By 1980, Booz Allen's annual revenues had climbed to $180 million, having more than tripled in a decade, and the company was running a close second in U.S. consulting service billings to Arthur Andersen. The Navy remained one of Booz Allen's principal clients during the 1980s, while Warner-Lambert Company also became an important corporate client, helping to launch the firm into health care consulting. Overseas, Booz Allen entered the decade engaged in oil and steel industry work in West Africa, Indonesia, and Nigeria, while also employed in Zambia to help consolidate that country's copper mining industry.

By 1983, recessionary conditions and an oil glut led to a profit slump for Booz Allen. The following year, Farley stepped down from his posts as chairperson and chief executive, returning to client work before becoming president of MONY Financial

Services. Before leaving Booz Allen, however, Farley established a firm-wide competition to select his successor in what proved to be, according to a 1988 *Forbes* article, a divisive and distracting ten-month process. Ultimately, Michael McCullough, president of PMTC since its 1978 reorganization, was chosen to succeed Farley. Under McCullough, PMTC had remained a bright spot in Booz Allen operations as commercial consulting lagged, generating annual billings of more than $100 million by 1984, while developing information systems for such clients as the U.S. Postal Service and the U.S. House of Representatives.

Also in the early 1980s, Booz Allen provided extensive services to AT&T, helping develop a strategic repositioning program for its divestiture of the local Bell operating companies.

During the mid-1980s, Booz Allen's commercial consulting work began to wane, and rival McKinsey & Company became the powerhouse of general management consulting, and Arthur D. Little grew into a leader in technology consulting. Booz Allen relied increasingly on government work. By 1987, government accounts—with the lowest profit margin in the consulting field—represented nearly one-third of Booz Allen's $340 in annual revenues at a time when defense spending was increasingly being targeted for budget cuts.

McCullough responded to Booz Allen's mid-1980s slump by restructuring the firm around industries rather than traditional geographic boundaries and emphasizing a multi-disciplinary approach to business problems, utilizing technical specialists in tandem with management consulting experts. McCullough's approach at the time was relatively untried, with most firms specializing in either management or technology. In 1989, the company launched a major expansion program of its computer systems integration (CSI) services for commercial clients, in an effort to expand its presence in the commercial computer systems and technology market. Booz Allen entered the commercial systems integration field at a time when CSI was the fastest growing segment of the consulting field, and also one of the toughest to crack; Booz Allen had to compete with both computer manufacturers and technology consulting firms.

In 1990, William F. Stasior, a senior executive from Booz Allen's technology business, was named president of the firm. The following year, Stasior assumed the additional duties of chairperson and chief executive, after McCullough returned to consulting as a senior partner, having spearheaded a six-year transition from a regional strategy to one increasingly focused on international operations and technology.

In 1991, Booz Allen acquired the major assets of Advanced Decision Systems Inc., a California-based artificial intelligence company, which became a Booz Allen division. By this time, Booz Allen's multi-disciplinary approach to business problems had become known in the firm as "Theory P." Named for its emphasis on integrating people and process, Theory P represented a problemsolving approach concerned less with how departments operated independently and more with how they worked together to produce goods and services. This strategy was adopted by other major companies, including Hewlett-Packard, Corning Glass Works, and Ford Motor Company.

During the early 1990s, Booz Allen also began offering its clients a type of corporate war game that simulated competition among companies and served as a business strategy tool. In 1993, Booz Allen was hired by the U.S. Agency for International Development to devise a strategy to lead a consortium of firms in the privatization of civilian and defense industries in 11 newly independent states of the former Soviet Union.

That year, two reports prepared by Booz Allen took center stage in the Delaware Supreme Court. The first, which Paramount Communications had used to inform their decision on whether to be acquired by Viacom Inc., revealed that Paramount and Viacom together would generate nearly ten times more profit than a Paramount merger with QVC Network Inc., which was also vying to acquire Paramount. In December 1993, the Booz Allen report on possible merger combinations—which included confidential data from Viacom but not QVC—was introduced as evidence in a legal battle between Viacom and QVC over the Paramount acquisition; Paramount sought a reversal of a court decision ruling that it had illegally rejected a QVC offer. Following the Delaware Supreme Court ruling in favor of QVC, Booz Allen prepared a subsequent report with confidential information from QVC, which resulted in the same conclusions as the first study.

As it moved into the mid-1990s, Booz Allen's business was equally split between technology services and systems development and commercial management consulting. While the firm had remained profitable (even in the sluggish 1980s, when its ranking among the top U.S. consulting firms fell from second to sixth or seventh), its percentage of the consulting industry's market in the future appeared to be dependent upon Booz Allen's ongoing merger of high-tech consulting and general management consulting.

Principal Subsidiaries: Booz Allen & Hamilton Health Care Inc; Booz Allen & Hamilton Acquisition Services.

Further Reading:

Baum, Laurie, "Is Booz Allen Having a Mid-life Crisis?" *Business Week,* March 9, 1987, pp. 76–80.
Berton, Lee, and Paul B. Carroll, "Booz Allen Plans a Major Expansion in Computer Systems Integration Work," *Wall Street Journal,* January 30, 1989, p. C5.
"Booz, Allen Tells Rich Inside Story," *Business Week,* December 20, 1969, pp. 22–23.
"Booz, Allen Tries to Cure Its Own Ills," *Business Week,* January 20, 1973, pp. 26–28.
Bowman, Jim, *Booz Allen & Hamilton: Seventy Years of Client Service,* New York: Kenner Printing, 1984.
Coy, Peter, "Oh, What a Lovely War Game," *Business Week,* February 1, 1993, p. 34.
"The Instant Executives," *Forbes,* November 15, 1967, pp. 27–41.
Machan, Dyan, "'Gladiators' Ball," *Forbes,* December 26, 1988, pp. 130–34.
"Management Experts Thrive on Own Advice," *Business Week,* April 23, 1960, pp. 104–18.
"The New Shape of Management Consulting," *Business Week,* May 21, 1979, pp. 98–104.

—Roger W. Rouland

Brinker International, Inc.

6820 LBJ Freeway
Dallas, Texas 75240
U.S.A.
(214) 980-9917
Fax: (214) 770-9593

Public Company
Incorporated: 1975 as Chili's Bar & Grill, Inc.
Employees: 40,000
Sales: $652 million
Stock Exchanges: New York
SICs: 5812 Eating Places; 6794 Patent Owners & Lessors

Brinker International, Inc. operates four popular American restaurant chains: Chili's Grill & Bar, Romano's Macaroni Grill, Grady's American Grill, and Spageddies. The mainstay of the company is Chili's, a chain of more than 300 eateries featuring Southwest decor and inexpensive meals. Under the direction of Norman E. Brinker, for whom the company was named, Brinker's expanded the Chili's chain and opened similar restaurants with different themes.

Brinker traces its origins to the first Chili's Grill & Bar, opened on Greenville Street in Dallas in March 1975. Chili's was established by Dallas restaurateur Larry Lavine, who sought to provide an informal full-service dining atmosphere with a menu that focused on different varieties of hamburgers offered at reasonable prices. Levine's concept proved successful, and 22 more Chili's restaurants, featuring similar Southwest decor, were opened in the late 1970s and early 1980s. In 1983, Levine's restaurant chain was taken over by Norman E. Brinker.

Brinker had a long and illustrious history in the restaurant business. He had begun his career in 1957 working for the Jack-in-the-Box fast food chain, which then had just seven outlets. Nine years later, Brinker left the greatly expanded Jack-in-the-Box operation to found Steak & Ale, an informal, full-service restaurant chain with a menu that emphasized inexpensive steak dinners and friendly service. Responsible for introducing the salad bar, an innovation which soon swept the restaurant industry, this new, casual dining concept became a favorite among the generation of "baby boomers."

By the 1970s, Brinker's nearly 200 restaurants, including the Steak & Ale and Bennigan's chains, were overseen by his S&A

Restaurant Corporation. When S&A was sold to the Pillsbury Company in 1976, Brinker became an executive at Pillsbury, in charge of that company's restaurant group, which now had four chains, including Burger King and Pillsbury's Poppin' Fresh Restaurants. Together, the operations of this group represented the second largest restaurant company in the world.

By 1983, however, Brinker had decided to leave Pillsbury in order to strike out again on his own. "I wanted to see if I could take a very small company and develop it against the big chains," Brinker recalled in a 1992 article in *Food & Service* magazine. Toward this end, Brinker purchased a significant share in the Chili's chain, becoming its chairperson and chief executive officer. At this time, Chili's had less than $1 million in equity, was $8.5 million in debt, and was earning less than $1 million a year. Planning to expand, Brinker took Chili's public in 1984, selling stock to the public under the ticker tape symbol "EAT." On the basis of Brinker's strong reputation in the restaurant industry, Chili's stock offering received strong support from the investment community.

In 1984, Chili's 23 restaurants were generating $40 million in sales from their menu of gourmet burgers, french fries, and margaritas. To improve the chain's profitability and thereby allow for expansion, Brinker began the process of fine-tuning Chili's operations. Seeking input from Chili's customers, as well as from customers of competing restaurants, Brinker made a practice of strolling around the parking lots of eating establishments, informally asking customers how they liked their meals and what changes they would like made. On the basis of this feedback, he began to shift the focus of Chili's menu away from burgers to include a broader array of salads and chicken and fish entrees.

Throughout the mid-1980s, Brinker and his associates expanded Chili's steadily, opening new restaurants across the country and further adapting the eatery's offerings. By the end of the decade, burgers accounted for just ten percent of the company's sales, as new items, such as ribs and fajitas, proved more popular. The company counted on its loyal customers, dubbed "chiliheads," to keep revenues high, while also striving to maintain its rapid rate of customer turnover; the average length of time a customer spent in a Chili's restaurant was just 35 minutes, which allowed for more profitable and efficient use of space and wait staff.

By the late 1980s, the company was ready to branch out into new restaurants and began to consider several different acquisitions. A plan to attempt regaining control of Brinker's former S&A Restaurant Corporation was vetoed, as was an idea to take on several fast food chains, such as Taco Cabana and Flyer's Island Express. Chili's eventually decided to focus on the casual, low-priced restaurant niche, in which it was already a strong player. In February 1989, the company purchased Grady's Goodtimes, a Knoxville, Tennessee-based restaurant chain owned by a family named Regas, who had been in the restaurant business in Tennessee since 1919. In 1982, the Regas's had opened the first of their Grady's Goodtimes outlets, which served primarily beef, seafood, salads, and sandwiches.

Since the Dallas restaurant market already had a chain called Grady's, Chili's executives decided to call their new chain

"Regas." However, this new name eventually proved unsuccessful, as some customers expressed confusion over its pronunciation and others associated it with "regal," leading them to suspect that it was an expensive restaurant. Moreover, Regas faced tough competition from established steakhouse chains in Texas. As a result, Chili's faced unexpected difficulties in expanding the acquisition.

Nine months after purchasing Regas, Chili's acquired another restaurant concept, which it also planned to expand into a chain. With $41 million in capital obtained through a stock sale, Chili's purchased the rights to the Romano's Macaroni Grill concept. Texas restaurateur Phil Romano had opened the prototype restaurant in 1988 in a location north of San Antonio, Texas. He based the eatery's atmosphere and menu on the communal style of dining that he remembered from growing up in an Italian family. Just as his grandfather had always kept a four-liter jug of wine on the dinner table, patrons in Romano's restaurant were provided with casks of house red wine. Customers were invited to serve themselves throughout the meal and then to inform their waiter of how much they had consumed; the waiter would then charge them accordingly. This "honor system" for wine was modified in areas where liquor laws forbid patrons to serve themselves, but on the whole, it helped to keep sales high at Romano's.

Other innovations at Romano's restaurants included glass walls through which patrons could see kitchen workers creating the evening's meals. The unique interior design of Romano's created a cavernous effect, with strings of bare lightbulbs illuminating high, wooden, vaulted ceilings and tables placed between fieldstone arches. Daily specials were displayed in deli cases near the restaurant's front door, and crates of wine and canned tomato products were hung on the walls, serving as decoration and storage space.

Chili's planned for Romano's to compete with the extremely successful Olive Garden chain of Italian restaurants owned by General Mills. Rapid expansion of Romano's and Regas was anticipated, and Brinker set a goal for the Chili's company to earn annual revenues of $1 billion by 1995. Brinker planned to pattern the growth of the new acquisitions after the Chili's chain expansion. In just seven years under Brinker's leadership, Chili's had grown to include 215 restaurants; although a large percentage of these were directly owned by the company, a franchising program had also proved useful in opening new restaurants.

To help Romano's and Regas achieve similar growth, Brinker decided to keep the identities and priorities of its three restaurant chains distinct, maintaining separate administrations for each. Each restaurant was designed to appeal to a middle class customer, between the ages of 25 and 55, and prices were kept reasonable: the average bill for a Chili's customer was $7.50; the average for a Regas customer was $9.50; and at Romano's, a slightly more upscale property, average bills per customer were $13.50. By the end of 1990, Chili's was operating 240 Chili's outlets, 14 Regas Grill restaurants, and three Romano's Macaroni Grill eateries. Together, these operations reported $438 million in revenues.

In May 1991, Chili's announced that it was changing its corporate name, to better reflect the newly diversified nature of its operations. The company's name became Brinker International, Inc., and Brinker told the Dallas Morning News that "this new name is a way to bridge our past with our future as a multi-concept corporation in the midst of international expansion." The first foreign countries targeted for Chili's operations were Canada and Mexico, where the company planned for restaurants to open in 1992.

Again, Brinker undertook extensive market research in order to adapt restaurant offerings to suit customer preferences. As U.S. demographic studies and customer feedback began to suggest that the average age of a Chili's customer had increased, the restaurant took steps to make itself more appealing to this segment of the public. The volume of music played over restaurant loudspeakers was lowered, the size of the print on Chili's menus was enlarged, sizes of some portions were reduced, and more low-fat entrees were added. At the same time, the company promoted Chili's as a friendly place for younger couples with children, providing fast and efficient service and low prices. "You have to stay in the energetic group of customers, but you try to tone it down enough so that you don't turn off the older group," Brinker explained to Food & Service magazine.

To keep the company's operations as efficient and cost effective as possible, Brinker also invested in an elaborate computer system. Computers were used to schedule workers' shifts and to help company headquarters determine the amount of supplies each restaurant needed. In addition, Brinker invested in extensive kitchen staff training programs, which were designed to minimize waste in company operations.

By the end of 1991, Brinker's had sales totaling $426.8 million and earnings of $26.1 million, a 44 percent increase over the previous year. Already operating a total of 271 restaurants by the spring of 1992, Brinker was opening one new restaurant a week, as the company chalked up a 23 percent rate of growth in sales, despite a general recession in the restaurant industry. Many of the Chili's restaurants opened in early 1992 showed a higher rate of sales than older properties, reflecting the company's growing expertise in the industry. Moreover, Brinker established Chili's restaurants in less populous areas, reflecting the widespread popularity of the Chili's concept.

Despite these strong signs of continuing financial health, Brinker executives estimated that the market for its Chili's chains would mature by the late 1990s. In order to take the pressure off the Chili's concept, and lessen the number of new restaurants openings needed to maintain brisk growth in corporate profits, Brinker looked for expansion in its newer properties.

By mid-1992, Brinker had opened 17 Regas restaurants, and, in response to the problems surrounding the chain's name, he had rechristened all of these outlets as Grady's American Grill. The company continued to experiment with different formats for the eatery, redesigning its interiors as more casual and being careful to distinguish Grady's from Chili's. As part of this effort, Grady's menu was centered on beef, seafood, and pasta, rather than the Mexican-based entrees that had become popular at Chili's.

Brinker also looked to Romano's to bolster corporate earnings. By May 1992, eight of these restaurants were in operation, contributing about $3 million a year in sales each, up from $2.4 million the year before. A Romano's restaurant cost no more to build than a Chili's, and brought in revenues that were twice as high, since its menu featured higher-priced items, and Brinker planned to nearly triple the number of Romano eateries over the next 12 months. The company's strategy was to enter as many markets as soon as possible, reap the rewards of novelty in areas without moderately priced Italian eateries, and then decide on which markets could support two or more Romano's outlets.

The success of Romano's prompted Brinker to test a second, less expensive Italian eatery concept, also developed by restaurateur Phil Romano. In July 1992, Spageddie's, a low-priced, casual pasta restaurant, was opened at a test location in Plano, Texas. The prototype restaurant seated 216 patrons, had a decor featuring bright colors, decorative canned goods, and colorful billboards, and included two bocci ball courts to keep customers amused while they waited for seats. As in Romano's restaurants, exhibition kitchens at Spageddie's allowed patrons to watch their food being prepared. With the two chains, Brinker hoped to flank its competitor Olive Garden, with Spageddies engaging a slightly less expensive niche and Romano's occupying a more costly segment of the market.

At the end of June 1992, Brinker posted annual revenues of $519.3 million, with earnings of $26.1 million; 300 Chili's Bar & Grills, 20 Grady's American Grills, and 17 Romano's outlets were in operation. Later that year, Brinker announced plans for further foreign expansion, signing an agreement with Pac-Am Food Concepts, based in Hong Kong, to franchise 25 Chili's restaurants in the Far East over the next 15 years. Pac-Am planned to duplicate the Chili's decor and menu in locations such as Jakarta, Indonesia, and Seoul, South Korea, with some changes to satisfy local tastes.

Brinker also began to test another theme restaurant, Kona Ranch Steakhouse, in Oklahoma City. A small, Tex-Mex restaurant in San Antonio, called Nacho Mama's, was also considered a possible avenue for expansion, although Brinker's executives vowed to change that restaurant's name in the event of an acquisition. In the midst of its aggressive plans to expand all four of its principal restaurant chains, the company encountered an unexpected obstacle on January 21, 1993, when Norman Brinker suffered a serious head injury while playing polo. Brinker was comatose for two weeks, during which time he was temporarily replaced at the company by his second in command. Despite an initially unfavorable prognosis, Brinker made a rapid recovery and returned to resume his positions of chairperson and chief executive officer in May 1993.

Shortly thereafter, Brinker International moved to expand its Spageddies property, buying out the interest of its partner Romano in the prototype Spageddie's restaurant and announcing that two more Texas locations, in Tyler and Mesquite, would be opened. To provide a corporate structure that would enhance growth in all areas of the company, Brinker reorganized its headquarters staff into concept teams, which were designed to act as small companies within the framework of the larger corporation. As Brinker approached the mid-1990s, it appeared well positioned for strong growth, enhanced by an experienced management team and a track record of success with a variety of different restaurant concepts.

Further Reading:

Bell, Sally, "Norm!," *Food & Service,* January, 1992.
Bernstein, Charles, "Brinker's Three-Way Combination: A Bid for Full-Service Dominance," *Nation's Restaurant News,* October 29, 1990.
Chaudhry, Rajan, "Ron McDougall's Winning Ways," *Restaurants & Institutions,* July 1, 1993.
Gutner, Toddi, "Norman Brinker Scores Again," *Forbes,* January 6, 1992.
Hall, Cheryl, "Brinker International Runs on Good Game Plan," *Dallas Morning News,* February 21, 1993.
Hall, Cheryl, "The Brinker Touch," *Dallas Morning News,* May 10, 1992.
Oppel, Richard A., Jr., "A Return Performance," *Dallas Morning News,* May 5, 1993.
Ruggless, Ron, "Brinker Inks Deal for Chili's Units in Asia," *Nation's Restaurant News,* November 16, 1992.
Ruggless, Ron, "Norman Brinker Hits the Comeback Trail," *Nation's Restaurant News,* March 29, 1993.
Sherbert, Felicia M., "Beyond Chili's," *Market Watch,* July/August, 1992.

—Elizabeth Rourke

Brown-Forman Corporation

850 Dixie Highway
Louisville, Kentucky 40210-1038
U.S.A.
(502) 585-1100
Fax: (502) 774-7876

Public Company
Incorporated: 1933 as Brown-Forman Distillery
Employees: 6,700
Sales: $1.69 billion
Stock Exchanges: New York
SICs: 2085 Distilled and Blended Liquors; 2084 Wines,
    Brandy, and Brandy Spirits; 3262 Vitreous China Table
    and Kitchenware; 3914 Silverware and Plated Ware; 3161
    Luggage; 3172 Personal Leather Goods, Nec; 2392 House
    Furnishings, Nec

Brown-Forman Corporation is a diversified producer, marketer, and exporter of upscale beverage alcohol and consumer products. The full-line distiller markets Jack Daniel's whiskey, Southern Comfort liqueur, Bols Liqueurs, Fetzer wines, Korbel champagne and brandy, Ushers scotch, and Early Times and Old Forester bourbon. Brown-Forman also owns, produces, and markets Lenox and Dansk branded crystal, china, giftware, and table linens, as well as Kirk-Steiff silver tableware.

George Garvin Brown and John Forman founded the Brown-Forman Distillery in Louisville, Kentucky in 1870. At the outset, Brown-Forman marketed Old Forester bourbon. Before Brown and Forman marketed their own brand, bourbon had been sold to taverns in barrels, and bartenders decanted the alcohol into special bottles with the name of the tavern on the label. Brown poured the bourbon into bottles at the distillery, he corked and sealed the bottles, labeled them, and warned taverns not to buy the bourbon if the seals were broken. As an additional innovation, all of the labels were handwritten and included a guarantee on the quality of the bourbon. Old Forester sold well as a result of these innovations—but Forman was dubious: in 1902 he sold his interest in the Brown-Forman Distillery because he believed that Brown-Forman's success would diminish as soon as the novelty of packaging began to fade. The Brown family purchased all of Forman's interest in the company.

In 1905 Brown-Forman continued their packaging innovations by bottling Old Forester in pear-shaped bottles. Old Forester's tavern sales increased significantly as a result. These increased sales led to a certain amount of bitterness among other distillers in Kentucky. Some competitors went so far as to slip iron nails into barrels of Brown-Forman whiskey to make it turn black.

Brown-Forman's bourbon was aged in barrels in large warehouses. At that time, warehouses were not heated, and labels on bourbon bore the expression "summers old," a reference to the fact that bourbon can age only in a warm climate. As a result, during the early decades of this century it took many years for the bourbon to be prepared for the market. Consequently, the word "old" became a common prefix in any brand name of bourbon.

Old Forester, produced, marketed, and distributed by Brown-Forman Distillers Corp., continued to be very successful under the private ownership of the Brown family, which had no plans to diversify. All the company's advertising concentrated on marketing Old Forester, which it promoted as a product that would restore health: "Many, many times a day, eminent physicians say, Old Forester will life prolong and make old age hale and strong." Although this advertising was effective, Prohibition threatened to close Brown-Forman. To prevent this from happening, Brown-Forman went public just prior to Prohibition, but the Browns maintained control of the majority of shares.

The pre-Prohibition advertising had been valuable: the Brown-Forman company was one of four distillers permitted by the government to sell alcohol for medicinal purposes during Prohibition. The marketing of Old Forester had saved the company from the kind of downfall that other distillers suffered as a result of Prohibition.

Brown-Forman spent the decade between the end of Prohibition and World War II readjusting to the fact that it could now legally sell Old Forester as bourbon. The bourbon now needed to be advertised as an alcoholic beverage rather than as a health tonic, in order to change the image it had acquired during Prohibition. However, the extensive advertising of the late 1930s and early 1940s was largely futile; the production of alcoholic beverages was once again severely curtailed during World War II. This time Old Forester could not be advertised as a health tonic since even this type of alcohol was now illegal. In spite of this development, the Brown family was not pessimistic about the future of their distillery. They investigated ways in which their alcohol could be used to help the war effort, and during the war Brown-Forman produced alcohol that was used in making both gunpowder and rubber. The Browns also continued to plan for the end of World War II and the future of the Brown-Forman company. They wanted their bourbon to have a head start in the postwar market.

During World War II Brown-Forman's executive committee considered the fact that it took at least four years to age a marketable bourbon. They attempted to predict when the war would end and correctly decided on 1945. By starting the aging in 1941, they could have Old Forester ready for sale immediately following the war. As the competition's bourbon would not be marketable until 1949, Brown-Forman could monopolize the bourbon market for the first four postwar years.

Because the executive committee's predictions were correct and resulted in impressive sales, Brown-Forman management decided to create a committee system of management. Finance, marketing, and production committees were created, in addition to the executive committee, to discuss and implement policies that could lead to the future success of the company.

In 1945 the management at Brown-Forman implemented an annual training course for ten to 20 selected individuals from outside the firm. These individuals worked in all areas of the company, from the lowest to the highest positions. Approximately half of them were then hired by other companies, and half continued with Brown-Forman in management positions. In this way, Brown-Forman created for itself an adequate supply of employees for management positions from outside the company itself. However, the remaining other employees were hired according to a policy of ''planned nepotism.''

Since George Garvin Brown founded Brown-Forman in 1870, the Browns have supported this type of company nepotism. In 1945 the executives at Brown-Forman publicly stated that nepotism was good for their business and would be encouraged. They believed that if a father enjoyed working at Brown-Forman, his son would feel just as comfortable working there. Brown-Forman executives, as a policy, encourage the children and grandchildren of good employees to work for the company.

One of the effects of the limited production of alcohol during World War II was that postwar consumers favored whiskey blends which did not have a strong alcohol taste. The executives at Brown-Forman, however, did not pay attention to this new trend. They continued to sell bourbon with high alcohol content. In 1956 Brown-Forman diversified into the premium rye whiskey business by purchasing the Jack Daniel Distillery in Lynchburg, Tennessee. Jack Daniel's had been founded in 1866 and enjoyed a popular, ''down-home'' image. The label of the ''Tennessee sipping whiskey'' featured men in overalls, coonhounds, and scenes from Lynchburg. Brown-Forman's confidence in the value of the Jack Daniel's franchise was evinced by the fact that the acquisition cost $20 million, a debt that exceeded the company's net worth. The deal also confirmed Brown-Forman's movement away from being a company that produced only bourbon. It was, however, the last time that the firm would incur debt to make an acquisition.

At the beginning of the 1960s, Brown-Forman continued its diversification program by purchasing the Joseph Garneau Co., an importer of scotch whiskeys and European wines. Although Brown-Forman had not followed consumer trends after World War II when blends were popular, they succumbed to the high demand for scotch in the 1960s. By 1962 scotch held 9 percent of the liquor market, and the popularity of wine was increasing steadily.

Despite the diversifications, Brown-Forman portrayed itself as a medium-sized company. This stance worked in favor of the company during the 1960s. Before 1963, 80 percent of all hard liquor in the United States was sold by the four largest distilling companies, and the remaining 20 percent was sold by Brown-Forman, Heublein, James B. Beam Distilling Co., and the

American Distilling Co.. However, in 1963 these smaller companies increased their sales by 70 percent while the larger companies did not increase their sales at all. Consumer tastes during the 1960s favored the small, independent distilling companies. One reason for this change was that consumers in increasing numbers were switching from blended whiskey, popular after World War II, to straight whiskey.

In 1964 in order to continue its expansion in the broader market for alcoholic beverages, Brown-Forman purchased all outstanding stock of the Oertel Brewing Co., a small Louisville brewery. This company produced beer which was distributed in Kentucky, Tennessee, Indiana, Ohio, and Alabama. The brewery later became unprofitable, and Brown-Forman sold its interest in the company during the late 1960s. Yet the purchase of Oertel was proof of Brown-Forman's willingness to diversify into new areas of the alcohol market.

In 1966 Daniel L. Street was appointed president of Brown-Forman, the first time that a man outside of the Brown family had been president of the company. Street joined Brown-Forman as a lawyer in 1938 and advanced to the position of executive vice-president in 1953. He continued Brown-Forman's program of diversification while president. In 1967 he authorized a merger with Quality Importers, which provided Brown-Forman with a ''top scotch and good gin,'' according to Street. Quality Importers produces Ambassador scotch, Ambassador gin, and Old Bushmills Irish whiskey. By 1968 sales had risen to $180 million as Brown-Forman continued to expand under the direction of Street.

Although Street effectively diversified Brown-Forman, William F. Lucas replaced him as president in 1969. Lucas was also not part of the Brown family. He had joined Brown-Forman as an engineer in 1935 and advanced through the ranks. Lucas concentrated on marketing Brown-Forman's premium-priced products—President's Choice, Jack Daniel's, Old Forester, and Early Times. Lucas did not spend large sums advertising Brown-Forman's low profit brands, because he felt that, as higher quality whiskey could be made for pennies more per fifth, and could be sold at a much higher price, only the expensive brands merited increased advertising expenditures.

In 1969 Lucas purchased the Bols line of liqueurs and Korbel champagne and brandy. These purchases expanded Brown-Forman's premium product line. In the early 1970s, as the demand for wine soared, Lucas initiated the purchase of Bolla and Cella Italian wines. This purchase was followed by the company's development of another product called Gold Pennant Canadian Whiskey. This whiskey was marketed specifically to women. Each bottle sold was accompanied by a horoscope pamphlet with ''love potion'' recipes for each astrological sign.

Lucas then bought six year old barrel-stored whiskey from Publicker Industries Inc. In the 1960s Publicker had decided to make light whiskey but had later, when it was unsuccessful, reversed this decision. Lucas used Publicker's misfortune to Brown-Forman's advantage by purchasing their light whiskey, triple filtering it, and marketing the clear 80 proof product. Light whiskey is a clear beverage because it is aged in used barrels that have already given color to the whiskey previously stored in them. The clear whiskey is then distilled at a higher proof so it is lighter in taste. The term "light whiskey" actually refers to the type or body of the whiskey and not to its color.

In December of 1970 Schenley Industries, National Distillers and Chemical Corporation, and American Distilling Co. filed an injunction against Brown-Forman to bar introduction and further distribution of Brown-Forman's light whiskey called Frost 8/80. Under government restrictions light whiskey was not permitted to be marketed until July of 1972. Although Brown-Forman's light whiskey was distributed before it was allowed to be, Brown-Forman's competition dropped its suit because Frost 8/80 was already on the market. As a result, Brown-Forman was free to advertise its new product as a "dry, white whiskey" with which "the possibilities are endless." By advertising the whiskey as easily combining with any mixers, Brown-Forman tried to capture a share of the vodka and lighter Canadian whiskey market. The difficulty was that consumers did not buy Frost 8/80; they were used to drinking whiskey with color and, moreover, they could not associate Frost 8/80 with identically colored vodka: the flavors were different.

By 1973, $6 million had been invested in Frost 8/80 without a profitable return. Brown-Forman had extensively researched the popularity of a white whiskey and had received positive consumer response in various areas of the United States. However, consumers were confused by the company's advertising promotions and did not purchase the product. The extensive market research which Lucas had consulted before distributing Frost 8/80 had been incorrect.

Although light whiskey was not successful, Lucas still believed that American tastes were turning to lighter alcoholic drinks. For this reason, in 1971, Lucas contacted Lester Abdson and Oscar Getz who owned Barton Brands of Canada. Barton Brands bottled Canadian Mist, a blended whiskey. Brown-Forman could not purchase the entire company because of strict antitrust laws, so Lucas negotiated an agreement with Getz and Abdson to buy Canadian Mist and its distillery without buying the entire company. (This was the first time that a major brand of liquor was sold separately from the remainder of the company.) Lucas' determination to satisfy the American taste for lighter drinks was not diminished by the strict antitrust laws or the failure of Frost 8/80. By 1973 sales of such products had significantly increased.

Brown-Forman's success dwindled in the late 1970s as the bourbon market declined. Lucas moved aggressively to concentrate on faster growing segments of the alcoholic beverage market. In 1979 Brown-Forman spent $35 million in advertising its full line of alcoholic products. Lucas significantly increased Brown-Forman's wine and liqueur revenue to 22 percent of total sales. Most importantly, in 1979 Lucas purchased privately held Southern Comfort for $90 million. This purchase provided Brown-Forman with greater access to foreign markets since one-fifth of Southern Comfort sales were overseas.

The acquisitions of Southern Comfort and Jack Daniel's were similar because both companies were small and privately held. Also, each company had developed a distinctive character for their single product. Unlike Jack Daniel's, Southern Comfort is a liqueur and does not need to be aged. It can be produced and sold at a much faster rate. Before the Brown-Forman acquisi-

tion, Southern Comfort was already the number one selling liqueur. Brown-Forman simply enhanced its success. The company was equally successful with Jack Daniel's: from 1970 to 1979 Brown-Forman tripled Jack Daniel's sales to 1.7 million cases by creating the image of a quaint distillery nestled in a Tennessee hollow.

In 1979, W. L. Lyons Brown, Jr. was appointed president of Brown-Forman. He was the great grandson of George Garvin Brown who founded Brown-Forman in 1870. After two presidents who were not related to the Brown family, W. L. Lyons Brown, Jr. reestablished the tradition of a Brown at the head of the business. The restoration of the family was a good omen: Brown-Forman advanced to sixth in the alcohol industry and became the fastest growing full-line distiller.

Despite overall growth, the company experienced a setback with Southern Comfort in 1982; as competition increased, the share held by Southern Comfort in the market decreased. Brown-Forman responded to this weakening market share with another innovative idea, one and three-quarter liter plastic bottles to replace the one-half gallon glass bottles. After petitioning the Bureau of Alcohol, Tobacco, and Firearms, the company was granted permission to begin using the plastic bottle in 1983. However, later tests indicated that a loose molecule of plastic could contaminate the alcohol, and the container was soon prohibited.

In 1983, Brown-Forman acquired Lenox Inc., even though Lenox fervently fought against the acquisition. Lenox made crystal, china, giftware, and luggage, products that presented special problems for Brown-Forman. Drastically different methods of distribution were needed to market the Lenox products. Yet management at Brown-Forman understood the need for a transition. This was apparent in their name change from Brown-Forman Distillers Corp. to Brown-Forman Corporation in 1984.

Subsidiary shuffling continued in the late 1980s and early 1990s, as the company worked to solidify its position in giftware. Brown-Forman sold Lenox's ArtCarved jewelry division to SGI Acquisition Corporation for $120 million cash in 1989, and sold the related Lenox Awards division to Jostens in 1990. The Lenox subsidiary acquired the Kirk-Stieff Co., a manufacturer and marketer of silver tableware, and Wings Luggage, Inc., in 1990 and 1991, respectively. Brown-Forman purchased Denver's Athalon Products Ltd., a manufacturer of travel and leisure products, in 1989, and supplemented its Lenox operations with the $70 million acquisition of premium giftware maker Dansk International Designs Ltd.

Nevertheless, the company's realignment did not exclude the rearrangement of other alcoholic products; Brown-Forman bought California Cooler Inc. in 1985 for $63 million, and sold Cella Italian Wines to Cosorzio Interprovinciale Vini, an Italian firm, at the end of the decade.

Unfortunately, a recession in the late 1980s—in combination with price and tax hikes—brought a halt to a burgeoning trend toward premium liquors, as consumers traded down to cheaper brands. Unit sales in the liquor industry fell 5.6 percent in 1991, which was widely characterized as "one of the worst years since Prohibition.'' The decline continued in 1992, when total sales dropped about 3 percent.

Rising health care costs came under fire in the early 1990s, especially after the Clinton administration came into power. This apparently unrelated situation came to bear upon Brown-Forman when some legislators determined to "kill two birds" with liquor tax increases. They surmised that the levies would help pay for health care costs and help lower "unhealthy" alcohol consumption. In his 1992 message to shareholders, CEO Brown railed against such charges, calling them "a proven failure as a device to increase federal collections." He cited recent history, noting that the federal government's 8 percent 1991 levy actually effected a $90 million decline in collections from distilled spirits.

Brown-Forman launched several ready-to-serve cocktails as extensions of its primary brands in the early 1990s. Jack Daniel's Country Cocktails, which were introduced nationally in 1992, soon became one of America's top twenty spirit brands. Southern Comfort Cocktails and Pepe Lopez Margaritas were introduced soon afterward. It was hoped that these products would serve as an alternative to beer, rather than erode or cannibalize their parent brands. In August of 1992, Brown-Forman acquired Fetzer Vineyards, an important producer of premium California wines, for about $80 million.

W. L. Lyons Brown, Jr. retired as CEO in 1993 and younger brother Owsley Brown II assumed the position. The new leader helped boost his company's stock through a Dutch auction wherein the company repurchased over 4.5 million shares.

In spite of the nagging issues of taxation and lingering recession, Brown-Forman marked successive sales and profits increases in its 1990 through 1993 fiscal years, enabling the firm to continue its four decade record of regular dividend payments. There was no reason to believe that the company would not extend that series into the 21st century.

Principal Subsidiaries: Jack Daniel Distillery; Lem Motlow, Prop. Inc.; Clintock, Ltd. (Ireland); Brown-Forman Beverage Co.; Wings Luggage, Inc.; Jekel Vineyards; Fetzer Vineyards; Canadian Mist Distillers, Ltd. (Canada); Joseph Garneau Company S.A.; Mt. Eagle Corp.; Brown-Forman International F.S.C. Ltd.; Thoroughbred Plastics Corp.; Longnorth Ltd.; Lenox Inc.; Early Times Distillers Co.; L-H Ltd.

Further Reading:

Levin, Gary, ''New Coolers Pouring It On,'' *Advertising Age,* August 3, 1992, pp. 3, 26.

''Liquor Sales Go Dry: Recession, Taxes Blamed for 5.6% Decrease,'' *Advertising Age,* February 10, 1992, p. 44.

Pearce, John, editor, *Nothing Better in the Market: Brown-Forman's Century of Quality, 1870–1970,* Louisville: Newcomen Society, 1970.

Pitturro, Marlene C., ''Bottoms Up!,'' *World Trade,* December, 1991, pp. 60–64.

—updated by April Dougal Gasbarre

Broyhill Furniture Industries, Inc.

One Broyhill Park
Lenoir, North Carolina 28633
U.S.A.
(704) 758-3111
Fax: (704) 758-3666

Wholly Owned Subsidiary of Interco, Inc.
Incorporated: 1926 as the Lenoir Chair Company
Employees: 6,700
Sales: $540 million
SICs: 2511 Wood Household Furniture; 2512 Upholstered
   Household Furniture

Broyhill Furniture Industries, Inc. is a leading American manufacturer of medium-priced wood and upholstered household
furniture. The company got its start making chairs in North
Carolina in the 1920s, and grew steadily under the hand of its
founder, who had first entered the furniture business under the
eye of his older brother, and who involved many members of his
family in the business as it flourished. In 1980, the Broyhill
family sold the company to a conglomerate, which made it part
of a group of furniture makers but retained the Broyhill name
and identity.

Broyhill was founded in 1926 by James Edgar Broyhill, known
as Ed. Broyhill had worked in his older brother's furniture
business as a salesman, bookkeeper, and clerk since 1919, when
he was 27 years old. The company had started out producing
single pieces of furniture, but had moved into the marketing of
multi-piece coordinated bedroom suites in 1920. Three of these
pieces, a chair, rocking chair, and bench, were supplied by
another manufacturer. In 1926, this company was destroyed by
fire. Seeing an opportunity, Ed Broyhill took out a loan for
$5,000, using his house as collateral, and founded the Lenoir
Chair Company, named after the North Carolina town where it
was located.

Broyhill started his company by buying a number of chair
frames, which he planned to upholster in his basement. Soon a
blacksmith and buggy shop near the railroad tracks became
available, and Broyhill moved his operations to this location.
The chairs were finished in the buggy shop and upholstered in
the dirt-floored blacksmith shop. In the summertime, upholstering work was done in the shade of a sycamore tree out back.

After two months, Broyhill took over a small ironing board
factory across the street, and used the woodworking machinery
he found there to make his own chair frames instead of purchasing them. In June of 1927, the fledgling company expanded its
physical plant further when it built a two-story building on the
site of the old blacksmith shop, which contained space for
upholstering, packing, and shipping, as well as two small offices. Throughout this time, Ed Broyhill continued to work full-
time for his brother's company. By the end of its first full year in
business, the company had produced more then $150,000 worth
of furniture.

Ed Broyhill joined with his brother Tom, who owned the Lenoir
Furniture Corporation, to buy the Harper Furniture Company,
another local business that made colonial-style bedroom suites,
secretaries, and desks, in 1929. With a more diversified line of
products, the Broyhills hoped to gain access to a greater number
of sales outlets. Later in that year, however, they came to regret
their hasty expansion, as the stock market crash brought on the
Great Depression.

Hard times, not surprisingly, caused a constriction in furniture
sales. Despite the general economic difficulties, however, the
Lenoir Chair Company's sales increased every year throughout
the 1930s, pushed by the efforts of the company's sales force,
which numbered 16 men by the end of the decade. Ed Broyhill
continued to sell furniture both for his brother's company and
his own up through 1938.

In 1932, the Broyhill brothers embarked on another joint venture with two other investors, when they bought the bankrupt
Newton Furniture Company in a nearby town for $12,500. This
company had been manufacturing a low-priced line of bedroom
furniture, which Ed Broyhill was convinced would be marketable in the current economic conditions. In late 1934, he bought
out his other three partners, and in 1935 he reopened the plant,
renaming it Lenoir Chair Company No. 2. Within six months,
over 100 men were working in the factory, making a newly
designed line of low-priced goods, which, along with the other
"Lenoir lines," were shipped in carload lots to dealers.

In an effort to reduce duplication of activity, all office operations for the four Lenoir firms were consolidated under one roof
in 1935. In the following year, after a series of heart attacks,
Tom, the older Broyhill brother, removed himself from active
involvement in the business, turning over responsibility for
many of the day-to-day decisions to Ed. Despite its steady
expansion, the Lenoir Chair Company had been under funded at
its inception, and it remained cash-poor throughout most of its
first decade of operation, a condition that forced the company to
take long-term loans and thus pay excessive interest. In 1939,
however, the company was finally able to arrange a $100,000
bank loan that enabled it to consolidate its debts and begin
paying its suppliers with cash.

On a firmer financial footing and with the American economy
starting to expand under the wartime demands for goods, the
Lenoir furniture enterprises moved to take on two additional
plants in 1941. The McDowell Furniture Company owned a
factory that made a line of furniture that fit in between the low-
priced Newton line and the medium-priced Lenoir goods, and
the Conover Furniture Company manufactured knee-hole

desks, a new product for Lenoir. For $110,000, Broyhill was able to obtain both operations. The following year, the Wrenn Furniture Company was acquired at a bankruptcy auction, and its antiquated facilities were converted into storage space. Ed Broyhill's enterprise had grown to include six different plants operating under five different names when the sales efforts for these operations were consolidated into the Broyhill Furniture Factories to reduce confusion.

After the entry of the United States into World War II, Ed Broyhill was named to head the Furniture Industry Advisory Committee of the Office of Price Administration. In this capacity, he helped the federal government decide how to allot precious resources between the civilian and military worlds. On November 3, 1941, prices for all furniture were frozen by the federal government for the duration of the war.

In 1943, Broyhill was also elected head of the Southern Furniture Manufacturers Association. In this position, he worked to get price controls on furniture lifted after the end of the war, since uncontrolled materials costs had virtually eliminated the sale of unprofitable low-priced furniture items. By the end of 1945, a five percent rise in prices had been granted.

In the later years of the war and the early postwar years, strong demand for the limited supply of consumer goods allowed Broyhill to sell its furniture on allotment, meaning that all of the pieces it produced were taken immediately by buyers. By the spring of 1948, however, this unusual situation had come to an end, as production caught up with demand. For the next year, the company's fortunes suffered severely. By the spring of 1949, Broyhill was forced to cut back its plant operation to three days a week.

To combat the company's declining profits, the company began to develop new lines of furniture in updated styles under the direction of one of Ed Broyhill's sons, Paul. Rather than the very elaborate and ornate "borax" style popular in the 1930s and 1940s, Broyhill began to market a more sleek, simplified, and modern series of products. Broyhill also made the transition from a sales force that worked on commission to one that was paid a salary, thus increasing the loyalty of its salesmen to the company.

The company had regained sufficient strength by the mid 1950s to expand operations again. In 1954, Broyhill built a new plant from the ground up for the first time. On a 65-acre tract outside Lenoir, the company designed and built a facility for upholstering chairs previously completed at the Lenoir Chair Company. In the following year, Broyhill purchased a plant, which it subsequently re-built and improved. In addition to the construction of new plants, Broyhill modernized many of its old factories, wrapping its old wooden buildings with a new steel and concrete structure then dismantling the old walls. In many cases, this transformation was completed while the plant was in operation.

As the American population grew steadily more affluent throughout the 1950s, Broyhill recognized that tastes in furniture were shifting. In the past, buyers of moderately priced furniture had sought massiveness and elaborate embellishment, but the company's executives felt sophisticated styling and quality were becoming more important. In 1957, in an effort to

meet this demand, the company established the Broyhill Premier line. The old Lenoir Chair Company plant was given over to production of these pieces, and a separate, additional sales force of 30 men was established. In addition, Broyhill began to institute a quality control program, complete with a lab, to insure that its Premier products lived up to their name. In 1958, Broyhill began an expensive national advertising campaign to support the introduction of its Premier products.

Although the new line won consumer acceptance, it did not turn a profit until the 1960s. Broyhill added upholstered products to its Premier line, as the concept began to bring in revenues. Once the Premier line had been established, the company grouped its remaining products under the label "Lenoir House," which included a variety of medium-priced, moderate styles of bedroom and dining room furniture that made up the bulk of the company's sales.

Of Broyhill's expansion throughout the 1960s, the gem was a three-story office and showroom building, which filled an entire acre. Set in a fifty acre park, the building was decorated on all sides with aluminum columns and fountains, which were lit at night. By 1966, when this site became a landmark in Lenoir, Broyhill's sales had topped $75 million a year.

As Broyhill entered the 1970s, its expanded in new ways. In 1970, the company entered the field of plastic furniture, opening a facility to manufacture these products. In 1976, Broyhill purchased a plant that manufactured upholstered furniture in Arcadia, Louisiana. With this move, Broyhill extended its operations to an area outside its geographical hub in North Carolina for the first time. In 1978, Broyhill expanded its product offerings to include a line of furniture that customers assembled themselves, and also a line of wall units, in an Early American style. In addition, the company set out to increase sales by emphasizing furniture in contemporary styles. In its upholstered furniture lines, Broyhill set out to upgrade its fabric patterns. By the end of the 1970s, Broyhill sales had reached $265.2 million a year. The company ran 20 factories with more than 7,500 employees.

The company, which had previously made acquisitions, turned the tables when it announced that it would be purchased by another company. Broyhill's new owner was St. Louise-based Interco, Inc., a manufacturer of shoes and clothing which had recently purchased another furniture company, Ethan Allen, Inc. In August 1980, Interco purchased Broyhill for $151.5 million. The company planned to use Broyhill and Ethan Allen as the foundations of a furniture and home furnishings group.

Under its new owners, Broyhill moved to shore up its market share. As part of this strategy, the company reintroduced its "Premier" brand name for furniture, which it hoped would help it to capture more of the market for upscale furniture. By 1984, Broyhill had turned its attention to marketing in its quest for higher sales. The company made changes in the way its distributed its products, reviewing its operations territory by territory. In addition, Broyhill began to focus more closely on competition from products manufactured overseas.

In 1987, Broyhill announced that it would close a bedroom furniture operation it had acquired in Austin, Texas, and seek to sell the property. Three years later, the company moved out of the furniture field for the first time, developing a line of products called "Accents 'n Stuff," consisting of decorative home accessories.

Throughout the 1980s, Broyhill's corporate parent, Interco, had expanded rapidly, buying up a number of other companies, including another Broyhill competitor, Lane, in April 1987. By the end of the decade, however, the company's resources had become overextended. At the end of June 1989, it was forced to sell its Ethan Allen furniture subsidiary, and in January 1991, the company declared bankruptcy, filing for protection from its creditors under Chapter 11 of the Federal Bankruptcy Code. One month later, Broyhill announced that its own revenues had fallen to $785 million.

Broyhill continued its efforts to increase its market share, despite the bankruptcy proceedings. As a result of its study of the most effective and efficient ways to distribute and sell its furniture, Broyhill began to contract with dealers to open outlets dedicated entirely to Broyhill products in the early 1990s. The company chose the name Broyhill Showcase Galleries for these facilities. By September 1991, eight Showcase Galleries had been opened in seven states, and the facilities had earned a positive response. These stores continued to open in the following year.

In March 1992, Broyhill announced that it had reorganized its corporate leadership, naming longtime employees to key posts to insure stability despite Interco's difficulties. At the same time, the company rolled out a further extension of its product line, called Comfort Time. These products were designed to recline and extend, without looking like typical recliners. Six months later, the company extended its Showcase Galleries concept, introducing Custom Sofa Gallery stores that were slated to open across the nation.

As it moved into the mid 1990s, Broyhill could look back on a solid history of growth in the furniture industry. Firmly ensconced in the market for medium-priced furniture, and skilled in efficient and low-cost manufacturing techniques, the company appeared well-suited to maintain its position in the American home furniture market for years to come.

Further Reading:

"Beck Industries Sells Furniture Subsidiary in Reorganization Step," *Wall Street Journal,* July 23, 1970.
"Broyhill Getting Positive Response in New Showcase Gallery Venues," *HFD,* October 7, 1991, p. 40.
"Broyhill's Business Is on the Recline," *Business North Carolina,* May 1993, p. 68.
"Interco Agrees to Buy Broyhill Furniture," *Wall Street Journal,* August 12, 1980.
Kelt, Deborah, "Broyhill's New Direction," *HFD,* November 23, 1992, p. 34.
"Real-Time Inventory Tracking Cuts Back Orders by 90%," *Modern Materials Handling,* September 1993, p. 58.
Stevens, William, *Anvil of Adversity: Biography of a Furniture Pioneer,* Popular Library, 1968.

—Elizabeth Rourke

Buffets, Inc.

10260 Viking Drive
Suite 100
Eden Prairie, Minnesota 55344
U.S.A.
(612) 942-9760
Fax: (612) 944-7362

Public Company
Incorporated: 1983
Employees: 10,500
Sales: $247.5 million
Stock Exchanges: NASDAQ
SICs: 5812 Eating Places; 6794 Patent Owners & Lessors

Buffets, Inc. is one of the most successful businesses in the restaurant industry, operating 166 eating establishments that serve more than 8,000 customers weekly. Among the company's best known restaurants is the Old Country Buffets chain, which pioneered several important concepts in buffet dining.

Buffets was founded by Roe Hatlen in 1983. Hatlen, a veteran of the restaurant industry, had spent nine years with International King's Table, Inc., an Oregon-based chain whose revenues were boosted to an annual $40 million with Hatlen's help. In 1982, Hatlen moved to Minnesota, where he took an executive position at the publicly held Pizza Ventures chain of restaurants. After only eight months at Pizza Ventures, however, he was let go when the company was acquired and reorganized by Godfather's Pizza.

During this time, Hatlen contacted his friend and former colleague at King's Table, C. Dennis Scott, an experienced restaurant operator responsible for running 22 King's Table restaurants. Hatlen persuaded Scott to leave the financial security of King's Table to pursue a new restaurant venture.

Hatlen and Scott decided to open a buffet style operation, which they expected to prove economical both for themselves and their customers. Without wait staff and bartenders, the buffet would necessitate a lower payroll than more formal operations and might appeal to customers who preferred not to' pay gratuities.

The partners divided responsibilities along the lines of their expertise, with Hatlen handling financial matters and Scott

overseeing the details of restaurant management. Hatlen was able to purchase Pizza Ventures' discarded computer system for five cents on the dollar and tapped his network of acquaintances in the restaurant business for investment capital, amassing nearly about three-quarters of a million dollars by the time Buffets, Inc. was incorporated on October 13, 1983.

Scott planned the restaurant's menu, designing a series of menus that centered on typical American favorites, such as fried chicken, baked fish, and hamburgers. With particular attention to the value-conscious diner, he made sure that each meal included salad and dessert. Also featured were pasta dishes and other fare that could be prepared fresh in small batches throughout the day by cooks rather than by highly trained and expensive chefs.

With a staff of 29, The Old Country Buffet opened in March 1984 in a small strip mall on the outskirts of Minneapolis. There, customers encountered a plain but comfortable decor, a buffet station with lines at either end, affording the customer a view of all food items, and a generous and varied menu. Customers prepaid the fixed rate before lining up at the buffet.

The restaurant was an instant success. Hatlen's and Scott's initially cautious projections for sales of $1 million during its first year were doubled by the end of 1984. By October 1985, nine Old Country Buffet restaurants were in operation around Wisconsin, Illinois, and Minnesota, requiring a total of 687 employees and netting sales of $59.5 million. Moreover, several investors were encouraging Buffets, Inc. to go public, which it did that year with an initial offering of 525,000 shares.

The cash flow generated by the offering allowed the company to expand over the next few years. By 1987, the Old Country Buffet chain had grown to include 11 restaurants in Minnesota, seven in Wisconsin, four in Illinois, and the remainder in new territories, including Missouri, Nebraska, Pennsylvania, and Oklahoma.

Public recognition of Old Country Buffets steadily increased. Moreover, *Restaurants and Institutions,* a food industry trade magazine, praised the buffets as "shipshape" and "financially responsible." The reviewer also observed that buffets were beginning to offer strong competition to the country's cafeterias.

While buffets and cafeterias offered similar menus, the buffet featured a fixed rate policy, which proved less costly to the customer than the pay-per-item policy common in cafeterias. Moreover, buffets began to offer an alternative to the standard straight-line cafeteria layout. Old Country Buffet restaurants adopted a new layout that featured individual food islands throughout, a system that hastened the self-service process and thereby allowed each restaurant to accommodate more customers. The number of restaurants in the chain rose to 70 by the beginning of 1990.

Buffets also became known for providing employment opportunities in the early 1990s, when economic recession led to high unemployment rates on a national level. During this time, Buffets placed a series of newspaper advertisements targeting potential managers seeking long-term employment. Emphasizing the rapid growth and continued success of Buffets, the copy received widespread attention and garnered the company the *Personnel Journal*'s Vantage Award for 1989.

In an effort to maintain employees knowledgeable in food production and personnel management, and to help curb its high employee turnover rate, Buffets opened a training center for managers at their Eden Prairie headquarters in Minnesota. There, employees underwent five weeks of seminars and three weeks of hands-on training in the headquarters restaurant.

Though at least 75 percent of Buffets employees were on part-time schedules in the early 1990s, graduates of the eight-week program helped established a solid managerial framework in almost all Old Country Buffets. Each restaurant retained two managers: one associate manager and one general manager in charge of operations. To maximize the profitability of each unit, the company based 50 percent of the general manager's annual salary on the profitability of his or her establishment.

In addition to enhancing the company's workforce, founder Hatlen also focused on procuring new restaurant locations left by unsuccessful retailers, whose incomplete leases gave him considerable negotiating power with desperate landlords. These cheaper rents helped make 1990 the seventh record year for earnings; sales soared 26 percent to $145.2 million, up from 1989's total of $115.4 million.

By the mid-1990s, Buffets operated a total of 90 restaurants, including those under the direction of two new subsidiaries. Gateway Buffets, acquired in 1989, came with a purchase price of $1.9 million, which the company was able to pay in cash. Evergreen Buffets was purchased for $1.7 million from C. Dennis Scott, who had left the company a couple of years earlier.

Firmly established as a leader in the restaurant industry, the company earned its fifth accolade from *Forbes* magazine as one of the 200 best small companies in America in 1992. Buffets' gross sales for 1992 reached $247.5 million, a figure that was bolstered one year later when the company discontinued its policy of employees with free meals. Charging employees $2 per meal, Buffets' added $300,000 to the sales total. Reforms in the American health care system were expected to affect operations at Buffets in the 1990s. If required to provide part-time workers with coverage, the company could offset increased costs by merging and eliminating its thousands of part-time positions.

Principal Subsidiaries: Southland Buffets, Inc.; Evergreen Buffets, Inc.; Texas Buffets, Inc.

Further Reading:

"Buffets, Inc. Planning Its Biggest Expansion Ever During 1991," *Wall Street Journal,* November 16, 1990.
"Buffets Inc. Profits Jump Despite Slowed Economy," *Nation's Restaurant News,* September 9, 1991.
"Corporate Performance: Buffets," *Fortune,* February 12, 1990, p. 118.
Fiedler, Terry, "Really Cookin'," *Minnesota Business Journal,* March 1986, p. 20.
Meeks, Fleming, and R. Lee Sullivan, "If at First You Don't Succeed," *Forbes,* November 9, 1992, p. 172.
"Old Country Buffet Plans to Sell 525,000 Shares," *Nation's Restaurant News,* October 7, 1985.
"Recruitment: Ads with Flair," *Personnel Journal,* October 1989, p. 50.
Weleczi, Ruth, "Buffets, Inc.," *Minneapolis-St. Paul City Business,* June 24, 1991, p. 31.

—Gillian Wolf

Burlington Coat Factory Warehouse Corporation

1830 Route 130 North
Burlington, New Jersey 08016
U.S.A.
(609) 387-7800
Fax: (609) 387-7071

Public Company
Incorporated: 1972 as Burlington Coat Factory Warehouse
Employees: 12,800
Sales: $1.20 billion
Stock Exchanges: New York Chicago Philadelphia
SICs: 5611 Men's and Boy's Clothing Stores; 5621
   Women's Clothing Stores

Touting itself as the largest outerwear retailer in the United States, Burlington Coat Factory Warehouse Corporation entered the early 1990s as one of the most successful retailers in the country. Diversifying beyond its original mainstay line of winter coats, Burlington Coat recorded exponential growth during the late 1980s by offering a complete line of men's, women's, and children's apparel, as well as children's furniture and linens, all at discount prices. In 1994, the company operated 185 stores scattered throughout 39 states, generated over $1 billion in sales, and stood poised for further expansion.

Belying its enormous size, Burlington Coat was essentially a family owned and operated business in the mid-1990s, as it was more than twenty years earlier, when Monroe G. Milstein, the patriarch of the Milstein family, opened the first Burlington Coat store in 1972. Over the ensuing twenty years, the family's grip on the operation of Burlington Coat was maintained by successive generations of Milsteins, led by Monroe Milstein and his wife, Henrietta.

Monroe's father, Abe, first linked the Milstein name to retailing when he opened a wholesale outerwear business in 1924. Nearly fifty years later, his son was drawn to the same type of business, selling outerwear at discount prices, but in a much different era, an era that would witness the rise in popularity of a particular breed of retailers and launch the Milstein name toward prominence in the U.S. retailing industry. Monroe Milstein acquired the first Burlington Coat facility in 1972, a coat factory located in Burlington, New Jersey, with an attached

retail outlet. Initially, Burlington Coat specialized in selling winter overcoats, a product line whose sales were heavily dependent on the weather, peaking in the winter and dropping off during the summer months as temperatures rose. Though first year sales reached $1.5 million, Monroe Milstein was wary of the company's reliance on the vagaries of the thermometer, and quickly realized that substantial growth could not be predicted on unpredictable climatic variations.

Milstein diversified into other apparel niches, thus laying the foundation for Burlington Coat's further growth. In its first few years, the company had assumed characteristics that would dictate its future success. The company's first facilities, the coat factory and the adjoining retail outlet, were purchased as existing properties, not constructed specifically for Burlington Coat, a practice the company would employ throughout its history, leasing existing retail spaces, rather than constructing its own. This strategic flexibility enabled Burlington Coat to expand rapidly when economic conditions were favorable and quickly halt expansion when conditions soured, an enviable ability in a frequently capricious retail market. Another precedent set in the first few years was the decision to display the company's merchandise in sparsely decorated surroundings, giving Burlington Coat outlets a bare, "warehouse feel," while enabling prices to be discounted 30 to 40 percent. The diversification of the company's product line also would prove to be a linchpin to its future success, lessening Burlington Coat's dependence on a particular market niche within the retail clothing industry and expanding the company's inventory outside apparel into furniture and linens.

These hallmarks of Burlington Coat's existence—leased, sparsely decorated stores offering a wide assortment of merchandise—were established policies by 1975, a benchmark year for discount retailers. Prior to 1975, manufacturers were allowed to fix their prices in collusion with the more entrenched, conventional retailers, such as department stores, that sold their merchandise at standard prices. Essentially left on the sidelines, discounters frequently could not stock the same products as their higher-priced competitors, and the merchandise they were able to obtain from manufacturers could not be offered to the public at prices low enough to attract their business. Under such an arrangement, manufacturers and the higher-priced retailers prospered while discount retailers were forced to traffic in inferior quality products. When federal antitrust legislation in 1975 made the agreements between manufacturers and retailers illegal, the door was opened to discount retailers, spurring their ascent to the top of the retail industry. For Burlington Coat, federal intervention arrived just as the company was gaining momentum and provided the defining difference between the two eras in which the father Abe and the son Monroe had hoped to succeed in the retail industry. For the son, it appeared the opportunity for success was now more readily attainable.

Success came, but at a moderate pace, at least in comparison to the rate of growth the company would realize later. By 1983 annual sales had climbed to nearly $300 million, and the company was becoming a giant in the retail industry. It went public that year, with the Milstein family purchasing a majority of Burlington Coat's stock and the company's name changing from Burlington Coat Factory Warehouse to Burlington Coat Factory Warehouse Corporation.

Two Supreme Court rulings in the early 1980s took much of the strength away from the 1975 decision that had essentially put an end to price fixing between manufacturers and traditional retailers. The new decision put the onus of proving vertical price fixing on the accuser, which invariably was the discounter. This greatly diminished the ability of discount retailers to mount a serious threat against the more established partnership between manufacturers and department stores; once a manufacturer terminated a contract with a discounter, the discounter was left with little recourse except to engage in lengthy and costly litigation. Perhaps more disturbing to discount retailers, such as Burlington Coat, was a shift in fashion trends toward high-priced merchandise, a potentially deleterious development that stifled growth throughout much of the decade. During the early 1980s, when consumers developed an affinity for high-priced, designer labels, Burlington Coat recorded modest sales growth, as the once bright prospects for discount retailers noticeably dimmed.

While sales growth was slow, it was better than average during these lean years for discounters nationwide. Sales barely eclipsed $300 million in 1984, then inched upward, climbing to $480 million by 1987. This lull in business, however, was only temporary, for in the next five years Burlington Coat's sales volume would more than double, as the company evolved into a retail empire. Several of the reasons for this exponential growth were attributable to strategic decisions made by Burlington Coat's management, but others were attributable to changing conditions within the retail industry that brought Burlington Coat and other discount retailers to the fore.

Efforts toward diversification were intensified, as the number of linen stores within Burlington Coat stores rapidly increased, growing from 55 in 1989 to over 140 by 1991. Men's apparel, particularly men's suits, became an important contributor to company sales, and stores began to offer merchandise entirely beyond the scope of many apparel retailers, including such items as children's furniture. Perhaps the most important contributor to Burlington Coat's dramatic growth was a recession in the late 1980s and early 1990s that arrested consumer demand for expensive, designer apparel. As the economy suffered and many consumers were left with significantly less discretionary income, discount retailers flourished. Burlington Coat, still continuing to lease its retail space, moved quickly to take advantage of the situation, quickly increasing the number of its stores.

As Burlington Coat's sales figures spiraled upwards, the company made two key moves to increase the efficiency of its operation. Burlington Coat improved inventory controls and took advantage of economies of scale by constructing a 438,000 square foot national distribution center in 1990. Located a mile and a half from the company's original coat factory and store in Burlington, the distribution center was supported by a new computer system Burlington Coat had instituted in 1988 in anticipation of the new distribution center. The computer system enabled Burlington Coat to process as many as 125,000 pieces of merchandise each day at its distribution center and helped position the company to continue to grow during a period that saw many other businesses fail.

Annual sales flirted with the $1 billion mark in 1992, then reached $1.2 billion the following year. There were 185 Burlington Coat stores in 1993, ranging in size from 16,000 square feet to 133,000 square feet, and plans were in place to continue expanding throughout the mid-1990s. Typical Burlington Coat stores offered 10,000 to 20,000 garments from as many as 300 different manufacturers at a 35 percent to 40 percent discount. In 1993, Burlington Coat signed an agreement with Mexican retailer Plaza Coloso S.A. de C.V., an operator of supermarkets and department stores, to open a Burlington Coat store in Juarez, Mexico, the company's first store outside the United States. The following year, after purchasing a ten-store discount chain called Mid-Island, Burlington opened an experimental freestanding men's store that offered men's outerwear, sportswear, and tailored clothing, a service not offered by many discount retailers.

As the company entered the mid-1990s expecting to open 25 to 30 stores between 1994 and 1996, an emphasis was placed on its men's apparel segment, particularly men's suits. Men's apparel increased its importance to the company during the early 1990s, largely because fewer and fewer retailers were offering men's formal attire. By the mid-1990s, men's apparel accounted for 35 percent of Burlington Coat's total sales, a substantial portion that nearly matched the sales garnered from outerwear. With this emphasis on men's apparel and another segment, children's furniture, which, it was hoped, would cultivate Burlington Coat customers at a younger age, the company entered the mid-1990s remarkably well-positioned for further growth.

Principal Subsidiaries: Burlington Coat Factory Warehouse of Reading, Inc.; Burlington Coat Factory Warehouse, Inc.; Monroe G. Milstein, Inc.; LC Acquisition Corp.; C.L.B., Inc.; C.F.I.C. Corp.; C.F.B., Inc.; Burlington Coat Factory International, Inc.

Further Reading:

Arlen, Jeffrey, "Burlington Coat Factory: Original Off-Pricer," *Discount Store News*, March 16, 1992, p. A10.
"Burlington Coat in Pact to Open Store in Mexico," *Women's Wear Daily*, October 11, 1993, p. 2.
Butler, Stacey, "Retail Industry Divided Over Bill to Protect Discounters," *Baltimore Business Journal*, May 27, 1991, p. 6.
"Coat Factory Takes Honors," *Chain Store Age Executive*, February 1994, p. 44.
Palmer, Jay, "Pipe-Rack Recovery," *Barron's*, March 23, 1992, p. 20.
Peres, Daniel, "Burlington Coat to Open Experimental Men's Store," *Daily News-Record*, March 3, 1994, p. 2.
Salfino, Catherine, "Burlington Coat Pins Star on Men's Suit Business," *Daily News-Record*, March 26, 1993, p. 8.

—Jeffrey L. Covell

Burlington Resources Inc.

5051 Westheimer
Houston, Texas 77056-5384
U.S.A.
(713) 831-1600
Fax: (713) 624-9645

Public Company
Incorporated: 1988 as Burlington Resources Inc.
Employees: 1,729
Sales: $1.25 billion
Stock Exchanges: New York
SICs: 1311 Crude Petroleum and Natural Gas; 1321 Natural
Gas Liquids; 4922 Natural Gas Transmission; 4610
Pipelines, Except Natural Gas; 6719 Holding Companies,
Nec

Burlington Resources Inc., the nation's largest independent natural gas exploration and production company, functioned in the mid-1990s as a holding company for its main operating subsidiary, Meridian Oil Inc. Originally created as a holding company for all of Burlington Northern's non-railroad assets, Burlington Resources quickly emerged as a powerful, domestically oriented energy company. After divesting properties deemed incongruous with its core operations, Burlington Resources entered the mid-1990s as a growing energy concern sharply focused on the exploration, production, and marketing of oil and natural gas. From its principal oil and natural gas properties located in the San Juan Basin in northwest New Mexico, the Willston Basin in North Dakota, the Permian Basin in Texas and New Mexico, and on the Gulf Coast of Texas and Louisiana, Burlington Resources stood poised to garner a substantial share of the country's future oil and natural gas market.

After nearly 130 years of existence, Burlington Northern, one of the pioneer railroad companies in the United States, had become many other things besides a railroad company. In 1849, the company's predecessors began laying a vast network of railroad track beginning in the midwestern United States and extending westward, acquiring along the way, both through its geographic growth and through its maturation as a corporate entity, many properties unrelated to the railroad business. The largest of these assets included the largest private coal reserves in the nation, one of the largest oil and natural gas reserves, 1.5 million acres of forestlands, and a number of real estate proper-

ties. These resources combined with its railroad operations made Burlington Northern a multi-billion dollar corporation by the latter half of the twentieth century.

By the 1980s, the management of this diversified giant, led by chairman Richard M. Bressler, decided to focus Burlington Northern's business on railroads, turning back the clock to more than a century earlier, when operating a railroad was Burlington Northern's sole function. This shift was prompted by looming railroad labor problems in the early 1980s, primarily the possibility of an extended strike by Burlington Northern's railroad workers that Bressler perceived would drain the company's profits. He decided to divide the company in two, reasoning that if indeed the imminent strike would adversely affect Burlington Northern's financial condition, it would only afflict the railroad-related assets of the company.

In 1988, a separate, publicly held corporate body was created to function as a holding company for the non-railroad assets of Burlington Northern. The aptly named Burlington Resources Inc. was thus born as a $1.75 billion resource and energy company. Burlington Northern sold a 13 percent stake in Burlington Resources in an initial public offering in July 1988, then distributed the remaining 87 percent to Burlington Northern stockholders five months later, on the last day of 1988. Initially, Bressler served as both Burlington Northern's and Burlington Resources' chairman, until he devolved his responsibilities at Burlington Resources to Thomas O'Leary, in 1989.

O'Leary had joined Burlington Northern in 1982, and was charged with building up the non-railroad business of the company. During his tenure, O'Leary added the El Paso Natural Gas Co., a pipeline concern that supplied 60 percent of the California market for natural gas, Southland Royalty Co., an oil and gas company, and several other interests to Burlington Northern's roster. By 1987, the company had amassed sufficient additional assets to mitigate the potential hazards of a labor strike, but in that year the U.S. Supreme Court upheld secondary boycotts by rail unions, which essentially enabled railroad labor to stage a nationwide strike and confer its settlement to U.S. Congress. Bressler's decision to divide the company was meant to protect the assets O'Leary had helped to acquire, and O'Leary was the ideal choice to head the new company.

One year after the company's creation, O'Leary stood at the helm and found himself in the midst of a hostile takeover, though he was now on the receiving end of an unsolicited purchase. Pennzoil Co., recently awarded $3 billion in a legal settlement with Texaco Inc., purchased eight percent of Burlington Resources' stock in February 1989, roughly one month after Burlington Resources became a separate company. O'Leary recognized the signs of a hostile takeover and adopted a corporate stock plan to prevent such an acquisition from taking place—commonly known as a "poison pill" stock plan—and filed a suit against Pennzoil declaring it had misrepresented its "true purposes." Meanwhile, Pennzoil maintained that its purchase of Burlington Resources' stock simply represented an investment in the company and did not reflect an attempt to gain control. In the end, either dissuaded by Burlington Resources outcry, or genuinely intending to merely invest in the company, Pennzoil sold its stake in Burlington Resources and realized a 20 percent net gain on its highly contested investment.

Against this backdrop, Burlington Resources had been trying to form its own identity, rather than just existing as an amalgamation of what Burlington Northern no longer wanted. Toward this end, Burlington Resources did essentially what Burlington Northern had done, selling or spinning-off unwanted assets and pursuing what it perceived as its core business. For Burlington Northern this meant focusing solely on the railroad business; for Burlington Resources the shaping of its new corporate identity meant focusing on gas and oil exploration, development, and production.

By 1990 Burlington Resources had collected more than $1 billion from the sale of assets deemed tangential or completely unrelated to its core business. Leading the departures were the Glacier Park Co., Burlington Resources' real estate subsidiary, which was sold for approximately $450 million, timber properties worth over half a billion dollars, and several subsidiary companies involved in mineral excavation. The proceeds from these sales were then funnelled into Meridian Oil Inc., Burlington Resources' primary operating subsidiary, for which Burlington Resources served as a holding company. In 1989, Burlington Resources spent $442 million on oil and gas capital expenditures; the following year, it spent $399 million to acquire all the producing properties of Unicon Producing Co., which amounted to more than 500 billion cubic feet of natural gas.

Although the company had substantial oil and natural gas assets, Burlington Resources had grown larger as a result of its aggressive pursuit of additional oil and gas properties. By the early 1990s, the company represented a powerful force in the energy market, ranking just behind the six major oil companies. For over a decade, the prospects for the natural gas market had been disheartening, as oversupply had lowered prices and forced many natural gas companies to abandon the business. Nevertheless, during this period Burlington Northern increased its presence in the natural gas market, acquiring properties while other companies sold properties. When Burlington Northern's stake in the natural gas market was later transformed into Burlington Resources, the company that emerged had a considerable lead over its competition.

As Burlington Resources became more entrenched in the oil and gas field, prognostications for the natural gas market improved significantly, at last justifying the company's investments during the 1980s. Industry pundits, looking forward from the early 1990s to the turn of the century, had several reasons to be optimistic, not the least of which was the expected greater demand for natural gas as an alternative fuel for the 1990s. As dictated by federal legislation, 70 percent of new vehicles purchased by large fleet owners were to be powered by alternative fuels by the year 2000. The number of natural-gas-powered automobiles was expected to increase from 30,000 in the early 1990s to 3.8 million by the end of the decade, and by the mid-1990s the amount of natural gas consumed by new gas-powered electric power plants was expected to double.

In the face of these encouraging figures, Burlington Resources stood in an enviable position, strengthened by its oil and gas

acquisitions during the late 1980s and early 1990s. By 1992, it was a $1.14 billion company, principally due to its Meridian Oil subsidiary, and represented the nation's largest independent natural gas exploration and production company. Divestiture of non-core assets continued as Burlington Resources spun-off or sold 1.5 million acres of timber land, nearly one million acres of real estate, a 22,000-mile network of gas pipelines, and an assortment of mining operations. In 1992, Hurricane Andrew caused the permanent loss of 600 million cubic feet of daily gas production from the Gulf of Mexico, but Burlington Resources was not the only natural gas concern adversely affected by the storm. Other natural gas production facilities were destroyed, which tightened supply and, in turn, engendered natural gas price increases, a boon for Burlington Resources despite its production loss.

In its fifth year of business, Burlington Resources recorded $1.25 billion in annual sales. Although sales were less than the $1.87 billion the company had generated three years earlier in 1990, the company's operating income had increased an average of 16 percent annually, overshadowing its decline in gross sales. Partly attributable to this increase was the technological superiority established by the company in the sophisticated yet cost-saving methods it used to locate and produce natural gas. Burlington Resources' cost were considered to be roughly half the industry average.

Burlington Resources' low operating cost earned it the reputation as the ''Wal-Mart'' of the natural gas industry by some observers, but the company's talent for finding and producing gas at substantially lower costs was not predicated on economies of scale as much as on its utilization of innovative, technologically advanced excavation methods. By adopting new horizontal drilling techniques and using advanced reservoir simulation technology, Burlington Resources was able to recover gas from fields abandoned in the 1950s and 1960s, giving the company an advantage its competitors did not enjoy.

Bolstered by its ability to locate and produce natural gas more efficiently than rival companies, and encouraged by its firm grip on domestic reserves, Burlington Resources entered the mid-1990s looking to expand further. In 1994, the company purchased an 87 percent interest in Diamond Shamrock Offshores Partners L.P., an offshore oil operation in the Gulf of Mexico, for $287 million from Maxus Energy Corp. With plans to acquire the remaining 13 percent of Diamond Shamrock, Burlington Resources, a comparatively recent entrant into the oil and natural gas market, was positioned as one of the industry's leaders and stood poised for further growth.

Principal Subsidiaries: Meridian Minerals Co.; Meridian Oil Holding Inc.; Meridian Oil Hydrocarbon Inc.; Meridian Oil Inc.; Meridian Oil Production Inc.; Meridian Oil Trading Inc.; PCTC Inc.; Southland Royalty Co.

Further Reading:

''BRI Fights Takeover Bid,'' *Seattle Daily Journal of Commerce,* February 24, 1989, p. 1.
''Burlington Resources Strikes Gold,'' *Seattle Daily Journal of Commerce,* November 29, 1988, p. 1.
''A Burlington Resources Takeover,'' *Seattle Post-Intelligencer,* February 7, 1980, p. B6.

Denne, Lorianne, "Burlington Resources Bets Heavily on Oil and Gas," *Puget Sound Business Journal,* July 2, 1990, p. 11.

Grunbaum, Rami, "Gas Ignites Burlington Resources' Growth," *Puget Sound Business Journal,* July 17, 1992, p. 1.

Impoco, Jim, "Feeling the Future," *U.S. News & World Report,* May 17, 1993, p. 54.

Lazo, Shirley A., "Speaking of Dividends," *Barron's,* January 18, 1993, p. 57.

Mack, Toni, "Blood from Turnips," *Forbes,* May 27, 1991, p. 338.

Norman, James R., "Divide and Prosper," *Forbes,* March 30, 1992, p. 45.

Solomon, Cales, "Tables Are Turned for Thomas O'Leary," *Wall Street Journal,* March 21, 1987, p. B12.

—Jeffrey L. Covell

Cabletron Systems, Inc.

35 Industrial Way
Rochester, New Hampshire 03867
U.S.A.
(603) 332-9400
Fax: (603) 332-7386

Public Company
Incorporated: 1988
Sales: $418.2 million
Employees: 3,065
Stock Exchanges: New York
SICs: 7372 Prepackaged Software; 3661 Telephone and
Telegraph Apparatus

Cabletron Systems, Inc. is one of the leading manufacturers of cables and other equipment for the Local Area Networking (LAN) industry, which enables all the computers in an office to exchange and share phone lines, power, and data. With a rapidly growing customer base of over 45,000 and 1993 record sales revenues of over $418 million, Cabletron has developed from a small two-man firm that initially manufactured Ethernet cable assemblies to a leader in the field of network management and connective solutions.

The Cabletron story starts in March of 1983 with then 25-year-old Robert Levine. For four years Levine had worked as an independent sales representative for such firms as Hercules Corporation and Insilco Corporation, selling cable, power supplies, and electronic equipment to various companies throughout the northeastern United States and Canada. One day he was called on by a customer who needed 1000 feet of highly specialized cable for one of his computer networks. Unfortunately, Levine's supplier refused to sell him cable in amounts less than 10,000 feet. When Levine told this to his friend, 28-year-old Craig Benson, there was little doubt in Benson's mind as to the next step. Benson had been a materials management specialist for three years at Interlan, an early manufacturer of local area network equipment, and a financial inventory analyst at Teradyne, Inc. before that. It took some time, but he finally persuaded Levine that it would not be much of a problem selling the other 9,000 feet of cable and doubling their money in the bargain.

The two friends purchased the 10,000 feet of cable for $30,000 on credit, and shipped it to Levine's garage in Ashland, Massa-

chusetts. During lunch breaks and evenings, Levine and Benson spliced a 1,000 foot section to meet their first order, and then sold the remaining 9,000 feet of cable to new customers. Not long afterward, Levine was selling wire and cable for his own company on a full-time basis, and Benson was taking care of the firm's finances during evenings and weekends. Levine's business was the only company supplying cable in less than 10,000 feet increments. To speed order processing, Levine hired ten part-time employees to splice and package cables. With the new employees, Levine and Benson could emphasize customer service, reducing the delivery time from 90 days to within 48 hours. By the end of one year's business, revenues amounted to nearly $120,000.

Disappointed over the amount of first year revenues, Levine and Benson were determined to make the company a much bigger success. In 1985, Cabletron was moved from Levine's garage to New Hampshire in order to take advantage of a lower tax rate and less expensive labor force. Another benefit included renting manufacturing space at half the amount for the same square footage near Boston. A stroke of good fortune also helped: lower housing mortgages attracted well-trained, highly creative software and hardware engineers from the failing computer businesses situated along Route 128.

After Cabletron's relocation, the two entrepreneurs quickly began to install networks in addition to selling cable and wire. Within a short time, they hired engineers to design and manufacture equipment for the networks. The most important and lucrative parts of the equipment were those that connected personal computers to telephones and to the computer network that manages the flow of data within a company's office. One of these connective parts was a small box which contained a circuit board that controlled all the information entering and leaving each of the personal computers within the network. To supply a network of 80 computers, a Cabletron contract might call for 80 of these small boxes, priced at $250 each. When Cabletron's engineers developed a box that not only controlled information input and output but allowed computer analysts to diagnose problems with connections into the network, both the product and the company were poised for success.

Levine and Benson decided to sell its box at nearly 15 percent below the market price. On the basis of this new product alone, Cabletron's sales skyrocketed from $4 million in 1986 to $25 million two years later. In 1988, Cabletron introduced another innovative piece of equipment named a "smart hub," a highly sophisticated and extremely reliable management system for networks. One of Cabletron's "smart hubs" might ordinarily monitor 90 personal computers on a network and, instead of searching from computer to computer to locate problems, it allows a technician to identify and locate faulty wires and computers immediately. With an initial sales price of $37,000 for the hub and an annual service fee of $4,400, Cabletron's revenues once again soared. Before long, smart hubs accounted for over half of the company's revenues.

Cabletron concentrated on developing more technological innovations for the networking industry to further the company's success. Company engineers introduced the Multi-Media Access Center (MMAC), the industry's first modular, intelligent wiring hub device for the central location of transmission media and data in 1988. The first entirely modular approach to comprehensive network integration, it soon became one of Cabletron's cornerstone network management technologies. Already having introduced LANVIEW in 1986, a diagnostic indicator for network systems, by 1988 it was redesigned and reintroduced as LANVIEW/Windows, the first Ethernet network management and control software package with diagnostic capabilities.

Cabletron decided to enter the PC card market in 1989, and although it entered the marketplace disadvantaged by its small product line, the company soon emerged as the fastest growing manufacturer of PC cards. Cabletron's plug-in network adapter cards for different kinds of computers allowed users to connect into Ethernet networks and thereby communicate and share information and data with other users on the network. In addition, Cabletron provided the LAN industry with a comprehensive approach to network management control with its SPECTRUM product, the first protocol independent multi-vendor network management system based on concepts derived from artificial intelligence.

Having focused almost exclusively on the Ethernet standard (which comprises 65 percent of the networking market) for the LAN industry, in 1990 Cabletron broadened its market by introducing its first products for IBM's "Token Ring" standard (which comprises the remaining 35 percent of the market). A "Token Ring" is a type of network where computer workstations are provided access to the network by means of a token that passes from station to station in a ring. Cabletron immediately began to make inroads on the $800 million "Token Ring" standard market that had been dominated by IBM.

With the success of its product line, Cabletron's revenues continued to grow rapidly. By 1989, sales had jumped to $55 million, and by 1990 sales had passed the $100 million mark. As sales increased dramatically, profit margins also soared from $189,000 in 1986 to almost $12 million by 1989. In light of these figures and the promising future for Cabletron that they indicated, Levine and Benson decided to take the company public. An initial public offering of $84 million was made in May of 1989. By 1990, the company's stock price had shot up from $16 to $23, giving it a market value of approximately $600 million. Not surprisingly, Levine and Benson profited handsomely; with a 36 percent ownership of Cabletron's stock, Levine's worth was estimated at $220 million while Benson, with a 29 percent interest, was estimated to have a stake worth over $170 million.

Throughout its short existence, Cabletron lagged behind its arch-rival SynOptics, a Mountain Valley, California, firm which was the leader in certain segments of the LAN equipment market. Initially, Cabletron trailed SynOptics because of its slowness in developing a smart hub. Yet Cabletron's continuing improvement and development of networking management software allowed it to finally surpass its competitor. By the end of 1991, Cabletron became the leader in the worldwide intelligent hub market, capturing a market share of nearly 17 percent, while SynOptics' market share fell to 15.9 percent. In the same year, Cabletron also became the world's leader in international

Ethernet hub shipments, with a 24.9 percent share of the market as opposed to a 23.3 percent share for SynOptic shipments.

Even though Cabletron's products outsold SynOptic's, many industry analysts speculated that Cabletron's success in surpassing SynOptics was not due merely to its product line, but also to its highly aggressive sales methods and its emphasis on technical support. Levine and Benson's unorthodox management style gives employees impetus to work hard. Levine and Benson describe themselves as corporate misfits, and encourage their employees to engage in rough games of market competition. Cabletron has no vice-presidents and almost no middle management; Levine and Benson discourage lengthy conference meetings by furnishing meeting rooms without chairs. The two men encourage an all-out, no-holds-barred aggressive sales technique to please the customer, a technique that proved so successful that by 1990 Cabletron had increased its work force by 90 percent, totaling approximately 2,300 employees, to keep up with company growth.

Cabletron expanded its services worldwide through a well-conceived strategy. During the 1990s, it opened offices in Canada, Mexico, Venezuela, Brazil, England, Ireland, Germany, France, Spain, Sweden, The Netherlands, Australia, Japan, and Singapore in order to capture high-profile multinational customers. Soon there were 25 sales and support offices located in Europe, South America, and the Pacific Rim. With the company's European headquarters located in Birkshire, England, and a 50,000 square foot facility in Limerick, Ireland, serving as the manufacturing and distribution base for all products sold on the continent, Cabletron's overseas revenues increased significantly. By 1993, over 60 percent of its revenues were generated from multinational corporations such as Philip-Morris, Motorola, Bank of America, and Mexico's largest bank, Bancomer, S.A.

In one decade, Cabletron has distinguished itself as one of the fastest growing companies in the world. In 1993, the company employed over 3,065 people worldwide, with 52 international direct sales/support offices. Marketing its products and services to end users and Original Equipment Manufacturers (OEMs), Cabletron lists 84 of the *Fortune* 100 as customers. Besides the *Fortune* 100 companies, Cabletron also provides products and services to a wide variety of financial institutions, federal and state agencies, industrial and manufacturing firms, and academic institutions.

Cabletron's international sales for the second quarter of 1994 amounted to $141.9 million, an increase of nearly 50 percent when compared to the second quarter of 1993. With an eight to one service to sales ratio, almost 70 percent of its revenue coming from existing customers, and the continued guidance of Levine and Benson, the company can look to the future with a good deal of confidence.

Further Reading:

Alpert, Mark, "A George Bush Kind of Company," *Fortune,* January 27, 1992, pp. 13–14.
Ignatius, Chithelen, "Work in Progress," *Forbes,* May 27, 1991, pp. 226–27.

—Thomas Derdak

Canal Plus

85–89, quai André Citroën
75015 Paris
France
(33) 1 44 25 10 00
Fax: (33) 1 44 25 18 23

Public Company
Incorporated: 1984
Employees: 1,697
Sales: $1.5 billion
Stock Exchanges: Paris
SICs: 4841 Cable & Other Pay Televisin Services; 7812
   Motion Picture & Video Tape Production

Canal Plus is among the most profitable and fastest-growing pay television channels in the world. With four million subscribers in France alone, and growing subscription rates in the rest of Europe and in Africa, Canal Plus has achieved success through state guidance, private capital, and innovative programming. Aggressive investments in Hollywood and the creation of its own production companies have also made Canal Plus an important player in both the American and European film industries, allowing the company to profit from its powerful involvement on both continents.

Canal Plus was the creation of André Rousselet, president of the French media and advertising giant Havas. While some observers were surprised that the top publicity group in France would become involved in a medium that needed no outside publicity, Havas hoped that the innovative move would open up a potentially profitable market. Rousselet decided to launch a subscription television channel in November 1984 to offer the French public an alternative to the comedies and variety shows typically featured on the three government-owned channels then in existence. Contending that no one would pay for television programming, critics dubbed the company "Canal Minus."

In fact, subscriptions were extremely low at the onset, and the company announced first year losses of FFr 330 million. Moreover, some politicians, including Laurent Fabius, France's prime minister, were not in favor of commercial television and petitioned for a retraction of Canal Plus' broadcasting license. Rousselet, however, was a personal friend, golf partner, and former chief of staff of President François Mitterand, and he

was able to acquire a government concession that gave Canal Plus an all but official monopoly on subscription television. In addition, Rousselet and Pierre Lescure, the company's director-general, put forth an aggressive spring schedule of blockbuster films, depleting all its programming for the next season, in an effort to attract viewers. Suddenly, subscriptions picked up. This initial success convinced Canal Plus that giving viewers what they were not able to get on government television—American hit comedies and French drama—was central to its future success.

In addition to Rousselet's effective political networking and the channel's innovative programming, Canal Plus benefited from lack of competition, high taxes on home video recorders, and a sluggish video market. The use of an existing broadcast channel and decoders allowed the station to avoid paying cable companies to broadcast shows and gave the station almost immediate national coverage. These advantages proved to be worth the expense the company incurred to improve early decoders, which were known for having technical problems.

Moreover, Canal Plus was exempt from regulations that required free channels to air films only three nights of the week and to wait three years to show a movie after its box-office release. Thus, Canal Plus was able to broadcast feature films only a year after their cinema releases. The channel also managed to use some restrictions to its own advantage. For example, the Socialist government's regulations required Canal Plus to broadcast a few hours a day with an unscrambled signal so that all television viewers could gain from the new service, and these unscrambled broadcasts were turned into ideal free promotion for the channel's regular programming. Two of every three subscribers first watched the channel during these free hours, according to Pierre Lescure. The government also required the channel to devote no more than 45 percent of its air time to films. This restriction encouraged Canal Plus to develop other interesting programming; as a result, sports programs became one of the channels specialties, gaining exclusive rights to national soccer matches and top-quality coverage of boxing and American football. When the government succumbed to pressure from the film industry to ban the company's movie broadcasting during peak cinema-going hours, the station expanded its programming beyond films to interview shows, documentaries, and soft pornography.

In 1985, Mitterand announced the opening of private commercial television stations. While these new stations offered serious competition to Canal Plus, the company managed to break even the following year. Growth since then remained around 25 percent annually, as each new subscriber added about FFr 2,000 in annual turnover, but required far less additional cost. Aggressive advertising and competent management of the viewer base kept subscriptions high. A policy of debiting fees from subscribers' bank accounts contributed to the extremely high viewer subscription renewal rate of around 95 percent. Canal Plus' financial stability was thus greatly increased, as subscriber fees accounted for almost 90 percent of all turnover. By the time the company's stock went on the market in 1987, and soared from FFr 275 to FFr 575 in just one year, the station was thriving, with profits at $100 million in 1988. The channel had penetrated 15 percent of the 18 million French households. By 1989, Canal Plus had almost three million subscribers, representing a comparable penetration rate in France as Home Box Office Inc. (HBO) had accomplished in the United States, without HBO's 12-year head start.

With a secure base in France, Canal Plus was looking to expand internationally. Its attempts to link up with Lausanne-based Telecine Romandie were thwarted by the Swiss government in 1988. However, the next year, Canal Plus launched a channel in Belgium, of which it controlled 33 percent, and entered into a consortium with Prisa, a media group, which gained a license to begin a private television station in Spain. In partnership with Bertelsmann and the Kirch Group, Canal Plus launched Germany's first national pay TV service, the Premiere channel.

While Canal Plus faced increased competition and had fewer political connections abroad, its local partners helped tailor its programming of films and sports to match local tastes. In France, as well, Canal Plus created new theme channels featuring specialized programming, including children's shows and old movies. While these new foreign and domestic channels initially lost money, they proved sound investments by edging out local competitors. By the time Canal Plus had expanded to Africa in 1990 with Canal Horizons, the channel had become the most successful subscription channel in Europe and was second only to HBO worldwide.

In the mid-1980s, Canal Plus began trying to acquire television rights to popular American television shows. Initially dismissed as a newcomer, the French channel soon won over Hollywood with its success and its international expansion, but remained very dependent on American film studios for the blockbusters which were essential to its programming. By 1991, Canal Plus was paying $100 million a year to acquire American movie rights. Unwilling to continue paying Hollywood's high prices, Canal Plus moved directly into film production, acquiring a five percent stake in Carolco Pictures, an independent U.S. studio, for $30 million in 1991. That year, the company also launched Studio Canal Plus, its own Hollywood production company, which had a working capital of $200 million and which later joined with Universal Pictures to co-produce films. Canal Plus also entered into a deal with Warner Brothers and the German media outfit Scriha & Deyhle to help finance Arnon Milchan's independent production company, Regency International. Through these various investments, Canal Plus contributed to the production of such movies as *Terminator 2, JFK,* and *Basic Instinct.*

The company's attempts to secure its position in the cinema industry did not all go smoothly, however, as it had to write off the $20 million it had invested in Carolco to help it out of bankruptcy. This loss lowered stock prices, and was not received well by investors. Canal Plus was also gradually withdrawing its equity partnership with Milchan, producer of the hit film *Pretty Woman.* Nevertheless, Canal Plus continued its investment in Carolco and did not stop buying the European rights to most Milchan films. The company, in fact, undertook another production venture in the form of Hexicon Films, a wholly owned production company, which released *Money Men.*

The important role of Canal Plus in both the American and French film industries became especially evident in the early 1990s. In 1992, Canal Plus was Europe's biggest purchaser of American movie rights and remained important to U.S. studios wishing to have access to the European Community market, in light of the increasingly protectionist attitude of the European film industry. At the same time, Canal Plus's management expressed the desire to play a leading role in modernizing and strengthening European film production. The company's obligations to spend ten percent of its revenue on French-made films increased its clout in the ailing French cinema industry, which had at first regarded the subscription channel as a competitor. With the increasing number of Hollywood movies entering the European market, Canal Plus came to be regarded as a savior for the French film industry, with its significant investments in French movies.

Canal Plus began to broadcast by satellite in 1992 to reach parts of France not hooked up to the cable network, developing subsidiaries to build satellite antennas and decoders. However, this venture produced conflicts with the government over the use of the D2-Mac standard for satellite broadcasting. The government's support of this standard broke the monopoly that Canal Plus had enjoyed in the decoder market. Nonetheless, Canal Plus was still reaching more and more viewers, passing the four million mark in France, which was long thought to be the saturation level.

The company continued its policy of European expansion, investing in such cable channels as European Sports Network and entering the market in Britain with a ten percent stake in TVS. In 1992, the channel joined with BSkyB, another powerful European subscription television service, to offer digital, multi-channel pay-TV to Europe. Canal Plus also teamed up with Rupert Murdoch's News Corp to develop new TV services throughout Europe in 1992.

Between 1988 and 1993, Canal Plus stock increased 378 percent, and sales rose to $1.5 billion. While the channel's earnings growth and return on capital were expected to decline slightly throughout the 1990s, due to its investment in cable television and foreign channels, continued growth patterns were expected to bolster profits once the company passed the break-even point in its new investments. Canal Plus's broadcasting license would come up for renewal at the end of 1995, and, with its investments in the French film industry, its ownership of a popular Paris-based soccer team, and its dominant position in French cultural life, Canal Plus was likely to receive a renewed contract from the government. Despite new competition in the form of Lyonnaise Communications' pay-per-view television in France and Taurus Programming Services's six-channel satellite service in Spain, the company's predominance in the market, as well as its flexibility, seemed likely to sustain its success.

In February 1994, Rousselet quit the Havas board, citing disagreement with equity moves. This development, however, was generally regarded as consistent with the continual reorganization necessary for competing in an aggressive market. Canal Plus's aggressive negotiations in Hollywood and its expansion across Europe had ensured its position as the premier financier of the European film industry and made it an ideal ally for American media giants. The pressure to supply good films and television to a growing audience of subscribers was continually increasing in the mid-1990s, and Canal Plus showed no signs of slowing down its efforts to meet this demand.

Principal Subsidiaries: Canal Horizons; Le Studio Canal Plus; Ellipse Programme (60.7%); Carolco (11.9%).

Further Reading:

Checketts, Peter, "News Corp., Canal Plus Are Partners," *Broadcasting,* October 12, 1992, p. 14.

Echikson, William, "The Big Payoff in French Pay-TV," *Fortune,* May 3, 1993, pp. 48–49.

Grantham, Bill, "Euromoguls," *Forbes,* December 9, 1991, pp. 140–46.

Jaques, Bob, "Swiss Govt Nixes Canal Plus Link with Troubled Telecine," *Variety,* March 16, 1988, p. 68.

Marcom, John, Jr., "TV de Triomphe," *Forbes,* October 16, 1989, p. 124.

Moore, Lisa, "Will Taurus' Pay-TV Plans Fly in Spain?," *Variety,* June 14, 1993, pp. 37, 39.

"Putting Europe on the Box," *The Economist,* July 11, 1992.

Riemer, Blanca, "Canal Plus: The Latest French Sensation," *Business Week,* May 13, 1991, p. 55.

Sasseen, Jane, "Return on Capital," *International Management,* January/February 1993, pp. 61–62.

Sasseen, Jane, "Star of the Small Screen," *International Management,* June 1991, pp. 42, 45.

"Stock Leap Leaves Top 12 Execs Sitting Pretty on a Pile of Coins," *Variety,* November 30, 1988, pp. 50, 60.

Williams, Michael, "New Broadcast Standard Threatens Canal Plus," *Variety,* March 9, 1992, pp. 40, 45.

Williams, Michael, "Paris Test Bodes Well for PPV," *Variety,* August 2, 1993, pp. 27, 48.

—Jennifer Kerns

CAREMARK

Caremark International Inc.

2215 Sanders Road #400
Northbrook, Illinois 60062-4791
U.S.A.
(708) 559-4700
Fax: (708) 559-4648

Public Company
Incorporated: 1979 as Home Health Care of America
Employees: 6,500
Net Revenues: $1.7 billion
Stock Exchanges: New York
SICs: 8082 Home Health Care Services

Caremark International Inc. is America's leading provider of health care products and services to patients requiring "alternate site" (out of hospital) treatment. The company's primary offering is infusion therapy, in which patients receive medication or fluids through a catheter for treatment of cancer, AIDS, cystic fibrosis, digestive disorders, and other conditions through 93 infusion therapy facilities nationwide. Caremark is the largest private provider of HIV/AIDS care in the United States and operates a network of 12 ambulatory care centers for the treatment of cancer patients. More than half of Caremark's branch care centers include a variety of health services specifically for women, particularly those involved in high risk pregnancies. Some Caremark facilities offer physical therapy and rehabilitation, and the company is also the largest provider of support services to people with hemophilia and other blood disorders, having been the first to offer these patients treatment in their homes. In addition to patient care, Caremark is a leader among mail-order pharmacy businesses in the country, providing prescription drugs at a discount to large corporate customers. Moreover, a pioneer in "managed care" for clinics, Caremark oversees the administrative and financial aspects of physicians' practices, helping these facilities keep health care costs low. Caremark manages several large clinics in the continental United States and runs one of the largest health cost management organizations in Puerto Rico, while its alternate site services have been established in Canada, Germany, the Netherlands, and the United Kingdom.

Caremark was established in 1979 as Home Health Care of America, based in Newport Beach, California. James M. Sweeney, a former executive of the giant health care firm Baxter

Travenol Laboratories, founded the company to provide home care for the seriously ill, prompted by advancements in technology and increasing interest in alternative site care. Many patients, particularly the elderly, preferred to receive care in their homes, whenever possible, and, as the elderly population in the United States began to burgeon after 1970, the federal government found that home care was a cost-effective way to treat its Medicare and Medicaid patients. Many private insurers concurred and began covering the costs of treatment at home, making home care a viable alternative to increasingly more patients. In the early 1980s, the home health care market grew by approximately 20 percent a year, and Home Health Care of America soon expanded. By 1985, when its name was changed to Caremark, the company ran 33 home care centers across the country.

During this time, the company became the first to offer at-home infusion therapy to its patients, and it formed a Hospital Partnership Program, offering its home health care services to patients of other providers. Acquiring Federal Prescription Service Inc., a $7.5 million mail order prescription business, the company continued to expand its offerings, and prescription drugs quickly became a major part of Caremark's business. In 1985, the company acquired the Health Data Institute, which sold software and management services to insurers and employers who wanted help controlling their health care costs. The Institute's clients included such large corporations as Chrysler and General Motors Corp.

Caremark grew explosively as alternative site care became the medical industry's fastest-growing segment, with overall annual revenues estimated at $10 billion. Caremark's own revenues climbed to around $250 million in 1987, almost double those of the year before. Moreover, the company had more than doubled its number of home health care outlets, from 33 in 1985 to 70 by 1987, and its success in this lucrative market soon made it an appealing acquisition. In 1987, Caremark was acquired by Baxter Travenol Laboratories (later Baxter International), a diversified health care supply company with revenues of $5.5 billion. Seeking to shore up its holdings in the home care market, Baxter paid for Caremark in a stock swap valued at an estimated $528 million, or nearly 37 times Caremark's 1987 earnings. Caremark then became a subsidiary of Baxter, and the strengths of each proved complementary to the other.

Baxter's small network of American home health care centers, which had generated about 15 percent of its revenues, were bolstered by Caremark's national presence; while Baxter was the leading manufacturer of devices for home intravenous drug use, Caremark was a leader in the service side of the same industry. Through Caremark, Baxter gained control of approximately 30 percent of the home infusion therapy market. Moreover, Baxter had just begun its own mail-order pharmacy, and with the addition of Caremark's established business, Baxter gained ownership of the second largest mail-order pharmacy in the country. Baxter was reportedly even more interested in Caremark's Health Data Institute, recognizing the strategic advantages of offering managed cost containment to some of its largest health care customers. Both Baxter and its new subsidiary prospered after the acquisition. By 1991, Baxter's sales were nearly $9 billion, while Caremark's had more than doubled in the four years since the merger, to $600 million.

During this time, around $130 million of Caremark's revenues came from the federal government's Medicare and Medicaid programs. When a doctor referred a patient to Caremark for home care, Caremark would then pay the doctor anywhere between $12 and $150 for monitoring the home treatment; if a patient was on Medicare, then Medicare reimbursed Caremark for the fee. However, in 1991, the Department of Health and Human Services began an investigation into Medicare payments to Caremark. The investigation concerned whether the reimbursement represented a legitimate fee-for-service arrangement or an incentive or "kickback" to encourage doctors to refer their patients to Caremark. This investigation surfaced in September 1991, and while new federal regulations regarding kickbacks to physicians were scheduled to go into effect October 1, the regulations did not address the particular home care situation in which Caremark was involved. Caremark complained that the law was too vague, denied allegations of wrongdoing, and ceased making the disputed payments. Nevertheless, the investigation of Caremark intensified in 1993, focusing on payments to doctors at a Minnesota hospital, and it had yet to be settled in 1994.

Although competitors emerged in the home care market, and, by the early 1990s, ten medium-sized companies and dozens of smaller home care practices had been established, Caremark continued to dominate the industry. Caremark contributed some 15 percent of total revenues to Baxter, and its mail-order pharmacy business was the parent company's fastest-growing area. In 1992, however, Baxter announced plans to spin off Caremark as a public company, hoping to use the cash to reduce its own large debt. Moreover, Baxter hoped to appease its large hospital customers, who had their own home care units and resented competition from Caremark.

The spin-off was formalized on November 30, 1992, and the Caremark unit became Caremark International, a mail-order pharmacy business and operator of traditional home care centers. Later in the year, Caremark launched an initiative to expand into managing large clinics, signing an agreement with Houston's Kelsey-Sebold clinic to take over the administrative and financial end of the multi-physician practice. Caremark soon signed another large clinic, the Oklahoma City Clinic.

That year, Caremark reported net revenues of $1.46 billion, up 22 percent from the previous year. Moreover, the company had a 20 percent share of the home infusion market, the top share in the industry. With its expertise in home infusion therapy, the company was able to work with pharmaceutical manufacturers to bring new treatments to patients at home. In an alliance with Genentech, for example, Caremark distributed a human growth hormone for home infusion to patients with growth disorders.

In alliance with Sandoz Pharmaceutical Corporation, Caremark also began distributing clozaphine, a new drug for treating schizophrenia. Because the drug had a potentially deadly side effect involving a blood disorder, clozaphine users required weekly blood monitoring to ensure safe use. Sandoz and Caremark thus established an agreement under which clozapine patients were required to purchase Caremark's blood monitoring service. The combined cost of the drug and Caremark's blood testing made clozapine one of the most expensive drugs

in the world; and a lawsuit ensued, filed by 33 states, charging Sandoz and Caremark of an illegal tie-in that made the price of the drug thousands of dollars higher than if hospitals performed their own blood testing. The suit was settled in late 1992 with no admission of wrongdoing by Caremark, and the two companies returned $10 million to individuals and hospitals using clozapine.

Home infusion represented about 25 percent of Caremark's business in 1992, and overall patient care provided about 60 percent of the company's revenues. Nevertheless, Caremark worked to expand its other businesses. By 1993, its prescription pharmacy service had enrolled nearly 900 corporations and insurance companies, including Sears, Roebuck & Co., United Airlines, Martin Marietta, PepsiCo, and Prudential Insurance. Moreover, Caremark's new chairperson, Lance Piccolo, moved the company more solidly into managed care, which he regarded as the most likely growth area for the future. Piccolo announced plans in 1993 to acquire as many as 20 clinics over the next three years, which Caremark would manage. Also that year, the company acquired the Regional Kidney Disease Program of Minneapolis, a network of 23 kidney dialysis centers. By the end of the year, the company predicted that the patient care division would grow by only about ten percent in the coming year, but that the managed care division (which included the mail-order prescription business) would increase revenues by 40 percent.

By early 1994, Caremark, and the home infusion industry as a whole, came under pressure from insurers and other managed care providers to contain costs. Toward that end, Caremark purchased the struggling infusion division of the second largest home care provider in the industry, Medical Care America, Inc. In March 1994, Medical Care America sold the unit to Caremark for $175 million, allowing Caremark to expand its patient services and cut costs in the process. Caremark seemed particularly well-positioned to respond to demands for cost containment as well as the health care reforms suggested by President Bill Clinton. Caremark's leading home care network would likely continue to gain patients, as its managed care services often proved less expensive than hospital care and its cost management services seemed integral to plans for reforming the American health care industry.

Further Reading:

Burton, Thomas M., "Baxter Considers Issuing New Stock in Home Care Unit," *Wall Street Journal,* April 28, 1992, p. A14.
Burton, Thomas M., "Caremark Probe Focuses on Transactions in Minnesota," *Wall Street Journal,* October 18, 1993, p. B4.
Deveny, Kathleen, "A Booster Shot for Baxter Labs," *Business Week,* May 25, 1987, p. 63.
Feder, Barnaby J., "Caremark Share Offer Set at $13.50," *New York Times,* December 1, 1992, p. D5.
Freudenheim, Milt, "A Squeeze Hurts a Health Niche," *New York Times,* September 2, 1991, p. D6.
Freudenheim, Milt, "Caremark a Spinoff by Baxter," *New York Times,* January 13, 1992, p. 37.
Freudenheim, Milt, "Sandoz and Caremark in Suit Settlement," *New York Times,* September 4, 1992, p. D3.
Kimelman, Johh, "Caremark International: Profits Begin at Home," *Financial World,* September 28, 1993, p. 22.
Marcial, Gene G., "A Slew of Suitors Wants to Shower Caremark with TLC," *Business Week,* October 18, 1993, p. 90.

Oloroso, Arsenio Jr., "Caremark Holds the Line," *Crain's Chicago Business,* August 2, 1993, p. 46.

Oloroso, Arsenio Jr., "Caremark's Mail-Order Drug Unit Delivers," *Crain's Chicago Business,* March 22, 1993, p. 1.

Palmeri, Christopher, "Buying Doctors," *Forbes,* June 7, 1993, p. 45.

Palmeri, Christopher, "Keeper," *Forbes,* November 23, 1992, p. 50.

Rosenberg, Hilary, "Prognosis for Home Health Care," *Financial World,* May 15, 1983, pp. 28–29.

Tomsho, Robert, "Medical Care America Planning to Sell Its Home-Infusion Business to Caremark," *Wall Street Journal,* January 17, 1994, p. A3.

"U.S. Inquiry Focuses on Baxter Subsidiary," *New York Times,* September 10, 1991, p. D4.

Wall, Wendy, "Baxter Agrees to Acquisition of Caremark," *Wall Street Journal,* May 22, 1987, p. 4.

—A. Woodward

Carolina Telephone and Telegraph Company

720 Western Boulevard
Tarboro, North Carolina 27886
U.S.A.
(919) 823-9900
Fax: (919) 554-7474

Wholly Owned Subsidiary of Sprint Corporation
Incorporated: 1895 as the Tarboro Telephone Company
Employees: 3,500
Sales: $552.9 million
SICs: 4813 Telephone Communications Excluding
   Radiotelephone

The Carolina Telephone and Telegraph Company (CT&T) is an independent telephone company serving large portions of North Carolina. The company was formed at the turn of the century and remained independent when most of the rest of the American telephone industry was consolidated. It continued to grow as the area it served was developed. At the end of the 1960s CT&T was purchased by a telecommunications holding company that eventually became the Sprint Corporation. With the advent of deregulation in the mid-1980s, CT&T expanded its services to include long distance calls.

CT&T got its start in the autumn of 1894 when a traveling salesman named G. A. Holderness united a group of businessmen to establish a telephone exchange in Tarboro, North Carolina. The group raised $2,500 and sold stock to nine additional citizens of Tarboro to gain further funding. In October, 1895, the exchange became operational. Its switchboard was located on the second floor of a building on Tarboro's main street. It had a capacity of about 50 lines, which served an initial pool of 30 subscribers. The new service quickly proved to be a success, and Holderness and his partners soon expanded operations to the nearby towns of Washington and Kinston. In addition, they purchased the previously existing exchange in Fayetteville.

During this time, an additional telephone exchange was set up independently in the town of Scotland Neck. In 1900 the five exchanges of Tarboro, Washington, Kinston, Fayetteville, and Scotland Neck were merged into one company, which was given the name Carolina Telephone and Telegraph Company. Over the next few years, this company purchased additional

exchanges in Maxton, Red Springs, Smithfield, Dunn, and Wilson. By 1905, the company had ten different operations in North Carolina and 1,645 customers.

CT&T's growth continued at the end of the decade, as three more properties in LaGrange, Benson, and Lillinton were added by 1912. The company's expansion was hampered somewhat by the American entry into World War I in 1916. Because of shortages of manpower and materials, the company was unable to provide service to all the customers who desired it. Citizens of several small towns who wished to be wired were required to wait until further materials became available at the war's end.

In the wake of the war, CT&T resumed its expansion. In 1919 the company bought six automatic dialing mechanisms, and the first of these was installed in the town of Pinetops in 1920. With the addition of this equipment, CT&T was better able to serve the small communities in its area. By the end of 1920, CT&T boasted 20 exchanges with a total of 7,775 telephones on line.

In the 1920s CT&T continued to grow and consolidate its operations. The telephone industry at that time was extremely fragmented, as each small town had developed its own exchange. These small operations were unable to provide updated service, and they were also not able to turn a profit. Because the structure of the telephone business at this time was inefficient, leaders in the industry recognized that a major series of mergers would have to take place.

In 1926 CT&T embarked on this process when it merged with the Home Telephone and Telegraph Company, headquartered in Henderson, North Carolina. This company ran exchanges in 24 towns, and together, the company served 42 exchanges. The base for both companies' activities was moved to Tarboro. In the immediate aftermath of this merger, CT&T also added telephone exchanges in Ahoskie, Windsor, Aulander, Winton, Williamston, Plymouth, Murferesboro, and Lewiston. By the end of 1927, the company could boast that nearly every town in eastern North Carolina had been provided with telephone service.

With the coming of the Great Depression, CT&T's economic fortunes took a nosedive, and the company was forced to relinquish 18 percent of its telephone stations by 1933. By 1934, however, the company's business had bottomed out, and it began to grow slowly once again. By 1937, CT&T had returned to its post-Depression size. And with the entry of the United States into World War II in 1941, CT&T experienced significant increases in demand for its services. Several major U.S. military installations were located within its service area, and the company was forced to make large additions to its central office staff and to its outside plant facilities in order to provide adequate telephone coverage to the military personnel in the area.

CT&T's rapid expansion continued at an even greater pace after the war. The cities and towns of the company's area experienced strong growth in population, and this new public clamored for phone service. In addition, the population of rural areas in North Carolina grew, as farmers were able to make a profit on their crops for the first time in many years. With this greater prosperity, many rural areas demanded to be wired for phones. During the five years after the war, CT&T worked to provide service to its rural customers, and by 1950, the company had extended its network to include 13,088 customers in outlying areas.

Throughout the late 1940s, CT&T struggled to meet the new demand for its services. The company experienced rising prices for its materials and was forced to ask for increases in telephone rates from the public utilities regulators on several occasions. With higher revenues, CT&T was able to finance further expansion, and by 1952, the company had installed its 100,000th phone. By the end of the year, CT&T had expanded to include 103 exchanges and 106,382 subscribers. At this time the company also began to computerize its operations, installing a rudimentary IBM accounting system for the tabulation of long-distance bills.

Further updating of company technology took place in the late 1950s. In 1957 CT&T installed a microwave system for communication between two towns. Later that year CT&T made direct distance dialing available to its subscribers in the town of Washington. With this advance, customers no longer had to go through an operator in order to reach customers in areas outside their local exchange. In 1958 a second direct distance dialing system was installed in Kinston, and 18 more towns received this service by the end of that year.

Also in 1958 CT&T introduced the first color telephones, which were installed in a motel in Kinston. This move signalled the advent of an era in which the telephone would become less a utilitarian device, and more a consumer object, with a wide variety of choices in styles and colors available. By marketing this wider range of products, CT&T was able to increase its earnings on its basic service.

By September, 1960, with the conversion of Maxton's exchange, all of CT&T's customers had received direct distance dialing, capping the greatest period of capital development in CT&T's history. The manually operated switchboard in Maxton was used for the last time on September 18, 1960.

Having completed phase one of this conversion, CT&T turned to the next technological innovation and began to alter its old five digit telephone numbers. First, the company announced that it would convert to "two-five" numbering, in which the name of an exchange's central office would be taken as the number's prefix, and its first two letters dialed. This system incorporated a word and five digits, such as "Plaza 6-5000." In February, 1960, however, just as this process was getting under way, CT&T called it off after realizing that there were not enough central office names available for use. Instead, the company moved to a new national seven-digit all-number standard. By the end of 1960, members of 83 exchanges had been given their new codes.

In addition to these changes in its operations, CT&T suffered two major natural disasters in 1960 when an ice storm in February downed large numbers of telephone poles, and then Hurricane Donna struck in September. Both of these events required extensive clean-up operations on the company's part.

The next year CT&T took the next step in automating its billing procedures when the company installed an IBM 1401 electronic data processing center. With this machine, CT&T was able to prepare 8,000 bills a day and rate 50,000 toll calls. In July, 1962, CT&T entered the satellite age, when the company arranged a symbolic call from New Bern, North Carolina, to Bern, Switzerland, by way of Telstar, a new communications satellite. In the following year, CT&T customers in the town of Rocky Mount, North Carolina, also gained the option of making person-to-person, collect, and special calls by dial.

By the end of 1963, CT&T had about 8,000 stockholders. The owner of one of the largest shares of the company was the Southern Bell company, an arm of American Telephone & Telegraph Company (AT&T). In December, 1963, Southern Bell sold its 18 percent holding in CT&T to the public, ending its involvement with the independent company. Five months later CT&T made its debut on the New York Stock Exchange.

In the following year CT&T introduced Improved Mobile Telephone Service, which allowed two-way dialing, and in the following year the company marked the completion of its seven-number conversion process. CT&T also installed a company-owned private automatic branch exchange at the Pope Air Force Base, which used the newest Centrex technology.

In 1968 CT&T broke ground for a new six-story headquarters building on St. James Street in Tarboro. Later that year the company signed a plan of merger with United Utilities, Inc., a holding company based in Kansas City. After a vote of the company's shareholders, CT&T became a wholly owned subsidiary of this company on March 28, 1969. Three years later CT&T's corporate parent changed its name to United Telecommunications, Inc., and 20 years after that it was transformed again, becoming the Sprint Corporation. Two months after its purchase, CT&T signed a contract with the Communications Workers of America, which covered employees in the company's Traffic and Plant departments. This move ushered in a period of new growth in the company's operations both internally and externally.

During the 1970s CT&T continued to modernize and upgrade its operations. In November, 1970, the company ended rural ten-party service, converting all party lines to groups of no more than four. In addition, the company continued to upgrade its long-distance equipment. In 1971 CT&T began the installation of a new electromechanical 4-A switching center in Fayetteville; this process was completed in the following year at a cost of $20.9 million. Two years later a second 4-A unit was installed in Rocky Mount for $14.8 million. Also in 1973, H. Dail Holderness, a descendent of CT&T's founder, was named the company's new chairman of the board.

In March, 1977, CT&T reached the 700,000 telephones installed mark, and the company also processed a record seven million long distance calls that month. In addition, the company began the move from the electronic to the digital age when it installed its first digital private automatic branch exchange for a mobile home manufacturer. Seven other clients signed up for this service by the end of the year. Also in the late 1970s CT&T merged with two other regional telephone companies, the United Telephone Company of the Carolinas, and the Norfolk Carolina Telephone Company. With this move, CT&T expanded its service area and added 50,000 new phones to its subscriber base.

In anticipation of greater competition in the telephone industry, CT&T opened a number of Phone Shops to sell telephone equipment in the late 1970s. This experiment did not flourish, however, and it was short-lived. In another move to prepare for greater competition, CT&T tried to shore up its bottom line by requesting rate increases from its regulatory agency. Beginning in 1978, the company requested three raises in three and a half years.

In the midst of its petitions to win higher rates, CT&T experienced a strike of its employees. In 1979 members of the Carolina Telephone union walked off their jobs for 60 days before an agreement was reached. Later that year, however, the company's employees joined together to move into CT&T's new headquarters building on Western Boulevard in Tarboro.

At the beginning of the 1980s, the telephone industry as a whole underwent widespread changes. Under court order, the longtime monopoly of AT&T was broken up, and wider competition was introduced to the industry. In addition, accompanying deregulation opened the door for telephone companies to compete in many areas in which they had previously been forbidden to act. To keep pace with these changes, CT&T expanded its services and products.

In 1983 the company began the installation of the next generation of telephone cables when fiber optic technology was introduced. On the first day of the following year, the new era in the telephone industry began. CT&T responded by consolidating its service centers into three and by establishing a new form of service, Carolina Business Services, which offered sophisticated products and systems to large business customers.

Three years later CT&T formed Carolina Telephone Long Distance. This subsidiary provided long-distance service to in-state areas that were outside the local calling area, and also hooked up callers to domestic and international long-distance services. The conversion of the company's exchanges to "equal access," which allowed customers to choose which long-distance service they preferred, also began in 1987.

In the following year CT&T established North Carolina Utility Services (NOCUTS). This division was responsible for locating and marking underground facilities for utilities, so that they would not be damaged in excavation. That year the company also installed new digital directory equipment, which meshed well with its other digital operations, after selling its previous operator directory assistance facility to AT&T. By 1989, CT&T's long distance operations had become profitable. In that year the company nearly doubled its number of access lines and its minutes of use, as its gross revenues more than tripled. By that time, CT&T was serving 145 exchanges with nearly 750,000 access lines.

With the advent of the 1990s, CT&T's corporate parent increased its visibility by changing its name to "Sprint" in early 1992. Later that year, Sprint announced that it would merge with Centel, another major independent telephone company, at a cost of more than $4.7 billion. After the merger was completed in 1993, operations of the two companies were combined into Sprint/Mid-Atlantic Telecom, which served four states and was headquartered in CT&T's old Franklin Street building.

On July 31, 1993, CT&T completed the last phase of its newest technological re-tooling when, after taking out of service the last of its electromechanical switches, the company became 100 percent digital. With this move, CT&T prepared itself to offer further services as telecommunications technology advanced. Backed by a large corporate parent with a long history of successful effort behind it, CT&T seemed likely to thrive in the coming years.

Principal Subsidiaries: Carolina Telephone Long Distance.

Further Reading:

Mollenkamp, Carrick, "Battle over Toll Calls Brewing in Raleigh," *The Business Journal-Charlotte,* January 19, 1989.
Mukherjee, Sougata, *Triange Business,* "CT&T's Plan," June 28, 1993; "CT&T to Issue $50M of Debt," December 7, 1982.

—Elizabeth Rourke

Carrefour ⟨C⟩

Carrefour SA

5, avenue du Général de Gaulle
91005 Lisses
France
1 60 86 96 52
Fax: 1 60 86 35 79

Public Company
Incorporated: 1959
Employees: 40,000
Sales: FFr 117 billion (US$21.7 billion)
Stock Exchanges: Paris New York
SICs: 5411 Grocery Stores; 5331 Variety Stores

One of Europe's leading retailers in supermarkets and hypermarkets, Carrefour SA oversees the operations of over 200 stores in France and abroad. The company's founders created the concept of the hypermarket, an expanded supermarket offering a wide variety of merchandise—including groceries, electronics, clothing, and automotive supplies—that allowed consumers to accomplish most of their shopping at one store. Hypermarkets became a rapid success, revolutionizing the retail industry in France and worldwide.

Carrefour emerged in 1959 as a collaboration between two entrepreneurs, Marcel Fournier and Louis Defforey, in Annecy, a city in eastern France that had become increasingly industrialized since World War II. Both men came from successful, enterprising families, and each was anxious to expand his own business by building large supermarkets. Fournier had already established the department store Grand Magasin de Nouveautés Fournier d'Annecy and had connections in the Casino supermarket company, while Defforey was president of Badin-Defforey in Lagnieu.

In the 1950s, the French grocery industry consisted largely of family operations. Traditional grocery stores, committed to providing a variety of high quality products, accounted for 83 percent of food sales. However, as fewer young people entered into family businesses, and grocers' unions, independent wholesalers, and food cooperatives increased in number, a need for alternatives to the smaller markets developed. At the same time, big department stores, generally located in the center of cities, often proved inconvenient, and the high prices they charged for luxury items and value-added services were prompting consumers to look elsewhere for nonfood items.

Moreover, the concept of free service was becoming increasingly popular. Free service, prevalent in retail by the 1990s, was invented in 1916. Prior to its institution, consumers relied heavily on assistance from sales clerks in selecting and obtaining merchandise. Under the free service system, however, customers used bags, carts, or baskets to collect their needs—placed within easy reach and individually priced—while sales clerks served primarily as cashiers.

The supermarket, which first appeared in France in 1954, used the concept of free service. With larger facilities located outside the center of cities, supermarkets could provide fresher produce, a greater variety of products, and lower prices than the traditional grocery store. However, by the end of the decade, only 33 free service supermarkets were in operation in France, and none of them were modeled after the large, discount supermarkets in the United States.

Thus, in May 1959, Fournier and Defforey decided to incorporate these virtually unexploited concepts for their store in Annecy. An offering of 7,000 shares of stock was made to ten stockholders, and a facility already under construction in Annecy was purchased. The ground floor of the building was to be used as the supermarket, while the upper floors, containing apartments, were to be sold to help finance the business. Marcel Fournier was elected president and Denis Defforey, Louis's son, was chosen as general director. Fournier named the business Carrefour, the French transliteration of the Greek word agora, or marketplace.

During this time, a businessman named Edouard Leclerc, who was establishing supermarkets in the Rhône-Alps region, announced plans to open a store in Annecy. Fournier and Defforey knew that they had to open their store before Leclerc opened his, in order to be able to compete. Thus, Fournier offered the basement of his department store, Grand Magasin de Nouveautés Fournier, for Carrefour's use. This annex was opened on January 7, 1960, six months before the opening of the larger store, and was an immediate success. In fact, four days after it opened, the annex was already out of goods and had to close for one day to restock. The threat of competition from Leclerc prompted Fournier and Defforey to offer the lowest prices they could, and, as it turned out, Leclerc never built the competitive supermarket in Annecy.

In order to familiarize the public with supermarkets, Carrefour embarked on an advertising campaign before opening its main store. The publicity was effective. The store opened on June 3, 1960, achieving sales that far surpassed expectations and drawing 15,000 customers in the first two days. In a little over three weeks, Carrefour had sales of FFr 290,000, a figure most independent grocers reported for an entire year. To prevent traffic jams, the store expanded its parking lot, but the company's management was soon convinced that supermarkets in urban areas were impractical.

Between 1961 and 1962, business at Carrefour increased 45 percent and salaries increased as well. The following year, another supermarket was opened in Cran-Gevrier, in the Annecy region, this time with a vast parking lot. Moreover, Carrefour installed its own discount service station in the parking lot of its first store, selling gasoline without a name brand for five centimes less per liter than the average price; making neither a profit nor a loss, the company's gas station was intended as a protest against the French government's high gasoline taxes. Carrefour's discounts angered smaller business owners, a reaction that would prove typical throughout much of Carrefour's history.

During this time, the company decided to expand into the Paris region, purchasing a tract of land 30 kilometers south of the capital in Sainte-Geneviève-des-Bois, where costs were lower and more space was available. Before construction began at the new site, Louis Defforey and his brother Jacques went to the United States to observe the American commercial structure. Seminars given by Bernardo Trujillo on such modern sales practices as free service, discount prices, and large facilities, convinced the Defforeys to completely modify Carrefour's initial plans for the store outside Paris. While Carrefour did not adopt the huge dimensions of American stores with many cashiers and large aisles, they did construct a relatively large facility and integrated the idea of low prices on every product by purchasing merchandise from wholesalers and producers. They also followed Trujillo's advice about investing less in luxury construction. The store opened in June 1963 and was referred to by the press as a hypermarket, reflecting its 2,500 square meters of space, 400 parking places, and abundance of both food and nonfood merchandise. The store was an immediate success, with each customer purchasing, on average, three times more than in a regular supermarket.

Carrefour's success was based on its discount prices, decentralization of power, reduced emphasis on aesthetics and equipment costs, and accelerated rotation of stocks. The hypermarket appealed to younger people and new suburban dwellers, as well as the budget-conscious consumer affected by the high inflation rates in the 1960s. Carrefour's innovations in weighing, pricing, wrapping, cashing, and refrigerating made its hypermarket integral to the ensuing revolution in French retail. However, not everyone was pleased with these developments. The company had an adverse affect on small businesses, and an independent butchers' union blocked Carrefour's trucks at an abattoir in 1964 to protest the store's discounts. Moreover, some complained that shopping at the hypermarket was an impersonal experience, lacking in the traditional rapport between shopowner and loyal customer.

In January 1965, to avoid government restrictions on expansion, Carrefour formed two divisions: Carrefour Supermarché was led by Marcel Fournier and Denis Defforey, while Grands Magasins Carrefour, a subsidiary, was led by Jacques Defforey and Bernard Fournier. A hypermarket of 10,000 square meters was opened near Lyon in 1966 as well as another of 20,000 square meters in Vitrolles. The following year, an office was opened in Paris to collect, compare, and distribute results from all the stores, and in 1968 Marcel Fournier moved his office from Annecy to Paris.

Carrefour also actively sought involvement with other companies in Europe, including Delhaize Frères-Le-Lion in Belgium, Mercure in Switzerland, Wheatsheaf Investment in Great Britain, and Italware in Italy, and made major efforts to expand into Mediterranean regions in Europe. During its international expansion, Carrefour was careful to appeal to new clientele by marketing local products, rather than exporting French products. Initially developing new stores through joint subsidiary companies in partnership with local retailers, Carrefour eventually acquired full interest in these stores. Competitors such as Auchan, Casino, and Euromarché followed Carrefour's lead over the next ten years, greatly increasing the number of hypermarkets in France.

In June 1970, Carrefour stocks went on sale at the Bourse in Paris. With high inflation in the mid-1970s, competition for food prices was fierce, and when the 1973 Royer law put restrictions on the development of large stores in France, Carrefour began to focus increasingly on expansion abroad. Between 1978 and 1982, the greatest number of new Carrefour stores were established outside of France, particularly in Latin countries. Profits proved high at its stores in Brazil, Argentina, and Spain.

By 1982 the hypermarket industry had matured, resulting in active competition for prices, standardization of product lines, and the closing of some parts of the market. The food market stagnated, and Carrefour reduced the size of some of its stores. During this time, the company entered into more partnerships with other companies, including one with Castrorama, through which it sought to satisfy increased demand for leisure and hardware products. While Carrefour reported sales nearly double those of its immediate competitors—Casino, Viniprix, and Nouvelles Galeries—the company's primary goal was to preserve existing markets and its commercial, financial, and developmental advantages.

Marcel Fournier, who had been awarded the Legion of Honor, died in 1985, and the institute of management founded by Carrefour was named after him. By that year, Carrefour had expanded to ten countries across three continents and had a net profit of FFr 520 million. As emphasis on brand image intensified on a national scale, Carrefour introduced its own private brands as a low cost alternative, while still emphasizing quality. In 1988, Carrefour was France's leading hypermarket merchant and the top retail company in Europe, with 65 hypermarkets in France and approximately 115 in Europe and South America. In February of that year, the company opened a 330,000 square foot hypermarket outside Philadelphia, Pennsylvania. Initial financial problems due to low customer volume were overcome, and Carrefour opened a second hypermarket in the Philadelphia area in 1991. Carrefour continued to provide autonomy to each department head through its successful policy of decentralization and continued to focus on long-term results rather than immediate successes.

In the early 1990s, all members of the founding families of Carrefour left the company's active direction and formed an advisory council. Carrefour sold its stores in Annecy and Cran-Gevrier to Casino, and, in return, Casino sold its hypermarket in Nantes to Carrefour, so that Carrefour only managed stores of more than 2,500 square meters. While France had reached the saturation point with 798 hypermarkets, Carrefour continued to expand in foreign markets, with its own stores or partnerships in Austria, Great Britain, the Netherlands, Switzerland, Germany, Belgium, Italy, Spain, Africa, Argentina, Brazil, and the United States.

In 1992, Carrefour planned to open two new stores in Great Britain in a joint venture with Costco, a warehouse club company. In addition, the company's discount food chain, known as Ed, was also established in Great Britain and Italy, providing a limited range of products at extremely low prices. Through the acquisition of Euromarché that year, Carrefour gained control of several stores throughout Europe. It also opened new stores in Spain, Brazil, and Argentina and began plans for stores in Taiwan, Turkey, and Malaysia.

In 1993, Carrefour faced further challenges to its expansion in France in the form of a government-enforced freeze on new hypermarkets in rural parts of the country. Nevertheless, accustomed to such legislative and noncompetitive restrictions, the company was expected to continue its pattern of growth, particularly in foreign markets. Moreover, the company would likely rely on its reputation for innovation, as well as its commitment to modification, decentralization, competitive prices, and flexibility in its selection of products to ensure success in the rapidly changing retail market of the late twentieth century.

Principal Subsidiaries: Carrefour (France); Immobilière Carrefour; Essodis; Carrefour Italia Finanziaria (Italy); Erteco; Carrefour Nederland BV (Netherlands; 91%); S2P (60%); Sogara (50%); Sogramo (50%); Superest (50%); Carma (50%); Carcoop SA (50%); Carfuel (50%); Carrefour Holdings, Inc. (United States; 40%); But (30%); Comptoirs Modernes (22%); Viniprix (15%).

Further Reading:

Bidlake, Suzanne, ''Ed's Cut Price Bonanza,'' *Marketing,* February 11, 1993, p. 19.
Johnson, Jay L., ''Carrefour Revisited,'' *Discount Merchandiser,* August 1990, pp. 24–30.
Sasseen, Jane, ''France: Balladur Halts March of the Hypermarché,'' *International Management,* June 1993, p. 24.
Toussaint, Jean-Claude, *La politique générale de l'enterprise, un cas concret: Carrefour,* Paris: Chotard & Associés, 1984.
Villermet, Jean-Marc, *Naissance de l'hypermarché,* Paris: Armand Colin, 1991.

—Jennifer Kerns

Central Newspapers, Inc.

135 N. Pennsylvania Street
Indianapolis, Indiana 46204-2400
U.S.A.
(317) 231-9200
Fax: (317) 231-9208

Public Corporation
Incorporated: 1934
Employees: 4,500
Sales: $470 million
Stock Exchanges: New York
SICs: 2711 Newspapers; 6719 Holding Companies Nec.

Central Newspapers, Inc. (CNI) is one of the 25 largest media companies in the United States. CNI and its subsidiaries publish and distribute popular newspapers in Indiana and Arizona, including the *Indianapolis Star,* the *Indianapolis Business Journal,* the *Phoenix Gazette,* and the *Arizona Republic.* The company also owns an interest in a newsprint mill in Usk, Washington.

The first edition of the *Indianapolis Star* was published on June 6, 1903. Among its contents were general stories on promised tax cuts by national politicians, reports of bad weather and serious flooding, stories on environmental damage to local waterways caused by manufacturing wastes, baseball scores, and charges of local political fraud. Other news in this first issue, however, was more reflective of the sensational journalism of the period. For instance, in one story, young William Hulyert, of Lawrenceburg, Indiana, was found buried up to his neck in clay in his backyard; a "voodoo woman" had reportedly buried Bill in an effort to cure his measles, and passersby were alerted to the boy's plight when a pig chewed off Bill's ear, and he screamed for help. Another article told of Anna McDonald, of Fort Wayne, who was suing the Poor Housemaids of Christ for $5,000, as a hot water bottle applied to her foot while she was under anesthesia had roasted off her flesh. Such stories proved popular, and citizens clamored for daily regional newspapers during the early 1900s, setting the stage for the entrance of the media moguls that arose throughout that period.

The *Indianapolis Star* remained the sole source of statewide news in Indiana until the *Indianapolis News* commenced publication in 1934. Publishers of the *News* hoped to benefit from the growing popularity of newspapers and the demand for an alternative viewpoint to that offered by the *Star.* The *News* and *Star* both increased subscribership during the 1930s and 1940s. Boosting readership during that period were: a drop in the cost of printing and distributing newspapers, which was largely the result of automation and new printing technologies; swelling urban populations; rising U.S. literacy rates; and the increasing influence of national and overseas events on the lives of many Americans.

Achieving a lock on the Indianapolis regional newspaper market, Central Newspapers Inc., incorporated in 1934, purchased the *Star* and the *News* in 1945 and 1948, respectively, under the direction of owner and publisher Eugene C. Pulliam. The Pulliam family would eventually dominate one other U.S. newspaper market, that of Phoenix, Arizona. Active in the Phoenix market since the 1930s, CNI published *The Arizona Republic* and the *Phoenix Gazette. The Arizona Business Gazette* was added to CNI's holdings in the late 1980s.

During the 1940s, a holding company, Central Shares Inc., was formed for the sole purpose of owning stock in CNI and was controlled by members of the Enid Goodrich family. Although CNI's newspapers dominated the market in Indiana and Arizona throughout the mid-1900s, CNI and the Pulliam family kept the company's financial and historical data private throughout most of the century. Because CNI was privately owned and all voting (class B) stock was held by the Pulliams, CNI was not required to divulge sales and profit data.

Nevertheless, the holding company's publications in both Phoenix and Indianapolis had clearly achieved a significant degree of success by the 1980s. The *Indianapolis Star,* for example, reached a circulation of 233,000 on weekdays and 350,000 on weekends during 1985. Weekly subscriptions that year were priced at $2.05 per week, resulting in apparent revenues of more than $500,000 each week from that publication alone. Circulation of the *Indianapolis News* was approximately 125,000, while sales of *The Arizona Republic* and the *Phoenix Gazette* roughly mirrored estimated revenues of the Indianapolis holdings.

When founder Eugene C. Pulliam died in 1975, after 31 years of leadership, he placed majority control of the stock in an irrevocable trust. Eugene C. was survived by his wife, Naomi, and their son, Eugene S., who became executive vice-president of CNI. The Eugene C. Pulliam Trust encompassed about 71 percent of the class B, or non-trading, stock, and Naomi Pulliam held 82 percent of all non-trading CNI stock.

In 1985, the *Indianapolis Business Journal (IBJ),* lacking cooperation from CNI management, sought to estimate the value of CNI's holdings. With help from consultants at two major brokerage firms, the *IBJ* estimated the value of all CNI's holdings at $746 million. CNI President Frank A. Russell commented in the September 9, 1985 issue of *IBJ* that "Formulas are fine. . . . But in the end, price depends on how bad the buyer wants to buy and how bad the seller wants to sell. There's a lot of bargaining before a price is finally hammered out." Eugene S. Pulliam declined to comment on the estimate, explaining "We don't make our results public," in the March 1988 issue of *Indiana Business.*

However, many of the answers to outsiders' queries about CNI's financial performance were answered later that year, when CNI went public with a stock offering. According to the Pulliams, the purpose of the offering was to create a market for CNI's holdings and to establish its value to owners and creditors. Shares of class A (non-voting) stock, owned by Central Shares, were sold, and CNI was obligated to divulge financial data to the public. In documents filed with the Securities and Exchange Commission, CNI reported net income of $38.5 million in 1989 from revenues of $436.2 million, the largest revenue and earnings figures in its 55-year history. This represented increases from $29.3 million in net income in 1988 and $32.8 million in 1987.

However, positive earnings and sales growth belied overall newspaper industry woes. Although revenues were up, the *Republic's* readership grew a meager three percent in 1989, while the *Gazette's* circulation dipped five percent. Furthermore, total advertising space dropped a disheartening 20 percent between 1987 and 1989. Similarly, circulation in the Indiana market fell 1.3 percent in 1989.

During this time, much of the newspaper industry faced a prolonged battle to retain subscribers and advertisers, as newspapers were increasingly losing readership to alternative media forms. In particular, the retail industry, which was the newspaper industry's largest advertising revenue source, was making a transition to other media forms. As a result, many publishers faced decreased earnings growth and industry consolidation.

Nevertheless, CNI entered into the 1990s poised for growth. While CNI was susceptible to many of the negative trends facing industry participants, it had several advantages over its competitors. Chief among those were demographic trends in both its geographic markets. Metropolitan Phoenix, for example, was the fourth fastest growing U.S. metro area in the early 1990s and was expected to become the nation's 16th largest by 1997. Moreover, CNI's irrevocable trust, established by Eugene C. Pulliam, precluded CNI's acquisition until well into the 21st century. "We get approached every now and then," said William A. Dyer, CNI's former general manager, in the September 9, 1985, *IBJ,* "but for the most part the word is out that the Pulliam papers can't be sold."

In addition to favorable demographics and regional market dominance, savvy management helped CNI minimize the effects of negative industry trends. For instance, CNI moved early to capitalize on the trend toward insert advertising, in which advertisements and coupons were inserted in newspapers delivered to specific demographic niches. In 1992, in fact, CNI opened a $130 million high-tech printing plant in Phoenix capable of producing high-quality inserts and providing greater efficiency and quality for its standard newsprint activities. Similar facilities were under consideration in Indianapolis in the mid-1990s. Such new production facilities, as well as management restructuring, had allowed CNI to reduce its workforce and increase its productivity.

CNI also sought profit growth through acquisition. In its first major newspaper purchase since 1948, CNI purchased Topics Suburban Newspapers Inc. of Noblesville, Indiana, in 1992. Topics was a publisher of 15 newspapers sold primarily in the lucrative north Indianapolis market. Although CNI did not disclose the purchase price, Topics added 97,000 readers to CNI's existing 500,000 subscriber base in Indiana. The acquisition distressed owners of smaller papers who feared CNI's growing strength. Jack McCarthy, publisher of the *Hendricks County Flier,* remarked in the November 23, 1992 issue of *IBJ*: "Thank God we have anti-trust laws in this country. . . . I have every confidence they won't [violate anti-trust laws], but just the same, I'm thankful small businesses have laws to protect them when I hear of acquisitions like this."

CNI sales and earnings increased throughout the early 1990s. The holding company's revenues jumped to $420 million in 1991, $434 million in 1992, and $467 million in 1993—the result of sales growth in both advertising and circulation. Similarly, operating income climbed 37 percent during that period, to $66 million. Furthermore, net assets rose 15 percent to about $465 million. CNI's price increases were the main factor in overcoming sluggish subscription growth—circulation for the *News* actually fell to 83,000 in 1994, while daily circulation of the *Star* remained at near-1985 levels. In addition, increased sales of Sunday editions buoyed subscription earnings.

Not all of CNI's ventures had been entirely successful, however. For example, the company's 13.5 percent interest in the Ponderay Newsprint Co. produced losses of $4.5 million in 1990 and $3.1 million in 1991. CNI originally invested in the plant with the intent of saving money on the cost of newsprint. However, oversupply, spurred by excessive Canadian imports, resulted in falling newsprint prices. "There's no way we could have looked into the crystal ball and seen that happening. . . . It was a bad deal," commented CNI Treasurer Wayne D. Wallace in the April 13, 1992 *IBJ.*

In the early 1990s, CNI demonstrated a commitment to the communities in which it operated. For example, Phoenix Newspapers, Inc. (PNI), CNI's Arizona subsidiary, launched the PNI Season for Sharing Fund in 1993 to raise money primarily for agencies that served children, but also for the homeless, the elderly, and the hungry. The effort garnered $790,000 in contributions from 10,800 individuals, which, when combined with corporate donations, totaled $1.58 million. Indianapolis Newspapers, Inc. (INI), CNI's Indiana subsidiary, was engaged in similar charitable and civic pursuits. "The first duty of citizenship is useful service to one's local community, and the newspaper wants to be a good citizen," stated the company's 1993 annual report.

In the mid-1990s, CNI worked to take advantage of shifting demographics and evolving trends in advertising. Much of its emphasis was on tailoring its newspaper distribution system to accommodate new niche marketing techniques. Toward that end, CNI introduced Indianapolis Market Penetration and Custom Targeting (IMPACT) in 1993, which allowed advertisers to select either targeted or complete coverage in *Star* and *News* markets. Similarly, AdSnap, a multi-media marketing package, was introduced in Arizona to help real estate agents prepare print ads. Other management strategies focused on increased manufacturing productivity and quality as well as more efficient distribution.

Principal Subsidiaries: Indianapolis Newspapers, Inc.; Phoenix Newspapers, Inc.

Further Reading:

Andrews, Greg, "Newspapers Commit to $17 Million Project, But Consider Much More," *Indianapolis Business Journal,* April 4, 1994, p. A3.

Andrews, Greg, "Newspapers Plot New Production Plant," *Indianapolis Business Journal,* March 14, 1994, p. 1.

Cavinder, Fred D., "A Star is Born," *Indianapolis Star,* June 4, 1978, pp. 10–14.

Felton, Meg, "Indiana's Newspaper Publishers," *Indiana Business,* March 1988, p. 10.

Fischer, Howard, "Central Newspapers Posts Strong Increase in 1989 Net Income," *Business Journal-Phoenix & The Valley of the Sun,* p. 13.

Higgins, Will, "How Much Are the Indianapolis Star and the Indianapolis News Worth?" *Indianapolis Business Journal,* September 9, 1985, p. 1.

Katterjohn, Chris, "Republic's Parent May Be Headed for Summer Public Offering," *Business Journal-Phoenix & the Valley Sun,* April 11, 1988, p. 7.

Kukolla, Steve, "Central Newspapers Loses Income but Pledges to Continue the News," *Indianapolis Business Journal,* April 13, 1992, p. A3.

Kukolla, Steve, "Will Star/News Parent Change Topics?" *Indianapolis Business Journal,* November 23, 1992, p. 1.

"Republic Parent to Buy Small Papers," *Arizona Republic,* November 18, 1992, p. C3.

Rush, Jill, "Hot Off the Presses!: Central Has Record Year; Predicts Flat '90," *Indianapolis Business Journal,* April 16, 1990, p. A1.

—Dave Mote

Century Communications Corp.

50 Locust Ave.
New Canaan, Connecticut 06840
U.S.A.
(203) 972-2000
Fax: (203) 972-2036

Public Company
Incorporated: 1986
Employees: 2,300
Sales: $350 million
Stock Exchanges: American
SICs: 8330 Broadcasting and Telecommunications

Century Communications Corp. is a major provider of cable television services in the United States. Through its subsidiary, Century Cable, the corporation served more than 900,000 subscribers in the United States and Puerto Rico in 1993. Centennial Cellular Corp., the company's publicly traded cellular telephone venture, served 76,000 subscribers across the nation and generated about 12 percent of Century Communications' 1993 sales.

Century Communications was founded by Leonard Tow, the company's majority owner, chief executive officer, and chief financial officer. Tow got his start in the industry in 1964, when he went to work for cable industry pioneer Teleprompter Corp. Still in its infancy, the subscriber television industry during that era primarily supplied nonurban areas with regular television broadcasting via antennae. Tow quickly worked his way up to vice-president of corporate development and planning. He played an important role in developing Teleprompter's subscriber base from 50,000 to more than one million by 1972, making it the largest cable television service in the nation.

Tow became frustrated with the management at Teleprompter in the early 1970s. Satellite broadcasting had emerged in 1972 as a promising technology for the future, and the cable industry was undergoing a pivotal transition from rural, network programming to urban, non-network services. Eager to capitalize on dawning opportunities and his knowledge of the business, Tow set out on his own in 1973 and formed Century Communications Corp. With $22,000 in capital and a $5 million line of credit—backed by his venture partner, Sentry Insurance Company—Tow attacked the cable market, buying up "dogs," or poorly managed cable companies.

Century Communication's first acquisition was four lagging cable TV markets in California, which were owned by Cablecom General. Tow and his innovative team, many members of which Tow had hired away from Teleprompter, quickly turned the markets into highly successful profit centers. These early successes gave Tow the credibility he needed to continue financing and improving new acquisitions throughout the 1970s and 1980s. In 1973, the company had just 15,000 subscribers, each of which paid $275 annually for service. By 1983, however, Century was generating more than $30 million in revenues per year from a subscriber base of nearly 200,000 households.

Part of Century Communication's recipe for success was its unique corporate culture. Disheartened by what he viewed as a traditional and oppressive corporate culture at Teleprompter, Tow decided early to structure his company as an extended family. Although workers had titles, they were allowed access to all levels of management and were told that at Century "everyone is viewed as a whole human being as good as anyone else." Some members of Tow's immediate family were involved in Century's management; son Andrew, for example, was president of the company's cable TV division in 1994, while Tow's wife, Claire, served as senior vice-president of human resources.

In addition to his unique management style and corporate philosophy, Tow credited his own initiative as a vital factor in the company's rampant growth. "The company grew as a function of my drive to build, through acquisition, a company," Tow asserted in the July 12, 1993 issue of *Fairfield County Business Journal* article, adding that "if every employee is devoted to giving their all and to giving their all to the customer base, you have all the ingredients for a successful business."

Century Communications's team continued to show strong results during the mid-1980s, as cable TV subscribership swelled to almost 250,000 in 1984 and to about 300,000 by 1986. Similarly, sales reached an impressive $40 million in 1984 and increased to approximately $55 million just one year later. By 1986, the company boasted 365,000 cable subscribers on 36 cable TV systems in 20 states. Seeking further growth, Tow took the company public on the NASDAQ exchange in February of 1986 in an effort to generate investment capital. Century effectively doubled its current (liquid) assets during that year to $16 billion.

Although Century managed its cable acquisitions from central and regional offices, it allowed each separate cable system to retain responsibility for its own operations and market strategies. In its 1986 annual report, Century described its cable network as a "mosaic of profitable and free-standing independent cable television service suppliers who are in tune with local markets and can customize the service for those local markets." Centralized management was primarily responsible for establishing and enforcing price and quality controls throughout the network.

During the late 1980s, the company acquired new markets and improved its existing operations. Its cable subscribership ballooned to 721 million in 1988 as company revenues soared past $160 million. Although the company lost money in 1987 and 1988, these losses were attributed to investments and expansions made to garner future profits. In 1987, the company absorbed several poorly performing cable companies which it planned to return to profitability, and, the following year, Century began purchasing cellular licenses, which would allow it to provide cellular telephone service to the regions it "owned."

Century was listed on the American Stock Exchange beginning in 1988, providing a new route to capital that would help continue its strategy of expansion into the cable TV industry over the next few years. Importantly, Century determined that its foray into cellular communications would become a major component of its long term growth strategy. Toward that end, Century purchased a cellular license in Yuma, Arizona, in 1989, and acquired cellular service providers in Nebraska and Texas during 1990. The company also arranged extensive lines of investment credit for cellular (and cable) expansion. Century's revenues from its cellular interests, which were about $3 million in 1989, shot up to nearly $12 million during 1990.

Century promoted and initiated numerous charitable and community development programs in the early 1990s. Paramount among such endeavors was the company's "Century Cares" program, which was started in 1988 to benefit nonprofit service organizations in the communities in which it operated. In 1990, for example, Century's 55 cable companies raised over $700,000 for programs ranging from battered spouse and children's shelters to senior day care and rehabilitation centers—customers that donated enjoyed reduced fees and free services.

As it entered the 1990s, Century continued to boost sales and expand its scope, despite a nagging U.S. economic recession. Company revenues in 1990 were over $275 million as its base of cable subscribers increased to nearly 900 million households. In 1991, Tow organized Century's cellular operations into a subsidiary called Centennial Cellular, intending to develop the wireless service provider into a major competitor in that burgeoning industry.

Tow also broadened his personal interests and activities in the early 1990s. In 1989, he served on the board of directors of Citizens Utilities, a provider of telecommunications and other utility services in 13 states. The following year, Tow served as the company's chief executive officer and chairperson before also assuming duties as CFO in 1991. Tow's affiliation with Citizens exemplified his knack for seizing an opportunity; denied a position at Citizens in the early 1960s, Tow had stayed in touch with the people he met at the company, eventually securing a seat on its board.

Tow's relationship with Citizens blossomed in 1992, when Century and Citizens joined forces in the Centennial Cellular venture. Citizens's subsidiary, Citizens Cellular Company, was absorbed by Centennial late in 1991, significantly expanding Centennial's market base. As a result of the merger, Century's revenues from Centennial increased to $31.3 million in 1992 from 57,300 subscribers. In 1993, moreover, cellular revenues jumped 38 percent to $43.2 million as subscribership surged to 76,000. By 1993, in fact, Centennial Cellular had become the ninth largest cellular service provider in the United States. Century retained more than 50 percent ownership of Centennial in 1994.

While Tow had gained a favorable reputation for leading Century to healthy growth during the 1970s and 1980s, he also had come under fire by some shareholders. Tow had been criticized, for instance, for his unusual role as both CEO and CFO of the company—most publicly traded companies separated the two spheres of responsibility as a means of insuring checks and balances regarding corporate operations. His wife's position on the company board as well as his son's role as senior vice president had also come into question.

The primary source of criticism surrounding Tow, however, was his high level of compensation. In Century's fiscal year ending in 1993, Tow received a hefty $2.95 million in pay, not including stock options and bonuses. Critics pointed out that this sum exceeded the salaries of CEOs running much larger companies in the industry; the head of AT&T, for example, received only $2.25 million in 1993. Furthermore, Century Communications had consistently lost money; its $37.8 million loss in 1993 capped a five-year string of losses resulting from beefy investments in the capital-intensive Centennial venture. Many shareholders were concerned by the fact that the company's combined debt and loss record had earned it a "C" ranking from Standard & Poors, indicating that Century was a risky investment.

Tow defended his compensation by pointing to Century's strong future profit potential, as well as healthy growth in revenues and operating profits. Indeed, revenues increased more than ten percent in 1993, to $345 million, and its operating income swelled 15.5 percent. Backing Tow's promise of future rewards was growth in Century Cable's subscriber base to about 950,000 in 1993 and extremely positive projections for increases in cellular revenues throughout the mid-1990s.

Also under criticism was another member of Century's management team, Bill Rosendahl, senior vice-president of Century Cable. Rosendahl achieved celebrity status in central and southern California during the late 1980s and early 1990s through his television talk show, *The Week in Review*. Because of Century's lock on the cable market in Los Angeles, Beverly Hills, West Hollywood, and surrounding regions, Rosendahl enjoyed a captive audience, and he used his forum to interview local celebrities and politicians.

Some industry observers maintained that the show represented a conflict of interest, providing a platform for politicians that ultimately voted on cable issues. However, in the July 1993 issue of the *Los Angeles Magazine*, Rosendahl maintained: "I'm a cable executive. I'm a TV journalist. I can do both things. Hey, it's the 1990s." Besides management experience in the cable industry, Rosendahl had also served in the State Department under the Carter administration. His half-hour show increased in popularity during the early 1990s, reaching 1.5 million households in 24 states by 1993.

Despite robust expansion of its cable operations, Century, like many other cable industry participants, suffered in the wake of federal legislation passed by Congress in 1992 and 1993. The legislation, which effectively restricted the rates that cable companies could charge, represented a serious blow to companies that were trying to raise money to develop more technologically advanced cable systems. "These changes are expected to slow dramatically revenue and cash flow growth in the coming year, and, absent new offerings, may indeed cause a reduction in fiscal 1994 cable television revenues and operating cash flow,'' wrote Bernard P. Gallagher, president and chief operating officer of Century Communications Corp., in the company's 1993 annual report.

Nevertheless, Tow forecasted continued growth for Century's cable division throughout the 1990s. In addition to many unexploited territories, Tow noted that only 60 percent of the potential customers in his existing markets had cable TV in 1993, a figure which he predicted would jump to 70 percent by the end of the century and 80 percent by 2010. ''Cable television will eventually be as universal as electric light and universal gas,'' Tow speculated in the July 12, 1993 issue of *Fairfield County Business Journal*. Advances in digital and data compression technologies would boost growth, according to Tow, as the capacity of cable TV service expanded to 500 stations or more.

In 1993, Tow expected revenues from Centennial Cellular to expand at a rate of 40 percent annually at least throughout the mid-1990s. Going into 1994, Centennial was planning vast capital investments in new cellular systems and was concentrating on cultivating several large markets in the Midwest, South, and Southwest. Of import to Century was the gradual integration of cellular, cable TV, and other communications technologies into a streamlined, interactive, multimedia network. Century was planning to capitalize on this transition through Electric Lightwave, a subsidiary of Citizens Utilities engaged in developing non-wire voice and data systems that could be offered as add-on services to cable customers.

Principal Subsidiaries: Century Cable; Centennial Cellular Corp. (53%).

Further Reading:

Gallagher, Bernard P., and Scott N. Schneider, ''Century Offers $200 Million 9¾ Senior Notes Due 2002,'' *Business Wire,* February 13, 1992.

Jefferson, David, ''The King of Cable: Why You're Seeing the Once-Maligned Century Cable's Bill Rosendahl All Over Your TV,'' *Los Angeles Magazine,* July 1993, p. 40.

Marshall, Cynthia, ''Tow Takes Century Communications to Forefront of Technology,'' *Fairfield County Business Journal,* July 12, 1993, p. 6.

Stepankowsky, Paula LaBeck, ''Century's CEO Earns Millions; Firm in Red Ink,'' *The Daily News* (Longview, WA), October 29, 1993.

—Dave Mote

CHIRON

Chiron Corporation

4560 Horton Street
Emeryville, California 94608-2916
U.S.A.
(510) 655-8730
Fax: (510) 655-9910

Public Company
Incorporated: 1981
Employees: 2,164
Operating Revenues: $317.54 million
Stock Exchanges: NASDAQ
SICs: 8731 Commercial Physical and Biological Research

One of the few independent biotechnology companies in the United States, Chiron Corporation is a world leader in biotechnological medicine. The company's five core businesses—The Biocine Company (a joint venture with Ciba-Geigy Ltd.), Chiron Vision, Chiron Diagnostics (a joint venture with Ortho Diagnostic Systems, Inc.), Chiron Therapeutics, and Chiron Technologies—each develops products that diagnose, prevent, and treat human diseases. Among Chiron's innovations in the pharmaceutical industry are the first genetically engineered vaccine, the first blood screening test for hepatitis-C, and the first drugs to treat multiple sclerosis, metastatic kidney cancer, and whooping cough. Chiron was also one of the first biotechnology companies to post a profit; after eight years of losses in the 1980s, Chiron's 1993 profits totaled $18.4 million, while revenues grew steadily from $47 million in 1989 to $317.5 million in 1993.

Chiron was founded by Dr. William Rutter, a biotechnology researcher at the University of California in San Francisco. In the late 1970s, Rutter led a team of researchers that made an important breakthrough in the relatively new science of genetic engineering: equipping bacteria with the ability to produce limitless quantities of insulin. Advances in the field rapidly ensued, and several companies sprang up in the early 1980s with the intent of developing these discoveries into marketable health care products. As the industry took off, new companies began recruiting the best scientists from university laboratories, including the one led by Rutter. Rather than see his best researchers work for other companies, Rutter chose to found his own biotechnology firm. As he told *Fortune* magazine, "It became obvious that I had to either get in or lose out."

In 1981, Rutter, Edward Penhoet, and Pablo Valenzuela founded Chiron Corp., which they named after the centaur in Greek mythology who taught medicine to Asclepias, the first physician. Soon after its founding, Chiron produced the first genetically engineered vaccine, another milestone in the burgeoning biotechnology industry. Chiron licensed this new vaccine, created for the prevention of hepatitis-B, to the pharmaceutical giant Merck & Co. Pending FDA approval, Merck would market the vaccine and pay royalties to Chiron.

Unlike many start-up biotech firms at that time, Chiron did not intend to become a fully integrated pharmaceutical company. Its marketing agreement with Merck became the first in a series of partnerships through which Chiron would bring new products to the marketplace while focusing primarily on biotechnological research into infectious diseases and viruses. In 1983, Chiron made another breakthrough when it became the first to clone epidermal growth factors—a genetically engineered protein which controls the way a wound heals. Funding for the project was provided by Ethicon, Inc. which, in return, gained the right to market the proteins once they received FDA approval. Also that year, although it had no products on the market, Chiron went public at $12 a share.

In 1984, Chiron became the first to clone a genome (genetic skeleton) of an AIDS virus called HTLV-3, the second step in developing a method of detecting and someday preventing infection by HIV. Two years later, Chiron won FDA approval to sell its hepatitis-B vaccine through Merck. Chiron also formed the first of its five divisions, The Biocine Company, a joint-venture with Ciba-Geigy, Ltd., focusing on the development and marketing of other new vaccines. In 1988, Chiron's Biocine division filed with the FDA for approval of an AIDS screening test and began research into an AIDS vaccine. The following year, The Biocine Company purchased Canada's Connaught BioSciences, a vaccine manufacturer to be owned 50 percent by Chiron and 50 percent by Ciba-Geigy.

Chiron researchers also continued to study hepatitis, and, in 1988, they discovered the hepatitis-C virus. Previously undetected, the hepatitis-C virus had caused approximately 150,000 people each year to become ill through infected blood transfusions. To market hepatitis-C screening tests, Chiron joined forces with Johnson & Johnson's Ortho Diagnostics Systems. Under the name Chiron Diagnostics, the division developed several blood tests to screen for various forms of hepatitis, and these tests were sold to blood banks and hospitals worldwide.

Primarily due to heavy outlays in research and development, Chiron posted losses for eight straight years. In the spring of 1989, Chiron raised $52 million through an equity offering and sold an eight percent share to Ciba-Geigy. While this move greatly increased the company's cash reserve, Chiron finished this year with a loss of $21.6 million on revenues of $35.4 million. In 1990, however, Chiron posted its first profit: $6.8 million on revenues of $78.5 million. Its products, including the hepatitis-B vaccine (marketed through Merck), its blood testing systems, and recombinant human insulin marketed through Novo/Nordisk brought in over $600 million in sales.

Chiron entered 1991 with a strong balance sheet. In July of that year, the company purchased a rival biotechnology firm, Cetus

Corp., for $650 million in stock. Cetus's major product was a highly touted cancer treatment called Proleukin or Interleukin-2, which its EuroCetus division had been selling in Europe for several years. However, the FDA had refused to approve use of the drug in the United States, and Cetus's chairperson resigned his post, leaving the company without direction and with a product whose image had been greatly tarnished. Chiron stepped in, continued testing Proleukin as the FDA had requested, and merged Cetus's projects with its own. With the purchase, Chiron also acquired a state-of-the art research facility, not far from its own headquarters in Emeryville, California.

By 1991, Chiron's operations had grown to include a complex network of joint ventures and marketing agreements with several pharmaceutical companies. Chiron thus reorganized its business into five units. Its cancer research department was merged with Cetus's oncology business under the umbrella of Chiron Therapeutics. Chiron Diagnostics, the joint venture with Ortho, absorbed Chiron's research on the HIV virus and began developing various forms of testing for that and other viruses. Chiron's burgeoning ophthalmic business merged with IntraOptics, Inc. to form Chiron IntraOptics, which manufactured a comprehensive line of surgical instruments used to correct cataracts and other vision problems. The Biocine Company purchased the children's vaccine division of Italy's Sclavo SpA, and renamed it Biocine Sclavo. A fifth business, Chiron Technologies, was created to absorb the company's Ethicon-funded research into growth factors, the development of a drug to treat multiple sclerosis (Betaseron), and also to develop and acquire new products and business.

Chiron posted a loss of $425 million in 1991, primarily due to its merger with Cetus, which had also been posting heavy losses. However, the next two years proved promising for the company. Biocine began the first phase of testing its AIDS vaccine under the sponsorship of the AIDS Vaccine Evaluation Group and the National Institute for Allergies and Infectious Disease. In 1992, Chiron Therapeutics finally obtained FDA approval to market Cetus's Proleukin, and, in 1993, Chiron Technologies received approval to market Betaseron, its first

genetically engineered drug to treat multiple sclerosis, and an agreement was reached with Schering A.G.'s Berlex Laboratories to market the new treatment, giving Chiron 25 percent of sales revenue. Buoyed by the successes of Proleukin, as well as strong sales of its blood-testing products, vaccines, and insulin, Chiron posted a 1993 profit of $18.4 million on revenue of $317.5 million.

Industry analysts considered 1993 a pivotal year in Chiron's rise to profitability, as products under development in the 1980s were beginning to pay-off handsomely. Betaseron alone brought in $10.5 million in the fourth quarter of 1993; Chiron Diagnostics also did well on sales of its blood-testing equipment. Furthermore, Chiron had the greatest number of products under development in the industry, working on vaccines for AIDS, genital herpes, and whooping cough. Its slow but steady growth in the volatile biotech industry was regarded as vital in establishing a secure foundation for greater success in the future.

Principal Subsidiaries: The Biocine Company; Chiron Technologies; Chiron Diagnostics; Chiron Therapeutics; Chiron Vision Corp.; Chiron Mimotopes, Pty. Ltd.; Chiron Mimotopes Peptide Systems, Biocine S.p.A; Magnum Diamond; Chiron Adatomed; Chiron Vision Australia; Chiron Vision Canada.

Further Reading:

Bronson, Gail, ''Beyond the Band-Aid,'' *Forbes,* June 1, 1987, p. 160.
Fisher, Lawrence M., ''Market Place: Chiron Investors Pay a Price for the Biotech Company's Success,'' *The New York Times,* March 25, 1994, pp. C6, D6.
Gannes, Stuart, ''Striking it Rich in Biotech,'' *Fortune,* November 9, 1987, p. 131.
Hamilton, Joan, O'C., ''Revenge of the Nerds in Biotech Land,'' *Business Week,* August 5, 1991, p. 26.
Savitz, Eric J., and Edward A. Wyatt, ''Fulfilling Their Promise: Wondrous Products and Even Profits Are in Sight for Biotech Firms,'' *Barron's News and Investment Weekly,* September 25, 1989, p. 6.
Zipser, Andy, ''Hit or Myth? Mutual Choice,'' *Barron's News and Investment Weekly,* May 25, 1992, p. 30.

—Maura Troester

CML Group, Inc.

524 Main Street
Acton, Massachusetts 01720
U.S.A.
(508) 264-4155
Fax: (508) 264-4073

Public Company
Incorporated: 1969
Employees: 5,000
Sales: $645 million
Stock Exchanges: New York
SICs: 3949 Sporting & Athletic Goods; 5961 Catalogue &
   Mail Order Houses; 5947 Gift, Novelty & Souvenir Shops;
   6719 Holding Companies

The CML Group, Inc. is the corporate parent of three specialty retailers: NordicTrack, an exercise machine company; Britches of Georgetowne, a men's clothing retailer; and The Nature Company, a company offering books and other objects relating to nature, as well as the products of Smith & Hawken, an upscale garden supply franchise. From its start, CML has grown by targeting the needs and desires of consumers with money and leisure time. The company reaps profits in small market niches by changing its group of subsidiaries to match shifts in demographic trends.

Charles M. Leighton founded CML and named the company with his initials. Leighton's partner in this venture was G. Robert Tod, who added a background in engineering to Leighton's marketing expertise. Before starting CML, Leighton had worked as a professor of management at the Harvard School of Business, and he and Tod had collaborated on an article for the *Harvard Business Review* called ''After the Acquisition: Continuing the Challenge.'' This article put forward ideas about how companies should manage new businesses after an acquisition. Although many companies were being bought and sold at the time, little thought had been given to how best to run them after the purchasing process had been completed.

Leighton and Tod decided to put their theories to a real-world test in 1969. To do so, the pair chipped in $40,000 of their own money, and raised $2 million in seed funds from nearly 100 different investors, including venture capitalists, the Ford Foundation, Reader's Digest, and the First National Bank of Boston.

When this process was complete, CML was launched as a holding company on June 3, 1969. The company's four employees were housed in offices set up in an old railroad depot in Concord, Massachusetts. Trains thundered by the building at regular intervals.

CML's founders planned to operate by two principles. First, they planned to use a light hand in managing the businesses they bought, keeping corporate interference to a minimum. Second, they sought out companies in the leisure products field, guided by the belief that a demographic shift was underway in which Americans would devote more and more of their time to leisure activities, and become increasingly willing to pay for equipment and paraphernalia to be used in those pursuits. CML sought out companies that produced ''ego-intensive products,'' as Leighton told the *Wall Street Journal.*

CML started out by making two purchases. First, the company bought Carroll Reed Ski Shops, Inc., a North Conway, New Hampshire-based retailer of ski equipment and clothing that was founded in 1936. Although the company's founder, Carroll Reed, had not initially wanted to sell out, Leighton and Tod convinced him that they would not interfere in the company's management. Nearing retirement, Reed turned over the business for $2.5 million. After acquiring Carroll Reed, CML set out to expand the company's operations and profits. It computerized the company's mailing list for its catalogue, sent out four times a year. A new building to house Reed's headquarters was built, and two new stores in Connecticut, one in Simsbury and a second in Westport, were opened.

CML made its second purchase a week after finalizing the Carroll Reed sale, when it bought Boston Whaler, Inc., a manufacturer of outboard motor boats. Boston Whaler products used rails to form their prows and a special fiberglass foam construction process to make the boats unsinkable, which provided safety and stability. Boston Whaler, founded 11 years earlier, had run into financial difficulties after attempting to enter the engine-manufacturing industry.

After this start, CML continued to acquire companies at a steady rate. Seeking out fast-growing fields, the company then investigated to discover which firms within that field had the highest reputation for quality. If they found one with a good product, potential for a growing market, and a management team—including a good president, marketer, and accountant—who wanted to stay with the company, then CML's leaders considered adding it to their roster of businesses. In this way two Massachusetts companies, Hood Sailmakers, Inc. and Madison & Sullivan, Inc., which sold kits to make grandfather clocks, were added to the CML Group in the early 1970s. Branching out from its New England base, the company soon added Kelty Pack, Inc., a backpack manufacturer; Sierra Designs, Inc., which made camping equipment; and Ericson Yachts.

This steady expansion was accompanied by growth in revenues. By mid-1970, sales stood at $12.2 million, with earnings of nearly $270,000. Two years later, revenues had more than doubled to $26.2 million, and earnings were approaching $700,000.

In the mid-1970s, CML continued to acquire companies and foster their growth through its management philosophy. In addition, some properties were dropped from its holdings, including Kelty Pack, Inc. Hood Sailmakers was sold back to its founder after CML refused to underwrite an entry for the company in the America's Cup race, believing that this venture would be an expensive and unwise risk.

In their stead, CML added a number of companies, bringing its list of subsidiaries up to 11. It purchased the Hoyt Archery Company, which made items such as an archery bow used in the Olympic Games; Gokey's, a maker of hunting boots and camping equipment; The Outdoorsman, Inc., which sold sporting goods; Country Store of Concord, Inc., a sportswear retailer; Mother Karen's, a skiwear designer; and the Sturbridge Yankee Workshop, Inc., which sold Early American furniture. Each of these companies had developed a loyal clientele and a reputation for quality. CML allowed them to retain their own names and identities, but made sure that the businesses were managed with computers, three year plans, and a steady expansion in sales.

These techniques showed results. Boston Whaler, for instance, saw sales grow from $5 million to $25 million in nine years, despite a strike at the company's main plant. Overall, CML's financial returns showed steady improvement. By the end of the 1970s, sales were topping $100 million a year, and profits had reached $2.7 million. Despite these gains, CML kept the number of employees at its corporate headquarters low. By the end of the decade, CML's staff consisted of just six executives and three secretaries. The company had by then moved out of its offices near the railway to new corporate headquarters at a wooded site in Acton, Massachusetts.

After fourteen years of steady growth, CML sold stock to the public for the first time in 1983. By 1984, sales had grown to $180 million. During the early 1980s, CML further refined its corporate identity to target customers between the ages of 35 and 50. This demographic group was projected to quadruple before the end of the century as the baby boom aged. The CML customer had a higher than average income and an active lifestyle. He or she sought out quality and convenience in products to purchase. In addition, CML sought to market products that were fun to use and did not harm the environment, ruling out such categories as snowmobiles and all-terrain vehicles. CML summed up its corporate philosophy with its name, suggesting that CML stood for ''customer, marketing, and lifestyle,'' as well as the initials of its founder.

To further appeal to its busy, high income target customers, CML also sought to make shopping easy. To do this, the company located its stores in specialty malls, where they would be surrounded by other exclusive retailers, and focused on providing full service to customers. In addition, CML emphasized catalogue shopping. By the mid-1980s, mail order operations made up about 20 percent of the company's sales. To further increase convenience, CML also began offering stockholders a credit card program for purchases in its stores.

In the early 1980s, CML also further refined its mix of product offerings. The company discontinued some unprofitable catalogues, and also sold off its Hoyt Archery subsidiary, after deciding that its products did not fit the image that CML was trying to project. To replace Hoyt Archery, CML founded a

company named Ingear, its only start-up. Ingear was a California sports equipment retail chain in which stores were arranged by ''pods.'' Each pod was dedicated to one activity, and contained the products that members of the store's staff had selected as the best in that category. Rather than a selection of brands, the stores offered an assurance of quality.

In addition, CML purchased two other companies: The Nature Company and Britches of Georgetowne. The Nature Company was a small San Francisco retailer which sold books, art, and other products with a naturalistic bent. CML helped the company to organize and finance a cross-country expansion in 1983. Britches of Georgetowne was a Washington, D.C., clothing retailer. Along with Boston Whaler and The Nature Company, this company provided the bulk of CML's profits in the early 1980s.

CML suffered one financial setback in 1982, when Gokey's, the company's midwestern sportswear chain, tried to computerize its accounting records. When the job was botched, orders went unfilled, bills went unpaid, and some debts were paid twice. The fiasco cost CML a $1 million write-off. Despite this setback, CML executives felt that overall their hands-off management philosophy gave companies the independence to succeed unhampered, even if mistakes were sometimes made. CML suffered another financial setback when a Canadian mail order subsidiary was forced to fold after an eight-month strike by the Canadian postal service. ''We lost money. There was nothing we could do. The strike didn't stop. We eventually had to liquidate that company,'' Leighton told *The Boston Herald.*

By the mid 1980s, however, profits were holding steady. Sales of clothing through Carroll Reed had grown to $45 million, and Boston Whaler revenues had reached $40 million. In addition, new units of CML, such as SyberVision, contributed profits. SyberVision produced audio and video self-help tapes, which showed experts playing various sports, such as skiing, golfing, and tennis, and also included other topics, such as weight loss. With a large advertising budget, SyberVision peddled its products through television and catalogues. In 1985, at the time of its purchase, SyberVision had annual sales of $2.5 million.

As it acquired SyberVision, CML also sold off Ericson Yachts. The company's executives had decided that the yacht business was too cyclical to provide steady profitability. It had also jettisoned its Sierra Designs unit after it became clear that the outdoorsy appeal of the company's products had diminished as the 1960s faded into memory. Despite these changes, CML revenues grew 26 percent in 1985, nearing $200 million. These sales were generated by 118 separate retail stores and more than 21 million catalogues.

In June 1986, CML made an acquisition that would prove to be key to the company's growth when it purchased NordicTrack, a Minneapolis-based exercise equipment manufacturer. CML installed an aggressive marketing manager at NordicTrack, which helped the company to double its sales of cross country skiing machines through television and direct mail advertising.

As CML continued to grow in size, reaching sales of $283 million in 1987, the scope of the company's operations made it difficult to continue searching out small companies that might make good investment prospects. To counter this difficulty,

CML developed a "farm team," late in 1987. This special division was assigned to seek out acquisition targets among small businesses earning about $3 million a year and investigate and develop them.

Despite these efforts, the potential for a little company to contribute significantly to the growth of CML, whose annual revenues had reached $326 million by 1988, was small. To offset this fact, CML announced in 1988 that it would also begin to fund a select number of marketing concepts, effectively floating start-up companies for a trial period. It's first experiment in this area involved an American designer named Lillian August. CML hoped that her designs would compete successfully with the lucrative British Laura Ashley franchise.

By 1989, CML's success and the debt it had taken on in the late 1980s to finance its acquisitions had attracted the interest of corporate stock speculators. In June 1989, one such corporate raider, Irwin Jacobs, bought 14 percent of the company's stock and announced that he might seek to take over the company. This threat forced CML to take defensive measures and maximize its financial health by selling off its less successful businesses.

In August 1989, CML's leaders announced that the company would undergo a radical restructuring which would halve its size. Four poorly performing units, Gokey's, SyberVision, Carroll Reed, and Boston Whaler, were sold. SyberVision's products fit poorly with the corporate profile CML was trying to build. Carroll Reed, with 54 stores, had suffered from low profitability for years. Boston Whaler, which had recently laid off one-fifth of its workforce and closed a plant in Rockland, Massachusetts, was sold for $30 million to Reebok International in August 1989. In addition, Britches' unprofitable women's stores were closed.

CML also announced that it would spend $36 million to buy the remaining shares of NordicTrack, giving the company an estimated net loss for the year of $13 to $17 million. With these moves, CML became the owner of three main units: NordicTrack, Britches of Georgetowne, and The Nature Company, as its other, smaller companies had been pared away over the years. The company planned to concentrate its energy on specialty store and mail-order retailing.

CML entered the 1990s with this new focus and an even more sizable debt, brought about through the company's prolonged battle with Jacobs, which did not come to an end until April 1990. Centering on the products of NordicTrack, CML announced that it would situate itself as a "wellness" company, stressing health and environmental awareness in the coming decade. As part of this push, the company planned to open NordicTrack fitness centers in shopping malls around the country.

This new direction proved to be in sync with the tenor of the times, and CML's profits, driven largely by the strong growth of NordicTrack, grew steadily. By the end of 1990, NordicTrack profits accounted for more than 90 percent of CML's overall earnings. On the strength of NordicTrack's earnings, CML was able to steadily reduce its debt.

By 1992, a quarter of NordicTrack's earnings were derived from retail outlets in malls, and the company had introduced new products, such as fitness chairs and body building machines, to supplement its cross country skiing machines. These products were also sold in a second chain of stores, called NordicSport by NordicTrack, which featured products with sleek styling to appeal to younger customers. NordicTrack had also developed a third line of less expensive machines, called ExerScience, that were sold through catalogues and television shopping channels.

In an effort to develop additional products, two CML executives traveled to Russia in the spring of 1993 to talk with people there about marketing products based on technology created for the Soviet Olympic and space programs. The company's efforts to develop new products were driven by the fact that NordicTrack's patent on the device that made its ski machines unique expired in 1994.

By May 1993, NordicTrack's success had spawned a number of imitators. In that month, CML won a $1 million settlement in a suit against a competitor, CSA, Inc., charging copyright infringement. By the middle of 1993, 43 stores and 45 mall kiosks selling NordicTrack's products had been opened nationwide. In the fall of that year, NordicTrack's first European store made its debut.

CML also moved to shore up the profits of its other divisions in 1993. Although Britches had shown erratic results for years, efforts to control costs had begun to show results, and the company ended 1993 with sales up 12 percent. The Nature Company, CML's third unit, forged an alliance with the National Geographic Society to market products with this prestigious imprimatur. In addition, in February 1993, CML added Smith & Hawken, a specialty garden retailer, to The Nature Company's franchise. CML believed that gardening, with its trendy ecological appeal, would grow in popularity as the American population continued to age.

As CML moved into the mid-1990s, it relied on the continuing strong popularity of NordicTrack for its robust financial health. If this market remained strong, CML appeared well situated to prosper along with it. If, however, the vogue for NordicTrack products proved to be a mere fad, CML would be obligated to re-imagine itself once again, as it had done twice before in its 25-year history, to preserve its status as a successful and growing venture.

Principal Subsidiaries: Britches of Georgetowne; The Nature Company; NordicTrack.

Further Reading:

Angrist, Stanley W., "It's All in the Earn-Out," *Forbes,* April 25, 1988.
Biddle, Frederic M., "The Profit Machine, " *Boston Globe,* June 8, 1993.
Bushnell, Davis, "Acton's CML Group Bullish on Itself after Shakeup," *Boston Sunday Globe,* June 3, 1990.
Dormer, Jean, "Former Harvard Prof Takes Aim at Middle-Aged Consumer," *Comprehensive Report on Industry and Economics in Central Middlesex County,* February 27, 1986.
Grisanti, Christopher, "One-Time Harvard Teacher Builds Group of Firms by Leaving His Managers Alone," *Wall Street Journal.*

Livingstone, Richard N., "Managing Leisure Markets at CML," *New Englander,* February 1973.

Lynch, Peter, "A Fad with Staying Power," *Worth,* April 1993.

Machlis, Sharon, "When Yuppies Grow Up, CML Will Be Waiting," *Middlesex News,* January 27, 1985.

McGlaughlin, Mark, "In Successful Acquisition Strategy, CML Asks about Lifestyles before It Acts," *New England Business,* March 21, 1988.

Mehegan, David, "CML Group to Sell 3 of Its 6 Subsidiaries," *Boston Globe,* August 3, 1989.

Rowan, Geoffrey, "CML Group Seems to Thrive on Diet of Well-Timed Acquisitions," *Boston Herald,* June 29, 1986.

—Elizabeth Rourke

Coach Leatherware

516 West 34th Street
New York, New York 10001
U.S.A.
(212) 594-1850
Fax: (212) 629-2602

Wholly Owned Subsidiary of the Sara Lee Corporation
Incorporated: 1941
Employees: 2,000
Sales: $150 million
SICs: 3171 Women's Handbags & Purses; 3172 Personal
    Leather Goods Nec; 2387 Apparel Belts

Coach Leatherware is a prestige marketer of handbags, brief-cases, luggage, and accessories. The company made its reputation selling sturdy leather purses in unchanging, traditional, classic styles. In the mid-1980s, the couple who had built the business and its solid reputation sold Coach to a much larger conglomerate, the Sara Lee Corporation, which set about expanding the market and profits of the company. Throughout the late 1980s and early 1990s, Coach steadily increased the number of products it made, as well as the number of outlets distributing them around the world, and its revenues grew exponentially.

Coach was founded in 1941 as a family-run workshop based in a loft on the edge of Manhattan's garment district. The company started with just six leather workers who made small leather goods, primarily wallets and billfolds, by hand. In 1946, Miles Cahn, a lifelong New Yorker, came to work for the company. By 1950, he was running the factory for its owners. The company's employees, members of Local 1 of the Pocketbook and Novelty Workers Union, continued to manufacture billfolds throughout the 1950s, producing small profits for the small concern.

By 1960, Cahn had taken notice of the distinctive properties of the leather used to make baseball gloves. With wear and abrasion, the leather in a glove became soft and supple. Following this model, Cahn devised a way of processing leather to make it strong, soft, flexible, and deep-toned in color, as it absorbed dye well. At his wife Lillian's suggestion, a number of women's handbags were designed to supplement the factory's low-margin wallet production. The purses, given the brand name Coach, were made of sturdy cowhide, in which the grain of the leather

could still be seen, instead of the thin leather pasted over cardboard that was used for most women's handbags at the time. This innovation marked the company's entry into the field of classic, long-lasting, luxury women's handbags that Coach would come to define.

In 1961, after more than a decade of running the leather workshop, the Cahns borrowed money to buy out the factory's owners and take possession of Coach. Throughout the next decades, Coach produced solid handbags in an assortment of basic styles. For the most part, the company steered clear of fast-moving trends, opting instead for traditional, conservative elegance and quality. Gradually, high-priced Coach products developed a reputation and a certain cachet. In the late 1960s, as fashion changed radically, Coach deviated somewhat from its traditional product line, introducing additional models that were designed to complement trendier styles in clothing. In 1969, the company began to market items such as a structured bucket bag, which was produced for only one season, and a fringe "shimmy" bag.

By the early 1980s, the Coach plant occupied four floors of a building on West 34th Street. The company was manufacturing purses, briefcases, billfolds, and belts, using skilled laborers, many of whom had emigrated from Argentina. Paying their workers wages that were a dollar or more higher than rates in other factories, the Cahns enjoyed good labor relations with their employees, which allowed them to produce a steady flow of Coach products.

In the late 1970s and early 1980s, Coach took two steps to diversify its channels of distribution. Under a new vice-president for special products, the company began a mail-order business, and also began to open its own specialty stores, to sell Coach products outside a department store setting. Sales of Coach products grew steadily throughout this period, until demand began to out-strip supply. Department stores were selling all the Coach bags that the company could produce, and by the early 1980s it had become necessary to ration the products to various vendors. Despite the potential for vast expansion of their market share, the Cahns continued to run their business in the same way that they always had. They had little desire to move their factory out of its urban Manhattan setting, to a place where rents and taxes might be lower, space more readily available, and wages cheaper. In addition, they did not want to change their methods of production so that goods could be made more quickly, at the expense of quality or workmanship. Instead, they continued to run their business on a personal level, maintaining first-name relationships with many of their workers, and inviting department store buyers from New York to tour their factory, to observe the craftsmanship that went into each Coach bag.

In 1983, the Cahns purchased a 300-acre dairy farm in Vermont, as a weekend diversion from their business in New York. Although the property was intended to provide a vacation home and retirement destination, the Cahns began to raise goats and market goat cheese under the brand name "Coach Farms" shortly after buying the farm. By 1985, they were commuting twice a week between Vermont and New York. In the summer of that year, after determining that none of their three children had any desire to take over the family leatherware business, the Cahns decided to sell Coach.

In July of 1985, they cemented an agreement with the Sara Lee Corporation, which also sold foodstuffs and hosiery. In return for a sum reported to be around $30 million, the conglomerate took control of the company's factory, its six boutiques, and its flagship store on Madison Avenue in New York. Sara Lee promised that it would continue to operate Coach in the way in which it had always been run. At the time of the sale, the Cahns split $1 million of the proceeds with 200 longtime employees, on the basis of their seniority.

Under its new owners, the company prepared for a rapid expansion. The basic strategy for this expansion was to add to the number of products that bore the Coach name, and to increase the number of customers buying these goods. Accordingly, the company added several new styles of handbag in an updated classics line, and also began a major expansion of its channels of distribution. In early 1986, new boutiques were opened in Macy's stores in New York and San Francisco, and in two Bamberger's stores. Additional Coach outlets were under construction in stores in Denver and Seattle, and agreements had been reached to open similar boutiques within other major department stores later in the year. And Coach opened its own stores in malls in New York, New Jersey, Texas, and California. By November, the company was operating 12 stores, along with nearly 50 boutiques within larger department stores. The company projected that the expansion would boost sales for 1986 to $25 million, a gain of 45 percent over the previous year.

A significant part of sales was expected to come from the newly-introduced Coach Lightweights line of products, which featured lighter weight leather and bags with new shapes. This line was intended to broaden the company's customer base by appealing to women who lived in the South and West, where warmer weather made lightweight handbags more desirable. The Lightweight line featured handbags in smaller sizes, for ease of access, and lighter spring colors, such as taupe, light brown, and navy. This line quickly came to comprise 15 percent of the company's overall sales.

To keep up with growing demand for Coach products, the company doubled its work force, leased additional space for factory operations, and expanded the work week to six days. Despite these measures, however, by the fall of 1987, Coach was again unable to meet all orders for its goods, and the company began to seek additional room for expansion. In addition, to better control the circumstances under which its products were sold, Coach slashed the number of department stores retailing its goods by 50 percent. Despite continued strong demand, the company did not increase its prices to keep pace with a sharp rise in the cost of leather. By the end of 1987, Coach had nearly doubled its revenues, despite its reduction of retailers and the increase in the price of leather.

In December of 1987, Coach opened a new flagship store on Madison Avenue, in New York. The two-story store, with a marble and mahogany interior, featured an atrium, and a gallery of leather art, as well as the full range of Coach products. The company expected to sell $5 million worth of handbags in the store's first year.

Coach solved its production problem by opening a plant near Miami, Florida, where its Lightweight collection was manufactured, in 1988. The plant's production supplied 22 free-standing stores and 300 different retailers, making Coach products available in more than 1,000 locations. Although the traditional line and the Lightweights products were emphasized, Coach further expanded its offerings to include more business items for men and women. Among the new products were briefcases, wallets, and diaries.

Coach's first non-leather product was introduced in 1988. Silk scarves, sold in four designs that related to leather goods, were planned to complement the other Coach products. Each of the 36-inch silk squares was manufactured in Italy, and priced at $60. Although the company estimated that first year sales of this line, which also grew to include men's ties and suspenders, would reach $2 million, the products were eventually discontinued, after it was determined that their equestrian designs, featuring bridles and stirrups, made them look too much like products from a Coach competitor, Hermès.

Coach took its first steps overseas in 1988. The company had long noted that many of the customers in its New York store were foreign tourists, and Coach executives believed that this indicated that demand abroad justified international expansion. The company began by opening Coach boutiques in England and Japan, setting up one outlet in Harrod's department store in London, and five in Mitsukoshi stores in Tokyo and other Japanese locations. These stores carried a full line of Coach products, and mimicked the look of Coach stores in the United States, with mahogany and brass fixtures and marble floors. The company planned to train foreign sales staff and hoped to take advantage of the low international value of the dollar to boost sales through lower prices.

As Coach continued its international push in 1989, opening a free-standing store on Sloane Street in London, company sales had quintupled to $100 million in a period of four years and the number of company stores had grown to 40. Coach established its first store in Continental Europe, with a 500-square-foot outlet in Stuttgart, Germany. By 1990, the Coach push to enter international markets had created 19 in-store shops in Japanese Mitsukoshi department stores, with six more slated to open in the next six months. Coach solidified its position in the Japanese market by renewing its agreement with Mitsukoshi, making it the exclusive distributor of Coach products in Japan. In addition, Coach joined with another company to open a boutique in a Singapore shopping area, and Coach opened a store in Taipei, Taiwan. With international sales making up ten percent of the company's revenues, Coach saw the Pacific basin as a key area for further growth.

The company's Far East push was driven by the popularity of Coach goods with Asian tourists in New York, and also by the belief that the company's understated style, lacking in logos or obvious status symbols, was beginning to supplant the vogue for flashy designer goods. To support sales of its products in the Far East, Coach began an advertising campaign to stress the ways in which Coach expressed the American spirit.

Coach's expansion overseas was coupled with domestic expansion, and production again was increased. In addition to its new facility in Florida, the company moved its New York area operations from Manhattan to Carlstadt, New Jersey.

Coach's success in expanding its brand awareness had caused other manufactures to imitate the company's trademark styles and shapes in their own products. To prevent this infringement of the company's unique designs, Coach sued a number of other manufacturers to stop them from imitating Coach styles. In 1990, the company won a suit in federal court against several other companies, including Ann Taylor and Laura Leather Goods. The ruling awarded the company damages for trade dress infringement.

Coach sales continued to grow in the early 1990s. By May 1991, revenues had increased by more than a fifth over the previous year, and annual sales had reached $150 million. The company continued to broaden its product line, while retaining the qualities identified with its prestigious brand name. Overall, Coach planned a dramatic shift in its identity in the 1990s. "We're going for positioning as Coach the brand, as opposed to Coach the leather company," the company's president told *Crain's New York Business.* "I can't see a limit to Coach's growth in the foreseeable future."

To bolster that growth, Coach hired a designer to lead a 16-person product development department, to create new objects that could be marketed under the Coach name. In its women's line, the company sought to introduce products in more fashionable colors, without watering down the Coach reputation. In this way, the company hoped to overcome the built-in drawback to high quality and timeless styling, which was that customers rarely needed to replace a product. It launched a line of desk accessories, and an all-leather travel collection was introduced.

In addition, the company began to sell a line of goods for men that included suspenders and socks. This fast-moving category had grown to provide 40 percent of the company's sales. Coach capped off its recent growth in products for men by opening two Coach for Business stores, which were devoted specifically to products for men, on Madison Avenue in Manhattan and in Boston. With these stores, the company hoped to shift its image, repositioning itself as a full-range accessory maker, rather than merely a handbag manufacturer.

Coach announced that it would move more aggressively into the leather accessories market, and also try to market its products to younger customers in 1991. To do so, the company hired a new, young advertising agency, which designed a campaign featuring descendants of famous Americans using Coach products, with the theme, "An American Legacy."

By early 1992, Coach had expanded its number of stores worldwide to 53, and had enhanced its line of men's and women's socks, to further exploit the appeal of the Coach brand name. Later that year, the company added gift items, including picture frames and belts. In the fall, Coach increased the scope of its handbag line, introducing the Sheridan collection, which featured textured, treated leather that would not burnish like other Coach items but was also more scratch resistant; and the Camden collection, which was styled with brass accents.

Coach stepped up its catalogue sales effort in the fall of 1992, mailing 10 million mail-order brochures to former customers and likely prospects. The company's catalogue operations, though small, were the most profitable of its branches. Coach turned to its mail-order operations to test market its latest innovation in November 1992, when the company began to offer leather outerwear. Providing five styles for men and women, made of soft, water-proof leather, the outerwear was joined by fabric luggage, another departure from Coach tradition, as the company tried to push the boundaries of its identity even further.

As Coach broadened its product offerings, it also broadened the variety of its handbags. Coach moved away from dark, staid colors to brightly-hued bags, introducing the Manhattan collection in the spring of 1993. To keep up with demand for this wide variety of new products, Coach expanded its manufacturing activities to Puerto Rico.

As Coach moved into the mid-1990s, the company appeared poised to continue its rapid growth. Supported by the resources of a large conglomerate as its corporate parent, and holding a trade name with a strong reputation for prestige and quality, the company was well-positioned to make good on its assets, provided that its push to expand and diversify did not dilute the value of the Coach identity, built by a line of traditional, classic, sturdy goods.

Further Reading:

Berman, Phyllis, "Goat Cheese, Anyone?" *Forbes,* September 18, 1989.
Fallon, James, "Coach Opens First Overseas Store in London," *Women's Wear Daily,* May 19, 1989.
Gault, Ylonda, "Buyers Riding Coach; Leather Maker Growing," *Crain's New York Business,* May 6, 1991.
Newman, Jill, "Coach Hits New Heights," *Women's Wear Daily,* January 8, 1988.
——, "Coach's International Approach," *Women's Wear Daily,* September 21, 1990.
Strom, Stephanie, "A Women's Chain Beckons to Men," *New York Times,* July 24, 1991.

—Elizabeth Rourke

 **Coca-Cola Bottling Co. Consolidated**

Coca-Cola Bottling Co. Consolidated

P.O. Box 31487
Charlotte, North Carolina 28231
U.S.A.
(704) 551-4400
Fax: (704) 551-4672

Public Company
Incorporated: 1980
Employees: 5,000
Sales: $655.78 million
Stock Exchanges: NASDAQ
SICs: 2086 Bottled & Canned Soft Drinks

Coca-Cola Bottling Co. Consolidated is the second largest Coca-Cola bottler in the United States. This manufacturer, marketer, and distributor of soft drinks, primarily products of the Coca-Cola Company, is the local Coke bottler for almost 15.5 million people and 120,000 retail outlets in 12 southeastern states.

Coca-Cola Bottling Co. Consolidated can trace its history to 1902, when three North Carolina entrepreneurs—J. B. Harrison, J. Luther Snyder, and J. P. Gibbons—set out to bring bottled Coca-Cola to the Carolinas. Before these pioneers got to work, the thirsty had to travel to drugstore soda fountains to enjoy a Coke. In the early days of bottled Coke, production workers washed refillable bottles by hand, used manually operated bottling machines to fill them, corked them by hand, and sold them from horse-drawn carriages. These efforts helped build a thirst for Coke that survived the Great Depression and the sugar rationing of World War I and World War II. By the early 1970s, hand-washed bottles and horse-drawn carts had given way to sophisticated bottling and distribution operations. The offspring of the first North Carolina bottling companies were beginning to consolidate and expand their territories.

Coke Consolidated traces its more recent history to 1972, when the Charlotte Coca-Cola Bottling Co. renamed itself the Coca-Cola Bottling Company of Mid-Carolinas and began trading its stock publicly. The following year, it acquired the Coca-Cola bottlers in Greensboro, Winston-Salem, Raleigh, and Hamlet. The fast-growing concern became Coca-Cola Bottling Co. Consolidated, which was incorporated in Delaware on May 14, 1980. James Johnson, who started working summers at the

Statesville Coca-Cola Bottling Company when he was 11, became president and chief executive officer of both Charlotte Coca-Cola Bottling Company and the Carolina Coin Caterers Corporation in 1969. Johnson saw the new Coke Consolidated through its incorporation as president and CEO; from 1980 to 1987, he was vice chairman of the board and director of public affairs.

In 1983, chairman J. Frank Harrison, Jr., hired Marvin Griffin, from Coca-Cola USA to be Coke Consolidated's chief executive. Under Griffin's leadership, Coke Consolidated began to expand its territory more aggressively. In 1984, it acquired three Georgia bottlers: Federal Coca-Cola Bottling Co. in Columbus, the Pageland Coca-Cola Bottling Works, and Waycross-Douglas Coca-Cola Bottling. The following year, Coke Consolidated purchased Wometco Coca-Cola Bottling Co. for $300 million, thereby acquiring new Coke franchise territories in Alabama, Tennessee, Virginia, and West Virginia. The sale of Consolidated Coin Caterers Corp. and 1.5 million new shares helped finance the Wometco purchase. In 1986 Coke Consolidated added bottling companies in Florida, Georgia, Tennessee, and Virginia. In 1987 and 1988, the company sold its Canadian subsidiary and added new territories in Tennessee, Kentucky, and North Carolina.

Several outside factors hurt Coke Consolidated's profitability in the mid-1980s. First, the introduction of New Coke in April 1985—and the public's emphatic assertion that it preferred the old Coke—brought big losses to Coke bottlers across the country. Coke Consolidated suffered along with everyone else. The same summer, the Coca-Cola Company began marketing a new line of clothes under the Coke label. Because the new line was manufactured abroad, it created a public-relations nightmare for Coke Consolidated, a company located in the heart of the depressed textile communities of the Carolinas. Coca-Cola responded to consumer protests with a $5 million donation to the textile and garment industries' Crafted With Pride campaign, but the damage was done. A $5 million settlement in a lawsuit brought by a local bottler also cut into profits. Heavy discounting was unable to raise profits. In April 1987, Griffin was out as CEO.

The difficulties did not impede Coke Consolidated's expansion. In 1989, the company obtained the Coca-Cola Bottling Company of West Virginia, Inc., from The Coca-Cola Company in exchange for 1.1 million shares of common stock and about $4 million. The same year it added the territories of Dickson, Tennessee, and Laurel, Mississippi. Coke Consolidated continued to acquire territories in North Carolina, Tennessee, and Mississippi in 1990 and 1991, including the franchise rights for Barq's and Dr. Pepper in the Jackson, Tennessee, territory.

Coke Consolidated was involved in two price-fixing cases in the late 1980s, winning a major decision in one and arranging a novel settlement in the other. In the first, a major antitrust case, the company was one of several accused of price-fixing by Sewell Plastics, Inc., an Atlanta company that pioneered the development of two-liter bottles for soft drinks. In 1986, Sewell sued Coca-Cola and bottlers in North Carolina, South Carolina, Georgia, Virginia, Tennessee, and Alabama for $17 million, alleging that Southeastern Container Inc., a cooperative the bottlers created in 1982 with the help of Coca-Cola, violated antitrust laws by setting prices for the plastic bottles that the cooperative produced. The U.S. District Court in Charlotte, North Carolina, dismissed the suit, ruling that the formation of the cooperative had actually increased competition and resulted in lower prices to consumers. In September 1990, a federal appeals court upheld the lower court's decision. In February 1991, the U.S. Supreme Court declined to renew the suit.

In a smaller price-fixing case, Coke Consolidated apparently became the first bottler to use coupons in a settlement. The West Virginia attorney general filed a price-fixing complaint against the company, alleging that it conspired to fix soft-drink prices from 1982 to 1985. Coke Consolidated, which said it acquired the offending bottler in 1985, agreed to settle the case by paying $50,000 to the state and attaching $50,000 worth of 20-cent coupons to two-liter bottles of Diet Coke, Diet Sprite, and Caffeine-Free Diet Coke. It distributed the bottles in areas of West Virginia where the alleged violations occurred.

In late 1991, analysts touted Coke Consolidated as a good stock bargain. Although a price war with PepsiCo's wholly owned bottling operation kept earnings down, Coke Consolidated per-share earnings were up after losing a cumulative $5.54 between 1986 and 1990. Analyst Joseph Frazzano told *Forbes* that although Coke Consolidated's stock was undervalued based on its cash flow, it was no target for an unfriendly takeover raid: the company had 9.2 million outstanding shares, Coca-Cola Co. held 30 percent of the equity, and the Harrison family controlled 86 percent of the votes.

The acquisition of Sunbelt Coca-Cola in 1991 for approximately $15.2 million in cash and company debt helped Coke Consolidated grow by 35 percent in 1991 and 1992. Before the acquisition, Coke Consolidated was the fourth-largest Coca-Cola bottler, with annual sales of $400 million. Adding Sunbelt, number eight with annual sales of $200 million, vaulted Coke Consolidated to second, behind only Coca-Cola Enterprises, Inc., an Atlanta company owned by Coca-Cola Co. By taking on the Charleston, South Carolina bottler, Coke Consolidated continued its growth strategy of purchasing bottlers in adjoining territories.

In 1993, a joint venture with the Coca-Cola Co. gave Coke Consolidated management responsibility for Wilmington Coca-Cola Bottling Works, Inc., Coastal Coca-Cola Bottling Co., and Eastern Carolina Bottling Company. Under the terms of the venture, named the Piedmont Coca-Cola Bottling Partnership, Coke Consolidated acquired new sales centers and territories in parts of South Carolina, North Carolina, and Virginia. The company reported that the joint venture would increase sales by 15 percent and reduce the company's outstanding debt by about 20 percent. In addition, it gave Coke Consolidated control of more than 90 percent of the territory in the Carolinas.

In the late 1980s, Coke Consolidated invested in advanced computer systems to provide management with timely and relevant data. All its route salespeople received handheld computers to record sales transactions. That innovation allowed salespeople to transmit the information via phone lines and, sometimes, by satellite, to the company's Charlotte computer center at the end of the business day. The following morning, managers could pull up freshly compiled volume, sales mix, selling price, and gross margin information. Another information innovation, the Lab Management System, allowed the company to store and analyze information on its extensive quality assurance program. Its computer system, Norand, also enabled Coke Consolidated to incorporate new acquisitions into the system almost as soon as it acquired them. The sales centers of the companies involved in the Piedmont Partnership were all operating on Norand in less than two months.

Other Coke Consolidated innovations have come in the areas of customer service and sales. A 24-hour toll-free number allowed customers to call the Consumer Response Center with questions and comments and provided information for the company to use in determining trends and consumer concerns. The "Cold Drink" organization made Coca-Cola products available in factories, entertainment venues, recreation areas, hotels, offices, and schools for on-site consumption. The "fast-lane merchandiser" put cold Cokes at check-out lines in retail outlets to encourage impulse buying.

Coke Consolidated's close relations with the Coca-Cola Co. have involved marketing collaborations as well as business opportunities. In the early 1990s, Coke Consolidated began working with Coke on the Mello Yello 500 NASCAR race at Charlotte Motor Speedway. In the weeks before the race, point-of-sale displays, visits by show cars and drivers to retail outlets, and tailored advertising drew attention to the race and boosted sales. On race day, 180,000 fans at the Speedway and millions more at home would see the event and the related advertising.

Coke Consolidated earned a record $14.8 million in 1993 on net sales of nearly $687 million, compared to a loss of $118.3 million (attributed to mandatory accounting changes) on sales of almost $656 million in 1992. The net income applicable to common shareholders was $1.60 per share. The company attributed the improvement in earnings to the 5 percent boost in revenues, in addition to lower packaging costs, improved operating efficiencies, and the tax and financing cost benefits of a refinancing of preferred stock in late 1992.

These results capped a five-year period during which the company's sales and operating cash flow nearly doubled, from $389 million in 1989 to 1993's $687 million. Income from operations during the period increased by approximately 20 percent each year, from $23.8 million to $57.3 million, and adjusted earnings per share (a measure that takes into account earnings per share plus amortization per share) grew by 30 percent annually. The return to shareholders during the five-year period averaged 13 percent.

Coca-Cola Consolidated, a *Fortune* 500 company, produced more than 343,000 cases of soda per day from its four manufacturing centers—Charlotte/Snyder Production Center, North Carolina; Roanoke, Virginia; Nashville, Tennessee; and Mobile, Alabama. From company headquarters in Charlotte, North Carolina, president and CEO James L. Moore oversaw 10 division offices, 74 distribution centers, and the work of approximately 5,000 employees. The company could boast steady growth, solid family ownership, and a strong relationship with the owner of perhaps the most recognizable brand name in the world. As it looked ahead, Coke Consolidated was confident that it would continue to generate volume growth from within and add new customers through the acquisition of additional territories.

Principal Subsidiaries: Columbus Coca-Cola Bottling Co.; Coca-Cola Bottling Co. of Nashville, Inc.; Dickson Coca-Cola Bottling Co.; Coca-Cola Bottling Works of Columbia, Tenn.; Coca-Cola Bottling Co. of Roanoke, Inc.; Coca-Cola Bottling Co. of Mobile, Inc.; Albany CCBC Inc.; Panama City Coca-Cola Bottling Co.; Case Advertising Inc.; CC Beverage Packing, Inc.; Tennessee Soft Drink Production Company; Coca-Cola Bottling Company of West Virginia, Inc.; Coca-Cola Bottling Company of Jackson, Inc.; Mrs. Sullivan's Pies, Inc.; Jackson Acquisitions, Inc.; Sunbelt Coca-Cola Bottling Company, Inc.; Palmetto Bottling Company; Fayetteville Coca-Cola Bottling Company; Coca-Cola Bottling Co. Affiliated, Inc.

Further Reading:

"Coca-Cola Bottling Consolidated: Concern Is Near Completion of Sunbelt Coca-Cola Deal," *Wall Street Journal,* December 19, 1991, p. A16.

Cone, Edward, "Are We There Yet?" *Forbes,* March 9, 1987, p. 110.

Kenneson, Kim, "Court Upholds Ruling for Bottlers," *Raleigh, North Carolina, News and Observer,* September 6, 1990, p. C7; "Coca-Cola Bottler's Deal Would Make It 2nd Largest," *Raleigh, North Carolina, News and Observer,* November 12, 1991, p. D1.

McCarthy, Michael J., "Coke Bottler to Use Coupons to Settle Price-Fixing Case," *Wall Street Journal,* January 18, 1990.

Sfiligoj, Eric, "For Coke Consolidated, Quality Is Job One," *Beverage World,* April 1992, p. 58.

"U.S. Supreme Court Won't Revive Suit Against Coca-Cola, Southeast Bottlers," *Raleigh, North Carolina, News and Observer,* February 20, 1991, p. C6.

"Where the Fizz Is," *Forbes,* October 28, 1991, p. 219.

—David B. Rice

The Coca-Cola Company

310 North Avenue, NW
Atlanta, Georgia 30313
U.S.A.
(404) 676-2121
Fax: (404) 676-6792

Public Company
Incorporated: 1892
Employees: 31,300
Sales: $13.96 billion
Stock Exchanges: New York Boston Cincinnati Midwest
   Pacific Philadelphia Frankfurt Zurich Geneva Bern Basel
   Lausanne
SICs: 2087 Flavoring Extracts and Syrups, Nec; 2037 Frozen
   Fruits and Vegetables; 2033 Canned Fruits and Vegetables

The Coca-Cola Company has consistently ranked among *Fortune* magazine's five most admired companies and, with a market value of $58 billion, stood as the fourth-largest company in America and the largest consumer goods company in 1993. That year, after over a century in business, the firm topped $2 billion in annual net income for the first time in its history. Coca-Cola's red and white trademark is probably the best-known brand symbol on earth; the firm's flagship product holds 57 percent of the worldwide cola segment. The company's family of brands held an overwhelming 44 percent of the global soft drink market and were advertised in over 80 different languages by the last decade of the twentieth century. Coca-Cola also operated the world's most pervasive distribution system, offering the Coca-Cola brand in over 195 countries worldwide. The company's success has been credited to proficiency in four basic areas: consumer marketing, infrastructure (production and distribution), product packaging, and customer (or vendor) marketing.

The inventor of Coca-Cola, Dr. John Styth Pemberton, came to Atlanta from Columbus, Georgia, in 1869. Since 1885, when he set up a chemical laboratory and went into the patent medicine business, Atlanta has been the headquarters of the Coca-Cola Company. Pemberton invented such products as Indian Queen hair dye, Gingerine, and Triplex liver pills. In 1886, he concocted a mixture of sugar, water, and extracts of the coca leaf and the kola nut. He added caffeine to the resulting syrup so that it could be marketed as a headache remedy. Through his re-

search Pemberton arrived at the conclusion that this medication was capable of relieving indigestion and exhaustion in addition to being refreshing and exhilarating.

The doctor and his business partners could not decide whether to market the mixture as a medicine or to extol its flavor for its own sake, so they did both. In *Coca-Cola: An Illustrated History,* Pat Watters cited a Coca-Cola label from 1887 which stated that the drink, ''makes not only a delicious ... and invigorating beverage ... but a valuable Brain Tonic and a cure for all nervous affections.'' The label also claimed that ''the peculiar flavor of Coca-Cola delights every palate; it is dispensed from the soda fountain in the same manner as any fruit syrup.'' The first newspaper advertisement for Coca-Cola appeared exactly three weeks after the first batch of syrup was produced, and the famous trademark, white Spenserian script on a red background, made its debut at about the same time.

Coca-Cola was not, however, immediately successful. During its first year in existence, Pemberton and his partners spent $73.96 advertising their unique beverage, but made only $50.00 from sales. The combined pressures of poor business and ill health led Pemberton to sell two-thirds of his business in early 1888. By 1891, a successful druggist named Asa G. Candler owned the entire enterprise. It had cost him $2,300. Dr. Pemberton, who died three years earlier, was never to know the enormous success his invention would have in the coming century.

Asa Candler, a religious man with excellent business sense, infused the enterprise with his personality. Candler became a notable philanthropist, incidentally associating the name of Coca-Cola with social awareness. He was also an integral part of Atlanta both as a citizen and as a leader. Candler endowed Emory University and its Wesley Memorial Hospital with more than $8 million. Indeed, the University could not have come into existence without his aid. In 1907, he prevented a real estate panic in Atlanta by purchasing $1 million worth of homes and reselling them to people of moderate income at affordable prices. During World War I, Candler helped to avert a cotton crisis by using his growing wealth to stabilize the market. After he stepped down as the president of Coca-Cola, he became the mayor of Atlanta and introduced such reforms as motorizing the fire department and augmenting the water system with his private funds.

Under Candler's leadership, which spanned a 26-year period, the Coca-Cola Company grew quickly. Between 1888 and 1907, the factory and offices of the business were moved to eight different buildings in order to keep up with the company's growth and expansion. As head of the company, Candler was most concerned with the quality and promotion of his product. He was particularly concerned with production of the syrup, which was boiled in kettles over a furnace and stirred by hand with large wooden paddles. He improved Pemberton's formula with the help of a chemist, a pharmacist, and a prescriptionist. In 1901, responding to complaints about the presence of minute amounts of cocaine in the Coca-Cola syrup, Candler devised the means to remove all traces of the substance. By 1905, the syrup was completely free of cocaine.

In 1892, the newly incorporated Coca-Cola Company allocated $11,401 for advertising its drink. Advertising materials included signs, free sample tickets, and premiums such as ornate soda fountain urns, clocks, and stained-glass lampshades, all with the words "Coca-Cola" engraved upon them. These early advertising strategies initiated the most extensive promotional campaign for one product in history. Salesmen traveled the entire country selling the company's syrup, and by 1895 Coca-Cola was being sold and consumed in every state in America. Soon it was available in some Canadian cities and in Honolulu, and plans were underway for its introduction into Mexico. By the time Asa Candler left the company, Coke had also been sold in Cuba, Jamaica, Germany, Bermuda, Puerto Rico, the Philippines, France, and England.

An event which had an enormous impact on the future and very nature of the company was the agreement made between Candler and two young lawyers that allowed them to bottle and sell Coca-Cola throughout the United States: the first bottling franchise had been established. Three years later, in 1904, the one-millionth gallon of Coca-Cola syrup had been sold. In 1916, the now universally recognized, uniquely-shaped Coke bottle was invented. The management of all company advertising was assigned to the D'Arcy Advertising Agency, and the advertising budget had ballooned to $1 million by 1911. During this time, all claims for the medicinal properties of Coca-Cola were quietly dropped from its advertisements.

World War I and the ensuing sugar rationing measures slowed the growth of the company, but the pressure of coal rations led Candler's son, Charles Howard, to invent a process whereby the sugar and water could be mixed without using heat. This process saved the cost of fuel, relieved the company of the need for a boiler, and saved a great amount of time since there was no need for the syrup to go through a cooling period. The company continued to use this method of mixing into the 1990s.

Although Candler was fond of his company, he became disillusioned with it in 1916 and retired. One of the reasons for this decision was the new tax laws which, in Candler's words, did not allow for "the accumulation of surplus in excess of the amount necessary for profitable and safe conduct of our particular business." (It has also been suggested that Candler refused to implement the modernization of company facilities.)

Robert Winship Woodruff became president of the company in 1923 at the age of 33. His father had purchased it from the Candler family in 1919 for $25 million, and the company went public in the same year at $40 a share. After leaving college before graduation, Woodruff held various jobs, eventually becoming the Atlanta branch manager and then the vice-president of an Atlanta motor company, before becoming the president of Coca-Cola.

Having entered the company at a time when its affairs were quite tumultuous, Woodruff worked rapidly to improve Coca-Cola's financial condition. In addition to low sales figures in 1922, he had to face the problem of animosity toward the company on the part of the bottlers as a result of an imprudent sugar purchase that management had made. This raised the price of the syrup and angered the bottlers. Woodruff was aided in particular by two men, Harrison Jones and Harold Hirsch, who were adept at maintaining good relations between the company and its bottling franchises.

Woodruff set to work improving the sales department; he emphasized quality control, and began advertising and promotional campaigns that were far more sophisticated than those of the past. He established a research department that became a pioneering market research agency. He also worked hard to provide his customers with the latest in technological developments that would facilitate their selling Coca-Cola to the public, and he labored to increase efficiency at every step of the production process so as to raise the percentage of profit from every sale of Coca-Cola syrup.

Through the 1920s and 1930s such developments as the six-pack carton of Coke, which encouraged shoppers to purchase the drink for home consumption, coin-operated vending machines in the work place, and the cooler designed by John Stanton expanded the domestic market considerably. And, by the end of 1930, as a result of the company's quality control efforts, Coca-Cola tasted exactly the same everywhere.

Considered slightly eccentric, Woodruff was a fair employer and an admired philanthropist. In 1937, he donated $50,000 to Emory University for a cancer diagnosis and treatment center, and over the years gave more than $100 million to the clinic. He donated $8 million for the construction of the Atlanta Memorial Arts Center. Under his leadership the Coca-Cola Company pioneered such company benefits as group life insurance and group accident and health policies, and in 1948 introduced a retirement program.

Woodruff was to see the Coca-Cola Company through an era marked by important and varied events. Even during the Depression the company did not suffer thanks to Woodruff's cost cutting measures. When Prohibition was repealed, Coca-Cola continued to experience rising sales. However, it was World War II that catapulted Coca-Cola into the world market and made it one of America's first multinational companies.

Woodruff and Archie Lee of the D'Arcy Advertising Agency worked to equate Coca-Cola with the American way of life. Advertisements had, in Candler's era, been targeted at the wealthy population. In Woodruff's time the advertising was aimed at all Americans. By early 1950, blacks were featured in advertisements, and by the mid-1950s there was an increase in advertising targeted at other minority groups. Advertising never reflected the problems of the world, only the good and happy life. Radio advertising began in 1927, and through the years Coca-Cola sponsored many musical programs. During World War II, Woodruff announced that every man in uniform would be able to get a bottle of Coke for five cents no matter what the cost to the company. This was an extremely successful marketing maneuver, and provided Coke with good publicity. In 1943, at the request of General Eisenhower, Coca-Cola plants were set up near the fighting fronts in North Africa and eventually throughout Europe in order to help increase the morale of American soldiers. Thus, Coca-Cola was introduced into the world market.

Coke was available in Germany prior to the war, but its survival there during the war years was due to a man named Max Keith who kept the company going even when there was little Coca-Cola syrup available. Keith developed his own soft drink, using ingredients available to him, and called his beverage Fanta. By selling this beverage he kept the enterprise intact until after the war. When the war was over the company continued to market Fanta. By 1944, the Coca-Cola company had sold one billion gallons of syrup, by 1953 two billion gallons had been sold, and by 1969 the company had sold six billion gallons.

The years from the end of World War II to 1980 were years of extensive and rapid change. Although Woodruff stepped down officially in 1955, he still exerted a great amount of influence on the company over the coming years. There was a series of chairmen and presidents to follow before the next major figure, J. Paul Austin, took the helm in 1970; he was followed by Roberto Goizueta in 1981. In 1956, after 50 years with the D'Arcy Advertising Agency, the Coca-Cola Company turned its accounts over to McCann-Ericson and began enormous promotional campaigns. The decade of the 1950s was a time of the greatest European expansion for the company. During this decade Coca-Cola opened approximately fifteen to twenty plants a year throughout the world.

The company also began to diversify extensively, beginning in 1960, when the Minute Maid Corporation merged with Coca-Cola. Four years later the Duncan Foods Corporation also merged with the company. In 1969, Coca-Cola acquired the Belmont Springs Water Company, Inc., which produced natural spring water and processed water for commercial and home use. The following year the company purchased Aqua-Chem, Inc., producers of desalting machines and other such equipment, and in 1977 Coca-Cola acquired the Taylor Wines Company and other wineries. These last two companies were sold later under Goizueta's leadership.

In addition to its diversification program, the Coca-Cola Company also expanded its product line. Fanta became available in the United States during 1960 and was followed by the introduction of Sprite, Tab, and Fresca, along with diet versions of these drinks. One reason that Coca-Cola began to introduce new beverages during the 1960s was competition from Pepsi Cola, sold by PepsiCo. Pepsi's success also motivated the Coca-Cola Company to promote its beverage with the slogan "It's the Real Thing," a subtle, comparative form of advertising that the company had never before employed.

Things have not always run smoothly for Coca-Cola. When Coke was first introduced to France, the Communist party, as well as conservative vineyard owners, did what they could to get the product removed from the country. They were unsuccessful. Swiss breweries also felt threatened, and spread rumors about the caffeine content of the drink. More consequential was the Arab boycott in 1967 which significantly hindered the company's relations with Israel. In 1970, the company was involved in a scandal in the United States when an NBC documentary reported on the bad housing and working conditions of Minute Maid farm laborers in Florida. In response, the company established a program that improved the workers' situation. In 1977, it was discovered that Coca-Cola, for various reasons, had made $1.3 million in illegal payments over a period of six years, mostly to executives and government officials in foreign countries.

During the 1970s, under the direction of chairman J. Paul Austin and president J. Lucian Smith, Coca-Cola was intro-duced in Russia as well as in China. To enter the Chinese market, the company sponsored five scholarships for Chinese students at the Harvard Business School, and supported China's soccer and table-tennis teams. The beverage also became available in Egypt in 1979, after an absence there of 12 years. Austin strongly believed in free trade and opposed boycotts. He felt that business, in terms of international relations, should be used to improve national economies, and could be a strong deterrent to war. Under Austin, Coca-Cola also started technological and educational programs in the Third World countries in which it conducted business, introducing clean water technology and sponsoring sports programs in countries too poor to provide these benefits for themselves.

Austin's emphasis was on foreign expansion. Furthermore, under Austin's management the company became more specialized. Where Woodruff was aware of all facets of the company, Austin would delegate authority to various departments. For instance, he would give general approval to an advertising scheme, but would not review it personally. Smith was responsible for the everyday operations of the company, and Austin would, among other things, set policies, negotiate with foreign countries, and direct the company's relations with the U.S. government.

Roberto Goizueta became chairman in 1981, replacing Austin. Less than a year later he made two controversial decisions. First, he acquired Columbia Pictures for about $750 million in 1982. Goizueta thought that the entertainment field had good growth prospects, and that it would benefit from Coca-Cola's expertise in market research. Secondly, without much consumer research, Goizueta also introduced Diet Coke to the public, risking the well-guarded trademark that until then had stood only for the original formula. Something had to be done about the sluggish domestic sales of Coca-Cola and the intense competition presented by Pepsi. In 1950, Coke had outsold Pepsi by more than five to one, but by 1984 Pepsi had a 22.8 percent share of the market while Coke had a 21.6 percent share.

In 1985, Goizueta took another chance. Based on information gathered from blind taste tests, Goizueta decided to reformulate the 99-year old drink in the hope of combating Pepsi's growing popularity. The move was not enthusiastically greeted by the American public. Apparently Goizueta did not take into account the public's emotional attachment to the name "Coca-Cola" and all that it stood for: stability, memories, and the idea of a "golden America." Within less than a year the company brought back the "old" Coke, calling it Coca-Cola Classic.

In September of 1987, Coca-Cola agreed to sell its entertainment business to Tri-Star Pictures, 30 percent of which was owned by Coca-Cola. In return, Coca-Cola's interest in Tri-Star was increased to 80 percent. Coca-Cola's holding in Tri-Star was gradually distributed as a special dividend to Coca-Cola shareholders until the company's interest was reduced to a minority, when Tri-Star changed its name to Columbia Pictures Entertainment and sought its own listing on the New York Stock Exchange.

In a 1984 article in the *New York Times*, Goizueta stated that he saw Coca-Cola's challenge as "continuing the growth in profits of highly successful main businesses, and [those] it may choose to enter, at a rate substantially in excess of inflation, in order to give shareholders an above average total return on their investment." Goizueta projected that by 1990 his new strategy would nearly double the company's net income to $1 billion. His prediction came true in 1988.

In the mid-1980s, Coca-Cola entered the bottling business, which had long been dominated by family-operated independents. Coke began repurchasing interests in bottlers worldwide with a view toward providing those bottlers with financial and managerial strength, improving operating efficiencies and promoting expansion into emerging international markets. The trend started domestically, when the parent company formed Coca-Cola Enterprises Inc. through the acquisition and consolidation of two large bottlers in the South and West in 1986. The parent company acquired over thirty bottlers worldwide from 1983 to 1993. By then, the market value of the company's publicly-traded bottlers exceeded the company's book value by $1.5 billion.

Called "one of the world's most sophisticated and powerful marketing organizations," the company's schemes for the 1990s included the 1993 global launch of the "Always Coca-Cola" advertising theme. The new campaign was formulated by Creative Artists Agency, which took over much of the brand's business in 1992 from longtime agency McCann-Erickson Worldwide. In addition to the new campaign, a 32-page catalog of about 400 licensed garments, toys, and gift items featuring Coke slogans or advertising themes was released. The 1994 introduction of a PET plastic bottle in the brand's distinctive, contour shape resulted from corporate marketing research indicating that an overwhelming 84 percent of consumers would choose the trademarked bottle over a generic straight-walled bottle. But the company's primary challenge for the last decade of the twentieth century came in the diet segment, where top-ranking Diet Coke was losing share to ready-to-drink teas, bottled waters, and other "New Age" beverages, which were perceived as healthier and more natural than traditional soft drinks.

In 1993, CEO Goizueta articulated Coca-Cola's three priorities: the creation of stockholder value, maintenance and building of trademark strength, and emphasis on the long-term. Although the company already had a substantial global presence, great potential for geographic development remained. Coca-Cola's 1993 annual report noted that the company's top 16 markets

accounted for 80 percent of its volume, but that those markets comprised only 20 percent of the world's population. Goizueta emphasized that "every single one of the world's 5.6 billion people [will] get thirsty" every day, and that Coca-Cola planned to do everything in its power to make its branded soft drinks "pleasantly inescapable."

Principal Subsidiaries: Bottling Investments Corp.; Carolina Coca-Cola Holding Co.; CRI Holdings, Inc.; Coca-Cola Financial Corp.; Coca-Cola Interamerican Corp.; Coca-Cola Overseas Parent Ltd.; CTI Holdings, Inc.; Coca-Cola Export Corp.; Refreshment Product Services, Inc.; Beverage Products Ltd.; S.A. Coca-Cola Beverages (1991) N.V.; Coca-Cola S.A. Industrial, Comercial Y Financiera; Coca-Cola Industries Ltda.; Recofarma Industria Quimica E Farmaceutica, Ldta.; Coca-Cola Ltd.; Atlantic Industries Ltd.; Conco Ltd.; Coca-Cola de Colombia, S.A.; Coca-Cola GmbH; International Beverages ltd.; Coca-Cola (Japan) Company, Ltd.; Coca-Cola Korea Company, Ltd.; Coca-Cola Nigeria Ltd.; Coca-Cola Poland, Ltd.; Minute Maid S.A.

Further Reading:

Candler, Charles Howard, *Asa Griggs Candler,* Atlanta: Emory University, 1950.

Coca-Cola Company, *The Coca-Cola Company: An Illustrated Profile of a Worldwide Company,* Atlanta: Coca-Cola Company, 1974.

Enrico, Roger, and Jessie Kornbluth, *The Other Guy Blinked: And Other Dispatches from the Cola Wars,* New York: Bantam, 1988.

Graham, Elizabeth C., and Ralph Roberts, *The Real Ones: Four Generations of the First Family of Coca-Cola,* New York: Barricade Books, 1992.

Harrison, DeSales, *"Footprints on the Sands of Time": A History of Two Men and the Fulfillment of a Dream,* New York: Newcomen Society in North America, 1969.

Kahn, Ely Jacques, *The Big Drink: The Story of Coca-Cola,* New York: Random House, 1960.

Oliver, Thomas, *The Real Coke: The Real Story,* New York: Viking Penguin, 1987.

Pendergrast, Mark, *For God, Country and Coca-Cola: The Unauthorized History of the Great American Soft Drink and the Company that Makes It,* New York: Macmillan, 1993.

Ramsey, Douglas K., *The Corporate Warriors: Six Classic Cases in American Business,* Boston: Houghton Mifflin, 1987.

Watters, Pat, *Coca-Cola,* New York: Doubleday, 1978.

Yazijian, Harvey Z., and J.C. Louis, *The Cola Wars,* New York: Everett House, 1980.

—updated by April Dougal Gasbarre

Cogentrix Energy, Inc.

9405 Arrowpoint Boulevard
Charlotte, North Carolina 28273-8110
U.S.A.
(704) 525-3800
Fax: (704) 529-5313

Private Company
Incorporated: 1983
Employees: 500
Sales: $362 million
SICs: 4911 Electric Services

One of the largest independent producers of energy in the United States, Cogentrix Energy, Inc. develops, owns, and operates independent electric power generation facilities. Like other "cogeneration" companies, Cogentrix utilizes a power generation process that produces two or more useful forms of energy, such as electricity and steam, from a single primary fuel source, such as coal or natural gas. Cogentrix operates ten cogeneration facilities across the United States, providing electricity to utility companies and selling thermal energy— primarily steam—to heavy industries and other users.

Cogentrix, was founded and incorporated by George T. Lewis, Jr., in Charlotte, North Carolina, in 1983. Lewis was one of the early participants in the independent power industry, the market for which was established when Congress passed the Public Utility Regulatory Policies Act of 1978, commonly known as PURPA.

Prior to the enactment of PURPA, the demand for power in the United States had traditionally been met by utilities constructing large, electric generating plants under cost-of-service-based regulation. PURPA removed most of the regulatory constraints relating to the sale of electric energy by nonutilities, and required electric utilities to purchase electricity from qualifying facilities. Therefore, nonutilities were encouraged to enter the electric power production market throughout the early 1980s. At the same time, the United States was undergoing a decline in the construction of new generating plants by electrical utilities, due mainly to regulations prohibiting the high costs of many large utility construction projects. Cogentrix and other cogeneration companies presented a cost-effective method for meeting the energy demands of the public and of large industrial users. As a result, a significant market developed for independent

power producers throughout the United States since the enactment of PURPA.

According to statistics compiled by the Edison Electric Institute, independent power producers were responsible for approximately 55,000 megawatts, or seven percent, of the nation's installed generating capacity in 1992. Between 1990 and 1992, independent power generation facilities accounted for 54 percent of total additions to electric generating capacity, with a ten percent increase during 1992. The Edison Institute reported that the generating capacity owned by electric utilities increased by less than one-half of one percent during the same year.

Construction of the Cogentrix's first generation facility began in September 1984. By 1994, Cogentrix had developed and constructed a total of ten generation facilities, all located in the United States. Nine of the ten were wholly owned subsidiaries, and the tenth—in Hopewell, Virginia—was owned equally by Cogentrix and another independent power producer. Each facility was located on a site which was owned or leased on a long-term basis by a project subsidiary. Unlike most of its competitors, which hired third-party contractors to run their plants, Cogentrix operated and managed each of its facilities, hiring its general plant managers early in the construction phases, investing in the hiring and training of operating personnel, and structuring its plant bonus program to reward efficient and cost-effective operation of the plants. The company's executive management group also established a policy of meeting several times a year with each plant manager to discuss individual facility issues and conduct on-site plant performance reviews.

Cogentrix became known for its efficient and reliable operations; its facilities averaged 95.71 percent "availability" in fiscal 1993 and 96.87 percent in fiscal 1992. The utility industry's measurement of availability is defined as the percentage of time a plant is available for operation in a given period, usually a year. For an independent power producer like Cogentrix, full capacity is defined as contracted-for electric generating capacity in megawatts. Cogentrix's availability statistics were regarded as high for the industry, and the company attributed this performance to several factors, including its utilization of standard design coal-fired technology, extensive employee training programs, the elimination of redundant practices at its facilities, and its comprehensive programs of preventative maintenance.

In September 1993, Cogentrix announced its intention to develop an eleventh facility in Michigan. The coal-fired Michigan plant was expected to be brought online in late 1996 and would generate enough electricity to light up a city of 35,000. Cogentrix expected the steam from the plant to be sold to James River Corporation's Parchment, Michigan-based paper mill. This new facility would mark Cogentrix's first experience with the new circulating fluidized-bed, a technology that combines pulverized coal with limestone particles in a hot bed. Calcium in the limestone combines with sulfur in the coal, reducing toxic sulfur dioxide emissions by as much as 90 percent, helping facilitate the company's compliance with regulations of the Clean Air Act of the early 1990s.

Since its founding in 1983, the company's competitive advantage has relied on its ability to construct coal-fired facilities at a lower total cost per kilowatt than most of its competitors. For example, the company's 240 megawatt facility in Richmond, Virginia, was completed within 17 months of groundbreaking at a total installed cost of less than $1,000 per kilowatt. Cogentrix has been able to achieve time and costs savings primarily by using standardized plant designs that incorporate proven technology and modular, as opposed to custom, construction. As a result, the construction and start-up of such facilities generally proceeded more quickly than for larger generating facilities.

While joint partnerships have been a part of only one out of ten of its past ventures, Cogentrix expected this arrangement to become a much larger part of future endeavors. By forming joint ventures with other independent power producers, equipment manufacturers, and fuel suppliers, Cogentrix hoped to gain technical expertise, greater knowledge of political and social conditions of the new region, and the ability to leverage the company's human and financial resources. Moreover, joint ventures would allow Cogentrix the luxury of sharing the risks associated with power generation projects.

In the mid-1990s, all of Cogentrix's generation facilities sold electricity to utilities under long-term sales agreements. A plant's revenues from such an agreement usually consisted of two components: energy payments and capacity payments. The energy payments generally covered the cost of electric generation—which varied according to current fuel and maintenance costs—and are based on a facility's net electrical output measured in kilowatt hours. Capacity payments, on the other hand, were intended to compensate for the plant's fixed costs—including debt service on the project's financing—and are calculated based on the declared capacity of a facility, that is, the amount in megawatts that the company's project subsidiary agreed to make available to a client in a sales agreement. In most cases, capacity payment rates varied over the term of a power sales agreement according to various schedules. Capacity payments comprised the majority of Cogentrix's sales revenues from power sales agreements.

With the exception of one facility, which produced thermal energy in the form of hot water for use by a commercial greenhouse, all of Cogentrix's plants produced "process steam" for use by industrial clients. These clients, or "hosts," include textile manufacturing companies, chemical producers, and synthetic fiber plants, all of whom use the process steam in their manufacturing operations. Cogentrix's steam sales contracts with these industrial hosts were generally long-term contracts that provided payment on a per-thousand-pound basis for steam delivered, in addition to a minimum annual payment in the event that the industrial host's plant is shut down.

Cogentrix's ten facilities also purchased fuel under long-term agreements. Nine of the company's projects in the mid-1990s were fueled with low-sulphur coal, while the other utilized natural gas. Under Congentrix's long-term supply agreements, coal-fueled plants were required to purchase all of their fuel for a particular plant from one coal sales company specified in each agreement. In turn, fuel suppliers were provided with a list of approved mines as part of the agreement. All ten of the company's facilities maintained fuel inventories that varied from a 15- to 20-day supply. Under normal circumstances, this level of inventory proved sufficient, and Cogentrix developed detailed contingency plans to deal with fuel shortages due to coal or rail strikes. Costs incurred under the fuel supply agreements and transportation agreements accounted for approximately 60 percent of Cogentrix's operating expenses in 1994.

In order to deal with the ash created by Cogentrix's coal-burning facilities, seven of Cogentrix's subsidiary facilities maintained contracts with ReUse, a wholly owned subsidiary of Cogentrix that handled the removal of coal ash. The company's other facilities employed a third party to remove coal ash. As an environmentally-conscious alternative to disposing of ash in landfills, ReUse developed a process in which coal ash could be used as structural fill material in the manufacturing and production of various products for resale. Most of the coal ash removed from the plants by ReUse was hauled to land located in nearby industrial/commercial areas, where it helped raise the existing grade of the land to a higher level, making the site more suitable for future development. The remaining coal ash was incorporated into such products as concrete blocks, concrete pavers, land plaster for peanut crops, and potting soil. At one site where coal ash was deposited as structural fill material for several years, ReUse established a composting operation to mix coal ash with wood byproducts and cotton gin waste to make potting soil. ReUse sold this potting soil in bulk to nurseries and other end users.

Experts in the energy field predicted that the future growth of Cogentrix's market would occur in the world's developing countries. According to several studies, the need for base-load generating capacity additions in developing countries between 1994 and 2004 would significantly exceed that of the United States. Many foreign markets, including Mexico, China, India, and Southeast Asia, adopted policies during the early 1990s that supported independent power producers. Those policies, as well as very high economic growth rates, ensured climates that would be ripe for the entry of companies like Cogentrix.

A dominant force in the United States, Cogentrix moved quickly to expand the company's presence worldwide. Management believed that by establishing relationships with large U.S. multinational companies, Cogentrix could develop reliable in-roads to new project developments. In May 1993, the government of India approved a Cogentrix proposal to develop a 1,000 megawatt coal-fired electric generating plant in the state of Karnstaka. The company expected to begin the first phase of construction in 1995, depending upon whether it could reach a long-term power sales agreement and obtain construction financing. The project would mark Cogentrix's first foray into the international arena.

Moreover, Cogentrix's management team considered Latin America as a great opportunity for development, following the enactment of the North American Free Trade Agreement (NAFTA), a comprehensive free-trade accord among the United States, Canada, and Mexico. In early 1994, Cogentrix was also actively investigating possible development opportunities in Mexico. However, such international projects have proven more difficult and expensive than domestic projects, since many foreign competitors had greater capital resources and local market expertise than Cogentrix.

The future market for Cogentrix and other U.S. independent power producers in the mid-1990s remained uncertain. Although many published forecasts reflected the need for continued growth among these companies, competition from regulated electric utilities was considered a threat. These utilities were making increasingly efficient use of their existing resources by improving plant availability, extending plant lives, repowering older facilities, and taking advantage of attractive bulk power purchases. Moreover, many regulated utilities have also initiated demand side management programs designed to reduce the need for new electric generating capacity.

In addition, obtaining a power sales agreement with a domestic utility has become progressively more difficult, expensive, and competitive throughout the late 1980s and early 1990s. As a result of this trend and other factors, consolidation of companies involved in the independent power industry has accelerated. Many state regulatory commissions now require or have policies in place that encourage power sales agreements to be awarded by competitive bidding. This process increases the costs and decreases the chances of obtaining such agreements.

Cogentrix's strategy is to avoid competitive bidding whenever possible and instead use negotiated power sales agreements.

In the future, Cogentrix intends to capitalize on the reputation it has established as a result of its high plant availability record and remain among the leaders in the rapidly-growing independent power industry. The company plans to accomplish this by developing and constructing or acquiring power generation facilities throughout the United States and selected foreign markets where the political climate is good for foreign development.

Principal Subsidiaries: Cogentrix Eastern Carolina Corporation; ReUse; Cogentrix of North Carolina Holdings, Inc.; Cogentrix of Pennsylvania, Inc.; Cogentrix of Richmond, Inc.

Further Reading:

Fralix, David, "Cogentrix Closer to Deal for Michigan Plant," *Business Journal,* May 16, 1994, p. 4.

—Wendy Johnson Bilas

COMPUCOM

CompuCom Systems, Inc.

10100 North Central Expressway
Dallas, Texas 75231
U.S.A.
(214) 265-3600
Fax: (214) 265-5275

Public Company
Incorporated: 1981 as CytoSystems Corporation
Employees: 1,541
Sales: $1.01 billion
Stock Exchanges: NASDAQ
SICs: 5045 Computers, Peripherals & Software; 7373
   Computer Integrated Systems Design

CompuCom Systems, Inc. is a leading personal computer (PC) dealer and computer network integration company. Serving as an authorized dealer of major PC lines, CompuCom markets and sells microcomputer hardware, software, and peripheral products to corporate customers through a direct sales force based in over 40 metropolitan locations. In addition to providing multivendor computing system solutions for corporate needs, CompuCom offers its customers a range of services including custom configuration of PC systems as well as network design, installation, training, and support services. Approximately two-thirds of CompuCom's common stock is owned by Safeguard Scientifics, Inc., a technology management company.

CompuCom Systems, Inc. traces its roots to the 1981 formation of CytoSystems Corporation, a Michigan company founded by Stanley Sternberg to capitalize on what was then a growing interest in the automation of manufacturing operations in the automobile and electronics industries. In 1983, the company changed its name to Machine Vision International Corporation (MVI), which principally served Detroit automakers, focusing its operations on the production of automated inspection guidance systems for industrial robots, which helped machines ''see'' in order to interpret data and control a manufacturing activity.

By the time MVI went public in the fall of 1985, the company was one of the largest machine vision operations in the United States with over $9 million in sales and nearly 200 employees. During this time, Safeguard Scientifics began investing several million dollars in MVI stock. However, Safeguard soon lost

millions on the machine vision company, when MVI was forced to cut back on its product line, due to technical problems in the development of its machines and reduced orders from automakers, including General Motors, which accounted for half of MVI's revenues. MVI lost $13.6 million on its operations in 1986, and industry analysts lost faith in near-term profitability for machine vision companies, suggesting that initial expectations for automation were too high and that difficulties in integrating robotic systems into factories had been underestimated.

In 1986, Safeguard Scientifics' chairperson Warren V. Musser was named chairperson of MVI. The following year, Safeguard Scientifics—which had helped finance the development of Novell Inc. earlier in the decade, transforming that firm from a struggling microcomputer manufacturer into a profitable local area network (LAN) software company—financed MVI's entrance into the business of selling microcomputers to corporate customers. Utilizing $15 million provided by Safeguard Scientifics, in July 1987, MVI acquired TriStar Data Systems, Inc., a regional computer reseller based in New Jersey, and purchased the computer retailer Office Automation, Inc. With the pair of acquisitions, MVI began marketing and selling branded microcomputer systems, including models manufactured by IBM, Compaq Computer Corporation, and Hewlett-Packard Company.

MVI's entrance into computer retailing marked the beginning of its exit from the machine-vision market. By August 1987, Stanley Sternberg had started a new, four-person operation in Ann Arbor, Michigan, called Machine Vision International Inc., which began work on a NASA contract to develop guidance systems for space robots. In October 1987, the original MVI formed the holding company CompuCom Systems, Inc. and relocated its offices to Cherry Hill, New Jersey, while retaining a Michigan machine vision division with a much-reduced payroll for fewer than 30 workers.

By December 1987, a shakeout in the machine vision industry was underway. While less than half the nation's machine vision companies were profitable, CompuCom, due to its diversified interests, earned $209,000 in 1987, the first time in the company's history that it showed a profit. In early 1988, CompuCom officially bowed out of the machine vision field, having been transformed into a substantially larger computer retailer.

In June of that year, CompuCom launched a national expansion strategy, purchasing the Dallas-based CompuShop Inc., a computer retailer and former CompuCom competitor, from Bell Atlantic Corporation. The $20.3 million acquisition helped create one of the computer retailing industry's largest outbound sales forces engaged in direct sales to corporate customers and gave CompuCom a national presence with 25 sales offices throughout the country.

After bringing CompuShop's operation into its fold, CompuCom relocated its headquarters to Dallas, and James Dixon, former CompuShop president, was named president of CompuCom, succeeding Ira Lubert, who then became chairperson. By the end of 1988, Safeguard Scientifics and Warren Musser controlled 46 percent of the company, and CompuCom's earnings had grown to $1.5 million on sales of $159 million. In

1989, Avery More succeeded Dixon as president of Compu-Com. That year, Safeguard Scientifics increased its interest in CompuCom to 66 percent while CompuCom's revenues climbed from $159 million to $270 million, and earnings inched up to $1.6 million.

CompuCom entered the 1990s with three self-declared strengths: an established base of corporate clients, products offered on an "a la carte" basis," and tight management controls over expenses. In April 1990, CompuCom acquired Data Access Systems Inc. (DASI), a Pennsylvania-based computer reseller and a former franchisee of Intelligent Electronics with $10 million in annual sales, which like CompuCom's revenues, came largely from corporate clients. Having successfully absorbed the larger CompuShop without losing profitability, CompuCom announced an agreement to acquire Computer Factory Inc., a one-time leading microcomputer retail chain with 63 outlets that had fallen on tough financial times. By the end of 1990, CompuCom was one of the fastest growing microcomputer dealers in the country and had more than doubled its earnings to $3.6 million on sales of $343 million.

In April 1991, CompuCom completed its $38 million acquisition of Computer Factory, which had prepared itself for the deal by reducing its number of retail outlets to 24, confined largely to the northeastern United States where CompuCom was seeking an expanded, direct sales presence. By the end of May, the Computer Factory chain had been pared down to 14 outlets, and Computer Factory's direct sales staff was integrated into CompuCom's corporate sales force.

In July of that year, CompuCom acquired the PC sales business of Photo & Sound Company, a west coast consumer electronics chain serving audio-visual and multimedia markets. The $9.4 million acquisition gave CompuCom—which had become the fifth largest PC dealer in the country with 37 offices—an expanded presence for its corporate sales in the western United States as well as a West Coast distribution facility.

Initially, CompuCom planned to use Computer Factory stores to explore new markets, but within six months of the acquisition that strategy changed. While the Computer Factory's corporate accounts were easily integrated into CompuCom's operations, its home computer market did not fit CompuCom's corporate-customer direct-sales strategy, particularly since the home computer sales market was increasingly dominated by mail order businesses and discount superstores. As a result, in November 1991, CompuCom backed away from the consumer retail market by first consolidating the former chain's remaining outlets into six New York locations and then discontinuing consumer operations altogether.

CompuCom's quick departure from the consumer market was welcomed by industry analysts, who had lauded the company for maintaining double-digit earnings in the face of a downswing in computer reselling. During 1991, CompuCom signed its first dealer agreement with Apple Computer Corporation, adding Apple computer systems to its multivendor product line of IBM, Compaq, and Hewlett-Packard systems. CompuCom's 1991 acquisitions, which had significantly expanded the company's direct sales force in northeastern and western states,

boosted annual revenues more than 50 percent, while earnings climbed to $5 million on sales of $528 million.

In April 1992, CompuCom entered the computer systems integration and computer related services market with the $2.7 million acquisition of the assets of CompuServe Systems Integration Group Southwest (formerly known as MicroSolutions) and CompuServe's LAN training facility in Dallas. CompuCom returned the "MicroSolutions" name to the Dallas-based computer systems integration business—which was a regional leader in providing technical network integration services for major corporations—and announced that MicroSolutions would serve as the company's first link in building a national network integration business.

That year, CompuCom began benefitting from a computer price war initiated by Compaq, which provided the brand name computer dealer with an opportunity to steal market share from clone retailers. And while some of its competitors were chalking up disappointing results, CompuCom—which had become Safeguard Scientifics' largest business unit, accounting for 80 percent of its revenues—earned $7.2 million on sales of $713 million as revenues rose 35 percent and net income grew by 45 percent.

Between 1992 and 1993, CompuCom enhanced its distribution operations to allow for low-cost, one-day delivery to most locations. The company expanded its West Coast distribution center in Stockton, California, and, the following year, relocated its eastern distribution center from Paulsboro, New Jersey, to a larger, modernized facility in nearby Woolwich, New Jersey.

In an effort to enhance customer support and further improve order processing, CompuCom also began a three-year program to centralize sales administration, support, and order processing activities—previously done by various offices throughout the country—at a new CompuCom Customer Center in Dallas. In 1993 CompuCom relocated its administrative offices to a new corporate headquarters, a six-story commercial office building in Dallas, which doubled as a showcase for the company's networking-based systems.

By 1993, CompuCom's business was booming as a result of its series of strategic acquisitions, while its bottom line was improving due to its four years of cost-control programs. In August of that year, Ed Anderson, a well-known computer industry veteran and former president of ComputerLand Corporation, was named chief operating officer of CompuCom. The management move, representing a step towards placing Anderson at the helm of the company the following year, was expected to help improve the company's following on Wall Street, which had been slow to actively monitor the company's progress because of Safeguard Scientifics large interest in CompuCom.

During 1993, CompuCom increased the number of its office locations to 41, and for the third consecutive year *Fortune* magazine listed the company among its "100 Fastest-Growing Companies." As demand for branded PCs increased, CompuCom's annual sales surged $300 million during the year, with revenues climbing 42 percent to more than $1 billion and earnings increasing to $11.4 million.

In January 1994, Anderson became president and chief executive, succeeding More, who remained a company director while moving on to form a new company, Eureka Ventures, a venture-capital and merchant banking firm. Eureka Ventures then agreed to acquire CompuCom's network training division and a 50 percent interest in CompuCom's PC Parts Express subsidiary, a computer parts distribution firm. Also during this time, the company sold off its government sales division, as it continued focusing on the expansion of its network support services for corporate customers.

In early 1994, CompuCom's financial position was bolstered by its expansion of customer credit lines to $150 million and by selling Safeguard Scientifics an additional $20 million in convertible preferred stock. During the same period, CompuCom's common stock—having risen from a first quarter 1993 high of $3.50 to $4.56 by the end of that year—continued to climb on the open market, and its listed price soared to a first quarter 1994 high of $7.25.

As CompuCom entered the mid-1990s, a period of increasing industry consolidation, the company planned to continue its policy of growth through acquisitions, while Safeguard Scientifics continued to maintain its role as the financial guardian. In response to a corporate trend of outsourcing computer and integration services, CompuCom planned further expansion of its network support services, through both acquisitions of regional service providers as well as internal growth. CompuCom appeared well positioned to gain ground in its market niche of selling brand-name computer products to corporations. The company was also poised to take advantage of price reductions by major computer manufacturers battling for business with clone makers and the increasing number of corporations abandoning mainframe and minicomputers systems in favor of networked personal computers.

Principal Subsidiaries: CompuCom Properties, Inc.; The Computer Factory Inc.; CompuCom Acquisition Corp; PC Parts Express, Inc. (50%).

Further Reading:

Armstrong, Michael W., ''Savvy Safeguard is Focusing on Computers,'' *Philadelphia Business Journal,* July 29, 1991, p. 3B.
Fisher, Susan, ''CompuCom Dismantles Retail Operations,'' *PC Week,* November 11, 1991, p. 134.
Lindstrom, John, ''Machine Vision Firms Aim for Lower-Cost Products,'' *Crain's Detroit Business,* December 7, 1987, p. 24.
Markoff, John, ''CompuCom Systems Puts Stores on Block,'' *The New York Times,* November 6, 1991, p. D4.
Melton, James, ''MVI: Industry Shakeout Killed Machine-Vision Biz, *Crain's Detroit Business,* December 12, 1988, p. 5.
Schuler, Joseph F. Jr., ''Safeguard Scientifics, Revisited: Flying Even Higher,'' *Pennsylvania Business & Technology,* July 1993, p. 23.
Vonder Haar, Steven, ''CompuCom Decides It Prefers Dallas Over New Jersey,'' *Dallas Business Journal,* June 6, 1988, p. 4.

—Roger W. Rouland

CompUSA, Inc.

14951 North Dallas Parkway
Dallas, Texas 75240
U.S.A.
(214) 383-4000
Fax: (214) 484-4276

Public Company
Incorporated: 1984 as Soft Warehouse
Employees: 2,492
Sales: $1.34 billion
Stock Exchanges: New York
SICs: 5734 Computer & Software Stores

CompUSA, Inc. is the largest operator of computer superstores in the United States, with 77 stores in more than 38 metropolitan markets. CompUSA stores offer more than 5,000 products, including microcomputer hardware, software, accessories, and related items, to retail, corporate, governmental, and institutional customers at deep-discount prices. Striving to offer its customers the lowest prices in the market, the company competes successfully with other large computer or electronics stores such as Circuit City and ComputerCity. CompUSA's sophisticated computerized merchandising and control systems connect each superstore to its suppliers; without intervening levels of distribution, the company is able to offer low prices and maintain a high inventory turnover rate. CompUSA superstores, each of which have approximately 25,000 square feet of retail space, offer technical support to their customers, repairing and servicing merchandise and providing training centers, where customers can learn how to use popular software. The company also operates a government sales division headquartered in Washington, D.C., that supplies computer products to federal, state, and local government agencies and government contractors. Corporate customers are serviced by the Direct Sales group, which also handles mail order and telephone sales. Among the many major brands of computers and equipment sold at CompUSA superstores is the company's own private label computer, Compudyne.

CompUSA began in Dallas in 1984 under the name Soft Warehouse, a company that initially sold software and hardware directly to corporate customers and within a year had opened its first retail store. During its early years, management explored the idea of opening a superstore, a large facility offering complete lines of low-cost merchandise. While the concept had proved successful for such retailers as Toys 'R' Us, Circuit City, and Office Depot, computer retail was generally thought to require a smaller sales staff expert in the technical nuances of the product. Soft Warehouse, however, speculated that as the public became more familiar with computers, the computer retail operation would broaden in scope, and with a staff and management more skilled in marketing than in computers, the company opened its first superstore in 1988. While retail chains such as ComputerCity and BusinessLand emerged during the early 1980s, Soft Warehouse developed the first chain of superstores in the computer market.

In January 1989, Soft Warehouse was acquired by a group of investors led by Ronald N. Dubin. Late that year, the company hired as its president and chief executive officer Nathan Morton, a former top executive of a leading retail chain called Home Depot. Morton had no background in computers, and he later recalled for a 1993 *New York Times* article that his friends and family were shocked that he took the leadership position at Soft Warehouse, some attributing the move to a mid-life crisis.

Morton, however, had a unique vision for the development of Soft Warehouse, which led to a period of explosive expansion for the company. Along with other new executives, who came to Soft Warehouse from Kmart, Hechingers, and Wickes Lumber, Morton planned the construction of a series of superstores that would provide the lowest prices in the industry and the largest selection available on a national scale. Eighteen superstores were in operation by the end of the 1980s, and sales increased dramatically from $66 million in fiscal 1988 to $600 million in 1990. The company became the largest chain of computer superstores in the country, changing its name to CompUSA in 1991.

The success of CompUSA was due in part to its finely honed system of merchandise flow. Rather than maintaining an expensive network of warehouses and trucking lines, CompUSA management used computer software to help track inventory and anticipate consumer demand, allowing them to stock the right amount of merchandise in the stores.

Through 1990, product lines at the CompUSA superstores consisted largely of IBM clone personal computers, including a private brand line known as Compudyne. In 1991, the company persuaded manufacturer Apple Computer, Inc. to allow the distribution of the Apple Macintosh personal computer through CompUSA. As Apple had never before allowed distribution through discounters, the company regarded this agreement as reflecting its reputation as a national marketing force. Soon thereafter, CompUSA gained the right to sell another major personal computer brand, Compaq.

While 35 percent of CompUSA's sales were to corporate buyers in 1991, a growing market of home computer users also fueled the company's expansion. In the early 1990s, an estimated 75 million Americans were using personal computers, and users were increasingly willing and able to install and maintain their own equipment without deferring to a computer expert. Moreover, dramatic increases occurred in the number of Americans either working from computers in the home or running home-based businesses as their primary occupation. Catering to this new market, CompUSA provided free information pamphlets throughout its stores to help consumers better understand product capabilities, and the stores featured low prices that were particularly appreciated by small business and home users.

In December 1991, CompUSA completed an initial public offering of its shares. Trading began at $15 and within a few months reached a high of $40 as investors leaped at the chance to buy into the burgeoning company. Losses reported in the prior year were attributable to control issues, and CompUSA's sales continued to increase. By the end of 1992, CompUSA operated 36 superstores across the country and had plans to add 12 more over the next six months. The company also introduced training centers in most of its stores, offering computer courses to its customers that generated nearly $700,000 a month, most of which was profit, helping offset low profit margins caused by heightened competition in the industry. The company's sales for 1992 reached $820 million.

In 1993, CompUSA decentralized its corporate structure in preparation for future growth. Nathan Morton was promoted from president to chairperson and CEO, replacing Ronald Dubin. Morton divided the company into three operating units responsible for the eastern, western, and central areas of the United States. An international unit was also formed to research expansion into Canada, Mexico, and Europe.

In spite of the company's expanding sales territories, however, profits lagged. Typical quarterly sales increases of 60 percent failed to generate similar increases in net income, and during the first quarter of 1993, CompUSA reported a 65.8 percent increase in sales and overall losses totaling $986,000. Operating expenses associated with opening new stores as well as high interest expenses contributed to the loss. At a board meeting in December 1993, Morton resigned.

Morton's replacement was CompUSA's president and chief operating officer James Halpin, who had come to the company six months earlier from the Home Base home improvement retail chain. Halpin oversaw the last weeks of the fiscal second quarter in which sales surged 65 percent and the company posted a loss of $5.5 million. He agreed that expenses had gotten out of hand. Rather than trimming expenses by slowing the company's growth, Halpin's plan included out-sourcing assembly of Compudyne computers, centralizing inventory management, and consolidating the management structure by eliminating several executive positions. With these measures, Halpin hoped to restore CompUSA to profitability, facilitating

his plan to open 30 new stores by June 1995, which would bring the total number of CompUSA superstores to nearly 80.

The precedent set by CompUSA, pioneer of the computer superstore concept, has prompted a wealth of competition. In 1991, Tandy Corporation opened a retail chain subsidiary called Computer City, and such discounters as Sears, Roebuck, & Co. and Wal-Mart also began selling computers and related equipment. Moreover, mail order services and warehouse clubs began catering to the computer shopper. Although CompUSA was no longer unique in the industry, it remained a market leader. The company's next challenge may lie in maintaining its place in a market it helped bring to its present maturity.

Further Reading:

Brammer, Rhonda, "Not-So-Super Concept? In Long Haul, CompUSA's Strategy May Not Compute," *Barron's,* March 9, 1992, p. 12.

Buckler, Arthur, "CompUSA's Morton Resigns Top Posts Amid Dissatisfaction over Profitability," *Wall Street Journal,* December 16, 1993, p. B13.

Collins, Lisa, "Computer Retailers Hacking Away," *Crain's Chicago Business,* July 22, 1991, p. 1.

"CompUSA Names Morton Chairman in a Reorganization," *Wall Street Journal,* May 14, 1993, p. B9.

"CompUSA Says Sales Have Been Growing, Margins Improving," *Wall Street Journal,* December 10, 1992, p. A13.

"Computer Superstores, Sign of the Times," *Fortune,* December 16, 1991, p. 48.

Forest, Stephanie Anderson, "CompUSA's New Boss: Damn the Torpedoes," *Business Week,* February 14, 1994, p. 38.

Hayes, Thomas C., "Compaq Deal to Expand Retail Sales," *New York Times,* September 9, 1992, p. D3.

Kimelman, John, "CompUSA: The Yellow Flag Is Out," *Financial World,* June 8, 1993, p. 18.

Mullich, Joe, "CompUSA Seeks Profit Boost," *Business Marketing,* January 1994, p. 3.

Mullich, Joe, "CompUSA's Morton Weds Retail, PCs," *Business Marketing,* June 1993, p. 26.

Pope, Kyle, "Compaq Computers Signs Accords with Three Big Retailers of PCs," *Wall Street Journal,* September 9, 1992, p. B4.

Strnad, Patricia, "Europe Enticing for Computer Superstores," *Advertising Age,* November 9, 1992, p. S3.

Strom, Stephanie, "CompUSA Chairman Ousted by Directors," *New York Times,* December 16, 1993, p. D4.

Strom, Stephanie, "CompUSA Starts Corporate Reorganizing," *New York Times,* May 14, 1993, p. D3.

Strom, Stephanie, "Will CompUSA, with $1.3 Billion in Sales, Be the Next Toys 'R' Us?" *New York Times,* May 30, 1993, p. F5.

—A. Woodward

CompuServe®

CompuServe Incorporated

5000 Arlington Center
Columbus, Ohio 43220-2913
U.S.A.
(614) 457-8600
Fax: (614) 457-0348

Wholly Owned Subsidiary of H & R Block Inc.
Incorporated: 1980
Employees: 2,200
Sales: $429.9 million
SICs: 7375 Information Retrieval Services; 7372
   Prepackaged Software; 7374 Data Processing and
   Preparation

Regarded as one of the world's leading computer information services, CompuServe Incorporated provides personal computer users in the home or office with a wide variety of online information services, communications opportunities, and software products. CompuServe prides itself on its technical sophistication; power stabilization and emergency systems ensure reliable service 24 hours a day from practically anywhere in the world.

CompuServe's primary division, CompuServe Information Service, provides personal computer users worldwide with videotex, a system for accessing electronic information. Members of the service can access CompuServe's more than 2,000 databases on their PCs, terminals, or word processors by using a telephone, a modem, and specially designed communications software packages. Contributing about 56 percent of the company's annual revenues in the early 1990s, the division had 1.8 million members, including more than 2,000 corporations and government agencies, by March 1993. Major competitors during this time included America Online Inc. and Prodigy, which is jointly owned by IBM and Sears, Roebuck & Co.

CompuServe also maintains a CompuServe Mail division, which oversees the operations of an electronic mail (e-mail) service and communication system tailored to businesses and associations. The e-mail system allows users to send messages, letters, documents, or other text to subscribers at any time of day or night and often proves more economical in the business community than traditional telephone communications. In the early 1990s, CompuServe Mail had the largest subscribership of

any electronic mail system in the world. For a fee, this mail system could also be linked up with other e-mail systems, including the Internet's system. Another division, the CompuServe Systems Integration Group, designs and installs local area network (LAN) computer systems in corporate settings and provides support and training in their use.

CompuServe was established in 1969 for the purpose of providing computer time-sharing services. Through its pioneering efforts in videotex technology, CompuServe introduced an online service, the CompuServe Information Service, in 1979. This network initially represented an extension of its core business; starting the information service was simply a matter of offering existing hardware to about 1,200 night time users in its first year. The following year, CompuServe became a wholly owned subsidiary of H&R Block, Inc., which provided the financial support to foster CompuServe's rapid growth through expansion as well as research and development.

Through videotex, CompuServe enabled users to perform banking and shopping transactions and access a wide variety of information from their homes. Using CompuServe, individuals could make travel reservations and order tickets for cultural or sporting events in the convenience of their homes, or access databases offering current news, weather forecasts, sports scores, and stock prices. The usage rate for many of these services initially fell below the company's expectations, however, as it proved difficult to change consumer behavior; many simply preferred to use the telephone or other conventional channels for acquiring their goods and services. Nevertheless, as personal computing and home office environments became more common in the United States, Americans became more willing to explore videotex transactions. CompuServe reported that sales made through its home shopping service, the Electronic Mall, rose 76 percent in 1990.

Other, more popular videotex applications involved communication networks facilitated by e-mail, electronic bulletin boards, and forums. These services, which allowed users across the country to communicate through their computers, quickly became the most popular of CompuServe's offerings. CompuServe played a particularly important role in developing online forums—its most heavily used service—that offer users the opportunity to share information on areas of common interest. The company's earliest forums consisted largely of shared information on personal computing technology and thus appealed primarily to specialists and technology buffs. As the concept gained popularity, however, forums for a wide variety of subjects and hobbies emerged, allowing users to electronically discuss music, gaming, auto racing, and science fiction, or more serious topics, such as law and medicine. By the early 1990s, CompuServe had become famous for its more than 450 technical support forums; every major software developer and computer manufacturer, including Borland, IBM, Microsoft, and 3Com Corporation, began hosting its own bulletin board to share information and entertain questions from their users. Forums also began serving as a point of access to the thousands of valuable public domain software programs in circulation.

In 1986, the market research organization LINK Resources published a report in which it characterized CompuServe's growth as "slow but steady." This reflected the company's marketing strategy of focusing on the enhancement of its popular services, while avoiding "quantum leaps" into new and untried areas. This strategy proved successful, as CompuServe was one of just a few profitable videotex companies by the early 1990s.

In 1987, CompuServe entered into a joint venture with Nissho Iwai Corporation and Fujitsu Limited to offer Nifty-Serve, a version of the CompuServe Information Service, in Japan. Licensing and distribution agreements were also made during this time to bring the CompuServe Information Service to Argentina, Australia, Chile, Hungary, Hong Kong, Israel, New Zealand, South Africa, South Korea, Taiwan, and Venezuela. After establishing access and support centers in the European population centers of Bristol, Munich, and Paris, CompuServe doubled its membership on the continent between 1992 and 1993, while Nifty-Serve claimed over 350,000 members.

In March 1989, CompuServe Information Service became the first general videotex service to garner a half million U.S. subscribers. Later that year, CompuServe completed the acquisition of Source Telecomputing Corporation, thereby expanding its membership by as many as 40,000 subscribers and eliminating a competitor. The following year, CompuServe acquired MicroSolutions Inc., a Dallas-based reseller of local area network and connectivity products. By 1991, CompuServe boasted over 620,000 subscribers and annual revenues of over $200 million. That year, CompuServe introduced new software providing colorful windows and icons to help users recognize and quickly select the service of their choice.

During this time, CompuServe was a litigant in a precedent-setting case involving censorship, liability, and libel in the electronic information age. The case involved Don Fitzpatrick, the coordinator of CompuServe's Rumorville forum for journalists, who was accused of posting defamatory remarks about Skuttlebutt, a rival forum. CompuServe was named as a co-defendant, but in November 1991, Judge Peter K. Leisure of the U.S. District Court likened CompuServe's responsibility to that of the owner of a bookstore, noting that the bookseller couldn't possibly be responsible for the editorial content of every book sold. Two years later, CompuServe was again involved in a lawsuit and was ordered by a federal judge to pay $4 million in compensatory and punitive damages to two Massachusetts businesses for breaching an agreement in connection with the purchase of a database system by CompuServe.

In the early 1990s, lower costs for computing and telecommunications technology made online services less expensive to operate. The savings were passed along to users, who were offered limited groupings of services for a single flat rate per month, regardless of the time spent using them. Spearheading flat-rate pricing, the Prodigy online service soon surpassed CompuServe as the leading videotex service in terms of acting members. Moreover, the Internet, a nonprofit, global network of more than 34,000 public and private computer networks, was becoming a potential threat to CompuServe's share of the market. Subsidized by the government and managed by volunteers, the Internet derived operating revenues from its members, who paid connection fees.

Although for-profit information services did not consider the Internet a direct competitor—and relied on a wider variety of services and appealing color graphics to maintain their market share—the issue of cost remained a factor in subscription rates. Dave Bezair, a senior product manager at CompuServe, Inc. told the *Wall Street Journal* in September 1993 that while "everyone wants to jump on this price issue . . . the reality is accessibility, ease of use, customer service and world-wide access." In fact, the company made major strides towards accessibility and ease of use by becoming the first in the industry to offer user interface software compatible with the popular Microsoft Windows operating system. Nevertheless, CompuServe did announce a subscriber fee reduction of as much as 40 percent, effective early in 1994. Hourly connect fees, which had ranged from $12.80 to $22.80 were dropped to between $8 and $16.

During this time, CompuServe also developed new products and services to meet competition. The Executive Service Option (ESO) was introduced, featuring business data enhanced by financial, demographic, and editorial information. Communications services designed especially for business users included online brokerage firms and electronic conferencing via computer. ESO also offered stock quotes and commodity information; historical market information; major market and industry indices; and national and international business news wires. In other fields, CompuServe created a public, online forum to help find missing children, which it made freely available to both customers and competing online services. Early in 1994, Vice-President Albert Gore, Jr., an avid promoter of the "information superhighway," gave one of the first online, interactive interviews by a major political figure on CompuServe.

CompuServe's revenues stood at $315.4 million in fiscal 1993, rising 12.3 percent above the previous year, while its membership increased 40 percent during the year, reaching 1.5 million. The CompuServe Information Service won the *PC Magazine* Editor's Choice Award in 1993 and was selected as the leading provider of public data network services in *Network World*'s reader survey that year. Billed in advertisements as "The Information Service You Won't Outgrow," CompuServe focused on developing and implementing new technologies to stay competitive in a rapidly changing marketplace.

Principal Subsidiaries: Compuplex Inc.; CompuServe Canada Ltd.; CompuServe U.K.; CompuServe Information Services GmbH (Germany); CompuServe Information Services SARL (France).

Further Reading:

Coursey, David, "The Cost of Information," *InfoWorld,* August 5, 1991, pp. 40–44.
"Gore Mistypes His Way Through On-line Forum," *Wall Street Journal,* January 14, 1994, p. B8.
Hawkins, Donald T., "Videotex Markets, Applications, and Systems," *Online,* March 1991, pp. 97–100.
Manning, Anita, "Shopping Comes Online with Computerized Ease," *USA Today,* October 25, 1990, p. D4.
O'Leary, Mick, "Product-Support Forums Fill Niche," *Link-Up,* May/June 1992, pp. 3, 16.

Picarille, Lisa, "BBS Not Liable for Libel, Court Says," *InfoWorld,* November 11, 1991, p. 130.

Schwartz, Evan, "Adventures in the On-line Universe," *Business Week,* June 17, pp. 112–13.

Stecklow, Steve, "Internet Becomes Road More Traveled as E-Mail Users Discover No Usage Fees," *Wall Street Journal,* September 2, 1993, p. B1.

Webb, Joseph A., "CompuServe Purchases the Source," *Information Today,* July/August 1989, p. 1–2.

—April Dougal Gasbarre

Computervision Corporation

100 Crosby Drive
Bedford, Massachusetts 01730
U.S.A.
(617) 275-1800
Fax: (617) 655-5090

Public Company
Incorporated: 1972 as Prime Computer, Inc.
Employees: 2,700
Sales: $827 million
Stock Exchanges: New York
SICs: 7372 Prepackaged Software

Computervision Corporation is a leading supplier of software for use in computer-aided design and computer-aided manufacturing (CAD/CAM), systems used by companies around the world to develop automotive, aerospace, and other engineered products. Computervision got its start as a computer hardware manufacturer in the early 1970s, and it continued to market minicomputers for 20 years. In the 1980s the company had begun to focus its efforts on the design and engineering fields, until the early 1990s, when it suffered a severe financial crisis and dramatically cut back its operations in order to focus exclusively on software and service.

Computervision's predecessor, Prime Computer, Inc., was founded in 1972 in the technology corridor outside of Boston, Massachusetts. Established by a number of computer science engineers, Prime's start-up was funded by venture capitalists. By 1974 Prime had become an engineering-driven company with sales of $6.5 million and losses of $541,000.

In 1975 Prime got a new president, Kenneth G. Fisher. With a background in marketing, rather than science or engineering, Fisher shifted the company's emphasis from research and development to the marketplace. The following year Prime introduced the super-minicomputer, which cost less than a conventional mainframe computer, but processed complex data much faster than a minicomputer. Prime pioneered the development of this innovative product, which blurred the line between the categories of mainframe computing and minicomputing.

Prime used a direct sales force to market its minicomputer to a small niche of customers, sophisticated users who put together their own computer systems and wrote their own software.

Using this strategy, along with stringent management and financial controls, the company achieved a high rate of growth in the late 1970s—between 1977 and 1980 Prime's annual sales grew at an average compound rate of 75 percent. In 1978 revenues hit $50 million, and a year later they had passed the $100 million mark, as the company reported sales of $153 million and earnings of $17 million. After doubling its profits each year for five years, Prime had become the seventh-largest minicomputer maker.

With this level of success, it became clear that Prime had outgrown its narrow market. The company needed to expand its product offerings and its customer base if it hoped to see its growth continue at the same rate. In April of 1980 Prime entered the office automation market when it unveiled a new line of computers designed to provide word processing, data processing, and electronic mail capabilities from a single terminal. The Prime system was designed to be a tool used by managers and professionals, and it was set up so that individual work stations would hook into a central computer. With this program, the company hoped to expand its potential pool of customers by 50 percent, including the 1,000 largest U.S. corporations.

In addition to its move into the office automation market, Prime also began to broaden its channels of distribution with another product. In May of 1980 the company introduced a new computer that cost less than half as much as its lowest-priced older models. This product was meant to be sold to computer systems builders, who customized Prime hardware with software programs and peripheral equipment for individual users. In addition, Prime signed up 29 computer dealers to market its products to unsophisticated first-time users.

By the end of that year, Prime's revenues had grown to $267 million, and its earnings had reached $31.2 million. Within six months, however, the tide of the company's fortunes had begun to turn. The company's core minicomputer offerings, once state of the art, had become outmoded and were facing heavy competition. In addition, because Prime had outgrown its loose, entrepreneurial style of management, the company had failed to introduce enough new products, a computer-aided design (CAD) program for example, in a timely manner. The company's practice of farming out software development to outside contractors had caused quality control problems with its office automation systems, and the company's overall marketing focus had slipped.

In July of 1981 Fisher left after a power struggle with the chairman and board of directors. In the wake of his departure, 15 other managers left the company. By year's end a new president had been appointed to fill the vacuum in leadership and, hopefully, stop the slide in the company's stock price. Sales growth had declined to 35 percent, half of what it had been a year before, and the company badly needed restructuring.

Late in 1981 Prime introduced a new super-minicomputer, the Model 850, in an effort to remain competitive in that market. The following year, the company also formed a special marketing task force to sell its products to large national corporations. In addition, Prime purchased the British government-owned Compeda, Ltd., a manufacturer of CAD software, in order to strengthen its offerings in that field. Compeda's products aided in the design of petrochemical plants and other processing facilities. With these efforts, revenues increased ten percent to $435 million by the end of the year, and income grew to $45 million.

Despite these gains, however, it had become clear by the spring of 1983 that retooling Prime for future success would not be an easy task. The company announced its first quarterly slump in income in ten years, as executives continued to leave for other jobs. In July, another six sales and marketing managers resigned from the company. Prime was forced to report a second straight quarterly drop in earnings, and its credibility with the investment community declined accordingly. In an effort to bolster profits, in July Prime introduced its newest minicomputer, the Model 9950, which carried a price tag of $392,500.

In hopes of fostering long-term growth, Prime invested heavily in research and development, upping its expenses in this area from 7.6 percent of sales in 1981 to ten percent of sales in 1983. The company concentrated its research efforts in fields that it considered to be the most promising for future growth: office automation, CAD/CAM, and commercial distributive data processing. With this effort, Prime hoped to introduce a large number of new products in a relatively short period of time.

These efforts started to pay off in May of 1984, when Prime introduced the Model 2250 super-minicomputer, which took up the same amount of space as just two desk-height filing cabinets. Designed to be used in a working office environment, the 2250 did not require the climate control of a data-processing center. In addition, this machine ran on the same operating system as the company's other computers, so it was able to use all the same programs, and it was moderately priced at $99,500.

In conjunction with this development, the company also began to stress its CAD/CAM business lines. Rather than sell its hardware to other companies, which then packaged it with software and sold it to manufacturers, Prime chose to market a complete CAD/CAM system directly to industrial designers and other users. To promote these sales, Prime increased its sales staff by 42 percent and its customer service unit by 87 percent. These efforts paid off as the company's CAD/CAM revenues doubled in 1984 to about $130 million, making up almost one-fifth of Prime's sales.

Prime's CAD/CAM initiative came as the company realized that it had missed the opportunity to make a significant splash in several other markets, including office automation and desk-top work stations. Also in May, the company entered into a joint venture with the Ford Motor Co. to market Ford's Product Design Graphics System—developed on a Prime minicomputer in 1980—which specialized in assisting the manufacture of curved and free-form surfaces, like those in cars, airplanes, and ships.

In June, Prime further increased its investment in the CAD/CAM market when the company became a joint owner of the Medusa design and drafting software package with its British developer, Cambridge Interactive Systems Ltd. The following month Prime introduced two new computers that strengthened its offerings in the CAD/CAM field, and by the end of the year the company had started to see some rebound in earnings.

In 1985 Prime's results improved even further, as sales rose 20 percent. This was due in part to the fact that the company doubled its sales force and enlarged its service and support divisions, adding 600 new employees to bring its total to 8,600. This push was part of Prime's effort to take market share away from its competitors as the computer industry as a whole underwent a shake-out.

In response to the industry turmoil, Prime's leaders decided that the structure of the minicomputer industry was in transition, and to survive, Prime would have to be enlarged, staking out a strong market niche. In order to do this, the company made a strategic decision to concentrate its efforts on the CAD/CAM market segment and began raising funds to purchase other companies in this field. By early 1987, $375 million had been gathered, and Prime's managers were shopping for likely acquisitions.

In addition to these long range plans, Prime continued its efforts to maintain its technological edge. In January of 1987 the company rolled out its newest super-minicomputer, the Model 2755. To keep the cost of developing this model down, the company had bought many of its components from other suppliers, rather than developing them itself. Two months later Prime also introduced its new graphics workstation, the PXCL 5500, for use by automotive, engineering, and aeronautical engineers. This product allowed designers to do three-dimensional work in color.

In April of 1987 Prime introduced a computer based on the latest micro-chip technology, which ran on the UNIX operating system, making it compatible with a variety of computers made by other manufacturers. In June Prime further pressed its campaign to keep its products on the cutting edge with the introduction of a new super-minicomputer, the Model 6350, which was followed by the Model 6550 at the end of the year. The company hoped to vanquish its competition and shore up its results, which had become depressed again in 1986, as buyers shied away from large investments in computer technology.

In October Prime made the first of its major CAD/CAM purchases when it bought the Versacad Corporation, which produced design systems for use on personal computers. However, the company's largest CAD/CAM acquisition came at the end of 1987, when Prime made a surprise $390 million bid for Computervision Corporation. Computervision offered Prime a new design workstation, a wide range of software applications, and 2,000 new clients. With the merger, Prime's 3.6 percent share of the CAD/CAM market quadrupled to 16 percent overnight, making it second in the field after IBM and tenth in the computer industry overall. By January 29, 1988, Prime had reached an agreement to purchase Computervision for $435 million, after the smaller company spent a month unsuccessfully shopping around for a better deal.

Prime reported 1987 revenues of $961 million, and profits of $65 million. The company made a third acquisition in the CAD/CAM field in October of 1988, when it bought the Calma Company from General Electric. With these three major acquisitions, Prime found itself facing the substantial task of integrating all of its new CAD-CAM operations.

Prime was in the midst of this project when MAI Basic Four, Inc. made a bid to buy the company for $970 million in a hostile takeover attempt in November of 1988. Prime instead arranged a leveraged buy-out in late 1989. In August of that year, DR Holdings, Inc., a company set up by the New York investment banking house J.H. Whitney & Company, purchased 79 percent of Prime's shares, and the following January, Prime formally merged with the holding company, completing the leveraged buy-out.

Although this tactic had enabled Prime to stay independent, the company had been forced to borrow a large sum of money in order to go private. The company found itself with an obligation to pay more than $125 million a year in debt service, at a time when the computer industry was undergoing a deep transition. In November of 1991 Prime introduced a new generation of CAD/CAM design workstations that offered additional capabilities but was also hampered by a number of drawbacks.

In the following year, Prime saw its operations further undercut as the market moved from reliance on specially-designed proprietary systems to open computing environments. In addition, a deep global recession cut into the buying power of its target customers in manufacturing. Finally, in August of 1992, Prime acknowledged the collapse of its hardware business and discontinued its minicomputer manufacturing operations. Instead, the company decided to concentrate its energies on its joint marketing agreements with Sun Microsystems and Digital Equipment for CAD/CAM systems.

That summer, Prime also moved to solidify its financial position by reducing its enormous debt. In order to do so, the company once again offered stock to the public, selling 25 million shares of common stock on August 13, 1992. Two weeks later, on August 26, 1992, Prime filed for bankruptcy and protection from its creditors under Chapter 11 of the U.S. Bankruptcy Code, in order to clear the way for its future viable operation.

In addition, Prime changed its name at this time to Computervision Corporation, to better reflect the scope of its newly reduced operations and capitalize on the market identity of its subsidiary's name. With the company's near-failure, customers had become reluctant to invest in its systems, concerned that service support and future advances in technology might not be forthcoming. Despite these efforts to revive the ailing company, Computervision reported in October of 1992 that losses for the quarter would be substantially worse than expected, totaling $88.1 million despite a $20 million gain from discontinuing its manufacturing operations. In March of the following year, Computervision reached an agreement in principle with its financial backers as part of its Chapter 11 proceedings.

Later that spring, Computervision's president was fired, and new management was installed in hopes that the company could

be saved, but by October the picture looked bleak. Business conditions in Europe and Japan, where the company did 70 percent of its business, had not improved. In an effort to cut costs, Computervision laid off 2,000 of its 4,500 workers, taking a $75.2 million charge for severance pay, and the company reported a third-quarter total loss of $543 million. Overall, the company's business plan at the time of its stock sale in 1992 had been a complete failure, and Computervision was hit by a number of shareholder suits alleging improper disclosure.

In its new incarnation, Computervision billed itself as a software and services company. The firm announced that it would no longer resell hardware made by Sun Microsystems, because customers did not want to operate through a middleman. Instead, the company would tell customers which hardware was necessary to run Computervision software, then take a commission on the sale to Sun.

With its new focus on software and services as well as its dramatically lowered overhead, which had been attained through staff cuts and sales of company property, Computervision hoped that its CAD/CAM products could keep the company afloat. In the spring of 1994 the company received a large contract from the Rolls-Royce Aerospace Group, brightening the outlook. Although Computervision appeared to have pared its operations to a manageable size, the company's large debt cast doubt upon its future chances. Whether Computervision would ultimately be successful in negotiating this acute crisis and moving forward into the late 1990s remained to be seen.

Further Reading:

"A Big Challenge at Prime Computer," *Business Week,* December 21, 1981.

Bulkeley, William M., "Computervision Reports Loss For 3rd Quarter," *Wall Street Journal,* October 22, 1993.

Campanella, Frank W., "Toward the High End," *Barron's,* August 27, 1984.

Davis, Bob, "Prime Computer Claims It Is on the Road To Recovery, but Major Problems Remain," *Wall Street Journal,* June 7, 1984.

"Did a clash of egos undo Prime's CEO?" *Business Week,* July 20, 1981.

Geipel, Gary, "Next Year May Be Prime's Time," *Business Week,* October 20, 1986.

Helm, Leslie, "The Merger Wave Bearing Down On Minicomputer Makers," *Business Week,* November 28, 1988.

——, "Two Could Be Prime's Number," *Business Week,* January 11, 1988.

"A Minicomputer Maker With Maxi Problems," *Business Week,* May 9, 1983.

"Prime Takes Aim at the Big Three," *Business Week,* April 21, 1980.

Roberts, Johnnie L., and Liz Roman Gallese, "Prime Computer, as Net and Credibility Wane, Says 6 Quit to Join Ex-Chief's Firm," *Wall Street Journal,* July 18, 1983.

—Elizabeth Rourke

Sophisticated Software Used Every Day

Compuware Corporation

31440 Northwestern Highway
Farmington Hills, Michigan 48334-2564
U.S.A.
(810) 737-7300
Fax: (810) 737-7108

Public Company
Incorporated: 1973
Employees: 2,600
Sales: $234.94 million
Stock Exchanges: NASDAQ
SICs: 7372 Prepackaged Software

Compuware Corporation is an international computer software organization. The company's activities include developing, marketing, and supporting systems software products. Historically, Compuware's principal emphasis has been on products designed to improve programmer productivity primarily for International Business Machines (IBM) and IBM-compatible mainframe computers. Compuware operates through two divisions—a product division and a services division. The product division tests, debugs, and maintains large-scale application software. The services division plans, develops, implements, and maintains computer systems for public sector clients and large corporate clients.

Compuware was established in 1973 by three co-founders: Peter Karmanos, Thomas Thewes, and Allen B. Cutting. According to a *Detroit News* report, Karmanos, Thewes, and Cutting pooled $9,000 to establish the company. Their original mission statement was: "We will help people do things with computers."

The first office occupied by the fledgling company was located in Southfield, Michigan. Originally, clients came to Compuware for data processing professional services and help with computer installations. In addition, Compuware provided "programmers for hire" to provide additional manpower for specific client projects or to create solutions to particular needs. Unlike other companies specializing in software and computer services for a specific industry, Compuware differentiated itself from competing companies by its emphasis on diverse applications of mainframe computer technology. Karmanos, quoted in the company's 20th anniversary publication, stated: "We were there to help them solve computer problems, not how to market their goods or services. We were a resource—a technology resource—to help our customers work smarter and be more productive."

Compuware continued in its original role as a provider of data processing professional services until 1977 when the company entered the software market with a fault diagnosis tool called Abend-AID. The name Abend-AID was derived from the term abnormal end, which referred to unexpected system errors or failures. These types of problems were often caused by faults in computer programs, changes in system environments, or other errors or failures.

Prior to the availability of Abend-AID, computer programmers confronted with abnormal end situations were required to use manual techniques to test and debug programs. The process involved preparing trial transactions through lengthy procedures such as manually creating experimental entries, writing special test programs, and reviewing program logic. Compuware called this process "tedious, time consuming, and errorprone." The Abend-AID program worked automatically. It intercepted system error messages during actual program execution. This enabled programmers to pinpoint precise error locations and identify the cause of the failure. Abend-AID also offered recommendations for necessary corrections.

Because mainframe computers were critical to business operations, time spent correcting problems often had a significant effect on a company's ability to conduct business. Quick remedies helped reduce the amount of downtime associated with computer problems and helped reduce programmer manpower costs. Abend-AID's success in the marketplace enabled Compuware to become established as a major force in the industry.

Following the introduction of Abend-AID, Compuware organized a products division to sell Abend-AID and other software packages. Although the company continued to provide services, the percentage of total revenue generated by the services division grew smaller as sales from the products division increased. The company's offerings focused on integrated systems software products designed to improve programmer productivity through program testing, data manipulation, interactive debugging, and fault diagnosis.

Interactive analysis and debugging products were tools to help programmers identify and correct errors in software by evaluating the quality of a program's code and logic. They worked by enabling a programmer to use either test or production data and progress through a program one statement or statement group at a time. Whenever an error was detected, the programmer could stop and make an immediate correction. Using this process, programs could be tested one step at a time until they were free from errors. The first software package in the interactive analysis and debugging product line, MBX Xpediter/TSO, was introduced in 1979. In 1983, Xpediter earned Compuware its first International Computer Program (ICP) award, granted in recognition of $1 million in sales.

File and data management software packages were used to automate test data preparation, thereby insuring the integrity of the data manipulated by programs. Compuware launched its line of file and data management products in 1983. The first offering in the line, File-AID, was originally sold under an exclusive marketing arrangement with another company, but rights to the program were purchased by Compuware in 1992. Using File-AID, programmers had immediate and direct access to the data necessary to conduct tests and analyze production work. Although early File-AID products were designed for IBM and IBM-compatible mainframe computers only, subsequent File-AID products were designed for other types of computers.

CICS-dBUG-AID, designed for use with IBM's CICS (Customer Information Control System) was introduced in 1985. The following year, Compuware introduced MVS PLAY-BACK, the company's first product in its automated testing line. PLAYBACK simulated an on-line systems environment that helped computer technicians execute transactions and check data created by manipulation. PLAYBACK streamlined testing procedures by reproducing a real-time environment without requiring that network users staff terminals or even that the communications network be active. Products in the PLAY-BACK family offered five phases of testing: the ability to test a single program from a single terminal; the ability to test a single program from more than one terminal; the ability to test the integration of more than one program; the ability to test a program's proficiency at varying production volumes; and the ability to confirm that programming changes made no unexpected consequences in other areas. Subsequent products in the PLAYBACK line permitted the creation of training sessions for network users.

Compuware entered a phase of rapid growth during the second half of the 1980s. In 1987, *Inc.* magazine ranked Compuware among the fastest growing privately held companies in the United States. Its premier product, Abend-AID received an ICP $100 million award, and IBM recognized Compuware as a business partner-authorized application specialist. In addition, Compuware expanded its global presence. Following a decision to operate in Europe through wholly owned subsidiaries, Compuware acquired European companies that had been distributing its software products in England, France, Italy, Spain, and West Germany.

To accommodate its expansion, Compuware announced a decision to build new headquarters in 1987. The $20 million facility, located in Farmington Hills, Michigan, provided 165,000 square feet of space in addition to a 4,000-square-foot satellite facility in Southfield, Michigan. When Compuware moved in, it employed 746 people and expected to increase its staff to 995 within a year. The company's annual compound growth rate for the previous five years stood at 34 percent. Software products accounted for 65 percent of revenues; professional data processing services contributed 30 percent; the remaining sales were generated from software developed for specific markets and from educational resources. As the 1980s ended, Compuware broke the $100 million mark in total annual revenue.

The 1990s brought an increased interest in expansion and growth through acquisition. For example, in 1991 Compuware merged with Centura Software in a move aimed at strengthening its interactive analysis and debugging product offerings. Compuware also increased the attention given to smaller computers. Although the company historically had focused on the sale of mainframe programming software, it released a version of File-AID able to test and edit mainframe data files on per-sonal computers (PCs). File-AID/PC enabled program developers to move blocks of data from mainframes to PCs where they could be scrutinized, copied, edited, modified, or printed. The technology provided a means for discovering programming flaws in a quick manner.

Other new products introduced in 1991 included DBA-XPERT for DB2 (a database management program) and Pathvu/2 (an OS/2 version of a previously released interactive analysis and debugging product). Like its mainframe counterpart, Pathvu/2 provided programmers working with COBOL an automated analysis and documentation tool to evaluate the structure of the programming code. In order to show what was happening within a program and to document missing elements in the code structure, Pathvu/2 created a graphic display of the program's organization. Compuware reported total revenues of $141.8 million in 1991.

In 1992, Compuware established Compuware Japan Corporation. Compuware Japan's main office was in Tokyo, and company officials hoped to add a branch in Osaka. Compuware Japan planned to focus on adapting existing products for Japanese programmers using Fujitsu and Hitachi hardware in addition to IBM mainframe equipment. The following year, Compuware further expanded its presence abroad with the establishment of Compuware Corporation Do Brasil. Brazil was estimated to be the fifth largest IBM mainframe market in the world. Compuware's move followed a policy change relaxing government imposed import restrictions on computers and software. Company officials expected the Brazilian subsidiary to be well positioned to serve the emerging Latin American market.

Compuware's first initial public offering of common stock occurred in 1992. The stock was offered at $22 per share and 5.5 million shares were sold by the company. Net proceeds (after underwriting discount and other expenses) totaled $111.5 million. In addition, existing shareholders sold 3.9 million shares of common stock.

Despite its successful stock offering, 1992 also marked the first year since its inception that Compuware failed to earn a profit. The company's reported net loss totaled $23.8 million. According to a published statement, the lack of profitability was attributed to special pretax charges of $52.6 million related to expenses surrounding its acquisition of XA Systems Corporation. XA Systems software products were primarily classified as file and data management tools.

In a move designed to augment its fault diagnosis product line, Compuware purchased the Eyewitness product line from Landmark Systems Corporation in 1993. The acquisition increased Compuware's product line to 27 software products. As of March 31, 1993, Compuware had licensed over 41,000 copies of its products to more than 5,700 customers around the world. Software license fees and maintenance fees produced 74 percent of the company's total revenues. The remaining 26 percent was generated from professional services.

Compuware's Professional Services Division operated branches in seven locations: Baltimore, Maryland; Columbus, Ohio; Colorado Springs, Colorado; Lansing, Michigan; Toronto, Canada; Detroit, Michigan, and Washington, DC. Most of the revenue generated from the services division was received from business application programming services. Business application programming services were those in which Compuware's programmers wrote original software to perform a particular function. Other services division operations included analyzing business problems and using computer techniques to overcome them; providing conversion services to organizations switching from one type of computer environment to another; systems planning, a service involved in identifying business objectives and information requirements in order to make recommendations for hardware and software; and consulting. Although revenues earned by the services division typically carried lower profit margins than did revenues earned by the products division, Compuware stated that it remained committed to providing services to its customers.

Despite its growth and expansion, Compuware's executives insisted that the company's basic mission remained unchanged: to help people do things with computers. They acknowledged, however, that the processing power of computers had changed vastly during the company's twenty years in business.

One significant change within the industry was the expanding presence of PCs. Some industry analysts had criticized Compuware's emphasis on mainframe computer technology. In response, Compuware noted that the 36,000 mainframe computers in operation were running "mission-critical systems" applications that were not suited to PC technology. These included credit card authorization services, airline reservations, and on-line banking. According to Compuware's data, only 13 percent of mainframe computer operators used software to diagnose faults. Even less used software for debugging, file and data management, and automated testing. Compuware's own analysts felt a sufficient base existed for expansion in the mainframe market.

Nevertheless, in 1993 Compuware turned its attention to the PC arena with its acquisition of EcoSystems Software, Inc. The EcoSystems product line included programs designed to be used in PC networks. The PC market differed significantly from the mainframe market because of the wide variety of computer hardware manufacturers and operating systems employed. Two new products were added to the EcoSystem line during the second quarter of 1994 to help network clients schedule batch jobs and better manage database environments.

In a similar move in early 1994, Compuware announced an agreement to acquire Uniface Holding B.V. Uniface, based in Amsterdam, Netherlands, was a supplier of client-server (network) application and development software. According to *Crain's Detroit Business,* industry watchers expected the acquisition to provide Compuware with a strong presence in the PC market at a time when its mainframe software licensing was still growing at a rate of about 30 percent. The acquisition was also expected to give Uniface a greater presence in the North American market.

Principal Subsidiaries: Compuware Nordic APS (Denmark); Compuware France; Compuware GMBH (Germany); Compuware Italy; Compuware System Software B.V. (Netherlands); Compuware Nordic AS (Norway); Compuware S.A. (Spain); Compuware Ltd. (UK); Compuware Corporation Do Brasil (Brazil); Compuware Japan Corporation; XA Systems Corporation; EcoSystems Software, Inc.; Uniface Holding B.V.

Further Reading:

Child, Charles, "Compuware: Riding the Dinosaur," *Crain's Detroit Business,* February 15, 1993.
"Compuware Acquires Hiperstation, Expands Automated Testing Business," *PR Newswire,* April 11, 1994.
Compuware: 20 Years of Helping People Do Things with Computers, Farmington Hills, Michigan: Compuware, 1993.
Cunningham, Cara A., "Pathvu/2 Taps OS/2 PM Graphics to Analyze COBOL Code," *PC Week,* January 6, 1992.
Maurer, Michael, "Compuware Merger Wins Raves," *Crain's Detroit Business,* March 28, 1994.
Olson, Lise, "In Software, Compuware's Got the Program," *Detroit News,* June 26, 1988.
Pallatto, John, "Compuware Moves Data Editor to PCs," *PC Week,* September 30, 1991.
"Software Growth: Compuware Corp. Keeps Expanding, Here and Abroad," *Detroit News,* January 28, 1987.

—Karen Bellenir

Conseco

Conseco Inc.

P.O. Box 1911
Carmel, Indiana 46032
U.S.A.
(317) 573-6100
Fax: (317) 573-6818

Public Company
Incorporated: 1982
Employees: 1,098
Sales: $2.64 billion
Stock Exchanges: New York
SICs: 6311 Life Insurance; 6719 Holding Companies NEC

Conseco, Inc. is a specialized financial services holding company that invests primarily in the insurance industry. It makes money by acquiring insurance companies and increasing their profitability and value through restructuring. The company also earns advisement and management fees from various financial institutions. Conseco was one of the fastest growing insurance holding company in the United States in the early 1990s.

Stephen C. Hilbert founded the company and guided its meteoric rise. The 48-year-old Hilbert has an unusual background for a chairman of a major financial institution. He was raised in a small rural community near Terre Haute, Indiana, and attended nearby Indiana State University. After only two years of college, however, Hilbert became restless. "I dropped out to sell encyclopedias," Hilbert explained to *Barron's* in 1991. "After I made $19,000 my first year as a 19-year-old, I knew I didn't need a college education to make a good living."

Hilbert drifted into the insurance business in the 1970s. After working for a small company for a few years, he got a taste of the corporate world at Aetna. Although Hilbert admired the muscle of Aetna and its corporate counterparts, he was frustrated by their lack of innovation. During this experience he conceived the idea for a new kind of enterprise—a life insurance company that would combine the flexibility and innovation of a small firm with the marketing savvy, financial strength, and computer systems of a big financial institution.

Just as he had done to sell encyclopedias in the mid-1960s, Hilbert started knocking on doors in the late 1970s. This time, however, he was looking for seed capital to fund his business start-up, Security National of Indiana Corp. Although several

regional securities firms laughed Hilbert and his five-page business plan back into the street, by the early 1980s he had raised $3 million in capital. In 1982, Hilbert acquired his first life insurance company, Executive Income Life Insurance Co., for $1.3 million. By slashing the fat and inefficiency out of his new purchase, Hilbert was able to return the ailing insurer to profitability after only one year.

True to his original concept of combining size with innovation, Hilbert established his enterprise in 1982 under two separate companies. Security National Corp. was formed to acquire and manage existing life insurance companies. To complement that holding company's subsidiaries, Security National of Indiana was established to develop and market new life insurance products and services. Although the two companies merged to form one holding company late in 1983, internal operations still reflected Hilbert's original concept.

Hilbert's company acquired Consolidated National Life Insurance Co. in August of 1983. In December of that year Hilbert's two holding companies were merged under the name Conseco, Inc. With about 25 employees and assets worth $3 million, Conseco substantially improved the performance of its two acquisitions during 1983 and 1984. The company then purchased Lincoln American Life Insurance Co. early in 1985 for $25 million. It quickly moved Lincoln's headquarters from Memphis to Conseco's burgeoning offices in Carmel, Indiana. Hilbert, now with a few successful acquisitions under his belt, took Conseco public in 1985 in an effort to boost its investment capital. By the end of the year the company's asset base had increased to $102 million.

Satisfied with its recipe for acquiring and improving insurance companies, Conseco stepped up its acquisition efforts in 1986. It purchased Lincoln Income Life Insurance Co. and Bankers National Life Insurance Co. for $32 million and $118 million, respectively. In 1987, it added Western National Life Insurance to its portfolio at a cost of $262 million. By the end of 1987, Conseco's assets had grown to a whopping $3.4 billion, and its work force had grown almost 20-fold since 1984, to nearly 500.

Conseco reorganized and caught its breath in 1988. It moved the balance of the operations from its largest purchase, Bankers National, to its ballooning Carmel headquarters. It also moved much of its Lincoln subsidiary from Kentucky. Although it increased the value of its holdings to more than $4 billion in 1988, Conseco was able to reduce its work force by almost 10 percent.

After nearly two years since its last acquisition, Hilbert raised $68 million in June of 1989 to purchase National Fidelity Life Insurance Co. It moved that concern's headquarters from Dallas to Carmel. To house its expanding staff and operations in Carmel, Conseco built a 40,000-square-foot data processing center in 1990.

Throughout the 1980s Wall Street perceived Conseco as young and inexperienced. However, the company's rapid growth finally began to pique the interest of industry analysts and mainstream investors. Hilbert's strategy seemed relatively simple to most observers: purchase troubled insurance companies with potential and increase their value by turning them around. When Conseco went hunting for acquisition candidates, it looked for organizations with sound asset portfolios. For example, it avoided the many companies that in the 1980s had invested heavily in risky real estate and junk bonds. In addition, Hilbert sought firms that had developed unique insurance and annuity products or had devised innovative distribution systems for their offerings.

Importantly, though, Hilbert also searched for insurers that were inefficient and bloated with excess personnel. He slashed the aggregate work force of the five companies he had purchased between 1985 and 1989, for example, from 850 to 450 by 1993. Conseco's 1989 annual report boasted that it had eliminated 83 percent of the employees from one of its acquisitions. Many of the cutbacks were accomplished by integrating Conseco's consolidated marketing, investment, and product development operations into the companies that it purchased. In addition, Conseco typically achieved significant efficiency gains by implementing advanced information and data processing systems.

By 1989, Conseco's assets were valued at $5.2 billion. Although Conseco's rise was impressive, rampant acquisition and expansion had a downside for the holding company. By the late 1980s, Conseco had accumulated about twice as much debt as equity. In order to continue acquiring new companies, Hilbert knew that he would have to find a new source of funding that was not linked to debt-burdened Conseco. Therefore, in 1990 Hilbert organized Conseco Capital Partners (CCP), a limited partnership that included several well-financed companies. The company was intended to serve as the primary vehicle for new life insurance acquisitions. CCP's first acquisition was Great American Reserve Insurance Co. for $135 million. It also purchased Jefferson National Life Group in 1990 ($171 million) and Beneficial Standard Life in 1991 ($141 million).

Continued gains in the value of Conseco holdings combined with the success of CCP investments resulted in dynamic growth during 1990 and 1991. Although many insurers suffered severe setbacks during the U.S. recession and experienced staggering declines in the value of their portfolios, Conseco swelled its asset base to $11.8 billion and doubled its work force to almost 1,100. Indeed, as the insurance industry weathered record insolvencies, Conseco expanded its headquarters and opened an entirely new hub, the Conseco Annuity Center, in Dallas. Entering 1992, the company was valued at over $800 million.

Because Conseco's performance contrasted so sharply with that of most of its competitors in the early 1990s, many analysts were skeptical. Critics charged that Conseco's amazing asset growth was largely the result of questionable accounting techniques. They pointed to the company's relatively low net worth, which was equal to only 2 percent of its total assets in 1991. Some analysts believed that it was just a matter of time before Conseco would fall prey to the asset devaluation that had plagued other fast-growing insurers of the 1980s.

Despite Hilbert's insistence that Conseco's success reflected a commitment to sound business practices, skepticism continued. Conseco endured a string of disparaging articles in major business journals in the early 1990s that questioned its integrity. Short-sellers—investors that had bet on Conseco's downfall— were enraged when its earnings continued to multiply. "This

(criticism) goes back to instinct and gut feeling, and no hard facts," said money manager Martin Lizt in a January 1993 issue of *Financial World.* "You have to ask the question, 'Have they found a new way to make white bread?'"

As detractors waited for Conseco's money machine to disintegrate in the early 1990s, Hilbert clung to his original guiding principles. As stated in the company's 1993 annual report, "Our operating strategy is to consolidate and streamline the administrative functions of the acquired companies, to improve their investment yield through active asset management . . . , and to eliminate unprofitable products and distribution channels."

Indeed, analysts familiar with Conseco's portfolios attested that the company's investments were much more liquid, of higher quality, and more conservative than those of most insurers. In addition to avoiding real estate and junk bonds, Conseco's portfolio managers steered away from other risky and trendy investment vehicles of the 1980s, particularly Guaranteed Investment Contracts. A study of the top U.S. insurers in 1991 showed that only 48 percent of their investments were fixed maturities, whereas over 50 percent were tied up in real estate and other less dependable assets. In contrast, more than 80 percent of Conseco's portfolio comprised fixed maturities, and only 2 percent consisted of real estate holdings.

In 1992, Conseco founded Conseco Capital Management, Inc. (CCM) to capitalize on its investment expertise. CCM provided a variety of financial and investment advisory services on a fee basis to both affiliated and nonaffiliated insurers. CCM was managing about $19 billion worth of assets going into 1994. Also in 1992, CCP shelled out $600 million to acquire Bankers Life and Casualty Co., one of the nation's largest writers of individual health insurance policies. In early 1993, Conseco acquired a controlling interest in MDS/Bankmark, a major marketer of annuity and mutual fund products.

The Conseco organization continued to add value to its holdings in the early 1990s and to achieve success with both CCM and CCP. In fact, it experienced stellar growth during 1992 and 1993. The company's net income increased 46 percent in 1992 to $170 million, and 75 percent in 1993 to $297 million. During the same period, the value of Conseco's assets ballooned from $11.8 billion to $16.6 billion—a gain of about 30 percent. As Conseco increased its value and expanded its asset base, suspicions about its performance began to wane in 1993 and 1994. Importantly, the company had eliminated much of its debt burden by 1994.

From an encyclopedia salesman in eastern Indiana, Hilbert had successfully boosted his status to that of corporate multimillionaire. In 1992, just ten years after starting his business, Hilbert was one of the highest paid executives in the United States. He received $8.8 million in pay and exercised stock options worth almost $30 million. Although some critics derided his benefits package and called it exorbitant, Hilbert was quick to point out that his compensation was tied to the company's performance. After all, a $100 investment in Conseco in 1988 would have returned $2062 in 1993.

Entering the mid-1990s, Conseco was poised for continued growth. Its goals for 1994 included increasing its assets under management by 30 percent. To help achieve this objective, Conseco formed a new limited partnership in early 1994, Conseco Capital Partners II, L.P. CCP II included 36 limited partners who had a combined investment potential of $5 billion to $7 billion. In contrast to CCP, the new partnership was designed to focus on the acquisition and improvement of larger companies valued at $350 million to $1.5 billion. The original CCP partnership was changed to CCP Insurance, Inc., in 1993, and began acting as a holding company for its three subsidiaries.

In addition to its insurance and financial management divisions, which accounted for more than 85 percent of Conseco's operations in 1993, the company was broadening its scope to include some nontraditional ventures. Conseco was investing tens of millions of dollars into new entertainment-related projects late in 1993 and 1994, including some river boat gambling proposals. In fact, in October of 1993 Hilbert formed Conseco Entertainment Inc., a holding company for Conseco's future entertainment investments. Other ventures included outdoor and indoor theaters in Indiana and Ohio. In addition, in 1992 the company paid $15 million for a 31 percent share of Chicago-based Eagle Credit Corp., an organization formed to provide financing to Harley-Davidson dealers and their customers. It also agreed to commit $5 million in 1993 to Rick Galles Racing, an IndyCar racing team in which Conseco owned a 33-percent share.

To its investor's chagrin, however, several of Conseco's past forays into nontraditional investments had not performed as well as its core insurance and financial holdings. In 1989, for instance, Conseco invested in a powdered drink mix developed by an Indiana doctor. The venture failed. Similarly, an investment in a restaurant chain that featured buckets of spaghetti fizzled. "You have to stay where your strengths are," acknowledged Ngaire E. Cuneo, Executive Vice President of Corporate Development, in the October 25, 1993, issue of the *Indianapolis Business Journal.* "We are going to stay away from food and beverage." Despite a few unwise choices, Conseco was recognized for its highly conservative approach to investing.

In May of 1994, CCP II made the first in a series of expected acquisitions when it agreed to purchase Statesman Group, Inc., for $350 million. Conseco planned to retain its proven strategy of using innovative management techniques to increase the value of acquired holdings. Hilbert moved his main personal office to New York, where he planned to direct Conseco's CCP II. However, Conseco's headquarters remained in Carmel, and Hilbert planned to sustain his active management role there. "This is what I love to do," Hilbert proclaimed in the June 7, 1993, issue of the *Indianapolis Business Journal.* "I think you'd hear the same thing if you were talking to Bill Gates or anyone else who has achieved success. . . . Its their baby."

Principal Subsidiaries: Bankers National Life Insurance Co.; Bankers Life Holding Corp. (56%); CCP Insurance, Inc. (40%); Conseco Capital Management, Inc.; Conseco Capital Partners II, L.P.; Lincoln National Life Insurance Co.; National Fidelity Life Insurance Co.; Western National Corp. (40%).

Further Reading:

Andrews, Greg, "Hilbert Takes a Bite of the Big Apple," *Indianapolis Business Journal,* November 15, 1993; "Conseco Move Marks Evolution," *Indianapolis Business Journal,* September 20, 1993; "Conseco Pouring Millions into Entertainment Ventures," *Indianapolis Business Journal,* October 25, 1993.

"Buoyed by Their Biggest Year Ever, Hilbert and Conseco Aim Higher," *Indiana Business Journal,* June 7, 1993.

Conseco Inc. 10th Anniversary 1992; Celebrating a Decade of Growth, Carmel, IN: Conseco Inc., 1992.

Feaver, Christopher, "Western National IPO Means More Big Bucks for Conseco," *Indianapolis Business Journal,* February 14, 1994; "Conseco Rolls Dice Again on Riverboat Gambling," *Indianapolis Business Journal,* December 6, 1993; "Conseco's New Partnership Will Stall Large Companies," *Indianapolis Business Journal,* January 17, 1994.

"Indiana's Highest Paid CEOs," *Indiana Business,* July 1993.

Laing, Jonathan R., "Deferred Risk? A Hard Look at Conseco, a Fast-Growing Life Insurer," *Barron's,* February 11, 1991.

Miller, James, "Conseco Partnership Agreement to Acquire Statesman for $350 Million," *The Wall Street Journal,* May 3, 1994.

Panchapakesan, Meenakshi, and Michael K. Ozanian, "Loaded for Bear: Why High-Flying Conseco Is Proving Its Numerous Detractors Wrong," *Financial World,* January 19, 1993.

Rosensteele, James W., "Corporate Profile for Conseco, Inc.," *Business Wire,* January 21, 1994.

—Dave Mote

Continental Grain Company

277 Park Avenue
New York, New York 10172
U.S.A.
(212) 207-5100
Fax: (212) 207-5043

Private Company
Incorporated: 1813
Employees: 15,000
Sales: $15 billion
SICs: 5153 Grain & Field Beans; 2048 Prepared Feeds, Not
 Elsewhere Classified

Continental Grain Company is one of the world's largest privately held companies and a primary player in the agricultural commodities business. The company has been owned and operated by one family throughout its history. The main component of Continental Grain's business consists of storing, selling, and shipping grains and oilseeds, but the company also runs a vast empire of holdings in more than 100 nations around the world, which produce and distribute meat, animal feeds, flour, petroleum, and financial services. Begun in Europe during the Napoleonic era, Continental shifted its operations to the United States in the wake of World War II and grew rapidly in the postwar years.

Continental Grain was founded by Simon Fribourg in 1813 in Arlon, Belgium. Legend has it that the business first took off during a Belgian drought in 1848 when Simon's son, Michel Fribourg, made the dangerous journey to Bessarabia in the Ukraine carrying several trunks of gold to trade for wheat. Upon his return to Belgium, Fribourg was easily able to resell the grain at a high return to his starving Belgian countrymen. From the beginning, the commodities trader thrived on the vicissitudes of nature and the ever-present need for food.

In addition to natural disaster, wars played a major role in the company's history. During the Franco-Prussian war, Belgium remained neutral and the Fribourgs' enterprise flourished. In the late 19th century, the company built flour mills in Luxembourg and Belgium. When World War I broke out in 1914, the Fribourgs moved their company to London in the wake of the German invasion of their country.

After the war was over, the Fribourgs returned to Antwerp, where they re-established their business under the name Cie Continental d'Importation. In 1921 the company opened a Paris office. At the same time the Fribourgs established an operation in Chicago, as the midwestern region of the United States emerged as a major source of the world's grain. The Chicago branch of the company was founded on February 5, 1921, and was capitalized with $50,000. Its purpose was to procure grains for export. To aid in this endeavor, Continental also opened a New York office in 1922.

In the course of the 1920s and 1930s, Continental expanded its operations to cities such as Rotterdam, Zurich, Bucharest, Genoa, Naples, and Madrid. In the United States the company began to establish grain elevators and corporate offices throughout the Midwest in the 1930s; by 1936 the company had a head office of 25 people in New York as well as a West Coast outpost, and fledgling domestic merchandising efforts were in place.

When Nazi leader Adolf Hitler marched on Paris in June of 1940, the Fribourgs made what would be a decisive break with Europe and their company's past. The family's patriarch at that time, Jules, gathered 13 relatives and close associates together to begin the journey over the Pyrenées to Portugal. His son, Michel, working in the company's London office, diverted one of Continental's freighters to Lisbon, where the family made their escape. Eventually, the Fribourgs found their way to the United States, where Jules began to run the family business from New York.

Michel Fribourg spent the war as an American soldier, working in army intelligence in France. In 1944 his father died, and stewardship of the company passed to his uncle. Upon Michel's return after the war, however, he took the reins; he was 31 years old. Faced with the fact that many of Continental's European operations had been decimated by war, leaving its American unit by far the strongest branch of the company, Michel Fribourg decided to make the United States the headquarters and primary arena of Continental's activities.

With European and Asian agricultural areas devastated by war, and the populations of these continents near starvation, American output of foodstuffs increased sharply in the late 1940s. To take advantage of this opportunity, Continental made substantial investments in a broad network of grain elevators and other aspects of commodity trading. The company's operations grew dramatically in the postwar years. By 1954, Continental's sales had reached $200 million. Despite this success, by the end of the 1950s, Fribourg came to recognize the limitations of a company focused on one field, and dominated by one family. To strengthen Continental, he inaugurated a number of changes in the company's operations. First, Fribourg extended the company's management pool beyond his own family, recruiting large numbers of young executives from top business schools and colleges.

In the mid-1960s Fribourg also began to widen Continental's spheres of operation, diversifying into different but related agribusiness fields. In 1966 the company bought a 53 percent interest in Allied Mills, Inc., of Chicago, an animal feed producer. This company subsequently bought four food processors:

Hilbun Poultry, Polo Food Corporation, Ful-O-Pep (an animal food company), and Central Nebraska Packing.

In 1970 Continental also entered the commodities brokerage field, establishing the ContiCommodity Services division. This branch of the company opened 14 domestic offices and one foreign location in an effort to become a worldwide commodity futures broker. In this way, Continental hoped to create a hedge against the risks it ran in the commodities market. The company also set up the Continental Milling Company on Long Island to export flour and animal feeds. In late 1971 Continental expanded its holdings further when it bought the Orowheat Baking Company, a specialty baker.

By the early 1970s more than 100 companies had been added to the Fribourg empire, including real estate concerns, ranches, and food processors and distributors. Continental had expanded its operations to nearly every corner of the world. The company's sales had increased to $2 billion, with 90 percent of them coming from grain trading, and its net worth had reached $100 million.

Continental handled about a quarter of the world's international grain shipments and about a fifth of the grain exports of the United States. The company boasted three million tons of domestic storage capacity and half a million tons abroad. To move the products it sold, Continental operated numerous country grain elevators, 13 river stations, 65 barges, and eight North American port elevators. In addition, the company leased hundreds of railroad cars and as many as 25 cargo ships.

In November 1971, in a deal personally arranged by Fribourg, Continental sold 900,000 tons of U.S. government surplus barley and 2 million tons of corn, worth $137 million, to the U.S.S.R. This sale followed the company's earlier 1963 sale of grain to the Russians, the first such deal between a Western company and the Soviets. In early 1972, Continental scored another Russian coup when it sold nearly 6 million tons of American grain and soybeans to the Soviets, plus an undisclosed proportion of the foreign foodstuffs bought by the country after Soviet crops failed because of bad weather. The value of this agreement was rumored to reach $3 billion. After then President Richard Nixon visited China in the early 1970s, Continental also became the first American commodities dealer to sell grain to that superpower.

Despite Fribourg's success in arranging these deals, by the early 1970s it had become clear that power in Continental needed to be decentralized. The company went through a series of reorganization plans and hired outside management consultants in an effort to restructure its lines of command, with limited success. These efforts were an attempt to respond to a changing climate in the commodities industry. Greater government control, in the form of subsidies to farmers, and investigations into trading practices were threatening to alter the age-old structure of the grain trading business. In 1973 the U.S. Congress launched an inquiry into Continental's Soviet deal, and the government charged the company with filing false reports. Despite these investigations, in 1975 Continental made another large sale of commodities, worth $640 million, to the Soviet Union.

In the mid-1970s Continental also found itself the object of government scrutiny in connection with its New Orleans grain elevator operations. In April of 1976, the company paid a $500,000 fine for shortweighting ships. On December 22, 1977, however, Continental suffered a much larger difficulty with its New Orleans operations when a massive series of explosions shortly after 9:00 a.m. obliterated the company's $80 million grain elevator in Westwego. Thirty-six workers were killed when static electricity set fire to grain dust, and 45 of the facility's 72 silos were destroyed.

Fires burned in the silos for nearly nine months after the explosion, and the company proved unable to demolish the steel-rimmed concrete structures with dynamite. Finally, Continental managed to level its remaining silos and spread out the grain in order to smother the flames. Although temporary facilities allowed some grain to be shipped from the site within a month, Continental faced lawsuits claiming more than $200 million in damages from the blast and received citations and penalties for safety violations by the Occupational Safety and Health Administration. In December of 1978, Continental announced that it would invest $200 million to rebuild its New Orleans site, constructing a new $30 million, fire-safe elevator.

In the late 1970s and throughout the early 1980s, Continental encountered a general slump in the agricultural industry, which depressed the company's revenues and earnings. The intervention of the federal government complicated the market domestically, and international trade also proved perilous. Continental had difficulty collecting large payments for grain shipments from both Turkey and Zaire in the late 1970s and went so far as to cut off the latter's supply of grain at one point in an effort to gain payment. In addition, in August of 1979, the company was cited for illegally cooperating with an Arab boycott of companies that did business with Israel.

Continental's decision to diversify into a broader range of financial functions came back to haunt the company early in 1980. Its commodities trading subsidiary, ContiCommodity Services, Inc., had moved into interest rate and currency futures in the mid-1970s, producing strong growth and profits. In the spring of 1980, however, the company found itself in an untenable position after the silver market collapsed, and Continental was forced to provide $81 million in additional funding for its subsidiary. By December 1980, ContiCommodity had also been forced to liquidate two of its mutual funds, McLean I and a successor fund, McLean II, after the spring silver debacle was followed by a two-week plunge in the markets.

Despite these difficulties, Continental promoted ContiCommodity's head to the newly created position of chief executive in March of 1981. He was joined in this spot by another top executive, as Continental continued in its effort to redistribute corporate power. In the wake of its difficulties, ContiCommodity saw many of its top executives lured away to other firms in 1982, and the company sued a competitor over the raid. In 1983 Continental toyed with the idea of selling the division, but then finally withdrew.

In April 1984, Continental did sell its Orowheat subsidiary, splitting the company into two parts, which were dispersed to the company's management and to General Foods. By the following year, Continental's troubled financial subsidiary had spun off four subsidiary companies: Conticapital Management, Conticurrency, Contifinancial, and Contiadvisory. ContiCommodity itself had begun to specialize in trading financial paper. Despite these measures, however, branches of the company continued to suffer heavy losses.

In September 1984, Continental announced that it had sold ContiCommodity to Refco, Inc., after admitting that it had made additional infusions of cash into the company after failures in two arbitrage trading programs. The company's high overhead, caused by its extensive network of offices, also contributed to its financial lack of health. With this move, Continental withdrew from the futures brokerage business entirely. The company did, however, remain liable for a fine of $1.5 million, assessed by the Commodity Futures Trading Commission in 1986 in connection with its late-1970s silver dealings. In addition, Continental paid an out-of-court settlement to the Peruvian government in connection with this matter.

In 1985 Continental continued the evolution of its corporate structure. The company divided its operations into five units and assigned each a head. The divisions were comprised of financial services, world meat, world milling, transportation and natural resources, and world grain and oilseeds processing. This last unit, which was headed by Michel Fribourg's son, Paul, accounted for 75 percent of the company's revenues, estimated to total $15 billion. Three years later, the company moved even further towards decentralized control when a non-Fribourg was named to succeed Michel Fribourg as chief executive.

In the late 1980s the agricultural industry began a slow revival from its slump, and this process began to enhance Continental's sales. In March 1990, the company announced that it would expand its infrastructure by purchasing 12 grain elevators, located throughout the Midwest. Also in the spring of 1990,

Continental named Paul Fribourg, the sixth generation commodities trader, to additional duties, as he made his way toward the pinnacle of the family company. On April 1, 1990, he took command of a consolidated World Grain, Oilseeds and Merchandising, and General Commodities group, which was called Bulk Commodities. The younger Fribourg was also elected a director of the corporation.

The process of transferring power from father to son was completed in July of 1994, when Michel Fribourg retired to become chairman emeritus, and his son Paul was named president and chief operating officer. Under his father's guidance for over 50 years, Continental Grain had grown to encompass a wide variety of businesses, including meat, milling, grain, oilseeds, rice, cotton, oil, gas, and financial services. The company operated in 100 different nations on six continents, and ships carrying its goods plied the world's seas. It remained to be seen how the sixth-generation Fribourg would guide the company.

Further Reading:

Blumstein, Michael, "ContiCommodity Being Sold to Refco," *New York Times,* September 9, 1984.
Eason, Yla, "ContiFocus: Financial Paper," *New York Times,* February 1, 1984.
"The Incredible Empire of Michel Fribourg," *Business Week,* March 11, 1972.
Maidenberg, H. J., "Harvest of Profits for Continental Grain," *New York Times,* August 5, 1973.
Morgan, Dan, "Continental Grain to Pay Fine Over Arab Boycott," *Washington Post,* August 29, 1979.
Polk, John, "Expansion of Grain Facilities Detailed," *Washington Post,* December 27, 1978.
"Shh . . . Hedging Going On!" *Forbes,* November 1, 1976.

—Elizabeth Rourke

Continental Medical Systems, Inc.

600 Wilson Lane
P.O. Box 715
Mechanicsburg, Pennsylvania 17055
U.S.A.
(717) 790-8300
Fax: (717) 766-8277

Public Company
Incorporated: 1986
Employees: 13,500
Sales: $901 million
Stock Exchanges: New York
SICs: 8051 Skilled Nursing Care Facilities

Continental Medical Systems, Inc. (CMS), is the country's largest provider of rehabilitative medical services. The company operates 36 rehabilitation hospitals, 120 out-patient clinics, and a wide range of contract rehabilitation and medical services in all 50 states. CMS got its start as a nursing home operator, but left this field quickly in order to concentrate on rehabilitative medicine. After embarking on a rapid and ambitious program of acquisitions and hospital construction, CMS slowed its spending to retrench in the early 1990s as high healthcare costs in general were called into question.

CMS was founded in 1986 by Rocco A. Ortenzio. Ortenzio got his start in the rehabilitation business in 1958, when he began working as an independent physical therapist. Over the next 25 years, he built and then sold two multi-million dollar rehabilitation companies. In 1985 the second of these enterprises, the Rehab Hospital Services Corporation, was sold to National Medical Enterprises.

In February 1986, Ortenzio incorporated CMS in a suburb of Harrisburg, Pennsylvania. On March 15, the new company commenced operations when it finalized a pact with the Continental Care Group, a consortium of nursing homes based in New Jersey that was struggling financially. CMS derived its name from this organization, and became the corporate successor to it. In the contract between the two companies, CMS agreed to manage ten of Continental's affiliated nursing facilities. These sites were located in six different states. In addition, CMS agreed to buy four of the nursing homes over the next twelve months, for a total of $15 million, and it received an option to buy the other six in the following year.

At the end of its first three-and-a-half months in operation, CMS reported a loss of $867,000 on its management of the ten nursing homes. The company attributed part of this loss to the expense of recruiting new personnel to work in these facilities.

On June 30, 1986, CMS also purchased the Riverdale Gardens Nursing Home for $9.6 million, to bring its total of owned medical facilities to seven. In July the company purchased California Physical Therapy, Inc., for $1.5 million in cash.

Five months later, on the last day of 1986, CMS bought the Braintree Rehabilitation Hospital, outside Boston, Massachusetts, and its affiliated properties, for $10.2 million. The Braintree property was a regional comprehensive medical rehabilitation facility. In business for just nine months, CMS had picked up seven nursing homes, two physical therapy services, and one hospital.

In February 1987 the company bought the Chestnut Hill Nursing Home, another medical facility in the Boston area, for $2.3 million. Later in that month, CMS bought the Hialeah Convalescent Center, Inc., located in Florida, for $2.4 million. On February 27, the company made further inroads into the California market when it paid $13.3 million for the Western Neuro Care Center, situated in the town of Tustin. This facility specialized in the care of head trauma, coma, and ventilator-dependent patients.

In the following month, CMS bought 50 percent of the South Dade Nursing Home, Ltd., further expanding its holdings in the Florida market. Because of Florida's large concentration of older residents, this area was key to CMS's plans for further growth.

At the end of June 1987, CMS acquired the Kentfield Hospital, a 60-bed medical facility specializing in rehabilitation which was located in Kentfield, California. CMS paid $9.5 million for this property and spent an additional $6.5 million for VTA Management Services, Inc., an affiliated business that served the New York metropolitan area. At the same time, CMA also purchased the stock of California Physical Therapy, Inc., its earlier acquisition.

In the fiscal year that ended on June 30, 1987, CMS generated $51.5 million in income. Fifty-seven percent of these profits were generated by the company's nursing home facilities. CMS used some of these profits to fund a 68,000-square-foot expansion of its Braintree Hospital, to be used for outpatient services. This facility opened in July 1987. In addition, CMS established seven satellite outpatient facilities of the hospital, serving various locations around Massachusetts.

In the fall of 1987, CMS continued its streak of acquisitions. On September 1, 1987, the company bought the Helen Wilkes Residence, an 85-bed skilled nursing home in Lake Park, Florida. With this purchase, CMA increased its holdings in the nursing home field to 16 different facilities with 1,711 beds. These nursing homes were located along the eastern seaboard, in Florida, Virginia, Maryland, Pennsylvania, New Jersey, and Massachusetts.

Although CMS had originally assumed that it would be able to prosper by converting money-losing nursing home properties into profitable operations through superior management and experience, the company had discovered that this was not the most efficient route to growth. In nine months ending in early 1988, for instance, CMS lost $1.2 million on four of its nursing homes in Florida, as an over-supply of nursing home beds kept revenues depressed. In 1987 CMS sued the Continental Care Group, from which it had purchased the bulk of its nursing home properties. At the end of the year, Continental settled the litigation, agreeing to cancel promissory notes worth $1.8 million and to pay $600,000 toward renovations of three separate nursing homes. With this agreement, the cost of CMS's further acquisitions from Continental was reduced by $2.4 million.

Before this settlement took place, however, CMS announced on October 13, 1987, that it would offer stock to the public. In this way, the company would be able to raise capital to fund further growth. Two weeks later, however, CMS announced that current stock market conditions had caused it to postpone indefinitely its initial public offering. Nevertheless, the company believed that its current financing was sufficient to pay for any further desired growth, and stock was sold a short time later.

In November 1987, CMA opened the Lakeview Rehabilitation Hospital in Elizabethtown, Kentucky. During this time, the company also completed its purchase of four other nursing homes that had originally been owned by the Continental Care Group.

In buying these properties, CMS sought to establish a nationwide presence in a highly fragmented market. By establishing a single, unified system, the company hoped to compete more effectively for patients and business. A young industry, rehabilitation services was being driven by the aging of the American population and by improved medical care that allowed people to live longer. The need for services such as therapy in the wake of a stroke or other catastrophic medical event would only increase. In addition, the market for rehabilitation was growing as it became clear that huge cost savings resulted from increasing the capabilities of people who had been disabled.

Accordingly, in 1988, CMS began to refocus its efforts. The company started to move out of the nursing home business, to emphasize its rehabilitation facilities exclusively. In March 1988, CMS augmented its rehabilitation operations by buying Pro Therapy of America, Inc., and its subsidiaries, for $9.1 million. This company contracted to provide physical, occupational, and speech therapy services to clients in ten states. It also had holdings in several joint venture outpatient clinics. With this acquisition, which joined the company's previously purchased California Physical Therapy and VTA Management Services, CMS became one of the largest contract therapy service providers in the United States.

To further strengthen its standing in the rehabilitation field, CMS broke ground on seven other rehabilitation hospitals in locations around the country. These new facilities were placed primarily in areas where CMS had not previously done business, moving the company into Arkansas, Louisiana, Kansas, Texas, Colorado, and California.

To build hospitals in these areas, Ortenzio turned to the construction company run by his son as the primary contractor on the projects. In seeking funding, the company entered into

partnerships with other hospitals, lining up many doctors as investors. This process raised the issue of ethics, as doctors would later refer patients to facilities in which they had a financial interest, arousing the interest of regulators.

CMS continued its move away from the nursing home industry in the spring of 1988, when it sold three long-term care facilities. In June 1988, the company announced a leveraged buy-out of the rest of its nursing home properties by the division's management. With this deal, which was not completed for another four years, the company essentially exited this segment of the healthcare industry.

By the end of June 1988, these efforts had reduced the portion of CMS's revenues derived from nursing homes to 33 percent. The other 67 percent were provided by rehabilitation, contract therapy, and development operations. Revenues for the previous twelve-month period at this point passed the $100 million mark, reaching $113 million. This represented an increase of 120 percent from the previous year. Earnings grew by 192 percent to reach $4.7 million.

CMS's strong growth in revenues had been driven by its brisk pace of acquisitions, and the company had grown into a nationwide organization in a relatively brief period of time. In mid-1988, CMS began to institute the changes in administration that would allow it to manage its operations and further growth efficiently. The company more than doubled the size of its corporate staff, and also opened regional offices in Denver, Colorado, and Sacramento, California.

In September 1988, CMS announced that it would embark on another building project, developing an 80-bed facility in Irvine, California, to be called the Irvine Rehabilitation Hospital. This project was a joint venture with American Medical International, Inc., which owned the hospital next to the site of the proposed facility.

Also at this time, CMS completed an agreement first made in 1986 to acquire the Drew Village Nursing Home. Despite this move, the company pushed ahead in early 1989 with its plan to exit the nursing home field and refocus its energies on rehabilitation services.

In May 1989, Ortenzio passed the baton of company leadership to his son, Robert A. Ortenzio, who became the company's president and chief executive officer, while his father remained chairman. By the following month, CMS had opened eight new rehabilitation hospitals, with 571 new beds. In doing so, the company tripled its number of such facilities to 12, with a total of 882 beds. With these additions, CMS became the largest independent provider of rehabilitation services in the United States.

Revenue from these operations climbed to $151 million in the twelve-month period ending in June 1989. Despite this gain, the company's earnings were depressed by losses associated with CMS's withdrawal from the long-term nursing care market, primarily an $8 million loss on the sale of three nursing homes.

In September 1989, CMS further expanded its operations in the contract rehabilitation services industry when it bought Rehab-Works, Inc., of Clearwater, Florida. This company employed over 418 therapists in seven states. Eleven months later, CMS made another acquisition in this industry when its purchased Communic-Care of America, Inc./Pro-Rehab, Inc., on August 31, 1990. With this move, the company established a presence in the contract rehabilitation market of 30 different states.

In addition, CMS continued its effort to build and open new rehabilitation hospitals. In July 1990, the Fort Worth Rehabilitation Hospital opened its doors. Later that year, CMS began construction on six other facilities in five states.

CMS began to see the fruits of these labors in 1991, as eight new rehabilitation sites in four states opened, bringing the company's total of hospitals to 19. In addition, CMS expanded its number of outpatient clinics to 50. On the basis of these operations, CMS's revenue reached $340 million, an increase by half from the previous year's total of $227 million. To finance further growth, CMS sold additional shares of stock to the public, and transferred its listing to the New York Stock Exchange on June 21, 1991.

CMS continued to grow rapidly throughout 1991 and early 1992. The company opened eight new rehabilitation hospitals spread across eight states, and nearly doubled the size of its network of outpatient rehabilitation centers, to 96. To staff these new facilities, CMS hired 3,500 new employees.

In addition, CMS moved to enhance its contract rehabilitation services area by buying CompHealth, Inc., in November 1991. This company, based in Salt Lake City, Utah, acted as a temporary agency for medical professionals. In May 1992, CMS purchased Advanced Care Medicine, Inc., of Louisville, Kentucky. This company provided respiratory therapy and ventilator programs. With these additions, CMS could boast that its contract health care branch operated in all 50 states. From these operations, and its other fields of activity, CMS reaped $658 million in revenues in fiscal 1992.

By the start of 1993, CMS had begun to feel the effects of a nation-wide re-examination of the nature of American healthcare. To counteract potential government efforts to reign in healthcare costs, the company began a public relations campaign to educate people about the need for its services.

In addition, CMS prepared for reduced future revenues by scaling down its planned expansion, significantly reducing the number of new hospitals it intended to build. As part of this change in strategy, the company scuttled 30 development projects it had embarked upon, incurring a one-time charge against earnings of $14.5 million in the process. Also, CMS rearranged its staffing plan at the hospitals it operated, in an effort to keep costs down.

In January 1993, CMS further responded to the growing need for economical health care by forming a Unit Management group. This sector of CMS was assigned to develop programs in which rehabilitation services would be offered within existing acute care hospitals, rather than in separate, free-standing facilities, such as the rehabilitation hospitals the company had been building for the bulk of its history. With this move, CMS acknowledged that the future of rehabilitation services might differ significantly from the industry the company's leaders had first imagined.

In February 1993, CMS acquired the Kron Medical Corporation, another provider of temporary medical help. This property was added to its Compuhealth operations, and filled a growing demand for flexible, cost-efficient medical staffing.

To better justify its costs to insurance companies or managed health care organizations, CMS also began a program to document the effectiveness of its rehabilitation programs for each patient. The company moved to upgrade its computer capabilities, as well, in an effort to gain further efficiency and economies in operations.

By June 1993, CMS's revenues had grown to $901 million, and the company anticipated that it would pass the $1 billion mark in the next year. Although the outlook of the healthcare industry as a whole remained an open question, CMS's solid record of growth and profitability suggested that the company would be a part of that industry in the late 1990s, regardless of the direction it took.

Principal Subsidiaries: Advanced Care Medicine, Inc.; Braintree Rehabilitation Ventures, Inc.; Communi-Care of America, Inc.; Pro-Therapy of America, Inc.; RehabWorks, Inc.

Further Reading:

Berkman, Leslie, ''Briefcase: Medical,'' *Los Angeles Times,* September 10, 1988.

Leonard, Jerry, ''Rehab Hospital to Open,'' *Pittsburgh Business Times & Journal,* May 11, 1987.

Sokol, Marlene, ''Caring for Elderly—Efficiently,'' *St. Petersburg Times,* August 22, 1988.

—Elizabeth Rourke

⊖⊋ CONTROL DATA

Control Data Systems, Inc.

4201 Lexington Avenue North
Arden Hills, Minnesota 55126
U.S.A.
(612) 482-2401
Fax: (612) 482-2388

Public Company
Incorporated: 1957 as Control Data Corporation
Employees: 3,285
Sales: $451 million
Stock Exchanges: New York
SICs: 3571 Electronic Computers; 3577 Computer Peripheral
Equipment Not Elsewhere Classified; 7372 Prepackaged
Software

Control Data Systems, Inc., (CDSI) provides computer systems integration services to businesses and governments around the world. In addition, the company provides services and software to owners of CYBER mainframe computers, once manufactured by the company's corporate parent. CDSI is one of two companies created from the ruins of the Control Data Corporation in the early 1990s. Throughout the 1960s and 1970s, Control Data was a worldwide leader in manufacturing scientific computer systems. Under the guiding hand of its strong-willed founder, the company gained a leading place in the market for proprietary mainframe computers used by the government, military, and large corporations.

Control Data also became involved in a variety of other endeavors that were idealistically intended to improve society. When the computer industry changed in the early 1980s, Control Data was caught off guard by the new technology, and the company suffered severe losses for nearly a decade before abandoning mainframe technology and splitting itself into two small and limited enterprises.

Control Data was founded in the late 1950s by William C. Norris and a number of partners. Norris had grown up on a Nebraska farm and trained as an engineer. During World War II, he joined the Navy and was assigned to a code-breaking team, where he first became familiar with the technology of digital computing. After the war Norris became a Navy contractor, starting a company that continued the work he had done during the war. When his firm was acquired by Remington Rand Inc., a much larger company, Norris stayed on but soon

found himself stifled by corporate bureaucracy. In 1957 he and a number of his fellow Remington Rand employees quit to found a new enterprise, Control Data Corporation.

To finance their venture, Norris and his colleagues sold stock on the open market, making Control Data the first computer company to be publicly financed. In a harbinger of later socially-oriented programs, Control Data sold its 600,000 shares at the rock-bottom highly inclusive price of $1 each.

With the funds they raised through the sale of stock, Norris and his colleagues set out to build the most powerful computer in the world, and in 1958 the company released its 1604 model. The prototype of this product was sold to the U.S. Navy Bureau of Ships a month after its creation. With this purchase, Control Data began a close relationship with the military and a long career as a defense contractor. Control Data also made its first acquisition that year. The company bought Cedar Engineering, which made peripheral equipment for computers. Within two years of this purchase, Control Data had released two further models of its computers.

In addition to its primary line of high-speed computers, Control Data also began to offer data services in the late 1950s. Because at that time many companies could not afford the enormous expense of a computer or did not generate enough work to make such a purchase economical, Control Data set up time-sharing programs on machines that it owned. In this way, companies were able to rent time on a Control Data computer at a more reasonable cost. Time-sharing and computer manufacturing made up the bulk of Control Data's business throughout the 1960s. The company dramatically expanded its time-sharing capacity in 1967 when it bought the software company CEIR, parent to the Arbitron Company.

In the following year, Control Data moved to seize a greater portion of the time-sharing market when it filed an antitrust suit against the International Business Machines Corporation (IBM). In bringing the legal action, Norris claimed that IBM discouraged potential buyers of Control Data mainframe computers by making claims about the superior qualities of an IBM machine which had not yet been built.

Defying the conventional wisdom of the financial community by filing the suit, Norris demonstrated his willingness to go his own way. At the time, Wall Street thought that Norris had "lost his marbles," as his biographer later recounted. The move paid off in the early 1970s, however, when IBM settled the suit out of court, and turned over its entire time-sharing operation, called the Service Bureau Corporation, to Control Data.

By the late 1960s Control Data's rapid expansion had depleted the company's financial resources. This process was exacerbated by the fact that Control Data's leasing arrangements made it necessary for the company to finance the build-up of the enormously expensive mainframes. Control Data was forced to take out loans, which contributed to the company's unfavorable balance sheet. In an effort to redress these structural difficulties, Control Data began making plans to acquire a finance company. In order to fend off a hostile takeover attempt, the Commercial Credit Company of Baltimore agreed to become a wholly owned subsidiary of Control Data in 1968.

While these arrangements were being made, social and political changes were sweeping American society. Norris first became aware of the upheaval when race riots erupted in Minneapolis and many other cities during the summer of 1967. That year Norris met with civil rights activist Whitney Young to discuss the situation. In the wake of that meeting, Control Data embarked on a series of ventures that Norris labeled "social projects." Although these activities seemed to be at odds with Control Data's status as a technology-driven defense contractor, Norris argued that "you can't do business in a society that's burning." Instead, Norris expanded Control Data's mission to include "addressing society's unmet needs," as his biographer later put it.

Norris believed that the methods of capitalism could be used to effect positive social change. To fulfill this philosophy, Control Data embarked on a wide variety of activities, including vocational training programs for prisoners, experimental farms in Alaska, projects to develop windmills as a power source, and an extensive range of education and training programs that incorporated computers. Believing in corporate urban renewal, Norris built a plant in a Minneapolis slum and poured a huge number of resources into its success. Later, Control Data began to provide financing and office services to struggling entrepreneurs, and the company set up consulting firms that advised municipal governments on inner city development.

Like Norris's suit against IBM, these efforts met with severe disapproval from the financial community. Despite Norris's claims that none of the company's efforts were philanthropy and that all were planned to become profitable businesses, he was branded a flake, and Control Data gained a reputation, according to *Inc.* magazine, as a "far-out firm."

By the end of the 1970s, Control Data's social engineering projects and its efforts to incubate small businesses had eclipsed the firm's bedrock activities in the public eye. Although it was better known for its high-profile, unorthodox moves, the vast majority of the company's business remained the production and sale of its family of proprietary CYBER computer systems. Control Data was the leading maker of computers used in scientific research, and by 1979 the company was fourth in the number of machines installed for these purposes around the world. In addition, Control Data was involved in hundreds of other ventures, ranging from technology components to real estate.

In the early 1980s, the structure of the computer industry began to change. American dominance in the field was seriously threatened by international competition, primarily from the Japanese, for the first time. In addition, new technology began to shift the industry's emphasis away from large, expensive, proprietary mainframe systems, like those created by Control Data, towards microcomputers operated on an open computing system. With open computing, an industry standard operating system enabled a wide variety of vendors to provide software and peripherals for use with smaller personal computers.

While other computer companies struggled to adapt to these changes as quickly as possible, Control Data remained slow to react, possibly distracted by its wide range of activities and social engineering goals. By the early 1980s, for instance, Con-

trol Data had lost its dominance in the supercomputer market to Cray Research, whose founders had initially worked at Control Data. In an attempt to regain its lost lead, Control Data began a new supercomputer development effort and spun the unit off to its employees in 1983. It was hoped the new unit, called ETA Systems, Inc., would circumvent the company's bureaucratic structure. Control Data retained an 89 percent stake in ETA Systems, in exchange for providing its development funds.

Despite this move, Control Data's revenues began to drop sharply in the early 1980s. In 1985 the company posted losses of $568 million on revenues of $3.7 billion, and defaulted on a $300 million loan. These ills were universally blamed on Control Data's refusal to stick to the business of computer making, and Norris was charged with corporate irresponsibility by the financial community. In January of 1986 he resigned his position at the head of the company, and Control Data began the process of trying to recover its profitability.

In mid-1986 Control Data floated a public debt offering, which allowed it to resolve its most immediate financial crisis. The company then turned to the task of shedding peripheral and money-losing units. Later that year Commercial Credit, whose profits had provided one bright spot in the mid-1980s, was also divested. During 1985 and 1986 Control Data lost $832 million, and by 1987 the overall staff had been cut by 25 percent, and top management had been halved. Administrators had not only been eliminated, many of them had been replaced with executives who brought a fresh perspective to the company. Norris's successor also reduced or sold dozens of subsidiaries, including most of the social engineering outfits, in order to narrow Control Data's focus to its computer and peripherals manufacturing and its service branch.

By January 29, 1987, these actions had started to show results, as Control Data posted its first profitable quarter in two years. Despite this bright spot, however, the overall situation looked bleak. Nearly 40 percent of Control Data's revenues were derived from its Computer Systems group, which held just 2.5 percent of the market. Concerned about Control Data's overall health, customers had become wary of purchasing big systems from the company. If it folded, they would be left with no support and no further development of compatible products. In an effort to revive this business, Control Data began to market a wider range of mainframe computers, and it also invested in software to join Control Data machines into networks. As a result, Control Data reported a profit for 1987 of $19.3 million on sales of $3.36 billion.

In 1988 Control Data continued its efforts to build greater profitability, despite adverse market conditions. While the company suffered withering price competition and weak demand for its conventional computer programs, its supercomputer subsidiary, ETA, was draining cash. Since 1984 ETA had soaked up an average of $50 million a year as the company developed its next generation supercomputer, called the ETA-10. When this product finally reached the market, however, demand proved to be less than expected, and the machine's software did not work properly. With these setbacks, the subsidiary's losses for 1988 reached $100 million.

By the end of the year, Control Data's total losses had mounted once again, and the company posted a five-year loss of $1.3 billion. Out of cash and in default on its loans, Control Data was forced by its bankers to appoint a new president, who moved to raise capital quickly. To do so, Control Data once again undertook a sweeping downsizing effort. The company laid off 3,100 workers and shut down ETA in April of 1989. In addition, it began to sell off its few profitable subsidiaries, a process that *Business Week* compared to "breaking up the furniture to feed the fire." In June Imprimis Technology Inc., a disk drive subsidiary ranked number two in the industry, was sold to market leader Seagate Technology, Inc. for $450 million. By the end of the year Control Data had also sold Ticketron, its money-making ticket broker. Control Data also made a fundamental shift in the direction of its computer business. Recognizing that its core mainframe business was a relic of the past, the company moved away from its hardware line towards manufacturing engineering and information management systems, which were run on the new open systems.

With this transformation under way, Control Data posted an annual profit in 1990 of $2.7 million on revenues of $1.7 billion. Abandoning its proprietary focus, the company's redefined mission was to be a provider of computing and systems integration services for a few core markets, including utilities and manufacturers. Government contracts for mainframes would be replaced by commercial clients who would purchase programs to be used with any computer hardware. With this shift, Control Data hoped to stem the tide of losses from its computer operations, which reached $119.4 million over the four years between 1987 and 1991.

In September of 1991 Control Data began restructuring its remaining units so that they could attract investment capital and forge competitive alliances with other companies. Finally, on May 27, 1992, the company announced that it would change its name to the Ceridian Corporation and spin off its computer operations into a separate company, to be called Control Data Systems, Inc. Ceridian retained the company's defense electronics operations and its information services, while CDSI became a computer systems integrator, developing technological solutions to business problems using a wide variety of hardware, software, and peripheral products.

In August, CDSI sold stock to the public for the first time, and the company subsequently embarked on a series of strategic alliances designed to increase its number of partners and suppliers. A joint venture called Metaphase Technology, Inc. was formed with the Structural Dynamics Research Corporation. The company also expanded its partnership with Silicon Graph-ics, Inc. and cemented an agreement with the Intergraph Corporation, along with Japan's NEC Corporation.

In 1993 CDSI joined with three computer makers, the Hewlett-Packard Company, the Acer America Corporation, and Sun Microsystems, to offer their products to its clients. In order to expand its Canadian business, the company bought Antares Electronics, Inc. and further added to its international operations with the purchase of the London-based MICHAEL Business Systems Plc.

At the end of 1993, CDSI reported a profit of $9.1 million, up from the previous year's loss. The company had moved aggressively to exit the computer manufacturing business, reducing CYBER's contribution to revenues to one-third. In addition, CDSI had worked to build its systems integration operations throughout the world. Seventy percent of CDSI's returns came from Europe, where the Control Data name had not suffered from adverse publicity, and CDSI moved to enhance its operations there. The company bearing the Control Data name was a very different enterprise from the business that had entered the 1980s as a leader in mainframe computer manufacturing. The company hoped its stripped-down and specialized operations would allow it to flourish in the highly competitive business climate of the late 1990s.

Principal Subsidiaries: Antares Electronics, Inc.; MICHAEL Business Systems Plc; Metaphase Technology, Inc.

Further Reading:

Gross, Steve, "The Big Fix at Control Data," *InformationWeek,* April 15, 1991.
Houston, Patrick, "Control Data is Moving Forward By Looking Back, " *Business Week,* April 18, 1989.
——, "How Bob Price is Reprogramming Control Data," *Business Week,* February 16, 1987.
Mitchell, Russell, "A Control Data Child That's an Underachiever," *Business Week,* October 10, 1988.
——, "Control Data May Finally Have the Right Stuff," *Business Week,* April 24, 1989.
——, "Fine Job, Larry—But Don't Get Too Settled," *Business Week,* October 16, 1989.
Pitzer, Mary J., "Do or Die Time for a Superfast Supercomputer," *Business Week,* December 22, 1986.
Wieffering, Eric J., "The Other Company," *Corporate Report Minnesota,* April, 1993.
Worthy, James C., *William C. Norris: Portrait of a Maverick,* New York: Ballinger, 1987.

—Elizabeth Rourke

Old Country Store

Cracker Barrel Old Country Store, Inc.

P.O. Box 787, Hartmann Drive
Lebanon, Tennessee 37088-0787
U.S.A.
(615) 444-5533
Fax: (615) 443-6780

Public Company
Incorporated: 1970
Employees: 18,035
Sales: $517.60 million
Stock Exchanges: NASDAQ
SICs: 5812 Eating Places; 5947 Gifts, Novelty & Souvenir
   Shops

Cracker Barrel Old Country Store, Inc., operates a chain of 182
country-style restaurants and gift shops located primarily along
interstate highways in the Southeast, Midwest, mid-Atlantic,
and southwest United States. The restaurants serve Southern
''down home'' fare, such as grits, catfish, and turnip greens, at
moderate prices. Cracker Barrel gift shops, considered by management to be an integral part of the restaurant's country atmosphere, sell reproductions of early American crafts and such
food items as preserves and old-fashioned candies. Cracker
Barrel ranks among the 12 largest family restaurant chains in
the United States. Its sales volume (more than $3 million per
existing unit since 1991) is the highest in its class.

The first Cracker Barrel Old Country Store was founded in
September 1969 by Dan Evins, a Shell gas station operator who
felt he could attract more customers if a restaurant and gift shop
were located on the station's lot. He borrowed $40,000 and built
his first combination gas station, restaurant, and store along the
interstate highway just outside Lebanon, Tennessee. Within one
month, Cracker Barrel Old Country Store began to make a
profit. Evins incorporated the company the following year and
sold half of the new business to a group of local businessmen,
raising $100,000 to open his second restaurant/gift-shop/gas
station. By 1974, Cracker Barrel was operating 10 units, all
located along interstate highways and all making a profit.

Although Cracker Barrel's restaurant and gift shop sales grew,
Evins's gasoline business was less profitable. When the gasoline crisis hit in the early 1970s, the company began building

new restaurants without gas stations attached. In 1974, Evins
ended his distribution contract with Shell Oil. The restaurants
did so well without gasoline service that by the late 1980s,
Cracker Barrel had eliminated gasoline service from all its
locations.

Cracker Barrel's solid growth began attracting the interest of
independent investors, prompting the company to register with
the Securities and Exchange Commission in 1974. Rapid expansion continued through the end of the decade. By 1983, the
company was operating 27 units located along interstate highways in Tennessee, North Carolina, South Carolina, Georgia,
Kentucky, Florida, and Alabama. Between 1978 and 1983, net
income and revenues increased at annual rates of 26 percent and
25 percent, respectively, resulting primarily from the addition
of new restaurants. In late 1981, when high interest rates threatened the company's expansion, Cracker Barrel went public,
selling shares on the NASDAQ exchange.

Despite Cracker Barrel's continued expansion, sales began to
slip. In 1985, Evins tried to stem the slide by making some
broad management changes. ''We had some people in our management who had grown up in this company, and we were
growing fairly fast for a small company,'' Evins told *Restaurant
Business* at that time. ''We realized that what we needed was
some heavier parts in our equipment, so to speak.'' Changes
included the establishment of a new marketing department and
the hiring of five executives, all with experience in larger
organizations. Net sales rose 20 percent to $80 million and net
income grew 49 percent in 1986, due in part to improved
operating efficiency and higher margins on sales.

Cracker Barrel also began opening restaurants near tourist destinations, including Opryland; Gatlinburg, Tennessee; and Hilton
Head, South Carolina. By the end of 1987, the Cracker Barrel
chain consisted of 53 stores in eight states, with annual net sales
slightly over $99 million.

Analysts cite several reasons for Cracker Barrel's success.
''One,'' said *Restaurant Hospitality* magazine, ''has been its
unrivaled ability to evoke nostalgia without being corny.
Cracker Barrel employees are simply warm and friendly. The
stores look old-fashioned but are never cute.'' This atmosphere,
reinforced by its inexpensive ''country cookin' menu,'' helped
Cracker Barrel carve out a niche for itself in the family restaurant business.

Cracker Barrel also instituted extensive manager and employee
training programs in the 1980s, which greatly improved store
efficiency and profit margins. Potential managers spend 10
weeks in an extensive training session, whereas hourly employees follow an on-the-job course, called the Personal Achievement Responsibility (PAR) program. Rewards, such as increased wages and cheaper benefits, are given for the successful
completion of company-set goals. The result has been a turnover rate among hourly employees of 160 percent, approximately half the industry average.

Cracker Barrel's tight management system helped it weather the
recession in 1990 and achieve existing per-unit sales of over
$2.7 million, almost double the per-unit sales of its nearest
competitor, Big Boy. Around the same time, however, the company got caught in a controversy when it fired a number of

homosexual employees. For a short time, it seemed the controversy would threaten Cracker Barrel's expansion into the northern states. Nationally televised protests against the firings sprang up in New York City, Atlanta, and a number of small towns. The City of New York, which held $3.6 million worth of Cracker Barrel shares in a pension fund, threatened to make waves if the company didn't change its policy. Cracker Barrel announced it would no longer fire employees based on their sexual orientation, although protesters claimed that discrimination continued covertly. Despite the controversy (or perhaps because of the publicity it generated), company profits jumped 50 percent in 1991 to $22.8 million. The number of Cracker Barrel units grew to 106.

In the early 1990s, Cracker Barrel opened new restaurants at a rate of over 20 units per year, and expanded into states such as Michigan, Wisconsin, and Missouri. For the first time in its history, however, Cracker Barrel faced some direct competition when Bob Evans Farms, Inc., opened seven Bob Evans General Stores with atmosphere and menu items that closely resembled those of Cracker Barrel. Bob Evans also opened the first of a chain of Hometown Restaurants, slated for development in towns with populations of 30,000 or less.

Analysts predicted heavy competition between the two restaurant chains because both intended to pursue the same market of "vacationers hungry for a homey atmosphere and comfort food." Cracker Barrel seemed well prepared for a market share battle. Net income in 1992 rose 48 percent to $33.9 million, and the number of units expanded to 127. A 1992 *Consumer Reports* survey gave the chain the top customer satisfaction rating, while a survey appearing in the February 1, 1994 issue of *Restaurant & Instition* magazine found that Cracker Barrel "has done the job better than all of its family-restaurant competitors." "Our goal is to become a national network," Evins said in 1987. With its strong management system and sales that led the industry, Cracker Barrel seemed in a position to do just that.

Further Reading:

"Cracker Barrel Set the Survey's Standard for Family Dining for the Fourth Straight Year," *Restaurant & Institution,* February 1, 1994.
Farkas, David, "Kings of the Road," *Restaurant Hospitality,* August, 1991, p. 118.
Ganem, Beth Carlson, "My Country, Right or Wrong," *Restaurant Hospitality,* February 1993, p. 73.
Gutner, Todd, "Nostalgia Sells," *Forbes,* April 27, 1992, p. 102.
Hayes, Jack, "Cracker Barrel Protesters Don't Shake Loyal Patrons," *Nation's Restaurant News,* August 26, 1991, p. 3.
Oleck, Joan, "Bad Politics," *Restaurant Business,* June 10, 1992, p. 80.
Rhein, Liz, "Along the Interstate with Cracker Barrel," *Restaurant Business,* June 10, 1987, p. 113.
Walkup, Carolyn, "Family Chains Beat Recession Blues with Value, Service," *Nation's Restaurant News,* August 5, 1991, p. 100.
Yanez, Luisa, "Food Fight on the Interstate," *Restaurant Business,* September 20, 1992, p. 50.

—Maura Troester

Curtiss-Wright Corporation

1200 Wall St. W.
Lyndhurst, New Jersey 07071
U.S.A.
(201) 896-8400
Fax: (201) 438-5680

Public Company
Incorporated: 1929
Employees: 1,550
Sales: $158.9 million
Stock Exchanges: New York
SICs: 3593 Fluid Power Cylinders & Actuators; 3398 Metal
  Heat Treating; 3492 Fluid Power Valves & Hose Fittings;
  3356 Nonferrous Rolling & Drawing Nec.

Curtiss-Wright Corporation is a diversified multinational manufacturing company, which produces and markets precision components and systems and provides highly engineered services to the aerospace, industrial, and flow control and marine markets. All of the company's core products and services, provided by four wholly owned subsidiaries, involve precision working of metals and alloys.

Curtiss-Wright Corporation was formed in 1929 as a holding company for a variety of aviation concerns, when the Curtiss Aeroplane and Motor Corporation and Wright Aeronautical Corporation merged, bringing together 18 affiliated companies and 29 subsidiaries. Bankers had tried for years to bring together the two rival companies, started by aviation pioneers and inventors Orville and Wilbur Wright and Glenn H. Curtiss, and the merger finally put an end to two decades of patent battles between the Wright brothers and Curtiss. Hailed upon its formation by Wall Street financiers as the world's most prodigious aviation concern, the company debuted with total assets of more than $70 million and stock valued at $220 million as it entered an industry battle with the recently created United Aircraft and Transportation Company.

While its namesakes had little to do with the creation of the new firm, Glenn Curtiss did serve as a member of the company's technical committee prior to his death in 1930, the year the Curtiss Condor—a civilian version of a two-engine bomber plane—was being introduced by some airlines. The Curtiss-Wright Corporation maintained a position of preeminence in aeronautics throughout the 1930s, although the aviation indus-

try remained relatively small and the firm's sales had reached only $49 million by 1939.

In 1940, the company created the Curtiss Propeller Division, a forerunner of the subsidiary Curtiss-Wright Flight Systems, Inc. Serving as a core source of government work after the United States entered World War II, Curtiss Propeller Division became one of the single largest defense contractors in the world. During the war, the company employed 180,000 workers and produced 146,000 aircraft propellers, 143,000 airplane engines, and more than 26,000 planes as Curtiss-Wright became the second largest manufacturer in the United States with annual sales surpassing $1 billion two years running. Curtiss-Wright engines powered the majority of American planes flown in World War II, including the B-29 that dropped the first atomic bomb on Japan and precipitated the close of the global conflict.

After the war, Curtiss-Wright was forced to deal with a rapid decline in military contracts, and enormous operational cutbacks were made as the company began converting military aircraft engines for use in commercial airliners. In 1949, Guy Vaughan, who had long directed the company's operations, was ousted in a management shake-up and replaced by Roy T. Hurley, who became president and chairperson. Hurley brought a reputation as a production cost-cutter to Curtiss-Wright, having served as a vice-president of production at Bendix Aviation Corporation and a director of manufacturing at Ford Motor Company.

With the United States' involvement in the Korean War during the early 1950s the company again benefitted from a new round of government contracts for aircraft engines. As a result, Curtiss-Wright remained among the top ten U.S. defense contractors during the first half of the decade, producing ram-jet engines for guided missiles, aircraft engines and propellers, and flight simulators for the military.

During this time, Hurley initiated a massive diversification drive, beginning in 1951 when Curtiss-Wright acquired a plant in Buffalo, New York, where it began a specialized metal extrusion business. The company also purchased another plant in Carlstadt, New Jersey, to serve as foundation for a new electronics division. During the mid-1950s Curtiss-Wright entered the Canadian market with the creation of the subsidiary Curtiss-Wright of Canada Ltd. (later renamed Canadian Curtiss-Wright). The company also established a scientific products and research division and began construction of a research and development center at Quehanna, Pennsylvania, where it established a nuclear materials laboratory to support defense and peacetime applications of atomic energy.

By the end of 1955, Hurley's diversification drive had helped propel Curtiss-Wright's annual sales from $475 million a year to more than $500 million, with commercial sales generating about 40 percent of the company's income. By 1956, Curtiss-Wright had 16 divisions, and the company's stock had risen to a high of 49⅜.

Curtiss-Wright utilized acquisitions and joint developments with other companies to bolster its engine business, acquiring Propulsion Research Corporation and Turbomotor Associates. The company began developing engines in the low-to-medium-range power categories for aircraft, helicopters, and missiles.

Curtiss-Wright also teamed up with Bristol Aeroplane Company to develop a series of commercial engines. The company's military engine production continued to consist largely of the J-65, initially licensed from Great Britain, while its principal commercial product was the 3350 Turbo Compound piston engine, used in the fastest commercial propeller airliners of the day.

In 1956, Curtiss-Wright agreed to loan $35 million to financially troubled Studebaker-Packard and provide management services for the automaker. In return, Studebaker-Packard sold Curtiss-Wright its subsidiary, Aerophysics Development Corporation, and leased the aviation concern its facilities in Utica, Michigan, and South Bend, Indiana, where Curtiss-Wright began producing the army's new Dart anti-tank missile, which Aerophysics Development had helped develop.

The following year, Studebaker-Packard received the rights to manufacture the Daimler-Benz engine from Germany's Mercedes-Benz in exchange for allowing the German automaker to produce a Curtiss-Wright plane. After two years of managing Studebaker-Packard, Curtiss-Wright terminated its management contract with the automaker and acquired the South Bend and Utica plants it had been leasing as well as the rights to manufacture and sell Daimler-Benz's diesel and multi-fuel engines, fuel injection systems, military vehicles, and buses.

By 1957, about two-thirds of Curtiss-Wright's sales were from government contracts, while about two-thirds of its profits stemmed from nonmilitary sales. Seeking to widen its commercial activities and steer clear of government contracts, the company focused on the development of ultrasonic equipment, new products for its Buffalo extrusion business, and new uses for its plastic material, Curon, which had applications as apparel lining, wall and floor coverings, soundproofing, upholstery, auto trim, and cushions.

In 1958, Curtiss-Wright began operating a nuclear research reactor at its Quehanna facility. The company also established a solar research laboratory in conjunction with New York University, resulting in an agreement with Hupp Corporation to jointly explore, develop, and sell devices in the solar energy field, including heat storage and cooking devices. In 1959, Curtiss-Wright also began producing industrial x-ray inspection equipment, which was added to the firm's lines of quality control equipment, inspection equipment, and measurement systems using ultrasonic, radiographic, and nuclear energy technologies. During this time, Curtiss-Wright entered the earth-moving business with the acquisition of a Continental Copper & Steel Industries division that manufactured such equipment.

Curtiss-Wright's experimental developments included a coal-based blacktop road paving material and an ''air car'' that could travel six to 12 inches above ground, as well as a lightweight internal combustion engine with only two main moving parts. The rotary engine, which became known as the Wankel, was designed to burn gasoline in such a way as to turn a triangular shaped rotor, rather than driving pistons up and down like conventional piston engines. Developed in conjunction with NSU Werke of West Germany, the engine—for which Curtiss-Wright attained exclusive world rights for aircraft uses and exclusive North American rights for all applications—stemmed from an invention by the German firm's Felix Wankel.

A series of defense cutbacks during the late 1950s hurt Curtiss-Wright's ramjet development business, and the company's earnings began to decline, falling from $25 million in 1958 to $14.3 million in 1959 as sales dropped from $388 to $329 million. In April 1960 Hurley was confronted by a hostile crowd at the firm's annual meeting and faced criticism over falling earnings, reduced dividends, high officer compensation, and insufficient information regarding the company's experimental developments. Hurley resigned as president and chairperson one month later and was replaced by one of his more vocal critics, T. Roland Berner. An attorney who had become a director at Curtiss-Wright after leading a nearly successful proxy battle against management in 1948, Berner had been instrumental in the 1949 shake-up that initially brought Hurley to power.

Berner quickly divested Curtiss-Wright of several divisions. The company donated its nuclear reactor to Pennsylvania State University and sold its South Bend and Utica facilities, Curon plastics business, West Coast research facilities, and its process for producing paving material from coal. Furthermore, the company's plant in Lawrence, New Jersey, which had been making ultrasonics as well as quality control and testing equipment, was closed, plans for commercial production of the air car were dropped, and operations at Quehanna ceased.

Seeking to return Curtiss-Wright to the status of a leading aircraft engine manufacturer, Berner shifted the firm's emphasis to defense and electronics products. During the early 1960s, Curtiss-Wright landed Air Force contracts for propellers, missile parts, and the modernization of the J-65 engine and began producing steel rocket casings for solid-fuel boosters for Titan III space launch vehicles. During the same period, Curtiss-Wright's electronics business was expanded through the acquisition of companies engaged in the manufacture of radar cameras and automatic timing controls for aircraft and missiles, as well as the manufacture of printed circuit board connectors for aircraft, missile, and computer applications.

Curtiss-Wright also expanded its activities in nuclear fields with the acquisition of an interest—and eventual complete control of—Target Rock Corporation, a manufacturer of hydraulic components and nuclear equipment. Curtiss-Wright also broadened its Canadian operations with the acquisition of companies engaged in the production of hydraulic equipment for oil companies and steel products for the building and mining industries.

In 1962, the company received a Federal Aviation Agency (FAA) contract to study compressor, turbine, and computer technologies for supersonic transport jet engines and began competing for a major government contract to develop and produce a supersonic commercial airliner engine. During the mid-1960s, the company sold its electronic fittings and components division at a time when it was plowing about $15 million of its own funds into the development of a supersonic transport plane engine.

Curtiss-Wright lost its bid to produce the supersonic engine, and, by 1967, the company had abandoned Berner's goal to build complete aircraft engines, opting to become a first-tier supplier, or subcontractor, for other companies involved in aerospace and other fields. By that time, when Curtiss-Wright landed a Boeing contract to provide flight actuators to extend and retract flaps on the wings of the giant Boeing 747 jet airliner, its "power hinge" mechanics were already in use on a North American Aviation supersonic research plane, a General Dynamic's fighter bomber, and a Boeing helicopter. Curtiss-Wright's relations with governmental and commercial customers continued to improve, and, by the late 1960s, Curtiss-Wright was supplying components for Lockheed's air bus and military transport plane and had become for many aerospace firms a preferred supplier of components for jet engines, helicopters and aircraft, as well a supplier of nuclear equipment and high precision products for firms in nonaerospace industrial fields.

In 1968, Curtiss-Wright began an expansion program at its Buffalo extrusion facility, adding new forging and machining equipment for building aircraft and aerospace components. That year, the company acquired Metal Improvement Company, Inc. (MIC), an industry leader in shot peening technology used to create aerodynamic curvatures in aircraft and other products. The company's operations were also expanded through acquisitions of domestic companies involved in the production of aircraft wing ribs and airframe parts and a Canadian manufacturer of metal-working equipment and supplies for the steel processing industry. In 1969, Curtiss-Wright acquired a majority interest in Dorr-Oliver Inc., a engineering firm that made mechanized equipment for airline cargo terminals; Curtiss-Wright eventually acquired complete control of Dorr-Oliver.

Curtiss-Wright entered the 1970s as a producer of components or systems for all new wide-bodied commercial jet airliners and most jet planes, at a time when cutbacks in defense and military spending resulted in fewer government contracts. When automakers and other firms began showing a growing interest in the Wankel rotary engine, Curtiss-Wright began extending licensing agreements for the engine. In 1970, General Motors Corporation paid $50 million to acquire a five-year nonexclusive license to develop and manufacture the rotary combustion engine in North America. Subsequent license agreements called for royalty payments to Curtiss-Wright for all sales of Wankel engines in addition to a licensing fee. Speculation on the potential for the development of the smaller, lighter, and more powerful Wankel intensified. By 1972, Wankel had become one of the hottest names on Wall Street, and Curtiss-Wright's stock was one of the most volatile and actively traded.

In 1972, Curtiss-Wright granted Wankel development licenses to Brunswick Corporation, a manufacturer of the Mercury line of outboard motors, and Ingersoll-Rand Company, for use in that firm's compressor, pump, and electric generator assemblies. The following year, American Motors Corporation became Curtiss-Wright's seventh Wankel licensee, about the same time that GM announced it would introduce the rotary engine in its 1975 Vega model. However, GM soon renegotiated its payment agreement with Curtiss-Wright after indefinitely postponing the debut of the Wankel in its vehicles, citing emissions and gas mileage difficulties as motivating factors.

As interest in the Wankel declined, due to hydrocarbon emissions concerns, Curtiss-Wright began acquiring the stock of Cenco Inc., a maker of pollution-control equipment and medical supplies and an operator of nursing homes and hospitals. By July 1975, Curtiss-Wright had acquired 16 percent of Cenco's stock. Upon learning that Cenco was entangled in allegations of fraudulent auditors reports and was on the verge of bankruptcy, Curtiss-Wright took control of the firm and placed Shirley D. Brinsfield, president of Dorr-Oliver, as Cenco chairperson. During this time, Teledyne Inc., a diversified firm with interests in electronic and aviation control systems and insurance, began acquiring Curtiss-Wright stock, and, by mid-1976, it held a 12-percent stake.

During this time, Curtiss-Wright was producing a wide range of military nuclear components, nuclear handling equipment, and nuclear systems devices, including special valves and regulators and seal weld fitting machines. The company also began actively developing turbine-powered generators, which were sold both domestically and internationally.

In 1978, Berner launched a proxy challenge to gain control of Kennecott Corporation, the nation's largest copper company. Having already acquired a 9.9 percent interest in the mining concern, Berner charged that Kennecott had wasted assets in its $567 million acquisition of the Carborundum Company, and he proposed a dissident slate of directors committed to selling Carborundum and distributing the proceeds among shareholders, including Curtiss-Wright. Kennecott's directors narrowly won the election, but a federal judge ordered a second vote. To stave off a rerun election, Kennecott convinced Thomas D. Barrow, an Exxon Corporation senior executive, to take control of the copper company, and within two weeks Barrow and Berner had agreed to a new Kennecott board, which would serve through the spring of 1981 and would give Berner's faction a voice in the mining firm's affairs.

Over the next two years, Curtiss-Wright boosted to more than 22 percent its stake in Lynch Corporation, a manufacturer of glass-forming machinery and flow instruments that Curtiss-Wright had controlled for about 15 years. Curtiss-Wright also entered the heat treating market in 1980 with the acquisition of Diebel Heat Treating Company, serving the automotive, oil exploration, and agricultural equipment markets.

By November 1980, Curtiss-Wright had increased its stake in Kennecott to 14.3 percent, and its truce with the company was about to expire. Consequently, the copper company made a bid to acquire Curtiss-Wright, setting off a second round of corporate warfare. Curtiss-Wright responded to the Kennecott threat by initiating a buyback of its own stock to block takeover attempts, spurring a Kennecott offer to buy up Curtiss-Wright's outstanding stock. As a result, Kennecott acquired nearly 32 percent of Curtiss-Wright and surpassed Teledyne as the largest Curtiss-Wright stockholder, though falling short of its objective for majority control. In January 1981, Kennecott and Curtiss-Wright signed a ten-year truce agreement, and Curtiss-Wright sold Kennecott its Dorr-Oliver subsidiary and its shares of Kennecott stock; in return, Kennecott gave Curtiss-Wright $168 million and the shares of Curtiss-Wright it held which, along with stock tendered in Curtiss-Wright's self-buyback, helped give Teledyne more than 50 percent control of Curtiss-Wright.

Curtiss-Wright's sale of Cenco—resulting in $9.8 million in earnings—along with a $52 million gain from the sale of Dorr-Oliver and Kennecott shares helped push Curtiss-Wright's 1981 earnings to $85 million. Next, the company began investing in Western Union Corporation, acquiring a 21.6 percent stake in the telecommunications concern. However, this investment proved unsuccessful; Curtiss-Wright lost $42 million on the company, and as its 1984 total earnings plunged to $1.9 million—down from $18.5 million a year earlier—the company sold its stake in Western Union. Also during this time, Curtiss-Wright abandoned its hopes for the Wankel, selling its rotary combustion engine business to Deere & Company after failing to discover a commercial application for the engines.

In 1986, Curtiss-Wright received an Air Force contract in excess of $40 million to provide wing-flap actuators for the F-16, leading to ongoing F-16 actuator business. The following year, Curtiss-Wright was forced to fire several Target Rock senior executives after discovering an embezzlement scheme that resulted in the indictment of several former employees and suppliers. Considered a victim of the embezzlements, Curtiss-Wright was not charged with criminal misconduct in the matter, although in 1990 the government initiated litigation against Target Rock Corporation related to embezzlements by former Target Rock officials and their alleged mischarging of government subcontractors.

In March 1990, Berner died and was succeeded by Shirley D. Brinsfield, an outside director and former chairperson of Cenco who pledged to focus Curtiss-Wright's operations on manufacturing rather than investments. Charles E. Ehinger was elected president and Berner's son, Thomas R. Berner, was elected to the company's board. Less than four months after Berner's death, Curtiss-Wright declared a special dividend of $30 a share. The primary beneficiaries were Unitrin Inc., an insurance company once owned by Teledyne with a 44 percent interest in Curtiss-Wright, and Argonaut Group (formerly owned by Teledyne) with an eight percent interest.

During the late 1980s, Curtiss-Wright's sales and income remained fairly stable, fluctuating between $21 million and $28 million in earnings and $188 million and $212 million in sales. In 1990, the company's revenues climbed to $214 million while earnings sunk to $6.8 million, largely due to a $13.8 million after-tax environmental charge related to soil and ground water contamination at the company's former Wood-Ridge facility. Over the next two years, however, earnings rebounded to more than $21 million. In July 1991, Ehinger resigned as president and Brinsfield assumed the duties of president. Curtiss-Wright sold the engine distribution business of its Canadian subsidiary and discontinued its remaining Canadian operations soon thereafter.

In early 1993, Curtiss-Wright announced that it would explore the sale of three of its four business units, including Metal Improvement Company, its Flight Systems Group, and its Buffalo Extrusion Facility. In May 1993, Curtiss-Wright's presidency was turned over to David Lasky, a former senior vice-president, and, two months later, Curtiss-Wright abandoned attempts to sell its Flight Systems subsidiaries, as offers did not meet expectations. By October of that year, Curtiss-Wright had reached an agreement to sell its extrusion business, while depressed conditions in the commercial and military aerospace markets led the firm to abandon the sale of MIC, which had garnered less than favorable offers.

At the end of the year, Curtiss Wright's Target Rock subsidiary agreed to pay the government $17.5 million to settle remaining litigation. The Target Rock settlement, coupled with environmental clean-up charges, contributed to an annual loss of $5.6 million on declining sales of $158.9 million in 1993.

Curtiss-Wright entered 1994 seeking expanded commercial markets in the area of pollution control, for which its electronic control valves were well suited. The company faced cutbacks in the production of commercial aircraft, a reduction in pricing levels and U.S. Air Force procurement of the Lockheed F-16 fighter plane, the recent termination of valve orders for the U.S. Navy's Seawolf program, and reduced production activity in the Navy's nuclear program. The future of Curtiss-Wright, which abandoned the sale of its subsidiaries in 1993 in favor of optimum shareholder value, appeared contingent on both the economics of the company's traditional markets and the company's success in broaching new markets. The company's future also seemed dependent on its ability and desire to maintain its business units under the Curtiss-Wright name in an era of increasing consolidation and cutbacks in the defense and aerospace industries.

Principal Subsidiaries: Curtiss-Wright Flight Systems, Inc.; Curtiss-Wright Flight Systems/Shelby, Inc.; Target Rock Corporation; Metal Improvement Company, Inc.

Further Reading:

Carley, William M., and Tim Metz, ''Proxy Pugilism: Curtiss-Wright's Bid for Kennecott Has David-Goliath Aspects,'' *The Wall Street Journal,* April 18, 1978, pp. 1, 39.

''Curtiss-Wright Engine Has Only 2 Moving Parts,'' *The Wall Street Journal,* November 24, 1959, p. 4.

''Curtiss-Wright Sees Its Earnings Growth Continuing this Year,'' *The Wall Street Journal,* February 18, 1969, p. 8.

''Curtiss-Wright, Studebaker-Packard Paths Marked by Mergers in Plane, Auto Fields,'' *The Wall Street Journal,* August 6, 1956, p. 4.

''Facing Reality,'' *Forbes,* November 15, 1967, pp. 24–25.

''Hurley Gives Up Curtiss-Wright Posts; Berner, a Director, Is Named Chairman,'' *The Wall Street Journal,* May 26, 1960, p. 9.

''Kennecott and Curtiss-Wright End Corporate Battle by Agreeing to 10-Year Truce Involving $280 Million,'' *The Wall Street Journal,* January 29, 1981, p. 3.

Martin, Richard, ''Wondrous Wankel: Engine Not Only Drives Vehicles, but It Also Puts Stocks Into Orbit,'' *The Wall Street Journal,* June 16, 1972, pp. 1, 25.

Shao, Maria, ''Kennecott's Battle With Curtiss-Wright Involves Ambitions, Strategies and Money, *The Wall Street Journal,* January 5, 1981, p. 19.

Stevens, Charles W., ''Curtiss-Wright Picks Top Officers After Berner Death,'' *The Wall Street Journal,* March 23, 1990, p. C18.

Tannenbaum, Jeffrey A., ''Curtiss-Wright Slates Payout of $30 a Share,'' *The Wall Street Journal,* July 13, 1990, p. C9.

''The Well-Deserved Decline of Curtiss-Wright,'' *Forbes,* November 15, 1967, pp. 24–26.

—Roger W. Rouland

Dana Corporation

4500 Dorr Street
P.O. Box 1000
Toledo, Ohio 43615-4033
U.S.A.
(419) 535-4500
Fax: (419) 535-4896

Public Company
Incorporated: 1916 as Spicer Manufacturing Company
Employees: 36,000
Sales: $5.46 billion
Stock Exchanges: New York London Pacific
SICs: 3714 Motor Vehicle Parts and Accessories; 3592
    Carburetors, Pistons, Rings, Valves; 3561 Pumps and
    Pumping Equipment; 3594 Fluid Power Pumps and
    Motors; 3492 Fluid Power Valves and Hose Fittings

Dana Corporation is a leading manufacturer and distributor of
vehicular and industrial products with 430 manufacturing and
distribution facilities in 27 countries around the world. Dana
operates in three principal business segments: vehicular, industrial, and financial holdings. The company's decentralized management system directs worldwide operations through four regional organizations in North America, South America, Europe,
and Asia Pacific. Developing concurrent to the automotive
industry, Dana has adapted to changes in that industry and has
remained a leader in its field. Another distinction of the corporation is its "consuming orientation toward people," a legacy of
former CEO Rene C. McPherson, known for his progressive
management techniques.

The Dana Corporation traces its origins to 1902, when Clarence
Spicer invented the Spicer universal joint and driveshaft to
replace the chain and sprocket devices then used in automobiles. Spicer founded the Spicer Universal Joint Manufacturing
Company in Plainfield, New Jersey, and served as president of
the company from 1910 to 1914, when he enlisted the well
known philanthropist, attorney, and legislator Charles A. Dana
as his successor. Dana would guide the firm for more than 50
years, and, in 1946, the Spicer Manufacturing Company was
renamed Dana Corporation in his honor.

Dana graduated from Columbia University with both bachelor
of arts and law degrees. After college, he practiced law for the
State of New York, advancing to the position of assistant prose-

cutor in 1907. Dana went on to serve as a state legislator for six
years before becoming president and then chairperson of Spicer
Manufacturing.

In 1930, the company moved its headquarters to Toledo, Ohio.
In the ensuing years, and during World War II in particular,
steel shortages forced Dana to make substantial cuts in its work
force; in 1945, the company laid off 4,000 workers because of a
steel shortage. Also during this time, the company faced labor
disputes. In 1945, 1,820 employees at the company's plant in
Pottstown, Pennsylvania, walked off the job, dissatisfied with
recent lay offs and subsequent rehirings of personnel with less
seniority. The strike lasted for 55 days before a settlement was
reached.

By 1952, Dana was considering closing the Pottstown plant
because it was no longer competitive. However, through careful
and lengthy negotiations with the United Auto Workers union,
the management agreed to a four-year, $5 million modern-
ization process that would enable the plant to regain its competitive edge. This meant several concessions on the part of the
UAW, including 21 revisions of its union contract, but, by 1959,
the plant was productive once again.

During the 1960s, the Dana Corporation became one of the
world's largest independent suppliers of automotive components and replacement parts with $500 million in sales. Charac-
terizing itself as a "growth company" rather than a conglomerate, the Dana Corporation sought expansion through acquisition
within the transportation industry. Early in the 1960s, Dana
purchased Perfect Circle Corporation, a manufacturer of piston
rings and related products, and, in 1963, Victor Manufacturing
and Gasket Company was acquired. By 1968, the company's
impressive customer list included General Motors, Ford, International Harvester, Chrysler, and American Motors.

In the late 1960s, Rene C. McPherson was appointed president
of the company. Described by *Fortune* magazine as a "maverick," McPherson was vital to the history of Dana Corporation
because of his progressive policies regarding management and
employee relations. He was also credited with turning a large,
somewhat unwieldy, auto parts manufacturer into a "model of
productivity." McPherson's first moves involved cutting 350
people from a staff of 500 at company headquarters and replacing the 17-inch stack of company operating manuals with a brief
policy statement. McPherson decentralized the corporate bureaucracy by requiring managers to assume more responsibility
in the decision-making process and encouraging personnel to
participate in a Dana stock plan. At his insistence, managers met
with employees instead of sending memos, time clocks were
abolished, and managers helped personnel to establish their own
production goals.

Another of McPherson's innovations was the establishment of
"Dana University," an in-house training program for employees who wanted to move up through the ranks of the company.
Moreover, Dana recruited "student teachers" to study excellence in manufacturing abroad and then return to their home
plants to disseminate the human relations strategies, manufacturing techniques, and philosophies they had learned. The progressive policies of the company led one security analyst to note

that McPherson brought "Japanese-style management to Dana before most people even knew what it was."

McPherson's business strategy was to make careful, small acquisitions while maintaining low costs and high productivity. As a result, Dana was considered one of the nation's best-run companies and maintained a sound financial record in the 1970s. During this time, McPherson shifted the company's focus away from its reliance on the original equipment market and toward the light trucks market, which ultimately represented 35 percent of its sales during the decade.

Moreover, Dana became known for its ability to turn unprofitable companies around. For example, in 1974, Dana acquired Summit Engineering Corporation, a manufacturer of numerical controls for machinery. At the time, the company's sales were at $900,000; under Dana's direction, sales increased to $18 million by 1979.

Between 1963 and 1980, Dana Corporation purchased 24 companies outside its original equipment vehicle business, and company profits rose from $62 million in 1975 to $164 million by 1979. By 1980, Dana had developed three distinct areas of business: original equipment auto and truck parts, replacement parts, and industrial machine components.

The changes implemented by McPherson were carried on by Gerald B. Mitchell when McPherson retired in 1980. Having started as a Dana machine operator at the age of 16, Mitchell understood and appreciated the company's commitment to its workers' concerns. However, economic recession during the early 1980s made it increasingly difficult to honor McPherson's personnel policies; when light trucks declined in popularity during the early 1980s, prompting drastic declines in company earnings, Mitchell was forced to close five plants and lay off one-third of its employees in its American operations. Some UAW officials regarded the company's treatment of its employees as unfair. Nevertheless, the company strove to offer its unemployed workers preferential hiring at other plants and assisted with relocation expenses. Lists of laid-off employees were sent to other manufacturers in the area, and a two-week job counseling program was provided when Dana plants were shut down.

In 1983, Dana's original equipment parts business had an unexpectedly profitable year, as earnings rose 119 percent to $112 million. However, Mitchell maintained that Dana's best prospects for the future remained in the replacement market for its auto and truck parts. In 1984, Mitchell anticipated that the replacement parts business would make up 40 percent of the company's net earnings within five years, while the original equipment business would account for only about 30 percent.

In 1984, Dana began manufacturing gears identical to those designed for a line of Clark Equipment Company truck transmissions. Through this tactic, Dana entered into direct competition with Clark's replacement sales, and Dana's success in this arena helped the company offset losses in other divisions. During this time, Dana also diversified into the financial service industry, acquiring the Cherokee Insurance Company, a small property and casualty insurance company. However, the venture proved unsuccessful, and Dana was forced to write off $6 million of its investment. While Dana considered its relation-

ship with Cherokee Insurance over, many of Cherokee's clients were unsatisfied that the subsidiary had been unable to fulfill reinsurance obligations. Dana was subsequently sued for $1.7 million by St. Regis Corporation.

In 1985, Southwood "Woody" Morcott, then a twenty-year veteran of Dana, advanced to the firm's board of directors and was subsequently elected CEO and president, positions he would hold into the 1990s. Morcott began focusing on streamlining operations and cutting costs at Dana, investing $120 million in "Project 90," a program for developing new technology, better facilities, and a new system of incentive payments which could be tied to higher productivity. The company hoped to reduce its costs to 90 percent of those of its major competitors.

However, in the late 1980s, global economic recession prompted increasing numbers of auto companies to manufacture parts in-house or to use less expensive foreign-made parts. Dana's earnings declined during 1989, 1990, and 1991, and, in 1992, Dana suffered a $382 million loss, despite a slight rebound in sales. Limiting its manufacture of passenger car components, Dana fortuitously expanded its production of engine parts for trucks. As that market segment, which constituted over 25 percent of Dana's business, rebounded in the early 1990s, the company was able to report net earnings of $80 million on 1993 sales of $5.46 billion.

As Dana's sales to Ford and Chrysler totaled 29 percent of its consolidated sales in 1993, Dana's future seemed inextricably linked to the fortunes of the automotive industry. Dana therefore focused on adapting its product lines in order to offset the effects of fluctuation in the industry. Management also persisted with its streamlining and cost-cutting measures and concentrated on penetration of international markets into the mid-1990s, with the goals of "Dana 2000" as incentive. According to the objectives stated in Dana's 1993 annual report, the company planned to earn 50 percent of sales from distribution markets and 50 percent of total sales from outside the United States. Distribution sales amounted to 36.6 percent of sales and foreign sales contributed 17.8 percent as of 1993.

Principal Subsidiaries: Albarus Inc.; DTF Trucking, Inc.; Dana Distribution, Inc.; Dana International Finance, Inc.; Dana International Ltd.; Dana World Trade Corp.; Flight Operations, Inc.; Gemstone Gasket Co.; Precision Specialties, Inc.; Swanton Air Three, Inc.; Results Unlimited, Inc.; Warner Sensors Corp.; Undercar International, Inc.; Krizman International, Inc.; Summit Fidelity Insurance Agency, Inc.; Diamond Financial Holdings, Inc.; Dana Venture Capital Corp.; Hayes-Dana Inc.; Air Refiner (Canada) Ltd.; Dana Japan, Ltd.; Dantean Co., Ltd.; Dana Asia (Thailand) Ltd.; Dana Industrial Co., Ltd.; Spicer Asia (Thailand) Ltd.; Dana Industrial Co., Ltd.; Dana Asia (Singapore)Pte. Ltd.; Dana Asia (Thailand) Ltd.; Dana Asia (Taiwan) APD Co., Ltd.; Spicer Asia Engineering Ltd.; Taiyiu Warner Industrial Ltd.; Dana Australia (Holdings) Ltd.; Warner Electric Australia Pty. Ltd.; Dana Europe Holdings B.V.; Warner Electric S.A.; Dana Holdings Ltd.; Superior Electric Engineering Services, Ltd.; Shannon Properties U.K., Ltd.; Shannon Finance Ltd.; Dana Commercial Credit Ltd.; Dana Commercial Credit (U.K.) Ltd.; Farnborough Properties Co.; Farnborough Airport Properties Co.; Dana S.A.; Superior Electric S.A.R.L. (France); Dana Finance S.A.; Warner Electric SpA; Spicer Italia Srl; Dana Italia SpA; Warner Electric Ltd.; Spicer Espana, S.A.; Dana A.B.; Warner Electric (International) S.A.; Warner Electric S.A.; Dana GmbH (Germany); Dana Equipamentos Ltda.; Warner Electric Do Brasil Ltda. Solar Insurance Company Ltd.; Astro Insurance Company Ltd.; Dana Foreign Sales Corp.; Fairway Captive Services Ltd.; DCC Spacecom Ltd.; Dana Asia (Hong Kong) Ltd.; Shui Hing Manufacturing company Ltd.; Technologia De Mocion Controlada SA de CV; Ubali S.A.; E. Daneri, ICSA; Dana Asia Pacific (Malaysia) SDN BHD; Dana Asia (Korea) Co., Ltd.; Industria de Ejes y Transmissiones S.A.

Further Reading:

Byrne, Harlan S., ''Dana Corp.: After a Sluggish '91, Parts Supplier Readies a Kick into High,'' *Barron's,* September 30, 1991, pp. 41–42.

McPherson, Rene C., *Dana: Toward the Year 2000,* New York: Newcomen Society in North America, 1973.

—updated by April Dougal Gasbarre

De La Rue PLC

6 Agar Street
London WC2N 4DE
United Kingdom
(071) 836-8383
Fax: (071) 240-4224

Public Company
Incorporated: 1896 as Thomas De La Rue
Employees: 8,600
Sales: £559.50 million (US$856.71 million)
Stock Exchanges: London
SICs: 6711 Holding Companies; 2753 Engraving and Plate
  Printing; 3574 Calculating and Accounting Machines,
  except Electronic Computing Equipment; 3555 Printing
  Trades Machinery and Equipment

The world's largest commercial banknote and security printing company, De La Rue has a presence in literally the four corners of the earth. With 90 percent of its sales outside the United Kingdom, it controls 31 manufacturing plants in 13 countries and has sales and marketing operations in 14 others. Its customers include commercial banks, central banks, other financial institutions, government departments, and major retail organizations. At the forefront of the move to automate retail banking processes, De La Rue is also the leader in payment systems, supplying cash handling equipment, producing cash dispensing machines, banknote sorting machines, and counting products. A company founded on and fueled by innovation, De La Rue has had a colorful and eventful history.

Thomas de la Rue was born in a small village in Guernsey, the Channel Islands, in 1793. A boy of little formal education but much ingenuity, he was apprenticed at the age of nine to a newspaper printer in Guernsey's capital, St. Peter Port. Immediately after his term of service ended in 1811, de la Rue entered into a partnership with Englishman Tom Greenslade to produce their own weekly ''journal politique et litteraire,'' the *Publiciste.* After only 13 editions, however, de la Rue, whose burning ambition was matched by an equally fiery temper, fell out with his partner and independently set up *Le Miroir Politique,* a forum from which he energetically attacked Greenslade and the other publishers in town.

From the beginning, however, de la Rue was more interested in publishing processes than in editorial content, and by the time he was 25 he had determined that provincial Guernsey offered too restricted a scope and moved to London. In order to support his family, de la Rue began his London career as a manufacturer of straw hats, but all the while he was experimenting with paper surfaces and printing processes. In 1829 he produced a deluxe edition of the New Testament, 25 copies of which were printed with pure gold powder. The result was universally admired, and book lovers judged it a marvel, but unfortunately, with a price tag of £15, only one copy was sold.

The foundation of the De La Rue company came in 1830, when de la Rue first went into the playing card business. Two years later de la Rue patented his ''Improvements to Playing Cards'' and produced the first modern cards. His printing technique, electrotyping on enameled paper, represented a notable achievement not only in playing cards but in the history of color printing. Within a few years De La Rue was acknowledged as the premier maker of playing cards in Britain. Although cards remained the backbone of the business until the 1850s, during the 1830s and 1840s De La Rue branched out into all aspects of the stationery business, establishing a brisk trade in elaborately designed Victorian stationery, visiting cards, wedding cards, fancy menus, and railway tickets (a handy way of using up odd pieces of pasteboard). In 1843 De La Rue established its first overseas trade, as de la Rue's brother Paul traveled to Russia to advise on the making of playing cards.

Meanwhile the burgeoning postal system was to supply De La Rue with its next major business avenue. In 1840 the system of prepaid postage was first introduced, and with it the idea of the envelope. The earliest envelopes were sold flat and unfolded; later they were cut and folded, but the whole laborious process was done by hand. In 1846 de la Rue's son Warren, an inventor like his father and in his later years a well-respected amateur scientist and astronomer, designed the first envelope-making machine, able to produce 2,700 envelopes in an hour. This proved to be a tremendous boost to De La Rue, particularly after 1851 when it caught international attention and acclaim at the Great Exhibition at the Crystal Palace in Hyde Park.

Two years later De La Rue scored another coup when it won a four-year contract from the Inland Revenue to produce adhesive fiscal stamps on drafts and receipts. The company's main competitor in this area, Perkins Bacon & Co., might have seemed the logical choice for this contract as it was already making Britain's first postage stamps, but De La Rue was pioneering a new method; instead of the old line engraved system, whereby each sheet was printed from a transferred plate, De La Rue's new process was typographical, or surface printed. The system was more economical and practical, and De La Rue promised, in addition, that they could provide a special ''fugitive'' ink which would disappear if anyone attempted to clean the stamps to reuse them.

De La Rue's first foray into security printing was thus a tremendous success. By 1855 the company was producing its first British postage stamp, the Fourpenny Carmine, and had begun supplying stamps to the East India Company. This was the start of a hugely lucrative contract; within a few years the company was supplying the entire colony with all its postal requirements.

A rival's bad luck and the uncertain temperament of a government official provided De La Rue's next big break. In 1858 Perkins Bacon inadvertently offended the Agent General in charge of the British colonies' stamps to such a degree that the Agent General relieved that company of the contracts for the Cape of Good Hope, Mauritius, Trinidad, Western Australia, Ceylon, Saint Helena, the Bahamas, Natal, and St. Lucia and awarded them all to De La Rue. This in turn led to another profitable avenue for De La Rue, as the same official contracted the firm to print the paper currency for Mauritius, giving De La Rue its first banknote printing contract. Success in the British colonies bred success at home, and by 1880 De La Rue had completely cornered the domestic postal market.

During the middle decades of the nineteenth century, De La Rue became an international force in security printing. As new countries emerged or different governments came to power, De La Rue was there to offer its expertise in postal and currency printing. During the U.S. Civil War, De La Rue was hired by the Confederacy to produce the only American stamp ever printed abroad: the Five Cents Blue, adorned with the head of Jefferson Davis. The business expanded into Italy, Portugal, Uruguay, and Ecuador, and as it expanded Thomas de la Rue and his sons Warren and William continued to make improvements in paper and processes.

In 1896 De La Rue converted from a family partnership to a private company. Now under third-generation leadership, the firm seemed to lose those qualities of ambition and innovation that had caused it to flourish under Thomas and his sons, and entered a long period of stagnation and decline. The company did enjoy a brief success with its Onoto pen, the first practical fountain pen. As its eccentric inventor George Sweetser enthused of his creation: "It can not only be filled in a flash and written with, but could be used to syringe your ears, spray the geraniums with insecticide, and it is ideal for 'ink-splashers' as it will carry across the road." Fueled by a £50,000 advertising campaign (an enormous sum at the time), the Onoto was a big success in the early years of the twentieth century, though not big enough to save the faltering fortunes of De La Rue.

As early as 1888 there had been some concerns expressed in Parliament about De La Rue's monopoly of the British postage stamp market. That incipient storm had blown over largely because De La Rue was able to convince the government that it was, simply, the best company for the job. By 1910, however, suspicions were rekindled, not least because, although production costs had gone down, De La Rue's prices remained as high as ever. The company was, in fact, making colossal profits and had grown complacent. The Inland Revenue proposed to split the contract between De La Rue and another firm, Harrisons. Reportedly, Thomas de la Rue's grandson, Thomas Andros de la Rue, was so incensed by this proposal that he stormed out of a meeting with the secretary of the Post Office after shouting that De La Rue would have the entire contract or it would have none of it. Thus De La Rue lost a contract it had held for 30 years. The consequences for the company were grave, with idle factories and redundant workers the result. Loss of face was added to loss of profits only months later when Thomas Andros de la Rue died and the rumor went around that De La Rue's workers were each to benefit by his will. The widely publicized rumor proved to be untrue, and De La Rue sank even further in the public's estimation.

With the outbreak of World War I, the company's fortunes were briefly revived with an important government commission to print one and ten shilling notes, but on the whole fourth-generation management fared no better than had third-generation. Indeed, the company started the war with £90,000 to its credit, and ended it £90,000 in debt. Part of the problem stemmed from Stuart de la Rue's too-eager embrace of the wartime government's suggestions that manufacturing firms should diversify. De La Rue diversified into everything from cricket bats to motor cars with mostly disastrous results. On one occasion, in a bid to prove De La Rue's security printing superiority, Stuart de la Rue forged one of the company's competitor's banknotes, successfully presented it to his bank, and triumphantly informed the government, only to be nearly imprisoned for counterfeiting.

By 1921, when the company went public, it was nearly ruined. Once at the forefront of new technologies and developing research, De La Rue's factories were degenerating into a jumble of antiquated machinery and outdated processes. Stuart de la Rue, as chairman, was the only family member left in the firm. When the government proposed that the company fulfill India's printing requirements on location rather than in London, Stuart refused to do so, with the result that within a few years the entire Indian contract—a mainstay of the business—was lost.

In 1923, Stuart de la Rue unwisely revealed that De La Rue had a secret private agreement with its competitor Waterlows over stamp interests. De La Rue held a monopoly on domestic and colonial stamps, Waterlows on foreign stamps. If the "wrong" tender were accepted, one company paid compensation to the other. There was a great public outcry at this revelation, and although Stuart received only a public admonishment in the inquiry that followed, the company's reputation was further discredited. Stuart de la Rue's own reputation was in tatters. It is said that, in desperation, he asked his employees what had gone wrong with the company, and one of them, Bernard Westall, a junior clerk who later became managing director, responded, "You." Stuart de la Rue left the company soon thereafter.

It took some time for De La Rue to recover from its troubles, but recover it did. Instrumental in the company's revival was its 1930 entry into the vast and lucrative Chinese market, which was to be for nearly 20 years a mainstay for De La Rue. Operations were frequently fraught with cloak-and-dagger style intrigue as international hostilities heightened and World War II drew near. A factory was secretly built in the French settlement of Shanghai with a back-up plant constructed in Rangoon, Burma, as a precaution against Japanese aggression. When France fell, De La Rue succeeded in moving its operations to Rangoon, and when Rangoon fell, to Bombay, India.

De La Rue's London factories at Bunhill Row were destroyed in the Blitz in December 1940, and the old ways of commercial printing were finished forever. De La Rue, however, quickly made arrangements to resume printing elsewhere by offset lithography and was able to honor all commitments.

Following the war, De La Rue embarked on a half century of acquisitions, developments, and expansions. In a strong postwar position, the company grew, establishing interests in Pakistan, Ireland, and Brazil. In 1958 the company set up Formica Ltd. (with 40 percent participation by American Cyanamid) and within a few years its factories were established in France, Germany, Australia, New Zealand, and India. Security Express, a carrier of valuables service, was created the following year.

In 1960 De La Rue's growing involvement in bank automation was signaled by its creation of a subsidiary, De La Rue Instruments. The following year the company acquired the de la Rue family's old printing rivals, Waterlow and Sons. The 150th anniversary of Thomas de la Rue's first edition of his own newspaper *Le Miroir Politique* coincided with the company's registration in New York as a security and financial printer to the New York Stock Exchange. In the late 1960s, the Rank Organisation made a bid for De La Rue but this was rejected by the Monopolies Commission as being against the public interest. In 1969 the early foundation of De La Rue, the playing card business, was finally sold.

The 1970s and 1980s were busy years of acquisitions and sales, with De La Rue divesting itself of interests that were not part of its core businesses (such as the sale of Formica in 1977) and consolidating its position in its chosen ventures (witness the 1982 acquisition of the U.S. payment card firm Faraday National Corporation). Also during the 1980s some of De La Rue's banknote export factories were opened, including those in Singapore and Hong Kong. Most significantly, however, the company moved increasingly into the area of payment systems, among other ventures, forming De La Rue Garny in Germany in 1983 and acquiring the Scottish-based Fortronic in 1987.

De La Rue has fared particularly well in the 1990s. To some extent this is due to Jeremy Marshall, chief executive since 1989. Taking over just after De La Rue had narrowly avoided a takeover bid by Norton Opax, Marshall continued and strengthened the trend toward concentration on De La Rue's strong core areas of currency, security printing, and payment systems, selling off loss-making subsidiaries and concerns not directly related to the firm's principal ventures.

De La Rue also profited from political events. The break-up of the Communist bloc resulted in some 26 countries requiring new currency. De La Rue got the lion's share of the business. Boosted by these new markets, the company's currency division remained strong in the 1990s. Of the world's countries whose governments do not print their own currency, De La Rue has 60 percent of the market share. The company has regained its traditional lead in technological innovation: specialized presses are continually being developed and marketed by its associated company, De La Rue Giori. Its patented Computer Aided Design System, Durer, is able to produce banknote designs in half the time formerly required.

Research and development are also keystones of De La Rue's security printing division: it supplies the Bank of Scotland with debit cards incorporating laser-engraved photographs, and in partnership with a Dutch electronics company, Philips, is developing microchip "smart cards." Plastic payment cards, checks, passports, travelers' checks, and bonds all play a part in De La Rue's security printing business, and the company is expanding into related ventures, moving increasingly into printed materials for elections and for national registration and identity card schemes.

De La Rue's payment services division, however, is the company's fastest growing areas of business. As banking becomes increasingly more automated, De La Rue is at the forefront of technological development. Its 1991 acquisition of Inter Innovation, a Swedish payment systems firm, caused the company's profits to rise sharply, and De La Rue is avowedly on the lookout for similar acquisitions to take full advantage of this rapidly expanding market. In the future, it seems likely that De La Rue will continue to uphold its status as the world's preeminent security printer while aiming to become a leading force in the creation of the automated banking world of tomorrow. Thomas de la Rue, that shrewd businessman and inventor, would surely applaud today the strategies of the company he founded so long ago.

Principal Subsidiaries: De La Rue Card Technology; De La Rue Giori (Switzerland; 50%); De La Rue Holographics (80%); De La Rue Identity Systems; De La Rue Inter Innovation (Sweden); De La Rue Numbering Systems; De La Rue Smurfit (Ireland; 50%); Garny (Germany; 93%); LeFebure Corporation (U.S.A.); Thomas De La Rue (Brazil); Thomas De La Rue (Hong Kong); Thomas De La Rue (Malta); Thomas De La Rue (Singapore); Thomas De La Rue and Company; Thomas De La Rue Kenya; Thomas De La Rue Lanka (60%); Thomas De La Rue International.

Further Reading:

"De La Rue Is Secret Bidder for Portals," *London Times,* May 15, 1994, sec. 3, p. 1.
"De La Rue's Future Looks Secure," *Management Today,* June 1991, p. 38.
"Excellent Results from World Leader," *Investors Chronicle,* June 4, 1993.
Houseman, Lorna, *The House that Thomas Built: The Story of De La Rue,* London: Chatto & Windus, 1968.
"In Line to Make a Mint," *Mail on Sunday,* April 4, 1993.
"The Lex Column: De La Rue," *Financial Times,* June 2, 1993.
"UK Company News: Ex-communists Help De La Rue Rise 34 Percent," *Financial Times,* June 2, 1993.

—Robin DuBlanc

Dentsply International Inc.

570 West College Avenue
P.O. Box 872
York, Pennsylvania 17405-0872
U.S.A.
(717) 845-7511
Fax: (717) 848-3739

Private Company
Incorporated: 1899
Employees: 4,400
Sales: $260 million
SICs: 3843 Dental Equipment and Supplies; 3841 Surgical
and Medical Instruments; 3842 Surgical Appliances &
Supplies

Dentsply International Inc. produces a complete range of equipment and materials designed for prosthetic, preventive, and restorative dentistry. It is the world's largest manufacturer of artificial teeth and consumable dental products and spends more on research and development than any other dental company. Products are marketed under the Ash, De Trey, Dentsply, and Caulk brand names and include artificial teeth, teeth implants, dental caulk, and surgical tools and appliances. They are sold in over 100 countries, on five continents, and are manufactured at plants located throughout Europe, Asia, and North and South America. A private company for most of its existence, Dentsply went public in 1993 when it merged with Gendex Corp., a publicly held entity.

Dentsply was originated around 100 years ago in New York City by Dr. Jacob F. Frantz, George H. Whiteley, Dean C. Osborne, and John R. Sheppard. In 1899 these four men (all with experience in the dental business) opened a retail dental supply service under the name The Dentists' Supply Co. of New York. At that time the dental supply business was highly competitive. The new company was battling to gain a foothold in New York's tightly controlled market when the four men received word that a small Pennsylvania manufacturer of porcelain teeth was going out of business. Convinced that their efforts would be better rewarded if they focused on manufacturing and selling only ceramic teeth—as opposed to retailing numerous types of supplies in New York—the four purchased the ailing company.

One of the four, George H. Whiteley, had considerable experience as a ceramist and was well versed in the process of manufacturing ceramic teeth. Whiteley was sent to oversee operations of the new company while the three others set up a marketing and distribution center in New York. At that time, the ceramic tooth industry in the United States was dominated by a few players with considerable experience and strong reputations in the business. Faced again with tremendous competition, the founders of the young Dentists' Supply Co. believed that their success depended solely on their ability to offer improved manufacturing services to the dental profession.

One of the first major improvements the company made was in the production of ceramic teeth. At that time, all artificial teeth were made of porcelain. In order to secure the tooth to the denture base, platinum pins were baked into the tooth's ceramic structure. These pins put undue stress on the tooth, and when unusual pressure was exerted while a person was chewing, the tooth would often break. Whiteley developed a patented process that solved the breakage problem. In his process, platinum split-ring anchorages were baked into the ceramic tooth. After the tooth was baked, the troublesome pins were soldered into the platinum rings. This greatly reduced pressure on the tooth's structure, and, according to company publications, "markedly reduced the frequency of breakage, lessened embarrassment to patients and saved dentists and dental technicians time, trouble and money." They named their new product Twentieth Century Teeth, in honor of the advent of the new century.

Armed with an innovative new product, the young Dentists' Supply Co. was able to carve out a niche for itself in the artificial tooth market. In just six years the company established a strong client base and a solid reputation as a provider of quality teeth. Fueled by the success of its new product, the company instituted a policy of continued professional service to the field of dentistry and began devoting a larger portion of its revenues to research and development. In 1906 Dentists' Supply instituted another "first" in the business when it hired a trained prosthodontist to lead a team working towards the development of stronger and more realistic-looking dentures.

Several years later, in 1914, Dentists' Supply Co. introduced another innovative new product—a series of different-sized teeth that could be selected and mounted into the denture in a manner that would be in harmony with the shape and size of a patient's face. Named the Trubyte System, the series was developed by Dr. James Leon Williams, a practicing dentist who was fed up with the awkward tooth sizes that had been produced up until that time. The company also underwrote the research of Dr. Alfred Gysi, a Swiss dentist involved in researching another first—the development of artificial posterior teeth that fit comfortably in the mouth. Together, the two doctors developed tooth size and placement standards that continue to form the fundamentals of dental teaching worldwide. In the 1920s the company introduced Twentieth Century Solila Vulcanite Gum Teeth, in which the teeth were imbedded in a strip of pink rubber that resembled natural gum tissue. The company also made important contributions towards selecting natural shades of teeth based on the age of the patient.

Early in its existence, Dentists' Supply Co. had entered into a distribution agreement with E. de Trey & Sons, an upstart dental distribution business founded by two young Swiss men whose father had invented an improved form of gold tooth filling called "Solila Gold." Caesar and August de Trey had come to the United States to sell their father's filling product, but soon realized that "American dental products matched the preeminence of American dentistry" and decided to export these products to Europe. They set up an office in London, from which the youngest of the two brothers, Caesar, sought to conquer Europe with American dental products. Within a decade, E. de Trey & Sons became Dentists' Supply Co.'s sole distributor. As Dentists' Supply continued to introduce new products, De Trey continued expanding its markets and by 1923 Dentists' Supply products could be found in Paris, Milan, Petrograd, Brussels, Zurich, New York, Moscow, Madrid, and London.

Sales slowed slightly when World War I brought about heavy tariffs on imports into European countries. This inspired Dentsply to establish tooth manufacturing operations overseas, the first of which was built in Paris in 1920. The postwar years were profitable ones, with De Trey making significant progress selling Dentists' Supply dentures and related products worldwide. However, when sales began to slacken, the manufacturing/distribution team found itself engaged in a fierce battle with London-based Ash Company, a leading producer of denture equipment. As they fought for control of the European and American dentures markets, the two rivals began slashing prices drastically. Dentists' Supply's Twentieth Century Tooth, marketed under the name Solila in Europe, had captured the largest market share, but both companies had cut prices so low that neither could generate a cash flow.

The war between De Trey and Ash became so grave and had such adverse effects on the dental industry as a whole, that in 1923 a group of independent dental professionals brought the two together to broker a settlement. The following year a solution was agreed upon: Ash and De Trey merged their distribution efforts to form the Amalgamated Dental Company Limited.

Around 1920, the international world of dental supply manufacturing consisted of only a handful of key players. Dentists' Supply had earned the position of being the world's largest producer of artificial teeth. Other companies dominated in the instrument and equipment fields. In 1925 Dentists' Supply purchased a 45 percent share of Zahnfabrik Weinand Sohne & Co. G.m.b.H., a German producer of artificial teeth that had been suffering from the combined effects of World War I and British and American domination of the dental supply market. The new Amalgamated Dental Co. purchased a 30 percent share in the company over a two year period. Soon after the purchase, Dentists' Supply reorganized the German factory to increase productivity and improve the quality of the teeth it produced.

After World War II, Dentists' Supply's close tie with Amalgamated Dental proved fruitful: when Zahnfabrik's Berlin sales and distribution offices were destroyed by Allied air raids, Dentists' Supply made distribution arrangements with Amalgamated's German subsidiary, De Trey Gesellschaft, to distribute its teeth. Furthermore, normal business operations in Germany had been thoroughly disrupted by the war, and both companies lost their Eastern European markets when the Soviet Union dropped the Iron Curtain, closing its borders to western busi-

nesses. Managers from both companies worked together to institute a postwar marketing strategy.

Based on the knowledge that "dental conditions in Germany [were] closer to other European countries than conditions in the U.S.," Dentists' Supply set up a new European research facility in Germany. The company hired a German dentist, Dr. Konrad Gatzka, to lead research operations. Within a few years, Gatzka had created Biodent, the world's first vacuum-fired porcelain tooth. Biodent soon grew to be the best-selling artificial tooth product in Europe, and continues to hold top market share.

As Dentists' Supply's teeth became known worldwide, the company continued to expand its manufacturing. Between 1920 and 1950, foreign factories were established in England, Germany, Italy, Australia, Argentina, Brazil, and Mexico, bringing the product closer to its market and avoiding potentially high tariffs on imported goods. In 1947 Dentists' Supply ventured into the Australian market, incorporating Dentsply Australia Pty. Ltd. to allow for the purchase of Natudryl Manufacturing Company, a specialist in the production of plastic teeth.

By 1950, the artificial teeth and dentures market had matured, and Dentists' Supply had dominated the market for years. At that time, management decided that if the company were to maintain a top portion in the rapidly changing market, it would have to make some changes. They began research into other growth areas of dentistry and collaborated with a Washington D.C.-based inventor named Dr. John V. Borden in the development of a new dental drill. Within a few years, Borden created a drill with rotational speeds of up to 250,000 R.P.M., a speed much faster than conventional drills, which rotated at 6,000 R.P.M. The Borden Airotor, as it was known, revolutionized the dental practice and soon dominated the market. In 1961 the company launched a worldwide introduction of another revolutionary dental tool, Dentsply Cavitron, the first ultrasonic teeth cleaning machine. On the foreign front, the company's Australian research laboratory introduced Neolux and Neolux Opearl in 1962 and 1969, respectively; these two lines of plastic teeth "incorporated pearlescence . . . in imitation of the pearlescent quality which can be seen in many natural teeth." Dentsply Australia also developed denture veneers that imparted denture bases with the natural colors of living gum tissue.

Organizational changes continued through the 1950s, and in the early 1960s the company developed a "three-point program of diversification." First, the company planned to diversify its product offerings and venture further into the dental equipment market. Secondly, the company sought to expand its fields of expertise through mergers with other dental product manufacturers; and lastly, management decided to venture into the optical business due to the similarities of the industry's market structure to that of the dental supply market.

In 1963 Dentists' Supply merged with The L. D. Caulk Company, of Milford, Delaware. L. D. Caulk enjoyed the reputation of being the best supplier of products used daily in dental offices, including restorative systems, dental cements, alloys, denture base materials, and a wide range of other products. A year later, Dentists' Supply merged with the Ransom and Randolph Company of Toledo, Ohio, a well respected manufacturer of ceramic materials, dental instruments, and dental burs. The company further reorganized its strategy in 1968, focusing on "related fields, markets or technology which were well managed and had growth potential equal to, or greater than, that of the industry as a whole." The first acquisition under this new philosophy was F. & F. Koenigkramer Company of Cincinnati, Ohio, a producer of hydraulic equipment, chairs, and stools used in the optical and dental industries.

Throughout its history, Dentists' Supply had developed a number of products under the "Dentsply" brand name, and over the years the company became more and more known by this name. So in 1969, Dentists' Supply Co. of New York simplified procedures by changing its name to Dentsply International Inc., linking the firm with its brand name and accurately reflecting the scope of its market. Also that year, the company further branched into the optical field and began purchasing several retail optical chains in the state of Kentucky.

Dentsply's largest merger came about in 1976, when it joined forces with its longtime worldwide distribution partner, Amalgamated Dental International. The merger gave Dentsply a highly developed worldwide distribution and marketing network, as well as control over A.D. International (Australia) Pty. Ltd., the largest retail dental supply chain in Australia. Under new ownership, the Australian subsidiary changed its name to Dental Houses/Dentsply. Market conditions changed in the early 1980s leading Dentsply to close its original Australian factory in 1981 and transfer production to its Brazilian operations, Dentsply Industria e Comercio Ltda. Dental House/Dentsply continued to import and distribute Dentsply's line, as well as products by other manufacturers, and grew to become the largest supplier in the country.

In 1982 Dentsply acquired the remaining shares of its German partner, Zahnfabrik, which then became a wholly owned subsidiary. Dentsply also sold off its optical business as well as its Koenigkramer equipment manufacturer. Throughout the 1980s and early 1990s, the company continued to broaden its product line through both laboratory developments and brand name acquisitions. Dentsply also ventured further into the Asian market, where large population groups and a booming economy promised enormous sales potential. In the late 1980s, Dentsply opened an Asian Distribution Center in Hong Kong and equipped it with an educational center to teach dentists, technicians, and sales personnel about Dentsply products and equipment. It also established several joint ventures in the People's Republic of China and in India. In 1991 Dentsply opened Dentsply Japan, K.K., a wholly owned subsidiary, opening the door to the enormously large, but tightly controlled, Japanese market.

Dentsply went public in 1993 when it merged with Gendex Corp., a young, publicly traded manufacturer of X-ray machines and equipment used in medical and dental practices. Gendex was founded in 1983 to purchase the dental X-ray branch of General Electric Company and in ten years had grown to become the leading supplier of dental X-ray equipment in the United States. The merger brought Dentsply a large share of the U.S. X-ray market, and provided Gendex with a highly developed international sales and distribution network. Dentsply also purchased Eureka X-Ray Tube, Inc., which conveniently supplied all the medical X-ray tubes used in Gendex systems. The company suffered a minor financial setback the first year it went public, caused primarily by the bankruptcy of Healthco, one of its major distributors. Dentsply absorbed the loss and established relationships with other distributors.

As it nears its 100th anniversary, Dentsply has great cause to be optimistic. It sees great sales potential in the Pacific Rim, and has already laid a strong foundation for growth as that region's economy continues to expand at a rapid rate. The company opened its first wholly owned subsidiary in Thailand in 1993 and seems to be devoting much of its energies to expanding that market. In the United States Dentsply also has cause to be optimistic: the percentage of the U.S. population covered by dental insurance rose by ten percent between 1980 and 1993, to 45 percent. Should a nationwide health care plan be approved, that number ought to increase even more. With its well-established relationships and good reputation in the dental community, Dentsply seems well poised to benefit.

Principal Subsidiaries: Dentsply Laboratory Division; Dentsply Equipment Division; Dentsply Specialty Products Division; Ash Dentsply; Latin America Export Division; Ransom & Randolph Division; L. D. Caulk Division; Ceramco Inc.; Dentsply Implant Division; Dentsply Canada, Ltd.; Dentsply Caulk de Mexico S.A. de C.V.; Ceramco Manufacturing Co.; Dentsply Industria e Comercio Ltda. (Brazil); Dentalina Comercial Ltda.; DeTrey do Brasil Industria e Comercio Ltda.; Dentsply Argentina S.A.C.e.l.; Dentsply G.m.b.H.; Ceramco Europe Limited; Dentsply Ltd.; DeTrey Dentsply, S.A.; DeArt s.r.l.; Dentsply International Inc.; Dentsply Japan K.K.; Dentsply (Australia); Dental House/Dentsply; Gendex; Rand Universal; Eureka.

Further Reading:

Dentsply International: First in Dentistry, York, PA: Dentsply International, 1993.
De Trey, Peter, "Heritage" series, York, PA: Dentsply International, 1980.

—Maura Troester

Detroit Diesel Corporation

13400 Outer Drive West
Detroit, Michigan 48239-4001
U.S.A.
(313) 592-5000
Fax: (313) 592-5058

Public Company
Incorporated: 1987
Employees: 3,700
Sales: $1.56 billion
Stock Exchanges: New York
SICs: 3519 Internal Combustion Engines

Detroit Diesel Corporation manufactures diesel and alternative fuel engines for use in trucks, buses, coaches, commercial and pleasure marine craft, power generation, the construction industry, and the military. Detroit Diesel products are distributed through more than 130 authorized distributors in 88 countries around the world. With 1993 annual sales of $1.5 billion, Detroit Diesel ranked 269th on the 1994 *Fortune* 500. For some time, the company was named Detroit Diesel Allison (DDA) and had strong ties with auto giant General Motors. In 1988 Penske Corp. purchased DDA's assets, and, as of 1994, auto racing legend Roger Penske served as CEO of the company. Penske turned the beleaguered company around, stretching its market share in the heavy-duty truck category from a meager 4 percent in 1988 to over 26 percent in 1993.

General Motors pioneered the development of practical, light-weight, powerful, and fast two- and four-cycle diesel engines. Initially the incentive to develop such engines came from the enormous profits available if diesel could replace steam in the locomotive industry. According to Alfred P. Sloan, president of GM during the 1920s and 1930s, Charles F. Kettering can be credited with the foresight and drive behind the practical application of diesel power. Kettering supervised experiments at GM as early as 1921 to develop a smaller, more efficient diesel. As Sloan tells the story in his memoirs *My Years With General Motors,* he dropped by Kettering's office at the research laboratories one day and said "Ket, why is it, recognizing the high efficiency of the diesel cycle, that it has never been more generally used?" Kettering explained that technical problems in diesel engine design up to that time had meant that the engines simply would not perform the way the engineers wanted them

to. Sloan replied in his typically forthright manner, "Very well—we are now in the diesel engine business. You tell us how the engine should run and I will see that available manufacturing facilities are provided to capitalize the program."

The small, practical GM diesel engine might never have been developed, however, if Kettering hadn't also been a yachtsman. Kettering's fascination with diesel engines led him to purchase a diesel engine built by Winton Engines for use in his personal yacht. Kettering was so impressed with the Winton engine that he convinced Sloan to buy the Cleveland Ohio company. Alexander Winton, one of America's pioneer auto makers, was reportedly enthusiastic about the sale of his company to GM. He wanted to see the potential of diesel realized but knew that the cost of developing such an engine was beyond his scope. The apparently happy takeover was almost derailed by the market crash of 1929, but the sale went through in 1930. Simultaneously, GM purchased another Cleveland-based company, Electro-Motive Engineering Company, which had worked closely with Winton in the 1920s in their endeavor to develop a diesel-powered locomotive engine. The purchase of these companies was a great risk for GM in those economically turbulent times. The risk paid off but only after a number of years of intensive and often distressing research and development.

The break for the two-cycle GM diesel engine came when the company decided to use it as the power source for its dramatic reconstruction of an assembly line for the 1933 Chicago World's Fair. The diesels required continual repairs, prompting Kettering's son to comment that "the only part of the engine that worked well was the dip-stick." Nonetheless, locomotive companies were impressed with the power and efficiency of the engines compared to the steam locomotives they had been operating for years. Demonstration runs showed that a diesel-powered locomotive could cut the running time from Chicago to the West Coast by more than twenty hours. Once the industry decided to convert to diesel, GM had a corner on the market. No other major manufacturer built a diesel locomotive engine until after World War II. The success of the locomotive diesel foray prompted GM in 1937 to set up Detroit Diesel Engine Division to research, develop, and promote smaller diesel engines for marine and industrial use.

The importance of the railroad began a precipitous decline after World War II, but Detroit Diesel had already moved decisively into the truck and industrial sectors. Its main competitor in the postwar years, Cummins Engine Co., began to fight seriously for market share in the 1960s. However, the trucking industry was booming and there appeared to be an almost limitless market for the powerful diesel engines.

In 1970, Detroit Diesel Engine division was consolidated with GM's Allison division. Allison had been added to GM in 1929, during the same period of expansion and diversification that had seen the founding of Detroit Diesel. Allison played an important role in developing engines for aircraft used by American and Allied forces during World War II, producing an estimated 70,000 aircraft engines during the war. After World War II GM decided that its future in the aircraft business rested with providing engines to other manufacturers and it merged its Detroit Diesel and Allison divisions. In spite of the recession in the auto industry in the mid-1970s, Detroit Diesel Allison continued to perform well. By the beginning of the 1980s, Cummins had assumed the top spot in the diesel engine market, but Detroit Diesel still controlled a respectable 30 percent of the domestic market.

Over the next six years, however, Detroit Diesel underwent a precipitous decline, and by 1987 its market share had dwindled to less than 5 percent. The reasons for this calamitous fall are complex. In a 1985 article in *Automotive News,* L. F. Koci, then general manager of DDA and later president of the independent Detroit Diesel, cited an influx of diesel engines from Europe and Japan as a major cause of the drop in DDA sales. Although imports certainly contributed to falling sales, Detroit Diesel had lost much of its market share to the American Cummins Engine Co. A spokesman for Detroit Diesel after it had become an independent company acknowledged in a 1988 article in *Financial World* that "in the late 1970s and early 1980s [DDA] was letting bad product out the door. The engines weren't performing well and we lost some good customers." Parent company General Motors had made some attempt to revitalize DDA; however, of the $50 billion spent on plant modernization by GM through the 1980s, only $100 million went towards the floundering DDA. It was a case of too little too late, and by 1987 GM began to look seriously for a buyer to take the beleaguered division off its hands.

The company didn't look long. Roger Penske, the famous auto racer and *wunderkind* of the auto business world, was immediately intrigued at the prospect of reviving the lumbering old giant of the auto industry. By early 1988, Penske and GM had signed an agreement wherein Penske obtained ownership of 60 percent of Detroit Diesel's stock and GM secured the remaining 40 percent. Penske retained much of the old personnel at Detroit Diesel, continuing to employ engineers and management who had a long association with GM. Rather than overhauling the company by purging it of its old brass, he simply realigned the corporate goals. As reported in *Financial World* in 1988, he eliminated redundant computer costs, and consolidated manufacturing operations in an effort to cut the operating budget by more than $70 million. However, he kept such long-standing Detroit Diesel employees as L. F. Koci, Detroit Diesel general manager at the time of the takeover.

In order to revive Detroit Diesel, Penske had to get results quickly. Within the first two years of independent operations Detroit Diesel had more than doubled its market share. By 1993, this share had risen to 26 percent, mostly at the expense of its arch rival Cummins. Although under Penske's management revenues grew by more than 60 percent, heavy investments in research and development reduced profits to only one percent of sales. This low level of earnings combined with a depressed American economy led to two consecutive years of losses in 1990 and 1991. In the long run, however, Penske's persistence seemed to pay off: the company rebounded in 1992 and had a net income of over $20 million in 1993.

Aside from some cost-cutting measures and reorganization of the company, the early success of Penske's Detroit Diesel came on the strength of one item: the Series 60 engine. According to *Business Week* in 1991, the electronically controlled Series 60 engine was "ground-breaking" and, in addition to offering "dramatically better fuel efficiency, it boasts nifty computer-

ized features that diagnose mechanical problems and can monitor engine use—and thus track driver productivity." The Series 60, the first engine of its kind to be electronically controlled, was introduced during the first quarter of 1987. It was the product of a "clean-sheet" design that applied the latest technology to every stage of the manufacturing process, including production, assembly, and testing. Detroit Diesel originally claimed the engine needed an overhaul only once every 500,000 miles; the company later extended this boast to 750,000 miles. Over the next several years the truck engines seemed to hold up well, and the $82 million that the Series 60 had brought the company by 1993 suggested that Detroit Diesel had overcome its reputation for unreliable products.

Joint ventures with other major manufacturers further consolidated the revival of Detroit Diesel. German giant Mercedes-Benz entered into an agreement with Detroit Diesel in 1991 to develop electronic fuel delivery systems. As part of an engine development financing agreement, Diesel Project Development, a wholly owned subsidiary of Mercedes-Benz, bought $20 million of Detroit Diesel debentures in 1993, giving the German firm an 11 percent stake in the company. Volvo Penta also came to an agreement in 1993 that promised Detroit Diesel exclusive rights to certain Volvo Penta marine diesel products within the NAFTA area. Perkins Engine, based in England, and Detroit Diesel made an agreement in 1988 that facilitated certain aspects of distribution. Perkins also agreed to manufacture some smaller engines for Detroit Diesel, providing them with a variety of engines ranging from 5 to 2,500 horsepower. In 1993 Detroit Diesel formed a joint venture company with RABA PLC of Gyor, Hungary. The new company, named RABA-Detroit Diesel Hungary, Kft., reportedly will use RABA as its Eastern European manufacturing center, opening up an extensive potential market for products. Finally, in a return to its roots, Detroit Diesel entered into a "technology coalition" with Republic Locomotive to build new electronically controlled locomotive engines.

These joint ventures represent a strategy that each of the major U.S. engine makers, Detroit Diesel, Cummins Engine, and Caterpillar, had begun to employ by the early 1990s. Rather than continuing to fight each other for a dwindling share of the American market, each company attempted to increase foreign sales. The U.S. manufacturers hoped that forging ties with foreign companies would open European and Japanese markets, where potential sales were double what could be had in the U.S. market. The management of Detroit Diesel believed that the NAFTA and GATT agreements would "provide opportunities for growth even after considering the cyclical nature of the North American heavy-duty truck market."

As Detroit Diesel faced the late 1990s, Environmental Protection Agency standards for bus and truck engines posed the greatest challenge. The company had gotten the jump on the competition after the EPA set emission standards for the 1990s by being the first manufacturer to come out with an entirely new model. Due to the high-tech production system used on the Series 60, less than 1 percent of the engine's components needed modifications to meet the steep reductions in particulate emissions stipulated by the EPA in 1991 and 1994. The company's engines could be depended on to meet emission standards through 1997, but the future was not assured after that date.

Detroit Diesel hoped that the impressive amount of research and development the company had factored into its operating budget would ensure the company's edge in fuel efficiency and emission standards. A great deal of their research since the introduction of the Series 60 focused on developing engines that would run on cleaner fuels. Some of these experiments led to test units that ran on natural gas as well as methanol, ethanol, and other alcohol-based fuels. If one of Detroit Diesel's competitors, however, developed a conventionally fueled model that could meet the emission standard before Detroit Diesel's experiments came to fruition, then the company would be set back considerably.

Despite the promising first few years of the Penske-owned Detroit Diesel, in the mid-1990s the company retained a large debt load from the lean and rebuilding periods. In an effort to offset this debt, the company completed an initial public offering (IPO) of 4.75 million shares of common stock in October of 1993. The result of the IPO was to offset the company's debt by $99 million. The ongoing series of joint ventures with companies both large and small, in the United States and overseas, positioned the company to broaden its market and product line. All of these joint ventures were closely tied to the company's goal of using high-tech advancements to stay ahead of the competition as the industry faced ongoing pressure about environmental issues. The company that seemed finished in 1985 appeared ready to fight for a place as an international leader a decade later.

Principal Subsidiaries: Detroit Diesel Remanufacturing Holdings, Inc.; Detroit Diesel Overseas Distribution Corp.

Further Reading:

Benoit, Ellen, "Jump Start," *Financial World,* November 1, 1988, pp. 42, 44.

Bohn, Joseph, "DDA Is Reorganizing Operations in Detroit," *Automotive News,* September 2, 1985, pp. 8, 42; "Detroit Diesel to Produce Natural Gas, Alcohol Engines," *Automotive News,* July 2, 1990.

Cochran, Thomas N., "On the Road Again: Why Mercedes-Benz Likes Roger Penske's Detroit Diesel," *Barron's,* September 27, 1993, p. 13–14.

"Detroit Diesel and Raba Form a New Joint Venture Company to Assemble Engines in Hungary," *Newswire Press Release,* December 20, 1993.

"Detroit Diesel and Volvo Penta Announce Strategic U.S. Agreement," *Newswire Press Release,* February 16, 1994.

Kelly, Kevin, "Does Cummins Have the Oomph to Climb This Hill?" *Business Week,* November 4, 1991, pp. 66, 68; "The Rising Rumble of American Diesels," *Business Week,* September 6, 1993, pp. 84, 86.

Lowell, Jon, "Roger Roars Ahead: Penske Fires Up GM's Dying Diesels; Profits Replace Problems," *Ward's Auto World,* November 1988, pp. 30–34.

Mele, Jim, "The First Look at 1991 Engines," *Fleet Owner,* November 1989, pp. 76–85.

Rowan, Roger, "Those Dazzling Diesels," *Automotive News,* September 16, 1983, pp. 425–26.

Schwind, Gene, "A Clean-Sheet Approach to Engine Design and Manufacture," *Material Handling Engineering,* May 1987, pp. 61–63.

Sloan, Alfred P., "Nonautomotive: Diesel Electric Locomotives, Appliances, Aviation," in *My Years with General Motors,* New York: Doubleday, 1964, pp. 341–53.

—Hilary Gopnik and Donald Cameron McManus

Dow Jones /telerate

Dow Jones Telerate, Inc.

200 Liberty Street
New York, New York 10281
U.S.A.
(212) 938-5200
Fax: (201) 938-2488

Wholly Owned Subsidiary of Dow Jones
Incorporated: 1969 as Telerate Systems Inc.
Employees: 2,500
Sales: $646 million
Stock Exchanges: New York
SICs: 7375 Information Retrieval Services

Dow Jones Telerate, Inc., is a leading purveyor of information concerning the financial industry to customers around the world. The company got its start listing prices for one type of financial instrument, and then grew rapidly when it made an alliance with another firm that allowed it to provide exclusive and vital information. During a period of rapid growth in the financial industry's boom years in the 1980s, Telerate was acquired by Dow Jones & Company, Inc. Subsequently, Telerate saw its growth slow as its competition became more formidable, and the· financial industry as a whole underwent a transition.

Telerate Systems Inc. was founded in 1969 by Neil S. Hirsch, a 21-year old college dropout who was working as a clerk in a Merrill Lynch brokerage office. While working at the firm, Hirsch became fascinated with the electronic stock quote monitors. He noted that stock quotes were readily available on computerized terminals, but that information about the prices of other money market instruments could only be obtained by calling around to various financial industry firms that bought and sold those instruments. Hirsch's innovation was to expand the computerized communications mechanisms to include other areas of the financial industry.

The field in which Telerate first began operating was the commercial paper market. This market was made up of I.O.U.'s issued by companies when they wanted to borrow money for a short period of time. If a company wanted a loan, the rate of interest which it paid was determined by current, general interest rates, which were set by the Federal Reserve, and by the company's credit rating, which estimated its overall reliability. Once a company had borrowed money, the value of the I.O.U. it

wrote, called "commercial paper," was fixed, but since markets and interest rates fluctuated constantly, its relative value went up and down. A complex market in these corporate debts had sprung up, in which other corporations, banks, insurance companies, and brokers bought and sold the debts. Although the market was extremely volatile, or "liquid," the only way to determine the going rates for corporate borrowing at any given time was to call around on the phone to firms or brokers buying and selling the debts, and ask them what they were paying.

Hirsch borrowed money to start Telerate, which made prices that had been gathered from commercial paper dealers available on computer terminals. In doing so, Telerate brought transparency to the commercial paper market, opening it up to outsiders, who were not part of the small, insular world of commercial paper brokers.

Within several years, Hirsch's fledgling company had lined up several dozen customers, but it had run out of money. The company was on the verge of selling stock to the public in late 1971, when it was approached by the Cantor Fitzgerald Securities Corporation. In 1972, Cantor bought a 25 percent interest in Telerate in exchange for $500,000 in debt. With this deal, Cantor also made it possible for Telerate to offer a new and lucrative service.

Cantor was an interdealer broker in U.S. Treasury securities. As such, it was one of five chief players in the market for Treasury bonds, notes, and bills. When the U.S. government wanted to borrow money, it did so by issuing these securities at various interest rates, and for various lengths of time. Cantor was one of five firms that acted as middlemen between the other brokers who sold Treasury securities to dealers, who, in turn, sold them to investors. Because of Cantor's position as a key link among the other main brokers within this hierarchy, it had access to the prices that other dealers were offering for the Treasury securities.

Because the market for U.S. Treasury securities was the largest debt market in the world, all other prices for money market instruments were set on the basis of this "gold standard." This factor meant that this information was extremely important and valuable to people active in the financial markets. Even people who were not directly involved in the market for Treasury securities needed to know what that market was doing, since it indirectly affected all others.

Before Cantor linked up with Telerate, the prices for government securities had been available only to a very limited and select group of companies—those within the inner circle of primary dealers in government bonds. Cantor wanted these prices more widely disseminated, in hopes that this would give it a competitive edge against other brokers, and so it hooked up with Telerate, which had already created the same conditions in the commercial paper market. In doing so, Cantor provided Telerate with access to the prices other brokers were offering for government securities.

When Telerate began to offer Cantor's price quotes on government securities as trades occurred among the dealers, it had a unique and extremely valuable piece of information to offer. Since the other four interdealer brokers refused to reveal their price information, Telerate had a monopoly on this essential information, and the company's alliance with Cantor marked the beginning of a remarkable growth spurt. By 1977, the company's earnings had increased to $1 million.

With the new availability of "executable" prices on Treasury securities, Telerate's sales boomed. Over time, Cantor increased its ownership share of the company, to nearly 70 percent. In 1977, Telerate formed another important alliance, when it joined with AP-Dow Jones. AP-Dow Jones was a joint venture of the Associated Press and Dow Jones that had been formed to deliver financial information and business news in Europe, Asia, and Latin America. Together, AP-Dow Jones and Telerate moved to expand Telerate's market to include customers overseas.

Four years after Telerate began to make inroads into the foreign market for financial information, Cantor sold its majority share in the company to a British investment group called Exco International. This London based consortium was made up of five partners: Guinness Peat, a financial group; Astley & Pearce, a money broker; Godsell, another money broker; the British & Commonwealth Shipping Company; and the Save & Prosper Group. In a complex transaction, the British investors acquired 89.6 percent of Telerate for $75 million. The firm's remaining shares were left in the hands of its executives. At the time of the sale, Telerate's annual earnings had increased to $13.6 million.

Two years after its sale to the British firms, shares in Telerate were offered to the public for the first time. The company was listed on the New York Stock Exchange in April of 1983, and Exco's stake in the company was reduced to 49 percent. At the time of the stock offer, Telerate's financial fortunes were booming, and the sale of stock made founder Hirsch's 7.6 percent stake worth $70 million.

The company's information service had been expanded to include price information and updates on a wide range of financial instruments, including fixed-income securities, foreign exchange rates, and precious metals. Every 24 hours, Telerate provided 10,000 electronic "pages" of information on commercial paper, certificates of deposit, Federal agency securities, mortgage market securities, financial futures, and energy quotes, among other facts. Telerate's bond and note quotations remained most important among this selection of information. For this service, customers paid from $540 to $700 a month. More than 8,000 terminals in the United States and Canada had already been installed to receive this information, along with 2,500 terminals in 21 foreign countries.

Three months after its stock offering, in July of 1983, Telerate updated its agreement with AP-Dow Jones, and the two companies agreed to form a new business together. This foreign subsidiary, to be called AP-Dow Jones/Telerate Company, would provide Telerate services overseas. It was to be 49.9 percent owned by Telerate, and 25.05 percent owned by Dow Jones and AP, separately. Two months later, Exco, the company's British parent, announced that it would increase its holding in Telerate to 51.5 percent, pushing its share just over the half mark.

Exco's interest in solidifying its possession of Telerate was justified by the company's strong financial results. At the end of 1983, Telerate posted pretax profit margins of greater than 55 percent. The company reported 90 percent growth in earnings in its last fiscal quarter, and annual revenues that had nearly doubled, from $11.1 million in 1982 to $20 million in the following year. Revenues had risen 61 percent, from $41.6 million to $67 million.

These financial gains were made possible by the general financial climate of the 1980s. As the United States government pursued a policy of deficit spending by borrowing large sums, trading in government securities increased dramatically. Interest rates, tied to rates on Treasury bonds, became more volatile, and investors began to seek sanctuary from the fluctuating rates. The Chicago Board of Trade introduced a futures contract that allowed investors to gain some measure of security against changes in the interest rate, and it became an extremely heavily traded item. All of this activity, as well as the entry of foreign investors into the market for Treasury securities in large numbers, made Telerate's service even more essential and widespread than it had been before. In five years, the company's customer base quintupled, and sales climbed six-fold.

By the beginning of 1984, Telerate had started to see the threat of competition for the first time, primarily from the British news service Reuters Holding PLC. In an effort to make its service more valuable, the company introduced Telerate II, software for use on IBM-compatible computers, which helped users to analyze and manipulate the information provided by the company. With these extra services, the company hoped to boost revenues by charging customers higher fees. In addition, Telerate introduced a handheld pocket display quote machine, which was portable, and received information via radio waves.

Despite this effort, Telerate's growth began to flatten in 1984, and its orders for installation of new terminals also started to slow. This process was exacerbated by difficulties involving the newly split-up phone company, which caused a large backlog of orders for installation which went unfilled. By September of 1984, the company's stock price had sunk well below its initial offering level, and Hirsch was complaining to the press that Telerate was underappreciated.

One company that did appreciate Telerate was its foreign marketing partner, Dow Jones. In 1985, the media conglomerate purchased a 32 percent stake in the company from Exco International for $285 million. This investment was justified as the government bond market continued to boom, driving Telerate to a 45 percent compound annual rate of earnings growth. To keep up with this growth, the company expanded its staff and office space.

At the end of 1986, Telerate bought back from its partners, AP and Dow Jones, the percentage of the group's foreign joint venture that it did not already own. Months later, in September of 1987, Dow Jones put an additional $416 million into Telerate, upping its stake in the company to 56 percent.

One month later, Telerate announced that it would join with the American Telephone and Telegraph Company (AT&T) to offer a foreign exchange transaction service. This move was designed to let Telerate to compete with its primary rival, the British giant Reuters Holding PLC, in the lucrative foreign currency trading industry.

Telerate also began to develop a system called Matrix that would allow personal computer owners to manipulate the data that the company supplied. This effort was a response to the introduction of a competing financial information system, called MoneyCenter, which had begun to gain customers rapidly during this time. Long the beneficiary of a monopoly, Telerate had fallen behind in customer service and cutting edge technology.

In the following year, Dow Jones increased its holding in Telerate further, paying $148 million to increase its share to 67 percent. In 1988, Telerate introduced its Matrix program, but the sales were disappointing, as customers judged its capabilities limited and its graphics weak. Also in that year, Telerate was weakened by the collapse of the savings and loan industry, which sharply reduced the number of potential customers for its service.

In September of 1989, Dow Jones moved to complete its piecemeal acquisition of Telerate. The company offered $18 a share for the rest of the company's outstanding stock, but Hirsch rejected this offer as too low. In November, Dow Jones increased its bid to $21 a share, and purchased another 25 percent of the company for $515 million. It then owned 92 percent of Telerate, and it was only two months later that Dow Jones finalized its acquisition, spending $161 million, for a grand total of $1.6 billion. This made Telerate the most expensive acquisition in the history of its venerable parent company.

In addition to its expenditures on Telerate, Dow Jones had spent $22 million buying out AT&T's half of the company's joint venture in foreign currency trading in December of 1989. Late in that year, The Trading Service (TTS) went on line, and Dow Jones began to absorb all of its start-up costs, which totaled $51 million in 1989.

Firmly in control of Telerate, Dow Jones began to make rapid changes in an effort to return what had once been a cash cow to its highly profitable ways. The company brought in new engineers to rebuild Telerate's technological capabilities, and it stepped up efforts toward customer service. When a group of Cantor's fellow interdealer brokers announced that they would make price quotes on government securities available, effectively ending Telerate's monopoly over this information, the company moved to counter the impact of this blow by negotiating the right to carry this information in addition to its long-standing Cantor rates.

Despite these efforts, the company reported earnings down significantly in mid-1990, and 41 workers were laid off. In addition, the two companies experienced a clash in corporate cul-

tures between the younger and more freewheeling Telerate and the older and more conservative Dow Jones.

In June of 1991, Telerate saw the final erosion of its exclusive Cantor franchise, when a consortium of three brokerage firms, 40 primary dealers, and five interdealer brokers began to disseminate real-time price information on trading of government securities in a service called GOVPX. This move was made in response to a 1990 government report that called for wider access to this data. In response to this threat, Telerate expanded its Treasury bill reporting at no charge to its customers. Nevertheless, the GOVPX price of $140, compared to Telerate's basic price of $600 a month, appeared to pose a serious threat to the company.

In April of 1992, Dow Jones restructured its on-line information services, forming Dow Jones Telerate, Inc., and two separate business news services. In the following year, the company moved to update its services by introducing a program that ran on the new Windows personal computer operating system, and by rolling out new TeleTrac financial software. In early 1994, Telerate announced that it would begin to list government bond prices from a major broker for primary dealers called Liberty Brokerage Investment Company. This information, from a company that specialized in short-term bonds, supplemented the company's Cantor figures, which were stronger in the long-term bond field. In addition, the company strengthened its Asian information services.

Although Telerate's days of flying high along with the rest of the government bond market in the 1980s had passed, and its once unique market niche had been invaded by an ever-growing number of competitors, the company's years of experience and its backing by Dow Jones, a giant in the financial information industry, seemed to insure that it would compete effectively in the coming years.

Further Reading:

Barker, Robert, ''Growing Pains: Telerate Faces New Rivals, Flattening Orders,'' *Barron's*, June 25, 1984.
Bremner, Brian, and Jeffrey Rothfeder, ''Dow Jones's $1.6 Billion Baby Is Hardly a Bundle of Joy,'' *Business Week*, September 10, 1990.
''A Company Most Traders Look at But Rarely See,'' *Business Week*, September 24, 1984.
Gilpin, Kenneth N., ''Data Service on Treasuries Challenges Dow Jones Unit,'' *New York Times*, June 17, 1991.
Guyon, Janet, ''AT&T, Telerate Unit of Dow Jones Plan Joint Venture,'' *Wall Street Journal*, October 21, 1987.
Eason, Yla, ''Telerate Girds for Challenge,'' *New York Times*, January 16, 1984.

—Elizabeth Rourke

Eaton Corporation

Eaton Center
Cleveland, Ohio 44114-2584
U.S.A.
(216) 523-5000
Fax: (216) 479-7014

Public Company
Incorporated: 1911 as the Torbensen Gear & Axle Company
Employees: 38,743
Sales: $4.4 billion
Stock Index: New York Midwest Pacific London
SICs: 3625 Relays and Industrial Controls; 3714 Motor
   Vehicle Parts and Accessories; 3823 Process Control
   Instruments

The Eaton Corporation is the United States' largest manufacturer of axles and transmissions for heavy-duty trucks. With operations in North America, Europe, Latin America, and the Pacific region, the company also manufactures automotive components, industrial controls, switching equipment, and defense systems. Eaton's greatest period of growth occurred during the 1960s, and the company has since sought to offset the cyclical nature of its traditional businesses through diversification.

In 1920, Joseph Oriel Eaton established a small machine shop in Bloomfield, New Jersey, manufacturing heavy-duty truck axles for the expanding automotive industry. Three years later, the Eaton Axle Company was acquired by the Torbensen Gear & Axle Company, and its operations were moved to Cleveland, in order to be closer to the auto manufacturers there and in Detroit. Over the next few years, the new company, Eaton Axle & Spring, acquired several smaller auto parts manufacturers; diversification of its product line also included a new line of parts for aircraft engines.

The company weathered the Great Depression, acquiring several companies that were nearing bankruptcy. By the late 1930s industrial growth was stimulated by President Roosevelt's New Deal program, and demand for products from the Eaton Manufacturing Company—a name change registered in May 1932—increased slowly and steadily. When the United States became involved in World War II, Eaton, as a primary manufacturer of vehicle parts, produced a variety of items for the war effort.

In 1946, Eaton purchased the Dynamatic Corporation and one year later established a joint sales and engineering company with two British firms, Rubry Owen and E.N.V. Engineering. These companies soon became suppliers of axles and gears to Ford Motor Co. and General Motors Corp. in England. In 1953, Livia, a small Italian manufacturer of engine valves, acquired technological assistance and a production license from Eaton. As a result, Livia become the exclusive supplier of engine valves for Simca of France as well as for all trucks built by Fiat. Livia was purchased by Eaton in 1961.

John C. Virden was named president of Eaton in 1958 and followed the company's diversification policy. A strong believer in "divisional autonomy," Virden ensured that Eaton's subsidiaries and divisions maintained a large degree of managerial independence. Under Virden, Eaton made 23 major acquisitions between 1958 and 1973, including Fuller Manufacturing, which produced automotive transmissions, and, perhaps more importantly, the Yale & Towne Manufacturing Company. Yale & Towne was founded in the 1870s by the inventor Linus Yale, Jr., who developed a revolutionary pin-tumbler cylinder lock, or padlock, which proved popular and has remained essentially unchanged since its invention. When Yale died in 1913 at the age of 47, Henry Towne took over the company and served as its leader for the next 50 years. Yale & Towne was acquired by Eaton on October 31, 1963, and a full merger occurred on January 1, 1966, under the name of Eaton Yale & Towne.

During this time, Eaton's auto parts division suffered a temporary setback when General Motors, one of Eaton's primary customers, reduced its orders after model changes and higher wages forced the auto manufacturer to scale down production. Nevertheless, Eaton Yale & Towne remained profitable, as its other divisions supported the company until demand for auto parts recovered. In 1966, Eaton Yale & Towne experienced record growth in sales and profits, largely as a result of an expansion in industrial growth.

Following the merger with Yale & Towne, the company executed a careful integration of managerial personnel; officials at Yale & Towne were given important permanent positions in the new company. Gordon Patterson, formerly president of Yale & Towne, was named vice-chairperson, and John Virden became chairperson, as Elliot Ludvigsen, a former president of Fuller Manufacturing, was named president. When Virden retired in 1969, E. Mandell de Windt, who had joined the company as a production clerk, was elected chairperson. The company's name was changed once again on April 21, 1971, to Eaton Corporation.

In the 1970s, decreased demand for American cars severely affected the three largest manufacturers of automobile components: Bendix, Rockwell, and Eaton. As a result, all three companies attempted further diversification of their operations. While Bendix acquired new product lines, and Rockwell added electronics products to its line, Eaton began to focus on the less volatile truck components market, as well as on expansion into foreign markets. Eaton also initiated a $470 million diversification program to develop a new line of factory automation products.

In 1978, with the automotive market still sluggish, Eaton made three acquisitions: Samuel Moore & Company, a manufacturer of hydraulic motors and transmissions; Kenway, a company specializing in robotic warehouse storage systems; and, most importantly, the electronics company Cutler-Hammer, whose AIL electronics division had developed the ALQ-161 advanced radar counter-measures system for Rockwell's B-1 bomber and had also been chosen by NASA to build the landing system for the space shuttles. Eaton intended to combine the resources of these three companies in order to develop a new line of factory automation products. However, during the development stage, high capital investments and low profit margins ensued, and Eaton began to struggle financially. Moreover, the Yale & Towne division's ventures in forest equipment and lift-truck manufacturing proved barely profitable; 1980 was a particularly bad year for Eaton.

The following year, Eaton sold or closed down 18 subsidiaries whose profits were marginal or nonexistent. The forestry equipment and lift-truck businesses were written off and sold in 1982 for $200 million. That year, Eaton registered its first loss in 50 years, $189.6 million on sales of $2.4 billion. Determined to reduce the company's exposure to the vagaries of the automotive components business, de Windt declared that Eaton had now dedicated itself to becoming a "high technology company servicing the growth markets of the 1980s."

Ironically, the automotive division generated most of the company's profit the following year. Eaton's major automotive customers, International Harvester (later renamed Navistar International Corp.), Ford, General Motors, and Paccar Inc., had fully recovered from the recession of the mid-1970s and were once again selling a wide range of trucks. Even so, automotive components, which had accounted for 79 percent of Eaton's sales in 1977, were down to 46 percent by 1983. In 1984, 12 of the company's automotive components plants were closed, and the work force was reduced to 41,000, down from 63,000 in 1979. During this time, sales from the electronic components division rose dramatically from 21 percent of turnover in 1977 to 54 percent in 1983.

Jim Stover, president and chief operating officer of Eaton since 1979, was named chairperson and chief executive officer when de Windt retired on April 23, 1986. Stover maintained de Windt's commitment to the company's substantial foreign markets, remarking that Eaton had learned from the recession that "you compete on a global basis or you don't compete at all." Stover took over after Eaton had reported a 1985 profit of $231 million on sales of $3.7 billion.

At the beginning of 1986, Eaton had $1 billion available for financing acquisitions, and, by July of that year, it had purchased three more companies: Consolidated Controls (precision instruments), Singer Controls (switches and valves), and Pacific-Sierra Research (defense and computer systems). At the end of the year, Stover unexpectedly placed the company's defense electronics business, AIL Systems, Inc., up for sale, noting quality control problems and reduced orders for the division's B-1B bomber systems. This segment of Eaton's business had suffered several other setbacks during this period as well. It was suspended from bidding on new Air Force contracts, and, in March 1988, AIL paid the Department of Defense $9.5 million to settle improper billing charges. Unable

to sell the subsidiary, Eaton sustained it as a discontinued operation until mid-1993, when it was "reconsolidated," according to that year's annual report.

From 1984 to 1993, Eaton invested almost $1.7 billion in capital improvements and $2.3 billion in research and development, which enabled it to introduce several new products in the early 1990s. One noteworthy innovation was the AutoSelect automatic transmission, the result of $10 million and six years of planning. Introduced in 1993, AutoSelect promised the trucking industry increased fuel efficiency, safer and easier driving, and drastically lowered training costs. An article in the June 1993 issue of *Forbes* magazine suggested that AutoSelect might also be intended to attract more female drivers to the shorthanded trucking industry, an allegation that Eaton strongly denied.

Eaton's global expansion resulted in annual sales increases from 13.4 percent in 1985 to nearly 30 percent by 1993. However, domestic sales from its automotive division continued to provide the largest share, over 50 percent, of Eaton's revenues. Still susceptible to market fluctuations, the company recorded rather meager profits from 1989 to 1991, and reported a loss in 1992. Nevertheless, profits rebounded the following year, fueled by surging sales in the North American market for sport utility vehicles.

That year, Eaton announced a plan to lessen its dependence on automotive components through the $1.1 billion acquisition of Westinghouse's Distribution and Control business unit. The purchase advanced Eaton to a top position in industrial control and power distribution markets, providing such products as circuit breakers. The company planned to pay off the $930 million debt it incurred for the acquisition by 1998. With heavy-duty truck backlogs of nearly 100,000 units and the addition of the Westinghouse business, Eaton's CEO William E. Butler hoped to stabilize Eaton's earnings throughout the 1990s.

Principal Subsidiaries: Eaton International Corp.; AIL Systems Holding Co.; Eaton Consulting Services Corp.; Eaton-Kenway, Inc.; Eaton I.C.S.A. (Argentina); Eaton Proprietary., Ltd. (Australia); Eaton S.p.A. (Italy); Eaton EST S.p.A. (Italy) (99%); Eaton Controls Verwaltungs GmbH (Germany); Eaton International, Inc. (Liberia); Eaton B.V. (Netherlands); Eaton, S.A. (Spain) (50.14%); Eaton, Ltd. (U.K.); Eaton, GmbH. (Germany); BAC Investments Ltd.; Eaton Administration Corp.; Eaton ESC Holding Company Inc.; Eaton USEV Holding Company Inc.; Eaton Leasing Corp.; Eaton IDT, Inc.; Eaton ETN Offshore Ltd.; Saturn Insurance Commune ltd.; Eaton Technologies S.A.; Eaton EST SpA (99%); Eaton Manufacturera S.A. de C.V. (53.9%); Eaton BV; Eaton Electrical Components Ltd., (99.98%); Eaton Ltd. (South Korea); Eaton Foreign Sales Corp.

Further Reading:

Ludvigsen, E.L., *Eaton Yale & Towne: A Corporate Portrait*, New York: Newcomen Society in North America, 1968.
Machan, Dyan, "Don't Clutch," *Forbes*, June 21, 1993, p. 46.
Verespej, Michael A., "Unfazed by the Challenge: Eaton Corp.," *Industry Week*, July 21, 1986, pp. 47–48.
Whitney, Allison A., "Eaton AIL Settles DOD Probe: Agrees to Pay $9.5 Million," *Manufacturing Week*, March 7, 1988, pp. 12–13.

—updated by April Dougal Gasbarre

Elder-Beerman Stores Corporation

3155 El-Bee Road
P.O. Box 1448
Dayton, Ohio 45401-1448
U.S.A.
(513) 296-2700
Fax: (513) 296-4586

Private Company
Incorporated: 1911 as Elder & Johnston Company
Employees: 8,500
Sales: $630 million
SICs: 5311 Department Stores

Elder-Beerman Stores Corporation is one of the largest regional retailers in the midwestern United States and one of the few remaining family-owned, independent department store chains in the country. The company's 49 Elder-Beerman department stores in Ohio, Michigan, Indiana, Illinois, Kentucky, Wisconsin, and West Virginia generate the vast majority of the corporation's total sales. The retailer's 130 El-Bee discount shoe store outlets help extend its geographic reach to Pennsylvania, Texas, Iowa, and Virginia, and its 72 Margo's La Mode women's ready-to-wear stores in the Southwest add Arkansas, Oklahoma, and New Mexico to the company's roster of states.

The Elder-Beerman Department Stores division is the company's most important business and primary source of growth. It operates 31 department stores and two furniture retailers in Ohio, nine department stores in Indiana, three in Illinois, four in Michigan, and one each in Kentucky, Wisconsin, and West Virginia. In total, this division generated 82 percent of the company's total sales for fiscal 1991. The stores are generally located in smaller, less competitive markets with populations of 20,000 to 60,000 people. There, Elder-Beerman is often able to garner an anchor location in medium-sized malls and become each community's primary supplier of soft goods. In the early 1990s, brand name products generated about 80 percent of total sales, with the remainder being private label or non-branded goods. Prominent brand names include Liz Claiborne, Esprit, London Fog, and Estee Lauder. The department stores' merchandise mix is approximately 77 percent apparel and accessories and approximately 23 percent home furnishings.

The Elder-Beerman Stores Corp. was formed through the 1962 merger of Beerman Stores, Inc., and the Elder Johnston Company. Known as "The Store with the Friendly Spirit," the Elder Johnston Company had roots in the pre-twentieth century Boston Dry Goods Store located on East Third Street in Dayton. William Hunter, Jr., Russell Johnston, and Thomas Elder, who had all worked as traveling salesmen for the venerable eastern retail firm, Jordan, Marsh and Company, founded the company in 1883. After scouting the Dayton retail environment, the three partners purchased all the stock and business of a firm that had suffered heavy losses in a fire.

The partners' Boston Dry Goods Store (it was popular in the Midwest to name retail stores after prominent eastern cities) stated its objective in its first advertisement as: "To present to the public good, dependable merchandise at sensible prices." The growing establishment moved into Dayton's first skyscraper, the Reibold Building, in 1896 and incorporated as the Elder Johnston Company in 1911. In the meantime, Johnston died and Hunter retired, leaving Elder to run the company until his death in 1936. Elder's son Robert had joined the company in 1908 after graduating from Princeton and, upon his father's death, became president. He served as president, and later chairman of the board, until retiring in 1955. Thomas Elder Marshall, a grandson of the founder, joined Elder Johnston in 1946 and succeeded Robert Elder as president in 1953. He advanced to chairman of the board in 1956. Marshall inaugurated a semiannual custom of giving each employee of Elder Johnston a red rose—he had a hobby of cultivating both roses and employee goodwill.

Beerman Stores, Inc., was founded in the late 1930s by Arthur Beerman, who had moved to Dayton from Pennsylvania in 1930 at the age of 22. He went to work for brothers Chester and Raymond Adler at their home furnishings and children's clothing stores. But Beerman would not be satisfied with being a mere employee. He founded Beerman Realty Co. in the mid-1930s and would parlay savvy real estate holdings into an Ohio retail empire. During the early 1940s, Beerman opened several neighborhood "Cotton Shops," offering house dresses and aprons. The entrepreneur soon added infants' and children's wear to boost sales in the winter months, and the business incorporated in 1945.

Through his realty venture, Beerman began acquiring and developing neighborhood strip shopping centers in anticipation of the suburban exodus. When a deal to rent a two-story shopping building fell through in 1950, he took advantage of the empty space and established his own Beerman Budget department store. His venture appealed to value-oriented shoppers with its "Beerman's for Bargains" slogan. In 1953, Beerman formed Bee Gee Shoe Corporation, a partnership with Max Gutmann, to operate leased shoe departments within the stores. In 1956, Beerman bought his former employer's Home Store and opened his first El-Bee Shoe store. Within three years, he had six stores located at shopping centers around Dayton. By 1961, Beerman had opened two additional stores and expanded into housewares.

Arthur Beerman acquired a controlling interest in, and the chairmanship of, Elder Johnston in December 1961. Although he had originally planned to keep the two ventures separate, he merged Elder Johnston with his own firm early in 1962 and closed the older retailer's flagship downtown store. Thomas E. Marshall, former president of Elder Johnston, became president and chief executive officer of the newly formed chain, and Max Gutmann became senior vice president and general manager.

The Elder-Beerman Stores Corporation's first-year sales were estimated at $30 million. The union facilitated the establishment of branch stores, and the firms' combined buying power helped transform Beerman's bargain image into a more fashion-oriented reputation. Public trading in Elder-Beerman shares began in 1966, but the Beerman family and insiders would continue to hold the vast majority of shares, over 70 percent.

The new alliance was embroiled in a retail rivalry throughout the 1960s that Arthur Beerman, who was known as "confrontational," took to the courts. In 1961, he filed a $15 million federal antitrust suit against Rike's, which was owned by retail giant Federated Department Stores. Beerman had offered to sell his stores to Rike's in 1959, but was rebuffed by the long-established rival. Although Beerman's stores had initially cultivated a budget orientation by offering lower-priced merchandise, executives hoped to transform the merged chain into a classier operation by offering brand-name goods. However, Arthur Beerman claimed that Rike's and Federated conspired with suppliers to keep many better quality brand names out of Beerman stores through "exclusive" contracts.

Beerman won a $3.8 million judgment, including triple damages (a stipulation of antitrust law), when the case came to trial in 1969, but the verdict was reversed on appeal. Before the appeal trial, a settlement was reached in which Rike's agreed to pay Elder-Beerman $1.2 million—the original judgment without treble damages. As part of the settlement, the Dayton Mall had to provide direct access from its parking lot to an adjacent Elder-Beerman store. Beerman had accused the mall, its developer Edward J. DeBartolo, and its major tenant, Rike's, of excluding his company from the mall. After defeating Rike's in court, Elder-Beerman supplanted its competitor as the Dayton area's preeminent retailer in the late 1970s.

Elder-Beerman continued to blanket the Dayton area throughout the 1960s and opened its first out-of-town store in 1968, just two years before Arthur Beerman's death. In 1970, Beerman's longtime partner, Max Gutmann, became president. A native of Germany, Gutmann and his family fled Nazi persecution during World War II. When he ultimately arrived in the United States, the teenager joined the Army and served in Europe. After the war, one of his first jobs was operating the leased shoe department at Dayton's Adler & Childs department store. Gutmann had joined Arthur Beerman to form the Bee Gee Shoe Co. in the early 1950s and rose in the executive ranks. He became chief executive officer and chairman in 1974, the same year that the chain crossed state lines and established a store in Richmond, Indiana.

Elder-Beerman grew dramatically under Gutmann's guidance. The leader expanded the retail chain internally, building seven local stores before the end of the 1970s, and pursuing an aggressive acquisitions policy. In 1969, Elder-Beerman bought Everybody's Office Outfitters and made it a wholly owned subsidiary, El-Bee Office Outfitters, by 1973. In 1978, Elder-Beerman acquired four of Cincinnati's Mabley & Carew stores, which boasted $20 million in sales the previous year. The 101-

year-old Mabley & Carew chain had previously been acquired by national retail powerhouse Allied Stores Corp., which operated the stores from 1961 to 1978.

Elder-Beerman purchased Texas-based Margo's La Mode chain of specialty stores from Alexander's Inc. for $7 million in 1981. Founded in the 1930s and owned by Alexander's from 1979 to 1981, Margo's operated 72 stores in Texas, Arkansas, Oklahoma, and New Mexico. The southwestern specialty chain Regan's was acquired in 1984, and its 20 stores were appended to Margo's. After a reorganization, the combined division encompassed 80 stores managed from Dallas. Twenty-six Spare Change discount junior sportswear stores in Ohio, Indiana, Kentucky, and West Virginia were acquired in 1982 and merged into the Margo's chain in 1986. In 1985, Elder-Beerman purchased three R. H. Macy & Co. stores in the Toledo, Ohio, area. Although the company had adopted a policy of avoiding larger urban markets beginning in the early 1980s, it entered Toledo with the assurance that it would begin as the city's number two department store in terms of volume.

Elder-Beerman celebrated its centenary in 1983 with the theme "100 years in the making and still something new every day." The company's sales grew 187 percent from 1975 to 1985, to $312 million, and net profit increased 236 percent to $7.3 million over the same period. Much of this growth was credited to Max Gutmann's dynamic leadership.

Elder-Beerman was taken private in 1987 by the E-B Acquisition Co., a vehicle of several executives and members of the Beerman family, including Jessie Beerman, Arthur's widow; Barbara Beerman Weprin, their adopted daughter; her husband, William S. Weprin; and Leonard Beerman Peal, a first cousin. The company purchased the remaining 30 percent of Elder-Beerman it didn't already own for an estimated $30.7 million, or $33 per share. The retail chain has been "closely held" since that time. According to its last annual report, for fiscal 1986, the company posted sales of $380.8 million and net profit of $6.3 million. As consolidation in the retail industry overall accelerated during the 1980s, Elder-Beerman found itself one of the few family-owned, independent department store chains. Local observer James Bohman, of the *Dayton Daily News,* noted that, by 1989, the Beermans ranked among Ohio's 25 wealthiest families.

Elder-Beerman acquired Meis of Illiana's 10-store chain, which operated locations in Indiana, Illinois, and Kentucky, from the Brown Group Inc. in 1989. The chain was founded by the Meis (sounds like "lease") family in 1924 and sold to the Brown Shoe Co. of St. Louis, Missouri in 1972. At the time of its sale to Elder-Beerman, Meis was considered one of western Indiana's leading retailers.

Max Gutmann retired in 1991. In addition to the dramatic growth that occurred during his watch, another legacy of Gutmann's leadership was the distinctive blue used in Elder-Beerman's logo—blue was one of the chairman's favorite colors. Gutmann was followed at Elder-Beerman's helm by Herbert O. Glaser, who had served as president of the department store unit from 1984 to 1989, and then as president and chief operating officer. He retained the post of COO only two years before retiring. Glaser was succeeded by Milton E. Hartley, chairman of the board and chief executive officer. The company continued to expand throughout these upper management shifts, opening 11 stores and a distribution center between 1991 and 1994. An April 1993 business brief in the *Dayton Daily News* noted same-store sales increases of over 8 percent and ''a record Christmas season,'' according to chairman Hartley. The private company is not required to disclose detailed financial information, and often declines to do so since going private in the late 1980s.

Principal Subsidiaries: El-Bee Chargit.

Further Reading:

''Beerman Buying Meis of Terre Haute, IN,'' *Dayton Daily News,* April 28, 1989, p. B9.

Bohman, James C., ''Max Gutmann's Master Plan Is Working Well for Elder-Beerman,'' *Dayton Daily News,* July 21, 1985, pp. E1, E3; ''Elder-Beerman Stores: Last of a Local Breed,'' *Dayton Daily News,* March 28, 1988, pp. S1, S2; ''The Beerman Boom,'' *Dayton Daily News,* March 6, 1989, p. S12; ''Is Cincy Elder-Beerman's 'Big League' Limit?'' *Dayton Daily News,* March 26, 1978, p. 12D.

''A Chronological History of the Elder-Beerman Stores Corp.'' Dayton: The Elder-Beerman Stores Corp., 1992.

Dayton Area Chamber of Commerce, *Sketches of Twelve Dayton Business Firms,* 1959.

''Elder's Diamond Jubilee Birthday Party,'' *Elder's Store Chat,* Elder Johnston Company: Dayton, February 1958; Dayton and Montgomery County Public Library, Dayton Collection.

Fisher, Doc, ''Beerman, Elder's Merge Operations,'' *Dayton Daily News,* January 30, 1962, p. 1.

Kelsey-Jones, Linda, ''Elder-Beerman: A Tradition of Success,'' *Dayton Daily News,* August 4, 1985, p. AA2.

''Ninety-year-old Founder of Store Ill Since August,'' *Dayton Journal Herald,* November 23, 1936, p. 1.

Sator, Darwin, ''Elder-Beerman to Add Four Cincinnati Stores,'' *Dayton Daily News,* March 20, 1978, p. 21.

Seemuth, Mike, ''Elder-Beerman's Share of Dayton Store Sales Grows,'' *Dayton Daily News,* June 7, 1980.

—April Dougal Gasbarre

Electronic Arts Inc.

1450 Fashion Island Blvd.
San Mateo, CA 94404
U.S.A.
(415) 571-7171
Fax: (415) 571-6375

Public Company
Incorporated: 1982 as Electronic Arts
Employees: 1,065
Sales: $418.29 million
Stock Exchanges: NASDAQ
SICs: 7372 Prepackaged Software

Electronic Arts Inc. (EA) is one of the world's leading publishers of video and computer games software. Better known video game companies, including Sega, Nintendo, and Atari, manufacture video game players but produce games only for their proprietary equipment. Electronic Arts, on the other hand, produces software for various manufacturers' hardware, whether computers, video game consoles, or CD-ROM players, and EA has specialized in just software. EA has experienced rapid growth in a swiftly expanding world market, with earnings increasing 60 percent annually between 1989 and 1994.

Electronic Arts was founded in 1982 by three former managers of Apple Computer: William M. (Trip) Hawkins III, who was a marketing director at Apple and at age 26 became head of the new enterprise; William Bingham (Bing) Gordon, who became the company's director of marketing; and Tom Mott. Both Hawkins and Gordon earned MBAs from Stanford University. The decision was made to form a company that specialized in developing and marketing software games for home computers at a dinner with four other friends at Hawkins's home. EA started with a team of 11 people and $5 million in capital from private investors.

EA was flexible from the beginning, developing its software for whatever computer hardware was most popular at the time, usually then producing multiple versions of programs to run on different systems. EA's first product, shipped in May of 1983, was a software game for the Atari 800 game player, but shortly thereafter the market shifted to the Commodore system. EA readjusted quickly, and in October 1983 it shipped six more games for the Commodore 64 computer. In 1984 its ''Skyfox'' computer game, designed for the Apple II computer, became a

best-seller. Two years later EA began producing games for the new Commodore Amiga, which turned out to be a very popular computer. By 1990 EA was investing an additional 50 percent of each product's development costs to retool the software so that it could run on a different hardware system.

Games software in the early 1980s was still a very new industry, as personal computers were not yet widespread. Thus, EA took a fresh approach to designing software, modeling the development and production more on the entertainment industry than on the software industry. Instead of hiring computer programmers, EA hired software graphic arts designers and project managers it called producers. Ideas for new computer games often came from freelancers, who proposed game scenarios just as independent scriptwriters submit their scripts to Hollywood studios. If an idea was approved by an in-house committee, the project was assigned to a ''producer.'' Later, more of the ideas were developed in-house, but EA continued to consider its software developers artists.

Like movie studios, EA produces many games to increase the chance of a success. Since 1984 EA has also acquired marketing rights to software packages developed by smaller outside companies through its Affiliated Labels program. EA even began contracting celebrities, especially sports stars, whose names and images were added to the software. These have included football star John Madden, basketball players Michael Jordan and Larry Bird, and chess champion Garry Kasparov. NASA's Chuck Yaeger was involved in the development of a flight simulation game.

Unlike many of its competitors, who use third-party distributors, EA took the strategic approach of establishing its own sales force. EA's salespeople sell directly to such retailers as Egghead Inc., Toys ''R'' Us, Wal-Mart and Target. In addition to permitting better control over sales and inventory, use of the sales forces has also helped EA keep better track of consumer trends.

Early on EA began selling its software overseas. In 1986 $1.5 million of its $30 million in revenues were from international sales. In 1987 EA established a manufacturing facility—which became part of what is known as EA Europe—in Langley, England. EA President and CEO Hawkins had begun to spend more time exploring strategic growth plans, particularly international expansion, and in 1987 much of the day-to-day administration of the company was turned over to his newly-hired senior vice president, Kenneth Zerbe. EA went public in September of 1989 with a market capitalization of about $84 million. Sales that year were $63.5 million, and net income had shot up from $1.3 million in 1988 to $4 million in 1989.

Having developed its software to run on a variety of computers, by 1986 EA had become the leading supplier of entertainment software in the United States, but this market was limited. In the late 1980s video game cartridges, which run on special players connected to television sets, were proving to be a more lucrative industry because most consumers had television sets but not computers at home. In 1989 the video game market was estimated at $3.4 billion in sales, as compared to $250 million for floppy disk computer games. It also comprised mostly children and teenagers, rather than the young adults who used computers. This market was dominated by the Japanese company Nintendo, with its own and compatible cartridges accounting for 80 percent of 1989 U.S. video game sales. Although EA had begun producing software for some cartridge game companies, it did not develop games for Nintendo's systems. EA was unwilling to abide by Nintendo's conditions, which would have involved agreeing not to provide the same games to Nintendo's competitors, such as Sega.

EA made its major move into the video game market by gambling on an unreleased game player from Sega. EA did not merely revise, but designed entirely new games for Sega's Genesis machine, which in 1989 was the first 16-bit video game player available to the U.S. market. The 16-bit players were almost twice as fast as the existing 8-bit machines. For the Genesis player, EA worked on eight to ten projects, each costing about $250,000, for a total product development investment of $2 million to $2.5 million. EA shipped its first games for Sega's Genesis in June of 1990, although sales of the machines did not really take off until 1991. Nevertheless, a quarter of EA's 1990 sales were from games for Genesis. The success of the Genesis, in fact, was partly due to the great popularity EA's sports games. EA was soon producing about 35 percent of the games that could run on Sega's Genesis, allowing EA to get a jump on the software competition in developing games for 16-bit machines.

The successes of Genesis spurred ever higher sales for EA. EA's net revenue increased 54.8 percent from $113 million in fiscal year 1991 to $175 million in 1992, largely due to a 215 percent increase in sales of cartridge games for the Sega Genesis, which totaled $77 million in fiscal year 1992. The following year, EA's total net revenues were up another 70.4 percent to $298 million, with sales of Sega games up 117 percent to $167 million.

It was also in 1990 that EA changed its position and began making games for Nintendo's 8-bit player for the first time. Nintendo did not introduce a 16-bit machine, the Super Nintendo Entertainment System (Super NES), to the United States until June of 1991. At this time, however, Nintendo reversed its policy and began letting software developers revise games they sold to competitors to also run on Nintendo machines. Thus, EA suddenly had a broader market for the 16-bit games it had developed for Sega.

In December of 1990 Lawrence Probst, who had joined the company as vice president of sales in 1984, took over Hawkins's post as president. Six months later Probst also assumed the position of CEO, which had been held by Hawkins, who remained as chairman and leading shareholder. In 1991 EA, originally incorporated in California, was reincorporated in Delaware and became Electronic Arts Inc.

EA quickly established itself as the leading independent developer of video games for 16-bit players. In fiscal year 1992, EA's sales of software for video game cartridges overtook its sales of software on floppy disks for personal computers for the first time. The following year 56 percent of EA's worldwide revenues were from Sega format games, while 18 percent was from Super NES games.

EA capitalized on its leadership in sports games by introducing the EA SPORTS brand name in 1991. Over the years, EA had purchased licenses for team and league names and logos from the National Basketball Association, the Professional Golf Association, the National Hockey League, the National Hockey League Players Association, and the Major League Baseball Players Association. Some of EA's most popular games were "John Madden Football," "NHLPA Hockey," "Bulls vs. Blazers and the NBA Playoffs," "Lakers vs. Celtics and the NBA Playoffs," and "PGA Tour."

In the early 1990s EA took great strides towards further international expansion. In 1991 EA acquired Vancouver, Canada-based Distinctive Software Inc. and renamed the subsidiary Electronic Arts Canada Inc. This acquisition doubled the company's games developers to about 115 people. In September of 1992 EA formed a joint venture with Japan's Victor Musical Industries Inc. The Tokyo-based company, called Electronic Arts Victor Inc., translated and distributed EA's games for the Japanese market and several other Asian countries. During the year following the establishment of EA Victor, EA's sales in Japan increased 140 percent. EA also established a manufacturing facility in Puerto Rico in 1992. Meanwhile, EA Europe had expanded its activities beyond manufacturing to include the translation of EA titles into up to seven languages and their distribution in 31 European and Mediterranean countries. EA Europe also developed original software games itself, and European sales doubled in both 1992 and 1993 before declining in fiscal 1994. International sales accounted for about one-third of EA's revenues in 1993.

In 1992 EA acquired Origin Systems Inc., a leading computer games developer based in Austin, Texas, with net revenues of $121 million. Origin was best known for its Ultima series of fantasy role-playing games in personal computer diskette and CD-ROM formats. These story games complemented EA's offerings in action, flying and driving simulation, and strategy games. EA subsequently diversified into educational games software for children, a category also known as "edutainment." In December of 1992 the EA*Kids brand and division was launched to provide software for children aged 3 to 14. Learning games introduced in 1993 included "Ping and Kooky's Cuckoo Zoo," "Eagle Eye Mysteries," "Peter Pan: A Story Painting Adventure," and "Scooter's Magic Castle." EA*Kids has also created versions of its software for schools. In April of the following year EA signed an exclusive long-term licensing agreement with the Children's Television Workshop to produce interactive multimedia software featuring the *Sesame Street* characters. A 1994 plan to merge with Broderbund Software, which was later cancelled, would have further expanded EA's involvement in the edutainment field. Part of the reason for EA's move into educational software was the aging of the company, whose employees were having children themselves.

Although EA has usually stayed out of developing hardware for running software games, it did introduce an innovative device in 1993 called a "Four-Way Play Adapter." It was the first device on the market that allowed up to four players, rather than just two, to simultaneously play a competitive game on a Sega Genesis game system. EA has also devised special performance-enhancing computer chips inside game cartridges.

An even more significant contribution to hardware development was EA's leading role in establishing a joint-venture technology company, 3DO Inc. 3DO was set up to license technology to hardware developers for the next generation of video game players, the 3DO Interactive Multiplayer, which has a 32-bit RISC microprocessor and a double-speed CD-ROM drive. EA was the largest of the original shareholders of 3DO, with approximately a 20 percent share. Other participants included Time Warner Inc.'s Time Warner Enterprises unit, Matsushita Electric Industrial Co., Ltd., MCA, AT&T, and two venture capital firms. EA helped develop 3DO's system software, and Hawkins, who was the driving force behind venture, became CEO of the new company, while remaining chairman of EA. The 3DO Interactive Multiplayer permitted quality of sound and graphics that was unmatched for video games played on a television set. In 1993 EA was one of the first companies to introduce games for the 3DO format, which would hopefully become the new standard for video games.

In addition to the 3DO CD player, EA began developing more products for the PC and Macintosh CD-ROM formats. Its first CD-ROM games were introduced in 1992. With the emerging base of computers with CD-ROM drives in homes, CD-ROM software was expected to be the fastest growing category in the mid-1990s.

As equipment became more advanced, EA pursued its Hollywood model of entertainment software publishing even further, developing more sophisticated software. In the fall of 1993 EA formed its Advanced Entertainment Group, which brought together animators, musicians, photographers, writers, and film makers. Through this venture, live actors have been filmed in Hollywood sound stages, and the videotaped performances have been digitized and integrated into the software. EA also began joint projects with Colossal Pictures, creators of the MTV show *Liquid Television*. Advanced Entertainment Group Senior Vice President Stewart Bonn explained in a company brochure: "We want to create a place where artists and craftsmen from various disciplines are inspired to gather and collaborate on exciting new forms and images." The resulting multimedia software combined CD-quality digitized stereo sound, full-motion video, and 3D-modeled animation. The more creative and realistic software helped extend EA's video game market beyond children and teenagers to adults.

To create these highly sophisticated games, EA increased its already deep investment in research and development. In 1994 the company was investing 14 percent of its revenues in R&D, up from around 12 percent the previous two years. EA's innovative development techniques have included its Artist Work Station, a computerized means of efficiently designing software and adapting it for multiple platforms. EA also came up with new ways to merge computer animation and live-action video. In 1993 the company formed a special group to oversee software development for the 32-bit hardware format, involving both the creation of entirely new games and the extensive redesign of existing games. Each new game for the 32-bit machine cost over $1 million to develop due to their complexity. Even if the 3DO were not to become the standard, the 32-bit system was expected to be the next trend, as Sega and Nintendo began developing 32-bit game players. Always looking toward the future, in the mid-1990s EA had other plans in the works, including interactive movies, travel-based entertainment, and access to its software through interactive cable television.

Principal Subsidiaries: Origin Systems; Electronic Arts Puerto Rico Inc.; Electronic Arts Canada Inc.; Electronic Arts Ltd. (U.K.); Electronic Arts Pty. Ltd. (Australia); Electronic Arts GmbH (Germany); Electronic Arts S.A. (France); Electronic Arts Victor, Inc. (Japan; 65%).

Further Reading:

Burstiner, Marcy, "Game Plan Pays Off; Software Maker Plays to Win in Competitive Field," *San Francisco Business Times,* May 21, 1993, p. 7A.

Carlsen, Clifford, "Electronic Arts Hires Zerbe, Looks to Future," *San Francisco Business Times,* July 27, 1987, p. 8.

Chakravarty, Subrata N., "The Best Job in the World?" *Forbes,* March 28, 1994, pp. 50–51.

Grant, Linda, "Plugging in to a New Game Plan," *U.S. News & World Report,* April 25, 1994, p. 74.

"King of the Nerds," *The Economist,* July 28, 1990, pp. 58–59.

Pitta, Julie, "Electronic Smarts," *Forbes,* May 27, 1991, pp. 10–12.

——, "'This Dog is Having a Big Day,'" *Forbes,* January 22, 1990, pp. 106–107.

Shapiro, Eben, "Jury Still Out on Video Games: Electronic Arts' Prospects Studied," *San Jose Mercury News,* June 24, 1991, p. 11E.

—Heather Behn Hedden

ENQUIRER / STAR
GROUP, INC.

Enquirer/Star Group, Inc.

600 S. East Coast Avenue
Lantana, Florida 33462
U.S.A.
(407) 586-1111
Fax: (407) 547-1017

Public Company
Incorporated: 1991
Employees: 1,330
Operating Revenues: $275.38 million
Stock Exchanges: New York
SICs: 2721 Periodicals

The Enquirer/Star Group, Inc. was incorporated in 1991 to serve as a holding company for the best-selling supermarket tabloids in the United States: the *National Enquirer, Weekly World News,* the *Star,* and *Soap Opera Magazine,* as well as Distribution Services, Inc., the group's marketing and merchandising operation. With investigative reporting on such sensational stories as alien spacecraft sightings in New Jersey and headlines such as "Cher: I haven't had sex for 10 months!," the $1.25-a-copy *National Enquirer* and *Star* enjoy a combined weekly circulation of seven million. Only *TV Guide* sells more copies.

The *National Enquirer,* the Group's flagship publication, traces its history to 1926, when newspaper magnate William Randolph Hearst lent his protege William Griffin money to found the *New York Evening Enquirer.* This Sunday afternoon paper was distributed throughout New York City. As partial payment of his loan, Hearst asked to use the *Enquirer* as an experimenting ground for new ideas. Hearst used the good ideas in his successful publications; the less successful ideas stayed with the *Enquirer,* and as a result the *Enquirer*'s sales never soared. They were further undercut during World War II, when Griffin wrote such fiery editorials against U.S. military involvement in the war that he was indicted for subverting the morale of U.S. troops. (Charges were later dropped.) By 1952, circulation had dropped to 17,000 copies.

In 1952, Generoso Pope, Jr., son of the founder of New York's Italian language daily newspaper *Il Progresso,* purchased the *Enquirer* for $75,000. Pope planned to gradually change the format of the paper to that of a national news-feature weekly. He dropped the paper's Democratic partisanship, increased its staff, and added a new, anonymously written "world-wide

intelligence column." Although Pope initially said the newspaper would not convert to the tabloid format, the paper became a tabloid in 1953.

The greatest change Pope instituted, however, was in the paper's editorial content. Gory stories of murder and mutilation became regular features. Confessions such as "I'm sorry I killed my mother, but I'm glad I killed my father," appeared. Headlines declared: "I say 'no' to passionate potentate and he has his half-men beat me into submission!" The *Enquirer*'s content was so salacious that New York City Mayor Wagner frequently voiced his displeasure, which eventually led to Pope's resignation from the city's Board of Higher Education in 1954. At that time, Pope also announced that he was handing control of the publication over to former general manager Roy Moriarity, although he did not disclose whether he still owned all or part of the paper.

In 1957, the paper was renamed the *National Enquirer.* Pope broadened its focus to include national stories of sex and sadism and also expanded its distribution. Sales grew steadily, despite content so offensive that the Chicago Transit Authority temporarily banned its sale at station newsstands. By 1966, however, sales had reached a plateau at 1 million copies per week, prompting Pope (who had once again taken control of the publication) to clean up the paper's image. "There are only so many libertines and neurotics," he told *Newsweek* in 1969. In defense of his earlier editorial choices he declared, "Every publication starts out by being sensational. I intended to make it a quality paper all along."

Analysts cite the declining number of newsstands as the real reason for the paper's stagnation. As mom and pop grocery stores and corner newsstands were gradually replaced by supermarket chains, outlets for the *National Enquirer* diminished. Pope sought to clean up the paper's image in order to tap into the enormous market of women who frequented supermarket check-out lines. He hired seasoned journalists, paying them some of the best salaries in the business. In keeping with the publication's new pristine image, company headquarters were moved from New York to Lantana, Florida (population 8,000), where the *Enquirer* soon gained acceptance in the community by sponsoring Little League teams and purchasing a new ambulance for the local fire station.

Pope also hired a vice-president for corporate planning and a public relations firm to broadcast the paper's new content. Stories such as "Poor Italian Immigrant's Son Starts Chinese Food Business in a Bathtub" were more zany than distasteful. The new *Enquirer* also began covering politics, albeit with its own special bent. Senator Edward Kennedy's much-publicized accident at Chappaquiddick, in which he survived a watery car crash that killed his female companion, received thorough coverage in the *Enquirer.* The paper even went so far as to hire clairvoyant Jeane Dixon to foretell the Senator's future.

Despite its improved image, supermarkets were initially reluctant to sell the *Enquirer.* Pope courted them by promising the supermarkets 22 percent of the cover price. Free subscriptions were given to wives of supermarket executives, and endorsements from Hubert Humphrey, Barry Goldwater, and Joan Crawford were made into a promotional film narrated by a well-known newscaster. When that didn't work, Pope claims that he enlisted the help of a friend, Melvin Laird, Secretary of Defense during the Nixon administration, who took supermarket executives on a private tour of the White House and allowed them to meet with the President for half an hour.

Within three years, the *Enquirer* was available in most supermarket chains across the United States. By 1969, circulation had climbed to 1.2 million copies per week, and the *National Enquirer* ousted *Reader's Digest* from the newsdealer's top-five bestseller's list. Sales continued growing to just below 4 million a week by 1974. Gross revenues in 1973 were $17 million; the next year they hit $41 million. Advertising sales were so good that the company allegedly turned down accounts, and analysts were calling the publication "outrageously successful."

In 1978 circulation peaked at 5.7 million copies, and slid to just under 4.6 million by 1981. The decline was attributed to the growing number of competing supermarket tabloids, including one created by Pope. In 1979, Pope launched *Weekly World News,* a black-and-white tabloid that published unusual stories similar to those found in the early days of the *Enquirer,* printed at the *Enquirer's* printing plant in Pompano Beach, Florida. Within two years of its debut, *Weekly World News* began making a profit, with a circulation of over 700,000. By 1984, Australian media mogul Rupert Murdoch introduced the *Star,* a four-color gossip sheet, to take advantage of consumer desire for naughty news.

In 1982, Pope raised the *Enquirer's* cover price by 20 cents, to 65 cents an issue. Circulation, fueled by an enormous advertising campaign, rose by 11 percent. Gross revenues climbed 54 percent to $140 million. Pope also sought to improve the bottom line by luring blue-chip companies such as General Motors, Procter & Gamble, and Sears to purchase advertising space in the paper. Until the early 1980s, approximately 12 percent of revenues came from advertising. Most were small, mail-order companies offering everything from biorhythm charts to seeds that grow six pound tomatoes. Calculating that revenues could increase by 25 percent if these small ads were replaced by full-page ads from major corporations, Pope began an all-out effort to woo advertisers, using the tag line, "You may not like the *Enquirer,* but 14 million people do."

Luring respectable advertisers prompted another change in editorial content, as Pope directed cutbacks in the gossip columns in an attempt to become "a service and entertainment publication for middle America." Pope used the same strategy he developed to get the *Enquirer* into supermarkets, giving free subscriptions to the wives of advertising executives, recording celebrity endorsements, and courting the approval of decision-makers. His strategy worked. By 1986, color ads for cigarettes, clothing, brand-name foods, and household products had replaced many of the smaller ads. Advertising revenues for 1985 were $31.1 million, up from $29.2 million in 1984.

Generoso Pope, Jr. passed away in October, 1988. Several of the world's leading publishing companies bid for the family-owned business, including Diamond Communications, Maxwell Communications Corp., and Hachette S.A. In June, 1989, GP Group Acquisition Limited Partnership (a partnership created by Boston Ventures Limited Partnerships III and IIIA and Macfadden Holdings, L.P.) purchased the operations for $413 million in cash.

GP Group Acquisitions instituted a number of reforms to boost revenues and cut costs. The *Enquirer's* outmoded printing plant in Pompano Beach, Florida, was closed, television advertising was discontinued, and editorial expenditures were reduced. In addition, mail order and classified advertising rates were increased substantially and the cover price of the *National Enquirer* was boosted to 85 cents in the United States, and 89 cents in Canada.

In early 1990, GP Group purchased the *Star, National Enquirer's* rival publication, from Rupert Murdoch's New America Publishing Inc. for $400 million in cash and stocks. At the time of purchase, the *Star's* 3.6 million weekly circulation was just below *National Enquirer's* weekly circulation of 4.1 million. That year, the company took the name Enquirer/Star Group, Inc. The Enquirer/Star Group went public in July 1991, with an initial offering of 13 million shares of Class A Stock. Also that year, the group launched *Soap Opera Magazine,* a weekly publication that provided in-depth coverage of daytime soap opera and was sold at supermarket checkout lines for $1.19 in the United States and $1.29 in Canada. Distribution of the *National Enquirer* and *Weekly World News* soon spread to the United Kingdom, Europe, and Asia.

Circulation declined across the publishing industry in the early 1990s, due to increased competition from television celebrity news programs. The Enquirer/Star Group responded by expanding its overseas market. The Group also entered into a number of other ventures in the early 1990s, including trademark licensing, story syndication, and the launch of *What People Are Wearing,* a monthly spin-off of the *Star* devoted to celebrity fashion and beauty. In 1993, the company entered into a joint venture with Brandon Tartikoff (former chairman of Paramount Studios) to begin production of a one-hour television program produced by the staff of the *Weekly World News* to be aired on network television. Stories on the one hour pilot include the usual *Weekly World News* fare, including a faith healer/mechanic who fixes cars by laying his hands on them and photos that "prove beyond a doubt" that humans live on Mars.

Although the Enquirer/Star Group may churn out some highly questionable stories, the company's bottom line remains solid. Net income grew by 15 percent to $19.4 million in 1993. With a strong cash flow and bold expansion strategies, Enquirer/Star Group's future as the world's primary news source on alien sightings and celebrity romances remains strong.

Further Reading:

Abrams, Bill, "*National Enquirer* Starts Drive to Lure Big-Time Advertisers," *Wall Street Journal,* March 18, 1982.
Byrne, John A., "Slugging It Out in the Supermarkets," *Forbes,* March 14, 1983.
Donaton, Scott, " 'Enquirer-Star' Team to Bring Both Clout," *Advertising Age,* April 2, 1990, p. 2.
"From Worse to Bad," *Newsweek,* September 8, 1969, p. 79.
Peer, Elizabeth, "The *Enquirer*: Up Front Smut," *Newsweek,* April 25, 1975.
"Pope Quits Board of City Colleges," *New York Times,* September 28, 1954, p. 26.
Wayne, Leslie, "Market Place," *New York Times,* May 3, 1993, p. C4.

—Maura Troester

Ethyl Corporation

330 South Fourth Street
P.O. Box 2189
Richmond, Virginia 23217
U.S.A.
(804) 788-5000
Fax: (804) 788-5618

Public Company
Incorporated: 1887 as Albemarle Paper Mfg. Co.
Employees: 5,500
Sales: $1.94 billion
Stock Exchanges: New York Pacific
SICs: 2824 Organic Fibers, Noncellulosic; 2869 Industrial
   Organic Chemicals, Nec; 2899 Chemical Preparations, Nec

With facilities in the United States, Japan, France, England, and Belgium, Ethyl Corporation was a leading manufacturer and marketer of value-added performance chemicals for the petroleum and plastics industries in the mid-1990s. The diversified company also produced high-tech chemical intermediates for detergents, polymers, electronics, agricultural chemicals, and pharmaceuticals. Through its subsidiary, Whitby Pharmaceuticals, Inc., Ethyl was also one of the United States' primary producers of ibuprofen pain relievers. Ethyl's history has been characterized by dramatic shifts in product and business focus that succeeded thanks to astute management.

The Albemarle Paper Company was founded in 1887 by a group of businessmen in Richmond, Virginia, who were convinced that paper was a growth area for the nineteenth century. Situated by the James River, the company's mill produced both kraft and blotter paper. The company's early history was uneventful until 1918 when Floyd Gottwald grew impatient with his job as an assistant paymaster for the Richmond, Fredericksburg and Potomac Railways and went to work for Albemarle. By the 1940s Gottwald was presiding over the company's plantation-style Richmond headquarters.

Floyd Gottwald, Sr., was once described by *Forbes* magazine as a "curmudgeon" with "a passion for anonymity," but what Gottwald lacked in congeniality he made up for in business acumen. Having cut his teeth staying ahead of the topsy-turvy market for blotter and kraft paper, Gottwald was prepared when, in the 1950s, launderers began using polyethylene bags for the clothes they dry cleaned rather than the Albemarle-supplied

paper bags. Rather than exit the business, Gottwald engineered the 1962 purchase of the Ethyl Corporation, a chemical company five times Albemarle's size, in part so that Albemarle could manufacture polyethylene bags. The headline in the *Wall Street Journal* read "Jonah Swallows the Whale," echoing the consensus among the business press that Albemarle's acquisition of Ethyl, the largest producer of anti-knock compounds for fuel, was the business coup of the decade. In another version of the buyout, Albemarle was interpreted as wanting to buy chemicals for bleaching paper from Ethyl, and the larger company was said to reject any agreement. "That made us mad, so we waited two years and bought Ethyl for ourselves," Gottwald was quoted as saying.

The Ethyl Corporation was created by General Motors and Standard Oil following the 1917 discovery that a lead additive in gasoline would prevent car engines from knocking. The additive, called tetra ethyl, allowed the Ethyl Corporation to hold a substantial share of the gasoline additive market for years, even in the 1950s when the patent expired. The obvious potential buyers for the Ethyl Corporation were large chemical companies like Dow Chemical or Du Pont, but they were prevented from buying from Ethyl under the stringent anti-trust laws of the time. Standard Oil, although happy to sell its share of Ethyl, had never put its shares up for sale for just this reason. When Standard Oil was approached by Albemarle, it sold Ethyl for $200 million.

Wall Street was surprised that Albemarle, a paper company with 1961 earnings of $1.8 million, could raise the necessary funds. It did so with the help of four insurance companies (including Prudential), several investment houses, and the Chase Manhattan Bank, each of which put up cash in exchange for notes. Albemarle immediately used Ethyl's depreciation to reduce its 100 percent debt to 80 percent. Nonetheless, the new Ethyl Corporation had a high debt to equity ratio.

The new company was reorganized so that Albemarle Paper became a subsidiary of the company it had recently purchased. The new company derived 60 percent of its sales from tetra ethyl and the rest from paper and plastics. In 1963 Gottwald bought Union Carbide's VisQueen, a major producer of polyethylene film used for food packaging. In 1966 it developed the capacity to produce plastic bottles and became a leader in the manufacture of polyvinyl chloride (PVC). These new acquisitions meant that Ethyl carried a burden of debt that would have been almost unthinkable in the 1970s or 1980s. But as one industry analyst pointed out, "In an economy where interest payments are tax-deductible, it makes sense to keep money in business rather than retire debt."

Ethyl Corporation soon entered the European market, selling its lead additives in bulk. In the first four years after Albemarle had purchased Ethyl, the company's profits went up 80 percent, setting the pace for Ethyl's subsequent growth. With the exception of an occasional year off, Ethyl has historically grown between ten and 20 percent a year.

Ethyl's acquisitions did not stop at plastics. In 1966 it bought the William Bonnel Company, a producer of shaped aluminum, and in 1967 it purchased the Oxford Paper Company. The managers of the old Albemarle Paper Company had always wanted to manufacture bleached paper; re-christened as Ethyl, they now owned one of the larger makers of fine printing paper and paper for books, as well as Oxford's 195,000 acres of timberland. The old Albemarle division was sold, along with Interstate Bag and Halifax Timber.

For many stock market analysts the radical, albeit successful, diversification policies of Ethyl during this period typified the business climate of the 1960s. In the period of a few years, a paper company of moderate size became a major force in markets as diverse as fuel additives, food wrap, and PVC, and had substantial aluminum holdings. In the late 1960s, however, Ethyl confronted another trend, namely, a growing concern for the environment. This led to the eventual extinction of Ethyl's main product, lead additives for gasoline.

In the mid-1960s, a Dr. Clair Patterson was tracing lead isotopes in the Arctic and the Pacific in order to discover clues about the formation of the Earth when he learned that air-borne lead was poisoning people. Patterson showed that urban dwellers had 50 percent more lead in their blood than their counterparts in rural areas. Scientist after scientist blamed leaded gasoline. Ethyl Corporation, which derived the bulk of its earnings from the leaded additives which many scientists claimed were polluting the atmosphere, was in a precarious position.

The Ethyl Corporation's official stance was that the studies of Patterson and other like-minded scientists were incorrect. Unleaded gasoline, the company said, would require expensive changes in automobiles and refineries, resulting in severe economic repercussions. In addition, one Ethyl advertisement claimed that, "Taking the lead out of gasoline can increase more than the price. It can increase the smog." This claim referred to the theory that inefficient, knocking engines would release more hydrocarbons than smoothly running engines which consumed leaded gas. Congress was not convinced and, in the Clean Air Act, mandated stricter emissions controls for cars. General Motors, Ethyl's old owner, signed the death warrant for tetra ethylene by opting for a catalytic converter on new cars rather than the lead converter that Ethyl proposed. Catalytic converters run on lead-free gas.

The planned elimination of leaded gasoline seemed to doom the Ethyl Corporation to failure, but while the price of Ethyl stock shares dropped precipitously, earnings did not. Because lead-free gas was phased in gradually, Ethyl had time to withdraw from its dependence on tetra ethylene. Moreover, a sizable European market for its lead additives buoyed company profits. Most of all, management at Ethyl had the intelligence to diversify. In 1970, for instance, the year after the decline in its stock, Ethyl bought a company that manufactured instruments to measure auto emissions. In 1971, despite a decline in lead sales, the company had a record year as paper and chemical sales surged. By 1975, chemical sales were so strong that the company sold its Oxford Paper division and focussed its attention on developing detergent intermediaries, more plastic products, and dispensers for personal care products. The advent of disposable diapers was also a boon, as Ethyl made the plastic lining for Pampers products. Despite the loss of its primary product, and despite several lean years, Ethyl Corporation survived and expanded in the 1970s.

Ethyl made another idiosyncratic acquisition in 1981 when it bought First Colony Life Insurance. At the time it made this purchase, Ethyl was deriving its income primarily from specialty chemicals and fuel additives, while First Colony was making a large amount of money by breaking all the traditional rules for selling insurance. For instance, it sold special policies to individuals in high risk groups, including diabetics and people with heart problems. Another innovation on the part of First Colony was to convince salespeople from other companies to sell First Colony life insurance when their own companies did not have a comparable policy. This meant that First Colony did not have to train career agents, which was an expensive project.

Floyd Gottwald, Jr., who had taken over the company from his father, defended the purchase by pointing out that it is good for a specialty chemical company to have some products that do not require expensive research and development. First Colony flourished under its new ownership; its earnings quadrupled between 1982 and 1984, going from $10.8 million to $39.4 million. With the addition of the newly acquired insurance company, Ethyl had a record year in 1984 as its earnings rose 25 percent. The company's chemical product mix was well balanced between bromides, semiconductor chemicals, herbicides, anti-oxidants, paper chemicals, and fuel additives. Not to be defeated in its old market, Ethyl persisted in selling a manganese substitute for lead as a fuel additive and had small investments in coal and oil. These last investments are referred to in the industry as "Ethyl's revenge."

The Ethyl Corporation of the 1980s looked quite different from its predecessors. Lead additives counted for only ten percent of profits and were easily eclipsed by the company's plastic and aluminum divisions. In the 1980s, Ethyl became a major supplier of reusable bottle caps and one of the primary U.S. manufacturers of ibuprofen, a pain killer approved for over-the-counter sales. Insurance was, after specialty chemicals, the company's most lucrative division, followed by plastics, aluminum, and energy. In fact, the company was so pleased with First Colony that it purchased the Barclay Group, a leader in life insurance policies paid for through payroll deductions.

In spite of the proliferation of environmental regulations prohibiting the use of lead as a motor fuel additive in the industrialized world, anti-knock additives continued to be one of Ethyl's significant product lines. In keeping with its history, however, the corporation adjusted to meet new imperatives. Ethyl ended its manufacture of lead anti-knock compounds with the 1993 closure of its Canadian plant, and instead marketed additives purchased from the Associated Octel Company Limited, the world's only remaining producer of tetraethyl lead (TEL).

Ethyl attempted to cover all its fuel additive "bases" with the creation and production of HiTEC 3000, an octane-boosting compound. Introduced in 1979 in Canada, HiTEC 3000 had captured a $30 million market there by 1990, and Ethyl hoped to create a $100 million market for the product in the United States. But there were many obstacles to the product's U.S. introduction. The National Institute of Environmental Health Sciences asserted that HiTEC 3000's use of manganese, a metal linked in some studies to nervous system disorders, could pose a health risk. Both Ford Motor Co. and Chrysler Corp. claimed that manganese deposits decreased the efficiency of catalytic converters. Ethyl has been unable to win Environmental Protection Agency approval for the product, despite the fact that HiTEC could save 30 million barrels of oil annually in the United States if used nationwide.

Ethyl's administration by members of the Gottwald family continued when Bruce C. Gottwald joined the company's executive committee as president and chief executive officer. Under a third generation of Gottwalds, the firm continued to transform itself as the business environment warranted, primarily through acquisitions and spin-offs. In 1989, the company spun-off its plastics, aluminum, and energy businesses to shareholders with the creation of Tredegar Industries, Inc. The company divested itself of First Colony Corporation through a tax-free spin-off in mid 1993, then focused on its chemicals and petroleum additives businesses. After reorganizing the Baton Rouge-based chemicals division, which produced olefins and derivatives, bromine chemicals, and specialty chemicals, Ethyl resurrected the Albemarle name and applied it to the chemicals businesses, which were distributed to shareholders early in 1994. These transactions reflected the fact that chemical stocks were trading below the replacement cost of assets.

Ethyl's success is a tribute to that venerable American institution, the family-run business. The Gottwald family owns 17 percent of the stock shares, and the directors and employees own another 15 percent. Says one insider, "They treat the company like it is their very own, and it is." In a 1986 feature story on executive salaries, *Business Week* singled out president Floyd Gottwald, Jr., as the most economical chairman of the board of an American company. With a $1.7 million salary, his personal financial future is bound up with that of his company; the chances he takes affect him, and not just shareholders. The Gottwald's personal commitment to their company has paid off handsomely for shareholders and should continue to do so. As the Gottwalds noted in their 1993 annual report, Ethyl hoped that it would be "leaner, more flexible and quicker in anticipating market needs and customer requirements" into the future.

Principal Subsidiaries: EID Corp.; Ethyl Asia Pacific Co.; Ethyl Canada, Inc.; Ethyl China Corp.; Ethyl Coordination Center S.A.; Ethyl Foreign Sales Corp.; Ethyl France SARL; Ethyl Interamerica Corp.; Ethyl Investments, Inc.; Ethyl Japan Corp.; Ethyl Mineraloel-Additive Gmbh; Ethyl Petroleum Additives, Inc.; Ethyl Petroleum Additives Ltd.; Ethyl S.A.; IMI-Tech Corp.; Potasse et Produits Chimiques S.A.; Whitby, Inc.; Whitby Pharmaceuticals, Inc.; Whitby Research, Inc.

Further Reading:

Ainsworth, Susan, "Ethyl, Cyanamid Catch Chemical Spin-off Fever," *Chemical & Engineering News,* September 27, 1993, pp. 7–8.
Cahan, Vicky, "This Octane-booster Could Use Some Boosters Itself," *Business Week,* November 12, 1990, pp. 98–99.
Robert, Joseph C., *Ethyl: A History of the Corporation and the People Who Made It,* Charlottesville: University Press of Virginia, 1983.

—updated by April Dougal Gasbarre

Federal-Mogul Corporation

P.O. Box 1966
Detroit, Michigan 48235-9988
U.S.A.
(313) 354-7700

Public Company
Incorporated: 1924
Employees: 14,400
Sales: $992.9 million
Stock Index: New York Pacific
SICs: 3714 Motor Vehicle Parts and Accessories; 3562 Ball
  and Roller Bearings; 3592 Carburetors, Pistons, Rings,
  Valves; 3452 Bolts, Nuts, Rivets, and Washers; 3053
  Gaskets, Packing and Sealing Devices

Federal-Mogul Corporation manufactures precision components for the automotive industry, marketing its products to original equipment manufacturers (OEMs) and aftermarket customers in the United States and around the world. The company rose to prominence through a series of expansions and acquisitions, which included the Bearing Company of America in 1953, the Bower Roller Bearing Company in 1955, and National Seal in 1956. In the early 1990s, Federal-Mogul sought to offset fluctuating demand in the OEM market by entering into aftermarket sales.

The history of Federal-Mogul may be traced to 1899, when J. Howard Muzzy and Edward F. Lyon, two mill supply vendors in Detroit, began searching for ways to produce better babbitt metal. Babbitt metal, an alloy of tin, antimony, and copper, had been patented in 1839 by Isaac Babbitt as an antifriction agent surrounding moving metallic locomotive parts. The use of babbit metal remained the principal means of preventing rotating metallic shafts from overheating and wearing out. However, the introduction of combustible engines early in the twentieth century prompted a need for new, improved babbit metal.

Having developed an alternative formula for babbit metal, Muzzy and Lyon left secure jobs at J. T. Wing and Company, a vendor of mill and factory supplies, where their friendship and business acumen had gradually matured. Determined to be their own bosses in the market they knew best, the two partners opened their first facility in 1900. During this time, the mill and factory supply business was highly competitive, and many producers offered shoddy merchandise at inexpensive prices. How-

ever, Muzzy and Lyon established a reputation for high quality products and were able to reinvest most of their profits back into the business. They used aggressive and imaginative advertising, providing money-back guarantees and coupons good for prizes ranging from pocket rulers to firearms.

Whatever time Muzzy could spare from his primary responsibility of managing the financial and manufacturing end of the business he devoted to experimentation with babbitt metals. Lyon, when not on the road selling company products, joined his partner in blending new formulas of tin, antimony, and lead. Their company soon garnered major orders from Clark Motor Company and the Sheffield Motor Company. As a result of the increased business, the partners formed a subsidiary company called the Mogul Metal Company.

During this time, the traditional method of making motor bearings was to pour molten babbitt metal directly onto the motor block and to shape the metal to fit by hand. Mechanics replaced worn bearings by laboriously gouging out the old metal and then pouring in the new. When Sheffield's parent organization, the Fairbanks Morse Company, inquired as to whether die cast metals could be manufactured to form standard size bearings, Muzzy and Lyon began working on a method. They purchased a typecasting machine, and, by modifying it, they were able to make some of the new parts themselves, while commissioning various machine shops to produce the rest. The design and construction of Muzzy's and Lyon's new machine remained a secret, and while the partners had limited mechanical and engineering experience, the machine proved successful.

The potential of the die casting machine so impressed the partners that they decided to drop the mill supply business completely. The company would devote its entire resources to manufacturing and mechanizing automotive bearings and babbitt metals. Orders for their die cast bearings began to arrive, and, in 1910, an important order was placed for 10,000 connecting rod bearings for the massive Buick 10. That year, the partners nearly lost a large order from the Hudson Motor Company when they refused to compromise their secret processes by allowing Hudson engineers to inspect the plant.

In 1923, Muzzy learned that Douglas-Dahlin, a large Kansas City-based parts distributor, stood in danger of bankruptcy while owing Mogul a large sum of money. S.C. Reynolds, vice-president of Federal Bearing and Bushing, which also stood to lose money, called Muzzy to discuss the situation, proposing a trip to Kansas City to protect their interests. When Muzzy and Reynolds began discussing their companies and assessing their relative strengths and weaknesses, they realized the advantages of a merger. The Federal Bearing employees were expert bronze foundrymen but lacked the capacity to produce babbitt. Muzzy-Lyon, on the other hand, operated a complete babbitt foundry but purchased bronze on the market. The companies merged in 1924, taking the name Federal-Mogul Corporation. To protect its investments, Federal-Mogul took over the near-bankrupt Douglas-Dahlin Company, entering the parts distribution business.

In 1927, Federal-Mogul purchased U.S. Bearings Company, an Indiana distributor that resold replacement bearings. The following year, Federal-Mogul's involvement in the service business increased substantially with the acquisition of the Watkins Manufacturing Company of Wichita, Kansas. Following this major expansion, Federal-Mogul also purchased the Pacific Metal Bearing Company in San Francisco, primarily to supply its West Coast branches. In 1936, the corporation acquired the Indianapolis-based Superior Bearings Company, and, in 1937, the service division went international with the acquisition of the former Watkins Rebabbitting Limited, with Canadian locations in Toronto, Montreal, and Winnipeg. By 1939, Federal-Mogul was operating 53 service branches across the North American continent.

World War II led to further expansion. By 1941, Federal-Mogul had over 50 facilities devoted to military production, turning out millions of bearings, bushings, and seals for military applications. The company's marine division won highly competitive U.S. Navy tests for PT boat propellers and secured orders for over 24,000 Super Equi-poise wheels for every PT boat propeller used by all the Allied navies, including that of the Soviet Union. The marine division grew from a work force of 50 in 1942 to nearly 1,000 by the end of the war. Moreover, from September 1939 to July 1945, the total area of Federal-Mogul plants increased nearly threefold, and annual sales were more than double the best prewar amounts.

Although postwar employee layoffs were necessary, the company continued to grow through acquisition. In 1953, Federal-Mogul merged with Bearings Company of America, marking the single largest acquisition in its history. The merger of the Bearings Company brought 610 new employees and approximately 121,000 square feet of manufacturing space into the organization. Even more significant growth occurred in 1955 when Federal-Mogul acquired the Bower Roller Bearing Company. Soon thereafter, the corporation announced its third major merger in as many years, when The National Motor Bearing Company joined the new Federal-Mogul-Bower Bearing Corporation in 1956. The acquisition earned the company its first listing among *Fortune* magazine's 500 largest American companies, ranking 350 with sales that exceeded $100 million that year. By the end of the 1950s, Federal-Mogul's service division had expanded from 58 to 96 branches, and the number of customers had doubled to over 10,000. The mergers and increased efficiency of the 1950s had increased annual sales to four times their 1949 level.

During the 1960s, the corporation's timely response to innovations in automobile production ultimately resulted in large dividends. One such development involved the steady expansion of foreign automobile manufacturers, facilitated by mass production technology and the development of the European Common Market. Observing a threat to American export sales, Federal-Mogul management began investing in foreign manufacturing operations and purchasing interests in various major European bearing firms. Domestic expansion also continued, and the firm began to focus on manufacturing parts for the highly sophisticated missile market. In 1964, Federal-Mogul opened a new oil seal facility that was publicized as the most highly mechanized plant of its kind in the world. The following year, the company purchased Steering Aluminum, a piston factory, and the Vellumoid Company, a manufacturer of gaskets and gasket materials.

The early 1970s marked a domestic expansion into the southern states. A highly automated new plant in Princeton, Kentucky, opened in late 1970, with 50,000 square feet devoted to producing super alloy metal powders. In 1971, a new plant in Virginia began manufacturing aluminum sleeve bearings, while another Federal-Mogul plant was introduced for the manufacture of bimetal bushings and bearings. The following year, an additional powdered metal parts plant was opened in Ripley, Tennessee, and, soon thereafter, a new 360,000 square foot plant in Hamilton, Alabama, began producing tapered rolling bearings ranging up to eight inches in diameter.

Economic recession in 1975 prompted management at Federal-Mogul to begin reassessing its long-term strategy. Although the company quickly recovered from the recession, recording its fourth consecutive year of record sales and earnings in 1979, management had found that the company's earnings were overly reliant on the fortunes of automotive OEMs. In the 1980s, chairperson and CEO Tom Russell placed increasing emphasis on a strategy of diversification. Toward this end, in 1985, Federal-Mogul acquired the Mather Company, a manufacturer of high performance sealing products for the automotive and industrial markets and a leader in Teflon technology. Moreover, the purchase of the Carter Automotive Company, a manufacturer of fuel systems, further strengthened Federal-Mogul's position.

Dennis J. Gorley, who assumed Federal-Mogul's chief executive office upon Russell's 1989 retirement, accelerated his predecessor's diversification scheme. Gorley spearheaded Federal-Mogul's expansion into the automotive aftermarket, which promised higher profit margins and more stability than the OEM market. From 1989 to 1993, the firm acquired some of the best-known brands in automotive replacement parts and divested some peripheral OEM businesses. Principal acquisitions included: Dietz Lighting, Glyco Engine Bearings, Brown & Dureau (Australia) and Sealed Power Replacement. The company made its largest purchase ever in 1992, when it bought TRW Inc.'s automotive aftermarket business (AAB). The former TRW operations expanded Federal-Mogul's European and Japanese penetration and constituted nearly 20 percent of annual revenues in 1993.

During this period, Federal-Mogul worked to improve efficiency through automation, capital improvements, and staff reductions. The company adopted bar code technology for inventory control and invested in guided vehicles, hand-held scanners, and computers for its Jacksonville, Alabama, worldwide distribution center. These modernizations cut order fulfillment time from three days to one. Federal-Mogul also moved to transform its export operations into international enterprises. By 1993, 21 percent of the company's sales were generated by businesses outside the United States and Canada, while another 13 percent of annual revenues still came from exports.

The transition was not entirely smooth; Federal-Mogul recorded net losses in 1991 and 1992 totaling $87.4 million. However, when the company reported a $40.1 million profit for 1993, *Financial World* praised the company's "sound acquisition strategy, good cost controls, and participation in international markets." Noting that the company's stock had outperformed the Standard & Poor's 500 Index, CEO Gorley maintained that recent progress was "just the beginning," telling shareholders in the company's annual report that Federal-Mogul was "positioning itself as a company capable of sustained earnings growth."

Principal Subsidiaries: Carter Automotive Company, Inc.; Mather Seal Co.; Metaltec, Inc.; Federal-Mogul Funding Corp.; Federal-Mogul World Wide, Inc.; Federal-Mogul Venture Corp. Federal-Mogual World Trade, Inc.; Federal-Mogual Bruss Scaling Systems (74%); Federal-Mogul Distribuidora SAC (66%); In-De-Co., H. Minoli S.A.I.C. (59%); Federal-Mogul Pty. Ltd.; Federal-Mogul Handelsgesellschaft MBH; Federal-Mogul World Trade E.C.; Federal-Mogul World Trade Ltd.; Federal-Mogul Boliviana, S.A.; Federal-Mogul Comercio International, S.A.; Glyco do Brasil; Federal-Mogul Canada Investment Co.; Federal-Mogul Canada Ltd.; Federal-Mogul Cayman Investment Company Ltd.; Federal-Mogul World Trade Chile Ltda (99%); Federal-Mogul de Costa Rica, S.A.; Federal-Mogul Dominicana, S.A.; Federal-Mogul del Ecuador, S.A.; Federal-Mogul S.A. (France); BHW GmbH; Federal-Mogul GmbH; F-M Motorentiele Holding GmbH: Glyco AG; Glyco KG; Glyco Antriebstechnik Gmbh: Federal-Mogul de Guatemala, S.A.; Federal-Mogul World Trade Hong Kong, Ltd.; Federal-Mogul SpA; Federal-Mogul Japan KK; Federal-Mogul World Trade SDN BHD; Conaba S.A. de C.V. (51%); Federal-Mogul S.A. de C.V. (61%); Manufacturas Metalicas Linan S.A.; Raimsa S.A. de C.V. (70%); Servicios Administrativos Industriales, S.A.; Sericios de Components Automotrices, S.A.; Subensambles Internacionales S.A. de C.V.; Femosa Mexico S.A. (90%); Glyco B.V.; Federal-Mogul New Zealand Ltd.; Federal-Mogul Panama, S.A. Villa Fane Auto Supply, Inc.; Federal-Mogul World Trade Pte. Ltd.; Federal-Mogul World Trade de Espana, S.A.; Federal-Mogul S.A. (Switzerland); Federal-Mogul Holding U.K., Ltd.; Federal-Mogul Ltd.; Federal-Mogul Westwind Air Bearings Ltd. (89%); Federal-Mogul Uruguay; Federal-Mogul de Venezuela C.A.

Further Reading:

Panchapakesan, Meenakshi, "Federal-Mogul: Shifting Gears," *Financial World,* January 18, 1994, p. 24.

—updated by April Dougal Gasbarre

Federal Signal Corp.

1415 West 22nd Street
Oak Brook, Illinois 60521-9945
U.S.A.
(708) 954-2000
Fax: (708) 954-2030

Public Company
Incorporated: 1901 as Federal Electric Co.
Employees: 4,426
Sales: $565 million
Stock Exchanges: New York
SICs: 3669 Communications Equipment, Nec.; 3993 Sign
   and Advertising Displays; 3545 Machine Tool
   Accessories; 3711 Motor Vehicles and Car Bodies

Federal Signal Corp., the nation's leading manufacturer of
emergency vehicles and street sweepers, also produces signaling and communications equipment, industrial tools, and
signs. Since its inception in 1901, Federal Signal has quietly but
steadily grown into a diversified international corporation, primarily through acquiring key companies for its four principal
divisions: commercial signs, alarm signals, industrial tools, and
emergency vehicles.

Federal Signal was founded as the Federal Electric Co. in
Chicago by brothers John and James Gilchrist and a partner
John Goehst. At the turn of the century, Goehst and John
Gilchrist worked for the burgeoning Commonwealth Edison
Co., Goehst as an electrical engineer and Gilchrist as assistant to
the manager of electricity sales. With $10,000 in capital,
Goehst's technical skills, and Gilchrist's sales savvy, the team
came up with the idea to develop and market store signs lit by
incandescent lamps. Incorporated in 1901, the Federal Electric
Co. was one of the first electric sign companies in the nation.

As electricity became common in businesses across the Midwest, Federal Electric's sign sales grew, and, in 1915, the
company diversified its product line by purchasing the patents
for an electrically operated siren. Federal Electric sold its sirens
primarily to police and fire departments as well as coal mines,
which needed an efficient way of warning miners of emer-
gencies, while its electric light signs were used primarily at
pharmacies, stores, and the kiosks of early nickelodeon movies.

During this time, Federal Electric came under the ownership of
Commonwealth Edison, eventually becoming a part of the
utilities empire owned by Commonwealth founder Samuel Insull. In the early 1930s, however, Insull's empire crumbled
under the weight of the Great Depression, and Federal Electric
was spun-off as an independent business under the name Federal Sign and Signal Corp.

The company's sales continued to grow, as new applications
were discovered for its signs and signals. During World War II,
Federal provided sirens to warn Londoners of incoming air
raids, and, after the war, the company's signs were used to
illuminate Las Vegas casinos. By 1961, Federal Sign and Signal
had gone public, trading on the NASDAQ market. Net income
reached $1 million that year, and sales hit a record $15 million.

During the 1960s, demand for illuminated signs increased dramatically. Over 4,200 independent businesses were in operation
by 1970, and Federal became the largest supplier of electric
signs in the United States. Unlike other companies in the industry, Federal leased its signs and also maintained them on a
regular basis; this value-added service bolstered Federal's profitability and stability. In fact, by 1970, the sign division accounted for 46 percent of Federal's total revenues of $59.8
million, and, of that 46 percent, the sign maintenance business
brought in 13 percent.

The market for protective fire equipment also grew considerably, and Federal's signal division profited from the growth.
Revenues from its fire warning systems, fire-truck lights, and
public address systems grew an average of eight to ten percent a
year. By the late 1960s, Federal's signal division was outpacing
its sign division, growing at a rate of 15 percent annually. Two
products that brought in considerable revenues for Federal were
its Autocall automatic fire warning system and VASCAR (Visual Average Speed Recorder and Computer), a speed detector
that Federal had sold to police in fifteen states within one year.

Federal adopted an acquisitions policy in the late 1960s, which
allowed the company to develop businesses in the transportation services industry. In 1968, Federal made four acquisitions:
Western Industries Inc. and Cullen-Friestedt (makers of rail bed
maintenance equipment, rail-road crossing gates, and other
safety devices); Aircraft Equipment Company (a manufacturer
of airport ground support equipment); and Autocall Company.
By 1971, the company operated four divisions: sign, signal,
aerosupport, and Western-Cullen rail. The company streamlined operations in 1973, selling Aerol Co., a maker of wheels
for its airport ground support equipment, and C. J. Anderson &
Co., an elevator equipment supplier.

In 1975, Federal appointed Karl F. Hoenecke president and
chief operating officer of the company. Hoenecke began focusing on developing Federal's niche markets, and the company's
name was changed to Federal Signal Corp. that year, in order to
reflect its business more accurately. Under Hoenecke, Federal
sold off holdings that proved slow or unprofitable, including the
relatively healthy but small Western-Cullen rail division, which
was sold for over $3 million to a group of investors in 1977.

During the 1970s, the majority of Federal's customers were
state, county, and municipal governments, which purchased
equipment by soliciting bids from independent contractors. In

1975, 70 percent of all civil defense warning systems sold in the United States were manufactured by Federal's signal division. Sales topped $29 million, providing 40 percent of the company's total volume. Three years later, however, the Federal Trade Commission (FTC) accused Federal of attempting to monopolize the market. Specifically, the FTC alleged that Federal had collaborated with local governments to devise the advertisements soliciting bids and providing job specifications, and that these advertisements were designed to prevent other companies from bidding successfully. While the charges were under investigation, Federal was prohibited from selling civil defense warning systems, radio equipment, sirens, and speed detectors to any government body. Ultimately, the issue was settled out of court.

In 1979, Federal established a vehicle division, when it acquired Emergency One Inc., a five-year-old Florida manufacturer that had pioneered the use of aluminum bodies for fire trucks. Three years later, this division also began overseeing operations of another new acquisition, the Elgin Sweeper Co., a leading manufacturer of high-powered, high-speed street sweeping machines. The company also established an industrial tools division during this time, with the purchase of a manufacturer of tools for cutting and stamping metal. Bolstered by high sales volume in its vehicle and signal division, Federal experienced rapid success in the early 1980s; in 1985, third quarter profits alone jumped 46 percent to $2.9 million, and the company appeared poised for further growth.

However, several challenges surfaced in 1986. That summer, union contract negotiations failed at Federal's Chicago-based signal plant, as well as at its Elgin street-sweeping plant. Workers walked out, production at both plants was severely curtailed for several months, and profits rose by only two percent, 11 percent below the company's average growth. In September, Federal replaced all striking workers at its Elgin plant. Although the strikes had a negative short-term impact on profits, management was able to reduce labor costs at both plants by 20 to 25 percent and announced that both production operations would remain profitable due to "lower, competitive labor costs."

Sales in the commercial sign business were also slow in 1986, due to the slumping economy, which greatly curtailed construction of new office and shopping centers. Although the commercial sign business had expanded its product line to offer electronic message boards and time and temperature indicators, the division—once Federal's strongest—brought in only 16 percent of company revenues, down from over 70 percent in the mid-1960s. Federal's new tool group was the company's strongest division, bringing in over 40 percent of earnings on 18 percent of company-wide sales.

Also in 1986, Hoenecke, a hemophiliac, died of AIDS after receiving a blood transfusion infected with the HIV virus. Joseph J. Ross, Federal's general counsel, was chosen to replace Hoenecke as president and chief operating officer. Finding that Federal's profits were tied up in excessive inventories, inefficient factories, and highly inflated working capital, Ross moved to ensure Federal's continued growth.

According to Ross, part of the problem in Federal's signal division was its outdated manufacturing facilities. At that time, the company relied on one assembly line to manufacture over 2,500 different products, and in order to begin manufacturing of one product, another had to be completed. This process greatly hindered Federal's ability to deliver goods to customers on a timely basis and resulted in excessive inventories ($24 million in 1988). Under Ross' leadership, Federal instituted a "work cell" process of manufacturing at its facilities; separate areas were created for building different products. With the new process, Federal was able to produce higher quality products, control inventory, and better respond to customer demands. By 1992, inventory in the signal division had fallen to $10 million from $24 million and operating margins were 12.5 percent, up from ten percent in 1986.

Between 1988 and 1992, Federal began a program of international expansion, purchasing four companies, including Dutch and Canadian fire truck manufacturers and a German producer of tool bits. By 1992, Federal's overseas sales had quadrupled to $120 million. Moreover, with a wide array of new products and a new financing service to attract buyers, Federal's vehicle division continued to grow despite a stagnant market. Emergency One's fire vehicles sales jumped six-fold from 1986 to 1989, with the light-weight, fuel efficient aluminum fire trucks becoming so popular that they drove its largest competitor, American La-France, into bankruptcy in the mid-1980s. Elgin street sweepers also led the nation in sales, and, by 1991, the vehicle unit held 30 percent of the U.S. market for both fire engines and street sweepers, a far greater percentage than any of its competitors.

In 1990, Federal's market position in all four divisions was strong. Despite the fact that its largest client base, city governments, experienced financial problems due to cuts in federal outlays for vehicles and signals, Federal had an order backlog of over $200 million. Revenues totaled $439 million, and net income hit a record $28.1 million. Federal increased its exports by 50 percent during this time and also received its largest contract: a $47 million order from the U.S. Air Force to furnish components for its rescue vehicles.

Although Federal controlled over one-third of the country's market for commercial signs, the sign division continued to perform poorly due to a continuing slump in commercial construction. As the recession continued into the early 1990s, the sign division posted a $1 million operating loss on sales of $59 million, and the tool group also showed lackluster growth. However, weak sales in the sign and tool groups were offset by a 37 percent gain in Federal's vehicle division. The signal division also performed well through the recession and continued to gain market share as several of its smaller competitors went out of business. In 1991, Federal reported an overall 12 percent gain in net income on revenues of $467 million.

In 1992, Federal acquired the Ravo Group, a Dutch street-sweeper manufacturer with annual sales of about $20 million, and, the following year, it purchased VAMA, a Spanish siren manufacturer. As the company continued purchasing foreign operations in its four main groups, international sales grew to comprise 20 percent of Federal's total sales volume in 1993, up from 13 percent in 1990.

Federal's sign group began to make a comeback in 1993 fueled by a swell in retail outlet construction and new business from riverboat casinos. Growth also picked up in the tool industry, both in the United States and abroad; income and sales grew ten and 12 percent, respectively. The vehicle and signal groups also continued to post impressive gains in both domestic and overseas market, leading Federal to once again post record earnings of $39.8 million on revenues of $565 million.

Anticipating stronger sales in foreign markets, particularly when the economic recession in the European Community abated, Federal planned to expand into other eastern European countries as well as in the Pacific Rim and Latin America. The company enjoyed practically no debt in the mid-1990s and continued to hold the top U.S. market position for signs as well as fire-fighting and street-sweeping equipment. Moreover, while these markets proved slow at times, Federal was sure of continued sales; Ross commented in a 1993 issue of *Forbes* magazine that government clients were not likely to say "We have no money so we won't put out fires."

Principal Subsidiaries: Federal Sign Co.; Emergency One Inc.; Elgin Sweeper Co.

Further Reading:

Autry, Ret, "Companies to Watch," *Fortune,* December 31, 1990, p. 98.

Byrne, Harlan S., "Federal Signal," *Barron's News and Investment Weekly,* April 27, 1992, p. 31.

Byrne, Harlan S., "Federal Signal: Despite Woes, Cities Still Need Fire Trucks and Sweepers," *Barron's News and Investment Weekly,* February 25, 1991, p. 45.

Byrne, Harlan S., "Federal Signal: Its Earnings—and Global Focus—Are on the Rise," *Barron's News and Investment Weekly,* February 28, 1994, p. 43.

Slutsker, Gary, "We Know Them All," *Forbes,* December 20, 1993, p. 240.

—Maura Troester

First Union Corporation

Two First Union Center
Charlotte, North Carolina 29288-0507
U.S.A.
(704) 374-6565
Fax: (704) 374-3425

Public Company
Incorporated: 1958 as First Union National Bank of North
    Carolina
Employees: 32,861
Total Assets: $72.6 billion
Stock Exchanges: New York
SICs: 6712 Bank Holding Companies; 6021 National
    Commercial Banks

First Union Corporation, with headquarters in Charlotte, North
Carolina, ranks as the nation's ninth largest bank holding company, based on total assets. Its employee base—nearly 35,000
strong—serves a customer group of more than 7 million people.
The bank's 1,314 banking branch offices in the economically
diverse South Atlantic states make it the nation's third largest
bank branch network. Together, they provide full-service investment banking, retail banking, commercial banking, and
trust services. First Union also has 215 diversified offices
throughout the United States to provide its customer base with
such financial services as mortgage banking, home equity lending, leasing, insurance, and securities brokerage services.

First Union traces its foundation to 1908 as the Charlotte-based
Union National Bank. The First Union name made its initial
appearance in 1958 following the merger between Union Na-
tional Bank and Asheville, North Carolina-based First National
Bank. At the time of the merger, the new bank became the first
Charlotte bank to own branch offices in another city.

Union National Bank's founder, H. M. Victor, would have a
difficult time recognizing the bank he founded in 1908. The
company's first offices were in the modest Buford Hotel on
Charlotte's main downtown thoroughfare of Tryon Street. Victor raised funds to start Union National Bank by selling 1,000
shares of stock at $100 each. Next, he set up his office at a
rolltop desk in the hotel's main lobby. Soon, Victor had earned
a reputation as a conservative banker who always confirmed his
customers' creditworthiness prior to issuing them any loans. For
many years, Victor even refused to make loans for the then-

newly invented automobile. Finally, he relented with a loan to a
customer for a Model-T Ford. Just to be safe, however, he held
the owner's keys and title until the loan was repaid in full.

As Union National grew, the company maintained the reputation Victor had established as being an institution of high credit
quality, strong financial performance, and excellent customer
service. It was this image and visibility that kept the bank open
during the troubled 1930s. The Great Depression forced many
of Union National's competitors to shut their doors permanently
during that era.

In the successful decades the followed the Depression, Union
National Bank stood out as a pioneer and leader in many areas
of the banking industry, and it developed an innovative approach to growth and diversification. For example, in 1947
Union National became the first Charlotte-based bank to open a
branch office. Later, it was the first bank to offer a flat-fee
checking account. Even before the development of MasterCard
and Visa, Union National was the first bank to offer a charge
card. Through the years, First Union has followed this legacy of
leadership, becoming the first bank in the United States to link
all of its branches by satellite for data transmission in 1993.

In 1958, a visionary leader at Union National by the name of
Carl McCraw, Sr.—then serving as president of the bank—
recognized that the future of American banking lay in a strong
branching network. With a young manager by the name of C. C.
Hope, McCraw traveled to New York to study mergers in depth.
McCraw was in very good company with the young Mr. Hope.
Hope was later to become vice chairman of the corporation,
president of the American Bankers Association, and director
of the Federal Deposit Insurance Corporation before his death
in 1993.

McCraw and Hope studied bank mergers diligently, and their
research paid off later that year when Union National merged
with First National Bank and Trust Company of Asheville. The
merger created the First Union National Bank of North Carolina. By 1964, the company had further diversified by acquiring
the Raleigh-based Cameron-Brown Company. Cameron-Brown
was one of the Southeast's leading mortgage banking and insurance companies. The acquisition propelled First Union to become one of only a few banking companies that was legally
empowered to offer a full line of insurance and mortgage
products to its customers in all 50 states. Cameron-Brown
changed its name to First Union Mortgage Corporation in 1986.
By 1994, the mortgage company stood as one of the nation's 11
largest mortgage banking companies based on mortgage servicing volume.

The late 1960s brought more organizational change to First
Union. During that time, the company formed a bank holding
company, and C. C. Cameron, the founder of Cameron-Brown,
became chairman of the newly-formed holding company. By
December 31, 1968, First Union formed a bank holding company with total assets of nearly $1 billion. In 1973, Edward E.
Crutchfield, Jr., became the nation's youngest president of a
major banking company when he was named president of First
Union at age 32.

From the 1960s to the mid-1980s, First Union expanded across
the state, merging with more than thirty banks and adding

branches to its statewide system. In 1985, the Supreme Court approved regional interstate banking, and First Union was among the first American banks to take advantage of this decision. At that time, the company expanded into other states and acquired banks in North and South Carolina, Georgia, Florida, and Tennessee.

Also in 1985, Crutchfield succeeded Cameron as chairman and chief executive officer of First Union Corporation. That year, he conducted an expansion program that encompassed Northwestern Financial Corporation of Greensboro, North Carolina. The merger was the largest in North Carolina's history, and it created the state's second largest bank. It also established First Union's flagship banking operation.

In 1988, First Union's national presence was sufficient to warrant listing its stock on the New York Stock Exchange. Prior to this event, the stock was traded only over the counter. Between 1985 and 1994, First Union used its powerful statewide foundation to complete 40 acquisitions and mergers with banks in North and South Carolina, Georgia, Tennessee, and Florida. In 1993, the company expanded its banking operations into Virginia, Maryland, and Washington, D.C. The corporation grew from $8.2 billion in assets on June 30, 1985, to $70.8 billion on December 31, 1993.

First Union's basic business strategy has been to seek other banking organizations with compatible management and philosophies. By merging with such similar companies, First Union maintained the reputation established by Victor at the original Union National. As of 1994, the bank held firmly to its image of strong financial performance and quality products and service. As the company consolidated the operations of its acquired banking partners, First Union managed to achieve efficiencies by standardizing products, policies, and procedures and by making full use of high technology automation systems.

During its growth years, First Union's transition was strengthened by such leaders as Frank H. Dunn, Jr., chairman and chief executive officer of First Union National Bank of North Carolina; Byron E. Hodnett, chief executive officer of First Union National Bank of Florida; Harald R. Hansen, chairman, president, and chief executive officer of First Union National Bank of Georgia; Sidney B. Tate, chairman, president, and chief executive officer of First Union Bank of South Carolina; Robert L. Reid, chairman, president, and chief executive officer of First Union National Bank of Tennessee, and Benjamin P. Jenkins, president and chief operating officer of First Union National Bank of Virginia. The banks' mergers also added the talents of B. J. Walker, formerly of Atlantic Bancorporation and by 1994 vice chairman of First Union Corporation, to First Union's arsenal.

Through the early 1990s, management of First Union's sales, marketing, and customer service fell under the jurisdiction of John R. Georgius, president of the corporation. Georgius helped develop the Quality Customer Service (QCS) program, which by 1994 had become an industrywide model. Under the Quality Customer Service program, First Union constantly trained employees on improved techniques for customer service and sales. Employees earned cash incentives for achieving the program's high standards of service. The corporation's incentive program

was just one example of its full commitment to providing quality service to its more than 7 million customers. It also served as a baseline for attracting new customers. As Georgius stated in First Union's Corporate Overview, "In the 1990s, there should be no question that First Union is one of the finest sales-driven, service-oriented organizations in the United States."

Other people have taken notice of First Union's success, on both the customer service front and the financial front. First Union Corporation was profiled as one of the "101 Companies that Profit from Customer Care," a book that cited role models "for the new American manager." The book praises First Union for its Quality Customer Service program, for its aggressive "mystery shopping" program by an independent firm, and for its in-depth market research into customer definitions of service.

In the 1990s, First Union also continued to build its product inventory. For example, the company built the most competitive foreign exchange operation in the southeastern United States, with a team of experienced traders who provided pricing and advice 24 hours a day. The foreign exchange operation assisted more than 350 corporate customers in some 54,000 transactions in 1993. This exchange operation became increasingly important in the North Carolina region as it attracted foreign-owned corporations at a rate that outpaced the rest of the nation.

Also, after nearly a decade of using derivatives to manage interest rate risk, First Union established a "derivatives products" business in 1993. That year, the company assisted 300 corporate customers in nearly 500 transactions to manage interest rate risk, reduce the cost of financing their businesses, and expand the financing opportunities available to them. The "capital partners" group was established in 1987 to provide merchant banking services to its southeastern communities. First Union also had financing specialists in such fields as trade finance, communications, health care, energy, lease finance, transportation, mortgage banking, and insurance.

That same year, First Union launched an aggressive new strategy to compete head-on with major brokerage and investment banking firms. The company estimates there are more than 100,000 corporations and entrepreneurs who need alternative financing solutions to traditional bank loans. Among those products First Union offered were syndicated loans, private placements, securitization of assets, mezzanine financing and equity capital. The company had recruited more than 60 capital markets experts from top money centers to spearhead the initiative.

After eight years of offering its own proprietary mutual funds, First Union began rapidly developing a licensed sales force to sell mutual funds in 1993. The company increased its range of financial offerings with the acquisition of Lieber & Company, advisor to the Evergreen Funds.

One element on First Union's side for future growth and success was its home region. The South Atlantic region of the United States has witnessed continued movement, or "in-migration," of people into the area from other parts of the nation. During the last decade, the South Atlantic states gained 3.3 million people in population in-migration. First Union's experts predicted that the rate will rise to 4.1 million people over the next decade. This rate is significantly better than any other region in the United States. Between 1991 and 1993, the South Atlantic region attracted more than 3,300 new or expanded plants and offices, 35 percent more than any other region and 29 percent of all new corporate locations in the United States. The South Atlantic region also attracted 45 percent of all new and expanded foreign-based facilities during this same time period. All of these statistics are even more remarkable when the region represents only 18 percent of the total United States population.

Banking opportunities increase with such rapid regional growth. First Union's banking region was projected to continue to outpace the rest of the nation in population, employment, and personal income growth throughout the 1990s. This situation, plus First Union's inherent financial strength, meant that the company was well positioned for growth, with resources, management talent, technological advantage, market posi-

tion, and products to continue to lead the pack in the banking world.

In the company's corporate profile, Chairman Crutchfield described First Union's mission ''to be the best place for companies and individuals to obtain the financial services and products they want—and then to delight them with our efforts to help them achieve their financial goals.'' He continued, ''When an individual wants an equity mutual fund, or a corporate treasurer seeks to hedge foreign currency exposure, or a state or municipality wants to issue general obligation bonds, or any customer has any financial need, our vision is for them to think, 'I bet First Union offers that.' ''

Principal Subsidiaries: First Union Mortgage Corporation; First Union Home Equity Corporation; First Union Brokerage Services, Inc.

—Wendy Johnson Bilas

FLAGSTAR

Flagstar Companies, Inc.

203 East Main Street
Spartanburg, South Carolina 29319
U.S.A.
(803) 597-8000
Fax: (803) 597-7538

Public Company
Incorporated: 1979 as Transworld Corporation
Employees: 105,000
Sales: $2.60 billion
Stock Exchanges: NASDAQ
SICs: 5812 Eating Places; 6794 Patent Owners and Lessors;
   6719 Holding Companies

Flagstar Companies, Inc. is one of the United States' largest restaurant companies, operating four popular restaurant chains, including Denny's and Hardee's. Originally part of a much larger and more diverse conglomerate, Flagstar was formed through a series of corporate mergers and divestitures, which ultimately produced a company focused on restaurants. The company's legacy of corporate restructuring, however, left it with large debts, which were not offset by its strong financial performance.

Flagstar emerged in the early 1990s from the Trans World Corporation, which was created in 1979 as a holding company for Trans World Airlines (TWA), Hilton International hotels, and the Canteen Corporation, a contract food-services company. Later that year, TransWorld acquired Century 21 Real Estate and Spartan Food Systems, which owned the restaurant chain Quincy's Family Steakhouse and is the largest franchisee of Hardee's restaurants. In the mid-1980s, TransWorld moved to streamline its diverse operations, spinning off TWA to its shareholders and selling Century 21 to the Metropolitan Life insurance company.

In 1986, Trans World's profits declined sharply after its purchase of American Medical Services, a nursing home operator in poor financial shape. As a result of this acquisition, the company's stock price dropped dramatically, attracting the attention of corporate raiders, who sought to buy up the inexpensive shares of Trans World stock, take over the company, and sell off its other valuable constituent parts for a profit. In order to ward off such hostile takeover attempts, Trans World was forced to restructure. The company's stock was liquidated on

December 31, 1986, and new stock, for a company called TW Services, Inc., was issued. This new entity included the assets of Canteen, Spartan, and American Medical Systems, along with other businesses.

The following year, TW Services moved to consolidate its operations further, and it sold its hotel operations, Hilton International, to Allegis, Inc. At the same time, TW Services expanded and strengthened its restaurant operations, purchasing Denny's, a restaurant chain with 1,200 outlets, and El Pollo Loco, another chain of 70 eateries specializing in chicken. After this process of corporate restructurings, TW Services emerged as an operator of chain restaurants and other food services. The company's five principal food-oriented businesses included Denny's, Hardee's, Quincy's Family Steakhouse, El Pollo Loco, and the Canteen Corporation.

The oldest of TW Services' units was Canteen, founded in July 1929 by Nathaniel Leverone and two other partners. Just before the onset of the Great Depression, Leverone acquired the Chicago Automatic Canteen Corporation, the vending operations of an American Legion chapter in Chicago. The company oversaw the operations of 100 five-cent candy bar machines stationed throughout the Chicago area. In 1930, Leverone changed the name of his company to the Automatic Canteen Company of America, and he began to seek out franchise operators, who would be given an exclusive contract to operate Canteen machines in different areas of the country. By 1931, 15 different franchises had been established.

Wartime shortages in the early 1940s challenged the abilities of Canteen's franchise operators. However, at the end of the war, a sharp increase in the manufacture of consumer goods proved a boon to Canteen operators, since many of their machines were located in factory lunchrooms. The company thrived throughout the 1950s, and, in 1960, its operations were expanded with the purchase of Nationwide Food Service, which also provided food services for people in their workplace. In the mid-1960s, American Canteen shortened its name to the Canteen Corporation. Three years later, the company was purchased by International Telephone and Telegraph (ITT).

Under ITT, Canteen's operations continued to expand, as it moved into the fields of hospital and college campus food services. In 1973, Canteen was sold to the Trans World Corporation, and, over the next several years, Canteen became involved in running food services for the National Aeronautics and Space Administration (NASA), as well as concession stands in national parks and at convention centers, sports arenas, and massive entertainment complexes.

The second oldest of the TW Services restaurant units was Denny's, founded as a doughnut stand in Lakewood, California, in 1953. Originally called Danny's Donuts, the shop was opened by Harold Butler, who planned to offer coffee and doughnuts 24 hours a day. By the end of its first year in operation, Butler's doughnut stand had garnered profits of $120,000. In 1954 Danny's Donuts became Danny's Coffee Shops, and Butler began expanding his operations, opening additional stores. Five years later the chain of coffee shops became Denny's restaurants, and doughnuts were phased out of the menu.

In choosing locations for his restaurants, Butler concentrated on major highway and freeway exits, where travelers would be plentiful at all hours of the day and night. The expansion of a national network of interstate highways during this time prompted increasing numbers of Americans to travel by car, and Denny's restaurants became a rapid success.

In 1967 Denny's opened its first foreign restaurant, located in Acapulco, Mexico, and eventually established additional outlets in Mexico as well as Hong Kong. In 1969, in an effort to streamline and centralize its food production, Denny's bought Delly's Food, changing the name of that concern to Proficient Food Company. This subsidiary was responsible for running warehouse and distribution operations to keep the company's restaurants supplied. Four years later, Denny's opened its own food processing facility, called Portion-Trol Foods, in Mansfield, Texas. In the mid-1980s, Denny's was purchased for $800 million by a group of investors in a leveraged buyout. Two years later, these investors sold the company to TW Services for $843 million.

TW Services also owned and operated the largest franchisee of Hardee's, one of the units of Spartan Food Systems. The first Hardee's franchise was opened in October of 1961 in Spartanburg, South Carolina. A second Hardee's franchise outlet was soon opened in another area of Spartanburg. This restaurant, which was a walk-up operation rather than a drive-in, was owned and run by Jerry Richardson and four other investors, who contributed a total of $20,000 and called their enterprise Spartan Investment Company.

Offering hamburgers, french fries, and beverages priced between ten and 15 cents, the franchised Hardee's was a success, and the Spartan investors soon opened other outlets. Within five years, they were running 15 different Hardee's restaurants. In 1969, the partnership changed its name to Spartan Food Systems and began to offer stock to the public. In 1976, Spartan was listed on the New York Stock Exchange for the first time.

The following year, with the money raised from this stock offering, Spartan purchased the Quincy's Family Steakhouse chain, founded in 1973 as the Western Family Steak House, a single restaurant located in Greenville, South Carolina. By 1976, nine Western Family Steak Houses were in operation, and the company's name was changed to Quincy's, in honor of cofounder Bill Brittain's grandfather. By 1978, the number of Quincy's restaurants had almost tripled, and this rate of rapid growth continued after Spartan was purchased by Trans World in 1979. Over the next five years, an additional 189 Quincy's steakhouse restaurants were opened throughout the Southeast.

TW Services also acquired El Pollo Loco, Spanish for "The Crazy Chicken," a company that got its start in Mexico in 1975. Francisco Ochoa opened a modest restaurant by the side of a road in the small town of Gusave, serving flame-broiled chicken that had been marinaded with his family's recipe of fruit juices, herbs, and spices. Ochoa's operation expanded rapidly in Mexico, as 90 outlets in 20 cities were opened during the 1970s.

At the end of 1980, the company opened its first restaurant in the United States, on Alvarado Street in Los Angeles, and, within three years, 16 more American restaurants were established. In 1983, the Ochoa family sold its American restaurants

to Denny's, retaining the El Pollo Loco Mexican operations. Under its new owner, the American El Pollo Locos were expanded to include several new outlets in California and Nevada, before being purchased by TW Services in 1987.

With a stable group of food service properties in place, TW Services announced in 1987 that it planned to invest $700 million in expanding and improving its operations in an effort to strengthen its presence in the food services industry. Toward this end, the company cut back the administrative staff at Denny's headquarters and simplified the chain's menus, improving the company's profitability.

Before other efforts had begun to take effect, however, TW Services found itself in the midst of another corporate takeover battle in the fall of 1988. Coniston Partners, an investor group known for breaking up and selling off parts of other big corporations, sought to buy TW Services for $1.14 billion. In response, the company put in place a "poison pill" defense intended to make it extremely expensive for any outsider to buy more than 20 percent of its stock. Coniston challenged this move in court, while continuing to purchase increments of TW Services stock. By mid-December 1988, 85 percent of TW Service's stock had been purchased by Coniston, and by the middle of the following year, the deal had been completed. Coniston bought TW Services for $1.7 billion. The company's new owners planned to keep its food services units and sell off its less profitable nursing home unit.

In 1990, American Medical Services was divested, along with two other smaller units, The Rowe Corporation and the Milnot Corporation. In addition, the company consolidated the administration of all of its restaurant chains, moving the headquarters of TW Services from Paramus, New Jersey, to Spartanburg, South Carolina, where its Hardee's franchises were based. In the months following, the headquarters of Canteen was moved from Chicago to Spartanburg as was Denny's administrative staff, which transferred from Irvine, California. Only El Pollo Loco, whose restaurants were located exclusively in the western states, retained its headquarters outside the new central company facilities.

These moves were intended to help TW Services run more efficiently, to offset its high debt, and stem its losses, which reached $67.8 million in 1990. The transfer of operations was completed in 1991, but the company still finished 1991 with losses of $67.6 million. Help for the beleaguered company came in 1992, when TW Services cut a deal with the venture capital firm Kohlberg Kravis Roberts & Company, which contributed $300 million in capital to TW Services, in return for a 47 percent stake in the company.

Hope for financial improvements was offset, however, by disturbing news on another front; African-American customers at Denny's restaurants in California began to complain that they had been discriminated against and denied service. Specifically, the customers alleged that some Denny's restaurants either refused adequate service or forced them to pay in advance for their meals, while white customers in the restaurants were not asked to do the same.

As the U.S. Justice Department began an investigation into Denny's, TW Services began an effort to control the public relations damage to its reputation. The company apologized to customers, made contact with civil rights groups, fired or transferred problematic employees, and implemented a cultural relations team designed to educate employees on issues of race. Negotiations with the Justice Department continued throughout 1992. In March 1993, TW Services signed a consent decree with the Justice Department that called for an end to prejudicial practices. The company agreed to initiate improved training guidelines for employees and to allow for the spot testing of Denny's restaurants for compliance with its nondiscriminatory policy.

Nevertheless, the company's legal troubles continued, as aggrieved customers pressed lawsuits. Moreover, in May 1993, six African-American Secret Service agents sued Denny's, claiming that they had been denied service at a restaurant in Annapolis, Maryland. The charges received extensive media exposure, as critics charged that Denny's employees exhibited such consistent racist behavior that it constituted a part of the company's culture.

In the midst of these image problems, TW Services changed its name in June 1993. Shedding all vestiges of its past association with Trans World, the company took Flagstar as its new moniker. Flagstar also hired its first African-American executive, a human relations administrator who vowed to tackle the problems at Denny's.

One month later, Flagstar announced an ambitious minority advancement program developed in conjunction with the NAACP. To demonstrate its good faith in its effort to stamp out racism, Flagstar announced that it would double the number of Denny's franchises owned by minorities to 107, hire 325 African-American managers, and pledge $1 billion to be earmarked for goods purchased from minority-owned contractors over a seven-year period. Moreover, the company promised to maintain a policy of designating 12 percent of its purchasing budget, ten percent of its marketing and advertising budget, and 15 percent of its legal, accounting, and consulting budget, exclusively for minority-owned firms.

Flagstar continued to suffer financial difficulties. Surveys showed the customer traffic in its Denny's chain, which contributed the bulk of its revenues, was down by seven percent. In an effort to draw more people into its restaurants, Denny's inaugurated an all-you-can-eat promotion, which had to be cancelled in the summer of 1993 when it became too expensive. By the end of the year, the company's losses had reached $1.7 billion, which included a $1.5 billion write-off of goodwill and other intangible assets. In addition in January 1994, Flagstar announced that it would take a $192 million restructuring charge in order to close or franchise 14 percent of its restaurants, primarily Denny's outlets. The company also announced that it would embark upon a modernization program for its 1,000 company restaurants, installing new facades and menus, additional lights, and contemporary logos in facilities that, in many cases, had not been updated in 20 years.

In May 1994, Flagstar agreed to pay $54 million to plaintiffs in three class action lawsuits against Denny's. This sum represented the largest and broadest settlement ever made in such a suit. With this move, the company hoped to settle 4,300 claims against it, contained in legal proceedings taking place in Maryland, Virginia, and California. At the same time, the company renewed its commitment to improving race relations at Denny's, setting up discrimination testing programs and monitoring employee behavior.

The following month Flagstar announced that it had completed the sale of the Canteen food and vending operations to London-based Compass Group PLC for $450 million. At the same time Flagstar began searching for buyers for its Volume Services and TW Recreational Services divisions. These efforts reflected the company's decision to focus on its restaurants, Flagstar's core business. With these steps in place, Flagstar hoped to move forward to more equitable and profitable operations in the years to come.

Further Reading:

Deveny, Kathleen, ''Do These Raiders Really Want to Start Flipping Burgers?'' *Business Week,* October 10, 1988.

Frank, Robert, ''Flagstar Loss Is $1.65 Billion on Big Charge,'' *Wall Street Journal,* January 25, 1994.

Holden, Benjamin A., ''Parent of Denny's Restaurants, NAACP Agree on Plan to Boost Minorities' Role,'' *Wall Street Journal,* July 1, 1993.

Labaton, Stephen, ''Denny's Restaurants to Pay $54 Million in Race Bias Suits,'' *New York Times,* May 25, 1994.

Ringer, Richard, ''Denny's Parent Has Loss After a Large Write-Off,'' *New York Times,* January 25, 1994.

Serwer, Andrew E., ''What to Do When Race Charges Fly,'' *Fortune,* July 12, 1993.

—Elizabeth Rourke

Fretter, Inc.

12501 Grand River Avenue
Brighton, Michigan 48116
U.S.A.
(810) 220-5000
Fax: (810) 220-5686

Public Company
Incorporated: 1951
Employees: 1,699
Sales: $545.51 million
Stock Exchanges: NASDAQ
SICs: 5731 Radio, TV & Electronics Stores; 5722 Household
   Appliance Stores

Fretter, Inc. is a major retail seller of home entertainment products, consumer electronics, and appliances. Fretter stores are typically located near major shopping malls and are open seven days and six nights a week. Fretter competes in the marketplace on the basis of price.

The Fretter name was taken from the company's founder, Oliver L. Fretter, who established the organization in 1951. Before moving to its new headquarters in Brighton, Michigan in 1994, Fretter was headquartered in Livonia, Michigan, a suburb of Detroit. The company's guiding philosophy was to offer consumers the choice of many brands, features, and options, at low prices and to maintain a full inventory for take-home purchases or quick delivery.

Most Fretter stores were laid out in a similar manner. They featured an open floor plan designed so that a consumer entering the door would be able to see the entire store without having his or her view obstructed by merchandise or displays. Products within the store were grouped together by categories such as audio, video, appliances, personal electronics, and home office equipment. Each of the product areas, designated a ''store within the store,'' was identified with signs and staffed with specialized sales people.

Between 1983 and 1986, Fretter underwent a period of rapid expansion, opening a total of 19 stores in three years. Company sales in 1984 totaled $152 million and yielded profits of $3.9 million; sales for 1985 reached $214 million and yielded profits of $9.9 million. By early 1986, the chain boasted 39 stores in

five states: 17 in Michigan; 8 in Illinois; 7 in Ohio; 5 in Indiana; and 2 in Massachusetts.

Fretter made an initial public stock offering in 1986. Company officials planned the offering in order to raise between $90 and $100 million to fund growth and expansion, particularly in markets outside Fretter's home state of Michigan. At the time of the offering Fretter sales per square foot, judged to be $721, was among the most impressive in the retail industry. In addition, the average Fretter store was producing about $7 million in sales per year. The largest segment, video products, accounted for 46 percent of sales.

Fretter's plans called for opening 11 new stores in 1986 and nine to 12 in 1987. The company also planned to spend up to $24 million over a two year period for land, buildings, improvements, and fixtures. Other anticipated changes included the relocation and renovation of some existing stores and the addition of two distribution centers in Massachusetts.

To help manage the expanding chain, Fretter began upgrading its computer system at an estimated cost of $2.6 million. The new system enabled point of sale information to be gathered in all Fretter stores. Capturing detailed information at the time each sale was made enabled Fretter's merchandisers to immediately assess developing trends and consumer buying patterns. Timely availability of data allowed stores to shift merchandise mixes and stocks to meet customer demand. Data also provided the company's managers with details necessary to monitor store activity and make plans for the future.

During the year following Fretter's public offering, however, the home electronics industry began to experience economic difficulties. Although Fretter's year-to-date sales were up 35.3 percent, the company's stocks dropped to a low in December of 1986. The drop was precipitated by an announcement of poor sales by Highland Superstores, one of Fretter's major competitors. According to industry analysts, investors interpreted Highland's lagging sales as a sign that the entire industry was going to experience a slowdown. Soft market conditions in the Midwest and Texas proved to be a forerunner of adverse industry-wide conditions during the late 1980s and early 1990s.

Between January 1988 and January 1991, Fretter company officials noted a downward trend in net sales. Several contributing factors were identified. Markets for many items, such as microwave ovens and VCRs, were reaching saturation. The percentage of U.S. households with color televisions had increased from 92 percent in 1986 to 96 percent in 1990, and VCR ownership had increased from 40 percent to 69 percent. Some industry analysts blamed lackluster sales on an absence of innovative products and noted that most new items were improvements or refinements of older technologies rather than devices offering new capabilities. Some popular consumer electronic goods with less than 50 percent market penetration in 1990 included answering machines (35 percent), cordless telephones (28 percent); compact disc players (22 percent), and camcorders (11 percent).

According to a *Detroit News* report, the consumer electronics industry experienced growth of only about two percent annually during the late 1980s. At the same time, industry participants faced increased competition. Sears launched its store-within-a-store, "Brand Central." In a similar move, Montgomery Ward inaugurated "Electric Avenue." Fretter, along with other consumer electronics and appliance specialty stores, lost market share to the department stores.

In 1989, Fretter reported employment of 1,317 and total sales of $224.6 million. The company's selling expenses represented 25 percent of sales and its profit margin was less than one percent. Finances tightened in 1990 following a move by Sears to reduce prices on major appliances by $500 and offer zero-percent financing on some items. Fretter also cut prices. Industry observers began to question the organization's financial health. According to one report, Fretter stopped buying store locations and turned to leasing. The company posted losses during the first six months of 1990 and stock prices fell.

Despite its difficulties, Fretter continued its expansion policy. During the fourth quarter of 1991, Fretter opened four new stores. At the same time, Highland closed its stores in the Massachusetts market. Some observers expected Fretter to benefit from Highland's troubles. Others felt that any benefit would be offset by increased competition in the Ohio market.

In fiscal 1991, Fretter reported net sales of $217.35 million but posted a net loss of almost $10 million. Most of the loss was attributed to a required change in the accounting method used for reporting service contract revenue. Financial Accounting Standards Board Technical Bulletin No. 90-1 specified the manner in which revenue from the sale of service contracts should be recognized. Fretter, in adopting the changes, posted a charge of $8.7 million representing the cumulative effect of the change. Other factors contributing to the loss included a sluggish national economy and a lack of consumer confidence attributed to the Persian Gulf War.

Fretter began looking west of the Mississippi for new growth opportunities. In September of 1991, Fretter purchased Fred Schmid Appliance & T.V. Co., Inc., Fred Schmid, Colorado's oldest consumer electronics dealer, operated 18 retail locations in Colorado, Montana, and Wyoming. Schmid, however, was on the brink of bankruptcy. Financing restrictions by Schmid's lenders had resulted in inventory reductions of 75 percent, workers had been laid off, and the company faced dissolution. Nevertheless, Schmid had a reputation for customer service and carried some upscale brands to which Fretter had previously not had access. These included Thompson's ProScan, Kenwood, Pioneer, KitchenAid, Mitsubishi, and Maytag. At the time, Fretter's top brands were Goldstar, GE, Magic Chef, NovAtel, Packard Bell, Panasonic, RCA, Sony, Toshiba, and Whirlpool. Fretter had also applied for a trademark registration to market speakers and components under the Audio Dimension label.

Although industry analysts expected Fretter to bring some changes to Schmid, including the adoption of a low-pricing strategy and an expansion of the organization's computer offerings, Schmid and Fretter were expected to maintain separate and distinct identities. Some industry watchers questioned whether Fretter would be able to control its stores effectively because of the large geographic gaps between its markets. Two months after the acquisition, however, Schmid was showing signs of recovery. The *Denver Business Journal* reported that the sales staff size had been restored, advertis-

ing spending was up, and inventory had more than doubled. Prices were down and sales were increasing, even achieving record breaking numbers. During fiscal 1992 Schmid locations were incorporated into Fretter's point of sale (POS) information system.

The Schmid acquisition positioned Fretter for future growth during the remaining years of the 1990s. Competition within the industry, however, remained intense. In 1992, for example, Best Buy challenged Fretter's low price dominance in Boston and Detroit. In addition, Best Buy planned to open 18 stores in the Chicago area. Other major competitors included Circuit City and McDuff.

Highland Superstores had been a stiff competitor during the 1980s, but was floundering during the early 1990s (and went out of business in 1993). According to a report in the *Detroit News,* Highland, based in Plymouth, Michigan, closed 42 stores in 1991. The chain's sales for the fourth quarter that year totaled $115 million compared with sales of $193 million for the fourth quarter of the previous year. When comparing the same two quarters, Fretter's sales increased 14.6 percent exclusive of sales attributed to Fred Schmid; including Schmid sales, Fretter reported revenues of $66.8 million for the quarter, up 26.1 percent over the same quarter for the previous year.

In the fiscal year ending in 1992, Fretter reported a return to profitability. The company's net earnings totaled $4 million. Net sales, including sales at Fred Schmid locations, were up 35 percent over 1991, reaching $293 million. Comparable store sales, a measurement comparing each store's sales in a current fiscal year to its sales in a previous fiscal year, increased 12.2 percent.

Fretter attributed its restored profitability to an aggressive pricing policy which included the institution of everyday low prices on all product lines, a new advertising campaign, new stores, and the success of its Schmid acquisition. Some of Fretter's competitors criticized the company's advertising campaign because it focused on specific price comparisons. Some filed lawsuits (Sears) complaining that the ads were unfair. According to a published account in *HFD,* Sears complained that Fretter's ads were misleading because they compared Fretter sale prices with Sears nonsale prices. Another suit filed in conjunction with the direct price comparisons by Montgomery Ward was expected to draw a countersuit from Fretter charging Montgomery Ward with libel and slander. *HFD* noted that the national attention created by the controversy helped Fretter gain market share and bolstered Fretter's image as a low-cost provider of products. Some industry analysts, however, questioned whether any long-term benefit would result.

Fretter continued its policy of controlled and steady growth. In fiscal 1992, three stores were opened and a fourth was relocated. By the year's end, Fretter operated a total of 64 stores under the Fretter name in Michigan, Illinois, Indiana, Ohio, Massachusetts, and New Hampshire and 18 Fred Schmid locations in Colorado, Montana, and Wyoming. The company planned to add five new stores in its existing markets during fiscal 1993. Although Fretter's markets reached from the East Coast to the Rocky Mountains, some industry analysts noted that the company was still considered a regional participant rather than a national force because of the gaps between its locations.

During 1993, Fretter's advertising strategy continued to draw controversy. According to a report in the *Wall Street Journal*, Fretter pulled its advertising from the Massachusetts market following charges that it violated Federal Trade Commission (FTC) rules by not disclosing the fact that the "real people" in the advertisements had been paid for their testimonials. FTC guidelines specified that when noncelebrities were paid for endorsements, the advertising needed to include an on-camera disclosure. Although Fretter made no direct comments on the situation to the *Wall Street Journal*, a spokesperson for its advertising agency pointed out that the company had reacted quickly to the concern by pulling the ads.

Fretter also began testing a "PriceTrac" system which permitted its customers and sales staff to compare the prices and features of Fretter's products with the products sold by the company's competitors. Fretter claimed that it was, and would continue to be, an industry leader in using state-of-the-art information technology to help better manage its stores.

Fretter's expansion program progressed in 1993 with the December purchase of Dixons U.S. Holdings, Inc. and its subsidiaries from Dixons Group plc, the largest consumer electronics retailer in the United Kingdom. Dixons U.S. Holdings included Silo Inc. and YES! Silo, with retail locations in 22 states that sold home entertainment products, consumer electronics, and appliances. The three YES! (Your Electronics Store) retail locations were in New York. The acquisition increased the number of stores operated by Fretter to 242. Net sales for fiscal 1994 reached $545.51 million.

According to a Fretter statement, after acquiring Silo, a review was necessary to consider store consolidations and relocations. In the process some locations with overlapping territories or low-performing stores were closed and the inventory liquidated. Other locations were upgraded. A Fretter competitor, Circuit City Stores, Inc. announced an agreement with Fretter in early 1994 to assume leases for 18 Silo stores in Los Angeles and to assume Silo extended service contracts covering items that had been sold from the stores.

Fretter's annual report for the fiscal year ending 1994 announced some changes in the organization's leadership. Company founder, Oliver L. Fretter, stepped down from the chairmanship although he still retained a position on the board. His son, Howard O. Fretter, resigned from the board. John B. Hurley remained company president, and Ernest L. Grove, Jr. assumed the responsibility of chairman.

According to a Fretter statement, "The company's strategy has always been focused on providing name brand products at favorable prices and a high level of customer service." Fretter's executives expected the company's acquisitions to provide a means for it to meet its objective.

Principal Subsidiaries: Dash Concepts; Fred Schmid Appliance & T.V. Co., Inc.; Dixons U.S. Holdings, Inc.; Dixons Group plc; Fretter Real Estate Company.

Further Reading:

Brauer, Molly, "Fretter Offering Heats Up Sales War," *Detroit News*, March 27, 1986.
"Circuit City Stores, Inc. Reports January Sales, Agrees to Assume Silo Leases in Los Angeles," *PR Newswire*, February 4, 1994.
"Crackdown on Testimonials," *Wall Street Journal*, July 13, 1993.
Deck, Cecilia, "Fretter Beats Highland in Quarterly Sales Report," *Detroit News*, December 14, 1991.
Harrington, Mark, "At 35, Is Fretter Better? Regional Powerhouse Moves toward Controversial National Status," *HFD*, January 20, 1992.
"Highland 'Hiccup' Gave Fretter Stock Sniffles," *Detroit News*, December 13, 1986.
"Hot They're Not: Superstores Hurting from Lack of Superstars," *Detroit News*, November 25, 1990.
"Sears Move May Hurt Highland, Fretter," *Detroit News*, December 8, 1990.
Wood, Christopher, "Schmid Plugs into Comeback," *Denver Business Journal*, November 22, 1991.

—Karen Bellenir

Gateway 2000, Inc.

610 Gateway Drive
North Sioux City, South Dakota 57049
U.S.A.
(605) 232-2000
Fax: (605) 232-2023

Public Company
Incorporated: 1985 as TIPC Network
Employees: 3,800
Sales: $1.7 billion
Stock Exchanges: New York
SICs: 3571 Electronic Computers; 5961 Catalogue and Mail
    Order Houses; 7371 Computer Programming Services

Gateway 2000, Inc., is the leading American seller of personal computers by mail. Started in the mid-1980s in a small Iowa town, the company grew by keeping its own costs at a rock-bottom level and undercutting its competitors on price. As its sales skyrocketed in the early 1990s, Gateway began to experience growing pains, as customers complained about low quality and poor service. The company moved to address these concerns while attempting to expand its market to include corporate buyers and European customers.

Gateway was founded in 1985 by Ted Waitt, who had attended two different colleges before returning to his family's cattle farm in Sioux City, Iowa. After spending nine months working at a computer store in Des Moines, Waitt felt that he had learned enough about the business of selling computers to allow him to carve out his own market niche.

Waitt noticed that computers tended to be either inexpensive models with extremely limited capabilities or top-of-the-line models with capabilities that few people would ever need. He decided that a middle path made more sense, and devised a "value equation," which stipulated that extra technology should not be added to a computer unless it provided extra value to a customer.

In addition, Waitt observed in his retail job that computers could be sold over the phone by an educated salesperson. This led to the idea that overhead could be virtually eliminated. Because he had no money to invest in his new business, Waitt took over some empty space in a farmhouse that his father's shrinking cattle brokerage business had left empty, and moved

in upstairs. Joining him in the business was Mike Hammond, the salesman who had trained him at his computer store job.

In September 1985, the two started up a mail order business that they called the TIPC Network. Waitt was 22 years old. Placing advertisements in computer magazines, TIPC sold peripheral hardware and software to people who owned Texas Instrument computers. Because these computers did not conform to the IBM-compatible standard, some considered them obsolete, and many computer stores did not offer additional features for the machines once they had been sold.

Waitt charged each of his customers a $20 membership fee, which gave him start-up capital. Because his costs were so low, he and Hammond could undercut competitors' prices, and within four months, the fledgling business had racked up $100,000 in sales. Six months after they started, Waitt's brother, Norman Waitt, Jr., bought half of the company and began to offer financial advice.

Waitt's goal in starting the company had not been to sell computer accessories, but to sell computers themselves. In 1986 TIPC Network experimented with assembling its own computers, and even sold them to local customers. Nevertheless, these made only a small contribution to the company's first-year revenues of nearly $1 million.

In mid-1987, however, TIPC was given an opportunity to break into the computer field when Texas Instruments inaugurated a program to let its buyers trade in their old machines for new, IBM-compatible units at a price of $3,500. Waitt and his partners decided that they could offer a similar IBM-compatible machine, put together from parts offered by other mail order dealers, for less than half as much. Employing Waitt's value equation, and his sense of what customers would be willing to pay for, the company created a machine with two floppy disk drives of different sizes, a color monitor, a large memory, and a keyboard with function keys, and a cursor keypad for $1,995. TIPC's competitors offered far fewer features for a similar price.

With the introduction of this computer, TIPC's sales took off. In 1987 the company had revenues of $1.5 million. In the following year, TIPC changed its named to Gateway 2000, and the company's sales exploded, hitting $12 million.

In expanding its product line beyond its initial Texas Instrument computer trade-in offer, Gateway eschewed research and development and a staff of designers. Instead, the company relied on Waitt's own sense of what customers would want. "We didn't do a whole lot of market research on it," Waitt told *Inc.* magazine. "A lot of it was instinctive." Hammond elaborated further: "The first question would always be, 'would I buy it,' " he told *Inc.* "Everyone wants smaller, faster, cheaper, so it's a fairly educated guess."

Gateway's clientele of sophisticated users did not make high demands for service or back-up support and shopped on the basis of price. Accordingly, despite its rapidly increasing sales, Gateway was not forced to increase its overhead, and the company was able to keep its prices low. With its growth in sales, the company moved from the Waitt family farmhouse to a 5,000-square-foot space in Sioux City's 100-year-old Livestock

Exchange building (which had piles of cow manure standing in the halls), paying $350 a month in rent. Gateway's offices were furnished with used furniture.

Because of Gateway's rural Midwestern location, Waitt discovered that he could pay his employees $5.50 an hour and experience virtually no turnover. In 1988 the company began to supplement these wages with monthly cash bonuses based on profits.

Gateway's advertising, too, was cut-rate, although effective. Eschewing the services of a professional advertising agency, the company's founders devised their own promotions. Gateway strove to present an image of reliability and trustworthiness to counteract customer fears that their low-priced products were being supplied by a fly-by-night outfit. In the company's first full-page ad, run in computer magazines in 1988, Gateway displayed a picture of Waitt's father's cattle herd, with the Sioux City water tower looming in the background. Playing on the novelty of the company's Midwestern location, the ad asked, "computers from Iowa?" In this way, Gateway was able to remind customers that their products were manufactured in the United States. In addition, the ad stood out in a magazine filled with pictures of computers.

Spurred by these promotional efforts, which consumed only 2.5 percent of company revenues, Gateway sales continued their meteoric rise, reaching $70.6 million in 1989. By that time, Gateway had expanded beyond the confines of its second office, and the company moved to South Dakota in January 1990. This location was selected in part because South Dakota collected no income taxes. In addition, the company's position near the exact geographic center of the United States helped to keep its phone bills lower.

In 1990 Waitt also hired an advertising manager, a local photographer, and a designer, and produced a series of eye-catching and humorous new Gateway ads that began appearing in computer magazines every few months to keep up momentum in the fast-changing industry. Rather than hiring models, the ads frequently featured company employees, particularly Waitt and his brother. An ad released in July 1990 showed Waitt dressed as an 1890s card shark, flashing a royal flush. Subsequent ads featured other company employees. One showed Gateway staffers standing in a pasture under the slogan, "we're out standing in our field." In a nod to its history, and in an effort to further play up its rural roots, Gateway adopted a cow as its mascot. The company began to ship all its products in white boxes spotted with black dots that looked like the markings on a Holstein. This black-and-white design also kept printing costs low.

By the end of 1990, Gateway's revenues had nearly quadrupled from the previous year, to $275 million. In just five years, the company had grown 26,469 percent. This extremely rapid expansion brought problems of its own, and Gateway was forced to confront some of the consequences of its new size. "The biggest challenge for us right now," Waitt told *Inc.* in 1991, "is figuring out how to add the necessary bureaucracy without becoming slow moving." To expand the company's executive pool, Gateway recruited six vice-presidents from large computer makers and a public accounting firm to help mastermind the company's future growth. In addition, Gateway set up a

number of new administrative branches. The company established a 20-member group to investigate new technology, and set up a "Road Map Group" to evaluate choices. Waitt began meeting with ten top assistants, known as the Action Group, every two weeks. Gateway hired a media buyer to systematize its advertising and established a five-member marketing department, which evaluated customer satisfaction by conducting telephone interviews.

To increase productivity in its manufacturing operations, Gateway built a new 44,000-square-foot building down the road from its headquarters in the summer of 1991. In constructing this facility, Gateway stuck to its low-cost, no frills philosophy, to create "the largest metal building I've ever seen," as Waitt told *Marketing Computers*. "It's a big ugly building, but its very functional," he added. Inside this structure, Gateway reorganized its computer-assembly workers into separate teams. This change was expected to increase output by 30 percent.

Gateway also began an effort in 1991 to expand into lucrative corporate accounts. In the fall of 1991, the company began to run ads that showed a group of conservative executives huddled around a Gateway computer, with the slogan, "because we've stood the test of time."

To further shore up its image as a legitimate computer dealer, Gateway began to divulge some quarterly financial results, in the form of press releases. The company also began to offer the more extensive customer service that corporate clients required, including training programs and troubleshooting procedures. By the end of 1991, Gateway's sales had reached $626 million, and the company was named the fastest-growing private company in America by *Inc.* magazine.

Gateway doubled the pace of its advertising schedule in the following year, releasing new promotions every month. Created by a nine-member in-house team, the ads ran in nine different computer industry magazines, two of which were published weekly. The faster pace was designed to keep up with the company's release of new products and changes in price for old ones.

With the vast increase in the volume of products it sold, Gateway had fallen somewhat behind in technological innovation. "We've been playing catch-up for the last two years," Waitt told *Marketing Computers* in 1992. "We're still not anywhere near where we want to be or need to be, but we're improving our processes continuously and we're learning from our mistakes." As part of its program to regain the lead in technology, Gateway released a notebook computer, called the HandBook, which weighed 2.7 pounds, in 1992. Rather than trying to manufacture this new technology itself, Gateway had the HandBook made by another company.

Gateway also moved to diversify its marketing strategy. Rather than assuming that all customers had the same needs—good value for a good price—the company set out to target the special needs of different segments of the market. "You won't see us introducing separate product lines, but you will see us doing separate sales and marketing efforts and a different level of customization," Waitt told *Marketing Computers*.

By the end of 1992, Gateway's sales had reached $1.1 billion, an increase of 76 percent over the previous year. At a time when other computer makers were reporting losses, Gateway's earnings reached $1.1 million, as the company took the lead in the mail order computer business.

Gateway's 1,500 employees were supplemented by 200 new hires at the end of 1992. These new workers were assigned to bolster Gateway's sales and support staff in hopes of alleviating some of the company's growing pains. The push to augment Gateway's staff came as the company discovered that finding and training a large number of technical support and computer assembly workers in the middle of South Dakota was not an easy task.

Starting in late 1992, Gateway found itself deluged by a wide variety of customer complaints, alleging problems ranging from delays in delivery to improperly constructed computers. Gateway buyers complained that the company's quality control had fallen apart, and that its efforts to address complaints were inadequate. The company blamed the shortcomings on extremely high demand for its products in the final quarter of 1992, which made it impossible for all orders to be filled.

Although Gateway's revenues for the first three months of 1993 remained strong, as the company moved to clear its back orders, during the second quarter the company reported its first drop in revenues. The slowdown was attributed to the company's quality control problems, and also to its aging merchandise, which needed to be updated with new products. Gateway responded with a color notebook computer and a sub-notebook based on a new computer chip, which had previously been in limited distribution.

In the fall of 1993, Gateway's competitors began an effort to capitalize on its problems: the Dell Computer Corporation started an ad campaign boasting "performance that blows the gates off Gateway." In addition, the company faced growing competition in the mail order field from industry giants such as IBM. To protect Gateway's market share, and to insure future growth, the company made plans to move more aggressively into the corporate market, and to enter foreign markets.

To increase the company's corporate sales beyond their 1992 level of 40 percent, Gateway formed a major accounts team, headed by a former IBM employee. The company's technical support staff was doubled to more than 400, and its on-line technicians were doubled to 14, in order to better service corporate clients. Late in 1993, Gateway inaugurated a separate phone line to provide support services to companies, in which each company was assigned its own personal service representative.

In the fall of 1993, Gateway also opened its campaign to move into the European market. Previously, foreign sales had ac-counted for just three percent of the company's revenues. In early October, Gateway opened a headquarters in Dublin, Ireland, with sales, marketing, support, and manufacturing facilities. From this base, the company began to sell mail-order computers in Britain. In the future, the company intended to branch out into France and Germany. This plan was complicated by well-established competitors and by the need to customize both machines and marketing programs for each country.

Both Gateway's corporate sales initiative and its expansion into Europe brought with them higher costs than the company had experienced in its South Dakota sales and marketing operations. In an effort to offset the impact of those expenses, Gateway surprised Wall Street by unexpectedly announcing its intention to sell stock to the public in October 1993.

In December 1993, Gateway went public, raising $150 million through the sale of 10.9 million shares, which accounted for 15 percent of the company. Waitt and his brother retained the other 85 percent of Gateway. With this infusion of capital, the company planned to finance current operations, as well as its European push, and also expand its range of products to include printers, networking products, fax modems, and software. In addition, Gateway announced that it would consider the acquisition of other companies in its field.

In the spring of 1994 Gateway moved to further enhance its corporate marketing effort. The company announced a multifaceted overhaul of its support operations to placate disgruntled customers and win new ones. This program involved a two-year extension of Gateway's one-year warranty, 24-hour-a-day phone lines for technical support, and one-day delivery for replacement parts. In May 1994, the company announced that it would continue to provide technical support free of charge, despite the fact that several of its competitors had begun to charge for these services.

Principal Subsidiaries: Gateway Europe.

Further Reading:

Hyatt, Joshua, "Betting the Farm," *Inc.*, December, 1991.
Impoco, Jim, "Why Gateway Isn't Cowed by the Computer Price Wars," *U.S. News and World Report*, July 26, 1993.
Smith, Dawn, "Home on the Range," *Marketing Computers*, December 1992.
Therrien, Lois, "Why Gateway Is Racing to Answer on the First Ring," *Business Week*, September 13, 1993.
Zimmerman, Michael R., "Gateway Seizes Moment," *PC Week*, November 1, 1993.
Zimmerman, Michael R., "Gateway Plots New Corporate Program," *PC Week*, April 25, 1994.

—Elizabeth Rourke

GEICO Corporation

One Geico Plaza
Washington, D.C. 20076
U.S.A.
(301) 986-3000
Fax: (301) 718-5234

Public Company
Incorporated: 1936 as Government Employees Insurance
    Company
Employees: 7,805
Sales: $2.08 billion
Stock Exchanges: New York
SICs: 6331 Fire, Marine & Casualty Insurance

The GEICO Corporation is a holding company for a number of
insurance companies, primarily the Government Employees Insurance Company, which writes auto insurance for good drivers. The company, which is the seventh-largest American auto
insurer, got its start during the Depression in Texas. Drawing
from the pool of government employees, the company grew
rapidly after World War II and gradually expanded its customer
base beyond its original franchise. After near failure in the
mid-1970s, GEICO returned to financial health in the 1980s and
1990s.

GEICO was founded in 1936 in San Antonio, Texas, by Leo
Goodwin. Goodwin was a 50-year-old employee of U.S.A.A.,
an insurance company that served the needs of officers in the
U.S. military. It was here that Goodwin got the idea of setting
up his own insurance company, which would select good drivers as customers. With a pool of better-than-average drivers,
and no insurance agents or salesmen as middlemen, he calculated that it would be possible to sell a policy that ordinarily cost
$36 or $37 for only $30 and still make money. At the time that
Goodwin formulated these plans, this discrepancy represented
a huge savings, since many people's weekly salary was less
than $30.

Goodwin sought out Fort Worth banker Cleaves Rhea, who
agreed to invest $75,000 in his company if Goodwin could put
up $25,000. After raising the money, Goodwin chartered the
Government Employees Insurance Company (abbreviated
GEICO) on September 1, 1936, at the height of the Great
Depression. He held one quarter of the company's stock, and

Rhea took possession of the other three quarters, in keeping
with the proportion of his contribution.

In seeking out a pool of good drivers, Goodwin targeted government employees as people who were likely to be responsible
and to have a steady income. Since the largest pool of government employees in one place was, logically enough, in Washington, D.C., Goodwin and his wife, Lillian, moved to the city
in 1937 and re-chartered their company on November 30, 1937.
GEICO set up offices in the Investment Building, at 15th and K
Streets in the northwest quadrant of the city.

Once in Washington, Goodwin and his wife worked tirelessly to
make their fledgling enterprise a success. They labored 12 hours
a day, 365 days a year, establishing principles to select good
drivers and sending out direct mail solicitations to government
employees and military personnel. GEICO's direct mail operations took the place of a sales force of insurance agents, and
helped to keep the company's rates low. On weekends,
Goodwin went out to local military bases and personally solicited customers, or hand-wrote responses to customer inquiries
and complaints. At the end of the company's first year in
business, GEICO had written $104,000 worth of premiums.

Each year, Goodwin's underwriting losses declined, until 1940
when the company showed a $5,000 underwriting gain and a
$15,000 profit. In an effort to strengthen these financial gains,
Goodwin stressed customer service. In 1941, for instance, a
large hailstorm severely damaged thousands of cars in the
Washington area. Goodwin arranged with repair shops to work
24 hours a day on the company's customer's cars, and he also
had automotive glass specially shipped to Washington to fill the
sudden demand. As a result of these efforts, his policyholders
had their cars repaired far sooner than many others.

The entry of the United States into World War II at the end of
1941 brought significant strain to GEICO, as its pool of military
and federally employed policyholders moved about the country
frequently and were shipped overseas. As the American economy was converted to wartime production, rationing, price
freezes, and shortages of essential goods resulted. Goodwin
relied on family members and a group of young female employees to keep GEICO afloat during the war years.

In the wake of the war, GEICO's business expanded dramatically as millions of soldiers returned home and purchased cars
and houses, which GEICO was able to insure. In 1946 the
company's net income quadrupled, and premiums reached $2.5
million, 50 percent more than the previous year. To handle this
new business, GEICO augmented its staff with a group of
young returning veterans who would form the backbone of the
company's management in the postwar years.

By 1948, GEICO's value had reached approximately $3 mil-
lion. At this time, Goodwin's original co-investor, the Rhea
family, sold its stake in the company to the Graham-Newman
Corporation of New York, E. R. Jones and Company of Baltimore, and David Lloyd Kreeger, a private investor who lived in
Washington, D.C. Later that year, Graham-Newman distributed
its portion of the company's 175,000 shares to its stockholders,
and GEICO became a publicly traded company. In the following year, GEICO bought a building to house its rapidly expanding operations, at 14th and L Streets Northwest, in Washington.

The six-story structure cost $725,000 to buy and renovate, offered 48,000 square feet of space, and was ready for occupation within a year.

Also in 1949 GEICO began to branch out, offering services beyond basic property insurance for the first time. The company incorporated the Government Employees Corporation (GECO), a Delaware finance company that made loans for the purchase of cars and boats. After GEICO customers began to ask if they could buy life insurance from the company, GEICO set up the Government Employees Life Insurance Company (GELICO) in Washington with $300,000 in capital raised from GEICO shareholders. In setting up these two spin-off companies, GEICO separated them from the parent company to avoid jeopardizing the financial health of GEICO by taking risks in unfamiliar fields. When each new company was formed, GEICO shareholders were offered the opportunity to buy stock in the new enterprises, so the three companies had many owners in common. Although their shares were traded separately on the stock exchange, they also shared services and office space, as well as key management with GEICO. By the end of 1949 the parent company of these new offspring had passed the $1 million mark in profits for the first time.

In 1950 GEICO expanded its geographical reach, winning a license to sell insurance in the key New York market as well as in nine other states. The company further expanded its potential market of policyholders in 1952 when it made all state, county, and municipal workers eligible for coverage. As a result of this change, over 41,000 new policyholders joined the company in that year. Written premiums jumped by more than 50 percent, to $15.2 million. To handle some of the influx of new customers, GEICO opened an information office in New York City, at 125 Broadway. This facility was so heavily used that an underwriting staff was added later in 1952 and a claims staff was installed the following year.

Also in 1953 GEICO purchased the old Federal Housing Administration Building at Vermont Avenue and K Street Northwest in Washington, D.C. Two years later, it was renamed the GEICO Operations Building. Also in 1955 GEICO expanded the types of insurance coverage it offered when it began writing fire insurance for dwellings and personal belongings in Washington, D.C., Maryland, and Virginia.

In 1956 GEICO took its first step toward automating its operations when it installed an IBM Type 500 Magnetic Drum Data Processing Machine at its operations facility. By the following year, premiums had increased to $36.2 million. In 1958 GEICO expanded its customer pool further when it added civilian professional, technical, and managerial occupation groups to those who were eligible for insurance coverage. With this enlargement, the company's number of policies rose to 485,443. Its customers were spread throughout the nation. The following year, GEICO moved again to a bigger facility; its 1,100 employees were transferred to a newly built Operations Center in Chevy Chase, Maryland, a suburb of Washington.

The company continued its technological innovation the following year when a new telephone system was installed in Chevy Chase that could handle up to 50 incoming calls at once. Also in 1960, GEICO extended the services it offered when it began to market a homeowners insurance package to its policyholders. By the following year, this package was being offered in 36 states and the District of Columbia. In 1961 GEICO also organized the Criterion Insurance Company to provide automobile insurance for enlisted military personnel who did not meet GEICO's good driver standards.

Along with this expansion in the types of coverage it offered, GEICO continued its geographical expansion in 1961 when it opened the company's first West Coast office, in San Francisco. Employees in this office handled sales, policy service, and claims settlement. A year later the company opened a second western office, in Denver. This facility was the headquarters of the Government Employees Finance Company (GEFCO), which was set up to make personal and educational loans. Nine years after its inception, this company was merged with the Government Employees Corporation (GECO), another loan outfit.

In 1964 GEICO pased the one million policyholders mark. In the following year, the company opened its first drive-in auto claim center in Chevy Chase, Maryland, to serve Washington-area policyholders. GEICO and its various subsidiaries continued to expand throughout the 1960s. By 1968, the company had offices in 24 states and three foreign sites: England, West Germany, and Okinawa. GEICO's foreign offices were located near large concentrations of U.S. servicemen.

By 1971, GEICO had become the fifth-largest publicly held auto insurance company in the United States. In the following year, the company passed the two million policy mark: its number of policies written had doubled in just eight years. After this remarkable postwar growth streak, however, GEICO began to lose its way as the structure of the insurance industry started to change.

In 1973 GEICO abolished the last of its occupational restrictions on eligibility for insurance. This step was only taken after a seven-month period of study, during which company executives decided that new computerized data bases, which provided information on an individual's driving record, provided sufficient means for determining who was a good driver. In place of reliable driver record information, the company had previously generalized on the basis of occupation about a driver's probability of mishap, but with access to new data, GEICO felt that it could safely expand its pool of potential clients. With this step, the company made its services available to the entire population. By the end of the year, this move had helped the company to become the fourth-largest publicly held auto insurer, with more than $479 million in annual premium income.

To solicit further growth in the population at large, GEICO ran advertisements, sent out 25 million pieces of direct mail a year, and relied on word of mouth from its current policyholders. In addition, the company had 123 field offices where salaried agents sold insurance policies. A network of regional offices with switchboards and operators was also being built, and the first center, a $13.1 million facility in Woodbury, New York, was dedicated in October, 1973. With a greater emphasis on regional operations, the company hoped to entice more customers west of the Mississippi, where only 20 percent of its policyholders lived.

Despite this push for new customers, GEICO continued to insist that it only insured good drivers. By this time, however, the company's reliance on good drivers to keep its claims down was becoming less and less feasible as no-fault insurance laws swept the nation. Under the old system, the insurer of the driver at fault in an accident paid for everything. Since GEICO drivers were rarely at fault, the company paid out little in fees, which enabled it to keep its premiums down. Under the new system, however, claims were determined by how much damage was done, not by who was at fault. In addition, GEICO found itself squeezed by regulatory restrictions on its rates, as public outrage about rising insurance costs caused states to pass laws limiting the amounts that companies could charge. These new laws, along with GEICO's headlong expansion, brought the company to the brink of disaster in the mid-1970s. The company had overestimated its own financial strength and discovered that it had underestimated its losses by $100 million. In 1975 GEICO reported a loss of $126.5 million, as high claims for hospital and auto repair fees battered its bottom line.

In May of 1976 GEICO appointed a new chairman, and the company undertook an aggressive program to stay afloat. With the assistance of the District of Columbia's Insurance Superintendent and the rest of the insurance industry, a rescue plan was devised for the company. A consortium of 27 insurance firms took over one-quarter of the company's policies, on a commission basis, so that the company would not fail and shake public confidence in the insurance industry. A stock offering of $76 million, to be used to pay off claims, was successfully completed, and GEICO also instituted a stringent cost-containment program, called Operation Bootstrap, in which policyholders in certain states were dropped and other high-risk drivers were eliminated, among other measures.

Although losses for 1976 equaled $26.3 million, by 1977 GEICO was proclaiming that it had returned to financial solvency, and the company began a period of retrenching and reorganizing. In 1978 GEICO began to acquire the stock of its three sister companies in an effort to diversify the company's lines of business. In January, 1979, a holding company for all the GEICO properties was formed and named the GEICO Corporation. By the start of the 1980s, GEICO was a much smaller company than it had been at its height in the 1970s, and it began to move cautiously into new areas. In 1981 the company formed Resolute Group, a reinsurance subsidiary set up to insure insurers. Also in that year, the company formed the GEICO Investment Services Company.

After selling off its 66 percent interest in GELICO, GEICO made a series of acquisitions. In 1982 the company bought a property casualty insurance company, which wrote standard insurance, and named it GEICO General. The company also bought the Garden State Life Insurance Company, and renamed it the GEICO Annuity and Insurance Company. The Criterion Casualty Company was also formed to write policies for young male drivers who could not obtain insurance elsewhere.

In 1984 GEICO increased its level of automation, and this investment was rewarded with lower costs and higher profits. Throughout the 1980s GEICO stuck to its core business of writing insurance policies for good drivers, and the company's financial position steadily improved. By 1991, its profits had reached $193.8 million, and the company had become the country's seventh-largest automobile insurer. In an effort to expand its market, GEICO formed an automobile club to compete with the American Automobile Association (AAA), and also tried to increase its market share in the homeowner's insurance field. In addition, the company continued its policy of buying up its own shares, strengthening its financial position further. As GEICO moved into the mid-1990s, the firm appeared to be well suited for continued financial stability. After its close brush with oblivion in the mid-1970s, the company had returned to its original franchise of low-cost insurance for good drivers, using no middlemen, and demonstrated that it could thrive in this niche.

Principal Subsidiaries: Government Employees Insurance Company; GEICO Indemnity Company; Criterion Casualty Company; GEICO General Insurance Company; Government Employees Financial Corporation; Merastar Insurance Company; Southern Heritage Insurance Company; Criterion Life Insurance Company.

Further Reading:

Bremner, Brian, ''GEICO's Acceleration Is No Accident,'' *Business Week,* March 30, 1992.
''Geico Builds on New Confidence,'' *New York Times,* August 16, 1979.
''GEICO's Financial Position Strong,'' *Journal of Commerce,* November 10, 1977.
''Is the Party Over?,'' *Forbes,* November 15, 1973.
''Why GEICO Is Acquiring More of Itself,'' *Business Week,* September 12, 1983.
Zonana, Victor F., ''Geico Says '77 Net May Top $32 Million, A Sharp Turnaround from Recent Losses,'' *Wall Street Journal,* March 31, 1977.

—Elizabeth Rourke

General Binding Corporation

One GBC Plaza
Northbrook, Illinois 60062-4195
U.S.A.
(708) 272-3700
Fax: (708) 272-1389

Public Company
Incorporated: 1947
Employees: 3,363
Sales: $376 million
Stock Exchanges: NASDAQ
SICs: 3579 Office Machines, Nec

General Binding Corp. (GBC) manufacturers office equipment and supplies to design, bind, laminate, shred, and protect a variety of paper products, such as books, magazines, annual reports, passports, and menus. GBC is a multinational company with 21 manufacturing plants in North and Central America, Europe, Australia, and Asia. Products are sold through an international network of direct sales and telemarketing personnel, dealers, distributors, wholesalers, and retail office supply outlets. GBC is considered a market leader in the United States for laminating and binding machines and supplies. Approximately 25 percent of GBC's sales come from the sale of business machines; the remaining revenue comes from sales of supplies and service related to GBC systems. GBC has one domestic subsidiary, U.S. RingBinder Corp., which produces metal rings for looseleaf binders.

GBC was founded in 1947 by William N. Lane and two business partners when they purchased a small trade bindery in Chicago, Illinois. First year sales totaled $250,000. GBC expanded operations in 1952, opening another domestic manufacturing plant and founding General Binding Corporation Canada, Ltd. In the 1950s GBC laid the groundwork for its international divisions, creating sales and distribution networks in Europe, Mexico, Canada, Venezuela, and Brazil. Sales were slow at first in the European market, where GBC's binding machines were readily available but supplies were not. In response to this situation, GBC established a manufacturing subsidiary in Switzerland in 1954 to produce a full range of plastic binding supplies as well as a limited number of binding machines. Wholly owned subsidiaries were then set up to market GBC machines and supplies throughout England, Germany, Holland, Italy, and France.

In 1958, the European Economic Community established a 30 percent tariff on goods produced in Switzerland and sold throughout Europe. To avoid hefty tariffs, GBC built a second European manufacturing facility in Germany, just across the border from its Swiss concern. One year later, when labor shortages in Switzerland sharply curtailed production at GBC's plant there, the company built a third European manufacturing facility in England.

In 1960, GBC introduced the Combo, its first combination punch/binding system. GBC also continued its international expansion, becoming one of the first foreign companies to set up operations in Japan. Three years later, the company established a fourth European manufacturing plant in Italy. Again, GBC's profits were threatened by high taxes, so the company built an automated plant in a newly created Italian economic development zone that had a lower tax rate. When the Australian government levied high import tariffs on GBC products in 1966, the company established an Australian manufacturing facility and purchased a Sydney-based firm to manufacture binding supplies from raw materials exported from the United States. This persistence in expanding its international sales garnered GBC an "E" Award for excellence in exporting from the U.S. government in 1964.

GBC also established a wholly owned subsidiary in Brazil in 1962. However, due to the unstable political situation in the country at that time, the company refrained from doing business there until 1971, when it entered into a joint venture with a Brazilian firm to distribute its products.

Sales from 1961 to 1971 rose an average of $2.1 million a year, 30 percent of which came from foreign markets. GBC's domestic sales also expanded greatly, fueled by growth in the office market as well as a surge in the printing and graphics industry. In 1962, GBC ventured into the lamination business with the purchase of Virginia Laminating, a designer and manufacturer of lamination machines. In 1969, GBC purchased Webtron Corp., a maker of specialty presses used for printing tags and labels, and set it up as a wholly owned subsidiary. GBC went public in 1966, listing its securities on the OTC (over the counter) market. Stocks split two-for-one in 1968 and again in 1971. The company declared its first cash dividend in 1975.

Sales in 1973 surpassed $50 million for the first time, and Therm-A-Bind, a revolutionary, heat-activated binding system was introduced. In 1977 GBC purchased U.S. RingBinder Corp. GBC founder, chairman, and CEO William N. Lane passed away in 1978. The Lane family retained control of 57 percent of the company and William N. Lane III was named chairman.

Sales in 1978 hit the $100 million mark but began to slip around 1981, due to the economic recession in the United States. In an attempt to boost earnings, GBC entered into an agreement with NorthStar Computers to sell its personal computers through GBC's well-established distribution and sales channels. The move proved to be nearly disastrous for GBC. Its sales force devoted the majority of its efforts towards selling new computers under the GBC name. However, IBM also ventured into the personal computer arena in the early 1980s and within two years cornered the market. In 1983, GBC sold less that 500 comput-ers. Earnings fell to $236,000 on sales of $145.7 million, compared to 1981 earnings of $7.5 million on sales of $149.6 million.

GBC's subsidiary U.S. RingBinder was facing competition from lower priced imports in the metal ringbinder industry. By 1983 U.S. RingBinder had resorted to selling its products at no gross margin in order to stave-off its eroding market share. GBC's second subsidiary Webtron was also feeling the squeeze of competition.

In 1984, Rudolph Grua was hired to replace John Preschlack as president and CEO. Under Grua, the company began a back-to-basics marketing effort, dropping its computer line and focusing on its core binding and lamination businesses. Faced with grow-ing threats from European and Japanese imports, Grua ear-marked $1.4 million for research and development of new binding and laminating systems and shredders. GBC introduced a number of new products and instituted a combined direct-mail, catalog, and telemarketing marketing drive for its binding and office supplies. U.S. RingBinder became competitive again by establishing a manufacturing plant in Singapore. 1984 sales rose 13 percent to $165 million; net earnings soared to $6.4 million.

In 1985, GBC entered into an agreement with VeloBind, Inc., to develop a new binding system that uses rigid plastic strips. The company broadened its marketing efforts, introducing an ex-panded product catalog named Sourcebook and establishing a telemarketing center at corporate headquarters in Northbrook, Illinois. The following year, telemarketing centers were estab-lished in England, Australia, and Canada. In 1987, with sales of over $200 million, GBC stocks split 3 for 2 and dividends increased by 20 percent. In 1988 stocks split 3 for 2 again; earnings jumped 55 percent to $14 million; sales hit a record $250 million.

GBC continued its expansion into the 1990s, establishing a new Film Products Division in 1989 and also purchasing Loose Leaf Metals Co., Inc., that year. The company also began tapping into the growing desktop publishing and home-office market. In 1991, the Film Products Division introduced a high-speed com-mercial laminating system, which established GBC as a com-plete marketer of paper finishing products. Also that year, GBC purchased VeloBind, Inc., for approximately $50 million. Re-search and development spending continued, resulting in the introduction of 14 new products in 1992, including binding machines, improved Therm-A-Bind systems, and shredding machines. The next year, GBC entered the office supply busi-ness with the acquisition of Bates Manufacturing Company.

As it moves toward the beginning of the twenty-first century, GBC plans to focus on improving its international markets, which have been hurt by recessions in the overseas operations. In 1993 international sales accounted for 45 percent of unit sales but only 36 percent of dollar sales. With a focus on developing its Mexican and Australian markets, GBC's continued growth and profitability seems likely.

Principal Subsidiaries: U.S. RingBinder Corp.

Further Reading:

"Back to Basics," *Barron's,* August 17, 1987, p. 45.
Byrne, Harlan S., "General Binding Corp.," *Barron's,* January 15, 1990, p. 40.
"GBC Cites Overseas Market 'Flexibility,' " *Industrial Marketing,* May 1974, p. 6.
Lashinsky, Adam, "Globetrotter Settles in at General Binding," *Crain's Chicago Business,* Sept. 6, 1993.
McCormick, Jay, "A Farewell to Puberty," *Forbes,* March 11, 1985, pg. 108.

—Maura Troester

GENERAL DYNAMICS

General Dynamics Corporation

3190 Fairview Park Drive
Falls Church, Virginia 22042-4253
U.S.A.
(703) 876-3000
Fax: (703) 876-3125

Public Company
Incorporated: 1925 as Electric Boat Company
Employees: 30,500
Sales: $3.19 billion
Stock Index: New York Chicago Pacific
SICs: 3721 Aircraft; 3761 Guided Missiles and Space
    Vehicles; 3728 Aircraft Parts and Equipment, Nec.; 3812
    Search and Navigation Equipment; 3483 Ammunition,
    Except for Small Arms, Nec; 3731 Ship Building and
    Repairing; 3795 Tanks and Tank Components

General Dynamics' contribution to the defense industry, through the production of nuclear submarines and armored vehicles, was identified by the federal Department of Defense as crucial to the U.S. Defense Industrial Base. The company also maintained interests in coal mining, ship management, and ship financing.

General Dynamics has a long history in weapons production, originating in the late nineteenth century with an Irish-American inventor named John Holland. Associated with the Fenians, a secret New York City organization sympathetic to the struggles of the Irish nationalists, Holland was commissioned to construct a submarine capable of destroying British naval vessels. While previous submarine designs had been attempted by other inventors, none were effective warships, and, in fact, several of Holland's first submarines sank. Moreover, his ill-conceived attempts at secrecy soon drew the attention of American law enforcement authorities, who prevented Holland from achieving his mission for the Fenians. Nevertheless, Holland remained interested in building a viable submarine, and, toward that end, he founded the Electric Boat Company in 1899, with financial backing from investors that later would include various members of Congress.

Once he developed a prototype, Holland had difficulty finding a market for his submarine, as the U.S. Navy wasn't initially interested in the project. Then, lawyer, financier, and battery and electronics magnate Isaac Leopold Rice offered to finance the development of subsequent Holland submarines in return for an interest in Electric Boat. Holland was persuaded to relinquish his patent rights and management authority to Rice, who successfully made sales to the U.S. Navy and several other foreign naval services. However, Holland effectively lost control of the company and found himself earning a salary of $90 per week as chief engineer, while the company he founded was selling submarines for $300,000 each.

Electric Boat gained a reputation for unscrupulous arms dealing in 1904–05, when it sold submarines to Japan and Russia, who were then at war. Holland submarines were also sold to the British Royal Navy through the English armaments company Vickers. Submarines, which had once been denounced in Britain as "damned un-English"—considered too sly and cowardly for use in a proper gentleman's war—were now legitimized as genuine naval weapons by the world's most powerful navy.

During this time, Holland lost patience with Rice and resigned in protest at being excluded from his company's affairs. A frail man plagued by a respiratory condition since birth, Holland died shortly thereafter in 1914. He was replaced as chief engineer by Lawrence Spear who, in close association with Vickers, redesigned the Holland submarine. Speed was improved, a conning tower and periscope replaced the Holland observation dome, and torpedo tubes were incorporated for the first time. The full potential of the submarine, however, was not fully recognized until World War I, when German U-boats caused serious disruptions in British shipping.

Isaac Rice died in 1915 and was replaced by his associate Henry Carse. Under Carse, Spear was given greater control over the company's operations. Electric Boat had a substantial backlog of profitable orders and was financially strong enough to purchase several companies, including Electro Dynamics (involved in ship propulsion), Elco Motor Yacht (builders of pleasure boats), and New London Ship & Engine of Groton, Connecticut (manufacturers of diesel engines and civilian ships). The company's name was changed to the Submarine Boat Corporation.

When the United States became involved in World War I, Carse made the crucial decision to devote the company's resources to the construction of disposable cargo vessels rather than submarines. Eventually realizing his mistake, Carse began to retool for submarine production; however, before the process could be completed, the war had ended, and the company had lost a great deal of money. Moreover, the U.S. Navy then decided to devote most of its reduced postwar budget to surface ships. Faced with bankruptcy, Carse reorganized the company, emphasized production of surface ships, and brought back the Electric Boat name.

On the eve of World War II, the business practices of Electric Boat came under investigation by the U.S. government and several independent groups; the company was accused of being a "financial beneficiary" of foreign wars. Electric Boat was also found to have inadvertently given design secrets to officials of the increasingly hostile government of Japan. In an investigation led by Senator Gerald Nye, Electric Boat was accused of profiteering, graft, and unethical business practices. Carse responded that, because the U.S. Navy had suspended all major contracts for ten years, Electric Boat had been forced to deal with foreign governments—many of which were corrupt—in order to remain financially solvent.

During this time, the German re-militarization and hostile Japanese activities forced the Roosevelt Administration to reassess its position on military preparedness. Consequently, the government placed orders for submarines and PT (patrol/torpedo) boats from Electric Boat facilities at Groton and the Elco plant in New Jersey. The new orders led to the revitalization of Electric Boat, now led by John Jay Hopkins, appointed by the retiring Lawrence Spear, who himself had taken over when Henry Carse retired. While Spear continued to offer advice from his retirement, Hopkins was thoroughly in charge and fully responsible for the company's strong re-emergence.

Following the American declarations of war against the Axis powers, Electric Boat and its Elco Yacht and Electro Dynamic subsidiaries mobilized for production at full capacity. This sudden expansion in output caused a serious labor shortage, which was filled by women, who took jobs as welders and riveters. During the war, the Electric Boat companies produced hundreds of submarines, surface ships, and PT boats, contributing greatly to the success of island fighting in the Pacific. When the war ended in 1945, the Navy reduced its orders for new vessels. Only 4,000 of the company's 13,000 wartime employees were retained after the war, and Electric Boat stock fell in value from $30 per share to $10.

As a result, Hopkins initiated another reorganization of Electric Boat, which included a diversification into related commercial and defense industries. Electric Boat purchased Canadair from the Canadian government for $22 million. Canadair produced flying boats and modified DC-4s during the war, but had greatly diminished sales during peacetime. A series of events, including the Berlin Blockade, Soviet detonation of an atomic bomb, and the war in Korea, stimulated demand for new aircraft, including the T-33 trainers, F-86 Sabres and DC-6's built under contract by Canadair. By the early 1950s, Canadair's success began overshadowing that of Electric Boat; some business advisers even suggested that Canadair purchase Electric Boat and operate it as a subsidiary.

With substantial profits from its Canadair subsidiary, Electric Boat purchased Convair from the Atlas Corporation. Convair manufactured a variety of civilian and military aircraft, including the 440 passenger liner, F-102 and F-106 fighters, Atlas and Centaur rockets, and the B-24, B-36, and B-58 Hustler bombers. On February 21, 1952, a new parent company called General Dynamics was established to manage the operations of Convair, Canadair, and Electric Boat.

Convair led the development of the American nuclear aircraft program, enthusiastically supported by the Pentagon. CEO Hopkins was a strong advocate of nuclear power and its numerous applications, but the nuclear airplane, or "N-bomber," was later found to be impractical, and the project was abandoned. Electric Boat enjoyed greater success with nuclear power; in 1955 it launched the first nuclear submarine, the *Nautilus*.

The company's development of commercial jetliners came near the end of Hopkins' tenure. While Douglas and Boeing were developing their DC-8 and 707 passenger jets, Convair was unable to introduce its jetliner because the company was delayed by contractual obligations to TWA and its eccentric and intrusive majority shareholder Howard Hughes. Specifically, Convair was bound to incorporate numerous design changes suggested by Hughes. As the result of a financial crisis that postponed TWA's purchase of jetliners, and eventually forced Hughes out of TWA, Convair was unable to recover from the delayed entry of its 680 and 880 models into the jetliner market. General Dynamics was forced to write off the entire passenger liner program with a $425 million loss.

The financial position of General Dynamics was so seriously weakened by the Convair jetliner program that the company was targeted for a takeover by Henry Crown, a Chicago construction materials magnate. Crown offered to merge his profitable Material Services Corporation with General Dynamics in exchange for a 20 percent share of the new company's stock, and the proposal was accepted in 1959. Two years later, Crown appointed Roger Lewis as chairperson of General Dynamics. Under Lewis, General Dynamics purchased the Quincy shipbuilding works from Bethlehem Steel in 1963 for $5 million. Quincy was then an outdated facility requiring costly improvements but held promise as a builder of surface ships.

In the early 1960s, the U.S. Defense Department invited American defense contractors to bid for the production of a new aircraft, the F-111, slated to replace the Department's aging fleet of B-52 bombers. General Dynamics entered the competition in partnership with the Grumman Corporation, against a design submitted by Boeing. Even though many regarded the Boeing F-111 as the better built and the more capable plane, the General Dynamics/Grumman version was consistently declared superior by Pentagon officials and industry experts. An investigation of impropriety in the selection process was interrupted when President Kennedy was assassinated in November 1963 and was not concluded until 1972.

General Dynamics continued to develop its version of the F-111 at its Convair facility in Fort Worth, Texas. The Air Force and Navy amended their design specifications and requested the addition of so many devices that the prototype could barely fly. With its utility as a replacement for the B-52 greatly diminished, the aircraft's role was reassessed, and the project was eventually identified by congressional critics as an example of gross mismanagement, organizational incompetence, and financial irresponsibility. The F-111 project consumed an inordinate amount of the defense budget and delayed by six years the introduction of Grumman's similar—and in many ways superior—F-14 Tomcat.

In 1966, Lewis removed Crown from the company by repossessing his 18 percent share of non-voting company stock. Crown was paid $120 million for his shares, but lost control of both General Dynamics and Material Services Corporation. Over the next few years, Crown continued to purchase substantial numbers of shares of voting stock, expanding his interest until he emerged in 1970 with control over the board of directors. Lewis was summarily fired and replaced by David Lewis (of no relation). Crown subsequently moved the company from New York to St. Louis in February 1971.

That year, the Electric Boat division of General Dynamics and its chief competitor, Newport News Shipbuilding, were awarded contracts to manufacture a new submarine, the 688, or *Los Angeles* class. Two years later, General Dynamics hired Takis Veliotis to take charge of the Quincy shipbuilding yard. Once in charge at Quincy, Veliotis concluded an agreement to build liquified natural gas tankers in conjunction with a cold storage engineering firm called Frigitemp.

During this period, the Defense Department announced a $200 million competition for the production of a new jet fighter. Careful to avoid the problems which plagued the F-111, General Dynamics initiated its development of the F-16. The F-16 program closely followed its development and budget schedules, and the first prototype exceeded specifications.

Although it was apparently chosen over the Northrop F-17 Cobra, the F-16 faced an unexpected challenge from McDonnell Douglas' independently developed F-15 Eagle. The lower-priced F-15 took a significant portion of the fighter market away from General Dynamics. However, the U.S. government compensated General Dynamics by promoting sales of the F-16 to NATO countries and other American allies. Canadair, which manufactured aircraft for Commonwealth countries, was sold back to the Canadian government in 1976 for $38 million.

The following year, Admiral Rickover publicly berated Electric Boat for poor workmanship and cost overruns on 18 *Los Angeles* class submarines. Rickover was particularly upset about the U.S. Navy's contractual obligation to absorb a large portion of the overruns, which were running as high as $89 million per vessel. A dispute then arose between the Defense Department and Electric Boat, wherein Electric Boat threatened to halt production of the submarines unless its share of the losses were covered as well. General Dynamics sought the protection of Public Law 85-804, which was originally intended to protect "strategic assets," such as Lockheed and Grumman, from bankruptcy due to cost overruns.

General Dynamics won a settlement from the Pentagon but soon realized that its problems at Groton were not merely financial. Productivity was seriously compromised by absenteeism and an employee turnover rate of 35 percent. Management lost control over inventories, and poor workmanship resulted in costly reconstruction. In October 1977, David Lewis transferred Takis Veliotis from Quincy to Groton, with instructions to reform the operation. Within months Veliotis had restored discipline, efficiency, and financial responsibility at Electric Boat.

Veliotis left Electric Boat in 1981 to take a seat on the General Dynamics board of directors and to serve as international salesperson and "company ambassador." Later that year, however, Veliotis resigned in protest over a dispute with David Lewis, whom Veliotis claimed had promised him the position of chief executive officer. Soon thereafter, Veliotis was indicted by government prosecutors for illegal business practices. He fled to Greece, maintaining that he had possession of damaging evidence of fraudulent overcharges made by General Dynamics.

In 1982, General Dynamics purchased the Chrysler battle tank division, with plants located in Warren, Michigan, and Lima, Ohio. The division, renamed Land Systems, had already secured a government contract to build the Army's next main battle tank, the M-1. Developed in response to newer Soviet tanks such as the T-72, the M-1 was to be powered by a jet turbine and capable of speeds of up to 50 miles per hour. The M-1 also included a computer-guided gun-aiming mechanism designed to assure a high degree of accuracy while the tank was traveling over rough terrain at high speeds.

When the first M-1 prototypes were delivered from Land Systems, several basic design flaws were noticed by Pentagon officials. First, exhaust from the engine was so hot that infantry could not come near the tank for cover under fire. Moreover, the M-1 was fast but prone to breakdown, and it required so much fuel that logistical support became questionable. Finally, the M-1's ammunition bay was too small to carry more than 40 shells. Critics recommended that the M-1 project be canceled in favor of its predecessor, the durable, battle-tested M-60. During this same period, General Dynamics won a government contract to service and maintain TAKX supply ships for the American Rapid Deployment Force.

During this time, Lewis and other company officials were called to testify before a congressional subcommittee, which suggested that the company had overcharged the government for supplies and personal expenses. The proceedings initiated separate investigations by the Justice Department and the Internal Revenue Service. Soon after Admiral Rickover was involuntarily retired by Navy Secretary John Lehman, General Dynamics was awarded a government contract to manufacture a number of new boats, including the $500 million Ohio class Trident submarine. The contract eliminated many of the company's disputed charges to the Pentagon and, as a result, led to the cessation of the congressional investigation. Wisconsin Senator William Proxmire criticized these developments by remarking that "defense contractors like General Dynamics have so much leverage against the government they can flout the laws that govern smaller companies and individuals."

David Lewis retired in 1985 and was replaced by Stanley C. Pace, formerly head of TRW. Oliver Boileau, president of General Dynamics, was passed over for the position at the insistence of the board of directors and the Crown family, all of whom wished to see an end to the policies of Lewis and his protégés. Pace made several changes at General Dynamics, even before Lewis had left the company. He sold the Quincy shipyard and founded a new division called Valley Systems, established to win contracts for the Reagan Administration's Strategic Defense Initiative. Pace also helped clean up General Dynamics' image by instituting an ethics program, which resulted in the firing of 27 employees.

Several external forces helped shape the conduct of business at General Dynamics in the late 1980s and early 1990s. The USSR's collapse revealed it a much weaker military foe than had previously been believed. The subsequent end of the Cold War soon brought Congressional and public pressure to cut domestic defense budgets. These factors compelled General Dynamics to transform itself into a smaller, more focused company with a higher concentration of international sales. The Persian Gulf conflict helped boost General Dynamics' tank and F-16 fighter sales to Turkey, Egypt, and Saudi Arabia and opened Middle East markets to the military manufacturer.

In January 1991, William A. Anders was assigned to reorganize General Dynamics according to the new market realities. He assumed the chief executive office, while Stanley Pace took a seat on the company's board of directors. Anders' strategy in the face of industry changes was to cut employees, trim research and development, divest peripheral businesses, and reduce capital spending. By June 1992, Anders had cut 25 percent of the work force (24,800 employees) and put $1.7 billion in assets up for sale. Gains from divestments were rolled back to shareholders, and, by 1993, almost $600 million in debt was paid, which helped boost the company's share price. General Dynamics, which had suffered a $578 million loss in 1990, recovered to realize a $305 million profit the following year.

Despite the improving financial picture, General Dynamics came under criticism from the Pentagon and Department of Defense for a lucrative executive Gain-Sharing plan that was tied to increases in the company's share price. In 1991 alone, as General Dynamics whittled away at its employee roster, *Business Week* reported that 25 top managers received $18 million in incentive bonuses.

Anders pronounced the transformation of General Dynamics complete in 1993's annual report. After selling its Texas aircraft operations to Lockheed for $1.5 billion, the company emerged with two primary business segments: nuclear submarines and armored vehicles. The corporate work force had shrunk from about 86,000 in 1991 to 30,500 in 1993, and debt decreased 94 percent during the period. Government contracts still comprised 94 percent of the company's annual sales, which remained essentially flat over the reorganization period. Operating earnings, however, increased by $98 million, from $211 million in 1991 to $309 million in 1993. That year, Anders relinquished the chief executive office to former president James Mellor and assumed General Dynamics' chair as a transitional measure through April 1994.

Principal Subsidiaries: Electric Boat Division; Land Systems Division; American Overseas Marine Corporation; Freeman Energy Corporation.

Further Reading:

Coulam, Robert F., *The Illusion of Choice: The F-111 and the Problem of Weapons Acquisition Reform,* Princeton, N.J.: Princeton University Press, 1977.

Ellis, James E., ''Layoffs on the Line, Bonuses in the Executive Suite,'' *Business Week,* October 21, 1991, p. 34.

Franklin, Roger, *The Defender: The Story of General Dynamics,* New York: Harper, 1986.

Goodwin, Jacob, *Brotherhood of Arms: General Dynamics and the Business of Defending America,* New York: Random House, 1985.

Tyler, Patrick. *Running Critical: The Silent War, Rickover and General Dynamics,* New York: Harper, 1987.

—updated by April Dougal Gasbarre

ⒼⒾ General Instrument

General Instrument Corporation

181 West Madison Street
Chicago, Illinois 60602
U.S.A.
(312) 541-5000
Fax: (312) 541-5019

Public Company
Incorporated: 1923
Employees: 9,200
Sales: $1.39 billion
Stock Exchanges: New York
SICs: 3679 Electronic Components, Nec; 3575 Computer
   Terminals; 3357 Nonferrous Wiredrawing & Insulating;
   6719 Holding Companies, Nec

The General Instrument Corporation is the leading American provider of cable television equipment. The company manufactures television set-top converters for cable transmission as well as scrambling devices for cable satellite signals. The company also provides fiber optic cables and coaxial cables for television transmission, as well as semiconductors. After decades as a multi-faceted manufacturer of parts for electronic equipment, primarily televisions, General Instrument began to narrow its focus in the mid-1970s, until, through a series of technological breakthroughs, it came to dominate the cable industry in the 1990s.

General Instrument got its start as an electronics manufacturer based in New York in 1923. It was not until the 1950s, however, that General Instrument embarked upon the series of acquisitions that would help it to become a technology conglomerate. Under the direction of company president Moses Shapiro, General Instrument bought a wide variety of electronics companies, most of them based in the New York area. Through these activities, the company moved into a number of different fields, including silicon transistor and semiconductor manufacturing.

In 1951 General Instrument merged a previous purchase, the F. W. Sickles Company, into General Instrument, making it a subsidiary. Three years later, in 1954, the company formed a Canadian subsidiary when General Instrument-F. W. Sickles of Canada, Limited, was created. This company subsequently purchased Watt Electronic Products, Limited, of Kitchener, Ontario. In 1955 the company returned to its geographic roots, buying the Automatic Manufacturing Corporation of Newark,

New Jersey. In the following year Micamold Electronics Manufacturing Corporation of Brooklyn and T. S. Farley, Limited, of Hamilton, Ontario, were added.

In April, 1957, General Instrument bought the Radio Receptor Company, Inc., of Brooklyn, and two years later the company bought the Harris Transducer Corporation. After purchasing these companies, General Instrument left their operations intact and made each a separate division of the company. In 1960 the company added the General Transistor Corporation of Jamaica, New York. One year later, the Pyramid Electric Company was acquired.

In June, 1962, General Instrument made its foray into the overseas market when it completed an agreement with an Italian firm, the Pirelli Group, to form a new company. This enterprise was called the Pirelli Applicazione Elettroniche, S.p.A., and it was set up to manufacture and sell General Instrument products throughout the European common market. General Instrument later bought this joint venture.

In 1963 General Instrument sold off one of its divisions, as the company's revenues fell by 3.6 percent. With these results, the company reported a loss for the year. In August, 1966, General Instrument acquired Signalite, Inc., and a year later it bought Universal Controls, Inc. By the mid-1960s, General Instrument had become a diversified electronics manufacturer, with an eclectic mix of products and businesses that had been collected by its free-wheeling president, Shapiro. The company's revenues and profits were highly dependent on demand for television components. Because televisions were luxury goods, their sales dropped during periods of economic downturn, and this in turn depressed General Instrument's financial results periodically.

In the late 1960s General Instrument made a number of acquisitions that diversified its product base and allowed it to somewhat stabilize its financial returns. In December, 1967, the company bought the Philadelphia-based Jerrold Corporation for $129 million. With this acquisition, General Instrument moved into the cable television equipment business. Also in 1967, General Instrument purchased the American Totalisator Corporation, the world's largest manufacturer of parimutuel betting machines. Both of these new lines of business would later play an important part in General Instrument's corporate strategy. Also in that year, General Instrument switched its stock listing to the New York Stock Exchange.

In 1968 General Instrument strengthened its holdings in the cable television industry. The company bought CATV, a cable television system in Texas, and the Telihoras Corporation, which ran cable TV systems in three New York counties. In the following year, the company also bought a half interest in Alpine Cable Television. Despite this strengthening in one area, General Instrument continued its policy of buying a broad variety of other companies. The company invested in three makers of miniature incandescent bulbs in 1969 and bought the Alliance Amusement Company of Chicago for $10 million.

By the early 1970s General Instrument's scattershot approach to the electronics industry had started to take its toll. The company began laying off employees in April, 1970: 27 percent of its micro-electronics division was let go. Further firings took place in May, August, and November. In January, 1971, the company began to withdraw from its participation in the cable television industry, when its Jerrold subsidiary sold its half-interest in a Florida cable venture. By November, Jerrold had divested itself of all its further cable television companies.

After these cost-cutting measures, General Instrument resumed its string of acquisitions, buying five more companies before 1975. At this time, the company remained a $500-million-a-year producer of a wide variety of electrical components, which left its bottom line vulnerable to recession. In addition, as a result of its rapid string of purchases, General Instrument was deep in debt. Its core business, supplying electronic components to manufacturers of consumer goods, was unlikely to help the company earn its way out of debt, since it showed little room for growth.

In 1975 General Instrument's president Shapiro retired and was replaced by Frank G. Hickey, the company's new chairman. Hickey brought a different management philosophy to General Instrument, and under his direction the company began to change its identity. Hickey embarked on a program to sell off General Instrument's poorly performing subsidiaries and to manage its cash flow. In addition, he strengthened the company's presence in two growth industries, cable television and gaming. By 1977, these efforts had begun to show fruit. In that year, General Instrument liquidated eight of its money-losing divisions. Instead, gaming machines accounted for 25 percent of the company's operating margins. Profits were up by 47 percent to $24 million, and the company's debt was reduced by 30 percent.

These trends continued in 1978, as first quarter earnings rose by a third. American Totalisator, the company's betting subsidiary, produced 40 percent of these returns. Long-term debt had been reduced to 36 percent of equity. In an unexpected stroke of luck, General Instrument also found that the fad for video games, such as Atari and Intellivision, drove demand for its specialized semi-conductor chips.

In October, 1979, General Instrument opened Teletrack, an $8 million closed-circuit television betting theater constructed in New Haven, Connecticut. With a giant 32-by-24-foot screen, patrons could watch live races at various local horse tracks and place legal bets on their outcomes. General Instrument received four to five percent of the revenues from this operation, which made up only a small part of its gaming activities. The company also supplied 80 percent of the on-track betting systems used in North America, 90 percent of the off-track wagering machines, and held a sizable chunk of the state lottery business. Overall, wagering systems accounted for 35 percent of General Instrument's 1979 profits of $50 million, up fivefold from $10 million in 1975.

By 1980, General Instrument had shed 11 business and facilities in areas around the world, and the company's debt level had shrunk from 100 percent of equity to about 20 percent. In addition to the growth of its wagering business, General Instrument saw its cable television operations explode. The company's growing dominance of this market drove its sales, earnings, and margins upward, while the price of its stock tripled.

By 1981, General Instrument's revenues were nearing the $1 billion mark, and its debt had been reduced to 9.3 percent of capital. Sixty-one percent of the company's earnings were contributed by cable equipment. General Instrument had come to dominate the market for head-end equipment, which transmitted cable programming; the company also came to hold half of the market for black-box converters. These devices, which sat on top of a customer's television set, decoded signals from the coaxial cable and put them on the television screen.

The increase in General Instrument's cable business came just as its strength in gaming was waning. Competitors such as Datatrol and Control Data had started to push down American Totalisator's profits in the early 1980s. To make sure that the company's cable dominance did not suffer the same fate, General Instrument took steps to remain on the technological cutting edge of this field. In February, 1982, the company formed United Satellite Television, a joint venture with the Allstar Satellite Network and Pop Satellite, that planned to offer direct satellite to home broadcasting via affordable 6-foot-wide satellite dishes. Through its exclusive contract with this service, General Instrument hoped to sell $1.5 billion worth of equipment to customers in remote areas. General Instrument was also exploring the potential of local-area networks, used to connect computers within an office, and interactive cable TV systems for the home. With these efforts, the company hoped to decrease its reliance on conventional cable gear.

General Instrument continued its strong returns throughout 1982. In October the company won a contract to supply $100 million worth of cable equipment to Telecommunication, Inc., a consortium of 300 cable systems. General Instrument increased its holdings in the cable television industry in December, 1983, when it bought Tocom, Inc., for $28 million. This company manufactured cable television converters and security systems.

By the spring of 1984, however, General Instrument's financial results had hit a snag, as the company posted a year and a half of flat or declining earnings, which ended with a 64.7 percent drop in profits for the year ended in February, 1984. Doubts plagued the company's joint satellite venture, and General Instrument suspended deliveries of equipment to this company in March because of questions about its finances.

General Instrument's financial difficulties continued in 1985 as the company reported revenues down 15.4 percent, to $848 million, and a $66.5 million loss. The company began to sell off a number of its units, including its money-losing semiconductor operations, and in February, 1986, General Instrument reorganized is upper management structure. This shuffle was the company's second difficult restructuring attempt in two years.

In the fall of 1986, searching for a new line of business that would help the company to rebuild, General Instrument paid $220 million for the cable television equipment operations of M/A-COM, a General Instrument competitor based in Massachusetts. This company's San Diego-based VideoCipher division had spent $20 million developing a scrambling and decoding device for use by satellite television operations. This company's VideoCipher II product was not only the industry standard, it had a monopoly on the production of these devices. By the end of 1986, however, these changes had not managed to stem the tide of General Instrument's losses, as the company reported a $80 million deficit on $788 million in sales.

In 1987 General Instrument continued to sell businesses in an effort to shore up its bottom line. In April, 1987, the company divested its interest in Sytek, its local area network partner, along with its optoelectronics division, its lamp division, an antenna manufacturing operation, and factories in Tucson, Arizona, and Post Falls, Idaho.

By the spring of 1987, however, General Instrument had finally started to get some good news. Demand for its VideoCipher II product was outstripping supply by 50 percent, and the company opened a second plant in Mexico to produce more than 50,000 units a month. Although it only cost $200 to make the devices, General Instrument was able to sell them for $325, reaping a hefty profit. Driven by the success of this product, General Instrument saw its revenues grow, posting sales of $1.16 billion at the end of 1987. In 1988 the company also began to increase its share of the market for addressable subscriber systems, which let cable operators control which pay channels and other services a viewer received in his home.

By the end of the 1980s, however, General Instrument was once again losing money. In the spring of 1990, the company began to seek a buyer. In August, 1990, General Instrument was purchased in a friendly leveraged buyout of $1.6 billion by the FLGI Holding Company, created for this purpose by Forstmann, Little & Company, a New York investment banking house. In October, 1990, General Instrument's new owners appointed Donald Rumsfeld, a longtime Washington insider, to head the company. Rumsfeld cut the company's costs by selling off peripheral businesses with annual sales of nearly $400 million.

In January, 1991, General Instrument announced that it would join with its chief contender in the race to develop high-definition television (HDTV), the next generation of television transmission. This teamwork paid off in June, 1991, when the company announced a breakthrough in its HDTV effort. This effort relied on digital compression technology to allow hundreds of channels to enter a viewer's home. With General Instrument manufacturing the equipment to compress signals for transmission, and then to decompress them for viewing, the company would have a lock on the next generation of cable equipment.

By August, 1991, however, General Instrument's revenues had dropped 14 percent, as cable companies cut their spending. Rather than cut funding to its promising research activities, the company cut its overhead to the bone in order to make its loan payments. Two-thirds of General Instrument's headquarters staff was let go, leaving a skeleton crew of 23 people, at a savings of $65 million a year. In addition, the company reduced inventories and instituted quality-control programs in its factories in an effort to increase productivity.

By the start of 1992, General Instrument's sales had started to revive, and in March the company gave a broadcast demonstration of its new all-digital HDTV technology. Shortly thereafter, the company won a contract for 100,000 HDTV compression devices from Tele-Communications, Inc., of Denver, the company's largest cable provider. This deal later provoked the scrutiny of the U.S. Justice Department, which launched an investigation to determine whether the company's dominance of the cable set-top industry constituted a stranglehold on competition.

In June, 1992, in an effort to reduce General Instrument's debt from its purchase, the company once again sold stock to the public, raising $307 million through the sale of 22 million shares. With this money, General Instrument restructured its balance sheet to reduce its interest payments. At the end of 1992, General Instrument reported an increase in sales of nearly 16 percent, to $1.07 billion, which nevertheless yielded a loss of $53 million.

In an effort to gain future sales, General Instrument announced in April, 1993, that it had joined with two other companies, Microsoft and Itel, to develop a cable box that combined the functions of a cable converter and a computer, allowing for interactive television. In July, 1993, General Instrument further strengthened its financial standing when it paid off the last $100 million of its debt to Forstmann, Little.

At the end of 1993, General Instrument merged its Jerrold Communications and its VideoCipher units into one division, GI Communications. The company reported year-end revenues of $1.39 billion, and a profit of $91 million. With these strong results, and General Instrument's central involvement in a number of the key communications technologies of the future, the company appeared well situated to thrive in the coming years.

Principal Subsidiaries: General Semiconductor Ireland.

Further Reading:

Andrews, Edmund L., "Antitrust Inquiry on Cable Gear," *New York Times,* March 9, 1994.
Block, Alex Ben, "The General," *Forbes,* June 29, 1987.
Blyskal, Jeff, "Fine Tuning," *Forbes,* March 29, 1982.
Kneale, Dennis, "General Instrument's Turnaround Seen by Some," *Wall Street Journal,* April 27, 1984.
"Mixing Luck and Knowhow," *Business Week,* October 18, 1982.
Palmeri, Christopher, "Act Three," *Forbes,* October 26, 1992.
Ringer, Richard, "General Instrument Moves to Pay Off Its Debt Early," *New York Times,* July 1, 1993.
Schuyten, Peter J., "Betting on Electronic Wagering," *New York Times,* March 12, 1980.
Stewart, Thomas A., "How a High-Tech Bet Paid Off Big," *Fortune,* November 1, 1993.

—Elizabeth Rourke

General Mills, Inc.

1 General Mills Blvd.
P.O. Box 1113
Minneapolis, Minnesota 55440
U.S.A.
(612) 540-2311
Fax: (612) 540-4925

Public Company
Incorporated: 1928
Employees: 121,300
Revenues: $8.1 billion
Stock Exchanges: New York
SICs: 2043 Cereal Breakfast Foods; 2045 Blended and
  Prepared Flour Mixes & Doughs; 2092 Fresh or Frozen
  Prepared Fish; 5812 Eating Places

General Mills, Inc. is one of the leading breakfast cereal companies in the world, with such well-known brands as Cheerios, Cocoa Puffs, Total, and Wheaties stocking the shelves of supermarket stores everywhere. In addition to its breakfast cereal products, the company also includes some of the best names in other food lines such as Gold Medal flour, Betty Crocker dessert mixes, Hamburger Helper dinner mixes, and Yoplait yogurt. Although General Mills derives nearly two-thirds of its revenues from cereal and other food products, the company also operates a restaurant business with the remaining revenues coming from its Red Lobster and Olive Garden restaurant franchises, and its Chinese food venture called China Coast.

General Mills was incorporated in 1928, but its origins go back to 1866, when Cadwallader Washburn opened a flour mill in Minneapolis, Minnesota. His business, which soon became the Washburn Crosby Company, competed with local miller C. A. Pillsbury. In 1869 they joined forces to form the Minneapolis Millers Association. Pillsbury and Washburn both wanted to find a way to make midwestern winter wheat into a higher grade of flour. Eventually, with the help of a French engineer, Washburn not only improved the method but made his product the best flour available in America. When Pillsbury adopted the same technique, Minneapolis became the country's flour milling center.

In 1878 the association was reorganized to appease farmers who found its business practices unfair. James S. Bell succeeded Washburn as head of the Washburn Crosby Company, ousting

Washburn's heirs. The mill prospered through the turn of the century. In 1928, the year General Mills was formed, the company had 5,800 employees and annual sales of $123 million. Its strongest products were Gold Medal flour, Softasilk cake flour, and Wheaties, a recently introduced ready-to-eat cereal.

Bell's son, James Ford, was responsible for creating General Mills in 1928 by consolidating the Washburn mill with several other major flour-milling companies around the country, including the Red Star Milling Co., the Sperry Milling Co., and the Larrowe Milling Co. Within five months Ford had collected 27 companies, making General Mills the largest flour-milling company in the world. As a part of General Mills, these mills kept their operational independence but left advertising and product development to General Mills headquarters. This consolidation was well timed, as it gave the company the strength to survive and even prosper through the Depression, when earnings grew steadily and stock in the company was stable.

Bell's research emphasis put General Mills in a strong position for the changing demands of increasingly urban consumers. The company soon introduced Bisquick, the first baking mix, and another ready-to-eat cereal, Cheerios, which 50 years later would be the best-selling cereal in America.

Bell's early interest in diversification and technology made mobilization for World War II easier. General Mills's factories were restructured to produce equipment for the navy, medicinal alcohol, and bags to make into sandbags, as well as the expected dehydrated food. In 1942 Donald D. Davis, president of General Mills since Bell moved to chairman in 1934, resigned to head the U.S. War Production Board.

Henry Bullis, who began at General Mills as a mill hand after World War I, replaced Davis. Following Bell's industrial lead, Bullis immediately entered the animal feed industry by processing soybeans, a venture which ultimately became General Mill's chemical division.

Postwar demand for consumer foods allowed the company to de-emphasize industrial activity and to concentrate on the success of its cereals and cake mixes. Consumers demanded less time in the kitchen and continued to buy foods that required less preparation. Ready-to-eat cereals, now the company's staple, grew dramatically, and more brands were introduced.

Throughout the 1920s Bell and his associates had invested heavily in advertising, which was becoming a significant force in selling products to a national market. Betty Crocker, created in 1921, was a legacy from Washburn Crosby. By 1928 Betty Crocker's name, signature, and radio voice had been introduced in connection with General Mills's consumer goods. General Mills also sponsored radio programs and pioneered the use of athlete endorsements on its own radio station, WCCO.

The postwar consumer's interest in convenience complemented General Mills's growing advertising efforts. The company continued to refine its advertising methods after World War II, and promotions like the *Betty Crocker Cookbook* and advertisements on TV, an exciting new medium at the time, helped to increase sales and consumer recognition of the company. Capitalizing on its research and media prominence, the company soon held the second position in breakfast food sales.

Another career General Mills man, Charles H. Bell, rose to the presidency in 1952. Since advertising had become the main force in marketing its various brands, centralization had crept into the organization. Bell found it necessary to reassign management decisions closer to operations. In 1958 he moved headquarters out of downtown Minneapolis and into suburban Golden Valley. Still stronger changes were needed, but the company was hesitant. General Mills's 1940s ventures into electronics and appliances had failed, and the company had recently begun to post losses in animal feeds and flour milling. Consumer foods remained the main moneymaker, but General Mills's stock value dropped to $1.25 a share in 1962, its lowest point in 12 years.

Bell recruited an outsider, Edwin W. Rawlings, in 1959, and two years later Rawlings was appointed president. Rawlings reevaluated company output and shook up management positions. The family flour market was declining 3 percent a year, and Rawlings decided consumer preferences had shifted once again. Although the company was then the largest flour miller in the world and flour made up the greatest volume of output, Rawlings closed half of General Mills's mills and renewed the company's commitment to packaged foods by introducing food service products for restaurants and hotels. He also divested its interests in electronics, appliances, formula feeds, and other smaller operations. These actions caused a short-term, five-year sales decline for the company.

Next Rawlings began a series of acquisitions that would alter corporate structure for the next 20 years and provide two decades of continual earnings growth. Snack foods entered the company's portfolio with the purchase of Morton Foods, Inc. in 1964. In 1966 came the Tom Huston Peanut Co., and in 1968 General Mills went abroad with the purchase of Smiths Food Group, Ltd. of England and Belgium. The French Biscuiterie Nantaise soon followed, as did snack food companies in Latin America and Japan.

Other major acquisitions were Gorton's, a frozen fish company, and an aggressive move into the toy and game industry with Rainbow Crafts (Play-Doh), Kenner and Parker Bros., all in 1968. In ten years international toy operations would comprise one-third of the company's sales, at $482.3 million. General Mills was no longer the world's largest miller, but it was now the world's largest toy manufacturer.

Early in 1969 the Federal Trade Commission (FTC) issued a consent order blocking General Mills from further acquisitions within the snack food industry. At the time of purchase, both Morton and Tom Huston were among the top ten producers of potato and corn chips.

During his seven years as General Mills chief, Rawlings managed to double the company's earnings and bring consumer foods to 80 percent of total sales, up from 45 percent. Although Rawlings wanted another outsider to succeed him, the board of directors chose James P. McFarland in 1969. General Mills was the only company McFarland had ever worked for, and in choosing him the corporation renewed its commitment to balance and stability.

Seeking controlled growth, McFarland slowed, but did not stop, acquisitions. The first of many clothing company purchases was

David Crystal, Inc. (Lacoste clothing) in 1969. Along with the purchase of Monet Jewelry in the same year, the purchase introduced General Mills to specialty retailing. Although the company missed the growth of fast food opportunities, purchasing and developing the Red Lobster restaurant chain would eventually make the new restaurant group General Mills's second largest division.

McFarland, an experienced salesman, involved himself with day-to-day operations and left long-term planning to operating chief James A. Summer. In his first two years as CEO, McFarland saw sales rise from $885 million to $1.1 billion and operating profits from $37.5 million to $44 million. His goal was to reach $2 billion in sales by 1976. Sales that year were actually $2.6 billion, four times the 1969 level, with earnings of more than $100 million. He then announced E. Robert Kinney as his successor.

Like most quickly expanding companies of this time period, however, not all of General Mills forays were successful. Between 1950 and 1986, General Mills made 86 acquisitions in new industries; 73 percent of those made by 1975 had been divested within five years. A profitable core business in consumer foods eased the burden of these failed efforts.

General Mills's advertising budget is typically as large as its earnings. Although spending less than it did in the late 1970s and early 1980s, General Mills still ranks as the thirteenth largest spender in all media, at $572 million a year. However, being such a highly visible company has not always provided favorable attention.

In the early 1970s the FTC attempted to dismiss General Mills 1968 acquisition of Gorton's. The block was lifted in 1973. Later, by allying itself with General Foods Corp., the firm succeeded in blocking a 1977 FTC proposal to forbid advertisements aimed at children. Late in 1980, the FTC again filed a complaint against cereal companies, this time an antitrust suit following a ten-year investigation. It charged that between 1958 and 1972 cereal manufacturers had an average after-tax profit of 19.8 percent, compared to a general manufacturing average of 8.9 percent and suggested that Kellogg Company, General Mills, and General Foods shared a monopoly over the cereal industry. The charges were dismissed in 1981 after the companies had lobbied for and won congressional favor.

By heavily promoting its brands, the company did well in the 1970s, reporting gains in the toy division and the tripling of sales for consumer foods. Between 1973 and 1978, sales increased $1.7 billion. Of this growth, 41 percent came from new products developed internally, 15 percent from acquisitions, and 18 percent from expansion of restaurant and retail centers. General Mills' management system, in which one manager oversees the production, marketing, and sales of each brand, also got credit for some of the increase. After the 1977 sale of the chemical division, General Mills divided its business into food processing, restaurants, games and toys, fashion, and specialty retailing.

In 1981 H. Brewster Atwater, Jr. became president of General Mills. The following year was a solid one for the company, as consumer foods, restaurants, toys, fashion, and retailing reported sales increases of between 12 percent and 24 percent.

However, retailing profit was half that of its previous year, and although the toy and game division had grown, the toy industry worldwide had decreased 2.9 percent.

Izod Lacoste also performed well. With $400 million in sales, General Mills intended to develop more items under the label. But by 1985 sales had dropped to $225 million, and the company hoped to cut overhead in order to break even at $180 million by 1986. In 1985 the largest toymaker in the world divested items representing over 25 percent of its sales, including toys, fashion, and nonapparel retailing. Former President Kinney became head of the spun-off Kenner Parker Toys Inc. The other spin-off, called the Fashion Co., consisted of Monet Jewelry, Izod Lacoste, and Ship 'n Shore. The company kept its furniture group (Pennsylvania House, Kittinger) for future sale. Also kept was Eddie Bauer Inc., despite its reported loss because of excess inventory. General Mills reported a net loss of $72 million due to the restructuring and a 21 percent increase in advertising expenses.

As expected by analysts, General Mills quickly recovered. Earnings were up to $222 million by 1987. Its core businesses were the Big G cereals, Red Lobster, and Talbot's in its consumer-foods, restaurants, and specialty retailing divisions.

The consolidation process begun in 1985 continued in the latter half of the 1980s. Pared down somewhat, the company originally planned to expand its remaining retailing operations. But the takeover climate of the late 1980s and a disappointing Christmas in 1987 forced the company to exit retailing altogether by selling Eddie Bauer and Talbot's.

General Mills has divested itself of many of its holdings since 1976, but its surviving businesses have a firm footing in their markets. More than 90 percent of the company's food sales come from products with a first or second place market share position. Streamlining has also allowed the company to keep up with the rapid pace of new product development. From 1985 to 1988, 24 percent to 29 percent of the food divisions' growth came from new products.

General Mills also increased its share in the fast-growing cereal market, boosted by the oat bran craze of the late 1980s (Cheerios' market share alone climbed 3.1 percent in one year) and the accompanying breakfast food boom. General Mills alone among top cereal producers was prepared for these trends. During the early 1990s, the company introduced Fingos, a cereal eaten by hand, and Ripple Crisp, a cereal which stays crisp in milk.

In 1989, General Mills began to expand into international markets, a sector which archival Kellogg has been exploiting for years. By forming Cereal Partners Worldwide with Nestle S.A., the Swiss-based food products giant, General Mills planned to cut into the European cereal market long dominated by Kellogg.

By 1991, the partnership was doing so well in Europe that it ventured into the Mexican market. In 1992, General Mills established Snack Ventures Europe, a $600 million partnership with PepsiCo, Inc. to take advantage of the growing market for snack foods in Europe.

After the growth in market share during the late 1980s and early 1990s, by 1993 General Mills experienced a slowdown in its core business of brand name cereal and food products. Nevertheless, in an unprecedented move, the company hired approximately 10,000 new employees during the same year. The reason for this was the growth of the restaurant business division. Having already acquired the Red Lobster seafood chain in 1970, General Mills attempted other formats including steak houses, Mexican, and health food eateries that didn't work. In 1983, the company came up with its own Italian restaurant chain called the Olive Garden Italian Restaurants and in 1991 launched China Coast, an attempt to fill the void in chinese food restaurant chains. At the end of 1993, there were 657 Red Lobster and 429 Olive Garden restaurants located throughout the United States, and nine China Coast units in Orlando, Indianapolis, and Fort Worth. With restaurant profits increasing rapidly, General Mills plans to open 100 new locations annually for next two or three years.

In a widely publicized decision amid growing consumer complaints, during 1993 General Mills decided not to increase its cereal prices to keep pace with Kellogg. Kellogg implemented a 2.1 percent increase on all its brand name cereals, but General Mills had previously hiked prices nearly 28 percent between 1988 and 1992. As a result, General Mills actually cut prices 11 percent to 16 percent on three of its most well-known brands. This discounting strategy increased volume sales on all three of the cereal brands.

General Mills reaped over $8 billion in sales during 1993, with the company's packaged goods accounting for two-thirds of its revenues and the restaurant division making up the remaining amount. With the highest return on equity of any company in the entire industry for the past five years—an impressive 42.8 percent compared to the industry median of 17 percent—management has been confident enough to predict an average growth in profits of 14 percent annually until the year 2000.

Principal Subsidiaries: Morton Foods, Inc.; Tom Huston Peanut Co.; Smiths Food Group, Ltd.; Gorton's; Rainbow Crafts; Kenner; Parker Bros.; David Crystal, Inc.; Monet Jewelry; Red Lobster Restaurants; Olive Garden Italian Restaurants.

Further Reading:

Kennedy, Gerald S., *Minutes & Moments in the Life of General Mills,* 1971.
"Long-Term Vision," *Forbes,* January 3, 1994.

—updated by Thomas Derdak

General Motors Corporation

3044 West Grand Blvd.
Detroit, Michigan 48202
U.S.A.
(313) 556-5000

Public Company
Incorporated: 1916
Employees: 750,000
Sales: $138.22 billion
Stock Exchanges: New York
SICs: 3711 Motor Vehicles and Car Bodies; 3714 Motor
   Vehicle Parts and Accessories; 3812 Search and
   Navigation Equipment; 3761 Guided Missiles and Space
   Vehicles; 3663 Radio and TV Communications
   Equipment; 6141 Personal Credit Institutions; 3743
   Railroad Equipment

General Motors Corporation is the world's largest full-line vehicle manufacturer and marketer. Its American nameplates include Chevrolet, Pontiac, Oldsmobile, Buick, Cadillac, GMC Truck, and Saturn. Opel, Vauxhall, Saab, and Isuzu comprise General Motors' international nameplates. The company's Automotive Components Group Worldwide brings vertical integration to General Motors' manufacturing, and also supplies components and systems to every major automotive manufacturer. Other principal businesses include GM Hughes Electronics Corporation, a manufacturer of automotive electronics, commercial technologies, telecommunications, and space and defense electronics; Electronic Data Systems corporation, a global information technologies company; and General Motors Acceptance Corporation and its subsidiaries, providers of financing and insurance to GM customers and dealers.

The beginning of General Motors can be traced back to 1892, when R. E. Olds collected all his savings in order to convert his father's naval and industrial engine factory into the Olds Motor Vehicle Company to build horseless carriages. For a number of years, however, the Oldsmobile (as the product came to be known) did not get beyond the experimental stage. In 1895 the first model, a four-seater with a petrol engine that could produce five horsepower and reach 18.6 mph, went for its trial run.

Olds proved himself not only an innovative engineer but also a good businessman and was very successful with his first model, of which relatively few were built. As a result of his success, he founded the first American factory in Detroit devoted exclusively to the production of automobiles. The first car was a luxury model costing $1,200, but the second model was introduced at a list price of $650 and was very successful. Two years later, at the turn of the century, Olds had sold over 1,400 cars.

That same year, an engineer named David Buick founded a factory under his own name in Detroit. A third factory for the Cadillac Automobile Company was also built in Detroit. This company was founded by Henry Leland, who was already building car engines with experience gained in the Oldsmobile factory, where he worked until 1901. By the end of 1902 the first Cadillac had been produced—a car distinguished by its luxurious finish. In the following year, tiller steering was replaced by the steering wheel, the reduction gearbox was introduced, and some cars were fitted with celluloid windscreens. Oldsmobile also reached their projected target of manufacturing 4,000 cars in one year.

By 1903, a time of market instability, so many different manufacturers were operating that the financially weakest disappeared and some of the remaining companies were forced to form a consortium. William Durant, a director of the Buick Motor Company, was the man behind the merger. The son of a Michigan governor, and a self-made millionaire, Durant believed that the only way for the automobile companies to operate at a profit was to avoid the duplication that occurred as many concerns manufactured the same product. General Motors was thus formed, bringing together Oldsmobile and Buick in 1903, and joined in 1909 by Cadillac and Oakland (renamed Pontiac). Positive financial results were immediately seen from the union, although the establishment of the company drew little attention.

Other early members of the General Motors family were Ewing, Marquette, Welch, Scripps-Booth, Sheridan, and Elmore, together with Rapid and Reliance trucks. General Motors' other U.S. automotive division, Chevrolet, became part of the Corporation in 1918. Only Buick, Oldsmobile, Cadillac, and Oakland continued making cars for more than a short time after their acquisition by GM. By 1920 more than 30 companies had been acquired through the purchase of all or part of their stock. Two were forerunners of major GM subsidiaries, the McLaughlin Motor Company of Canada (which later became General Motors of Canada Limited) and the Fisher Body Company, in which GM initially acquired a 60 percent interest.

By 1911 the company set up a central staff of specialists to coordinate work in the various units and factories. An experimental or "testing" laboratory was also established to serve as an additional protection against costly factory mistakes. General Motors' system of administration, research, and development became one of the largest and most complex in private industry.

About the same time that General Motors was establishing itself in Detroit, an engineering breakthrough was taking place in Dayton, Ohio: the electric self-starter, designed by Charles F. Kettering. General Motors introduced Kettering's invention in its 1912 Cadillacs, and with the phasing out of the dangerous and unpredictable hand crank, motoring became much more popular. Kettering's Dayton Engineering Laboratories were merged into General Motors during 1920 and the Laboratories were relocated in Detroit in 1925. Kettering later became the scientific director of General Motors, in charge of its research and engineering programs.

During World War I General Motors turned its facilities to the production of war materials. With no previous experience in manufacturing military hardware, the American automobile industry completed a retooling from civilian to war production within 18 months. Between 1917 and 1919, 90 percent of General Motors' truck production was for the war effort. Cadillac supplied Army staff cars, V-8 engines for artillery tractors, and trench mortar shells, while Buick built Liberty airplane motors, tanks, trucks, ambulances, and automotive parts.

It was at this time that Alfred Sloan, Jr., who went on to guide General Motors as president and chairman until 1956, first became associated with the company. In 24 years, Sloan had built a $50,000 investment in the Hyatt Roller Bearing Company to assets of about $3.5 million. When Hyatt became part of General Motors, Sloan joined the corporate management.

General Motors suffered greatly under the effects of the Depression, but it emerged with a new, aggressive management. Coordinated policy control replaced the undirected efforts of the prior years. As its principal architect, Sloan was credited with creating not only an organization which saved General Motors, but a new management policy that was adopted by countless other businesses. Fundamentally, the policy involved coordination of the enterprise under top management, direction of policy through top-level committees, and delegation of operational responsibility throughout the organization. Within this framework management staffs conducted analysis of market trends, advised policy committees, and coordinated administration. For a company comprised of many varied divisions, such a system of organization was crucial to its success.

By 1941 General Motors accounted for 44 percent of the total U.S. automotive sales, compared with 12 percent in 1921. In preparation for America's entry into the Second World War, General Motors retooled its factories. After Japan struck at Pearl Harbor in 1941, the industrial skills that General Motors had developed were applied with great effectiveness. From 1940 to 1945 General Motors produced defense material valued at a total of $12.3 billion. Decentralized and highly flexible local managerial responsibility made possible the almost overnight conversion from civilian production to wartime production. General Motors' contribution included the manufacture of every conceivable product from the smallest ball bearing to large tanks, naval ships, fighting planes, bombers, guns, cannons, and projectiles. The company manufactured 1,300 airplanes and one-fourth of all U.S. aircraft engines.

Car manufacturing resumed after the war, and postwar expansion resulted in increased production. The decade of the 1950s was characterized by automotive sales records and innovations in styling and engineering. The public interest in automatic gears convinced General Motors to concentrate their research in this field; by 1950, all the models built in the United States were available with an automatic gearbox. Car body developments proceeded at the same time and resulted in better sight lines and improved aerodynamics.

During the Korean war, part of the company's production capacity was diverted into providing supplies for the United Nations forces (although to a smaller extent than during the Second World War). The reallocation reached 19 percent and then leveled off at about five percent from 1956 onwards. Between 1951 and 1955 the five divisions which today form General Motors—Buick, Chevrolet, Pontiac, Oldsmobile, and Cadillac—all began to feature a new V-8 engine with a higher compression ratio. Furthermore, the electrical supply was changed from six to the more reliable 12 volts. Power assisted steering and brakes appeared on all car models and the window dimensions were increased to further enhance visibility. Interior comfort was improved by the installation of the first air-conditioning systems. Also during this period General Motors completely redesigned its classic sedans and introduced front seat safety belts.

The period between 1950 and 1956 was particularly prosperous in the United States, with a rise in demand for a second car in the family. However, Americans were beginning to show real interest in smaller European cars. By 1956, a year of decreasing sales, Ford, Chrysler, and General Motors had lost some 15 percent in sales while imports were virtually doubling their market penetration. The longer Detroit's automobiles grew, the more popular imports became. In 1957 the United States imported more cars than it exported, and despite a recession, imports accounted for more than eight percent of U.S. car sales. Although General Motors promised that help was on its way in the form of smaller compact cars, the new models failed to generate much excitement; the company's market share slipped to just 42 percent of 1959's new car sales.

The 1960s were difficult years in Detroit. Riots in the ghettos surrounding General Motors' facilities forced management to recognize the urban poverty that had for so long been in their midst and they began to employ more workers from minority groups. Much of the new hiring was made possible by the expansionist policies of the Kennedy and Johnson administrations. General Motors prospered and diversified; its interests now included home appliances, insurance, locomotives, electronics, ball bearings, banking, and financing. By the late 1960s after-tax profits for the industry in general reached a 13 percent return on investment, and General Motors' return increased from 16.5 percent to 25.8 percent.

Like the rest of the industry, General Motors had largely ignored the importance of air pollution control, but new, costly federal regulations were mandated. However, by the early 1970s, the high cost of developing devices to control pollution was overshadowed by the impact of the oil embargo. General Motors' luxury, gas guzzling car sales were down by 35 percent in 1974, but the company's compacts and subcompacts rose steadily to attain a 40 percent market share. Ford, Chrysler, and General Motors had been caught unaware by a vast shift in consumer demand, and General Motors suffered the greatest losses. The company spent $2.25 billion in 1974 and 1975 in order to meet local, state, and federal regulations on pollution control. By the end of 1977 that figure had doubled.

Under the leadership of president F. James McDonald, and chairman Roger Smith, General Motors reported earnings declines from 1985 to 1992. The only respite came from an accounting change in 1987, which effected an earnings increase. McDonald and Smith attempted to place these losses in perspective by arguing that they are necessary if General Motors is to develop a strong and secure position on the worldwide market. Since the start of the 1980s, General Motors had spent over $60 billion redesigning most of its cars and modernizing the plants that produce them. The company also acquired two major corporations, Hughes Aircraft and Electronic Data Systems (EDS). Though expensive, the EDS purchase provided General Motors with better, more centralized communications and backup systems, as well as a vital profit center.

General Motors' market share dropped steadily from 1982 to 1992. In 1987 Ford's profits exceeded GM's for the first time in sixty years. From 1990 to 1992, the corporation suffered successive and devastating annual losses totaling almost $30 billion. Problems were myriad. Manufacturing costs exceeded competitors' due to high labor costs, over capacity, and complicated production procedures. GM faced competition from 25 companies, and its market share fell from almost 50 percent to about 35 percent.

In 1992 Jack Smith, Jr. advanced to General Motors' chief executive office. He had earned respect as the engineer of GM Europe's late 1980s turnaround, and quickly applied those strategies to the parent, focusing on North American Operations (NAO). During 1993, Smith simplified the NAO, cut the corporate staff, pared product offerings, and began to divest GM's parts operations. He was hailed for his negotiations with the United Auto Workers. In 1993 he pledged $3.9 billion in jobless benefits, which raised the blue-collar payroll costs about 16 percent over three years. But at the same time the contract gave Smith the ability to cut 65,000 blue-collar jobs by 1996 in conjunction with the closure of nearly 24 plants. Salaried positions were not exempted from Smith's job-cutting scalpel: staffing at the corporate central office was slashed from 13,500 to 2,300 in 1992.

In the early 1990s GM began to recapture the automotive vanguard from Japanese carmakers, with entries in the van, truck, and utility vehicle markets and the launch of Saturn Corp. GM also gained an advantage in the domestic market because the weak dollar caused the price of imported cars to increase much faster than domestics. Market conditions along with Smith's strategies effected a stunning reversal in 1993, when GM recorded net income of $2.47 billion on sales of $138.22 billion. The CEO noted his corporation's strategic advantages:

"a large customer base; a large and excellent car and truck dealer network; strong brands; a global presence in engineering, manufacturing, and marketing; a management team with broad international experience; and, most of all, a worldwide team of diverse, capable, and motivated employees."

Principal Subsidiaries: Electronic Data Systems Corp.; GM Hughes Electronics Corp.; General Motors Acceptance Corporation; Saturn Corp. The company also has subsidiaries in the following countries: Australia, Austria, Belgium, Brazil, Canada, Chile, Colombia, England, Finland, France, Greece, Ireland, Italy, Japan, Luxembourg, Mexico, The Netherlands, New Zealand, Norway, Portugal, South Africa, Sweden, Switzerland, Uruguay, Venezuela, Germany, and Zaire.

Further Reading:

Cray, Ed, *Chrome Colossus: General Motors and Its Time,* New York: McGraw Hill, 1980.
Dassbach, Carl H. A., *Global Enterprises and the World Economy: Ford, General Motors, and IBM, the Emergence of the Transnational Enterprise,* New York: Garland, 1989.
De Lorean, John Z., *On a Clear Day You Can See General Motors,* London: Sidgwick and Jackson, 1980.
Hamper, Ben, *Rivethead: Tales From the Assembly Line,* New York: Warner Books, 1992.
Jacobs, Timothy, *A History of General Motors,* New York: Smithmark, 1992.
Keller, Maryann, *Rude Awakening: General Motors in the 1980s,* New York: Morrow, 1989.
——, *Rude Awakening: The Rise, Fall and Struggle for Recovery of General Motors,* New York: HarperCollins, 1990.
Kuhn, Arthur J., *GM Passes Ford, 1918–1938: Designing the General Motors Performance-Control System,* University Park: Pennsylvania State University Press, 1986.
May, George S., *R.E. Olds, Auto Industry Pioneer,* Grand Rapids, MI: Eerdmans, 1977.
Ramsey, Douglas K., *The Corporate Warriors: Six Classic Cases in American Business,* Boston: Houghton Mifflin, 1987.
Rothschild, Emma, *Paradise Lost: The Decline of the Auto-Industrial Age,* New York: Random House, 1973.
Sloan, Alfred, Jr., *My Years with General Motors,* New York: Doubleday, 1964.
Smith, Roger B., *Building on 75 Years of Excellence: The General Motors Story,* New York: Newcomen Society of the United States, 1984.
Weisberger, Bernard A., *The Dream Maker: William C. Durant, Founder of General Motors,* Boston: Little Brown, 1979.

—updated by April Dougal Gasbarre

Giddings & Lewis, Inc.

P.O. Box 590
Fond du Lac, Wisconsin 54935
U.S.A.
(414) 921-4100
Fax: (414) 929-4455

Public Company
Incorporated: 1895 as The Giddings & Lewis Manufacturing
    Company
Employees: 4,041
Sales: $622.9 million
Stock Exchanges: NASDAQ
SICs: 3541 Machine Tools, Metal Cutting Types; 3559
    Special Industry Machinery

Giddings & Lewis, Inc. is the leading manufacturer of industrial automation products and machine tools in the United States and ranks as the fourth largest producer of machine tools in the world. The company's major product line includes automated assembly systems, industrial measurement and control systems, programmable industrial computers, high-precision automated machine tools, and flexible inspection systems. Providing its products to manufacturers from 250 different industries, including the aerospace, automotive, construction, defense, appliance, electronics, and energy industries, Giddings & Lewis serves customers in 70 countries.

Giddings & Lewis traces its history to 1859, when John Bonnell established a machine shop in Fond du Lac, Wisconsin, a focal point of agricultural development and industrial activity during the mid-nineteenth century. Fond du Lac was located at the foot of Lake Winnebago, in close proximity of the railroad lines, and was therefore an ideal location for lumbering operations. Logs were stripped and sawed in preparation for shipment to the growing American markets, and a large number of saw mills were established throughout the area. Moreover, the surrounding farmland proved extremely fertile, prompting the establishment of grist mills to prepare grain for shipment to other states. Such industrialization led to the need for machining and repair work, which Bonnell supplied.

In 1866, having successfully run his shop for six years, Bonnell sold it to George and Horace Trowbridge. The two brothers added a gray iron foundry—the first in Wisconsin—to meet the growing demand for repairs and machinery from local saw mills

and farmers; they named the business Novelty Iron Works. In 1874, the Trowbridge brothers sold the business to Colonel C. H. DeGroat, A. E. Bosworth, and Walter Bigelow. When Bigelow died in 1877, his share of the investment was placed with his estate, and Bonnell sold his interest in the company to David Giddings, who in turn sold it to a relative, George Giddings. In 1880, Giddings purchased Bigelow's interest after his estate was settled, and subsequently sold it to O. F. Lewis.

During this period, the company changed its name from Novelty Iron Works to DeGroat, Giddings & Lewis. Having continued its saw mill machinery business and having expanded into the manufacture of steam engines, the company was rapidly becoming an industry leader. A standard practice for the firm was to make complete installations whenever it was contracted for business. With an emphasis on the quality of its products and a willingness to serve its customers well, the company soon gained national recognition and made installations in Michigan, Minnesota, Maine, Texas, and Washington, as well as Canada. In 1895, due to failing health, Colonel DeGroat sold his share to Giddings and Lewis. Now in partnership, the two men changed the name of the company to The Giddings & Lewis Manufacturing Company, which incorporated under state laws that year.

In 1897, the lumber industry peaked and began to rapidly decline. By the turn of the century, almost all the lumbering activity in the region had ceased, and the company decided to sell its saw mill machinery operation. Shortly thereafter, Giddings & Lewis began to manufacture other machine tools while continuing its foundry and machine shop businesses. Contracted by the municipal government of Fond du Lac, the company provided the city's casting needs for lamp posts, catch basins, and a variety of other items. The firm's first machine tools were also produced during these years, including 17- and 19-inch engine lathes.

In 1910, a controlling interest in Giddings & Lewis was acquired by the Rueping family. The Ruepings had lived in Fond du Lac for years and had built one of the largest tanneries in the country. Under the new president, F. J. Rueping, the company continued manufacturing machine tools, concentrating on different types and sizes of lathes; in addition, Giddings & Lewis manufactured hydraulically-operated shapers, small planers, and six-spindle vertical turret lathes. During the early years of World War I, the British government contracted the company to make a large amount of shell lathes. In addition, the firm began to manufacture horizontal boring, drilling, and milling machines. When the United States entered the war, Giddings & Lewis were contracted by the American government, and the company's staff increased to almost 300.

Immediately after World War I, Rueping reorganized the company under the name Giddings & Lewis Machine Tool Company. Under his direction, the firm expanded its line of boring mills and horizontal lathes to include floor and table type machines with $2\frac{1}{2}$-inch to five-inch spindle diameters. In 1921, Giddings & Lewis purchased the exclusive rights to an automatic internal grinder upon which it made improvements; this product soon became one of the company's best selling items. During this time, H. B. Kraut was appointed general manager and immediately implemented a program for modernizing the plant's equipment and developing several new product lines.

By the end of the 1920s, Giddings & Lewis was the envy of many struggling machine tool companies. Brand new, state-of-the-art machine tools and shop equipment had been installed along with a redesign and expansion of the company's full line of horizontal boring, drilling, and milling machines to include machines with 2½-inch to eight-inch spindle diameters, and floor, table, multiple, and planer head types that ranged from approximately 10,000 to 275,000 pounds.

In spite of the company's success, however, the Rueping family decided to withdraw from active management of the company. Kraut's financial acumen and administrative abilities impressed management, and he was asked to serve as board chairperson and president. Under his direction, the company initiated a thorough modernization of its buildings with the construction of a power house and modern assembly facility. As part of this modernization strategy, Giddings & Lewis decided to discontinue its foundry operations since the variation in casting sizes made it more economical to purchase from outside foundries.

The stock market crash of 1929 and the Great Depression of the 1930s had little effect on the company. In 1934, to continue its program of expansion and modernization, Giddings & Lewis initiated their first public stock offering. The additional capitalization helped the company to complete construction on the machine shop and provided the financial resources for updating machine tool equipment. By 1939, the firm was able to introduce an entirely new and modern design of unusually large horizontal machines with main spindle diameters of six and seven inches, available in floor, table, and planer types.

In 1940, the company's old administrative building and several shop buildings were torn down and replaced with newer structures. Even before the United States entered World War II, Giddings & Lewis was asked by the government to expand its facilities in order to prepare for the amount of material necessary for the war effort. When the war started, the government contracted the company to build a War Department Emergency Plant Facility adjacent to its own plant for the purpose of increasing production of large horizontal drilling, boring, and milling machines. One of the most modern and sophisticated machine tool plants in the United States during that time, the plant covered seven acres and had approximately 150,000 square feet of working space. Business boomed for Giddings & Lewis during the war, and by its end there were nearly 700 full-time employees.

The 1950s were successful years for the company. The American economy was expanding, and Giddings & Lewis benefited from the demand for machine tools from the airline, automotive, and agricultural industries. Having purchased the Davis Tool Company in the mid-1940s, sales of its product line of double cutter block-type tools, rotary tool holders, and boring bars began to increase dramatically. Relocated to Fond du Lac from St. Louis in 1957, the Davis Tool plant underwent a major expansion to meet the ever-growing demands of machine tool manufacturing.

Despite a small recession during the late 1950s, Giddings & Lewis entered the 1960s on a very positive note. The company's financial success was indisputable, and Kraut's leadership kept its facilities running at an extremely high level of production. In 1966, the firm acquired Gisholt Machine Company, located in Madison, Wisconsin. A very old and well-known machine manufacturing operation with its own foundry, Gisholt helped Giddings & Lewis to increase its production capacity by one-third, while adding balancing machinery to the company's product line. Kraut also helped the company win larger and larger contracts with airline manufacturers; in 1966, the product line expanded to include aircraft profilers for 747s, DC-10s, and the brand new SuperSonic Transport. Over 4,300 were employed at Giddings & Lewis by the end of the decade.

In 1970, however, the company began to suffer from one of the worst recessions to hit the machine manufacturing industry. The collapse of Rolls-Royce in England hit metal cutting firms hard and, with regular customers no longer buying tools, Giddings & Lewis began to lose money. Inventory and accounts receivable began to increase, but the company could only collect upon delivery. Sales fell to $95 million, a decrease of $8 million from 1969. With a net loss of $3.3 million, 1970 saw the worst annual financial performance in the company's history. For the first time since the Depression, the board of directors was unable to pay a dividend on its stock.

Kraut immediately implemented drastic cost-cutting measures to weather the recession. Manufacturing payroll was almost cut in half from approximately $13 million to $7 million. Salaries for the company's upper management were reduced by nearly 50 percent; sales related salaries were also halved. Reluctantly, Kraut decided to sell Gisholt in order to save over $3 million in overhead costs, and 1,200 people were put out of work. While this move resulted in a decrease of the company's domestic production capacity by one-third, Kraut ensured that primary manufacturing was not interrupted. Widespread layoffs continued at all levels until the work force was reduced 56 percent to 1,900.

The industry-wide collapse of tool manufacturing continued throughout the decade. Moreover, American manufacturers were challenged by overseas competitors, who had more modern equipment available. Attempting to diversify in 1978 with the acquisition of Basic Electronics Manufacturing Company, Giddings & Lewis still struggled to survive. By the time of Kraut's departure, the firm was in deep financial trouble and without the experienced leadership to turn it around.

In 1982, with increasing debt and antiquated machinery, Giddings & Lewis was acquired by AMCA International, Ltd., a Canadian manufacturing firm. While retaining the facilities in Fond du Lac, AMCA management restructured the tool manufacturer and then ran its operations as a division referred to as the Industrial Automation Segment. Giddings & Lewis drew on the financial resources of its parent company and began to update its equipment, and in 1989 AMCA decided to spin off the firm in a public offering. William J. Fife, Jr., chair and chief executive officer, was given the responsibility of reinvigorating the company in order to lead it back to manufacturing competitiveness.

Fife's stewardship was dramatic: he immediately invested in research and development and started an aggressive campaign to expand the company's customer base. From the time he was hired in 1987 to 1991, sales shot up from $125 million to

$327 million, and operating income increased from $6 million to over $30 million. New orders rose from $143 million to $410 million. The new CEO even paid the company's entire debt of $16 million within the first eight months of the spinoff from AMCA International. In a significant move to promote the company's international competitiveness, Fife also began to market Giddings & Lewis as one of the world's leaders in heavy-duty metal cutting machinery and automated industrial systems.

The resurgence of Giddings & Lewis was facilitated by a general upturn in the manufacturing industry during this time. Manufacturing productivity in the United States increased at an annual rate of 3.6 percent, nearly triple the rate of growth during the entire decade of the 1970s. However, the United States represented only a little over ten percent of machine tool purchases, while Europe, and especially eastern Europe, represented nearly 45 percent of machine tool consumption worldwide. Giddings & Lewis therefore began a campaign to invade the overseas market. In order to bring this campaign to fruition, Fife decided that he needed to increase the productive capacity of his company; the logical decision to make was to acquire another machine tool manufacturer.

In 1991, the company bought Cross & Trecker Corporation, a tool manufacturing firm nearly double the size of Giddings & Lewis. Located in Bloomfield Hills, Michigan, Cross & Trecker had been losing money for years, but its small lathes and auto-parts machining lines complemented Giddings & Lewis's core products. The combination of the two companies catapulted Giddings & Lewis to a number four ranking in the list of machine-tool manufacturers. With its concentration on custom-designed, high-value machines, and its focus on developing into a "total service" automation company, sales for Giddings & Lewis grew to over $500 million in 1992.

In April 1993, due to a disagreement with the board of directors over his financial decision-making, Fife unexpectedly resigned from his position as chair and chief executive officer and was replaced by Joseph R. Coppola. The new leadership honored Fife's strategy of investing in research and development and moving into eastern Europe in order to expand the company's customer base. Comprised of four divisions—Automation Technology, Integrated Automation, Automation Measurement and Control, and European Operations—sales continued to mount for the company. In 1994, Giddings & Lewis ranked as the largest North American industrial automation and machine tool company and one of the largest firms in the world.

Further Reading:

"Hard Times Is Their Best Teacher," *Business Week*, August 14, 1971, pp. 80–1.
Pouschine, Tatiana, "Give It the Gas," *Forbes*, September 16, 1991.

—Thomas Derdak

golden corral

RESTAURANTS

Golden Corral Corporation

P.O. Box 29502
Raleigh, North Carolina 27626
U.S.A.
(919) 781-9310
Fax: (919) 881-4485

*Wholly Owned Subsidiary of Investors Management
    Corporation*
Incorporated: 1972 as Golden Corral Corp.
Employees: 14,000
Sales: $511 million
SICs: 5812 Eating Places

Having started with one small steakhouse, Golden Corral Corporation has grown into one of the nation's strongest family restaurant chains. The ability to adapt to changing tastes has allowed Golden Corral to continue growing as changes in eating habits and increased competition have brought drastic change to the family steakhouse business.

Golden Corral was born in 1973, when James H. Maynard and William Carl were unable to convince Ponderosa, Bonanza, Western Sizzlin', or any of the other major chains that they were financially worthy of a franchise. Undaunted, they mapped out the plans for their first steakhouse in a North Carolina library and raised money by selling shares to friends from high school and college. The first Golden Corral opened in 1973 in Fayetteville, 40 miles from the company's Raleigh headquarters. The motif was western and the emphasis was on meat and potatoes. Patrons raised their hands for their orders when the waitresses, or ''steerettes,'' called out their numbers. During the 1970s, about 90 percent of Golden Corral customers raised their hands for red meat.

The new company counted on freshness to separate itself from other budget steak houses. From the beginning, each Golden Corral restaurant cut its own steaks from fresh, USDA Choice beef. ''Nobody in America at the time was doing that,'' Maynard told *Restaurant Hospitality.* ''We started with a seven-ounce sirloin and ran up to a 12-ounce. We cut top butts, tenderloins, filets, and ribeyes.'' Golden Corral charged only slightly more for its fresh steaks than the other budget chains did for their frozen, imported steaks. The company also set itself apart by focusing on small-town America, opening most of its units in markets with almost no direct competition. Golden

Corral also distinguished itself by avoiding franchising agreements; many Golden Corral managers became partners, owning 20–30 percent of the units they ran.

They may have started on a shoestring, but Golden Corral's cofounders had big plans. ''We set out from day one to do multiple units,'' said Maynard. Using money from sales and lease-backs, bank loans, and internally generated cash, the young company grew rapidly. By 1979, Golden Corral owned more than 100 restaurants. By the end of 1980, the total was 151. The 1982 purchase of 193 restaurants from Sirloin Stockade, a Kansas-based competitor, further swelled the ranks. Approximately 100 Sirloin Stockades became Golden Corrals, either owned outright by the privately held company or managed under the Golden Corral banner through a leasing agreement with parent company Investors Management Corp. By the mid-1980s, there were 430 Golden Corral restaurants. Each unit averaged about 5,000 square feet in size and about $1 million in annual sales.

The company continued to add restaurants and make a profit throughout the 1980s, but increased competition, the recession, and changes in American eating habits threatened to make the steak house a dinosaur. As consumption of red meat dropped and demand for fresh green foodstuffs grew, Golden Corral and its competition first added salad bars and then expanded them. Some Golden Corral units gave up more than 30 seats to make room for salad bars up to 27 feet long. Expanding the dining room added 75 seats but reduced parking. Waste and spoilage shrank profit margins because employees were not trained to handle fresh fruits and vegetables. On top of that, market researchers reported that family steakhouse chains were losing market share to fast-food restaurants and to more upscale chains like TGI Friday's and Chili's.

By 1987, Golden Corral had more than 500 restaurants in 38 states; revenues reached $457 million in 1988. The company never lost money, but as its market share and profit margins grew leaner, Golden Corral—like competitors Bonanza, Western Sizzlin', Quincy's, and Western Steer—began trimming money-losing units. It eventually cut 87 restaurants (although several would reopen as Ragazzi's, an Italian chain also owned by Investors Management). The company also began taking a long, hard look at what it would take to begin growing again.

Leading the company in its new direction were Maynard, now chairman and treasurer, and Theodore M. Fowler, president and soon-to-be CEO. Fowler, who started as an area supervisor in 1977, succeeded Maynard as president in 1982 and as CEO in 1989. (Cofounder Carl left Golden Corral in 1984, but remained a director.) Following a series of strategy sessions in 1988, Golden Corral decided to ask its customers which way it should go. The company hired market researchers to poll current and potential customers on their attitudes about every aspect of ''the experience of eating in a restaurant,'' Fowler told *Business/ North Carolina.* ''We wanted to design a concept better than anything else in the market.''

Golden Corral's late eighties' soul-searching resulted in a number of changes of direction for the company. Most readily apparent to customers was the Metro Market concept. The company hired architect Jerry Cook to design a prototype based on its market research. The first Metro Market, in Lawton, Oklahoma, was a far cry from the dark, wagon-wheeled decor of the earlier Golden Corral. It was light, airy, and large, although at 7,800 square feet it fell about halfway between the older units and the model the company eventually would adopt. Most importantly, it replaced the old salad bar with a U-shaped buffet court that took up about a third of the floor space.

The first seven Metro Market, or GC-10, restaurants opened in 1991. At approximately 10,000 square feet and able to seat 400–440 customers, the new units dwarfed the old, which averaged 5,000 square feet and 175 seats. The centerpiece of the new units was, of course, the food bar, dubbed the Golden Choice Buffet. Entering a cafeteria-style line, customers could still order a fresh-cut USDA choice-grade steak; now, however, they could also opt for any of up to 170 all-you-can-eat items. A typical Golden Choice Buffet might include Salisbury steak, chicken pot pie, fried chicken, shrimp, and meatballs and gravy among the entrees and corn, green beans, carrots, turnip greens, creamed potatoes, and baked potatoes with six different toppings among the vegetables. A health-conscious diner could balance the many fried items with fresh fruit and salad fixings. At the Brass Bell Bakery, the ringing of a brass bell every 15 minutes signaled that more fresh bread, rolls, and pastries were coming out of the oven. For those who saved room, there were plenty of choices for dessert, too.

To many, the new Golden Corral hardly seemed to be a steakhouse anymore. About 80 percent of the customers ordered the food bar, either alone or with an entree. Only about 30 percent still ordered steak. "That's why we call it a steak, buffet, bakery concept," Fowler told *Business / North Carolina.* Whatever they called it, it worked. The average customer spent $5.45 at the first Metro Markets, down from the $6 average at the older units. The combination of menu management and sheer volume, however, boosted annual earnings at the best performing of the newer restaurants to nearly $3 million, close to triple the $1 million average of the old restaurants. In *Restaurant Hospitality,* Fowler explained why the food bar worked. "The genius is to have a lot of great tastes at four cents an ounce, which then allows you to offer more expensive items like chicken wings or shrimp at ten cents an ounce." A large, well-trained staff that kept large numbers of people moving through the lines also helped.

The location of the new restaurants marked another departure for Golden Corral. Moving away from its almost exclusive commitment to small communities, the company designed its GC-10 units for markets of 50,000 or more, although it planned a limited number of smaller and medium-sized restaurants for areas of 18,000 to 35,000 and 35,000 to 50,000 people. In 1993 and 1994, the company estimated that 60 percent to 70 percent of its new units would be Metro Markets. Most of the first wave of new units were located in the southern states of Texas, Oklahoma, North Carolina, and New Mexico.

Another major change was Golden Corral's decision to hitch its growth plans to an aggressive franchising effort. The company took its first tentative steps in this direction between 1988 and 1991, when it franchised some 55 troubled outlets to its most talented general managers. In 1991, it awarded seven new franchises. The franchising effort began in earnest in 1992.

Larry Tate, vice president of franchising, told *Southeast Food Service News* that Golden Corral intended to award 40 franchises that year. "But the concept took off so well," Tate said, "that we closed the year with 102 new franchises." The company planned to open two new franchises and one company store per month in 1993, and boost the total to three franchises and one company store per month in 1994.

To insure that a commitment to franchising did not compromise Golden Corral's reputation for quality and value, the company said it would award franchises only to qualified applicants, train them well, offer them support, and continue to adapt to shifts in customer tastes. The company set its franchising fee at a modest $40,000, but estimated the total commitment involved in opening a new Golden Corral at about $2 million per location. Golden Corral requires potential franchisees to have $300,000 in liquid assets and a net worth of $1.5 million. Previous restaurant experience is necessary, as is the completion of a 12-week training program that teaches a franchise operator every task performed at a Golden Corral restaurant.

As Golden Corral remodeled and expanded, it also reorganized. In 1991, Fowler's management team completed three years of examining the company's corporate structure by giving more decision-making authority to restaurant managers and their regional supervisors. The company added two geographic divisions, for a total of six, and moved the positions of marketing manager, human resources and training director, division administrator, and district manager from its Raleigh, North Carolina, headquarters to the six divisional offices. The changes resulted in Golden Corral division headquarters in Raleigh; Washington, D.C.; Tampa, Florida; Kansas City, Kansas; Dallas; and Houston. Golden Corral's divisional offices also offer support to franchises.

Golden Corral also opened a Center for Training and Development in 1991 to train restaurant managers, prospective managers, and training professionals. The center marked the company's effort to standardize training, which in the past had varied from restaurant to restaurant. It also indicated a growing trend in the restaurant industry. In an economy with a shrinking number of young job-seekers and increased competition, the possibility of training and advancement helps companies attract people with the potential to move into management.

The early returns on Golden Corral's reinvention were promising. Following several years of near-nil growth, Golden Corral's systemwide sales were $449 million in 1991, up 27 percent from 1990. Total sales increased to $481 million in 1992 and to $514 million in 1993. In July 1992, *Restaurants and Institutions* cited the company's emphasis on value when it named Golden Corral one of "10 Great Growth Chains." Earlier that year, the same magazine's "Choice in Chains" survey of 2,500 U.S. households named Golden Corral the best steak chain. According to *Southeast Food Service News,* Golden Corral had also become the largest privately owned company in North Carolina.

In February 1993, Golden Corral celebrated its twentieth anniversary in Fayetteville, the site of the company's first restaurant. During the celebration, company executives emphasized their plans to open 500 new restaurants and triple revenues to $1.7 billion within five years. By the end of the decade, the company planned to celebrate the opening of the 1,000th Golden Corral restaurant. "We want to make Golden Corral the largest family restaurant chain in the world," Larry Tate said.

Later in 1993, IMC announced a five-year development deal that would bring Golden Corral 47 units closer to its goal of 1,000 restaurants. Under the terms of the agreement, Corral Midwest, Inc., agreed to purchase 26 existing Golden Corral units and open up 47 new Metro Market units. Corral Midwest, the largest Golden Corral franchisee, planned to open the new units in Indiana, Illinois, Iowa, Kentucky, Missouri, Kansas, Oklahoma, Nebraska, and Tennessee. IMC, Citicorp Venture Capital, and several members of the Corral Midwest management have ownership stakes in the franchise concern. Golden Corral also announced a 14-restaurant deal with the Winston Group of Atlanta and an 18-unit agreement with Golden Partners of Fort Smith, Arkansas.

The first international Golden Corral opened in Juarez, Mexico, in July 1993. A Juarez investor planned to open five restaurants, and a franchisee in Monterrey, Mexico, planned eight more. The south-of-the-border Golden Corrals will differ from their northern siblings in one important respect—they will serve alcohol.

The many challenges Golden Corral faced as it entered the mid-1990s included maintaining uniform quality as it took on new franchises and planning how to break into the nation's largest markets with a restaurant concept that required 2.5 acres of space. Just above its niche loomed the more upscale steak chains; the cheaper fast-food joints lurked below. The obstacles were many and its goals ambitious, but Golden Corral's ability to recreate itself to meet its customers' desires boded well for its chances of growing into the largest family restaurant chain in the world.

Further Reading:

Carlino, Bill, "Golden Corral Parent Agrees to Franchise Acquisition Plan," *Nation's Restaurant News,* August 30, 1993, p.3; "Down-scaling Concepts to Upscale Profits," *Nation's Restaurant News,* August 30, 1993.

Carlson, Eugene, "Golden Corral Bucks Slowdown With Shift in Direction," *Raleigh, North Carolina, News and Observer,* May 2, 1993, p. F1.

Chaudhry, Rajan, "10 Great Growth Chains," *Restaurants and Institutions,* July 22, 1992.

Douglas, Linda Brown, "Restaurant Chain to Get 47-Store Franchise," *Raleigh, North Carolina, News and Observer,* August 20, 1993, p. C7.

Farkas, David, "The Reincarnation of Golden Corral," *Restaurant Hospitality,* February 1992.

Marshall, Kyle, "Breaking 'Em In at Golden Corral," *Raleigh, North Carolina, News and Observer,* September 25, 1991, p. C8; "Golden Corral Revamps Operations; Restaurants to Get More Authority," *Raleigh, North Carolina, News and Observer,* March 7, 1991, p. C6; "Healthy Vittles at the Corral," *Raleigh, North Carolina, News and Observer,* February 9, 1992, p. 1F.

"North Carolina Restaurant Chain on Aggressive Growth Track," *Southeast Food Service News,* March 1993, p. 1.

Williams, Bob, "Revved Up for Fast Move into Mexico," *Raleigh, North Carolina, News and Observer,* November 14, 1993, p. F1.

Wittebort, Suzanne, "Golden Corral Relishes Lean Times," *Business/ North Carolina,* May 1992, p. 47.

—David B. Rice

the good guys!

The Good Guys!, Inc.

700 Marina Blvd.
Brisbane, California 94005-1840
U.S.A.
(415) 615-5000
Fax: (415) 615-6287

Public Company
Incorporated: 1973
Sales: $503.9 million
Employees: 2,474
Stock Exchanges: NASDAQ
SICs: 5731 Radio, TV & Electronics Stores

As one of the top consumer electronics retailers in the country, and a leading specialty electronics retailer in California, The Good Guys!, Inc., is a dominant force in an extremely competitive field. The company sells televisions, video equipment, laser discs, car and home stereo components, telephones, cellular phones and pagers, cameras, and personal computers. Despite challenges from such powerful competitors as Circuit City Stores Inc. and a recession that damaged many California businesses, The Good Guys! rallied and maintained its edge in the marketplace.

The company was founded in 1973 by Ronald A. Unkefer, who would ultimately become chairman of the board. Unkefer opened his modest television shop in San Francisco's Marina district, a fashionable area frequented by tourists. At first, The Good Guys! was a one-man operation, which led a vendor to ask, "There's only one of you, so how can you be The Good Guys?" The name did not derive from the number of employees, but from a catch phrase Unkefer borrowed from a favorite radio station. As he expanded his staff, he encouraged customers to think of his salespeople as "good guys" who could help them get the best deal on the latest equipment.

Initially, Unkefer did not have ambitions to become a major player in the field of consumer electronics. The Cleveland native had moved to California simply because he wanted to live in the state and run some sort of business. However, as time wore on and new technologies, such as VCRs and state-of-the-art stereo systems, were introduced, he began to see growth opportunities. "It certainly wasn't a grand plan at the time to grow as big as we are now," he reflected in an interview with the *San Francisco Business Times* in 1991, when there were 33

Good Guys! locations. "When I opened up the second store in 1976 I was almost talked into it by a very determined real estate developer."

Unkefer decided to launch the second store to help pay his advertising bills at the *San Francisco Chronicle.* The Good Guys! was well positioned to take advantage of the growth in consumer demand for stereo components in the 1970s, and sales increased steadily each year. Unkefer maintained his low-key approach to business—by 1983, there were only four Good Guys! stores in San Francisco. The company continued to expand its product offerings, adding video cassette recorders for consumers eager to create their own home entertainment centers.

In 1985, the company reported net sales of about $71 million, and a pretax income of $2.25 million. A year later, Unkefer took his company public to fund further expansion beyond the existing eight stores. The Good Guys! had already opened stores outside San Francisco, and was targeting San Jose as the location for its next new store.

The formula for success at The Good Guys! was simple and straightforward from the outset. The company used a combination of extensive promotions and advertising, along with competitive pricing and a broad selection (offering 20 percent more models than rival stores). From the early days, customer service was a cornerstone of the company's strategy. The motto at The Good Guys! was "Our name is our way of doing business."

During the late 1980s, The Good Guys! kept up an aggressive program of growth and expansion. In 1987, the company made its first foray outside the Bay Area when it opened two stores in Sacramento. By this time, The Good Guys! was targeting a decidedly upscale consumer base. According to one retail specialist quoted in Sacramento's *Business Journal,* "It's the type of store in which you would find the owner of a BMW searching for an audio system for his car."

However, even yuppie consumers did not prevent The Good Guys! from having a bad year in 1986. Earnings dropped by nearly 40 percent from the previous year, and the company's net income fell from $2.2 million to $1.4 million. At one point, the stock plunged $3.125 per share. According to Unkefer, the soft market for durable goods—particularly VCRs—and stiff competition were to blame.

For the balance of the decade, The Good Guys! took several steps to boost sales. Feedback from customers revealed that the company's practice of haggling over prices was unpopular and contributed to a "sleazy salesman" stereotype in the minds of consumers. So, in 1987, the company stopped negotiating prices and introduced a lowest-price guarantee. If a competitor offered the same piece of equipment at a lower price, The Good Guys! promised to beat that price. The company also instituted a 30-day, no-questions-asked return policy and upgraded its merchandise mix, focusing on higher-end brands.

These fundamental changes produced the desired results. Net income for 1987 was back up, to $2.6 million. By the end of 1988, sales had increased 24 percent and net income was $3.3 million. The company had 17 stores and planned to open an 18th in Reno, Nevada. The company retained its impressive sales and income figures through the end of the decade, despite the appearance of arch rival Circuit City Stores Inc. in San Francisco in 1989. Circuit City opened a store two blocks from one Good Guys! location. The move worked for, rather than against, The Good Guys!, however. Company President Unkefer noted in the *San Francisco Business Times* that, "We do better where people can compare," adding that his company offered more upscale merchandise and did not offer appliances.

The Good Guys! entered the 1990s flush and prosperous. The company had grown to 30 stores, and sales had increased 51 percent. Net income increased 86 percent over 1989, hitting $7.4 million. The company broke new ground by opening six stores in Los Angeles, a billion-dollar consumer electronics market that is one of the hottest and most competitive in the country. The move brought The Good Guys! toe-to-toe with a dozen major competitors, including Circuit City. Unkefer was confident that The Good Guys! could hold its own, however, noting that the company's success rested on its dedication to customer service.

However, the consumer electronics market is generally among the first to suffer when recession hits, as it did in California in 1990 and 1991. Analysts predicted difficult times in the wake of a shocking 11 percent, industrywide decline in the sale of color televisions during the second quarter of 1990. The Good Guys! did not feel the effects of the recession immediately. Unkefer predicted sales growth of 25 percent per year for the next several years. By the end of 1991, the company had 33 stores and sales of more than $427 million. In addition to such basics as televisions and stereos, The Good Guys! now offered fax machines, video cameras, telephones, and answering machines. With the highest sales per square foot of any consumer electronics chain, it looked like the company might emerge relatively unscathed from the recession.

Sales and net income did continue to increase in the early 1990s, but the gains were more modest than they'd been in the past. In 1992, for example, same-store sales went up only two percent. "The company's goals in this difficult retail climate are to continue to build market share and maintain our sales momentum," Robert A. Gunst, the company's president and new chief operating officer, said in an interview in early 1992.

A softer market didn't curb expansion. The Good Guys! grew to number 44 stores by late 1993, the company's 20th anniversary year. By this time, The Good Guys! was well established as one of the top consumer electronics retailers in the country. In keeping with its customer service credo, The Good Guys! stores featured special listening rooms for speakers and on-site installation of car stereos and speakers, cellular phones, and car alarms. The Good Guys! was consistently ranked as one of California's top companies. In 1993, sales for the now 48-store chain were $552.4 million, a 10 percent increase over the previous year. Net income was $7.6 million.

In a move to further boost sales, reinvigorate growth, and meet consumer demand, the company began selling personal computers in 1993, concentrating on such name brands as IBM, Apple, Compaq, and Packard Bell. With the increase in home offices and advances in information technology, The Good Guys! hoped to catch a wave of demand, as it did in the 1980s with home video products. "We feel it is essential for consumer electronics to participate in the information superhighway, and we believe interactive technology is going to be a substantial part of consumer electronics," said Tom Hannah, senior vice president of stores, in a 1993 interview with the *San Francisco Business Times*. The move was a daring one, given the vagaries of the computer industry and the lingering effects of the state's worst economic problems since the Great Depression. One analyst predicted that the move would ultimately hurt The Good Guys! by diluting the company's focus. After one month, however, The Good Guys! reported that computer sales had exceeded projections.

As The Good Guys! entered the mid-1990s, its future seemed to brighten further. The company opened three new stores in San Diego and repaid customer loyalty with a "90 Days Same as Cash" credit plan for holders of a "Preferred Customer Card." To stimulate consumers to buy electronics, The Good Guys! stepped up its targeted direct mail campaign and offered cross-promotions with the California State Lottery and Tower Records, a regional chain.

The company was rewarded with record second-quarter earnings in 1994. Earnings rocketed up 691 percent over the same quarter for the previous year, and sales increased 37 percent. Cellular phones were a top-selling item, and computer sales were stronger than predicted. As the decade progressed, The Good Guys! remained committed to its aggressive policy of expansion, with plans to open stores in Las Vegas and the Pacific Northwest.

Further Reading:

Carlsen, Clifford, "Good Times for The Good Guys: Addition of Computers Expected to Reboot Growth," *San Francisco Business Times,* November 5, 1993, p. 1; "The Good Guy!: Unkefer Built Chain by Staying Close to Home," *San Francisco Business Times,* October 25, 1991, p. 12.

Glover, Kara, "Two New Consumer Electronics Retailers Will Enter Super-Competitive Southland Market," *The Los Angeles Business Journal,* October 22, 1990, p. 6.

Groves, Martha, "Good Guys Comes South," *Los Angeles Times,* June 25, 1990, p. 1.

Gunst, Robert A., "The Good Guys! Announces First Quarter Earnings and New Chief Financial Officer," *Business Wire,* January 29, 1992.

Martin, Patricia, "Good Guys, Another Electronics Retailer, Rides In," *The Business Journal—Sacramento,* March 30, 1987, p. 3.

Oppenheimer, Richard, "The Good Guys! Reports Record Year-End and Fourth Quarter Results," *Business Wire,* November 12, 1990.

Power, Gavin, "Good Guys Reports Best Second Quarter," *San Francisco Chronicle,* April 26, 1994, p. B1.

Rechtin, Mark, "Future Bright for Good Guys, Despite Tight Field," *Orange County Business Journal,* September 10, 1990, p. 6.

Shaw, Jan, "Who's Going to Go Public? Who Else? The Good Guys!," *The Business Journal—San Jose,* December 30, 1985, p. 1; "Good Guys and Tower Records Combine Forces," *San Francisco Business Times,* May 16, 1988, p. 3.

Soltesz, Diana, "The Good Guys! Are Ready to Ride into San Diego County," *Business Wire,* September 23, 1993.

Weston, Barry, "The Good Guys! Report Financial Results," *Business Wire,* November 14, 1988.

—Marinell James

The Governor and Company of the Bank of Scotland

The Mound
Edinburgh EH1 1YZ
United Kingdom
(031) 442-7777
Fax: (031) 243-5437

Incorporated: 1695
Employees: 17,150
Sales: £1.25 billion
Stock Exchanges: London
SICs: 6012 Recognized Banks; 6111 Financial Institutions

The Bank of Scotland's long history reaches back to 1695 when, uniquely among Scottish banks, it was founded by an Act of the Scottish Parliament; it is today one of the few remaining institutions to be created by that body. The main components of the Bank of Scotland consist of the NWS BANK plc, the group's financial house; the British Linen Bank (acquired in 1971), a merchant banking institution; the Bank of Wales, which serves primarily corporate customers; Kellock, which provides factoring; and the New Zealand Countrywide Banking Corporation. The bank has the reputation among the United Kingdom's financial community as a prudent, conservative bank that confines itself to core banking services while other banks explore new and various operations. At the same time, however, the bank is known as a pioneer of innovative technological services to its customers, making this small but respected bank an unusual blend of tradition and progress.

Scotland in the seventeenth century, with its sparse population of approximately one million people, was economically backwards compared with other European countries. The country's limited economic activity centered on the exporting of such goods as wool, grain, fish, linen cloth, and plaiding, and the importing of such luxury goods as wine, brandy, fine cloths, and lace. Commercial "banking" consisted of Edinburgh's merchants transacting business at the cross in the High Street and of the activities of the city's goldsmiths, who gave loans and bought and sold foreign coins at their booths near St. Giles Kirk. Economic development was also held back by the fact that the country had very little currency of its own; most of the coinage in circulation was foreign, obtained from trade with other European countries, particularly Flanders and France. Otherwise, people used gold, silver, and bills of exchange (prototypes of banknotes), which were drawn on London banks.

As the century drew to a close it became increasingly clear that if Scotland's economy were to grow and prosper to match its European counterparts, a more sophisticated system of raising capital and credit was needed. To that end a group of prominent Edinburgh merchants, aided by John Holland, a prosperous English merchant based in the City of London, proposed the foundation of a bank of Scotland. Although the proposal enjoyed little public support, it was strongly backed by men of influence, including the Lord High Chancellor of Scotland, and so came into being. Unlike the Bank of England, which had been created by the English Parliament the year before, the Bank of Scotland was envisioned principally as a trading bank, established to develop the country's North Sea trade.

On July 17, 1695, the Scottish Parliament passed an act creating The Governor and Company of the Bank of Scotland. With the avowed intention of giving Scotland's first bank a good start in life, the new body was accorded monopoly status and its proprietors (as the shareholders were known) were granted limited liability and allowed tax-free dividends for 21 years. The new bank opened in January 1696, authorized to lend money, discount bills, transmit money to other cities (primarily London and Rotterdam in practice), and issue banknotes from £5 to £100.

Given such a solid foundation by Parliament, the bank nonetheless had a relatively slow start, primarily due to Scotland's shaky political atmosphere at the time. The bank did receive a boost from international tensions in 1705, however, when a French fleet appeared in the Forth. Although it was later dispersed by a storm, its ominous presence led many people to deposit their valuables at the bank for security, thus helping to establish safekeeping as one of the bank's roles.

The Bank of Scotland widened its activities after the 1707 Act of Union with England, overseeing the Scottish Mint and supervising the changeover from Scottish coinage to sterling.

The bank's government-granted monopoly expired in 1716, but it wasn't until 1727 that a rival appeared on the scene—the Royal Bank of Scotland. The clash between the two banks was bitter and long, as each tried to drive the other out of business; however, neither succeeded. In any event, the spread of new banks was inevitable as the Scottish economy improved dramatically: by 1772 there were 31 different banks, each issuing its own banknotes. About this time the Bank of Scotland began to establish branch offices, opening facilities in Dumfries and Kelso in 1774 and in Glasgow in 1787. By 1793 the bank had some 18 branches throughout the country. Despite the ever-growing competition, the Bank of Scotland prospered during the nineteenth century and was prominently involved in Scotland's economic development, helping to build Edinburgh's New Town and playing a significant role in the rapid development of Glasgow as an important industrial center.

Scotland's banks proved their growing power and influence in 1826 when they were threatened by the government's proposal to limit the number of notes in circulation by allowing only the Bank of England to issue banknotes with a value of under £5, requiring other banks to use gold or silver. The move would have been disastrous for Scottish banks, including the Bank of Scotland, as many branches would have been unable to hold such reserves. Such was the resistance to the plan, however (even Sir Walter Scott, writing under the pseudonym Malachi Malagrowther, defended the Scottish £1 note), that the government retreated and Scotland retained its paper money.

By the latter half of the nineteenth century the bank was ready to move beyond Scotland's borders; it established its first English office in the City of London in 1865. Expansion remained severely limited, however; the Bank of Scotland's plans to move into England were thwarted by the 1875 Bank Act, which forbade the establishment of Scottish bank branches in England and vice versa. In 1868 the Bank of Scotland acquired the Perth-based Central Bank of Scotland, the first of a series of acquisitions and amalgamations designed to consolidate and further its position in Scottish banking. In 1907 it acquired the Caledonian Bank, ensuring that it began the twentieth century in a very strong position.

The bank suffered during World War I, not least from a dramatic loss of personnel—it is estimated that of the 4,198 employees who served in the war, 617 never returned. (The bank was even forced to employ women for a time, though it carefully stipulated that it did so only as a temporary emergency measure.) Following a short-lived postwar boom, economic difficulties engulfed the nation. However, the Bank of Scotland not only survived but in the 1920s enjoyed a reputation for being at the forefront of technological modernization of banking procedures. During the 1930s and 1940s this trend continued, as the bank was among the first to make efficient use of telephones, typewriters, adding machines, and the like.

The 1951 Bank of Scotland Act freed the bank from the old system under which it could raise capital only through an act of Parliament, allowing it to operate freely in the commercial market. As the decade progressed, further amalgamations and increasingly sophisticated technology brought success to the bank. In 1955 it merged with the Union Bank of Scotland. Founded in 1830, this bank had itself been active in acquiring other financial institutions, so that, with the merger, the Bank of Scotland gained an additional 200 branches. Three years later the bank acquired North West Securities (which became NWS BANK plc in 1989), a hire purchase finance house, through which it acquired the Industrial Bank of Scotland. In that same year the Bank of Scotland became the first bank in the United Kingdom to employ a centralized electric accounting system.

The 1960s saw little of note in the bank's history, but its course of quiet consolidation and prosperity during these years left the bank poised to take full advantage of the new and superbly profitable opportunity of the 1970s—oil. Via its prominent involvement with North Sea Oil and Gas, the Bank of Scotland became known as the United Kingdom's "oil bank," establishing a department joining oil and banking expertise—and bringing the bank to the international stage for the first time. Prominent involvement with the worldwide energy industry led the way to participation in international banking, and the bank opened offices in New York; Chicago; Houston; Los Angeles; Jacksonville, Florida; Moscow; and Hong Kong.

The 1970s were notable for the Bank of Scotland not only because of what it did but also because of what it did not do. In 1971 the long-standing cartel agreement that had prevented Scottish banks from penetrating into English markets lapsed, but the Bank of Scotland, unlike its old arch-rival the Royal Bank of Scotland, made the decision not to establish a branch network in England. Nonetheless, the bank recognized the need to move beyond Scottish boundaries, and in the 1980s began a campaign of expansion in the South, thus beginning what the *Guardian* termed "one of the extraordinary growth stories of the British banking scene." The bank maintains more than 20 offices in London and in carefully selected provincial financial centers in the South, but prefers to offer services electronically, or provide products, such as the bank's Money Market Cheque Account, which do not require a branch presence. Such is its electronic sophistication that the bank is able to provide banking services accessed from distant locations, frequently arranged through agreements with other financial and retail organizations, including the Automobile Association and Renault. Although in some respects an Edinburgh-based bank perforce suffers drawbacks in the United Kingdom, whose financial heart is London, the Bank of Scotland's strategy was clearly a success; indeed, from the early 1980s to 1993 the Bank of Scotland's share of the U.K. market rose approximately from 2 percent to 7 percent.

The 1980s were a time of expansion in another significant way as, continuing its history of technological awareness, the Bank of Scotland introduced a series of new services. In 1985 it established the first Home Banking System, whereby customers could call up their account details onto their television screens or a computer. The service was expanded the following year to include businesses, creating HOBS (Home and Office Banking Service). In 1987 the bank introduced TAPS (Transcontinental Automated Payment Service), which provides electronic links to worldwide banking systems. In 1986 the bank pioneered the first major credit card to be processed in Scotland.

Despite its name, in the mid-1990s the Bank of Scotland was essentially a U.K. bank maintaining headquarters in Scotland. It operated chiefly as a retail banking service in its native land, with over 500 branches throughout Scotland. International profile notwithstanding, the Bank of Scotland remained committed to its origins. Among other functions, the bank's International Division was active in bringing foreign investment to Scotland. The bank retained strong links with all aspects of Scottish industry, providing financial services and funding to work for a healthy domestic economy. In England, where its customers were principally in the corporate sector, it was known as a financial specialist, well respected for its expertise in project financing and management buyouts. Internationally, the bank provided specialist services. In 1988 it established a subsidiary, FISCOT, created with the three-fold aim of identifying opportunities in international trade and finance; introducing client companies to new markets and bringing them together with new business partners; and facilitating financial transactions across international borders.

Progressing into the 1990s, the Bank of Scotland continued its dual policy of steady but unspectacular advancement and creative technological improvement. Active in commercial lending, the bank continued to finance projects at home and abroad.

It increased its international presence through further joint ventures, including its financing of a retirement community in Florida, a joint agreement with the German Quelle Bank to sell credit cards to Quelle's mail order customers, and an arrangement with a Milan-based company to move into the mortgage market.

In 1993 the Bank of Scotland was the first Scottish bank to introduce banking by telephone services, and also became the first British Visa member to offer customers the opportunity to make international telephone calls using their credit card. The following year the bank improved HOBS, making it possible for customers to conduct their own transactions via a Screenphone. Among other developments the bank also introduced statements in large print or in braille for visually impaired customers.

The bank suffered in the recession of the early 1990s along with every other British bank, but, as the *Financial Times* put it, the "Bank of Scotland has achieved an enviable reputation . . . of being both less accident prone than others, and of running operations efficiently." Still, the bank was particularly hard hit by bad debts in the early 1990s; its subsidiary the Bank of Wales suffered acutely. Its fortunes were once again on the upswing, however, by 1994, as the setback was overcome and profits rose healthily once more. Indeed, the bank was much admired—and envied—for its cost/income ratio, which, alone among U.K. banks, fell under 50 percent.

For the future, the Bank of Scotland planned a course of primarily internal growth, though it had not ruled out the option of further acquisitions—indeed, in 1994 there was much speculation that the bank would acquire a building society. Any such decision, however, would be weighed very carefully by this bank, which has, according to one of the bank's senior managers (as quoted in the *Independent*), "rather a Presbyterian attitude, trying to improve bit by bit without any great leaps forward."

Principal Subsidiaries: Bank of Scotland Treasury Services plc; Bank of Wales plc; British Linen Bank Group Ltd.; Countrywide Banking Corporation Ltd.; Kellock Holdings Ltd.; NWS BANK plc.

Further Reading:

"Bank of Scotland Pioneers Visa Phone Service," *Scotsman,* September 14, 1993.

"Banks Get Phone Message," *Sunday Telegraph,* April 3, 1994.

"Bottom Line: Bank Shares May Have Gone Too Far," *Independent,* October 7, 1993.

A Brief History of Scotland's First Bank, Edinburgh: Bank of Scotland.

Cameron, Alan, *The Bank of Scotland: An Illustrated History, 1695–1995,* Edinburgh: Mainstream, forthcoming.

"Good Growth, Bad Debts for Bank of Scotland," *Guardian,* May 7, 1993.

Hamilton, Fiona, "Scotland in Europe," *Investors' Chronicle,* March 12, 1993, pp. 73–74.

Malcolm, C. A., *The Bank of Scotland, 1695–1945,* Edinburgh: privately published, 1948.

"Markets: Bank that Stuck to Banking," *Financial Times,* May 7, 1994.

"Profits Expected to Improve at Bank of Scotland," *The Times,* May 7, 1993.

"Quality Shines Through," *The Times,* May 6, 1994.

Saville, Richard V., *The Bank of Scotland, 1695–1995,* Edinburgh: Edinburgh University Press, forthcoming.

"UK Company News: A Late Victim of the Recession," *Financial Times,* May 7, 1993.

—Robin DuBlanc

Great Western Financial Corporation

9200 Oakdale Avenue
Chatsworth, California 91311-6519
U.S.A.
(818) 775-3411
Fax: (818) 775-3471

Public Company
Incorporated: 1955 as Great Western Corporation
Employees: 16,016
Total Assets: $38.4 billion
Stock Exchanges: New York London Pacific
SICS: 6712 Bank Holding Companies; 6036 Savings
Institutions Except Federal; 6162 Mortgage Bankers &
Correspondents

True to its name, Great Western Financial Corporation is one of the largest financial services companies in the western United States. It is the parent company of the nation's second-largest savings and loan institution, Great Western Savings Bank. Great Western engages primarily in retail banking and the origination of small residential mortgages, but it also runs operations in consumer finance, insurance underwriting, commercial leasing (a business de-emphasized since 1987), and real estate brokerage. The company has also engaged in a great deal of high-profile advertising in California media markets; it has employed actors John Wayne and Dennis Weaver in successful television and radio commercials, and in 1988 it bought the right to rename the Los Angeles Lakers' home arena, the Forum, the Great Western Forum.

Great Western traces its history back to a savings and loan that began operation in California in 1919. In 1955 a holding company, Great Western Corporation, was formed in Los Angeles to oversee its assets and pave the way for a dramatic burst of acquisition activity. The next year, Great Western changed its name to the Great Western Financial Corporation. It expanded northward when it acquired Bakersfield Savings and Loan (later renamed Great Western Savings of Central California) and southward into Orange County when it acquired Santa Ana Savings and Loan. At the end of its second year in existence, Great Western posted a profit of $4.4 million and had $206 million in outstanding loans.

However, its growth spurt did not stop there. In 1957 Great Western acquired Sacramento-based West Coast Savings and Loan. Over the next two years, it continued to expand its presence in California's Central Valley, acquiring San Jose-based Guaranty Savings and Loan in 1958 and San Luis Obispo-based Central Savings and Loan in 1959. Also in 1959, it acquired First Savings and Loan of Oakland. Thus, within five years, Great Western had gained at least a marginal presence in almost every significant metropolitan area in California.

Soon after, however, the company began to struggle as it digested its new acquisitions. In 1961 Great Western stopped paying its stock dividend. Delinquent loans and foreclosures rose dramatically, reaching $23.2 million in 1964. By 1965, however, the foreclosure rate had dropped just as sharply. Great Western also cut costs that year by merging its three northern California subsidiaries into a single association, First Savings and Loan. In 1965 the company also merged Santa Ana Savings and Loan with Great Western Savings and Loan.

By the late 1960s Great Western had recovered well enough to embark on another dramatic course of expansion. In 1968 it acquired Santa Rosa Savings and Loan in a stock swap. The next year it bought out Los Angeles-based Safety Savings and Loan. In 1970 the company paused to consolidate its three major subsidiaries, merging Great Western Savings and Loan, Central Savings and Loan, and First Savings and Loan.

The pause did not last very long, however, nor did it indicate that Great Western had in any way sated its appetite for growth. Less than a month later, the company acquired Belmont Savings and Loan in a stock swap. In June 1970 it acquired Santa Barbara-based Citizens' Savings and Loan in a stock swap and North Hollywood-based Victory Savings and Loan for $6 million in cash. At the end of the year, Great Western merged with LFC Financial, parent company of Equitable Savings. In 1971 it acquired San Diego-based Sentinel Savings and Loan. Between 1972 and 1974, Great Western merged all of its savings and loan operations into a single subsidiary, Great Western Savings and Loan. In 1973 it liquidated its escrow operations.

Also in the early 1970s, Great Western, along with every other institution engaged in mortgage banking, found its ability to turn a profit challenged by radical changes in the economy. Rising inflation, worsened by the oil price shock, sent interest rates on a steep climb that would last into the next decade, catching mortgage lenders with outstanding loans booked at fixed interest rates that were suddenly below their current cost of funds. Mortgage lenders were faced with the conundrum of how to book 30-year loans in an environment in which interest rates were not only unstable but, it seemed, always on the rise. Great Western responded by pioneering the concept of the variable-rate mortgage, which gave lenders the flexibility to cope with wide variances in interest rates over the long term. By the end of the decade, 60 percent of the company's mortgages were variable rate. Great Western was also quick to jump on the bandwagon when federal regulators approved adjustable-rate mortgages in 1981; by the early 1980s all of the company's new mortgages featured adjustable rates.

In 1979 James Montgomery, a former Price Waterhouse accountant, became CEO. Under Montgomery, Great Western remained decidedly untrendy in a very important way during the 1980s. While other savings and loans expanded aggressively by gobbling up weaker competitors and coped with deregulation of the industry by making high-risk loans and investing in junk bonds, Great Western remained conservative and stuck mainly to booking small residential mortgages. To be sure, the company expanded and diversified some: in 1982 it merged with Northern California Savings, and the next year it acquired the brokerage and real estate services firm Walker & Lee. Nonetheless, Great Western seemed like a stick-in-the-mud compared to the adventurousness of many of its competitors.

By the end of the decade, however, Great Western's decision to stick to what it had always known best had made Montgomery look very astute. While many savings and loans came to grief when their houses of financial cards collapsed, Great Western still stood on a solid foundation. In 1987 the company's equity base was valued at $2 billion, an exceptionally strong 6.9 percent of its assets. That year, it sold off its life insurance subsidiary, John Alden Life Insurance, and terminated its fledgling commercial real estate business. However, it also acquired a profitable consumer finance company, City Finance, and prepared for major expansion throughout the western United States and into Florida. In 1988 Great Western acquired Phoenix-based First Commercial Savings and Loan and a Bellevue, Washington-based near-namesake, Great Western Saving Bank.

Great Western also scored some public relations points in the latter half of the decade. In 1988 it applied to the FDIC to recharter itself as a savings bank, and promptly changed the name of its primary subsidiary from Great Western Savings and Loan to Great Western Savings Bank. The change was largely a semantic one; James Montgomery publicly acknowledged that Great Western was, essentially, a bank that specialized intensely in mortgage lending. However, the change disassociated the company from the growing stigma attached by the general public to the savings and loan industry, which by then had become the beneficiary of a massive federal bailout and the center of some notorious scandals involving institutions that allegedly squandered depositors' funds.

In 1989 the company paid nearly $4 million for the right to place its name on the Forum, the home arena of the NBA's Los Angeles Lakers and the NHL's Los Angeles Kings. As a result of the transaction, the Forum's maroon exterior was repainted blue to match Great Western's logo. A less visible result of Great Western's sponsorship was a friendship between James Montgomery and Forum and Lakers owner Jerry Buss, who gave Montgomery one of his NBA championship rings.

As the 1980s gave way to the 1990s, Montgomery had earned the right to be a little smug about his success. As a guest speaker at a conference sponsored by Michael Milken in the late 1980s, Montgomery took a wry dig at the assembled junk-bond adherents when he noted that he had "built a company, if you'll pardon the expression, with an investment grade." He later said of the audience, who made their livings by hawking non-investment-grade companies to investors, "I'm not sure they all appreciated it." Under Montgomery, Great Western had shunned the opportunity to buy failed savings and loans as a cheap

and dirty way to expand. Instead, when it did acquire competitors, Great Western chose healthy ones and was careful to sell off all nonperforming assets as soon as it could.

As a result, Great Western found itself with a strong balance sheet that allowed it to take advantage when the Resolution Trust Corporation offered two high-profile opportunities for sale. In 1990 it acquired Miami-based CenTrust Federal Savings for $86 million, even after its initial bid of $100 million was refused as too low. The deal gave Great Western 46 branches in its most important new target market. The next year, it acquired Charles Keating's Lincoln Savings, which came to the RTC by way of the most spectacular and scandal-ridden savings and loan failure to come out of the industry's period of crisis, for a mere $12.1 million. Between 1990 and 1992, the company also acquired a handful of other properties: New Jersey-based Carteret Savings Bank in 1990, Florida-based City Savings in 1990, Pioneer Federal Savings in 1991, The First in 1991, and Miami-based Amerifirst Federal Savings in 1992.

Industry observers suddenly realized that Great Western had begun the process of building a national financial services empire centered on mortgage banking. At the same time, a major warning sign had arisen. The slowdown in the California economy, precipitated by major cutbacks in the defense industry, hit homeowners in that state with terrible force. Nonperforming loans rose 30 percent just in the first quarter of 1992, and profits fell 37 percent in the same period. Sluggish demand for consumer loans also magnified the cost of keeping over 1,000 branches and consumer credit offices open.

The company's problems quickly turned some industry analysts against James Montgomery's leadership. They noted that Montgomery, an avid collector of Western art and artifacts, had begun building a log cabin-style third house in Utah, and asserted that he was not paying enough attention to business matters. Problem loans, expressed as a percentage of total assets, rose steadily in the early 1990s, to nearly 5.5 percent in 1993. Much of the problem stemmed from the precipitous drop in Southern California home prices. In order to dominate the low end of the market, Great Western sold heavily mortgages requiring only a 10 percent down payment. The drawback of such loans was that a mere 4 percent drop in the house's value would wipe out the borrower's initial equity, and home prices fell as much as 35 percent in Southern California during this period. As a result, Great Western received defaults at a rate of $100 million per month during 1993.

Nonetheless, the company found the wherewithal to strengthen its position in the San Diego market in December 1993 when it won the bidding for nearly all of the assets of HomeFed Bank and purchased them from the RTC. Great Western had long desired HomeFed's branches and deposits as a way of bolstering its presence in a key California market.

Undeniably, Great Western suffered a setback in the early 1990s on account of the sharp and sudden slump in California real estate prices. As of 1994, its future depended in large part on how effectively and quickly the state's no-longer-golden economy could recover. The company's moves toward geographical diversification, made in anticipation of the day when all restrictions against interstate banking would be lifted, should help reduce its dependence on a single regional market. It may also be said that for a savings and loan company to be left standing at all, much less to be standing large and relatively strong after the debacles of the 1980s, is an achievement to be saluted.

Principal Subsidiaries: Great Western Savings; Consumer Finance Group; California Reconveyance Company; Great Western Financial Insurance Company; Great Western Investment Management Corporation; Great Western Mortgage Corporation.

Further Reading:

Carson, Teresa, ''How Playing It Safe Worked for Great Western,'' *Business Week,* September 7, 1987.

Grover, Ronald, ''Great Western Is Keeping Its Branding Iron Red-Hot,'' *Business Week,* May 11, 1992.

King, Ralph T., ''Great Western Financial Seeks to Chart a Fresh Course,'' *Wall Street Journal,* May 17, 1993.

Lawrence, John F., ''How to Succeed in a Lousy Business,'' *Fortune,* July 3, 1989.

—Douglas Sun

H. F. Ahmanson & Company

4900 Rivergrade Road
Irwindale, California 91706
U.S.A.
(818) 960-6311
Fax: (818) 814-3676

Public Company
Incorporated: 1928 as the H.F. Ahmanson and Company
Employees: 10,318
Assets: $48.1 billion
Stock Exchange: New York
SICs: 6712 Bank Holding Companies; 6035 Savings
   Institutions, Federally Chartered.

H. F. Ahmanson & Company is the holding company for the largest savings and loan institution in the United States, Home Savings of America. Ahmanson has accrued more than $48 billion in assets, almost all of which is derived from Home Savings with its emphasis on financing residential real estate loans. The company weathered the difficulties that many savings and loan institutions fell victim to during the 1980s, but recovered to continue its expansion into heavily populated urban areas throughout the United States.

Howard Fieldstead Ahmanson, the company's founder, was born in 1906. Considered by his father to be a genius by the age of five, H.F. Ahmanson founded the company that bears his name in 1927, even before graduating from the University of Southern California that year at the age of 22. Ahmanson's company specialized in casualty insurance and quickly became the largest underwriter in California. During the Depression, the company prospered by dealing with foreclosures. Ahmanson once remarked that he felt like an undertaker: "the worse it got, the better it was for me." In 1943 Ahmanson bought control of the North American Insurance Company, the company his father had owned but which the family had been ousted from after his father's death in 1925.

After World War II, the housing market took off. Nowhere was this more evident than in California. In 1947, Ahmanson purchased Home Savings of America, a savings and loan association with assets of less than $1 million, for $162,000. Founded in 1889, Home Savings is today the cornerstone of its parent company, H.F. Ahmanson. In the decade that followed, Ahmanson acquired 18 additional institutions, merged them under the name Home Savings, and turned the group into a financial giant. So meteoric was its growth, in fact, that the Department of Justice's antitrust division launched an investigation of the conglomerate in the mid-1950s that was soon dropped.

While involved in this burgeoning savings and loan association, H.F. Ahmanson also formed the Ahmanson Bank and Trust Company in 1957, the National American Title Insurance Company in 1958, and the National American Life Insurance Company of California in 1961.

The company continued to grow at a furious pace until the 1960s, when the housing market began to falter and the federal government began to pass legislation designed to regulate the savings and loan industry. In 1965, the Ahmanson Company wisely shifted its mortgage emphasis from tract housing to apartment buildings and was able to avoid most of the problems that other savings institutions faced. Howard Ahmanson viewed the collapse as good for the industry because homes were being built too quickly. In his plain-spoken way, he likened this industry-wide correction to "a good laxative that cleaned out the system when it could afford to be cleaned."

In 1968, while traveling in Belgium with his wife and son, Howard Ahmanson suffered a heart attack and died. *Fortune* estimated Ahmanson's financial worth at the time at between $200 and $300 million, most of it controlled by trust funds and foundations. The Ahmanson company has been known for keeping a tight lid on the status of its operations, so it is not clear who succeeded Ahmanson as head of the then-private corporation. However, the executives that Ahmanson left in charge of his empire were carefully chosen, and even after his death, the company's reputation for aggressive and shrewd management continued, as did its ability to weather downswings in the economy.

The late 1960s and early 1970s were lean years for the savings and loan industry. A frantic building spree had led to many foreclosures in California and money was tight. Out-of-state money had poured into California because interest rates there were much higher than in the rest of the nation, but as other states began to match California's rates, the money was withdrawn.

By the latter part of the 1970s, investors were beginning to put their money in California institutions again, but in general at this time people were spending more and saving less than past generations. Savings and loans began to look for alternative ways to make money, through consumer lending (such as appliance financing) and loans on properties other than single-family homes. Ahmanson had foreseen these difficulties and had been making loans on apartment buildings since 1965 as a cushion against the failing mortgage market. But Ahmanson did not diversify to the point that would cause the failure of many thrift institutions in the years to come—even into the 1990s the company still did not make auto or consumer loans, leases, or unsecured commercial loans, which tend to be riskier.

Several federal regulations passed during this period proved advantageous to H.F. Ahmanson & Company. A 1968 law ended a nine-year freeze on takeovers by holding companies, and a 1971 rule allowed financial institutions to make loans within 200 miles of each branch office—whereas the old rule had restricted lending to within 200 miles of an institution's headquarters only. Spurred by the easing of restrictions, the Home Savings network soon covered the whole state of California, as four offices were acquired in northern California.

In the 1960s, there was intense competition among savings and loan associations centered around sky-high interest rates and offers of expensive premium items for customers who opened new accounts. In 1966, legislation ended the so-called "rates wars," leaving institutions to rely on their advertising budgets to attract new customers. Not surprisingly, the larger institutions with more advertising dollars to spend prospered and the giants, including Home Savings, gained the power to set loan rates.

The Tax Reform Act of 1969, which called for a reduction of concentrated holdings by foundations, resulted in several stock offerings by H.F. Ahmanson, but the company's financial base was so solid that the sales had minimal effect. A $100 million stock offering in 1972 was a record for the time, yet it only represented 6.4% of the firm's $4.4 billion in assets. After the Bank Holding Company Act of 1970, it was necessary for Ahmanson to sell the Ahmanson Bank, which it did in 1976 to private Philippine investors. However, Ahmanson was able to retain its trust operations as a subsidiary, Ahmanson Trust Company.

Ahmanson's insurance operations, the original business of the company, continued to grow, as Stuyvesant Insurance Group was acquired from GAC Corporation in 1974 and Bankers National Life Insurance Company was purchased in 1981.

Having saturated the California savings and loan market, Ahmanson began to merge out-of-state institutions into the Home Savings network under the name Savings of America. In December of 1981, three mergers were completed in Florida and Missouri; six more in Texas and Illinois followed in 1982. A New York merger was completed in 1984. Subsequent mergers included institutions in Ohio (1985), Arizona (1987), and Washington (1987). At the end of 1987, Home Savings reported $27 billion in assets.

These forays outside California often included expensive, and very successful, direct-mail campaigns. One promotion in Texas reportedly brought in $60 million in one month. But Ahmanson's interstate mergers have also generated some opposition. When Savings of America announced plans to open an office in Berwyn, Illinois, a community known for its proliferation of financial institutions, critics in the industry questioned Ahmanson's motives. An earlier protest to the Federal Home Loan Bank by Illinois officials had been dropped after the company convinced the protesters that Illinois money would not be used for California investments. In any event, as one official said, protests rarely affect regulatory approvals, and the Savings of America branches continue to attract savers by offering interest rates as much as 2% higher than local competitors.

Further penetration outside California continued when, in January of 1988, Ahmanson acquired the Bowery Savings Bank, an institution that was established in 1934 in New York. The 25 Bowery offices continue to operate under their original name.

Ahmanson also strengthened its loan operations in the 1980s by opening lending offices under the name of Ahmanson Mortgage Company in Colorado, Connecticut, Georgia, Maryland, Washington, D.C., Massachusetts, Minnesota, North Carolina, Oregon, Tennessee, and Virginia. Two regional loan-service centers, in California and North Carolina, provided support for the offices.

Richard H. Deihl became chairman and CEO of H.F. Ahmanson in 1983. A company veteran, he joined Home Savings as a loan agent in 1960 and was elected CEO of the subsidiary in 1967. Under Deihl's leadership, Ahmanson avoided the temptation to jump on the bandwagon for the high returns from junk bonds during the mid-1980s, preferring to rely on the safer 1 to 1.5 percent earnings garnered from a home loan. It was a prescient decision. From 1988 to 1990, when hundreds of savings and loans throughout the United States were failing because of their involvement with junk bonds, Ahmanson's deposits grew by 75% and its assets increased by more than 65%. The company's net earnings during the same period averaged more than $200 million per year.

Part of Deihl's success was due to his strategy of streamlining Ahmanson's operating costs. First, the company moved its headquarters to Irwindale, California to take advantage of more space for less money. Secondly, more than 700 employees were eliminated at staff and administrative levels and, as a result, the company lowered its ratio of general expenses to 1.5% of its average assets, nearly one-half point below the industry ratio for the larger savings and loan institutions. Deihl also insisted on adhering to strict criteria for home loans. The average borrower at Home Savings carried a personal debt of 33% of his total income, almost 3% below the standard set by the Government National Mortgage Association. In 1991, approximately 95% of the company's entire loan portfolio was secured by residential real estate properties.

In light of such favorable numbers, Ahmanson continued to expand. In 1990 and the following year, the company purchased Home Savings Bank of New York and also acquired numerous branch offices from Coast Savings' San Diego operation. In 1992, Ahmanson acquired County Bank of Santa Barbara and also changed the names of its savings and loan operations in New York and Connecticut to Home Savings of America. In 1993, the company purchased 24 branch offices from HomeFed Bank.

Yet even with this expansion Ahmanson felt the effects of California's recession during the early 1990s. In 1992, earnings fell to $156 million, partially due to falling property values in the state which led to a substantial increase in nonperforming assets. During the same year, 61% of its mortgage business resulted from refinancings.

Despite these setbacks, Ahmanson remains a successful giant in the savings and loan industry. With a long and distinguished history, and an effective but low-keyed advertising strategy, Ahmanson has garnered a reputation for dependability and safety. Astute and conservative management policies helped the company avoid the catastrophes that hit many savings and loans in the 1980s. Indeed, the company actually prospered in those years by concentrating on what thrift institutions were chartered to do: take in savings and provide loans to people buying homes. If it continued to provide this service, H.F. Ahmanson & Company's role as a leader in the industry seemed assured heading into the late 1990s.

Principal Subsidiaries: Home Savings of America; Savings of America; Ahmanson Mortgage Company; Ahmanson Marketing, Inc.; Griffin Financial Services.

Further Reading:

Barrett, Amy, ''Can A Superthrift Survive On Safety?'' *Business Week,* August 23, 1993.

Murray, Tom, ''It's A Wonderful Life,'' *Financial World,* April 30, 1991.

—updated by Thomas Derdak

Havas, SA

136, avenue Charles-de-Gaulle
92522 Neuilly-sur-Seine Cedex
France
(33) 1 47 47 30 00
Fax: (33) 1 47 47 32 23

Public Company
Incorporated: 1835
Employees: 12,430
Sales: FFr 28 billion
Stock Exchanges: Paris London
SICs: SIC 4833 Television Broadcasting Stations; SIC 2711
    Newspapers: Publishing, or Publishing and Printing; SIC
    7011 Hotels and Motels; SIC 7311 Advertising Agencies;
    SIC 4724 Travel Agencies

As France's largest media and communications group, with a diverse range of businesses and investments in France and abroad, including audiovisual and other media, advertising, tourism, and publishing, Havas has played a remarkably powerful role in the control of information in Europe. In the early 1990s, Havas was the fourth largest pan-European media company, owning France's top tourism agency, retaining a 25 percent interest in Europe's top pay-TV channel, Canal Plus, and having a 45 percent interest in Euro-RSCG, the world's seventh largest advertising group, among other investments. The company has consistently been a major player in news and publicity since its conception in 1835.

The history of Havas may traced to its founder, Charles Havas, a former supply officer in Nantes who, from a very early age, recognized the importance of information as a commodity. While working as a banker and importer in the international cotton trade, Havas gained exposure to the governmental business of translating foreign newspapers, becoming co-proprietor of the newspaper *Gazette de France* from 1813 to 1815. When Louis-Philippe proclaimed freedom of the press in 1830, Havas was convinced that the traffic of news could be organized and made public.

In 1832, Havas founded Bureau Havas in Paris to supply the rapidly growing number of French newspapers with translations of foreign publications. In 1835, he added the service of translating French publications for foreign newspapers, and the bureau was renamed Agence Havas, an international press agency. From the onset, the agency recognized the importance of being the quickest to supply news to the press and was constantly exploring new methods of transporting information, from carrier pigeons to the electric telegraph. Moreover, Havas founded his company with a belief in cooperating with the government in order to gain financial support, avoid conflicts, and have exclusive access to governmental information. This status as official government supplier of news both facilitated the company's enormous success over the following 150 years and caused much corruption, exploitation, and public mistrust of the media until the end of World War II.

In 1851, in addition to operating a successful press agency, Havas founded the first publicity agency in France. Despite the limits imposed upon the press under the Second Empire, Havas prospered during the great commercial and industrial expansion of the era. The company's success and power stemmed from the faith that the French government, business community, and press had in its services, as well as from its expansion into newspaper circulation, improvements in the telegraph, and the increasing importance of public opinion. When Charles Havas died in 1858, his sons assumed control of the business and inherited their father's belief in the need to be a loyal instrument of the state in order to retain the agency's monopoly on information. In 1862, Auguste Havas finalized an agreement with the Minister of the Interior to make Havas the exclusive diffuser of official news.

During this time, Paul-Julius Reuter, a former employee of Havas, opened a press agency in London, while another former Havas worker, Bernhard Wolf, opened a similar office in Berlin. By 1856, Havas, Reuter, and Wolf had signed an accord to exchange information and cooperate to exploit future markets, while still retaining monopolies in their respective regions. Following attempts by German statesman Otto von Bismarck to retain control of the German-language press, Havas, Reuter, and Wolf signed a new agreement in 1869, establishing new geographic domains for each agency. Wolf controlled Austria, Scandinavia, and Russia, while Reuter covered England, Holland, and their dependencies. France, Italy, Spain, and Portugal became the domain of Havas. Reuter expanded into Australia, Egypt, the Antilles, and the Far East, while Havas established itself in South America and Indochina. Since 1867 when the transatlantic telegraph cable linked London and New York, the United States was declared neutral, with each agency establishing relationships with clients and collecting news independently. Each agency signed a separate accord with the American Associated Press. The three agencies retained close ties to one another in order to discourage the foundation of competition.

During the Franco-Prussian War, the exchange of news between Havas and Wolf took place through Reuter in London. With the siege of Paris by the Prussians, Auguste Havas installed himself in Tours, and Havas Paris depended upon Gambetta's hot-air balloons to communicate the news of the besieged capital to the rest of France and abroad. The Prussians released falcons to intercept the messenger pigeons used by Havas Paris to get news from Tours. During the Paris Commune of 1871, the insurgents took control of the Havas dispatches. Auguste Havas returned to Paris immediately after the Commune fell. By this time, 24 of 164 parts of Havas's press agency division were controlled by Auguste Havas and his son. The remaining divisions were in the hands of industrialists, politicians, and businessmen, whose connections played a large role in Havas's success.

Auguste Havas sold the business to Emile d'Erlanger, an international financier, and, in 1879, the company sold stocks to the public. The agency's international network expanded yearly and was enjoying exceptional prosperity by 1881. Havas's threefold function as press agency, publicity agency, and liaison between the government and the business community made the company very appealing to investors. The company was expanding in France, adding newspapers in Lyon, Lille, Marseilles, Toulouse, and Dijon. Havas's commercial activity increased tenfold, and its connections to influential financiers were augmented by its involvement with the Banque de Paris et des Pays-Bas (Paribas). This period in the company's history was marked by efforts at discretion in relation to its customers and at trying to follow government objectives without losing journalistic credibility, despite a climate of journalistic corruption.

During this time, the publicity division of Havas made an agreement with the Compagnie Générale de Publicité Étrangère, facilitated by an American, John Jones. Like the accord between Reuter and Wolf in 1856, the new agreement divided the publicity market geographically to avoid a price war. Havas won exclusive rights to publicity in Spanish, Portuguese, and Russian newspapers, while Jones retained rights in Dutch, Scandinavian, Danish, and Austrian journals. Hungarian, Swiss, and Belgian customers were shared equally so that competition remained only for British customers.

In the figure of Léon Rénier, Havas found a natural leader who played a major role in establishing the company as a powerful and diversified news monopoly. Under Rénier, Havas and Paribas invested in telegraph communications linking France with northern Europe, the Antilles, and the United States. Rénier played a large role in Havas's contract for exclusive advertising in the Parisian subway system and at kiosks in Paris. As the number of daily newspapers with large circulations increased and the business of publicity grew larger, Rénier made Havas a more dynamic enterprise and became one of the most powerful men in France.

The immense power Havas wielded in the media was evidenced by the fact that most newspapers depended so completely on Havas dispatches for national and international news that they did not maintain their own offices in Paris. The philosophy of efficiency and speed of dispatches upon which Havas was founded continued through the agency's progressive use of the telegraph and the telephone. One example of the company's commitment to efficiency involved the dispatching of news on the Dreyfus affair at Rennes in 1899. To obtain news about the trial of the alleged traitor, Alfred Dreyfus, Havas employed cyclists to pedal between the Palais de Justice and the central telegraph agency, and maintained a telephone at the stock exchange, incurring costs of Ffr 1 million.

Around the turn of the century, Havas became the privileged intermediary for financiers and foreign governments seeking to influence French public opinion discretely through the press. For example, after Russia borrowed money from French banks in the last years of the nineteenth century, the revolutionary events of 1905 in Russia were smoothed over by reassuring dispatches by Havas. The banks, including Paribas, made big profits by avoiding public anxiety about the loans, which amounted to 80 percent of Russia's public debt. Havas also received FFr 1.5 million from Banque Périer and Banque Impérial Ottomane to assure support in Parisian newspapers for loans to the Turkish government. According to Antoine Lefebure in *Havas, les arcanes du pouvoir,* Havas was one of the principal instigators of corruption of the French press by foreign governments. This corruption had limited political consequences during the time, but that was not to be the case in the next century.

In January 1914, Société Générale des Annonces, a joint stock publicity company, became part of Havas, which then came under the control of the Syndicat Central de Publicité, whose sole purpose was to control the publicity of the four big Paris newspapers. In each of these four papers, *Le Journal, Le Matin, Le Petit Journal,* and *Le Petit Parisian,* the Syndicat Central de Publicité and Léon Rénier played major roles. With Rénier's election as head of both Havas Information and Société Générale des Annonces, press and publicity became even more united within the company. With the beginning of the war in 1914, the need to control public opinion became all the more important. Havas took part in propaganda campaigns against the Germans and received FFr 6 million from the French government for propaganda distribution. The agency received money from Greece in 1919 and from Yugoslavia in 1920 to influence the French press in their favor against Italy.

The postwar period was very profitable for Havas, despite the corruption scandals and the high amount of government involvement in the press. The agency added newspapers in Mulhouse, Nice, and Bordeaux to its publicity administration. Paribas increased its influence in Havas and took part in that company's move to increase capital by selling stocks. While the agency did by no means have a monopoly on the publicity market, it did expand its business after the war by combating a general mistrust of advertising in France. In 1931, advertising budgets in France were eight times less than in the American market. Havas therefore took a more subtle approach with its clients by avoiding newer media, such as radio. Big businesses did not want to appear to be directly controlling the press, and so Havas played the role of intermediary between the press and the business community, protecting the anonymity of companies. The agency also influenced the contents of a newspaper to benefit such clients as the government, banks, and small companies. The French government, which relied on the press for its own electoral motives, did not intervene in these manipulations of publicity.

After World War I, Rénier convinced the publishers of the five largest Parisian dailies that competition for publicity could damage their profitability, and the five papers gave over to Havas their publicity offices, with a percentage of their capital being put aside for operations of common interest. As the meeting point of political groups and powerful financiers, Havas and this publicity consortium played a powerful role in French politics between the wars. One formidable competitor was François Coty, who had made a fortune in perfumes before he began to construct a newspaper empire. When Havas and its consortium refused to distribute, print, or sell any of Coty's journals, they was forced to pay FFr 14 million in damages for unfair competition. By 1934, however, Coty's empire had disintegrated, and Havas bought him out.

The hegemony of this consortium limited the diversity of the press, which was mostly controlled by political conservatives. A Socialist movement, led by Léon Blum, who served as premier from 1936 to 1938, denounced Havas for its omnipotence, manipulation, and corruption. Citing the American example, Blum called for a separation of news and publicity and for the publication of newspaper budgets without secret financing by foreign governments. Rénier agreed to the latter regulation and agreed to cooperate with Blum's government if the agency was not dismantled. Blum accepted, and Havas received the contract for the publicity of the 1937 World Exposition.

With the beginning of World War II, the accord between Havas, Wolf, Reuter, and Associated Press ended. Wolf became a propaganda office for the Nazi regime, and Havas's correspondent in Germany was expelled from the Reich by the Gestapo. Abroad, Havas's offices became press agencies for the French embassies. The consortium of five Parisian dailies was dismantled, and Havas came upon difficult financial times. By 1940, many of its former clients were no longer advertising; on June 9, 1940, the French government retreated to Tours, and the next day Havas suspended its news service.

The occupying German forces considered Havas an agent of French propaganda and forbade its operations in the occupied zone while taking over a large share of its stock. Moreover, Havas was forced to agree to the harsh regulations imposed upon it by the Vichy government in 1940. The agency was both careful not to offend Hitler or Mussolini and anxious to reinforce its ties to Vichy, creating an ''official propaganda'' service to run ministerial publicity. Despite the adverse conditions, Havas's capital increased from FFr 300 million in 1942 to FFr 400 million in 1943. The company's collaboration with the Vichy government and the Germans was an effort to protect the company's interests and investments, which had increased before the war. However, in the postwar movement of nationalization, Havas and Rénier were seen as open participants in economic collaboration with the occupiers, as well as instigators of corruption under the Third Republic. Called a traitor, Rénier was replaced by Jean Schloesing, who set about reestablishing Havas's reputation. In 1944, Havas was nationalized, with the French government controlling the stocks previously held by the Germans.

By 1947, the agency had a FFr 62 million deficit and was competing with Publicis for advertising clients. In these difficult years, Havas finally eliminated editorial work from its press agency and separated information activity from publicity. The final split between news and publicity came in 1959, when Jacques Douce was named commercial publicity director. Havas's president Jean Chevalier focused the agency's opera-

tions on private industry to offset the business it no longer conducted with the government. The company also invested in travel agencies, cinema, and radio.

By 1952, Havas's publicity contracts reached 1938 levels, and from then on, contracts doubled every ten years. By 1972, the publicity market in France was seven times larger than prewar levels, due to the explosive expansion in television, radio, news weeklies, and industrial investment in publicity. In 1974, Douce created Eurocom, a publicity subsidiary of Havas, and, in 1978, Havas agreed to develop new media interests with its direct competitor, Publicis.

On November 4, 1984, Havas president André Rousselet launched Canal Plus, the first cable television station in France. While some observers were surprised that the top publicity group in France would become involved in a medium that needed no outside publicity, Rousselet hoped that the innovative move would open up a potentially profitable market. In 1985, President François Mitterand announced the opening of private commercial television channels, and Canal Plus's subscription rate declined sharply. However, the channel continued in operation, and, with aggressive advertising and competent management, Canal Plus became one of the biggest French audiovisual successes of the 1980s.

In 1986, with French President Edouard Balladur's plans for massive privatization, publicity contracts poured into Eurocom. Havas, itself, was privatized in 1987, ending 40 years of government control. In 1988, American Robert Maxwell bought almost five percent of Havas in his quest for a French communications acquisition. Also that year, Rousselet left Havas to head Canal Plus, in which Havas had gained a 25 percent interest by 1992. Publicity skyrocketed for Havas in the 1980s, as revenues from television advertising doubled between 1983 and 1989. The company showed less expansion in areas in which it had traditionally been successful, such as information and newspaper publicity.

During this time, Havas made investments in cinema through Canal Plus and took part in several large acquisitions, including the publicity group RSCG (Roux, Séguéla, Cayzac, Goudard) in 1992, which made Euro-RSCG the seventh largest publicity group in the world. In the early 1990s, with the international recession, business slowed, and the publicity market weakened due to depressed consumer spending.

Nevertheless, in 1992, Havas was France's largest media and communications group, comprising a wide range of business and investments, including local and audiovisual media, international multimedia sales, tourism, full-service advertising, and publishing. With the deregulation of European television markets, Havas emerged as one of the top four pan-European companies. While Europe remained the company's first priority, Chairperson Paul Dauzier announced plans to expand aggressively outside of France. Euro-RSCG opened an office in Poland in 1992 and reorganized its offices in the United States. Havas's publicity department took part in a joint venture with Czechoslovak Television to bring Western commercials and programming to Czechoslovakia and made similar arrangements with Magyar Television in Hungary.

The flexibility and diversity that Havas exhibited in the second half of the twentieth century were expected to help ensure its future success in the industry. Moreover, the company's position at the forefront of communications in France and throughout Europe seemed stable, due largely to the wide range of business in which it was involved, the broad geographical spread of its activities, and its continual innovation in new media.

Principal Subsidiaries: Havas Voyages; Avenir Havas Media Group (97%); Euro RSCG (45%); Eurocom (44%); C.E.P. Communications (40%); Canal Plus (25%).

Further Reading:

Bruner, Richard W., "E. Europe Attracts Media Magnates," *Advertising Age,* July 16, 1990, p. 27.

Kasriel, Ken, "Feeling Heat in Hungary: Havas Unit's Media Venture Sucked into Power Struggle," *Advertising Age,* January 18, 1993, pp. 1–6.

Lefebure, Antoine, *Havas, Les arcanes du pouvoir,* Paris: Bernard Grasset, 1992.

Rosenbaum, Andrew, "Havas to Know No Boundaries," *Advertising Age,* June 25, 1990, p. 36.

—Jennifer Kerns

HILLENBRAND INDUSTRIES

Hillenbrand Industries, Inc.

700 State Route 46 East
Batesville, Indiana 47006
U.S.A.
(812) 934-7000
Fax: (812) 934-6630

Public Company
Incorporated: 1969
Employees: 9,800
Sales: $1.45 billion
Stock Exchanges: New York
SICs: 2599 Furniture and Fixtures; 3429 Hardware, Nec;
  3841 Surgical and Medical Instruments; 3995 Burial
  Caskets; 7352 Medical Equipment Rental and Leasing;
  6311 Life Insurance; 6719 Offices of Holding Companies,
  Nec

Hillenbrand Industries, Inc., is the largest manufacturer of caskets and hospital beds in the world, and also supplies a variety of health care equipment and funeral planning services. Teamwork and product innovation were key elements in the dynamic growth that brought company revenues to $1.45 billion by 1993. Hillenbrand is among the 300 largest industrial corporations in the United States.

"The first generation starts a company, the second builds it, and the third generation destroys it," recalled August (Gus) Hillenbrand, president and CEO of Hillenbrand Industries, in the *Cincinnati Business Courier* in 1993. A family friend had offered those words in jest to Hillenbrand when he was boy. "That has just stuck with me all my life . . . and that's why we work so dang hard." Indeed, in the mid 1990s Hillenbrand was sustaining a legacy of success which his grandfather, John A. Hillenbrand, initiated in the late 1800s.

John A. Hillenbrand's father, a German immigrant and woodworker, settled in the German-speaking community of Cincinnati, Ohio, before the Civil War. He was soon drawn, however, to the enormous timber stocks of southeastern Indiana. Shortly after moving to Batesville, Indiana, in 1861, the 16-year-old Hillenbrand found himself orphaned with two infant sisters. Realizing that timberland was abundant and inexpensive in comparison to farmland, he abandoned his family's unprofitable farm and began purchasing small sections of woodland. He cut

and sold the rich hardwood to the railroads for track ties, and then sold the cleared land to farmers.

Like his father, John A. Hillenbrand combined hard work and ingenuity to create several Hillenbrand family enterprises, including a general store. In 1906 Hillenbrand seized an opportunity to rescue the Batesville Casket Company, a local casket manufacturer, from bankruptcy. He employed German woodworkers, carvers, and cabinet makers to craft his high quality coffins, and used his business acumen to turn the company around. Steady coffin demand, a swelling population, and Hillenbrand's success at increasing his share of the regional casket market allowed the company to realize healthy profit growth throughout the early twentieth century.

Part of John A. Hillenbrand's unique recipe for success was close cooperation with his four talented sons. For example, John W., the eldest son, eventually assumed his father's role as president, and guided company expansion during the mid-twentieth century. George C. became the company's manufacturing genius. His numerous patents and his insistence on continuous product improvement made innovation a Hillenbrand hallmark. Daniel A., the youngest son, is credited with extending the company's reach nationally and, during the late twentieth century, globally.

William A., the second oldest son, vastly broadened the scope of the Hillenbrand operations into the health care field. In an attempt to start a furniture business, he founded the Hill-Rom Company in 1929, during the Great Depression. Determined to set himself apart from other furniture makers, William decided to enter the hospital market. He spent almost a full year visiting hospitals throughout the United States to determine how he could improve furniture in patient's rooms. The end result was his development of the first wood and metal hospital bed, which soon replaced the prevailing white tubular steel beds.

Hill-Rom, a division of Hillenbrand Industries, prospered along with the Batesville Casket Company during the 1930s, and especially during the post-World War II economic expansion in the United States. The company combined high-quality hardwoods, including cherry, mahogany, oak, and walnut, with expert craftsmanship and design to broaden its share of regional casket and hospital bed markets. Importantly, though, it was the companies' completely new product innovations that vaulted them past their competitors.

In 1940, for example, Hillenbrand pioneered the mass production of metal caskets, which became considerably less expensive to manufacture than traditional wooden coffins. The company eventually integrated stainless steel, bronze, and copper into its products. Metal caskets, many of which are warranted against corrosion for 75 years, grew to dominate U.S. coffin sales. By the 1990s, wood caskets represented only 15 percent of global industry sales.

Hillenbrand also led changes in the hospital furniture business. In 1950, for instance, Hill-Rom introduced the first electronically-controlled bed. A slew of advancements followed, such as beds that monitored patients, maternity beds, and special beds for burn victims. The company boasts that it has developed virtually every meaningful innovation in the hospital room furniture and equipment industry since World War II.

Besides high-quality materials and craftsmanship, inventiveness, and family cooperation, other important factors influenced Hillenbrand Industries' success. For example, the company prides itself on a heritage of fiscal responsibility. Prudent management allowed the Hillenbrand brothers to expand the company almost entirely from cash flow instead of debt. Even during the 1980s, when many other corporations were assuming large debt loads, Hillenbrand minimized its debt ratio. The Hillenbrand family retained a 60 percent ownership share of the corporation in 1993.

The company attributes its past achievements to a strong work ethic and a cooperative relationship between management, labor, and the local community. Hillenbrand has poured millions of dollars into the local community, and in 1993 employed about 60 percent of Batesville's 4,500 residents. "If it weren't for the Hillenbrands, this wouldn't be the town that it is," remarked Mary Gauck, a 20-year Hillenbrand veteran, in the *Cincinnati Business Courier.* "We wouldn't have the YMCA, the swimming pool, or the library." In explaining his company's success, Gus Hillenbrand complemented Gauck's remark: "The work ethic [in Batesville] is phenomenal."

After serving as president of the Batesville Casket Company for seven years, Daniel took the reins from his eldest brother in 1971 when he became chairman of the board of Hillenbrand Industries. In an effort to continue his brother's successful leadership and to parlay the company's numerous competitive advantages into new achievements, Daniel sought to expand Hillenbrand's market presence.

Besides taking the company public in 1971, Daniel led the company into completely new arenas. The company purchased American Tourister, Inc., of Warren, Rhode Island, in 1978. American Tourister was a major U.S. luggage manufacturer with a reputation for producing high-quality, affordable goods. In 1984, Hillenbrand made Medeco Security Locks, Inc. of Salem, Virginia, the fourth company operating under its corporate umbrella. Medeco was a leading producer of high-performance locking devices and security systems.

In 1985, Hillenbrand entered the insurance business when it organized the Forethought Group, Inc. This group of companies was established to provide advance funeral planning services, in the form of insurance policies, through funeral homes. In a bid to increase its health care presence, Hillenbrand also purchased SSI Medical Services, Inc. of Charleston, South Carolina, in 1985. SSI was a leading provider of specialized therapeutic products and services. By 1994, SSI and Hill-Rom were being integrated under the Hill-Rom name.

Hillenbrand's diversification strategy began to pay off in the late 1970s and early 1980s. As revenues multiplied from about $60 million in 1970 to over $325 million in 1980, the company's net income surged from less than $10 million per year to $25 million. Moreover, by 1985 the company netted almost $35 million in income from about $440 million in sales.

Besides new lines of business, Hillenbrand's profit growth during the 1980s reflected the continued success of its core casket and hospital furniture segments. New products and manufacturing techniques allowed both Hill-Rom and Batesville Casket Company to achieve greater market dominance. Hill-Rom

broadened its product line to include items such as infant warmers, special stretchers, and nurse communication systems. Its hospital bed offerings grew to encompass a variety of specialty devices, like critical care beds, sleep surfaces for ulcer patients, and birthing beds.

Like Hill-Rom, the Batesville Casket Company increased its offerings during the 1980s to include over 400 products sold to more than 16,000 funeral homes. By the end of that decade, the company was manufacturing caskets in several states, including Kentucky, Mississippi, New Hampshire, and Tennessee. Its Kentucky plant, which employed advanced robotics, was one of the world's most automated metal casket production facilities.

Hillenbrand also developed new marketing techniques during the 1970s and 1980s, emphasizing customer service and satisfaction. The company's sales pitch to prospective hospital furniture clients often entailed a trip to Batesville, a stay at a company farm and conference center, and product demonstrations between rounds of food and drink. Similarly, the company hosted thousands of funeral directors annually at its Batesville headquarters.

As Hillenbrand widened its scope, improved its products, and boosted marketing efforts during the 1970s and 1980s, it also benefitted from favorable demographic and economic trends. The number of annual deaths in the United States rose about 12 percent between 1970 and 1990, resulting in gradual growth in the combined demand for caskets and cremation products and services. Furthermore, U.S. expenditures on hospital beds and other medical equipment rose at a rate of roughly 15 percent per year throughout much of the 1970s and 1980s.

When Gus Hillenbrand replaced his uncle as president and CEO of Hillenbrand Industries in 1989, he presided over the culmination of 83 years of immense growth and prosperity. His grandfather's fledgling casket business had grown into a national corporation with six separate operating companies and nearly 10,000 employees. Hillenbrand's 1989 net income topped $71 million, as revenues vaulted past $870 million, up an extraordinary 98 percent since 1985. Furthermore, the Hillenbrand umbrella could boast dominance of over 90 percent of the entire U.S. hospital bed market and over 30 percent of the total casket business.

In addition to its business accomplishments, the Hillenbrand organization had also achieved success in its local community. Aside from donating money for various recreational and educational facilities and contributing the lion's share of Batesville's operating budget, Hillenbrand prided itself on emphasizing employee satisfaction and personal development. Indeed, the Hillenbrand family was credited locally with having a direct and positive impact on the lives of the Batesville citizenry.

Motivated in part by the prophetic jest of his childhood—that the third generation destroys a company—Gus Hillenbrand entered the 1990s determined to quash that Germanic myth. To boost sales in its casket division, for example, Hillenbrand initiated an aggressive campaign in the early 1990s to expand into its first line of cremation products and services. It also strove to elevate its presence in the African-American and Hispanic burial market.

To jump-start shipments in the slowing hospital furniture market, Hill-Rom focused on the development of niche products. One of the company's most notable achievements in 1993 was its introduction of the first voice-activated control system for hospital beds. Using a new high-tech attachment, a quadriplegic patient, for example, could operate the bed, call a nurse, adjust a television or radio, make a telephone call, or activate a light switch. The system was designed to pick up sounds from only one direction, and can be trained to respond only to the patient's voice.

In 1991 Hillenbrand acquired Block Medical, Inc., of Carlsbad, California, a leading manufacturer of infusion pumps. Block introduced a portable home infusion pump and was experiencing significant productivity gains under Hillenbrand management.

Perhaps Gus Hillenbrand's greatest aspiration was the globalization of Hillenbrand Industries. To continue the 16 percent revenue growth rate that the company had averaged since 1972, he believed that Hillenbrand would have to expand its international presence. In 1991, Hill-Rom acquired French manufacturer Le Courviour S.A., a leading European supplier of hospital beds and furniture. In 1993 Batesville Casket Company acquired leading casket producers in both Canada and Mexico, strengthening its dominance of the North American market, and in 1994 Hill-Rom bought L. & C. Arnold S.G., a major German hospital manufacturer.

Although burgeoning domestic markets and proliferating global opportunities boded well for the company, a few impediments threatened to slow Hillenbrand's momentous growth. Federal proposals for government intervention in the U.S. health care system, for example, meant that technological advancements in the Hill-Rom and SSI subsidiaries might require more extensive government approval before health care providers could purchase their equipment. In addition, the entrance of Michigan-based Stryker Corp. into the hospital bed market posed a potential threat to Hill-Rom's command of that segment.

Hillenbrand jettisoned its lagging American Tourister division in 1993, while its Medeco lock company benefitted from renewed consumer spending and concerns about crime during that year. Late in 1993, Hill-Rom became the target of a federal antitrust probe. Noting its almost unequaled reputation for integrity, analysts suspected the charges were of little relevance.

Despite minor hindrances, Gus Hillenbrand's multi-faceted growth strategy successfully guided the corporation through the perilous early 1990s. Indeed, Hillenbrand's unprecedented growth and profitability between 1989 and 1993 seemed almost staggering, particularly in light of a relentless world economic recession that lingered into 1993. Sales jumped an impressive 13 percent in 1990 and 10 percent in 1991, to $1.08 billion, and 1991 net income jumped 18 percent, to more than $89 million. In 1992, moreover, net income rocketed 30 percent as sales ballooned to more than $1.30 billion. Explosive growth continued in 1993, as sales jumped 11 percent to $1.45 billion and net income soared 25 percent to $146 million. About 40 percent of the company's revenues came from its funeral-related subsidiaries, while the other 60 percent were derived from health care divisions.

As the company prepared to enter its ninth decade, management was focused on sustaining Hillenbrand's legacy of growth and profitability. Hillenbrand's corporate vision was based on four equally weighted and fundamental principles: niche market leadership, total customer satisfaction, continuous improvement, and individual worth. The company's strong equity position and market dominance added credence to these goals.

Principal Subsidiaries: Batesville Casket Company, Inc.; Block Medical, Inc.; The Forethought Group, Inc.; Hill-Rom Company, Inc.; Medeco Security Locks, Inc.

Further Reading:

Boyer, Mike, "Hillenbrand Plans to Sell American Tourister," *Cincinnati Enquirer,* August 4, 1993; "Hill-Rom Aids Immobilized Patients," December 22, 1992.

Faris, Charlene, "Batesville Casket Co.: The Nation's Largest Casket Manufacturer," *Indiana Business,* April 1993.

"Hillenbrand Hospital-Bed Unit, German Company Link," *Indianapolis Business Journal,* June 28, 1993.

Larking, Patrick, "Analysts Downplay Inquiry of Hill-Rom Co.," *Cincinnati Post,* October 19, 1993.

Lundegaard, Karen M., "At Home with Hillenbrand," *Cincinnati Business Courier,* June 28, 1993.

Song, Kyung M., "Indiana Hospital-Bed Maker Is Target of Probe," *Louisville Courier-Journal,* October 20, 1993.

—Dave Mote

Honda Motor Company Limited (Honda Giken Kogyo Kabushiki Kaisha)

1-1, Minami-Ayama, 2-chome
Minato-Ku, Tokyo 107
Japan
81-3-3423-1111
Fax: 81-3-3423-0511
U.S. Headquarters: Honda North America, Inc.
1290 Avenue of the Americas
Suite 3330
New York, New York 10104
U.S.A
(212) 765-3804
Fax: (212) 541-9855

Public Company
Incorporated: September 24, 1948
Employees: 28,000
Sales: US$33 billion
Stock Exchanges: Tokyo Osaka Niigata Nagoya Kyoto
Fukuoka Supporo Hiroshima New York
SICs: 3751 Motorcycles, Bicycles & Parts; 3711 Motor
   Vehicles & Car Bodies

Prior to 1960 the image of the motorcyclist in America was that of an unsavory teenager who belonged to a group of unruly characters known by such names as "Hell's Angels" and "Satan's Slaves." In general, motorcyclists were regarded by the American public as troublemakers who wore leather jackets. By the mid-1960s, however, Honda Motor Company Limited and its American subsidiary had successfully transformed that image, and at the same time established the company as the leading motorcycle manufacturer in the world. During the 1970s and 1980s, Honda also established itself as one of the world's preeminent car manufacturers. With its best-selling Honda Accord, the popular Civic, and the upscale Acura, the company became a sales leader in the American automotive industry.

In 1959 Honda established an American subsidiary, named the American Honda Motor Co., which was in sharp contrast to other foreign manufacturers who relied on distributors. Honda's strategy was to create a market of customers who had never given a thought to owning a motorcycle. The company started its enterprise in America by producing the smallest, lightweight motorcycles available. With a three speed transmission, an automatic clutch, five horsepower (an American cycle had only two and a half), an electric starter and step-through frame for female riders, Honda sold its unit for $250 retail compared to $1,000–$1,500 for the American machines. Even at that early date Honda was probably superior to other companies in its productivity. By 1959, with sales of $55 million, Honda was already the largest motorcycle manufacturer in the world.

Honda followed a policy of developing the American market region by region. The company started on the West Coast and moved eastward over a period of five years. During 1960 2,500 machines were sold in the United States. In 1961 it established 125 distributors and spent $150,000 on regional advertising. Honda's advertising campaign, which was directed to young families, included the slogan, "You meet the nicest people on a Honda." This was a deliberate attempt to disassociate their motorcycles from the image many American's had of motorcylists. Honda's success in creating a demand for lightweight motorcycles was impressive. Its U.S. sales skyrocketed from $500,000 in 1960 to $77 million in 1965. By 1966 the market share revealed the ascendancy of the Japanese manufacturer and its success in selling lightweight motorcycles.

Any description of the company's success must take into account the unusual character of its founders Soichiro Honda, and his partner, Takeo Fujisawa. Soichiro Honda's achievements as a mechanical engineer are said to match those of Henry Ford's. Working in his machine shop in 1938, Honda concentrated his efforts on casting a perfect piston ring, and finally succeeded in casting a ring that met his standards. Two years after rejecting Honda's first batch of piston rings, the Toyota Corporation placed a large order, but because the country was preparing for war, Honda was unable to obtain cement to construct a factory to mass produce piston rings. Undaunted, he built the plant by learning how to make his own cement.

Honda's factories survived the bombing attacks during World War II but were then destroyed by an earthquake. Undaunted, Honda sold his piston ring operation to Toyota and went on to manufacture motorbikes. He had designed his first bike in the early postwar years when gasoline was very scarce and the need for a low fuel consuming vehicle was great.

To form a company, Honda joined efforts with Takeo Fujisawa. Honda and Fujisawa had known one another throughout the 1940s and in 1949 Fujisawa provided the capital, as well as the financial and marketing strategy. Honda's motivation for establishing this company was not purely commercial but to provide a secure financial base so that he might pursue other ambitions. In 1950, after his first motorcycle had been introduced in Japan, Honda stunned the engineering world by doubling the horsepower of the conventional four-stroke engine. With this technological innovation, the company was poised for success. By 1951 demand was brisk, yet production was slow. It was primarily due to design advantages that Honda became one of the four or five industry leaders by 1954 with 15 percent of the market share.

The two owners of the company had different priorities. For Fujisawa, the engine innovation meant increased sales and easier access to financing. For Honda, the higher horsepower engine opened the possibility of pursuing one of his central ambitions in life—motorcycle racing. Indeed, winning provided the ultimate confirmation of his design abilities. Success came quickly, and by 1959 Honda had won all of the most prestigious motorcycle racing prizes in the world.

Fujisawa, throughout the 1950s, attempted to turn Honda's attention away from racing to the more mundane tasks of running a successful business venture. By 1956, as the technological innovations gained from racing began to pay off in vastly more efficient engines, Fujisawa prompted Honda to adapt this technology for a commercial motorcycle. Fujisawa had a particular segment of Japanese society in mind. Most motorcyclists in Japan were male and the machines they used were primarily an alternative form of transportation to trains and buses. There were, however, a large number of small commercial establishments in Japan that still delivered goods and ran errands on bicycles. The finances of these small enterprises were usually controlled by Japanese housewives who resisted buying conventional motorcycles because they were expensive, dangerous, and difficult to handle. Fujisawa suggested to Honda that, with his knowledge of racing, he might be able to design a safe and inexpensive motorcycle that could be driven with one hand (to facilitate carrying packages).

In 1958 the Honda 50cc Supercub was introduced. It featured an automatic clutch, three-speed transmission, automatic starter, and the safe, friendly look of a bicycle. Its inexpensive price was due almost entirely to its high horsepower but lightweight 50cc engine. Overwhelmed by demand, the company arranged for an infusion of capital in order to build a new plant with a 30,000 unit per month capacity. By the end of 1959 Honda had climbed into first place among Japanese motorcycle manufacturers. The company's total sales that year of 285,000 units included 168,000 Supercubs.

Honda had experimented with local southeast Asian markets in 1957 and 1958 with little success. The European market, while larger, was heavily dominated by its own name brand manufacturers, and their popular mopeds dominated the low price, low horsepower products. Fujisawa decided to focus attention on the United States market.

In the spring of 1963 an undergraduate advertising major at University of California, Los Angeles submitted, in fulfillment of a course assignment, an advertising campaign for Honda. Its theme was: ''You meet the nicest people on a Honda.'' Encouraged by his instructor, the student submitted his work to a friend at Grey Advertising. Consequently, the ''Nicest People'' campaign became the impetus behind Honda's sales. By 1964 nearly one out of every two motorcycles sold in the United States was a Honda.

As a result of the growing number of medium-income consumers, banks and other consumer credit companies began to finance the purchase of motorcycles. This involved a shift away from dealer credit, which had been the traditional purchasing mechanism. Seizing the opportunity created by a soaring demand for its products, the company set in motion a risky plan. Late in 1964 Honda announced that soon thereafter it would cease to ship motorcycles on a consignment basis and would

require cash on delivery. Management prepared itself for a dealership revolt. Yet, while nearly every dealer either questioned or complained about the decision, not one relinquished his franchise. By this one decision, Honda transferred the financial authority (and, the power that goes with it) from the dealer to the manufacturer. Within three years this method became the basic pattern of the industry and the Honda motorcycle had the largest market share of any company in the world. By 1981 Honda's total motorcycle production reached some 3.5 million units and one-third of those were produced or sold outside of Japan.

As early as 1967, when Honda was on its way to becoming the world's leading motorcycle manufacturer, it also began to produce cars and trucks. In addition, the company started to manufacture portable generators, power tillers, lawn mowers, pumps, and outboard motors. In 1967 and 1968 the company introduced two lightweight passenger cars which performed poorly in both the Japanese and American markets. It was not until 1973 and the introduction of the Honda Civic that the company became a real presence on the international automobile market. The world was in the grip of the oil crisis, and the energy-efficient Japanese compacts suddenly found a worldwide market.

In 1976, as sales of the Honda Civic surpassed the one million mark, the company introduced an upscale, higher priced model named the Accord. Sales of the Accord grew rapidly, not only in Japan, but especially in the United States. In 1982, as a result of the burgeoning American market for Japanese cars, production of the Accord was started at Honda's Marysville, Ohio, manufacturing plant. As the Accord became more and more popular with middle-class Americans looking for high-quality, reliable, and affordable cars, management was convinced that the company could succeed in entering the luxury car market. In 1986, Honda introduced the Acura, which immediately garnered large sales throughout Japan and the United States. By the end of the 1980s, Honda had developed into one of the leading car manufacturers in the world.

Honda's success continued into the early 1990s. The Accord was the most popular and best-selling car in America from 1990 to 1992. Sales were astronomical, with two cars sold in the United States for every one sold in Japan. No one could have predicted that by 1993 Honda would have passed Chrysler Corp. to become the third largest seller of cars in the United States. In addition to car sales, the company's motorcycle unit even broke new ground: in 1992 Honda organized the first joint venture to make motorcycles in China. Many industry analysts say this agreement will give Honda an initial foothold in what could become the world's largest and most lucrative motorcycle market.

Yet Honda's success in such a competitive market as the automotive industry could not continue indefinitely. With increasing sales of Pontiac's Grand Am, Ford's Taurus, and Toyota's Camry, sales of Honda's Accord slipped 35 percent in 1993. In the luxury car market, sales of Honda's Acura decreased 17 percent, battered by competition from Toyota's Lexus and Nissan's Infinity. Honda even lost a significant portion of its share of the Japanese market. Exacerbating its loss of market share was the widely publicized scandal that high-ranking Honda managers accepted payoffs as high as $100,000 from dealers who wanted Honda franchises and certain types of special treatment.

With over 40 percent of its worldwide sales in the United States, Honda started to fight back on American soil. After Soichiro Honda died in 1991, the company initiated a comprehensive reorganization. Led by Nobuhiko Kawamoto, the company's president and chief executive officer, Honda reorganized its Japanese, European, and North American units into autonomous operations to improve cost effectiveness. In order to introduce more Americans into company management, Honda arranged for 50 employees from its Ohio plant to spend two to three years working in Japan. The company has also expanded its sales training in the United States, and introduced dealer incentives of up to $1000 per car in order to move some of its inventory. Finally, Honda introduced its first four-wheel drive vehicle to compete with already established models such as Isuzu's Rodeo.

Honda products are manufactured by 43 plants in 40 countries. BL Ltd. (formerly British Leyland), Britain's largest car manufacturer, which is owned by the government, decided to manufacture one passenger car model under license from Honda. In this particular case, Honda sold a technical license to BL Limited. The company also has joint agreements with South Africa, Yugoslavia, France, and China.

Although Honda has trimmed its overhead, incorporated more Americans into management of the company, and introduced new models, none of these changes will alter one salient fact—namely, that the worldwide car industry is saturated and will remain extremely competitive for both the short and long term. Ironically, Honda might have to get used to the squeeze American car manufacturers felt during the 1970s and 1980s, when Japanese competition almost forced them out of business.

Principal Subsidiaries: Honda Research and Development Co. Ltd.; Honda Engineering Co. Ltd.; Honda International Sales Corp.; Honda SF Corp.; Honda Minami Tokyo Co. Ltd.; Honda Motor Service Co. Ltd.; ACT Trading Corp.; Press Giken Co. Ltd. (98.2 percent); Seiki Giken Co. Ltd. (98 percent); Honda and Co. Ltd. (86.6 percent); Honda Research of America, Inc.; Honda Sogo Tatemono Ltd. (70 percent); American Honda Motor Co.; Honda of America Mfg., Inc. The company also has subsidiaries in the following countries: Australia, Belgium, Canada, France, The Netherlands, Thailand, United Kingdom, and West Germany.

Further Reading:

Ramsey, Douglas K., *The Corporate Warriors: Six Classic Cases in American Business,* Boston: Houghton Mifflin, 1987.
Sakiya, Tetuus, *Honda Motor: The Men, The Management, The Machine,* Tokyo: Kadonsha International, 1982.
Taylor, Alex, "The Dangers of Running Too Lean," *Fortune,* June 14, 1993.

—updated by Thomas Derdak

HOUGHTON MIFFLIN COMPANY

Houghton Mifflin Company

222 Berkeley Street
Boston, Massachusetts 02116
U.S.A.
(617) 351-5000
Fax: (617) 227-5409

Public Company
Incorporated: 1864 as Hurd & Houghton
Employees: 2,096
Sales: $462.9 million
Stock Exchanges: New York
SICs: 2731 Book Publishing; 7372 Prepackaged Software

The Houghton Mifflin Company is a leading publisher of textbooks for the elementary, secondary, and college market. In addition, the company produces testing materials, reference books, children's literature, and a small line of adult trade books of interest to the general public. Formed in the nineteenth century as a printing house, the company grew and diversified, playing an important part in the intellectual life of the United States through its purchase of a distinguished competitor. With time, Houghton's focus shifted to more profitable educational publications, and it became a major presence in the educational market.

Houghton was founded by Henry Oscar Houghton, a printer born into poverty in Vermont in 1823. At age 13, Houghton was apprenticed to a printer in Burlington, Vermont. In 1842, he entered the University of Vermont, earning his way through college by working in various printers' offices. In an effort to pay off the debts he had amassed while in school, Houghton moved to Boston after his college graduation in 1846, where he held a series of jobs in journalism and printing.

In 1848, having paid off his debt from college, Houghton bought out one of the partners in one of Boston's premier printing businesses for $3100, to be paid in installments, and formed Bolles & Houghton. The business had changed its name by 1851 to Houghton & Haywood, as Houghton exchanged his former partner for one of his cousins. The company moved the following year to an expanded printing plant on the banks of the Charles River, and began to call itself the Riverside Press. In 1852, the business changed hands again, and took the name H.O. Houghton & Company.

Five years later, in 1857, Houghton was shaken by a widespread economic panic, the lingering effects of which wore on for the next four years. As banks and other businesses closed and paper money lost its value, Houghton found itself in possession of the stereotype plates, used to print off new copies, for a number of books. These assets were given to the printer in lieu of payment by insolvent publishers. Soon after, Houghton purchased the stereotype plates for a 39-volume book on English law from the Boston publisher Little, Brown & Company. With these moves, Houghton took the first step in the process of changing from a printer into a publisher. In order to exploit the value of the stereotype printing plates it owned, it was necessary for Houghton to use them to print books, which then needed to be distributed.

By 1863, Houghton had amassed enough plates to flesh out a basic publisher's list: law books, general classics, and a lucrative arithmetic textbook. When one of his press' primary clients, Little, Brown & Company, terminated their contract with Houghton, the company was forced to diversify its activities in order to insure its continued financial health. Accordingly, in 1864 Houghton entered into a partnership with Melancthon M. Hurd, a wealthy New Yorker with whose firm Houghton had previously produced a series of books by Charles Dickens. Houghton planned to handle the printing, advertising, and distribution aspects of the business, leaving authors, manuscripts, and editors in the hands of his partner, Hurd. The new New York-based company, called Hurd & Houghton, took as its colophon a shield with two interlocked ''H's.''

The first catalogue of books published by the new firm included the texts for which Houghton owned the stereotype printing plates, works by Englishmen, and several books written by Americans. In January 1865, the company purchased an additional 20 titles, including works by James Fenimoore Cooper. Later that year, the fledgling enterprise found itself the object of a suit by Hurd's former partners over the rights to publish the Dickens books. Eventually, this was resolved to Houghton's satisfaction.

In 1866, Hurd & Houghton was reorganized, as one of Houghton's brothers contributed additional capital. With this money, the company moved to newer, more stylish offices in New York and expanded its Cambridge printing facilities. After purchasing the Riverside Press site, the company added a new four-story building and ten new presses. These new facilities, inaugurated at the end of 1867, allowed the press to keep up with demand for its most popular product, the Merriam Webster Unabridged Dictionary, as well as to print newspapers and periodicals and the books of Hurd & Houghton's line. These included law books, school books, Bibles, prayer books, theological works, and children's literature.

While Houghton's Massachusetts-based printing operations were turning a profit, its New York publishing arm languished. Hurd & Houghton's periodicals, such as the *Riverside Magazine for Young People,* suffered from stiff competition, and were expensive to produce. Nonetheless, by the end of the firm's second year in operation it remained profitable overall.

In 1872, Hurd & Houghton took on several additional business partners, among them Horace Elisha Scudder, who worked on the children's magazine, and George Harrison Mifflin, a rich young man who had joined the firm in 1868. In the 1870s, Houghton & Hurd expanded steadily, acquiring publications in a number of fields, including the *Atlantic Monthly,* and garnered a number of lucrative government contracts. Gradually, it was becoming the predominant Boston publishing house.

Boston suffered a devastating fire in 1872, worsened by the fact that all the fire department's horses had an equine illness. This catastrophe, in which the premises of many paper manufacturers and printers were destroyed, was followed by a prolonged economic slump, in which many businesses failed. These events had forced one of New England's oldest and most illustrious publishing houses, Ticknor & Fields, in its present incarnation as James R. Osgood & Company, into dire economic straits. This publisher had begun in 1832, and had published such leading intellectual lights as Ralph Waldo Emerson, Henry David Thoreau, Nathanial Hawthorne, Mark Twain, Henry Wadsworth Longfellow, Harriet Beecher Stowe, John Greenleaf Whittier, and others. In 1878, Houghton bought out the older firm, and formed Houghton, Osgood & Company, moving his company more firmly into the realm of literary publishing, away from the lucrative printing and textbook publishing with which it had begun.

By the start of the 1880s, Houghton, Osgood was operating under the burden of heavy debts assumed under the Osgood takeover. In order to ameliorate this dangerous situation, the company was reorganized in 1880, to become Houghton, Mifflin & Company. The company spent the next ten years striving to reduce its debt. Houghton published books by such authors as Henry James, and Kate Douglas Wiggins, who wrote the children's classic *Rebecca of Sunnybrook Farm,* during this time.

In 1882, Houghton also established an educational department, which worked to update the company's educational offerings. Chief among the company's school books was the Riverside Literature Series, also inaugurated in 1882, which made unabridged American classics, annotated with study guides, available to schools as cheaply as possible. One version of the project was printed on opaque paper, with inexpensive paper covers, and sold for 15 cents a volume.

In 1895, Houghton's founder, Henry Oscar Houghton, died and control of the firm passed to his younger partner, George Harrison Mifflin. Houghton left the firm in strong, if not invincible, economic shape, as it faced slowing profits in response to another general economic depression. In the late 1890s, in addition to the firm's standard list of children's works and educational tomes, Houghton added a number of novels that were designed to attract public attention. Several of these books sold well, moving well over 10,000 copies. In addition to its fiction, Houghton also offered newly updated school books, and the *Atlantic Monthly.*

In 1901, Houghton Mifflin opened a book shop in downtown Boston. In the windows, the company mounted displays promoting its best-selling novels, and inside, samples of the fine printing and binding of the Riverside Press were available. Seven years later, in 1908, after a series of deaths among the firm's original partners, Houghton, Mifflin & Company restructured itself, changing from a partnership into a corporation,

under the name Houghton Mifflin Company. At this time, the firm sold its journal, *The Atlantic Monthly,* to a group of investors who planned to install new editors while maintaining some ties with Houghton.

By 1914, George Mifflin's desire to publish novels that would win widespread popularity had brought about a decline in the overall literary quality of Houghton's offerings. One of the publisher's most prominent poets, Amy Lowell, quit the house for another, charging that the company had suffered a decline in prestige through its practice of publishing second-rate fiction.

Houghton lost further literary currency when World War I broke out in Europe in 1914. Under the leadership of its Anglophilic editor-in-chief, the company avidly supported the Allied war effort, working with Wellington House, the propaganda division of the British Foreign Office, a policy which later earned Houghton the suspicion of many intellectuals. Between 1914 and 1918, Houghton published more than 100 books related to the war effort.

Many of Houghton's books concerning the war proved profitable. An additional, unexpected positive side-effect of World War I was a large increase in the size of the reading public, and thus, the market for books. Programs to put inexpensive books in the hands of servicemen during the war had introduced the habit of reading to a vast number of men.

In the years following the war, American letters underwent a renaissance, as new authors introduced new literary movements. Despite its heritage of having published many of the leading literary lights of the nineteenth century, however, Houghton was largely left out of the new movements. The company had a strong reputation for conservatism, a product of the archaic tastes of several of its key editors, who sought uplifting works with pleasant themes and found the new stark realism unpalatable. In addition, Houghton's editors perceived themselves to be handicapped in the publication of radical material by their location in Boston, where local authorities frequently banned books found objectionable or dangerous. The company feared that Boston police could seize the entire print run of an offending work as it came off the presses in Cambridge, preventing a book from ever even entering circulation.

Although the literary tumult of the 1920s passed by Houghton, the company did show more success with its nonfiction offerings. In addition, its educational books division thrived. It had begun publishing intelligence quota, or ''I.Q.,'' tests in 1916, and continued to update these best sellers for decades. Houghton relied on its perennial sellers and its solid lists of educational publications throughout the economic depression of the 1930s. A key part of this approach was the development of the market for standardized tests. Working with educators at the University of Iowa, the company developed the *Iowa Tests of Basic Skills.*

Also during the 1930s, Houghton Mifflin added Adolf Hitler's *Mein Kampf* to its non-fiction list. All royalties from this work were paid to the Office of Foreign Litigation of the U.S. government. After publishing Hitler, the company went on to publish the works of his adversaries in the wake of World War II. In the late 1940s, Houghton paid its largest advance ever for Winston Churchill's six volume account of World War II, for which he was later awarded the Nobel Prize in Literature. In addition, the company published the works of General George Patton and Field Marshall Bernard Montgomery.

Following World War II, the U.S. government passed the G.I. Bill, promising a free college education to all who had fought in the war. This move dramatically increased the market for college textbooks, and Houghton's operations in this area expanded greatly. In 1949, the company also introduced the McKee readers, which taught young children how to read, and were purchased by school systems expanding to accommodate the baby boom of the 1950s. In addition, Houghton increased its participation in the standardized testing field.

Houghton grew in size throughout the 1950s and 1960s, adding such works as Rachel Carson's controversial *Silent Spring* to its non-fiction list. In 1967, Houghton sold stock to the public for the first time, listing its shares on the New York Stock Exchange. Two years later, Houghton introduced the best-selling *American Heritage Dictionary,* one of the first such works to be created using a computerized word base. In 1971, the company moved further into the field of computer publishing when it began working with a small New Hampshire-based firm called Time-Sharing Information to develop computer programs for use in schools. Four years later, Houghton purchased this company, to better integrate its operations with its textbook division.

Also in that year, Houghton was sued by three women and charged by the Massachusetts attorney general with discrimination against women in hiring and promotions. Two years later, the company agreed to pay $750,000 to its female employees and increase its affirmative action program. In a separate settlement in 1981, Houghton paid an additional $325,000.

By the late 1970s, as the number of school-age children dwindled, Houghton began to shift its emphasis in educational publishing. The company started to move away from primary and secondary school texts toward college texts, particularly business course and professional offerings. In 1977, it purchased the Pinecliff Publishing Company, a California-based medical publisher.

By 1978, Houghton had compiled a record of steady success in the text book industry, racking up ten years of growing sales and profits. These gains attracted the attention of Western Pacific Industries, a railroad conglomerate, which announced that it had acquired 6.7 percent of the company's stock in March, 1978. Concerned about a possible corporate takeover, Houghton authors such as John Kenneth Galbraith and Arthur Schlesinger organized an Author's Guild inquiry into the matter, wrote letters of protest to the buyer, and announced that they might quit the publisher if it was not able to remain independent. This campaign worked, and Houghton was able to buy back its shares from the conglomerate.

In the following year, the company continued its growth. In 1979, Houghton established a Chicago subsidiary, The River-side Publishing Company, to produce reading text books with a new approach. To sell this line, the subsidiary was given its own separate sales force. In addition, in its trade books division, Houghton reintroduced the Ticknor & Fields imprint, which had belong to the distinguished Boston publisher the company had purchased long ago. This division of Houghton was set up to publish a small list of distinguished authors on politics, biography, and historical fiction. In addition, the company added the imprint J.P. Tarcher, Inc., for science books, before consolidating all its trade activities into one division, in the hope of increasing profits.

In 1980, Houghton moved to solidify its dominance of the textbook market by purchasing educational publishing operations of Rand McNally & Company for 11.6 million. These activities remained separate from Houghton's other businesses. Throughout the 1980s, Houghton's textbook business remained strong, growing at a rate of more than ten percent a year.

In the early 1990s, Houghton sought to strengthen its position in educational publishing by making a series of acquisitions and divestitures. Under the leadership of a new chief executive officer, the company purchased the special needs testing products of the Assessment Division of DLM, Inc., for $17 million in cash. Also in October 1992, the company bought a part of Cassell, PLC, a British publisher of foreign language dictionaries. Three months later, Houghton acquired the publishing operations of College Survival, Inc. During this time, it also shed certain operations, reorganizing its foreign publishing operations along more profitable lines.

In January 1994, Houghton bought McDougal, Littell & Company, another textbook publisher, for $138 million, in an effort to enhance its products for the secondary school market. At the same time, the company announced that it would fold its prestigious Ticknor & Fields imprint, and merge its 20 or so trade books into the company's general line, in an effort to stem losses at the imprint. In another effort to streamline, Houghton spun off its computer software division into a separate company, of which it retained 40 percent, renaming it InfoSoft International. As Houghton moved into the mid 1990s, the company's strong textbook operations, as well as its illustrious history in other areas, indicated that it would continue to prosper in the ever-changing publishing climate.

Principal Subsidiaries: The Riverside Publishing Company; HMR, Inc.; HMF, Inc.

Further Reading:

Ballou, Ellen B., *The Building of the House: Houghton Mifflin's Formative Years,* Boston: Houghton Mifflin, 1970.
Gallese, Liz Roman, "Houghton Mifflin's New Trade Book Boss Expands Lines, Cuts Costs, Manages 'Ideas,' " *Wall Street Journal,* December 5, 1980.
Jereski, Laura, "Making Book," *Forbes,* March 7, 1988.
"Textbook Case," *Forbes,* July 9, 1979.

—Elizabeth Rourke

information resources inc

Information Resources, Inc.

150 N. Clinton
Chicago, Illinois 60661
U.S.A.
(312) 726-1221
Fax: (312) 726-0360

Public Company
Incorporated: 1977
Employees: 4,700
Sales: $334.5 million
Stock Exchanges: NASDAQ
SICs: 8732 Commercial Nonphysical Research; 8742
   Management Consulting Services; 7372 Prepackaged
   Software

Information Resources, Inc. (IRI), the world's second largest market research company, provides customers with a broad range of services designed to assist in making marketing decisions. The company's Information Services Group develops and maintains computerized databases that enable consumer packaged goods companies to accurately monitor the effectiveness of their marketing, as well as their coupon promotion and television advertising. IRI's InfoScan, a weekly research service that collects sales information on all brands using scanners placed at 2,700 supermarkets, 500 drugstores, and 250 mass merchants nationwide, is the core of the Information Services Group. InfoScan generated $180.6 million of IRI's $334.5 million in 1993 revenue. IRI's Software Products Group sells decision support software and information systems for a diverse range of industries and government agencies. Software sales accounted for $95.4 million of the company's revenues in 1993.

IRI was founded in 1977 by market research veteran John Malec and University of Iowa marketing professor Gerald Eskin. Their inspiration to create IRI came from two sources: a pioneering market research company called Adtel, Inc. and the emergence in the early 1970s of bar codes and supermarket scanners. Adtel used purchase diaries kept by consumers to compare the effects of alternate TV ads run by separate cable systems. The main drawback of the Adtel system was that it took rather long to decipher the data. Malec figured that if scanners could be used as a tool for collecting the same types of information, that problem would be solved. In 1978, they enlisted the company's third founder, William Walter, to de-

velop the necessary computer models to make their idea a reality.

Unfortunately, the trio did not have enough money to get the company off the ground. After numerous banks rejected their pleas for financing, a new strategy was adopted. They approached prospective customers directly, and by 1979, IRI had $2 million in contracts for future services with 11 companies, including such big-names as Coca-Cola, Quaker Oats, Kraft, and Procter & Gamble. IRI then bought $2 million worth of scanners from National Semiconductor, and operations were begun in earnest.

In January 1980, IRI launched BehaviorScan, its first scanner-driven market research service. Marion, Indiana, and Pittsfield, Massachusetts, were chosen as the initial test markets. IRI provided scanners free of charge to 15 supermarkets in those two towns, and 2,000 households in each town were recruited to participate. Each time a member of a test household went shopping, the universal product code (UPC) on each item purchased was scanned, and the information fed to IRI's computer in Chicago. In addition, devices were attached to the television sets of test families, enabling IRI to not only monitor what advertising was being watched, but also to test different versions of commercials by cutting into cable programs and replacing the preprogrammed ad with a different one. BehaviorScan created shock waves in the market research industry, and sent competitors like A.C. Nielsen scrambling to improve their own technology, particularly in the area of scanner-based services.

By 1982, IRI's net income reached $2 million on revenue of $12 million, 60 percent of which came from its ten largest clients, a list including General Foods, Campbell Soup, Nabisco, and R.J. Reynolds. IRI went public in March 1983. On the first day of the offering, the price of IRI stock shot up from $23 to $43 a share, and $20 million was raised to pay off the company's long-term debt. By that time, BehaviorScan was tracking the purchases of 15,000 households in eight cities. Drugstores were also added in several of IRI's test cities. Sales for 1983 jumped to $21 million.

IRI continued to grow at a brisk pace in the mid 1980s. In 1984, it was ranked 15th on *INC.* magazine's list of the 100 fastest-growing public companies in the United States. That year IRI registered sales of $35 million. Revenue more than doubled to $75 million the following year when IRI acquired Management Decision Systems, Inc., a company specializing in decision support software. In 1986, president and chief operating officer Gian Fulgoni, who had come over from Adtel in 1981, took on the additional position of chief executive officer. Malec retained his board chairmanship.

Increasingly, IRI was seen by industry observers as the young, aggressive alternative to Nielsen, the world's largest market research company and the industry's sluggish dinosaur. IRI's technology was perceived by many as a step ahead of Nielsen's. Long-time Nielsen clients were beginning to defect in growing numbers after InfoScan, the first nation-wide supermarket tracking service based on UPC scanning, was introduced in 1987.

In August 1987, Nielsen's parent company, Dun & Bradstreet Corporation, proposed a $590 million takeover of IRI. The offer was accepted, but in November the Federal Trade Commission challenged the acquisition, asserting that such a merger would hinder competition in the consumer tracking industry. Dun & Bradstreet immediately withdrew the offer, and IRI remained independent.

The aborted deal was fairly damaging to IRI, however. Its stock price plummeted, leaving the company with a sizable debt. Clients who had put off using InfoScan in anticipation of the merger had to be won over anew. In spite of this setback, revenue continued to soar, reaching $105 million for the year. InfoScan was tracking the purchases of 65,000 households by this time, and IRI's reputation among potential customers remained stellar.

In 1988, IRI developed VideOcart, a shopping cart equipped with a video screen that displays product promotion information, as well as recipes, item locations, and trivia games. In order to avoid the high cost of developing VideOcart, IRI spun it off in 1990. Meanwhile, large-scale customer defections from Nielsen continued. Among the companies that began subscribing to InfoScan in 1988 were Frito-Lay, Procter & Gamble's Soap Sector, and ConAgra.

IRI was the third largest marketing research company in the United States by 1989, capturing 40 percent of the national tracking market with InfoScan in only two years. Software was beginning to play a more prominent role as well. IRI bolstered its software business with the acquisition of Javelin Software Corporation, a promising company that had fallen on hard times. Although IRI's revenue reached $136 million in 1989, the company still suffered from growing pains, recording a net loss of $2.9 million. Pepsi-Cola, Nabisco, and Reynolds Metals were among the high-profile companies that began using the InfoScan service during that year.

In 1990, IRI's upper management structure was revised. When Malec departed with the newly spun-off VideOcart, the new office of chief executive, a combination of chief executive officer and chief operating officer, was created. Fulgoni and James Andress, who had been serving as president and chief operating officer, became the co-holders of the new post.

IRI took a large bite out of Nielsen's industry lead by acquiring the recently folded SAMI service from Arbitron, a unit of Control Data Corporation, in 1990. The absorption of SAMI, which tracked products through scanners and warehouse withdrawals, left IRI and Nielsen as the only significant competitors in the product tracking field. For $7 million, IRI assumed all of SAMI's customer contracts. Equally important was the access gained to SAMI's Drug Warehouse Withdrawal historical data base. This enabled IRI to become instantly competitive in the drugstore arena at a cost much lower than would have been spent expanding InfoScan. The alliance with Arbitron made InfoScan information available to Arbitron's clients, mainly broadcasters and ad agencies, in exchange for IRI's access to Arbitron's television and radio audience ratings. During the year, Ore-Ida, Lever Brothers, Ralston Purina, and Tropicana all became InfoScan users.

IRI introduced two new software products, SalesPartner and CoverStory, in 1990. SalesPartner's analytical abilities enabled clients to exploit data from InfoScan more efficiently. These

additions increased the share of IRI's revenue generated by software to 30 percent. Checkout counters at 2,700 supermarkets in 75 cities were equipped with InfoScan scanners, giving the company over half the U.S. supermarket scanner tracking market. Five hundred drug stores and 250 mass merchandisers were also contributing information to the system, which by this time was tracking 2.5 million UPC-coded items. During that year, IRI released a study with the sweeping title *How Advertising Works*. The study was one of the most comprehensive ever done on the subject, and was well-received by many major advertisers. IRI's sales continued to soar, reaching $208 million in 1991.

By 1992, the head-to-head battle between IRI and Nielsen for market research clients had become remarkably fierce. IRI was perceived by many industry analysts as having an edge in technology, while Nielsen's major strength was its international presence. During 1992, IRI snatched the gigantic Procter & Gamble account away from Nielsen, a major coup by any measure. Previously, IRI was tracking only six of Procter & Gamble's product categories, while Nielsen controlled the remaining 50.

The focus of the battle between IRI and Nielsen shifted to Europe, where Nielsen held a decided advantage. Late in 1992, IRI began offering InfoScan in England as part of a joint venture with two European companies that led to the acquisition of NMRA Retail Audit, formerly part of Robert Maxwell's AGB empire. Although IRI picked up ground in the turf war over Europe, the company's scanner-based systems were slower to catch on there due to the continued consumer preference for mom-and-pop groceries.

As the 1990s continued, IRI maintained the pace of its European expansion, opening offices in Germany, France, and Holland. The company continued to expand its line of scanner-driven services as well. One system added was QScan (short for Quality Scanning Information), a program which provides retailers with direct access to scanner data and software applications. QScan is capable of providing data for all of a retail chain's stores, rather than just a sample. Another system recently introduced by IRI is LogiCNet, which stands for ''logistics communications network.'' LogiCNet assists manufacturers and retailers in efficiently monitoring the chain of product replenishment. QScan and LogiCNet are both part of an initiative called Efficient Consumer Response (ECR) whose aim is to improve the supply system efficiency of grocery chains.

Meanwhile, U.S. customers continued to flee Nielsen for IRI in large numbers. New clients in late 1992 and early 1993 included Kellogg Co., Campbell Soup's Pepperidge Farm, Keebler Co., and Sara Lee Corporation's L'eggs division. One defection that went in the other direction was that of a key executive. George Garrick, president of IRI's European Information Services, left the company in July 1993 to become president of Nielsen's U.S. market research division. But Nielsen received a shock when Garrick moved back to IRI after four months. The degree of intrigue that accompanied Garrick's recruitment and counter-recruitment is usually reserved for fiction, not corporate America. Ploys associated with the episode included the release of a booklet containing anti-Nielsen memos written by Garrick over the years.

In 1994, IRI announced it was acquiring the Survey Research Group, Asia's largest market research company. The company continued to focus on international expansion, and by that year its services were being marketed in 26 different countries throughout the world. Although the battle for clients was no longer as one-sided as it had been a few years earlier, IRI's list of new customers was impressive. Between October of 1993 and March of 1994, Dole Foods, Seagram Beverages, and Tetley were among the new companies in the IRI camp.

In only a decade-and-a-half of existence, IRI has attained a position of prominence in its industry. By using cutting-edge technology, IRI has been able to grow at a brisk pace. The company has had a history of aggressive customer recruitment throughout its head-to-head competition with Nielsen. If IRI's success in closing the gap in the global market approaches that of its domestic campaign, it is entirely plausible that it will eventually overtake Nielsen as the leading company in the market research business.

Principal Subsidiaries: Towne-Oller & Associates Inc.; Catalina Information Resources, Inc. (50%); Shopper's Hotline, Inc.; Information Resources S.A. (France); Information Resources GmbH (Germany); InfoScan NMRA Limited (U.K., 60%).

Further Reading:

Byrne, Harlan, "Information Resources," *Barron's,* September 6, 1993, p. 42.
——, "Information Resources," *Barron's,* September 7, 1992, p. 31.
——, "Information Resources," *Barron's,* February 11, 1991, p. 37.
Feder, Barnaby, "Scanning Sales with an Eye on Rival," *New York Times,* December 2, 1993, p. C1.
Here's How We Made It Happen . . . ., Chicago: Information Resources, Inc., 1992.
Hume, Scott, "IRI Aces Nielsen in Battle for P&G's U.S. Scanner Biz," *Advertising Age,* July 6, 1992, p. 4.
——, "IRI, Arbitron Team Up on Nielsen," *Advertising Age,* October 8, 1990, p. 82.
——, "IRI Prepares to Battle Nielsen in U.K.," *Advertising Age,* November 16, 1992, p. 42.
——, "Nielsen vs. IRI: Battle of the Research Titans," *Advertising Age,* October 12, 1992, p. 1.
Information Resources, Inc. 1992 Annual Report, Chicago: Information Resources, Inc., 1993.
Kreisman, Richard, "Buy the Numbers," *INC.,* March 1985, pp. 104–112.
Labate, John, "Information Resources Inc.," *Fortune,* December 27, 1993, p. 79.
Lowenstein, Roger, and Scott Kilman, "Dun & Bradstreet Drops Plan to Acquire Information Resources, Citing U.S. Move," *Wall Street Journal,* November 18, 1987, p. 7.
"Market Research by Scanner," *Business Week,* May 5, 1980, pp. 113–114.
Much, Marylin, "Information Resources Gains Edge in Data Fight," *Investor's Business Daily,* March 2, 1994.
Schlossberg, Howard, "IRI, Nielsen Slug It Out in 'Scanning Wars'," *Marketing News,* September 2, 1991, p. 7.
Schumer, Fern, "The New Magicians of Market Research," *Fortune,* July 25, 1983, pp. 72–74.
Stern, Gabriela, and Richard Gibson, "Data Raids," *New York Times,* November 15, 1993, p. A1.
Teinowitz, Ira, "Research War Takes New Turn as Garrick Bolts IRI for Nielsen," *Advertising Age,* July 5, 1993, p. 4.
Wylie, Kenneth, "IRI Bounces Back via Scanner Data," *Advertising Age,* June 3, 1991, p. 31.
Yates, Ronald, "A Victory for Global Presence," *Chicago Tribune,* March 9, 1994, sec. 3, p. 1.

—Robert R. Jacobson

INFORMIX®

Informix Corp.

4100 Bohannon Dr.
Menlo Park, California 94025
U.S.A.
(415) 926-6300
Fax: (415) 926-6593

Public Company
Incorporated: 1980 as Relational Database Systems Inc.
Employees: 1,445
Sales: $352.9 million
Stock Exchanges: NASDAQ National Market System
SICs: 7372 Prepackaged Software

Informix Corp. is one of the world's top three developers of relational database software for computers using the UNIX operating system. The other two companies are Oracle and Sybase, Inc. While the company also provides other kinds of business and programmers' development software, Informix has been most successful with its core database products. The young company emerged at the right time to take advantage of the trend among corporate computer users to switching from mainframe computer systems having proprietary software to networked microcomputers (workstations and personal computers) running various forms of UNIX.

The software company, originally named Relational Database Systems Inc., was founded in 1980 by 25-year old entrepreneur Roger J. Sippl with a $200,000 investment. Sippl, who earned an B.A. in computer science from the University of California, Berkeley, had previously been manager of database research and development at Cromenco, a manufacturer of microcomputers. Sippl became the president, chief executive officer, and chairman of his new company.

Relational Database Systems was one of the pioneers in developing fully relational database management systems (RDMS) for multiuser computers with its product line called INFORMIX. RDMS programs link multiple files together and permit the comparison and analysis of the data in these files. For example, a customer database file, an order file, and a product list database may be linked so that a company may determine what customers ordered which of its products. RDMS software had existed since the 1970s, but it was typically customized or was proprietary software for mainframe computer systems, and

was not considered commercially viable in other forms. Relational Database Systems was one of the first companies to specialize in offering RDMS software packages designed to run on the UNIX operating system, which is used on many different makes of minicomputers and microcomputers. The company began distributing its first UNIX RDMS in 1981.

Relational Database Systems quickly became a leader in the new field of UNIX-based database management software. The company gained a technological edge over its competitors by developing its products specifically for workstations and personal computers. Oracle and Relational Technology Inc., another leading RDMS company at the time, had instead revised software they had originally developed for mainframes and minicomputers.

In summer 1985 Relational Database Systems introduced a significant new product, INFORMIX-SQL, a RDMS that featured an ANSI-standard query language that was based on International Business Machines Corporation's (IBM) Structured Query Language (SQL). Although the software was for UNIX, the use of IBM's SQL opened up a potential market of IBM computer users familiar with that query format. The company also introduced INFORMIX-ESQL/C, which offered additional programmable features in the C language.

Also in 1985 the company introduced the first SQL-based RDMS software version for local area networks of DOS-based personal computers. The design of separate "front-end" and "back-end" components of the company's SQL software, developed several years prior, made it most efficient when running on client/server networks, whereby multiple users at individually networked computers share database files kept on a designated computer known as a server.

The company moved further into providing software for programmers and not just end-users when in February of 1986 it introduced INFORMIX-4GL, a fourth generation programming language designed especially for developing databases. It was the first application-building language that combined all the needed fourth generation application programming features along with SQL and could be used under all versions of UNIX. Later in 1986, versions of INFORMIX-4GL and INFORMIX-SQL were introduced that ran on the VMS operating system of Digital Equipment Corporation's VAX minicomputers and MicroVAC workstations. Also in 1986, the company began development of INFORMIX Datasheet Add-In, a product that added true RDMS capabilities to Lotus 1-2-3.

By the mid-1980s Relational Database Systems had developed a broad marketing network comprising original equipment manufacturers (OEMs), value-added resellers (VARs), dealers, and distributors. By 1986, OEMs had packaged the company's software products with over 150 different kinds of midrange computer models and contributed to 22 percent of Relational Database Systems' sales. VARs, which customized the company's software for specific industry markets and also combined it with hardware, accounted for about 13 percent sales. International distributors were responsible for 13 percent of sales, up 200 percent from 1985.

The company's own direct sales force was significantly expanded through the opening of six regional domestic sales offices between mid-1985 and the end of 1986, and the sales staff increased from 12 to 84 people. Direct sales to corporate end-users made up the largest share, at 32 percent, of the company's sales in 1986. Another 12 percent of sales was to the government sector.

Relational Database Systems had $2.1 million in revenues and $169,000 in earnings in 1983. Over the next three years the business grew over tenfold. Revenues in 1986 were $21.1 million, and earnings were $2.4 million. The number of employees grew from 22 in 1983 to 214 in 1986. Much of the company's success over these three years has been attributed to the compatibility of its database products with IBM's SQL database language standard.

In August of 1986 the company changed its name to Informix Corp. in anticipation of an initial public offering. The company was reincorporated under the new name in Delaware as a holding company, and an operating subsidiary, Informix Software Inc., was created and headquartered along with Informix Corp. in Menlo Park, California. Informix Corp. went public on September 24, 1986, by selling 969,446 shares at $7.50 per share, raising $6.7 million. The company raised an additional $2.3 million by selling 330,554 shares to Altos Computer Systems, which put Altos' investment in the company at 23 percent. The shares held by officers and directors of Informix were thus reduced from 66 percent to 56 percent.

In February 1988 Informix made the significant strategic decision to acquire Innovative Software Inc. of Lenexa, Kansas. It was hoped that Innovative's microcomputer software products, and especially its front-end applications, would complement Informix's RDMS software so as to offer clients integrated office automation software. Innovative, which had 1987 revenues of $18.8 million, had developed a package of integrated software applications for the personal computer called SmartWare. The two companies first considered a joint venture, but then decided in fall of 1987 that a merger would be more advantageous. Michael Brown one of the two founders of Innovative, was made president of the merged Informix, while Sippl retained the posts of chairman and chief executive.

The merger, however, did not go well. The companies had very different products, markets, corporate cultures, and geographic locations, and were difficult to integrate. Furthermore, the decision to retain dual headquarters led to confusion and inefficiency. The employment increased from 350 to 1,200, and expenses doubled. There was significant turnover of sales and marketing personnel, and two vice-presidents of sales left the company in 1988. Earnings, excluding merger costs of $800,000, steadily declined from $2.5 million in the first quarter of 1988 to $1.5 million second quarter, to $98,000 third quarter, followed by the company's first loss of $2 million in the fourth quarter. Furthermore, Informix's accounting methods had to be revised due to criticisms from investors and auditors. To top it all off, in late 1988 Informix was the subject of a class action lawsuit by shareholders charging company officers with inflating the company's stock price. The company ended 1988 with a $46.3 million loss.

Problems in managing the merger contributed to delays in introducing new products, which led to further financial troubles. Release 4 of Informix's database engine was delayed from early 1989 to the end of the year. An upgrade to SmartWare was also many months late. A new spreadsheet software package called Wingz, which Innovative had begun developing in early 1987, was announced in January of 1988 and supposed to be on the market by June, but did not ship until spring of 1989. It was Informix's first product for the Macintosh, and debugging the software took much longer than anticipated. Thus losses continued in 1989 and 1990.

Despite innovative features and favorable reviews, Wingz never had a reasonable chance to become a successful product. It was impossible to compete with Microsoft Corporation's Excel, which held an estimated 70–90 percent of the market share for Macintosh spreadsheet programs. Some industry observers cited the decision to launch Wingz as a major mistake. Likewise SmartWare II was not a big success, not because of the quality of the program, but because integrated software—a single package that combines word processing, spreadsheet, database management, and other capabilities—has not been popular in the United States. SmartWare was relatively successful in Europe, however.

Meanwhile Sippl had turned over the management of the company to a new chief executive with more professional management experience, while staying on as chairman. At the beginning of 1989 Informix hired Phillip E. White as CEO of Informix. Until then White was president of Wyse, and prior to that spent 15 years at IBM and then two years as vice president of sales and marketing at Altos.

Indeed it took a new chief executive to turn Informix around. White announced a corporate reorganization in January of 1989. He laid off about 200 employees, or 15 percent of the staff. He eliminated the dual nature of the company, which since the acquisition had had two sales forces, two manufacturing operations, and two marketing operations. Instead he created two product divisions, the Workstation Products Division in Lenexa and the Advanced Products Division at the headquarters in Menlo Park. White took over the presidency of Informix and the management of the Advance Products Division and made former Informix president Michael Brown president and general manager of the Workstation Products Division. The Advanced Products Division was responsible for Informix's traditional database, network, and application-development software, while the Workstation Products Division was made responsible for Wingz and other office productivity software. In 1990 White relocated some of the manufacturing operations to Kansas, where labor costs were lower.

By the end of 1989 office automation software, developed primarily by the Workstation Productions Division, was accounting for 27 percent of Informix's revenues, while database management software accounted for 36 percent. Software development tools, such as INFORMIX-4GL, made up 37 percent of sales.

At the beginning of 1990 Informix introduced a new, high-end RDMS product for enterprise-wide use called INFORMIX-

OnLine. Designed for on-line transaction processing, it featured distributed processing, fault tolerance, and multimedia capabilities permitting the storage and retrieval of digitized sounds and graphics. Transaction processing capabilities were especially important to Informix's clients in the retail industry.

Sippl gave up day-to-day control in 1990 and left in 1992, feeling that his start up company had grown too big to manage himself. White thus succeeded Sippl in the post of chairman in addition to those of president and chief executive.

White's turnaround of Informix proved to be spectacular. The company returned to profitability in 1991 after losses of $46.4 million in 1990. The following year, 1992, sales increased 46 percent to reach $283 million, and net income quadrupled from $12.2 million to $47.8 million. Contributing to 1992 sales was a single $26.8 million contract for the Army National Guard and Army Reserves. Informix's stock price, which fell as low as $1.31 a share in January 1992 shot up to around $38 a share by spring of 1993. The market capitalization of the company rose 24 times in the same period to reach $1.2 billion. Informix was credited with one of the lowest expense ratios in the industry. Manufacturing costs dropped from 13 percent of revenues in 1989 to only 5 percent in 1993.

Most significantly though, Informix was able to continue its growth by taking advantage of the accelerating demand for UNIX-based business software applications among corporations switching from mainframe computers to networks of personal computers and workstations that share files from servers. Database management software, moreover, is among the best suited for such client/server computing structures, whereby multiple users access shared data stored on a server. In 1989 Informix introduced INFORMIX-STAR, software that enables users of its new INFORMIX-OnLine RDMS to retrieve data from not one but multiple network servers.

Under White Informix followed a new strategy of investing in its core databases and software developers' tools while contracting out the rest. It delegated providing add-on software applications and greater marketing responsibilities to its growing network of about 2,000 value-added resellers. It increasingly was sharing the costs and credit for developing new products with other corporate partners. For example, Informix began working with Sequent Computer Systems Inc. on a parallel processing data query product, with Siemens A.G. on a data dictionary, and with Symbol Technologies Inc. on programming tools to aid in the development of applications for wireless networks. Informix also licensed Hewlett-Packard Company's SoftBench framework for third-party computer-aided software engineering tools. Having learned its lesson from the Innovative merger, Informix did not pursue any more acquisitions, but rather engaged in strategic investments in other companies. As a result of these strategies, Informix was able to maintain operating margins in the early 1990s of over 20 percent.

Meanwhile, Informix began to deemphasize its office automation software, such as Wingz, to concentrate on its original core products of database management software of programming development tools.

Informix was also expanding its overseas sales faster than its competitors. For example, its first quarter 1993 European sales increased 48 percent, whereas Oracle's increased only 4 percent. In 1993, through 30 overseas sales offices, foreign sales accounted for 58 percent of Informix's revenues, up from 54 percent the previous year. Informix's lower-end RDMS, IN-FORMIX-SE, sold through international VARs, did especially well in Europe.

In early 1993, 80 percent of Informix's sales were for software running on the UNIX operating system, and the company claimed to be the world leader in number of installed RDBSs on UNIX computers. At the same time, however, Informix decided to further expand its offerings for other operating systems and platforms. It increased its marketing efforts for a version of its RDMS to run on Novell Inc.'s Netware Loadable Module, which it had launched in 1992. Informix began making its INFORMIX-OnLine available for Microsoft's Windows NT server operating system. It also entered a joint marketing deal with Microsoft for a software package consisting of the IN-FORMIX-SE Client/Server Software Developer's Kit and Microsoft Windows NT, which began shipping in January of 1994. In addition, it was looking into more support for the Macintosh platform.

A new pricing system was introduced in December of 1993, which aimed at setting the software price according to the value that its customers derive from it. This user-based pricing model replaced a pricing structure based on machine class. While emphasizing value to the customers, the new pricing system was also expected to raise revenues on average slightly. Shortly thereafter, competitors began to follow Informix's example in pricing methods.

Informix developed a new product technology in late 1993 called Dynamic Scalable Architecture, the first database management design to combine parallel-processing capabilities, data replication, and connectivity in a single product, while also being adaptable to a user's growing needs. Dynamic Scalable Architecture was first incorporated into INFORMIX OnLine Dynamic Server 6.0, introduced in December of 1993. In March of 1994 Informix shipped OnLine 7.0, it first true multiprocessing database. It featured parallel data query, co-designed by Informix and Sequent Computer Systems Inc., which automatically splits user queries into several parts to run simultaneously across multiple processors.

Staying at the forefront of technology in its chosen field of specialization, and specializing in a software product category upon which corporate clients are increasingly relying, Informix's future looked bright through the end of the 1990s.

Principal Subsidiaries: Informix Software Inc.

Further Reading:

Bozman, Jean S., ''Informix Diversifies UNIX Portfolio,'' *Computerworld,* February 15, 1993, p. 109.

Doler, Kathleen, ''Informix to Undergo Restructuring, Delays Its Database Engine,'' *PC Week,* January 30, 1989, p. 54.

Houston, Patrick, ''Backseat Strategist,'' *PC Week,* July 26, 1993, p. A5.

——, and Karen D. Moser, "Enjoying the Sippl Life," *PC Week*, March 7, 1994, p. A4.

Kaberline, Brian, "Merged Informix Yet to Find Wingz in Software Market," *Kansas City Business Journal*, January 23, 1989, pp. 1, 34.

Karon, Paul, "PC Efforts Stalling Informix's Growth," *PC Week*, December 26, 1988, p. 59.

Lineback, J. Robert, "Sippl Wants to Help UNIX Hook onto the Business Market," *Electronics Week*, March 11, 1985, p. 47.

McCoy, Charles, "Informix Rides High-Tech Wave with UNIX System," *The Wall Street Journal*, May 3, 1993, p. B4.

Rauber, Chris, "Prime Times: Database Company Bounces Back," *San Francisco Business Times*, May 21–27, 1993, pp. 8A, 10A.

—Heather Behn Hedden

Intel Corporation

2200 Mission College Blvd.
P.O. Box 58119
Santa Clara, California 95052-8119
U.S.A.
(408) 765-8080
Fax: (408) 765-1402

Public Company
Incorporated: 1968 as N M Electronics
Employees: 29,500
Sales: $8.87 billion
Stock Exchanges: New York NASDAQ
SICs: 3674 Semiconductors and Related Devices; 3577
   Computer Peripheral Equipment, Nec.; 7372 Prepackaged
   Software; 3571 Electronic Computers

Intel Corporation is the largest semiconductor manufacturer in
the world, with major facilities in the United States, Europe, and
Asia. Intel has changed the world dramatically since it was
founded in 1968; the company invented the microprocessor, the
"computer on a chip" that made possible the first handheld
calculators and personal computers. By the early 1990s, Intel's
product line included: microcontrollers, memory chips, computer modules, and boards for original equipment manufacturers; network, communications and personal conferencing
products for retail sale; and high-performance parallel su-
percomputers. Intel remained competitive through a combination of clever marketing, well-supported research and
development, a vital corporate culture, and legal proficiency. In
1993, the market research firm Dataquest estimated Intel's chip
sales at almost 30 percent higher than those of its closest
competitor.

Intel's founders, Robert Noyce and Gordon Moore, were among
the eight founders of Fairchild Semiconductor, established in
1957. While at Fairchild, Noyce and Moore invented the integrated circuit, and, in 1968, they decided to form their own
company. They were soon joined by Andrew Grove, a Hungarian refugee who had arrived in America in 1956 and joined
Fairchild in 1963. Grove would remain president and CEO of
Intel into the 1990s.

To obtain start-up capital, Noyce and Moore approached Arthur
Rock, a venture capitalist, with a one-page business plan simply
stating their intention of developing large-scale integrated cir-

cuits. Rock, who had helped start Fairchild Semiconductor, as
well as Teledyne and Scientific Data Systems, had confidence in
Noyce and Moore and provided $3 million in capital. The
company was incorporated on July 18, 1968 as N M Electronics
(the letters standing for Noyce Moore), but quickly changed its
name to Intel, formed from the first syllables of "integrated
electronics." Intel gathered another $2 million in capital before
going public in 1971.

Noyce and Moore's scanty business proposal belied a clear plan
to produce large-scale integrated (LSI) semiconductor memories. At that time, semiconductor memories were ten times more
expensive than standard magnetic core memories. However,
costs were falling, and Intel's founders felt that with the greater
speed and efficiency of LSI technology, semiconductors would
soon replace magnetic cores. Within a few months of its startup,
Intel produced the 3101 Schottky bipolar memory, a high-speed
random access memory (RAM). The 3101 proved popular
enough to sustain the company until the 1101, a metal oxide
semiconductor (MOS) chip, was perfected and introduced in
1969. The following year, Intel introduced the 1103, a 1 Kilo-
byte (K) dynamic RAM, or DRAM, which was the first chip
large enough to store a significant amount of information. With
the 1103, Intel finally had a chip that really did begin to replace
magnetic cores; DRAMs eventually proved indispensable to the
personal computer.

The company's most dramatic impact on the computer industry
involved its 1971 introduction of the 4004, the world's first
microprocessor. Like many of Intel's innovations, the microprocessor was a byproduct of efforts to develop another technology. When a Japanese calculator manufacturer asked Intel to
design cost-effective chips for a series of calculators, Intel engineer Ted Hoff was assigned to the project; during his search for
such a design, Hoff conceived a plan for a central processing
unit (CPU) on one chip. The 4004, which crammed 2,300
transistors onto a one-eighth- by one-sixth-inch chip, had the
power of the old 3,000-cubic-foot ENIAC computer, which
depended on 38,000 vacuum tubes.

Although Intel initially focused on the microprocessor as a
computer enhancement that would allow users to add more
memory to their units, the microprocessor's great potential—
for everything from calculators to cash registers and traffic
lights—soon became clear. Their applications were facilitated
by Intel's introduction of the 8008, an 8-bit microprocessor
developed along with the 4004 but oriented toward data and
character (rather than arithmetic) manipulation. The 8080, introduced in 1974, was the first truly general purpose microprocessor. For $360, Intel sold a whole computer on one chip,
while conventional computers sold for thousands of dollars. The
response was overwhelming. The 8080 soon became the industry standard and Intel the industry leader in the 8-bit market.

In response to ensuing competition in the manufacture of 8-bit
microprocessors, Intel introduced the 8085, a faster chip with
more functions. The company was also developing two more
advanced projects, the 32-bit 432 and the 16-bit 8086. The 8086
was introduced in 1978 but took two years to achieve wide use,
and, during this time, Motorola produced a competing chip (the
68000) that seemed to be selling faster. Intel responded with a
massive sales effort to establish its architecture as the standard.

When IBM chose the 8008, the 8086's 8-bit cousin, for its personal computer in 1980, Intel seemed to have beat out the competition.

During the 1970s, Intel had also developed the erasable programmable read-only memory (EPROM), another revolutionary but unintended research byproduct. Intel physicist Dov Frohman was working on the reliability problems of the silicon gate used in the MOS process when he realized that the disconnected, or "floating," gates that were causing malfunctions could be used to create a chip that was erasable and reprogrammable. Since conventional ROM chips had to be permanently programmed during manufacture, any change required the manufacture of a whole new chip. With EPROM, however, Intel could offer customers chips that could be erased and reprogrammed with ultraviolet light and electricity. At its introduction in 1971, EPROM was a novelty without much of a market. But the microprocessor, invented at the same time, created a demand for memory; the EPROM offered memory that could be conveniently used to test microprocessors.

Another major development at Intel during this time was that of peripheral controller chips. Streamlined for specific tasks and stripped of unneeded functions, peripheral chips could greatly increase a computer's abilities without raising software development costs. One of Intel's most important developments in peripherals was the coprocessor, first introduced in 1980. Coprocessor chips were an extension of the CPU that could handle specific computer-intensive tasks more efficiently than the CPU itself. Once again, innovation kept Intel ahead of its competition.

Intel's rapid growth, from the 12 employees at its founding in 1968 to 15,000 in 1980, demanded a careful approach to corporate culture. Noyce, Moore, and Grove, who remembered their frustration with Fairchild's bureaucratic bottlenecks, found that defining a workable management style was important. Informal weekly lunches with employees kept communication lines open while the company was small, but that system had become unwieldy. Thus, the founders installed a carefully outlined program emphasizing openness, decision making on the lowest levels, discipline, and problem solving rather than paper shuffling. Moreover, the company's top executives eschewed such luxuries as limousines, expense account lunches, and private parking spaces to establish a sense of teamwork with their subordinates.

In an interview with the *Harvard Business Review* in 1980, Noyce remarked on the company's hiring policy, stating, "we expect people to work hard. We expect them to be here when they are committed to be here; we measure absolutely everything that we can in terms of performance." Employee incentives included options on Intel stock, and technological breakthroughs were celebrated with custom-bottled champagne— "Vintage Intel" marked the first $250 million quarter, in 1983—the year sales reached $1 billion for the first time.

During the 1974 recession, Intel was forced to lay off 30 percent of its employees, and morale declined substantially as a result. Thus, in 1981, when economic struggles again surfaced, instead of laying off more employees, Intel accelerated new product development with the "125 Percent Solution," which

asked exempt employees to work two extra hours per day, without pay, for six months. A brief surge in sales the following year didn't last, and, again, instead of more lay offs, Intel imposed pay cuts of up to ten percent. Such measures weren't popular among all its work force, but, by June 1983, all cuts had been restored and retroactive raises had been made. Moreover, in December 1982, IBM paid $250 million for a 12 percent share of Intel, giving the company not only a strong capital boost, but also strong ties to the undisputed industry leader. IBM would eventually increased its stake to 20 percent before selling its Intel stock in 1987.

During the early 1980s, Intel began to slip in some of its markets. Fierce competition in DRAMS, static RAMS, and EPROMS left Intel concentrating on microprocessors. While competitors claimed that Intel simply gave away its DRAM market, Moore told *Business Week* in 1988 that the company deliberately focused on microprocessors as the least cyclical field in which to operate. Customer service, an area Intel had been able to overlook for years as it dominated its markets, became more important as highly-efficient Japanese and other increasingly innovative competitors challenged Intel's position. In addition, Intel's manufacturing record, strained in years past by undercapacity, needed fixing. Fab 7, Intel's seventh wafer-fabrication plant, opened in 1983 only to face two years of troubled operations before reaching full capacity. Between 1984 and 1988, Intel closed eight old plants, and in 1988 it spent some $450 million on new technology to bring its manufacturing capacity into line with its developmental prowess.

Despite these retrenchments, the company continued to excel in the microprocessor market. In 1982, Intel introduced its 80286 microprocessor, the chip that quickly came to dominate the upper-end PC market, when IBM came out with the 286-powered PC/AT. The 286 was followed in 1985 by Intel's 80386 chip, popularized in 1987 by the Compaq 386, which, despite bugs when it first came out, became one of the most popular chips on the market. While the 286 brought to the personal computer a speed and power that gave larger computers their first real challenge, the 386 offered even greater speed and power together with the ability to run more than one program at a time.

In 1989, Intel introduced the 80486, a chip *Business Week* heralded as "a veritable mainframe-on-a-chip." In designing the i486, Intel resisted an industry trend toward RISC (reduced instruction-set computing), a chip design that eliminated rarely used instructions in order to gain speed. Intel argued that what RISC chips gained in speed they lost in flexibility and that, moreover, RISC chips were not compatible with software already on the market, which Intel felt would secure the 486's position. However, a new chip, the 64-bit i860 announced in early 1989, did make use of RISC technology to offer what Intel claimed would be a "supercomputer on a chip."

Also in 1989, an important lawsuit that Intel had filed against NEC Corporation five years before was decided. Intel had claimed that NEC violated its copyright on the microcode, or embedded software instructions, of Intel's 8086 and 8088 chips. Although Intel had licensed NEC to produce the microcode, NEC had subsequently designed a similar chip of its own. At issue was whether microcode could be copyrighted. The court ruled that it could but that NEC had not violated any copyright in the case at hand. The suit made public some issues surrounding Intel's reputation. Some rivals and consumers, for example, claimed that Intel used its size and power to repress competition through such tactics as filing "meritless" lawsuits and tying microprocessor sales to other chips. Other observers, however, praised Intel's protection of its intellectual property and, subsequently, its profits. The Federal Trade Commission conducted a two-year investigation of Intel's practices and did not recommend criminal charges against the company, but two rival companies—Advanced Micro Devices Inc. and Cyrix Corp.—filed antitrust lawsuits against Intel in 1993.

Intel's annual net income topped $1 billion for the first time in 1992, following a very successful, brand-building, marketing campaign. Intel ads aggressively sought to bolster consumer interest in and demand for computers that featured "Intel Inside." By late 1993, the company's brand equity totaled $17.8 billion—more than three times its 1992 sales. Also during this time, Intel began to branch out from chipmaking. In 1992, the company's Intel Products Group introduced network, communications, and personal conferencing products for retail sale directly to PC users.

In 1993, Intel released its fifth-generation Pentium processor, a trademarked chip capable of executing over 100 million instructions per second and supporting, for example, real-time video communication. The Pentium processor was up to five times more powerful than the 33-megahertz Intel 486 DX microprocessor, but, in an unusual marketing maneuver, the company

suggested that "all but the most demanding users" seek out PCs powered by the previous chip.

The company enjoyed a dramatic 50 percent revenue increase in 1993, reaching $8.78 billion from $5.84 billion in 1992. Moreover, Intel's net income leaped 115 percent to $2.3 billion, repudiating Wall Street's worries that competition had squeezed profit margins. While Intel faced strong competition both from chip makers like giant Motorola's PowerPC and former partner IBM, its place at the leading edge of technology was undisputed and expected to continue. As it entered the mid-1990s, Intel looked to address potential challenges in the form of leadership transitions, as founders Moore and Grove neared retirement.

Principal Subsidiaries: Intel Japan K.K.; Intel Corporation S.A.R.L. (France); Intel Corporation (U.K.) Ltd.; Intel GmbH (Germany); Intel Semiconductor, Ltd. (Hong Kong); Intel Semiconductor of Canada, Ltd.

Further Reading:

Clark, Tim, "Inside Intel's Marketing Machine," *Business Marketing,* October 1992, pp. 14–19.
Defining Intel: 25 Years/25 Events, Santa Clara: Intel Corporation, 1993.
A Revolution in Progress . . . A History of Intel to Date, Santa Clara: Intel Corporation, 1984.
Ristelhueber, Robert, "Intel: The Company People Love to Hate," *Electronic Business Buyer,* September 1993, pp. 58–67.

—updated by April Dougal Gasbarre

International Controls Corporation

2016 N. Pitcher St.
Kalamazoo, Michigan 49007
U.S.A.
(616) 343-6121
Fax: (616) 343-1660

Private Company
Incorporated: 1959
Employees: 5,055
Sales: $909 million
SICs: 3715 Truck Trailers; 3465 Automotive Stampings;
    6719 Holding Companies Nec

International Controls Corporation (ICC), is the holding company of Checker Motors Corp. and Great Dane Trailers Inc. Reporting sales of $909 million in 1993, from which it earned a ranking among *Fortune* magazine's top 500 American companies, ICC had net losses of $43 million, due primarily to circumstances surrounding its large debt load. ICC had at various times during its history controlled over 50 companies— including an electronics firm, a defense contractor, a trucking company, and an auto parts manufacturer—under an expansion plan initiated by the notorious financier, Robert Vesco. However, the company was forced to liquidate many of its holdings in the aftermath of a debacle involving charges of securities fraud against Vesco. Thereafter, the company spent years trying to rebuild its reputation and financial condition.

ICC was founded in 1959 as a small producer of electronic devices for aircraft and computers. Although the electronics industry was beginning to flourish during this time, ICC remained a small company, grossing about $300,000 per year and netting virtually nothing. By 1965, ICC was struggling to survive, when a buyer, Robert Vesco, promised to provide a much-needed infusion of capital.

Vesco, the son of a Detroit autoworker, dropped out of engineering school in his early twenties to go to work for an investment firm. After a brief foray in a minor position at the firm, Vesco decided to go it alone. With an $800 stake, he began matching buyers and sellers in the aluminum market, until he eventually acquired a portion of the profits of a floundering aluminum plant. By 1965, he was in a position to borrow enough money to acquire ICC, and Vesco's notorious rise to wealth began.

At ICC, Vesco established a business strategy of borrowing heavily to make acquisitions. The revenues generated from these investments were, in turn, used to gain increasingly larger loans to further expand the company's holdings. Vesco, extremely adept at cultivating investors, including bank presidents and experienced entrepreneurs, reportedly emphasized ICC's impressive sales figures and downplayed its substantial debts. While ICC's sales rocketed to $6.8 million in only two years as a result of Vesco's acquisitions, rising interest rates began to take a heavy toll on ICC's large debts.

In 1969, Vesco launched an unfriendly takeover bid against Electronic Specialty, a West Coast manufacturer of aircraft parts and electromechanical components, which had annual sales of over $100 million. After a succession of lawsuits initiated by ELS shareholders, Vesco managed to gain control of 55 percent of ELS stock, incurring another $20 million in debt in the process. Nevertheless, banks continued to lend ICC money based primarily on its annual sales figures, which included sales from the recently acquired Intercontinental Industries, a Dallas weapons manufacturer. The original owner of Intercontinental sued Vesco for control of the company, noting in a 1969 article in *Forbes:* "I never saw the likes of this guy . . . I haven't been paid for it, even though Vesco has consolidated it in his figures." The two companies eventually reached a settlement, which again further raised ICC's debt load.

Still, Vesco remained committed to his acquisition policy, noting in an article in *Forbes:* "The main thing is the future. . . . Now that we are a $100 million-plus company, we can look at a $300 million one. I plan to do a billion by 1971." Toward that end, in 1970, Vesco began a successful takeover bid for Investors Overseas Services (IOS), a mutual fund investment firm with holdings of $1.5 billion run by financier Bernard Cornfield. The investment service provided the funds Vesco needed to further expand ICC's network of holdings but eventually proved integral to his undoing.

According to later allegations, Vesco began to move money from IOS's mutual funds out of blue-chip stocks and into various offshore enterprises controlled through ICC. By 1972, the Securities and Exchange Commission (SEC) and some IOS investors had become suspicious of Vesco's activities, and an inquiry was launched. In an attempt to squelch the investigation, Vesco reportedly delivered $200,000 in cash to President Richard Nixon's re-election campaign—a move that, once uncovered, brought the investigation onto the front pages of the nation's newspapers.

In February 1973, with criminal charges against him imminent, Vesco took the corporate jet and fled to Costa Rica along with about $200 million worth of IOS's investments, according to SEC allegations. Vesco would continue to wage a legal battle from Costa Rica and the Bahamas to try to maintain control over his 26 percent of ICC stock, but, with five outstanding indictments for securities fraud against him, he could not return to the United States.

When Vesco fled the country, he left behind him a corporation that was not only at the center of the biggest financial scandal of the decade but that also had posted a loss of $38 million in the previous year and was in debt for more than $48 million.

Moreover, ICC was named in several lawsuits related to the Vesco debacle. The company was immediately placed under court supervision, and all stock was suspended from trading. The court appointed a board of five directors, who, in turn, appointed Allen Shinn, a retired U.S. Navy Admiral, as chairperson of ICC.

Elmer Sticco was named chief operating officer and company president. Sticco had been a senior manager at Electronic Specialties when ICC acquired that company in 1969. After the acquisition, Electronic Specialties became an ICC division, with Sticco as its leader. Although he was aware that Vesco's dealings were not always above board, Sticco deliberately avoided any direct involvement with his boss's decisions and was cleared of any wrongdoing during the SEC investigations. With his thorough understanding of the company's strengths and failings, Sticco was in a perfect position to assume management of ICC.

The first step in bringing ICC back to viability was to reduce its huge debt. The company sold 11 of its divisions, including Portland Heavy Industries, which was acquired by Boeing for $16 million. When the major pruning was done, ICC was left with only two major subsidiaries, Datron Systems and American Industries. Long term debt was reduced from $48 million to a more manageable $22 million, and stockholders' equity rose from $7 million to $18 million. Next, Allen Shinn toured the country trying to reassure suppliers and customers who were reluctant to deal with the tainted company. By 1976, ICC was recording net profits of almost $2 million, and, by 1980, sales had climbed to $117.9 million with earnings of over $7 million.

Despite this dramatic turnaround, ICC struggled to shake off Vesco's legacy. In 1977, at the first stockholders meeting following the court takeover, a three-way fight for election to the board of directors ensued. Two groups of shareholders staged competing attempts to topple the court-appointed board of directors, claiming that Sticco had received an unduly large salary and bonuses, and that ICC lawyers were deliberately slow to reinstate stockholder control of the company in order to continue collecting their large retainer fees. The third party in the struggle was Robert Vesco, who filed a suit, through his daughter, to regain control of the 25 percent of shares that had been confiscated from him and placed in the hands of a court-appointed trustee. Both Vesco's lawsuit and the stockholders' revolt were ultimately unsuccessful, but the controversy and publicity surrounding the event did little to bolster ICC's reputation.

By 1981, ICC appeared close to severing its ties with Vesco. A final payment of $11 million to IOS settled the company's liability for Vesco's dealings. In addition, ICC regained control of the outstanding 25 percent share in the company by paying $640,000 to Vesco's family. In an article in *Forbes* that year, Sticco remarked, "There is a real possibility that after next year we can put out an annual report without the name Vesco in it."

During this time, ICC's defense related industries blossomed under the Reagan administration's increased defense budget. With the U.S. government as its largest customer, ICC looked forward to several years of multi-million dollar contracts for its military hardware. Total sales in 1980 topped $117 million, and

earnings rose to $7.2 million, almost doubling the previous year's performance. Moreover, for the first time in the company's 20-year history, ICC directors began discussing the possibility of declaring a cash dividend for stockholders. Based on the company's improved financial condition, three banks established a $10 million credit line for ICC, which hoped to make some large acquisitions over the next few years. "If we're sitting here with quality management, there's nothing I could get involved with that I couldn't handle," Sticco commented in *Forbes* during this time.

However, in the mid-1980s, an unexpected and unwelcome takeover bid was initiated by financier Arthur Goldberg. Referred to by *Forbes* magazine writer Phyllis Berman as "an accomplished greenmailer," Goldberg had a history of investing heavily in companies and then selling out at a profit either to corporate raiders or to company management, who sought to avoid a takeover. Goldberg began to buy up ICC stock in 1984, and, the following year, he teamed up with Bear, Stearns, an investment firm, to acquire 22 percent of ICC stock. His takeover bid was at first flatly rejected by Sticco. However, after suffering a series of crippling heart attacks, Sticco agreed to resign his post in favor of the newcomer. The ICC board was apparently unaware of Goldberg's investment history; one ICC director was reported to have asserted, "He's not a raider type. He's not in it for a quick kill, at least it doesn't seem so to me."

Goldberg's first move, taken within days of assuming control at ICC, was to convince the board to designate $100 million in bonds for acquisitions. Within a matter of months, ICC made an offer to acquire Transway International Corp., a huge trucking firm with annual sales of nearly $900 million. With the acquisition, which one *Journal of Commerce* analyst compared to "a minnow swallowing a whale," ICC's revenues swelled from about $166 million to almost $1 billion, and its stock rose from $16 to $28 per share. While stock and revenues were up, the company was $427 million in debt from the Transway deal.

Next, Goldberg decided to take ICC private. In early 1987, he directed the company to offer $32 per share for the 71 percent of the publicly held stock. Stockholders balked at the low figure, and five separate class action suits were filed. Goldberg and the stockholders finally agreed on $44 a share, and ICC borrowed more money to pay for the privatization of its stock. In 1988, Goldberg's ICC, again heavily in debt, began to sell off its divisions, and, by the end of the year, Great Dane Trailers Inc., a company bought in the Transway deal, was the only remaining ICC subsidiary. While ICC remained in debt for $360 million, the divestitures had brought in some $157 million in cash with which Goldberg and his partners could arrange further financing.

Next, Goldberg arranged one of the intricate financial deals for which he had become known. His associate in the deal was Martin Solomon, a former IOS financial advisor to Robert Vesco and a government witness in the Vesco case. Along with some partners, Solomon had recently undertaken a $60 million buyout of the Michigan-based Checker Motors, at one time the top manufacturer of taxicabs. The once powerful company had given up its cab manufacturing business in the early 1980s to focus on automotive stampings and the operations of its two subsidiaries, the Yellow Cab Co. of Chicago and an insurance firm. Solomon and Goldberg arranged for ICC to acquire Checker Motors for $135 million in cash, available from ICC's divestitures. Solomon and his three partners then formed a new company, Checker Holding, which in turn acquired all of the equity in ICC for $45 million. Finally, Checker Holding was merged into ICC, leaving ICC in control of two subsidiaries, Checker Motors and Great Dane Trailers Inc., all of which were overseen by Solomon and his partners. After only four years, Goldberg ended his involvement with ICC, which was then nearly $400 million in debt.

In the early 1990s, ICC focused on alleviating its huge debt burden. In 1992, *Standard & Poor's* dropped its rating of the company's stock from CC to CCC-, in response to ICC's large debt ratio and the depressed truck and auto industries, which were now ICC's chief business sectors. Despite large revenues from Great Dane Trailers, which placed ICC in the Fortune 500 list of top grossing companies, ICC still recorded a net loss of $43 million in 1993. With new corporate headquarters in Kalamazoo, Michigan, the volatile company strove to overcome its financial burdens and a reputation that prompted mistrust among investors.

Principal Subsidiaries: Checker Motors Corp.; Great Dane Trailers Inc.

Further Reading:

Anreder, Steven S., "Vesco's Legacy: International Controls Corp. Hopes to Live It Down," *Barron's,* April 17, 1978, pp. 9, 16–18.

Baker, Thomas, "De-Stalinization, Corporate Style," *Forbes,* June 8, 1981, pp. 78–80.

Berman, Phyllis, "Let 'Em Eat Junk," *Forbes,* April 16, 1990, pp. 72–74.

Burgess, William H., "The Remarkable Recovery of the Company Vesco Left Behind," *Management Review,* May 1982, pp. 31–32.

"Company On the Make," *Forbes,* March 1, 1969, p. 29.

Donnelly, Christopher, "Trouble Seen for International Controls," *Investment Dealers' Digest,* January 13, 1992, p. 1.

Greer, Philip, and Mike Kandel, "Vesco Seeks to Regrip Reins of Intl. Controls," *The Insiders' Chronicle,* September 8, 1977, p. 9.

"If At First . . . ," *Forbes,* September 7, 1987, p. 8.

"International Controls: Struggling to Dissipate the Post-Vesco Clouds," *Business Week,* November 13, 1978, pp. 165–68.

"International Controls: The Lively Corpse," *Forbes,* October 15, 1977, pp. 63–64.

"Life After Vesco," *Barron's,* September 7, 1981, pp. 34–35.

Marcial, Gene G., "Raider Goldberg Tries a Lowball Tactic," *Business Week,* December 16, 1985, p. 79.

Slutsker, Gary, "Come Right In, You Cur You," *Forbes,* October 7, 1985, p. 84.

Sterne, Larry, "Analysts Eye Acquisition of Transway," *Journal of Commerce,* October 3, 1985, p. 7A.

"What Robert Vesco is Doing in the Bahamas," *Business Week,* March 30, 1974, pp. 78–80.

—Hilary Gopnik

the freezer and the soft ice cream flowed into three-gallon containers. The containers were covered with lids, frozen at −10 degrees Fahrenheit, and delivered to customers. When an ice cream store was ready to serve the product, the ice cream was put into a dipping cabinet and the temperature increased to 5 degrees Fahrenheit.

The ice cream was frozen solid, not for the pleasure and enjoyment of the customer, but for the convenience of the manufacturer and store owner. Yet the elder McCullough had known for a long time that ice cream at colder temperatures numbed the tastebuds and resulted in a much less flavorful product; soft, fresh ice cream drawn from a spigot at approximately 23 degrees Fahrenheit tasted best. He began to wonder if there was some way to dispense semifrozen ice cream that kept its shape, but soon realized that the batch freezers in use during the 1930s were unsuitable. An entirely different type of freezer was required and, moreover, every ice cream store that wished to dispense the new product would have to purchase at least one of the new freezers. Faced with these difficulties, Grandpa McCullough decided to give up the idea as impractical.

After a few years, however, Grandpa McCullough was still thinking about soft ice cream, and he convinced his son that they should find out whether or not the product would capture people's tastebuds. They asked one of their customers, Sherb Noble, if he would arrange a special offering of soft ice cream at his store in Kankakee, Illinois. With an advertisement of "All you can eat for 10 cents," the sale was held in early August of 1938. Using an ordinary commercial batch freezer, the men put the soft ice cream into five gallon containers and then hand-dipped the product into 16-ounce cups. In two hours, Noble and the McCulloughs dished out over 1,600 servings. A short time later, another sale of soft ice cream was offered at Mildred's Ice Cream Shop in Moline. The response from the public was the same. With such overwhelming success, the McCulloughs began searching for the type of freezer that would make dispensing soft ice cream a reality.

The McCulloughs approached two manufacturers of dairy equipment and asked if they would be interested in designing a machine that dispensed semifrozen dairy products into dishes or ice cream cones. The first manufacturer immediately rejected their proposal, while the second firm, Stoelting Brothers Company in Kiel, Wisconsin, thought the idea lacked potential. With no where else to go, the McCulloughs seemed to arrive at a dead end. But one day while Grandpa McCullough was casually paging through the want ads in the *Chicago Tribune* he noticed an advertisement for a continuous freezer that would dispense soft ice cream. The ad had been place by Harry M. Oltz.

Oltz and the McCulloughs met in the summer of 1939. Having already received the patent for his freezer in 1937, Oltz extended the production rights to his new partners, as well as rights for the exclusive use of the freezer in Illinois, Wisconsin, and all the states west of the Mississippi River. According to the agreement, Oltz kept exclusive rights to use of the freezer in all states east of the Mississippi, and would receive continuous royalties based on the number of gallons of soft serve ice cream processed through all the dispensing freezers produced under the patent. Oltz then moved to Miami, Florida, and established

International Dairy Queen, Inc.

5701 Green Valley Drive
Minneapolis, Minnesota 55437
U.S.A.
(612) 830-0200
Fax: (612) 830-0270

Public Company
Incorporated: 1962
Sales: $297.1 million
Employees: 518
Stock Exchanges: NASDAQ
SICs: 5046 Commercial Equipment; 2023 Dry Condensed and Evaporated Dairy Products

International Dairy Queen, Inc. licenses, services, and develops over 5,400 Dairy Queen stores in the United States, Canada, and numerous foreign countries, including operations in Austria, Slovenia, China, Oman, and Guam. In addition to selling its famous diary desserts, many of the stores also sell hamburgers, chicken, hot dogs, and a variety of beverages. The company also owns Karmelkorn Shoppes, Inc., a franchisor of over 100 retail stores that sell popcorn, candy, and other items, and Orange Julius, a franchisor of nearly 500 stores which feature blended drinks made from orange juice, various fruits, and fruit flavors.

The founders of Dairy Queen, J. F. "Grandpa" McCullough and his son Alex, originally established the Homemade Ice Cream Company in 1927. Located in Davenport, Iowa, the two men sold a variety of ice cream products throughout the Quad Cities area, which includes Moline and Rock Island, Illinois, and Bettendorf and Davenport, Iowa. In order to expand their operations, during the early 1930s the McCullough's decided to move their business to Green River, Illinois, and purchased a former cheese factory in which they located their ice cream mix plant.

When the McCulloughs made ice cream at their plant in Green River, it was a complicated process. Butterfat, milk solids, sweetener, and stabilizer were first combined, then mixed, and finally put into a batch freezer where the combination was chilled, given a specific amount of air (technically called "overrun"), and flavored. The product was denser and richer with less overrun. At 23 degrees Fahrenheit, a spigot was opened in

AR-TIK Systems, Inc., a firm that would find stores to serve soft ice cream in the eastern United States. Meanwhile, the McCulloughs returned to the Stoelting Brothers and reached an agreement with them to manufacture a soft-serve ice cream freezer for their own company.

The first Dairy Queen store opened in Joliet, Illinois, on June 22, 1940. Jointly owned by the McCulloughs and Sherb Noble, the partners contracted Jim and Elliot Grace to manage the store for them. By the end of the summer, the store had grossed $4000, and Noble decided to buy out the McCulloughs' interest. On April 1, 1941, the McCulloughs opened another store in Moline and once again contracted the Graces to manage it for them. Additional stores were opened in Aurora, Illinois, and Davenport, Iowa, and by the end of 1942 there were a total of eight Dairy Queen businesses in operation. But with the advent of World War II, manufacturing materials used for building the freezers were reassigned to the war effort. Without new freezers, no new stores were able to open for the duration of the war.

Despite the inability of the McCulloughs to open more stores, they remained active. During the war, father and son sold rights to would-be store owners to use the Dairy Queen freezer and mix, and develop businesses in certain geographical areas of the country. Since they both thought the popularity of Dairy Queen would be brief, it was more sensible to the McCulloughs to sell territories outright rather than to arrange an ongoing royalty system. All profits were up front, and if the product lost its appeal there was no fear of losing any income. Unfortunately, the McCulloughs' method of contracting the development of new territories was extremely informal—sometimes scribbled on a napkin, paper sack, or daily newspaper—and this led to a host of problems later on.

Impressed with the long lines at the Dairy Queen store in Moline, Harry Axene, a sales manager for a farm equipment company, approached Grandpa McCullough and soon became a 50–50 partner in the mix company. He also purchased the territory rights for Illinois and Iowa at a price of $12,000. By the end of the war, Axene had purchased the remaining interest in the mix company and, more importantly, had seen the future of Dairy Queen in franchising. In November of 1946, Axene organized a meeting with 26 potential investors at the LeClaire Hotel in Moline. Excited about organizing a national Dairy Queen franchise system, Axene introduced the idea of selling territories based on a royalty system where territory store owners would pay Axene an initial fee plus an ongoing royalty fee for the soft serve mix. Even though no formal organization resulted from this meeting, interest in Dairy Queen stores grew at a tremendous pace. With only eight stores in operation at the end of the war, by the end of 1946 there were 17, and by the end of 1947 there were over 100 Dairy Queen stores operating throughout the United States.

In 1948, Axene arranged for 35 store owners and territory operators to meet in Minneapolis with the purpose of establishing a national organization. In December of the same year, the first official meeting of the newly incorporated Dairy Queen National Trade Association (DQNTA) was held in Davenport, Iowa. Organized as a not-for-profit corporation, with C. R.

Medd as its first president, national offices were soon established in the city. The DQNTA was created in order to standardize cones, plastic goods, and all other materials used in Dairy Queen stores, along with coordinating all the various kinds of advertising for Dairy Queen products. By the early 1950s, membership in the DQNTA had grown to nearly 900 dues-paying members.

There were 1,400 Dairy Queen stores open for business in 1950, and up until that time the menu was limited to sundaes and cones for immediate consumption, and pints and quarts to take home. When supermarkets began to sell ice cream at low prices and when air conditioning and television began keeping people home on sultry summer evenings, sales in Dairy Queen stores across the country began to suffer. In order to keep attracting customers, most stores responded to requests for an expanded menu. In 1949, milkshakes and malts were made available, and banana splits were added in 1951. Toppings for sundaes were expanded to include hot fudge, chocolate, strawberry, pineapple, butterscotch, and other flavors. Take home novelty products were also introduced, including the Dilly bar, a soft-serve, chocolate dipped confection with a wooden tongue depressor inserted for the customer to hold while eating.

During the 1950s, Dairy Queen stores were also challenged by the emergence of fast food outlets that offered hamburgers, hot dogs, french fries, and various soft drinks. Since these outlets served full meals, they remained open the entire year; Dairy Queen stores were put at a disadvantage since they were boarded up for most of the winter season. In order to stay competitive, store operators in different parts of the country began to offer various food products, from bowls of chili to pork fritters. Yet the lack of a standardized menu brought complaints from customers, until the Brazier system of broiled burgers, hot dogs, barbecued beef, french fries, and onion rings was introduced in 1958. With the introduction of this system, the quality control and standardization of meat products helped to increase profits for store owners.

Though the Dairy Queen National Trade Association was formed in 1948 to standardize products and services for store operators, its not-for-profit status rendered it unable to enforce any of its policies. As a result, the DQNTA was reformed in 1955 and made a for-profit corporation. Renamed the Dairy Queen National Development Company, its members gave it more latitude and authority to implement uniform products, operating practices, standards, and services to all Dairy Queen stores, though it had no franchising rights. Relocating its offices to St. Louis, Missouri, the new company immediately initiated a consumer research program and lobbied for a standardized mix formula for all soft serve products.

After years of involvement, the family members who had started Dairy Queen slowly left the company. Grandpa McCullough had retired during the late 1940s, while his son retired in 1953. Harry Oltz also retired during the late 1940s, while his son Hal continued the family's involvement with the Dairy Queen system. Harry Axene presented the idea of an automatic continuous freezer to the Dairy Queen store operators convention in 1949, but when his proposal was rejected he severed ties with the system and formed the Tastee Freeze business, which he operated on the Pacific coast for 20 years. Only Alex's son, Hugh, remained to look after the McCullough family interests during the 1950s, and by 1960 trouble was brewing on the horizon.

Harry Oltz's patent on his continuous freezer expired in 1954, and a number of store operators refused to continue paying royalties. Hugh McCullough responded with a lawsuit to prove that franchisees were not only paying royalties for use of the freezer, but for use of the trade name. The dispute became even more complicated when a group of store owners who had acquired their territory and franchise rights from Harry Axene filed suit to prove that people who had purchased territory rights from Axene had the right to use the Dairy Queen name because it was Axene and not the McCulloughs who owned the rights.

As the legal battles dragged on and on in the courts, Hugh McCullough grew more and more weary, and finally agreed to sell all his holdings and the rights to the name Dairy Queen. For $1.5 million in cash, McCullough relinquished his claim to all territory and trade name rights. Thus in March 1962, a new corporation, International Dairy Queen, was formed by a group of investors led by Burt Myers, who served as chairman of the board, and Gilbert Stein, who became president.

Headquartered in Minneapolis, management immediately created a wholly-owned subsidiary, American Dairy Queen Corporation, to take care of trademarks, collect royalties, and sell store franchises. More importantly, the new management quickly cleared up all the remaining lawsuits and established undisputed ownership of the name Dairy Queen. In addition, management inaugurated a standardized food program, implemented a national advertising and marketing program, created a national training school, imposed product uniformity at over 60 percent of Dairy Queen stores, revised contracts to cover percentages of sales rather than gallons of soft serve mix, and increased the number of employees in the national office from five to 125.

During the mid 1960s, International Dairy Queen consolidated its domestic operations by purchasing the franchising rights of Harry Oltz's AR-TIK Systems, including seven southeastern states, and by securing the development rights for territories in numerous states. The confusion over who owned territory in what state, and whether fees were outstanding or not, was due to the McCulloughs' tendency during the early years to sell territories and prospective store locations in a haphazard manner. Management's intention was to provide more effective services and standardize products by ironing out these problems. At the same time, management launched an aggressive acquisition strategy by purchasing interests in franchise operations within the recreation industry. A ski-rental firm in Denver was bought first, and was soon followed by a franchise for camping equipment.

The company's consolidation of operating territory and its acquisition strategy proved costly, and a $2 million loss was forecast for fiscal 1970. With a growing cash flow problem that made it a potential take-over target, company management decided to accept the overtures of a new investment group. Headed by men who were part of the development of National

Car Rental System, Inc., the group offered $3 million in cash with $2 million in credit to provide financing for working capital and expansion needs. In return, the investors assumed both majority interest and effective control of International Dairy Queen. Bill McKinstry became executive committee chairman and chairman of the board of directors and Harris Cooper was named president.

McKinstry's and Cooper's reorganization strategy had immediate effects. By discontinuing one of the company's divisions, closing 16 accounting and regional offices, and standardizing operating procedures and product lines, International Dairy Queen soon became profitable once again. In 1972, the company began trading its stock on the over-the-counter market; during the same year, its stock price increased from $1.50 per share to $22.75.

In May 1972, the first Dairy Queen store was opened in Tokyo. While 75 stores were operating outside the United States and Canada in 1976, more than 150 stores in Barbados, Guatemala, Iceland, Japan, Panama, Puerto Rico, Trinidad, the United Arab Emirates, and Hong Kong were operating by the end of the decade.

International Dairy Queen's total revenues in 1979 amounted to $956 million; as the system celebrated its 40th anniversary in 1980 total revenues came to $1.2 billion. Within the fast food industry, Dairy Queen ranked fifth in total sales volume behind McDonald's, Kentucky Fried Chicken, Burger King, and Wendy's; the company ranked third in total number of stores behind McDonald's and KFC. In the United States, Dairy Queen had 4,314 stores in operation, with 365 in Canada, 123 in Japan, and over 30 in eight other foreign countries.

John Mooty had replaced McKinstry as chairman of the board of directors in 1976, and Mooty began working just as well with Cooper. Due to a sharp fall in stock prices during the mid 1970s, Mooty implemented a stock repurchasing plan to provide more stability for the company. By the early 1980s, International Dairy Queen had used nearly $40 million to buy back two-thirds of its outstanding shares on the stock market. At the end of the decade, the performance of the stock was widely regarded as one of the best; an individual who had invested $10,000 in Dairy Queen stock in 1980 would have a portfolio worth $470,000 in 1990.

Under Mooty's and Cooper's stewardship, International Dairy Queen had introduced both the Peanut Butter Parfait and Fudge Brownie Delight, both of which were highly successful novelty products. It was the introduction of the Blizzard, a concoction of soft-serve and various items such as candy, cookies, and fruit, that secured Dairy Queen's ranking as the number one treat chain during the 1980s, however. In 1985 alone, the year it was introduced, over 100 million Blizzard treats were sold to customers. Along with the success of the Dairy Queen stores, the company's purchase of Golden Skillet, a chain of fried chicken restaurants; Karmelkorn Shoppes, Inc., a 60-year-old popcorn and candy franchise; and Orange Julius, a franchise selling fruit-flavored blended drinks and various snack products, secured its position as the eighth ranked fast food chain in the United States.

As the company entered the 1990s, John Mooty remained chairman of the board of directors and Mike Sullivan had replaced Harris Cooper as president. Yet Cooper's departure did not slow domestic growth or international expansion of Dairy Queen. Within the United States, the company is developing opportunities to open stores in shopping malls, office complexes, railroad stations, airports, and other non-traditional markets. In the international arena, International Dairy Queen has initiated development programs in Thailand, Cyprus, Kuwait, Oman, Taiwan, and Indonesia, and plans a major campaign to open stores in Western and Eastern Europe. With a potential market of over 324 million people in Western Europe, a third of them under the age of 30, International Dairy Queen plans to extend one of the most recognizable advertising symbols in the world: "The Cone with the Curl on Top."

Further Reading:

Otis, Caroline Hall, *The Cone with the Curl on Top: The Dairy Queen Story, 1940–1980,* Minneapolis, MN: International Dairy Queen, Inc., 1990.

—Thomas Derdak

International Game Technology

520 South Rock Boulevard
P.O. Box 10580
Reno, Nevada 89510-0580
U.S.A.
(702) 688-0100
Fax: (702) 688-0120

Public Company
Incorporated: 1980
Employees: 3,000
Sales: $478 million
Stock Exchanges: New York NASDAQ
SICs: 3999 Manufacturing Industries, Nec

International Game Technology (IGT) is the world's leading designer and manufacturer of video slot machines, blackjack, keno and poker games, and proprietary software for computerized game monitoring. Its product line is the most extensive of any gaming equipment manufacturer and holds the top share of gaming machine sales in Nevada and New Jersey. IGT is also the only manufacturing company licensed to sell its machines in every regulated gambling jurisdiction in the world. The company has two major divisions: IGT-North America covers markets in Nevada and New Jersey, river boats, American Indian reservations, and sales to the Canadian government and Canadian First National. IGT-International, founded in 1993, covers markets in Latin America, Australia, Europe, Asia, and Africa.

The company was founded by William S.(Si) Redd in 1975 under the name A-1 Supply. Redd, the son of a Mississippi sharecropper, began his career in the gaming industry at age 18, when he bought a used pinball game and convinced a hamburger stand operator to keep the machine in his establishment in exchange for 50 percent of its revenues. After working as a distributor for Wurlitzer jukeboxes in New England, Redd was hired by Bally Manufacturing in 1967 to distribute slot machines in Nevada. He founded his own affiliate, Bally Distribution, and became known throughout the state as "The Slot Machine King." In 1975, Redd founded A-1 Supply and one year later entered into a deal with Bally Manufacturing through which he acquired sole rights to the company's burgeoning video business.

Redd devoted a large amount of resources to research and development. As a result, A-1 Supply became a pioneer in the video gaming industry, developing a line of video poker, blackjack, keno, and slot machines, which Redd sold to casino operators throughout Nevada and New Jersey. Redd changed the name of his company to SIRCOMA (from "SI Redd COin MAchines") in 1979. In 1980, SIRCOMA changed its name to International Game Technology and went public on NASDAQ in October 1981. Annual sales had grown from less than $3 million in 1975 to over $61 million in 1982. By 1982, approximately 9 percent of gambling machines in Nevada were video machines, and IGT held 90 percent of that market.

IGT also began developing its lottery game technology and by 1986 was one of the top six players in the $1 billion industry. That year it purchased a 36 percent stake in Syntech International, Inc., a rival manufacturer of lottery ticket vending machines and manager of several state lottery games. Revenues dropped precipitously in 1986, however, due to a slump in the Nevada gaming industry and growing competition from Japanese manufacturers. To help his struggling company, Redd hired Charles W. Mathewson to take over as chairman. Soon after, Mathewson was named president.

When Mathewson took over as president in 1986, he boasted that IGT stock prices (then trading at 11 cents a share) would double within two years. The company's heavy R&D spending paid off in 1987 when it introduced Megabucks, a computerized slot machine network that allowed any number of participants across the state to play for the same progressive jackpot. Within a year, IGT had sold Megabucks to over 30 casinos throughout Nevada and had obtained rights to sell the system in New Jersey. Mathewson's boasting had been proved correct. Fueled by strong sales of Megabucks, IGT's sales hit $81 million in 1987, and earnings rose to 71 cents a share. Share prices climbed, hitting 26.875 in September 1988, and rose further to 29 cents in 1990.

By 1988, IGT's Megabucks and other newly developed progressive jackpot systems had captured 60 percent of the Nevada slot machine market. IGT had also secured 25 percent of the international gaming market, with gaming machines in Australia, Portugal, the Netherlands, Turkey, and Monte Carlo. 1988 sales were $95 million, 25 to 30 percent of which came from international markets. The following year, revenues soared 50 percent to $151 million as earnings jumped to $1.73 a share.

In the early 1990s, the U.S. gaming industry began a growth spurt that sent IGT sales soaring. The Federal Government passed a law permitting native Americans to own and operate casinos on Indian reservations. Many other states, particularly those along the Mississippi River, began permitting riverboat gambling. IGT was well positioned to serve these emerging markets. Over half the river casinos built in the early 1990s were stocked solely with IGT machines. The nation's largest Indian reservation casino purchased 80 percent of its machines from IGT, and the new Luxor, Treasure Island, and MGM Grand casinos in Las Vegas purchased a minimum of 70 percent of their machines from IGT.

European gaming markets also expanded, and, in 1991, IGT opened a European division, with plans to establish an assembly factory, a product distribution center, and a direct factory sales center in Europe. After a long and arduous attempt to break into the Japanese gambling market, IGT received approval to sell slot and *paschisuro* machines there in April of 1993.

In 1993, IGT reorganized its corporate structure, establishing IGT-International to oversee manufacturing and sales outside of North America, and creating the corporate "Office of the President" to direct strategic planning worldwide. 1993 sales were $478 million, with earnings over $100 million. Stock prices continued to climb, trading at $38.75, three times its expected earnings.

As IGT entered the mid-1990s, analysts predicted that it would remain the leader in the gaming machine industry throughout the decade. IGT had been able to stay on top of the booming gaming market by regularly introducing new games and quickly adapting to changes in the market. As the *Wall Street Journal* stated, IGT machines "tend to get played much more heavily than machines by competitors." As the number of casinos worldwide swelled, IGT's profits followed.

Further Reading:

Clements, Jonathan, "IGT Stock Is Riding High on Gambling Boom, and the Bells Could Keep Ringing for a While," *The Wall Street Journal,* September 20, 1993, p. C2.
Lane, Randall, "Back into the Breach," *Forbes,* November 9, 1992, p. 96.
Paris, Ellen, "Call and Raise," *Forbes,* August 30, 1982, p. 50.
Schlesinger, Jacob M., "Tough Gamble: A Slot-Machine Maker Trying to Sell in Japan Hits Countless Barriers," *The Wall Street Journal,* May 11, 1993, p. A1.

—Maura Troester

J. I. Case Company

700 State Street
Racine, Wisconsin 53404
U.S.A.
(414) 636-6011
Fax: (414) 636-6432

Wholly Owned Subsidiary of Tenneco Incorporated
Incorporated: 1842 as Jerome Increase Case Machine
    Company
Employees: 18,600
Sales: $3.7 billion
SICs: 3523 Farm Machinery and Equipment; 3531
    Construction Machinery

J. I. Case Company, a subsidiary of Tenneco, Inc., is one of the United State's largest industrial companies with concerns in natural gas production, automotive parts, packaging, and chemicals. Case is the second largest maker of farm equipment, trailing John Deere Company, and third in construction equipment sales, following Caterpillar Inc. and Deere. After celebrating its 150th year in business, Case undertook an extensive restructuring to return it to profitability after the recession of the 1980s.

Case's history is merged with the Industrial Revolution's impact on farming. Jerome Increase Case grew up threshing wheat by hand on his father's farmstead in the early 1800s. Wheat was cut with scythes, then beaten by hand to remove the grain. The blistering work meant that one person produced about half a dozen bushels a day, so farmers necessarily limited their acreage to prevent bottlenecks in production of their wheat. When Case was 16, he took his father to a demonstration of a crude, mechanized thresher patented around 1788 by Scotsman Andrew Meikle. His father was sufficiently impressed by the machine and applied for a franchise to sell them.

For five seasons, Jerome Case operated the machine for his father and his father's clients. During that time, Case became aware of the machine's flaws, as well as its indispensability to farming. In 1842, Jerome Case moved to Rochester, Wisconsin, then the growing heart of the wheat culture in the United States. He sold five thresher machines along the way, reserving one for himself.

Rochester was a village when Case arrived. That autumn, he did custom threshing and worked on his modifications of the machine. Case envisioned a machine that was both separator and thresher, constructed so that the straw would move to one end while grain fell underneath the machine. Such a machine had already been patented by inventors in Maine in 1837, but Case had not seen their invention. His machine differed in its operation. Case was helped by Stephen Thresher, a carpenter he met where he boarded in Rochester. The two were advised by Richard Ela, who made fanning mills and hailed from New Hampshire.

After a successful first demonstration of his new thresher-separator, Case decided to concentrate on manufacturing rather than custom threshering. When Rochester balked at his petition for water-power rights, Case moved to Racine, Wisconsin, in 1844, playing a part in that town's explosive growth. Within three years, he had gone from renting a building to constructing his own factory. First named Jerome Increase Case Machinery Company, the name was changed to Racine Threshing Machine Works. By 1848, Case was producing 100 threshers a year and claimed he was meeting only half of the orders received. By 1854, water power was supplanted by a steam boiler and engine within the factory.

It was difficult to deliver such cumbersome equipment in the 1800s. There were no railroads in Wisconsin until the 1850s. Most roads were widened Indian trails, and rain could make them treacherous to wheels. Timely delivery of the heavy machines was not always possible and timing is as essential as rain to farmers. In addition, Case spent much time traveling to distant farms to collect back payments, credit being another necessity of his clients' business.

Many complementary farming products were appearing around the same time that the wheat belt of the Midwest and the Great Plains was burgeoning. Around the same time Case's business was growing, John Deere and Major Andrus were developing a steel plow in Illinois, and a reaper had been developed by Cyrus McCormick. Case purchased rights to the thresher and fanning mill invented before his, then he added improvements. Acknowledging that his own strength was business and seeing the applications of machines, Case often acquired and improved upon the inventions of others. Case was established as a leading thresher manufacturer by the early 1850s. The company has long been noted for leasing or buying the patents of inventions it recognizes as promising.

Business was steady enough to allow Case to pursue civic interests; he was elected three times to the State Senate and served twice as Racine's mayor. The poor harvest and financial panic of 1857 did not prevent the company, then still specializing in threshers, from introducing new products. In 1862, Case began selling the "Sweepstakes," a thresher capable of producing 300 bushels of wheat a day. Pressures, including the Civil War, drove Case to create a co-partnership by 1863, established as J.I. Case & Co. The partnership included Case, Massena Erskine, and Stephen Bull until 1880.

The same year that Alexander Graham Bell won a bronze medal at the Philadelphia Centennial Exhibition, Case's new thresher, the 1869 Eclipse, also won a bronze and a commendation. The thresher took the gold medal at the World's Fair in Paris two years later. With the Homestead Act of 1862, farming burst into a new era, requiring equipment that could keep up. In 1878, Case produced its first steam traction engine, and by the following year had sold 109 of them. Sales doubled in 1878, reaching the one million dollar mark by 1880. The partnership was incorporated as J.I. Case Threshing Machine Company in 1880. By 1890, Case was offering nine different horsepowers of steam traction engines, and continued improvements. Production peaked the same year the first gasoline tractor was introduced, 1911. Most steam engine products were eclipsed by the gasoline tractor by 1924. At that point, Case had built about one third of this country's farm steam engines. But it took time for tractors to become standard farm equipment; as a power source on U.S. farms, draft animals outnumbered tractors until 1952.

Case died in 1891 at the age of 73. Leadership of the company was passed to one of his former partners, Stephen Bull, who was assisted by his son Frank. Between 1893 and 1924, the company expanded to Europe, South America, and Australia. Competition between thresher manufacturers lead to the dissolution of the Thresher Manufacturers Association in 1898 and increased rivalries. A depression between 1893 and 1897, a warehouse fire, and a Great Plains drought contributed to a decline in Case profits of nearly three quarters between 1892 and 1896. Stockholder dissatisfaction lead to new ownership, which resulted in Frank Bull as president. Bull became chairman of the board in 1916 and was succeeded in presidency by Warren J. Davis. The company name was changed to J.I. Case Company after further reorganization around 1928.

Case was advertising a full line of road machinery by 1912. The gasoline tractor became one of the company's most important products. Since 1902, many firms were fighting to produce the gasoline-powered successors to steam-powered engines. International Harvester began making them in 1905, and Ford in 1907. The design and manufacture of lighter, smaller versions of the engines made Case a major player in the gasoline tractor market by the 1920s. By the late 1920s, Case had become a full-line manufacturer, aided by its 1919 acquisition of Grand Detour, a tillage equipment company. Case also made expensive automobiles from 1912 to 1927: roadsters, coupes, and sedans in 14 different models over the years. Because of low profitability, the auto lines were phased out.

The depression in the American economy in the wake of World War I greatly impacted the farm equipment industry. By 1929, only 18 of the 157 manufacturers of farm equipment operating 12 years earlier remained. Case's profits fell steadily, despite the addition of a combine to its line in 1923. The company was especially challenged by the dealer network of International Harvester. Case did not keep up with competitors' improvements while it was enjoying the sales of its steam traction engines and threshers. Between 1920 and 1922, annual gross sales plunged from $34 million to less than $16 million. In 1924, Case's new president, Leon R. Clausen, assumed the reigns after leaving John Deere Company. He would remain president until 1948, and chairman of the board until 1958.

Clausen brought many ideas with him from Deere, including faith in aggressive marketing and the value of being a full-line manufacturer. He established three primary goals: improve trac-

tor designs, establish a full line, and modernize the factories. The Model C tractor was introduced in 1929, and a tricycle tractor appeared in 1930. A line of "Motor Lift" implements arrived in 1935. Lines were expanded by acquisition as well as invention: Case purchased through the Emerson-Brantingham Company a line of farm equipment that included binders, mowers, reapers, and corn planters. The Rock Island Plow Company was acquired in 1937, adding drills, spreaders, and plows to the company's offerings.

Case also purchased that year a factory in Iowa to make small combines, sales of which had been growing steadily since they were introduced to the market. Case, Harvester, and Deere were responsible for three quarters of the farm machinery sold in the United States by 1937. Although Case had, since 1912, offered an array of road building machinery, these products were not promoted under Clausen and it was not until the mid 1950s that Case became serious about marketing its construction equipment.

Clausen set to work on revamping the sales department and restructuring manufacturing. He is credited with building Case's dealer network. Although severe cutbacks were necessary to weather the Great Depression, Case managed to increase sales by 1936 on the strength of their tractor sales. In 1939, a new tractor line was introduced, as well as a small combine, hammer feed mills, and farm wagon gears.

With the start of World War II, Case's tractors were in even greater demand. More than 15,000 of its tractors went to the military between 1941 and 1945. New tractors were designed and manufactured with war-needs in mind. Case was also producing items such as shells, aircraft wings, and gun mounts for the war effort. Case devoted much more wartime engineering to federal production than did Deere or Caterpillar, which left it at a disadvantage at the war's end. Nonetheless, the postwar demand for farm machinery outpaced supply and Case's lost wartime share soon seemed recoverable.

Regaining lost market share, however, was interrupted by a strike in 1945 that lasted 440 days. It was, at that time, the nation's longest strike. Clausen's animosity for unions—first noted when he was still with Deere—was mutual. Depleted by the strike and its aftermath, Clausen stepped down as president in 1948, staying on as chairman of the board. The strike hurt Case on every level: in its relationship with dealers, customers, and its union, and in its research and development, where it was already lagging behind its competitors.

With the Marshall Plan and the lifted export restrictions, devastated Europe's hunger for working machinery became a fresh market for Case. In addition, stateside farm machinery was in disrepair. There was a shortage of manpower on farms, due to deaths in the war, which increased the need for machinery. Sales growth on the west coast led to a plant purchase in California in 1947. This purchase expanded Case's range into a new tobacco harvester. These factors helped Case post a profit through 1949, despite its costly strike.

Profits declined between 1950 and 1953, in part because of outdated products. Competitors introduced lighter models of tractors in the late 1930s, and these units became popular after the war. Case, on the other hand, had at the end of the war roughly the same heavy series it had at the beginning. Poor engineering hurt Case during the early 1950s as well, as did a propensity to blame the dealer rather than the product. Items such as Case's hay baler, which had topped the market in 1941, lagged to less than 5 percent of baler sales in 1953 because Case failed to respond to a competitor's improvements.

All of these problems added up to a crisis in leadership at Case. According to Case's own published history, *J.I. Case: The First 150 Years,* Clausen consistently made decisions opposed to change: he opposed diesel engines for domestic sales; he believed farmers preferred "dependability" to changes such as a foot-operated clutch, a cab, and an oil filter—all of which a 1946 survey of farmers specified as desired. When Clausen left the presidency in 1948, Theodore Johnson took over. Johnson was 66 and had never worked outside of Case. The company continued to drift, with a lackluster response to competition, and no notable innovations. Johnson was replaced in 1953 by John T. Brown.

Under Brown's direction, Case released a multitude of new or improved implements, including the 500 series tractor, which would become a popular line. The 500 had a six-cylinder, fuel-injected, diesel engine, power steering, and a push-button start. Two manure spreaders were unveiled in 1956. That same year, however, Case reported its second loss since 1953. For the first time, bankruptcy seemed a possibility. Diversification seemed the only remedy.

Case launched its industrial equipment line in 1957 as though it were new, but it had been making industrial units based on agricultural models for three decades. Street and highway builders, national forests and parks, and others had come to rely on industrial tractors adapted from farm use. Case applied itself to expanding this sector of its line, and turned to Caterpillar Company for marketing assistance. To revitalize its industrial line, Case acquired American Tractor Corporation (ATC) in 1957. ATC's volume around purchase time was $10 million, but the company was in debt due to recent rapid growth. Its assets included a vigorous president, Marc Bori Rojtman; a strong line of distributors and dealers; and a sturdy line of crawler tractors and loader backhoes—the company's star product. Under Rojtman, Case's manufacturing capacity improved, new retailers were attracted, and the company moved confidently into the construction equipment business.

Rojtman's showman's personality led to dazzling regional shows to promote new product lines. Deliberate showmanship in marketing resulted, despite criticism, in huge increases in orders. New product invention and marketing and overseas expansion proved financially taxing. But sales rose 50 percent in 1957, reaching $124 million. Income the following year was more than tripled. Clausen, head of the board, strongly opposed Rojtman's presidency and his debt load, and resigned in 1958. An economic downturn in 1958 left the company in a precarious position. William Grede replaced Rojtman in 1960.

Case's debt load in 1959 was $236 million. It had become the country's fourth largest farm and construction equipment producer. Grede's first order of business was to reduce debt and consolidate manufacturing. A new offering of accessories such as batteries, oil, and hydraulic fluid proved successful. Between

the new offering and special discounts, Case sales were still strong in 1960. A six-month strike occurred that same year. Unable to met a $145 million bill due on short-term notes in 1962, a bank agreement was negotiated which called for reorganization and deferment of most of the interest until 1967, so Case could focus on paying down principal. Reorganization included the ousting of Grede. He was succeeded by Merritt D. Hill, who had previously worked in Ford's Tractor and Implement Division.

Hill brought talent with him from Detroit, including a chief product engineer. He completely restructured Case. Separate divisions were created for marketing, manufacturing, and engineering. Hill also ushered in a new era of labor-management relations, being the first of Case's presidents sympathetic to issues of labor and race. Money constraints impeded the development of new product lines, but Case managed to stay in the ring with competitors such as Ford and Deere, as the new head of its engineering department insisted. In 1964, Case introduced the 1200 Traction King, a 4-wheel drive, 120 horsepower giant that marked the company's entry into the large agricultural tractor market.

Case's operating loss had declined and its production levels were up. The company seemed on solid business ground by 1964, but was still not in a position to meet the terms of the 1962 agreement and have enough left over to fuel growth. Case shopped for a cash-rich partner to whom it could offer the use of its agreement's tax loss carry-forwards.

In May 1964, the Kern County Land Company (KCL) of California acquired majority stock in Case. KCL was founded in 1874 and began as a cattle-raising venture that branched into petroleum royalties after oil was discovered. It diversified into hard minerals, real estate, and businesses such as its Racine, Wisconsin-based parent company, the Walker Manufacturing Company. KCL was cash-rich and agreed not to dictate Case's growth or internal decisions. These circumstances allowed Case to expand between 1964 and 1967, in accordance with a booming demand for existing products and the itch to produce new ones. Around 1965, the 450 crawler and a 1150 dozer debuted. A new series of loader backhoes were introduced around this time also, among them Case's mainstay, the 580. By 1966, Case's income decline had been reversed. Hill became chairman of the board and Charles A. Anderson became president. Anderson had been with KCL and Walker.

Suddenly KCL, under threat of a hostile takeover by Armand Hammer, wooed a friendly buyer instead, and ended up being acquired by Tenneco Company of Houston. Gardiner Symonds, Tenneco's president, was familiar with KCL's natural resources but had no experience with manufacturing. Tenneco was a holding company. The deal closed in 1967. It was thought that Tenneco would quickly sell Case.

When investors began inquiring about Case's stock, Tenneco decided to run an analysis of the company and found it well-run, but too low on liquid assets to grow. This shifted Tenneco's plan. Case would prosper from a shift to construction equipment, so Tenneco decided not to sell it. In 1968, Tenneco acquired Drott Manufacturing Company in Wisconsin and leased it to Case. Case had been buying loader buckets from

Drott for years. That same year, Tenneco also bought Davis Manufacturing Company of Wichita, Kansas, a producer of crawler and rubber-tire mounted trenchers and cable-laying equipment. Tenneco allowed Case to expand by two product lines: log skidders for timber harvesting, through Beloit Woodlands of Wisconsin, and a "skid steer" loader, manufactured by the Uni-Loader Division of Universal Industries.

James Ketelsen succeeded Anderson as Case's president in 1967. Tenneco deferred to Case's manufacturing experience, but both agreed that the company's future was in construction equipment. The agricultural market had slowed to replacements and larger machinery to accommodate fewer, huge farms. Case essentially exited the farm implement business by 1970. And though Case dropped its combine business in 1972, an acquisition in 1985 returned harvesting equipment to Case's line.

After dropping so many of its lines, Case thought it could survive without being a full-line company. The farm economy was dire in the early 1970s, especially for smaller farmers. Case shifted its focus not away from agricultural implements altogether, but toward the large tractor market. Tenneco "loaned" Case $60 million from 1969 to mid 1970, giving the company enough fiscal strength to deal with healthy competitors such as Deere. Even Deere did not have access to such resources. By 1971, Case's entire construction equipment line had been replaced and that year it unveiled more new machinery than any of its competitors. Tenneco's faith was repaid, as Case led all of Tenneco's companies in earnings gains the following year.

In 1972, Case bought David Brown, Ltd., a British agricultural equipment firm founded in 1860. Brown had a large distribution system in Britain and Case concentrated its small tractor production in Brown. Thomas Guendel took over company presidency in 1972 and commanded a chapter of unprecedented growth until he left Case seven years later. Sales quadrupled during that time and earnings improved more than 600 percent. The phenomenal growth was due largely to increased success in construction equipment and overseas markets.

The company reentered the military market during the 1970s. It was awarded a $55 million contract with the Army and Air Force in 1978. The economy was improving after the recession between 1974 and 1975, and Case was the country's third largest producer of construction equipment by 1975. By the late 1970s, 45 percent of Case's sales were overseas, while 80 percent of its production was domestic. France's Poclain Company, the largest manufacturer of hydraulic excavators in the world, was purchased by Case in 1977. Because Drott's excavators could not be sold in Europe due to trade restrictions, Poclain was a savvy purchase; it was a recognized world-wide market leader.

When Jerome K. Green replaced Guendel in 1979, Case passed the $2 billion mark in revenues. Case started the 1980s with 28,000 employees, but it did not anticipate the recession that would shatter the farming community. Shifting to the construction product line was no rescue, as that industry was equally hard hit. New general purpose tractors had been introduced in 1983 and were languishing. Four more 94 series tractors were unveiled in 1984, but by that point, farms were in a real crisis. Case cut production to 55 percent of capacity and it still ex-

ceeded demand. Although overseas sales of construction equipment remained strong during the 1980s, Case's overseas sales did not balance the wounds of the recession in the United States: in 1983, Case lost $68 million, and followed that with a deficit of $105 million in 1984.

Case acquired International Harvester's production facilities, product line, and distribution system in 1985. The history of Harvester was as long and as distinguished as Case's. Harvester retained and renamed its trucking business. Case shut down its own factories for the start of 1985, reducing production to 45 percent of retail sales, and went on to close several Brown plants, and to retire the oldest and least efficient of Case's home plants. Trimming its agricultural product line to such things as tractors, tillage equipment, crop production, and combines, Case was prepared to compete head-on with John Deere, dominator of the farm equipment market.

Losses in 1986 were down to $1 million, despite the deepening farm recession. And Case was among the top three farm equipment manufacturers in Germany, France, and the United Kingdom. Nevertheless, Tenneco was unhappy with Case's bad financial showing and unacceptably tardy production in 1987. Green was replaced by James K. Ashford that same year. About 35 new agricultural products were introduced in 1987, while nine factories were closed or closing. Case was assisted by *Fortune*'s listing of its combines, planters, and loader backhoes as among the best U.S. products in 1988. Ashford oversaw aggressive cutbacks and revamping, including the elimination of 300 jobs in Racine and an intended worldwide cut of 3,000 employees.

By 1989, Case had gone from a $142 million loss to a record profit of $228 million. The recovering farm economy and improved construction equipment sales were cause for celebration. Case's confidence was sufficient to announce a new headquarters complex, but the recovery was short-lived and sales began to weaken. Though John Deere was cutting back production, Ashford gambled that the recession was over and that Case would gain from a preparatory inventory.

This decision was disastrous. The market did not rebound. In the fourth quarter of 1990, Case's earnings were off by nearly $100 million and the year ended with a $42 million decline in operating profits. Part of this decline was due to a weakened dollar, which raised imported parts costs. Though Ashford was credited for Case's turnaround in 1989 and for replacing 80 percent of its divisions' managers and reviving a sluggish management, he resigned suddenly.

Losses continued in 1991 as Case scrambled to cut personnel by 5,000 and production schedules by as much as 23 percent. Sales were up, but discounts cut deeply into profits. Case ended 1991 with a $618 million operating loss.

Case had become a serious problem for Tenneco when Robert J. Carlson assumed the presidency in 1991. Carlson had spent nearly 30 years at Deere and inspired confidence at Case. The company announced extended factory shut-downs at all of its 10 domestic plants and closure of some of its European facilities. Case had restructuring charges variously reported from $461 to $522 million in 1991. Added to Case's operating losses for that year, the loss was a staggering $1.1 billion. While Deere and Caterpillar had suffered from the extended recession as well, their trimmed production left them in better shape than Case.

Talk of further reducing the workforce by 4,000 employees started in 1992, when Edward J. Campbell assumed the presidency of Case. Campbell's approach to downsizing was different: he didn't just slash, he reorganized and he cut from the top, dismissing 21 of the company's 43 officers. Various European factories were closed or sold, including the Poclain plant at Carvin. An agreement was made with Sumitomo Heavy Industries of Japan to make mid-sized excavators for the North American market. Japan was an increasing presence in the agricultural and construction equipment industries.

These measures helped reduce losses for 1992, but revenues were also down. Operating losses were reduced by about 75 percent while agricultural equipment sales were down by about 30 percent. The year closed with revenues of $3.8 billion, and operating losses of $260 million, not including restructuring charges. From a high of 30,000 in 1990, Case's employees now numbered 18,600.

The farm economy appeared to have stabilized at the end of 1992, but construction equipment sales were sluggish. All manufacturers suffered from weak pricing, lower unit volume, the economic slump overseas, and cautious dealers. Caterpillar had a sales increase, but Deere and Case both reported losses. Though Case's performance improved, its progress was uneven, with profits in the second quarter of 1992 and losses in the third. Tenneco announced a $2 billion restructuring plan to revamp Case into three divisions: sales and marketing, manufacturing, and engineering. Jean-Pierre Rosso became president and chief executive of Case in 1993.

Case launched a $920 million restructuring program in March of 1993, to be completed in 1996. Proposed were further plant closings and consolidations and new product development. Some of the changes included plans to privatize the 150 Case dealerships owned by Tenneco. Sales of farm equipment were up by the summer of 1993, especially large tractor sales. Most farmers hadn't purchased new tractors or combines since the farming boom in the 1970s. Case announced that its 1993 combine production was sold out by June, but its Racine tractor plant was closed for 17 weeks following a $17 million loss in

the first quarter of that year. The heavy equipment markets were proclaimed healthy by the end of 1993, but it remained to be seen how healthy Case was. The year ended well for Case: operating income was $82 million in 1993, an improvement over its operating loss of $260 million the previous year, and revenues were $3.7 billion. Case was aided by a vast reduction in inventories, higher retail pricing, and increased demand for new products late in the year.

Case's first quarter of 1994 was strong, with production up 14 percent over the first quarter of 1993. Rosso appeared committed to Case's comeback, and to developing markets overseas. In addition, Tenneco appeared committed to Case.

Further Reading:

"Agricultural Equipment," *Standard and Poor's Industrial Surveys*, October 1993, pp. S34–S35.
"Construction Equipment," *Standard and Poor's Industrial Surveys*, October 1993, pp. S36–S37.
Deutsch, Claudia, "Former BMC Chairman Assumes Post at Case," *New York Times*, July 23, 1991, p. D4.
Eiben, Therese, "How the Industries Stack Up," *Fortune*, July 12, 1993, p. 102.
Fisher, Lawrence, "Tenneco Names Head of Its J.I. Case Unit," *New York Times*, December 7, 1991, p. 39.
Gilpin, Kenneth, "Chief at Troubled J.I. Case Stepping Down," *New York Times*, September 16, 1992, p. D4.
Hayes, Thomas, "Head of Tenneco Unit to Quit All His Posts," *New York Times*, March 16, 1991, p. 33; "J.I. Case Plans to Cut Work Force by 4,000," December 5, 1991, p. D4.
Holmes, Michael, *J.I. Case: The First 150 Years*, Racine, WI: Case Corporation, 1992.
Johnson, Robert, "Tenneco Restructuring Is Over, but Doubts Remain," *Wall Street Journal*, September 8, 1992, p. B4.
——, "Tenneco's Plans to Restructure Case Unit Include $843 Million After-Tax Charge," *Wall Street Journal*, March 23, 1993, p. A3.
McKanic, Patricia Ann, "Tenneco's Ashford to Resign as Chief of Case Unit, which He Turned Around," *Wall Street Journal*, March 18, 1991, p. B8.
McMurray, Scott, "Farm-Equipment Sales Are Running at Full Throttle," *Wall Street Journal*, June 15, 1993, p. B4.
Osenga, Mike, "Case Corporation," *Diesel Progress Engines & Drives*, June 1992, p. 102.
"Tenneco in Plan to Revamp Case," *New York Times*, January 23, 1992, p. D4.

—Carol I. Keeley

PERSONAL WEIGHT MANAGEMENT

Jenny Craig, Inc.

445 Marine View Drive
Del Mar, California 92014
U.S.A.
(619) 259-7000
Fax: (619) 259-2812

Public Company
Incorporated: 1983
Employees: 4,570
Sales: $444 million
Stock Exchanges: New York
SICs: 6794 Patent Owners & Lessors; 7991 Physical Fitness
   Facilities; 8742 Management Consulting Services.

Among the four largest diet companies in the United States, Jenny Craig, Inc. is also the only publicly held company in the industry. Through its chain of weight management centers, Jenny Craig sells a meal plan, based on the purchase of its own prepared foods, and provides advisory and motivational services to its customers. The chain experienced rapid growth during the 1980s, and, by 1993, it was operating 588 company owned and 220 franchised centers in 45 states, as well as in Australia, New Zealand, Canada, and Mexico. During this time, the company reported a client base of approximately 155,000 in the United States and 25,000 in foreign markets. However, the company also showed signs of slower sales and growth, reflecting the national economic recession and several unfavorable reports on the safety and health benefits of many diet programs.

Co-founder Jenny Craig developed an interest in the fitness industry in the 1960s, through her efforts to lose weight following a pregnancy. She operated a gym in her hometown of New Orleans, before joining the staff at the Body Contour fitness center in 1970. Body Contour was headed by Sid Craig, who maintained a 50 percent interest in the company. Jenny and Sid married in 1979, and together they helped turn the struggling company into a thriving business that reported $35 million in sales by 1982.

In 1982, the Craigs sold Body Contour to a subsidiary of Nutri/System Inc. With the $3.5 million they made from the sale, the Craigs formed Jenny Craig, Inc. in 1983. Initially barred from entering the U.S. diet industry by a noncompetition clause, the company opened its first weight loss center in Australia. By 1985, 69 Jenny Craig Weight Loss Centers were in operation in

Australia, and the company became one of the biggest players in that country's diet industry. That year, the Craigs returned to the United States, opening 13 centers in the Los Angeles area, which were soon followed by six additional facilities in Chicago.

By 1987, the company had established 46 centers in the United States and 114 in foreign countries; of these 160 units, 45 were franchised operations. Seeking capital from outside investors, the Craigs considered taking their company public but were discouraged by a weak market for initial public offerings. Instead, Michael Tennenbaum, vice-chairman of investment banking at Bear Stearns, stepped in. Tennenbaum brought together a group of investors that included his partners at Bear Stearns, the New York Life Insurance Co., and TA Associates, an investment and venture capital firm, among others. Together they invested $50 million in Jenny Craig, and two bank loans contributed another $50 million to the company's recapitalization. The successful expansion left the Craig family with a $108 million dividend.

Marketing was integral to Jenny Craig's success. In the early 1990s, ten percent of sales went into commercial advertising each year, and franchises were required to spend the higher of ten percent of sales or $1,000 a week on advertising for their centers. The company's television campaigns featured celebrities, such as actors Elliot Gould and Susan Ruttan, who had achieved success with the Jenny Craig program. Moreover, ads provided a toll free number which automatically connected callers to the center nearest to them. In 1991, the company also began a direct mail campaign based on its extensive database of two million current and former clients.

The Jenny Craig program was designed by its staff of registered dieticians and psychologists and approved by an advisory board consisting of health and nutrition research experts. The three principal tenets of the program were behavior education, proper nutrition, and exercise. Central to the program was Jenny's Cuisine, portion and calorie controlled foods that participants were required to purchase. Jenny's Cuisine was created by suppliers in compliance with standards set by a board of dieticians; suppliers included Overhill Farms, Magic Pantry Foods, Truitt Bros., Campbell Soup Company, Carnation, and Vitex Foods. The program made available 60 different breakfast, lunch, dinner, dessert, and snack food items, including apple cinnamon oatmeal, teriyaki beef, and chocolate mousse. Menus were updated to include microwaveable entrees and canned foods in 1986. The company's gross revenues from food sales increased from 60 percent in 1986 to 91 percent in 1993.

Another important part of the Jenny Craig program was its twice-weekly meetings. New clients met with a counselor, who would monitor their progress and sell them installments of Jenny's Cuisine. At subsequent group meetings, participants attended classes covering such subjects as "dining out," "asserting yourself," and "dieting as a team." In 1989, video cassette programs were introduced into counseling classes to ensure consistency at all centers. After viewing video cassettes, participants engaged in discussion facilitated by their counselor.

In 1991, under improved market conditions, Jenny Craig was taken public, issuing 3.5 million shares at $21 share. The offering generated $73.5 million in capital, which was used to satisfy the company's bank loans and its debt to the investment group. During this time, the Craigs sold another 1.65 million of their own shares for $36 million, and the banks and investors garnered $11.5 million for the 550,000 shares they sold. As a result, the Craigs retained 59 percent of the company, while banks and investors controlled 20 percent and the public claimed 29 percent.

Sid Craig's expectations for company revenues to grow by 15 to 20 percent a year through expansion proved unrealistic. After a period of remarkable growth in the weight loss industry as a whole during the 1980s, public attention focused on the potential health risks involved in dieting during the early 1990s, and enrollment at diet centers dropped. In 1990, Jenny Craig and its rival Nutri/System Inc. were named as defendants in a class action lawsuit alleging that weight loss programs, like those promoted by the companies, had resulted in cases of gallbladder disease. Moreover, Jenny Craig was named in 11 other personal injury cases during this time. The disputes were settled, and the alleged link between gallbladder problems and the Jenny Craig program was never proven. However, the cases prompted a Federal Trade Commission investigation into the validity of the claims for successful weight loss made by Jenny Craig and other companies in the diet industry.

The company terminated its operations in the United Kingdom, due to their lack of profitability, and, in 1992, a secondary offering of public stock was postponed indefinitely, due to weak market conditions and a decline in profits linked to a failed promotional campaign. Nevertheless, Jenny Craig continued the expansion of its diet center chain, opening 89 new centers and repurchasing 41 franchises.

During 1993, the ongoing FTC investigations into the advertising and promotional practices of the diet industry generated more negative publicity. Specifically, the FTC questioned whether advertising was leading consumers to mistakenly believe that maintaining weight loss after finishing the diet program would be easy. Moreover, medical journals and newspapers reported that "yo-yo dieting"—the repeated gain and loss of weight—caused more health problems than simply remaining slightly overweight.

Jenny Craig and four other major commercial weight loss companies—Weight Watchers, Nutri/System, Diet Center, and Physician's Weight Loss Center—petitioned for standard advertising rules for the industry, but the petition was rejected.

When Nutri/System reported severe financial setbacks in April 1993 and was forced to close its headquarters and 283 of its centers, Jenny Craig immediately began an advertising campaign offering Nutri/System clients the opportunity to continue their weight loss programs at Jenny Craig at no additional service fee. In its open letter to Nutri/System clients, Jenny Craig emphasized its financial strength as a "debt-free, $500 million New York Stock Exchange Company with ten years of proven success." However, neither Jenny Craig nor Weight Watchers, which had launched a similar campaign, saw a significant increase in enrollments.

Increased competition in the industry, largely by "do-it-yourself" diet companies, also began to cut into Jenny Craig's

market by emphasizing the high costs of membership in diet center programs. Typical Jenny Craig clients—women wanting to lose thirty or more pounds—could spend over $1,000 as clients of Jenny Craig, paying an initial start-up fee and about $70 a week for meals. Companies like Just Help Yourself began offering self-administered diet plans, marketing themselves as cheaper, more convenient alternatives to diet centers.

Despite the shrinking market, the Craigs continued to expand. In 1993, Jenny Craig added 100 new centers and bought back 48 franchises, bringing its total outlets to 794. The company also introduced a program for those living in areas beyond the reach of its centers, allowing customers to order products by telephone and receive direct shipments.

Some shareholders disagreed with the company's expansion policy. Stock purchased at $21 in 1991 sunk below $15 the following year. In October 1993, three shareholders filed a suit against the company, alleging that the expansion was designed to bolster sales figures, overshadowing the company's financial difficulties. While Jenny Craig's total revenues for the year ended June 30, 1993 were $490.5 million, up six percent from 1992, average revenues for each company-owned center declined ten percent from the previous year. Moreover, although the company's southern California centers remained profitable, these outlets experienced a 26 percent decline in revenues.

When Ronald E. Gerevas, chief operating officer and president, departed unexpectedly in November 1993, Jenny Craig stock dropped to $11.75 a share. Gerevas' replacement, Albert J. DiMarco, left after just four months; William R. Lewis, a former business associate of DiMarco's who had just been appointed chief financial officer the month before, left with DiMarco. By this time, confidence in the company was declining, and its stock was trading at about $6.25 per share, less then a third of its original price. In April 1994, hoping that new management would help restore investor confidence, the company appointed C. Joseph LaBonté as president and CEO, and Ellen Destray was made chief operating officer. Sid Craig remained as the company's chairperson.

Jenny Craig introduced modifications to its original program in 1994. A wider variety of meetings were offered, and clients were allowed to choose the classes most pertinent to their lifestyle. The company's video programs were also updated and made available for home use. Perhaps most importantly, the program was modified to reflect current trends in popular psychology that suggested that overeating was a result of emotional distress. Accordingly, Jenny Craig encouraged clients to discover, address, and overcome individual emotional issues that might impede the success of their dieting. Given the rapidly changing nature in health and fitness beliefs and practices in the United States, Jenny Craig's future will likely depend on its ability to adapt its programs accordingly.

Further Reading:

Bird, Laura, "Jenny Craig Kicks Off a Database Program," *Adweek's Marketing Week,* January 7, 1991, p. 8.
Barret, Amy, "How Can Jenny Craig Keep on Gaining?" *Business Week,* April 12, 1993, p. 52.
Berman, Phyllis, "Fat City," *Forbes,* Feburary 17, 1992, pp. 72–73.

Craig, Jenny, *Jenny Craig's What Have You Got to Lose?* Villard Books, 1992.

Goldman, Kevin, ''Ads Dished up for Nutri/System Dieters,'' *Wall Street Journal,* May 7, 1993, p. B8.

Holden, Benjamin A., ''Financial Officer Quits Jenny Craig After Brief Tenure,'' *Wall Street Journal,* March 10, 1994, p. B10.

''Jenny Craig Inc.,'' *Wall Street Journal,* November 30, 1993.

Lippert, Barbara, ''Weighty Matters,'' *Adweek,* January 10, 1994, p. 28.

Rundle, Rhonda L., ''Jenny Craig Inc. Delays Planned Stock Offering,'' *Wall Street Journal,* May 28, 1992, p. A8.

Saddler, Jeanne, ''Three Diet Firms Settle False-Ad Case; Two Others Vow to Fight FTC Charges,'' *Wall Street Journal,* October 1993, p. B5.

Valeriano, Lourdes Lee, ''Diet Programs Hope Broader Services Fatten Profits,'' *Wall Street Journal,* August 5, 1993, p. B4.

—Elaine Belsito

KPMG Worldwide

P.O. Box 74111
1070 BC Amsterdam
The Netherlands
011-31-20-656-6700
Fax: (212) 909-5299

Private Company
Incorporated: 1897 as Marwick, Mitchell & Company
Employees: 76,200
Sales: $1.8 billion
SICs: 8721 Accounting, Auditing & Bookkeeping

KPMG Worldwide is a global federation of accounting firms that together comprise the world's largest accounting partnership. KPMG Peat Marwick, the company's American subsidiary, is the fourth-largest American accounting firm. Founded in New York in the late 19th century, the company made a strategic international alliance early on in its history and grew rapidly to become one of the eight premier accounting firms in the United States. Peat Marwick's steady expansion overseas was capped by its alliance with a firm of almost equal size based in the Netherlands.

KPMG got its start in 1897, just a few years after the first American accounting firm had been set up. The company was formed by James Marwick and Roger Mitchell, who had both immigrated to the new world from Scotland. They set up their new partnership, called Marwick, Mitchell & Company, in New York City. Eight years after its founding, Marwick, Mitchell & Company launched a banking practice, focusing its efforts on one industry for the first time. This effort proved so successful that the firm later went on to offer tailored services to companies in the insurance industry, the thrift field, and to mutual fund brokers.

In 1911 Marwick, Mitchell & Company merged with a British accounting firm headed by Sir William B. Peat. The new transatlantic company was called Peat, Marwick, Mitchell & Company. Through the merger, Marwick, Mitchell & Company strengthened its operations in Europe, while Peat gained greater access to the rapidly growing North American market. This configuration of the company remained in effect for the next three-quarters of a century.

During that time, Peat Marwick grew steadily, becoming one of the eight major public accounting firms in the United States. In the late 1960s and early 1970s, Peat Marwick's business and revenues began to grow dramatically, along with those of the rest of its profession. This boom in demand for accounting services came as a result of increasingly complex tax laws, securities laws, and industry regulations. Between 1973 and 1976, for example, the Securities and Exchange Commission (S.E.C.) added 16 new disclosure requirements for publicly held companies. With the ever-increasing mandated need for accounting services, Peat Marwick's revenues grew steadily as demand outstripped supply.

In addition to the welter of new federal regulations, accounting industry standards became more exacting. The Accounting Principles Board and the Financial Accounting Standards Board issued a wide variety of directives to members of the industry in response to complaints that the accounting industry was not fulfilling its watchdog role in corporate American stringently enough. Like the rest of its peers in the industry, Peat Marwick suffered a number of suits charging it with failing to prevent or expose financial malfeasance. In 1970 the company settled a suit filed in 1965 in connection with its audit of the Thor Power Tool Company from 1960 to 1964. Together, Thor and Peat Marwick agreed to pay stockholders $475,000 to settle the case.

In 1971 a similar suit produced a landmark court decision on an auditor's responsibilities, as the courts and the government groped their way toward a more thorough understanding of the nature of an accountant's obligations. After the president of the Yale Express trucking company was convicted of mail fraud for making false financial statements, which Peat Marwick had certified, the firm was sued by the company's stockholders. A judge ruled that Peat Marwick was eligible to be sued for stock fraud and common-law deceit because the company had discovered false financial statements from 1963 that it did not disclose until May, 1965. After the court ruled that Peat Marwick had had a duty to disclose the information immediately, the accountants paid $650,000 to settle the suit.

Peat Marwick faced an even larger legal difficulty in 1972, when the S.E.C. included several of its employees, among them the partner in charge of the firm's Washington, D.C., office, as well as a number of lawyers, in charges of violations of federal securities laws in connection with stock offerings of a company called the National Student Marketing Corporation. In 1970 this company's stock had collapsed, costing investors well over $100 million. The government's inclusion of lawyers and accountants in its indictments marked a landmark attempt to expand the apportionment of blame in a case of financial wrongdoing. Previously, charges by the S.E.C. had generally been limited to people actually employed by offending companies.

Peat Marwick was charged with failing to insist that the company's financial statements be revised in accordance with reservations about the company's financial health that Peat Marwick had identified. In addition, the firm was charged with failing to publicize the company's financial improprieties to its stockholders, and with failing to notify the S.E.C. of them.

In the spring of 1972, the steady drumbeat of lawsuits in connection with Peat Marwick's work continued, as, indeed, all the members of its industry found themselves plagued by legal actions. In May the Raytheon Company sued the accounting firm over its audits of the Visual Electronics Corporation from 1968 to 1970, charging that its work failed to show how bad the company's financial straits were. Further legal complications came in October, 1973, when the S.E.C. charged Peat Marwick in connection with its audit of Talley Industries, Inc. By this point in time, though, Peat Marwick had become the largest public accounting firm in the nation. The company had grown by providing services to corporations and also by winning government contracts. In 1972, for instance, it won a Department of Transportation contract to analyze the department's planning techniques.

In 1974 the Peat Marwick partner charged by the S.E.C. in connection with the National Student Marketing collapse, along with another former Peat Marwick employee, were indicted by a grand jury on federal charges of making false and misleading statements, as the government pressed its attempt to hold accountants liable for the actions of their clients. This marked only the third such prosecution of an accountant for a Big Eight firm. At the time, a Peat Marwick public statement protested that "we believe the allegation of criminality of these two professionals is unjustified, unsupported and unprecedented," as the *Wall Street Journal* reported.

The trial of the two auditors opened in October, 1974, with the entire accounting industry watching to see whether the government would be successful in extending enforcement of securities laws to accountants. Peat Marwick was charged with allowing National Student Marketing to use an inappropriate accounting method, as well as with hiding the fact that certain sales had been written off as non-existent in a proxy statement. In November, 1974, the two Peat Marwick accountants were convicted of stock fraud in the case.

In response to this unexpected blow, and a general consensus that the financial industry was moving toward greater accountability, Peat Marwick took steps in 1975 to shore up the controls on its accounting practice. "We have a little bit of an image problem, and we'd better start doing something about it," Peat Marwick's senior partner told the *Wall Street Journal.* The firm was concerned that its recent bad publicity was causing local government units, highly sensitive to public opinion, to seek other firms for their auditing business.

Hoping to clear its name, Peat Marwick engaged another Big Eight accounting firm, Arthur Young & Company, to audit its quality control procedures and make the results available to its clients and staff. In taking this step, Peat Marwick became the first public accounting firm to inaugurate a peer review process. The audit was scheduled to begin in June, in place of an earlier planned process that would have been conducted by the American Institute of Certified Public Accountants. Peat Marwick abandoned its plan for this review because it wished to make the results of the audit public.

Despite this move toward greater rigor in examining its accounting practices, Peat Marwick received the most severe rebuke ever dealt to a major accounting firm by the S.E.C. in July, 1975. The government completed a lengthy inquiry into the firm's operations and harshly criticized its auditing practices in connection with five clients, all of which had suffered severe financial reverses. Along with the National Student Marketing Corporation and Talley Industries, Inc., these included the Penn Central Company and Stirling Homex Corporation, both in bankruptcy, and the Republic National Life Insurance Company. In censoring Peat Marwick, the government banned the firm from taking on any more publicly held clients for the next six months. Peat Marwick agreed to the settlement in an effort to clear up controversies with the S.E.C. and countered in its own defense that the problem cases made up an extremely small part of its client base of 25,000 companies, handled by nearly 100 U.S. offices. The company agreed to further review of its audit practices by the S.E.C., and to outside reviews in the next two years.

In November, 1975, Peat Marwick released the study of its operations by Arthur Young & Company in an effort to bolster its battered reputation for reliability. The report, which cost the company more than half a million dollars, was favorable in its account of the company's activities. In April, 1976, the company revised its audit manual to include more use of internal auditors.

Despite this effort to redress weaknesses in it operations, Peat Marwick was named in yet another lawsuit in October, 1976, in connection with the bankruptcy of a New York based-company called the Investors Funding Corporation. In May, 1977, the review of Peat Marwick's procedures mandated by the S.E.C. reported that the company's "prescribed policies, procedures, and practices are comprehensive, effectively communicated, and appropriate," as the *Wall Street Journal* reported. Overall, the report was qualified in its assessment, pointing out a number of areas for improvement.

Just two months after this report, Peat Marwick won a major new governmental client when it was selected to audit New York City, a job that brought with it an annual fee of nearly $1 million. In addition to its other big clients, the firm numbered the General Electric Company, whose audit required 429 employees in 38 different offices.

In 1978 Peat Marwick formed Peat Marwick International to oversee the firm's activities outside the United States. With this change, the company set up a multi-national umbrella partnership of different firms in locations around the world. By doing this, Peat Marwick hoped to prepare itself for further globalization of the world economy and financial markets by combining a single firm image with well-respected and established local accounting organizations.

In 1979 Peat Marwick reported record revenues from its worldwide operations, which yielded $673.8 million in revenues over a twelve-month period, an increase of 15 percent from the previous year. As Peat Marwick entered the 1980s with this strong financial performance behind it, the company began to face a maturing market for its services and growing competition from the other Big Eight firms. In addition, under pressure from the federal government, the accounting industry was forced to abandon its self-enforced prohibition on advertising. This resulted in a far more hotly contested market for accounting services.

In 1981 the company moved to counter this competition by automating the audit process. As a first step in this process, Peat Marwick developed a program called SeaCas, an abbreviation for Systems Evaluation Approach-Computerized Audit Support. Three years later, the company switched to the Apple Macintosh for all its future computer applications. Also in 1984, Peat Marwick purchased another accounting firm, W. O Daley & Company, based in Orlando, Florida. With this move, the company added eight new partners to its worldwide tally of 1,284.

Two years later the company made a much larger alliance when it agreed to merge with Klynveld Main Goerdeler (KMG), a Dutch accounting firm. Combined, the two firms made up the world's largest accounting firm. In its new configuration, Peat Marwick enhanced its ability to attract big U.S. companies with multinational operations as audit clients. After approval by Peat Marwick's 2,733 partners and KMG's 2,827 partners, the joined companies were to be known as Klynveld Peat Marwick Goerdeler, or KPMG, and were to be headquartered in Amsterdam. In September, 1986, Peat Marwick announced that it had opened negotiations to buy a public relations company and a consulting business, both with ties to the high-tech industry. In the wake of its proposed merger with KMG, this move was seen as a bid by the company to enhance its profile in the consulting field.

On January 1, 1987, the merger between Peat Marwick and KMG was officially completed, capping the largest merger in the history of the accounting business. The new firm instantly inherited worldwide revenues of $2.7 billion, with $1.7 billion contributed by Peat Marwick. In the United States, the operations of both KMG, with 79 U.S. offices, and Peat Marwick, with 91, were combined into one organization, which was to be known as Peat Marwick. This company would have duplicate organizations in 50 cities, and some cutbacks were anticipated, although all partners were given a three-year guarantee of employment.

As the 1980s came to an end, the accounting business once again found itself in a period of transition. During the previous decade, booming business conditions had produced brisk growth for accounting firms, and Peat Marwick had expanded rapidly along with the rest of the industry. By the end of the decade, the firm's client base had started to shrink as a result of changes in the financial world, such as the collapse of the savings and loan industry. Peat Marwick found itself the object of a sweeping inquiry into its audits of savings institutions by the Office of Thrift Supervision as a result of the firm's involvement with the San Francisco Savings and Loan Association. In addition, the wave of bankruptcies that followed the frenzy for mergers and leveraged buyouts in the 1980s resulted in a reduction in need for accounting services, and also generated a large number of lawsuits for public accounting firms as a result of their participation in these activities.

These factors combined to flatten KPMG's revenues in 1988 and 1989. In late 1990 the partnership elected a new chief executive, and KPMG began to implement changes to improve its profitability. In February, 1991, the company announced that 265 partners, or one in seven, would be removed from the firm in a streamlining effort. KPMG predicted that severance costs would amount to $52 million. Despite this drain on U.S. earnings, the company's worldwide returns remained strong, as it posted annual revenues of $6 billion.

In March, 1992, Peat Marwick began to reorganize its operations under the aegis of a Future Directions Committee. Relying on input from the company's Client Service Measurement Process, a survey of customer satisfaction inaugurated in 1989, the firm chose six lines of business: financial services; government; health care and life sciences; information and communications; manufacturing, retailing, and distribution; and special markets and designated services. In addition, Peat Marwick divided the country into ten separate geographical practice areas. The company then organized accountants, tax specialists, and consultants into industry-specific teams. Within this framework, Peat Marwick sought to develop specialists with certain areas of expertise who would entice new clients and bring high-paying tax and consulting jobs.

In September, 1993, as growth in the company's targeted industries remained sluggish, Peat Marwick launched an advertising campaign for the first time. Focusing on the company's international stature, the ads urged companies to "go global—but not without a map." Whether or not this campaign significantly enhanced Peat Marwick's American business, KPMG Worldwide appeared to be solidly entrenched in the top ranks of its industry, backed by a long history and a broad array of operations worldwide as it moved into the mid-1990s.

Principal Subsidiaries: KPMG Peat Marwick (United States).

Further Reading:

Andrews, Frederick, *Wall Street Journal,* "Peat Marwick Is the First Big CPA Firm to Submit to 'Quality Review' by Peers," June 17, 1974; "Fraud Trial of Peat Marwick Attracts Anxious Attention of Other Accountants," October 29, 1974; "Two Auditors Are Convicted of Stock Fraud," November 15, 1974.

Berton, Lee, "Peat Marwick and KMG Main Agree to Merge," *Wall Street Journal,* September 4, 1986.

Cowan, Alison Leigh, "Regulators Investigate Peat on Its Auditing of S.&L.'s," *New York Times,* May 23, 1991.

Minard, Lawrence and Brian McGlynn, "The U.S.' Newest Glamour Job," *Forbes,* September 1, 1977.

Stodghill, Ron, "Who Says Accountants Can't Jump?," *Business Week,* October 26, 1992.

Weiss, Stuart, "Peat Marwick Merges Its Way to the Top," *Business Week,* September 15, 1986.

—Elizabeth Rourke

L.L.Bean®

L. L. Bean, Inc.

Casco Street
Freeport, Maine 04033
U.S.A.
(207) 865-4761
Fax: (207) 797-0047

Private Company
Incorporated: 1934
Employees: 4,044
Sales: $870 million
SICs: 5651 Family Clothing Stores; 5941 Sporting Goods
and Bicycle Shops; 5961 Catalog & Mail-Order Houses

L. L. Bean, Inc., is a leading U.S. catalog company and the largest supplier of outdoor gear in the world. The L. L. Bean catalogs, a tradition since the company's founding, are the engine that drives company sales; in 1993 the company took in $745 million from catalog sales alone. The 1993 catalogs, 30 in all, offered approximately 6,700 different items, most tied to the pursuit of outdoor, active lifestyles. For the solitary fisherman or the fun-seeking yuppie, the name L. L. Bean stands for quality, value, and enduring style—so much so that each year more than 3.5 million visitors make pilgrimages to the company's original retail store, in Freeport, Maine, to soak up the Bean ambiance and the Bean bargains. Retail sales for 1993 (including those for five factory outlet stores and two independently owned retail stores in Japan) reached $125 million. L. L. Bean also enjoys a high reputation, among its corporate peers as well as its customers, for order fulfillment.

The founder of the company was a 40-year-old Maine outdoorsman named Leon Leonwood Bean. Orphaned at age 12, Bean began to develop his entrepreneurial skills by doing odd jobs and by selling soap door-to-door. He also earned money by trapping. "Although he was a natural salesman," writes Robert B. Pile, "he was never really satisfied in one job and drifted about from place to place." Finally, Bean went to work for his older brother, Otho, in a Freeport dry goods store. There Bean sold overalls to manual laborers and earned $12 a week. However, his true love was hunting and fishing in the Maine woods and streams, a love that would eventually lead to the development of one of the most popular and enduring products in American retailing.

Like most outdoorsmen in the early 1900s, Bean frequently suffered the problem of hiking with waterlogged boots. In 1912 he decided to add leather tops to a pair of ordinary rubber boots. He sought the services of a local shoemaker, and, after a few pairs of the boots had been sewn together, he penned a circular entitled "The Maine Hunting Shoe." A model of early direct-mail advertising, the circular began: "Outside of your gun, nothing is so important to your outfit as your foot-wear. You cannot expect success hunting deer or moose if your feet are not properly dressed." Bean mailed the letter to sportsmen from outside Maine who had purchased Maine hunting licenses and touted his original shoe as "light as a moccasin, with the protection of a heavy hunting boot." He priced his product at $3.50 per pair and, to further entice his fellow hunters, offered a money-back guarantee.

Bean's marketing was flawless; however, his product was not. Of the 100 pairs of his Maine Hunting Shoes that were ordered and sent, 90 were returned because the tops had separated from the bottoms. Rather than give up his fledgling enterprise, though, Bean honored his guarantee and then borrowed $400 to redesign and perfect his boots (Bean also perfected his guarantee, making it unconditional and, in fact, the essence of Bean's customer service culture through the present day). His determination to satisfy himself and his customers paid off after he traveled to Boston to meet with representatives of the U.S. Rubber Company, who were able to fulfill his original design intentions. Bean redoubled his boot-making efforts and his commitment to the mail-order business, fortuitously in the same year that the U.S. Post Office began its parcel post service.

Bean's revamped footwear quickly became successful, and he soon expanded his marketing push into other states. A *Fortune* "Hall of Fame" article records that when another of Bean's brothers, Guy, became the town postmaster, Bean established his factory directly over the post office and facilitated the mailing process with a system of chutes and elevators. "He never lost his touch. Knowing that hunters from out of state often drove through Freeport in the middle of the night on their way to some hunting camp in the far wilds. Bean opened for business 24 hours a day. Night customers found a doorbell and a sign that read: 'Push once a minute until clerk appears.' "

Bean's name spread during the 1920s, due to word-of-mouth as well as print advertising and the founder's continuing innovations. In 1920 Bean opened a showroom store adjacent to his workshop, in accession to the demands of visitors. In 1922 Bean reengineered the Maine Hunting Shoe by adding a split back-stay to help eliminate chafing. Within two years, sales rose to $135,000 annually. In 1923 the company received welcome publicity when its boots were used to outfit the Macmillan Arctic Expedition.

The catalog expanded in 1927, adding fishing and camping equipment to the Bean line of clothing and hunting equipment. Typical of the ad copy was the inducement: "It is no longer necessary for you to experiment with hundreds of flies to determine the few that will catch fish. We have done that experimenting for you." For years, in fact, Bean insisted on personally testing all of the products the company planned to sell. Perhaps this is why the Maine Hunting Shoe, as innovative as it was, proved to be simply the first in a string of classic Bean products, like the Maine Guide Shirt, the Chamois Cloth Shirt, Bean Moccasins, the Zipper Duffle Bag, and Bean Cork Decoys. (The company also included high-quality non-Bean products, beginning with the Hudson Bay "Point" Blanket in 1927.)

During the Great Depression era, the mail-order house managed not only to survive but to thrive, passing the million-dollar mark in sales in 1937. According to Pile, "Bean invested nearly every dollar he made back into the business, with his eye on building it for the long term." The secret to L. L. Bean's success during these growth years was a threefold emphasis on quality products, fair pricing, and creating a timeless appeal to the Bean catalogs, which always featured paintings of outdoor Maine scenes and stories that underscored the strong link between Bean products and an outdoor lifestyle. In addition, Leon Leonwood instituted a postage-paid policy, further strengthening the company's reputation for catering to the customer. By the post-World War II era, both Beans, the man and the company, had become living legends. And the list of Bean customers was fast becoming a collection of legends itself, as such names as Calvin Coolidge, Franklin Roosevelt, Jack Dempsey, John Wayne, and Ted Williams were added.

In 1951 Bean, still at the helm as he approached 80, announced that the Freeport retail store would begin operating 24 hours-a-day, 365 days-a-year. Another important innovation during this decade was the introduction in 1954 of a women's department. Yet, despite the now-famous Bean name, as the company entered the 1960s its sales volume was not as high as might have been expected. Pile asserts that "dark clouds loomed on the horizon as [Bean] became older.... No longer did annual sales increase 25 percent or more each year; dollar volume actually began to flatten. Merchandise in the catalog and in the store was no longer up-to-the-minute, and even worse, orders were being slowly filled by part-time people who had little interest in doing the best possible job." The downhill course the company appeared to be on was steepened by the inception of other sports specialty marketers. However, this course was altered following Bean's death in 1967 when ownership of the company fell to the Bean heirs. Only one was interested in management: Leon A. Gorman, grandson of the founder.

Gorman was first hired by the company in 1960. In 1967 he became president of a languishing business, with $3.5 million in annual sales and $65,000 in profits. Strong leadership and redirection were required and Gorman filled the need. His first decisions included expanding the advertising budget and demographic target group and making prices more competitive. He refrained from seeking growth through more retail outlets for fear of jeopardizing the catalog business. During his first full year as president, sales rose to nearly $5 million. The company had gotten back on track just in time to enjoy a huge recreation boom that was spreading across the country. By 1975 sales had reached $30 million and the company was employing more than 400 people. During the 1970s, the computerization of many business segments and the relocation of manufacturing to a new building further speeded the company's growth.

Several trends contributed to Bean's substantial growth in the 1980s. Among them was the accidental, or perhaps inevitable, affiliation of the Bean label with prep culture and clothing. According to Milton Moskowitz, Lisa Birnbach's *Official* *Preppy Handbook,* tongue-in-cheek or not in its declaration of the Bean store as "nothing less than prep mecca," helped fuel a 42 percent rise in 1981 sales. A new health and fitness boom contributed to Bean's growth, as well as a surge in mail-order shopping. First-time Bean customers, nearly 70 percent of which were women, increased rapidly during the 1980s.

However, as the 1990s approached, the country experienced a serious recession; sales slowed, returns rose, and a 30 percent postal increase loomed on the horizon. For a time, Bean suffered along with the other major catalog marketers and was forced to lay off ten percent of its hourly and salaried workforce over a two-year period. In a 1992 *Forbes* article, Phyllis Berman placed the problem in a more serious context: "What went wrong? To some extent L. L. Bean is the victim of success. A whole generation is already outfitted with L. L. Bean leisurewear and camping equipment. Its durable, high quality clothing lines have spawned many imitators. Meanwhile, similar items turn up in discount stores.... Bean carried relatively few styles and introduced new products slowly. But today's trend-conscious and jaded consumers want variety and novelty."

Berman, who continued by questioning Gorman's management decisions, may have been premature in her analysis; by the end of 1992, the company's 80th anniversary, sales had risen by 18 percent to $743 million. The same year, L. L. Bean opened its first store in Japan, a ripe market that also contributed high year-end catalog revenues. A second Japanese store was added in July 1993; both are jointly owned by Seiyu and the Matsushita Electric Industrial Co. More L. L. Bean Japan stores were scheduled to open in the mid-1990s.

Despite its problems in the late 1980s and early 1990s, Bean still had great strengths from which to draw, including its mailing list, which is thought to be approximately 15 million names strong, and its heritage. Of the latter, Gorman commented: "In running L. L. Bean on a daily basis, we have been most successful by applying what my grandfather called his Golden Rule: 'Sell good merchandise at a reasonable profit, treat your customers like human beings and they'll always come back for more.'" Of the catalog, the very embodiment of the Bean heritage, James R. Rosenfield wrote in *Direct Marketing:* "When you look at a great painting, you sometimes get the feeling that a kind of perfection has been reached, where nothing could be added or subtracted. In a more mundane way, that's how I feel about the L. L. Bean catalog. It gets a perfect 10." Whether that perfection will lead to a repetition of Bean's strong 1980s growth remains to be seen.

Further Reading:

Alpert, Mark, "Yuppies Want More Than Most Catalogues Offer," *Fortune,* October 22, 1990, p. 12.
"Bean Sticks to Its Backyard," *Economist,* August 4, 1990, p. 57.
Berman, Phyllis, "Trouble in Bean Land," *Forbes,* July 6, 1992, pp. 42–44.
Bonnin, Julie, "In L. L. Bean Store, the Catalog Fantasy Lives," *Minneapolis Star Tribune* (Cox News Service), December 13, 1993, p. 1E.
Brown, Tom, "Worried About Burnout? Try Fly Fishing," *Industry Week,* January 17, 1994, p. 29.
"For Your Information," *Minneapolis Star Tribune,* February 23, 1993, p. 8D.
"Leon A. Gorman," *Chain Store Age Executive,* December 1992, p. 57.

de Llosa, Patty, ''The National Business Hall of Fame (Leon Leonwood Bean),'' *Fortune,* April 5, 1993, pp. 112, 114.

Moskowitz, Milton, et al, ''L. L. Bean,'' in *Everybody's Business: A Field Guide to the 400 Leading Companies in America,* New York: Doubleday, 1990.

Pile, Robert B., ''L. L. Bean: The Outdoorsman Who Hated Wet Feet,'' in *Top Entrepreneurs and Their Businesses,* Minneapolis: Oliver Press, 1993, pp. 29–43.

Port, Otis, and Geoffrey Smith, ''Beg, Borrow—and Benchmark,'' *Business Week,* November 30, 1992, pp. 74–75.

Rosenfield, James R., ''In the Mail: L. L. Bean,'' *Direct Marketing,* February 1992, pp. 16–17.

Sterngold, James, ''Young Japanese Like Rugged American Look of L. L. Bean,'' *Minneapolis Star Tribune (New York Times),* March 4, 1993, p. 6E.

Tucker, Frances Gaither; Seymour M. Zivan; and Robert C. Camp, ''How to Measure Yourself Against the Best,'' *Harvard Business Review,* January/February 1987, pp. 8–10.

Vannah, Thomas M., ''A Most Bucolic Business,'' *New England Business,* May 1990, pp. 64, 63.

—Jay P. Pederson

Lechmere Inc.

275 Wildwood Street
Woburn, Massachusetts 01801
U.S.A.
(617) 935-8320
Fax: (617) 935-2980

*Wholly Owned Subsidiary of Montgomery Ward & Co.,
   Incorporated*
Incorporated: 1948 as Lechmere Tire & Sales Company
Employees: 5,000
Sales: $800 million
SICs: 5722 Household Appliance Stores; 5731 Radio, TV &
   Electronics Stores; 5719 Miscellaneous Home Furnishings
   Stores; 5941 Sporting Goods and Bicycle Shops

Lechmere Inc. is a retailer of electronics, appliances, and other
goods, with 24 stores located throughout New England and
New York. The company was founded in the early twentieth
century and expanded during the postwar years as a family
business offering an eclectic mix of products. Upon its sale to
Dayton Hudson in the late 1960s, Lechmere underwent rapid
expansion into five states in the Southeast. In the late 1980s,
however, Lechmere's executives took the company private and
closed some of its newer facilities in order to focus on the New
England market. In early 1994, Lechmere was once again purchased by a national chain, as Montgomery Ward acquired the
business.

Lechmere traces its origins to 1913, when Abraham Cohen, a
Russian immigrant who had settled in Massachusetts, purchased the harness-making shop at which he worked. The A.
Cohen Harness Maker shop was located in a district of Cambridge known as Lechmere, named after Lord Lechmere, a
British Tory who had helped to develop the area during the
eighteenth century. Cohen soon changed the name of his business to Lechmere Harness Shop.

Over the next ten years, as automobiles began to replace horse-
drawn carriages, the need for harnesses declined. In response,
Cohen decided to shift the focus of his business to include tire
sales. To reflect this new emphasis, the company's name was
changed to the Lechmere Vulcanizing Company. In 1945,
Cohen brought his three sons, Maurice, Norman, and Philip,
into the Lechmere business, and the company became a partnership.

After World War II, when demand for a wide variety of consumer goods increased dramatically, the Cohens moved to
broaden their product line beyond tires. They began to offer
small appliances, and, in 1948, the company's name was
changed to Lechmere Tire & Sales Company. Also that year,
the business was incorporated.

In the early 1950s, Lechmere expanded its operations further.
The company began to offer a wider variety of household
goods, devoting more display space to televisions and other
popular appliances. Additional floors were added to the store,
and the expanded showroom began to feature cameras, luggage,
silver and other flatware, sewing machines, toys, and lawn and
garden tools.

In an effort to distribute its wares more efficiently to customers,
Lechmere introduced the concept of the "pick-up counter" in
the early 1950s. Customers would examine models of the various products available on a showroom floor, and then go to
another location in the store to pick up one of the items they had
selected. In 1956, the Cohens bought an old bus garage at 88
First Street in Cambridge, around the corner from their store.
This property was converted into the company's main retail
store. With this additional space, Lechmere expanded its product line even further, offering records, jewelry, sporting goods,
and additional appliances and household wares, along with its
standard line of televisions and large appliances.

To draw the large client base needed to maintain its high-
volume operation, Lechmere became one of the first local
retailers to advertise extensively on television. In order to help
people remember its address at 88 First Street, Lechmere
adopted the gimmick of setting all of its prices at a dollar
amount, plus 88 cents. This signature pricing policy was later
adopted by other discount retailers.

Lechmere became known in the Boston area for its unusually
diverse selection of merchandise as well as the visible involvement of the Cohens, who often walked about the store meeting
customers and inviting their comments. By the early 1960s, the
company was ready to expand its facilities again. In 1963,
construction of a new, modern building at the 88 First Street
location was completed. This steel-framed facility encompassed
100,000 square feet and provided room for the Cohens to
branch out into the retail of office equipment, hardware, accessories for the bath, books, greeting cards, and tobacco. Lechmere also opened a four-bay auto servicing garage in its new
building.

Two years after this expansion, Lechmere opened its first store
outside of Cambridge, in Dedham, Massachusetts. When this
venture proved successful, the Cohens began to explore the
possibility of further geographical expansion, and, by 1967,
they had developed a plan to open three more stores over the
next five years. The Cohens soon recognized, however, that
they would need a significant infusion of capital to pay for the
construction of new stores. To gain access to the funds necessary for expansion, they decided to sell Lechmere to another
department store chain, the Dayton Corporation of Minneapolis.

Under the agreement, Dayton would hold Lechmere as a separate subsidiary, leaving much of the day-to-day operations
under control of the Cohens and their store managers. On

February 28, 1969, the sale was completed, and Lechmere became a subsidiary of the newly formed Dayton Hudson Corporation, after Dayton merged with the J.L. Hudson Company. With the financial resources of a much larger company behind it, Lechmere embarked upon a program of geographical expansion in the 1970s, and, by the end of 1971, the company had added two more stores, in Danvers and Springfield, Massachusetts

During the 1970s, the Cohens gradually began ceding control of the firm's day-to-day operations, and Lechmere's product line began to change, focusing increasingly on traditional discount store fare, which was inexpensive and frequently of lower quality. As a result, the company's reputation for offering unique merchandise began to suffer, and sales began to decline. In an effort to counteract this trend, Lechmere embarked upon a program in the late 1970s to boost sales by cutting prices dramatically. With this strategy, sales at the chain's stores began to increase. In 1977, Lechmere opened a fifth store, in Manchester, New Hampshire, and, the following year, a sixth store was opened in Framingham, Massachusetts.

In 1980, Lechmere's corporate parent began to take a more active interest in the future of the chain. Two new executives were dispatched to take over the company and move it in new directions. A team of entrepreneurs was recruited to help redirect Lechmere, whose operations at that time were generating only $135 million a year. "The store had drifted from the course set by the Cohens," Lechmere's chairperson, C. George Scala, recalled in HFD, a trade journal, commenting that the Cohens had "emphasized value in quality electronics and appliances. They wanted to sell steak cheap, not cheap steak. However, after they left, new managers . . . indulged in a series of undisciplined diversifications. They really didn't possess a strategic position in the marketplace."

To reposition Lechmere, Scala and his associates commissioned a large-scale study of customer preferences, which took place between 1980 and 1981. From this survey, Lechmere learned that many customers found shopping in Lechmere stores unpleasant and time-consuming, that customers were frequently frustrated by items being out of stock, and that the chain's focus was unclear. Moreover, the survey indicated that customers went to Lechmere to buy major appliances, not smaller decorative goods, and that they were interested in items to use in their leisure time. "Those recommendations became our guidelines," Scala told HFD.

The new management began by streamlining Lechmere's offerings. Automotive accessories, furniture, grandfather clocks, fireplace fixtures, bath-related wares, books, greeting cards, gourmet foods, cigarettes, ski clothing, jewelry, Christmas trim, and other merchandise, totaling $15 million, were eliminated from the company's product line. Lechmere then focused on the items important to its initial success under the Cohens, which included televisions, major home appliances, audio equipment, records and tapes, photography and sporting goods, housewares, and seasonal and lawn equipment. Redefining itself as a marketer of equipment for communication, education, entertainment, preparation, recreation, and information, the company set up four "worlds" in which it planned to operate: Home Electronics, Major Appliances, Housewares-Hardware, and Leisure and Sporting Goods. Thus, Lechmere hoped to better focus its identity in the industry, while also providing new lines of business, such as video equipment, tape rental, personal computers, telephones, and physical fitness equipment. "We don't focus on product," Scala explained to HFD, "but rather on adding value to the lifestyles of our customers, which we track by observation and by communicating with them."

In 1981, Lechmere changed its name to better reflect its new identity, dropping "Tire and Sales" to become, simply, Lechmere, Inc. At this time, the company also undertook an effort to improve the quality of the customer's shopping experience in its stores. Customers had complained about Lechmere's cumbersome check-out process and outmoded conveyor belt pick-up system. To expedite sales transactions, Lechmere invested in an entirely new computer system, which tracked its merchandise from ordering to purchase.

In 1982, Lechmere completed the renovation of its store in Manchester, New Hampshire, to conform to its new business prototype, with each merchandise category being adequately represented. Lechmere's plan to become a high-volume, low-margin retailer required that sales-per-square-foot in all of its stores be unusually high. The new Lechmere's Manchester store proved successful, and the company moved quickly to renovate its other five stores on this model. By 1983, sales in Lechmere's six outlets had reached $221 million, an increase of 40 percent in two years. The company then decided to open two more stores, and, in 1984, a new outlet in Woburn, Massachusetts, opened its doors at a former K-Mart location, while an eighth Lechmere store was inaugurated in Seekonk, Massachusetts.

Lechmere's continuing market research during this time indicated that one-quarter of the American population would be working at home by the mid-1990s. Therefore, the company decided to add a home office category, offering a large selection of telephones, answering machines, computers, software, and ready-to-assemble furniture. Lechmere also began a program of rapid expansion in the mid-1980s. From 1985 to 1986, the company opened nine new stores, moving into areas outside New England for the first time. In 1986, the company began operating in the Atlanta market, opening four stores simultaneously to make a big impact in this new arena.

In 1987, Lechmere opened seven new stores, including outlets in Raleigh, North Carolina, Clearwater, Florida, and Sarasota, Florida. The Sarasota store, with 60,000 square feet of selling space, 20,000 less than other Lechmere stores, became the company's new store prototype, as it made more efficient use of space. With a total of 24 stores, Lechmere posted profits of $22.7 million on sales of $636.3 million for 1987.

The following year, the company's total number of stores rose to 27, which were spread across nine states, including North Carolina, South Carolina, Georgia, Florida, and the states of New England. In June 1989, Lechmere opened a completely new flagship store in Cambridge, next door to its original structure, which had been demolished to make way for a mall. The three-story facility had 122,000 square feet of space, making it the largest in the chain. Two more Lechmere outlets were also opened in Birmingham, Alabama.

Despite its geographical expansion and steady increase in sales, however, Lechmere's profits remained flat, due to the company's low-margin operations and stiff competition in the consumer electronics, sporting goods, and home office supplies markets. This performance, out of line with the returns from other Dayton Hudson properties, prompted some to suggest that Dayton Hudson would put Lechmere up for sale. These rumors were confirmed in July 1989, when Lechmere announced that it was being purchased by a group of investors that included Berkshire Partners, a Boston-based leveraged buy-out firm, eight Lechmere executives, and two local shopping mall executives. The price for the chain was reported at $600 million, and the deal would allow Lechmere to retain its autonomy.

Three months after leaving Dayton Hudson, Lechmere announced plans to close eight of its ten stores outside New England on December 24, 1989, putting 1,200 employees out of work. The closings affected stores in Georgia, North Carolina, South Carolina, Alabama, and Florida, while two stores in Georgia and North Carolina were slated to remain open only until they could be sold. Two days after this announcement, Lechmere made public additional plans to sell its credit operation, letting 115 more workers go. With these moves, Lechmere hoped to streamline its business for more efficient, profitable operations in areas such as distribution. By the end of 1990, Lechmere's 17 remaining stores had notched sales of $627 million, despite a general recession in retailing.

Lechmere resumed its expansion in 1991, focusing on areas closer to its home base, such as New York. Stores were opened in Syracuse and Buffalo, bringing Lechmere's total to 20. During this time, sales increased to $672 million, after Lechmere turned in a strong holiday season performance, despite heavy competition from nationwide discount electronics chains, such as Circuit City. In 1992, Lechmere opened outlets in Kingston, Taunton, Attleboro, and Manchester, Connecticut, and also remodeled its Springfield, Massachusetts store. By early 1994,

Lechmere's locations totaled 24, and its annual sales had reached $800 million.

In February 1994, Lechmere announced that it had been purchased by Montgomery Ward & Co., a Chicago-based retailing giant, for $100 million plus the assumption of a $106 million debt incurred when the company had been taken private four years earlier. Although Montgomery Ward soon announced that one of its executives would take over as head of Lechmere, it vowed that Lechmere would retain its corporate identity and separate operations, and that no stores would be closed or employees let go. With the resources of its giant corporate parent behind it, as well as a strong regional identity and an unusual merchandise mix, Lechmere appeared well-situated to compete effectively in the crowded electronics and appliances market as it moved into the mid-1990s.

Further Reading:

Epstein, Gady, "Scala Retires from Lechmere," *Boston Globe,* June 23, 1992.
Gilbert, Les, "Lechmere Diversifies Carefully," *HFD—The Weekly Home Furnishings Newspaper,* October 17, 1988.
Kimbrough, Ann Wead, "Two Years Later, Lechmere Stays Status Quo," *Atlanta Business Chronicle,* August 15, 1988.
Levine, Martin, "Lechmere Challenged in Beantown OAH Battle," *Consumer Electronics,* September 1988.
Mehegan, David, "Big Bang at Lechmere," *Boston Globe,* June 2, 1989.
Mehegan, David, "Lechmere Bought Back," *Boston Globe,* July 20, 1989.
Mehegan, David, "Lechmere to Close Ten Stores in South," *Boston Globe,* September 29, 1989.
Mehegan, David, "Through the Season's Uncertainty," *Boston Globe,* December 18, 1990.
Reidy, Chris, "Lechmere Sale Complete," *Boston Globe,* March 31, 1994.
Zuckoff, Mitchell, "Lechmere Agrees to Takeover," *Boston Globe,* February 2, 1994.

—Elizabeth Rourke

LEGENT

Legent Corporation

575 Herndon Parkway
Herndon, Virginia 22070-5226
U.S.A.
(703) 708-3000

Public Company
Incorporated: 1989
Employees: 2,400
Sales: $442 million
Stock Exchanges: NASDAQ
SICs: 7372 Prepackaged Software

One of the largest software companies in the world, Legent Corporation develops and markets software to facilitate the management of enterprise-wide computer systems. Legent offers more than 130 products designed to increase the efficiency, reliability, and security of distributed management in the areas of systems, network, application, and data management. Marketed to large manufacturers, major financial institutions, and government agencies, Legent's products work across mainframe, work station, and client/server platforms.

Legent was formed in 1989 by the merger of Duquesne Systems and Morino Associates, two leading providers of systems management software for mainframe computers. Separately, the companies had both exhibited notable growth: during the 1980s, each had revenues increase by 50 percent and earnings by 60 percent. Combined, they offered 40 types of prepackaged software, including popular programs that automated software development and that made mainframe data bases more efficient. After the merger, analysts expected Legent's sales to grow 39 percent, to $173 million in 1990, and to continue to rise by 30 percent annually for several years thereafter.

The two companies' former heads began by sharing the decision making, with Morino's Mario M. Morino as chairman and Duquesne's Glen F. Chatfield as chief executive. Merging the companies' disparate management systems proved difficult; Chatfield wanted to retain Duquesne's centralized, conservative management, whereas Morino endorsed his former company's dispersed management. Unable to resolve their differences, the two agreed to drop their titles and take staff jobs. Joe M. Henson, a Legent director, took over as chief executive officer in November of 1989. Within a few months, Chatfield had resigned his staff position, although he remained a director of the company.

Henson's first job was to complete the consolidation of the two companies, a job that took 14 months from the time of the merger. "It's been no piece of cake," Henson told *Business Week* in 1990. With the merger completed, he then concentrated on the company's growth, which he intended to maintain at a high rate through acquisitions. He had already promoted that strategy as a director of the company when, in August 1989, he approved Legent's acquisition of Business Software Technology for $47 million in stock. With $3 million in profits on $14.7 million in sales that year, the company sold for a substantial sum. However, Henson told *Business Week,* "You're talking big-time payoff." He expected Business Software Technology, a leader in application management, to make $30 million in profits on $100 million in sales within a few years. Henson planned to execute similar acquisitions in the next few years, using stock rather than cash to buy other small software companies poised for large growth.

Until 1991 Legent offered software products for mainframe computers exclusively. With the company's acquisition of Spectrum Concepts that year, it moved into the larger arena of distributed computing. Spectrum's key product, the XCOM 6.2, gave Legent the most advanced product of its kind yet on the market. The software connected disparate systems, both to one another and to the IBM host processor, allowing information to be distributed among heterogeneous platforms. The acquisition contributed to the 20 percent rise in Legent's revenues in 1991. Although its growth did not reach the 30 percent expected by some analysts, Legent revenues did grow to $208 million.

Until the acquisition of Spectrum Concepts, Legent's organization reflected its history of mergers, with three divisions that corresponded to the original Morino, Duquesne, and Business Software Technology companies. An unwieldy system, it was changed in 1991 to one based on function. The company created four business areas: systems management, which focused on the delivery of data center and distributed systems management solutions; networking, which provided complete applications necessary to run a distributed network; applications management, which developed software for managing the applications and databases involved in distributed computing; and services, which not only supported the company's products but also eventually offered management consulting services in system resource planning.

In 1992, Legent vastly accelerated its growth by merging with Columbus, Ohio-based Goal Systems International Inc., a leading provider of data center management, network performance, and software distribution products. The combined enterprise, still operating under the name Legent, stepped into line behind IBM and Computer Associates International Inc. as the third largest supplier of mainframe systems software. Legent's staff jumped from 1,200 to 2,000, and its customer base grew from 4,500 to 10,000. Combining the operations of the companies was expected to take two to three years.

Legent's latest merger required combining not only two hierarchies, but also two products lines which overlapped in critical ways. Both companies had popular mainframe products in automated systems operations (ASO) and in automated output management. ASO products automatically respond to mainframe system messages and handle routine console tasks, and automated output management products facilitate the distribution of printed reports and allow end users to view reports on line. Rather than choose one product in each area, gradually phasing the other out, Legent combined the competing products. A "core" product was chosen from each overlapping pair, to which key features of the "losing" product would be added. This method ensured that existing customers would not give up any functional investments they had already made in the previous versions. New customers would presumably have the best of what made the previous versions popular. The new superset products stood a good chance of dominating both the ASO and the automated output management markets.

By 1992, Legent had 40 offices in 14 countries, and its rapid growth warranted new buildings in its principal locations. In April of that year, the company began construction on a new 240,000-square-foot facility in Pittsburgh, Pennsylvania. It also purchased a 130,000-square-foot building in Herndon, Virginia, and had moved its headquarters there from Vienna, Virginia, by 1993.

Legent's merger with Goal Systems helped boost its already impressive sales growth. Legent president and CEO John Burton told *Datamation*, "Our average order size has risen from $30,000 to $100,000 since the merger." The two company's premerger revenues in 1991 equaled $364 million combined; 1992 postmerger revenues reached $446 million. Legent's net income rose 80 percent in 1992 to $65 million.

In the early 1990s, companies increasingly chose local area networks over mainframes for their computing needs, which many saw as the death knell for mainframe software companies like Legent. However, industry analyst Rich Edwards gave a different assessment of Legent's future to *Datamation:* "In contrast with the general perspective that, if mainframe system sales are not growing, then the mainframe software opportunities therefore must be limited, Legent is generating solid revenue growth through a multi-pronged strategy."

That strategy included offering products that worked across a variety of hardware platforms, including mainframes, work stations, and client/servers. Legent also devoted increasing attention to products that facilitated the use of a variety of operating systems. The trend away from host-based computing to a client/server model of computing created opportunities for companies able to help those making the transition. In October 1993, Legent announced a comprehensive program, called Cross Platform Environment (XPE), that was designed to help customers integrate and use systems management solutions throughout their client/server computing environments. Legent had devoted three years and $50 million to develop XPE through internal product development, strategic partnerships, technology licensing agreements, and acquisitions. Legent's XPE initiative addresses eight systems management functions: distribution management, software administration, network problem management, resource management, distributed operations management, distributed backup and recovery, user administration, and distributed database management.

Legent's products for distributed management were primarily acquired through its purchase of Spectrum Concepts in 1992. The XCOM product line allowed file transfers between more than 20 computer and operating system environments. The acquisition was also instrumental in Legent's development of DistribuLink, a product that distributes both custom and prepackaged software to a broad range of hardware platforms. Legent's acquisition of Corporate Microsystems, Inc. in September 1993 extended the capabilities of Legent's products for distributed management. CMI provided technology for software distribution and file transfer for UNIX and IBM OS-2 platforms.

The company's software administration products, called Endevor, help customers manage the software development lifecycle, eliminating many time-consuming manual tasks. Although Endevor products had been offered by Legent for several years, the company gained important technology to expand Endevor's capabilities when it acquired TeamOne Systems, Inc. in 1994. The new technology will integrate configuration management capabilities across all major computing platforms. Legent acquired the technology for the network problem management area of XPE when it purchased Networx, Inc. in September 1993. The company's problem management applications for client/server computing helped Legent move into this targeted area of expertise. Legent also offers the distributed operations management products AutoMate/XC, which manages multiple IBM and non-IBM systems, and OPS/MVS, which collects, organizes, and evaluates host-based operations information and automates mainframe system activities.

Legent's resource management products help companies use their existing resources and personnel to their fullest by addressing the areas of capacity management, performance management, financial and asset management, storage management, and resource integration. The company introduced the performance management application Paramount in April 1993; it offered common, single-point access to critical information about systems resources and streamlined trouble-shooting and resource management tasks. An alliance with Hewlett-Packard, initiated in September 1993, is expected to integrate Legent's Paramount with HP UNIX performance products to allow single-point management control between data centers and distributed computing environments. The alliance will also enable Legent to license, distribute, and support HP's performance products. The company's MICS products offer enterprise-wide data collection, analysis, management reporting, and operational reporting.

Legent introduced its first distributed backup and recovery product in November 1993, the Enterprise Storage Manager (ESM). ESM provided both local and off-site backup and recovery for LAN-based servers connected to mainframes. Phil Carrai, a Legent vice-president, said at the product's introduction, "Many of our customers have been waiting for industrial-strength storage solutions before deploying client/server technology, and ESM provides the solution." Legent first offered distributed database management products late in 1993 after its acquisition of Performance Technologies, Inc. and its alliance with Bridge Technology, Inc.

Legent's revenues in 1993 were $442 million; net operating income reached $60 million, despite somber predictions for mainframe software vendors. Not only do Legent's mainframe software products continue to sell well, but the company's move into products for client/server computing is keeping the company abreast of changes in the industry. With 24 percent of its revenues in research, development, and support, and its commitment to gaining and refining new technology through acquisition and strategic alliances, Legent seems positioned to maintain its impressive profitability and to increase its market scope.

Principal Subsidiaries: Duquesne Systems Inc.; Morino, Inc.; Business Software Technology, Inc.; CMA Software A/S.

Further Reading:

''Legent,'' *Washington Technology Almanac,* 1993, p. B-79.

Miles, Gregory L., ''Legent Plans to Buy and Buy—Then Buy Some More,'' *Business Week,* April 2, 1990, pp. 68–70.

Semich, J. William, ''Application Development Control!'' *Datamation,* June 1, 1991, pp. 28–31.

——, ''The Datamation 100 North American Profiles,'' *Datamation,* June 15, 1993, p. 114.

Taber, Mark, ''The Legent/Goal Merger: What It Means to Users,'' *Datamation,* November 1, 1992, pp. 91–95.

—Susan Windisch Brown

Louis Vuitton

54, avenue Montaigne
75008 Paris
France
(1) 40 90 32 00
Fax: 1 45 61 46 95

Public Company
Incorporated: 1854 as Louis Vuitton SA
Employees: 3,400
Sales: FF 7.2 billion
Stock Exchanges: Paris
SICs: SIC 5099 Durable Goods, NEC; SIC 3161 Luggage;
   SIC 2396 Automotive Trimmings, Apparel Findings, and
   Related Products; SIC 3429 Hardware, NEC; SIC 2211
   Broadwove Fabric Mills, Cotton

Louis Vuitton has been the supplier of luggage to the wealthy and powerful for well over 100 years and is known for combining quality fabrication with innovative designs to reflect the needs of customers and the ever-changing modes of world travel. In 1987, the company became part of Moët-Hennessy Louis Vuitton (LVMH), the world's largest luxury goods conglomerate.

Louis Vuitton left Anchay, his birthplace in the Jura, for Paris in 1835 at age fourteen. After one year of traveling on foot, he reached the capital and soon became an apprentice packer and trunkmaker. The son of a carpenter, Vuitton mastered the skill of woodworking and designing trunks and, within ten years, had become an expert. During his apprenticeship, Vuitton gained experience in packing by traveling to the homes of wealthy women, where he was employed to pack their clothes before they embarked on long voyages. With his master, Monsieur Maréchal, Vuitton went regularly to the Tuileries Palace, as the exclusive packers to the Empress Eugénie and her ladies-in-waiting.

In 1854, Vuitton opened his own business at 4 rue Neuve des Capucines, very close to the couture houses around Place Vendôme. Due to his familiarity with wood, silk, and satin, he became well respected by the couturiers, who hired him to pack their creations. His invention of flat-topped trunks, which were more easily stacked for travel than the traditional domed trunks, established his reputation as a master luggage-maker. Vuitton

began covering his trunks in grey Trianon canvas, which was both elegant and waterproof when varnished.

As the business grew increasingly successful, Vuitton built workshops outside Paris in Asnières, where transportation of wood from the south was convenient. When his original store became too small, business was transferred to 1 Rue Scribe, and Vuitton began focusing on trunk-making rather than packing. Vuitton became the supplier of luggage to many of the most famous people of the era, from King Alfonso XII of Spain to the future Czar Nicholas II of Russia. He created special trunks for Ismail Pacha, the viceroy of Egypt, for the inauguration of the Suez Canal as well as a trunk-bed for Savorgnan de Brazza, who discovered the source of the Congo in 1876. The quality of the materials, the arrangement of interiors, and the finishings made Vuitton's deluxe trunks far superior to anything that had previously been produced.

In an attempt to discourage copying of the Trianon grey canvas in 1876, Vuitton introduced new designs featuring red and beige stripes and brown and beige stripes to cover his trunks. By 1888, these striped canvases were imitated, and a patented checkered material was implemented. A large part of the company's success was its ability to respond to the changing modes of travel which emerged at an astonishing rate in the second half of the nineteenth century. Vuitton designed classic wardrobe trunks for sleeping cars and lighter versions of the suitcase traditionally used by the English aristocracy. His son Georges played an important role in the managing of the business, opening the first Vuitton branch abroad in London in 1885.

In 1890, Georges invented the theft-proof five tumbler lock, which provided each customer with a personal combination to secure all his luggage. Two years later, the company's first catalog presented a wide range of products, from very specialized trunks for transporting particular objects to simple bags with the typical traveler in mind. Four years after the death of Louis Vuitton in 1892, Georges introduced a new canvas design in another attempt to thwart counterfeiters. In memory of his father, Georges' new design featured Louis Vuitton's initials against a background of stars and flowers; it was patented and became an immediate success.

Travelling to America for the Chicago Exposition of 1893, Georges became convinced of the importance of a sales network abroad. By the end of the century, John Wanamaker began representing Louis Vuitton in New York and Philadelphia, and the London store was transferred to New Bond Street, in the heart of London's luxury commerce. The company also expanded its distribution to Boston, Chicago, San Francisco, Brussels, Buenos Aires, Nice, Bangkok, and Montreal in the early twentieth century.

Georges also foresaw the importance of the automobile as a form of transport and began designing automobile trunks, which imitated the lines of the car, to protect travelers' effects from rain and dust. Contending that one should be able to take in a car what one could take on a boat or train, he created iceboxes, canteens, and light and flexible steamer bags. Other efforts to adapt to the changes in the travel industry included the manufacture of airplane and hot air balloon trunks and cases for spare tires. In 1914, the company erected a new building on the Champs-Elysées as the center for its growing network of distribution; this store became the world's largest retailer of travel goods.

During World War I, production was modified to the needs of the war effort, as simple and solid military trunks replaced delicate and luxurious models. Part of the factory in Asnières produced folding stretchers which were loaded directly into ambulances leaving for the front. With the 1918 German offensive 60 kilometers from Paris, Georges had difficulty supplying his factory with materials and assuring the safety of his workers. After the war, the Vuittons struggled to supply their stores with what remained of the factory. Although the company supplied Prince Youssoupov with a jewel case to transport precious stones to America before the Bolshevik revolution, such personal orders were less common after the war, and the factory devoted more time to producing showcases for traveling salesmen.

As economic times improved, and Louis Vuitton regained its stylish clientele, special orders increased. The workshop at Asnières worked to produce orders for Coco Chanel, the Aga Khan, Mary Pickford, the Vanderbilts, and the president of the French Republic, among others. Charles Lindbergh ordered two suitcases from Vuitton for his return trip to America after his famous flight to France. During this time, the company provided some packing services for foreigners who came to buy garments from the Paris couture collections. In the early 1930s, exoticism was in vogue, and Vuitton used tortoise shell, lizard skin, ebony, and unusual woods in its fabrications.

As economic conditions deteriorated worldwide, however, the Vuittons realized the necessity of increasing the company's profitability. Georges's son, Gaston, worked with his father to increase efficiency. An advertising agency was set up and a design office was created to make detailed sketches of products to show customers before fabrication. By the time Georges Vuitton died in 1936, special orders had dramatically declined, and the company's sales depended more than ever upon its catalog offerings, which were expanded to include trunks for typewriters, radios, books, rifles, and wine bottles.

During World War II, when delivery of Vuitton products was curtailed, overseas contracts were terminated, and the Vuitton factory and stores closed. The post-war period involved resupplying the stores, rebuilding business to pre-war levels, and restructuring operations. Three of Gaston's sons played important roles, Henry in commercial management, Jacques in financial administration, and Claude in factory management. The first important post-war order at the company was for the President of the Republic, Vincent Auriol, who made an official visit to the United States.

In 1954, the company's 100th anniversary, Louis Vuitton moved from the Champs-Elysées to Avenue Marceau. As travel times were cut with the development of trains, cars, and airplanes, the company created and improved its soft-sided luggage. In 1959, Gaston perfected a system of coating his motif canvases, making them more durable, waterproof, and suitable for shorter journeys. These lightweight, practical bags signified a new standard in luggage. Gaston invited well known artists to take part in the design of accessories. From 1959 to 1965,

an average of 25 new models of Vuitton luggage were created each year.

With the company's success and reputation for luxury came a vast wave of counterfeit Louis Vuitton products. One year before his death in 1970, Gaston Vuitton decided to take action against the counterfeiters by opening a store in Tokyo; by offering the real Vuitton product in the Asian market, he hoped to better inform customers and discourage the purchase and manufacture of imitations. The company also undertook a successful advertising campaign to battle the increase in counterfeiting.

Henry Racamier, the husband of Gaston Vuitton's daughter Odile, took over management of the company in 1977. Racamier had founded Stinox, a steel manufacturing business, after the Second World War and had sold it at a huge profit before coming to Louis Vuitton. Under Racamier, the company's sales soared from $20 million in 1977 to nearly $1 billion in 1987. Racamier recognized that the major profits were in retail and that to succeed on an international level, Louis Vuitton had to expand its presence in stores and distributors in France. As a result, Louis Vuitton stores were opened all over the world between 1977 and 1987, and Asia became the company's principal export market. Moreover, product diversification ensued, and in 1984, at the urging of financial director Joseph Lafont, the company sold stock to the public through exchanges in Paris and New York.

The 1980s were profitable years for Louis Vuitton, as the Vuitton name was prodigiously promoted. In 1983, Louis Vuitton became the sponsor of the America's Cup preliminaries. Three years later, the company created the Louis Vuitton Foundation for opera and music. Also in 1986, the central Paris store moved from avenue Marceau to the posh avenue Montaigne. Production at the factory at Asnières incorporated the use of lasers and other modern technology during this time, and a distribution center was opened at Cergy-Pontoise, north of Paris. The company allocated two percent of annual sales revenue to the unending battle against counterfeiters.

Under Racamier, Louis Vuitton began to acquire companies with a reputation for high quality, purchasing interests in the couturier Givenchy and the champagne house Veuve Cliquot. Louis Vuitton's takeover philosophy was personal, courteous, and discreet, rather than systematically aggressive. In June 1987, Racamier signed a $4 billion merger of Louis Vuitton with Moët-Hennessy, a conglomerate with interests in the production of champagne, cognac, wine, and perfume. The merger allowed Louis Vuitton to expand its investments in the luxury business, while saving Moët-Hennessy from the threat of takeover. Moreover, the merger respected the autonomy of each company over its own management and subsidiaries.

As Moët-Hennessy was three times the size of Louis Vuitton, its president, Alain Chevalier, was named chairperson of the new holding company, Moët-Hennessy Louis Vuitton (LVMH), and Racamier became executive vice-president. Massive disagreements and feuding followed, however, as management at Louis Vuitton believed that Moët-Hennessy was trying to absorb its operations. The 60 percent ownership that Racamier and the

Vuitton family had held in Louis Vuitton became a mere 17 percent share of LVMH.

After several disputes and legal battles between Racamier and Chevalier over the running of the conglomerate, Racamier invited the young property developer and financial engineer Bernard Arnault to acquire stock in the company. Hoping to consolidate his position within LVMH with the help of Arnault, Racamier soon saw, however, that Arnault had ambitions of his own. With the help of the French investment bank Lazard Frères and the British liquor giant Guinness PLC, Arnault secured a 45 percent controlling interest of LVMH stock for himself.

An 18-month legal battle ensued between Racamier and Arnault, after Chevalier had stepped down. Despite Louis Vuitton's strong performance, accounting for 32 percent of LVMH sales, Racamier could not hold onto his stake in LVMH against Arnault, who had the support of the Moët and Hennessy families. The courts eventually favored Arnault, and Racamier stepped down to create another luxury goods conglomerate, Orcofi, with the backing of French investors such as Paribas and L'Oréal. Arnault weeded out Vuitton's top executives and began to bring together his fragmented luxury empire.

Guinness had originally been brought into LVMH by Alain Chevalier, who had hoped to find an ally in his feuding with Racamier, in a deal to exchange one-fifth of the two companies' equity capital. Guinness then united with Arnault to control LVMH. In 1990, when Racamier left, Arnault increased his interest in Guinness from 12 to 24 percent, fueling rumors that Guinness would be his next target. Takeover speculation was also encouraged by the fact that Guinness directors had little power in LVMH, while Arnault had by far the largest shareholder vote in Guinness. However, Arnault's percentage in Guinness was proportionately equal to the 24 percent Guinness controlled of LVMH. In the early 1990s, Arnault controlled the world's largest luxury empire, with about $5 billion in worldwide sales. His holdings were structured as a pyramid of interconnected companies with control of LVMH central to his power, as it had a market capitalization of $10 billion in 1990.

The ubiquity of the Louis Vuitton monogram in the mid-1980s had damaged its reputation as a status symbol, and both profits and sales declined in the early 1990s. However, demand for luxury goods was expected to rise again, especially in Japan, Korea, and Chiana, where buying power was growing rapidly. However, the American market, which accounted for 17 percent of LVMH sales, was not expected to remain strong as an upheaval in upscale retail outlets was hurting sales. Arnault planned to create data processing and advertising sharing among his luxury retailers, including Louis Vuitton, Dior, Givenchy, Lacroix, and Loewe.

In the early 1990s, Yves Carcelle, a former textile executive, became president of Louis Vuitton and broadened the range of products distributed to the company's 150 stores in an attempt to increase sales. Rampant counterfeiting, a difficult world economy, and its own flagging image were Louis Vuitton's nemeses in the early 1990s. The company's success in the twenty-first century seemed to depend on its ability to exploit the enormous capital of its holding company and the dynamism of Bernard Arnault, while maintaining the high quality of construction and materials which had established the company's reputation in the past.

Further Reading:

Berman, Phyllis, and Zina Sawaya, ''Life Begins at 77,'' *Forbes,* May 27, 1991, pp. 160–67.

Carson-Parker, John, ''Dese, Doms and Diors,'' *Chief Executive,* November/December 1989, pp. 34–7.

Caulkin, Simon, ''A Case of Incompatibility,'' *Management Today,* February 1993, p. 88.

''Fashionable Takeover,'' *Economist,* July 16, 1988, p. 66.

''French Capital Markets: Bags of Bubbly,'' *Euromoney,* January 1987, p. 40.

''Guinness: Stout Fellows,'' *Economist,* June 9, 1990, pp. 66, 68.

Monnin, Philippe, and Claude Vincent, *Guerre du luxe - L'affaire LVMH,* Paris: François Bourin, 1990.

Sebag-Montefiore, Hugh, *Kings on the Catwalk: The Louis Vuitton and Moët-Hennessy Affair,* Chapmans, 1992.

Toy, Stewart, ''Avant le Deluge at Moët Hennessy Louis Vuitton,'' *Business Week,* April 24, 1989, p. 16.

Toy, Stewart, ''Meet Monsieur Luxury,'' *Business Week,* July 30, 1990, pp. 36–40.

Vuitton, Henry L., *La malle aux souvenirs,* Paris: Editions Mengès, 1984.

—Jennifer Kerns

Marvel Entertainment Group, Inc.

387 Park Avenue South
New York, New York 10016
U.S.A.
(212) 696-0808
Fax: (212) 576-9289

Public Subsidiary
Incorporated: 1939 as Timely Publications
Employees: 775
Sales: $415.2 million
Stock Exchange: New York
SICs: 2721 Periodicals

The Marvel Entertainment Group, Inc., is the largest American publisher of comic books. The company got its start during the Depression and grew rapidly during the 1930s and 1940s when comic books were in their heyday. Its industry suffered a setback in the 1950s, but grew stronger in the 1960s as a new crop of popular characters appealed to the children of the baby boom. After another slump in the 1970s, Marvel rebounded in the 1980s, growing even larger and more popular. The company began to diversify in the 1990s, as it sought to reap full value from its stable of enduring and beloved superheroes through licensing arrangements and other media outlets.

Marvel was founded in the late 1930s by Martin Goodman, a New York publisher of pulp magazines. In 1939, Goodman was convinced by a sales manager for Funnies, Inc., a collection of artists and writers who produced complete comic book packages to be printed and distributed by publishers, that comic books would be a good investment. Funnies, Inc., provided Goodman with material featuring a super-hero character, the Sub-Mariner, who was part man and part fish. The title of this experimental venture would eventually become the banner of a pulp empire: Marvel Comics.

In addition to the Sub-Mariner, the first issue of Marvel Comics also featured the Human Torch. Priced at ten cents, it was published in October, 1939, and reprinted the following month. Providing colorful, action-packed escapism at the Depression-era price of ten cents an issue, Marvel comic books were an instant success.

Both the Torch and the Sub-Mariner exhibited traits that many Marvel heroes would come to share. They were both flawed protagonists and angry young men. Unlike other comic heroes such as Superman, they were rebels rather than upstanding role models for the youth of America. The Torch and the Sub-Mariner spoke in slang and exhibited adolescent traits, making flip comments while they wreaked havoc.

With the success of his first issues, Goodman became his own one-man staff and formed a new company, Timely Publications. He began publishing two new lines of comics, *Daring Mystery Comics*, and *Mystic Comics*, searching endlessly for marketable superheroes who would sell comics issue after issue. In addition, as a result of Goodman's concern about the threat posed by Hitler's Germany, Timely Publications' characters began to combat the Nazis even before the United States formally entered the war. In February, 1940, for instance, the Sub-Mariner took on a Nazi U-Boat.

In March, 1941, Marvel pushed this concept one step further, introducing Captain America to fight the Nazis. With the arrival of this character, Timely's comic books sky-rocketed in popularity, as the first number sold nearly one million copies. Flush with this success, the company inaugurated four new titles in 1941. With the actual U.S. entry into the war that Timely's heroes had been fighting for over a year, much of the company's staff joined the military. Despite the general shortage of manpower, and a later shortage of paper, the comics business boomed during the war.

Around this time, Timely branched out from superheroes to humor, adding *Comedy Comics*, *Joker Comics*, and *Krazy Komics*. In addition, the company produced a number of lines featuring funny animals, which appealed to younger children more than the violent super-heroes comics. With this success, Timely expanded its staff and moved its offices to the Empire State Building.

In 1943, the company expanded its audience further when it discovered that teenage girls would purchase comic books directed to them. *Miss America* featured a female superhero in its first issue, but turned to teen beauty tips in its second, attaining lasting popularity along with *Patsy Walker* , a serial about dating and dances.

In the wake of the war, the super-hero franchise weakened, and the comic book industry as a whole went into a slump. In an effort to revive sales, Timely tried crime comics, cowboy comics, romance titles, and finally, cowboy romance. The old super-heroes, the Torch, the Sub-Mariner, and Captain America, were "retired" by 1950.

Despite the death of the old heroes, Timely's operations overall were still going strong. In 1950, the company was producing 82 separate titles—written and drawn by a "bullpen" of company talent—each month. At this time, with the outbreak of the Korean War, Timely also began to produce a new generation of war comics. Created by actual veterans, these issues portrayed war in a new way, showing the pain and misery experienced by the average soldier.

Early in the 1950s, Goodman decided to increase his profits by setting up his own national distribution system, which he called the Atlas News Company. To raise money for this expensive venture, he cut back on office overhead, and switched his staff of writers and artists to freelance status. By the end of 1951, Timely had been converted to Atlas Publishing, and a black and white globe logo was appearing on the front of the company's comic books. In addition to war comics, Atlas published a large number of horror issues, with titles like *Adventures into Weird Worlds*.

In the mid-1950s, the comic book industry came under attack from groups that saw it as a pernicious influence in society. In 1954, the U.S. Senate formed a Subcommittee to Investigate Juvenile Delinquency, which heard testimony in April of that year that comic books were causing violence in society. In a brief spasm of hysteria, customers boycotted stores, comic books were publicly burned, sales plummeted, and a number of comic book producers went out of business. Atlas saw its revenues shrink drastically, and the company moved from its offices in the Empire State Building to smaller quarters at 655 Madison Avenue.

The comic book publishers who survived this crisis, including Atlas, formed the Comics Magazine Association of America in 1955. Immediately, the association set up a censorship board, the Comics Code Authority, whose seal of approval on the front of a comic book guaranteed inoffensiveness (and, many readers believed, blandness). After attaining an all-time high in popularity in the early 1950s, sales of comic books began to drop precipitously.

By 1957, with little product to distribute, Atlas' distribution operations had become a drain on income, and they were shut down. Goodman turned instead to American News Company, another distributor, to place his products in stores and newsstands. With the overall depression in the industry, however, this company soon failed as well, and Goodman was left with no means of distributing his comic books. In desperation, he made a deal with archrival D.C. Comics, which agreed to distribute just eight of Goodman's titles a month.

The company limped along on this basis for three years, until late 1961, when a new idea for a comic book series won widespread popularity and returned the company to financial health. In November, 1961, Goodman's top writer and artist produced *The Fantastic Four*, which featured a superhero group and concentrated more on the complex personalities of the characters and less on the machinations of plot. Featuring The Thing, Mr. Fantastic, Human Torch, and Invisible Girl, *The Fantastic Four* was an immediate hit, and fan mail began to pour in.

The debut of the Fantastic Four was followed by the introduction of the Incredible Hulk and Spider-Man, in short order. By 1962, Goodman's company was once again thriving, as baby boomers discovered a new generation of comics heroes. Although the word "Marvel" was not yet appearing on comic books, the company's work bore a small "MC" insignia, and was conceptually linked by the idea that the "Marvel universe" contained all the super-heroes, who knew each other and interacted.

In May, 1963, Goodman's comic books began bearing the words "Marvel Comics Group" on the cover of its issues in a vertical box, surrounding the head of the superhero in question. Marvel had been the name on the first series of comics the company published, and it now became the focus of the company's promotional efforts.

Throughout the mid-1960s, Marvel continued to introduce new characters, such as the Avengers, the X-Men—and Daredevil, a blind attorney—among others. To capitalize on the popularity of its large stable of superheroes, the company began to merchandise products that featured their images, such as T-shirts, board games, and model kits. In 1966, a half-hour television show featuring "The Marvel Super Heroes" was syndicated to stations around the country. In the following year, Saturday morning cartoons featuring The Fantastic Four and Spider-Man were introduced on the ABC television network.

By 1968, Marvel was selling 50 million comic books a year. With this strong performance, the company was able to revise its distribution arrangement with D.C. Comics, which had limited production of its own comics, to put out as many different titles as demand warranted. With his valuable franchise established, Goodman sold his businesses in the fall of 1968 to the Perfect Film and Chemical Corporation, which soon changed its name to the Cadence Industries Corporation. Within the structure of Cadence, Goodman's properties were grouped together under one name, Magazine Management.

By 1969, it had become clear that the most recent boom in the comics industry was over. Marvel began to shed titles as sales weakened. In an effort to increase its flexibility, Marvel ended its distribution agreement with D.C. Comics and signed with the Curtis Circulation Company, a large magazine wholesaler, which allowed the publisher greater independence.

Marvel experienced a period of instability in the early 1970s, as the company's old guard of editors and corporate executives retired and their replacements came and went. In an effort to shuck off the outdated Comics Code restrictions, Marvel published three anti-drug theme Spider-Man issues that had been suggested by the U.S. Department of Health, Education, and Welfare. When the Comics Code board rejected the issues because rules forbade any mention of drugs at all, Marvel published the comics without the Comics Code seal of approval. This move eventually led to a loosening of restrictions—and was important because comics had begun to lose ground to television and other media.

With fewer prohibitions on subject matter, Marvel began to feature such previously forbidden characters as vampires and werewolves as heroes and villains. The company also began an affirmative action push, including more black characters and more strong female figures. In an effort to make a place for more artistic efforts, Marvel also began to offer black-and-white comics magazines, which were pitched to an older audience than its color comics.

In May, 1975, Marvel published *Giant-Size X-Men*, a special large-format issue that re-introduced the characters which would become the company's most popular franchise. Featuring characters from around the world, the X-Men were designed to be marketed in foreign as well as domestic markets.

Despite the success of this new line, however, Marvel had lost $2 million by the middle of 1975. The company was in bad financial shape. Although Marvel's sales remained strong, its profits had dropped. The comics industry's traditional retail outlets, small community stores, were being replaced by big chain grocery stores which did not carry comics. The number of distribution outlets was shrinking. In addition, paper prices had risen, cutting into earnings. In response to this financial crisis, Cadence installed a new company president, who pared the number of titles produced, firmed up publishing schedules, and reorganized sales and distribution. Throughout the late 1970s, Marvel cut back on expenses and new publications in an effort to remain profitable.

Among Marvel's bright spots during this time was the 1977 hit television series featuring the Incredible Hulk. This suggested that fertile ground for Marvel's future growth might lie in spin-offs from the company's core comics business. In the late 1970s, a number of television shows featuring Marvel characters were created, and Marvel also licensed characters and stories from other sources for its own comics. These moves were motivated as much by desperation as they were by expansionism, because by 1979 the market for comic books had shrunk to an all-time low.

In the early 1980s, Marvel reorganized its somewhat chaotic corporate structure in an effort to recover from this slump, and began to increase its staff and its output. The company had a steady hit with the X-Men franchise, and was also starting to benefit from a change in the way comics were distributed. In the past, comics had been sold on newsstands with a lot of other publications; but with the rise in comic book collecting, stores devoted exclusively to sales of comic books began to open. Between 1981 and 1982, this direct sales market came to account for half of Marvel's sales. Noting this increase, Marvel began to produce special issues to be sold in this market. In addition, the company continued to publish graphic novels, which provided longer and more sophisticated tales of featured heroes.

In 1985, Marvel also moved to include younger children in its market when it produced Star Comics, which featured humor, talking animals, and child characters. These comics were sold to children in mall bookstores, a new outlet for comic book distribution. By the mid-1980s, Marvel was starting to see its circulation rebound, reaching 7.2 million a month by the end of 1984. Sales were driven by the network of 3,000 comics specialty shops that had sprung up. By the end of 1985, Marvel's revenues had reached $100 million, driven in part by licensing agreements for products featuring its characters.

This success attracted the attention of members of the financial industry. In 1986, Marvel was sold to New World Pictures, a movie company that wanted the publisher's stable of characters and animation studio, for $46 million. This move touched off a series of corporate transformations for the company. In November, 1988, New World announced that a series of losses had caused it to sell Marvel to the Andrews Group, Inc., for $82.5

million. The Andrews Group was a subsidiary of a holding company called the McAndrews & Forbes Group, which was owned largely by investor Ronald Perelman.

In June, 1991, in an effort to raise $48 million, Marvel announced that it would sell stock to the public for the first time. With this money, the company planned to pay off bank debts and increase publishing, distribution, and licensing operations. As a publicly held company, Marvel also began to step up its marketing activities and diversified into a number of different fields related to its publishing empire.

In September, 1992, Marvel purchased the Fleer Corporation, a trading card company, for $265 million. In the spring of 1993, Marvel also invested $7 million to buy 46 percent of Toy Biz, Inc., a New York-based toy manufacturer. The company then hired a top toy designer to make successful action hero toys out of familiar Marvel figures. These characters demonstrated booming popularity in the early 1990s.

By late 1993, Marvel was publishing nearly twice as many titles as it had in 1989. The company's revenues had increased steadily during that time, as distribution expanded to new venues, like record stores and drug stores, and overseas markets opened up. In addition, the company stepped up its efforts to sell space in comic books for advertising, and kicked off a licensing campaign to extend its market into Europe, Africa, and the Middle East. Marvel also signed a number of movie deals to support this effort.

In 1993, Marvel declared its ambition to be among the world's top five licensors. With a stable of popular characters, and the potential to invent more when the need arose, Marvel appeared to have successfully made the transition from children's publisher to marketing monolith. Its continued success in the children's entertainment industry seemed assured.

Principal Subsidiaries: Marvel Comics, Inc.; Fleer Corporation; Toy Biz, Inc. (46 percent); Dubble Bubble Confectionery Products.

Further Reading:

"A Marriage of Corporate Celebrities," *Mergers & Acquisitions*, September, 1992.

Anderson, Richard W., "BIFF! POW! Comic Books Make a Comeback," *Business Week*, September 2, 1985.

Cuff, Daniel F., "Publisher Expects Sale to Aid Marvel Comics," *New York Times*, November 28, 1986.

Daniels, Les, *Marvel: Five Fabulous Decades of the World's Greatest Comics*, New York: Harry N. Abrams, Inc., 1991.

Dwek, Robert, "Marvel Takes License with Spider-Man," *Marketing*, August 19, 1993.

Henry, Gordon M., "Bang! Pow! Zap! Heroes are Back," *Time*, October 6, 1986.

Kanner, Bernice, "Comics Relief," *New York*, October 25, 1993.

—Elizabeth Rourke

Maxtor Corporation

211 River Oaks Parkway
San Jose, California 95134
U.S.A.
(408) 432-1700
Fax: (408) 432-4510

Public Company
Incorporated: 1982
Sales: $1.4 billion
Employees: 8,900
Stock Exchanges: NASDAQ
SICs: 3572 Computer Storage Devices

Maxtor Corporation is one of the world's leading manufacturers of computer disk drives. Along with Conner Peripherals, Quantum Corporation, Seagate Technology, Western Digital, and Micropolis, Maxtor shares in dominating the 1.8 to 5.25 magnetic and optical disk drive market. However, due to the cyclical nature of the disk drive market, a failure to introduce new products in a timely fashion, and poor management decisions, Maxtor has been plagued by severe financial problems for most of its existence.

Established in 1982 by a group of computer and computer-marketing whiz kids, Maxtor was soon dominated by co-founder James McCoy, who became the central figure in Maxtor's early development and success. McCoy, who had held positions at Verbatim and Exabyte and had been a marketing manager at Shugart Corporation and a vice president at Quantum Corporation, possessed valuable experience in the computer storage device industry. He immediately set out to make Maxtor a leader in the magnetic disk drive market by engineering and manufacturing 1.8-inch (105MB) to 5.25 (1.2GB–1.7GB) Winchester magnetic disk drives.

The company's sales increased rapidly and soon Maxtor was competing with the biggest names in the computer disk drive industry. By 1984, it was in direct competition with Seagate Technology over the introduction and market share of high-capacity 5.25-inch Winchester rigid-disk drives. However, the competition took place in the realm of company press releases rather than in the marketplace. Seagate, the originator and leading manufacturer of 5.25 Winchesters, boasted that it would soon introduce the ST412 High Performance interface, which would make it easier for high-volume computer manufacturers

to enhance their disk drives in a shorter period of time. Maxtor responded by publicizing that it would soon introduce its Enhanced Small Disk Interface, which would transfer high-rate data in large memory systems. With the demand for 5.25 high-capacity Winchesters increasing, it seemed as though the first company to ship its product in volume would be declared the victor.

Yet even with such high stakes, Maxtor could not avoid delayed production shipments of the high-capacity 5.25 Winchesters and allowed Seagate to reach the market first with its product. Maxtor's shipment problem originated with its decision to contract Read/Rite Corporation, a components manufacturer and supplier for the computer disk drive industry. Read/Rite was experiencing financial, production, and management difficulties that prevented the company from supplying Maxtor's order according to the schedule stipulated in the contract. As time elapsed, and no product was yet in sight, Maxtor began to suffer severe financial losses. Once the management at Maxtor ironed out its problems with Read/Rite and contracted other suppliers, the company reversed its losses.

From 1985 through 1987, Maxtor held undisputed dominance in the disk drive market above 100MB. The company's gross profits, which approximated 19 percent of total revenues, jumped to nearly 30 percent by the end of 1986. During these years, Maxtor had developed into a market leader primarily because it was able to identify industry trends quickly and improve its manufacturing efficiency. These two factors gave the company an edge over its closest competitors. However, after 1987, Maxtor's success began to unravel once again. Manufacturing problems with its most recent SCSI and ESDI drives plagued the company, and an increase in both domestic and foreign competition crowded the disk drive industry. Compounding the company's problems was the retirement of almost all of the founding management, and the discontinuity in both strategy and financial management that this departure caused.

By the middle of 1988, Maxtor was losing its market position within the industry. The company's continuing dependence on five-year-old products, its inability to solve its supplier problems, and its involvement in a price war contributed to plunging profits. At the end of the fiscal year, Maxtor's gross profits had dramatically decreased to a mere 3.4 percent of total revenues. Yet the new president and chief executive officer of Maxtor, a 17-year management veteran of Advanced Micro Devices named George M. Scalise, was optimistic that economies of scale in manufacturing products could return the company to the profitability of earlier years.

Initially, the new CEO's strategy seemed to work; manufacturing efficiency began to generate much needed cash for Maxtor's research and development program. In 1988, Maxtor sold approximately $300 million worth of conventional hard disk drives alone. One year later, with the little cash he had on hand, Scalise decided to challenge both Sony and Matsushita by manufacturing an optical disk drive that could put one billion bytes—the equivalent of 2,800 floppy disks—on one optical disk the exact 5.25-inch size of most floppy disks. In one move, Maxtor planned to exceed by more than half the capacity of competing disk drives manufactured by the Japanese computer giants. The optical disk drive was attractive for a number of reasons: it featured high storage capacity, it was erasable, and it was as easy to remove as a regular floppy disk, a feature no hard disk drive had at that time.

Following this bold move, Scalise entered into an agreement with Kubota Corporation of Japan to jointly acquire and manage Maxoptix Corporation, a California-based manufacturer of optical storage devices. During this time, Maxtor also purchased MiniScribe Corporation, a disk drive manufacturer located in Colorado. The acquisition of MiniScribe brought Maxtor two foreign subsidiaries, but the company was insolvent and required a huge outlay of cash by Maxtor. Despite the possible financial trouble these new ventures might bring to a company with a severe cash-flow problem, Scalise pointed with pride to an unbroken string of 13 profitable quarters under his leadership. At the end of 1990, management was proud to report a $10.8 million profit for the year.

Yet the storm clouds that had been gathering during Scalise's tenure as CEO suddenly let loose a torrent of problems. Maxtor, which had been the leader in the high-capacity 5.25-inch disk drive market, lost its position because of production delays with its Panther series of subsystems. Micropolis replaced Maxtor as the new 5.25-inch market leader, and intense competition from such companies as Seagate and Hewlett-Packard contributed to the company's eroding market share. At the same time, nearly 15 engineers who worked on the Panther development team resigned from their positions, citing mismanagement of the project. This turn of events led to a further delay in production of the Panther series of subsystems.

In addition, Maxtor's acquisitions were soon found to be not as profitable as Scalise had first thought. After a very short time, Maxtopix, the joint venture between Maxtor and Kubota, was running its operations in red ink. The optical drive program, the pet project that Scalise had hoped would make Maxtor the pre-eminent disk drive manufacturer in the industry, also experienced production delays. Maxtor's purchase and consolidation of MiniScribe, which the company had counted on to help improve its cash flow, took twice the amount of money that management initially anticipated. The combined problems of large staff defections, components shortages, production delays, and intense competition both in the international and domestic markets led to a loss of $65.7 million in fiscal 1991.

Scalise resigned in January of 1991, after receiving a poor performance review by Maxtor's board of directors. Scalise, and most of the upper-level positions that he had filled upon his arrival at the company, were replaced by many members of the old management team, including James McCoy. McCoy was immediately appointed chairman of the board, and Lawrence R. Hootnick, a former president of the embedded controller and memory division at Intel Corporation, was chosen as the new president and chief executive officer. Together McCoy and Hootnick devised a strategy to stop Maxtor's financial hemorrhaging by introducing new products and by selling some of the firm's assets.

Maxtor's new management quickly introduced Tahiti II, the company's 1-gigabyte erasable optical disk drive. It followed with a new product line of Apache disk drives for Apple Computer's PowerBook notebook, and shortly thereafter offered a line of new disk drives for NetWare local area networks. Maxtor then sold its assembly plant in Malaysia to Read/Rite Corporation for $17 million, and placed on the market its Storage Dimensions Inc. subsidiary, a manufacturer of optical and magnetic subsystems. The company laid off 140 domestic workers and permanently eliminated approximately 130 positions at its manufacturing plant in Singapore. Through what McCoy and Hootnick described as an aggressive strategy to reduce costs, control inventory, and manage the company's cash flow, Maxtor recovered from its financial difficulties and headed for profitability. By the end of the new management's first year, Maxtor had turned a profit of $4 million.

In 1992, Maxtor celebrated its 10th birthday by surpassing the billion-dollar mark in total revenues; the company reported an $89 million profit on revenues of $1.40 billion, a complete turnaround from just two years earlier. This dramatic change of fortune was partly caused by the improvement in the disk drive industry and the growing demand for disk drives geared toward Windows applications. However, management also took the appropriate measures to build upon its core business, improve its quality control, and provide better service to customers. Maxtor's No Quibble service plan guaranteed that it would replace a customer's disk drive in less than 48 hours. At the same time, Maxtor introduced new products such as drives for high-end personal computers and high-end notebooks. The company also increased its quarterly research and development budget from a mere $5 million to just over $29 million. Finally, in an effort to financially strengthen the company, management sold its Storage Dimensions subsidiary to a private investment group for a $4 million note, $18 million in cash, and a 30 percent interest in the company.

According to every economic indicator, Maxtor was back on track. During the first half of fiscal 1993, sales increased almost 50 percent and net income jumped to $66 million, compared to the same period a year earlier. Yet the past acquisition of MiniScribe came back to haunt the company. The purchase and subsequent merging of Maxtor's and MiniScribe's operations were executed poorly, and continued to drain the company of cash that needed to be spent elsewhere. Combined with an unexpected pricing war, these financial difficulties resulted in Maxtor's revenues dropping 24 percent and a net loss of over $72 million for the first quarter of fiscal 1994.

With Maxtor in such a precarious financial situation yet again, management sought a long-term solution to the company's problems. An agreement was reached with Hyundai Electronics Industries Corporation, a gigantic South Korean-based firm, to purchase a 40 percent interest in Maxtor. Under the terms of the agreement, Hyundai would put up $150 million and receive almost 20 million shares of common stock in Maxtor at a price of $7.70 per share. Furthermore, the agreement would entitle Hyundai to representation on Maxtor's board of directors and voting rights proportional to its ownership of Maxtor stock. The deal pleased both companies: Maxtor would gain desperately needed cash, and Hyundai would benefit by Maxtor's presence in the international disk drive market.

At the end of 1993, the agreement between Maxtor and Hyundai was still awaiting approval by Maxtor shareholders and the governments of the United States and South Korea. This delay meant that Maxtor had still not received the cash as stipulated in the agreement, although it appeared likely that the money would be forthcoming. In addition, Maxtor's difficulty in getting its products to market in a cost-effective, timely manner still hampered the company's ability to improve its financial condition. Maxtor's 2.5-inch, 250-megabyte disk drive, for example, was experiencing severe production problems. According to Chief Executive Officer Laurence Hootnick, Maxtor's future viability depended on an infusion of capital and an ability to bring products to market on time. As of mid-1994, whether or not Maxtor could get the cash it needed to stay afloat and solve its seemingly intractable production delays, according to many people within the disk drive industry, was sheer speculation.

Further Reading:

Alpert, Mark, ''500,000 Pages on One Erasable Disk,'' *Fortune,* January 2, 1989, pp. 99–101.

Deagon, Brian, ''Three Makers' Missteps May Prolong Industry Troubles,'' *Electronic News,* December 19, 1988, pp. 10–11; ''Maxtor Aftermath,'' *Electronic News,* February 4, 1991, pp. 11–14.

—Thomas Derdak

Mead Data Central, Inc.

9393 Springboro Pike
Miamisburg, Ohio 45342-4424
U.S.A.
(513) 865-6800
Fax: (513) 865-7476

Wholly Owned Subsidiary of Mead Corporation
Incorporated: 1968
Employees: 3,700
Sales: $551.5 million
SICs: 7375 On-Line Data Base Information Retrieval

Mead Data Central, Inc. is a leading database service headquartered near Dayton, Ohio, with 50 sales offices in the United States and overseas. The company's primary services, LEXIS and NEXIS, serve over 650,000 active subscribers through nearly 5,000 databases. LEXIS, a legal research service, and NEXIS, a full text news and business information service, rank among the world's top computer-assisted resources. Mead Data Central also offers legal publishing through its Michie Company subsidiary; infobase management software through the Folio Corporation subsidiary; legal software through the Jurisoft division; and manual searching, filing, and retrieval services through its LEXIS Document Services division. A LEXIS twentieth anniversary publication noted that "if someone were to read all the information online, reading 24 hours a day at average speed, it would take approximately 360 years to read today's [February 1993] LEXIS/NEXIS library. For each year of reading, new data being added would cause the person to fall behind by another 30 years."

Mead Data Central began as the Data Corporation in the 1960s, when the concept of computer-assisted legal research (CALR) was being developed through projects in Pennsylvania, New York, and Ohio. In 1967, Data Corp. was contracted by the Ohio State Bar Association to provide a "free-text" search and retrieval system. As a result, the Ohio Bar Automated Research (OBAR) system was developed, through which Ohio attorneys could pay a fee for printouts of Ohio statutes, which they received within hours. Improvements to the system eventually allowed lawyers to access OBAR directly from their offices.

During this time, Data Corp.'s pioneering activities in the fields of digitized scanning and printing attracted the attention of forest products manufacturer Mead Corporation, which ac-

quired Data Corp. for $6 million in 1968. Two years later, Mead Data Central was spun off as a subsidiary of Mead. In 1971, the company established its own phone communications network linking New York and Washington, D.C. The network tripled the speed of phone communications and evolved into MEADNET, which grew to serve over 75 cities by the early 1990s.

LEXIS, the world's first commercial online legal research service, was launched in April 1973. The new service offered electronic, full-text copies of federal statutes, case reviews, and other legal information. Initially, the LEXIS database contained general information on cases from the U.S. Code and Supreme Court, the U.S. Court of Appeals, and District courts, as well as a federal tax library, specialized information on cases specific to Ohio and New York, and a service known as the National Automated Accounting Research Service (NAARS). By the early 1990s, however, LEXIS had grown to incorporate major archives of codes and regulations, annotations, professional journals and directories, public records, corporate filings and financial statements, analyst reports, and patents. Moreover, it offered material from 45 libraries specializing in tax, securities, banking, labor, environmental, and insurance law.

In 1975, Mead Data Central launched an innovative marketing strategy that would ensure a future generation of subscribers. By offering LEXIS usage free to law schools, the company promoted CALR as an essential part of many curricula, and the interns or associates who had utilized the system in school helped push law firm usage to unequaled heights each succeeding year. Consequently, the use of traditional research sources—large, expensive law books—became less popular, and LEXIS emerged as the new standard. LEXIS allowed attorneys to narrow their searches to strictly relevant and manageable material, providing a substantial savings of time and expense.

NEXIS general news service was launched in 1979 as a complement to LEXIS. Initially, NEXIS offered the full text of articles from four news publications and two wire services. Eventually, however, the service incorporated over 450 business and general publications, including *Business Week, Fortune,* and *The Washington Post,* as well as Tass, the Soviet press agency. NEXIS also became the exclusive electronic carrier of complete articles from *The New York Times.* By 1993, NEXIS ranked as the world's leading news and business service with more than 1,000 full-text sources and 2,000 sources of abstracts. The appeal of both LEXIS' and NEXIS' speedy, thorough searches quickly became clear to those who had used manual periodical indexes.

By the end of the 1970s, Mead Data Central was bringing in $23 million in annual revenues, and once case law for all 50 states was completed in 1980, the venture experienced even more rapid growth. Mead Data Central's proceeds reached $47 million in 1981 and increased by more than 20 percent annually from 1983 through the end of the decade. LEXIS accounted for the vast majority of the company's income, representing $215 million of its $307.6 million total revenues in 1988, for example.

Much of the company's swift growth during the 1980s was overseen by Jack W. Simpson, a former executive at IBM who became president of Mead Data Central in 1982. Under Simpson, the company made several acquisitions. In 1985, the company purchased Micromedex, Inc. a vendor of information on poisons and emergency medicines, which it marketed on compact disks. Two years later, Mead Data Central gained increased exposure in the Canadian market by purchasing one of that country's largest financial online services, Dataline, Inc. Dataline offered brokerage firms such computer systems as Canquote, Teledat, Knight-Ridder's MoneyCenter, and Insider Trading Monitor. The Illinois Code Company was acquired in 1988 and became the LEXIS Document Services division, providing manual searching, filing, and retrieval services for Uniform Commercial Code (UCC) liens, corporation records, and tax liens filed throughout the United States.

The Michie Co., a small legal publisher with annual revenues of $34 million, was also acquired in 1988. This addition, which sold printed statutes from 23 states to law firms, courts, corporate legal departments, and electronic publishers, was the company's first attempt to diversify beyond electronic publishing. Although some observers, including Simpson, found the $226.5 million price tag prohibitive, parent Mead Corporation considered the acquisition important in helping to broaden the scope of Mead Data Central. In 1989, the company acquired Jurisoft, a leading developer of legal software based in Cambridge, Massachusetts. The company became a division of Mead Data Central, offering such products as CiteRite II, FullAuthority, CompareRite, and CheckCite, which allowed users to verify citations and establish definitive source lists quickly.

Joint ventures during the 1980s included a partnership with a Ford Motor Co. subsidiary, BDM, to create the Electronic Data Gathering Analysis and Retrieval System (EDGAR), a public online database of Securities & Exchange Commission filings. Although Mead Data Central expected only moderate success from the system, it hoped that the diversification of services would draw more financial and corporate subscribers to its LEXIS Financial Information Service. Known as "Exchange" until 1988, this offspring of LEXIS received mixed reviews; a reviewer in *Business Week* called the system a "sputtering spinoff," while the *Wall Street Computer Review* regarded it as a "successful online financial information service."

In 1988, Mead Data Central sued Toyota for trademark infringement over the latter's use of the name Lexus for its new line of luxury cars. A U.S. district judge in New York ruled that the automaker's use of the brand would dilute the effect of Mead Data Central's trademark, and Toyota was restricted from advertising its Lexus nationally, although it was allowed to feature the name at auto shows in Los Angeles, Detroit, and Chicago. However, in 1989, the U.S. Second Circuit Court of Appeals overturned the ruling, and the car was launched in showrooms that fall. Since that time, some analysts have suggested that the situation was of mutual benefit to Mead Data Central and Toyota; the Lexus name achieved a reputation for high quality and prestige in both arenas.

After a decade of dramatic revenue and profit increases, Mead Data Central experienced a slower growth rate in the late 1980s and early 1990s, which it attributed to economic factors and increased competition. The economic recession that began in 1989 hit the legal profession especially hard; for the first time in recent memory, partners were being laid off and law firms were restricting hiring. Moreover, competition intensified dramatically in the late 1980s. From 1985 to 1990, the number of computerized services available increased from about 300 to 800. Encouraged by industry-wide annual revenue increases of 18 percent, major competitors included Knight-Ridder, Inc.'s Dialog subsidiary; Reuters Holdings, PLC; Thomson International; Reed Elsevier; and Dow Jones & Company, Inc.

However, the strongest competition came from West Publishing Co. and its Westlaw electronic retrieval service for legal documents. West was already a dominant player in the field of legal texts and research volumes, and its Westlaw service was credited with cutting LEXIS's share of that market from an early 1980s high of 95 percent to 60 percent by 1993. Westlaw achieved this by introducing time-based fees as an alternative to the fixed per-search charges imposed by LEXIS. Furthermore, West began offering Knight-Ridder's Dialog general news retrieval service to compete with NEXIS.

Perhaps the greatest challenge offered by West was its September 1992 introduction of a more user-friendly search system that offered associative retrieval technology, or natural language searches, rather than the Boolean searches required by LEXIS. A January 1993 article in *Forbes* provided a comparison of the two technologies: "to search West's database for cases involving travel agents' liability, a lawyer might type in *Can a travel agency or book publisher be held liable for injuries sustained by a tourist while visiting a recommended place?* But to give the same instructions to LEXIS, a lawyer must type in the following Boolean sequence: *(travel w/15 agen! or guide or brochure or literature) w/25 (injur! or accident or death) w/25 (tourist or traveler).*" Through associative retrieval technology, the West system was able to parse sentences, rank and give weight to various words, and chose synonyms to search as well. As a result, many industry experts regarded LEXIS as outdated. The expense of catching up coincided with the economic downturn and heightened competitive environment, putting Mead Data Central at a disadvantage.

In 1992, a new CEO at Mead Corporation, Steven Mason, effected fundamental changes at Mead Data Central. The parent had previously run its debt to capital ratio up to 46 percent, counting on Mead Data Central to be the "cash cow" that would help pay that debt down to more normal 30 percent to 40 percent levels. But this practice became hazardous when growth at Mead Data Central slowed from 30 percent annually in the 1980s to less than ten percent per year in the 1990s. Under Mason, LEXIS president David Berger was fired, and shortly thereafter Jack Simpson left the company. According to the *Wall Street Journal,* Simpson left due to "a disagreement with executives about how to proceed with the business operations of the unit." Simpson was succeeded in April 1993 by Rodney L. Everhart, who had served Mead Data Central as vice-president of finance and administration and corporate controller.

Everhart brought a new corporate focus on customer service to Mead Data Central, calling himself a "change agent" in an interview for *Online* magazine. Rather than simply increasing the amount of information provided by its databases, Everhart emphasized the process of making that information easier to use. Furthermore, in response to customer demands and Westlaw's initiative, Mead Data Central revised its pricing structure to include transaction pricing, hourly pricing, zero connect pricing, subscriptions, and modified subscriptions in the early 1990s.

Another plan that the company hoped would generate sales involved modifying its databases to allow subscribers to import LEXIS and NEXIS files into their own work space as manipulable information. A cooperative alliance with Microsoft Corp. to coordinate LEXIS/NEXIS and the popular Windows interface was a primary step toward this goal. Mead Data Central's December 1992 acquisition of Folio Corporation—a pioneer and market leader in the development of information management software products located in Provo, Utah—was another key step toward this goal. Everhart planned to continue Folio's retail sales of such applications as Folio VIEWS and simultaneously integrate its programming proficiencies into the LEXIS/NEXIS online systems.

The company also planned to add an e-mail system and expand its international operations. In addition to developing products specifically for the international market, Mead Data Central set up a remote processing facility in London to make closer connections with licensers in Europe and thereby get data online more quickly. The company also established sales offices in London, Germany, Hong Kong, Latin America, and Toronto.

In the fall of 1993, Mead Data Central announced the elimination of 400 headquarters employees, or 9.5 percent of the company's total staff. During this time, rumors began to circulate that the subsidiary was for sale. Patricia Lane, of *Information Today,* speculated in September 1993 that the firings were part of an appeal to Wall Street, "the theory being eliminate jobs—your stock goes up."

Principal Subsidiaries: Mead Data Central International, Inc.; The Michie Company; Folio Corporation.

Further Reading:

Berss, Marcia, "Logging off Lexis," *Forbes,* January 4, 1993, p. 46.

Griffith, Cary, "Mead Data Central: New President, New Focus," *Information Today,* May 1993, pp. 1, 16.

Lane, Patricia, "Mead Data Central Downsizes," *Information Today,* September 1993, pp. 1, 16.

"LEXIS Started with a Handful of Clients, Scant Material Online," *LEXIS 20th Anniversary,* Dayton, Ohio: Mead Data Central, Inc., 1993, pp. 12–17.

Low, Kathleen, "Spotlight: Mead Data Central," *Link-Up,* September/October 1993, pp. 6–7.

Mallory, Maria, "Mead Tries a Newfangled Medium: Print," *Business Week,* April 10, 1989, pp. 81–2.

Matthew, Janet, "Booming Service Gives Way to One with More Bang," *Wall Street Computer Review,* August 1988, pp. 8–10, 59–60, 74–5.

McGill, G. M., "Mead Data Central's Vision of the Future," *LEXIS 20th Anniversary,* Dayton, Ohio: Mead Data Central, Inc., 1993, pp. 9–11.

"Mead Data Central Debuts New Features, Library, and Software for the Lexis/Nexis Services," *Information Today,* April 1993, p. 74.

"Mead Data Trying to Stay on Top," *New York Times,* May 9, 1990, p. D20.

Ojala, Marydee, "Rod Everhart, Change Agent at Mead Data Central," *Online,* September 1993, pp. 16–24.

Putterman, Nancy, "U.S. Firms Acquire CMQ, Dataline," *Computing Canada,* December 28, 1987, pp. 1, 4.

Williams, Linda, "Toyota Can Use the Lexus Name on New Care Line, Appeals Court Rules," *Los Angeles Times,* March 9, 1989, Sec. IV, p. 1.

—April Dougal Gasbarre

MERVYN'S

Mervyn's

25001 Industrial Boulevard
Hayward, California 94545
U.S.A.
(510) 785-8800
Fax: (510) 786-7791

Wholly Owned Subsidiary of Dayton Hudson Corporation
Incorporated: 1949
Employees: 38,000
Sales: $4.4 billion
SICs: SIC 5611 Men's and Boys' Clothing and Accessory
   Stores; SIC 5621 Women's Clothing Stores; SIC 5632
   Women's Accessory and Specialty Stores; SIC 5641
   Children's and Infants' Wear Stores

Mervyn's, one of the largest retailers in the western United States, operates over 280 department stores throughout the country. While most Mervyn's stores are located on the Pacific Coast and in the Southwest—nearly half in California, with just over half of those concentrated in the greater Los Angeles and San Francisco Bay areas—the company also operates outlets in Michigan, Florida, and Georgia. Mervyn's is a middle-market department store offering "trend-right" apparel and home fashions at moderate prices.

Mervyn's was founded in 1949 in northern California by Mervin Morris, who took the advice of those who told him that exchanging the "i" in his first name for a "y" would add flair to the department store that he named after himself. The centerpiece of Mervyn's merchandise was a line of private-label family apparel, which Morris sold in season at prices higher than a discount retailer's but still below what his customers would pay for similar goods in other department stores.

Morris relied on rapid inventory turnover to secure profits, maintaining a loyal customer base by ensuring that Mervyn's products represented good value. Innovative advertising also helped keep Mervyn's in the public eye. For many years, it was the only retailer in California to publish its own tabloid advertisement. The tabloid, which was distributed in the stores and through the Sunday newspapers, pushed weekly promotions and helped establish Mervyn's reputation as a value-oriented retailer.

This emphasis on providing customers with value, rather than on offering a luxurious shopping experience, was an unusual concept at a time when the full-service department store was still the standard in general merchandise retailing. However, it proved profitable, and Morris gained a reputation as a pioneer in the industry. By the early 1970s the company was in a position to expand considerably. In 1971 it went public, raising $5.4 million over the counter to retire all of its outstanding debt. Then, between 1972 and 1978, Mervyn's nearly quadrupled in size, opening 31 stores, all of them in California and Nevada. In 1977, the company earned $11.8 million on sales of $264 million.

Mervyn's success attracted the interest of Dayton Hudson, a midwestern retailer known primarily for operating the upscale Dayton's and Hudson's store chains. Both Dayton's and Hudson's had venerable histories as big-city department stores. Hudson's began as a haberdashery established in Detroit in 1881 by Joseph L. Hudson, who was looking for a way to rebuild his fortune after going bankrupt in the panic of 1873. In 1954, the company built Northland, then the largest shopping center in the United States, in suburban Detroit. Dayton's was founded in Minneapolis in 1902 by George Dayton, a former banker. In 1956, the company built Southdale, the world's first fully enclosed shopping mall, in Minneapolis. In 1962, Dayton's created two subsidiaries that would prove highly successful, the Target chain of discount retailers, and the B. Dalton chain of bookstores.

Dayton's went public in 1966, acquiring Hudson's, which was then still privately owned, three years later. Dayton Hudson promptly expanded by acquiring shopping malls and specialty retailers. Despite this aggressive course of expansion, however, the company was not well known outside the upper Midwest. With its B. Dalton stores well established in California, Dayton Hudson sought to introduce its department stores on the West Coast, and, in 1978, the company acquired Mervyn's in a stock swap valued at over $280 million.

Mervin Morris became a director at Dayton Hudson, and his family became one of the company's largest stockholders as a result of the deal. John Kilmartin replaced Morris as CEO of Mervyn's, overseeing a period of impressive growth. Backed by Dayton Hudson's financial resources, Mervyn's embarked on a remarkable course of expansion. By the mid-1980s, the chain was operating 148 stores. In 1984, Mervyn's opened nine stores in Texas—its first adventure outside the western United States—and posted a $223.3 million profit on sales of over $2 billion. The following year, Mervyn's contributed 37 percent of Dayton Hudson's operating profit. Impressed with this success, Dayton Hudson planned to allocate approximately half of its capital investment budget from 1986 through 1990 for new Mervyn's stores.

Mervyn's was highly regarded in the retail industry in the mid-1980s, when many of its competitors for the mid-range department store customer were floundering. During this time, many of Mervyn's rivals retooled themselves, adopting many of Mervyn's best ideas. Most notably, J.C. Penney abandoned its old identity as a full-line department store, and, like Mervyn's, focused on apparel and soft goods. Moreover, competitors began publishing their own tabloid advertisements, imitating the marketing tactic Mervyn's had used for decades. Perhaps most importantly, several retailers all across the retailing spectrum began selling department store-quality goods at discounted prices. Faced with increased competition, Mervyn's business began to taper off, particularly when factory outlet stores started becoming popular.

During this time, Mervyn's made no aggressive moves to stay ahead of the competition. Dayton Hudson executives later admitted that they did not pay close enough attention to their star performer. Mervyn's profits sank sharply in 1986 and remained depressed in 1987, despite continuing strong revenues. Earnings at Dayton Hudson sank correspondingly, and speculation surfaced in the financial press that the company might become a takeover target as a result of this weakness.

In 1986 Mervyn's centralized its buying operations, which had previously been split between its stores in the West and its fledgling stores in Texas. Consolidating buying operations in California speeded up inventory replenishment and cut costs. The chain also contained costs by focusing more of its resources on product quality control and by installing checkout scanners to help manage inventory, among other things.

More importantly, though, Mervyn's began to recalibrate its merchandise lines. Since low prices and good values no longer made Mervyn's unique, in an era when Kmart became the largest retailer in the United States and intramural rival Target prospered, the company had to find a way to distinguish itself once more. The chain responded by focusing its attention even more closely on apparel, which had largely been responsible for founder Morris' success in the first place. "We dropped toys, infants' furniture and draperies because we couldn't be dominant in them without sacrificing potential in our core businesses," Walter Rossi commented. Even within its apparel lines, Mervyn's sacrificed variety to concentrate on its bestsell-

ing items. For instance, it pared in half the number of women's blouses that it offered, leaving only the most popular ones.

Mervyn's also responded to heavy price competition from its rivals by trying to upgrade the quality of its clothing, even when that meant raising prices slightly. One of the chain's most popular clothing lines was its men's and women's sweat clothes. Mervyn's sweats, however, tended to shrink substantially in washing and did not have a reputation as high-quality garments. Mervyn's decided to size them more generously and upgrade the fabric and the sewing, even though it meant a price increase of nearly 20 percent. To compensate for the price hike, Mervyn's offered a broader range of colors and more fashionable designs.

As a result of these changes, Mervyn's sales and profits rebounded in 1988 and 1989. In the 1990s, however, the chain's recovery stalled, hurt by the sharp downturn in the California economy. Sales flattened out during the first half of the decade, and profits dropped sharply from $284 million in 1991 and 1992 to $179 million in 1993. During this time, Rossi was succeeded as CEO by Joe Vesce, and then Mervyn's received five new top executives, including three transfers from Target.

Mervyn's continued to struggle in the mid-1990s. Dayton Hudson's 1993 annual report characterized Mervyn's performance as disappointing, and that year Moody's announced that it was considering lowering Dayton Hudson's debt rating due to Mervyn's financial problems. Some analysts were skeptical as to Mervyn's ability to overcome its losses. Despite its reputation for innovation in the industry, Mervyn's faced a formidable challenge in seeking to survive the competition.

Further Reading:

Barmash, Isadore, "A Turnaround at Dayton Hudson," *New York Times,* May 28, 1989.

—Douglas Sun

Mestek, Inc.

260 N. Elm Street
Westfield, Massachusetts 01085
U.S.A.
(413) 568-9571
Fax: (413) 562-8437

Public Company
Incorporated: 1946 as Sterling Radiator Company
Employees: 2,900
Sales: $231 million
Stock Exchanges: New York
SICs: 3585 Refrigeration & Heating Equipment; 3535
   Conveyors & Conveying Equipment; 8711 Engineering
   Services; 7372 Prepackaged Software

Mestek, Inc., is a leading manufacturer of heating, ventilating, and air conditioning systems for industrial, commercial, and residential spaces. The company also manufactures steel-manipulating equipment for factories, and produces computer systems for use in the medical industry. The company got its start in the wake of World War II as a manufacturer of heating components for commercial spaces, and it grew steadily in this field through the early 1980s. In the mid-1980s, it joined with a bankrupt steel-making machinery company, changed its name, and expanded its scope of business into the waste management field, before returning to its core operations.

Mestek's predecessor was the Sterling Radiator Company, founded in 1946. The enterprise was first conceived during the previous year, when John E. Reed, the company's founder, had dinner in Albany with a businessman who described to him the possibilities of a new technology: fin tube radiation. After a long conversation, and additional research, Reed joined with partner Gustave H. Stenner to launch the Sterling Radiator Company in February of the next year.

A few weeks later the new company began operations in rented quarters located off Bartlett Street in Westfield, Massachusetts. Sterling boasted three employees, who worked in the company's small garage space. By July 1946, they had manufactured their first products: 1¼ inch and 2 inch steel tubes equipped with either 32 or 24 metal fins per foot. These devices, which had been developed before World War II, were originally used to heat railroad passenger cars. In the wake of the war, finned tubes were adapted to heat commercial buildings through

the use of hot water or steam. Reed remarked to friends as his business got under way that he had chosen this enterprise because it was so simple.

Sterling fin tubes were available only in black. The company purchased brackets for installation and simple expanded metal covers from another supplier. A one-page sales brochure was produced to describe all of Sterling's products. Throughout 1946 and 1947, the company's business expanded steadily. By the end of 1947, Sterling's activities had expanded beyond the size of the company's quarters on Bartlett Street, and Reed purchased a small building that had once been a milk plant on Birge Avenue in Westfield.

In its new quarters, the company continued to expand the range of commercial heating products it offered to include a wider selection of fin tubing and louvered covers. In addition to these products for use in stores and other industrial spaces, the company began to experiment with products for use in the home. Sterling's plant was expanded to accommodate these new activities in the late 1940s.

By 1950, Sterling had grown so large that an additional manufacturing facility was needed. The company purchased land and a building at 260 North Elm Street in Westfield. A short time later, Sterling branched into its first new line of business, when the Sterling Heat Specialties Company was established to put together and sell gas-fired unit heaters, for use in commercial and industrial buildings.

Four years later, the company more than doubled its factory space when a new addition was completed. In addition to its continuing efforts to expand the number and kind of products it offered, Sterling also began to develop a network of salesmen in locations across the country, to facilitate distribution of its products nationwide.

These efforts were underway in August 1955, when Sterling suffered a major setback. A torrential downpour caused a railroad embankment near Sterling's plant to dissolve and be washed away, releasing a torrent of water that destroyed many of the plant's buildings and left a thick layer of mud on top of all of its equipment. It took ten days of intensive cleanup operations before the factory was able to produce fin tubing, and several more weeks before other products were being manufactured in volume.

The effects of the flood lingered into 1956, but the massive rebuilding made necessary by the deluge offered Sterling the opportunity to expand its facilities and rearrange them for greater efficiency. Within four years, the company again required greater capacity and new facilities were built; this process was repeated again in 1964.

In that same year, Sterling began a process of expansion through the acquisition of companies in its own field or complementary fields. In 1966, Sterling purchased the Carl G. Peterson Company, a manufacturer of coil-handling machinery founded in 1946. This purchase grew out of the close cooperation between Sterling engineers and Peterson workers, who sought together to make more efficient and sophisticated machines for metal-stamping.

By 1967, Sterling's work force had grown to 220 employees. Two years later, the company entered the fire and smoke damper business (a field related to its core heating industry operations) when it purchased Phillips Aire. This company made fire dampers—safety systems used in commercial or industrial buildings which detected flames or smoke and responded to the threat of fire by sealing off air ducts and sending smoke out through a ventilation system. Because of Reed's previously developed expertise in metal forming, and Sterling's network of sales agents and distribution channels, the fire damper industry was a natural avenue for expansion.

In 1975, Sterling substantially augmented its operations in the gas-fired heater industry when it purchased a manufacturing plant in Farmville, North Carolina. This factory allowed the company to offer an improved and greatly expanded line of products that included gas unit heaters, rooftop duct furnaces, and steam unit heaters. With the purchase of the Farmville facility, Sterling became one of the three leading companies in the gas-fired unit heater market.

One year later, Sterling also moved to expand its operations in the metal-stamping machinery field, when it purchased Cooper-Weymouth, a New England-based firm that made machinery for use in factories. Cooper-Weymouth equipment handled giant rolls of steel sheets known as "coil stock." This purchase complemented Sterling's earlier acquisition of the Peterson company, and Sterling combined the two into a unit known as its Cooper-Weymouth, Peterson division. At this time, the company also changed its name from Sterling Radiator Company to the Reed National Corporation, which better reflected its broadened scope of activities.

Two years later, Reed took a leading place in the damper industry when it purchased Air Balance, Inc., a fire safety company, in 1977. With this move, the company substantially broadened its line of products and acquired another prestigious name brand in the fire damper field. Air Balance manufactured its fire damping equipment in plants in Wren, Georgia, and Los Angeles, California, giving it an important toe-hold in the burgeoning West Coast building market. Later in the 1970s, Reed also broadened its holdings in the steel-manufacturing machinery field, acquiring the Dickerman Company, which made machines to feed coiled steel into other machines for stamping and other forms of manipulation.

Despite this diversification, the core of Reed's business continued to be fin-tube manufacture for use in hot water or steam heating. In 1982, the company expanded its scope of operations in this industry when it bought one of its competitors, Beacon/Morris, which made steam-unit heaters, convectors, and heaters marketed under the brand name Twin-Flo. As part of Reed's Specialty Hydronic Heat Distribution division, Beacon/Morris unit heaters were used to heat warehouses, stores, factories, and other large open spaces. In addition, the company offered forced hot water and two-pipe steam heating convector products for use in hospitals, hotels, office buildings, schools, or apartments.

Two years later, Reed also bought Vulcan Radiator, the company which had first pioneered the use of finned-tube heating for commercial and industrial spaces. At the end of that year, 1984, Reed purchased Pacific Air Products from a company called PAPCO, for $1.4 million. Pacific Air developed and marketed energy-efficient dampers for use in the air-conditioning systems of commercial buildings. In addition, the company developed products to cool air in power plants.

In addition to these acquisitions, Reed also bought another company, to expand its operations in the coil stock machinery business. With the purchase of the Coil-Matic line of air feeds for sheets of steel, Reed's Cooper-Weymouth, Peterson division was able to offer the widest selection of such machinery in the industry.

By the mid-1980s, Reed's operations had expanded to the point where the company set up a special engineering group. This arm of the company was responsible for designing and developing new products, and also for locating new sources of raw materials and monitoring their quality.

At the end of 1985, Reed completed an agreement to complete a reverse-merger with another company, Mestek, Inc. Mestek was a publicly held manufacturer of steel mill equipment based in Pennsylvania that had been known as the Mesta Machine Company until, having been driven into collapse by its heavy debt burden and high overhead, it declared bankruptcy on February 9, 1983. Subsequently, the company was re-organized. It's heavy steel mill equipment business, which had been badly battered by the cheap costs of labor for its foreign competition, was pared away, and its two profitable subsidiaries, an engineering services unit and a computer operation, emerged from bankruptcy on February 20, 1985, under the name Mestek, Inc.

Under the terms of the reverse merger, Reed's owners took over ownership of more than half of Mestek, and the combined operations of the two companies were called Mestek. The deal was completed on July 31, 1986. Mestek in its transformed state consisted of the old heating, ventilating and air conditioning operations of Reed National; Cooper-Weymouth, Peterson, Reed's steel coil machinery arm; and two units contributed by Mestek: the Chester Engineers, and MCS, Inc.

The Chester Engineers were a consulting firm that specialized in environmental engineering. The firm concentrated on waste management projects, and wastewater treatment. The company had extensive computer-aided design facilities, as well as an environmental laboratory to detect minute particles of contaminants in water. MCS, Inc. developed and marketed computer systems for order processing and accounts receivable for companies in the durable medical equipment industries, and for retail lumber and building material dealers.

In the wake of the merger, the new company moved rapidly to make two acquisitions. In November 1986, Mestek bought Alton/Applied Air from the Hussmann Corporation. This company made large industrial forced air heating units, evaporative coolers, and specialized heating-cooling units for use on rooftops. Its operations were complementary to those of Mestek's Gas-Fired Products Division.

One month later, Mestek bought the American Warming and Ventilating Company, which manufactured air control dampers and louvers. First founded in 1904, this company fit well with Mestek's existing Air Balance fire and smoke damper operations. At the end of 1986, after its rapid transformation, Mestek posted profits of $5.2 million on sales of $87 million.

In the following year, Mestek continued its policy of acquiring companies which enhanced and complemented its standing in the industries in which it operated. In January 1987, Mestek acquired Arrow Louver and Damper, a company based in New York which fit well with its other damper operations. In the middle of the year, Mestek bought the L.J. Wing company. Founded in 1875, this firm made heaters for commercial and industrial buildings. Aided by revenues from these two properties, Mestek finished 1987 with sales of $135 million.

By 1988, however, Mestek's program of rapid growth through acquisitions had begun to demonstrate some drawbacks. In an effort to keep the costs of the companies it purchased down, Mestek typically sought out companies in financial trouble, with significant operational or administrative hurdles, confident that it could make the companies profitable through superior management and expertise. This process, however, was not always instantaneous, and Mestek found its operating revenues fluctuating greatly during 1988.

This unexpected slowdown in financial performance made it necessary for the company to borrow $7 million in order to finance further acquisitions. With this money, Mestek bought Keystone Environmental Resources, a company that doubled its capacity in the municipal and industrial waste treatment field; the company then added Arrow United Industries, Inc., a louver manufacturer based in Pennsylvania and New York.

Despite these additions to the company's operations, Mestek experienced a second year of flat earnings in 1989. Three out of five of the company's damper and louver units reported losses, and the costs of integrating Keystone Environmental Resources acquisition turned out to be unexpectedly high. As a result, the pace of Mestek's further acquisitions slowed somewhat in 1989. The company bought a small Los Angeles-based manufacturer of specialty heating and air conditioning equipment, Air Fan Engineered Products, which strengthened its position on the West Coast. It also purchased nearly half of the common stock of H.B. Smith Company, a cast-iron boiler manufacturer founded in Westfield, Massachusetts, in 1853.

By 1990, Mestek's financial fortunes had rebounded strongly, despite a slump in the housing market. The company's commercial and industrial heating units, machine tool operations, and waste management arm all contributed strongly to revenues which topped $200 million for the first time. Mestek limited its acquisitions to firms in the company's fastest-growing area of operations, waste management. Its Chester Environmental Group, which had quadrupled in size in just four years, was augmented by two new units. NEA, Inc. was a Portland, Oregon, company that specialized in air quality control. GeoSpatial

Solutions was a small firm that developed satellite imaging and mapping to enhance land use planning.

By 1991, Mestek had nearly tripled in size in the five years since its merger. The company made an ambitious number of acquisitions, despite a general recession in the building market, which hurt its heating, ventilating, and air conditioning operations, and caused a drop in profits. Mestek purchased Kamber Engineering, which supplemented its Chester group; the Hydrotherm Corporation, which made boilers and other heating products; and Temprite Industries, which manufactured heat-recovering devices, and, with its base in Ontario, helped Mestek to penetrate the large Canadian heating market. In addition, the company bought Dynaforce, which made air curtains.

In the following year, Mestek enhanced its research and development facilities when it began work on the Reed Institute, in Westfield, Massachusetts, to train members of the heating, ventilating, and air conditioning industry. Also inaugurated was a 15,000 square foot lab in Westfield, for testing products for this industry. This foundation for long-term growth did not prevent the company's profits from dropping for the second straight year, however, as the costs of absorbing recent acquisitions depressed earnings.

By 1993, however, a resurgence of activity in the building industry had helped Mestek to enhance its bottom line. In a move to consolidate its operations and focus on the heating industry, Mestek sold 70 percent of its interest in the environmental engineering unit, Chester Environmental, Inc., to Duquesne Enterprises. In its newly streamlined state, with the building market booming, and with a long history of solid management behind it, Mestek appeared to be well situated to prosper as it moved into the late 1990s.

Principal Subsidiaries: Alapco Holdings, Inc.; HBS Acquisition Corporation; Hydrotherm Corporation; MCS, Inc.; Pacific Air Balance, Inc.; Peritek, Inc.; TEK Capital Corporation; Temprite Industries; Vulcan Radiator Corporation; Westcast, Inc.; West Homestead Joint Venture Corporation.

Further Reading:

Cairns, Linda, and Seward, Hilary, "Tender Mercies and Small Increases," *New England Business,* June 1990.

Richards, Frank, "Pittsburgh's Top Ten Growth Companies," *Executive Report,* December 1990.

Robb, Charles C., "From the Ashes," *New England Business,* June 1990.

Tascarella, Patty, "On Top," *Executive Report,* December 1993.

Tascarella, Patty, "Board Games," *Executive Report,* July 1993.

Thompson, Donald B., "Executives on the Spot: Mestek, Inc.," *Industry Week,* September 1, 1986.

Thompson, Donald B., "Chapter 11: An Offensive Weapon," *Industry Week,* August 4, 1986.

—Elizabeth Rourke

Midas International Corporation

225 N. Michigan Ave.
Chicago, Illinois 60601
U.S.A.
(312) 565-7500
Fax: (800) 621-4562

Wholly Owned Subsidiary of Whitman Corporation
Founded: 1956
Employees: 2,000
Operating Revenues: $485.6 million
SICs: 3714 Motor Vehicle Parts and Accessories

A private subsidiary of the Whitman Corporation, Midas International is the leader in the automotive service industry. In 1993 Midas accounted for 20 percent of Whitman Corporation's total sales. The company has nearly 1,900 Muffler and Brake Shops located in the United States and over 700 outlets in Australia, Austria, The Bahamas, Belgium, Canada, France, Honduras, Mexico, New Zealand, Panama, Spain, and Switzerland. Over 300 stores are operated by Midas; the rest of the shops are part of the company's extensive franchising network.

In the early 1950s, the founder of Midas International Corporation, Nate H. Sherman, operated a family business in Chicago that manufactured car mufflers. As president of International Parts Corporation, Sherman was well aware of the developments in the automotive industry during the 1950s: The American economy was expanding rapidly, making the average person more prosperous than ever before. This prosperity translated into increased consumer demand for cars, and between 1950 and 1956 almost 40 million new automobiles were purchased. Technological innovations, such as 18-month mufflers and dual exhaust systems, were also changing the way cars were serviced. Sherman recognized that the independent service stations—the "mom and pop" corner gas stations—would no longer be able to meet the growing demand for automotive services. These developments convinced Sherman that he could develop a new type of service station where he could sell his mufflers directly to consumers and eliminate the need for distributors.

Sherman correctly predicted that consumers would prefer fast, efficient automotive service to the slower "mom and pop" service station. He felt that the best way to take advantage of the dramatic changes in the automotive market was to create a network of independent businesses that would be supported by a central company—in short, to begin franchising. In 1956, the entrepreneur formed the Muffler Installation Dealers' Association (M.I.D.A.S.) and convinced long-time friend Hugh Landrum to open the first Midas Muffler franchise shop. Located in Macon, Georgia, the shop installed and replaced mufflers as quickly and as efficiently as possible. In order to differentiate Midas from other service stations and to encourage return business, Sherman guaranteed to replace any muffler his shop had installed in a domestic car for as long as the motorist owned it. By the end of 1957, there were 100 Midas Muffler franchise shops independently operated in 40 states.

With his flair for marketing, Sherman began to revolutionize the automotive service industry. Consumer surveys taken throughout the 1950s indicated that most people didn't understand how their own cars worked; because of their lack of mechanical knowledge, many of these people believed that they were overcharged or charged for unnecessary repairs at service stations. In addition, a large number of people were angry with the inadequate service or poor workmanship evident in fixing their cars. Sherman's marketing strategy was to directly involve the customer in making decisions about repairing the car. He instructed Midas Muffler shop owners to invite the motorists into the service bays to educate them about their cars and what needed repair. A written estimate that included an itemization of the repair work was given to each customer before the repairs were begun. Finally, Sherman suggested that all Midas shops install large windows to an area where customers could watch the repairs made on their cars.

The accuracy of Sherman's predictions about the automotive industry and his marketing savvy helped Midas become one of the fastest growing franchises in the United States. By 1960, there were 319 Midas Muffler Shops in operation and a growing number of competitors both locally and regionally. In order to protect and increase its share of the automotive services market, Midas introduced shock absorber service in 1960. The company continued to grow, and in 1968 Midas purchased Huth Manufacturing Corporation, a firm that produced made-to-order bender machines. The benders provided automation to cut and weld tubing for a car's exhaust system. The Huth machines proved to be time savers, and, as muffler installers increased their demand for the benders, Midas' marketing network grew both in the United States and in foreign countries. The first Midas Muffler "Silencer" Shop opened in 1968 in Harlesden, England. By 1970, there were 577 Midas Muffler Shops operating throughout the United States, England, and Canada.

In 1972, Midas International was purchased by IC Industries, Inc., which subsequently renamed itself the Whitman Corporation. At that time, under the leadership of William Johnson, IC Industries divested most of its railroad holdings and began the transformation into a multinational conglomerate. Diversification into consumer goods and services was indicated by three major acquisitions: Pepsi-Cola General Bottlers, a soft-drink bottler located in the Midwest; Midas International; and Pet Inc., an evaporated milk company operating out of St. Louis.

As a wholly owned subsidiary operating within IC Industries' consumer products division, Midas benefited from the financial resources of its parent company. In 1974, Midas created the

Midas Institute of Technology in Palatine, Illinois. This facility was designed to serve as a training center for new franchisees, managers, and automotive mechanics. In order to ensure the best service throughout its franchise network, emphasis was placed on developing good consumer relations and improving the technical skills of Midas employees. In 1978, Midas opened its 1,000th shop in the United States; during the same year, Midas also extended its muffler guarantee to customers with foreign cars. In 1979, Midas announced that it would provide brake service in all its shops. By 1980 there were 1,350 Midas Muffler and Brake Shops, with franchises in Australia, Belgium, Canada, England, France, Mexico, and Puerto Rico.

Midas continued to grow during the 1980s. The company manufactured its 50 millionth muffler in 1983 largely due to improvements in production. The company initiated a major expansion at its manufacturing facilities in Bedford Park, Illinois, and Hartford, Wisconsin, where it produces exhaust systems and other automotive parts for domestic and foreign cars, vans, light trucks, and even antique autos. With over 1,400 franchise outlets in the United States by 1985 and over 400 shops in foreign countries, Midas was three times larger than its closest competitor. Record revenues of $298 million were reported in 1984, an increase of 10 percent over the previous year. Also in the same year, Midas opened 74 shops in the United States alone. In the exhaust replacement market, Midas accounted for approximately 12 percent of the outlets but garnered about 25 percent of the business.

Near the end of 1984, *Entrepreneur* ranked Midas as one of the top-ten franchisers in the country. Although the automotive products and services market was growing at an annual rate of over 10 percent, the market was far from saturated. Research had shown that as consumers kept their cars longer and as traditional service stations provided fewer automotive repairs, the demand for special repair stores continued to increase. Midas' own marketing research indicated that the company had the highest profile and best name recognition of all the competitors in the exhaust replacement industry. By taking advantage of these trends, Midas opened its 2,000th shop in 1986. In contrast, Car-X and Speedy Muffler King (both franchises are controlled by Toronto-based Tenneco), Midas' closest competitors in the automotive services franchise business, operated 434 shops combined. Meinecke Muffler Company, with 400 shops located primarily in the southern and midwestern parts of the United States, ranked third.

In 1986 Midas opened its New England Training Center in Taunton, Massachusetts. Because of the large number of appli-

cations for Midas franchises in the eastern part of the United States, the company duplicated the training services it had established in 1974 at the Midas Institute of Technology in Palatine. At the company's Hartford and Bedford Park manufacturing facilities, highly automated and computerized assembly lines were producing more than 1,000 mufflers per hour for both the domestic and foreign markets. In 1989, Midas manufactured its 100th million muffler. Midas also introduced computerized suspension and alignment services in all its shops during this time. With the increasing popularity of four-wheel-drive vehicles, the addition of smart suspension systems, and the use of four-corner struts by most car makers, Midas anticipated that the suspension market would ultimately grow larger and more financially rewarding than either the exhaust or brake markets.

In 1991, Midas celebrated its 35th year of operation by continuing to expand its franchise network. During the early 1990s Whitman Corporation began acquiring muffler shops in Europe for Midas to operate and increased its name recognition in the United States through a major advertising campaign. By continuing to expand both in the United States and in such countries as England, Switzerland, and Austria, sales for the company grew rapidly. In 1992, sales and services provided by Midas shops accounted for 20 percent of Whitman Corporation's total sales.

Spurred by its franchising success, in 1993 Midas initiated an expansion campaign in Mexico. Under a franchise contract with Interamericana de Talleras SA de CV, Midas began opening retail and service outlets in major metropolitan areas. Management expected these outlets to grow at a rate of 10 shops per year for the first few years and then increase rapidly. The goal was to open over 140 shops to service the nearly 10 million registered automobiles and light trucks in the country.

The most recognized name in the muffler service and repair business, Midas is poised to take advantage of the growing used car market. The unpredictable state of the world's economy has resulted in people holding onto their cars longer than at any time in the past, and Midas plans to provide the repairs and services necessary to keep these cars on the road. With its continually expanding franchise operation and its ready access to the financial resources of its parent company, Midas seems positioned to remain the industry leader for many years to come.

Further Reading:

Strazewski, Len, "Muffler Shops Search for Golden Touch," *Advertising Age*, May 16, 1985, p. 15.

—Thomas Derdak

National Association of Securities Dealers, Inc.

1735 K Street, NW
Washington, D.C. 20006-1500
U.S.A.
(202) 728-8000
Fax: (202) 728-8882

Nonprofit Corporation
Incorporated: 1939
Employees: 2,500
Sales: $332.1 million
SICs. 6231 Security and Commodity Exchanges

The National Association of Securities Dealers, Inc. (NASD), is a self-regulating association that runs NASDAQ, an automated over-the-counter stock market which lists the shares of more than 4,600 companies. NASDAQ is the second largest stock market, in terms of dollar values of trade, in the world, and the fastest growing securities market in the United States. NASD got its start during the Depression as the federal government tried to re-establish order in the American financial industry. In the early 1970s, it instituted a technological breakthrough in stock trading with the introduction of NASDAQ. The association has refined this system as its market has grown.

NASD was founded in 1939 in the wake of the 1938 Maloney Act amendments to the Securities Exchange Act of 1934. In cooperation with the United States Congress and the Securities and Exchange Commission (S.E.C.), the nation's dealers and brokers in over-the-counter securities joined together to regulate themselves, under the government's supervision. The market in over-the-counter (OTC) stocks was made up of transactions conducted between investors and "market makers" who were authorized to trade a company's stock. Between the association's founding in 1939 and 1970, it functioned primarily as a regulatory body for the activities of buyers and sellers of OTC stocks.

During this time, trades were carried out through a cumbersome process. In order to buy stock, it was necessary to shop around by phone among the various market makers, in order to see who was offering the best price. With this system, it was impossible to give a fixed price for any stock at any given time, so it was also impossible to keep track of whether a stock's price was rising or falling.

In 1971 NASD introduced an automated system that recorded all price quotes for a given stock by the different market makers authorized to sell it. "Bid" and "ask" quotes, the prices for which a dealer was willing to buy or sell a stock, along with volume figures, were updated once a day, in the same way that mimeographed stock listings had previously been left at each broker's door every morning. The new computerized system was called the National Association of Securities Dealers Automated Quotations (NASDAQ) stock market. With this move, NASD brought market transparency to the OTC stock market.

With NASDAQ, the association brought an end to the need to shop around for the lowest price on a stock. The OTC stock market became an electronic dealer's market, a fully automated exchange which operated without a trading floor. NASD began to compete with the older New York Stock Exchange and the American Stock Exchange to list companies that were offering stock to the public for the first time, and to win investors.

Although it competed with the older exchanges, NASDAQ operated in a somewhat different way because of the presence of the market makers. Instead of one dealer authorized to sell a stock, NASDAQ had multiple dealers. Each OTC stock was typically carried by seven to 11 market makers, which included some of the world's largest securities firms, who competed for an investor's order by posting prices on NASDAQ.

This competitive system provided efficient pricing, and also increased the capacity of the stock market to handle high volumes of orders, eliminating the trading halts that were periodically instituted in traditional exchanges. Market makers also produced research reports on the stocks they handled, raising visibility in the investment community, and provided distribution services through a retail arm.

Despite these technological advances, the OTC stock market in the early 1970s was considered "a moribund backwater of the security industry," as NASD's president Gordon S. Macklin told *Forbes* magazine at the time. Requirements for joining the NASD stock market were extremely loose. Companies were required only to have stock that was publicly traded, and to pay their NASD fees faithfully.

Every day, NASD published a listing of its stocks in newspapers around the country, which was based on volume of shares traded. Because this was the sole criterion for appearing in the printed list, small companies with very cheap stocks could make a big splash simply by having a lot of their shares moved around. Under this system, companies also enjoyed the benefit of appearing in the newspaper very shortly after going on the exchange.

Four years after NASD established NASDAQ, stocks listed on the system were purchased by five million different investors. With a high capital gains tax in place, activities in all stock markets were slowed during the 1970s.

During the 1980s NASD began a push to increase the size and prestige of NASDAQ. At the end of 1981, the association changed the way its stocks were listed in daily newspapers.

Rather than judge by volatility, NASD established a two-tiered system for ranking its 3,600 companies. Those in the top tier, who met certain financial criteria, such as market value, net worth, length of time in operation, and profitability, were put on the NASDAQ National Market list. The selection criteria for these companies was nearly as rigorous as that for the older American Stock Exchange. "It's a pretty swanky list," Macklin told *Forbes* at the time. "You have Berkshire Hathaway, 500 or 600 New York Stock Exchange-eligible companies and hundreds of banks."

Companies that did not meet these new stringent criteria were put on a supplemental list, which came to be called the NASDAQ SmallCap Market, and was carried by far fewer newspapers than the main tally. With this step, NASD moved to make its biggest and best-established companies happy, at the expense of smaller, less mainstream members of the association.

By 1982, NASDAQ had grown to encompass 25 percent of all trading done in the markets. In addition, the system had attracted a significant number of institutional investors, which made up 50 percent of the exchange's volume. As the capital gains tax had dropped, investment in all stock markets had increased dramatically, and NASDAQ's tally of investors had doubled in five years to reach 10 million by 1980.

NASDAQ had also become more popular with companies looking to raise capital. Although half of the 3,400 companies listed with NASD qualified for bigger stock exchanges in 1982, they had chosen to stay with NASDAQ because of the advantages it offered over competing markets. Popular companies such as Apple Computer Inc., MCI Communications Corporation, and Intel Corporation started out on NASDAQ and then stayed. Decisions like these helped to make NASD the fastest-growing stock exchange in the early 1980s. With the presence of larger companies and institutional investors, however, NASDAQ began to resemble its big siblings more closely, becoming more volatile and more closely tied to the performance of other markets.

To foster further growth, NASD upgraded its computer systems in the early 1980s. In April 1982, the association introduced the National Market System (NMS). This advance, which started with 40 companies, meant that the price and volume of popular securities was updated on NASDAQ computer screens 90 seconds after a transaction occurred. This "last-sale" reporting, which made the system's information more timely, helped NASDAQ come closer to duplicating the up-to-the-minute trading conditions of the other two major exchanges.

This advance, plus the large number of new companies coming to market to sell stocks, helped to fuel NASDAQs growth in the mid-1980s. In 1983 NASDAQ's listings grew by 60 percent to reach 3,901. Since many of the new companies started during this time were computer makers or other high-tech firms, NASDAQ gained a reputation as the stock market with cutting edge companies on its list.

NASDAQ was also popular with start-up companies because of its looser regulations. Many firms founded by an entrepreneur set up unequal stock structures when they sold shares to the public, in which the original owners retained almost all of the control of the company, even though other people had contributed money. This unequal arrangement was forbidden on the New York Stock Exchange, which held to a one share, one vote standard.

NASD made another significant technological breakthrough in December 1984, when the association introduced its Small Order Execution System. With this program, brokers could place an order for a stock without having to pick up the phone and call a dealer. Instead, the dealer offering the lowest price for a stock was automatically given the sale. For large orders, however, the old, telephone-based system remained, since brokers liked the flexibility it gave them, which allowed them to maximize their profits in the market.

In December 1984, NASD won a ruling from the S.E.C. that gave it the right to expand the number of companies linked by its NMS from 1,102 to 2,600. The New York Stock Exchange and the American Stock Exchange vociferously objected to this ruling, since it narrowed the distinction between their operations and NASDAQ.

Despite these advances, in 1985 NASD encountered an extremely irate investor, who raised a controversy about the way the market worked. This investor discovered that his NASDAQ broker was dealing primarily in his own interest, and only secondarily in his client's, and that this practice was permitted by the exchange. Although NASD asked its brokers to alert their customers to the rules of the exchange, and to follow their fiduciary responsibility to their customers, the structure of the market, which benefitted the large broker over the individual investor, was not substantially changed. This dispute was a harbinger of a much larger number of complaints which would erupt later in the decade.

In April 1985, NASD won a further ruling from the S.E.C. expanding the limits of its activities. This move, however, proved to be a double-edged sword. After NASD petitioned for the right to trade options on six of its most popular shares, as well as the shares themselves, the other stock markets were granted the same privileges. In this way, NASD lost the exclusive right to deal in shares of Apple Computer, Convergent Technologies, Digital Switch, Intel, MCI Communications, and Tandem Computers, which were among its hottest stocks.

By 1987, when Macklin resigned and a new head took over NASD, two issues had come to the forefront. The association needed to strengthen its self-regulatory posture, to better protect investors, and also to move more forcefully into the market for foreign capital. As a start in this direction, NASD set up a quotation link with London early in 1987, and added a second tie to Singapore by the end of that year. At the same time, the association extended its regulatory oversight to include 60 government securities dealers, and considered including investment advisors as well.

Before these steps could be fully implemented, however, the NASD suffered a severe blow on October 19, 1987, when all of the American stock markets crashed on one day, Black Monday. In the chaos of the crash, a number of the weaknesses of the NASD system which had led to abuse were revealed, and the association later received more than 4,000 complaints from investors. After the shock, amid the soul-searching that ensued, NASD made a number of changes in its operations.

Because investors had accused OTC stock brokers of not answering the phone while the crash was in progress, so that shareholders were unable to bail out of the market, the association eliminated phone ordering altogether. Instead, in effect, it forced all market makers into its previously instituted Small Order Execution System. To do this, NASD instituted a computer-to-computer purchasing system called Order Confirmation Transaction, which was designed to handle large orders. By the end of January 1988, this program had replaced the telephone with software which electronically transferred orders, offering greater efficiency and capacity than the phone-based system.

In July 1988, NASD moved to put the last price quotes of penny stocks, previously listed on the "pink sheet," on line, in an effort to better police the market. In addition, NASD stepped up its market surveillance overall, searching out embezzlement, misrepresentation, and unauthorized trading on its own, rather than waiting for an investor complaint to act. The association began to refer criminal violations to the Justice Department, and made brokers' NASD disciplinary proceedings part of the public record. With all of these moves, NASD hoped to rebuild the public's confidence in the financial markets.

By the end of the 1980s, these efforts had proven largely successful, and NASDAQ resumed its strong growth. In March 1991, the association moved to branch out into another aspect of the financial industry when it developed a system to provide price quotations and trading data on high-yield debt and other fixed income securities, known colloquially as junk bonds. Called Fixed Income Prototype System (FIPS), this system was developed at the behest of the S.E.C.

Two years later, NASD began a push to expand into other markets, when it petitioned the S.E.C. for the right to trade index warrants on the NASDAQ indices. A few months later, the association also moved to enter the market in derivatives and hybrid products. If the proposals were approved, NASD would be taking on the other exchanges in these fields.

In May 1993, FIPS began operating, bringing enhanced transparency to the junk bond market. With the NASD system, trading in these securities was made more straightforward and easy to police, since the computer retained an audit trail of all transactions. At its start, FIPS covered 50 bonds. With this service, smaller profits on bond sales were anticipated. Brokers hoped that higher volume, with the increased credibility of the market, would offset this decrease.

Three months later, NASD also tried to refine its Small Order Execution System. Over the years, NASD had discovered that the system was being abused in a number of ways. To prevent outsiders from using it to break the monopoly of the market makers, the association proposed that the maximum order be cut from 1,000 shares to 500. In addition, NASD requested permission to partially dismantle the system, removing the mandatory lowest bid feature, and replacing it with an order routing and execution system that would give market makers wider latitude in trading.

In addition to fine-tuning its computerized stock market at home, NASDAQ worked to export its proprietary technology and programs to other countries seeking to set up capital markets. In 1993 the London Stock Market announced that it was considering a purchase of NASDAQ's system. Markets in Paris, Frankfurt, Sydney, and Toronto had also moved toward a screen-based, rather than trading floor-based, system. National markets in Argentina, Korea, and Taiwan were also set up on the NASDAQ model. Whether or not these would indeed become the "Stock Market for the Next 100 Years," as the company's advertising campaign proclaimed, it seemed clear that automated trading in general and the markets regulated by NASD in particular would continue to grow and thrive in the coming years.

Further Reading:

Antilla, Susan, "Battle of the Stock Exchanges," *Working Woman,* September 1984.
Cahan, Vicky, "Hardiman Could Be Just What the NASD Needs," *Business Week,* July 6, 1987.
Carmichael, Jane, "Getting Listed," *Forbes,* May 24, 1982.
Hughey, Ann, "Wall Street Says, 'Me First,' " *Newsweek,* April 22, 1985.
Sloan, Allan, "NASDAQ Goes Upscale," *Forbes,* December 21, 1981.
P.B.B., "The Institutionalization of NASDAQ," *Forbes,* November 8, 1982.
Yang, Catherine, "The Man Who Would Make Securities More Secure," *Business Week,* July 18, 1988.

—Elizabeth Rourke

National Car Rental System, Inc.

7700 France Avenue South
Minneapolis, Minnesota 55435
U.S.A.
(612) 830-2034
Fax: (612) 830-2548

Private Company
Incorporated: 1947
Employees: 8,000
Sales: $700 million
SICs: 7514 Passenger Car Rentals

National Car Rental System, Inc. (or National Interrent, the corporate tagline), is one of the foremost car rental businesses in the world. Privately held National features vehicles made by General Motors (which owns an 81.5 percent share in the company) and functions as a leading partner—with Tilden Interrent, Europcar Interrent, and Nippon Interrent—of the Interrent network, with more than 5,000 rental locations in 130 countries. Over the years, National has bounced from owner to owner, but perhaps no transition proved as unsettling as the leveraged buyout (LBO) engineered by former National chairman Vincent A. Wasik in 1986. Ultimately forced out by GM executives in 1992, Wasik left the company as it was losing market share and $100 million annually. National was still in the midst of turning itself around in 1994.

National was formed in St. Louis, Missouri, on August 27, 1947, by 24 independent car rental operators who hoped to broaden their market influence by teaming together. Among the original owners was Joe Saunders, who is generally credited with launching the car rental business back in 1916. One of National's most important early moves was the international service agreement it formed with Tilden Interrent, the largest and oldest Canadian car rental firm, in 1959. Two years later National's headquarters were moved to Jackson, Mississippi, when a Minneapolis-based investment group took charge of the corporation. In 1965 National relocated to Minneapolis and was a less-than-promising, seven-employee operation with $12 million in annual revenues and $2.77 million in losses.

However, National was in improved financial shape by 1968, the year in which it became the first car rental company to install a centralized computer system. This same year, National, then held by Greatamerica Corporation, was purchased by Ling-

Temco-Vought (LTV Corporation), a Dallas-based conglomerate. National closed the decade with yet another change in ownership, this time by Illinois-based Household International. Revenues and earnings for the subsidiary stood at $71 million and $5 million, respectively.

In 1970 National created its own subsidiary, National Car Rental System International, Ltd., in order to accommodate the company's growing international business. By the end of 1972 National was operating 1,700 rental stations nationwide and also had licensing agreements with a network of 700 locations in 57 countries around the world. Two years later National signed its first agreement with Europcar Interrent, the largest car rental network outside the United States, serving all of Western Europe and much of Eastern Europe, as well as Russia, the Middle East, and Africa. A number of other ventures characterized the decade, including the operation of an E Z Haul Division of trucks and trailers, and a growing emphasis on fleet sales to the general public.

By 1980 National was selling approximately 20 percent of its fleet annually, or about 12,000 cars per year, compared to just 5 percent in 1974. Assessing the situation in 1980, Bob Tamarkin wrote: ''For years the car rental companies were content to wholesale the used cars from their fleets . . . at any prices they could get in order to make way for new models.'' However, soaring car prices during the 1970s, coupled with wholesalers' tendencies to pay below fair market price for late-model rentals, spurred first Hertz, and later Avis and National, to approach used car sales as a profit-making sideline. The practice continued until it ultimately threatened new car sales and led GM and other carmakers to extract concessions in the form of buy-back requirements from the rental agencies before the delivery of new fleets. When an economic recession hit, National was forced to sell its 120 used-car lots for a write-off of $90 million.

In 1985 National's owner, Household International, began a large-scale and probably overdue divestiture program so that it could refocus on its original financial services businesses. The investment firm Paine Webber recruited Vincent A. Wasik to head a leveraged buyout of National, for which his reward was a 25 percent equity stake and chairmanship of the company. According to David Brauer, Wasik increased his holdings to 36.5 percent the following year by orchestrating the sale of Paine Webber's interest to General Motors. When the original deal was completed in 1986, National was in an apparently strong number three position, with earnings of $16.2 million on revenues of $889 million (including franchisees, which accounted for around 25 percent of sales) and a reputation as the industry's service leader.

However, the company had its problems, according to Steve Weiner, ''As operated by Household, National sometimes was profitable mostly because of tax breaks.'' During his first year, Wasik, a former vice-president and director of Hertz, chopped a whopping $1.6 billion in debt in half and also ruthlessly cut expenses through fleet reductions, closings of unprofitable locations, and other measures. Although Wasik claimed credit for ''a phenomenal turnaround in profits,'' Weiner pointed out that the company had given up market share; in particular, airport market share, a key index, was down from 20 percent to 17 percent.

Wasik's core strategy was to boost sales to the business segment, especially those customers renting 10 or more times per year. To this end, he launched the Emerald Club, a pioneering frequent car renter program that charged an up-front fee and then rewarded members through free trips, cars, and other prizes for their amount of rental usage. In 1987 this group represented 10 percent of National's revenue. This same year the company dramatically streamlined its rental agreement, foreshadowing the Emerald Aisle, which offered "entirely paperless transactions" through Smart Key Machines.

In 1988 National solidified its worldwide network through an agreement with Nippon Interrent, which brought the company into contact with Japan, Asia, and the Pacific Rim. National closed the decade on a high note by expanding its relationship with Disney, which stretched back to 1975. The new, 10-year agreement named National the official car rental company of Disney and the beneficiary of high-profile exposure not only at the entertainment giant's resorts but also, periodically, in its movies (in the film *Beaches,* for example, the character played by Bette Midler rented a National car).

Despite such publicity coups, National was suffering internally from the effects of the 1987 deal between Paine Webber and GM. Aside from creating annual interest payments of $100 million, part of that agreement obligated National to purchase a fixed number of vehicles from GM, whether the company required them or not. Other costly situations included failed ventures in limousine and classic car rentals. "To careful observers," wrote David Brauer, "the first clear sign that National was failing to meet the GM loan covenants came in early 1991, when the rental company signed a 10-year, $500 million contract to have the GM unit Electronic Data Systems Corporation (EDS) manage its data processing and communications services." The contract was unnecessary from National's standpoint, for information systems was one of its greatest strengths. However, GM needed to stem the losses caused by its troubled holding.

Until 1992, according to Brauer, Wasik ruled National autocratically. Ultimately, GM executives forced his resignation, though not until the company had fallen to fourth largest and was losing $100 million annually. In 1992 GM bought out Wasik's Fidelco Capital Group for $28 million and took a $744 million restructuring charge; this same year, National regained its third slot in the industry.

In early 1993 Jay Alix, a turnaround specialist, was brought in to join newly installed chairman and CEO Thomas Murphy (who had earlier served as a GM executive-on-loan) to return National to profitability. In April 1993 Murphy stepped down as chairman and was replaced by fellow GM executive William Hoglund. Alix was named CEO at the same time. By December 1993 National had found a new advertising partner in W.B. Doner & Company and was charting a renewed, high-profile course with greater attention to finding the right balance between the business and leisure markets. Some observers predicted a sale of National, but whether it would occur remained to be seen in mid-1994.

Further Reading:

Brauer, David, "Taken for a Ride," *Corporate Report Minnesota,* January 1993, pp. 31–35.
Heitzman, Beth, "U-Turn: National Car Rental System Inc. Changes Its Decision on Media Advertising," *ADWEEK Eastern Edition,* September 27, 1993, p. 1.
Hirsch, James S., "Renting Cars Abroad Can Drive You Nuts," *Wall Street Journal,* December 10, 1993, pp. B1, B7.
"In Brief: National Car Rental/Interrent," *Minneapolis Star Tribune,* April 6, 1994, p. 3D.
Levin, Doron P., "GM to Post $23.5 Billion Loss for 1992," *Minneapolis Star Tribune,* February 2, 1993, p. 1D.
Magenheim, Henry, "National Car's 'Global Deal' Expands," *Travel Weekly,* June 20, 1991, p. D3.
Peterson, Susan E., "National Car Rental System Names Thomas Murphy as Chief Executive," *Minneapolis Star Tribune,* January 28, 1993, p. 1D; "After 3 Months as CEO at National Car Rental, Thomas Murphy Steps Down Amid Restructuring," *Minneapolis Star Tribune,* April 8, 1993, p. 1D.
Tamarkin, Bob, "Buy Where You Rent?" *Forbes,* February 18, 1980, pp. 150–51.
Teinowitz, Ira, "National Car Rental Eyes Consumers," *Advertising Age,* June 15, 1992, p. 54.
Underwood, Elaine, "Budget, National Take Different Directions," *Brandweek,* July 27, 1992, p. 5.
Weiner, Steve, "First, Kick the Tires," *Forbes,* October 5, 1987, pp. 50, 52.

—Jay P. Pederson

National Gypsum Company

2001 Rexford Road
Charlotte, North Carolina 28211
U.S.A.
(704) 365-7300
Fax: (704) 365-7218

Public Company
Incorporated: 1925
Employees: 3,000
Sales: $511.1 million
Stock Exchanges: NASDAQ
SICs: 3275 Gypsum Products

The National Gypsum Company, the second largest producer and supplier of gypsum wallboard and related products in the United States, emerged from bankruptcy and legal difficulties in 1993 as a leaner and financially stronger company. With eight mines and quarries, 24 manufacturing and processing plants, and a network of chartered rail, sea, barge, and truck transportation, National Gypsum controls the production of wallboard and related products virtually from the mine to the walls of homes around the country.

Melvin Baker, Joseph Haggerty, and Clarence Williams incorporated National Gypsum Company in Delaware on August 29, 1925, to develop Haggerty's new brand of wallboard, a mixture of newsprint, a mineral called gypsum, and starch. During this time, composite wallboard was replacing the plaster and lath method of making interior walls and ceilings, and Haggerty's concoction was lighter and stronger than the gypsum products then on the market. Baker contributed a plan to market and sell Haggerty's wallboard, while Williams had an option on a gypsum deposit near Buffalo. The three set about raising the $2.5 million they needed to mine gypsum products, build a plant, and organize a sales and marketing force.

At the heart of the new company's marketing campaign was its "gold bond," a certificate included with every shipment of wallboard that offered $5,000 to anyone who could prove that the product was not lighter and stronger than any other gypsum wallboard on the market. Soon the wallboard became known as Gold Bond Wallboard, and the product name was better known than the manufacturer's name.

In 1927, the young company established a new plant in Iosco County, Michigan. It also barely survived the loss of two patent-infringement suits. Baker, who became president of National Gypsum upon Haggerty's death in 1928, ensured the company's survival by agreeing to pay U.S. Gypsum and Universal Gypsum, the competitors who filed the suits, a percentage of National Gypsum's profits until U.S. Gypsum's patent on covering the edges of wallboard with paper and Universal's claim to Haggerty's formula expired.

National Gypsum also managed to survive the Great Depression, largely because Baker struck a deal to become the sole supplier of wallboard to the Century of Progress Exposition in Chicago, the only significant building project in the country in 1932. In 1934, the company acquired a subsidiary of Bethlehem Steel that made metal lath, used to support wallboard, establishing a policy of developing new products and acquiring companies that were in the gypsum business or made products that could be used in the business.

In 1935, National Gypsum acquired its adversary Universal Gypsum in a stock swap. The acquisition of a company twice its size gave National Gypsum new plants in Texas, Iowa, Pennsylvania, and New York, in to addition several valuable mines, while also establishing the company in the Midwest. The following year, as National Gypsum's sales reached $8 million and profits were a record $1 million, the company also acquired Atlantic Gypsum and its New York, New Hampshire, and Nova Scotia plants.

In 1937, National raised $1.5 million to build a factory in Alabama, where it could take advantage of a new process to convert waste pine into insulation board. A stock split and listing on the New York Stock Exchange raised new investment capital, with which the company acquired Keene's Cement, a manufacturer of hard white plaster used as a background for setting tile and in making moldings. As a part of the deal, National Gypsum gained access to a 30 million-ton mine of pure white gypsum near Medicine Lodge, Kansas. That year, the company also moved into the rock wool insulation line.

National Gypsum's sales reached $24 million in 1940. In fact, between 1930 and 1940, the company's sales and earnings had increased more than 500 and 2,800 percent, respectively. When Universal Gypsum bought Windsor Paper Mills Inc., of Newburgh, New York, for $200,000 in the early 1940s, the company realized its goal of manufacturing all the major items it needed to make its own products. During World War II, National Gypsum produced ordnance, designed, and manufactured acoustical units to dampen the noise of testing aircraft engines, as well as interlocking metal landing strips and insulation for refrigerated cargo ships, products that later proved useful during the Korean and Vietnam wars. By the end of the 1940s, National Gypsum owned 16 plants.

Anticipating a postwar building boom, National Gypsum borrowed $18 million to help finance a $50 million expansion intended to double prewar capacity. A round of aggressive fundraising allowed the company to exceed Baker's goal of doubling production, and still the company could not keep up with demand. Once primarily a southern and southwestern product, wallboard was now needed nationally. To increase its capacity, the company modernized its three paper production plants, purchased three new cargo ships to carry gypsum from Nova Scotia, and enlarged plants in New York and Portsmouth, New Hampshire.

By 1950, National Gypsum controlled 27 percent of the gypsum market—producing more than 150 building products and reporting $75 million in sales—while competitor U.S. Gypsum's market share, 85 percent in 1925, shrunk to 33 percent. In 1951, National Gypsum acquired National Mortar and Supply Company and built a paper mill as well as a wallboard and plaster plant. The following year, the company made a brief and ultimately unsuccessful attempt to break into the water-based latex paint market with the acquisition of Wesco.

In 1954, National Gypsum purchased Abestone Corporation and an asbestos cement plant in Millington, New Jersey. While the company's asbestos business never accounted for more than ten percent of total sales, it would later involve the company in long and expensive legal battles over the dangers of asbestos. Also that year, the company began a covert project to mine for gypsum 500 feet below the surface in Shoals, Indiana, the first effort to mine the inexpensive ore below the earth's surface. The following year, the company's engineers and geologists discovered one of the largest gypsum deposits on the continent near Halifax in Nova Scotia. At the end of the decade, National Gypsum established its presence in the tile business, continuing its working relationship with Olean Tile in New York and acquiring American Encaustic Tile and Murray Tile.

Following a year of negotiations, National Gypsum acquired Huron Portland Cement Company in 1960 in exchange for more than one million shares of stock. The move gave National Gypsum the largest cement plant in North America, a 200-year supply of limestone, and a 125-year supply of shale. Moreover, Huron also provided distribution plants at 12 ports throughout the Great Lakes. To provide cement for its eastern market, National Gypsum acquired Allentown Portland Cement Company in Allentown, Pennsylvania.

In 1964, National Gypsum entered into a joint venture with the French company Lafarge Cement and Victor Hosp of England's Clark and Fenn to establish a wallboard plant in Carpentras, France. Like the company's asbestos acquisitions, this relatively small deal would play an important part in the company's later history. At the end of the year, Baker retired after nearly 40 years at the helm of National Gypsum. Colon Brown, who started his career with National Gypsum in 1936, became chairperson and chief executive on January 1, 1965. Brown's first task was to reorganize National Gypsum's divisions so that each functioned almost as a separate company. The primary result of this five-year effort was the creation of Gold Bond Building Products Division as a separate entity. Brown also strengthened National Gypsum's ties with Lafarge Coppee.

In the late 1960s, National Gypsum was named in a civil suit alleging impropriety in the pricing practices of several gypsum manufacturers. Although the company paid $19 million to settle in 1973, the civil suit led to a U.S. Department of Justice investigation into pricing practices in the gypsum industry. Criminal indictments filed in federal court in Pennsylvania later that year alleged that the company and two employees partici-

pated in a conspiracy to fix prices in the gypsum industry. The case eventually reached the Supreme Court, which upheld an appeals court reversal of a guilty finding against National Gypsum and the two employees.

In 1975, National Gypsum celebrated its fiftieth anniversary. Colon Brown retired, and John P. Hayes replaced him as president while William A. North took over as company chairperson. During his brief tenure as chairperson, North moved National Gypsum's corporate headquarters from Buffalo to Dallas, and a year later stepped aside for another long-time employee, Robert Scifres. Scifres took over a company with seven divisions, 13,000 employees, and about 50,000 shareholders. National Gypsum had just taken on new debt to fund expansion, and building was down.

In 1978, Scifres announced that the Gold Bond division would also leave Buffalo for Charlotte, North Carolina, and he oversaw the closing of the company's first plant, near Buffalo at Clarence Center. As recession loomed, Scifres announced the formation of an international division to push the company's products overseas. He also decided to go ahead with a $279 expansion, gambling that National Gypsum could gauge the end of the recession and be ready to exploit it. The move paid off with record profits during the early years of the Reagan administration.

National Gypsum's president, John Hayes, a 36-year veteran of the company, succeeded Scifres as chairperson in January 1983, taking over as the building business was entering its worst slowdown since the depression. During this time, corporate raiders were in search of strong but undervalued companies, such as National Gypsum. In January 1984, attempting to make itself less attractive to raiders, National Gypsum purchased The Austin Company—a family-owned design, engineering, and construction firm, whose business cycles differed from the residential building business—for 789,000 of its common shares.

After acquiring Austin, National Gypsum set out to divest itself of any division that didn't meet at least one of three criteria: serving as the low-cost producer in its field, having a proprietary product or service, or occupying a special niche in the marketplace. Between 1986 and 1991, the company sold its glass window business and glass distribution division; the decorative products division, which made and sold wall coverings; the National Gypsum Energy Company, an oil and gas producer the company had formed in the 1970s as a hedge against fuel shortages; American Olean Tile; its vinyl siding operations; much of its cement holdings; and a 40 percent share in the French gypsum producer Compagnie du Platre.

Housing starts, one of the principal indicators of the demand for wallboard, picked up in 1984, and National Gypsum's earnings increased to $95.1 million. The following year, earnings increased 22 percent to $116.1 million. National bought back 531,000 shares of its common stock and declared a 3-for-2 stock split in the form of a 50 percent stock dividend. Despite these maneuvers, however, rumors flew in November 1985 that the Belzburg family of Canada was planning a hostile takeover.

The company's executives decided that a leveraged buyout on their part was the best way to maintain control. In November 1985, Aancor Holdings, Inc., a management-led investors group, offered to purchase all National Gypsum shares for a combination of cash and debentures. A decline in interest rates, an increase in new home construction, and a hostile takeover bid by Wickes Companies, one of National's largest customers, complicated the buyout process. Lafarge Coppee's last minute decision to join the investors allowed Hayes to complete the $1.55 billion deal. At the time of the buyout, in April 1986, the book value of National Gypsum's debt was $1.5 billion, the face value $2.1 billion. In 1988, Lafarge Coppee increased its stake in the company to 50.1 percent, but while retaining its position on the board, the French company but did not become involved in operating National Gypsum.

Already critically in debt, National Gypsum suffered through a five-year decline in housing starts; in 1986, total housing starts reached 1.81 million, and, by 1991, they had fallen to 1.01 million, the lowest level since World War II. The slowdown in housing starts was accompanied by a seven-year annual decline in average wallboard prices, from $122 per thousand square feet in 1985 to $72 per thousand square feet in 1992. Ironically, the volume of sales remained high, with National Gypsum holding on to about 25 percent of average annual sales of 20 billion square feet. Prices declined, however, because the company had to ship wallboard from the overstocked southwest into the understocked north and northwest areas.

The threat of large legal losses also hung over the company, prompted by its asbestos holdings. By the early 1990s, approximately 200,000 individuals had filed suits against companies that made or used asbestos, alleging that they exposed their workers to the mineral despite knowing that it could cause cancer and lung diseases. National Gypsum, which used asbestos in the production of insulation until the 1970s, faced approximately 45,000 unresolved asbestos cases in 1992.

In October 1990, 69-year-old John Hayes retired as CEO of National Gypsum and Aancor Holdings, Inc. Peter C. Browning, an executive at Continental Can, was selected as the company's new president and chief executive. Soon thereafter, Browning became chairperson as well. During this time, Browning caught many investors by surprise when he announced that the company was filing for Chapter 11 bankruptcy because it could not find a lender to replace an expiring $75 million credit line with Citibank. Although the company had $75 million on hand at the end of the third quarter and had paid off about half of the debt it owed after the buyout, it still carried $1.02 billion in debt. New lenders were scared off, Browning said, by declining prices in the wallboard market and concerns about the company's asbestos lawsuit liability.

Bankruptcy and deterioration in the industry brought tough times for National Gypsum. The company posted net losses of $40.7 million in 1989, $522.9 million in 1990, and $95.7 million in 1991. While it lost $71.4 million in 1992, its wallboard volume had increased to five billion square feet, and prices began to creep up again.

Following a series of battles over its value, National Gypsum emerged from Chapter 11 bankruptcy proceedings in July 1993. Under the plan, the old National Gypsum was replaced by a new company with the same name, and Aancor ceased to exist. The former company's creditors received common stock in the new

National Gypsum, in addition to cash, senior notes, or warrants. Moreover, the new company announced that it would issue 20 million common shares worth $12.50 each, warrants for another 2.2 million shares, and $100 million of ten-year, ten percent senior notes. The bankruptcy court, agreeing with National Gypsum and its senior creditors, valued the company's total debt and equity at $350 million.

That year, National Gypsum also completed a $75 million revolving credit line with General Electric Capital Corporation, which the company initially used for letters of credit. In August, the common stock and warrants of the new company began trading on the NASDAQ national market. Under the reorganization, the former operating company, the stock of Austin Company, $5 million in cash, and more than $600 million in insurance policies covering asbestos claimants were transferred to the NGC Settlement Trust. All of these assets were slated for settling asbestos-related claims, leaving the new company free from outstanding asbestos property damage claims and current asbestos bodily injury claims.

Six months after National Gypsum emerged from bankruptcy, housing starts, which had begun to rebound in 1992, continued their rise, and the price of wallboard exceeded $80. The company's shares were suddenly trading for $34, giving National Gypsum a market value of $680 million and fueling discussion among critics who had accused the company of undervaluing its assets. National Gypsum had enough cash on hand to retire half of the $100 million in senior debts, and the new company posted net revenues of $511.1 million for 1993, a 9.3 percent increase over the old company's $467.7 million the previous year. Net income was $672.9 million, compared to a $71.4 million loss in 1992. Moreover, National Gypsum produced and sold 5.1 billion square feet of wallboard in 1993, including a record 1.35 billion square feet during the fourth quarter.

In October 1993, chairperson and CEO Peter Browning resigned. Soon thereafter, the company announced that it would lay off 360 of its 3,000 employees by the end of the year, continuing a consolidation that had eliminated 900 jobs since 1990. Later in October, Lafarge Coppee, which had owned more than half of the old company, announced plans to purchase four million shares of National Gypsum from Water Street Corporate Recovery Fund, an entity controlled by Goldman, Sachs. The acquisition gave Lafarge Coppee about 20 percent of the shares outstanding and a seat on National Gypsum's board.

In 1994, Stephen Humphrey, formerly of Rockwell International Corporation, became the president and chief executive officer of National Gypsum. Most of the top management was also new, as was the company's headquarters: in July 1993, it moved from Dallas to Charlotte to join the former Gold Bond Products division. Gold Bond, no longer a separate operating unit, became the brand name for the National Gypsum's products.

National Gypsum entered the mid-1990s confident that it could continue the profitable trend it began in 1993. With interest rates low and wallboard prices rising, the company believed that its position as a fully integrated, low-cost producer with its own supply of gypsum rock and paper and a nationwide network of plants would allow it to thrive despite the highly cyclical nature of the business.

Further Reading:

Blumenthal, Karen, "National Gypsum and Parent Seek Chapter 11 Status," *Wall Street Journal,* October 30, 1990, p. A12.

Bockmon, Marc, *Turning Points: The National Gypsum Company Story,* Dallas: Taylor Publishing Company, 1990, 145 p.

"Commercial Union to Cover Some Claims at National Gypsum," *Wall Street Journal,* October 29, 1992, p. C13.

Dorfman, John R., "Heard on the Street: Pickup in Housing Starts Spells Good News for USG and National Gypsum, Manager Says," *Wall Street Journal,* November 29, 1993, p. C2.

"Four More Concerns Settle in Major Asbestos Trial," *Wall Street Journal,* July 6, 1992, p. 14.

"National Gypsum Co.: Bankruptcy Court Judge Confirms Reorganization," *Wall Street Journal,* March 10, 1993, p. A4.

"National Gypsum Co. CEO Resigns to Take Sonoco Products Post," *Wall Street Journal,* October 1, 1993, p. B8.

"National Gypsum Co.; Wallboard Maker to Lay Off About 360 by Year's End," *Wall Street Journal,* October 6, 1993, p. B4.

"National Gypsum Co.," *Wall Street Journal,* August 7, 1990, p. C10.

"National Gypsum Leaves Chapter 11, Arranges Credit Line," *Wall Street Journal,* July 12, 1993, p. B4.

"National Gypsum Picks CEO," *Wall Street Journal,* March 4, 1994, p. B6.

"National Gypsum Says It Won Ruling in Case of Claims Coverage," *Wall Street Journal,* December 24, 1992, p. 3.

Norman, James R., "A Matter of Opinion," *Forbes,* January 31, 1994, p. 98.

Norman, James R., "Mountain Climbing Is Easy," *Forbes,* November 23, 1992, p. 48.

—David B. Rice

NationsBank

NationsBank Corporation

NationsBank Corporate Center
100 South Tryon Street
Charlotte, North Carolina 28202
U.S.A.
(704) 386-6699
Fax: (704) 386-5000

Public Company
Incorporated: 1960 as North Carolina National Bank
Employees: 57,000
Total Assets: $165 billion
Stock Exchanges: New York Stock Exchange
SICs: 6712 Bank Holding Companies; 6021 National
  Commercial Banks

NationsBank is one of the United States' largest banking and financial companies. Based in Charlotte, North Carolina, the company grew at breakneck speed through the late 1980s and early 1990s to claim a spot as one of the nation's top five financial institutions. Industry analysts credit this phenomenal growth to the company's foundation of bold, aggressive management and thorough, professional planning. They also credit the company's success to the personality and leadership of Hugh L. McColl, Jr., who has served as NationsBank's CEO since 1983. McColl's style, that of a southern-born and bred ex-Marine, contrasts sharply with that of most members of the banking community, and has contributed to NationsBank's image as one of the mavericks of the banking world.

NationsBank was officially formed on December 31, 1991, with a merger between the $69 billion asset North Carolina National Bank Corporation (NCNB) and the $49 billion asset C&S/Sovran Corporation. The merger created the fourth-largest banking company in the United States. McColl became the first president and chief executive officer of NationsBank, and Bennett A. Brown became the first chairman.

The two companies entered the merger having both completed a decade of rapid growth that was typical of the banking industry in the 1980s. NCNB and C&S/Sovran both followed the common industry pattern of numerous mergers and acquisitions in the 1980s. After expanding into South Carolina and Florida in the early to mid-1980s, Charlotte-based NCNB took an unprecedented leap forward through a unique expansion into Texas in 1988. The FDIC selected NCNB to manage the restructured

subsidiary banks of First RepublicBank Corporation of Texas. Atlanta-based C&S Bank had banking offices throughout Georgia, Florida, and South Carolina. In 1990, this company merged with similarly sized Sovran Financial of Norfolk, Virginia. Sovran had banking offices throughout Virginia, the District of Columbia, and Maryland, as well as in Tennessee and Kentucky. After these two companies merged, the resulting organization established dual headquarters in Atlanta and in Norfolk.

NCNB traces its illustrious history back to the Commercial National Bank, which was organized by several prominent Charlotte citizens in 1874. Its initial start-up capital was $50,000. A series of mergers with other North Carolina financial institutions in the 1950s ultimately led to the creation of North Carolina National Bank on July 1, 1960. At the time of its formation, NCNB had 1,300 employees, 40 offices in 20 North Carolina communities and assets of $480 million. The bank continued to acquire smaller institutions, and by 1969 NCNB had grown to 91 offices in 27 North Carolina counties with deposits of more than one billion dollars. Ten years later, it stood as the state's largest bank.

In the mid-1950s, however, when the nation talked about banking in the state of North Carolina, most people were talking about Wachovia Bank and Trust Company, NCNB's arch-rival. Based in Winston-Salem, Wachovia had offices from the mountains to the coast and exercised considerable political clout in the capitol city of Raleigh. Bankers at other institutions stood in envy of Wachovia. Many bankers thrived on the competition, and some, such as Addison Reese at American Commercial Bank—one of NCNB's predecessor institutions—in Charlotte, considered that competition the reason for going to work each morning.

At the time, Reese believed that North Carolina banking was poised for a change and nothing could stop him from meeting Wachovia's threats. North Carolina's banking laws were more liberal than in most states. They had been on the books since the early 1800s, when a Wilmington, North Carolina, bank appealed to the state legislature for permission to open an office about ninety miles away in Fayetteville. The legislature complied with the bank. Unlike in most states, the North Carolina legislature saw no reason to restrict branch banking during the intervening 150 years. In retrospect, many people believe that it was the close competition with backyard rival Wachovia that spurred NCNB's rapid growth.

North Carolina National Bank broke new ground when it expanded into Florida in 1981 with its purchase of First National Bank of Lake City, Florida. At the time, it became the first non-Florida bank to expand its retail services into the state. After a quick approval of the purchase by the Federal Reserve Board of Governors, NCNB rapidly purchased several other Florida banks.

In 1986, NCNB benefited from a change in North Carolina's interstate banking laws. With the advent of reciprocal interstate banking in the Southeast, North Carolina National Bank moved into South Carolina with the purchase of Bankers Trust Company. In 1985, it acquired Southern National Bankshares of Atlanta and Prince William Bank of Dumfries, Virginia, in 1986. North Carolina National Bank moved into Maryland in

1987 with the purchase of CentraBank of Baltimore. In 1989, NCNB acquired full ownership of First RepublicBank in Texas. During this period of growth, North Carolina National Bank established several "firsts" in its industry. For example, NCNB was the first U.S. bank to use commercial paper to finance the activities of nonbank subsidiaries; to open a branch in London; to operate a full-service securities company; and to list its common stock on the Tokyo Exchange.

The C&S/Sovran side of the NationsBank puzzle traces its roots back to the 1860s. The company that would eventually become Sovran opened its doors in Richmond during that decade. At the time, its customer base included Confederate Army commander Robert E. Lee. More than a century later, in 1984, two major institutions—Virginia National Bankshares and First and Merchants—merged to form Sovran Financial Corporation. At the time, it was the largest banking merger in Virginia's state history.

Sovran's management team decided to merge with D.C. National Bancorp, headquartered in Bethesda, Maryland, in 1986. By November of 1987, Sovran was moving west by merging with Commerce Union, a 71-year-old bank holding company based in Nashville. Commerce Union's business at the time spanned Tennessee and had a presence in Kentucky. The merger gave Sovran strongholds in both of those states.

Around the time Sovran Bank's foundations were being laid, the Citizens Bank of Savannah, Georgia, opened its doors in the temperate coastal city on November 2, 1887. At the time, the bank had $200,000 in startup capital. In 1906 it merged with its crosstown rival, Southern Bank, to form Citizens and Southern Bank. The resulting organization became the state's largest financial institution. It began to spread rapidly across the state of Georgia. Citizens and Southern began opening offices in South Carolina in 1928, but the company sold its operations there in 1940 when it anticipated federal rules preventing banks from owning branches in multiple states. The resulting C&S Bank of South Carolina was rejoined with Citizens and Southern in 1986 when the Georgian giant bought them back. That acquisition, along with the purchase of Landmark Banks of Florida in 1985, helped Citizens and Southern doubled its size within eighteen months during the mid-1980s.

C&S can also claim several firsts in the industry. Among the highlights in C&S history are being the first bank to figure "to the penny" balances; offering one of the first checking accounts in the South; being among the first banks to issue its own credit card; and being the first bank in the nation to offer 24-hour access to its services via automated teller machines. The nation's first ATM machine was set up in Valdosta, Georgia, under the C&S banner.

In spring of 1989, C&S was successful in resisting a takeover bid by NCNB. At the time, C&S cited what it considered a low price offer and concerns about NCNB's recent entry into the then-depressed Texas banking market. Soon thereafter, C&S and Sovran merged in a deal finalized on September 1, 1990.

The banking environment, however, was in the midst of tremendous change. Large banks were continuing to consolidate. As a result, smaller banks were under constant pressure to find new ways to improve their efficiency and productivity and reduce their workforces. In addition, the nation as a whole experienced a downturn in the real estate market—an area responsible for much of an average bank's business. The newly merged C&S/Sovran (the merger was announced in the spring of 1989 and consummated in the fall of 1990) was suffering from the recession in the Southeast, and it had been particularly hard hit by mounting losses on loans in the District of Columbia metropolitan area. Real estate loans made up 32 percent of the bank's $34 billion portfolio at the end of 1990, with Washington, D.C., accounting for 21 percent of the real estate total. C&S/Sovran's stock price had dropped from $35.88 at the close of the first quarter in 1989, when NCNB announced its merger intentions, to $15.63 at the close of the fourth quarter in 1990. Under these circumstances, North Carolina National Bank renewed its offer to merge with C&S/Sovran.

Prior to reissuing his offer, McColl gathered with his advisors. According to Howard Covington and Marion Ellis in the book *The Story of NationsBank: Changing the Face of American Banking,* McColl told Senior Vice-President C. J. "Chuck" Cooley, "I am going to buy C&S/Sovran. I don't know when. I don't know how." He instructed Cooley to hire the best talent available and deliver a complete psychological profile on C&S/Sovran's key players, including Bennett Brown and Dennis Bottoroff. Cooley handled the job himself, and several weeks later, he handed McColl a profile of Brown as well as a profile of McColl himself, as seen by Brown.

Cooley told his boss that the keys to Brown's relationships with people were honesty, sincerity, warmth, and friendliness. To McColl's chagrin, however, each of those traits was opposite the characteristics that McColl portrayed to Brown. From Brown's vantage point, McColl was arrogant, crude, and ungentlemanly. After hearing Cooley's report, McColl and several other advisors began an intense series of role-playing sessions. McColl was schooled to avoid the use of militaristic terms and other verbal and nonverbal examples of his usual aggressive style. His staff coached him to become softer, more receptive, and friendlier in his approach.

Meanwhile, McColl's confidence was growing as C&S/Sovran's problems continued to multiply. The credit problems in the D.C. area increased, and the bank's board split badly between an Atlanta faction and a Tennessee and Virginia faction. News filtered down to the NCNB leaders that although both factions preferred to remain independent, a merger with NCNB was the second choice among those on both sides. With this knowledge, McColl renewed his merger efforts with Brown.

On June 20, McColl departed Charlotte in the NCNB plane for Atlanta to make Bennett Brown a second offer. The two banking leaders sat down in Brown's home to discuss the terms of the deal. Brown's concerns were predictable: he wanted to know about leadership, cuts in personnel and staff, the name of the new bank, and—most important—the price.

McColl supplied the right answers to all of Brown's questions. The merged bank would carry the name NationsBank, which eased concerns about the North Carolina flag flying over Georgia. Shortly after NCNB's Texas acquisitions, the marketing group began experimenting with new names that would better reflect the company's size and geographic diversity, as well as be more acceptable in new markets. At that time, the company began working with the Naming Center in Dallas. The Naming Center enlisted the work of academic linguists who worked with Latin teachers and poets to develop names rather than generating them by computers.

On the list of prospective names was the word "Nation." Using poster-sized flash cards, the company combined two of them to create the single word "NationsBank." Everyone was surprised when lawyers determined that the new name was not in use anywhere else in the world, and it soon cleared marketing surveys conducted nationwide. Ironically, NationsBank consistently scored as one of the most recognized and highly regarded names in banking, although it had never been used before. The corporate identity firm of Seigel and Gale in New York then developed a graphic look for the word that would reinforce its characteristics.

As for the issue of leadership, McColl wanted Brown to take the chairmanship, while he retained the title of CEO and president. McColl also pulled a sheet of paper from his coat that illustrated an exchange of 0.75 shares of NCNB stock for each share of C&S/Sovran. That exchange would mean a total payout of $3.99 billion for C&S/Sovran's shareholders. Brown was re-.ceptive to the deal, but could not supply McColl with a firm answer.

It was on June 25 that the news about the probable merger broke in the Charlotte community. Even the national media focused on the possibility of a megabank deal in the South. C&S/Sovran's leadership soon received the second offer with enthusiasm. Among other issues, NCNB had proven the wisdom and success of the large Texas acquisition, and C&S/Sovran was seeking the efficiencies and economies of scale inherent in a merger of this magnitude. The merger was approved by the Federal Reserve on November 29, 1991, and NationsBank officially opened its doors on January 2, 1992. At the time of the union, North Carolina National Bank was the tenth-largest bank in the United States, and C&S/Sovran was the twelfth largest. Together, they thrust each other to a position among the top three banking leaders in the United States.

The new entity quickly went to work to establish its presence in its chosen corporate headquarter city of Charlotte. Already, NCNB's office buildings jutted into the southern skyline, but as NationsBank, the company decide to build a new headquarters building. The result of this goal was the new NationsBank Corporate Center, a pristine sixty-story tower designed by architect Cesar Pelli. At the time it was built, it became the tallest building in the Southeast, and NationsBank firmly established itself as one of the nation's financial heavyweights. As tribute to the man who led this building effort, many Charlotte onlookers began to call the new Corporate Center the "Taj McColl."

The new bank had more domestic deposits than New York's Citibank, market capitalization to rival J.P. Morgan & Company, more branch offices than almost any other competitor, and assets of nearly $120 billion. In addition to serving as a leader in the financial world, in the early 1990s NationsBank served as a role model to the larger corporate community as well. Nationwide, it was known as a company that exercised not only sound management practices, but cultural consciousness as well. Under McColl's leadership, NCNB had already established flexible hours for working parents and a pretax child care expense reimbursement fund. Maternity leave was extended to six months, and the concept was expanded to include time off for new fathers. These ground-breaking policies attracted the attention of the *Wall Street Journal,* which in its centennial issue edition in 1989 selected NCNB as one of twelve companies in the world to watch in the future. *Fortune* magazine also chose McColl as one of the year's twenty-five most fascinating business people—the only one selected from the banking industry—in its January 1989 issue.

The company's financial strength also served as a resource for the many communities it supported. Charlotte itself was one of the nation's fastest growing metropolitan areas, due largely to the growth and visibility of NationsBank. In 1994, the company had 1,800 branch offices, which made it the second-largest branch network in America. By providing traditional banking products to retail and corporate customers, as well as investing in innovative products and services, the company's assets had grown to $165 billion.

Principal Subsidiaries: NationsBank of Florida; NationsBank of Georgia; NationsBank South Carolina; NationsBank of Tennessee; NationsBank of Texas

Further Reading:

Covington, Howard E., and Marion A. Ellis, *The Story of NationsBank: Changing the Face of American Banking,* Chapel Hill: The University of North Carolina Press, 1993.

—Wendy Johnson Bilas

Navistar International Transportation Corp.

Navistar International Corporation

455 North Cityfront Plaza Drive
Chicago, Illinois 60611
U.S.A.
(312) 836-2000
Fax: (312) 836-2159

Public Company
Incorporated: 1966 as International Harvester
Employees: 13,612
Sales: $4.69 billion
Stock Exchanges: New York Chicago Pacific
SICs: 3711 Motor Vehicles and Car Bodies; 3713 Truck and Bus Bodies; 3519 Internal Combustion Engines, Nec; 5511 New and Used Car Dealers; 6159 Miscellaneous Business Credit Institutions; 6719 Holding Companies, Nec

Navistar International Corporation is America's largest manufacturer of medium- and heavy-duty diesel trucks. Until 1986, Navistar was known as International Harvester, a leading manufacturer of agricultural and construction machinery, with 47 manufacturing plants comprising 38 million square feet. Years of dramatic financial losses, however, forced the company to sell off these primary businesses to focus on the production of diesel trucks, a move that necessitated the lay off of thousands of workers and resulted in a reduction in sales by more than 50 percent. With a new name and a new "diamond road" symbol, the company looked forward to more successful years. Although the company ranked 126th among *Fortune* magazine's top 500 industrial companies in 1993, Navistar had yet to turn an annual profit in the 1990s.

Navistar traces its history to 1831, when Cyrus Hall McCormick invented a machine for reaping grain. McCormick's reaper did not gain immediate acceptance among American farmers; in fact, ten years passed before he sold his first reaper, and, by then, his patent had expired. To stay ahead of the competition, McCormick developed such sales techniques as the warranty and the extended guarantee. Early reapers were bulky and noisy, and, at the Great Exhibition in 1851, the *Times* of London disparagingly referred to McCormick's entry as a "cross between ... a chariot, a wheelbarrow, and a flying machine." Soon thereafter, however, the reaper became increasingly popular; the reaper and The McCormick Harvesting

Company would eventually prove to have a dramatic impact on the farming industry.

While McCormick died in 1884, his company continued to experience rapid growth. In 1902, McCormick Harvesting was merged with four other struggling agriculture machinery manufacturers to form International Harvester. This merger was contested by critics who charged that the new firm represented a monopoly on the industry, and, for more than 20 years, the company would be involved in several antitrust suits. However, Cyrus H. McCormick, descendant of the inventor and the company's first president, defended the merger by arguing that it gave the new company opportunities and resources that were beyond the reach of smaller companies. "Presently," he wrote, "there was afforded to the business world the unique spectacle of five competitors in one line coming together for the preservation of their concerns and of the industry, and for the fulfillment of their hopes of a future that was to count for much in the swelling total of American enterprise."

The courts eventually agreed that Harvester neither raised prices nor stifled competition, and that the conglomerate actually helped farmers by developing and marketing new equipment. Harvester's product line expanded to include a wide range of tools used to speed the production of food, including disk harrows, harvester combines, feed grinders, and manure spreaders. In 1907, Harvester introduced a new piece of farm equipment called the auto wagon, a high-wheeled, rough vehicle designed to carry a farmer, his family, and his produce over rutted mud roads to the marketplace. Prompted by the success of the auto wagon, the company eventually designed new models with water and air-cooled engines as well as lower, rubber tires rather than wooden wheels.

The company also began marketing its machinery abroad, and, between 1903 and 1912, sales climbed from $53 million to $125 million, capitalization more than doubled, and foreign sales rose 388 percent to $51 million. By 1912, more than 36,000 dealers in 38 countries were selling McCormick products. During this time, the company's work force grew to 75,000, and management invested in iron mines, coal mines, and acres of forest property, all of which provided the raw materials for producing farm machinery. Although the company suffered a huge loss during the 1917 Russian Revolution, when its Russian interests were taken over by the new government, Harvester's growth continued into the 1920s, as the U.S. economy expanded, new roads were built for trucks, and the international demand for agricultural equipment increased.

While Harvester continued to enhance its offerings—introducing a line of walk-in freezers in the 1930s, for example—the company sought to promote competition in the agricultural machinery industry by refusing to invoke tariffs and by protecting its patents for no more than five years. The company also experienced vigorous competition in both the construction and the truck industries, while building up a vast dealer and supplier network. Eschewing any corporate restructuring during this period of rapid growth, Harvester simply added new divisions, over which managers had relatively little control and had to clear even minor decisions with the central offices. As a result, Harvester became a rather large and unwieldy collection of businesses, gaining a reputation for conservatism, antiquated management techniques, and strictly in-house promotions. Nevertheless, this form of organization saw Harvester through the Great Depression and into World War II.

In 1940, Harvester accepted $80 million in defense contracts from the government. Even before the Japanese attack on Pearl Harbor, which prompted U.S. entrance into the war, 20 percent of the company's total output was defense-related. Harvester employed its dealer network to haul in millions of tons of ferrous scrap from the fields of farmers and also sent its mechanics into the army in order to service and maintain military vehicles. Moreover, Harvester subsidiaries in Great Britain during the war were able to raise agricultural production there by one-third. Wartime production accounted for $1 billion in sales, and the company's contributions to the war effort garnered a *Business Week* cover story and several awards.

However, the war left Harvester financially weakened, and the company was unprepared for the postwar years. High taxes and a concentrated research effort cut profits; in 1945, the company reported $24.4 million profit on $622 million in sales, a significant decrease from 1941's earnings of $30.6 million on $346.6 sales. Moreover, one Harvester official noted in *Forbes* that "the company's leadership in many articles of farm equipment [was] almost too well-established to bear expansion without charges of monopoly."

Nonetheless, the company continued to expand whenever possible. Harvester entered the consumer market for air conditioners and refrigerators, introduced a mini tractor, the Farmall Cub, for small farmers, and manufactured an 18-ton crawler tractor for the construction market. A mechanical cotton-picker, introduced in 1942, sold well, as did a self-propelled combine and pickup baler. Furthermore, the company's overall market changed, and, by 1948, farm equipment accounted for less than half of the company's total sales. Trucks were the company's single largest item; construction equipment and refrigeration equipment comprised the remainder of its product line.

These new units and a capital improvement program improved profits, which peaked at $66.7 million in 1950, representing a performance that Harvester would not match for nine years due to an overextended budget, conservative management, and intransigent unions. Harvester's efforts to reduce labor costs were opposed by some of its 80,000 workers and 28 unions. An innovative pension fund program and in-house promotions placated workers, but even more difficulties arose when Harvester tried to reduce wages during the McCarthy era. During this time, the company accused the leaders of the Farm Equipment Workers union of communist sympathies, while the workers accused Harvester of using such "red smoke screens" to cover up wage cuts. Nevertheless, Harvester won an "Industrial Statesmanship Award" from the National Urban League during this time for establishing racially integrated plants in Memphis and Louisville; "Fair employment," remarked one Harvester manager, "is good business."

The company's profit margin remained dangerously low, however, due to high labor costs, poor management, an inadequate organizational structure, and its failure to introduce innovative products, many of which, competitors claimed, were merely redesigns of existing machines. Moreover, Harvester's much-

touted policy of in-house promotions was actually stifling research and technological advances; most Harvester officers stayed with the company for as long as 30 years.

In 1955, Harvester sold its line of refrigeration equipment but kept its other losing ventures and failed to modernize antiquated plants. Intent on conserving its resources, the company failed to emphasize growth and began a slow and steady decline. "For too many years, as long as there was cash to cover the dividends, few executives really cared about how much the company made," one Harvester director later observed. Moreover, tradition was valued to a fault at Harvester; although sales for one of its truck models remained poor, for example, the truck was kept in production. And although Harvester retained its market share, competitors alleged that it did so only by making government and fleet deals at cost.

Beginning in the late 1950s, a series of company presidents attempted to reverse the economic fortunes of the company. Frank W. Jenks, president from 1957 to 1962, standardized production, reduced district offices by half, reduced the number of dealers from 5,000 to 3,600, and increased expenditure for research and development. In 1961, Harvester re-entered the consumer market with a jeep called the Scout and a small lawn and garden tractor named the Cub Cadet. The company also expanded its promotional campaign for a station wagon, the Travelall, which resembled a scaled-down truck.

All three of these new products could be produced inexpensively, as the company did not have to retool its plants to manufacture them and they could be sold through the company's already existing distributor network. While new products increased sales, profits only rose temporarily before Harvester found itself ranked the second in the farm machinery industry, having been surpassed by John Deere & Company. In response, management tried to improve upon Harvester's ten to 15 percent share of the construction industry but failed to gain any ground on Caterpillar and other competitors. By 1964, Harvester's truck line was its only viable product, comprising close to half the company's total sales. Harvester had the largest market share of the heavy-truck market—31 percent.

Throughout the 1960s, Harvester's profits declined, as the company expended more capital and went deeper into debt. Its labor costs were higher than General Motors; its management had poor communication channels; and low-selling products, such as the in-city truck, named the Merco, continued to be produced at high volume. Moreover, Harvester's decentralization policy failed to allow plants in different countries to share research or manufacture interchangeable parts. Although these plants would eventually work more closely during the 1970s, Harvester's construction products were still sold under several brand names, in direct competition with one another. In 1974, such products were combined under the PayLine name to present "a united front to the industry."

Even though Harvester was larger than most of its competitors, it ranked second or lower in each of its three industries. In 1968, Cyrus H. McCormick's grandnephew, Brooks McCormick, took charge of the company, closing several inefficient plants, including the famed McCormick Works in Chicago. Under McCormick, younger executives were hired, dealerships were reduced, and a Chrysler executive named Keith Mazurek was appointed head of advertising. Mazurek promptly doubled the advertising budget, put the best-selling models on the main assembly lines, and reorganized the district dealer network along regional lines. However, profits continued to decline. While sales in 1971 passed $3 billion, profits reached a mere $45 million. *Forbes* described the company as virtually all sales and no profits and warned that Harvester's profits were far behind all its main competitors.

In 1977, Harvester brought in Xerox executive Archie R. McCardell, who quickly reduced costs and engineered a profit increase from $203.7 million to $370 million in his first year. However, McCardell's cutbacks led to a crippling strike in 1979, and, over the next year, the company suffered more than $1 billion in losses, falling $4.2 billion into debt. When McCardell resigned in 1982, industry experts predicted that the company would soon file for bankruptcy. New managers tried to restructure the company, but, as one observer noted, "The new management is doing some very good things, but it is like putting a band-aid over a massive stomach wound."

Moreover, Harvester's share in the construction and farm markets continued to decline, and it fell to a number two ranking in heavy trucks, after Ford Motor Co. Although the company had cut its employment from 98,000 to 15,000 and shuttered all but seven of its 42 plants, it still lost $3.3 billion from 1979 to 1985. Troubled by soft markets and persistent creditors, Harvester entered a period of continuous restructuring. The corporation sold its construction line and then its agricultural holdings. The sale of its agricultural line to Tenneco for $488 million in 1985 helped the company reduce its long-term debt to less than $1 billion.

In 1986, Harvester was renamed Navistar International Corporation, a name that management hoped would reflect its new focus on high technology. The company also left the gasoline powered truck market, relying primarily on its line of diesel powered medium- and heavy-duty trucks. Navistar manufactured diesel engines for the medium trucks and used engines from other companies for the heavier trucks. The emphasis on fuel-efficiency, along with the solid construction and reliability of the trucks, prompted Navistar to advertise them as "LCO," or lowest cost ownership. That year, after recording its first annual profit since 1979, chief financial officer James Cotting petitioned investors for a 110 million share, $471 million stock offering. The cash infusion helped Navistar retire a significant amount of its high-interest debt and thereby avoid bankruptcy.

In the late 1980s and early 1990s, Navistar held one-fourth of the heavy- and medium-duty truck market (the leading share) but continued to face several challenges. Fallout from reorganizational divestments included a $14.8 million settlement with 2,700 employees of former subsidiary Wisconsin Steel, who had charged that their parent company had deliberately spun them off to a purchaser who had no experience in the steel business. Moreover, intense competition from better-funded domestic and international rivals in a declining truck market—which sunk to a five-year low in 1990—also hindered Navistar's efforts to realize consistent earnings gains.

One of the most costly problems faced by the corporation evolved in part from its drastic labor cuts of the 1980s. The pension plan that was regarded as innovative in the 1950s became unacceptable in the 1990s, as Navistar found itself with 3.3 benefit-consuming retirees for every active employee. Health benefits squandered seven percent of the company's annual sales. In 1992, Navistar made an innovative move to revamp its benefits structure by filing a declaratory judgment action in federal court. The legal maneuver, which was immediately countersued by the United Auto Workers, asked the court to sanction the company's plan to reduce benefits to 40,000 pensioners and their 23,000 dependents. Navistar held out what amounted to half-ownership of the company in exchange for the benefits concessions. In August 1993, under the supervision of the federal court, labor and management agreed on a two-tier plan, which actually reduced overall costs and improved benefits. The settlement slashed Navistar's liability from $2.6 billion to $1 billion but compelled the company to engineer a one-for-ten reverse stock split.

During this time, Cotting, who had become Navistar's chairperson, invested in modest overseas expansion, product development, automation, and plant renovation. While these investments brought product and production improvements, they did not result in profits; in 1994, Navistar had still not recorded an annual net income and had reported losses $889 million. Nevertheless, Cotting expressed his unflagging confidence in the company's ability "to translate Navistar's traditional strengths—a broad product line and a strong and capable distribution network—into bottom-line results."

Principal Subsidiaries: Navistar International Transportation Corp.

Further Reading:

Ozanne, Robert W., *A Century of Labor-Management Relations at McCormick and International Harvester,* Madison: University of Wisconsin Press, 1967.
"Settlement Reached in Suit Against Navistar," *Employee Benefit Plan Review,* July 1988, pp. 68–69.
Winninghoff, Ellie, "US: When Giving Employees Half Saves the Whole," *Global Finance,* July 1993, pp. 13–14.

—updated by April Dougal Gasbarre

Nextel Communications, Inc.

201 Route 17N
Rutherford, New Jersey 07070
U.S.A.
(201) 438-1400
Fax: (201) 438-5540

Public Company
Incorporated: 1987 as Fleet Call, Inc.
Employees: 368
Sales: $53.0 million
Stock Exchanges: New York
SICs: 4812 Radiotelephone Communications; 5999
  Miscellaneous Retail Stores, Nec

Nextel Communications is one of the most promising small companies in the telecommunications industry. It was founded to develop mobile telephone service on existing radio bands, providing competition not only for wireline telephone networks, but also conventional cellular systems.

Nextel managed to skirt regulations that restricted the allotment of increasingly sparse radio bands by making better use of others that already existed. The company developed an all-digital system to operate within underutilized radio bands that were previously used only to dispatch taxicabs. Rather than lobbying a regulatory commission for rights to new frequencies, Nextel merely purchased those that were already there. In doing so, the company established a mobile telephone system that works like cellular, but is not subject to the regulatory morass that has precluded new start-up companies from entering the market.

Mobile radio systems have been in use since the 1930s, enabling police, firemen, and taxi and delivery drivers to stay in touch with dispatch operators. The Federal Communications Commission (FCC) allotted special frequencies for these systems, but their limited bandwidth made them practical only for mobile fleets and not for the average motorist. During the 1970s, AT&T developed a system using a network of local transceivers that could switch a mobile telephone from one antenna, or "cell," to another as it moved from one area to the next. Technological developments greatly expanded the capacity of this service, making widespread commercialization possible. Accordingly, the FCC designated new frequencies for these "cellular" phone systems.

With the break-up of AT&T in 1984, local telephone companies inherited the rights to develop cellular telephone networks. To ensure speedy development, the FCC limited each market area to only two cellular companies. In such places as San Francisco, Denver, Chicago, and New York, customers were allowed a choice, but only between two cellular companies.

The companies best suited to develop cellular systems often were those with the most resources, in other words, established telephone companies, such as BellSouth, Southwestern Bell, Ameritech, and GTE. Many smaller companies in the industry, unable to compete or raise financing, were steamrollered into mergers with these companies. What resulted was a regime in which pairs of competitors locked up virtually every market in the country. The entry of third competitors was precluded by FCC rules aimed at nurturing the market and conserving capacity on the airwaves.

Thousands of other radio wavelengths had been reserved for some future use. Others had been set aside decades before for mobile radio, using an old and highly inefficient analog signaling system—an accident of history and technology that provided the seed for a new form of mobile telephony that could operate in competition with cellular systems. These specialized mobile radio networks could be converted to use digital signals, which require only a fraction of the bandwidth of conventional capacity-hogging analog signals. By going digital, previously limited radio bands could be opened up to handle thousands of calls.

The FCC recognized that its policies had successfully allowed the cellular industry to mature to a point where greater competition could be allowed. Rather than further crowd existing cellular frequencies by allowing more competitors into each market, the commission chose instead to back the development of specialized mobile radio.

Hundreds of radio frequencies were put into play as entrepreneurs began a mad scramble for SMR frequencies. One of the key players in this trade was Morgan O'Brien, a telecommunications lawyer who represented major SMR operators in proceedings with the FCC. In 1987, O'Brien decided to get into the industry himself. He established a partnership with Brian D. McAuley, an accountant and former executive with Millicom and Norton Simon. In April of that year, O'Brien and McAuley founded a company called Fleet Call specifically to acquire SMR properties.

Within the next 12 months, Fleet Call had financed the acquisition of ten mobile radio companies and began laying plans for the construction of communications networks in large markets. At this early stage, Fleet Call concentrated only on acquiring SMR licenses. The task of turning SMR frequencies into a new type of cellular system was still years away.

The SMR business had for years been dominated by Motorola, which not only manufactured the radio systems, but also operated dozens of networks. O'Brien and McAuley feared that Motorola would oppose their plan to build a new communication network within the SMR frequencies and, with its substantial resources, persuade the FCC to stop them. O'Brien and McAuley arranged a meeting with Motorola chairman George Fisher at which they would reveal their plans. They expected

Fisher to tell them that he wouldn't allow Fleet Call to so radically upset Motorola's SMR business, one of its oldest enterprises. To their astonishment, Fisher not only supported the idea, he asked if Motorola could become a partner in the venture. The two companies worked out an equity stake in Fleet Call for Motorola, and developed plans for the electronics giant to build parts of the new system.

A month after the meeting with Fisher, Fleet Call had acquired 74 mobile radio businesses in such metropolitan areas as Los Angeles, San Francisco, New York, Chicago, Dallas, and Houston. It continued to operate them as radio dispatch systems using old analog transmission technology, and provided service to more than 120,000 subscribers.

However, in April 1991, Fleet Call formally requested permission from the FCC to design and build digital communications systems that would operate on the SMR bands. The systems would continue to accommodate existing fleet dispatchers but, by going digital, would allow thousands more calls to be placed. The FCC unanimously voted to allow Fleet Call to proceed with its plans in February of 1991. In its opinion, the Fleet Call system would provide a healthy form of competition for entrenched and technologically limited cellular companies, while providing customers with new options only available with digital technology.

Fleet Call decided to use a digital technology called time division multiple access. Simply described, this system makes use of periods in which no data is being transmitted (such as during pauses in conversation) by temporarily lending communication capacity to other calls. Statistically, all calls will have such pauses more or less evenly distributed. TDMA, as the technology is called, ensures that every available "channel" is not squandered by transmitting silence.

With the radio bands in its possession, and having decided on a technology for the system, Fleet Call brought in other partners to build the network with Motorola. One of them was Northern Telecom, a Canadian manufacturer of telecommunications network equipment. In December 1991 another company joined, the Japanese consumer electronics giant Matsushita, manufacturer of the Panasonic and Technics brands and the company that bought the Quasar line from Motorola some years earlier. Matsushita agreed to supply subscriber units (basically handsets) for Fleet Call's digital mobile networks.

In January of 1992, O'Brien and McAuley took Fleet Call public. The initial offering of 7.5 million shares raised $112.5 million, which was used to fund construction of the company's first network cell site in Los Angeles. Fleet Call also got $345 million in equipment financing from Motorola, Northern Telecom, and Matsushita. Finally, Fleet Call got a $230 million investment commitment from Comcast, a large cable television provider with significant cellular operations, in exchange for a 30 percent interest in the company.

Investor interest in Fleet Call increased dramatically when details of the company's plans—and information about its partners—got out. Share prices nearly doubled as investors clamored to get in on the business.

The company completed work on its Los Angeles cell site in May of 1992, using a system that operated in the 800-megahertz band. This frequency could accommodate mobile phone service, two-way radio dispatching, alphanumeric paging and messaging, and dozens of other future applications—all clearly beyond the capability of conventional cellular systems. In addition, the combined functionality of the Fleet Call system would allow customers to receive a single bill for paging, cellular, and mobile data services, rather than the three they would receive under the existing systems.

The only downside to Fleet Call's system was that it was incompatible with other cellular networks, precluding "handoffs" to and from other cellular operators outside Fleet Call's service territory. Recognizing that Californians are married to their cars and spend hours on freeways, Fleet Call expanded the Los Angeles site to cover Santa Barbara, Palm Springs, and San Diego County. Plans were expanded to provide seamless service throughout California by mid-1994. The company also turned its system incompatibility into a marketing advantage by touting its superior privacy and anti-billing fraud characteristics.

Much of Fleet Call's expansion was made possible by its December 1992 merger with Dispatch Communications, another mobile radio company with the same plans as Fleet Call. The combined operation gave Fleet Call coverage in nine of the country's 10 largest markets, covering a potential user population of 95.5 million people.

The company scored something of a coup in January 1993 when it hired John Caner, director of wireless data development at PacTel Cellular. In Fleet Call, Caner saw an opportunity to build an entirely new communications system without the burden of aging legacy systems and Bell-related regulatory problems.

In March of 1993 the company changed its name to Nextel Communications. The Fleet Call name was deemed inappropriate because it referred to the old radio dispatch technologies. By contrast, "Nextel" cleverly suggested to consumers that, with wave after wave of new technologies, this was the next new thing in communications.

The company established numerous service trials in California during 1993, offering service to 500 customers. This enabled the company to conduct live testing of the system, establish traffic engineering patterns and perfect billing mechanisms. A great deal had been written about Nextel up to this point, but the company didn't actually begin to offer service until August of 1993, when the system was formally "turned on."

Nextel remained on the hunt for radio bands in new territories, but many of these had already been snapped up by other companies. However, few of these companies had developed as far as Nextel, making them prime merger targets for the company.

In October of 1993 Nextel concluded merger agreements with Questar Telecom and a subsidiary of Advanced MobilComm that brought the company operating rights in the strategically important San Diego region, as well as in Utah, Nevada, and other mountain states. Through a second merger agreement,

Nextel exchanged certain of its Rocky Mountain and Midwestern SMR properties for an equity stake in CenCall Communications. The agreement gave CenCall access to Nextel's digital communications technology, and Nextel gained a 37 percent stake in CenCall. Through a third merger agreement that same month, Nextel absorbed the operations of PowerFone Holdings, a company with SMR properties in Cleveland, Cincinnati, Pittsburgh, and other Midwestern markets. These developments greatly increased Nextel's service area and potential customer base.

Perhaps the most important acquisition made by Nextel came in November of 1993, when the company acquired the SMR licenses of Motorola in exchange for an additional interest in the company. These properties encompassed 21 states, covering 180 million "pops," or potential customers. This transaction positioned Nextel to seriously challenge cellular communications duopolies across the country.

This flurry of activity late in 1993 significantly diluted Nextel's investor base but succeeded in establishing a platform in which the company could offer nearly seamless digital mobile radio services nationwide.

The company's largest potential competitor came not from within the digital mobil radio market but, understandably, from the conventional cellular market. Numerous cellular companies formed joint marketing agreements in an effort to build nationwide brand identities.

The competitive landscape came into clearer focus in 1993 when AT&T announced its intention to acquire McCaw, the nation's largest cellular communications company. In addition to providing AT&T a position in the rapidly growing mobile communications market, McCaw would give AT&T direct access to millions of local telephone customers. As a long distance company, AT&T was dependent on local telephone companies for access to these customers. Additionally, by merging with AT&T, McCaw would have access to AT&T's substantial financial and technological resources.

By contrast, although Nextel had substantial backing from leading equipment manufacturers, it had as yet no link-up with a long distance provider. In order to ensure nationwide coverage to rival the AT&T/McCaw combination, Nextel began negotiations with MCI, the nation's second-largest long distance carrier and AT&T's fiercest rival. A formal alliance between Nextel and MCI was announced on February 28, 1994. MCI purchased a 17 percent stake in Nextel for the right to market wireless phone, data, and dispatching services under the MCI brand name, using the Nextel network.

Although Nextel lost $10 million on only $34 million in revenue during 1993, its market value was a staggering $9.5 billion. This indication of investor confidence was based on the formidability of Nextel's emerging alliances.

Perhaps the greatest asset to Nextel's network came from its involvement with Motorola, which provided the advanced digital cellular technology under which the system would operate. By using the Motorola Integrated Radio System, or MIRS, Nextel entered the communications market with a state-of-the-art platform that provided far greater capabilities than any existing system. In fact, cellular companies remained divided over which digital system to use in their own upgrade from analog to digital technology, delaying implementation of systems that could compete effectively with MIRS.

The Nextel consortium contained every element necessary to ensure successful entry into the wireless market. Nextel possessed the frequency licenses and network equipment, Motorola the engineering and manufacturing expertise, Comcast the experience with cellular networks, and MCI the long distance capability, billing systems and, perhaps most importantly, a nationally recognized and highly valued brand name.

The alliance was particularly important to MCI, which early in 1994 unveiled a new business strategy called *networkMCI*. As part of this strategy, the long distance carrier announced its intention to establish partnerships with other communications and information industry companies to provide seamless voice and data communication to customers anywhere. With about 95 percent of the nation's population covered by the Nextel system, MCI possesses the ability to market communication services directly to nearly 250 million people. By contrast, companies such as Sprint and AT&T are relatively restricted to the limited coverage of their cellular systems or obliged to deal with local telephone companies and competing cellular operators for access to customers.

It is difficult to predict where Nextel will take MCI and its other partners, but with the wireless communications market growing at more than 20 percent annually, even conservative estimates indicate that the venture will be tremendously successful. The only possible negative variable lies in the ability of the alliance's competitors to establish an equally expansive digital system on an equally ambitious schedule. It will, however, take several years for Nextel to build its network to a point where it can actually deliver services to the market. As this process continues, Nextel will surely be an important company to observe.

Further Reading:

"Fleet Call Changes Name," *Wall Street Journal,* March 24, 1993, p. A5.
"Fleet Joins Communications Consortium," *Journal of Commerce and Commercial,* March 2, 1992, p. 3B.
"A Leap into the Digital Future," *Management Review,* October 23, 1993, p. 24.
"Motorola to Sell 42% of Licenses in Mobile Radio," *Wall Street Journal,* October 25, 1993, p. A2.
"Nextel Communications, Inc.," *Los Angeles Times,* November 19, 1993, p. D2.
"Nextel Goes Digital, Mounts Threat to Cellular Providers," *Telephony,* September 6, 1993, p. 8.
"Nextel Keeps Making the Right Connections," *Business Week,* March 14, 1994, p. 31.
"Nextel, Motorola Deal Throws Open Wireless Market," *Business Marketing,* December 1993, p. 4.
"Nextel's Deal with Motorola Advances Wireless Vision," *Wall Street Journal,* November 19, 1993, p. B4.
"The Taxicab as Phone Company," *Forbes,* January 6, 1992, p. 41.
"A Wireless Communications Wonder," *Forbes,* April 12, 1993, p. 55.

—John Simley

NL Industries, Inc.

3000 North Sam Houston Parkway East
P.O. Box 60087
Houston, Texas 77205
U.S.A.
(713) 987-5000
Fax: (713) 987-5189

Public Company
Incorporated: 1891 as National Lead Company
Employees: 3,600
Sales: $893.4 million
Stock Exchanges: New York
SICs: 2816 Inorganic Pigments; 2819 Industrial Inorganic
    Chemicals Nec.

NL Industries, Inc. is one of America's largest manufacturers of titanium dioxide pigments, which are used to brighten and add opacity to paints, plastics, paper, textile dyes, and ceramic glazes. The company also produces rheological additives, which control the flow and leveling properties of paints, inks, greases, sealants, adhesives, and cosmetics. Having undergone several reorganizations during its history, as technological developments dictated changes in its markets, NL Industries came under the control of entrepeneur Harold Simmons in the late 1980s.

The history of NL Industries may be traced to 1891, when 25 lead mining and smelting operations, unable to compete with larger manufacturers by themselves, teamed up to form a general holding company called the National Lead Company. The parent organization ensured that each member company's resources were efficiently employed while effectively eliminating competition between the affiliates.

National Lead was primarily a mining company consisting of several dozen lead pits. The company quickly became one of the country's largest producers of bulk refined white and red lead and lead oxides, which it sold almost exclusively to foundries and paint manufacturers. During this time, white and red leads were commonly used in paint, providing a durable and inexpensive covering considered necessary for preserving wooden structures. When mixed with linseed oil, white lead helped the paint mixture hold other pigments; red leads proved the least expensive paints and became commonly used on barns and railroad structures.

National Lead marked several years of steady growth, and, because of its size and the constant demand for lead by paint companies, it withstood the commodity gluts and financial panics that destroyed its smaller competitors. The most serious challenge to the company's survival occurred during the Great Depression of the early 1930s, when most consumers could not afford paint, and demand for lead plummeted.

During this time, National Lead prepared to diversify, using whatever capital it could spare to invest in the rights to titanium mines. Titanium was discovered to have applications as a pigment, producing brighter whites and a clearer base for other pigments than was possible with lead. Moreover, titanium dioxide had applications in the manufacture of paper, denture material, ceramics, and even whitewall tires. National Lead set up a brokerage operation for the new product, becoming the country's largest supplier of the mineral. Thus, by 1934, when the national economy began to recover, National Lead was able to withstand declines in demand for lead and was prepared to take advantage of growth in the titanium market.

By 1939, National Lead had regained earnings stability. The following year, as the country began a modest armament program to meet the growing threat from Germany, titanium paints were increasingly used in upgrading military installations. At the onset of World War II in 1941, titanium was found valuable in strengthening steel and other metal alloys, and the company's chief product came under government control. Since National Lead remained a supplier rather than a mining operation, sales stalled. Nevertheless, at the end of the war, National Lead emerged as the leading dealer in titanium ores. Industrial uses of titanium increased, particularly in equipment for drilling oil wells, die castings, and metal bearings for the railroad and other industries. During this time, National Lead also entered the consumer market for titanium paints, creating a product line under the name Dutch Boy. Dutch Boy paints competed with other brands that contained mineral products supplied by National Lead.

In 1950, in order to strengthen and protect its leading position in the titanium ores market, National Lead entered into a partnership with Allegheny Ludlum Steel. Called the Titanium Metals Corporation of America, this joint venture developed new applications for titanium alloys, produced various grades of the product, and marketed both raw titanium and zinc alloys made with the mineral.

By the 1950s, National Lead supplied roughly 40 percent of the nation's titanium. Alloys made from the metal were used in aircraft, which were produced in tremendous numbers during the Korean War. When aircraft production was scaled back in the late 1950s, sales of titanium were buoyed by demand in the production of missiles and other weapons. Acquisitions during this time included Doehler-Jarvis, a die cast company acquired in 1953, and the R-N Corporation, acquired in 1957.

National Lead decided to widen the scope of its operations to include products useful in drilling for petroleum in the 1960s. The company's line of new products included muds—the lubricants used in drilling operations—as well as the alloys, drill bits, and other assemblies used in burrowing through thousands of feet of earth in search of oil deposits. As a result, National

Lead became a competitor of oilfield equipment suppliers like Schlumberger and Halliburton. Moreover, through the Titanium Metals Corporation, National Lead secured access to vast mineral reserves in the United States and Norway, and the company initiated its own mining operations. Thus, National Lead became involved in every aspect of the titanium industry: mining, refining, finishing and, in the case of Dutch Boy, retailing.

By 1964, paints, pigments, and oils comprised 38 percent of National Lead's business. Fabricated lead products, primarily used in the automotive industry, provided 23 percent of revenues, and die castings, zinc alloys, and metal forming dies accounted for 17 percent. Oil well drilling materials and bearings used by the railroad industry contributed the remainder. The company's agressive acquisition activity helped achieve this dynamic product line, but by the late 1960s, its increased holdings prompted criticism that the company had spread itself too thin.

By this time, National Lead's subsidiaries included: Morris P. Kirk & Sons and Pioneer Aluminum, companies engaged in the production of aluminum products for the aircraft industry; Baker Castor Oil, a farming operation that raised castor oil used in paint and cosmetics; and Enenco, Inc., a partnership with the National Dairy Products Corp., that produced a line of fatty amines for gelling agents used in paints and water softeners, as well as in the textile, oil, and mining industries.

The diversification of National Lead was strategically intended to consolidate as many applications for its products as possible under one management. However, the plan lead to an unmanageable diversification of its markets, as National Lead supplied products to oil companies, airplane builders, shirt makers, painters, and costmetic companies. Investors lost their enthusiasm for National Lead as its profitability began to slide. Once considered a growth company with glowing management, National Lead was finally seen for what it was: an industrial stock.

As a result, investors lost enthusiasm for the company, and profitability began to decline. The company's chairperson, Joseph Martino, curtailed the acquisition policy, and the decentralized management structure the company had maintained since its inception was reformed. Because it derived more than 60 percent of its income from titanium operations, National Lead became NL Industries on April 15, 1971. The following year, the company reorganized its operations, creating five divisions that oversaw operations in chemicals, metals, industrial specialties, pigments, and fabricated products. The company's paint and magnesium unit, including the Dutch Boy enterprise, and its Lake View Trust Savings Bank subsidiary continued to operate independently, in preparation for a possible spin-off.

Perhaps the greatest changes in NL Industries came after 1972, when Ray C. Adam, a former Mobil Oil executive, joined the company's management team. Well versed in the oilfield equipment business, Adam was convinced that this was the one area in which NL might enjoy faster growth. He began an effort to dispose of NL's non-core operations, maintaining that the company had attempted to be in too many businesses at once and that "the only thing NL didn't make was money." Replacing Martino as CEO in 1974, Adam sold off 38 of NL's 79 subsidi-

aries, including Dutch Boy, the bank, and a citrus peeling operation. He also sold off the company's magnesium and lead businesses, declaring that NL should stand for "no lead."

The sales yielded more than $400 million, and, with the proceeds, Adam invested heavily in oilfield equipment manufacturing and related services. This proved timely, as the OPEC cartel's 1973 embargo created a worldwide energy crisis that caused oil companies to renew oil exploration on a massive scale.

Central to Adam's strategy was NL's 1976 acquisition of the Rucker Company, a leading manufacturer of oil tools, drill bits, blowout preventers, hydraulic equipment, and drilling muds, for $165 million. Adam retained NL's metals and chemical groups, which provided steady income that could be used for further investment in the petroleum equipment business.

By 1980, the petroleum services division accounted for more than 50 percent of NL Industries' sales and two-thirds of its profits. The chemicals group, which included titanium products, contributed 30 percent of sales, while the metals operation comprised 24 percent of sales. Under Adam, the company had undergone radical transformations; with 5,000 fewer employees, it was seven times more profitable.

In the mid-1980s, Adam was succeeded as CEO by Theodore Rogers, during a slump in the oil industry that severely affected NL's oilfield support business. Failing to downsize quickly, the company's oil division incurred a $324 million operating loss, prompting a rapid undervaluation of the company. This undervaluation—along with the clean-up of NL's debt and streamlining of operations facilitated by Adam—created a tremendous opportunity for a corporate raider.

Harold C. Simmons, a relentlessly inventive takeover artist with a brilliant record of acquiring undervalued companies and turning them around, was aware of an unusual company bylaw dictating that the board not consider more than one tender offer at a time, thereby preventing the company's shares from being put into play (a policy enacted by NL to rebuke an earlier bid by Coniston Partners). Simmons purposely triggered NL's takeover defense mechanism by purchasing 20 percent of the company's shares. Rather than amending its policy to accomodate other investors who might have helped stave off the hostile takeover, NL's board launched its own stock repurchase plan and sought a court enjoinder to prevent Simmons from buying any more shares. To fund the repurchase plan, the board issued tracking stock of the NL's chemical operations which traded separately from NL's common shares.

Simmons defeated NL in court, winning the right to buy a majority of the company's shares, and, after only eight weeks, he emerged with a 51 percent share of NL, as well as a 20 percent share of NL Chemicals. Moreover, he achieved this level of control with an investment of only $250 million, about a third as much as his original tender offer.

The investment vehicle for Simmons' investment in NL was Valhi, Inc., a conglomeration of diverse businesses, such as refined sugar, forest products, hardware products, and fast food chains, that had no obvious synergies with NL. Simmons proposed a merger of Valhi with NL, but was prevented by outside directors from acquiring the 49 percent of the company not already owned by Valhi. Simmons did finally win board approval to spin off the company's oilfield services subsidiary, Baroid Corporation, and redeem the tracking stock of NL's chemical operations. Following the spinoff and redemption, Valhi's ownership in NL was 66 percent. Valhi's control of NL gave Simmons access to about $1 billion in loans for further acquisitions.

NL's operations were subsequently revamped by Simmons and his management team, which included his long-time associate J. Landis Martin, who became president and CEO of NL. NL was divided into two operating divisions, Kronos, which encompassed the titanium dioxide business, and Rheox, which supplied solvent- and water-based rheological additives for paints, inks, lubricants, sealants, adhesives and cosmetics.

In 1993, NL Industries remained an extremely vital player in the titanium and rheological additive markets. The company established a new titanium dioxide pigments plant at Lake Charles, Louisiana—the first such facility to be built in America since 1979. To help pay down the substantial debt incurred to build the facility, NL negotiated the sale of 50 percent of the operation to Imperial Chemical Industries, PLC (ICI) for $200 million. Some analysts suggested that further cooperation between NL and ICI might provide new competitive opportunities for NL's titanium operations in Europe, where much of the Kronos division is headquartered.

Principal Subsidiaries: Rheox, Inc.; Abbey Chemicals, Ltd. (Scotland; 70%); Bentone-Chemie GmbH (Germany; 70%); Kronos, Inc.; Kronos International, Inc. (Germany); Kronos-Titan GmbH (Germany); Kronos Titan A/S (Norway); Kronos Canada, Inc.; Kronos World Services, S.A./N.V. (Belgium); Kronos Europe S.A./N.V. (Belgium/Netherlands); Kronos Lou-isiana, Inc.; Kronos UK, Ltd.; Societe Industrielle du Titan, S.A. (France; 93%); Titania A/S (Norway).

Further Reading:

Brockinton, Langdon, "Simmons Takes on a Bite of Georgia Gulf," *Chemical Week,* July 12, 1989, pp. 12–13.

Brown, Paul B., "Life without Dutch Boy," *Forbes,* July 20, 1981, pp. 40–42.

Kelly, Kevin, "If Simmons Boards Lockheed, Can He Fly It," *Business Week,* April 2, 1990, pp. 77–78.

Marcial, Gene G., "Harold Simmons is Set to Roll Another Seven," *Business Week,* October 5, 1987, p. 106.

Mason, Todd, and Jim Hartoel, "Meet Harold Simmons: Mr. Ice Guy," *Business Week,* September 1, 1986, pp. 74–76.

Mason, Todd, "Harold Simmons is Coming Out to Play Again," *Business Week,* January 9, 1989, pp. 44–46.

Morris, Gregory, "Still on NL's Mind," *Chemical Week,* February 28, 1990, p. 11.

"National Lead to Paint Bright Profits Picture," *Barron's,* July 27, 1964, p. 20.

"A New Look at National Lead," *Financial World,* September 11, 1963, pp. 10–11.

"NL Industries Lines Up in Five Product Rows," *Chemical Marketing Reporter,* October 2, 1972, p. 22.

"NL Industries, Rucker Reach Merger Accord," *Wall Street Journal,* September 8, 1976, p. 4.

Robinson, Charles, "National Lead and American Smelting & Refining," *Magazine of Wall Street,* February 8, 1964, pp. 526–28.

Rowe, Frederick, E., Jr., "The Harold Simmons Bet," *Forbes,* August 2, 1993, p. 148.

"Searching for a New Multiple," *Financial World,* April 15, 1980, pp. 36–37.

"The Worm Turns," *Forbes,* January 1, 1961, pp. 82–84.

"Good—But Not That Good," *Forbes,* March 1, 1967, pp. 52–53.

Zukosky, Jerome, "NL's Raider Gets His Prize—Minus a Few Marbles," *Business Week,* August 25, 1986, p. 37.

—John Simley

Norsk Hydro A.S.

Bygdøy allé 2,
N-0240, Oslo 2
Norway
(47) 243-2100
Fax: (47) 243-2725

U.S. Headquarters:
Norsk Hydro U.S.A. Inc.
800 Third Ave.
New York, New York 10022-7671
(212) 688-6606
Fax: (212) 750-1252

Public Company (51% owned by Kingdom of Norway)
Incorporated: 1905 as Norsk Hydro-Elektrisk Kvaelstofak-
tieselskab (Norwegian Hydro-Electric Nitrogen Corporation)
Employees: 34,957
Sales: NOK 58,06 billion (1992)
Stock Exchanges: New York
SICs: 2873 Nitrogenous Fertilizers; 2879 Pesticides and Agri-
cultural Chemicals, Nec; 3354 Aluminum Extruded Products;
2821 Plastics Materials and Synthetic Resins, Synthetic Rubber,
Cellulosic & Other Manmade Fibers, Except Glass; 2834 Phar-
maceutical and Biological Research; 1311 Crude Petroleum and
Natural Gas; 1321 Natural Gas Liquids

Norsk Hydro was Norway's largest publicly owned industrial
group in the early 1990s, with multinational activities in the
production of fertilizers, light metals aluminum and magnesium, petrochemical raw materials and plastics, industrial
chemicals, and oil and gas. The company also controlled interests in aquaculture, biomedicine and pharmaceutical research,
and hydroelectricity. Hydro's head offices were located in
Norway and 51 percent of the company was owned by the
Kingdom of Norway. Ninety percent of sales were made to
international markets, with approximately 83 percent of sales
made to western European countries, including Norway. During
the 1990s, the company made efforts to expand sales in such
regions as Vietnam, Russia, Sri Lanka, and the United States.

Norsk Hydro was founded in 1905 by Norwegian entrepreneurs
Sam Eyde and Kristian Birkeland as Norsk Hydro-Elektrisk
Kvaelstofaktieselskap (Norwegian Hydro-Electric Nitrogen
Corporation). Originally, the company exploited the hydro-
electric resources of waterfalls to generate electricity used in the
production of nitrogen fertilizers. Initial output was mostly limited to Scandinavian markets until after the World War II, when
the Norwegian government took a 48 percent stake in the company and ushered in an era of multinational expansion and
diversification. In 1969, the company name changed to Norsk
Hydro A.S. By the 1990s, the company's size justified a decentralized organization plan grouping the company into four business segments, each serving as the strategic and financial center
for its composite divisions: agriculture, oil and gas, light metals,
and petrochemicals. Combining these segments with a growing
number of other activities—from alginate production to pharmaceutical research, seafood, and insurance—Hydro proved
that its origins in fertilizers laid fertile ground for almost a
century of lush business growth.

Hydro's original business continued to play a leading role in the
company's agriculture segment. By the 1990s, Hydro had become a western European leader in the production and sale of
mineral fertilizers. Principal ammonia and fertilizer production
plants were located in Norway, Germany, France, the Netherlands, the United Kingdom, Trinidad, and Tobago, with additional partnerships in Qatar and the United States. In addition to
the marketing and distribution of fertilizers in over 100 countries, the agriculture segment also produced a wide variety of
industrial gases and chemical products—mostly related to fertilizer manufacture—through its industrial chemicals division.

Hydro's oil and gas segment began its rapid ascent after the
discovery of oil and gas in the Ekofisk field in 1969, giving the
company interests in roughly two-thirds of the wells drilled on
the Norwegian shelf by the early 1990s. Gas and oil production
expanded beyond the Ekofisk and Frigg fields developed in the
1970s, into the Gullfaks and Oseberg fields in the late 1980s,
and into development of other fields, including the Troll
Oseborg Gas Injection Project offshore, and the Brage, Snorre,
Sleipner East, Sleipner West, and Heidrun oilfields, as well as
growing interests in Denmark, the Netherlands, Egypt, Gabon,
Angola, Syria, Yemen, Namibia, Vietnam, and Russia. The oil
and gas segment also marketed and distributed its products
throughout Scandinavia.

Hydro's light metals segment included hydro aluminum and the
magnesium and energy divisions. Metal was produced in the
form of rolling slabs, billets, wire rod, and foundry alloys, as
well as semi-fabricated extruded and rolled products, with
particular emphasis on aluminum and magnesium extruded
products for such industries as automobile manufacturing. Just
as the division's metal production was increasingly used for
Hydro's own semi-fabricating facilities, most of its hydro-electric energy fueled Hydro's own internal operations.

In the petrochemical segment, Hydro entered the 1990s as a
leading producer of ethylene, plastic resin polyvinyl chloride
(PVC), and vinyl chloride monomer (VCM), the main ingredient in PVC production. In addition to its PVC leadership in
Scandinavia and the United Kingdom—with a 1992 market
share of about 40 percent and 25 percent respectively—Hydro
manufactured and sold VCM to other PVC producers in Europe
and the Far East. With the growing global PVC market at about
18.4 million tonnes in 1992, and with studies suggesting that the
material was environmentally preferable to many other plastic

products, PVC production augured positive growth for the petrochemical segment, despite lagging sales in the early 1990s.

Despite Hydro's tremendous diversity by the 1990s, the company never lost sight of its historical origins in fertilizers. In fact, the initial objective of diversification into oil and gas was to garner raw materials for fertilizer production; subsequent growth into light metals, petrochemicals, pharmaceutical research, and seafood development—yielding products from PVC pipes to packaged salmon—also branched out of fertilizer interests.

As early as World War II, Hydro's fertilizer activities fueled widely divergent enterprises; in this case, German occupying forces made use of the company's plant in Rjukan, Norway to produce heavy water (deuterium oxide) for use in nuclear reactor research. The Rjukan plant produced ammonia, which yielded heavy water as a by-product. With its use as an atomic brake fluid, heavy water was a key tool in atomic fission experiments and the development of the atomic bomb, a device that was considered a key determinant for the outcome of the war. Fearing German access to heavy water for their escalating research program, the Allies chose 11 saboteurs, trained them in the British Isles, and on February 1943 parachuted them onto the Hardanger plateau, from where the renowned "Heroes of Telemark" descended to Vemork by combining skiing, treacherous climbing, and sheer willpower to destroy the plant. Though the definitive impact of the sabotage on the outcome of the war remained a point of historical debate, the mission's unquestionable adventure appeal energized numerous books and documentaries and two feature films.

World War II brought far more change than the destruction of the Rjukan plant. After the bombing of Hydro's Herøya plants in 1944 and the financial losses that resulted, the company moved to consolidate much of its business in Norway and to expand the scope of its interests. While 97 percent of the company's shares were owned by foreigners at the outbreak of World War II, after armistice the Norwegian government seized German holdings and took a 48 percent stake, which along with additional purchases and reparation rose to a 51 percent government stake in the company.

Starting in the 1950s, Hydro expanded into a number of new businesses, both directly and indirectly related to its core fertilizer production. In 1951, Hydro began production of magnesium metal and polyvinyl. In 1967, the company opened an aluminum reduction plant and semi-fabricating facility at Karmoy, Norway, and constructed the Rldal-Suldal hydro-electric facility to power the Karmoy works. The company also made preliminary steps in seafood with its fish-arming subsidiary, MOWI, in 1969. With Hydro's 1965 and 1967 opening of two Norwegian ammonia plants using naphtha (a liquid mixture of hydrocarbons distilled from petroleum, coal tar, and other hydrocarbon-rich substances) and heavy fuel oil feedstocks in the production process, the company became dependent on outside suppliers of raw materials. Attempting to supply its own hydrogen for ammonia production, Hydro began investigating opportunities in gas and oil production in the late 1960s. These initiatives, paired with a new management strategy starting in the late 1960s, spurred tremendous growth that transformed the company into an industrial group.

Under the leadership of Johan B. Holte (president from 1967 to 1977 and chairman of the board from 1977 to 1985), Hydro restructured not only its policies on employee relations but its overall organizational structure. Holte set new standards for cooperation between management and workforce at all levels of Hydro; and those levels multiplied rapidly, as Holte initiated aggressive moves to expand and diversify core business beyond domestic fertilizers and into light metals, gas and oil, and eventually other segments on an international scale. In a 1990 retrospective article, Holte's successor as president, Odd Narud, summarized the organizational strategy for Hydro's in-house publication, *Profile Magazine*: "The company has concentrated on growth in its core areas; agriculture, oil and gas, light metals and petrochemicals. It is the sustained efforts to improve in these areas which have created the basis for serious involvement in new product areas."

By the early 1970s, oil and gas constituted one such "new product area." In 1965, when Norway granted licenses for offshore petroleum exploration, Hydro obtained concessions and formed partnerships with foreign companies on numerous fields. In 1969, the Phillips Petroleum-operated drilling rig *Ocean Viking* struck oil in the Ekofisk field, in which Hydro owned a share. The company's success with North Sea oil and gas continued with the Elf-Aquitaine-operated Frigg discovery in 1971. In an attempt to combine Hydro's success with a stronger petroleum policy, the Norwegian government increased its share of Hydro to 51 percent and created Statoil, a state-owned company, in 1972. Hydro began operating its oil refinery at Mongsted, Norway in 1975. Experience from these projects in the 1960s and 1970s would prove extremely beneficial for Hydro's innovative contributions to oil and gas development in the late 1980s and early 1990s.

Building on its natural gas liquids resources, Hydro began investing large amounts of capital in the petrochemical industry in the early 1970s, with the decision to build the Rafnes petrochemical complex, which began production of ethylene and vinyl chloride in 1978. Falling in the wake of the international oil crises, however, Hydro's petrochemical activity incurred losses until the late 1980s. Nevertheless, the company implemented ongoing growth strategies through the 1980s: in 1982, the company formed Norsk Hydro Polymers Ltd., one of two PVC manufacturers in the United Kingdom, after acquiring BIP Vinyl's Aycliffe facility and the last 50 percent of Vinatex; in 1984 the company acquired KemaNord's facility in Stenungsund, Sweden, and formed Norsk Hydro Plast AB; in 1987 Hydro bought 47 percent of Singapore Polymer to better target Asian markets (increasing its holdings to 60 percent a year later); and in 1989, Hydro Polymères was formed in France to produce PVC and engineering plastics in continental Europe. By 1990, the company announced development of a new PVC plant at Rafnes. And in March of 1991, Hydro announced a joint venture with BFGoodrich Company to market vinyl-based injection-molding compounds for use in applications such as business machine components, telecommunications equipment, and construction products.

The company also covered new ground in fertilizers, with the acquisition of NSM, a Dutch firm (1979); 75 percent of the Swedish firm, Supra (1981); a British firm renamed Norsk Hydro Fertilizers Ltd. (1982); a West German company renamed Ruhr Stickstoff AG (1985); and 80 percent of the French Compagnie Francaise de L'Azote (1986), along with the remaining 20 percent the following year. After restructuring its fertilizer division in 1987, the other divisions in Hydro's agriculture segment shifted as well, with sales of industrial gas operations in Finland and Sweden and formation of a new company, Hydrogas AS, the largest company in the industrial chemicals division. By 1990, Hydrogas sold the whole range of industrial gases in Norway and held about 10 percent of the carbon dioxide market in Europe. In 1991, the agricultural segment continued to acquire fertilizer facilities: one in Rostock, Germany; another in Green Bay, Florida; another in the United Kingdom; and three ammonia plants facilities in Trinidad and Tobago.

Hydro expanded its light metals segment in the 1980s. First it acquired five aluminum extrusion plants in Europe from Alcan Aluminum Limited. Then, in 1986, the group merged with Ardal og Sunndal Verk AS (ÅSV), a government-controlled aluminum company, and consolidated its interests in May 1988, renaming the merged entity Hydro Aluminum AS (ranked as the world's fifth largest aluminum company in 1990, with sales of 15 billion NOK). Hydro positioned its growing aluminum extrusion business to supply growing demand in strategic market segments, such as the automotive industry (a separate automotive aluminum unit was established in Munich, the German automotive capital, in 1990) and tubing for air conditioning systems in the United States. The company's purchase of Bohn Aluminum & Brass in 1990 further strengthened its position in the American extruded products market.

Just as aluminum's light weight and high strength characteristics made it suitable for automotive parts ranging from frames to tires, magnesium was characterized by similarly useful formability and lightness. In addition to the construction of a new magnesium plant in Canada in 1986, Hydro collaborated with the automotive industry in the development of magnesium components. By the early 1990s, these efforts were disrupted by a stagnant economy—which led to depressed prices and high inventories of magnesium—and by reverberations from the United States Commerce Department International Trade Administration's 1991 claim that Canada and Norway were unfairly dumping magnesium in the United States, and its imposition of anti-dumping duties to deter continuation of the practice. That same year, Hydro announced reduction of magnesium production in its Norwegian and Canadian plants, resulting in 1992 levels between 25,000 and 30,000 tonnes less than 1991 levels.

Expansion and internationalization of its core businesses increasingly exposed Hydro to opportunities in the less related, though no less promising spectrum of "other activities," including seafood and salmon farming and processing. While Hydro's involvement in salmon farming began with its 50 percent acquisition of MOWI in 1959, not until the end of the 1970s did Hydro's stake reach 75 percent, and not until 1980 did MOWI operate internationally. In 1980, MOWI acquired 44 percent of the Icelandic ocean ranching company, ISNO, and 75 percent of Fanad Ireland, a near-bankrupt trout farming operation that became a world leader in fish farming. Other developments included the acquisition of Golden Sea Produce (1983), with Sea Life Centre aquariums in Scotland and England; new

fish farms at Haverøy and Turøy (1985 to 1986); the establishment of the Prodemar turbot farming facilities, in cooperation with the Bank of Bilbao in Spain (1987); the establishment of Biomar, a joint venture between Norsk Hydro, Dyno Industrier a.s., and KFK (1988); and the acquisition of the Danish fish smoking companies Pescadana and B&H Fish Export (1990).

Starting in the mid-1980s, Hydro also aspired to become a leading company in bio-polymers, fatty acids, and pharmaceuticals. A series of acquisitions toward that end started in 1985, when Hydro bought a majority share (and later acquired over 90 percent) of Carmeda AB, a producer of biologically active surfaces for medical equipment. In 1986, Hydro Pharma AS was established to develop pharmaceutical activities, including the products of drug delivery systems by Biogram AB, diagnostic ultrasound equipment by Vingmed Sound A/S, enzymes by Marine Biochemicals, and fatty acids by Johan C. Martens. In 1987, Hydro Pharma acquired all the shares of NAF Laboratories, a leading Norwegian pharmaceuticals supplier. Hydro's Pharma and Biomarine Divisions were merged into the Biomedical Division in 1988. And in 1989, the company increased its stake in Securus, a company listed on the Oslo stock exchange, to 77.3 percent. By 1990, these diversified activities were all brought under one umbrella with Securus's takeover of Hydro's Biomedical division.

The 1980s represented a period of growth that virtually transformed Hydro into a multinational giant. The company's operating revenue of 14 billion kroner in 1980 soared to over 60 billion in 1990; its 13,000 employees increased to 42,000 over the same period.

A picture of Hydro with nothing but such positive growth figures, however, would be misleading; suffering from international economic recession in the late 1980s and early 1990s—compounded by low-priced competition from the changing economies of Eastern Europe and the former Soviet Union in areas such as light metals and fertilizers—Hydro was forced to consolidate operations and manage cost reductions to remain competitive into the 1990s. As early as April of 1991, efforts began to pay off, with Moody's upgrading Hydro senior debt ratings to A3 from Baa1, reflecting the company's good positioning in the face of possible economic slowing in Western Europe. In 1992, the company president, Egil Myklebust, announced a two-year plan to reduce fixed costs by NOK 1,500 million. In the third quarter of 1991, the magnesium and fertilizer businesses were extensively restructured, with plant closures and rationalization of Swedish fertilizer interests. In December 1991, Hydro's UK North Sea oil and gas interests were sold to British Borneo Petroleum, and Dutch exploration and production assets were also put up for sale. In June of that year, Japan's Nippon Steel Chemical Co. and Nichimen Corp. jointly took over the resin compound manufacturing division of Hydro's chemical division.

In the early 1990s, Hydro also implemented a strategy of internationalization in its core businesses. In 1992, the company's oil and gas division was made operator for the first offshore license in Namibia. It was also awarded blocks in Vietnam, Angola, and continued to negotiate numerous feasibility contracts in Russia (such as the 1990 gas discovery in Schtockmanskoye in the Barents Sea). In 1993, Hydrogas A.S.

negotiated the acquisition of 70 percent of the Polish state-owned Plgaz Gdansk as part of that firm's privatization process.

Major gas and oil development continued to distinguish Hydro as a major technical innovator and a big player in improved petroleum markets projected for the later 1990s. Hydro applied state-of-the-art technology as an operator in the Oseberg field, which quickly became a major source of oil and gas after it began production in 1988. Building on Oseberg's transport system, the Troll-Oseberg gas injection (TOGI) project, and later on the Troll oil project, Hydro demonstrated the advantages of remote-controlled subsea systems to develop and control deep-water projects. Much of the technology was used in the Phillips Petroleum Company's 1993 project to plan and build new facilities called Ekofisk II at the Ekofisk field, of which Hydro held a 6.7 percent share. After acquiring 300 Danish gasoline stations from UNO-X in 1990 and Mobil Oil's Norwegian marketing and distribution system in 1992, Hydro also became a major player in on-land gas and oil marketing.

Moving into the mid-1990s, the outlook for the Hydro group would depend on many complex factors: the success of the fertilizer industry in a European agriculture scene under the flux of freer world markets; the long-term demand for Norwegian gas and oil; the demand for PVC products and their resistance to concerns over their environmental impact; and the continuation of research and technology to develop new products and technologies in the group's strategic segments. Hydro's power lay largely in its diversity; and that diversity stemmed from years of success related to its original success in hydro-electric power. If the adage that power begets power holds true, the Hydro industrial group will remain as a powerful and growing force in multinational agriculture, light metals, oil and gas, petrochemicals, and beyond.

Principal Subsidiaries: Freia Marabou a.s. (Norway; 38.3%); Dyno Industrier a.s. (Norway; 39.2%); Hydrogas a.s. (Norway); Hydro Aluminum a.s. (Norway); Pharmala a.s. (Norway); Securus Industrier A-S (Norway); Hydro Seafood A/S (Norway); Ammonia A/S (Denmark; 29%); Norsk Hydro Azote SA (France); Hydra Supra AB (Sweden; 95%); Hydro Aluminum Automotive Inc. (USA).

Further Reading:

"BFGoodrich and Norsk Hydro Complete Formation of Joint Venture," *PR Newswire,* March 21, 1991.

"ITA Preliminary Finds Canada and Norway Are Dumping Magnesium," *International Trade Reporter,* February 19, 1992, p. 308.

"Japanese Firms to Buy Resin Division of Norwegian Corp.," *Agence France Presse,* June 14, 1991.

Norsk Hydro a.s., "Hydro Between 80 and 90," *Profile Magazine,* December 1990.

"Norsk Hydro in the Polish Privatization Process," *Warsaw Voice,* July 25, 1993.

"Norsk Hydro Reports Stronger Third Quarter," *Business Wire,* October 25, 1993.

"Phillips Norway Group Submits Plan for Long-term Ekofisk Operation," *Business Wire,* July 1, 1993.

"U.S.S.R. Joint Venturing Offshore Areas," *Offshore,* November, 1990, p. 27.

—Kerstan Cohen

Northern Foods PLC

Beverley House
St. Stephen's Square
Hull HU1 3XG
North Humberside
United Kingdom
(0482) 25432
Fax: (0482) 226136

Public Company
Incorporated: 1949 as Northern Dairies
Employees: 30,219
Sales: £2.02 billion
Stock Exchanges: London
SICs: 6711 Holding Companies; 2026 Fluid Milk; 2021
   Creamery Butter; 2013 Sausages and Other Prepared Meat
   Products; 2051 Bread and Other Bakery Products; 2041
   Flour and Other Grain Mill Products

Northern Foods is one of the United Kingdom's leading manufacturers of high-quality fresh foods, supplying the country's preeminent retail outlets. It has the reputation of being one of the most adventurous, idiosyncratic, and successful companies in the United Kingdom. Its oddball reputation is perhaps due more to the high-profile personalities of the company's leaders—whose left-leaning politics and cheerful candor are deemed eccentric in the United Kingdom's conservative business climate—than to Northern Foods' track record of steady, respectable growth.

In 1932 Alec Horsley joined his father's condensed milk business, Pape and Co., Ltd., a small Hull-based concern importing Dutch condensed milk for wholesale. From the beginning, however, Horsley was convinced that strength lay in size; he was eager to expand and saw his opportunity in 1936. Amid the growing threat of war and rumors that new import duties might affect their business, Horsley, with his father's support, determined to change the focus of the business to production of their own supply. To that end he convened a meeting with six other small dairy firms in Hull, suggesting that they should merge for their mutual benefit. Only one of the six proved interested: Southwick's Dairies, a wholesale and manufacturing concern. The two entered into a partnership with the object of building their own condensery. Foreshadowing the energy and determination which were to characterize the growth of Northern

Foods, Horsley and his partner managed to choose the site, prepare the plant, and build the factory in only four and a half months. By October of 1937 the new factory at Holme-on-Spalding-Moor was up and running.

The onset of the war radically altered the face of the dairy trade in Britain. The need to change to meet wartime conditions proved fatal to many small dairies, but Horsley, a reformer at heart and quick to see opportunity in adversity, eagerly adapted to and profited from the altered circumstances. Due to wartime shortages, the Ministry of Food discouraged the use of cans and sugar—necessary in the making of condensed milk—and supported the sale of liquid milk. Horsley therefore saw the need to move into retail, a shift he had long wanted to make but which had been resisted by his partner George Southwick.

The prewar system of doorstep delivery had been haphazard and circuitous. A dozen small dairies might service different addresses on the same street, then each travel separately to another neighborhood to make more deliveries. The wartime shortages of labor and material, particularly gasoline, made this complicated network of delivery routes unacceptable. The government suspended free competition and insisted upon "rationalization" of dairy delivery. Established routes were disrupted, sometimes drastically altered; in many cases small dairies were forced to completely swap their customers with other businesses.

Recognizing that the time of the small dairyman was over, Horsley embarked upon an energetic and ambitious campaign of expansion, acquiring other dairies one by one. The larger the business grew, the more attractive it became to small firms beset by the bombing (Hull was very hard hit during the war), the chronic shortages, and the difficulties of adapting to rationalization. As the firm expanded it actually became more efficient with each new addition, as Horsley chose the best dairies and plants when consolidating operations. By 1942 Horsley controlled a considerable network of retail and wholesale businesses scattered throughout Humberside and Yorkshire, and the retail end of the company was renamed Northern Dairies to reflect this (although the wholesale operations continued to be known by their individual names).

As the war progressed, Northern Dairies found itself in the enviable position of having to decline to take over several businesses due to the sheer volume of the requests for amalgamation. Horsley and his associates decreed that three of four conditions must be met before they could consider acquiring a business: (1) the town in which it was situated must be flat for ease of delivery; (2) the proposed firm had to be near enough to another of Northern Dairies' depots to allow for convenient exchange of plant or vehicles, or to act as a shadow dairy in areas where bombing was a problem; (3) there was to be no other sizable dairy in the area with the exception of the Co-operative; and (4) there had to be the possibility of future expansion in the area.

The wartime strategies which had proved so advantageous to Northern Dairies were equally successful after the war. Indeed, to a considerable extent the exigencies of wartime business provided the bedrock of the company's future corporate philosophy, particularly the importance of acquisition as well as organic growth and the significance of the concept of rationalization. Horsley established principles of rationalization with other large dairy concerns—in 1950 alone, for example, Northern Dairies sold its Sutherland trade to Craven Dairies in part exchange for its Middlesborough trade, struck a deal to avoid overlapping trade in County Durham, and exchanged Huddersfield and Barnsley for Mansfield in an agreement with Express Dairies. Northern Dairies' amalgamation with the Hull- and Bridlington-based Riley/Granger dairy group also happened in 1950.

Ironically, Riley/Granger, then two separate entities, had attended Horsley's meeting in 1936, when they had both declined to merge with Pape and Co. Riley's had at that time been the market leader in Hull. When it finally joined Northern Dairies in 1950 it was half the size of the company it had once rejected. This amalgamation, significant to Northern Dairies because of the size of the parties involved, was also important in that it brought the center of the company's operations, grown rather dispersed, back to its origins in Hull.

Expansion of product line was a natural corollary of Northern Dairies' growth; in 1946 it had entered the ice cream market through the acquisition of Kingston Ices and Harmers Ices, and soon expanded into cheese, curd, whey, and chocolate crumb. Nevertheless, the firm's original product of condensed milk was not neglected. As soon as the government allowed it after the war, Northern Dairies moved back into milk processing, expanding its condensing operations at Holme-on-Spalding-Moor, and in 1950 established another, more modern plant, able to condense 20,000 gallons per day as compared with the original plant's 8,000.

Northern Dairies became a public company in 1956. Its expansion continued, making its name a misnomer as the company moved into the Midlands and Northern Ireland. Northern Dairies expanded throughout the dairy trade, and its profits surpassed the one million mark by 1970. In that year Alec Horsley retired as chairman and was succeeded by his son Nicholas. Under second-generation leadership, Northern Dairies began its rapid expansion into new and lucrative fields of business. Cream cakes, yogurts, desserts, sandwiches, recipe dishes, pizza, pasta, meat, fish, soups, hors d'oeuvres, cheeses, fresh produce: throughout the 1970s and 1980s the product line continually expanded.

The year 1970 was a watershed for Northern Dairies in another highly significant way: a chance meeting sent the company onto a new and phenomenally successful path. Christopher Haskins—Alec Horsley's son-in-law, later to become chairman of Northern Foods after Nicholas Horsley stepped down—found himself sitting next to an executive from Marks and Spencer (the ubiquitous and well-respected department store with a high-quality, upmarket grocery division) on a plane: from their chat was built a successful and mutually rewarding business relationship.

Throughout the 1970s the relationship with Marks and Spencer was a major focus for the company, which was renamed Northern Foods in 1972 to reflect the expanding nature of its business. From its relatively humble beginnings as manufacturer of the St. Michael (Marks and Spencer's own brand) trifle, Northern Foods grew to become Marks and Spencer's biggest supplier,

employing its typical enthusiastic blend of acquisition and innovation. As part of this two-pronged approach, Northern Foods set out on a policy of acquiring existing suppliers to Marks and Spencer wherever it could (witness, for example, its purchase of Park Cakes in 1972 and Fox's Biscuits in 1977); equally, the company concentrated on creating new products for its favored customer: by 1988 Northern Foods was producing a range of 250 products for Marks and Spencer.

Northern Foods' unique business relationship with Marks and Spencer is best illustrated in the construction of the sophisticated Fenland Foods factory in 1986. As a gesture of its goodwill and enthusiasm, Northern Foods built this Marks and Spencer dedicated plant—at a cost of £8 million—before it had yet been established what products were to be made there. Echoing Alec Horsley's 1937 achievement with his first milk processing plant, Fenland Foods, which has been hailed as Europe's most advanced food factory, was built in 40 weeks—and was selling to Marks and Spencer three weeks later.

Northern Foods continued its dual policy of aggressive acquisition and organic growth into the 1990s, concentrating on its four main areas: dairy, convenience foods, meat products, and groceries. In a clear sign that it meant to stay true to its roots, the company acquired the dairy companies Express and Eden Vale in 1992, consolidating its position as the United Kingdom's leading liquid milk company, and holding 24 percent of the market in England and Wales. Doorstep delivery, although an anachronism in the modern world, remains a staple with Northern Foods, which serves some three million households throughout the country. Hedging its bets, the company is also the leading supplier of milk to U.K. supermarkets. Although the effects of the government's proposed abolition of the Milk Marketing Board in 1994 are far from clear, the company's move to supplying supermarkets will leave Northern Foods free to buy milk direct from purchasers. To that end, the company helped to establish the Northern Milk Partnership in 1993 as a means of negotiating collectively with dairy producers.

Northern Foods produces an extensive line of fresh convenience foods sold under the labels of the United Kingdom's most prominent retailers, including Marks and Spencer and supermarket giants Sainsbury's, Tesco, Safeway, and Gateway. The company's meat products range encompasses hot and cold meat pies, some sold as retailers' own labels and others under the well-known brand names Pork Farms, Bowyers, and Hollands. Northern Foods' grocery line is grandly named, considering it consisted in the mid-1990s primarily of biscuits, and would seem to signal plans for future expansion. The upmarket Fox's Biscuits are produced under their own brand name while the less expensive Elkes Biscuits generally produces for stores' private labels.

Rationalization remained a priority for Northern Foods in the 1990s, as the company sought to simplify and consolidate wherever possible, concentrating on the aggressive rationalization policies which made its fortune in the first place. The company has invested heavily in new facilities and technologies, and as a sideline of its main business Northern Foods operates its own chilled distribution services, for itself and for other food manufacturers, including a dedicated transport operation for Sainsbury's. Bread products are one new focus for the future, as the company began in the 1990s to expand into specialty bakeries and flour mills.

The company's rise has not been uniformly smooth; it has had its share of well-publicized (and ruefully admitted) fiascoes. Some of its forays into new lines of business have proved unwise. Its move into consumer finance with the purchase of British Credit Trust was initially profitable (at one point it accounted for 40 percent of the company's profits), but in the banking crisis of the mid-1970s it lost all its deposits and nearly went under, which came as "a bloody shock," according to chairman Chris Haskins. The company sold the British Credit Trust in 1978. A failed attempt to move into the brewing industry in 1972 strengthened the firm's subsequent resolve to stay within its bounds as a food company.

Particularly embarrassing, however, was Northern Foods' attempt to enter the American market with the acquisition of Bluebird Inc. and Keystone Foods Corporation in 1980 and 1982, respectively. Legal problems with the former and philosophical differences with the latter prompted Northern Foods to withdraw from the American market quickly. With characteristic forthrightness, Chris Haskins referred to the experience as Northern Foods' "American cock-up." A sortie into the chicken market with the 1986 acquisition of Mayhew Foods was equally unfortunate, preceding the first recorded falling-off of chicken consumption in the United Kingdom. The venture, Haskins admitted, "has been a disaster. . . . We will probably have to get rid of it."

Monumental though a few of its blunders have been, that there are so few in Northern Foods' astonishingly long list of acquisi-

tions—more than 40 new businesses between the 1970s and the 1990s—is testimony to its generally sound business principles and good judgment. Ironically for a company whose own name is never seen on its products, Northern Foods is the largest fresh food manufacturer in the United Kingdom. The company's 1993 sales figures elevated it to the coveted status of membership in the "two billion club," proving that Northern Foods' emphasis on continual product development, strategic acquisition, consistently high quality, and solid personal links with its customers are successful policies for the future.

Principal Subsidiaries: Batchelors Ltd.; Bowyers (Wiltshire) Ltd.; Convenience Foods Ltd.; Dale Farm Dairy Group Ltd.; Edmonds Eccles Cakes Ltd.; Express Dairy Ltd.; Falconis Ltd.; Fleur de Lys Pies Ltd.; Fox's Biscuits Ltd.; NFT Distribution Ltd.; Northern Dairies Ltd.; Northern Foods Grocery Group Ltd.; Pork Farms Ltd.

Further Reading:

Caulkin, Simon, "Northern Foods' Changing Recipe," *Management Today,* February 1988, pp. 48–52.
"Champion Who Bats Well for the North," *Yorkshire Post,* February 21, 1994.
Hamilton, Sally, "Food's Clean Bill of Health," *Business,* March 1991, pp. 105–108.
Horsley, Alec, *The Story of Northern Dairies,* Hull: Northern Dairies, 1953.
"Wicklow's Big Bite," *Business & Finance,* June 3, 1993.

—Robin DuBlanc

Pacific Dunlop Limited

101 Collins Street
Melbourne, Victoria 3000
Australia
(03) 270 7270
Fax: (03) 270 7300

Public Company
Incorporated: 1920 as Dunlop Rubber Company of Australia
    Ltd.
Employees: 48,000
Sales: A$5.8 billion
Stock Exchanges: Sydney Tokyo London
SICs: 2281 Yarn Spinning Mills; 2329 Men's and Boys'
    Clothing, NEC; 3069 Fabricated Rubber Products, NEC;
    3089 Plastics Products NEC; 6719 Offices of Holding
    Companies, NEC

Pacific Dunlop is a multinational company that manufactures, distributes, and markets a wide range of products; its eight divisions market everything from car batteries to pacemakers, and sporting goods to condoms.

The roots of Pacific Dunlop reach back to Belfast, Ireland. It was there that John Boyd Dunlop based his prosperous veterinary practice. In the course of his work, Dunlop traveled throughout the countryside on often bumpy roads. In order to suffer less the "unsprung weight" of his bicycle and thus ease his travels, Dunlop attached pneumatic tires to his tricycle in 1889. In July of that year he applied for a patent. Dunlop was soon approached by two businessman who expressed an interest in forming a company. They purchased the rights to Dunlop's patent and asked William Harvey Du Cros, the president of the Irish Cyclists Association, to serve as president of the new company. He agreed, providing that he could "assume complete control, appoint the directors, write the prospectus, and make the issue to the public."

In November 1889, the Pneumatic Tyre Company and Booth Cycle Agency of Dublin was created with £25,000. Dunlop was allotted 3,000 shares and £500 and was named to the board of directors. Uncertain of the venture's future, however, Dunlop soon returned 1,500 shares.

To the surprise of the newly formed company, Dunlop's patent application was refused—the principal of a pneumatic tire had been patented in 1845, although it remained unused. The name of the company was changed to the Dunlop Pneumatic Tyre Company Ltd. of Dublin, but the business soon moved from Dublin to Coventry, England, and eventually to Birmingham, England. By 1892, the company had offices in Europe and North America.

In 1893, a branch office and factory of the Dunlop business was established in Melbourne, Australia. Semi-assembled tires were sent to the factory, where they were completed. The manager of the factory was 18 years old, and Dunlop's general manager for Australasia was 19 years old. In 1896, the Melbourne factory gained a contract for making hand-assembled pneumatic tires for the Thomson steam car. The offices in England did not see any future in making tires for automobiles, however.

By 1899, financial speculation by the parent company as well as the decline of bicycling's popularity led the parent company to sell off its interests in North America and Australasia. In August of that year, the Dunlop Pneumatic Tyre Company of Australasia Ltd. went public on capital of £170,000; 80,000 shares priced at £1 each were offered to the general public. Only 23,000 shares were sold, however, and the unsold stock was purchased by one of the company's backers. The company was registered on August 31, 1899, and was listed on the stock exchanges at Melbourne, Sydney, and Adelaide.

The company grew as the popularity of the automobile grew, and Dunlop expanded its production facilities. In 1906 the company changed its name to the Dunlop Rubber Company of Australasia Ltd. With the coming of World War I, there was a new demand for Dunlop products.

On August 20, 1920, the company was incorporated in Victoria, Australia. By 1927, Dunlop U.K. took a 25 percent equity in its Australasian relative when it purchased 500,000 shares and was given a position on the board of directors. (The equity was reduced over time, however, and the relationship was completely severed in 1984.) Dunlop continued to expand. In 1929 it merged with the Perdriau Rubber Company, a manufacturer of general rubber products that was based in Sydney. That company was founded in 1888 after Henry Perdriau was contracted to supply rubber parts to the railroads of New South Wales. Because of an incorrect invoice he was sent five times the amount of rubber he had ordered. Perdriau quickly opened a retail store to sell the surplus, and in 1904 he took the business public with £40,000 in capital. By the time it merged with Dunlop, the Perdriau Rubber Company had expanded into a large venture valued at A$3 million. The newly formed company was named Dunlop Perdriau Ltd.

Dunlop Perdriau quickly acquired a controlling interest in Barnet Glass Rubber Company Ltd. Barnet, founded in 1876, originally manufactured waterproof clothing. It expanded to produce other rubber products, and in 1910 it began to make automobile tires. In 1941, Barnet Glass became a wholly owned subsidiary of Dunlop, which again changed its name to Dunlop Rubber Australia Ltd.

After World War II the company expanded its range of consumer goods in an effort to profit from increased postwar demand; for example, in 1948 Dunlop opened a factory to produce footwear. During the 1960s the company initiated a continuing effort to diversify, and in 1967 it was renamed Dunlop Australia Ltd. By the end of the decade it had branched into the manufacture of clothing, textiles, footwear, bedding, and other rubber products. Like many other manufacturers, Dunlop began to move some of its operations offshore—its first such venture was the Dunlop Papua New Guinea Pty. Ltd., which was established in 1969.

Also in 1969 Dunlop made an acquisition that would later prove to be of central importance to its operations when it purchased the Ansell Rubber Company. Ansell had been founded in Richmond, Australia, in 1905 by a former Dunlop employee, and its first products were balloons and condoms. In 1925 Ansell started to make household rubber gloves, and by 1945 Ansell had created an automated process that could turn out 300 dozen pairs of gloves every eight hours. Ansell actively sought clients in North America and Europe. The advent of disposable surgical gloves in 1964 proved to be a boon for Ansell and the company's profits soared; Ansell won an export award in 1967 from the Australian Department of Trade and Industry.

During the 1970s the company consolidated many of its burgeoning operations and streamlined its corporate structure. These moves readied it for another major expansion program that took place throughout the 1980s. In 1980, Dunlop Australia Ltd. renamed itself Dunlop Olympic Ltd. after it acquired Olympic Consolidated Industries Ltd. for A$92.5 million. Olympic, like Dunlop, was a major tire manufacturer in Australia with its own chain of tire stores; the company also made other industrial products. Founded in 1922 and incorporated in 1933 (as the Olympic Tyre and Rubber Company Pty. Ltd.), Olympic started producing tires in 1934 and had expanded to other industrial products by 1949. By the time of its merger with Dunlop, Olympic held 169 tire-store outlets and its post-tax profit had reached A$10.2 million. The tire stores would later come together under the name Beaurepaires for Tyres.

Along with Olympic Consolidated Industries came a 50 percent interest in Olex Cables Ltd.; Dunlop Olympic acquired the remaining 50 percent in 1981 for A$56.8 million. Olex had been founded in 1940 in an effort to meet the wartime demand for insulated cable.

Dunlop Olympic continued to grow when in 1984 it acquired Dunlop New Zealand Ltd. (which manufactured tires, industrial products, and sporting goods) and Olex Canzac Cables, New Zealand's second largest cable manufacturer. By the end of the year the company had severed its ties with Dunlop U.K. and the technical agreements that had been in effect since 1899 were halted.

In 1986 Dunlop Olympic Ltd changed its name to Pacific Dunlop Ltd, thus reflecting the company's region-wide aspirations. The company's stock began trading on the London Stock Exchange on December 31st of that year. Pacific Dunlop entered into a joint venture with Goodyear Tire and Rubber Company in 1986 that consolidated the two companies' tire manufacturing, marketing, and retail operations in Australia, New Zealand, and Papua New Guinea under the name South Pacific Tyres. However, the brand names Dunlop, Olympic, and Goodyear were still used, and the tire services—Beaurepaires for Tyres and Goodyear Tyre, Brake, and Clutch Service—

continued to be operated independently. In February 1987 shares of Pacific Dunlop Ltd began to be traded on the Tokyo Stock Exchange.

Also in 1987 the company acquired clothing and textile manufacturers and marketers Bonds Industries, which brought under the Dunlop wing many brand names well-known in Australia, including Chesty Bond, Grand Slam, and Gotcha. Pacific Dunlop then acquired a 60 percent interest in GNB Batteries, which was to become a division of the company. Dunlop had first manufactured batteries in 1949, and in 1985 it had acquired the Chloride Group PLC, which had operations in the United States, Canada, Mexico, New Zealand, and Australia, as well as its own manufacturing facilities. With the purchase of GNB Batteries Dunlop became one of the world's largest manufacturers of automotive, traction, and stationary batteries. In 1989 it acquired the U.S. battery manufacturers Standard Batteries and Southern Batteries.

Furthering its diversification program, the company in 1988 purchased Nucleus Ltd. and also Telectronic Holdings Ltd., a manufacturer of such health care products as pacemakers and hearing aids. The company went on to acquire a controlling or complete interest in a vast array of manufacturers, including Repco Automotive Parts, Repco Leisure Cycles, Red Robin Industries, Mates Healthcare Ltd., Derby Bicycles, and Slumbertime Bedding. Also in 1988 the company created a manufacturing facility in Colombo, Sri Lanka to make gloves and condoms, and started construction of a balloon-manufacturing plant in Thailand—examples of the company's efforts to move production offshore.

In 1990 Pacific Dunlop and Goodyear entered into a second joint venture, forming Tecbelt Pacific to manufacture steel-cord conveyor belting. By 1991 Dunlop's Ansell division had become the world's largest producer of medical, industrial, and household gloves. Dunlop diversified further that year by entering the food-manufacturing business when it acquired Petersville Sleigh Ltd., a leading Australian food company, for A$374 million. Petersville Sleigh carried with it many well-known brand names, including Edgell-Birds Eye, Peters Ice Cream, Herbert Adams Bakeries, and Socomin International. Dunlop named its new food division the Pacific Brands Food Group. The following year the company restructured its food division to better position it in the international market—its strategy being to enter growing markets armed with strong brand names on high-profit items. The company also sold a string of Petersville assets (for example, Pacific Dunlop sold off Eastman, the U.S. stationary and furniture concern, for $142 million in December 1992).

Dunlop quickly added to its stable of food products. In July 1992 it purchased a 75 percent interest in Pasta House and took 100 percent ownership of International Se Products. In July 1993, Dunlop purchased the Plumrose food-products business in Australia for A$225 million. The agreement carried with it the rights to market several brand names, including Yoplait and Silhouette. At the same time the food division launched its arrival in the Japanese premium ice cream market when, in a partnership with a Japanese company, it sent a shipment of ice cream to Japan worth A$5 million. Dairy and pasta products were examples of upper-end items with high export value.

The company signaled its intention to become a force in the Pacific region when it created the Pacific Rim Advisory Board—which is mandated to seeking ways to take advantage of the burgeoning Pacific Rim economy—in 1991. By 1992 Dunlop had investments of more than A$400 million throughout the region, and its total exports were A$144 million.

A major element of Pacific Dunlop's strategy was to strengthen and expand its presence in Asia from A$500 million in 1992 to A$1 billion in the year 2000. A significant component of its Asian ambit was China, where in 1992 its investments totaled A$120 million. Olex Cables held two factories in China that produced cable for its own exploding market as well as for export. In May 1992 Olex Cables won a A$22 million contract to supply optical-fiber cable to link the cities of Chengdu, Xi'an, and Zhengzhou. The next year it won a A$70 million contract to supply 3,150 kilometers of optical-fiber cable between the Chinese cities of Lanzhou and Yining in northwestern China. By 1993 its factory in the Shenzen economic area, which had started production in 1992, was manufacturing near capacity—nearly 2,500 kilometers of cable daily.

In May 1993 Pacific Dunlop registered a holding company in China—Pacific Dunlop Holdings (China). The Shanghai-based entity was at that time only the third foreign company that had earned the approval to do so. The holding company was created to oversee Pacific Dunlop's investments in that country, which then comprised nine factories. The company sought at least a controlling 51 percent interest in its Chinese ventures. It looked to its Chinese partners to secure the land to build its factories, staff them, and procure orders for them.

By the mid-1990s, Pacific Dunlop Ltd was one of the twenty largest companies in Australia. Its operations spanned more than twenty countries. In 1993, Pacific Dunlop reported sales of A$6.3 billion for the year ending June 30. The company's profits climbed to A$260.4 million, up from A$185.6 million.

The company was comprised of eight divisions. The Pacific Brands division, which focused on consumer products such as footwear (with names such as Grosby, Candy, Pro-Sport, Dunlop, and Hollandia); sporting goods (Dunlop, Repco, Speedwell, Raleigh, and Slazenger); clothing (Chesty Bond, Red Robin, Baby Gro-Wear, Grand Slam, Berlei); and bicycles (Tuf, Adidas, Jockey, Dunlop, Speedwell, Raleigh, and Holeproof).

Pacific Brands Food Group, the food-products division, manufactured and marketed products with brand names such as Edgell-Birds Eye, Plumrose, Big Sister, Four 'n Twenty, Leggo, Vitari, and Herbert Adams. Food products were distributed in Australia, New Zealand, and other Pacific Rim nations.

The Distribution division distributed a wide range of electrical products (e.g., cables) and industrial goods (such as transmission and rubber products). The Medical Group—the health care division—produced pacemakers, implantable defillibrators, and ultrasound equipment. Ansell International produced latex products such as condoms, balloons, and household and medical gloves.

South Pacific Tyres, the automotive division, manufactured and marketed tires under the names Dunlop, Goodyear, Kelley, and Olympic. Tires and other automotive parts were sold through Beaurepaires for Tyres and other outlets. GNB Batteries manufactured and marketed batteries under the brand names Chloride, Dunlop, Masse, Marshall, and Exide in Australia and New Zealand and the Champion, National, Stowaway, and Marshall brands in North America. Industrial Foam and Fibre, the division that manufactured products to be used in building and construction, made industrial rubber products as well as plastics, transmission hoses, foam and fiber products, plastics, and bedding (including the Sleepmaker, Serta, and Slumberland brands).

Principal Subsidiaries: GNB International Battery Group (Australia); Industrial Foam & Fibre (Australia); Pacific Brands (Australia); South Pacific Tyres (Australia); Telectronics Pacing Systems (United States); GNB U.S.A. (United States); Pacific Dunlop Holdings, Inc. (United States); Ansell Canada Inc. (Canada); Pacific Dunlop Holdings (China)

Further Reading:

Jacques, Bruce, "Pacific Dunlop Sells Eastman Stake to U.S.," *The Financial Times,* December 8, 1992, p. 23.
Walker, Tony, "Firm Chinese Foothold for Pacific Dunlop," *The Financial Times,* May 8, 1993, p. 24.
"Major Australian Food Groups Map Plans for Stagnant Market," *South China Morning Post,* June 29, 1993, p. 9.
"Pacific Dunlop Pushes up Profit," *South China Morning Post,* September 11, 1993, p. 2.

—C. L. Collins

Peabody Coal Company

P. O. Box 1990
Henderson, Kentucky 42420-1990
U.S.A.
(502) 827-0800
Fax: (502) 827-6166

Wholly Owned Subsidiary of Peabody Holding Company, Inc.
Incorporated: 1890
Employees: 4,500
Sales: $900 million
SICs: 1221 Bituminous Coal & Lignite—Surface; 1222 Bituminous Coal—Underground

As a subsidiary of Peabody Holding Company, Inc., the largest coal producer in the United States, Peabody Coal Company operates ten coal mines in western Kentucky, Illinois, and Indiana, an area known collectively as the Illinois Basin. Ninety percent of the company's coal is sold to electrical generation plants, chiefly in the Midwest, while the remaining ten percent is purchased by industries engaged in generating their own electricity and steam power. The transportation of coal from mines to consumers is accomplished primarily by river barges and railroad, although the development of conveyor belt systems that haul coal directly to power plants has proved expedient and increasingly popular.

Peabody Coal was founded in the 1880s by Francis S. Peabody. The son of a prominent Chicago attorney, Peabody graduated from Yale University with the intention of studying law in Chicago. Displaying little aptitude for the profession, however, he opted for a career in business, working at a bank for a brief period before embarking on a private retail venture in 1883. With a partner, $100 in start-up capital, a wagon, and two mules, the 24-year-old Peabody established Peabody & Company, which sold and delivered coal purchased from established mines to homes and small businesses in the Chicago area. Capitalizing on the social and business relations cultivated by Peabody's father, the company attracted a large customer base and experienced success from the onset. As Peabody's sales continued to increase, the company rose to prominence among the major coal retailers in Chicago.

In the late 1880s, Peabody bought out his partner's share of the business, and in 1890 the company was incorporated in the state of Illinois under the name Peabody Coal Company. Five years later, in order to meet increasing customer demand, Peabody began its own mining operation, opening Mine No. 1 in the southern Illinois county of Williamson. This venture represented the first step in Peabody's transition from coal retailer to mining company.

At the turn of the century, coal-burning fireplaces and furnaces composed the chief source of heat for both private residences and public buildings. Moreover, the railroad and shipping industries relied heavily on coal to power their steam engines. Over the next ten years, however, the increasing popularity of alternative fuels—including natural gas, which had applications in home heating, and diesel fuel, which could be used to power locomotives—led to a greatly reduced demand for coal in what had been its primary markets. Nonetheless, coal became an important commodity for another developing industry during this time; as electricity was brought to homes and businesses in urban and eventually rural parts of the country, the operation of electrical utility plants demanded large amounts of coal. In 1913, Peabody Coal won a long-term contract to supply coal to a major electric utility, and, realizing the growing importance of this market, the company began focusing on obtaining similar high-volume, long-term supply contracts, while acquiring more mining and reserve property to meet expected demand.

Having anticipated and adapted to changes in the marketplace, Peabody Coal thrived, gaining a listing on the Midwest Stock Exchange in 1929 and becoming known as a coal producer rather than retailer. Despite adverse economic conditions during the Great Depression and disputes and strikes involving the unionization of mine workers, the company continued to realize profits and growth. In 1949, Peabody Coal was listed on the New York Stock Exchange. During this time, Francis S. Peabody retired and was succeeded as company president by his son, Stuyvesant (Jack) Peabody, who later ceded control to his son, Stuyvesant Peabody, Jr.

By the mid-1950s, Peabody was ranked eighth among the country's top coal producers. Long dependent on its underground mines, however, the company began losing market share to competitors engaged in surface mining, a less expensive process that yielded a higher volume of coal. Heavy losses at Peabody ensued in the early 1950s, and the company engaged in merger talks with Sinclair Coal Company, the country's third largest coal mining operation. Peabody management believed that Sinclair could offer the company access to greater financial resources and surface mining operations that would help it to remain competitive.

Like Peabody, Sinclair was founded in the late nineteenth century as a retail operation, providing customers in the vicinity of Aurora, Missouri, with coal for heating their homes and businesses. During the 1920s, Sinclair president Grant Stauffer was approached by Russell Kelce, an ambitious coal miner who sought to put his years of practical experience to use in an executive capacity. Born into a long line of coal miners, Kelce had begun working in the mines of Pennsylvania while in his teens. He later moved to the Midwest, where his father had established a mining operation. Stauffer and Kelce reached an agreement in which Stauffer would be responsible for cultivating a large customer base and long-term contracts and Kelce would oversee mining operations. By 1926, Kelce had purchased a significant share of the Sinclair Coal Co., and he became president when Stauffer died in 1949.

Kelce was also named president of the new company that resulted when Sinclair and Peabody merged in 1955. That year, Sinclair acquired 95 percent of Peabody's stock and moved Peabody's headquarters to St. Louis. However, the Peabody name, familiar to investors due to its listing on the NYSE, was retained. Under the leadership of Russell Kelce, and, later, his brothers Merl and Ted, Peabody doubled its production and sales by opening new mines and acquiring established mines in the western states, including Arizona, Colorado, and Montana. By the mid-1960s, the company had opened a mine in Queensland, Australia, its first venture outside North America.

In 1968, Peabody's assets were acquired by Kennecott Copper Corporation. Although Peabody became the largest coal producer in the United States during this time, its position under Kennecott was made tenuous by an antitrust suit. The Federal Trade Commission (FTC) ruled that Kennecott's purchase of Peabody was in violation of The Clayton Act, a decision that Kennecott challenged. In 1976, after eight years of litigation, the FTC ordered Kennecott to divest itself of Peabody Coal Company. That year, a holding company, Peabody Holding Company, Inc., was developed, and the following year it bought Peabody Coal for $1.1 billion.

Edwin R. Phelps presided over Peabody during these years of litigation, and in 1978 he was named the company's chairperson. The presidency was then transferred to Robert H. Quenon, a former executive in the coal division of the Exxon Corp. Quenon met with several challenges at Peabody, including poor labor relationships, low employee morale, financial losses, and outdated plants and equipment. However, he later recalled in an interview for Peabody's *Pulse* magazine that he was encouraged by the fact that the company "had a very good management team. They understood coal, and made things happen."

Quenon oversaw a reorganization of Peabody that resulted in separate divisions for sales, marketing, mine operations, resource management, and customer service. By selling off several of its properties, the company was able to finance more modern facilities and equipment. Moreover, Quenon was able to capitalize on the OPEC oil crisis by renegotiating longer term contracts with customers who feared that coal prices, like oil prices, would soon increase dramatically.

Although Peabody became more financially stable, it also faced union strikes and litigation over safety issues during the 1970s and 1980s. The longest strike took place from December 1977 through March 1978, ending when mine workers throughout the country accepted a new three-year contract. The 110-day strike could have led to power shortages and industrial layoffs; however, this threat to the nation's economy was avoided largely due to the stockpiling of coal that occurred before the strike commenced. Nevertheless, this strike and another in 1981 that lasted for 75 days proved costly to Peabody, and the company strove to improve its relations with its employees.

The safety of Peabody mines was called into question beginning in 1982, when the company was charged with tampering with the results of safety tests at its mine in Morganfield, Kentucky.

The tests, made mandatory for all coal mines by the Mine Safety and Health Administration (MSHA), measured the amount of coal dust to which miners were exposed, since excessive amounts of the dust were linked to pneumoconiosis, commonly known as black lung disease. Peabody plead guilty to 13 charges of tampering with the test results in December 1982 and paid fines totaling $130,000. Also during this time, MSHA found the company's Eagle No. 2 mine in Illinois in violation of safety standards, having failed to provide adequate roof support beams, which resulted in the accidental death of a foreman. Reacting to these and other similar disasters, Peabody focused its attention on safety, designating teams of engineers to design stronger roofs and better ventilation systems at its underground mines. In addition, the company patented its invention of a "flooded bed scrubber," which operated in conjunction with mining machinery to reduce the amount of coal dust in the mines.

In 1983, Quenon was made president and CEO of Peabody's parent company, Peabody Holding Co., and Wayne T. Ewing was named president of Peabody Coal. Two years later, when Ewing moved to the Peabody Development Company, another subsidiary of Peabody Holding, he was replaced at Peabody Coal by Howard W. Williams. Improved labor relations at Peabody were reflected in the successful negotiations of contracts with the United Mine Workers, allowing the company and its miners to avoid strikes in 1984 and 1988. Growth in Peabody's operations continued, and, in 1984, the company acquired the West Virginia coal mines of Armco Inc. for $257 million, resulting in new contracts with northeastern utility companies. During this time, Peabody's headquarters were relocated in Henderson, Kentucky, which offered closer proximity to its central mines.

The passage of The Clean Air Act by Congress in the early 1990s forced many coal producers, including Peabody, to reassess their operations. Phase I of the Act mandated that American industries work to reduce the amount of sulfur dioxide emissions produced by their plants. Although the installation of scrubbers at coal-burning power plants would enable such companies to modify the effects of high-sulfur coal themselves, most customers preferred to switch to a low-sulfur coal product. As a result, Peabody's competitive status hinged on its ability to renegotiate customer contracts and provide a product lower in sulfur content. Some Peabody mines, including Eagle No. 2, lost major contracts and were forced to close, whereas others were able to implement new equipment and procedures that produced low-sulfur coal. The prospect of the stricter clean air requirements required by Phase II of the Act, scheduled to go into effect by the year 2000, prompted Peabody to invest heavily in technology, hoping to be better prepared for eventual shifts in demand.

In 1991, G. S. (Sam) Shiflett became the company's 13th president. In addition to the responsibilities of containing costs and implementing substantial changes in the company's Illinois Basin mines, Shiflett faced the threat of a strike by United Mine Workers during the first year of his presidency. Several developments in the coal industry contributed to dissatisfaction among mine workers. Technological advancements, including the computerization of some mining operations, led to reductions in the work force. Moreover, new nonunion mining operations emerged, offering stiff competition through lower coal prices, which unionized miners feared would lead to wage cuts. Finally, as coal companies were increasingly acquired by large, international conglomerates, the lines of communication between labor and management became convoluted, and the potential for rifts increased.

The costly, extended strike and over a year of negotiations ended in December 1993, when the union agreed to a new four-year contract. The contract included provisions for an improved health care plan as well as the establishment of the Labor Management Positive Change Process (LMPCP). LMPCP, an effort to resolve future problems through cooperation rather than confrontation, invited employees to voice concerns regarding mine conditions and job security and suggest solutions. As chairperson of the Bituminous Coal Operators' Association (BOCA), Peabody president Shiflett was instrumental in designing and negotiating the contract to resolve the strike.

In the mid-1990s, Peabody continued to rely on the utility industry as its primary customer base. With analysts predicting steady increases in the country's demand for coal in the 1990s, bolstered by rising demand at electric generation plants, Peabody Coal looked forward to renewed profits and expansion throughout the 1990s.

Further Reading:

Brown, Mike, "Mine-Safety Chief Backs 'Judgment Call' in Note," *Louisville Courier-Journal,* September 23, 1986.
Eubanks, Ben, "Standing Up at Peabody," *St. Louis Business Journal,* January 14, 1985, pp. 1A, 13A.
Lenhoff, Alyssa, "Miners Wonder What Coal Talks Will Produce," *Charleston Gazette,* January 5, 1988.
Schneider, Keith, "Coal Company Admits Safety Test Fraud," *New York Times,* January 19, 1991, p. 14.
Smothers, Ronald, "Union Prepares for Long Strike at Coal Mines," *New York Times,* February 6, 1993, p. 6.

—Tina Grant

PepsiCo, Inc.

Purchase, New York 10577-1444
U.S.A.
(914) 253-2000
Fax: (914) 253-2070

Public Company
Incorporated: 1919 as Loft, Inc.
Employees: 423,000
Sales: $25.02 billion
Stock Exchanges: New York Chicago Basel Geneva Zurich
    Amsterdam Tokyo
SICs: 5812 Eating Places; 2086 Bottled and Canned Soft
    Drinks; 2087 Flavoring Extracts and Syrups, Nec; 2096
    Potato Chips and Similar Snacks; 2099 Food Preparations,
    Nec; 2052 Cookies and Crackers; 6794 Patent Owners and
    Lessors

PepsiCo, Inc. is a diversified consumer products company with
some of the world's most important and valuable trademarks.
By the early 1990s, the company's system dispensed $30 mil-
lion in snack foods, $43 million in fast food, and $77 million in
beverages each day. At that time, snack foods from PepsiCo's
Frito-Lay division, which included Doritos tortilla chips,
Ruggles and Lay's potato chips, Fritos corn chips, and Rold
Gold pretzels, contributed the majority (39 percent, or $1.19
billion) of the conglomerate's operating profits. Incidentally,
Frito-Lay also held 50 percent share of the $8 billion snack food
market. Beverages, including the venerable Pepsi-Cola, and
newer Slice and Mountain Dew, comprised 36 percent (or $1.11
billion) of PepsiCo's operating profits. While the restaurant
division's Taco Bell, Pizza Hut, and KFC chains brought in the
majority of PepsiCo's sales, they added the minority of operating profits, 25 percent, or $778 million. As PepsiCo neared its
centennial, its soft drinks were distributed in 166 countries, its
snack foods were available in almost 90 countries, and its
restaurant chains had operations in 88 countries and territories.

When Caleb D. Bradham concocted a new cola drink in the
1890s, his friends' enthusiastic response convinced him that he
had created a commercially viable product. For twenty years,
"Doc" Bradham prospered from his Pepsi-Cola sales. Eventually, he was faced with a dilemma; the crucial decision he made
turned out to be the wrong one and he was forced to sell. But his
successors fared no better and it was not until the end of the

1930s that Pepsi-Cola again became profitable. Sixty years
later, PepsiCo, Inc. was a mammoth multinational supplier of
soft drinks, snack food, and fast food. PepsiCo's advance to that
level was almost entirely the result of its management style and
the phenomenal success of its television advertising.

Doc Bradham, like countless other entrepreneurs across America, was trying to create a cola drink similar in taste to Coca-
Cola, which by 1895 was selling well in every state of the union.
On August 28, 1898, at his pharmacy in New Bern, North
Carolina, Bradham gave the name Pepsi-Cola to his most popular flavored soda. Formerly known as Brad's Drink, the new
cola beverage was a syrup of sugar, vanilla, oils, cola nuts, and
other flavorings diluted in carbonated water. The enterprising
pharmacist followed Coca-Cola's method of selling the concentrate to soda fountains; he mixed the syrup in his drugstore then
shipped it in barrels to the contracted fountain operators who
added the soda water. He also bottled and sold the drink
himself.

In 1902 Doc Bradham closed his drugstore to devote his attention to the thriving new business. The next year, he patented the
Pepsi-Cola trademark, ran his first advertisement in a local
paper, and moved the bottling and syrup-making operations to a
purpose-built factory. Almost 20,000 gallons of Pepsi-Cola
syrup was produced in 1904.

Again following the successful methods of the Coca-Cola company, Bradham began to establish a network of bottling franchises. Entrepreneurs anxious to enter the increasingly popular
soft drink business set themselves up as bottlers and contracted
with Bradham to buy his syrup and sell nothing but Pepsi. With
little cash outlay, Pepsi-Cola reached a much wider market.
Bradham's first two bottling franchises, both in North Carolina,
commenced operation in 1905. By 1907, Pepsi-Cola had signed
agreements with 40 bottlers; over the next three years, the
number grew to 250 and annual production of the syrup exceeded one million gallons.

Pepsi-Cola's growth continued until World War I, when sugar,
then the main ingredient of all flavored sodas, was rationed. Soft
drink producers were forced to cut back until sugar rationing
ended. The wartime set price of sugar—5.5 cents per pound—
rocketed after controls were lifted to as much as 26.5 cents per
pound in 1920. Bradham, like his rivals, had to decide whether
to halt·production and sit tight in the hope that prices would
soon drop, or stockpile the precious commodity as a precaution
against even higher prices; he chose the latter course. But
unfortunately for him the market was saturated by the end of
1920 and sugar prices plunged to a low of 2 cents per pound.

Bradham never recovered. After several abortive attempts to
reorganize, only two of the bottling plants remained open. In a
last ditch effort, he enlisted the help of Roy C. Megargel, a Wall
Street investment banker. However, very few people were willing to invest in the business and it went bankrupt in 1923. The
assets were sold and Megargel purchased the company trademark, giving him the rights to the Pepsi-Cola formula. Doc
Bradham went back to his drug dispensary and died 11 years
later.

Megargel reorganized the firm as the National Pepsi-Cola Company in 1928, but after three years of continuous losses he had

to declare bankruptcy. That same year, 1931, Megargel met Charles G. Guth, a somewhat autocratic businessman who had recently taken over as president of Loft Inc., a New York-based candy and fountain store concern. Guth had fallen out with Coca-Cola for refusing the company a wholesaler discount and he was on the lookout for a new soft drink. He signed an agreement with Megargel to resurrect the Pepsi-Cola company, and acquired 80 percent of the new shares, ostensibly for himself. Then, having modified the syrup formula, he canceled Loft's contract with Coca-Cola and introduced Pepsi-Cola, whose name was often shortened to Pepsi.

Loft's customers were wary of the brand switch and in the first year of Pepsi sales the company's soft drink turnover was down by a third. By the end of 1933, Guth had bought out Megargel and owned 91 percent of the insolvent company. Resistance to Pepsi in the Loft stores tailed off in 1934, and Guth decided further to improve sales by offering 12 ounce bottles of Pepsi for a nickel—the same price as six ounces of Coke. The Depression-weary people of Baltimore—where the 12 ounce bottles were first introduced—were ready for a bargain and Pepsi-Cola sales increased dramatically.

Guth soon took steps to internationalize Pepsi-Cola, establishing the Pepsi-Cola Company of Canada in 1934 and in the following year forming Compania Pepsi-Cola de Cuba. He also moved the entire American operation to Long Island City, New York, and set up national territorial boundaries for the bottling franchises. In 1936, Pepsi-Cola Ltd. of London commenced business.

Guth's ownership of the Pepsi-Cola Company was challenged that same year by Loft Inc. In a complex arrangement, Guth had organized Pepsi-Cola as an independent corporation, but he had run it with Loft's employees and money. After three years of litigation, the court upheld Loft's contention and Guth had to step down, although he was retained as an adviser. James W. Carkner was elected president of the company, now a subsidiary of Loft Inc., but Carkner was soon replaced by Walter S. Mack, Jr., an executive from the Phoenix Securities Corporation.

Mack established a board of directors with real voting powers to ensure that no one person would be able to wield control as Guth had done. From the start, Mack's aim was to promote Pepsi to the hilt so that it might replace Coca-Cola as the world's best-selling soft drink. The advertising agency Mack hired worked wonders. In 1939, a Pepsi radio jingle—the first one to be aired nationally—caught the public's attention: "Pepsi-Cola hits the spot. Twelve full ounces, that's a lot. Twice as much for a nickel, too. Pepsi-Cola is the drink for you." The jingle, sung to the tune of the old British hunting song "D'Ye Ken John Peel," became an advertising hallmark; no one was more impressed, or concerned, than the executives at Coca-Cola.

In 1940, with foreign expansion continuing strongly, Loft Inc. made plans to merge with its Pepsi-Cola subsidiary. The new firm, formed in 1941, used the name Pepsi-Cola Company since it was so well-known. Pepsi's stock was listed on the New York Stock Exchange for the first time.

Sugar rationing was even more severe during World War II, but this time the company fared better; indeed, the sugar plantation

Pepsi-Cola acquired in Cuba became a most successful investment. But as inflation spiraled in the postwar U.S. economy, sales of soft drinks fell. The public needed time to get used to paying six or seven cents for a bottle of Pepsi which, as they remembered from the jingle, had always been a nickel. Profits in 1948 were down $3.6 million from the year before.

In other respects, 1948 was a notable year. Pepsi moved its corporate headquarters across the East River to midtown Manhattan, and for the first time the drink was sold in cans. The decision to start canning, while absolutely right for Pepsi-Cola and other soft drink companies, upset the franchised bottlers, who had invested heavily in equipment. However, another decision at Pepsi-Cola—to ignore the burgeoning vending machine market because of the necessarily large capital outlay—proved to be a costly mistake. The company had to learn the hard way that as canned drinks gained a larger share of the market, vending machine sales would become increasingly important.

Walter Mack was appointed company chairman in 1950, and a former Coca-Cola vice-president of sales, Alfred N. Steele, took over as president and chief executive officer, bringing 15 other Coke executives with him. Steele continued the policy of management decentralization by giving broader powers to regional vice-presidents, and he placed Herbert Barnet in charge of Pepsi's financial operations. However, Steele's outstanding contribution was in marketing. He launched an extensive advertising campaign with the slogan "Be Sociable, Have a Pepsi." The new television medium provided a perfect forum; Pepsi advertisements presented young Americans drinking "The Light Refreshment" and having fun.

By the time Alfred Steele married movie star Joan Crawford in 1954, a transformation of the company was well underway. Crawford's adopted daughter Christina noted in her best seller *Mommie Dearest*: "[Steele had] driven Pepsi into national prominence and distribution, second only to his former employer, Coca-Cola. Pepsi was giving Coke a run for its money in every nook and hamlet of America. Al Steele welded a national network of bottlers together, standardized the syrup formula . . . , brought the distinctive logo into mass consciousness, and was on the brink of going international." In fact, Pepsi-Cola International Ltd. was formed shortly after Steele's marriage.

Joan Crawford became the personification of Pepsi's new and glamorous image. She invariably kept a bottle of Pepsi at hand during press conferences and mentioned the product at interviews and on talk shows; on occasion she even arranged for Pepsi trucks and vending machines to feature in background shots of her movies. The actress also worked hard to spread the Pepsi word overseas and accompanied her husband, now chairman of the board, on his 1957 tour of Europe and Africa, where bottling plants were being established.

Steele died suddenly of a heart attack in the spring of 1959. Herbert Barnet succeeded him as chairman and Joan Crawford was elected a board member. Pepsi-Cola profits had fallen to a postwar low of $1.3 million in 1950 when Steele joined the company, but with the proliferation of supermarkets during the decade and the developments in overseas business, profits reached $14.2 million in 1960. By that time, young adults had become a major target of soft drink manufacturers and Pepsi's advertisements were aimed at "Those who think young."

Al Steele and Joan Crawford had been superb cheerleaders, but a stunt pulled in 1959 by Donald M. Kendall, head of Pepsi-Cola International, is still regarded as one of the great coups in the annals of advertising. Kendall attended the Moscow Trade Fair that year and persuaded U.S. Vice-President Richard Nixon to stop by the Pepsi booth with Nikita Khrushchev, the Soviet premier. As the cameras flashed, Khrushchev quenched his thirst with Pepsi and the grinning U.S. Vice-President stood in attendance. The next day, newspapers around the world featured photographs of the happy couple, complete with Pepsi bottle.

By 1963, Kendall was presiding over the Pepsi empire. His rise to the top of the company was legendary. He had been an amateur boxing champion in his youth and joined the company as a production line worker in 1947 after a stint in the U.S. Navy. He was later promoted to syrup sales where it quickly became apparent that he was destined for higher office. Ever pugnacious, Kendall has been described as abrasive and ruthlessly ambitious; beleaguered Pepsi executives secretly referred to him as White Fang. Under his long reign, the company's fortunes skyrocketed.

Pepsi-Cola's remarkable successes in the 1960s and 1970s were the result of five distinct policies, all of which Kendall and his crew pursued diligently: they advertised on a massive, unprecedented scale; they introduced new brands of soft drinks; they led the industry in packaging innovations; they expanded overseas; and, through acquisitions, they diversified their product line.

The postwar baby-boomers were in their mid- to late-teens by the time Kendall came to power. "Pepsi was there," states a recent company flyer, "to claim these kids for our own." These "kids" became the "Pepsi Generation." In the late 1960s Pepsi was the "Taste that beats the others cold." Viewers were advised "You've got a lot to live. Pepsi's got a lot to give." By the early 1970s, the appeal was to "Join the Pepsi people, feelin' free." In mid-decade an American catch-phrase was given a company twist with "Have a Pepsi Day," and the 1970s ended on the note "Catch the Pepsi Spirit!"

The Pepsi Generation wanted variety and Pepsi was happy to oblige. Company brands introduced in the 1960s included Patio soft drinks, Teem, Tropic Surf, Diet Pepsi—the first nationally distributed diet soda—and Mountain Dew, acquired from the Tip Corporation. Pepsi Light, a diet cola with a hint of lemon, made its debut in 1975, and a few years later Pepsi tested the market with Aspen apple soda and On-Tap root beer. The company also introduced greater variety into the packaging of its products. Soon after Kendall's accession, the 12-ounce bottle was phased out in favor of the 16-ounce size, and in the 1970s Pepsi-Cola became the first American company to introduce one-and-a-half and two-liter bottles; it also began to package its sodas in sturdy, lightweight plastic bottles. By the end of the decade, Pepsi had added 12-pack cans to its growing array of packaging options.

The company's expansion beyond the soft drink market began in 1965 when Kendall met Herman Lay, the owner of Frito-Lay, at a grocer's convention. Kendall arranged a merger with this Dallas-based snack food manufacturer and formed PepsiCo, Inc. Herman Lay retired soon thereafter but retained his substantial PepsiCo shareholding. The value of this stock increased dramatically as Frito-Lay products were introduced to Pepsi's nationwide market.

In the late 1960s and early 1970s, Kendall acquired two well-known fast-food restaurant chains, Taco Bell and Pizza Hut; naturally, these new subsidiaries became major outlets for Pepsi products. But Kendall also diversified outside the food and drink industry, bringing North American Van Lines, Lee Way Motor Freight, and Wilson Sporting Goods into the PepsiCo empire.

Overseas developments continued apace throughout Kendall's tenure. Building on his famous Soviet achievement, he negotiated a trade agreement with the USSR in 1972; the first Pepsi plant opened there two years later. Gains were also made in the Middle East and Latin America, but Coca-Cola, the major rival, retained its dominant position in Europe and throughout much of Asia.

By the time PepsiCo greeted the 1980s with the slogan "Pepsi's got your taste for life!," Kendall was busy arranging for China to get that taste too; production began there in 1983. Kendall put his seal of approval on several other major developments in the early 1980s, including the introduction of Pepsi Free, a non-caffeine cola, and Slice, the first widely distributed soft drink to contain real fruit juice (lemon and lime). The latter drink was aimed at the growing 7-Up and Sprite market. Additionally, Diet Pepsi was reformulated using a blend of saccharin and aspartame (NutraSweet). "Pepsi Now!" was the cry of company commercials, and this was interspersed with "Taste, Improved by Diet Pepsi."

In 1983 the company claimed a significant share of the fast-food soft drink market when Burger King began selling Pepsi products. A year later, mindful of the industry axiom that there is virtually no limit to the amount a consumer will buy once the decision to buy has been made, PepsiCo introduced the 3-liter container.

By the mid 1980s, the Pepsi Generation was over the hill. Kendall's ad agency spared no expense in heralding Pepsi as "The Choice of a New Generation," using the talents of superstar Michael Jackson, singer Lionel Richie, and the Puerto Rican teenage group Menudo. Michael Jackson's ads were smash hits and enjoyed the highest exposure of any American television commercial to date. The company's high profile and powerful presence in all of the soft drink markets—direct results of Kendall's strategies—helped it to weather the somewhat uncertain economic situation of the time.

On only one front had Kendall's efforts failed to produce satisfactory results. Experience showed that for all its expertise, PepsiCo simply did not have the managerial experience required to run its subsidiaries outside the food and drink industries. A van line, a motor freight concern, and a sporting goods firm were indeed odd companies for a soft drink enterprise; and Kendall auctioned off these strange and ailing bedfellows, vowing never again to go courting in unfamiliar territories.

With his house in excellent order, the PepsiCo mogul began to prepare for his retirement. He had bullied and cajoled a generation of Pepsi executives and guided them ever upward on the steep slopes of Pepsi profits. But he had one last task: to lead PepsiCo to victory in the Cola Wars.

Hostilities commenced soon after the Coca-Cola Company changed its syrup recipe in the summer of 1985 and with much fanfare introduced New Coke. Pepsi, caught napping, claimed that Coca-Cola's reformulated drink failed to meet with consumer approval and pointed to their own flourishing sales. But serious fans of the original Coke were not about to switch to Pepsi and demanded that their favorite refreshment be restored. However, when blindfolded, it became manifestly apparent that these diehards could rarely tell the difference between Old Coke, New Coke, and Pepsi; indeed, more often than not, they got it wrong. In any event, the Coca-Cola Company acceded to the public clamor for the original Coke and remarketed it as Coca-Cola Classic alongside its new cola.

Some advertising analysts believed that the entire "conflict" was a clever publicity ploy on the part of Coca-Cola to demonstrate the preeminence of its original concoction ("It's the Real Thing!"), while introducing a new cola—allegedly a Pepsi taste-alike—to win the hearts of waverers. More interesting perhaps than the possible differences between the colas were the very real differences in people's reactions. Four discrete fields were identified by Roger Enrico and Jesse Kornbluth in their book, *The Other Guy Blinked: How Pepsi Won the Cola Wars*: the totally wowed (possibly caffeine-induced); the rather amused; the slightly irritated; and the distinctly bored.

The latter group must have nodded off in front of their television sets when Pepsi took the Cola Wars beyond the firmament. "One Giant Sip for Mankind," proclaimed the ads as a Pepsi "space can" was opened up aboard the U.S. space shuttle Challenger. Presumably, had a regular can been used, Pepsi-Cola would have sloshed aimlessly around the gravity-free cabin. This scientific breakthrough, together with the almost obligatory hype and hoopla, and more mundane factors such as the continued expansion in PepsiCo's outlets, boosted sales to new heights, and Pepsi's ad agency glittered with accolades. The debate still continues, at least within Coke and Pepsi corporate offices, as to who won the Cola Wars. The answer would appear to be that there were no losers, only winners; but skirmishes will inevitably continue.

D. Wayne Calloway replaced Donald M. Kendall as chairman and chief executive officer in 1986. Calloway had been instrumental in the success of Frito-Lay, helping it to become PepsiCo's most profitable division. The new chairman realized that his flagship Pepsi brand was not likely to win additional market share from Coca-Cola, and focused his efforts on international growth and diversification.

Calloway hoped to build on the phenomenal success of the Slice line of fruit juice beverages, which achieved $1 billion in sales and created a new beverage category within just two years of its 1984 introduction. From 1985 to 1993, PepsiCo introduced, acquired, or formed joint ventures to distribute nine beverages, including Lipton Original Iced Teas, Ocean Spray juices, All Sport drink, H2Oh! sparkling water, Avalon bottled water, and

Mug root beer. Many of these products had a "New Age" light and healthy positioning, in line with consumer tastes, and higher net prices. In 1992, PepsiCo introduced Crystal Pepsi, a clear cola that, while still a traditional soda, also tried to capture the momentum of the "New Age" beverage trend.

In the restaurant segment, PepsiCo's 1990 acquisition of the Hot 'n Now hamburger chain continued its emphasis on value priced fast foods. But the company strayed slightly from that formula with the 1992 and 1993 purchases of such full-service restaurants as California Pizza Kitchen, which specialized in creative wood-fired pizzas, Chevys, a Mexican-style chain, East Side Mario's Italian-style offerings, and D'Angelo Sandwich Shops.

Pepsi lost a powerful marketing tool in 1992, when Michael Jackson was accused of child molestation. Although the case was settled out of court, Pepsi dropped its contract with the entertainer. The firm launched its largest promotion ever in May 1992 with the "Gotta Have It" card, which offered discounts on the products of marketing partners Reebok sporting goods, Continental Airlines, and the MCI telephone long distance company. The company also launched a new marketing (or, as the company phrased it, "product quality") initiative early in 1994, when it announced that packaged carbonated soft drink products sold in the United States would voluntarily be marked with a "Best if Consumed By" date.

Although Pepsi had commenced international expansion during the 1950s, it had long trailed Coca-Cola's dramatic and overwhelming conquest of international markets. In 1990, CEO Calloway pledged up to $1 billion for overseas development, with the goal of increasing international volume 150 percent by 1995. At that time, Coke held 50 percent of the European soft drink market, while Pepsi claimed a meager 10 percent. But Pepsi's advantage was that it could compete in other, less saturated segments. The company's biggest challenge to expanding its restaurant division was affordability. PepsiCo noted that, while it took the average U.S. worker just 15 minutes to earn enough to enjoy a meal in one of the firm's restaurants, it would take an Australian 25 minutes to achieve a similar goal. Pepsi still had other options, however. In 1992, for example, the company forged a joint venture with General Mills called Snack Ventures Europe which emerged as the largest firm in the $17 billion market. By 1993, PepsiCo had invested over $5 billion in international businesses, and its international sales comprised 27 percent, or $6.71 billion, of total annual sales.

In January 1992, Calloway was credited by *Business Week* magazine with emerging from the long shadow cast by his predecessor "to put together five impressive years of 20 percent compound earnings growth, doubling sales and nearly tripling the company's value on the stock market." Calloway was also working to reshape PepsiCo's corporate culture by fostering personal responsibility and a decentralized, flexible management style. PepsiCo is one of America's true corporate giants, and seems likely to continue its tradition of well-chosen acquisitions and astute marketing into its second century of business.

Principal Subsidiaries: A&M Food Services, Inc.; Ainwick Corp.; Anderson Hill Insurance Ltd.; Atlantic Soft Drink Company, Inc.; Beverages, Foods, & Service Industries, Inc.; Collin

Leasing Corp.; CPK Acquisition Corp.; Davlyn Realty Corp.; East Kentucky Beverage Company, Inc.; Embotelladoa del Uruguay S.A.; Equity Beverage, Inc.; Frito-Lay of Puerto Rico, Inc.; Frito-Lay of Hawaii, Inc.; Hostess-FL NRO Ltd.; Hot 'n Now, Inc.; Japan Frito-Ltd.; Kentucky Fried Chicken of California, Inc.; National Beverages, Inc.; PepsiCo Capital Corporation N.V.; PepsiCo China Ltd.; PepsiCo Holdings Ltd.; Pizza Management, Inc.; Recot, Inc.; PepsiCo. Overseas Corp.; PepsiCo Overseas Finance N.V.; PepsiCo Services Corp.; PepsiCo World Trading Company, Inc.; Pepsi-Cola (Bermuda) Ltd.; Pepsi-Cola Bottling Company of Los Angeles; Pepsi-Cola Chile Consultores Ltda.; Pepsi-Cola Commodities, Inc.; Pepsi-Cola de Espana S.A.; Pepsi-Cola France S.N.C.; Pepsi-Cola Equipment Corp.; Pepsi-Cola Far East Trade Development Company, Inc.; Pepsi-Cola Interamericana S.A.; Pepsi-Cola International Ltd. (Bermuda); Pepsi-Cola International Ltd. (U.S.A.); Pepsi-Cola Mamulleri Limited Sirketi; Pepsi-Cola Metropolitan Bottling Company, Inc.; Pepsi-Cola Mexicana S.A. de C.V.; Pepsi-Cola Personnel, Inc.; Pepsi-Cola San Joaquin Bottling Co.; Pizza Hut, Inc.; Redux Realty, Inc.; Rice Bottling Enterprises, Inc.; Sabritas S.A. de C.V.; Taco Bell Corp.; Taco Enterprises, Inc.; TFL Holdings, Inc.; Von Karman Leasing Corp.; Wilson International Sales Corp.

Further Reading:

Dietz, Lawrence, *Soda Pop,* New York: Simon and Schuster, 1973.
Enrico, Roger, and Jesse Kornbluth, *The Other Guy Blinked: How Pepsi Won the Cola Wars,* New York: Bantam, 1986.
Lousi, J. C., *The Cola Wars,* New York: Everest House, 1980.
Mack, Walter, and P. Buckley, *No Time Lost,* New York: Atheneum, 1982.
Martin, Milward, *Twelve Full Ounces,* New York: Holt Rinehart, 1962.

—updated by April Dougal Gasbarre

PictureTel Corp.

222 Rosewood Drive
The Tower at Northwoods
Danvers, Massachusetts 01923
U.S.A.
(508) 762-5000
Fax: (508) 762-5245

Public Company
Incorporated: 1984 as PicTel Corp.
Employees: 670
Sales: $141.4 million
Stock Exchanges: NASDAQ
SICs: 3669 Communications Equipment Nec

PictureTel Corp. is the world's leading manufacturer of video communications systems for use over conventional telephone lines. The company offers several systems, including relatively inexpensive models that provide audio/visual surveillance, more complex models that enable personal computer (PC) users to view each other on their computer screens, and complex multipoint systems that allow people in several locations to communicate at once.

The concept of video communications emerged during the 1960s, when American Telephone and Telegraph Company (AT&T) developed a telephone capable of sending a series of snapshots simulating motion over its lines, which were then displayed on an accompanying video screen. The device was originally intended for use in residential markets, but when market research indicated that users were uncomfortable with the idea of being seen during telephone conversations, plans to continue with the development of the "picture telephone" were stalled.

Video communications would later have more practical applications in the business community, which welcomed less costly and time-consuming alternatives to the travel involved in corporate meetings. In the 1970s, AT&T again tried to exploit its video network by establishing studios in major cities, where video communications were made available to businesses for a rental fee. However, the costs involved in operating the system, reflected in the rental fees, proved exorbitant, discouraging demand for the service. Opportunities for companies other than AT&T to develop and manufacture video communications systems were limited during this time, as the Federal Communica-

tions Commission (FCC) imposed regulations and specifications for equipment that interconnected with the public telephone network. In 1984, however, with the divestiture of AT&T, barriers to entry in the telephone equipment market came down.

Improvements in video communications were also contingent on modifications to the country's telephone network system. Designed only for voice communication, conventional telephone lines had an extremely limited bandwidth that provided only a narrow frequency range; for proper transmission, video images required enormous bandwidths. The development of digital electronics technology helped overcome this problem. Digital electronics created more data transmission space by using algorithms to replace repetitive or superfluous signals with simpler, shorter codes, a process known as data compression.

Two experts in this technology were Brian L. Hinman and Jeffrey G. Bernstein, long-time friends and colleagues in the electrical engineering graduate studies program at the Massachusetts Institute of Technology during the 1970s. At MIT, Hinman and Bernstein focused on the science of image processing through visual data compression, gaining valuable technological guidance from their faculty advisor, Dr. David Staelin. The three conceived of a plan to develop and market a line of video communication devices based on a 56-kilobit per second translating interface, or "codec," they had assembled. This system would allow images to be sent over telephone wires.

Hinman, Bernstein, and Staelin gained financial backing from Robert Sterling, an entrepreneur specializing in high-technology ventures, and the PicTel Corporation was formed on August 13, 1984. PicTel established a corporate office and laboratory in Peabody, Massachusetts, where work commenced on software and hardware for the 56-kilobit per second codec.

The company drew its management team from some of the country's most prominent corporations. Robert Bernardi and Dr. Norman Gaut were recruited from companies in Massachusetts' high-tech industrial corridor. Dr. Ronald Posner, former head of the Harris Corporation's satellite division, became president and CEO, and Thomas Spaulding, formerly of Multilink, Inc., became chief financial officer.

Before it had even developed a product, the company went public on November 8, 1984, selling 2.2 million shares at $2 per share. On December 4, the company's underwriter, S. D. Cohn & Company, purchased 330,000 shares, reflecting growing confidence in PicTel's project. Product development continued through 1985 without a single sale. Early in 1986, however, PicTel developed its MCT algorithm, which reduced the bandwidth necessary for transmission of an acceptable video image from 768 kilobits per second to just 224.

In July, the company introduced its first product based of the MCT algorithm, a software-based codec called C-2000. While the device's applications were limited, few other companies were as far along with this technology as PicTel, and work continued on improvements in the product through 1987. During this time, the company changed its name to PictureTel in order to better reflect its focus on picture transmission and to distinguish its name from the technical term "pixel," which referred to the picture elements in a video image.

In 1988, PictureTel developed a new image coding system, called hierarchical vector quantizing, which required a bandwidth of only 112 kilobits per second, a rapid rate made possible by the system's ability to weed out redundant image transmissions, or those that reflected little or no movement. The company also introduced two new products that year: the C-3000 video codec and the V-2100 videoconferencing system. The C-3000 was compatible with the C-2000 and performed as well as any competing system on the market, at half the price and half the size. The V-2100 system was enclosed in a wheeled cabinet that enabled users to set up a video conference from any room that was properly wired.

In January 1989, AT&T chose PictureTel as the equipment vendor for an international video conference it held. The demonstration provided two-way, full-motion voice and video connection between PictureTel headquarters and an AT&T office in Paris. Other PictureTel demonstrations followed, including one for its remote-control V-3100 videoconferencing system and another that featured the Px64, which allowed PictureTel systems to be connected to those developed by other manufacturers. By the close of 1989, PictureTel had shipped more than 70 percent of the videoconference systems in use throughout the world. While the company's revenues tripled between 1987 and 1988, to $18.6 million, PictureTel had yet to turn a profit.

Several other product extensions were introduced in 1990, incorporating larger monitors and more rugged construction. PictureTel developed a one-way transmission system for surveillance use, enabling security groups to monitor remote locations through inexpensive, simple telephone connections. The company's Software Generation 3 system provided better picture quality and seven kilohertz of audio bandwidth at the same 112-kilobit per second switched data rate. By marketing entire video systems, rather than just the codec devices, PictureTel reaped a larger margin on each system sale. Shipments of videoconferencing systems increased by 40 percent over 1989, to 770 units. Revenues increased a further 99 percent over the previous year, to $37 million.

In January of 1991, PictureTel introduced a new family of videoconferencing systems under the System 4000 name. The line included four models, ranging from small consoles to large conference room devices. System 4000 included a proprietary audio technology called Integrated Dynamic Echo Cancellation (IDEC), which helped prevent feedback that could produce annoying echoes. The System 4000 became PictureTel's flagship product line. At two-thirds the cost of competing systems, it also had considerable demand.

PictureTel's primary customer base consisted of large corporations with offices in multiple locations. These customers laid out in excess of $20,000 for each system and also paid for the special switched data links necessary to form a network. While a substantial investment, the PictureTel videoconferencing system could pay for itself in as little as a year. Executives who formerly convened in person, incurring substantial airline and hotel costs, could now meet in the comfort and convenience of their own offices.

However, by 1991 PictureTel had nearly exhausted its market among the large Fortune 500 companies that could afford such a system, and the company began making efforts to boost sales of videoconferencing equipment to smaller companies. Key to this effort was a marketing partnership with North Supply. Under the terms of the agreement, PictureTel products were sold through North Supply dealerships. The company soon introduced a new low-cost product line, which could be used by companies of modest means or added to enhance existing networks.

In April 1991, with investor enthusiasm in the company running high, PictureTel issued another 2.3 million shares, raising more than $40 million in equity capital. In September, PictureTel introduced its M-8000 multipoint bridge, a device that enabled users to conduct as many as eight simultaneous videoconferences among 16 users.

While PictureTel led the industry in videoconferencing technologies, it remained a small company with limited marketing resources. To increase its capital, PictureTel established a joint marketing agreement with IBM, which welcomed the opportunity to leverage PictureTel's products into its own flagging line of computer products. As an IBM "multimedia business partner," PictureTel provided full-motion color video technologies that enhanced IBM's personal computers, allowing videoconferences to be conducted from individual work stations. PictureTel ended the year with record earnings, due primarily to the success of the System 4000 product line. Reporting a profit for each quarter, the company's revenues grew to $78 million and net income reached $6 million.

PictureTel sealed another series of important joint marketing agreements in January 1992. In one agreement, AT&T agreed to handle sales and service of an AT&T videoconferencing product based on PictureTel technology. A separate arrangement was established under which Bell Atlantic's seven telephone companies would directly handle sales and service of PictureTel products. The company also established a Japanese subsidiary to handle sales of videoconferencing products in Japan. A month later, the company finalized similar agreements with Mercury Communications in the United Kingdom, as well as with the U.S. telecommunications corporation Sprint. PictureTel videoconferencing technologies were also marketed as part of the Lotus Notes software application.

Total revenue for 1992 exceeded $141 million, net income grew to $10.7 million, and shipments numbered more than 2,850 units, marking a second year of profitable operation for PictureTel. However, with such success in the marketplace, PictureTel showed signs of vulnerability to price competition from such rivals as Vtel Corporation and Compression Labs. To prevent losses, PictureTel reduced prices on its System 4000 family by 20 percent and introduced an entry-level product called the Model 150E. Priced at $18,500, the system could be leased for only $500 per month, making videoconferencing affordable for even the smallest and lowest-margin businesses. Other low-cost videoconferencing products included the new PictureTel LIVE, PCS 100 desktop, and System 1000 lines, all of which were compatible with international standards and, therefore, operable with any standard-based system.

In an effort to enhance its existing product line, PictureTel acquired KA Teletech, a Baltimore-based developer of scheduling, reservation, accounting, and network management software for the videoconferencing industry. The enterprise was subsequently relocated to PictureTel headquarters in Danvers, Massachusetts.

During this time, PictureTel launched its first national advertising campaign, featuring such taglines as: "Over 70 percent of dial-up videoconferences are PictureTel. Get the Picture?"; "This isn't an ad for videoconferencing. It's a wake-up call"; and "We don't move people, we move ideas. And ideas are what move companies."

At the close of 1993, PictureTel unveiled a new product that converted PCs into videophones. Regarded as substantially higher in quality than a competing system from AT&T, the PictureTel product sold for $6,000, or $1,000 more than the AT&T model. Despite increasing competition, PictureTel was expected to realize the greatest growth from the emerging videoconferencing market, a segment that has been described as the "fax of the '90s."

Principal Subsidiaries: PictureTel AG (Switzerland); PictureTel Japan K.K.; PictureTel GmbH (Germany); PictureTel UK Ltd.

Further Reading:

Bulkeley, William M., "PictureTel to Introduce $6,000 System to Make PCs Work as Video Telephones," *Wall Street Journal,* July 16, 1993, p. B8.
Clark, Tim, "PictureTel Sharpens Brand Image," *Business Marketing,* June 1993, p. 33.
"PictureTel, AT&T Vie for Videoconferencing Growth," *Electronic News,* May 17, 1993, p. 15.
"PictureTel Shrinks Size and Price of Video-Conferencing Suite," *PC Week,* July 20, 1993.

—John Simley

Quantum Corporation

500 McCarthy Blvd.
Milpitas, California 95035
U.S.A.
(408) 894-4000
Fax: (408) 894-3207

Public Company
Incorporated: 1980
Operating Revenues: $1.69 billion
Employees: 2,455
Stock Exchanges: NASDAQ
SICs: 3572 Computer Storage Devices

Quantum Corporation is one of the world's largest suppliers of high-performance 2½-inch and 3½-inch hard disk drives for personal computers, workstations, notebook computers, fax machines, and printers. In addition to its 20 percent share of the 3½-inch drive market, Quantum holds a large segment of the market for storage enhancement devices, with increasing sales of its Quantum DriveKit, Hardcard, and Passport XL. With a comprehensive and highly efficient distribution network in over 40 countries worldwide, Quantum sells its product line to original equipment manufacturers (OEMs), systems integrators, small-scale OEMs, value-added resellers, and retail stores. Through able management, Quantum has established a reputation as a growing, financially stable company in an industry that is well known for its volatility.

Quantum's first president was James L. Patterson, an experienced engineer with an astute business acumen. Making decisions based on a collegial rather than a hierarchical management model, Patterson inspired confidence and a hard work ethic. By 1984, four years after its incorporation, Quantum was leading the market in mid-capacity 5¼-inch disk drives, having jumped ahead of Priam Corporation, Micropolis Corporation, and Control Data. Nearly 20 percent of the 473,000 5¼-inch drives sold in 1985 were made by Quantum. The company's financial statement reflected its growing leadership position in the disk drive market. From 1984 to 1985, revenues increased from $106.2 million to $126.6 million, a growth of almost 20 percent, and earnings increased from $18.1 million to $21.5 million, a jump of over 18 percent. Without any long-term debt, the company was able to concentrate on developing a new line of 5¼-inch OEM products.

The company's revenues remained at the same level in 1986, but production delays with its new generation of 3½-inch disk drives led to a loss of all but two of its customers. Displeased with what they regarded as complacent management, Quantum's board of directors replaced Patterson with Stephen M. Berkeley, the head of the company's subsidiary, Plus Development Corporation. In addition to a new chief executive officer, the board also appointed David A. Brown, a former associate of Berkeley at Plus Development, as Quantum's new president. Realizing that Quantum had fallen behind its competitors in the market for hard disk drives, Berkeley and Brown were determined that their company should take the lead in the industry-wide move toward smaller computers. This decision meant that Quantum would have to phase out its production of 5¼-inch disk drives in order to concentrate on the 3½-inch disk drive market.

The two men immediately plotted a strategy that was unusual for companies within the disk drive industry. Ordinarily a firm either buys the components it uses to build disk drives or it manufactures its own. Either road has both benefits and liabilities: if a firm buys its components it avoids high fixed costs, but it may run short of parts when demand increases; conversely, if a firm makes its own components, it can outfit production easily to meet an increase in demand, but if demand slows then high fixed costs take their financial toll. Having already established a working partnership with Matsushita Kotobuki Electronics Industries, Ltd., a Japanese firm that had grown into the largest manufacturer of videocassette recorders, Berkeley and Brown hired MKE to facilitate Quantum's entry into the 3½-inch disk drive market. The two companies reached an agreement whereby Quantum took on the responsibility of designing and marketing new products while Matsushita manufactured them. Although the Japanese company had never built a disk drive before, its skills in manufacturing electromechanical equipment had already been proven.

Quantum's arrangement with Matsushita instantly led to benefits for both companies. Matsushita required Quantum to completely redesign and overhaul the manner in which it developed disk drives, which led to the implementation of design by robotic assembly. Although this redesign frustrated some of Quantum's engineers, the end result was more than the company could have hoped for. Since Matsushita spent nearly $150 million in developing automated plants, Quantum derived all the benefits of manufacturing in-house without any of the usual fixed costs. In contrast with most of Quantum's competitors, over 95 percent of all the disk drives built on Matsushita assembly lines needed no reworking. This efficiency meant that Quantum had one of the highest gross margins in the entire disk drive industry—even after what was paid to Matsushita.

Quantum's leadership was correct in anticipating a quick rather than slow transition toward more compact drives. Not surprisingly, the company's efforts to create the new generation of 3½-inch disk drives resulted in record sales. In 1989, Quantum increased its revenues to $394.2 million and reported a net income of $41.3 million. These figures catapulted Quantum to the top of the compact drive market. The company's contract with Apple Computer Inc. significantly helped it achieve its leadership position. At the time, approximately 40 percent of company sales were going to Apple, which used Quantum's

3½-inch ProDrive in its Macintosh SE30 and Macintosh IIcx computers. Other firms that bought Quantum disk drives included Sun Microsystems Inc., Hewlett-Packard, and Next Inc.

In 1991, Quantum passed one of its most important milestones—revenues of over $1 billion. Revenues increased an amazing 50 percent over the previous year, the amount totaling $1.07 billion. With its burgeoning revenues, its focus on quality control, and its efficient distribution network, Quantum was also listed in the ranks of the Fortune 500 for the first time during the same year. Quantum was Apple Computer's leading suppler of disk drives; Apple used the drives in its newly introduced Macintosh Classic and LC desktop computers. Even though the company continued to ship its disk drives to Apple at the same level through the entire year, sales to Apple actually fell as a percentage of Quantum's total sales, decreasing from 40 percent to 15 percent. Quantum's impressive revenue growth stood on a widening customer base.

Quantum's strong revenue growth was partially due to the introduction of new products and the upgrade of existing ones. The company brought out 11 new models of its 3½-inch and 2½-inch drives and improved its product line of Passport removable disk drives. The company also put a significant effort into reducing the amount of development time for a particular product, cutting the development process from 24 months to 15. The most important element contributing to Quantum's revenue growth, however, was the company's expansion of its distribution network. Quantum signed agreements with Rein Elektronik, a leading distributor in Germany, and Inelco Peripheriques, one of the leading distributors in France. These two distributors provided Quantum with a reliable flow of cash from the European market. The company also merged its Plus Development Corporation subsidiary into its Commercial Products Division. Plus Development, a manufacturer of hard disks on adaptor cards, otherwise known as "hard cards," was reorganized to better serve the growing demands of the distribution network that included retail outlets and computer superstores.

In 1992, Quantum brought in new leadership. Berkeley and Brown, who had directed the company to unparalleled growth and record revenues, relinquished their day-to-day control of operations to the new chief executive officer, William J. Miller, an 11-year management veteran from Control Data Corporation. The momentum that Berkeley and Brown had created continued under the new CEO. At the end of 1992, Quantum's revenues were reported at $1.54 billion, a whopping 43 percent increase over the previous year's figures. The company's increase in net income was even more impressive, from $49.6 million to $84.7 million—a leap of approximately 71 percent. Quantum appeared to be doing everything right.

Yet throughout 1992 and 1993 there were indications that Quantum's market share was eroding, and that companies such as Conner Peripherals, Seagate Technologies, and even cash-strapped Maxtor were carving out a larger piece for themselves. In late 1992, Quantum sales nearly came to an abrupt halt, as the company found itself unprepared to meet the demand for its products. Matsushita, with whom Quantum had contracted to manufacture its product lines, was unable to build the required disk drives quickly enough for the company to maintain its share of the market. Thus, in spite of its increase in revenues, Quantum spent most of the latter part of 1992 and early 1993 expanding its production base in order to meet demand. The new management quickly entered into a long-term agreement with Matsushita that gave Quantum the right to design and market its product line worldwide and gave the Japanese company the right to worldwide manufacturing. The two companies also arranged for Matsushita to build a state-of-the-art plant in Ireland at a cost of $40 million to help Quantum quicken the pace of distributing products throughout its European network.

Quantum's management had corrected the incipient problems, and the company once again achieved record revenues—$1.7 billion by the end of fiscal 1993. Net income for the first nine months of the fiscal year rose an astonishing 128 percent. Sales to original equipment manufacturers, such as Apple, accounted for more than 33 percent of Quantum's total figures. Although Quantum was still heavily dependent on its business with Apple, the company had increased sales to other OEM customers, including AST Research, Dell Computers, Compaq, and Hewlett-Packard.

The company's strategy to increase its worldwide distribution network had also paid off handsomely. Sales from the international sector accounted for over 45 percent of the company's total annual sales, and accounts with such well-known foreign firms as Fujitsu, ICL, Lucky Goldstar, NEC, Olivetti, Peacock, Philips, Sharp, and Siemens assured long-term financial stability. Quantum also decided to improve upon its burgeoning international operations by relocating its European headquarters to Neuchatel, Switzerland. With a new factory in Ireland and an expanding distribution network, Quantum had developed its operations to provide the best possible service and support to its multinational customers.

As of 1994, Quantum's continuing success depended on the development of its product line and its ability to bring these items to market in a timely manner. The company's ProDrive ELS, a low-priced disk drive targeted at entry-level systems, was doing very well, and the 240 ProDrive LPS 1-inch high-capacity disk drive was one of the best-selling products Quantum had ever introduced. Along with its Maverick 270 and 540 AT/S, a high-capacity disk drive for larger systems, and its Daytona and Go-Drive GLS drives for portable systems, primarily notebooks, Quantum was not only keeping abreast of the market in 1994, but continuing to position itself as one of the top companies in the industry.

Further Reading:

Catalano, Frank, "James L. Patterson: The Drive to Succeed," *Electronic Business,* April 1, 1986, p. 50.
Hof, Robert D., "Quantum Has One Tough Hurdle to Leap," *Business Week,* July 8, 1991, pp. 84–86.
Lindholm, Elizabeth, " 'Quantum Corporation,' The Datamation 100," *Datamation,* June 15, 1992, p. 86.

—Thomas Derdak

R. L. Polk & Co.

1155 Brewery Park Blvd.
Detroit, Michigan 48207-2697
U.S.A.
(313) 393-0880
Fax: (313) 393-2862

Private Company
Incorporated: 1870
Employees: 6,000
Sales: $250 million
SICs: 2741 Miscellaneous Publishing, 7375 Information
   Retrieval Services

R. L. Polk & Co. is a worldwide provider of information, particularly automotive and demographic statistics, made available through published directories, custom reports, and online interactive computer services. In addition, Polk manages direct marketing programs and is one of the largest U.S. manufacturers of calendars and other advertising specialties. Polk's activities include publishing 1,300 city directories, compiling data covering 95 million consumer households, and reporting information about 197 million motor vehicles. Polk operates facilities in the United States, Canada, England, Australia, and Barbados.

R. L. Polk & Co. was established in 1870 by Ralph Lane Polk. After serving in the Union Army during the Civil War, Polk earned a living by selling patent medicines door-to-door. During his travels, he met an enumerator in Ohio who was collecting information for a directory publisher. Fascinated, Polk took a job with the publisher and served several years in the Midwest before he moved to Detroit, Michigan, at the age of 21 to establish his own company.

Polk set up an office in the Tribune Building at 40 Larned Street. His first publication was a directory of towns located along the Detroit and Milwaukee Railroad that included town populations and the names of about 17,500 residents and 600 professionals and tradespeople. Other early publications included a gazetteer and business directory for the State of Michigan, which included the names and addresses of shopkeepers within walking distance of railroad depots. Because Polk had exhausted his own funds in compiling the information included in his first directories, publication expenses were financed by James E. Scripps, owner of the *Detroit News.*

Following his initial success in Michigan, Polk began producing other directories. His first city directory, was compiled for Evansville, Indiana. It included 375 pages of names and addresses, a listing of post offices, and a miscellaneous section giving information about courts, stage lines, steamboat companies, and other organizations. A Detroit city directory was published in 1874. Other early directories covered cities in Indiana, Michigan, Ohio, Minnesota, Montana, Oregon, Wisconsin, Washington, Iowa as well as the Canadian province of Ontario. By 1888 Polk's reputation as a national provider of directories was well established; at that time the company was producing gazetteers for 29 states.

Polk's expansion continued through the turn of the century with the addition of directories for cities in geographically diverse locations. The company also began publishing directories for special fields such as medicine, architecture, grain, and real estate. In 1913 Polk moved into new headquarters—a two-story building located at 431 Howard Street in Detroit. As the company grew, however, so did the building: a third story was added to make room for Polk's printing division, and later its size was increased by six more floors.

In 1916 Polk published its first bank directory, which had been purchased from Anthony Stumpf Publishing Company in New York City. The *Bankers Encyclopedia,* renamed *Polk's Bankers Encyclopedia* underwent subsequent renovations and emerged as *Polk's Bank Directory,* a standard reference in the banking industry.

The company's involvement with automotive statistics began in 1920 with the compilation of data from motor vehicle records in Michigan. The following year, Polk began collecting registration data in other states. In 1922, at the request of General Motors Corp., Polk began generating car registration reports; new truck registrations were first reported in 1926. Initially, data for all states was not listed, but by 1927 all of the 48 states and the District of Columbia were represented, and car model and make was added in 1928. Polk's reports were an important tool for car manufacturers because they provided unbiased statistical information with which to make marketing and production decisions.

The 1920s brought many other changes. Following the death of Ralph Polk in 1923, his son Ralph Lane Polk II, who had been working in the business full time since 1901, ascended to the presidency. Under his leadership, the company established a Direct Mail Division (later renamed the Marketing Services Division) using lists developed from directories and previously published gazetteers as well as those obtained from purchased list companies. By 1927 the division was mailing more than 20 million pieces on behalf of such customers as Willard Battery Company, Ford Motor Co., General Motors, Reo Motor Car Company, and others.

The company underwent a reorganization in 1928, when a holding company was formed to consolidate all Polk operations. Prior to that year, activities had been conducted by subsidiary corporations, partnerships, and individual proprietorships. Through the Depression years, Polk maintained about 80 percent of its directory business but abandoned the publication of state gazetteers. As the company emerged from the Depression, another reorganization in 1935 dissolved the surviving subsidiaries and consolidated them into one operating company, R. L. Polk & Co. The 1930s also brought tremendous expansion to Polk's City Directory Division. By the decade's end Polk was producing more than 1,000 city and suburban directories.

Collection of automotive statistics was suspended during World War II, when civilian auto production halted, but the process was resumed in 1945. During the war years, Polk provided mass mailing services for government departments and agencies. The company's efforts included assisting the Federal Food Administration in its efforts to distribute regulations and instructions to food product manufacturers. By the end of the 1940s, Polk operated several printing plants and had branch offices in more than 40 cities. The company's City Directory Division was publishing 750 directories and the Direct Mail Division was processing up to two million pieces of mail per day. Employment stood at about 5,000.

The 1940s closed with a change of leadership—following the death of Ralph Lane Polk II, Ralph Lane Polk III assumed the presidency. Previously a manager in the City Directory Division, the new president led R. L. Polk into the computer era. The company's first computers, installed in 1956 and 1958, were used to compile motor vehicle statistical data and facilitate direct mail activities. Prior to the beginning of electronic processing, reports were produced by hand-sorting information and manually tabulating it. Improvements in printing technology also helped make the job of producing documents more efficient. As a result, employment within the Statistical Services Division peaked at 745 in 1955. Although the division's workload continued to increase, fewer employees were needed.

Polk's foreign expansion began in 1956 with the purchase of a Canadian directory company, Annuaries Marcotte Ltd. Annuaries Marcotte published directories for Quebec city and other smaller communities. The company name was changed to R. L. Polk & Co. (Canada) Ltd. Later Polk Canada served as a holding company for subsequent Canadian acquisitions.

Polk's growth continued. In 1958 the company established a Bank Business Development Division to use list information generated by the billing operations of its Bank Services Division. The new division performed promotional, research, and syndicated marketing services for banks and other financial institutions. In 1960 Polk's City Directory Division built a new printing plant in Hutchinson, Kansas. The plant was the company's first to include in-house bindery capabilities.

Based on the obvious benefits, the company was also expanding its computer applications. Polk's National Vehicle Identification Number File was computerized in 1961, the same year computer operations were converted to magnetic tape. The Eureka, California, city directory was the first one published with data processing techniques. A programming language developed by Polk's staff, called Market Area Report Generator (MARG), aided in the production of complex automotive reports.

In 1963 Ralph Lane Polk III moved out of the president's office in order to serve as company chairman. Walter J. Gardner, who had been executive vice-president since 1955, became the first non-family member to hold the position of president. Under Gardner's direction, the company achieved international recognition as a leader in the information industry. Gardner also continued his predecessor's policy of pursuing technological modernization.

Some activities of the late 1960s included an expansion within the Bank Services Division to accommodate the production of annual custom bank directories and the adoption of innovative computer technology within the Marketing Services Division to permit computer letter printing and improved list services. Demand for automotive information increased following a 1966 federal law that required manufacturers to notify vehicle owners of safety-related defects in automobiles. Car manufacturers turned to Polk for assistance in sending recall notifications. Polk's Auto List II, a semiannual auto list, replaced the company's annual list in 1967.

During the 1970s Polk expanded and improved its existing services. Enhanced computer processing power enabled Polk's staff to generate more detailed statistical profiles of major automotive markets. Polk's ability to create reports by census tract as well as by postal zone helped motor vehicle dealers defend their markets in the wake of state franchise legislation.

The 1970s also marked the beginning of Polk's activities in Australia. In 1972 Polk acquired Direct Mail Services Pty. Ltd. (DMS) of Melbourne, Australia. The company's name was changed to R. L. Polk & Co. (Australia) Pty. Ltd. and subsequently served as a holding company for later Australian acquisitions in the Melbourne, Sidney, and Canberra areas. In Australia, Polk pioneered the fully personalized computer letter and successfully lobbied for postal acceptance of poly bag mailers.

In the United States, the 1980s marked a period of aggressive growth and challenge. In 1981 Ralph Lane Polk IV was elected president, but he served only four years before his sudden death in 1985. Polk was succeeded by John M. O'Hara, who faced the challenge of a nationwide trend toward consumer privacy and resulting restrictions in the availability of motor vehicle records for commercial purposes. Under O'Hara's leadership, Polk maintained its relationship with motor vehicle departments in all 50 states.

In 1987 Polk acquired Advertising Unlimited, Inc. (AUI), the largest U.S. manufacturer of promotional calendars and a leading provider of specialty advertising products (low-cost objects suitable for custom imprinting or personalization intended for use as corporate giveaways). AUI, incorporated in 1961, originally sold Yellow Page advertising and White Page maintenance services to small and medium-sized independent telephone companies. AUI began supplying merchandise to the specialty advertising industry in 1967. Following federally-mandated restructuring within the telephone industry, AUI's telephone directory business declined, and the company increased its emphasis on specialty advertising and calendars. At the time of Polk's acquisition, AUI operated three facilities, two in Minnesota and a third in London, Ontario. Stock included such items as calendars, planners, first aid kits, personal care products, and Anchor/Wallace worship bulletins.

Another major acquisition occurred in 1988 when Polk purchased National Demographics & Lifestyles Inc. (NDL), a Denver-based provider of demographic data. NDL, founded in

1975, collected lifestyle information to create an enormous database by using product registration questionnaires. In 1990, NDL's Lifestyle Selector included 25 million names. NDL was able to provide its clients with targeted mailing lists according to customer profiles.

Other acquisitions made during the late 1980s included North Winds Trading Company, the Fordan calendar line of National Press Inc., Talbot Communications (located in London, Ontario) and a 40 percent interest in Geographic Data Technology Inc. (GDT) headquartered in Lyme, New Hampshire. Polk acquired complete ownership of GDT in 1994.

GDT was founded in 1980 to prepare computerized maps. Its first digital maps were used for defining political and census boundaries in Florida. By 1983 GDT had completed boundary files for all U.S. counties and towns. Computerized maps were used to predict store site values, plan election campaigns, target direct mail promotions, and establish routes for buses and delivery vehicles. The company generated revenue by selling long-term licenses for the use of its files.

In other areas, existing products were upgraded and new products were developed. For example, Polk's REGIS (Registration Information System) database, which was first developed in 1982, made information accessible to customers who were linked to Polk's mainframe computers using PC network technology. By 1990, Polk reported that 40 companies subscribed to REGIS and its other interactive databases. Interactive databases gave users the flexibility needed to look for specific information on a task-oriented basis.

Another interactive product, TELE-PLAN, made information from Polk's National Vehicle Population Profile (NVPP) available to subscribers. Users of TELE-PLAN included suppliers to the automotive aftermarket industry. By combining information from the NVPP database with their own parts catalog and inventory, suppliers were better able to make accurate inventory decisions. Benefits included reducing the number of returns based on obsolescence and reducing back orders.

To accommodate its growth, Polk's corporate, executive, and accounting divisions moved into new headquarters in 1990. The offices were slated to occupy the top two floors of a new $32 million building, constructed during the second phase of a three-phase office project at a 20-acre complex formerly occupied by Stroh Brewery in Detroit. In addition, in 1990 the Polk family returned to the presidency with the election of Stephen R. Polk. Stephen R. Polk, a great-grandson of the company's founder, had served as executive vice-president since 1985.

Under Stephen Polk's direction, the company moved toward providing full-service data and marketing services. In 1980 revenues had been split equally between automotive and non-automotive customers, however, according to one estimate, by 1990 automotive accounts represented about one-third of the company's total revenues, judged to be $285 million. A reorganization of the Statistical Services Division and Marketing Services Division led to the formation of a new Automotive Marketing Group and a Direct Marketing Service division. The Automotive Marketing Group was able to provide coordinated services to automotive customers while the Direct Marketing Service met the needs of the company's non-automotive clients. Hoping to improve the efficiency of its interactive services, Polk also began a centralization process aimed at combining its four databases at one site in Taylor, Michigan.

In 1992, Polk introduced a new information product called Decision Point. Decision Point was designed to help large retailers locate new stores or dealerships by coordinating census, income, and auto registration information. Special software, licensed from the University of Leeds in England, enabled users to retrieve needed data and analyze it.

A service designed to help combat fraud associated with auto salvage was unveiled in 1993. Auto fraud was sometimes perpetrated by operators who purchased wrecked cars, rebuilt and repainted them, and then transferred them to states where new titles without salvage designations could be obtained. The rebuilt cars were then resold as non-salvage vehicles. According to a report in *Crain's Detroit Business,* approximately 3 million wrecked cars were resold annually. Consumers who unwittingly purchased salvage vehicles faced increased repair bills and potential safety hazards. In a test of a limited version of Polk's title database conducted by Anglo American Auto Auctions of Nashville, Tennessee, 15 vehicles per week (out of 1,000) were identified as having improper titles. After the auction company's ability to discover bad titles was made known, the number reportedly fell to about five per week.

Polk's leaders expected the company to continue to grow. Although they anticipated some growth would be achieved through acquisition, they also looked to internal development to provide the rest. This included making the company's vast information databases available in a greater variety of formats.

Principal Subsidiaries: Advertising Unlimited, Inc.; National Demographics & Lifestyles Inc.; Geographic Data Technology, Inc.; R. L. Polk & Co. Ltd. (Canada); R. L. Polk & Co. Pty. Ltd. (Australia).

Further Reading:

Child, Charles, "Facts to the Max," *Crain's Detroit Business,* August 2, 1993.
——, "Polk Attacks Car Fraud," *Crain's Detroit Business,* June 14, 1993.
Doll, Lesa, "Data Deluge," *Corporate Detroit Magazine,* December 1991.
A History: R. L. Polk & Co., Detroit: R. L. Polk, n.d.
Prater, Constance, "Publishing Firm Relocates to Stroh Site," *Detroit News,* December 7, 1988.
"R. L. Polk & Co.," *Automotive Marketing,* December 1991.
"R. L. Polk & Co. Since 1870: A Brief History," Detroit: R. L. Polk, n.d.
"R. L. Polk—Triad Contract Will Lead to New Automotive Database," *PR Newswire,* January 27, 1994.

—Karen Bellenir

READ-RITE ℞

Read-Rite Corp.

345 Los Coches Street
Milpitas, California 95035
U.S.A.
(408) 262-6700
Fax: (408) 956-3205

Public Company
Incorporated: 1981
Employees: 10,488
Sales: $515.6 million
Stock Exchanges: NASDAQ
SICs: 3679 Electronic Components, Nec.

Read-Rite Corp. is the world's top supplier of thin-film recording heads, a component used in Winchester disk drives to read data stored on a computer's hard disk. Read-Rite also manufactures the head stack assemblies that house these thin-film recording heads, holding a small but growing market share in that segment. The company's client base consists of other manufacturers of computer components, including Western Digital, Maxtor Corp., Conner Peripherals, Inc., Digital Equipment Corp., NEC, Quantum, and Micropolis Corp. Demand for Read-Rite's highly specialized product has been bolstered by the computer industry trend towards obtaining higher performance from increasingly smaller components. Moreover, competition in the company's market was slight; in 1994, there were fewer than five similar manufacturers in the world. However, analysts predicted that more companies would enter the arena in the late 1990s.

Read-Rite was founded by a group of computer scientists and venture capitalists in California's booming Silicon Valley. Well versed in the ways of the computer industry, this group responded to a perceived trend towards increasingly smaller hard drives and a corresponding need for technology that would allow data to be accessed quickly and efficiently. The group believed thin-film recording technology was the key. With an initial investment of $23 million provided by Hambrecht & Quist, Citicorp Venture Capital Ltd., and several other financial partners, Read-Rite was established in November 1981, in Milpitas, California, to begin producing thin-film recording heads.

By November 1984, Read-Rite has shipped its first thin-film recording head. During its first year of operations, the company

shipped approximately 100,000 thin-film heads, one of the highest first-year volumes in the burgeoning thin-film head industry. As other component manufacturers experienced sales slumps during this time, Read-Rite sales grew, bolstered by an increasing demand for thin-film products. Between February 1985 and February 1986, the company's order backlog quadrupled. Although it was far from making a profit, the company had a strong balance sheet, resulting from additional funding that amounted to $14 million over two years.

In November 1986, Read-Rite merged with Cybernex, the world's largest producer of thin-film head. Cybernex had recently suffered from a trade secret suit filed against it by IBM, the result of which was an out-of-court settlement stating that Cybernex could no longer continue as an independent business. Through a stock-swap, Read-Rite absorbed all of Cybernex's assets, including its production facilities, staff, and technology patents.

By June 1987, Read-Rite had shipped its one-millionth head and had established accounts with several key components manufacturers, including Maxtor Corp. and Conner Peripherals. However, with Read-Rite's increased sales came a host of manufacturing problems. In early 1987, imperfections appeared in the chemical compounds used in manufacturing head assemblies. Originally intending shipments to be temporarily delayed as the company rectified the problem, Read-Rite found the situation to be more severe than expected. Two of its key customers, Micropolis and Maxtor had to delay hard drive production, generating some bad publicity for Read-Rite. Furthermore, its own production delays stopped up cash flow. The company was forced to lay off over 30 percent of its work force, and Chairperson John R. Osborne and President Wade Meyercord were replaced by a "turn-around" team assembled by Hambrecht & Quist, Read-Rite's principal financial partner. The company posted a total loss of $34 million in 1987 and 1988, on combined revenues of $39.5 million.

The following year, however, Read-Rite's sales hit $38 million, and the company experienced its first profitable year. Business began booming, and, in 1990 alone, the company shipped seven million thin-film heads, resulting in an almost 50 percent increase in sales to $73 million. When Cyril J. Yansouni joined Read-Rite in 1991 as chairperson and CEO, company sales and profits were beginning to take off.

The first project Yansouni undertook was to help reach a joint-venture agreement with Japan's Sumitomo Metal Industries to establish thin-film head operations in Japan. Sumitomo, a leading steelmaker, had been attempting to break into the data storage industry with its own thin-film heads, producing 50,000 heads monthly and having difficulty breaking into the American market. Conversely, Read-Rite, which was putting out two million heads monthly and held the top market share in the United States, was badly in need of a cash infusion. In the venture, Sumitomo put more than $20 million towards the construction of an assembly plant near Osaka and also invested another $20 million in Read-Rite in exchange for a ten percent stake in the company. Scheduled to begin production in 1994, the venture put Read-Rite in an advantageous position to profit from an expected boom in Winchester disk drives in the Japanese market. Sumitomo and Read-Rite each held a 50 percent stake in the venture, named Read-Rite SMI.

Read-Rite had earlier attempted to enter into the head stack assembly (HSA) business, which would allow the company to immediately integrate its thin-film heads into head stack assemblies and sell the two components as one unit. This first attempt had proved unsuccessful, however, and the company allegedly garnered a $2 million loss in the process. Read-Rite withdrew from the market, regrouped, and founded a new Head Stack Assembly group, headed by Marty Horn and Richard Stubberfield. In September 1991, the group purchased a two-year-old HSA plant in Penang, Malaysia, from Conner Peripherals and also began construction of a new plant in Thailand. Two months later, the group paid $17 million to acquired the Malaysian HSA operations of Maxtor Corp. Given Read-Rite's existing sales ties with the two companies, the move proved fortuitous and improved competitiveness against Read-Rite's top rival, Dastek Inc. In the midst of this tremendous growth, Read-Rite went public on the NASDAQ exchange on October 18 at $11.50 per share and raised $50 million in its initial public offering.

During this time, personal computer prices plunged and worldwide sales increased dramatically, while use of thin-film head in the disk drive industry swelled from 20 percent in 1990 to 70 percent in 1992. As a result, Read-Rite captured 50 percent of the market, and its sales hit $177 million in 1991. To handle growing demands for its components, Read-Rite began building a new manufacturing facility near its headquarters in the Santa Clara County and also began construction of a manufacturing facility in Thailand. In September 1992, Read-Rite SMI began production of thin-film heads, two years ahead of projections, and its sales for the year totaled $398 million.

In May 1993, Fred Schwettmann, former vice-president of Hewlett-Packard Co.'s circuit technology group, joined Read-Rite as chief operating officer and president. Schwettmann assumed these posts at a time when the industry was heading towards a major realignment, for which Read-Rite had not been entirely prepared. Read-Rite's customers in the hard-drive industry had not foreseen a market trend towards newer, high-

capacity drives, and, as a result, were suffering from a glut of unwanted low-capacity drives. Drive makers began cancelling their contracts with component makers and concurrently put pressure on them to reduce prices. Read-Rite's net income plummeted 89 percent in the third quarter of 1993 to $1.3 million, down from $12.2 million in third quarter of 1992. Although overall sales climbed from $389 million in 1992 to $482 million in 1983, net income plunged $47 million to hit $884,000, due to this sharp decline in the fourth quarter of 1993.

Sales at Read-Rite continued to fall in the first half of 1994, although the company picked up several new contracts with leading component manufacturers. During this time, Read-Rite merged its head stack assemblies operations with Sunward Technologies, Inc., a leading producer of rigid disk recording head products, preparing to face growing competition from emerging alternative technologies. Some industry analysts contended that Read-Rite's financial declines in the early 1990s reflected the company's failure to anticipate and develop technology for the new high-capacity drives. Others, however, maintained that the declines were simply the result of market cycles, suggesting that the company would report more promising figures once the market realigned itself.

Principal Subsidiaries: Read-Rite SMI.

Further Reading:

Deagon, Brian, "Conner Thin-Film Stack Unit in Malaysia Sold to Read-Rite," *Electronic News,* September 9, 1991, p. 13.

Deagon, Brian, "Read-Rite, Sumitomo in Venture," *Electronic News,* July 8, 1991, p. 11.

Detar, Jim, "Head Snag Still Delaying Maxtor Drives," *Electronic News,* August 17, 1987, p. 19.

Khermouch, Gerry, "Read-Rite to Buy Head-Stack Plant in Malaysia from Maxtor for $17M," *Electronic News,* November 25, 1991, p. 14.

Krey, Michael, "Cyril Yansouni: Unassuming CEO Keeps Read-Rite Out Front of Pack," *The Business Journal-San Jose,* June 8, 1992, p. 12.

Marsh, Gary, and Jim Nash, "Read-Rite's Once-Bright Star Starts to Grow Dim," *The Business Journal,* August 9, 1993, p. 1.

—Maura Troester

REICHHOLD

Reichhold Chemicals, Inc.

P.O. Box 13582
Research Triangle Park, North Carolina 27709-3582
U.S.A.
(919) 990-7500
Fax: (919) 990-7711

Wholly Owned Subsidiary of Dainippon
Incorporated: 1927
Employees: 2,200
Sales: $540 million
SICs: 2821 Plastics Materials & Resins

Reichhold Chemicals, Inc. (RCI) is a leading producer of chemicals used for coatings, adhesives, emulsions, and reactive polymers, with 31 factories located throughout North America. The company was started in the 1920s by a German immigrant who provided new, fast-drying paints to the automotive industry. From this basis, Reichhold grew steadily, acquiring new plants and adding new products. In the mid-1980s, RCI was purchased by a large Japanese chemical company with which the firm had long done business.

RCI got its start in the United States after its founder, Henry Helmuth Reichhold, who was born the youngest of seven children near Berlin, had emigrated to America. His father, Carl, was a chemist, and a principle in one of the leading European paint companies of the day. As a youth, Helmuth Reichhold spent time in child labor camps in Germany during World War I. After the war, he studied at the universities of Berlin and Vienna, and, at the age of 20, followed his older brothers into his family's business in Vienna.

Three years later, after his father had advised him that staying in Europe meant seeing a business destroyed every 25 years by the depredations of war, Reichhold emigrated to the United States. In 1924, he went to Detroit to study surface finishing methods used in the American automobile industry. Speaking only a few phrases of English, Reichhold was hired as an assistant in the paint laboratory of the Ford Motor Company, earning $4.80 a day.

Within a year, with his chemistry background, Reichhold had been made technical head of the department. At this time, applying the lacquer finish to an automobile was a time consuming process. Ford used "coach-and-carriage" finishes that were based on natural resins and gums for adhesiveness, and took days to dry. This created a bottleneck in production, and a stubborn obstacle to the true mass production which Henry Ford desired.

Meanwhile, and despite his meteoric rise at Ford, Reichhold had always had his eye on his own business. When he heard from his brother Otto in Germany during the winter of 1925 that his father's old company had developed a heat-hardening and oil-soluble phenolic resin that dried in hours rather than days, Reichhold's experience at Ford enabled him to recognize what an important breakthrough this was.

Reichhold asked his brother to ship him 20 100-pound bags of the new substance, which he bought on a loan of $10,000. He stored the bags in the garage of his friend Charles J. O'Connor, who sold paint. Calling the new substance "Beckacite," after Beck, Koller, & Company, the name of his father's firm, Reichhold went into business as its distributor, selling the product to Ford. He hired his friend O'Connor as a salesman and reduced his hours at the factory. When Ford refused to give him a 40-cents-a-day raise, Reichhold quit altogether.

In 1927, Reichhold borrowed $10,000 from his father to buy a 4,000-square-foot paint and varnish factory in a Detroit suburb. He also opened a sales office in the General Motors Building in Detroit. In order to simplify the importation of his main product from Germany, Reichhold set up his company as Beck, Koller, & Company, U.S. In 1928, the company took delivery of its second paint shipment from Europe.

Also in that year, two scientists arrived from Germany to help Reichhold set up his own manufacturing facility for Beckacite. In its first full year in business, the fledgling company had $532,000 in sales. The bulk of these sales went to Ford, who refused to buy paint from the DuPont chemical company because they also supplied General Motors. Using Reichhold's products, Henry Ford was able to fully implement his plan of mass production for cars in colors other than black. In 1926, Ford's Model T came in blue, gray, and brown. By 1927, with Reichhold's input, that palette had been expanded to include maroon and green.

In 1929, Reichhold made his first acquisition, buying the Synthe-Copal Company, of Buffalo, New York. This company manufactured ester gums, a raw material used in the production of synthetic resins. Then, however, the American economy took a steep plunge, entering the Great Depression. In 1930, Reichhold and O'Connor incorporated their venture in the state of Delaware, calling it Beck, Koller, & Company. During the economic downturn, Reichhold worked to develop his products. In 1931, he established research laboratories to develop synthetic resins, using phenols and other chemicals. By the following year, the company's output had reached $1.5 million pounds of chemicals.

To protect his market share, Reichhold sought to become a complete supplier for the needs of paint formulators. He sought efficient manufacturing processes, and economies of scale in order to keep prices low. In addition, Reichhold stressed sales efforts, to increase the company's volume. To improve distribution, he began to place his factories near the markets he hoped to penetrate. In 1934, for instance, he had the Synthe-Copal plant in Buffalo dismantled and moved to Michigan, where his automotive customers were. Once reassembled and expanded, this facility became the largest individual ester gum/resin plant in the world. In 1935, a plant was built in San Francisco, but it burned down the following year. By that time, Reichhold had set aside a quarter of a million dollars for factory expansion. With these funds, an East Coast plant was constructed from 1935 to 1936, in Elizabeth, New Jersey. It made resins for coating the surface of woods, and maleic anhydride.

By late 1937, Reichhold had come to expect shortages of his raw materials, and he began an effort to become his own supplier, manufacturing the chemicals used to make the resins he sold. In 1934, the company had begun production of alkyd resins; three years later, it also began to make urea-formaldehyde. Around this time, Reichhold had also linked up with a number of resin manufacturers in Europe, a natural expansion of his firm's roots in his father's Austrian company. By 1937, operations had been established in Great Britain and Austria.

Reichhold's brother Otto was traveling to America to discuss these foreign ties in 1937 when he died in the explosion of the Hindenburg blimp in New Jersey. With this symbolic severance of the tie between Reichhold and his family's European firm, Reichhold dropped the Beck, Koller, & Company name in 1938, re-naming his enterprise Reichhold Chemicals, Inc. (RCI). By that time, the company's three production plants were producing sales of more than $3 million annually.

RCI increased its East Coast manufacturing facilities further when it purchased a Brooklyn producer of chemical pigments. By the following year, this had been established as RCI's Chemical Color Division. With the outbreak of World War II, and the switch of the American economy to war-time production, RCI's Brooklyn facility became the source of one-third of the U.S. military's rust prevention primer. The company went on to produce coatings for tanks, battleships, bombers, ground vehicles, and more prosaic products, such as radios and furniture. In response to war-time shortages, the company opened new plants and developed substitute chemicals. In 1942, a factory in Tuscaloosa, Alabama opened to make synthetic phenol. In addition, RCI's Detroit plant was expanded. By 1943, RCI's founder had Americanized his name, from the German "Helmuth Reichhold" to Henry H. Reichhold.

In the wake of the war, Reichhold moved to raise its public profile, particularly in the Detroit area. The company became a major sponsor of the Detroit Symphony Orchestra. It also sponsored radio broadcasts and, in the 1950s, a television program called "America's Town Meeting of the Air." During the late 1940s, RCI also expanded its production capabilities, to keep pace with rising demand in the postwar boom years. The company opened a plant in Seattle, Washington, and built a resin facility in Weston, Ontario, the foundation for Reichhold Chemicals (Canada) Limited. In 1950, factories in Argo, Illinois, and Azusa, California, were also added, and in the following year a plant in Charlotte, North Carolina came on line.

In response to this rapid expansion, RCI moved its corporate headquarters from Ferndale, Michigan to Rockefeller Center in New York City in 1951. This move repositioned the company for greater ease in making international alliances, and RCI entered into a number of joint agreements. In 1951, the company agreed with a Swiss company to manufacture resins, and more importantly, formed a joint venture with a Japanese firm, the Dainippon Printing Ink Manufacturing Company, Limited. Renamed Japan Reichhold Chemicals, Inc., this enterprise supplied Reichhold's technology to Japanese facilities and personnel.

By 1952, Reichhold's international push had resulted in facilities and licensees in 13 countries: Australia, Brazil, England, France, Germany, Holland, Israel, Italy, Japan, Spain, Sweden, and South Africa. After seeing its Austrian operations seized by Russian forces during World War II, the company reestablished operations in that country in another location. By 1953, RCI's sales were nearing the $100 million mark.

Throughout the early 1950s, RCI added manufacturing facilities at the rate of nearly one per year. In 1954, the company revealed plans for further expansion, pledging to spend $10 million on improvements to its American factories. Two years later, RCI went public, raising capital through the sale of 200,000 shares in the company. With these funds, further facilities were added in the late 1950s, as the strong demand for materials continued. Between 1957 and 1960, RCI built or bought nine different chemical plants, in keeping with Reichhold's philosophy that products should be produced near their intended market. In keeping with this theory, RCI also established a Mexican subsidiary, and assumed control of its German branch, Reichhold Chemic AG, which had suffered total destruction during World War II.

In 1962, RCI's Japanese partner, Dainippon, bought out the company's interest in their joint venture, but retained a 20-year license with RCI for use of its technology. In the early 1960s, RCI continued to expand rapidly, adding plants at the rate of more than one per year. From its base in resins and polymers, the company branched out to include plastics and fiberglass. In 1965, RCI acquired Structoglas, a Cleveland-based company, which joined with an earlier RCI acquisition to produce reinforced plastics.

Two years later, the company purchased a Blane Chemicals factory in Manfield, Massachusetts, which made thermoplastics, and then bought Cooke Color & Chemical, based in Visalia, California and Rockport, New Jersey, which also manufactured these substances. In 1968, RCI entered the rubber latex field, purchasing a Cuyahoga Falls plant in Ohio from the Rubber Latex company. At this time, RCI had 30 domestic factories and 32 licensees in 24 countries outside the United States.

In the next seven years, RCI added 12 more plants that specialized in various aspects of its industry. In 1975, the company established the Reichhold Energy Corporation as a subsidiary. Also in that year, RCI acquired half of the Fibron Corporation as an investment. With plants in Portland, Oregon, St. Louis, Missouri, and Seattle, Washington, this company recycled wood fibers and produced plywood. Next, RCI acquired Reichhold Chemie, AG, the German firm that the company had taken over in 1959. At the same time, Reichhold bought Standard Brands Chemical Industries, which became the company's Emulsion Polymers Division. With plants in five states, this branch of RCI made textile products, adhesives, leather finishing products, paper chemicals, and rubber products.

In 1979, the company signed a licensing agreement with Exxon Chemicals to supply modified polyolefins. By 1981, RCI's sales had reached nearly $1 billion, and the company had joined the ranks of the Fortune 500. Henry Reichhold retired as chief executive officer of the company the following year, passing leadership of the firm to younger executives. At the time of his retirement, Reichhold had been at the head of a Fortune 500 company longer than any other chief executive. During his time as leader of the company, he had traveled tirelessly to inspect facilities, and strived to maintain a familial atmosphere at the company, despite its ever-growing size.

In the wake of Reichhold's departure, RCI continued its policy of growth through acquisition and international expansion. In 1985, the company bought its Canadian subsidiary Reichhold Limited, and also acquired Swift Adhesives from the Eschem company, moving strongly into the adhesives production industry. Headquarters of the Swift company, which became a subsidiary of RCI, were based in Downer's Grove, Illinois; Swift also ran 20 factories in the United States. In addition, Swift brought significant foreign operations to RCI, with six plants in Canada, an equal number in Great Britain, two in France, and one in Spain. In the same year that RCI purchased Swift, the company expanded its operations in this field further when it bought the adhesives production operations of the Peter Cooper Corporations.

In the mid-1980s, RCI began an effort to bring some form of order to its sprawling operations, which had grown so rapidly and so steadily over the last three decades. In 1986, the company sold off one of its divisions, which produced specialty phenolics. This part of the company was bought by BTL Specialty Chemicals. At the same time, RCI established a strategy of focusing on four main markets. These areas were adhesives, paper chemicals, coatings, and plastics.

In the wake of this reorganization, RCI's long-time Japanese partner, Dainippon Ink & Chemicals, Inc., based in Tokyo, launched a bid to buy the company. After the Japanese firm successfully purchased all of RCI's outstanding shares, it ceased to be a publicly held corporation, and became instead a wholly owned subsidiary of Dainippon. RCI's foreign operations were split off from the company to form a separate unit of Dainippon. At the time of the takeover, RCI's retired founder expressed acquiescence with the deal, noting that the Japanese stress on long-term company growth over the short-term gains demanded by Wall Street accorded with his philosophy on the proper way to build and run a business.

Under its new corporate owners, RCI again underwent a number of operational shifts. In 1989, the company announced that it would leave the New York metropolitan area to relocate its headquarters and research activities in Research Triangle Park, North Carolina. In the following year, ground was broken for a new $50 million headquarters building, and company personnel started to relocate to the area. The move was completed a year later and the company was reorganized into groups based on function. Instead of dividing responsibility according to the type of product that was being manufactured, RCI split itself up into groups that performed either operations, technology, or sales and marketing.

In the early 1990s, RCI moved to strengthen itself in the latter area, sales and marketing. The company strove to improve customer service, to upgrade its computer operations, and to enhance its distribution systems. In 1994, RCI further centralized its administration when the corporate headquarters of the Swift Adhesives Division moved to North Carolina from Illinois. With operations centralized, and the company reorganized for more efficient operation, RCI appeared to be well-situated to continue its steady success into the late 1990s.

Principal Subsidiaries: RBH Dispersions, Inc.; Reichhold Ltd.; Reichhold Quimica de Mexico, S.A. (Mexico); Surface Technologies, Inc.; Swift Adhesives, Inc.; Swift Adhesives, Ltd.; The Product Design Center, Inc.

Further Reading:

"Henry Helmuth Reichhold, 1901–1989," New York: New York Community Trust, 1989.

—Elizabeth Rourke

REX Stores Corp.

2875 Needmore Rd.
Dayton, Ohio 45414-1918
U.S.A.
(513) 276-3931
Fax: (513) 276-2713

Public Company
Incorporated: 1984 as Audio/Video Affiliates, Inc.
Employees: 829
Sales: $298.17 million
Stock Exchanges: New York Boston Midwest Pittsburgh
    Pacific
SICs: 5722 Radio, Television and Consumer Electronics
    Stores; 5731 Household Appliance Stores

REX Stores Corp. is a prominent retailer of consumer electronics and appliances in the Midwest and Southeast. REX has grown from a 4-store chain in Dayton, Ohio, to a 132-store retailer with locations in 23 states. This growth has occurred primarily through acquisition. Although the chain is headquartered in Ohio, the highest concentration of REX stores (20) is in Florida. The chain extended its reach into Kansas, Oklahoma, and Wisconsin in fiscal 1994. The company changed its name from Audio/Video Affiliates, Inc., in August 1993 to more accurately connect the holding company with its retail affiliates. REX has expanded its product mix significantly from its initial focus on radios to include a broad selection of brand name televisions, camcorders, and video and audio equipment (known in the industry as "brown goods"), as well as major household appliances (known in the industry as "white goods"), including microwaves, air conditioners, refrigerators, washers, dryers, and ranges. The company ventured into jewelry sales in the early 1990s.

Key elements of REX's business strategy include an emphasis on small- and medium-sized "niche" markets, depth of selection within key product categories, the ubiquitous "everyday low price" policy, extensive local newspaper advertising, and efficient operations. Although other chains in the industry concentrated on such hard-fought markets as New York and Chicago, REX has placed its outlets in small communities. The chain's concentration on smaller cities and towns accomplished several corporate objectives. Rents and other overhead expenses are often lower in these markets and, at the same time,

competition from major consumer electronics chains is frequently not as intense, enabling REX to bring discounting to these markets and still earn high profit margins. The chain offers national brands at a variety of price points, including General Electric, Hitachi, JVC, Magnavox, Panasonic, Pioneer, RCA, Sharp, Toshiba, and Zenith. REX offers a "low price guarantee" that is almost mandatory in the consumer electronics environment of the 1990s. The chain promises to refund at least 125 percent of the difference between its own and any competitor's lower price found within 30 days of the sale.

REX Stores Corp. was founded as REX Radio, a single outlet in a Dayton hotel storefront, in 1926. During the 1950s, the company expanded into televisions and subsequently changed its name to REX Radio & TV. The store established a long-standing volume-buying strategy in the 1960s when it became a founding member of the NATM Buying Corporation. In the late 1980s, REX joined Silo, Highland, and Circuit City in the formation of a new purchasing organization, Group 4. By the early 1990s, REX continued to employ its volume-oriented strategy, but did so independently.

Significant developments in REX's recent history began in 1980, when the Dayton-area four-store chain was acquired by Stuart Rose, a merger and acquisition broker at Niederhoffer, Cross and Zeckhauser. The owner of REX had hired the New York firm to find a buyer for the business. Rose was interested, but relatively cash poor: he had saved $150,000 ("by skipping meals and living in a run-down apartment," according to a 1986 *Business Week* article), but the purchase price was $4.3 million. At the same time, his prospects for a loan weren't good either. Interest rates were rising fast and lenders were not eager to go out on a limb for a 24-year-old entrepreneur. So Rose bypassed traditional funding sources in favor of large-scale financial techniques to acquire and promote his relatively small business. First, he borrowed against the REX stores' own inventory and upped their mortgages, thereby raising almost half of the necessary capital. He was then able to persuade CMNY Capital Co., a New York investment firm, to buy a 6.6 percent stake in REX for $350,000 and convinced H.A. Armstrong to loan him $1.5 million at 22 percent interest.

Although Rose had no experience in consumer electronics, he soon realized that the only way his newly acquired business would succeed was through expansion. By anticipating and participating in the consolidation of the consumer electronics industry, REX would be able to survive and take advantage of the trend. Early growth came from significant acquisitions. In 1981, REX purchased TV & Stereo Town, a 16-store electronics chain with locations in Des Moines, Iowa, and Largo, Florida. This heavily leveraged deal utilized $500,000 borrowed from Stereo Town's own line of credit and another half million from the chain's former owner. The next year saw the acquisition of Kelly & Cohen, a 36-store chain in Pittsburgh, Pennsylvania. By this time, Rose's credit record was well established, and he was able to borrow the entire purchase price, $3.5 million. The original REX chain, Stereo Town, and Kelly & Cohen were operated as affiliates.

Faced with massive debt and still eager to expand, Rose elected to take his chain public in 1984 under a holding company,

Audio/Video Affiliates, Inc. The initial public offering raised $18 million at $5 per share, $10 million of which was used for working capital. Sales rose 36.7 percent in fiscal 1984 (which ended in January 1984), to $118.7 million.

By the late 1980s, the consumer electronics chain numbered over 100 stores, but such rapid expansion required a retrenchment. Late in 1988, a reorganization plan had been created; its primary element was Audio/Video Affiliates, Inc.'s acquisition by a newly created unit of Citicorp, AV Holdings. The transaction, valued at $98 million, was for all of Audio/Video's 11.5 million shares. By the end of the year, however, the deal was canceled, due to skyrocketing interest rates on the junk bonds that would have financed about half of Citicorp's purchase. Citicorp did, however, acquire about 15 percent of Audio/Video's stock, which it agreed to sell back to the company in 1991.

In 1989, REX started a more orthodox reorganization: the company reduced its outstanding shares by over half, from 15.7 million to 6.2 million through a stock buyback and self-tender. Personnel reductions and cost-cutting measures in distribution and advertising helped the chain achieve much-touted operational efficiencies. The reorganization also involved the closing of 25 stores and one warehouse, as well as the sale/leaseback of 50 other stores and two other warehouses. These transactions raised $59 million, 66 percent of which was used for debt retirement, mortgages, and taxes. By 1990, REX's total number of stores had been reduced by over 40 percent, from 125 to 73. The company recorded a net loss of almost $2 million for fiscal year 1991, then bounced back the following year to earn profits of over $3 million. This retrenchment did not last long; it only prefaced a period of dramatic growth.

In 1993, REX raised $17 million on the sale of stock to fund its biggest expansion in over a decade. The company added 25 new stores in 1993 and planned to open 30 to 35 more in 1994 as it moved westward across the United States. Texas, Georgia, Ohio, Tennessee, South Carolina, Pennsylvania, Wisconsin, North Carolina, Kansas, and Oklahoma were targeted for expansion. Net income at REX increased 80 percent during fiscal 1994, to $8.6 million from $4.8 million in fiscal 1993. Same-store sales increased 8 percent over the year.

REX faced more intense competition from Circuit City and warehouse clubs in the early 1990s. In line with industry trends, REX reported that its fastest-growing product segment was big-screen televisions. REX experimented with offering jewelry at "stores-within-a-store" in the early 1990s, hoping to take advantage of the higher margins of the trade. By April 1994, six stores participated in the fledgling program. During fiscal 1995, REX planned to begin test marketing personal computers and related accessories in 20 selected markets with a view toward adding them chainwide. The company had avoided this highly competitive niche until that time.

Further Reading:

Gelfand, Michael, "Consumer Electronics Superstores," *Discount Merchandiser,* January 1993, pp. 60–66, 70.
Levine, Jonathan, "Turning Points in the Lives of Companies: How Big-League Techniques Paid Off for Stuart-Rose," *Business Week,* November 3, 1986, p. 124.
Pinkerton, Janet, "Mining the Boondocks," *Dealerscope Merchandising,* August 1993, pp. 50–53.
Stricharchuk, Gregory, "Audio/Video Says Plan to Acquire It Has Been Dropped," *Wall Street Journal,* December 16, 1988, p. C5.

—April Dougal Gasbarre

RHÔNE-POULENC

Rhône-Poulenc S.A.

25 quay Paul-Doumer
F 92408
Courbevoie CEDEX
France
(33) 1.47.68.12.34
Fax: (33) 1.47.68.19.11

Public Company
Incorporated: 1895 as Société Chimiques des Usines du
   Rhône
Employees: 81,678
Sales: FFr 80.6 billion
Stock Exchanges: New York Paris London
SICs: 2834 Pharmaceutical Preparations; 2836 Biological
   Products Except Diagnostic; 2869 Industrial Organic
   Chemicals, Nec.; 2865 Cyclic Crudes and Intermediates;
   2819 Industrial Inorganic Chemicals, Nec.; 2879
   Agricultural Chemicals, Nec.

Rhône-Poulenc S.A. ranks among the world's ten largest chemical companies, with interests in: agricultural chemicals; human and veterinary pharmaceuticals; fibers and polymers; specialty chemicals; and organic and inorganic intermediates. Rhône-Poulenc's business was dramatically internationalized through myriad acquisitions in the late 1980s and early 1990s. By the end of 1993, the company had operations in 140 countries and almost eighty percent of its income came from outside of France.

Rhône-Poulenc traces its history to the formation of two separate companies established in the nineteenth century: the Société Chimiques des Usines du Rhône and the Etablissement Poulenc-Frères. In 1858, a pharmacist named Etienne Poulenc purchased a small drug store in Paris. Soon thereafter, Poulenc's interests extended to more than apothecary supplies, and he began to produce his own specialty products, featuring a line of photographic supplies and products. This early interest in diversification became characteristic of the firm as it grew.

In 1900, Etienne Poulenc's two brothers joined him in his business, and the company became known as the Etablissement Poulenc-Frères. Over the next twenty years, they became associated with other firms in France and abroad. The brothers first joined forces with the Comptoir des Textiles Artificielles (CTA), founded by the Gillet and Carnot families. Collabora-

tion between Poulenc chemists and doctors from the CTA led to the production of many drugs used to treat soldiers during World War I. The 1922 acquisition of the British firm May and Baker strengthened the Poulenc-Frères position in the pharmaceutical industry.

In 1895, while the Poulenc brothers were building their chemical company, the Société Chimiques des Usines du Rhône was being formed in Lyons for the manufacture of dyestuffs and of raw materials for perfumes. This company faced several obstacles during its early years. At the turn of the century, for example, German domination of the chemical industry caused difficulties for this and many other French firms. The Usines du Rhône was forced to stop production of its dyestuffs line, and the company was taken over by the banks, which, in turn, put the company's management into the hands of Nicolas Grillet, one of their chemical engineers. New products then began emerging from the company, among them Rhodine, which became aspirin, and a perfume called Rodo. The latter, exported to Rio de Janeiro for Carnival, brought in as much as three-quarters of the company's profits during this period. Another major development of the firm prior to World War I was the manufacture of cellophane. A 1922 merger between the Gillet family's CTA and the Usines du Rhône produced the firm known as Rhodiaceta.

By the 1920s, a union was developing between Poulenc-Frères and the Usines du Rhône, due largely to their shared association with CTA. It seemed that even greater benefits were to be found in combining their resources. Thus, in 1928, the two firms merged to form the Société des Usines Chimiques Rhône-Poulenc (SUCRP). Two new subsidiaries, Prolabo and Spécia, were created at approximately the same time.

The early growth of the new firm was hampered by the worldwide depression beginning in 1929, which forced SUCRP to consolidate its laboratories into two sites and reduced the company's holdings to three factories. Nevertheless, the company's English subsidiary May and Baker continued with its research and production; a notable discovery of this period was a sulfamide drug made in their laboratories, which was used to cure Winston Churchill of pneumonia. While the firm was able to continue production through the depression, the onset of World War II nearly ten years later limited options even further by creating a shortage of supplies. Even with these limitations, however, SUCRP was involved in two important chemical developments: nylon, which was in only limited production during the war, and the first French production of penicillin. These two innovations gave SUCRP the capital it needed after the war in order to finance the restart of many of its factories.

After the war, Rhône-Poulenc's policies exhibited a growing commitment to research and development. Research became a high priority, as the company relegated four-and-a-half to five percent of its new sales for research. Over time, the firm was divided into five groups, including chemistry, health, textile, agricultural chemicals, and films. This last group, a relatively new endeavor, hearkened back to the days of Etienne Poulenc.

Elsewhere in the industry, there were changes which would again reshape the corporate structure of SUCRP. The Gillet family, whose firm CTA had been so important for Rhône-

Poulenc's early development, formed a holding company known as CELTEX in 1952 to consolidate their various interests. Meanwhile, SUCRP continued its moves into pharmaceuticals with the 1956 acquisition of Théraplix, another manufacturer of health products. These two groups were brought together in a critical merger during 1961, with the formation of a holding company to combine SUCRP and its various subsidiaries. Also forming part of this company was CELTEX. Additions in the areas of textiles and films were immediately apparent; the new group's sales were about 60 percent in the textile area.

Rhône-Poulenc continued to build its resources. Between 1963 and 1968 it acquired majority interests in two research facilities, the Laboratoire Roger Bellon and the Institut Mérieux. Two smaller chemical firms, Progil and Péchiney Saint Gobain, were acquired in 1969. These moves strengthened the group's position in the basic products area, as well as in heavy and agricultural chemicals; the former in particular provided the company with a long overdue branch in petrochemicals. These acquisitions prompted further internal restructuring, with the formation of Rhône-Progil from the two most recent additions, and that of Rhône-Poulenc Textile, from CTA and Rhodiaceta. The distribution of sales once again shifted, as chemicals moved to the forefront. By 1969, Rhône-Poulenc had become the largest company in France. This series of mergers, acquisitions, and restructurings helped to establish a corporate identity that would remain throughout the mid-1970s.

Despite its size and position, however, Rhône-Poulenc faced several challenges. The company maintained a strict policy of anonymity, as well as a rather provincial attitude towards expansion. As long as French tariffs remained high, this strategy was effective; its business was conducted internally, and it retained the largest share of the French market for many of its products. Yet tariffs began to fall with the advent of the Common Market, international competition in the French market increased, and Rhône-Poulenc's market position within the industry began to decline.

The company management had also made some grave policy mistakes during this period, the effects of which began to surface. One such decision involved the company's licensing of the major tranquilizer Thorazine, widely used in the treatment of the mentally ill. Instead of manufacturing Thorazine in the United States, where its sales were very high, the company accepted royalties on the product from American pharmaceutical manufacturers Smith Kline & French Co., for whom it was enormously profitable.

Some of the problems in Rhône-Poulenc's market position were solved by the acquisitions of the late 1960s, which shifted the company's emphasis away from a textile market which was slipping in profitability. However, the move towards international expansion initiated at this time was much too late; had it been carried out some time before, it might have assured long-lasting financial health for the company. The delay in making such a move left the company with a very small international market share. In addition, Rhône-Poulenc had the misfortune to expand internationally at the time of an industry-wide slowdown. Attempts to turn around the company's downward slide were severely hampered by a combination of management pro-

crastination and bad timing. The French government's attempts to lower inflation added a further strain on the firm, which was one of many important French manufacturers to show a large deficit by the mid-1970s. The strain necessitated the layoff of 20,000 workers in 1974.

The downward trend continued throughout the 1970s, despite impressive profits from several licensing deals. Moreover, a new managing director, Jean Gandois, failed to effect a notable change after his appointment in 1976. However, a change in the French government during this time changed operations at Rhône-Poulenc dramatically. Determined to reverse the fortunes of what it perceived as a failing French economy, the new socialist government opted for nationalization of many industries. In February of 1982, Rhône-Poulenc's management was assumed by the government.

Among the major changes made by the government in its nationalization of Rhône-Poulenc was the appointment of a new chairperson, Loïk Le Floch-Prigent. His predecessor, Gandois, resigned after the nationalization, due to his irreconcilable differences with the Socialist program. While Le Floch, a former civil servant, had no such ideological conflicts, his was a surprising appointment; Le Floch was only 39 years old and had no experience as an industrialist, having worked as a researcher for the Industry Ministry.

Le Floch's background had a clear influence on his policy, giving research a high priority in his plans for the future of the company. At the time he assumed control, he acknowledged that the firm would need large infusions of government cash if it were to return to prosperity. He also made extensive changes in top management, replacing older executives with younger ones. Another key to Le Floch's strategy was to work more effectively with the unions, whose leaders had earlier criticized Rhône-Poulenc for the massive layoffs.

Le Floch's was not the sole voice dictating company policy. One of the government's primary concerns in its nationalization program was the reorganization of the chemical industry by means of redistributing product lines among different companies. In the process, Rhône-Poulenc lost its status as the largest chemical company in the nation, giving up its fertilizer and petrochemicals divisions. However, the company gained several specialty chemical and pharmaceutical product lines, helping give the company a clearer focus.

A combination of business changes and good fortune strengthened Rhône-Poulenc's prospects for renewal in the following year. The good fortune involved the European market, which began showing a greater demand for chemicals. The additional influences of new management and restructuring, along with extensive financial input from the government, gave rise to a noticeable improvement in the company's financial condition. By the end of 1983, Rhône-Poulenc was making a profit for the first time since 1979. Le Floch began making plans to realize what he saw as the company's full potential. He began closing plants in profitless areas and reducing the workforce, in part through an emphasis on early retirement plans. New areas of production included high-growth products such as the recently strengthened pharmaceuticals division. The company also devoted a large amount of funds for research in these areas, as well as for investment in foreign countries. With this new vitality, Rhône-Poulenc planned on making a significant profit by the government's deadline of 1985.

Although Le Floch's policies were in many ways an extension of those purported by Gandois, new management and the favorable economic conditions paid off for Le Floch. A key factor in this economic revival was the company's expansion into foreign markets, particularly in the United States and Japan. In the mid-1980s, Rhône-Poulenc began several diverse ventures in Japan, in such areas as agricultural chemicals, pharmaceuticals, and rare earth materials. Many of these projects were made as joint ventures; Rhône-Poulenc and Mitsui Petrochemical cooperated to produce computer print boards, while Sumitomo Metal Industries was the firm's partner in its rare earths venture.

In the summer of 1986, Loïk Le Floch-Prigent left Rhône-Poulenc, and its chair passed to Jean-René Fourtou, another government appointee. Fourtou continued the trend of investment outside France. The company's most significant expansion at this time occurred in its farm chemicals area, with the acquisition of all related interests of the Union Carbide Corporation. A large investment for the still struggling company, the purchase was made feasible at least in part by the fall of the U.S. dollar, and through the first U.S. dollar-denominated perpetual floating rate note for a corporate borrower. This transaction provided Rhône-Poulenc with the needed size and influence in the competitive U.S. market, the largest farm chemical market in the world. The move was particularly favorable given the two firms' complementary product lines. Rhône-Poulenc's line was left much more complete than it had been, giving it an additional edge in the U.S. market. Notably, the acquisition did not include Union Carbide's assets in India, where a gas leak at Bhopal had killed some 1750 people two years earlier.

Despite a slight earnings slip, by late 1986, Rhône-Poulenc appeared to be financially healthy once again. One of the best indicators of the company's revival was Fourtou's advocation of early privatization by the government. Before the company returned to the private sector, Fourtou engineered a reorganization with the eventual goal of making Rhône-Poulenc one of the world's five largest chemical companies by the turn of the century.

Toward that end, Fourtou tied his corporation's fortunes to the large American market. From 1986 to 1992, Rhône-Poulenc spent more than $7 billion on acquisitions and sold at least 80 subsidiaries. The purchases hiked Rhône-Poulenc's debt up as the company floated what David Lanchner of *Global Finance* called "a variety of bizarre securities." Major acquisitions included Canada's Connaught Laboratories, the United Kingdom's RTZ Chemicals, and America's GAF and Rorer Group. By 1992, 75 percent of Rhône-Poulenc's business was outside France, and the corporation had operations in 140 countries. Sales doubled from about $7.5 billion in 1986 to $15.4 billion in 1992. Rhône-Poulenc's U.S. sales increased from 11 percent of its 1987 total to 18.4 percent in 1993.

Fourtou was recognized for his stunning turnaround and globalization of Rhône-Poulenc by the American section of the Societe de Chimie Industrielle, when that group awarded him its Palladium Medal in April 1993. That year, Rhône-Poulenc's long-heralded privatization was realized when French Prime Minister Edith Cresson ended President Francois Mitterand's ban on privatizations and nationalizations. The transfer was made in two stages. In February, the French State sold six million shares (which were later adjusted to 25.8 million after July's 4-for-one stock split), reducing its share of Rhône-Poulenc's capital from 56.9 percent to 43.4 percent. This well-received offering was oversubscribed by a factor of four, and shares sold for a healthy 27 times earnings despite Rhône-Poulenc's large debt (up to Ffr24 billion in early 1994). Total privatization was completed in November 1993 with the sale of 103.2 million shares. By the end of the year, nearly three million people had become new shareholders, and employees held six percent of the company's capital.

Rhône-Poulenc recorded a 36.5 percent decline in net income for 1993, as sales slid 1.4 percent to Ffr 80.56 billion. The contraction was attributed to the effects of a European economic recession and the reform of Europe's Common Agricultural Policy. Fourtou's plans for the newly autonomous company included reducing its debt and developing its Asia/Pacific operations so that they would comprise ten percent of group sales by the end of the 1990s. Rhône-Poulenc planned to focus on China, Southeast Asia, and Japan, utilizing joint ventures to break into those markets.

Principal Subsidiaries: Rhône-Poulenc Chimie; Rhône-Poulenc Chimie N.V. (Belgium); Rhône-Poulenc Quimica SA (Spain); Rhône-Poulenc Italia; Donau Chemie (Austria); Thann et Mulhouse; Texel; Industries Chimiques Mulhouse Dornach; Meyhall A.G. (Switzerland); Rhodiamul (Spain); Rhône-Poulenc Geronazzo (Italy); Scanlates (Sweden); Siliconas Hispania (Spain); Rhône-Poulenc Fibres; Rhône-Poulenc Films; Rhône-Poulenc Rhodia AG (Germany); Rhône-Poulenc-Viscousuisse (Switzerland); Rhône-Poulenc Fibras (Spain); Rhône-Poulenc Nutrition Animale; Rhône-Poulenc Biochimie; Institut Mérieux; Pasteur Mérieux Sérums et Vaccins; Rhône Mérieux; Institut de Sélection Animale (I.S.A.); Connaught BioSciences Inc. (Canada); Rhône-Poulenc Rorer Inc. (U.S.A.); Rhône-Poulenc Agrochimie; Rhône-Poulenc Jardin; Rhône-Poulenc Agro GmbH (Germany); Rhône-Poulenc Agriculture (U.K.); Rhône-Poulenc Agro SpA (Italy); Rhône-Poulenc Agro (Spain); Rhône-Poulenc Agro KK (Japan); Rhône-Poulenc Ltd (U.K); Rhodia S.A. (Brazil); Rhône-Poulenc Inc. (U.S.A.).

Further Reading:

Smith, John Graham, *The Origins and Early Development of the Heavy Chemical Industry in France,* Oxford: Clarendon Press, 1979.

—updated by April Dougal Gasbarre

Safeguard Scientifics Inc.

Safeguard Scientifics, Inc.

800 Safeguard Building
Wayne, Pennsylvania 19087
U.S.A.
(610) 293-0600
Fax: (610) 293-0601

Public Company
Incorporated: 1953 as Lancaster Company
Employees: 2,500
Sales: $845 million
Stock Exchanges: New York
SICs: 7372 Prepackaged Software; 3577 Computer Peripheral
    Equipment, Nec.

Safeguard Scientifics, Inc., is one of the few publicly traded venture capital firms in the United States. Like most venture capital firms, Safeguard offers financial backing to fledgling businesses. The company is regarded as unique, however, for its policy of entering into partnerships with its acquisitions and providing extensive support in the forms of administrative, legal, marketing, and entrepreneurial training in return for an administrative fee. Once the young company is strong enough to stand alone, Safeguard makes its profits by either taking the company public or spinning it off to its shareholders.

Safeguard began as the Lancaster Company, which was founded by Warren Musser and a business partner, Frank Diamond, in 1953, for the purpose of raising money from independent investors to fund small, promising businesses. Primarily a venture capital holding company, Lancaster was considered an unusual business for its time. After raising $300,000 from private investors, Musser and Diamond backed two companies. The first, a fledgling cable television company called Jerrold Electronics, built a cable television network in Tupelo, Mississippi. In 1963, Lancaster's share of the business was sold to entrepreneur Ralph Roberts, who later developed the business into Comcast.

The second investment, Safeguard Industries, proved more successful and became Lancaster's principal subsidiary. A printing operation founded in 1900, Safeguard attracted the attention of Lancaster through its invention of a highly successful check-writing machine that imprinted checks with the dollar amount by perforating the paper. Safeguard also successfully marketed

an accompanying bookkeeping system that automatically recorded the dollar amount each time a check was printed.

As Safeguard sales grew steadily through the 1950s and 1960s, profits from Lancaster's initial investment were used to purchase interests in automotive parts, business forms, and merchandising service companies. Fueled by frequent acquisitions and a business forms market that grew by 15 percent annually in the mid-1960s, Lancaster's total sales grew from $5 million in 1963 to $20.4 million in 1968. During this time Lancaster also acquired Display Manufacturers, Inc., in 1967; DeMarco Business Forms, Inc. and Central Business Forms in 1968; and Butler Industries, Inc. in 1969. Lancaster went public in 1967, and the following year its name was changed to Safeguard Industries Inc. The original Safeguard Industries became known as Safeguard Business Systems in order to help distinguish it from Lancaster's new name.

Safeguard spent much of the 1970s regrouping from its buying spree of the 1960s. Butler Industries was sold in 1972, and the company began focusing on its core operations in automotive replacement parts and business systems. That year, Safeguard Business Systems expanded its distributions and product lines. Net earnings for 1972, including automotive operations, totaled $1.8 million on sales of $73.9 million. During the first half of the decade, sales and earnings from Safeguard's Business Systems remained strong, growing at a rate of 32 percent annually, while Safeguard Industries' auto parts and other businesses grew at an annual rate of ten to 15 percent.

In 1977, Musser suggested to his board that spinning off Safeguard Business Systems would allow stock market pressures to raise its per-share value to an amount that properly reflected its strong sales growth. Given that Safeguard Industries had a sizeable debt, and that Safeguard Business Systems brought in 60 percent of company revenues, board members and bankers were reluctant to approve the plan, fearing that Safeguard's other businesses could not survive on their own. Nevertheless, by 1979, Musser had convinced the board that the businesses would survive, and the following year a tax-free spin-off was completed in which stockholders received one share of Safeguard Business Systems for each share of Safeguard Industries. Safeguard Industries was then named Safeguard Scientifics, Inc. Within a year, shares of Safeguard Business Systems split three-for-two and were trading at 16¾, while the new Safeguard Scientifics traded at 15⅜.

During this period, Safeguard Scientific's combined sales dropped from $46 million to $39 million, while earnings dropped 50 percent. Musser, however, remained optimistic, and, convinced he had a great idea, he began looking around for other up-and-coming companies that he could finance, help grow, and then spin off as he had with Safeguard Business Systems. In 1981, Musser identified two such companies: Imreg, a new biotechnology concern that had developed a drug with potential to restore damage created by the HIV virus, and Novell Data Systems, Inc. (NDSI), a fledgling computer firm based in Utah. Safeguard entered into a partnership with both, allocating $1.2 million to Imreg and $7 million to NDSI. In addition to financing, Safeguard began its unique process of entrepreneurial consultation, providing administrative, management, legal, and marketing support where needed. The company also held, beginning in 1982, regular "senior partner councils," where heads of Safeguard's different partnerships could exchange ideas and information.

After Safeguard entered the partnerships with NDSI and Imreg, the company's share price jumped by 78 percent in three months, and trading of its stock was suspended. Investigations by the Securities and Exchanges Commission revealed that Gary V. Lewellyn, an independent stockbroker, had covertly acquired a 58 percent share in the company by embezzling $16 million from his father's bank, First National Bank of Humbolt. When news of the fraud hit the markets, Safeguard's share prices dropped from around $16 a share to $5. Angry brokers attempted to take control of Safeguard and boost share prices, but Musser held on. In the summer of 1983, Safeguard agreed to buy shares back for $4.50 apiece. Shareholders were appeased, but the incident, Musser told *Barron's* in 1986, "cost us about two years of our lives."

In the meantime, Safeguard's investment in NDSI was deteriorating under the weight of strong competition from IBM and Japanese manufacturers. In 1983, Safeguard took a $6 million write-off and closed NDSI. Using NDSI's tax carryforward, Safeguard created a new corporation, replacing NDSI's executive management with a team headed by Raymond Noorda. Noorda quickly turned the company around by developing a software system to connect local area network (LAN) system that became known as the best in the industry.

Novell became Safeguard's biggest success. It continued to prosper, and, in 1984, Safeguard offered its shareholders a "rights offering" of Novell stock. Through the rights offering, holders of Safeguard securities were allowed to purchase one share of Novell at $2.50 a share for every two shares of Safeguard they held. The remaining shares were sold on the market, which dictated a price of $5 on the first day, giving Safeguard shareholders who had purchased Novell stock an immediate 100 percent profit.

Safeguard realized $5.3 million from the transaction, as its share in Novell dropped from 51 to 24 percent. The company then took these profits and liquidated a failed enterprise that produced computer systems for the automotive industry, leaving an after-tax profit of $1.26 million. In 1985, Safeguard reported earnings of $3.3 million on sales of 58.8 million.

During the 1980s, the company took several fledgling information technology companies under its wing. In 1984, Safeguard purchased a 31.5 percent share of Machine Vision International Corp. (MVI), a systems integrator that endowed computers with a simulated sense of vision. The company was in need of a strong cash infusion, so Safeguard made a rights offering in 1985. Due to an industry-wide slump, MVI continued to lose millions of dollars annually. When it posted a $13 million loss in 1987 and laid off two-thirds of its employees, Safeguard focused the company in another direction. MVI changed its name to CompuCom Systems Corp., moved its corporate offices from Ann Arbor, Michigan, to Dallas, and began supplying microcomputers and accessories to corporate clients. By 1990, CompuCom was Safeguard's biggest operation, with earnings of $3.6 million on sales of $343.3 million.

Not all of Safeguard's acquisitions attained the success of Novell and CompuCom. Premier Systems, a developer and marketer of software to manage bank trust accounts, founded in 1980, lost its major customer, Bank of America, in 1988. Unwilling to give up on its investment, Safeguard refinanced Premier in 1989 and replaced its senior management early the following year. CenterCore, an office furniture company that Safeguard bought into in the early 1980s, made its first rights offering to Safeguard shareholders in 1988, but fell well below Safeguard's expectations for profits.

Some partners, such as Rabbit Software Corp., never had a profitable year. Rabbit, which designed and marketed units that allowed microcomputers to communicate with a mainframe computer, made a rights offering to Safeguard shareholders in 1986. When it failed to turn a profit by 1990, Safeguard replaced members of the company's executive team with management from Novell and Safeguard. Under new management, the company began improving its product lines and seemed poised to improve its bottom line.

One risky partnership from which Safeguard withdrew involved Unison Technologies, Inc., a producer of uninterruptable power sources and supplies. Safeguard invested in the company in 1987, but Unison was slow to bring its products to market. By the time Unison was ready to begin selling, competition had already captured much of the market. Unwilling to invest in a heavy marketing operation, Safeguard sold Unison to Trippe Manufacturing Co. for $1.8 million in 1991.

In 1990, Safeguard entered into a partnership with another venture capital fund, Radnor Venture Partners, LP. Radnor and Safeguard invested in Cambridge Technology Partners—a designer, integrator and developer of corporate computer systems—and Micro Dynamics, Ltd.—a developer and marketer of document imaging systems.

By 1993, Safeguard was managing partnerships with 15 different companies. With the exceptions of Sky Alland Research (a market researcher for the automotive industry), Pioneer Metal Finishing (a metal anodizing operation), and The Nichols Company (office and commercial leasing), all Safeguard's partnership were with information technology firms. Safeguard controlled three publicly traded firms: Tangram Enterprise Solutions (formerly Rabbit Software), CenterCore, and CompuCom.

While analysts expected Safeguard to realize impressive growth through the 1990s, all venture capital firms involved considerable risks. The company enjoyed tremendous success with Novell, offering investors an 800 percent return on their investment, and in 1993, industry analysts cited CompuCom as Safeguard's "next Novell," ranking CompuCom sixth on *Fortune* magazine's list of the fastest-growing public companies. But for every success like Novell, Safeguard nurtured a dozen or more companies whose future was uncertain. Nevertheless, known for its creative financing and loyalty, Safeguard has proven its ability to realize profits from risk.

Principal Subsidiaries: Cambridge Technology Partners; CenterCore; Coherent Communications Systems; CompuCom Systems Corp.; Diamond Technology Partners; Laser Communications; Micro Dynamics Ltd.; New Paradigm Ventures; The Nichols Company; Pioneer Metal Finishing; Premier Solutions; Radnor Venture Partners, LP; Sanchez Computer Associates; Sky Alland Research; Tangram; XL Vision Inc.

Further Reading:

Alpert, William, M., ''Bigger than a Bread Basket: Safeguard Scientifics Is a Very Unusual Company,'' *Barron's News and Investment Weekly,* February 3, 1986, p. 11.

Armstrong, Michael, ''Safeguard Scientifics Lends Premier a Hand,'' *Philadelphia Business Journal,* February 20, 1989, p. 4.

Armstrong, Michael, ''Savvy Safeguard Is Focusing on Computers,'' *Philadelphia Business Journal,* July 29, 1991, p. 3B.

Chapman, Francesca, ''PictureWare rings up $2.2 M Financing Deal,'' *Philadelphia Business Journal,* November, 23, 1987, p. 11.

Huron, Richard L., ''SEC Charges Lewellyn Manipulated Stocks of Safeguard Scientifics and Bilked Bank,'' *The Wall Street Journal,* April 5, 1982, p. 4.

Liedman, Julie, ''For Pete's Sake,'' *Business Philadelphia,* April 1993.

—Maura Troester

SAS Institute

SAS Institute Inc.

SAS Campus Drive
Cary, North Carolina 27513
U.S.A.
(919) 677-8000
Fax: (919) 677-8123

Private Company
Incorporated: 1976 as SAS Institute, Inc.
Employees: 3,200
Sales: $420.3 million
SICs: 7372 Prepackaged Software

Privately held SAS Institute Inc. is one of the largest independent software companies in the world. Installed in 27,000 businesses, universities, and government agencies worldwide, the SAS System—the Institute's flagship product—is a modular, integrated, and hardware-independent suite of software products for enterprise-wise information delivery that provides organizations with tools to access, manage, analyze, and present their data within an applications development environment.

Headquartered in Cary, North Carolina near the Research Triangle Park, the Institute maintains regional offices in Austin, TX, Irvine, CA, Washington DC, New York, NY, Seattle, WA, Kansas City, KS, Atlanta, GA, Orlando, FL, Denver, CO, Pittsburgh, PA, and Cincinnati, OH, as well as established offices, subsidiaries, and distributors in about 60 countries around the world.

SAS Institute was founded and incorporated in 1976 by North Carolina State University professor, Dr. James Goodnight and John Sall. The two academics had developed a statistical analysis software package for their own research use that had become popular with faculty at NC State and a number of other universities throughout the South. "Eventually, our fledgling operation grew too big to run out of our offices at State, and they invited us to leave," Goodnight told *Business Leader* magazine. "So, we moved across Hillsborough Street, and that's how it all started."

Over the next 18 years, Goodnight's and Sall's single software package grew into a modular information delivery system used by 98 percent of the Fortune 100 companies. In 1994, the company could boast over 3 million users in 120 countries, 12 U.S. regional offices, subsidiaries in 29 nations, and distributors

in 20 others, and over 3,000 employees worldwide. In 1993, the company recorded sales revenues of $420.3 million, which marked a 15 percent increase over the year before. The figure also established the company's 17th consecutive year of double-digit growth in revenue.

These figures represent financial success that any company would envy. Most members of the SAS "family" attribute the Institute's success to a single philosophy: listen carefully to your customers and give them exactly what they want. "Here at SAS, we do software development by users for users," vice president of North American Sales and Marketing Barrett R. Joyner told *Business Leader*. "While we certainly need to be profitable in order to stay in business, our primary focus isn't making money; it's solving problems. We want to provide our users—business people, researchers, scientists—with advanced technology that will enable them to access, manage, analyze, and present their data effectively so that they can make sound business decisions."

This approach is obvious in the company's flagship software product, the SAS System for Information Delivery, which can be used in almost every computing environment, from the laptop computer to the data center. The system is an integrated suite of software products that provides users with a wide range of capabilities that they can set up in whatever combination they require. At the heart of the SAS System is a single software package called "Base SAS," which provides data management, analysis, and report writing. The rest of the system comprises more than 20 modular software packages that link with the base software. These packages enable users to add specialized functions, such as spreadsheets, graphics, quality improvement, project management, cooperative processing, applications development, and more, depending on the needs of their company.

Another component behind SAS's financial success is its commitment to research and development investments. In 1993, SAS Institute heralded its eighth consecutive year of leading the software industry in the percentage of revenue devoted to research and development. That year, the company reinvested a record-setting $143 million, or 34 percent of revenue, to improving its array of products. On average, the top 100 revenue-generating software companies reinvest less than 20 percent of revenue in R&D. SAS Institute's management team said that its commitment ensured that the company would continually provide its customers with software that exploits the latest technology. To support its massive R&D effort, the Institute built a five-story research and development building with a virtual data center in each of its 1,100 offices.

SAS Institute's researchers have some unconventional methods for problem-solving. With roots based in Goodnight's and Sall's former campus offices, most of the researchers at the Institute take a "technological garage" approach to their work. Their style is similar to two entrepreneurs in their garage who start out with a crazy idea and end up with a product that earns millions of dollars. The Institute's management team encourages its developers to follow up on all promising ideas, even if they seem to have no immediate practical applications. The company conducts usability studies to determine the value of each piece of research. Many such projects—which may have never been initiated in other companies—end up becoming real money-earners for SAS Institute. The Institute's leadership firmly believes that this type of strategy encourages developers to start projects even though they may not lead to end products and fosters the creativity and freedom that can lead to tremendous product innovation.

SAS Institute's marketing group also has its own distinct business philosophy. Rarely does the group resort to such marketing standbys as market penetration studies or competitive analysis. Instead, the company's marketing team prefers to rely on the SAS customers themselves via users groups. Since SAS Institute's inception, the direction of its research and development has been largely driven by Institute customers, who are encouraged to express their opinions about the company's software products and services through formal and informal channels. To keep up with changing demands, SAS sponsors a network of more than 200 local, regional, national, international, in-house, and special-interest users groups. In 1993, the Institute experimented with the most extensive usability test ever performed on software. Preparing for major enhancements to the menu-driven interface to the SAS System—SAS/ASSIST software—marketing, training, and software development staff teamed up to conduct a three-phased study. They invited computer users of various experience levels to put the new version of SAS/ASSIST software through its paces and provide feedback. The company's annual SASware Ballot, a survey distributed to all SAS users, also provides a way for users to provide feedback to the Institute's management and influence development efforts, from general issues to specific enhancements.

In addition, SAS Institute holds frequent users group conferences to provide a forum for Institute developers to meet directly with SAS System users. This free-flowing exchange of ideas leads to software enhancements and new services that address the real computing issues that organizations face. For example, in 1992, SAS introduced a series of Information Delivery Strategy conferences for information systems executives. These conferences gave the participants the chance to see the software operating in simulated vertical market settings and to voice their opinions to members of the Institute's marketing and development staffs.

As Joyner told *Business Leader:* "We're not a marketing-driven company. Throughout the eighties, when a lot of other software companies were mesmerized by market share, we focused on talking face-to-face with users and meeting their needs. The competition saw us as a bunch of naive yokels who just fell off the turnip truck. In the last couple of years, though, many of our competitors have realized the value of being customer-driven." The ultimate measurement of the company's responsiveness is that the overwhelming majority of SAS software sites renew their annual software licenses year after year. According to the company's 1993 annual report, 95 percent of Fortune 500 companies that licensed SAS software that year elected to renew their licenses.

SAS Institute also makes a concerted effort to develop close relationships with other firms in the field. The company believes that this strategy helps them to bring cutting-edge products to market rapidly. SAS Institute, for example, was one of the early participants in Microsoft Windows' NT development and one of the first vendors to work with Digital Equipment Corporation

on their ALPHA AXP project for RISC-based processors. In 1991, SAS struck a formal business partnership with Intel, one of the world's leading computer chip manufacturers. The agreement allows for technology exchanges between the Institute and Intel and ensures that the two companies will forge a strong alliance between future generations of SAS software and Intel chips. In 1993, SAS Institute completed the development of an internal compiler that exploits the ground-breaking "Pentium" processor.

The business relationship with Microsoft Corporation was sealed in 1989 to give SAS access to Microsoft's operating system development information. The result of this deal was the delivery of releases of the SAS System for Windows and Windows NT in 1993. The relationship between the two companies became even stronger when SAS representatives sat on Microsoft's Independent Software Vendor Advisory Council. In addition to these two major agreements, SAS also has close working relationships with database companies, including Oracle, Sybase, Informix, and Ingres to ensure that its customers have easy access to the data they need regardless of the manufacturer.

SAS Institute also stands firmly by its commitment to quality. Although "quality assurance" became one of the buzzwords of the early 1990s, SAS Institute had a long-standing reputation for producing software products that were reliable and high quality. "Quality is part of the culture here," Lynne Fountain, manager of public affairs, told *Business Leader.* "Everyone who works here is really proud to be a part of SAS, and it shows in everything we do—from the quality of our products to the attractiveness of our campus and the gourmet food in our cafeteria."

SAS Institute also differentiates itself by its sales strategy. Its sales employees do not earn commission because the company wants them to concentrate on finding the best way to solve a customer's problem. Instead of "selling" its products the way its customers do, SAS licenses the base SAS software and modules on an annual basis. Prices vary according to the platform the customer decides to use. At the end of the licensing period, a customer can add or drop components to accommodate changing business requirements or decline to renew at all.

From the time it was founded in 1976, SAS Institute has displayed a commitment to its work force, as well as to its customers. Like most high-technology firms of the late 20th century, SAS Institute understands that its continued success lies in its ability to attract and retain high-quality, intelligent, competent employees. As a result, the Institute makes sure that its workers enjoy bright, airy, well-equipped office buildings and can use an on-site recreation and fitness center along with an on-site health care center. The Institute also offers its employees two on-site Montessori child care centers and the "Generation to Generation" program, which helps employees cope with the needs of aging relatives. In recent years, these types of employee amenities helped SAS to earn a place on the list of "100 Best Companies for Working Mothers," by *Working Mother* magazine for seven consecutive years. Most important, however, they help SAS Institute to maintain an average annual turnover rate of a mere three percent. The national industry average is 22 percent.

SAS Institute's business strategy for the future is to continue to exploit a variety of new technologies to meet its customers' needs. A good example of this is SAS Executive Information Systems (EIS). This software package was introduced in 1992 on an experimental basis as part of a SAS System upgrade. This new module makes highly complex data very "user friendly." With it, developers can make corporate data very accessible to even the most computer-illiterate executives among the customer base. According to Goodnight, who serves not only as president, but also as director of research and development, "SAS/EIS is one of the most important products in our history. It provides our customers with the tools to deliver information to anyone in their organization quickly and efficiently, allowing them to make better, more informed business decisions."

SAS/EIS software and other new SAS products incorporate cutting-edge technologies and applications, such as object-oriented programming technology, which allows objects built for one application to be reused in others. This technology dramatically increases the efficiency and productivity of software development. SAS is also breaking new research ground in such areas as imaging, geographic information systems, and online user documentation. The company is also hard at work developing several new products for niche markets. In 1992, for example, SAS introduced its first vertical market product for the pharmaceutical and biotechnology industries.

Principal Subsidiaries: SAS Consulting Services, Inc.

Further Reading:

Romani, Jane Hairston, "SAS Institute: 21st Century Technology . . . Today," *Business Leader,* December 1993.
SAS Institute, Inc., *SAS Communications,* First Quarter 1994.

—Wendy Johnson Bilas

Scholastic Corporation

555 Broadway
New York, New York 10012-3999
U.S.A.
(212) 343-6100
Fax: (212) 343-6928

Public Company
Incorporated: 1920
Employees: 2,850
Sales: $552 million
Stock Exchanges: New York
SICs: 2721 Periodicals; 2731 Book Publishing; 7372
   Prepackaged Software; 6719 Holding Companies

The Scholastic Corporation is the largest publisher of books and magazines for children in the United States. In addition to printed materials, the company also produces software and videos, many of which are educational and are sold through schools. Started as a newsletter for Pennsylvania high school students in the early 1920s, Scholastic struggled throughout its first three decades, gaining steady profits only in the postwar years, when it expanded its offerings and channels of distribution.

Scholastic was founded in 1920 by Maurice R. Robinson, whose experience in journalism was enhanced during his tenure as a staff member on the Dartmouth College student newspaper. Upon graduation from Dartmouth, Robinson returned to his hometown of Wilkinsburg, a suburb of Pittsburgh, and took a job at the Pittsburgh Chamber of Commerce. There he came across statistics indicating that the high school student population was expected to increase steadily throughout the decade, and he decided that a newspaper dedicated to students' interests would be a good prospect. The first edition of *The Western Pennsylvania Scholastic,* providing articles on topics of general interest to students, including a feature on the Western Pennsylvania Interscholastic Athletic League, was published on October 22, 1920. Robinson designed the four-page paper from a desk in his mother's sewing room, and he sold it for five cents a copy.

The following year, Robinson arranged for office space in Pittsburgh and hired a clerk to serve as office manager and assistant editor. In order to finance the publication of *The Western Pennsylvania Scholastic* during this time, Robinson continued to work at various jobs in public relations. Although the paper did not turn a profit during the 1921 to 1922 school year, its circulation reached 4,000.

In 1922 Robinson decided to widen the scope of his student newspaper. Over the summer, he distributed a brochure describing his proposed publication, the *Scholastic,* to those present at the National Education Association convention in Boston. The publication's new format was to resemble that of a magazine and would include articles relevant to classroom work in English, social studies, science, and foreign languages. Preparing for increased business, Robinson hired a circulation manager and incorporated his venture as the Scholastic Publishing Company. The first issue of the *Scholastic,* which billed itself as ''The National High School Bi-Weekly'' was published on September 16, 1922 and sold for 15 cents per copy.

In order to stimulate circulation, sell advertising space, and generate copy of interest to students across the nation, Robinson assembled an advisory board of high school teachers and administrators and a staff to sell ads and push subscriptions to teachers and their students. Moreover, he began selling shares of Scholastic stock in order to raise funds. In 1924, Scholastic began to sponsor the Scholastic Creative Writing Awards as well as a contest to provide cover designs by high school art students, programs that proved extremely popular. As a result of these activities, circulation of the *Scholastic* reached 33,000 by the spring of 1925, a figure that would nearly double by the end of the decade. Despite the publication's popularity, Scholastic continued to struggle financially, never realizing a profit in the 1920s. Moreover, its seasonal distribution generated no income during the summer months.

In the early months of 1929, Robinson acquired a weekly social studies periodical, *The World Review,* which he paid for with Scholastic stock. When the stock market crashed in October, he was able to sell this property to a competitor, giving his company a much-needed infusion of cash. Shortly thereafter, Scholastic acquired the children's magazine *St. Nicholas,* and the company's name was changed to Scholastic-St. Nicholas Corporation.

Continued financial strains brought on by the Great Depression, however, prompted Robinson to seek the economic resources of another publishing firm. During the 1931 to 1932 school year, Scholastic entered into a joint venture with competitor American Education Press, in which Scholastic gained control of four publications: *The Magazine World, World News, Current Literature,* and *Looseleaf Current Topics.* Temporarily bolstered by increased business, Scholastic opened offices on East 44th Street in New York and launched another new publication, *Scholastic Coach.*

In April 1932, Scholastic bought out American Education Press, and, two months later, the company's name was changed to Scholastic Corporation, as plans were made to sell *St. Nicholas* before the end of the year. By the fall of 1932, circulation of the company's publications had dropped sharply, and salary cuts for all staff members at Scholastic were necessary. Focusing on the potential of its original publication, the *Scholastic,* Robinson cut costs by doing away with its expensive cover art and printing the entire magazine on less expensive paper. Hoping to increase revenues, he also put the *Scholastic* on a weekly publication schedule.

Scholastic reported slight gains in circulation in 1934 and 1935, and the following year, the company reported its first annual profit ever, $2,400. A magazine for junior high school readers, entitled *Junior Scholastic,* was introduced during this time, and the company's underpaid staff received salary increases. By the spring of 1938, however, the circulation of the mainstay *Scholastic* (which eventually became known as *Senior Scholastic* in order to distinguish it from its junior counterpart) had dropped precipitously, and projections for the success of *Junior Scholastic* proved overly optimistic. Consequently, Robinson was forced to suspend payment of his staff for a month. The losses were attributed, in part, to the fact that many Scholastic publications came under the scrutiny of disapproving parents and politicians during this time. Facing charges that the material was unsuitable for young people, some schools were forced to ban Scholastic magazines. In two widely publicized cases, in Washington D.C. in 1936, and Topeka, Kansas, in 1938, *Senior Scholastic* was accused of promoting communism.

In the early 1940s, Scholastic's two principal stockholders, hoping to recoup their investment, sought a buyer for the company. When no suitable offers were forthcoming, they brought in an outside management consultant to evaluate Scholastic's operations. The study was completed in 1941 and recommended that the company either be liquidated or that Robinson be replaced as its head. Instead, however, Scholastic's backers agreed to finance the company on a long-term basis, provided some economizing measures were taken.

At the onset of World War II, Scholastic introduced a new magazine devoted to current events. *World Week,* first published in September 1942, was promoted as "The New All Social Studies Classroom Magazine Graded to Meet Your Wartime Teaching Requirements." When wartime rationing of paper went into effect on January 1, 1943, however, Scholastic was forced to produce thinner publications and turn down subscribers.

After the war, Scholastic moved to expand its circulation and the number of titles it offered. In 1946, *Scholastic Teacher, Practical English,* and *Prep* were introduced. Two years later, *Literary Cavalcade* was added to the fold as was the Teen Age Book Club, a joint endeavor with Pocket Books formed to market paperback books to young people in school. To boost circulation, company executives divided up their sales territory into 180 "Scholastic Districts," hiring part-time sales staff, referred to as Resident Representatives, to work on commission in each district. By 1951, Scholastic was able to pay a dividend on its stock for the first time.

Problems concerning the political views reflected in Scholastic publications resurfaced in the late 1940s and 1950s. In 1948, the city of Birmingham, Alabama, issued a ban on *Senior Scholastic,* finding articles advocating racial equality unacceptable; this ban was lifted three years later. Perhaps the most widespread controversy surrounding Scholastic publications developed when Senator Joseph McCarthy and others serving on the House Committee on Un-American Activities began a program of accusing American citizens of communist affiliations. In

1952, a Scholastic editor was ordered to explain his involvement 20 years prior with a short-lived youth magazine under suspicion of promoting Communist sympathies. While he did so satisfactorily and was exonerated, several similar charges were leveled against Scholastic over the next few years.

By the end of the decade, Scholastic had added several new publications to its roster, including *Practical Home Economics,* acquired in 1952, and *JAC/Junior American Citizen,* which was renamed *Newstime.* Moreover, two new book clubs, the Arrow Book Club and the Campus Book Club, were introduced. The growth of Scholastic's book club operations, which distributed paperback books to students through the classroom, created the need for a warehouse to hold goods for shipping. In 1959, the company completed construction of such a facility in Englewood Cliffs, New Jersey.

During the 1960s, Scholastic explored new markets, introducing two book clubs for young children, Lucky and See-Saw, and adding 13 new periodicals to its line. Furthermore, the company began publishing various instructional materials and books, including a series of books adapted for different age levels intended to develop reading skills and introduce young people to the short story and poetry. In 1962, the World Affairs Multi-Text series was offered for use in social studies classes, and a series of arithmetic booklets were promoted for individual study at home.

In 1965, Scholastic introduced its hardcover book publishing division, the Four Winds Press. This unit eventually became central to Scholastic's Library and Trade Division, which marketed publications to libraries and book wholesalers and distributed a new line of Scholastic/Folkways Records, the company's first audio offerings. By 1968, a series of short films, entitled *Toute la Bande,* had been designed for instruction in the French language.

The company continued to expand its audiovisual offerings in the early 1970s, introducing Enrichment Records; Art & Man Filmstrips, which supplemented a Scholastic periodical published under the direction of the National Gallery of Art; Bill Russell's Basketball Films; Clifford Filmstrips; and Margaret Court Instructional Films.

Another area of concentration at Scholastic during this time reflected the country's increased awareness of the need for remedial reading instruction at all age levels. For those students regarded as slow learners, Scholastic offered several textbook programs and magazines, some of which featured easy-to-read articles and stories that would appeal to older students. In addition to exploiting a new and growing market, such material helped offset the declining popularity of *Senior Scholastic.*

Scholastic stock was first offered to the public through the New York Stock Exchange in 1969, and the 1970s began a period of steady financial growth at Scholastic. With the scope and complexity of its operations expanding, the company underwent several corporate reorganizations in the 1970s. In 1971, a School Division was created to oversee operations involving the company's book clubs and magazines. This division was headed by M. Richard Robinson, Jr., son of the company's founder, and four years later, Robinson took over as president of the company, initiating another period of reorganization.

By 1980, budget cuts and declining school enrollment rates posed a challenge to Scholastic. Unable to raise prices to meet the rapidly increasing costs of publishing books and periodicals, the company saw its revenues decline. To offset this trend, the company decided to enter the highly competitive textbook market, investing more than $5 million in an effort to make significant inroads. Within two years, however, the venture had failed to provide the expected returns, and the company resumed its focus on supplementary educational materials.

During this time, Scholastic also explored the burgeoning market for educational material related to computers, introducing its first consumer magazine, *Family Computing,* a line of software for children entitled Wizware, a magazine on disk, called *Microzine,* and two publications for educators, *Electronic Learning* and *Teaching and Computers.* By issuing more stock, consolidating its distribution operations, and selling off some of its facilities, Scholastic funded the costly process of computerizing its operations and developed a new division, known as Scholastic Productions, to enter the field of television programming production.

However, these new ventures had resulted in losses of $13.8 million by May 1984, and the company's stock price plummeted. When new management and reorganizations failed to alleviate the financial burden, Robinson decided to take Scholastic private. In 1986, he reestablished control over the company by creating SI Holdings Inc., which maintained a 51 percent share of the company's stock. In July 1987, SI Holdings paid $84 million for the remaining Scholastic shares.

Five years later, back on solid financial ground, Scholastic again went public, offering $90 million worth of stock in February 1992. Backed by profits from "The Babysitters Club," a phenomenally successful young adult fiction series, which developed into a cable television program, the company planned to invest $20 million for another venture into the textbook market, this time emphasizing a more diverse format. In the mid-1990s, Scholastic's strong presence in children's publishing consisted of 32 magazines and a broad range of books sold in schools and other outlets. With demographic studies projecting a sharp increase in the population of children, Scholastic appeared poised for continued success.

Principal Subsidiaries: Scholastic Canada Ltd.; Scholastic Publications Ltd. (United Kingdom); Ashton Scholastic Pty. Ltd. (Australia); Ashton Scholastic Ltd. (New Zealand).

Further Reading:

Bhargave, Sunita Wadekar, "Scholastic Gets Ready to Hit the Books," *Business Week,* August 24, 1992.
Elliott, Stuart J., "Scholastic's Talents Put to High-Tech Field," *Advertising Age,* March 28, 1983.
Gold, Howard, "Go to the Back of the Class," *Forbes,* October 22, 1984.
Lippert, Jack, *Scholastic: A Publishing Adventure,* New York: Scholastic Book Services, 1979, 562 p.

—Elizabeth Rourke

Sega of America, Inc.

255 Shoreline Drive
Second Floor
Redwood City, California 94065
U.S.A.
(415) 508-2800
Fax: (415) 802-3802

Wholly Owned Subsidiary of Sega Enterprises Ltd.
Incorporated: 1986
Employees: 1,300
Sales: $2.5 billion
SICs: 5092 Toys & Hobby Goods & Supplies; 5045
   Computers, Peripherals & Software

Sega of America, Inc. is a wholly owned subsidiary of publicly-held, Japan-based Sega Enterprises, Ltd. and a leading manufacturer and distributor of video games and accessories in the American marketplace. The company oversees Sega Enterprises' operations in Canada, Mexico, and the United States. Sega of America markets and distributes trademarked Genesis home video game systems, Game Gear hand-held portable video game systems, and Sega CD systems through its consumer products division. It also manufactures half of all the software it distributes domestically in addition to supplying 70 percent of the parent company's branded software worldwide.

Sega of America traces its roots to two companies—Service Games Company and Rosen Enterprises, Ltd.—both founded in Japan by Americans during the 1950s. In 1951, Raymond Lemaire and Richard Stewart started Service Games to develop and market amusement-type games and machines, and within a few years the company was importing jukeboxes and slot machines to supply American military bases in Japan. In 1954, David Rosen, who had been stationed in Japan with the Air Force, returned to Tokyo and launched a two-minute photo booth business which quickly grew into a nationwide chain in Japan, where residents needed numerous identification pictures.

While developing his instant photo booth business, Rosen made invaluable contacts in theaters and departments stores where his booths were located. In 1957, Rosen started tapping those contacts again after he began importing mechanical coin-operated arcade games which were popular on U.S. military bases in Japan but largely unfamiliar to the Japanese public. Within a

few years, Rosen Enterprises had a nationwide chain of 200 arcades and only one principal competitor, Service Games.

Rosen, not satisfied with the mechanical games he was importing from Chicago's leading manufacturers in 1965, orchestrated a merger with Service Games, which by that time had its own factory. Rosen became chief executive of the new firm, Sega Enterprises, which derived its name from the first two letters of the words "Service" and "Games." Sega began its transformation from an importer to a manufacturer the following year, after Rosen designed a game called Periscope—with then-innovative sound and light effects—in which players lined up chain-mounted cardboard ships through periscope sights and then torpedoed the targets by pressing a button. Periscope became a quick hit in Japan and was soon exported to Europe and the United States, where it became the first 25-cent game and helped revitalize a sinking arcade game industry.

In 1969 Rosen, by then the sole owner of Sega, sold his company to the U.S.-based Gulf & Western Industries (G&W), becoming a millionaire in the deal while remaining with Sega as chief executive. Two years after Atari Inc. had launched a new era in video games with its 1972 release of Pong, a version of table tennis played on a video screen, G&W made Sega Enterprises a subsidiary and took the arcade game manufacturer public.

Sega rode the wave of a booming arcade industry during the late-1970s—facilitated in part by Atari's Space Invaders video game and home video-game system—and in 1979 Sega's annual sales skyrocketed from $37 million to more than $100 million. Sega joined other game manufacturers in the move into electronics and then microprocessors as its sales climbed to $150 million in 1981, and nearly $215 million by 1982, the year it introduced the industry's first three-dimensional (3-D) video game, SubRoc 3-D, in Japan. By 1983, when a surplus of mediocre games caused a crash in the arcade business that reduced Sega's revenues to $136 million, Sega had pioneered the use of laser disks in its "Astronbelt" video game and developed its first video game console, the SG-1000.

After spinning off part of its arcade game subsidiary, G&W bought back the part of Sega it did not own in 1983 and then sold Sega's U.S. manufacturing operations to Bally Manufacturing Company, an electronic game, casino, and amusement park company. In January of 1984, Rosen resigned his post as president of Sega Enterprises and was replaced by Hayao Nakayama, who had been heading up Sega's Japanese operations since Nakayama's arcade game distribution company, Esco Trading, had been acquired by Sega five years earlier.

In May of 1984, Rosen became re-involved in the company he founded after G&W sold the research and software design remains of Sega Enterprises for $38 million to a partnership which included Rosen, Nakayama, and CSK, a large Japanese software company which helped finance the buyout. CSK became owner of 20 percent of Sega while CSK's chairman, Isao Ohkawa, became chairman of the new Japanese firm, renamed Sega Enterprises, Ltd.

In 1986, Sega Enterprises went public in Japan and established Sega of America, Inc. as a wholly owned subsidiary to adapt Sega's video game products to the American marketplace.

Nakayama was named chairman and Rosen president and chief executive of Sega of America, which entered the home video game business that same year with the introduction of its first home video system, the 8-bit color Master System. (The machine was called an 8-bit system because its computer chips processed data in chunks of eight bits of electronic instructions.) Sega's Master System immediately faced stiff competition from another Japanese-based company, Nintendo, which had single-handedly revitalized and gained control of the U.S. home video-game industry in 1985 after introducing its 8-bit Entertainment System.

In 1987, Sega of America signed a distribution agreement with Tonka Corp. that boosted the presence of Sega's Master System, which came to be supported by more than 100 software video game titles (which were sold on cartridges that plugged into a game player, with that system in turn plugged into a television on which the game was viewed and played). For Sega's 1988 autumn battle with Nintendo, Tonka helped roll out 22 new titles for Master System, including adventure games based on the popular arcade titles ''Double Dragon, Shinobi'' and ''Thunderblade'' as well as a sports games promoted by baseball great Reggie Jackson and Chicago Bears running back Walter Payton, whose pictures were featured in store displays.

Sega's strategy took a major shift in 1989 after the company developed the industry's first 16-bit color video-game home entertainment system, named Sega Genesis in the United States. Aimed at breaking Nintendo's hold on 80 percent of the then-$3 billion American video game market, Genesis offered better sound and graphics, faster action, and more difficult challenges than 8-bit game players. With games more three-dimensional and characters appearing more human and less robotic, the Genesis 16-bit system quickly changed the landscape of the video game industry while establishing Sega as a technological leader and the second largest vendor of consumer game products. Targeting the market niche of older teenagers, young adults, and Nintendo players looking for a tougher game challenge, Sega utilized popular arcade titles such as ''Altered Beast'' and sports games featuring the names of Arnold Palmer and Tommy Lasorda to sell Genesis. Genesis was launched with a $10 million advertising and promotional blitz that included commercials on MTV and shopping mall tours.

Sega entered the 1990s using its 16-bit technology to deliver games that simulate race car driving, flying, and submarine navigation, as well as the dance steps of Michael Jackson, who was featured in a new game called ''Moon Walker.'' Sega of America began developing its own software products specifically for the American market in 1990. That same year, Thomas Kalinske, a former executive with toy makers Mattel and Matchbook International, became president of the American subsidiary after Rosen was named co-chairman.

In the summer of 1991, Sega entered the two-year-old hand-held video game system market and debuted its 8-bit portable video-game system, Game Gear, which featured a color screen designed to better Nintendo's monochrome Game Boy. In August 1991—anticipating a new Nintendo product to compete with Sega's 16-bit machine—Sega launched an aggressive comparative advertising campaign, describing itself as the de-

veloper of the ''fastest game in the world'' while branding Nintendo as a children's toy maker.

While Sega's Genesis soon attracted older teenagers and advanced game players, it also caught the attention of retailers and third-party software game developers alienated by Nintendo's higher licensing fees. By the time Nintendo jumped into the 16-bit market with its Super NES system in the fall of 1991—18 months after Sega rolled out Genesis—Sega already had 150 16-bit software titles on the market and had come up with a character to rival Nintendo's well-known Super Mario: Sonic, a blue hedgehog who rescued his friends from an evil scientist by maneuvering his way through a 3-D obstacle course. Nintendo suffered from its late debut in the 16-bit market, its failure to follow Sega's lead and have its 16-bit machine support 8-bit titles, its pricing of Super NES 25 percent more than Genesis, and its failure to respond to Sega's comparative ads.

While Nintendo was launching its 16-bit machine, Sega was readying itself for the development of its next round of hardware and by mid 1991 Sega had reached an agreement with Victor Company of Japan—a major audio-video company manufacturing products under the JVC label—to develop a home entertainment system which would read video-game software from a compact disk. To develop such software, Sega Studios was founded and began to develop, film, and produce CD-ROM-based interactive games in October 1991.

By the end of 1991, Sega had sold 1.6 million copies of Genesis and emerged from the Christmas season as the leader in the 16-bit market, outselling Super NES in most stores. Sega had doubled its 1990 share of total video game market sales to 20 percent, primarily as a result of an expanding library of software titles and the growing popularity of Sonic the Hedgehog.

Nintendo responded to Sega's gains by cutting the prices of its 16-bit player by 10 percent in a move industry analysts labeled as a retreat for Nintendo, which had built its marketing edge largely by limiting the supply of its products while keeping prices relatively high. As the market for video games softened, Nintendo reduced the price of Super NES three times since 1992, and Sega soon matched its rival's hardware price of $99.

Sega helped launch a new era of video games in the fall of 1992 when it released Sega CD, a $299 compact disk multimedia peripheral for Genesis that could play standard music CDs or live-action video-game software. With 100 times more memory than 16-bit cartridges, Sega CD carried the ability to play to both Genesis cartridges and new Sega CD games, which were displayed in movie-like images rather than simple cartoon-like graphics.

Sega's first CD games, such as ''Night Trap,'' featured human actors, compressed full-motion video, special effects, and high-fidelity sound, with players having the ability to alter the action and effect the outcome of real B-grade movies. Sega's new CD software library also included a game in which players could make their own video to the soundtrack of popular songs by selecting video cuts and special effects and then overlaying lyrics. Despite complaints that Sega CD was too costly for the consumer masses and the quality of games too inconsistent, the new peripheral helped to continue Sega's position as a technological leader in the eyes of consumers.

To boost sales of its CD peripheral and bolster its image as the hip game maker, in the fall of 1992 Sega hired a new advertising firm, Goodby, Berlin & Silverstein, and released a new group of games, including "Sonic 2" and Sega's in-house-developed "Streets of Rage II." In less than four months, the company aired 35 variations of a commercial aimed at branding Sega's name into the mind of consumers by flouting conventionality; the advertising spots utilized rock soundtracks and concluded by having people with a crazed looks in their eyes shout "Sega" into the camera.

Between 1989 and 1992, Sega of America's pre-tax profits rose 50 to 70 percent a year while its staff grew from 35 to several hundred as the American subsidiary became the dominant arm of Sega Enterprises. In 1993, Sega of America began overseeing the newly-established Sega of Canada, Inc., formed to market Sega products in the growing $340 million Canadian video game marketplace, and Sega of Mexico, a Latin American marketing and distribution wing.

By 1993, competition in the video-game industry had broadened to include such newcomers as 3DO, which developed the industry's first 32-bit game player, a $700 CD-ROM based game machine displaying near 3-D images that doubled as an compact disk audio system. Atari Corporation followed suit with the development of a low-cost, $200 32-bit machine, with both companies debuting the new game players later that Christmas season. In an effort to enhance the technology of its products, in 1993 Sega formed a number of strategic alliances designed to—as the company advertised—take video gaming to "the next level."

Sega joined with Time Warner Inc. and Tele-Communications Inc. in 1993 to offer Sega's video games through cable systems under a premium channel system called Sega Channel. Planned to debut in mid-1994, the Sega Channel was expected to allow subscribers to download video games from the cable channel into their game machines while also offering new game previews and game play tips. The channel was additionally viewed by Sega as a chance to test its potential in the undeveloped interactive television market.

Sega expanded its group of strategic allies in June 1993 when AT&T agreed to help Sega create a low-priced hardware product. Dubbed Edge 16, the product would serve as a Genesis peripheral device and allow for multi-person gameplay over normal phone lines. Plans for Edge 16 also included special ports on the peripheral, which would provide for the addition of a computer keyboard and expansion upgrades.

In another diversification move designed to give Sega a difficult-to-duplicate edge, the company announced plans to build as many as 50 Virtual Reality (VR) theme parks in the United States. The parks would feature VR "rides" and games—simulating such "worlds" as the Wild West and outer space—within the small confines of windowless capsules. To perfect some of those games, Sega signed an agreement with Martin Marietta Corporation allowing Sega to tap the expertise of the defense contractor by using its tank-simulation technology to develop a battlefield game with realistic action.

In the fall of 1993, Sega opened Sega VirtuaLand, an experimental arcade and forerunner of Sega's VR parks in the new Luxor, a Las Vegas entertainment complex/hotel. By the time VirtuaLand had opened Sega had also lined up a team of major players to help develop its next home video-game player, a 32-bit machine code-named Saturn. Included in Sega's group of Saturn allies were Hitachi Ltd., a micro chip maker; Victor Company, a manufacturer of video image circuitry; and Yamaha Corporation, a sound chip builder.

Sega entered the 1993 Christmas season with an edge in the crucial 16-bit market of the $6 billion American home video-game industry, holding 43 percent of total cartridge-based video-game sales, compared to Nintendo's 55 percent share. Sega's greatest yuletide sales came from "Sonic the Hedgehog" games and its best-selling "Mortal Kombat," an explicitly violent game that Nintendo also sold in a censored version.

In response to growing criticism and concern over Sega's "Mortal Kombat" game, in which heads were cut off and hearts torn out, and Sega's "Night Trap" game, which featured vampires who drilled holes in the necks of scantily-clad sorority sisters, a Sega-led group of video game companies—which Nintendo declined to join—went before an unsympathetic Congressional committee to announce it would police itself in 1993. Within a week after the Congressional hearings and a subsequent increase in publicity over violent video games that followed, Toys R Us, America's largest toy retailer, decided to pull "Night Trap" from its shelves. Soon, Sega itself pulled the game from all stores.

After reaching distribution agreements in mid-1993 with Kmart and Wal-Mart, which put Sega's distribution on par with Nintendo, Sega's sales began to soar and the company ended the year claiming to have beaten Nintendo in total sales, capturing a 51 percent share for the six months leading up to Christmas. For the Christmas-buying season, Sega claimed a sales advantage in the 16-bit, CD-ROM, and portable game categories while Nintendo held a slight overall sales lead, largely on the strength of its edge in the hand-held market and its virtual lock on the declining 8-bit game segment.

In January 1994, Sega signed a pact with the world's largest computer software company, Microsoft Corp., which agreed to develop an original operating system for Sega's forthcoming Saturn system which would make it easier for game developers to design compatible software for the 32-bit machine. Sega's alliance with Microsoft opened the door to Sega's possible entrance into the much-heralded realm of "convergence" of personal computers, communications, and entertainment and offered the additional prospect of Saturn becoming a "set-top box," or operating system that could serve as an "on-ramp" to the so-called "information superhighway" by allowing owners access to multimedia realms such as interactive television.

With its new generation of games relying increasingly on human characters, in January 1994 Sega expanded the role of its Hollywood production office, adding script evaluation, casting, and production functions to the office's licensing and character development activities. Sega also expanded its hand-held offerings to include a new Sports Game Gear unit, announced the addition of video games for three-to-six-year-olds, and introduced its first line of toys, including the $160 educational game called Pico, which utilized an electronic pen that enabled a picture children touched on a cardboard book to appear on their television screen.

In one of the largest marketing campaigns in video game history, Sega launched a $20 million promotion of its new ''Sonic The Hedgehog 3'' for Genesis, tapping corporate promotions involving McDonald's, Betty Crocker, LifeSavers, and Cracker Jack in 1994. In addition, Sega expanded its market by targeting serious game players and older, more affluent game enthusiasts, when it debuted its Genesis CDX, the first integrated 16-bit cartridge and CD-ROM multimedia gaming system. At a price of $395, Genesis CDX offered players access to nearly 500 Genesis games and dozens of Sega CD titles while doubling as a portable CD music system.

Sega moved toward mid-1994 with several new trend-setting hardware releases planned before year's end, including Edge 16, the 32-bit compact-disk Saturn system, and Sega VR, which was billed as the first full-color virtual reality home game unit offered on a mass-market price level. Expected to be available as an adjunct of the 16-bit Genesis system, the planned features of Sega VR included a 3-D head-mounted display helmet and tracking system with built-in headphones for stereo surround sound.

Looking beyond 1994, Sega's plans for the future included becoming one of the first international video game companies to successfully move consumers onto the information superhighway by offering a wide range of entertainment opportunities, including VR parks, electronic toys, and interactive entertainment games. To get to the ''next level,'' the game maker was banking on the expertise of such companies as Time Warner and Tele-Communications to help it in its move into cable television. To keep its customers playing Sega games, the company was looking to alliances with such firms as AT&T, Hitachi, Yamaha, JVC, Microsoft, and Martin Marietta to help Sega expand its technology base.

Standing in Sega's way of becoming the clear sales leader in home video-games and accessories, which most market analysts and numerous industry insiders predicted would occur by 1995, was Nintendo, which promised a 1995 release of a 64-bit machine. Additionally, Sega faced competition in the 32-bit machine arena from 3DO and Atari, as well as competition in the CD-ROM market from Commodore International, Phillips, and Sony, which had access to the expertise of its Hollywood movie studio.

As it moved towards 1995, Sega's plans for dominance in the video-game market were grounded in its evolving process of diversifying and reinventing itself as the company which would provide on-ramps to the information superhighway, as well as various means to traverse through the worlds of entertainment and information. Or, as Sega of America's senior vice-president, Joseph B. Miller III told *Business Week,* Sega was not just along for the video-game industry's ride, it had placed itself ''in position to help design the look and feel of the [information super] highway.''

Further Reading:

Battelle, John, ''Seizing the Next Level: Sega's Plan for World Domination,'' *Wired,* December 1993, pp. 3–11.

Brandt, Richard, ''SEGA!: It's Blasting beyond Games and Racing to Build a High-Tech Entertainment Empire,'' *Business Week,* February 21, 1994, pp. 66–74.

——, ''Pow! Bam! Sock!,'' *Business Week,* September 6, 1993, p. 28.

——, ''Video Games: Is All that Gore Really Child's Play?'' *Business Week,* June 14, 1993, p. 38.

Carlton, Jim, ''Sega, Aided by Hedgehog, Is Gaining on Nintendo,'' *Wall Street Journal,* November 5, 1993, pp. B1, B14.

Dumaine, Brian, ''When Delay Courts Disaster,'' *Fortune,* December 16, 1991, p. 104.

Ernsberger, Richard Jr., ''Get Out Your Earplugs!: Sega Issues a CD Challenge to Nintendo,'' *Newsweek,* November 2, 1992, pp. 87–88.

Fannin, Rebecca, ''Zap?,'' *Marketing and Media Decisions,* November 1989, pp. 35–40.

''For Video Games, Now It's a Battle of Bits,'' *Wall Street Journal,* January 9, 1990, pp. B1, B6.

Pereira, Joseph, ''Nintendo Faces a Tough Rival in Sega's Genesis,'' *Wall Street Journal,* December 30, 1991.

Pollack, Andrew, ''Sega Takes Aim at Disney's World,'' *New York Times,* July 4, 1993, sec. 3, pp. 1, 6.

''Sega v. Nintendo: Sonic Boom,'' *Economist,* January 25, 1992, p. 69.

—Roger W. Rouland

THE SHARPER IMAGE®

The Sharper Image Corporation

650 Davis Street
San Francisco, California 94111
U.S.A.
(415) 445-6000
Fax: (415) 445-1574

Public Company
Incorporated: 1978
Employees: 800
Sales: $147.44 million
Stock Exchanges: New York
SICs: 5399 Miscellaneous General Merchandise Stores; 5961
   Catalog & Mail Order Houses

The Sharper Image Corporation is a specialty retailer, selling
apparel and gift items through 74 stores and a catalog that is
issued monthly. Offering a line of unique and often expensive
products, the company grew rapidly in the 1980s, bolstered by a
booming demand for luxury goods that appealed to a generation
of affluent young consumers that came to be known as young
urban professionals or yuppies. By 1990, however, the company's popularity and profitability dropped dramatically,
prompting The Sharper Image to widen the scope of its retail
operations to include less expensive merchandise that would
appeal to a new, broader customer base.

The Sharper Image was founded in 1977 by Richard Thalheimer. Thalheimer put himself through law school in San
Francisco by selling office supplies, and three years after his
graduation, he hit upon a potentially profitable marketing idea
that led to a full-time career in retailing. An avid runner, Thalheimer speculated that high-tech stopwatches might prove popular among others who enjoyed the sport. After lining up a
supplier, he invested $1,000 in a magazine ad offering digital
wristwatches with a stopwatch mechanism for sale by mail.
Thalheimer's venture coincided with the onset of a national
jogging craze; he was able to sell out his entire stock of watches.

Realizing that a large American market existed for high-priced
gadgetry, primarily among the country's growing yuppie community, of which he was a member, Thalheimer used his profits
from the watch venture to run similar ads for telephones, miniature calculators, and other devices. In 1978, he incorporated his
mail order business, calling it The Sharper Image, and the

following year, he compiled his product line in a lavish, glossy
mail order catalog.

Profits from The Sharper Image's mail order operations rose
steadily throughout the early 1980s. Eschewing market research, Thalheimer based his product line on his own instincts
about what people like himself might buy, and the company's
catalogs featured pictures of Thalheimer using the items offered
for sale. Product lines were expanded to include a wide variety
of unique, often peculiar, items, including a $250 imitation Uzi
submachine gun.

As a mail order operation, The Sharper Image was able to keep
its overhead low. By purchasing its inventory on delayed credit
and paying suppliers after collecting from customers, the company could maintain limited inventory and operate with relatively little ready cash. In 1981, the company reported revenues
of $28 million and profits of $1.4 million. In 1982, revenues
reached the $51 million mark, and three years later, The Sharper
Image was issuing 42 million catalogs annually and reporting
sales of $69 million. Commenting on the increasingly whimsi-
cal and nonutilitarian merchandise offered in the company's
catalogs, for a 1986 article in *Forbes,* Thalheimer recalled: ''I
think I got a little fixated on toys.''

In the mid-1980s, orders from The Sharper Image catalogs
began to decline slightly, and the company explored new marketing techniques. When The Sharper Image advertisements on
cable television proved unsuccessful, the company focused on
appealing to customers who preferred not to purchase items
through mail order, opening The Sharper Image retail stores
around the country. In 1985, 12 stores were introduced in such
urban centers as New York, St. Louis, and Honolulu. Twenty
more stores were opened the following year, primarily in affluent areas, including Beverly Hills and Stamford, Connecticut.
The addition of in-store retailing involved a significant transformation of the company's business practices as well as increased
costs for maintaining inventory and leasing store space. Nevertheless, the new The Sharper Image stores contributed strong
sales to the company's overall performance, and by the end of
1985, revenues from all operations had risen to $87 million.

However, financial growth over the next two years stagnated.
As new The Sharper Image retail outlets emerged, the costs they
incurred, as well as markedly slower sales, contributed to a first
quarter loss of $72,000 in 1987. To offset its lackluster perform-
ance, the company went public in April 1987, selling shares
over the counter on the New York Stock Exchange. The Sharper
Image raised $12 million by selling 1.4 million shares of stock.
Thalheimer retained a 72 percent interest in the company, which
immediately became worth millions. During this time, Thalheimer reduced his involvement in the company, gradually
allowing management to oversee daily operations and make
merchandising decisions.

With its infusion of capital, The Sharper Image forged ahead
with plans for rapid expansion. The number of retail outlets was
increased to 42 in 1987, and the company reported gains in the
second and third quarters of the year. Moreover, after an extremely successful holiday season, the company finished 1987
with profits of $5.6 million on overall revenues of $161 million.
Despite this strong finish to the year, The Sharper Image experi-

enced losses again in 1988. While first quarter losses totaled $1.2 million, and were expected to continue for the next three months, the company continued its rapid expansion into conventional retailing, opening several more stores that year.

Increased competition from department and electronics stores, as well as an unfavorable currency exchange rate, which led to low profit margins on goods manufactured in Asia, contributed to the company's mounting losses, which were reported at $2 million in September 1988. Some analysts pointed out that any growth reported on the part of The Sharper Image merely reflected the company's aggressive expansion policy and not higher sales at existing outlets. Sales at previously opened stores, in fact, dropped seven percent between 1986 and 1987.

As a result, The Sharper Image set out to modify its product offerings. During this time, the company was known for its pricey gimmicks and gadgets, including a suit of armor that sold for $3,800, collector's sport cars selling for $80,000, a $7,700 old-fashioned Coca-Cola vending machine, and a $649 toy model of a Ferrari. While such novelties drew people into The Sharper Image stores, the company began to rely on more practical, moderately priced products, such as briefcases and cordless telephones, for the bulk of its sales. Among its more popular items, for example, was a non-fogging shaving mirror for use in the shower, which retailed for $39; the company sold more than 70,000 of these mirrors.

In addition, the company focused on controlling costs and improving management relations, which reportedly suffered due to that fact many employees and executives found Thalheimer a difficult and demanding boss. In fact, The Sharper Image experienced a high degree of employee turnover and had gone nine months in 1988 without a chief financial officer, due to disputes within the company. By providing a more cohesive managerial team, the company hoped to better control the costs incurred by its previously ''loose'' organization.

By the end of 1989, the company's earnings had fallen to $4.7 million, despite sales of $209 million that represented a ten percent increase over the previous year. Having become closely associated with the yuppie generation, the company saw its profits decline as the yuppie ethic of consumerism declined in popularity. In an effort to bring new customers into its stores, The Sharper Image increased its catalog mailings to 39 million in 1989, incurring a cost of $25 million, or $6 million more than it had spent on promotional mailings the year before. With fewer people in the market for luxury gadgets, however, even this big push failed to significantly increase the company's sales, 80 percent of which now took place in retail stores.

The Sharper Image introduced catalogs aimed at several new types of customers in 1990. Sharper Image Kids featured video games and other toys for children. Catalogs designed specifically for customers over the age of 50 were introduced as were home furnishings catalogs, prompted by a perceived trend among Americans of spending more time in the home. In a joint promotional venture, The Sharper Image began to feature celebrities on the cover of its catalogs, in exchange for advertising tied in with movie ads.

The company also planned to market more functional products, such as devices for measuring cholesterol levels in food. ''We want to move away from the disposable glitz of the 80s,'' Thalheimer told *Business Week* in 1990.

During this time, the company sought to reduce its spending on catalog operations, reducing its yearly mailings to 32 million and trimming its mailing list by dropping customers who had not recently made purchases. Cheaper catalogs, with fewer pages, were produced, and a practice of distributing a condensed version of the catalog through Sunday newspapers was established. Other cutbacks at The Sharper Image included a two-year freeze on salary increases, initiated in May 1990, and a lay off of 110 employees in September of that year.

Like most retailers, The Sharper Image suffered a heavy blow at the end of 1990, when holiday sales declined precipitously. The Sharper Image reported losses of $3.6 million, as sales dropped 13 percent to $181 million. In the spring of 1991, the company's merchandise buyer was let go, and Thalheimer returned to a more active role in the business. To cut costs, Thalheimer directed the renegotiation of some store leases during a time in which the real estate market was depressed. He also renewed the company's commitment to providing less expensive products, particularly those that could be sold for less than $50. Cutting down on the number of low-margin electronic products offered, he began exploring a new area of high margin goods: men's clothing. Since surveys indicated that 65 percent of the company's customers were men, and Thalheimer believed that most men preferred not to shop in department stores, The Sharper Image began to offer designer ties, silk shirts, leather jackets, and comfortable walking shoes for men. This simple selection of stylish goods soon accounted for more than ten percent of Sharper Image sales. By the end of 1991, The Sharper Image was still struggling. Several banks refused to increase the company's credit lines, as sales fell to $142 million and losses reached $5.2 million during its second year of poor performance.

After this low point, the fortunes of The Sharper Image began to rebound slowly in 1992. The company began to a run full-page promotional ads in local newspapers, and ads run in two test cities—Kansas City, Missouri, and Buffalo, New York— prompted an 80 percent increase in foot traffic in The Sharper Image stores in one week. The company hoped that the ads, which were relatively inexpensive to run in major metropolitan areas, would familiarize more customers with its stores' new low-priced product offerings.

In April 1992, The Sharper Image began to market its products through mall carts, inexpensive, freestanding units, which required only one employee. Mall carts, offering a small selection of reasonably priced items, were installed in 17 locations. ''It's an easy way to expand the business without opening new stores,'' Thalheimer noted later that year in *Forbes*. Moreover, in August 1993, the company announced that it had finalized marketing deals with several department stores, including, most notably, Bloomingdales, to sell its products at boutiques in their stores.

Later that year, The Sharper Image saw its stock price surge, when it announced that it would market its wares through a cable television home shopping channel. During two hour-long promotions on the QVC network, the company sold as much merchandise as a small The Sharper Image store typically sold in six months. Earnings from this endeavor were particularly high since most of the products marketed were manufactured by The Sharper Image, and those goods carried a 75 percent profit margin. In December 1993, The Sharper Image announced a second major department store deal, as it sealed an agreement with Dillard's, a department store chain with 200 outlets in the Midwest and Southwest, to sell The Sharper Image merchandise.

As a result of such innovative marketing strategies, The Sharper Image reported profits during 1992 and 1993. In January 1994, the company joined with five other retailers and media giant Time Warner Inc. to launch a new 24-hour cable shopping channel. With more functional and affordable merchandise, The Sharper Image had made strong strides in its effort to refashion itself for the 1990s. Future success depended on its ability to adapt to changes in the marketplace through creative and aggressive marketing.

Further Reading:

Greenberg, Herb, "A Clearer Picture of Sharper Image," *San Francisco Chronicle,* January 24, 1994.

King, Ralph, Jr., "Richard Thalheimer's Toy Chest," *Forbes,* February 10, 1986.

Morgenson, Gretchen, "The Sharper Image's Sharper Image," *Forbes,* October 26, 1992.

Shao, Maria, "Sharper Image: Where Have All the Yuppies Gone?" *Business Week,* July 23, 1990.

Shao, Maria, "The Sharper Image May Need to Refocus," *Business Week,* November 21, 1988.

Strom, Stephanie, "Sharper Image Begins Its First Campaign in Newspapers," *New York Times,* February 28, 1992.

—Elizabeth Rourke

Spiegel, Inc.

3500 Lacey Road
Downers Grove, Illinois 60515-5432
U.S.A.
(708) 986-8800
Fax: (708) 769-2823

Public Subsidiary of Spiegel Holdings Ltd.
Incorporated: 1893 as Spiegel House Furnishings Company
Employees: 14,000
Sales: $2.6 billion
Stock Exchanges: NASDAQ
SICs: 5961 Mail Order Houses; 5621 Women's Clothing
  Stores; 5651 Family Clothing Stores; 5399 Miscellaneous
  General Merchandise Stores; 6141 Personal Credit
  Institutions; 5611 Men's and Boys Clothing Stores; 5941
  Sporting Goods Stores

Billing itself as "the nation's dominant multi-channel specialty retailer," Spiegel, Inc. is perhaps best known for its distribution of over 80 different catalogs with a total circulation of over 313 million. The target market for the apparel and home furnishings featured in Spiegel's catalogs consists primarily of working women, ranging in age from 21 to 59 with an average household income of $51,000. The company also operates several specialty retail stores, including Eddie Bauer, Inc., which sells men's and women's casual and sports apparel through catalogs and retail outlets. Nearly 300 Eddie Bauer stores were in operation in 1993, and that year the subsidiary's revenues topped $1 billion for the first time. Another subsidiary is New Hampton, Inc., a specialty catalog company that markets moderately priced women's apparel. Although a portion of Spiegel's stock is traded publicly in the United States, the company is controlled by members of Germany's Otto family, whose Otto-Versand GmbH is the largest catalog retailer in the world. Spiegel was purchased by Otto-Versand in 1982, and those shares were transferred to various family members two years later.

For the first 100 years of its history, Spiegel was largely a family business. The company was founded in 1865 by Joseph Spiegel, the son of a German rabbi. After spending the last several months of the Civil War in a Confederate prison camp, Spiegel settled in Chicago, where his brother-in-law, Henry Liebenstein, ran a successful furniture business. With Liebenstein's assistance, Spiegel opened J. Spiegel and Company, a small home furnishings retail operation located on Wabash Avenue in Chicago's loop. The business was quite successful in its early years. In 1871, however, the Great Chicago Fire destroyed most of the area's business district, including the Spiegel store.

After the fire, Spiegel and partner Jacob Cahn rebuilt the business, and by 1874, the company was prospering again, this time under the name Spiegel and Cahn. When Cahn retired from the business in 1879, the name reverted to J. Spiegel and Company. The company grew impressively through the 1880s. In 1885, Spiegel began running regular advertisements in several Chicago newspapers, and the following year the company moved to a larger building on State Street. Spiegel's two oldest sons, Modie and Sidney, were also brought into the business during this time.

Spiegel issued its first catalogs in 1888. The catalogs were made available to potential customers who lived outside the city. While a mail order system did not yet exist, the catalogs served to lure people into the downtown store from further away. By 1892, however, business had taken a turn for the worse, as many customers were slow to pay for their purchases. With debts mounting, the company went bankrupt. At Modie Spiegel's urging, the company reinvented itself as Spiegel House Furnishings Company of Chicago in 1893. The principal difference was that the new company, like many others in the furniture business, sold on credit. The decision to offer installment plans, and the timing of the decision, made possible Spiegel's remarkable expansion over the next several decades.

The new Spiegel was an instant hit, and the first branch store was opened on Chicago's South Side in 1898. Another South Side branch went into operation three years later. The company's slogan—"We Trust the People!"—reflected its emphasis on credit merchandising. In 1903, Joseph Spiegel's third son, Arthur, entered the business with a plan to develop mail-order operations for Spiegel. After a couple years of lobbying, Arthur convinced the company hierarchy to open a mail-order department, and in 1905 Spiegel became the first company to offer credit through the mail. The new service was reflected by the addition of a word to the company motto, which now read: "We Trust the People—Everywhere!" The response was phenomenal, and soon a huge, previously untapped base of customers was ordering from Spiegel's mail-order catalog.

In 1906, Spiegel's mail-order sales were nearly $1 million, far beyond anyone's expectations. To handle the overwhelming success of the mail-order operation, a new company—Spiegel, May, Stern and Company—was formed, allowing the Spiegel House Furnishings Company to devote its limited resources to conventional retailing, rather than assume the debts associated with building up the mail-order segment. Arthur was named president of the new company. Spiegel then began to diversify its line of products, offering apparel for the first time in 1912. After a couple of unsuccessful partnerships with independent clothing manufacturers, Spiegel, May, Stern began offering its own line of women's apparel. The "Martha Lane Adams" line, named after its fictional designer, was so successful that it quickly became a wholly owned subsidiary of Spiegel, May, Stern, with its own catalog. Martha Lane Adams' sales had grown to nearly $2 million by 1916, when Arthur Spiegel died of pneumonia at age 32.

Spiegel's next marketing breakthrough came in 1926, when company executive Ed Swikard introduced a promotional idea involving Congoleum floor covering. Swikard engineered a mailing to over nine million residences, offering a pre-cut Congoleum package at a low cost. The response was again overwhelming, and company sales reached a record $16 million for the year, with a net profit of $4 million. In 1928, Spiegel, May, Stern went public for the first time, although the Spiegel family retained its controlling interest. The following year, just as the Great Depression was setting in, the Spiegels began gradually liquidating their retail furniture business, and by 1932, the last Spiegel furniture store in Chicago had closed.

After experiencing considerable economic losses in the early years of the Depression, Spiegel entered a period of terrific growth and profits beginning in 1933. During this time, M. J. Spiegel, son of Modie, took over the leadership of the company. Spurred by a remarkably liberal credit policy (''No Charge for Credit''), the company's sales rose from $7.1 million in 1932 to over $56 million in 1937. Furthermore, a $300,000 net loss was transformed into $2.5 million in profits. The strategy behind this growth involved the aggressive marketing of easy credit as the company's most important commodity. When sales began to level off in 1938, Spiegel reacted by shifting its attention to consumers in a higher income bracket. The company began adding dozens of brand names with national reputations to its catalog. The new approach was referred to as the ''quality concept.''

The onset of World War II was disastrous for Spiegel. Because so much manufacturing had been shifted to wartime production, many of the products that were popular catalog items were no longer available in large quantities. Moreover, a shortage of labor affected the company's operations, and when buying on credit was officially discouraged by the U.S. government, Spiegel management had to discard its ''No Charge for Credit'' policy. For 1942 and 1943 combined, the company lost $3.8 million. In order to reverse this trend, Spiegel began to open retail outlets once again in 1944, hoping to mimic the success of its larger competitors Sears, Roebuck & Co. and Montgomery Ward. That year, Spiegel acquired 46 Sally dress shops in Illinois. Several other chains were purchased over the next few years, and by 1948, Spiegel was operating 168 retail stores featuring a wide range of merchandise, including clothing, furniture, and auto supplies.

After initial success, the costs of retail operations began to outweigh the benefits, and by the mid-1950s, Spiegel was again concentrating on its former mainstay, mail-order sales on credit. While nearly all of the company's retail outlets were sold off by 1954, several catalog shopping centers were retained so that customers could ask questions and place orders with company representatives. The following year, Spiegel unveiled its Budget Power Plan, a liberal policy under which customers were offered a line of credit sometimes as high as $1,000, with very low monthly payments. The idea was to add as many names as

possible to the Spiegel customer list. The company also began to include an ever-widening range of products in its catalogs; by 1960, Spiegel was even shipping pets. By that time, sales were well over $200 million, and nearly two million people had Spiegel credit accounts.

In 1965, after a century of operation as a family business, Spiegel was purchased by Beneficial Finance Company. Spiegel stockholders received shares of Beneficial stock, and Spiegel became a wholly owned subsidiary. During the early 1970s, several charges were leveled against Spiegel by the Federal Trade Commission (FTC) regarding some of the company's marketing tactics. In 1971, the FTC accused Spiegel of failing to adequately disclose credit terms in some of its statements and catalog ads. The company was also cited for its handling of credit life insurance policies, as well as for offering free home trials without informing customers that credit approval was required before a product would be shipped. Moreover, in 1974, the FTC charged that Spiegel's debt-collection policies treated customers unfairly. Most of the complaints brought by FTC during this period were settled by minor changes in company practices, and serious action by the government was generally avoided.

Rising interest rates in the mid-1970s made financing credit accounts costly. Also during this time, Spiegel began to feel the pressure of competition from discount stores such as Kmart, which were rapidly establishing a national presence. In 1976, to help turn the company around, Beneficial hired Henry ''Hank'' Johnson, a veteran of the mail order operations of Montgomery Ward and Avon. One of Johnson's first moves was to streamline company management. Dozens of executives were let go, and overall employment was cut in half over the next five years, from 7,000 in 1976 to 3,500 in 1981. Johnson also closed Spiegel's remaining catalog stores.

Perhaps more importantly, Johnson sought to change Spiegel's image to that of a ''fine department store in print.'' Accordingly, the Spiegel catalog was completely revamped, and low-budget items were replaced by upscale apparel and accessories for career women. Merchandise bearing designer labels began appearing in 1980, when the company introduced a line of Gloria Vanderbilt products. Spiegel soon became a trendsetter in the catalog business, which was booming as a whole during the early 1980s. The company's sales grew at an impressive pace of 25 to 30 percent a year. Although Spiegel still ranked fourth in catalog sales during this time, trailing Sears, J. C. Penney, and Montgomery Ward, the company's moves were being followed closely by its larger competitors.

In 1982, Beneficial sold Spiegel to Otto-Versand GmbH, a huge, private West German company prominent in catalog sales. Between 1982 and 1983, Spiegel's revenue shot from $394 million to $513 million, and the company's pre-tax profits more than doubled, reaching $22.5 million in 1983. The following year, control of Spiegel was transferred from Otto-Versand itself to members of its controlling family, the Ottos. Under its new ownership, Spiegel's transformation into an outlet for higher-end products continued. In 1984, Spiegel began distributing specialty catalogs in addition to its four primary catalogs; 25 of these specialty catalogs were in circulation by 1986, featuring Italian imports, plus-sized clothing, and other specialty items. That year, Spiegel mailed a total of 130 million catalogs, at a cost of $100 million, and company sales surpassed the $1 billion mark for the first time. Also during this time, a new president and CEO, John Shea, was named.

In 1987, six million shares of nonvoting stock was sold to the public, the first time since 1965 that Spiegel was not completely privately held. The following year, Spiegel acquired Eddie Bauer, Inc., a retail chain specializing in sportswear and outdoor equipment. Eddie Bauer, which also maintained a catalog operation, had annual sales of $260 million. In the first year following the acquisition, the chain was expanded from 60 to 99 stores.

By 1989, Spiegel had become the number three catalog retailer in the United States, with a total circulation of about 200 million catalogs, including 60 different specialty catalogs, and an active customer base of five million. In 1990, Spiegel acquired First Consumers National Bank, which began issuing credit cards and statements to Spiegel and Eddie Bauer customers. That year, the company enhanced its image as the catalog for career women through an advertising campaign that featured actress Candice Bergen, who portrayed a career woman on the situation comedy "Murphy Brown." The campaign also featured a specialty catalog promoted by Bergen, emphasizing the inconvenience of department store shopping and the relative ease of shopping by catalog. The company also began to expand its retail outlet operations based on lines from its catalogs. Spiegel stores included For You From Spiegel, which offered large-sized women's apparel, and Crayola Kids, providing a line of children's apparel first launched in 1991. In spite of these innovations, the company's growth stagnated due to national economic recession, and earnings declined sharply in 1991. Slight gains were realized the following year as Spiegel's revenue topped $2 billion. Eddie Bauer performed particularly well, having grown to 265 stores.

In August 1993, Spiegel announced its purchase of New Hampton, Inc., a catalog company specializing in moderately priced women's clothing. Later that year, Spiegel unveiled a new specialty catalog, E Style, featuring a clothing line aimed at African-American women. Moreover, Spiegel formed a joint venture with Time Warner Entertainment to create two home shopping services for cable television. Spiegel reported total revenues of $2.6 billion in 1993. Sales at Eddie Bauer stores reached $1 billion that year, bolstered by the 30 new outlets opened over the past 12 months. Between Spiegel and Eddie Bauer, 81 different catalogs, with a total circulation of over 313 million, were distributed in 1993. The company's specialty retail stores also performed well in 1993, generating $840 million in net sales.

By the mid-1990s, having spent many decades in the shadow of Sears, Roebuck & Co. and Montgomery Ward, Spiegel was regarded as a leader in the catalog shopping industry. Relying on its proven ability to adapt to changes in customer tastes and trends in competition, the company was expected to maintain this status, which would no doubt further benefit from the increasing use of home shopping through catalog and television.

Principal Subsidiaries: Eddie Bauer, Inc.; New Hampton, Inc.; First Consumer's National Bank; Spiegel Acceptance Corporation; Cara Corporation.

Further Reading:

"Aggressive Approach to Credit Sales Pays Off in Bigger Net for Spiegel," *Barron's,* January 2, 1961, pp. 20–1.

"Beneficial Finance and Spiegel, Inc., Propose Merger," *Wall Street Journal,* June 1, 1965, p. 30.

"Beneficial Sets Spiegel Merger," *New York Times,* August 6, 1965, p. 33.

"Beneficial's Spiegel to Close Remaining 131 Catalog Stores," *Wall Street Journal,* February 10, 1978, p. 16.

"Besieged Spiegel," *Business Week,* June 15, 1946, p. 92.

Byrne, Harlan, "Spiegel Inc.," *Barron's,* August 14, 1989, pp. 102–3.

Collins, Lisa, "Spiegel's Big Order: Salvage Lousy Year," *Crain's Chicago Business,* October 21, 1991, p. 1.

Cornell, James, Jr., *The People Get the Credit,* Chicago: Spiegel, Inc., 1964.

Fitzgerald, Kate, "Spiegel Expands Retail Holdings," *Advertising Age,* July 15, 1991, p. 12.

Fitzgerald, Kate, "Spiegel Pans Department Stores," *Advertising Age,* April 2, 1990, p. 41.

Johnson, Henry, "Spiegel's New, Winning Spirit Based on Target Marketing," *Direct Marketing,* August 1982, pp. 58–63.

"Montgomery Ward, Spiegel Cited by FTC on Credit Charge," *Wall Street Journal,* February 11, 1971, p. 30.

Oneal, Michael, "Wall Street Isn't Buying Spiegel's High-Gloss Look," *Business Week,* October 19, 1987, p. 62.

Palmeri, Christopher, "Indoor Outdoorsman," *Forbes,* March 29, 1993, pp. 43–4.

"Resurgent Spiegel," *Business Week,* May 18, 1946, pp. 86–8.

Smalley, Orange, and Frederick Sturdivant, *The Credit Merchants,* Carbondale: Southern Illinois University Press, 1973.

Strom, Stephanie, "Home Shopping Plans for Spiegel-Time Warner," *New York Times,* September 28, 1993, p. D5.

Veverka, Mark, "Spiegel Broadens with Catalog Buy," *Crain's Chicago Business,* September 6, 1993, p. 9.

Williams, Winston, "The Metamorphosis of Spiegel," *New York Times,* July 15, 1984, p. F8.

—Robert R. Jacobson

SPX Corporation

SPX Corporation

700 Terrace Point Drive
P.O. Box 3301
Muskegon, Michigan 49443-3301
U.S.A.
(616) 724-5000
Fax: (616) 724-5720

Public Company
Incorporated: 1911 as The Piston Ring Company
Employees: 8,600
Sales: $756.15 million
Stock Exchanges: New York Pacific
SICs: 3714 Motor Vehicle Parts and Accessories; 5013
   Motor Vehicle Supplies and New Parts; 3546 Power
   Driven Handtools; 3492 Fluid Power Valves & Hose
   Fittings; 3542 Machine Tools, Metal Forming Types; 3561
   Pumps and Pumping Equipment; 3829 Measuring and
   Controlling Devices Nec

SPX Corporation is the world leader in the specialty service tool and equipment market and a North American leader in the production and marketing of automotive parts and components. From its headquarters in Muskegon, Michigan, SPX monitors subsidiaries and affiliates in 14 nations worldwide. SPX became a Fortune 500 company in 1983 when its sales topped $400 million. By 1993 sales had climbed to over $800 million and its specialty service tools were being used by professional service technicians in more than 120,000 vehicle repair facilities around the world. The specialty service tools segment of SPX, which accounted for 54 percent of its revenues in 1993, is operated through its Kent-Moore, Power Team, Dealer Equipment and Services, OTC, Robinair, and Automotive Diagnostics divisions. SPX's original equipment components group, previously called Sealed Power Technologies, was separated from its parent in 1989 but was reacquired in 1994. This group of companies, which in 1994 included SPX's Contech, Hy-Lift, Acutex, Sealed Power, and Sealed Power Europe divisions, together posted 1993 annual sales approaching $460 million.

SPX's foundations were laid on December 20, 1911, when two friends, Charles E. Johnson and Paul R. Beardsley, each deposited $1,000 in the National Lumberman's Bank of Muskegon, Michigan. The money was to serve as the initial working capital of their new single product firm, The Piston Ring Company. Johnson, a mechanic, and Beardsley, a salesman, foresaw the need for automotive parts for the burgeoning automotive industry in Michigan. The two partners personally delivered the first piston rings manufactured in their rented 30 by 60 foot factory to the firm's first customer, Continental Motors Corporation. In its first years, the aptly named The Piston Ring Company devoted itself entirely to the production of piston rings for leading engine builders. The advent of the first World War brought a huge increase in the demand for engine parts for the war effort, and The Piston Ring Company responded by undertaking a major plant expansion.

In the years between the two World Wars, The Piston Ring Company began a series of acquisitions and expansions, a pattern of growth for the company for the next 60 years. In 1923 they bought the No-Leak-O Piston Ring Company, which allowed the firm to further increase its production of the crucial engine component. By 1925, they were able to begin exporting their product and to enter the increasingly lucrative replacement parts market. The acquisition in 1931 of the Accuralite Company, a maker of pistons and cylinder sleeves, would mark a crucial step for the growing firm. This diversification of their product line would become a fundamental component of the company's strategy in later years. In order to reflect this new diversity, the company also changed its name from the simple "The Piston Ring Company" to the more evocative "Sealed Power Corporation."

The post-World War II years were a period of major expansion for Sealed Power. In 1946 the company opened its first plant outside Muskegon with the construction of a piston ring machining facility at St. John's, Michigan, closer to the huge Detroit automakers that were its primary customers. Two years later the company built a cylinder sleeve machining facility in Rochester, Indiana, and in 1957 it added a Replacement Distribution Center in LaGrange, Indiana. This distribution center, which serviced 33 smaller distribution outlets in key cities throughout the United States and Canada, was indicative of the growing role of replacement parts marketing in the company's business strategy. By 1959, replacement parts accounted for about 50 percent of Sealed Power sales and served as an important hedge against the highly cyclical original equipment market. The automotive aftermarket is not only relatively free from the sharp ups and downs of the original parts industry but actually tends to increase during downturns in the original automotive market. When people are not in a position to buy new cars they have their old ones repaired instead.

Sealed Power's relatively rapid expansion in the 1950s led to the company's first public offering of common stock in 1955. The company also increased exports, distributing their original and replacement parts in 78 countries by the end of the decade. Even more significantly for their global presence, by the dawn of the 1960s Sealed Power had opened plants in Stratford, Canada, and in Mexico City. This expansion in both production and market diversity was accompanied by a major product breakthrough in 1956 when Sealed Power introduced the first stainless steel piston ring. The ring quickly achieved 100 percent original and replacement market acceptance, according to company sources.

At the beginning of the 1960s, in spite of product diversification over the previous 50 years, the sale of piston rings for both the original and replacement markets still accounted for over 65 percent of Sealed Power's sales. These sales made up about one quarter of the total U.S. market for piston rings and made Sealed Power the second largest manufacturer of piston rings in the country. Cylinder sleeves and pistons made up the bulk of the company's remaining sales, although by this time it was also producing a variety of small engine parts, such as valves and tappets. By the end of the decade, Sealed Power, determined to decrease its reliance on a single product, implemented a planned program of product diversification. In 1968 the company acquired another cylinder sleeve plant in Mexico as well as the Consolidated Die Cast Corporation (since renamed Contech), a Michigan firm that produced precision die castings. During the next six years it acquired a manufacturer of valve tappets (since renamed the Hy-Lift Division), a manufacturer of transmission fluid filters (since renamed the Filtran Division), and a manufacturer of small alloyed castings. It had also opened a sealing ring plant in Franklin, Kentucky, a tappet facility in Zeeland, Michigan, and a new piston ring plant in Liege, Belgium, to serve the European market.

Sales rose steadily during the 1960s and 1970s as Sealed Power expanded. From annual sales of $25 million in 1960, the company's sales had grown to over $200 million by 1977. Although sales grew, earnings remained heavily dependent on fluctuations in the auto industry. In 1974, for instance, a year in which American car and truck production plummeted, earnings fell to $1.46 per share from the previous year's $2.19. Diversification had meant that piston rings made up a smaller percentage of sales than it had in the early 1960s; nonetheless, Sealed Power's original engine parts group, which now included sealing rings, valve tappets, and transmission filters in addition to the company's long standing engine products, still accounted for 42 percent of sales in 1975. With over three quarters of these sales coming directly from the auto industry, Sealed Power's fortunes were inextricably tied to that of the major American automakers. In a 1980 press release, company president Edward I. Schalon stated that "as a supplier of engine parts to the motor vehicle industry we are adversely affected by the proliferation of cars and trucks imported into the United States. This situation is compounded by the growing number of vehicles which bear domestic nameplates, but are powered by engines manufactured overseas."

Diversification continued to dominate Sealed Power's long-term business strategy in the 1980s. In early 1982, the company acquired Kent-Moore Corporation in a cash and stock transaction valued at $70 million. Kent-Moore, headquartered in Warren, Michigan, was a major manufacturer of specialized service tools, equipment, and diagnostic instrumentation for the transportation industry. An important step in Sealed Power's campaign to diversify its product line, the acquisition of Kent-Moore provided a new direction for Sealed Power's relationship with the auto industry. Although Kent-Moore dealt directly with the same automakers that Sealed Power had supplied since its beginnings in 1911, the specialty tools that it produced relied on the introduction of new automotive models rather than on the volume of production. Each new car model requires a set of specialized tools with which dealers can service the vehicles,

and the Kent-Moore division works directly with manufacturers before new vehicles are introduced. Kent-Moore also had significant overseas operations, including a partnership in Japan, that allowed Sealed Power to expand its foreign presence. In 1982, the first year of the acquisition, Kent-Moore contributed some $86 million to Sealed Power's $366 million sales total.

Sales continued to grow during the 1980s, topping $400 million in 1983 and placing Sealed Power on *Fortune*'s "500" listing. Earnings, however, continued to fluctuate. In 1983 and 1984, when domestic automobile production soared, Sealed Power earnings rose an impressive 27 percent and 17 percent only to fall back again in 1985 and 1986 when both the original equipment and replacement markets flattened out. By 1985, as it became clear that the American auto industry would be unstable for at least the immediate future, stock analysts began to stress the advantages of the aftermarket. "At this point in the automobile cycle," a parts industry analyst for Merrill Lynch was quoted as saying in a 1985 *New York Times* article, "we believe that the aftermarket is more attractive than the original equipment segment." After the Kent-Moore purchase the proportion of sales contributed by each of Sealed Power's product groups began to shift. In 1982, the year of the Kent-Moore acquisition, aftermarket sales made up 39 percent of total sales, original equipment contributed 35 percent, and specialty service tools took over 22 percent of total revenues.

In 1985, Sealed Power further expanded its specialty tool product segment through the acquisition of the Owatonna Tool Company and its subsidiaries, now the Power Team and Truth divisions of SPX. Owatonna, a producer of specialty tools and electronic repair equipment, allowed Sealed Power to expand its market in this area. Power Team and Truth further diversified Sealed Power's product line with the addition of high-pressure hydraulic pumps and other equipment for industrial applications as well as window and door hardware for the home construction industry. Also acquired in 1985 was the V.L. Churchill Group of Daventry, England, a major supplier of specialty tools and service products in Europe, further expanding Sealed Power's overseas presence. In order to respond to the growing threat of Japanese automobile imports, Sealed Power also set up a joint agreement with the Riken Corp., Japan's largest manufacturer of piston rings, to allow Sealed Power to distribute Riken's engine parts for repair and maintenance of Japanese cars in the United States. Sealed Power continued its program of diversification and expansion through acquisitions into the late 1980s. In addition to a number of smaller companies, the company purchased the piston ring operations of TRW in 1987, resulting in a reorganization and consolidation of Sealed Power's piston manufacturing plants and the laying off of some 400 employees.

The late 1980s were a critical period for Sealed Power. By 1988 Sealed Power's products ranged from piston rings to door hardware and were sold to a wide range of markets. Original equipment motor parts sales had fallen to only 28 percent of total company revenues, whereas replacement parts constituted 36 percent of sales, service products and specialty service remained steady at 22 percent of corporate volume, and window and door hardware now assumed 14 percent of total sales. In recognition of the changing nature of the company, the decision was reached to change the company name from the Sealed Power Corporation to the SPX Corporation. Robert D. Tuttle, then company chairman and CEO, stated in a press release that the name change was necessary because the Sealed Power name did not reflect the scope of the company's diversity in products and markets nor the range and depth of its vision of the company's future.

Acquisitions had greatly increased SPX's total sales, which rose from $250 million in 1980 to $632 million in 1989. Net income, however, failed to rise as consistently and the still considerable original equipment segment continued to be tied to the fluctuations in the automobile industry. The acquisition in 1988 of Bear Automotive Service Equipment Company increased SPX's presence in the specialty service equipment field. In 1989 the company reached a major crossroads as it became apparent that diversification had transformed them from an engine parts maker with some other interests, to a replacement parts and specialty service tool manufacturer who also made piston rings.

A rumor was reported in early 1989 that corporate raider Arthur Goldberg was making a move towards SPX and had actually purchased a 4 percent stake in the company. Whether or not these rumors were heeded by SPX management, they clearly felt that strong action was needed to maintain shareholder confidence in the now diffuse company. That action came in April of 1989 when it was announced that the company would undergo a major restructuring. The key component of this restructuring would be the sale of a majority stake in all of SPX's original equipment operations.

A new partnership, to be called Sealed Power Technologies Limited Partnership, would be formed from four Sealed Power divisions specializing in original equipment manufacture. The partnership would be controlled by a joint agreement between Sealed Power, who would retain a 49 percent stake in the companies, and Goldman, Sachs & Co., a New York securities firm who would assume control of 49 percent of the partnership. The remaining 2 percent stake would be owned by company management. This partnership would operate independently of SPX's other operations and would leave SPX free to concentrate more heavily on its replacement and specialty service tools segments. In addition, SPX would establish an employees stock ownership plan, in an apparently defensive move, to make unfriendly takeovers more difficult. "The restructuring will allow SPX to concentrate fully on a market segment that has higher margins and is more resistant to recessions than the original equipment business," CEO Robert Tuttle was quoted as saying in an article in the *Grand Rapids Business Journal.*

The resistance to recession that SPX felt it would gain from concentrating its resources on the automobile aftermarket and construction industries failed to materialize. Instead, 1990 proved a very poor year for all sectors of SPX, with the exception of such environmentally driven products as refrigerant recycling equipment from their Robinair division. Net income dropped from $23.6 million in 1989 to only $17.7 million in 1990 (not including income or losses from Sealed Power Technologies), mostly due to a weak demand in the automotive replacement business and a major downturn in the housing

industry. If 1990 was disappointing for the reorganized SPX, 1991 was disastrous. For the first time in over 50 years SPX recorded a net loss, totaling $19.4 million. Sales were down in all sectors, but continued losses in their Bear Automotive Service Equipment division were particularly worrisome.

Faced with increasing pressure to restabilize the company, Dale A. Johnson, SPX CEO since 1989, essentially reversed the restructuring that had taken place in the late 1980s. The first step in the repositioning of the company was the sale of their automotive replacement parts division to Federal-Mogul in September of 1993. Then, in late 1993, the company decided to repurchase the outstanding 49 percent stake in the Sealed Power Technologies Partnership. With the reacquisition of the four divisions that had made up the partnership, in addition to the sale of SPX's door and window hardware division, SPX was firmly back into the original automotive equipment market. The restructuring itself had, however, demanded a substantial outlay, and SPX faced another substantial loss by the end of 1993. Johnson, commenting on the $40.6 million loss in a press release, maintained that "operating performance for 1993 was sharply impacted by steps taken to complete the strategy for transforming the company into a global market leader in specialty service tools and original equipment components for the motor vehicle industry."

As the new SPX emerged in 1994, its operations were tightly focused in two distinct arenas. Specialty Service Tools made up 54 percent of sales and were produced and distributed by the Automotive Diagnostics (created by the merging of Bear Automotive with the newly acquired Allen Testproducts), Dealer Equipment and Services, Kent-Moore, OTC, Power Team, and Robinair divisions of SPX. The Original Equipment Components Group, formed by the Acutex, Contech, Hy-Lift, and Sealed Power divisions, contributed 46 percent of revenues. A substantial recovery in the motor vehicle industry occurred in 1994, making SPX's re-entry into the original equipment market seem well timed.

Principal Subsidiaries: Acutex; Contech; Hy-Lift; Power Team; Automotive Diagnostics; Dealer Equipment and Services; Robinair; Filtran; Kent-Moore Corporation; Sealed Power; OTC; Allied Ring Corporation (50%); Jurubatech (Brazil); Bear (Germany, Italy, United Kingdom); Euroline (Germany, Spain, Switzerland, United Kingdom); Sealed Power Europe (Germany; 70%); V.L. Churchill—OTC (England); Jatek (Japan; 50%); Promec (Mexico; 40%); RSV Corporation (Japan; 50%).

Further Reading:

Blake, Laura, "SPX Sees Profit with Acquisition," *Grand Rapids Business Journal,* July 5, 1993, p. B7.

"Car Parts: A Replacement Bias," *New York Times,* April 15, 1985.

Dorfman, Dan, "Money Follows Goldberg's Moves," *USA Today,* March 3, 1989, p. 4B.

"Greater Efficiency, New Items Spark Advance in Earnings of Sealed Power," *Barron's,* November 6, 1961, p. 21.

Maher, Tani, "SPX Cannot Unseal Its Past," *Financial World,* September 6, 1988, p. 16.

"Sealed Power Corp. Extends Solid Earnings, Recovery of Final Half of Last Year," *Barron's,* March 16, 1959, p. 28.

"Sealed Power Corp. Reports 1980 First-Quarter Sales," *PR Newswire,* March 18, 1980.

"Sealed Power Corp. Reports 1982 Sales and Earnings," *PR Newswire,* February 16, 1983.

"Sealed Power, Engine Parts Maker Revved Up for Record Earnings," *Barron's,* May 10, 1976, pp. 32, 34.

"SPX Corporation Reports 1990 Sales and Earnings," *Business Wire,* February 12, 1991.

"SPX Corporation Reports 1992 Financial Results," *Business Wire,* February 16, 1993.

"SPX Corporation Reports 1993 Financial Results," *Business Wire,* February 23, 1994.

"SPX to Consolidate Bear, Allen Divisions," *Tire Business,* July 12, 1993, p. 5.

Turner, Mike, "The New Look of Muskegon's SPX," *Grand Rapids Business Journal,* April 17, 1989, p. B1.

—Hilary Gopnik

Staples, Inc.

100 Pennsylvania Avenue
P.O. Box 9328
Framingham, Massachusetts 01701
U.S.A.
(508) 370-8500
Fax: (508) 370-8955

Public Company
Incorporated: 1985
Employees: 3,234
Sales: $883 million
Stock Exchanges: New York
SICs: 5112 Stationery and Office Supplies

Staples, Inc. is the country's third largest operator of office supplies superstores, which offer a vast selection of products at very low prices to small business owners. Staples pioneered this concept in 1986 and grew rapidly after opening its first store in the Boston area. The company has subsequently expanded to areas outside the Northeast, opening hundreds of outlets across the nation and beginning joint ventures overseas.

Staples was founded in November of 1985 by Thomas G. Stemberg and Leo Kahn, who had previously competed against each other in the Boston grocery market. Stemberg had worked in the New England food business since graduating from Harvard Business School in 1973. After his employer fired him in 1985 because of "philosophical differences," he used his year's worth of severance pay to explore other business opportunities.

Stemberg was interviewing for a job at a generalized warehouse club retailer when he noticed that the aisle featuring office supplies was in disarray, attesting to the popularity of the products, which moved quickly out of the store. When he learned that this small category of goods accounted for seven percent of all warehouse store sales, Stemberg recognized a niche market that would provide him with the opportunity he wanted.

In formulating his concept for an office supplies warehouse, Stemberg drew on several demographic factors. As large corporations cut their workforce, small businesses were taking up the slack in the American economy, signalling a quickly expanding, lucrative market. In addition, the service sector of the economy was growing rapidly, and such businesses typically used a good deal of office supplies.

Stemberg's plan called for the elimination of the middleman in office supply distribution. Traditionally, manufacturers of paper and other items sold their goods to one of six major wholesalers around the country. The wholesalers then sold their goods to office supply dealers and stationary stores. The dealers sold supplies to large corporations, while stationers catered to small businesses and individuals. However, along the way, the two layers of middlemen between the factory and the customer drove up costs dramatically.

With his Staples store, as he planned to call the outlet, Stemberg would collapse those two layers into one. Because supplies would be purchased directly from manufacturers, the store would be able to offer much lower prices than its competitors in the heavily fragmented retail environment. With this new idea, Stemberg hoped to gain a significant enough portion of the office supply market to justify purchasing in bulk. Stemberg expected that imitators would quickly copy his idea if it proved successful, so he set out to raise a large amount of capital to finance his company, hoping to expand Staples rapidly after its start-up and avoid losing ground to its competitors.

To do so, Stemberg approached his old nemesis Leo Kahn, who invested $500,000. In addition, Stemberg made presentations to venture capitalists in the Boston area and was met with an enthusiastic response. In the first round of financing, the company raised $4 million. With this money, Stemberg set out to recruit a management team. Looking for people who shared his philosophy of how to run a business, he sought out those with a similar background, bringing in people who had worked at the same national grocery chain that he had. By the spring of 1986 everything was in place.

The first Staples Office Superstore opened its doors in May at 1660 Soldiers Field Road in Brighton, Massachusetts, a suburb of Boston. Consisting of one vast, open 14,000-square-foot space, the Staples store had a typical warehouse decor, with concrete floors and an unfinished ceiling. A huge array of goods was stacked on metal shelves, and shopping carts were provided for customers at the front. More than 40 workers were deployed to ring up sales at six cash registers. In an effort to provide customers with one-stop shopping, the store stocked everything that could conceivably be used in an office, from paper and pens, to office furniture, to microwave ovens. Most products were offered at a price half as low as that of Staples's competitors.

To drum up business, Staples gift certificates were sent to 35 local small business office managers, who would be surveyed on their reactions to the store when they made a purchase. After five weeks, only nine of the certificates had been redeemed, and Stemberg learned that he had a sizable marketing task ahead of him.

The marketing push began with an effort to differentiate Staples from other stationery outlets, in order to draw the company's targeted customers into the store. The company invested more than $1 million in several linked minicomputers and a staff of three computer programmers and began amassing a database of small businesses. The database became part of a sophisticated multi-step marketing program. Through telemarketing, Staples identified customers and enticed them into the stores. Customers then became a part of an extended database that tracked their purchases, enabling Staples to offer special discounts and encourage repeat business. With these strategies, Staples was able to begin building a solid customer base. In November of 1986 the company opened its second store in Woburn, Massachusetts, another suburb of Boston. A third location came on line in Providence, Rhode Island, the following year, and the company began to plan for its expansion into the New York area.

As Staples broadened its geographical scope throughout the Northeast, the company decided to invest in a centralized distribution facility. Rents tended to be high in the crowded urban areas where Staples stores were located, and the company hoped that this move would allow it to offer a fuller selection in smaller facilities because fewer products would have to be stockpiled on site at each location. With the distribution center, the company believed that it could replenish its shelves faster than competitors who had to rely on manufacturers for supplies. In addition, the central depot cut down on freight costs, as manufacturers were able to ship large amounts of goods to one location. It also kept payroll costs low. Staples began work on their 136,000-square-foot processing and distribution center in Putnam, Connecticut, in 1987. The decision to go ahead with this project aroused controversy among Staples's management because the investment meant that the company would postpone becoming profitable for an even longer period of time.

In June of 1987 Staples made its first foray into the New York market, opening a store in Port Chester. By the end of the year the company had opened a total of nine stores that were clumped in the New York and metropolitan Boston areas. The following year Staples moved into the other major East Coast markets of Philadelphia and Washington, D.C. This was done in conjunction with the opening of the $6 million distribution center.

In the winter of 1988, Staples stepped up its marketing efforts by sending potential customers a special catalog. Wrapped around this brochure was a coupon promising a free pen and pencil set with a purchase of $10 or more. Of those who redeemed this offer, company data indicated that more than half would return to make future purchases.

By May of 1988 Staples had opened 16 stores, and the company's revenues had risen to $40 million. In its rapid Northeastern expansion, the company sought to lock up prime retail locations throughout the region so that competitors would have difficulty establishing their own stores. To support this rapid growth, Staples solicited three more rounds of financing from the investment banking community, raising a total of $32 million.

The number of Staples stores had grown to 23 by the beginning of 1989. Whenever Staples opened a new store, the company bought a list of all the small businesses located within a 15-minute drive of the outlet. Buyers of office supplies from these firms were then contacted by telemarketers who announced the store's opening and garnered data about the buyers' purchasing habits. In return they received a coupon for free copy paper that would hopefully bring them into the store and spur word-of-mouth advertising.

In addition, the company offered customers a free Staples card that offered discounts on goods purchased. When customers filled out a card application, the company got data about the nature of their businesses. The numeric code on the card also enabled Staples to track their purchases precisely. All of this information was collated at the company's headquarters on a daily basis.

In February of 1989 Staples introduced its Private Label products—generic office supplies at exceptionally low prices. This strategy was one that Stemberg had first implemented in the grocery business, when he introduced company-label groceries for Star Markets. In April Staples sold stock to the public for the first time, raising $37 million to fund its further expansion. By the end of that month, the company's sales had reached $120 million. Despite this strong growth in revenue, Staples had yet to make any earnings, although the company did turn in its first profitable quarter at the end of January, 1989. Overall, losses since Staples' founding had reached $14.1 million.

These losses were caused by the high costs of the company's start-up and expansion as well as the strong competition the company faced. As Stemberg had predicted, Staples had quickly been joined in the office supplies market by a host of imitators around the country. In mid-1989 the company slipped to second place in revenues behind Office Depot Incorporated; Office Club was making a strong showing in California; and retail giants Kmart and Ames were also deliberating a move into the stationary field. To counter these threats, Staples continued its rapid pace of new store openings. By the end of the year the company was operating 38 stores, and it had racked up sales of $182 million.

Building on these gains, the following year Staples moved to centralize its Northeast delivery operations through a hub-and-spoke system set up with its Putnam facility at the center. This warehouse was augmented with a 32,000-square-foot delivery distribution center. This new system allowed Staples to set up a toll-free telephone line for orders, which were then shipped for delivery the next day. This operation was dubbed Staples Direct.

In July of 1990 the company also commenced operations in a new market, Southern California. Staples made its inroad into this competitive field with three stores located in Orange County, California, and a separate California distribution facility. Staples had targeted Orange County because of its high number of small businesses and growing economy, viewing its move into this area as the first step of a planned 34-store California roll-out.

Staples followed its West Coast expansion with the introduction of a new retail concept, called Staples Express. The first of these stores was opened on Court Street in the heart of Boston's financial district. With a space only a third as large as the company's suburban stores, this facility stocked 2,700 items, or half of the usual complement, which were sold at the same low prices. Staples Express was designed to appeal to the small business operator in an urban area and was geared to quick trips and impulse buying on lunch hours and after work. Customer purchases were typically small, being no bigger than what a person could carry.

The unveiling of this prototype was part of the company's strategy was to dominate the office supplies market through three distribution channels: the suburban superstore, the urban ministore, and phone-in direct delivery service. Also in 1990 Staples began to buy its products overseas. To conduct international buying the company formed a subsidiary called Total Global Sourcing, Inc.

By the end of the year, the number of Staples stores had doubled to 74, including nine in California, and the company's sales had nearly reached the $300 million mark. Staples accelerated its California operations the next year when it bought ten Los Angeles stores from defunct superstore operator HQ Office Supplies Warehouse and converted them to Staples stores.

At the same time, Staples entered its first foreign venture, investing in Business Depot, Limited, a new Canadian office superstore. In the United States, Staples celebrated the opening of its 100th store, an outlet on Long Island in New York. By the end of the year, sales had risen 83 percent to reach $547 million, and earnings grew by 117 percent.

In June of 1992 Staples expanded into another region of the U.S. with the purchase of Office Mart Holdings Corporation for $3.1 million. This company owned ten WORKplace stores in Florida. Staples had now moved into direct competition with its biggest rival, Florida-based Office Depot.

That year Staples made additional progress in its campaign to expand overseas. The company bought a 48 percent interest in MAXI-Papier, operators of five office superstores in cities around Germany. Staples also signed a partnership agreement with Kingfisher plc to open office superstores in the United Kingdom. Sales at the end of 1992 reached $883 million. In 1993 Staples celebrated the opening of its 200th store, and at that time the company announced plans for an additional 130 store openings over the next two years.

This ambitious schedule was set despite fluctuations in the price of Staples's stock. Wall Street had lost confidence in the com-

pany in early 1993 after its two largest rivals embarked upon a rapid string of acquisitions, while Staples demonstrated difficulty rolling out a new line of personal computer products. To redress these problems, Staples pared down the number of machines and software programs it offered, to create a more manageable department. In addition, the company began to make a number of acquisitions of its own. Staples arranged to buy out its Canadian partner in the Business Depot for $32 million in early 1994. The company also signed agreements to buy two contract stationers: New Jersey-based National Office Supply Company, Inc., which cost $99 million, and Spectrum Office Products, of New York. The former company boasted a nationwide distribution system.

In April of 1994 Staples bought seven former Office America stores based in Virginia and began to convert them to Staples outlets. In July, the company announced that it would buy D.A. MacIsaac, Inc., a regional contract office supplier. These moves were all designed to increase Staples's size and penetration of the office supplies business as the company moved into the late 1990s. Although its market had become more competitive than ever, Staples appeared to be well-situated to continue its strong growth in the future.

Principal Subsidiaries: Office Mart Holdings Corporation; Total Global Sourcing, Inc.

Further Reading:

Charm, Robert E., "Thomas G. Stemberg of Staples, Inc.," *New England Business,* May 2, 1988.

Galanie, Mary Ann, "Staples Plans to Open Four Stores Here," *Los Angeles Times,* December 12, 1989.

McConville, James A., "Staples Targets Urban Niche," *HFD—The Weekly Home Furnishings Newspaper,* October 22, 1990.

——, "Fla. Retail Showdown Looms," *HFD—The Weekly Home Furnishings Newspaper,* March 9, 1992.

Solomon, Stephen D., "Born To Be Big," *Inc.,* June, 1989.

Teitell, Beth, "Office Supply Supermarkets: A Future Staple?" *Boston Business Journal,* March 17, 1986.

—Elizabeth Rourke

Stratus Computer, Inc.

55 Fairbanks Boulevard
Marlboro, Massachusetts 01752
U.S.A.
(508) 460-2000
Fax: (508) 481-8945

Public Company
Incorporated: 1980
Employees: 2,600
Sales: $513.7 million
Stock Exchanges: New York
SICs: 3577 Computer Peripheral Equipment; 7372
   Prepackaged Software

Stratus Computer, Inc. is a leading producer of computer systems that offer continuously available, or fail safe, applications. The company sells its hardware and supporting software to customers in industries, such as financial services, telecommunications, and healthcare, where reliable non-stop computing power is essential. Started in the early 1980s by three experienced engineers, the company rapidly achieved profitability and steady growth, which slowed in the 1990s as the nature of the computer industry shifted.

Stratus was founded in 1980 by William E. Foster, who had worked in the research and development department of the Hewlett-Packard Company in the 1970s. When co-workers he supervised left the company to start their own company making computers that never broke down, Foster declined their invitation to join them, only to see the company they founded, Tandem Computer, become highly successful. By the end of the 1970s, after changing to a job at the Data General Corporation, Foster had become convinced that he could do the job his friends at Tandem were doing, only better. Joining with Gardner C. Hendrie and Robert A. Freiburghouse, who also had experience in the computer industry, Foster formed Stratus Computer in May 1980. On the strength of their reputations, the three men raised $6.7 million from seven different venture capital firms to start the company.

Computers made by Foster's rivals relied on software to provide their users with fail-safe operation. When their system was first developed, this had been the most economical way to design such a system, since parts, or hardware, had been very expensive. In the intervening years, however, the cost of hardware had come down. With this in mind, Foster and his cohorts set out to design a computer system that relied on duplication of hardware to insure reliability.

Twenty-one months after Stratus was founded, the company was ready to ship its first product. It marketed its effort as a computer with more fail-safe aspects than Tandem's, which nevertheless cost less. The Stratus/32 machine had two central processors, which worked on the same tasks at once. Inside each Stratus Continuous Processing System, two computers were nestled side by side, like Siamese twins. Each processor was able to check its own operation, since duplicate logic circuitry had been wired into it. If one computer failed, the other took over automatically, avoiding a breakdown in service. Unlike the Tandem product, Stratus' processors did not need to spend time checking on each other, so they were able to work more quickly. This advance was made possible by the fact that semiconductors cost just a fraction of their former price.

In January 1982, Stratus shipped a computer system to its first customer, the West Lynn Creamery, a dairy located near company headquarters in Massachusetts. The creamery used its $148,000 system to handle orders and to route its milk trucks. Although this customer was a small start, Stratus was confident that the market for fail-safe, or "fault tolerant," computers would grow, as businesses became more dependent on computers for much of their day-to-day operations.

To increase sales, Stratus embarked on diverse marketing campaigns in the United States and abroad. Aggressive marketing efforts in the United States, in which Stratus attempted to set itself apart from Tandem, brought the company a lawsuit charging the company with false advertising. To sell computers in Italy, Stratus signed a $40 million marketing agreement with Ing C. Olivetti & Company, an Italian typewriter and computer company which had been an early investor in Stratus. Under this arrangement, Olivetti sold Stratus computers in Italy under the Olivetti name; by the mid-1980s, ten percent of Stratus' products were sold through Olivetti. By the end of 1982, sales of Stratus products had reached $5.5 million.

On the strength of its early success, Stratus sold shares to the public for the first time in July 1983. The company used the revenue generated by its stock sale to buy equipment for new product development, testing, and demonstrations. When software to link its fault-tolerant systems to IBM computers was introduced in 1983, the company tapped into a new customer pool. By the end of 1983, sales of Stratus products had nearly quadrupled to $20.6 million. With these gains, the company reported its first profit, of $2.2 million.

By 1984, Stratus had increased its customer base to include financial services companies, such as Morgan Stanley, which used its products to report stock prices, and Merrill Lynch, a brokerage house. Other buyers of the Stratus system included the Bank of America, Ford, and Xerox. These companies used Stratus products to perform on-line transaction processing, in which computer operations took place in real time, frequently in conjunction with a customer interaction. Automatic teller machines, for instance, needed to be available to customers at all times, so that banks could avoid embarrassing breakdowns.

Stratus tried to broaden its customer base by providing numerous products and using different marketing avenues. Stratus was marketing three models of its computer by 1984, the most popular of which sold for around $200,000. But by 1986, Stratus marketed entry-level and mid-range models of its standard 32-bit based computer, and the company's products then ranged in price from $100,000 to about $1 million. In November 1984, Stratus introduced a version of its operating system called Virtual OS, which was designed for use with UNIX mainframe computers. In addition, the company unveiled new software to facilitate communication between IBM personal computers and its fault tolerant machines in August 1986. Stratus entered into a strategic marketing alliance with IBM in 1985 which licensed the computer giant to resell its products. IBM named its Stratus offering the System/88, and it became the only non-IBM product to be sold by that company's enormous sales force. By 1986, Stratus' sales had risen to $125 million, an increase of more than 50 percent from the previous year. In addition, earnings had grown to $13.5 million.

Despite its impressive record of growth, Stratus remained a small company, winning just a small portion of a small niche in the computer market. By 1987, no more than four percent of the country's on-line transaction processing was handled by fault tolerant computer systems. Major potential customers, such as airline reservation systems, remained unwilling to give up their crash-prone IBM or DEC mainframe systems, and Stratus found itself bidding for contracts against competitors who were many times larger.

In an effort to enhance its competitiveness in the cut-throat computer marketplace, Stratus unveiled a new generation of computers in 1987. The company's XA2000 was designed to process transactions three times as fast as its older models. This speed was made possible by the computer's use of new, more powerful computer chips, which were strung together in groups of up to four. Comparable in power to Tandem's top of the line machine, the Stratus model was priced at 40 percent less. By the end of the first three months of 1987, sales to IBM made up 15 percent of the company's revenues. Within three months of the introduction of its new line, that percentage had risen to 25 percent, as IBM cemented deals with customers such as telephone companies MCI and Southwestern Bell.

Overseas, Stratus found that its linkage with IBM gave it credibility in markets where its own name was not well known. To expand its markets overseas, Stratus Computer GmbH, a computer sales company based in West Germany, was opened in December 1985. Stratus continued its push overseas in 1986, when the company cemented an agreement with the C. Itoh company of Japan to market its products and inaugurated Stratus Taiwan to tap into another Asian market. By 1987, it formed a subsidiary to market its products in France. Stratus finished 1987 with sales of $184.1 million, as its revenues continued to grow sharply.

In January 1988, Stratus enhanced its new XA2000 line by producing an additional two models to be marketed. The XA2000 Model 50, priced at $79,000, was designed to handle 10 transactions a second. The XA2000 Model 70 had the capability of performing 12 operations a second, and was sold for $110,000. Each of these computers was compatible with older, more powerful models. With these offerings, Stratus hoped to broaden its customer base to a wider range of customers.

In June 1988, one of Stratus' original investors liquidated its investment in the company, as Olivetti sold its 9.3 percent stake in Stratus for $52 million. This did not indicate a severing of ties between the two firms, however, since Olivetti renewed its marketing agreement with Stratus at the same time. By the end of the year, Stratus was once again reporting dramatically improved financial results, with revenues of $265.3 million in 1988. Growth continued the following year, as this figure rose to $341.3 million, a gain of nearly a third.

Despite this continued good news, however, the first signs of trouble for Stratus were beginning to appear. By the late 1980s, orders for its three-year-old product line slowed as customers waited for newer products to be introduced. This anticipation caused a flattening in the company's sales for several quarters.

The company's introduction of 13 new models of its XA2000 Continuous Processing Systems line of computers in 1990, however, moved the company into the highly competitive mainframe computer market. Among the customers Stratus won with its new line were US West Communications, which used the company's fault tolerant computers to run 911 emergency telephone systems; First Florida Banks, which used Stratus technology in automated teller machines; and the Mt. Sinai Medical Center in New York.

In addition to the introduction of new, more up-to-date products, Stratus began an effort to widen its channels of distribution. Throughout the late 1980s, the company had relied on sales of its products by IBM for a significant portion of its revenues. By the early 1990s, Stratus' continuing growth was being threatened by declining sales of its products by IBM. Where it had once relied on IBM to move a significant portion of its products, the company now found sales to its partner stagnant. To protect itself against this fall-off in revenues, Stratus began to diversify its business partnerships, entering into a flurry of marketing agreements. Some of the agreements included leasing worldwide marketing rights for its operating software to Sanderson Computers, signing a joint marketing pact that allowed software sellers to bundle their products with Stratus computers, and signing an agreement with Perception Technology to develop its voice processing capabilities.

The most significant deal in this string of alliances was an agreement with the Japanese computer company NEC. Beginning in 1991, Stratus gave NEC the right to sell its computers throughout the world. NEC planned to package Stratus' fail safe computers with its own telephone switching and networking products, in an effort to win contracts from telephone companies in many countries. In addition, Stratus granted NEC the right to use its basic operating software in its own computers.

The alliances enabled Stratus to continue its profitability throughout the early 1990s, despite a general downturn in the American economy. Stratus revenues grew to $403.9 million in 1990, and climbed again to $448.6 million over the course of 1991. By the end of 1992, sales had risen to $486.3 million.

These gains belied the problematic transition that Stratus, along with the rest of the computer industry, was undergoing. Rather than continuing to market computers that ran on its own proprietary operating system, Stratus decided in the early 1990s to switch over to an industry standard operating system developed by Unix. In an effort to compensate for the difficulties and delays caused by this change, which brought about a slowdown in revenue, Stratus also decided to invest in the development of a new generation of products based on a new computer chip, called PA-RISC. Manufactured by Hewlett Packard, this chip used "Reduced Instruction Set Computing," rather than the older "Complex Instruction Set Computing," or CISC, in its operations. The company introduced a family of products called XA/R, which incorporated its RISC-based operating system, in 1992, and they were fully available by the following year.

By the middle of July 1993, Stratus' sales had flattened, and its net income had begun a slight decline. The company announced that its earnings for the year would be down. The biggest source of Stratus' problems was a sharp drop in sales of its products by its marketing partners. IBM moved 62 percent fewer Stratus machines than it had a year earlier, and Olivetti sold only 22 percent of its previous year's allotment in the second quarter of the year. Overall, growth had slowed in Stratus' flagship fail safe computer line, and additional company models, which were less expensive and also slightly less reliable, were unable to make up the slack.

In an effort to take greater control of its destiny in a competitive and rapidly changing market, Stratus announced a new corporate strategy in the fall of 1993. Rather than concentrate exclusively on the manufacture of computer hardware, the company decided to diversify into software as well, in order to provide a more complete package to customers. To do so, Stratus announced a $100 million plan to invest in small software makers in the field of on-line transaction processing, the area where most Stratus computers were used. Stratus planned to specialize in a few industry niches, such as healthcare, telecommunica-tions, banking, retail, travel, and gaming, and it looked at nearly 100 small software companies in these fields, shopping for acquisitions. In September 1993, Stratus made its first purchase: Shared Financial Systems, Inc., a privately owned company based in Dallas, Texas, that made software for credit card authorization and other banking and retail functions. The company paid $15 million for its first acquisition, which it renamed Shared Systems Corporation. Other acquisitions included Bell-South Systems Integration, Inc. (renamed SoftCom Systems, Inc.), a unit of BellSouth Corporation which created software to link older mainframe computers and newer, small computer systems, and Isis Distributed Systems, Inc., a privately owned software maker.

As it moved into the mid-1990s, Stratus faced a computer market that had evolved dramatically from the one in which it began. With a solid history of profitable operation behind it, and a strenuous effort to restructure and refocus its operations on a more precise segment of its original market for fail safe computing, the company appeared well suited to prosper in the coming years.

Principal Subsidiaries: SoftCom Systems, Inc.; Isis Distributed Systems, Inc.; Shared Systems Corporation; Stratus Computer Corporation (Canada); Stratus Computer S.A. (France); Stratus Computer GmbH (Germany); Stratus Computer Ltd. (Hong Kong); Stratus Computer Japan Co., Ltd. (Japan); Stratus Computer Ltd. (United Kingdom).

Further Reading:

"A Fail-Safe Entry That's a Bargain," *Business Week,* November 16, 1981.

Kleinfeld, N. R., "Stratus' Nonstop Computers," *New York Times,* July 11, 1984.

Wiegner, Kathleen K., "Mixed Blessings," *Forbes,* September 21, 1987.

—Elizabeth Rourke

Sun Television & Appliances Inc.

1583 Alum Creek Drive
Columbus, Ohio 43209-2713
U.S.A.
(614) 445-8401
Fax: (614) 444-0849

Public Company
Incorporated: 1949
Employees: 1,070
Sales: $398.64 million
Stock Exchanges: NASDAQ
SICs: 5731 Radio, Television and Consumer Electronics
Stores; 5722 Household Appliance Stores; 7699 Repair
Services, Nec; 6719 Holding Companies, Nec

Sun Television & Appliances Inc., Ohio's leading consumer electronics and appliance discounter, expanded its operations to include Pennsylvania, western New York, and West Virginia in the late 1980s and early 1990s, establishing nearly 40 stores in the region by the end of 1993. In a September 1992 article in *Barron's* magazine, the company's president, Robert Oyster, maintained that Sun held more than a 50 percent share of the Columbus, Ohio, market for consumer electronics and appliances and had captured between 20 and 25 percent of that market in its other metropolitan areas. Sun's management credits its low price guarantee, broad selection, aggressive local newspaper advertising, and well-trained service staff for its dramatic growth during the late 1980s and early 1990s.

Sun Television was founded in 1949 by Macy T. Block and a partner as a subsidiary of ZS Sun Limited Partnership. In May 1991, Sun Television was taken public, with an initial offering of two million common shares. Still, nearly 60 percent of the company's shares remained under the control of management, including Block, who was elected to the posts of chairperson and chief executive officer. This high proportion of inside ownership contributed to the company's tight-lipped policy on financial and historical information.

Presumably beginning operations as a retailer and repair service for televisions and other relatively simple electronic appliances such as radios and hi-fi systems, the company was offering a wide variety of merchandise through a chain of stores by the early 1980s. Sun distributed merchandise to its stores from a warehouse it maintained in Columbus, using its own fleet of trucks. Although most retailers of electronics began contracting with manufacturers for repair services during this time, Sun continued to offer customers its own repair service, which reportedly generated about six percent of annual revenues.

During this time, Sun established a catalog division complete with a toll-free number through which customers could purchase name-brand office equipment. Sun's offerings expanded to include facsimile machines, word processors, copiers, typewriters, printers, projectors, transcribers, and other items popular for home and office use. Home computers were introduced to the Sun product line in 1990. Committed to maintaining a sales staff knowledgeable in the company's merchandise, Sun employees underwent extensive training seminars in an effort to provide customers with quality service. Sun's "lowest price in town" guarantee proved popular among price-conscious consumers.

In April 1980, Sun Television filed a $500,000 lawsuit against a Lancaster, Ohio, firm that called itself Sun Furniture, claiming that the smaller company's name infringed on Sun Television's trade name and confused consumers. The litigation was settled in May of the following year, when Sun Furniture agreed to remove the word sun from all advertising material and from its building, equipment, and motor vehicles by July 1. The district court judge in charge of the case also permanently enjoined Sun Furniture from using "sun" in connection with any other operation of the business.

Sun began to expand rapidly in the late 1980s and early 1990s, more than tripling in size from 1988 to 1994. Eschewing expansion through acquisitions, Sun continued to focus on establishing new stores in small communities rather than in urban areas, where competition was great. Elliot Schlang, an analyst with Kidder Peabody, noted in a 1993 *Fortune* article that this strategy proved advantageous for the growing company, commenting that although Sun's "concentration has been in smaller communities, . . . there are hundreds of them."

Sun also preferred to "cluster" new stores near existing outlets, which allowed for advertising and distribution efficiencies. Some analysts observed, however, that this policy tended to promote "cannibalism" among the stores, retarding sales growth at individual stores. Nevertheless, Oyster told *Fortune* that this regional focus helped the company avoid "the boom-and-bust cycles of the coasts," allowing them to enjoy "moderate but solid growth." When scouting sites, the company sought high-traffic areas, either at strip shopping centers or in freestanding locations at regional malls. Most of the new stores were "superstores," with net selling space of 20,000 square feet. The firm crossed the Ohio state line in 1988, adding a superstore in Mars, Pennsylvania, near Pittsburgh.

Sun proceeded to exploit the territory between Pittsburgh and Columbus, building at least six stores near northeast Ohio's metropolitan areas of Cleveland, Akron, and Youngstown beginning in 1990. This move soon brought Sun into an intense rivalry with Livonia, Michigan-based Fretter Inc. Fretter and Sun each made similar advertising claims, guaranteeing the lowest prices available, and in 1992, Fretter sued Sun, accusing that latter of airing "false, malicious and defamatory" television commercials. Sun promptly filed a countersuit to the same effect. By the end of the year, both Sun and Fretter had agreed to drop their suits.

Sun's geographical expansion soon necessitated the construction of a satellite distribution center to cater to northeast Ohio.

The company's sales increased over 250 percent from 1989 to 1993, from $157.24 million to $398.64 million, while net income grew even faster over the same period, from $2.26 million to $11.6 million. In 1992, Sun was named one of *Forbes* magazine's 200 best small companies, a ranking that took into account a company's five-year average annual returns on equity as well as sales and earnings growth. At that time, Sun had reported a 12.5 percent average annual return on equity from 1986 to 1991.

Sun successfully completed two common stock offerings during fiscal 1993. The net proceeds from these issues totaled $46.88 million, or over 1.5 million common shares. These funds, combined with increased cash flow from earnings, were used to pay off all the company's bank debt and position it to pursue future expansion opportunities. By the end of fiscal 1993, Sun had a bankroll of over $45 million with which to continue its growth strategy. That year, Sun established a superstore in Syracuse, New York, and planned to open a total of eight locations in its target region in May 1993. According to a March 1993 *Fortune*

brief, Sun aimed to become "the dominant consumer electronics and appliance retailer in northern Ohio and western Pennsylvania." The company established its first store in West Virginia in March 1994.

Further Reading:

Byrne, Harlan S., "Sun Television & Appliances," *Barron's,* September 1, 1992, pp. 47–48.

"Computer, Health Firms Top 200 List," *The Columbus Dispatch,* October 26, 1992, p. 1E.

Phillips, Jeff, "Sun TV Expanding into Home Computer Market," *Business First—Columbus,* March 5, 1990, p. 4.

Sabath, Donald, "Sun Appliance Chain Plans to Open Stores in Northeast Ohio," *The Plain Dealer,* October 6, 1990, p. 3F.

"Selection, Low Prices at Sun TV," *The Columbus Dispatch,* January 29, 1989, p. 3G.

Solo, Sally, "Sun Television & Appliances," *Fortune,* March 22, 1993, p. 91.

" 'Sun' Companies Settle Dispute on Trade Name," *The Columbus Dispatch,* May 7, 1981, p. 7D.

Thompson, Chris, "Ad Battle Goes to Court," *Crain's Cleveland Business,* February 17, 1992, p. 1.

Truck, Julie, "Aggressive Sun Spars with New Competitor in Cleveland Market," *Business First—Columbus,* March 2, 1992, p. 1.

—April Dougal Gasbarre

Sybase, Inc.

6475 Christie Avenue
Emeryville, California 94608
U.S.A.
(510) 922-3500
Fax: (510) 922-4468

Public Company
Incorporated: 1984
Employees: 2,800
Sales: $427 million
Stock Exchanges: New York
SICs: 7372 Prepackaged Software

Sybase, Inc., is the world's second-largest creator of relational database management systems. The company develops and markets tools for building client/server computer systems, which allow companies to manage and manipulate data efficiently. Founded in the mid-1980s in Silicon Valley, the company has grown steadily, establishing a strong market share and a worldwide network of customers.

Sybase was founded in 1984 by Mark Hoffman and Robert Epstein. Hoffman had previously worked as an executive at a company called Britton Lee, which pioneered the field of database computing. He joined with Epstein, who had helped to create an early relational program called Ingres while working toward his Ph.D. at the University of California at Berkeley. Together, the two set out to market a cutting-edge relational database management system (RDBMS), which would organize information and make it available to many computers in a network.

After gathering a corps of experienced programmers, the company spent more than two years working on its debut product. During this time, Sybase's activities were funded by a consortium of venture capital firms, including Hambrecht & Quist and Kleiner Perkins Caufield & Byers. In late 1986, Sybase shipped its first test programs, entering a market that others had pioneered five years earlier. In May 1987, Sybase formally released the SYBASE system, the first high-performance RDBMS for on-line applications. Rather than having a vast central bank of data stored in a large mainframe computer, the SYBASE System provided for a client/server computer architecture.

Client/server computer systems logically broke up monolithic applications into separate components that inter-related over a network for faster processing. The system linked hardware and software into a complex web in which information resources were distributed over multiple computer systems. Clients (individual desktop computers) and servers (databases) moved information and tools back and forth between themselves in order to most efficiently fulfill a company's needs. With the SYBASE system, companies could maintain the integrity of and control over their information that a mainframe gave them, but could also make use of that information in a much more widespread and efficient manner.

The SYBASE system was based on Structured Query Language (SQL), a standard IBM computer programming language, and consisted of two parts, the DataServer and the DataToolset. The first component allowed a network of computers to all gain access to a database at the same time. The second provided the building blocks for programs that developed applications, wrote reports, and performed queries. In its use of SQL, the company provided an advance in computer software that no other company had made.

In order to give its program the greatest possible capabilities, Sybase made the decision to limit its use to a small number of strategic hardware platforms. The company chose to market SYBASE for use only on DEC, IBM, and UNIX-based computers. Sybase invested heavily in training for its technical support staff to reassure its potential customers that they could rely on the company for help in using its products. Eschewing middlemen or software dealers, the company relied on direct sales to distribute SYBASE, establishing a network of sales offices across the United States and an office in London.

In the first year after its release, Sybase's software formed some important alliances. In September 1987, the Pyramid Technology Corporation began selling its own hardware and Sybase software as a package deal. In October 1987, Sun Microsystems, Inc., another computer maker, bought 40 copies of the Sybase program for its own internal use. After seven months of sales, Sybase was able to report revenues of $6 million, as its product notched quarterly sales of $3 million. The company had moved from losses to a profit in the third quarter of the year. At that time, Sybase also received an infusion of $3.3 million in capital from Apple Computer.

In January 1988, software giant Microsoft revealed that it had made an agreement with Sybase in 1986 that would allow Microsoft to license the company's technology. As a result of this agreement, Microsoft SQL Server for the company's OS/2 computer operating system was released. SQL Server retrieved information faster than similar programs, and was the first to update all outlying databases in a network instantaneously if the central databank was revised.

With this partnership, Microsoft helped to establish Sybase in the industry by co-developing and selling versions of the company's products for use on its operating systems. The first arrangement of this kind came shortly after Microsoft's announcement, when the Ashton-Tate software company moved to release SQL Server for use on machines that ran on DOS, the IBM-standard operating system. This program would be known as Ashton-Tate/Microsoft SQL Server, and would be marketed both individually and in conjunction with the company's dBase product.

Within a year of SYBASE's release, the program had established a strong following in the corporate and government world. Because of its power, Sybase targeted its sales in part to customers who required on-line transaction processing, or real-time computer operations, such as banks. At the end of 1988, Sybase formed Sybase Canada; three months later the company also set up a French subsidiary.

In March 1989, Sybase toyed with the idea of selling stock to the public, but finally announced that it would postpone this step to a later date. Six months later, the company announced that it had, instead, received additional funding from the Lotus Development Corporation, a software company that acquired 15 percent of Sybase's stock.

In October 1989, Sybase released additional products, introducing the SYBASE Open Client/Server Interfaces, new software programs that provided generic client/server communication, allowing for greater connectivity within computer networks. With these offerings, and its earlier system, Sybase notched sales of $56 million in the course of 1989.

In January 1990, Sybase paid $3.5 million for D&N Systems, Inc., an integrated database consulting firm which it renamed SQL Solutions, Inc. Sybase increased its penetration of the government market in early 1990, when the company successfully marketed its products to NASA, the Army, and the Air Force's Military Airlift Command. These clients made particular use of the Sybase program's capacity to keep data secure and confidential. In June 1990 Sybase formed a joint venture with HCL America, called HCL Sybase, to sell its programs in Singapore.

Despite this growth, Sybase's earnings slowed in the late 1980s, and the company reported several quarters of loss. In August 1990, Sybase cut its staff by five percent, laying off 50 members of its 800-member work-force in an effort to cut costs. To shore up its returns, the company also began to seek out clients in the financial services field. Offering customers the ability to process transactions in real time, Sybase had lined up 20 of Wall Street's 22 largest brokers within the next few years.

In the next month, Sybase introduced new products that were designed to help IBM mainframe computers become part of a client/server system. These programs were the first to join local area network (LAN) technology to mainframe technology. In addition, Sybase introduced joint marketing ventures with its investor Lotus, creating interface software for Lotus 1-2-3 and packaging the company's spreadsheet with its own SQL Server. At the end of the year, Lotus increased its ownership of Sybase from 15 to 25 percent by buying Ashton-Tate's shares in the company.

In March 1991, Sybase made its second acquisition, purchasing Deft Software, Inc. Five months later, the company made its initial public offering of stock. In the wake of this move, with the new accountability to Wall Street investors that it brought, Sybase saw its European sales fall short of expectations. In an effort to redress this failing, the company set out to unify and upgrade its European operations, eliminating country managers and instituting other changes.

With its new infusion of capital, Sybase merged with SQ Software, Inc., in June 1992, and purchased Gain Technology, Inc., a vendor of object-based, multi-media application development tools, in September of that year. This company's principal product was GainMomentum, a software program that allowed different forms of data to be included in the company's client/server computer architecture.

Two months after this purchase, Sybase announced its latest generation of software. Dubbed the System 10 product family, these programs were designed to provide a framework for companies to switch over their computer operations from older mainframe models to client/server systems. At the end of 1992, Sybase posted revenues of $265 million.

In April 1993, Sybase introduced the first component of System 10, called OmniSQL Gateway. This program connected up the various parts of a computer network, enabling users at any point to gain access to changes being made anywhere on the system. This quality was known as ''transparent interoperability.'' Building on the program of its acquisition, Gain Technology, the company introduced a family of products called ''Momentum.'' These included Build Momentum and Enterprise Momentum, both environments for building applications. With these tools, programmers could create visually appealing programs for corporate employees to use when negotiating their company's computer system.

In the summer of 1993, Sybase also completed a re-organization of its operations. With more than 2,000 employees, the company had grown rapidly, and it needed to better define its corporate goals. In order to do this, Sybase divided its activities into two groups, the Tools Technology Group, and the Server & Connectivity Group.

In October 1993, Sybase completed its roll-out of the System 10 components, which included SQL Server 10 and Back-up Server; Open Client/Server APIs, and SQL Monitor and SA Companion, which were used to manage computer systems. In the next month, Sybase also released its Replication Server, which allowed computer users to build reliable systems to keep computer operations running for on-line transaction processing.

By the end of 1993, Sybase's revenue had reached $427 million, and earnings were $44 million. The company's growth rate for this year was 61 percent, which made Sybase the world's second-largest supplier of enterprise client/server RDBS software. With this gain, the company moved ahead of its competitor Informix, and came up on the heels of industry leader Oracle.

Sybase had achieved this growth by emphasizing customer service and prompt delivery of new software. During the course of 1993, the company had dramatically increased the size of its customer service and support divisions. Sybase also opened three new technical support service centers in Burlington, Massachusetts, Tokyo, and Mexico City. Including the employees hired to staff these outposts, Sybase increased its staff by 1,400 people during 1993.

Sybase's strong growth had also been driven by the company's rapid international expansion. After its successful revamp of foreign operations, overseas sales had doubled in 1993, boosted by 82 percent growth in Europe and an extremely strong 182 percent gain in Asia and Latin America. These operations accounted for more than a quarter of the company's revenues. Over the course of 1993, Sybase added new subsidiaries in Belgium, Italy, Spain, Switzerland, and Mexico. Overall, it had ten foreign subsidiaries and 39 international distributors.

On the first day of 1994, Sybase purchased Oasis Group P.L.C., a British firm that helped companies choose and build computer systems. With this alliance, Sybase positioned itself as a provider of a complete range of services for customers upgrading their computer operations. Later in January, Sybase also announced that it would purchase Micro Decisionware, Inc., a producer of networking software. With this merger, Sybase hoped to become the market leader in this field.

One month later, Sybase enhanced its software offerings to government agencies when it released Secure SQL Server 10, which offered secure and practical RDBMS applications. In April 1994, Sybase announced a new generation of software that would expand a company's computer network over telephone lines to take in other businesses and clients. Sybase embarked upon this project with its partner Tele-Communications, Inc., to produce programs to control the traffic over such large-scale extended enterprise systems. In addition, the company rushed to release its Navigation Server, a program that implemented the newest parallel-processing technology.

With nearly 20 percent of the rapidly growing market for relational database management systems, Sybase was firmly established in a field laden with opportunity. The company's strong record of past performance indicated that it would continue to succeed in the competitive software programming market of the late 1990s.

Principal Subsidiaries: SQL Solutions, Inc.; Deft Software, Inc.; Oasis Group P.L.C.

Further Reading:

Brandt, Richard, ''Sybase Steps Out of the Shadows,'' *Business Week,* April 18, 1994.

Davey, Tom, ''Three Bay Area Companies Lead Pack in Database Race,'' *San Francisco Business Times,* June 17–23, 1994.

Eisenhart, Mary, ''Connectivity Solutions in Data Base Management,'' *Microtimes,* March 1988.

Garner, Rochelle, and Houston, Patrick, ''Inside People,'' *P.C. Week,* September 20, 1993.

Houston, Patrick, ''Learning from a Rival's Reorg,'' *P.C. Week,* June 13, 1994.

Knowles, Anne, ''A Software Start-up with Hardware Back-Up,'' *Electronic Business,* January 15, 1988.

Siegmann, Ken, ''Data Management Takes Off,'' *San Francisco Chronicle,* May 9, 1994.

—Elizabeth Rourke

Symantec Corporation

10201 Torre Avenue
Cupertino, California 95014-2132
U.S.A.
(408) 253-9600
Fax: (408) 253-4694

Public Company
Incorporated: 1982
Employees: 1,100
Sales: $267 million
Stock Exchanges: NASDAQ National Market System
SICs: 7372 Prepackaged Software

Symantec Corporation is the leading software company providing utility programs for personal computers and is also a key player in other specialty software categories. It does not have one dominant product, but has pursued a strategy of developing or acquiring various product technologies that are leaders in their respective market segments. Symantec has expanded rapidly, primarily through acquisitions, which have averaged two per year.

Symantec was founded in 1982 by 34-year-old Dr. Gary Hendrix, a prominent expert in natural language processing and artificial intelligence. He brought together a group of Stanford University researchers in the field of natural language processing to form the company, which had various ideas for innovative software, including a database program. The enterprise's initial funding was a National Science Foundation grant. When that grant ran out, Hendrix obtained financing from venture capital firms that were interested in investing in the field of artificial intelligence, even though the company in 1983 was still far from creating a product.

In 1984 Symantec was acquired by another, even smaller computer software startup company, C&E Software, founded by Dennis Coleman and Gordon E. Eubanks, Jr., and headed by Eubanks. The merged company retained the name Symantec, and 38-year-old Eubanks became its chief executive officer. Eubanks, formerly a nuclear submarine commander, had studied computer engineering at the Naval Post-Graduate School in Monterey, California. For his master's thesis, Eubanks had developed an innovative microcomputer tool for the CPM operating system called EBASIC. At the time of the merger, C&E Software was also working on a database program, but the

different fields of expertise of the two companies complemented each other. Whereas Symantec's founders were strong in high-technology innovation, C&E had more experience writing tight computer code and working out program bugs. The merger received significant support by venture capitalist John Doerr, who went on to become a member of the board of directors. Doerr was the first to see the potential in the merger and helped bring it about through his urging and financial backing.

Symantec shipped its first major product, Q&A for the IBM-compatible PC, in 1985. Q&A was a flat-file database program and was one of the few database management software packages for personal computers that used natural language query, based on an internal vocabulary of nearly 600 words. In order to obtain lists or statistics based on a data file, the user types in queries as ordinary English sentences instead of as arcane commands. Hence the name Q&A for the process of question and answer. The use of natural language query in this product was a significant step in making computers more user-friendly. Symantec's sales for 1985 totaled $1.4 million.

Despite the modest success of Q&A, it soon became clear that the product would not be able to compete with the major personal computer database program on the market, Ashton-Tate's dBase, or Lotus Development Corp.'s spreadsheet program Lotus 1-2-3. Although innovative, Q&A managed to bring in only $8 million in sales in its first two years combined, which was far short of its expectations. Eubanks realized that the market had changed in such a way that Symantec could no longer be a one-product company relying solely on Q&A like other, established software companies, such as Ashton-Tate, Lotus Development, or WordPerfect Corp. Thus, Symantec took the strategic move of broadening its product base, particularly in specialty niche software categories.

To take advantage of such software developments of other, smaller firms, Symantec formed its Turner Hall Publishing division to publish third-party software. In October of 1985, Turner Hall introduced Note-It, a notation utility for Lotus 1-2-3. More significantly, Eubanks decided that the company would expand its product offerings through acquisitions of other software companies. This involved not only obtaining a company's products but also retaining the company's programmers (in order to continue to develop new products in the given category) and its marketing staff (who had established client relationships).

At the same time, Eubanks decided to structure Symantec's organization into complete teams for each product. This involved establishing product groups comprising all the functions of product development, quality assurance, marketing, documentation, and technical support. Subsequently, when other companies were acquired by Symantec, product autonomy was maintained. This way, employees of acquired companies who were accustomed to working in small companies were able to maintain a sense of the small company culture.

Symantec began its acquisition campaign in 1987. In January that year Symantec acquired Breakthrough Software, located in Novato, California. Breakthrough had developed Time Line, the leading project management program for the IBM-compatible PC. In July Symantec acquired Living Videotext, based in nearby Mountain View, California. Living Videotext was the developer of ThinkTank, a presentation graphics program for the Macintosh, and Grandview, an information management program for the PC. In September Symantec acquired Think Technologies of Bedford, Massachusetts. Think had developed THINK C and THINK Pascal, both programming language compilers for the Macintosh, and InBox, an electronic mail system.

As a result of these acquisitions Symantec's sales doubled between 1987 and 1988, to reach $19.6 million. The number of employees likewise nearly doubled, to reach 180 in 1988, with 90 percent of the acquired companies' employees staying on. Direct sales representatives increased from 20 to 45. The portion of Symantec's sales to large corporations rose from 18 percent to about 35 percent in 1988. Symantec's existing products also benefitted from the acquisitions through the ability to provide complementary software package combinations.

For a relatively small company, managing such acquisitions was not easy. Although sales doubled, Symantec suffered net losses due to the costs of the acquisitions. While product management was kept separate, the acquired companies' finance, administration, personnel, and public relations functions all had to be merged. The restructuring was complicated by the loss of top managers. The founders of acquired companies Videotext and Think Technologies decided to leave Symantec. More significantly, in 1988 Chief Financial Officer Michael Perez and Vice President of Business Development Spencer Leyton both left the company. Eubanks proceeded to reorganize the company to reduce the number of top executives and give more authority to middle managers. These management and financial difficulties all contributed to the postponement of an initial public offering, which Symantec had originally planned for May of 1988.

After six years of losses, Symantec finally became profitable in 1988, or fiscal year 1989 (ending March 31, 1989). On June 23, 1989, the company made its initial public offering. A stock split went into effect in September, 1991. By November of that year the stock price was five times higher than it was when it went public, and it was selling at 64 times earnings. The high stock price supported Symantec's acquisitions, which were usually bought in exchange for Symantec stock.

Meanwhile, Q&A continued to be successful in its own smaller market of flat-file database programs. Flat-file databases, in contrast to relational database programs, require all the data to be in a single file. In fiscal 1989, Q&A accounted for one-third of Symantec's $50 million in revenues. In 1991 Q&A was the leader in the $60-million flat-file database market.

Symantec made its biggest acquisition to date in August of 1990 when it purchased the highly successful Peter Norton Computing Inc. of Santa Monica, California. Norton Computing became a pioneer in DOS-based utilities software with its introduction of The Norton Utilities in 1982. This software package historically has been the market leader in PC utilities software. Utilities are programs that perform functions such as backing up and compressing files, checking for viruses, and restoring lost data. The acquisition gave Symantec a 34 percent share of the $410-million utilities market.

The purchase also helped Symantec, whose utility products were more heavily weighted towards the Macintosh platform, expand into the PC utilities market. Peter Norton, the founder and owner of the acquired company, was given one third of Symantec's stock, worth about $60 million, and a seat on Symantec's board of directors. The acquired company became a division of Symantec and was renamed Peter Norton Computing Group. Most of Norton Computing's 115 employees were retained. The merger also helped Norton Computing regain the market share it was losing to competitors, especially Central Point Software. Norton Computing's revenues tripled between June of 1990 and September of 1991, and by November it appeared to have regained the market lead over Central Point. Norton Computing's merger with Symantec has since been cited as one of the most successful acquisitions in the software industry.

Symantec made three more acquisitions in 1991. In June it acquired Leonard Development Group, which had developed GreatWorks, an integrated applications program for the Macintosh. In August it acquired Zortech Inc., a developer of cross-platform C++ programming language compilers. Zortech had been the first company to introduce a C++ compiler for microcomputers. Symantec's acquisition of Zortech, with 32 employees for $10 million in stock, thus brought the company into the business of object-oriented programming and multiple platforms. Also in 1991 Symantec acquired Dynamic Microprocessor Associated Inc., which had developed pcANYWHERE, the leading remote control communications software product for personal computers.

Even during the recession of the early 1990s, which was especially severe in California, Symantec continued to grow. Revenues increased from $75 million in fiscal 1990 to over $116 in fiscal 1991, and the number of its employees increased by 28 percent between June of 1990 and June of 1991.

Symantec also expanded in Europe. The company opened a European manufacturing facility outside of Dublin, Ireland, in October of 1991. The facility subsequently began supporting Symantec's customers outside of North America. In May, 1991, Symantec began selling Norton Utilities and certain other software packages in the Soviet Union through three official distributors. To combat rampant software piracy in Russia, Symantec also offered after-sale services and technical support to registered users. Taking a more active role in international distribution, Symantec acquired its exclusive distributor in the United Kingdom, Symantec U.K., in March of 1992. By 1994 Symantec had a network of over 150 partner companies worldwide and had produced over 120 translated versions of various software products into different foreign languages.

Symantec moved towards becoming a significant provider of programming tools for corporate software developers when it acquired two more companies in June of 1992 for a total of about $2.1 million. The acquired companies were Whitewater Group of Evanston, Illinois, a developer of object-oriented programming tools and a provider of a collection of graphics libraries, and MultiScope Inc. of Mountain View, California, a developer of innovative debugging programs for the DOS, Windows, and OS/2 platforms. In 1992 only 5 percent of Symantec's sales were in programming languages software, but Symantec hoped to expand its market by offering programming tools that could be used for multiple computer platforms.

In late 1992 Symantec officers were sued by rival software company Borland International Inc. over Symantec's hiring of former Borland vice president Eugene Wang. Borland charged that Wang had passed on trade secrets via electronic-mail to Symantec CEO Eubanks before leaving Borland. This was the first legal case in which a high-level executive had been implicated based on electronic-mail messages as evidence, and thus the case attracted a great deal of attention even outside the software industry.

The next major product category that Symantec pursued was business project management software. In the early 1990s this was seen as one of the fastest growing software areas. Symantec introduced Guide Line, an easy-to-use project scheduling software, and provided improved versions of Time Line, a leading project management software package.

To expand in other areas of business software, Symantec made its largest acquisition since Norton Computing, purchasing Contact Software International Inc. for $47·million in exchange for 2.7 million in common shares. Contact Software, which had sales of about $20 million, was the maker of Act!, the leading contact management database program for executives and sales staffs. The acquisition also boosted Symantec's sales, which had been flat for the first nine months of fiscal 1993. In addition, Symantec finally centralized the separate marketing activities of each of its four product groups at its Cupertino, California, headquarters in 1993 in order to be more efficient. Product development, though, remained autonomous.

Despite forays into different software categories, Symantec remained dedicated to utilities programs ever since gaining that market's leadership with the acquisition of Norton Computing. In 1992 utility programs accounted for about 65 percent of revenues, whereas applications programs, such as Q&A, accounted for only 30 percent. In October of 1993 Symantec acquired Certus International Corp. of Cleveland, Ohio, which had developed antivirus and security software for the PC. In the fall of 1993, Symantec acquired Fifth Generation Systems Inc. of Baton Rouge, Louisiana, a developer of DiskLock, FastBack, Safe, and other software utilities for various platforms. Both companies, while remaining in their respective locations, were administratively merged into the Peter Norton Computing Group in Santa Monica, which in 1992 accounted for 75 percent of Symantec's revenues. Finally, in the spring of 1994, Symantec made a $60-million bid to acquire its leading competitor in utilities programs, Central Point Software of Beaverton, Oregon, whose 1993 revenues were estimated at $80 million. The two companies combined held 60 percent of the $440-million

market for utilities software, but competition had forced prices and profits down.

Symantec's latest major strategic move was to broaden its product offerings to include software for client/server systems and local area networks. Despite its dominance in the field of software utilities, the market was shrinking as the leading supplier of PC operating system software, Microsoft, was increasingly combining utilities into later versions of its DOS operating system. Microsoft, however, was less dominant in the field of network software. Thus, Symantec purchased the NetDistributor Pro product and other technology from Trik Inc. in 1993. To aid its product development technology, in January of 1994 Symantec acquired the Rapid Enterprises division from DataEase International Inc., based in Shelton, Connecticut, for $7.5 million. Rapid Enterprises had been developing a fourth-generation software development tool for client/server applications. These tools helped Symantec to revise its existing software products so as to be able to run on enterprise-wide networks. Symantec began offering a line of network utilities in early 1994 and later combined them in a common management program, Norton Administrator for Networks. These programs permit central monitoring and execution of utilities functions on a number of computers over a network. Symantec also planned to redesign the product foundations for better integration when used over wide area networks, but its competition was tougher in this field.

Principal Subsidiaries: Symantec Ltd. (Ireland); Symantec (UK) Ltd.; Symantec GmbH (Germany); Symantec SARL (France); Symantec Canada Ltd.; Symantec Srl. (Italy).

Further Reading:

Bowen, Ted Smalley and Jai Sigh, ''Symantec on Prowl Again: Eyes Relationships with DataEase and Fifth Generation,'' *PC Week,* August 30, 1993, p. 6.

Cunningham, Cara A., ''Symantec Makes Play for Tools with Acquisition of Two Firms,'' *PC Week,* June 15, 1992, pp. 147–48.

Heinlein, Susan W., ''Gordon Eubanks Jr.: Intense Drive and Focus Distinguish Symantec Corp. Leader,'' *The Business Journal-San Jose,* pp. S7–S8.

Heinlein, Susan W., ''Symantec: The Pride and the Passion,'' *The Business Journal-San Jose: Software Magazine,* September 1991, p. 14.

Lyons, Daniel J., ''Stumbling Blocks Put Symantec's IPO on Hold,'' *PC Week,* September 5, 1988, p. 133.

Morrissey, Jane and Karen D. Moser, ''Symantec's REI Acquisition Fuels Enterprise Push,'' *PC Week,* January 10, 1994, pp. 107–08.

Pitta, Julie, ''Talk to Your Computer,'' *Forbes,* July 23, 1990, pp. 281–82.

Rebello, Kathy, ''This Boss Measures 6.0 on the Richter Scale,'' *Business Week,* April 20, 1992, pp. 96–98.

Shaffer, Richard A., ''Symantec's Little Hits,'' *Forbes,* November 25, 1991. p. 196.

—Heather Behn Hedden

SynOptics Communications, Inc.

4401 Great America Parkway
Santa Clara, CA 95054
U.S.A.
(408) 988-2400
Fax: (408) 988-5525

Public Company
Incorporated: 1985
Employees: 1,255
Sales: $388 million
Stock Exchanges: NASDAQ
SICs: 3661 Telephone and Telegraph Apparatus; 3577
  Computer Peripheral Equipment

SynOptics Communications, Inc. pioneered computer communications through the use of telephone lines and is one of the world's leaders in local area networks (LANs). SynOptics controls one-third of the market for "intelligent hubs," which are used to link personal computers. SynOptics attained its leading position in the market quickly; in less than a decade, from 1986 to 1992, the company's revenues increased astronomically, from $1.8 million to over $388 million.

The foundation for the company was laid in 1983, when Andrew K. Ludwick and Ronald V. Schmidt first shook hands at Xerox's highly-regarded Palo Alto Research Center (PARC) near San Francisco, California. As an employee at Xerox, Ludwick's task was to identify new technologies developed at his company which were suitable for commercialization and market distribution. While working at this assignment Ludwick met Schmidt, who was developing Ethernet applications at PARC. Like Ludwick, Schmidt was also interested in applications of new technology for commercial development, and the two men spent a good deal of time discussing what kinds of products might be brought to market.

It was not until 1984 however, that Ludwick and Schmidt both recognized a development which signaled enormous consequences for the industry. IBM announced its introduction of a shielded twisted pair cabling system, which provided support for the entire range of IBM communications products, and at the same time introduced the "Token Ring," a new LAN access method that would operate on IBM's new structured cabling system. Since this system employed a star configuration, the entire network activity of an office, for example, could be concentrated in selected control points, such as a building's wiring closet. The advantages of IBM's new product and what distinguished it from other cabling systems at the time was its physical layout—not only would there be improved network performance but system maintenance would be drastically simplified.

While people within the industry were trying to figure out the implications of these developments, Ludwick and Schmidt quickly recognized the importance that IBM's new cabling system and Token Ring would have on Ethernet. Ethernet, a widely used a coaxial-based network access system created by Xerox, Digital Equipment, and Intel, was in danger of being eclipsed by IBM's new product. Because Ethernet's system ran on the linear bus topology used by coaxial cable, while IBM's new cabling system ran on a star topology, IBM's cabling system would not support Ethernet. Long one of the most overlooked aspects of computer networking, IBM's announcement made it clear to the two young men that computer network cabling systems would play an important role in the development of the industry.

Without losing any time Schmidt, confident that he could come up with a competitive response to IBM's cabling system and save Ethernet at the same time, began working non-stop in his PARC lab. In the course of his research over the previous few months, Schmidt already had Ethernet running in a star topology over fiber optic cables. He now devoted himself to creating a simplified version of Ethernet operating on a shielded twisted pair cabling system, similar to IBM's. After Ludwick was notified of Schmidt's work, Ludwick immediately devised a business plan to revitalize and develop Ethernet by using the IBM cabling system.

The crucial part of Ludwick's business plan focused on the assumption that local area networks (a local area network is a collection of personal computers, printers, file servers, and work stations operating on a common system), which were used in a minor capacity for workgroups at the time, would ultimately expand to become part of the necessary framework for all future business communications. Moreover, Ludwick and Schmidt correctly predicted that the star topology cabling structure they were now concentrating on would soon become the essential factor as the reliability and financial aspects of local area networks grew more important.

With such a grand opportunity knocking at the door, Ludwick and Schmidt decided to commercialize the new technology and convinced management at Xerox to help them set up their own company. Xerox agreed to back the new venture, and created a spin-off company to bring the new product to market. By June of 1985, the two men were able to procure enough funding to open a small operation with 12 employees and headquarters located in a trailer. Christening the new company "SynOptics," work began immediately on its first product, LattisNet. Lattisnet was a concentrator designed to support Ethernet running on a shielded twisted pair cabling system and meant for installation in an office building's wiring closet. From the very first day of company operations, Ludwick and Schmidt focussed on cabling systems for computer networking, which they both were convinced would herald a revolution in the industry.

As Ludwick worked on the production and marketing needed to bring LattisNet to market, Schmidt was developing a project that would allow Ethernet to run on unshielded twisted pair cabling, otherwise known as ordinary telephone wire. When it became known that Schmidt was working on this cutting-edge technology, many experts within the industry doubted that he could bring it to fruition. Although unshielded-pair cabling is already installed and used in most office buildings throughout the United States, with the added benefit of being extremely inexpensive, it was nonetheless assumed that this type of cabling would be too easily affected by environmental factors such as interference from common radio frequencies and electromagnetic transmissions for Ethernet to operate effectively. Even the people at Xerox who agreed to spin-off the new company doubted the technological feasibility and the market prospects of linking computers over telephone wire.

In 1987, SynOptics surprised industry experts and naysaying pundits by introducing the first ever unshielded twisted-pair cabling that would support Ethernet products. It was immediately recognized as a revolution within the industry; local area networking would never be the same. First of all, this technological breakthrough meant that unshielded twisted-pair cabling—normal telephone cables already installed in office buildings—could provide businesses with the ability to use Ethernet for their networking needs. Secondly, and even more importantly, since SynOptics' unshielded twisted-pair product line was configured in a star topology and employed an electronic concentrator found in the wiring closet of any office building, there was no need to rip out walls in order to install the special coaxial cables then in use. With its emphasis on focusing network activity in a wiring closet, suddenly the efficiency and inexpensive cost of using unshielded twisted-pair cabling for computer networking became obvious to everyone in the industry.

SynOptics' revenues shot through the roof when their line of LattisNet unshielded and shielded twisted pair products was introduced on the market. In 1987, company revenues amounted to $6.1 million, but by 1988 revenues reached $40.1 million. There was such growing demand for the company's LattisNet product line during the same year that management procured over $4 million in new financing to expand its manufacturing base. Along with the financing came a decision to implement an international distribution network, which had an immediate affect on company sales. When Xerox and other investors lobbied SynOptics to make a public stock offering, the resulting 1½ million shares brought in more than $20 million. Management wisely used the money to continue expanding its production facilities, and improve its international distribution network in order to deliver products to customers even more quickly and efficiently.

Ludwick and Schmidt's prediction that local area networks would dominate modern business communications surpassed their expectations. By 1988, personal computers were not only found on the desks of employees in the corporate world, but on the desks of individuals working for all kinds of organizations, from not-for-profit foundations to government agencies. As these organizations grew, they turned to LANs to help provide them with the ability to share information throughout their offices. Unfortunately, LANs were growing more rapidly than

anticipated, and the amount and flow of information within these systems was increasing at unmanageable rates. Soon there were numerous LAN overloads and failures, some of which had catastrophic consequences in Wall Street brokerage firms.

In order to solve the problem of system-wide network failures, organizations turned to either client-server computing or added bridges and routers to their LANs. The client-server model of computing was an attempt to distribute computing power equitably throughout the network so that computer failures or downtime would be less likely. Yet this model did not solve the problem of increasing the distributed computing power on an entire system. In short, the client-server model lacked a mechanism for systematically controlling and developing the computer network. In a similar fashion, the attempt to add bridges and routers to connect LANs and then reorganize them into more manageable subnetworks in order to control the flow and amount of data worked well, but these devices increased the complexity of an already overwhelmingly complex system.

SynOptics' management believed that both these solutions were inadequate. The two co-founders had earlier envisioned the development of ''intelligent hubs''—concentrators located in wiring closets—that accommodated any combination of Ethernet connections. In December of 1988, SynOptics introduced its LattisNet Network Management system, a combination of both software and hardware that controlled hubs and related physical elements of local area networks. The company's new product provided a means for integrating different LAN types and services and, equally as important, provided a foundation for the systematic growth and control of LANs. On the cutting edge of new technology once again, SynOptics' introduction of its intelligent hub signaled another milestone in the industry.

The company's LattisNet Network Management system propelled it to the forefront of the market. In 1989, SynOptics brought out the LattisNet System 3000, an intelligent hub product line that allowed customers to adapt their network systems in order to meet specific needs. As the company continued to add to its intelligent hub line of products, revenues continued their upward climb. With sales of over $77 million in 1989 and $176 million the following year, SynOptics was confident enough to declare a two-for-one stock split in June of 1990.

SynOptics' success, however, soon attracted numerous competitors, and the company's market share began to erode rapidly. In 1988, SynOptics possessed an undisputed monopoly on the market, yet by the end of 1991 its share had diminished to about 40 percent. Along with the loss in market share, the company's profits decreased and its stock plunged from a price of $51 to $14 per share. The company most responsible for cutting into SnyOptics' hold on the market was Cabletron, a New Hampshire-based operation which implemented an aggressive advertising campaign and emphasized lower prices for intelligent hubs.

Management at SnyOptics moved quickly to counteract the growing perception in the industry that the company had given up its leadership in the intelligent hub market to Cabletron. SynOptics reduced prices on most of its networking products by approximately 40 percent, cut back the number of value-added resellers that marketed and sold its product lines, increased the amount of funds designated for research and development, and substantially increased its marketing budget while at the same time revamping the company's advertising strategy. SynOptics also relocated its production facilities to Santa Clara, California, in order to lower the cost of manufacturing. The company was soon back on track. Revenues for 1992 reached $388 million and SynOptics' stock jumped to $83 per share.

The most important factor in SnyOptics' revival, and in its continuing success and leadership in the intelligent hub market, is the company's commitment to developing new products. Nearly 60 percent of the firm's total sales in 1992 were due to products which were introduced during the previous year. Syn-Optics introduced its own LattisNet Token Ring System Products, and also entered into a joint venture with IBM to manufacture LattisRing workgroup hubs. Along with the continued expansion of its product line in the Ethernet field, the company has brought out a Fiber Distribution Data Interface (FDDI), which has become the standard for high speed data transmission. All these products are designed to reduce the cost and complexity of installing and managing local area networks, while simultaneously ensuring compatibility with different networking environments.

As long as SynOptics continues to introduce the kind of cutting-edge products that first established its reputation, the company will not have much difficulty maintaining its leadership position within the highly competitive computer networking products industry. Indeed, with Ludwick still president and chief operating officer of the company and Schmidt acting as the chief technical officer, SynOptics is poised for whatever vagaries the future might bring.

Further Reading:

Gianturco, Michael, ''Two Networking Stocks to Own,'' *Forbes*, December 9, 1991, p. 318.
Kindel, Stephen, ''LAN War in America,'' *Financial World*, October 29, 1991, p. 58.

—Thomas Derdak

System Software Associates, Inc.

500 West Madison
Chicago, Illinois 60661
U.S.A.
(312) 641-2900
Fax: (312) 641-3737

Public Company
Incorporated: 1981
Employees: 1,700
Sales: $263.4 million
Stock Exchanges: NASDAQ
SICs: 7372 Prepackaged Software; 7379 Computer Related
Services, Nec; 3577 Computer Peripheral Equipment, Nec

System Software Associates, Inc. (SSA) is one of the world's leading providers of software for industrial businesses. It is the single largest supplier of software for the AS/400 line of minicomputers manufactured by IBM. The flexibility of SSA's software products allows them to be reconfigured to meet specific customer and business demands in any industry. The company maintains its global presence through offices and business affiliates in 67 countries, while support for clients is provided by a network of over 5,000 professionals.

SSA's core product line is the Business Planning and Control System (BPCS), a group of integrated software products for industry that includes applications for manufacturing, distribution, and financial operations. The company is also a leader in computer-aided systems engineering (CASE) technology. Its AS/SET line uses CASE technology to allow clients to build their own applications. Electronic Data Interchange (EDI), which enables businesses to communicate electronically with trading partners, is another area in which SSA has developed advanced products. The company's Main/Tracker line automates maintenance, safety inspection, and warranty tracking, and is the leading maintenance management system in the world.

SSA sprouted from a humble home business into a major international player in less than a decade. The company was founded in 1981 by Roger E. Covey. At age 26, Covey was already experienced in selling software manufacturing systems, having previously worked for Chicago, Illinois-based Professional Computer Resources, Inc. For mid-sized manufacturing concerns, he noted a need for an integrated software product that could handle every stage of operations, from raw materials to the distribution of finished goods. Convinced that he could

develop such a product, Covey launched his own firm, initially running it from his mother's dining room table. With his first three employees, Covey developed SSA's Business Planning and Control System (BPCS), which ran on the IBM System/34 computer. BPCS was essentially an umbrella product for about 20 applications modules, each compatible with the others, which enabled customers to easily adapt the system for their own requirements. The company's first customer was Best Chairs, a chair manufacturer based in southern Indiana.

The key to the company's early growth was its unique distribution system. Covey had determined that selling through retail channels made it difficult to find customers, while selling though a direct sales force and providing extensive servicing made it difficult to turn a profit. Therefore, SSA instead developed a network of local affiliates, trained by SSA, that would sell, install, and service the products for a commission. This enabled the company to expand at an impressive rate while keeping its overhead costs low. Within a year, SSA was big enough to move to a new location in Chicago's loop.

Early on, Covey and his employees decided to concentrate on improving the company's specialty, integrated software packages for industry, rather than search for ways to diversify its product line. By 1984, SSA had sales of $3.9 million. And SSA continued to grow rapidly through the mid 1980s by continuing to cater to medium-sized companies, which often needed to expand their computer system capacities and software capabilities without adding programming personnel to their payrolls.

In 1986, SSA began to expand by acquiring smaller companies, first acquiring Syncrocom, Inc. for about $540,000. SSA went public in February 1987. Its stock, which was initially offered at $13 a share, was hovering around $20 within a few months. The proceeds from the offering were used to finance the acquisitions of three of its affiliated companies by the end of 1987: Outlook, Inc., ASE Services, Inc., and portions of the Australian-based EDP Pty. Limited.

SSA's scope was international by 1987. The company had 40 affiliates in 25 countries, and half of its sales were generated outside the United States. Its customer list had reached 1,500 and was dominated by companies with annual sales between $5 million and $300 million. Of SSA's $31 million in sales for 1987, about 22 percent were on software for financial operations. Manufacturing and distribution applications each accounted for about half of the remaining share. For the year, sales increased 92 percent, and the company's net income jumped 88 percent to $3.3 million.

In 1988, IBM introduced a new mid-sized computer, the AS/400 (also known as Silverlake). Companies that had been taxing their System/36 and System/38 computers eagerly awaited the appearance of the new minicomputer, and SSA was among the handful of companies ready and waiting with software for the new system. Despite fierce competition from a group of companies that included IBM, Chicago's Pansophic Systems, and Arthur Andersen, SSA was able to carve out a sizable chunk of the new software market for itself. On the strength of its new BPCS/400 system (essentially the old BPCS revamped for the AS/400), SSA was able to nearly double its net income to $5.9 million on sales of $61.5 million in 1988. That year, it was ranked number 23 on *Inc.* magazine's list of the 100 fastest-growing small public companies. SSA was also ranked number 25 on the list of 100 Best Small Companies published by *Business Week.*

By 1989, SSA had nearly 400 employees and over 4,000 customers in 30 countries. The company was producing software in eight languages, including Chinese, Japanese, French, German, and Italian. Twenty-six integrated software products were being offered by this time, ranging in price from $50,000 to $500,000, depending on the size of the computer on which the applications were to run. SSA's network of affiliates had grown to 52 by the middle of 1989, penetrating nearly every major market in the world. Although competition remained tough, particularly IBM's improved integrated software package, the market for integrated software for medium-sized companies remained somewhat under-penetrated, and SSA was able to sustain its rapid growth rate through the year. For 1989, the company's sales made another jump, to $95 million, with net income reaching $11.1 million.

SSA was able to continue its remarkable growth into the beginning of the 1990s. In 1990, the company recorded net income of $16.4 million on sales of $124.2 million. That year, SSA launched SSA Mid Atlantic, Inc., a 50–50 joint venture with its New Jersey-based affiliate Software Plus, Inc. The company entered another joint venture the following year with the stockholders of Solid Beheer B.V., a Dutch company. Later in 1991, SSA founder Covey resigned as company president and CEO to pursue an academic career. He remained on the board of directors as vice chairman, and kept his 30 percent stake in the company. The void left by Covey's resignation was filled by Larry J. Ford, an IBM vice-president in charge of marketing the AS/400. Ford, who had been with IBM for 28 years, assumed the posts of president, chairman, and chief executive of SSA.

Under Ford, SSA continued to prosper. Increasing emphasis was placed on the company's CASE products, which assist clients in adapting software for their own purposes as business conditions change. By 1991, SSA had over 4,000 customers, more than half of them overseas. The company's net income finally began to level off during that year, although sales continued to climb, reaching $146 million.

SSA's growth jumped back into high gear in 1992. By the middle of the year, the company's CASE tool, AS/Set, was bringing in about 10 percent of its revenue. SSA continued to benefit from the trend in business away from the use of large mainframes toward the use of minicomputers such as the AS/400. The acquisition of two overseas companies helped spur growth in 1992. Comat Services Pte. Ltd. was purchased through the company's SSA Asia Pty. Ltd. subsidiary, and SSA acquired an Italian affiliate, CSA Sistemi Software, renaming it SSA Italia. For 1992, SSA's revenue shot up to nearly $229 million, with profits of $26.6 million.

By 1993, SSA software was being translated into 20 languages. The company continued to expand its global network, strengthening its operations in Asia, Africa, Scandinavia, Eastern Europe, the Middle East, and Latin America. In February 1993, the company launched a new joint venture with DAT GmbH, a German affiliate. SSA acquired Elke Corporation, a maker of maintenance tracking software, in August.

Although the company's network of affiliates continued to work well in keeping marketing and servicing costs down, it became apparent that this system was not particularly well-suited for its large, multinational clients, which were left in the position of working with different affiliates at different locations. SSA began to enhance its own support staff to improve its service to those clients. SSA's net income slipped to $23.4 million for 1993, on sales of $263.4 million.

Through the end of 1993 and into 1994, SSA focused its attention on a new strategy for supporting open-system client server computing environments. Using its CASE technology, SSA began offering more flexible software than was previously available. The company's new version of its flagship BPCS series was called BPCS/AS (for "advanced solution"). BPCS/AS consists of over 40 integrated applications, which can be easily manipulated to keep up with rapid changes taking place in both the hardware on which they are run and the business climates in which they are used. The company announced that its new client/server application products could be run on Unix-based systems as well as on the AS/400.

In a relatively short period of time, SSA has maneuvered itself into a dominant position in its niche market. Whether the company can sustain its tremendous growth record remains to be seen. If its management continues to make the kinds of decisions it has made in the past, such as its early commitment to CASE technology and its early jump onto the AS/400 bandwagon, SSA's chances for continued growth will certainly be enhanced.

Principal Subsidiaries: SSA Services Pty. Ltd. (Australia); System Software Associates Ltd. (England); System Software Associates Co., Ltd. (Japan); System Software Associates Asia Pte. Ltd. (Singapore); System Software Associates Caribbean, Inc. (Puerto Rico); System Software Associates Nederland B.V. (Netherlands); System Software Associates, New Zealand Ltd.; General Business Solutions S.A. (Spain); Comat Services Pte. Ltd.; System Software Associates Italia (Italy).

Further Reading:

Bozman, Jean S., "Support Net Keys SSA's Big Growth," *Computerworld,* April 18, 1988, p. 111.

Bucken, Mike, "SSA Harnesses AS/400 Growth," *Software Magazine,* June 1992.

Cleaver, Joanne, "System Software Joins Rush for IBM Gold," *Crain's Chicago Business,* June 27, 1988, p. 66.

Dutton, Barbara, and Larry Stevens, "Strong Support for Diverse Operations," *Manufacturing Systems,* September 1993.

Lashinsky, Adam, "High-Tech Firm in Low Gear," *Crain's Chicago Business,* February 15, 1993, p. 38.

Merrion, Paul, "Why Bears Like System Software," *Crain's Chicago Business,* May 22, 1989, p. 1.

Oloroso, Arsenio Jr., "Sustained Strength Confounds System Software's Naysayers," *Crain's Chicago Business,* April 23, 1990, p. 13.

Strahler, Steven R., "Piggy-Backing Distribution, Software Firm Hits Bedrock," *Crain's Chicago Business,* September 28, 1987, p. 33.

Sulski, Jim, "Software Firm Zeroes In on Success," *Chicago Tribune,* November 19, 1989, sec. 19, p. 22.

"System Software Taps IBM Exec as CEO," *Chicago Tribune,* August 20, 1991, sec. 3, p. 4.

—Robert R. Jacobson

TARGET.

Target Stores

33 S. Sixth Street
P.O. Box 1392
Minneapolis, Minnesota 55440-1392
U.S.A.
(612) 370-6073

Wholly Owned Subsidiary of Dayton Hudson Corporation
Incorporated: 1962
Employees: 120,000
Sales: $11.74 billion
SICs: 5331 Variety Stores

Target Stores, Inc., the largest division of Dayton Hudson Corporation, is the third of the "Big 3" in discount retailing, behind Wal-Mart and Kmart. Target accounts for 61 percent of all Dayton Hudson revenues and 60 percent of the parent company's operating profits. At the end of 1993 Target operated 554 stores in 32 states. Curiously enough, Target opened its first store the very same year as did Kmart and Wal-Mart, 1962. For much of the time since then, Target's growth has been nothing short of meteoric. Several analysts look upon Target as the healthier of Wal-Mart's two chief rivals, despite Kmart's considerably larger size. Part of that confidence lies in Target's ability to combine bargain prices with fashionable, branded merchandise and excellent customer service; revealingly, the company motto is "Expect More. Pay Less." Target operates distribution centers in Minneapolis; Los Angeles and Sacramento, California; Indianapolis, Indiana; Little Rock, Arkansas; Pueblo, Colorado; and Tifton, Georgia.

The Dayton's department stores began planning a Target discount chain in 1961 when they foresaw a rising public demand for lower-priced, mass merchandise available in a convenient, friendly environment. According to company literature, the Target name and red-and-white bull's-eye logo were selected for their visual impact and underlying message to consumers: that the stores would be aimed at offering the best prices. When Target was incorporated in 1961, there were a handful of high-volume, low-margin discount retailers doing business around the country; nonetheless, Target claims to be the first to offer quality national brands in a comfortable, attractive setting. As Target expanded during the 1960s, consumer attitudes toward discount retailers changed dramatically, from mild disdain to enthusiastic acceptance.

The first Target store actually opened in 1962 in Roseville, Minnesota, a northern tier suburb of Minneapolis and St. Paul. The test store conformed to later Target stores, which generally ran between 80,000 and 135,000 square feet and emphasized wide aisles, well-marked displays, ample checkout lines, and a clean, inviting atmosphere. While plans for Target were still in an embryonic stage, the management of Dayton's consulted with the management of another fashionable, upscale department store chain in Georgia named Rich's, which was planning a similar new retailing entry in its home market, Richway stores. According to a 1989 Target advertisement/retrospective, "the two teams shared ideas and strategies" and "did not see themselves as competitors, but as collaborators." Central to the strategy of each parent company was locating its discount offspring in major markets near major thoroughfares. The Minnesota-Georgia planning sessions obviously rewarded Target during the short term but also in the long term: In 1989, when Target was prepared to enter the Southeast, the Richway chain proved an ideal acquisition candidate that facilitated a strong Target entry into the region.

By the end of Target's introductory year, four stores had been opened. By 1966 the subsidiary had made its first foray outside of Minnesota with the opening of two stores in Denver. In four more years, Target had 17 stores in four states. The company closed the decade with heady, 40 percent average annual growth over four years and annual sales of $100 million. During the 1970s the discounter reached maturity not only in terms of size (80 stores in 11 states by 1979, with $1.12 billion in sales) but also in terms of technology (electronic cash registers for improved inventory control) and corporate identity (toy safety campaigns, shopping events for seniors and the disabled, and various outreach programs). The tone for Target's aggressive expansion was set in 1971 when the subsidiary acquired a 16-store retail chain serving the markets of Colorado, Oklahoma, and Iowa. It was through such opportunistic purchases as well as the regular addition of new stores that Target was able to become Dayton Hudson's top revenue producer by 1975. In addition, changes in the attitudes of premier brand-name manufacturers, formerly accustomed to establishing exclusive relationships with department stores, helped fuel the success of discount retailing, for Target as well as its competitors.

However, Target's ascendancy was not without its problems. In 1973 the chain stood at 46 stores and was facing two consecutive years of decreased earnings. New management, in the form of replacement president Stephen Pistner and merchandising executive Kenneth Macke (who eventually became president of Target and then chairman and CEO of Dayton Hudson, retiring in 1993), arrived and took stock. In a 1986 *Star Tribune* article, Macke commented, "Target had grown very fast and they'd forgotten a little about the most important person: the customer." In 1974 Target initiated a rapid turnaround that began with a one-year halt to new store additions. Other steps included the creation of a management team to review Target's objectives; the creation of a quality assurance committee to review the manufacture and pricing of private-label products; the addition of new brand-name selections; the renovation of store interiors and displays; and the advent of color promotional inserts in Sunday newspapers, all of which was designed to demonstrate to customers Target's high reputation and uncommon commitment to good products at low prices.

Thus revitalized, Target continued its transition from an expanding subsidiary to the central growth division of Dayton Hudson, a transformation that became especially overt between 1977 and 1982. At the beginning of this five-year period, Target's operating profits represented just 26 percent of overall corporate profits; by 1982, department-store profits had plunged from 58 percent to 25 percent, while Target earnings had risen to a solid 33 percent, approximately the same as the Mervyn's chain (acquired by Dayton's in 1978).

Target launched into the 1980s with the acquisition of Ayr-Way Stores, a 40-outlet chain operating in Illinois, Ohio, Indiana, and Kentucky; the last three states were new territories for Target. Three years later the company acquired 33 FedMart sites in southern California and Arizona. According to Neal St. Anthony, analysts were particularly worried about Target's acquisition of 28 closed FedMart stores in the highly competitive region of southern California. Some believed that to compete there, Target would have to follow other mass merchants and begin offering liquor and groceries as well as clothing and household items. In addition, FedMart employed union workers, Target did not. However, these and other obstacles were overcome and California became, by the 1990s, the state in which Target had by far the most stores, retail square feet, and revenue (some 25 percent of Target's total take).

In addition to catapulting Target firmly into the "Big Three," the successful California expansion won the approval of Wall Street and kudos from a number of others. In 1984 the University of California's School of Business Administration named Dayton Hudson Corporation, of which Target formed no small part, the "best managed company in the U.S.A." Target closed the decade with several highlights, including a large expansion into the Southeast, recognition as the Discounter of the Year, and sponsorship of the International Trans-Antarctica Expedition. By 1989 the company operated 399 stores in 31 states and boasted annual sales of $7.52 billion.

In 1990 Target opened its first Target Greatland, a megastore featuring wider aisles, color-coded signs and graphics, broader product offerings, and "Food Avenue" and "Guest Services" areas. The Greatland concept continued to be implemented in 1994 and also served as a guide for the approximately twice-per-decade remodeling of existing stores. During 1990 Target also unveiled a small market strategy to introduce Target stores to smaller cities (exactly the opposite strategy of giant rival Wal-Mart), as well as total quality and micromarketing programs. This last was designed to capitalize on the unique needs and interests of different communities and regions through merchandise reflecting, for example, the local climate or local sports teams.

In 1991 Bill Saporito, writing for *Fortune*, posed the question "Is Wal-Mart Unstoppable?" According to him, the stage for a three-way showdown in discount retailing was now set: "In the next five years the three biggest outfits—the Marts, K and Wal, as well as the less well known Target stores . . . will be on one collision course after another. . . . [By 1995] the three, which now control 70 percent of the discount department store business, will overlap in about 40 percent of their territories, up from 15 percent today." The outcome was by no means any clearer in 1994, though Kmart appeared to be experiencing the

greatest difficulty in maintaining profits, a situation that led to a shareholder revolt and divestiture request in mid-1994, initiated by certain large institutional investors.

However, a glimpse of the mounting battle in the form of price wars was offered in 1993 by articles in the *Star Tribune* and *U.S. News & World Report*. Both reported on a skirmish between Wal-Mart and Target, in which certain Wal-Mart stores apparently used flawed price comparison advertising. Target retaliated with ads headed "This Never Would Have Happened If Sam Walton Were Alive," charging that Wal-Mart was posting inflated or misleading prices on Target items. Wal-Mart responded in kind, and Target requested an investigation by the Better Business Bureau. The whole price brouhaha was underscored in May 1993 when Wal-Mart began phasing out its slogan "Always the low price. Always" to "Always low prices. Always," perhaps confirming the belief that price wars in discount retailing are ultimately unsustainable. Experts admit that not even the largest companies in the industry can conceivably hope to offer the best prices on all the products all of the time.

A primary focus for Target during the 1990s was a reinvestment in its employees. Beginning in 1989, Target staff were trained through an intensive course called "Target U." to treat customers as guests and to generate a "fast, fun, friendly" shopping environment. According to Ronald Henkoff in *Fortune*, "The new training has had a dramatic impact on employee turnover, which peaked at 89 percent among hourly workers in 1989—the year Target U. was born—and dropped to 59 percent in 1992. Customer service, as measured by the stores' semiannual surveys, has been on a steady upward trend." The 1993 Target Annual Report announced the company's commitment to institute this "Guest Culture"—"modeled on the practices of premier customer services companies such as Disney"—nationwide.

Target's most prominent goal in the mid-1990s was to seek out opportunities for new growth. During 1993 the company entered the Chicago market with 18 stores. Another 32 stores were added to existing markets in the Midwest, Southeast, and Southwest. By March 1994 the Target tally stood at 567 stores in 32 states. Plans for 1994 included adding 61 new stores. One of the most imitated mass merchandisers in the country, Target's strategy has been a model of simplicity: provide customers with quality products at low prices. In 1986 Target's first president, Douglas Dayton, remarked that Dayton Hudson "would have been a fading retail entity" without Target.

Further Reading:

Apgar, Sally, "Target Accuses Wal-Mart of Not Playing Fair When Posting Comparative Prices," *Minneapolis Star Tribune*, March 25, 1993, p. 1D.

"Big Three Discounters Top Big Builders List," *Chain Store Age Executive*, December 1993, pp. 114, 116, 118, 124.

Fitzgerald, Kate, "Bob Thacker: Target," *Advertising Age*, July 5, 1993, p. S18; "In Retailing, Price Stranglehold Lessens," *Advertising Age*, November 1, 1993, pp. S6, S18.

Grant, Linda, and Warren Cohen, "Shopping's Big Chill," *U.S. News & World Report*, July 12, 1993, pp. 44–46.

Hendrix, Kimberly D., "Discount Stores Fared Well During Recession," *Chain Store Age Executive*, August 1992, pp. 19A, 22A, 23A.

Henkoff, Ronald, "Companies That Train Best," *Fortune*, March 22, 1993, pp. 73–74.

Ortega, Bob, "Wal-Mart Bows to Pricing Reality by Changing 4 Letters," *Wall Street Journal*, May 21, 1993, p. B1.

Papa, Mary Bader, "William Andres: Executive of the Year," *Corporate Report Minnesota*, January 1984, pp. 57–63.

St. Anthony, Neal, "Target Stores Have Made Their Mark: Discount Offspring Now Powers Parent Firm," *Minneapolis Star Tribune*, April 7, 1986, pp. 1M, 8M.

Saporito, Bill, "Is Wal-Mart Unstoppable?" *Fortune*, May 6, 1991, pp. 50–59.

Schafer, Lee, "The Best Defense," *Corporate Report Minnesota*, June 1989, pp. 31–35.

Stavig, Vicki, "A Sight to be Sold," *Corporate Report Minnesota*, April 1986, pp. 37–38, 42.

—Jay P. Pederson

Tech Data Corporation

5350 Tech Data Drive
Clearwater, Florida 34620
U.S.A.
(813) 539-7429
Fax: (813) 538-7050

Public Company
Incorporated: 1974
Employees: 1,400
Sales: $1.57 billion
Stock Exchanges: NASDAQ
SICs: 5045 Computers and Peripheral Equipment

Tech Data Corporation is one of the largest distributors of personal computer products in the United States. With an 11 percent market share, Tech Data is third largest among the nation's microcomputer wholesalers, behind Ingram Micro and Merisel. The company's customer base consists of over 50,000 value-added resellers and retail dealers located in the United States, Canada, Europe, Latin America, and the Caribbean. Its product line contains more than 18,000 different items, including computers, printers, monitors, disk drives, networking equipment, and software. Apple, Compaq, IBM, AST Research, and Toshiba are among the over 600 manufacturers and publishers whose products are distributed by Tech Data. The company also provides technical training and support to computer resellers through authorized classes and other support programs. Products are shipped from the company's ten distribution centers in Chicago, Atlanta, Dallas, Miami and other cities. No single customer accounts for more than three percent of Tech Data's sales, and no single supplier accounts for greater than a ten percent share. Steven Raymund, CEO and son of company founder Edward Raymund, owned 12.7 percent of Tech Data's stock in 1994.

When Tech Data was founded in 1974, it bore little resemblance to the industry giant the company has grown to become. The company was started by Edward Raymund to market computer supplies to large institutions in central Florida. Its customers at that time were end-users rather than resellers, primarily hospitals and government agencies. From Tech Data, these end-users purchased disk packs, tape, and other data-processing paraphernalia for use with their mainframe and mini computers.

By the early 1980s, the company had annual sales of about $2 million. Around that time, several developments both inside the company and in the computer industry as a whole led to profound changes in the way Tech Data was to do business. The emergence of personal computers (pcs) in 1980 created an exciting new market niche that was wide open for exploitation. When Raymund decided to pursue a share of the market for pc supplies, however, he met with resistance on the part of his field sales force. Raymund's plan involved the expansion of the company's telemarketing operation, and the field sales staff, which relied on large institutional customers, perceived this as a threat to their dominant position in the company.

Also during this time, Steven Raymund, Edward's 25-year-old son, came to work for the company. Put to work on the upcoming Tech Data catalog, Steve initially had no intention of making the situation permanent. Gradually, however, his interest in the company's operations increased. As the elder Raymund began spending less time at Tech Data to concentrate on his other company, Tech Rep Associates, Steven Raymund took on more responsibilities, eventually becoming operations manager at Tech Data. This development did not sit at all well with the sales force, which had hoped to buy the company out from Raymund in the near future; Steven Raymund's sudden rise to prominence meant that a buyout was unlikely.

About a month after Steven Raymund received his new title, a group consisting of Tech Data's key salespeople staged a coup of sorts. The group of five gathered at the office on a Saturday and proceeded to photocopy all of the company's customer records and vendor information. The following Monday, Raymund found letters of resignation on his desk from the five, who then went to work for a nearby competitor. The impact of this mass desertion at Tech Data was immediate and brutal. It quickly became apparent that the salespeople had taken many of the company's best customers with them. Monthly sales figures dropped by more than 50 percent, and the company began losing money. In fact, the situation became so bad that the elder Raymund considered shuttering Tech Data so that he could devote more resources to his other company, which was thriving.

Instead, the Raymunds undertook a radical shift in strategy. Rather than replace the departed field sales force, they beefed up their telemarketing staff, which was much less expensive to support. They then began to aggressively court computer dealers in addition to end-users. The company also began to pay more attention to direct mail, purchasing mailing lists and sending out catalogs in greater numbers. By the middle of 1983, Tech Data was once again making money. About that time the company began dealing in pc products such as disk drives, printers, and keyboards. Selling to dealers rather than users proved so successful that by the end of fiscal 1984 the company had withdrawn from the end-user market entirely, and its transformation into a wholesale distributor was complete. That year, Steve Raymund was named chief operating officer, and the following year he became chief executive officer.

In 1986, Tech Data offered its stock to the public for the first time, entering the market at $9.75 a share. Annual sales had reached $37 million by this time. Marketing primarily to value-added resellers, which sold computer equipment and supplies to small and medium-sized businesses, Tech Data grew at a remarkable rate through the rest of the 1980s. Sales nearly doubled in 1987, reaching $72 million. The company doubled its sales again, to $149 million, the following year.

In 1989 Tech Data made its move northward with the acquisition of ParityPlus, a modest Canadian microcomputer distributor. The Canadian operation, purchased for just over $1 million in cash, was subsequently renamed Tech Data Canada, Inc. By the end of fiscal 1989, the company's coast-to-coast network of ten distribution centers was in place, and its work force had grown to 430. Sales for the year were $247 million.

After reporting impressive earnings for several years in a row, Tech Data stumbled slightly in 1990. Although its sales grew to $348 million for the year, the company's net income was cut in half. This off year was attributed in part on the bankruptcy of a major customer, Bulldog Computer Products of Atlanta, which cost Tech Data $1 million. Mismanagement and theft of inventory, including accounting errors and reported thievery at the company's Los Angeles warehouse, resulted in another $4 million in red ink. Raymund reacted to these problems with a combination of tightened inventory controls and cost-cutting measures. The company's executive rank was thinned out, and the frequency of inventory checks was switched from yearly to quarterly.

By 1991, Tech Data had turned things back around. That year, Steve Raymund succeeded his father as chairman of the company's board of directors. Tech Data had settled in among the top five computer distributors in the United States and was an acknowledged leader in the distribution of local area network (LAN) and network products. For the year, Tech Data reported earnings of $6.7 million on sales of $442 million. The company began stocking the products of several well known manufacturers around this time. Among the companies whose wares Tech Data began selling in the early 1990s were Compaq, Conner Peripherals (a leading maker of disk drives), Toshiba, and Lexmark (a typewriter and printer spin-off of IBM).

By 1992, the company had about 25,000 customers, 70 percent of which were value-added resellers. The rest consisted of large national retailers. In March 1992, Tech Data added software to its line for the first time, helping to close the gap between Tech Data and its largest competitors, Ingram Micro and Merisel, where software was already generating about 40 percent of those companies' revenues. Forty software companies were quickly added to Tech Data's list of suppliers.

Tech Data also benefited increasingly from the desire on the part of pc manufacturers to cut distribution costs. Since selling to a distributor required less effort than selling directly to dealers, more and more producers of computer equipment were drawn to companies like Tech Data as the most efficient channel for selling their goods. Eventually, even the largest companies in the computer industry began to feel that selling through wholesale distributors was necessary if they were to remain competitive with such up-and-coming concerns as AST Research and Dell.

For fiscal 1992, revenues at Tech Data rose to $647 million. In January 1993, Tech Data made an important breakthrough when it received authorization to begin selling certain Microsoft system and application software products to value-added resellers. IBM and Apple were also added to the list of companies whose products were available through Tech Data. With these major producers in the fold, Tech Data's numbers jumped impressively once again. The company reported earnings of $19.8 million on sales of $979 million for 1993. During that year, Tech Data also sought to expand internationally, and toward that end, an export division was established early in the year. Based in Miami, the division was designed to serve the Latin American market.

For fiscal 1993, Tech Data's sales increased 57 percent to $1.53 billion. Record earnings of $30.2 million were reported as well. In a flurry of activity, the company announced the addition of several major software companies to its line of offerings. In January 1994, Tech Data completed the acquisition of Software Resource Inc., a software distributor based in Novato, California. This acquisition enabled the company to begin offering several well known software lines, most importantly those of Borland International and WordPerfect Corporation. In March, Tech Data beefed up its international operations with the acquisition of Softmart International, S.A., a privately-held French distributor of pc products. The list of software companies represented in Tech Data warehouses again during the first half of 1994, with the inclusion of Lotus, Aldus, and Computer Associates.

In the mid-1990s, Tech Data appeared to be narrowing the margin by which it trailed its larger competitors, Merisel and Ingram. By devoting a greater share of its work force to customer support and shoring up its software business and international operations, Tech Data stood to increase its overall market share, further solidifying its position as a leader among distributors of computer products.

Principal Subsidiaries: Tech Data Canada, Inc.

Further Reading:

Doyle, T. C., and Longwell, John, ''Tech Data to Expand Reach via Software-Signing Spree,'' *Computer Reseller News,* February 14, 1994.

Dubashi, Jagannath, ''Tech Data: There's Gold in Them VAR Hills,'' *Financial World,* May 12, 1992, p. 14.

Finegan, Jay, ''Turning Point,'' *Inc.,* April 1989, pp. 106–07.

''Inside Tech Data,'' *Tampa Tribune,* June 28, 1993.

Quickel, Stephen W., ''Tech Data Muscles onto Others' Turf,'' *Electronic Business Buyer,* September 1993, p. 32.

Rooney, Paul A., ''Tech Data Mastering Growth,'' *Tampa Bay Business Journal,* April 12, 1991, p. 1.

Scholl, Jaye, ''Cool Cat with a Hot Hand,'' *Barron's,* January 6, 1992, pp. 16–7.

—Robert R. Jacobson

Teledyne, Inc.

1901 Avenue of the Stars
Los Angeles, CA 90067
U.S.A.
(310) 277-3311
Fax: (310) 551-4365

Public Company
Incorporated: 1960
Employees: 21,000
Revenues: $2.4 billion
Stock Exchange: New York
SICs: 3724 Aircraft Engines and Engine Parts; 3812 Search,
   Detection, Navigation, Guidance, Aeronautical, and
   Nautical Systems and Instruments

Teledyne is a diversified manufacturing corporation with 21 operating companies focused in four business sectors, including aviation and electronics, specialty metals, industrial manufacturing, and consumer products. Within these four areas, the company's product lines range from electronic warfare systems to commercial uses of zirconium, and from machine tools to Water Pik shower massages. Unfortunately for Teledyne, however, from the late 1980s onward the company has been at the center of a legal maelstrom and burdened with shareholder lawsuits, whistle-blowing revelations in its defense business, and allegations that it has cheated on government contracts.

Ever since he was a boy Henry A. Singleton wanted to build a large corporation: "A company like GM, AT&T, Dupont—I want to build a company like that," he would say. In 1960, after earning three degrees from MIT and rising to vice-president and general manager of Litton, Singleton decided the time was right. He quit his $35,000 a year job and convinced his assistant and old friend, George Kozmetsky, who had earned a doctor of commercial science from Harvard, to join him in a new business venture.

Singleton, who in five years had helped raise Litton Industries Incorporated's electronics equipment division to $80 million in sales, decided that success lay in the semiconductor business. Despite an already crowded market, he nevertheless believed that producing semiconductors, the "basic building block of electronics," would lead to other high-technology and high-growth inventions.

Using the money they earned from their Litton stock options, Singleton and Kozmetsky each invested $225,000 to start their business. Singleton became chairman and president of the company they named Teledyne, and Kozmetsky became executive vice-president. Their backgrounds in high-technology and innovative ideas quickly paid off. The company achieved first year sales of $4.5 million and employed nearly 450 people. Second year sales of $10.5 million confirmed their success. Sales continued on an upward trend when the company embarked on a series of acquisitions, first in electronics and then in geophysics, to increase the company's strength in businesses related to semiconductors. In 1966 Teledyne bought Vasco Metals Corporation, which started a third wave of acquisitions, in specialty metals. Vasco, with sales of $43 million, specialized in titanium, molybdenum, beryllium, and vanadium alloys.

Later that year Kozmetsky, whose 130,000 shares of Teledyne were by then worth well over $20 million, retired from the company to become dean of the College of Business Administration at the University of Texas. George A. Roberts, formerly president of Vasco, replaced him as president of Teledyne. Singleton continued on as chairman and chief executive officer. By the end of 1966 Teledyne broke into the 293rd spot on the *Fortune* 500 ranking with sales of more than $256 million— nearly triple the total of just one year before.

In 1967 Teledyne continued its impressive growth. The company's 16,000 employees were busily making microelectronic integrated circuits, microwave tubes, aircraft instruments, miniature television camera transmitters, hydraulic systems, computers, seismic measuring devices, specialty alloys, and a large variety of other sophisticated products. More good news arrived when the company bettered IBM and Texas Instruments in a government defense contract contest and became the prime contractor for the development of the Integrated Helicopter Avionics System (IHAS). The IHAS was a helicopter control system that used computers to provide the "precise navigation, formation flight, terrain following, and fire control" in virtually any kind of weather. Also that year, in a move *Business Week* magazine called a "coup," Teledyne purchased the Wah Chang Corporation, a leading producer of tungsten and columbium, and the world's top producer of hafnium, zirconium, and other exotic metals. And, to increase the company's assets and provide it with more leverage for future acquisitions, Teledyne moved into the insurance business by purchasing 21 percent of United Insurance Company for $40 a share.

In 1969 Teledyne's sales surpassed the $1 billion mark. The company subsequently stopped its aggressive acquisition program and paid off its short term debts. Wall Street analysts predicted that the acquisition phase was over and that Singleton was turning Teledyne into an operating company. Teledyne's financial condition was quite strong. For the ten years previous to 1971, the company led the *Fortune* 500 ranking in earnings and earnings per share growth. And in the early 1970's, while many conglomerates were experiencing financial difficulties, Teledyne weathered the recession well. Sales increased somewhat with inflation, but net profits remained near $60 million.

In 1972, Argonaut, one of Teledyne's six financial companies, decided to expand from the worker's compensation field into the medical malpractice insurance business. At the same time, the frequency and size of malpractice claims were growing—but premiums didn't keep pace. By 1974 Argonaut took a $104 million pretax writeoff, resulting in a $31.2 million net loss in insurance operations and a reduction of Teledyne's net profit for the year to $31.5 million. Nine of Argonaut's 11 top officers were fired, and Singleton began running the operations from headquarters in Los Angeles. Argonaut, one of the last large companies in the malpractice market, discontinued underwriting individual policies for the 20,000 physicians it covered. It continued to offer coverage to the 25 percent of the nation's hospitals it covered, but at higher rates and covering fewer risks. In the meantime, the company collected $170 million in reserves against malpractice cases.

Teledyne's problems were compounded in 1973 when the consumer products division lost $1.8 million, mostly because of its Packard-Bell television production unit's failure to capture a large enough share of the West Coast television market. Teledyne reduced production and narrowed the loss to $500,000 the next year.

With the insurance unit and consumer unit problems solved, Teledyne's outlook had improved markedly. Net income soared to $101.7 million on sales of $1.71 billion in 1974. The largest share of profit came from industrial products such as diesel and gasoline engines and machine tools. Insurance operations had improved and were contributing $19 million. The consumer products division showed a healthy profit of $13.1 million because of Water Pik, which had sold a million shower heads at $25 to $40 each. The closing of the Packard Bell television unit had little effect on earnings; it was accomplished so successfully that no final writedown was taken.

In 1976 the company attempted, for the sixth time since 1972, to buy back its stock in order to eliminate the possibility of a takeover attempt by someone eager for the cash reserves the company had accumulated. Altogether, Teledyne spent $450 million buying back its stock, leaving $12 million outstanding, compared to $37.4 million at the close of 1972. With many of the company's divisions showing stronger results and fewer shares outstanding, Teledyne's stock increased from a low of $9.50 per share to $45 per share, becoming the largest gainer on the New York Stock Exchange. Singleton wasn't content to buy back his own stock, however. Teledyne then purchased 12 percent of Litton's stock, becoming that company's largest shareholder.

By 1978 Singleton's strategy of bringing in new management to replace underachievers appeared to be working. Only one of the 130 profit centers into which the company was divided was losing money. Without a single acquisition, company sales had soared to $2.2 billion, the result of internal growth at an annual rate of 7 percent. Nearly all of Teledyne's units were reporting continued growth and strong positioning in the marketplace. Sales from the company's offshore drilling rig had grown to $80 million from $10 million in 1966. Water Pik's sales reached $130 million, up from $8 million in 1966. Teledyne had also become an important producer of specialty metal. Allvac, which vacuum-melts metals, had surpassed $40 million in sales compared with $1.5 million in 1964. And Merla Manufacturing, purchased for only $80,000 with monthly sales of $30,000, had grown to $7 million in sales. Chang had grown from near

bankruptcy in 1967 to over $100 million in sales in 1977. And Packard Bell's business was greater than when it sold televisions.

In the meantime, over a two-year period, Singleton took advantage of the company's regained financial strength and used $400 million of the company's earnings to purchase surprisingly large stakes in 11 companies. By 1978, through Teledyne, Singleton had gained effective control of six companies, owning 22 percent of Litton's common stock, 28.5 percent of Curtiss-Wright, nearly 20 percent of Walter Kidde, 22 percent of Brockway Glass, and 20 percent of Reichhold Chemicals. In addition, he purchased eight percent of GAF, 5.5 percent of Rexnord, seven percent of Federal Paper Board, five percent of Colt Industries, and eight percent of Eltra.

Most of the money for these purchases was funneled through Unicoa and Argonaut. Almost all insurance companies keep some of their assets in stock, but most have stock holdings less than their net worth. Argonaut, on the other hand, had accumulated seven times its net worth in stock holdings, which is very unusual in the insurance business. Singleton's action quickly caught the attention of the business press and of the management of the companies whose stock he purchased. Rumors abounded about his possible intentions, some of which speculated that he wanted to merge the companies into Teledyne, particularly his former employer, Litton.

In the end, the merger attempts never materialized. What soon became apparent was that Singleton had actually purchased a number of difficulties. As earnings were being channeled into the stock market, Teledyne was putting only 1.5 percent of manufacturing sales back into research and development and plant and equipment maintenance, more than 25 percent below the average industry investment. Manufacturing operations, cut off from corporate resources, started to lose competitiveness. As a result, Teledyne's divisions lost market shares, contracts, and technological advantages.

One of the worst problems the company was confronted with occurred in 1980. Until then, its Continental Motors division in Muskegon, Michigan, supplied diesel engines to all U.S. military tanks, an important contributor to Teledyne's earnings. When the turbine-powered M1 was introduced that year, however, Continental was relegated to the replacement-engine market for existing tanks.

In addition, Wah Chang, which had once enjoyed a virtual monopoly on the free-world production of zirconium, a crucial metal in building nuclear reactors, had lost a large portion of its market share to French companies, which controlled 40 percent of the market. And Westinghouse Electric Corporation's completion of a new plant threatened to reduce Chang's market share to less than half of the $150 million free-world output. In 1981 the insurance operations, which contributed 25 percent of Teledyne's total revenue, were once again in trouble. These companies, which were not performing well within their industry, lost $79.2 million before taxes.

The stock portfolio, which had been built up at the expense of the rest of the company, was also in trouble during 1982. Overall, Teledyne's stock portfolios had dropped $380 million during the previous year. That unreported loss almost matched the company's earnings of $412 million on sales of $4.3 billion. Part of Teledyne's stock problems were due to its 16 percent investment in International Harvester, which over the previous year and a half had lost $100 million on paper.

The manufacturing plants and service companies continued to perform poorly in several important markets. Water Pik was showing a profit, but only by reducing product development, advertising, and marketing expenditures drastically. And Ryan Aeronautical, formerly the premier producer of robot aircraft used for military target practice and reconnaissance, lost most of its market share. Ryan's Firebee model controlled 75 percent of the market in the early 1970's, but Teledyne's emphasis on accumulating cash opened the field to more innovative competitors. Northrop Corporation, for instance, introduced less expensive and easier to launch alternatives that used sophisticated electronics to match the Firebee's capabilities.

With the company financially weakened, Teledyne management appeared to adopt a more aggressive strategy in 1982 by making its first large acquisition bid in 13 years. Continental tried to purchase Chrysler's tank division, which was the prime contractor for the M-1 tank. However, General Dynamics Corporation won the bid with a $336 million offer, exceeding Teledyne's offer by $36 million. According to *Business Week*, Pentagon officials were relieved that Continental lost the bid because they considered Continental to be ''stagnating.''

In 1983 Teledyne's sales fell from $3.24 billion to $2.86 billion, while net profit fell 37 percent to $248.7 million. That same year, Teledyne took a $49.1 million loss on its stake in GAF, and in December of 1985 Teledyne sold its 6.7 percent share in GAF.

With Teledyne's financial troubles fully apparent, discord also began to appear in management. High level executives complained increasingly that Singleton, who once claimed to have no specific business plan for the company, was only involved in management when problems developed. Due to the rumbling in management ranks, and because he was increasingly out of touch with the demands of strategic corporate planning, Singleton remained chairman but handed over the day-to-day management operations to George Roberts in 1986. Roberts, formerly the head of Vasco Metals and part of the company's specialty metals business, jumped in as chief executive officer and attempted to right Teledyne's financial difficulties.

Teledyne seemed to rebound almost immediately under Roberts' leadership. In 1986 the company spun off Argonaut Insurance and began to divest some of the numerous operations it had acquired over the previous 15 years. By 1988, Teledyne was back on track when it reported a profit of $392 million on revenues of $4.5 billion—an impressive return on equity of nearly 20 percent. In 1990, the company spun off its Unitrin insurance group to shareholders and then disposed of its industrial rubber and oilfield equipment units. Even though the employee payroll had been reduced from 43,000 to 24,000, Roberts was a long way from completing the company's restructuring. In 1991, he announced that Teledyne planned to either close or sell 24 of its facilities.

Mounting legal problems, however, began at this stage to undermine the company's reputation, reduce profits, and interfere with its restructuring strategy. Numerous lawsuits were filed against Teledyne, including accusations of falsifying test results on missile relays, selling defective equipment, lying to cover up commissions on sales of military goods to Taiwan, and bribing both Saudi Arabian and Egyptian officials to procure contracts. Due to a U.S. government investigation into its Relays Division, the company was temporarily prohibited from bidding for any government contracts. Although Teledyne denied most of these charges, the sheer number of them indicated something was wrong with company management.

While continuing his plans to restructure the company, Roberts also began to deal straightforwardly with Teledyne's legal woes. Since 1992, Teledyne has pleaded guilty to many accusations cited in the lawsuits brought against it, and has paid nearly $30 million to settle charges. The settlement of a federal probe into its Relays Division significantly reduced profits in 1992, but management thought this move was necessary because the U.S. government accounted for more than one-third of Teledyne's business that year. In short, Teledyne didn't want to take any chances of losing any future government contracts, especially with the economic upheaval in the defense industry signaled by the end of the Cold War.

In 1993, Roberts retired and was replaced by William P. Rutledge. The new chairman and chief executive officer was from FMC Corporation and had worked at Teledyne in specialty metals since 1986. Rutledge brought in Donald Rice, a former secretary of the U.S. Air Force, to serve as president and chief operating officer. Immediately, the two men set out to repair Teledyne's damaged reputation. While Rutledge began to speed up the final phases of Teledyne's restructuring, ice supervised the company's internal probe of ethical compliance. Under Rutledge and Rice, Teledyne's operations were consolidated from 65 units into 21 companies, reduced from a high of 130 in 1990. Wholesale layoffs of 1,200 executives followed, which brought the payroll down to almost 22,000.

Going into the middle 1990s, forecasts by Wall Street analysts for Teledyne's consumer products line, commercial use of specialty metals, industrial factory systems, and aviation electronics were very positive, as were conjectures that Teledyne could survive its legal problems. They also warned that Teledyne must repair its reputation, restore its credibility, and narrow its corporate focus. If Teledyne is to remain a successful high-technology manufacturer in the post–Cold War era, especially as competition for government contracts becomes more intense, the company must overcome both the business and ethical problems of its recent past.

Principal Subsidiaries: Teledyne Industries, Inc.; Teledyne Exploration Co.; Teledyne Isotopes, Inc.; Unicoa Corp. (98.4%).

Further Reading:

Norman, James R., ''A New Teledyne,'' *Forbes*, September 27, 1993.

—updated by Thomas Derdak

Telxon Corporation

3330 West Market Street
Akron, Ohio 44333-3352
U.S.A.
(216) 867-3700
Fax: (216) 873-2058

Public Company
Incorporated: 1967 as Electronic Laboratories, Inc.
Employees: 1,425
Sales: $238.41 million
Stock Exchanges: NMS
SICs: 3571 Electronic Computers; 3577 Computer Peripheral
    Equipment, Nec; 7372 Prepackaged Software; 7378
    Computer Maintenance and Repair

Telxon Corporation is a world leader in the design, manufacture, integration, and marketing of portable and wireless tele-transaction computers and systems. The Akron-based company designs, develops, manufactures, markets, integrates, and services several types of portable microprocessors, associated software, and peripheral devices for on-site data collection processing and communications. Its systems can be found in a wide variety of business environments, including retail, wholesale, manufacturing, utility, service, transportation, and government. The company dominates the industry's supermarket niche; 24 of the top 25 grocery chains in America utilize Telxon portable tele-transaction computers and systems. Telxon maintains subsidiaries and branches in Canada, the United Kingdom, Germany, France, Belgium, Italy, Australia, Japan and Singapore, and distributors in other parts of Europe, Asia, Africa, South America and the Middle East. By 1993, over 7,000 companies in 47 countries utilized Telxon products.

First incorporated in Texas in 1967 as Electronic Laboratories, Inc., the company went through several restructurings and was renamed Telxon Corporation in 1974. Telxon began to design order entry and inventory systems for retailers and wholesalers in the grocery, drug, and hardware industries in the early 1970s. Demand for these systems increased after 1973, when the universal product code (or UPC barcode) identification system was adopted as a standard in the grocery industry. Telxon's computer products also met a growing need for timely, accurate information, which helped reduce costs, improve productivity, and enhance service. These devices transmitted data through direct-connect (dedicated) telephone lines, thereby eliminating redundant and often erroneous data entry.

Unable to pay $500,000 in commissions owed to an independent sales company, Telxon was taken over by the creditor in 1978. Robert F. Meyerson became chief executive officer, a post he held until 1985. With the help of President Raymond Meyo, Meyerson helped Telxon recover from the brink of bankruptcy, and took the company public in 1983. Telxon flourished under its new leadership, which emphasized smaller, faster, programmable computers and custom application software for the retail market. During its first year of incorporation, the company introduced TCAL (Telxon Common Application Language), a proprietary computer language that featured specialized capabilities designed expressly for the portable computing environment.

The company soon captured the top rank in the estimated $400 million portable tele-transaction computer (PTC) industry, surpassing industry leader MSI Data by building better hardware and developing specialized software for such mass retailers as Revco, Winn-Dixie, and Lucky Stores. Telxon's revenues increased from $33 million to $160 million during its first five years as a public entity, and its stock (adjusted for splits) more than quadrupled, from $6 to $25, returning $4,000 on a $1,000 initial investment.

Meyerson was succeeded as president and chief executive officer in 1985 by the 41-year-old Meyo. A career salesman, Meyo sensed growing competition in the retail sector—Telxon's biggest market—in 1987, and set out to diversify the company into new markets. He quartered Telxon's sales force to focus on new areas, including manufacturing, warehousing, and government. Meyo concurrently expanded Telxon's custom software program and attempted to build a field service staff to support it. He planned to develop most of the software for each market internally, as the company had done with products intended for its retail customers. But without sophisticated, industry-tailored software generating programs, Telxon's endeavors to customize each client's software package soon overwhelmed the company's programmers. Selling into three vastly different new markets swamped the company's program writers, while cost overruns and delivery delays were largely disregarded as Meyo turned his attention to the acquisition of rival MSI in fall 1988. By the end of the year, Telxon had lost MSI to another top PTC producer, Symbol Technologies. Moreover, during this time, Telxon was compelled to settle patent-infringement and unfair competition lawsuits brought by Symbol with $7 million in prepaid royalties and the purchase of $40 million of Symbol's scanning hardware over five years.

Although Telxon's sales continued to grow, its manufacturing costs increased 45 percent between 1988 and 1989 as the company reconfigured its assembly lines to accommodate individual markets' requirements for keyboards, screens, scanning wands, and other options. Sales climbed 28.9 percent from year to year, while net income only rose 9.7 percent.

Acknowledging that his expansion scheme wasn't working, Meyo initiated a reorganization in June 1989. He cut costs by trimming the company's work force by eight percent, or 110 people. The staff reductions extended all the way to the top;

from September to December 1989, all four of the company's vice-presidents and its chief financial officer either resigned, were reassigned, or were fired. The old, decentralized management structure was replaced with a more manageable team of four executives, and Meyo brought in a management consulting firm to assess Telxon's administration.

However, the independent evaluators traced some of Telxon's problems to Meyo, who, they contended, had relied too heavily on sales gains and ignored areas in which the company was struggling. Repetitive personal computer products and unnecessary options were eliminated after evaluators found that Telxon could satisfy over 90 percent of its customers' needs with ten percent of the options it had been offering. The company's four separate sales forces were reunited, and sales commissions were awarded in relation to profits instead of sheer dollar volume. Still, Telxon ended fiscal year 1990 with a loss of $14.44 million and no order backlog.

Meyo responded by delegating more responsibilities, and he capped off his reorganization with a risky, unique, and admittedly impulsive, pledge: if Telxon's performance did not improve within a year of the fall 1989 annual meeting, he would step down. This bold move prompted criticism in the media. Jeffrey Sonnenfeld, director of the Center for Leadership and Career Change at Emory University, commented that "When things are bad and a CEO makes himself the target, he achieves heroic stature which encourages others to take risks." On the other hand, Warren Bennis, a leadership and motivation consultant from the University of Southern California told *The Wall Street Journal* that Meyo's pledge was "ridiculous." Nevertheless, Meyo's gamble paid off in the short term: during fiscal years 1991 and 1992, Telxon posted profits of about $17 million, as new product introductions and joint ventures buoyed the struggling company.

In the early 1990s, wireless communication emerged as one of the fastest-growing segments of the portable microcomputer industry. Telxon introduced its DATASPAN 2000 wireless radio network during its 1991 fiscal year. The integrated system included PTCs, base station communication controllers, and other coordinating equipment that could instantly transfer data, thereby enhancing mobility and flexibility. In 1992, one of America's largest mass merchandisers, Wal-Mart Stores, Inc., adopted Telxon's DATASPAN 2000 network for merchandising and customer service areas in the chain of over 1,800 stores, implementing the largest installed base of spread spectrum, wireless data communication systems in North America. Contracts with Wal-Mart accounted for over ten percent of Telxon's annual revenues by 1993.

In 1992, Telxon paid $10 million in cash and stock to acquire 95 percent of Telesystems SLW Inc., of which the company already owned the remaining five percent. This Canadian developer and supplier of wireless data communications products and local access networks (LANs) was the first company in the industry to receive the approval of both the U. S. Federal Communications Commission and Canada's Department of Communication for its spread spectrum radios. That year, Telxon also purchased Retail Management Systems Corp., of Des Moines, Iowa, a supplier of store-level software programs.

When, in October 1992, Telxon announced that it would likely report a loss for the fiscal year ending in March 1993, Wall Street reacted swiftly. Within two days of the October 8 news release, Telxon lost about $101.8 million, or 34.8 percent, of its market value, as its stock dropped $3.625 to $13.375. Meyo resigned that month, Robert Meyerson returned to the posts he had previously held, and chief operating and financial officer Dan R. Wipff added the responsibilities of the presidency to his duties. The following spring, Telxon recorded a loss of over $12 million on continually rising sales of $238.41 million in its annual report for the 1993 fiscal year.

In December 1992, four class action suits were filed in the U.S. District Court, Northern District of Ohio, by stockholders who purchased Telxon common stock between May 20, 1992 and January 19, 1993. The suit accused Meyo, Wipff, and Telxon as a whole, of fraud on the stock market and negligent misrepresentation of the company's financial performance and prospects. A Motion to Dismiss filed on behalf of the defendants was denied in June 1993.

Telxon undertook what it referred to as a preemptive reorganization late in 1992, creating strategic business groups (SBGs), each addressing key vertical markets and their particular requirements. The Retail Technology Group, Inc., Telxon's first SBG, was organized as a wholly owned subsidiary in January 1993 to focus on Telxon's primary market segment. Business from supermarkets, mass merchandisers, drug stores, and specialty chains represented about 50 percent of the company's 1993 revenues. Applications of the company's products in this SBG included receiving, price management, returns, transfers, and computer-assisted ordering.

One of Telxon's newest product lines for the retail market was its trademarked POS-XPRESS series. Unveiled early in 1992, these clipboard-sized, self-contained, full-function point-of-sale (POS) registers incorporated barcode scanning, magnetic stripe reading, electronic signature capture, and on-the-spot receipt printing. Along with competitor Symbol Technologies, Telxon's introduction of the hand-held registers at the National Retail Federation's annual expo captured the interest of attendees and the press. Although the devices could only accommodate debit or credit card transactions, not cash, they promised to help alleviate long lines during busy shopping seasons and facilitate remodeling without rewiring traditional cash registers.

The March 1993 acquisition of the Itronix Corporation, based in Spokane, Washington, was central to Telxon's second SBG. Itronix was a leading manufacturer of rugged portable microcomputers primarily for the mobile work force and field service automation markets. Itronix products were environmentally sealed to protect delicate computer components against the effects of water, shock, temperature extremes, dust, and rough handling. This SBG would concentrate on serving mobile work force and field service markets, including telephone company field service personnel.

Telxon formed an Industrial Systems Group SBG to cater to manufacturing, warehousing, and distribution markets during 1993. This SBG adapted already existing components to fit the specific functions of a warehouse, such as receiving, inventory put away, replenishment, picking, shipping, and cycle counting of inventory. Telxon's warehouse automation systems consisted of handheld or vehicle-mounted PTCs that communicated in real time via wireless data communications to various warehouse software packages running on a host computer. The company's Realtime Distribution Manager system of hardware, software and technical support was expected to become a key product of this SBG. Among The Industrial Systems Group's customers were Nike, Inc., Ocean Spray Cranberries, Inc., and The Trane Company.

One of the company's newest product groups, pen-based portable tele-transaction devices, was developed with Teletransaction Corp., which Telxon acquired in February 1993. Telxon hoped to utilize the new line, dubbed PTC-1100, to penetrate existing retail and other emerging mobile work force markets, including transportation, manufacturing, health care, insurance, and financial services. Shipments of the PTC-1100 series were expected to begin in early 1994.

The company's 1993 annual report to the Securities and Exchange Commission put forth a plan for future growth: "First, the company plans to continue to penetrate its traditional retail and wholesale markets by offering more comprehensive integrated system solutions to new and established customers. Second, Telxon plans to sell new PTCs and new wireless integrated systems to new markets as their needs are identified through market research." Telxon identified logistics, transportation, health care, insurance, and financial services as target markets throughout the 1990s.

Principal Subsidiaries: Telxon Australia PTY, LTD.; N.V. Telxon Belgium S.A. (Belgium); Telxon France S.A.; Telxon Italia S.R.L.; Telxon MDE GmbH (Germany); Telxon Limited (United Kingdom); Telxon Japan; Telxon Canada Corp., Inc.; MicroOffice Systems Technology, Inc.; Telxon Europe B.V.; Telxon Data Systems AG; Itronix Corporation; Telxon Foreign Sales Corp.; New England Data Systems, Inc.; PTC Airco, Inc.; The Retail Technology Group, Inc.; Teletransaction Corp.; Telesystems SLW Inc. (Canada).

Further Reading:

Fox, Bruce, "Will Wireless Take Off? Mervyn's Eddie Bauer Test Concept," *Chain Store Age Executive,* July 1992, p. 50, 52.

Fritz, Michael, "The Little Company that Had Trouble Growing Up," *Forbes,* December 25, 1989, p. 118, 120.

Mula, Rose, "The Long Arm of the Portable," *Computerworld,* June 15, 1987, p. 55, 59.

Radding, Alan, "Sturdy Personal Computers Built to Take Beating," *Computerworld,* June 8, 1992, p. 105.

Robins, Gary, "Auto ID Technologies: An Update," *Stores,* May 1993, pp. 54–7.

Stricharchuk, Gregory, "Should a CEO Bet His Job on an Upturn?" *Wall Street Journal,* May 10, 1990, p. B1.

"Telxon Shows Sharp Loss in Market Value," *New York Times,* October 10, 1992, p. A36.

—April Dougal Gasbarre

Tenneco Inc.

Tenneco Building
P.O. Box 2511
Houston, Texas 77252-2511
U.S.A.
(713) 757-2131
Fax: (713) 757-2777

Public Company
Incorporated: 1947 as Tennessee Gas Transmission
   Company
Employees: 75,000
Sales: $14.5 billion
Stock Exchanges: New York Toronto
SICs: 3523 Farm Machinery and Equipment; 3531
   Construction Machinery; 3731 Ship Building and
   Repairing; 3714 Motor Vehicle Parts and Accessories;
   2653 Corrugated and Solid Fiber Boxes; 4923 Gas
   Transmission and Distribution; 6719 Holding Companies,
   Nec.

Tenneco Inc. is one of the largest diversified companies in the
world, ranking among the United States' 30 largest industrial
companies and among the top 100 industrial companies worldwide. Tenneco's holdings include Case Corporation, one of the
world's largest manufacturers of agricultural and construction
equipment; Tenneco Gas, one of the natural gas industry's
largest and most profitable companies; Tenneco Automotive, a
global manufacturer of automotive parts; Newport News
Shipbuilding, a primary supplier to the U.S. Navy; Packaging
Corporation of America, one of the world's leading packaging
manufacturers; and Albright & Wilson, an international manufacturer and marketer of chemicals. During the early 1990s,
these companies became the focus of Tenneco, as it divested
other interests in pulp and paper chemicals; oil exploration,
production, processing and marketing; and life insurance.

Much of the company's early success was attributed to its first
director, Henry Gardiner Symonds. Acquiring a degree in geol-
ogy from Stanford University in 1924 and an MBA from Harvard three years later, Symonds began his career in Chicago as a
banker with what eventually became the Continental Illinois
Bank and Trust Company. In 1930, Symonds began work with a
small investment firm and bank subsidiary called the Chicago

Corporation, and his success there led to his appointment as
vice-president of the division in 1932.

In 1938, oil was discovered on land that the Chicago Corporation had purchased for natural gas deposits, near Corpus Christi,
Texas, and Symonds was dispatched to Texas to manage the
property. Later that year, he became a board member of the
firm. The Chicago Corporation was unable to fully exploit the
large reserves of natural gas it had developed in Texas, due to
national shortages of pipeline materials essential for gas transmission. When a shortage of fuel for defense plants in West
Virginia developed in 1943, the Chicago Corporation was able
to obtain a Federal Power Commission (FPC) license to operate
a pipeline, in addition to a priority order for pipeline materials.
Symonds was placed in charge of the construction of a 1,265-
mile pipeline, which linked the gas fields of the Gulf states with
factories in the eastern United States.

A company called the Tennessee Gas and Transmission Company, founded in 1940 and acquired by the Chicago Corporation
in 1943, was placed in charge of the pipeline. The project was
completed in October 1944; however, the day after the pipeline
went into operation, the FPC moved to regulate the pipeline and
ordered the company to reduce its transmission rates. Symonds
protested, contending that the FPC had led him to believe that
the Chicago Corporation would be allowed to operate without
such regulations. Regarding the FPC's actions as unfair,
Symonds declared that he would never again become involved
in projects subject to government regulation. Nevertheless,
when the Chicago Corporation promptly divested itself of Tennessee Gas after World War II, Symonds remained with the
company and was subsequently named its president.

Tennessee Gas continued to add pipelines to its network, planning 3,840 additional miles in 1946. A long coal strike that year
increased demand for oil- and gas-burning furnaces and other
devices, and Tennessee Gas applied for rights to build more gas
lines as well as to pump oil through the government-sponsored
''big-inch'' and ''little inch'' oil pipeline programs. On July 18
of the following year, the company was reincorporated in
Delaware as the Tennessee Gas Transmission Company, while
its headquarters remained in Houston.

Symonds used profits from the pipeline operations to establish a
separate but complementary subsidiary business in oil and gas
exploration. He advocated the acquisition of existing oil companies during the 1950s, including Sterling Oil, Del-Rey Petroleum, and Bay Petroleum, and oversaw acquisitions of several
petrochemical companies, diversifying the product base and
involving Tennessee Gas in industrial plastics. Fifteen Oil,
acquired in 1960, was one of several subsidiaries engaged in oil
and gas exploration and production in places as diverse as
Alaska, Canada, Latin America, and Africa. A subsidiary called
the Tenneco Corporation was formed that year to coordinate the
management of several company subsidiaries.

During this time, Tennessee Gas received some unfavorable
publicity, when reports surfaced that company's general counsel had met with FPC officials, including FPC chairperson
Jerome Kuykendall. Critics alleged that the group had privately
discussed legally restricted matters, but Symonds denied any
wrongdoing.

In February 1961, a corporate restructuring occurred that placed the company's non-utility subsidiaries, principally Tennessee Gas and Bay Petroleum, under the managerial authority of Tenneco. Acquisitions in the chemical industries continued through the 1960s and included the Heyden Newport Chemical Corporation, which formed the core of what later became Tenneco Chemicals, Inc. in March 1965. Moreover, the Tenneco division added a new line of business in June 1965 when it purchased the Packaging Corporation of America, a manufacturer of paperboard and packaging materials, with over 400,000 acres of timberland resources. Between September 1950 and March 1966, Tennessee Gas had acquired 22 companies.

A second corporate restructuring took place in April 1966, in which Tenneco assumed control over all the assets of Tennessee Gas, which then became a Tenneco subsidiary. Symonds was promoted from president and board chairman positions in which he had served since 1958, to chief executive officer and chief policy officer, in addition to being named the company's chairperson "for life."

Tenneco's most significant acquisition under Symonds came in August 1967, when it purchased the Kern County Land Company for approximately $430 million. Kern was established in California around 1850 by two lawyers from Kentucky, Lloyd Tevis and James Ben Ali Haggin, who intended to purchase land for resale to prospectors drawn to California in search of gold. Although the scheme failed, the subsequent development of irrigation systems transformed the 2.5 million acres of arid wasteland into arable cropland. Moreover, some of the land was later found to contain oil deposits. While the Kern Company lacked the expertise to develop these oil deposits, Tenneco was perfectly suited to develop the sites. At the same time, Tenneco had no immediate interest in Kern's agricultural businesses, but, as those businesses were profitable, they could easily be assimilated into Tenneco's existing land management group. The acquisition also included Kern's 53 percent interest in J.I. Case, a manufacturer of farm and construction machinery located in Wisconsin, and Walker Manufacturing, which produced automotive exhaust systems.

After the acquisition, Tenneco divided its subsidiaries along geographical lines, resulting in Tenneco West (formerly Kern) and Tenneco Virginia, which had grown out of the company's gas transmission business. In September 1968, Tenneco Virginia purchased Newport News Shipbuilding & Drydock Company for about $140 million. Newport News was engaged in the construction of nuclear-powered submarines and aircraft carriers, as well as merchant and commercial ships. The company also repaired and reconditioned ships, and refueled nuclear vessels. The nation's largest privately owned shipyard, Newport News was also in serious financial trouble.

Symonds died of a heart ailment on June 2, 1971. His method of expansion through diversification had been based on three rules: seeing that the company he wished to acquire would benefit from Tenneco management; choosing companies whose operations would complement those of Tenneco; and enforcing standards which kept each division "big enough to stand on its own two feet." Under Symonds's successor, James Lee Ketelsen, Tenneco continued to operate on these precepts, but the number and size of subsequent acquisitions were noticeably reduced.

The application of Tenneco management methods to Newport News had transformed the shipbuilding division into a successful venture by 1971. Over a period of several years, Tenneco invested nearly $100 million in the company, and, by 1973, the division had accumulated an order backlog of $1 billion. As a result of increased demand for imported petroleum products, Newport News engaged in the construction of large ships capable of carrying crude oil and liquefied natural gas.

In the course of restructuring Newport News Shipbuilding, Tenneco encountered strong opposition from organized labor and the Occupational Health and Safety Administration (OSHA). Eventually, after a three-month strike, all 16,500 employees of Newport News gained representation by the United Steelworkers. OSHA levied a fine of $786,190 on Newport News, citing 617 cases of deficient medical care, unsafe working conditions, and excessive noise. It was the largest fine OSHA had ever imposed on any company.

Wall Street analysts had consistently advised Tenneco to sell Newport News, warning that the division would require costly modernization and reorganization. Despite such problems, however, Tenneco officials recognized the subsidiary's potential, particularly after Navy Secretary John Lehman declared his intention to establish a 600-ship navy in 1981. Thereafter, Newport News abandoned commercial shipbuilding in favor of government defense contracts. Much of its initial work in this area centered on the Los Angeles -class attack submarine, which it designed and consistently delivered at a profit. Newport News was also the world's only manufacturer of nuclear-powered aircraft carriers, including the Carl Vinson and Theodore Roosevelt, launched in 1982 and 1986, respectively. Newport News also planned to construct servicing berths for the larger Trident submarines, then built exclusively by the Electric Boat division of General Dynamics.

Between 1968 and 1976, Tenneco acquired an additional 13 companies, including the British chemical company Albright & Wilson Ltd., and consolidated its ownership of J.I. Case. The automotive parts division of Tenneco experienced strong growth during the 1970s through the acquisition of AB Starlawerken of Sweden in 1974, Monroe Auto Equipment (best known for their line of shock absorbers) in 1977, and Lydex, a Danish company, in 1978. Tenneco started to purchase insurance companies in 1978, including Philadelphia Life and Southwestern Life Insurance.

Ketelsen, who was named chairperson and chief executive officer in 1978, was instrumental in the company's decision to convert its refinery at Chalamette, Louisiana, to process lower grades of crude oil from Venezuela and Mexico. In response to the reduction in oil prices, Tenneco redirected capital expenditures from oil and gas exploration into finding ways to produce oil at lower prices.

During the early 1980s, Tenneco sold its petrochemical and polyvinyl chloride production facilities to Occidental Petroleum. In 1984, to combat low gas prices and the adverse trends in the gas industry, Tenneco formed a new subsidiary called Tenngasco, which was responsible for sales of spot market gas in unregulated intrastate markets. Also that year, the Tenneco Packaging Corporation of America acquired Ecko Housewares and Ecko Products from the American Home Products Corporation.

In 1985, Tenneco purchased the farm machinery division of International Harvester, which had been forced to restructure as a result of a severe crisis in the American farming industry. Paying $430 million for the division, Tenneco then combined these operations with its Case subsidiary, which was also losing money. Tenneco officials believed that Case could benefit from Harvester's broader product line and stronger dealer network. The new combined group commanded a 35 percent market share for large tractors, a figure second only to Deere & Company's 42 percent. As a result of restructuring efforts and the temporary closure of several tractor plants, the new Case division registered a modest profit by the end of the year.

Having survived a 1982 attempt by stockholders to separate and sell the company's various divisions, the company was again considered a prime takeover target in 1987, given its high debt, rich assets, and record of underperformance. The company had previously insisted on paying stock dividends rather than reducing its debt or, in some other way, reducing its exposure to corporate raiders. But in the late 1980s, Tenneco began boosting its stock through massive repurchasing programs and debt retirement. From 1988 to 1990, the company bought back 26.3 million shares and paid off $5 billion in long- and short-term debt.

In 1986, Tenneco divested its five insurance companies to I.C.H. Corporation for about $1.5 billion. The company's late 1980s efforts to refocus its business interests included the sale of all its precious metals operations, the agricultural operations of Tenneco West, Tenneco Oil Company, and the retail muffler shops of Tenneco Automotive. At the same time, a new holding company, Tenneco Inc., was organized to serve as the corporation's principal financing vehicle.

Fine-tuning continued through the early 1990s under new leadership; in August 1991, Tenneco replaced James L. Ketelsen, who had lead the company for 13 years, with Michael H. Walsh. The new president, who soon became CEO as well, found a company in far worse shape than he had been led to believe. Earnings and cash flow were falling short of targets in nearly every division, and debt stood at 70 percent of capital—"unacceptable" results, as Walsh's 1991 letter to shareholders candidly observed. By the end of the year, Walsh had instituted a $2 billion action plan that incorporated several retrenchment initiatives in the face of a lingering global recession. Walsh, dubbed a "tough boss for tough times" by *Business Week*, cut Tenneco's dividend in half, eliminated 8,000 jobs, divested three short-line railroads and other non-core assets, issued $512 million in new equity, and reduced capital spending for the two-year period by $300 million.

Walsh instituted additional reorganizational measures in 1992, focusing on divestments and consolidation. Tenneco Minerals company was sold for $500 million, and Albright & Wilson's pulp chemicals business was spun off to Sterling Chemicals. Although the latter sale brought $202 million to the corporation, it also eliminated 54 percent of Albright & Wilson's annual profit. Tenneco's plans for the ensuing three years included consolidation and "resizing" of production capacity, divestment of unprofitable product lines, and privatization of company-owned retail outlets. After just 18 months at Tenneco's helm, Walsh had reversed potentially dangerous trends and instilled a "no excuses" policy in its corporate culture.

In January 1993, Walsh announced that he had been diagnosed with inoperable brain cancer. Walsh elected to stay on at Tenneco and see the conglomerate through the reorganization he had begun. He designated a new recruit, Dana G. Mead, head of the Case Corporation subsidiary, as his successor and began delegating more authority to Mead and the rest of Tenneco's senior management. In February 1994, Walsh yielded Tenneco's presidency and chief executive officership to Mead and accepted the post of chairman. By that time, Tenneco was a $13 billion conglomeration, having gone from two successive years of losses totaling over $2 billion to a 1993 net income of $426 million and having reduced its debt from 70 percent of capitalization to 49.3 percent. Mike Walsh died in May 1994.

Principal Subsidiaries: Tenneco Gas; Case Corporation; Tenneco Automotive; Newport News Shipbuilding; Packaging Corporation of America; Albright & Wilson (England).

Further Reading:

Bremner, Brian, "Tough Times, Tough Bosses," *Business Week,* November 25, 1991, pp. 174–79.

Huey, John, "Mike Walsh Takes on Brain Cancer," *Fortune,* February 22, 1993, pp. 76–77.

Sobel, Robert, *The Age of Giant Corporations,* Westport, Connecticut: Greenwood, 1972.

Tenneco's First 35 Years, Houston: Tenneco Inc., 1978.

—updated by April Dougal Gasbarre

Trizec Corporation Ltd.

855-2 Street SW
Calgary, Alberta T2P 4J7
Canada
(403) 263 7120
Fax: (403) 265 7301

Public Company
Incorporated: 1960
Employees: 9,120
Assets: C$1.23 billion (US$920.60 million)
Stock Exchanges: Toronto

Trizec Corporation Ltd. is a leading Canadian property development company, with approximately 160 income properties comprising about 75 million square feet of office and retail space spread across North America. Trizec also owns eight hotels and a 70 percent stake in Bramalea Ltd., the Toronto-based property development company with a $5 billion office and retail portfolio in Ontario and California. Its other holdings include full control of nursing home chain Central Park Lodge; 100 percent ownership of the Hahn Company, the U.S. shopping center developer with 50 retail sites; and a 23 percent stake in the Rouse Company, the U.S. publicly listed development company with $1.85 billion in assets.

Trizec was founded in 1960 by William Zeckendorf, one of North America's most colorful property developers of the postwar era. Born in 1905 in Paris, Illinois, Zeckendorf worked in his father's general store and then attended New York University. Before acquiring a degree, however, Zeckendorf dropped out of school and took a job as a real estate agent in New York City, where he worked for 13 years.

Then, in 1938, Zeckendorf went to work for Webb & Knapp, a New York City real estate firm. There he managed Vincent Astor's $50 million property portfolio while Astor served in the navy. Before long, Zeckendorf added $5 million in assets to the Astor portfolio, securing for himself a reward check in the amount of $350,000 and requesting that Webb & Knapp "send him a bunch of flowers." The real estate company did more than that; when Zeckendorf offered to buy the company, Webb & Knapp assented.

In 1946, Zeckendorf sold 17 acres of land on New York's east side to John D. Rockefeller for what would eventually become the site of the United Nations Building. In 1953, the wealthy businessman, whose empire had grown to $300 million in assets, bought a group of buildings in New York City, including the Chrysler Building, an art deco landmark on Lexington Avenue. Soon Zeckendorf began redeveloping property in downtown Denver, Washington, and Chicago.

In 1956, he turned to the Place Ville Marie development in Montreal, which Zeckendorf sought to model after New York's Grand Central Station and Rockefeller Center. The development was ambitious: the $1.5 million project was to be built on 23 acres of land in downtown Montreal owned by the Canadian National Railway, the country's major rail carrier. However, the development proved financially inviable, and too much time was spent looking for retail and commercial tenants for the complex. By 1960, Zeckendorf looked to outside partners to carry the development. Webb & Knapp (Canada) Ltd. formed a partnership, called Trizec Ltd., with Eagle Star Insurance, a British insurance company, and Eagle Star's property arm Second Covent Garden Property. The name Trizec in fact combined "Tri", for three, "Z" for Zeckendorf, "E" for Eagle Star, and "C" for Covent Garden.

Zeckendorf originally held a 50 percent stake in Trizec. But, in 1963, Webb & Knapp backed out of the Montreal development, and Eagle Star stepped in for Zeckendorf to take a larger share of Trizec for itself. By 1965, Zeckendorf's empire began to crumble as Webb & Knapp was put into U.S. bankruptcy court. That forced Zeckendorf from the head of Trizec, and he was replaced that year by James Soden, a Montreal lawyer. Joined by Bill Hay, another Toronto lawyer, the two built Trizec up through acquisition and construction of properties in Toronto.

By 1968, Trizec had become Canada's largest publicly owned real estate company, with assets of $241 million. That portfolio was up from assets worth $179 million a year earlier. Chief among those assets were several suburban shopping malls, including Yorkdale Plaza, a giant development in North Toronto.

In 1970, Trizec acquired Cummings Properties Ltd, a Montreal-based property concern, with assets of $115 million. Cummings had formed a few joint ventures with Great West International Equities Ltd., founded by Calgary developer Sam Hashman. Trizec moved quickly to take control of Great West, and because Edward and Peter Bronfman maintained a large interest in Hashman's dealings, the two brothers were brought onto the Trizec board, and given nine percent of the property company's equity.

Brothers Edward and Peter were the nephews of Sam Bronfman, founder of the mighty Seagram liquor empire. While much of the Bronfman inheritance had gone to older brothers Edgar and Charles, Edward and Peter Bronfman hired well-known Touche Ross investment analysts Trevor Eyton and Jack Cockwell to join their organization, Edper Investments, in 1969. Together, Eyton and Cockwell would build Edper Investments into a labyrinth of crossholdings among Canada's largest corporations.

Property was to figure prominently in the Edper empire. Trizec had been expanding into the U.S. property market through Trizec's 51 percent owned subsidiary, Tristar Developments Inc. But, in 1975, Peter Bronfman asked James Soden of Trizec whether the company would consider allowing Edper to "Canadianize" Trizec. While Eagle Insurance of Britain still held a majority stake in Trizec, it had become concerned with the Canadian government's Foreign Investment Review Agency (FIRA), introduced in 1974, to regulate overseas investment. The British insurer feared FIRA would make raising money in Canada difficult for foreign companies. So Edper offered to leave Eagle Star with a controlling interest in Trizec, while effective control would move to a new holding company, Carena Properties, in the Edper camp.

The deal was concluded, and in 1976 the Bronfmans took control of Trizec, moving quickly to depose Soden from the company boardroom. Shortly thereafter Soden was fired, and Bill Hay left the company to join Olympia & York, then controlled by the Reichmann brothers, rival Canadian property developers. Edper appointed Harold Milavsky, who had come up through the Hashman empire, to replace Soden as president and chief executive of Trizec. Milavsky, an Alberta executive, would eventually see the move of Trizec's head office to Calgary, away from Montreal, because he preferred to live in the oil city where he had most of his business contacts.

By 1979, Trizec's assets surpassed the $1 billion mark. The company had become so strong that in January of that year the Reichmann brothers considered Trizec a possible takeover target. That month, brothers Paul and Albert Reichmann visited the offices of English Property, in which Eagle Star held a 21 percent stake, and met with executive Stanley Honeyman. They were informed that for the right price Honeyman might sell them English Property.

A bidding war for English property ensued between Olympia & York, NV Beleggingsmaatschppij Wereldhave—a Dutch real estate company—and Eagle Star Insurance. Having worked hard to build Trizec up, the Bronfman brothers feared that the Reichmanns were looking to take the company away from them by buying English Property. Edper therefore considered Olympia & York's interest in English Property unfriendly. By February 22, 1979, the Reichmanns had paid for 7.6 million shares in English Property and launched a 50 pence per share bid for all remaining shares. Eagle Star had already tendered to the Reichmanns their 21 percent stake in the company.

The Bronfmans encouraged the Dutch real estate company to offer 56 pence per share for all outstanding English Property shares. The Reichmanns responded by upping their bid to 60 pence per share and announced "... it is not Trizec we are bidding for but English Property." While Olympia & York let the current arrangements between Edper and Trizec stand, the Bronfmans were not consoled. In March, Edper prepared plans to enter the bidding war for English Property, which by now had driven up the price of shares on the London stock market above the Reichmann's 60 pence per share offer.

According to one account, Trevor Eyton and Harold Milavsky were dispatched to London, and while seated in their hotel lobby, they saw Paul Reichmann enter the hotel to check in. The two Edper executives walked over to greet Reichmann, who in turn suggested that they might sit down and talk. Ten minutes later, the three men reached a general agreement on how Trizec would be run, an arrangement that would be finalized a week later in Montreal. The agreement stipulated that the Bronfmans would not challenge Olympia & York's bid for English Property, and the Reichmanns would in turn allow Edper to increase its stake in Trizec. Moreover, Olympia & York and Trizec agreed to avoid conflicts of interest between Canada's two largest property development concerns. Thus, two families gained control of Trizec, with the Reichmanns and the Bronfman brothers receiving an equal 37 percent stake in the property company.

In November 1980, Trizec completed its acquisition of Ernest W. Hahn Inc. Paying $267 million for the regional shopping center developer and owner, Trizec financed the purchase by a mixture of equity and debt, including a note of $88 million issued to Hahn shareholders. With the Hahn acquisition, Trizec's own asset base rose to the $2 billion mark. That year the developer completed $113 million worth of new property construction, most in western Canada and the southwestern United States. Furthermore, most Trizec properties were located in prime downtown sites in major North American cities.

In 1981, the company bought 20.5 percent of the common shares belonging to The Rouse Company of Columbia, Maryland. Rouse, like Hahn, developed shopping centers and specialty retail centers, most in the eastern part of the United States. That year, Trizec reported more than $700 million worth of property scheduled for completion in the next 24 months, as well as $1.5 billion worth of developments to come onboard by 1986. This growth was important because shareholders measured the worth of property companies by the rental income they derived from properties they own or manage. Therefore the more developments they have in the works, the more income shareholders can expect from the company's asset portfolio, providing a potentially stable growing source of cash flow from ongoing leases and renewals.

In June 1982, on the steps of Place Ville Marie, Trizec celebrated the 20th anniversary of the downtown Montreal office complex that prompted the formation of the company. By the following year, the Rouse and Hahn stock acquisitions had ensured that 82 percent of Trizec's rentable properties were in the U.S. market. Nevertheless, the company did not neglect the Canadian market, and in 1983 Trizec bought a further 50 percent interest in Lougheed Mall in Burnaby, just outside Vancouver, British Columbia. This purchase took the company to full ownership of the shopping mall. At the same time, Trizec sold its 50 percent stake in Brentwood Mall, also in Burnaby. In August of that year, Trizec sold its mobile home division and bought three nursing homes in Philadelphia, bringing tenant capacity in Central Park Lodges, its nursing home division, to 4,930 people.

The mid-1980s brought an improved economic climate for Trizec. In the company's 1983 annual report, President Milavsky commented: "We are experiencing a gradual return to economic health in 1984. Trizec enters 1984 having established itself as the premier public real estate company with the largest portfolio of income producing properties in North America."

In 1985, Trizec expanded by increasing its interest in rival Canadian property developer Bramalea Ltd. to 31 percent, with an option from a major shareholder to increase that stake to 43 percent. For shareholders, the purchase meant gaining an impressive one-third stake in a rival property developer with more than $2 billion worth of assets in its portfolio. Specifically, Bramalea's assets included more than 20 million square feet of retail, commercial, and industrial real estate in 95 buildings across North America. In addition, Bramalea was also a community developer, home builder and, through Coseka Resources Ltd., had oil and gas interests.

In the company's 1985 annual report, Milavsky warned shareholders that major urban centers in North America were "overbuilt," and that Trizec would have to be aggressive in pursuing specific opportunities. By 1986, Trizec's own asset base had topped $4 billion, with investments in more than 136 properties across North America. Among the company's developments that year were a retail center in Escondido, California, and two office buildings and the Horton Plaza in San Diego.

During this time, Trizec exercised its option to increase its stake in rival Bramalea to 43 percent. And by November of that year, Trizec had gained control of Bramalea by pushing its ownership stake to 65 percent. This prompted both companies to combine their retail assets in a new entity, Trilea Centers Inc. Trilea would own and operate 28 shopping centers across Canada comprising in total 13.4 million square feet.

Trizec also expanded on the residential real estate front. Adding Florida Life Care Corporation of Sarasota, Florida, to its portfolio, Trizec moved beyond operating homes for senior citizens to providing rental accommodation and housing as well.

Unprecedented expansion was facilitated when Trizec completed an issue of $100 million of preferred shares, bumping up its shareholders equity to $1 billion on a book basis, a measure of the company's asset base. In 1987, an additional $100 million preferred share issue was completed, as was an issue of ordinary shares worth $171.25 million, bringing shareholders' equity to $1.1 billion on a book value basis. The company's market capitalization at the time reached $3 million.

That year Trizec announced plans to build the Bay-Adelaide Financial Center in a 50–50 joint venture with Markborough Properties, a development with office and retail rental properties. Furthermore, in July 1988, Trizec's interest in Bramalea was raised to 70 percent after a purchase of 3.65 million Bramalea shares. The company opened eight new developments that year—three office buildings and five retail shopping centers, comprising 3.5 million square feet.

However, while Trizec was enjoying unprecedented property development and rental income growth, the Canadian economy was heading for a severe recession. By 1990, decreased consumer spending had affected retail sales, which reflected on Trilea's shopping center performance. Furthermore, rising operating costs and competition in the senior citizens' housing market undercut margins in that industry for Trizec, while reduced housing prices owing to recessionary pressures affected housing sales for the company.

The threat of too much commercial and retail space coming on the market, creating a buyer's market in which rents plunged, loomed large. Nevertheless, Trizec company chairperson Milavsky remarked in the company's 1991 annual report: "Our office portfolio continued to generate stable cash flow, although several new properties, which are still in the lease-up stage, were added to the rental stream during the year."

As a result of the difficult economic climate, construction work on the joint venture Bay-Adelaide Center was delayed until late 1994, as a glut of space in Toronto's financial district dramatically undercut leasing of the project. In the interim, a development that was to become the centerpiece of Trizec's Toronto property holdings remained little more than a multilevel parking lot.

In 1991, Trizec sought to strengthen its balance sheet by reducing its overhanging debt levels. Plans included selling nonstrategic property holdings and reducing land holdings. However, the company looked to sell into a buyer's market, where prices for property, especially in the Toronto and New York markets, were falling steadily. Trizec also looked to streamline its own operations to reduce business overheads. It announced it would delay new developments until market conditions improved and current projects had a chance to contribute to cash flow, rather producing a drain on the company's profit line. In addition, asset sales were made to reduce the company's debt, and in September 1992, Trizec sold 9.5 million of the 11 million shares it held in The Rouse Company to U.S. investors for around $140 million.

Of particular concern to the Trizec board was the failing fortunes of subsidiary Bramalea. For the first six months of 1992, rental income for Trizec, excluding Bramalea, was up three percent to $683.7 million, compared with $664.3 million in the same period a year earlier. But Bramalea, in the same period, posted a loss of $34 million in its rental income, and a negative cash flow of $22.3 million. In addition, Trizec had to make welltime asset purchases of Bramalea to prevent it from falling into the bankruptcy court, a move that required extra borrowing.

Milavsky commented in September 1992: "In addition to the ongoing challenge of maintaining profitability during these uncertain times, considerable time has been devoted to supporting Bramalea with its restructuring efforts. We continue to believe that a consensual restructuring of Bramalea is in the interest of shareholders, bringing about greater stability and the opportunity to share in renewed growth in the years ahead."

By the end of 1992, Trizec's own $5.1 billion debt load prompted the departure of Milavsky after 16 years at the company helm. He was replaced by Willard L'Heureux, who became Trizec president as well as co-chief executive officer. He would act in that position alongside existing CEO Kevin Benson.

In addition, Trizec's boardroom was completely revamped. The number of board members was cut from 25 to 16. Furthermore, another seven board members belonging to the insolvent Olympia & York Developments Ltd. departed. That company's 36 percent stake in Trizec would go to a cluster of international banks whose loans to O&Y were secured by Trizec shares. Also in December 1992, Trizec announced a $669 million writedown on its investments in Bramalea.

Writedowns figured large in Trizec's profit line. Rental income in 1992 was posted at $419 million, up slightly from $415 million the year before. But the company provided $175 million for losses on its undeveloped properties, reflecting the steep fall in property values during the recession. That, and its Bramalea writedown, produced a loss for 1992 of $544 million, against a profit of $62 million a year earlier.

Trizec's stock price continued to fall from a high of nearly $28 a share in 1989 to $1.80 currently. Analysts speculate that resolving Trizec's problems will depend on management's ability to solve the company's outstanding problems and the banking community's return to providing loans to property companies. Trizec faces $2.39 billion worth of debt maturing over the next three years. That figure will need to be refinanced, and the company's scramble for cash will be difficult at a time when international banks are taking a hard line on real estate lending after the O&Y debacle.

If Trizec finds it too difficult to sell assets in a buyer's market, the company will have little alternative but to open talks with its creditors to restructure its debt. In March 1993, Trizec sold its remaining 1.5 million shares in The Rouse Company for $24 million. Trizec also faced $56.6 million worth of Swiss franc debentures coming due in October 1993 and $149.9 million worth of preferred shares due to be redeemed by the end of the year. Like Bramalea, Trizec may propose to defer or reduce the financial pressure of these payments. Then the company's shareholders and creditors will know whether Trizec's financial problems are insurmountable or whether continuing rental income and asset sales can provide help it stay afloat.

Principal Subsidiaries: Trizec Equities Ltd.; Trilea Centres Inc.

Further Reading:

Peter Foster, *The Master Builders,* Toronto: Penguin, 1986.
''Trizec Asking Lenders for 'Half a Chance','' *Globe and Mail,* February 26, 1993.
''Trizec Changed, Problems Persist,'' *Globe and Mail,* March 31, 1993.
''Trizec's Debt Troubles Prompt Shuffle,'' *Globe and Mail,* February 5, 1993.

—Etan Vlessing

USSC ™

United States Surgical Corporation

150 Glover Avenue
Norwalk, Connecticut 06856
U.S.A.
(203) 845-1000
Fax: (203) 845-4125

Public Company
Incorporated: 1964
Employees: 8,100
Sales: $1.2 billion
Stock Exchanges: New York
SICs: 3841 Surgical & Medical Instruments; 3842 Surgical
   Appliances & Supplies

The United States Surgical Corporation (USSC) is a leading producer of tools for use in surgery, including staplers, sutures, and laparoscopic instruments. The company was founded in the 1960s by an entrepreneur who had no background in medicine but had an idea about how to use staples in surgery and pioneered the development of this market in the United States. In the late 1980s USSC introduced another innovation in surgical techniques when it began to market tubes and other devices that allowed operations that were far less invasive than conventional procedures. On the strength of this new technique, the company's fortunes soared in the early 1990s, only to be deflated in the mid-1990s as uncertainty in the health care industry as a whole set in.

USSC was founded in 1964 by Leon Hirsch, the owner of a small, unsuccessful dry-cleaning equipment business. With only a high school education, Hirsch nevertheless had an avid interest in gadgets and in biology, and he often stopped by the office of a patent broker in New York City, where he lived, to see what was around. One day in the spring of 1963 he happened across a wooden device on the man's desk that looked like a shillelagh. Hirsch was told that the mystery object was used by doctors in Hungary and Russia to make stitches, instead of silk thread, as was used in the United States.

The surgical stapler, as it was known, had first been invented in Hungary in 1908, at a time when many surgery patients died of infection from contamination of their wounds. With the stapler, an area inside the body could be clamped off before any cutting was done, which cut down dramatically on the loss of blood and other fluids. However, the stapler was extremely cumbersome

and time consuming to use. It took two hours to assemble, and a second person had to feed individual stainless steel staples into it with tweezers in order for a surgeon to use it.

Looking at the stapler, Hirsch had the inspiration that a disposable cartridge of staples would simplify the instrument's use enormously. In the basement of his house, he made a prototype cartridge stapler out of balsa wood, and then spent $75,000 of his savings to have a metal version of his model made. Two surgeons at Johns Hopkins medical school in Baltimore tested the new device, and on the basis of their strong recommendation, Hirsch was able to line up $2 million in financing from two other investors to develop and market the product. In 1964 he incorporated the United States Surgical Company, with four employees.

From 1964 to 1967 Hirsch and his partners worked to refine their prototype and to develop a variety of other surgical instruments. They made this effort so that they would be able to spread the costs of their marketing activities among a number of different products. In 1967 USSC finally began to sell its products, distributing them through wholesalers of surgical supplies. The company's main product, the surgical stapler that Hirsch had first developed, looked like a stainless steel wrench. It had a hooked end, and a slot for a staple cartridge. A surgeon placed the hooked end around the area to be closed, tightened the clamp, and then pulled a trigger to insert the staple. With this device, blood loss and injury to tissue was minimized, and time spent in surgery was sharply reduced. The device was used primarily for abdominal and thoracic surgery when it was first introduced.

In its first two years, USSC successfully sold staplers to a large number of surgeons. In 1967 sales totaled $350,000. By 1969, the company's sales had reached $1 million. However, the company had also racked up $1 million worth of losses. Surgeons were buying the stapler, but they weren't using it; USSC had counted on making its money from sales of the staple cartridges, which were disposable and had to be purchased again and again.

The company found that surgeons were instinctively cautious and conservative in the operating room, reverting in an operation to the techniques they knew best and had been trained to use. Only those surgeons who had been personally trained in the operating room by one of Hirsch's employees had made the switch to regular staple use. USSC tried a number of different solutions to the problem of how to combine sales with training. First, 20 registered nurses were hired to act as technical instructors, training surgeons in the use of staplers in the operating room. This method worked, but it proved too expensive to be practical.

Then, Hirsch hired medics and paramedics leaving the army, and asked them to sell the stapler and to train surgeons. Although they had a sound medical background, Hirsch found that they were poor salesmen. Finally, in 1972 USSC hit upon the solution of hiring experienced salespeople, and then giving them medical training. The company developed a 240-hour course that covered many aspects of basic medicine, which was supplemented by 40 hours of training in an animal laboratory, where actual surgery was done. Overall, the training of each salesperson cost $8,000. To motivate its sales force, the company paid no regular salaries to salespeople, but only commissions, and dismissed employees quickly if they failed to perform well.

By the late 1970s, these efforts, as well as a high pressure corporate culture, had driven USSC's sales to new heights, allowing the company to grow rapidly. From a base line of 20,000 patients who had operations with staples in 1969, the company's market had grown to include 700,000 patients. In addition, the company had expanded its operations to Europe, training sales representatives to begin introducing surgical staples in that market.

At this time, however, clouds began to appear on the horizon. As USSC had contracted out its manufacturing when demand for its product grew, the company's standards of quality control had slipped. To ameliorate this problem, USSC began to build new factories for its products in Puerto Rico and North Haven, Connecticut.

For many years, USSC had had the surgical staple market largely to itself. In 1977, however, one of its main competitors, Johnson & Johnson's Ethicon division, entered the surgical staple market with a disposable stapler, which eliminated the need for the costly cleaning and maintenance of the re-usable stapler. The Ethicon stapler immediately became popular, and temporarily captured a large portion of USSC's external wound closure market.

To counter this threat, USSC launched a four-year, $100-million development program to make up lost ground. The company announced that it would market its own disposable stapler, and that it would also move into new areas of medical supplies, like intravenous feeding sets and electronic vital signs monitors. These new products would have their own sales force.

Also in 1977 USSC decided to replace its network of independent distributors with its own operations. In response, one of its unemployed distributors moved to Australia and set up a competitor to USSC called Hospital Products, Inc., which began to market very similar products in the United States and Australia. USSC responded by suing Hospital Products, Inc., for a variety of infractions, including patent violations and misrepresentation. Hospital Products responded with legal action of its own, charging unfair competition and anti-trust violations, and the cluster of suits provoked a frenzy of backbiting and name-calling that went on as the legal actions dragged on into the mid-1980s.

Despite its rapid growth throughout the 1970s, USSC allegedly began in 1979 to engage in a series of illegal practices that were designed to inflate its sales figures. As the Securities and Exchange Commission (S.E.C.) later claimed, the company used fraudulent accounting practices and shipped faked or non-existent orders in order to pump up its sales figures. In 1981, for instance, USSC claimed profits of $12.9 million, when in fact the S.E.C. calculated that it had earned only $200,000. In February, 1984, under pressure from the Securities and Exchange Commission, USSC agreed to cut its earnings claims by a total of $26 million for the years 1979 to 1982, and some of its managers agreed to give back bonuses they had earned in earlier years for fraudulently computed sales gains.

In addition, USSC was charged with a variety of illicit sales practices, all of which pointed to an atmosphere of extreme pressure within the company to sell. Salespeople complained that they were forced or encouraged to dump USSC products on hospitals and to engage in a number of dishonest practices, such as hiding products, stealing them, wasting them, writing phony orders, adding zeros to numbers on order forms, and sending products that hadn't been ordered and then refusing to take them back. In 1980, in response to complaints from hospitals about overshipment, USSC revamped its sales management and fired 20 employees. In 1983 the company also moved to reduce pressure on its sales force by changing the structure of its payment from 100 percent commission on increase in sales, to half salary.

Despite these difficulties, by 1982 USSC's sales had risen to $160 million. Although the company's growth slowed in the following year, as cost-conscious hospitals cut back on inventory, the company's sales nonetheless rose to $180 million. By 1984, USSC controlled 90 percent of the market for internal surgical staples and the majority of the market for external, skin staples.

USSC had diversified its product line to include 13 more products in 1981, and in 1984 it introduced a new technological breakthrough: absorbable staples, which made staple removal unnecessary. While absorbable suture thread had existed for years, the company's new product introduced this quality to the stapling procedure. In the mid-1980s USSC also embarked on a program to enter the suture market. In 1987 the company won a ruling from the Food & Drug Administration streamlining the process for approval of new suture materials, and it announced plans to introduce its suture materials by the early 1990s.

By far the most important development of 1987 for USSC, however, was the introduction of the Surgiport trocar, a disposable tube-like device through which other surgical instruments were inserted into the body. The company had purchased exclusive rights to this technology from a company called EndoTherapeutics in the previous year. This gadget eventually opened the door to laparoscopic surgery, in which very small incisions were made in the body so that a camera could be inserted, enabling a surgeon to operate using instruments channeled through narrow tubes. This technique reduced the need for large incisions, which required long periods of recovery for the patient.

In the late 1980s USSC came under fire from animal rights activists for its use of dogs as laboratory animals. For years, the company had used hundreds of dogs to train its sales force in surgical techniques, and also to train doctors in the use of its instruments. Activists complained that these practices were unnecessary and constituted cruelty to animals, and the company was plagued by a number of vociferous protest demonstrations. In 1988 a bomb was placed neared Hirsch's parking place by an animal rights protestor, but USSC's company security had infiltrated the movement and was able to prevent the bomb from doing any harm.

Contrary to the wishes of the animal rights protestors, USSC's financial fortunes skyrocketed in the early 1990s. Although the company sold only $10 million worth of laparoscopic tools in

1987, three years later the company introduced the "Endo Clip," which allowed laparoscopic gall bladder removal, and the market for these tools began to grow rapidly. Soon, laparoscopy was also being used for hernia operations, appendectomies, hysterectomies, and other types of abdominal surgery.

With a virtual monopoly on sales of the equipment for these operations, USSC saw its sales grow by 50 percent in 1990 and 75 percent in the first half of 1991. Earnings during that time grew by 78 percent, and by the end of the year, they had nearly doubled since 1990. USSC sold more than $300 million worth of laparoscopic equipment in 1991, to become one of the fastest-growing companies in America, with profits of $91 million. The company's stock price kept pace with its spectacular increase in business, and many of USSC's executives who owned stock found themselves millionaires.

Hirsch predicted ample room for growth in the laparoscopic field, as the technique was adapted to an ever greater number of surgical tasks, and USSC set out to market a package of laparoscopic tools, surgical staples, and sutures. In addition, the company began a major push to market its products in Europe, building a new sales and distribution center in France. Overall, one quarter of USSC's revenues came from foreign sales.

By 1992, 85 percent of all gall bladder procedures in the United States were performed using laparoscopic techniques. At the end of that year, USSC's revenues had topped a $1 billion, of which half was contributed by laparoscopic products. The company's stupendous success with these instruments had attracted a competitor: industry giant Johnson & Johnson formed Ethicon Endo-Surgery and vowed to introduce 40 competing products. In response to this threat, and the presence of other competitors in the field, USSC brought suit alleging patent infringement.

In January, 1993, USSC won a suit against a subsidiary of Eli Lilly & Company in which its opponent was ordered to stop making and marketing its products. By the middle of the year, however, the company's luck had changed, as its sales dropped dramatically in the face of price competition from its other competitor, Ethicon. In July, 1993, USSC reported a quarterly loss of $22 million. A switch in distribution practices, to a more prompt just-in-time delivery system, caused an unexpectedly sharp fall-off in sales, as hospitals used up the back-log of

products that had stockpiled on their shelves, confident that they could acquire more when they needed them.

By September, 1993, USSC was still struggling with the effects of a vast oversupply of its products, and its stock price had gone into a steep slide. Anxiety over the possible effects of health care reform, as well as the maturation of the market for gall bladder instruments and a drop-off in popularity of other laparoscopic procedures, also helped to depress USSC's sales. The company's heavy investments in manufacturing capacity, which had caused it to go into debt, further damaged USSC's financial results, and the company embarked upon a plan to reduce expenditures.

In October, 1993, USSC announced another quarter of losses and specified the cost-cutting procedures it would adopt. The company planned to lay off eight percent of its work force (700 people), cut executive pay, and reduce its stock dividend. In an effort to reduce the oversupply of its products, USSC announced that it would shut down its factories for two weeks in the fall and then re-open them on a four-day work week. In December, 1993, the company announced further cuts as its financial woes continued, and it took a $130 million charge against its earnings to pay for its restructuring.

In February, 1994, USSC began to seek investors to infuse badly needed cash into the company. This move came after USSC lost a suit it had brought against Ethicon for patent infringement, removing the possibility of a big cash settlement to strengthen its balance sheet. With uncertainty about the future of the health care industry continuing into the mid-1990s, USSC's ultimate fate also appeared to be up in the air.

Further Reading:

Driscoll, Lisa, "U.S. Surgical Has Hearts Beating Faster," *Business Week,* August 12, 1991.

Feder, Barnaby J., "Feuding by Hospital Suppliers," *New York Times,* August 25, 1981.

Kleinfeld, N. R., "U.S. Surgical's Checkered History," *New York Times,* May 11, 1984.

Smart, Tim, "Will U.S. Surgical's Cutting Edge Be Enough," *Business Week,* September 21, 1992.

Smith, Geoffrey, "The guts to say 'I was wrong,' " *Forbes,* May 28, 1979.

Teitelman, Robert, "Case Study," *Forbes,* May 7, 1984.

—Elizabeth Rourke

United Technologies Corporation

United Technologies Building
Hartford, Connecticut 06101
U.S.A.
(203) 728-7000
Fax: (203) 728-7944

Public Company
Incorporated: 1934 as United Aircraft Company
Employees: 168,600
Sales: $20.74 billion
Stock Exchanges: New York London Paris Frankfurt Geneva
   Lausanne Basel Zurich Brussels Amsterdam
SICs: 3585 Refrigeration and Heating Equipment; 3534
   Elevators and Moving Stairway; 3724 Aircraft Engines
   and Engine Parts; 3721 Aircraft; 3812 Search and
   Navigation Equipment; 3714 Motor Vehicle Parts and
   Accessories; 3764 Space Propulsion Units and Parts

United Technologies Corporation is one of the largest conglomerates in the U.S. military/industrial complex. The company's reputation for keeping a low profile is primarily the result of its diversified holdings, which include Pratt & Whitney aircraft engines, Carrier Corp. air conditioners, the Otis Elevator Co., automotive parts for original equipment manufacturers, and Flight Systems helicopters and flight controls. Despite economic struggles in the early 1990s, United remained profitable, with its Pratt & Whitney engine division powering almost three-fourths of the world's commercial aircraft.

United traces its origins to Fred Rentschler, who founded the Pratt & Whitney Aircraft Company in 1925 as one of the first companies to specialize in the manufacture of engines, or "power plants," for airframe builders. Pratt & Whitney's primary customers were two airplane manufacturers, Bill Boeing and Chance Vought. Interested in securing a market for his company's engines, Rentschler convinced Boeing and Vought to join him in forming a new company called the United Aircraft and Transportation Company. The company was formed in 1929, and thereafter Pratt & Whitney, Boeing, and Vought gave exclusive priority to each other's business.

Early in its history, United Aircraft became so successful that it was soon able to purchase other important suppliers and competitors, establishing a strong monopoly. The group grew to include Boeing, Pratt & Whitney, and Vought, as well as

Sikorsky, Stearman, and Northrop (airframes); Hamilton Aero Manufacturing and Standard Steel Prop (propellers); and Stout Airlines, in addition to Boeing's airline companies.

The men who led these individual divisions of United Aircraft exchanged stock in their original companies for stock in United. The strong public interest in the larger company drove the value of United Aircraft's stock up in subsequent flotations. The original shareholders quickly became very wealthy; Rentschler himself had turned a meager $253 cash investment into $35.5 million by 1929.

During this time, U.S. Postmaster William Folger Brown cited United Aircraft as the largest airline network and the most stable equipment supplier in the country. Thus, the company was assured of winning the postal service's lucrative airmail contracts before it applied for them. The company's airmail business required the manufacturing division to devote all of its resources to expansion of the airline division. Soon United Aircraft controlled nearly half of the nation's airline and aircraft business, becoming a classic example of an aeronautic monopoly.

In 1934, Senator Hugo Black initiated an investigation of fraud and improprieties in the aeronautics business. Bill Boeing was called to the witness stand, and subsequent interrogation exposed United Aircraft's monopolistic business practices, eventually leading to the break-up of the huge aeronautic combine. Thereafter, Boeing sold all of his stock in his company and retired. In the reorganization of the corporation, all manufacturing interests west of the Mississippi went to Boeing Airplane in Seattle, everything east of the river went to Rentschler's United Aircraft in Hartford, and the transport services became a third independent company under the name of United Air Lines which was based in Chicago.

Chance Vought died in 1930, and his company, along with Pratt & Whitney, Sikorsky, Ham Standard and Northrop, became part of the new United Aircraft Company. Sikorsky became a principal manufacturer of helicopters, Pratt & Whitney continued to build engines, and Vought later produced a line of airplanes including the Corsair and the Cutlass.

At the onset of World War II, business increased dramatically at United's Pratt & Whitney division. The company produced several hundred thousand engines for airplanes built by Boeing, Lockheed, McDonnell Douglas, Grumman, and Vought. Over half the engines in American planes were built by Pratt & Whitney. After the war, United Aircraft turned its attention to producing jet engines. The Pratt & Whitney subsidiary's entrance into the jet engine industry was hindered, however, as customers were constantly demanding improvements in the company's piston-driven Wasp engine. In the meantime, Pratt & Whitney's competitors, General Electric and Westinghouse, were free to devote more of their capital to the research and development of jet engines. Thus, when airframe builders started looking for jet engine suppliers, Pratt & Whitney was unprepared. Even United Aircraft's Vought division had to purchase turbo jets for its Cutlass model from Westinghouse.

Recognizing the gravity of the situation, United Aircraft began an ambitious program to develop a line of advanced jet engines. When the Korean War began in 1950, Pratt & Whitney was again deluged with orders. The mobilization of forces gave the company the opportunity to re-establish its strong relationship with the Navy and conduct business with its newly created Air Force.

In the early 1950s, United Aircraft experienced a conflict of interest between its airframe and engine manufacturing subsidiaries, as Vought's alternate engine suppliers—Westinghouse and General Motors' Allison division—were reluctant to do business with a company so closely associated with their competitor, Pratt & Whitney. On the other hand, Pratt & Whitney's other customers, Grumman, McDonnell, and Douglas, were concerned that their airframe technology would find its way to Vought. As a result, both of United Aircraft's divisions were suffering, and, in 1954, the board of directors voted to dissolve Vought.

In 1959, Fred Rentschler died, following a long illness, at the age of 68. Commenting on Rentschler's role in developing engine technology to keep pace with that of the Soviet Union, a reporter in the *New York Times* stated: "This nation's air superiority is due in no small measure to Mr. Rentschler's vision and talents." Rentschler was succeeded as president of United Aircraft by W. P. Gwinn, while Jack Horner became chairman of the company's subsidiary, Pratt & Whitney.

United Aircraft continued to manufacture engines and a variety of other aircraft accessories into the 1960s. Much of its business came from Boeing, which had several Pentagon contracts and whose 700-series jets were capturing 60 percent of the commercial airliner market. When Horner retired in 1968, he was succeeded by Gwinn. While this change in leadership was of little consequence to United Aircraft, which was running smoothly, Pratt & Whitney was about to enter a period of crisis.

First, there was considerable trouble with Pratt & Whitney's engines for Boeing's 747 jumbo jet. The problem, traced to a design flaw, cost Pratt & Whitney millions of dollars in research and redevelopment. Moreover, it also cost millions of dollars for Boeing in service calls and lost sales. Commercial airline companies suffered lost revenue from cancelled flights and reduced passenger capacity.

By 1971, the performance of the Pratt & Whitney division had begun to depress company profits. The directors of United Aircraft acted quickly by hiring a new president, Harry Gray, who was drafted away from Litton Industries. Harry Gray was born Harry Jack Grusin in 1919. He suffered the loss of his mother at age six and was entrusted to the care of his sister in Chicago, when his father's business was ruined in the Depression. In 1936, he entered the University of Illinois at Urbana, earning a degree in journalism before serving in Europe with General Patton's Third Army infantry and artillery during World War II. After the war, he returned to Urbana, where he received a Master's degree in journalism. In Chicago, Grusin went through a succession of jobs, working as a truck salesperson and as a manager of a transport company. In 1951, he changed his name to Harry Gray, according to the court record, for "no reason." He moved to California in 1954 to work for the Litton Industries conglomerate, and he spent the next 17 years at Litton working his way up the corporate ladder.

Hindered in promotion at Litton by superiors who weren't due to retire for several years, Gray accepted an offer from United Aircraft. While at Litton, Gray had been invited to tour General Electric's facility in Evandale, Ohio. Litton was a trusted customer of General Electric, and consequently Gray was warmly welcomed. He was made privy to rather detailed information on GE's long range plans. A few weeks later, officials at GE read that Gray had accepted the presidency at their competitor United Aircraft. The officials protested Gray's actions but were casually reminded that Gray had asked not to be informed of any plans of a "proprietary" nature during his visit to the GE plant.

One of Gray's first acts at United Aircraft was to order an investigation into and re-engineering of the Pratt & Whitney engines for Boeing's 747. He then sought to reduce United Aircraft's dependence on the Pentagon and began a purchasing program in an effort to diversify the business. In 1974, United Aircraft acquired Essex International, a manufacturer of wire and cables. One year later, the company purchased a majority interest in Otis Elevator for $276 million, and, in 1978, Dynell Electronics, a builder of radar systems, was added to the company's holdings. Next came Ambac Industries, which made diesel power systems and fuel injection devices.

United Aircraft changed its name to United Technologies (UTC) in 1975 in order to emphasize the diversification of the company's business. Acquisitions continued, as UTC purchased Mostek, a maker of semiconductors, for $345 million in 1981. Two years later, the company acquired the Carrier Corporation, a manufacturer of air conditioning systems. In addition, UTC purchased several smaller electronics, software, and computer firms.

Gray was reportedly known to maintain a portfolio of the 50 companies he'd most like to purchase; virtually all of his targets, including the ones he later acquired, viewed Gray's takeovers as hostile. Some of the companies which successfully resisted Gray's takeover attempts were ESB Ray-O-Vac (the battery maker), Signal (which built Mack Trucks), and Babcock and Wilcox (a manufacturer of power generating equipment).

During the 1980s, UTC operated four principal divisions: Power Products, including aircraft engines and spare parts; Flight Systems, which manufactured helicopters, electronics, propellers, instruments and space-related products; Building Systems, encompassing the businesses of Otis and Carrier; and Industrial Products, which produced various automotive parts, electric sensors and motors, and wire and printing products. The company, through its divisions, built aircraft engines for General Dynamic's YF-16 and F-111 bomber, Grumman's F-14 Tomcat, and McDonnell Douglas' F-15 Eagle. In addition, it supplied Boeing with engines for its 700-series jetliners, AWACs, B-52 bombers, and other airplanes. McDonnell Douglas and Airbus also purchased Pratt & Whitney engines.

Gray, who aimed to provide a new direction for UTC away from aerospace and defense, proved to be one of the company's most successful presidents. He learned the business of the company's principal product, jet engines, in a very short time; upon his appointment as president of United Aircraft, sales for the year amounted to $2 billion, and, by 1986, the company was recording $16 billion in sales. A year after he joined the company, Gray was named CEO, and soon thereafter he became chairman as well. In his 15 years at UTC, Gray completely refashioned the company. As Gray's retirement drew near, however, UTC's directors had a difficult time convincing him to relinquish power and name a successor. When a potential new leader appeared to be preparing for the role, Gray would allegedly subvert that person's power. One former UTC executive commented, ''Harry equates his corporate position with his own mortality.''

One welcome candidate to succeed Gray was Alexander Haig, who had served on UTC's board. However, Haig left the company after being appointed Secretary of State in the Reagan administration. The members of the UTC board then created a special committee to persuade Gray to name a successor. Finally, in September 1985, Robert Daniell (formerly head of the Sikorsky division) was appointed to take over Gray's responsibilities as CEO of UTC. Nevertheless, Gray remained chairman.

In light of the poor performances posted by the company's various divisions, some industry analysts were beginning to question Gray's leadership. His refusal to step aside threatened the stability of UTC. With the $424 million write-off of the failed Mostek unit, many analysts began talking of a general dissolution of UTC; the divisions were worth more individually than together. But these critics were silenced when Gray announced in September 1986 that he would retire and that Daniell to take his place.

Even before the official departure of Gray, Daniell had moved quickly to dismantle the company's philosophy of ''growth through acquisition.'' Hundreds of middle-management positions were eliminated, and there was speculation that some of the less promising divisions would be sold. Daniell told *The Wall Street Journal,* ''This is a new era for United Technologies. Harry Gray was brought here to grow the company. But now the company is built, the blocks are in place and growth will be a secondary objective.'' Daniell then had to prove that neither Gray's overstayed welcome nor his departure would affect the company adversely.

Daniell also had more pressing challenges. The USSR's collapse in the late 1980s revealed that it had been a much weaker military foe than previously believed. As a result, the end of the Cold War brought Congressional and public pressure to cut domestic defense budgets. While some other leading defense companies moved to carve out niches in the shrinking market, UTC worked to strengthen its interests in more commercial industries.

UTC's transition was not smooth, and Pratt & Whitney suffered the most. While in 1990 Pratt & Whitney had brought in one-third of UTC's sales and an impressive two-thirds of operating profit, the subsidiary's losses from 1991 to 1993 reached $1.3 billion. Pratt & Whitney was hampered not only by defense cuts, but also by the serious downturn in the commercial airline industry, intense global competition, and a worldwide recession. Moreover, saturation of the commercial real estate market during this time caused declines in demand for elevators and air conditioners, products manufactured by UTC's Otis and Carrier subsidiaries. These companies also recorded losses for 1991. That year, UTC also faced six charges of illegal dumping against its Sikorsky Aircraft division. In the largest penalty levied under the Resource Conservation & Recovery Act up to that time, UTC agreed to pay $3 million in damages.

In 1992, Daniell brought George David, who had been instrumental in the revival of both the Otis and Carrier units, on board as UTC president. David, in turn, tapped Karl Krapek, who was called a ''veteran turnaround artist'' by *Financial World,* to lead the beleaguered Pratt & Whitney subsidiary. Krapek quickly reduced employment at the unit from a high of 50,000 to 40,000 by the beginning of 1993. The divisional reformation also focused on manufacturing, with the goals of shortening lead times, reducing capacity, and expedite processes. Overall employment at UTC was cut by 16,500 from 1991 to 1993.

By the end of 1993, Daniell was able to report positive results; UTC made $487 million on sales of $20.74 billion. In April 1994, after leading the corporation for nearly a decade, Daniell appointed David as the company's CEO, retaining his position as UTC's chairman.

Principal Subsidiaries: Pratt & Whitney; United Technologies Automotive Holdings, Inc.; Carrier Corp.; Otis Elevator Co.

Further Reading:

''EPA Levies Record RCRA, CWA Fines,'' *Environment Today,* June 1991, p. 14.

Fernandez, Ronald, *Excess Profits: The Rise of United Technologies,* Reading, Massachusetts: Addison-Wesley, 1983.

Norman, James R., ''Welcome to the Real World,'' *Forbes,* February 15, 1993, pp. 46–47.

Smart, Tim, ''UTC Gets a Lift From its Smaller Engines,'' *Business Week,* December 20, 1993, pp. 109–10.

Velocci, Anthony L., Jr., ''United Technologies Restructures in Bid to Boost Profitability, Competitiveness,'' *Aviation Week & Space Technology,* January 27, 1992, p. 35.

—updated by April Dougal Gasbarre

UNIVERSAL FOREST PRODUCTS

Universal Forest Products Inc.

2801 E. Beltline N.E.
Grand Rapids, Michigan 49505
U.S.A.
(616) 364-6161
Fax: (616) 361-7534

Public Company
Incorporated: 1955
Employees: 1,900
Sales: $661 million
Stock Exchanges: NASDAQ
SICs: 2421 Sawmills & Planing Mills, General

Universal Forest Products Inc. manufactures, treats, and distributes lumber products for the manufactured housing, wholesale lumber, industrial, and do-it-yourself markets. The largest producer of pressure-treated lumber in the United States, the company is also North America's leading manufacturer of engineered roof trusses for the manufactured housing market. Other major product lines include dimension lumber and value-added lumber products such as lattice, fence panels, deck components, and various kits for individual home renovation projects. With 28 manufacturing, treating, and distribution plants in the United States and Canada, Universal ranked among *Fortune* magazine's list of 500 top grossing American companies in 1994, for the first time in its 49-year history. Moreover, Universal's 43 percent increase in sales represented one of the top 20 largest gains among ''Fortune 500'' companies.

Universal Forest Products was established in 1955 to distribute lumber to the burgeoning postwar mobile home manufacturing industry. In its early years, the company's major stockholder, William F. Grant, also served as its only salesperson. Universal initially relied solely on the railway system to distribute the lumber it sold. However, as the country's railway system began to decline in the 1960s, and demand for the company's product increased, Universal sought to gain greater control of its distribution process. Toward that end, in 1970, the company purchased the assets of a component yard in Georgia; the following year, the company acquired a second component yard, in Pennsylvania. The establishment of such distribution centers was part of plan to meet the demand for lumber wherever it most frequently arose; the company therefore became less dependent on the railway system and was able to pass on its rail service

savings to the customer. After the success of the first two component plants, others were opened in Florida and North Carolina, and Universal made its first direct business acquisition, Lumber Specialties of Granger, Indiana.

In 1971, Universal reported sales of $12 million. That year, company vice-president Peter F. Secchia, who had joined Universal upon graduation from Michigan State University in 1962, purchased a controlling share of the company. Soon thereafter, Secchia initiated a plan which would allow salaried employees to share in the equity of the corporation; by 1994, employees owned approximately 18 percent of Universal. Secchia also introduced a policy of remanufacturing Universal's inventory as supply needs changed.

Expansion continued through the 1970s, and, by 1983, a reorganization along geographic lines became necessary. The new Universal divisions oversaw manufacturing and distribution in the Atlantic, Midwest, Northeast, Southeast, and Southwest. Affiliate companies, such as Lumber Specialties, also adopted the name of the parent company in hopes of enhancing Universal's national presence and public recognition.

The U.S. market for manufactured housing units experienced substantial declines during the 1980s. In an effort to offset similar declines in the company's growth rate, Universal began to offer a more varied array of manufactured products, including re-graded items, mixed loads of lumber, particle board, and plywood. Moreover, a research and development department was introduced, comprised of a full-time engineering staff.

Also during this time, Universal entered the wood treating business, representing an investment that fortuitously coincided with the rise of the do-it-yourself market. The do-it-yourself revolution, beginning in the 1980s, had a profound effect on the lumber industry, as smaller lumber yards were replaced by huge retail warehouses catering to individual home renovation projects. Universal's distribution network proved well suited to this change in the industry.

Manufactured housing, which had represented 90 percent of Universal's sales in the late 1970s, was responsible for only 35 percent of sales in 1985. By 1989, Universal had become the nation's largest producer of CCA-preserved lumber. Over the next five years, the company established 15 treating plants and planned for two more. With 28 locations in 18 states and two in Canada, Universal focused on guaranteeing customers stock availability, which smaller suppliers often could not supply. Seeking to never let a customer down by not having available product, Universal also remained committed to curbing the financial loss involved in overstocking merchandise.

In 1989, President George Bush appointed Universal board chairperson and CEO Peter Secchia as U.S. Ambassador to Italy. Secchia, the son of Italian immigrants, had a long association with the National Italian-American Foundation. He had also been active in Republican politics in the Midwest, acting as vice-chairman of the Republican National Committee for the 13 states of the Midwest and campaigning for George Bush during the 1988 elections. Universal President Bill Currie, hired by Secchia in 1972, replaced Secchia during his tenure as American Ambassador to Italy. After President Bush was defeated in the 1992 election, Secchia's tenure as ambassador came to an end, and he returned as chairperson of Universal.

Under the Clinton administration, Universal and others in the lumber industry faced stricter limitations on annual timber harvests. The short term effect of Clinton's environmental policy actually helped companies with large inventories, such as Universal, by creating a temporary shortage in the lumber industry that prompted a sharp rise in prices. Moreover, unusually wet conditions in the country's forests during this time, as well as a public debate over the effects of logging on the preservation of the spotted owl, inflated lumber prices further. Nevertheless, the long term effects of Clinton's policy were regarded as potentially harmful to the lumber industry. In May 1993, an inevitable dip in lumber prices occurred.

Meanwhile Universal continued to grow, making new acquisitions of smaller companies that were less well positioned to adjust to the changing lumber industry. Although growth through acquisitions clearly became an important part of Universal's strategy for the 1990s, Secchia preferred to downplay this aspect of their business plan. In a 1993 article in the *Grand Rapids Business Journal,* for which he was questioned about the aggressiveness of the company's acquisition strategy, Secchia commented, ''I'm very reticent about that because some of our acquisitions have not been that successful.''

Between 1992 and 1993, Universal had a remarkable 43 percent rise in sales from $449.5 million to $643 million. During this time, Universal acquired Chesapeake Wood Treating Co., a division of Chesapeake Corp., a deal that included five wood treatment plants. With $90 million in sales in 1991, Chesapeake Wood Treating Co. accounted for approximately ten percent of Chesapeake Corp.'s consolidated net sales. The acquisition was the largest in Universal's history, and it came just one month before the company went public.

Universal's exceptional gains, as well as the return of Secchia as chairperson, boosted investor confidence in Universal. The company went public in November 1993, offering 5.2 million shares of common stock at $7 per share, and gaining approximately $33.4 million from its initial public offering. These funds were used to reduce notes payable to banks and to invest in new machinery connected with the acquisition of Chesapeake. By 1994, Universal was in an excellent position for continued growth. The previously depressed manufactured home market was again on the rise, and Universal's share of that market remained strong. Moreover, Universal's reputation for adapting to changes in the lumber market was expected to ensure its success, even if the do-it yourself segment declined.

Further Reading:

Blake, Laura, ''Lumber Prices Dip,'' *Grand Rapids Business Journal,* May 17, 1993, p. 1.

Boyer, Kerry, ''Universal Forest Opening Lumber Plant in Hamilton,'' *Greater Cincinnati Business Record,* August 2, 1993, p. 4.

Clabrese, Dan, ''Secchia May Take Universal Public,'' *Grand Rapids Business Journal,* August 2, 1993, p. 1.

Clabrese, Dan, ''Universal's IPO Move Shows Initial Promise,'' *Grand Rapids Business Journal,* November 22, 1993, p. 6.

La Franco, Robert, ''Forest Products and Packaging,'' *Forbes,* January 3, 1994.

''A Living Story: How Universal Forest Products Rose to its Current Prominence in the DIY Market,'' Universal Forest Products, Inc., Grand Rapids, 1992.

Turner, Mike, ''New Universal Chief Harbors Presidential Ambitions,'' *Grand Rapids Business Journal,* July 17, 1989, p. 3.

—Hilary Gopnik and Donald Cameron McManus

USAA

USAA Building
San Antonio, Texas 78288
U.S.A.
(800) 531-8100
Fax: (210) 498-0030

Private Company
Incorporated: 1922 as United States Army Automobile
   Association
Employees: 16,000
Sales: $6 billion
SICs: 6311 Life Insurance; 6331 Fire, Marine, and Casualty
   Insurance; 6035 Federal Savings Institutions; 6022 State
   Commercial Banks; 6282 Investment Advice; 6211
   Security Brokers and Dealers; 6531 Real Estate Agents
   and Managers

USAA is a diversified insurance and financial services company
patronized primarily by officers in the U.S. military and their
dependents. The country's fifth largest auto insurer and fourth
largest home insurance company, USAA was founded in Texas
in the 1920s as a mutual association, so that military officers,
who moved frequently, could obtain automobile insurance. Led
by a series of retired officers, who managed its assets and
operations conservatively, USAA grew steadily throughout the
century, as successive wars and military build-ups increased its
pool of eligible members. In the 1970s and 1980s, USAA began
to branch out into additional financial services related to its
insurance business, and with its customer base of loyal and
reliable members, the company grew rapidly in size and financial strength.

USAA was founded in 1922, when Major William Henry Garrison called together 24 of his fellow Army officers at the
Gunter Hotel in San Antonio, Texas. The purpose of the meeting was to discuss solutions to the problem of automobile
insurance for army officers. Because of their frequent moves,
officers often found that their policies were extremely expensive and prone to cancellation. Moreover, many insurance companies were unreliable and failed with some regularity, leaving
their former policyholders without insurance.

The 25 men present at Garrison's meeting decided to form a
mutual company, in which they would insure each other. They
took as their model the Army Cooperative Fire Insurance Com-

pany—based at Fort Leavenworth since 1887—and called the
new enterprise the United States Army Automobile Association. An agreement was signed, and a president, vice-president,
and board of directors were established, all of whom were
active duty army officers. Shortly thereafter, a manager named
Harold Dutton was also hired, and he set up an office at Kelly
Field in San Antonio. The new firm issued its first policy to
Major Walker Moore for his 1922 Elcar. He was charged
$114.47.

Within two months, USAA had enrolled 142 members, and
proceeds from their policies totaled $820. Ten months later,
however, USAA had a deficit of more than $3,000, caused by its
failure to accurately estimate the cost of an insurance policy. In
an effort to compensate for the shortfall in funds, USAA's
board voted at its first annual meeting to extend membership to
all active duty and retired officers of the U. S. Navy and Marine
Corps. The company's name was changed to reflect this broader
constituency, becoming the United Services Automobile Association.

The 1924 annual meeting also resulted in a vote to adopt an
industry standard for insurance premiums, minus a discount of
20 percent. In addition, the company's leaders applied for a
Texas license, declared an eight percent dividend, and established a reserve for losses. By the end of the year, the company
had more than 3,300 members and assets exceeding $85,000.

Two years later, in an effort to foster growth, USAA's board
designated funds for advertising. With $1,500, the company
mailed a flier to all eligible officers and put an ad in the *Service
Journal*. In addition, the company bought 6,000 company em-
blems which it sold to members for display on the hoods of their
cars. These symbols soon became popular among members and
served to promote the company.

By 1927, USAA's business was thriving. Its management,
however, was in chaos. The board of directors had split, and a
break-away group had begun meeting in secret, plotting to
overthrow the company. At the same time, USAA's secretary-
treasurer and general manager were engaged in struggle for
control of the company. After a six-hour board meeting, during
which power changed hands repeatedly, it was determined that
a new leader was needed from outside the company to restore
member's faith in USAA's leadership. Thus, on January 1,
1928, Major General Ernest Hinds, commanding general of Fort
Sam Houston in Texas, became both the general manager and
secretary-treasurer of USAA. Assured that he would have complete control of the company, Hinds took over. The company
then had 7,500 members and more than $300,000 in assets.

Less than two years after Hinds assumed command, the crash of
the stock market plunged the United States into the Great
Depression. Under Hinds' leadership, USAA invested its
money in government securities early on in the financial crisis.
These safe bonds prevented the company from losing large
sums of money in the volatile financial markets. When USAA
did invest in the stock market, it did so conservatively, limiting
its exposure to $20,000.

An unexpected side effect of the Depression was that cars
bearing the USAA hood emblem became the special targets of
thieves, causing the company to discontinue distribution of the

symbols. USAA adopted another preventive measure in 1938, introducing its first Safe Driver Reward Plan, which enrolled a majority of the company's members.

By 1941, at the onset of World War II, USAA's membership exceeded 22,000, and its assets had increased five-fold over the last decade. The company continued to grow throughout the war and instituted a practice of sending telegrams and updating policies when soldiers who had been declared missing in action or had been taken prisoner resurfaced. As a result of the war, and the vast number of men conscripted into the military, the number of potential USAA members grew exponentially. By 1947, the company's annual business had doubled over the last six years, and its membership had increased by more than a third.

In 1948, USAA opened its first office outside San Antonio, in New York City. This step was taken in order to qualify the company to write insurance policies for people who lived in New York. Even further afield, USAA opened an office in Frankfurt, to serve members of the American occupation forces in Europe.

During the late 1940s, USAA's business grew rapidly, aided by the cold war and compulsory ROTC programs on the campuses of land-grant colleges. The company's revenues doubled between 1948 and 1949, and then doubled again by 1952. The following year, when the company's offices on Grayson Street in San Antonio had become badly overcrowded, USAA's board of directors agreed to spend $6 million to construct a new facility in the city. With a modern new facility, containing such amenities as an employee cafeteria, the company hoped to lessen its employee turnover rate of more than 100 percent a year. By 1956, the new building on Broadway was complete, and the company's 802 employees, nearly all of whom were female, had been installed.

That year, USAA's bylaws were altered to modernize the company's corporate structure. The company's general manager was named president, and his assistants were named vice-presidents. This change was made to accommodate USAA's ever-expanding operations, after the company's business had doubled again by 1955. In 1957, USAA installed an IBM 650 computer, the first move in the drive to automate its cumbersome operations.

Within five years, the company's new facilities were again deemed inadequate. In 1962, USAA added 110,000 more square feet to its building and began conversion to a newer, larger computer system, the IBM 7074-1041. Also during this time, the board of directors amended the bylaws to enable the company to offer life insurance, along with property and casualty insurance. With $5 million in seed money, the company began to organize the USAA Life Company.

By 1967, USAA's assets had reached $206 million, and its membership topped 650,000, a rapid rate of growth attributed to the mass mobilization of troops to fight in Vietnam. In 1969, the company's presidency was assumed by Robert F. McDermott, a retired Air Force brigadier general who had previously been Dean of the Faculty at the Air Force Academy. McDermott set out to reform the company, instituting more modern, streamlined procedures to improve employee morale and customer service.

Such reform was necessitated largely by USAA's failure to implement adequate computer systems. For example, in the late 1960s, the company was still keeping separate claims and underwriting files on each of its members. In order for a new insurance policy to be issued, 55 steps had to be performed, in 32 different locations, spread across four separate floors. Files piled up on employees' desks and were continually misplaced. The company hired dozens of college students to come to its offices every night to search, often in vain, for missing folders.

Moreover, the many separate units of USAA had poor lines of communication, and personnel problems at the company were rampant. Managers were promoted solely on the basis of seniority, which often caused friction, and many jobs were regarded as repetitive and boring, as some people were assigned such tasks as unsealing envelopes and pulling staples. Not surprisingly, the annual turnover rate stood at 43 percent.

Under McDermott, numerous changes were made. The company reduced its number of employees by more than 800 through attrition by the end of 1969. Those employees who remained were given much broader job descriptions, in an effort to increase their interest in their work. To make sure they were able to perform new tasks, USAA inaugurated a new program of extensive employee training.

In addition, USAA invested heavily in computers and telecommunications to improve service to its members. With new computers, USAA was able to make several important changes. Instead of writing a separate insurance policy for each car, for instance, the company began to write multi-car policies. With this shift, USAA was able to eliminate hundreds of employee slots and also reduce the cyclical nature of its business, spreading its workload more evenly throughout the year.

Furthermore, USAA restructured its organization, dividing members by geography, rather than by type of policy issued. Under this new structure, company leaders devised a 20-year plan for growth prompted by the results of a member survey, which asked whether a more diverse line of services would be appreciated. Respondents to the survey indicated that they would be interested in several additional financial services, including mortgage loans, auto financing and leasing, mutual funds, and a bank. Car-related services, such as an auto travel club, were also deemed desirable. This data paved the way for USAA's eventual diversification into several fields outside the insurance business. However, development of these new fields would not begin for several years, since the company's board of directors balked at this radical revision of the company's scope.

In 1973, USAA bylaws were revised to allow officers in the National Guard and the military reserves eligible for membership, as well as military dependents. Members from these groups soon made up a large part of the company's business. A centralized training and education facility was developed during this time, and the company moved from its overcrowded offices to a new building, situated on 286 acres in northwest San Antonio. This facility became the world's largest private office building. With tennis courts, picnic tables, four cafeterias, and a company store, it was designed to enhance employee satisfaction on the job. The company also instituted a four-day work week to provide its workers with more flexible hours.

Along with the main San Antonio facility, USAA opened several smaller, satellite offices in areas around the country with large concentrations of military personnel, including Sacramento, Seattle, Colorado Springs, Tampa, and the Virginia cities of Norfolk and Reston. A second overseas office was opened in London.

After an amendment in the company's by-laws, USAA finally moved to provide a greater number of services for its members. Organizing new functions under subsidiaries, the company added the USAA Life Insurance Company and the USAA Investment Management Company, or IMCO, which managed a number of mutual funds. USAA also began to offer a discount brokerage service.

In the 1980s, the USAA Federal Savings Bank was founded, establishing lucrative Visa and MasterCard operations, mortgage and home equity loans, deposit services, and consumer loans. USAA also set up a travel agency and began to offer real estate investment opportunities. The move directly into the real estate market was realized with the completion of USAA Towers, a 23-story retirement community, and USAA Parklane West, a medical care facility. Each of these new enterprises made a broader range of services available to USAA members and also contributed to the company's overall net worth.

By the early 1990s, USAA's diversified business lines were thriving. The Life Insurance Company, carrying policies total-ing more than $46 billion, was the country's 43rd largest life insurance company; within three years, it ranked 37th on the list, with $57.4 billion worth of policies written. The company's bank, USAA Federal Savings Bank, reported over $3.5 billion in assets, had issued more than 1.5 million credit cards, and had become one of the five largest savings and loan institutions in the United States. In addition, USAA had also inaugurated a joint program with Sprint, to provide discount telephone services to its customers.

By 1993, USAA's owned and managed assets had reached $33 billion, as the company, in its broadened guise, became the 21st largest American diversified financial services company in the Fortune Service 500. USAA's attention to employee morale and training had also won praise, and it was named one of the ten best companies to work for in America. With a loyal and well-trained corps of employees, and a smooth-running operation that ran with precision, USAA appeared well situated to continue its growth and solid financial success well into the 21st century under the leadership of new chairman and CEO, Gen. Robert T. Harris, USAF (Ret.).

Principal Subsidiaries: USAA Life Insurance Company; USAA Investment Management Company; USAA Federal Savings Bank.

Further Reading:

Levering, Robert, and Milton Moskowitz, *The 100 Best Companies to Work for in America,* New York: Doubleday, 1993.

—Elizabeth Rourke

Viking Office Products, Inc.

13809 South Figueroa Street
Los Angeles, California 90061
U.S.A.
(213) 321-4493
Fax: (310) 327-2376

Public Company
Incorporated: 1960
Employees: 1,067
Sales: $449.7 million
Stock Exchanges: New York San Francisco
SICs: 5961 Catalog and Mail-Order Houses

Viking Office Products, Inc., is a leading mail order seller of office supplies to small- and medium-sized businesses. The company relies on sophisticated computerized mailing systems to send customized catalogs to its potential buyers, and then provides them with a high level of customer service in order to keep their business. Founded as a small California stationery store, Viking began to expand dramatically in the mid-1980s and has attained high levels of revenue and income growth ever since.

Viking got its start in 1960 as a small office supply retailer located in Los Angeles, California. The store was opened on January 7, 1960, by Rolf Ostern, who hired an assistant to round out his two-man staff. From the beginning, Ostern supplemented his retail operations with a small catalog, but it was not until five years after going into business that he mailed his first catalog featuring the store's full line to his customers. In 1969 Ostern changed the name of his store to Viking Office Supplies and moved to a new location. At this time, the company also purchased its first computer, to keep track of its growing operations.

By the mid-1970s, Viking had established itself as a West Coast mail-order retailer of discount office supplies to small and medium-sized businesses. At that time, the company began a geographic expansion. In August, 1976, a division of Viking opened in Dallas, Texas, and began shipping orders. Three years later a third location was added when operations commenced in Cincinnati, Ohio.

In 1983 Viking hired Irwin Helford as president of the company. Under his direction, Viking's revenues began to expand at a dramatic rate, as he introduced new marketing and merchandising techniques. Helford stressed customer service as a way to set Viking apart from its competitors in the office supplies market. Customers received courteous service while ordering on the phone, and then their supplies were delivered to them as soon as possible, often in just one day. In addition, the company embarked on an aggressive program to increase its customer base. In 1985 Viking mailed 15.4 million catalogs, the vast majority of them to potential customers who had never ordered from the company.

At the end of 1985 Viking reported revenues of $42.5 million, derived from sales to 215,000 active customers. These sales more than tripled the company's previous year's sales, which totaled $15 million. Viking's sales figures continued to rise in the next year, as an additional 42,000 businesses phoned in orders, and revenues increased to $57.5 million.

In 1987 Viking opened a fourth distribution center to better serve another segment of the country. The company's East Windsor, Connecticut, facility was designed to fulfill orders coming from the East Coast states. With the addition of this new facility, Viking's revenues rose to $81 million in 1987, as its customer base climbed to 335,000. Viking's growth mimicked the growth of the office supplies industry overall in the 1980s, as the market for these products expanded steadily.

With its record of strong growth throughout the mid-1980s, Viking's original owner, Ostern, and his financial partners decided to cash in their ownership in the company. Accordingly, on September 1, 1988, Viking was sold by its founders in a leveraged buyout to the VOP Acquisition Corporation. This company had been founded by Viking's management and the New York investment banking house of Dillon Read & Company, along with some of their affiliates, for the express purpose of purchasing Viking. At that time, Helford became chairman of the company's board of directors.

In the year that Viking changed hands, the company's revenues continued to grow. Sales topped the $100 million mark for the first time, reaching $105.1 million, and 364,000 customers ordered from the 28 million catalogs that the company mailed. In October, 1988, Viking introduced a new line of merchandise, office furniture, with its own separate catalog and program.

In the following year Viking opened its fifth operations center, a facility in Jacksonville, Florida, strengthening the company's East Coast operations. In October, 1989, the company also introduced its second new catalog operation, rolling out a line of computer supplies targeted to the needs of small- and medium-sized businesses. By the end of the year, these products were accounting for eight percent of the company's overall sales.

In the course of 1989, Viking's owners put in motion the steps to sell stock in the company for the first time. At the start of December, 1989, VOP was merged into its subsidiary, Viking Office Products, in preparation for the company's initial public offering of stock. On March, 14, 1990, Viking offered stock to the public on the NASDAQ stock exchange, selling 2,300,000 shares at a price of $10.50 per share to raise $25 million. Much of this money was used to repay debts incurred in the 1988 buyout of the company. With this move, Viking was able to significantly lower its interest payments.

Three months after the stock sale, in June, 1990, Viking once again reported record annual revenues, posting $157 million in sales over the previous twelve months. These sales came despite fierce competition in the office supplies industry. The emergence of low-priced office supply warehouses, or superstores, and the disappearance of the traditional stationery dealer, meant that price competition in the industry had grown extremely strong. Viking's market research indicated that approximately one quarter of the company's customers were located in areas where superstores also did business, and the company instituted elaborate monitoring procedures to determine the effect of this competition on its business.

With prices kept low by this competition, and a general recession that caused businesses to cut back on expenditures, Viking faced a real threat to its profits. In an effort to maintain its competitive edge, the company stepped up its customer service activities, vowing to provide "fanatical" attention to those who bought from its catalogs, while controlling its own costs and overhead.

As part of its campaign to contain costs, Viking defeated a local Teamsters union attempt to unionize its Los Angeles work force in late 1990 and early 1991. The company also ended its financial obligations associated with its buyout in April, 1991, when it fulfilled the terms of an agreement with Glenfed Capital. This helped to keep costs associated with financing down.

In the spring of 1991 Viking experimented with a program of personalized, private discounts for its customers. Using its database of previous purchases, the company sent clients catalogs that featured reduced prices on certain key items. This program was made possible by new ink jet printers and publishing technology. In its early trials, it proved successful in enhancing sales. Viking also sought out new, less competitive markets. Its product line extensions in the furniture and computer supplies fields grew to contribute almost a quarter of the company's sales in 1990. In addition, Viking turned its attention to foreign shores.

The company made its first move overseas in September, 1990. At that time, Viking established a United Kingdom subsidiary, Viking Direct Limited, and opened a facility in Leicester, England. In making this move, Viking hoped to gain a toe-hold in the European Economic Community before the planned unification of that market. Viking rolled out its first European facility without resorting to acquisition, partners, or consultants, and the startup costs for this venture were high. Part of these costs were related to lawsuits filed by the company in order to win exclusive rights to the use of the "Viking Direct" name. By June, 1991, Viking Direct had racked up sales of $41 million, a promising start, and the operation had become profitable on a day-to-day level, although it was far from recouping its initial costs. Nevertheless, in a brief time, Viking Direct had become the largest mail order marketer of office supplies in the United Kingdom.

Domestic sales at this time reached $226.3 million, an increase of 43 percent over the previous year. Viking attributed its ability to win new customers and keep old ones during this time in part to its sophisticated database management. This database was contained on eight IBM AS/400 computers, which used special-ized software to keep track of every sale the company had made since 1984. In addition, Viking monitored how much it cost to attract each customer, what items the customer typically ordered, and the total amount of that customer's business, and also cross-referenced these statistics by mailing, region, and size and type of business. With this information, Viking phone operators were able to increase the size of a customer's order by suggesting items that the client had ordered in the past.

Viking also discovered that it could retain customers even if its prices were not the rock-bottom lowest in the market. "We've found we don't have to be the lowest every time on every item the way the superstores are," Helford told *Catalog Age* in August, 1991. This factor allowed Viking to protect its bottom line without losing customers. In addition, in early 1992, Viking stepped up its efforts to use catalog mailings most efficiently. The company installed computer programs that allowed it to mail more catalogs to customers who were more likely to respond favorably, and to make sure that no two catalogs mailed to a customer were ever the same. With 50 different version of each catalog that it printed, the company was able to select the best format or product mix for each client.

In January, 1992, Viking's stock split two-for-one as a result of the company's rapid growth and its strong performance in the stock market. To fuel future growth, Viking opened its sixth distribution center in Seattle, Washington, early in 1992. This facility was designed to provide overnight delivery to customers in the Pacific Northwest. On June 1, 1992, Viking expanded its geographical reach further when it began operations in France. The company set up a subsidiary based in Paris to enter the highly competitive French office supplies market. Within one month of its inauguration, this operation had reported more than $1 million in sales, and it had lined up 5,000 French businesses as customers.

At the end of June, 1992, Viking reported year-long revenues overall of $320 million, an increase of more than 41 percent from the previous year. These sales yielded income of $12.8 million. Viking had shown strong growth in active customers, increasing its list of buyers more than 30 percent, to 700,000. A significant portion of the company's growth came in the relatively immature British market, where sales more than doubled to $100 million. Another source of Viking's steady growth was its state-of-the-art database and catalog customizing technology. The company sought to offer the broadest possible array of products, and to tempt customers with catalogs as often as possible. At the start of each year, Viking mailed its "big book," known as the Spring Buyer's Guide.

Outside of the annual buyer's guide, however, Viking believed that the future of mail order operations depended not on mass mailings directed at a general population, but on customized offers made to individual customers. In creating its other mailings, Viking strove at all times to take notice of the different needs of its clients, and to provide them with targeted offers of the products they had ordered in the past. Although this tactic proved successful overall, it backfired in one instance when Viking Direct sent a British company a catalog with a notice on the front calling attention to the large quantities of toilet paper the company used.

Viking also personalized mailings with a message on the cover directed to its customer by name, mentioning the company's line of work, or previous purchases the customer had made. "We get far better response rates by tailoring the message to the customer," Helford told *Fortune* magazine. In one special case, Viking used its computerized database to cull the names of customers located in southern Florida after the area was devastated by Hurricane Andrew in the summer of 1992. The company sent these customers a special catalog that included a $100 gift certificate. This effort resulted in a 52 percent response rate, along with letters of gratitude and pledges of long-term business.

As part of its overall effort to segment its business, Viking also introduced a number of new, focus catalogs, which offered a separate line of merchandise. In addition to its older furniture and computer supply programs, the company added office machines, a wide variety of papers, and custom printed stationery. "We're constantly asking ourselves, 'what are our customers buying from our competitors that we could be offering ourselves?' " Viking's director of marketing explained to *Catalog Age* in August, 1992. "The specialty catalogs are a way to get more than existing customers." The new items also offered less price competition and higher margins than Viking's staple products, which still accounted for 85 percent of the merchandise it sold.

By August, 1992, Viking's efforts toward high-level customer service had improved the company's fulfillment time for its office supply orders. In 1989, 70 percent of all company orders had gone out the same day they were received. By the summer of 1992, that number had increased to 98 percent. This overnight service was free for orders above $25. In addition, Viking offered toll-free ordering and an iron-clad one year guarantee on all its goods, which even extended to its stationery printing operations. The company had an extremely liberal return policy. For instance, Viking offered to replace orders of printed goods if they were inaccurate, even if the error was the customer's fault.

Driven by these policies, Viking's growth remained strong in the first months of 1993, although the company experienced some adverse effects from it foreign operations. A devalued British pound depressed earnings from its United Kingdom operations, and the company wrote off a $6.3 million loss on its subsidiary in France. As the French Viking operations gained customers, however, its losses steadily slowed.

By the end of June, 1993, Viking's annual revenues had increased $449.7 million, a gain of more than 40 percent from the year before. A significant portion of this increase came from the company's European operations, which grew 88.6 percent in twelve months. With these strong returns, the company began to plan operations in other European countries, including Germany, Spain, and Italy. Viking also began to explore the feasibility of enlarging its European market by shipping goods across national borders. Despite its steady gains, Viking's Paris subsidiary had still not reached the break even point by July, 1993, and the company fired its French head of these operations. In September of that year, the French Viking unit finally began to turn a profit.

Further geographic expansion took place in October, 1993, when Viking commenced operations in Australia. The company opened a full-service distribution center in Sydney, and it began to ship orders in November. By the end of January, this operation was reporting revenues of $2.8 million, exceeding expectations. As Viking moved into the mid-1990s, the company's strong record of growth and profitability, driven by its stringent attention to customer service and its sophisticated catalog mailing operations, suggested that Viking would continue to thrive.

Principal Subsidiaries: Viking Direct Limited (United Kingdom); Viking Direct S.A.R.L. (France); Viking Pty., Limited (Australia).

Further Reading:

Frey, Nathaniel, "Office Suppliers Fight Back," *Catalog Age,* August 1991.
Moreau, Katherine, "Viking Office Products: Close Up," *Catalog Age,* August 1992.
Scussel, Patricia A., "Segmenting Business Buyers," *Catalog Age,* February 1992.
"Viking Office Products," *Fortune,* November 30, 1992.
"Viking Office Products, Inc.," *Financial News,* September 11, 1990.
"Viking Pioneers Direct-Mail Office Supplies," *California Business,* May 1993.

—Elizabeth Rourke

Vitro Corp.

45 West Gude Drive
Rockville, Maryland 20850-1160
U.S.A.
(301) 738-4300
Fax: (301) 738-4323

Wholly Owned Subsidiary of Tracor Inc.
Incorporated: 1950 as Vitro Manufacturing Co.
Employees: 4,000
Sales: $315 million
SICs: 7373 Computer Integrated Systems Design; 8711
   Engineering Services

Vitro Corp., a wholly owned subsidiary of Tracor Inc. since 1993, is one of the Washington D.C. area's largest defense contractors, providing systems and information engineering for the Department of Defense (DOD), the National Aeronautics and Space Administration (NASA), Federal agencies, defense contractors, international governments, and the intelligence community. Vitro's subsidiary, Quality Systems, Inc. (QSI), headquartered in Fairfax, Virginia, complements Vitro's primary business by providing customers with software development services, which consist of analyzing and designing new computer systems and providing technical support and training programs.

Company data traces Vitro's formation to 1948, the onset of the Cold War, a period characterized military build-ups resulting from increasing ideological conflict and mistrust between the United States and the Soviet Union. During this time, Vitro developed test systems for military applications. With headquarters in New York City, Vitro was incorporated in 1950 as Vitro Manufacturing Co. That year, Vitro acquired Kellex Corp. and a J.R. Simplot plant, and, in 1953, these subsidiaries were merged with the parent to create Vitro Corp. of America. The corporation established significant and long-standing connections with the U.S. Navy during this time and later affirmed that it had "provided services for virtually every guided missile system installed by the U.S. Navy on its ships since 1948." The Navy remained one of Vitro's primary customers in the 1990s.

Vitro built an on-site laboratory at Elgin Air Force Base in Florida in 1951, where the company surveyed test ranges and designed, installed, operated, and maintained ground-based test instrumentation and equipment. The company also designed, manufactured and installed precision tracking and meteorological radar systems and intrusion detection systems. In the mid-1950s, Vitro acquired Thieblot Aircraft Co., Inc. and NEMS-Clark, Inc., and Vitro's headquarters were moved to Silver Spring, Maryland. Vitro's sales increased rapidly, while Cold War defense and military budgets multiplied; by the late 1960s, the company's annual sales stood at over $70 million.

Vitro operated independently until 1968, when it was acquired by Automation Industries, Inc. through an exchange of stock. As a subsidiary of Automation Industries, the company was renamed Vitro Engineering Corp. When Automation Industries and General Cable Corp. merged a decade later, Vitro was included as part of the agreement. The new conglomeration, named GK Technologies Incorporated, had interests in a wide variety of concerns, including cable and wire manufacture and household products.

In 1981, GK Technologies and Vitro were acquired by Penn Central Corp., which had survived bankruptcy by selling its rail properties to the federal government and diversifying into energy, defense, and manufacturing. Significant Vitro projects during the 1980s included ship communications and air support systems for such projects as the Polaris, Poseidon, and Trident ballistic missiles as well as the Tomahawk cruise missile system. As the federal government opened increasingly more of its contracts to competitive bidding during the decade, Vitro increased its marketing capabilities and expenditures to maintain and obtain business from the Air Force and Army.

During the mid-1980s, Vitro became involved in a legal battle with a subcontractor, California-based Systems Exploration Inc. (SEI), which specialized in software. SEI sued Vitro in 1985, alleging, according to *The Washington Post,* that Vitro's "entire purpose was to lure SEI into teaming agreements so that SEI's expertise and availability could be held out to the government in order to win the proposals and to then give SEI as little work as possible, thus keeping the work and profit in-house." After four years of depositions, Vitro paid SEI a settlement of over $707,000, without admitting any wrongdoing.

By the early 1990s, Penn Central had shifted its focus from manufacturing industries to service industries, such as insurance. Vitro, which had 1991 sales of $419.7 million, was put up for sale in 1992. At the time, Vitro's book value was estimated at $100 million by *The Washington Post.* Tracor Inc., based in Austin, Texas, purchased the defense contractor for $94 million the following year. Tracor, a 37-year-old electronics and technical services firm, had recently emerged from bankruptcy after racking up nearly $500,000 in losses for the 1988, 1989, and 1990 fiscal years. Vitro became Tracor's largest subsidiary.

Cuts in defense budgets in the early 1990s prompted a decline in the defense industry, and Tracor planned to focus on "those portions of the defense market which will support a smaller military force, upgrade current systems for longer operation before replacement, and develop new technologies to provide advanced capabilities in the event they are required." Moreover, the company was also encouraged to court business from foreign countries, with which the United States was on friendly terms, such as Egypt.

Principal Subsidiaries: Quality Systems, Inc.

Further Reading:

Sugawara, Sandra, ''Penn Central Looking to Sell Silver Spring-Based Vitro,'' *Washington Post,* December 11, 1992, p. D1.
Tucker, Elizabeth, ''Vitro Corp. Settles Suit by California Subcontractor,'' *Washington Post,* January 21, 1989, p. D12.

—April Dougal Gasbarre

Warner-Lambert Co.

201 Tabor Road
Morris Plains, New Jersey 07950-2693
U.S.A.
(201) 540-2000
Fax: (201) 540-3761

Public Company
Incorporated: 1920 as William R. Warner & Co.
Employees: 34,000
Sales: $5.6 billion
Stock Exchanges: New York Zurich Paris London Frankfurt
   Brussels
SICs: 2834 Pharmaceutical Preparations; 2836 Biological
   Products Except Diagnostic; 2835 Diagnostic Substances;
   2844 Toilet Preparations; 2067 Chewing Gum; 2064
   Candy & Other Confectionery Products; 3421 Cutlery

The Warner-Lambert Co. manufactures and markets pharmaceutical, consumer health care, and confectionery products, including such popular brands as Listerine antiseptic mouthwash, Chiclets gum, Halls lozenges, Certs mints, Rolaids antacids, and Schick razors.

The product of a long history of mergers and acquisitions, the Warner-Lambert name reflects the combined assets of two businesses: the William R. Warner Company, a pharmaceutical and cosmetic concern, and Lambert-Pharmacal, manufacturers of Listerine oral antiseptic, which merged in the 1950s. Thereafter, Warner-Lambert became a large multinational corporation under the leadership of Elmer Holmes Bobst.

Bobst arrived at William R. Warner & Company in 1945, already a veteran executive of the pharmaceutical industry and a multimillionaire. As president of Hoffmann-La Roche's U.S. office, he had proved instrumental in acquiring for the Swiss company a large share of the U.S. drug market. Many observers were surprised that Bobst accepted the position at Warner; he was then 61 years old, wealthy, and could have settled into a comfortable retirement.

However, when Gustave A. Pfeiffer, Warner's chairperson and the only surviving member of the original founding family, approached Bobst with an offer of the presidency, he accepted. Nearly 30 years earlier, Bobst had been asked to join Warner as the head of its pharmaceutical division but declined when the Pfeiffer family refused to sell Bobst any of the company stock (the family held all the common stock). By the mid-1940s, however, Bobst had proved his abilities, and Pfeiffer readily offered the job on Bobst's terms; Bobst was hired and allowed to purchase 11 percent of the common stock. By 1955, Bobst's holdings were worth over $3 million.

What Bobst inherited with his new position was a family operated company suffering from an aging product line and antiquated facilities. Although Pfeiffer's 1916 acquisition of the Hudnut cosmetic line accounted for most of the company's $25 million sales, that product line was barely turning a profit. In an effort to improve the image of the cosmetics production, Bobst renamed the firm Warner-Hudnut in 1950.

Warner had a long history of growth through acquisition. Warner was founded in the mid-nineteenth century by William Warner, a Philadelphia pharmacist who had earned a fortune by inventing a sugar-coating for pills. In 1908, the company was acquired by the Gustavus A. Pfeiffer & Company, a patent medicine company from St. Louis. Pfeiffer retained the Warner company name, moved its headquarters to New York, and began a series of acquisitions that included the Hudnut line and the DuBarry cosmetic company. By the time Bobst assumed the presidency, some 50 companies had been acquired during the 99 years of the Warner company's history.

Bobst's managerial style was well suited to this company acquisition policy. Moreover, his experience with high-level industry and political affairs enabled him to hire a new management team of accomplished executives and public figures. Successful investment bankers, business executives, and political officials were brought in, notably Anna Rosenberg, the company's manager of industrial and public relations, who was once the U.S. Assistant Secretary of Defense, and Alfred Driscoll, later Warner's president, who had served as governor of New Jersey for seven years.

In 1952, Bobst made his first major acquisition, purchasing New Jersey Chilcott Laboratories, Inc. Chilcott earned its reputation as a manufacturer of ethical drugs largely through its development of Peritrate, a long-acting "vasodilator," which enlarged constricted blood vessels. By 1966, an estimated 56 percent of 3.1 million people afflicted by heart disease used Peritrate. While the sales of the drug became Warner-Hudnut's mark of excellence in the pharmaceutical industry, its success was also cause for some controversy.

Peritrate proved useful in a wider application of treatments than originally allowed, and the Food & Drug Administration (FDA) approved of Peritrate's "new drug" usages in 1959. Over the next several years, however, Warner embarked on a controversial Peritrate advertising campaign. Appearing in several medical journals, including the *Journal of the American Medical Association,* ten page ads advocated the use of Peritrate not only for the treatment of angina, but as a "life-prolonging" prophylactic for all cardiac patients. The advertisement, based on the results of one study, was released at a time when the FDA had initiated an increasingly aggressive policy of evaluating claims for drug effectiveness. Even as the director of the study refuted the advertisement claims, Warner-Lambert executives stood by the claims for the effectiveness of their drug. However, by 1966, the government, under the directive of the FDA, seized a shipment of the drug, bringing charges against the company's unapproved advocacy of an even wider usage for the drug.

Also during this time, Bobst arranged a merger between his company and Lambert-Pharmacal. Bobst had met the president of Lambert, Edward Williams, at a meeting of the American Foundation for Pharmaceutical Education, and the two decided that their operations, each producing different but reputable products, would complement one another. Bobst was particularly interested in gaining access to Lambert's well-organized distribution network, which incorporated modern marketing techniques previously unavailable at Warner-Hudnut's. Furthermore, Williams brought a strong background in the management of pharmaceutical companies, enhancing Bobst's accomplished executive team, which had little experience in the pharmaceutical industry. When Warner and Lambert merged, former governor Alfred Driscoll was named president of the new company.

Lambert's Listerine product, which had accounted for over 50 percent of Lambert's total sales, guaranteed Warner a large share of the oral antiseptic market.Listerine was developed in the nineteenth century and became widely popular, particularly under the advertising strategy of Gordon Seagrove, who joined Lambert in 1926 after leaving his job as a Calliope-player in the circus. Seagrove made Listerine a household staple by promoting its ability to cure halitosis, sore throats, and dandruff. The advertising copy for one magazine ad depicted a man encouraging a woman to continue massaging Listerine into his head, with the tagline "Tear into it, Honey—It's Infectious Dandruff!"

Listerine continued to increase in popularity under its new ownership; by 1975, the oral antiseptic held a sizeable portion of the $300 million market. Warner-Lambert continued to invest heavily in advertising for Listerine. For years, Listerine had been advertised as a preventative measure against colds and sore throats, and, during the Asian flu epidemic of 1957, Bobst personally placed an ad in *Life* magazine promoting Listerine's ability to resist the sickness. The company's advertising agency had earlier rejected the ad, since its claims were unsubstantiated, but the promotion resulted in sales increases of $26 million for the year.

By 1975, the Federal Trade Commission (FTC) had begun to investigate the Listerine advertisements. The FTC disputed the cold prevention claims of Listerine as insupportable and ordered the company to embark on a disclaimer ad campaign amounting to $10 million, a figure equal to the company's average annual advertising expenditure between 1962 and 1972. The FTC argued that only corrective disclaimers could educate the consumer, and, in 1978, the Supreme Court upheld the FTC's order.

During the 1970s and 1980s, Warner-Lambert made several acquisitions, including Emerson Drug, which made Bromo-Seltzer, cough drop manufacturer Smith Brothers, American Optical, and Schick Shaving. To acquire American Chicle,

makers of Chiclets chewing gum, Warner-Lambert used 7.8 million of its own stock, which was then worth about $200 million. Many industry analysts criticized the high price paid for American Chicle; in 1962, the company's net income for the year was under $10 million. By 1983, however, after expanding into foreign markets, Chiclet sales were reaching the $1 billion mark. Ward S. Hagan, chairperson of American Chicle, called its gum and mint business "the largest in the world."

Another merger during this time involved Parke, Davis & Co. However, Warner-Lambert's proposal to merge with Parke, Davis was investigated by the Antitrust Division of the Justice Department. According to the chair of the House Judiciary Committee, the merger would raise "serious problems" because it had the potential to limit competition and create a monopoly. Upon approval, the merger would result in a combined revenue of $1.7 billion and would rank the new company among the 100 largest industrial companies in the United States.

On November 12, 1970, the Justice Department announced it would not challenge the merger despite the Antitrust Division's recommendation to the contrary. The department referred the matter to the FTC, which held concurrent authority to enforce the Clayton Act. A day later, the merger was completed. By 1976, however, the FTC ordered the company to sell several units of its Parke, Davis subsidiary that produced specified drugs. Those units producing thyroid preparations, cough remedies, cough drops and lozenges, normal albumin serum, and tetanus immune globulin would have to be sold in order to restore competition in those product lines.

Satisfied with the FTC's actions, S. Burke Giblin, chair and chief executive officer of Warner-Lambert at the time of the ruling, nevertheless faced several other challenges in the ensuing years. In 1976, Warner-Lambert disclosed figures to the Securities and Exchange Commission (SEC) concerning illegal payments abroad, announcing that more than $2.2 million "in questionable payments" had been uncovered in 14 of the 140 countries in which Warner-Lambert conducted business.

Only months later an explosion at an American Chicle plant in Queens, New York, killed six people and injured 55. After a year of investigation, a grand jury indicted the company and four of its officials on charges of reckless manslaughter and criminally negligent homicide. The charges were based on reports that the fire department had warned the company about the explosive potential of magnesium stearate dust used as a gum-machine lubricant. Contending that the charges were "outrageous" and unwarranted, company executives appealed the case. In 1978, a state judge dismissed the charges citing "crystal clear and voluminous evidence" that the company had tried to eliminate the danger of an explosion. The following year, however, the New York State court's appellate division voted to restore the indictments. Finally, in 1980, the state's highest court once again dismissed all charges in connection with the explosion.

Another controversy involved Warner-Lambert's Benylin cough syrup product, which was made available without a prescription in 1975. In response to questions regarding the cough syrup's effectiveness, the FDA ordered the drug back on a prescription-only status, and, after seven years of deliberation, a settlement was finally reached in which the FDA approved the reinstated over-the-counter sale of the drug.

In 1978, Warner-Lambert purchased Entenmann's Bakery for $243 million in cash. By 1982, Entenmann's had become Warner-Lambert's most profitable consumer division, with sales reaching $333 million and an annual growth rate of 19 percent. However, during this time, a rumor was started that Entenmann's profits were supporting Reverend Sun Myung Moon's Unification Church. Since the source of the rumor was said to come from Westchester county in New York, Warner-Lambert took out an ad in the county newspaper denying the alleged connection. Nevertheless, the rumor continued to circulate and actually received a large amount of publicity in the Boston, Massachusetts, area. It was reported in some places that Entenmann's delivery and sales staff were being harassed, and one Rhode Island church urged a boycott of the baked goods. When sales growth began to slip, Warner-Lambert mailed a letter to 1,600 churches in New England describing Entenmann's history as a family-owned business for 80 years before it was purchased. As Entenmann's profits continued to slip, Warner-Lambert sold the bakery to General Foods for $315 million in 1982.

The late 1970s had proved financially unstable for Warner-Lambert. Profit margins were off by 40 percent in 1979, the majority of revenues came from the sale of consumer goods, and the company was considered a potential takeover candidate. One critic characterized it a "floundering giant." That year, Ward S. Hagan replaced Bobst as chairperson, while Joseph D. Williams assumed the chief executive office. Hagan and Williams then embarked on a restructuring program with the goal of revitalizing the pharmaceutical operations and trimming unprofitable and non-core businesses.

Five unprofitable subsidiaries, including American Optical and Entenmann's, were divested between 1982 and 1986, providing Warner-Lambert with capital of nearly $600 million. At the same time, such company programs as the "Total Production System" aimed to increase productivity by cutting downtime, reducing paperwork, and creating a more flexible work environment. Hagan and Williams closed or consolidated 24 plants in foreign and domestic locations, while reducing the company labor force by almost half, from 61,000 to 32,000. Research for new drugs at the Parke, Davis division was supported by a 20 percent increase in budgetary funds during 1983 to $180 million.

Despite its improved financial condition, Warner-Lambert came under criticism, particularly for its 1982 purchase of IMED Corp., a small hospital supply manufacturer. Many found Warner-Lambert's $468 million purchase, 23 times IMED's earnings, exorbitant. IMED was the market leader, with 35 percent of sales in the hospital supply field and continued annual sales growth of 50 percent. However, the company was beset with problems. IMED's executives apparently concentrated on short-term sales goals, at the expense of new product development. In fact, a management conflict between IMED's manufacturing and research and development executives caused many important employees to resign in frustration. In 1986, Warner-Lambert sold IMED and some of its affiliates to The Henley Group, Inc. for $163.5 million.

Williams, who was given the additional duties of chairperson during Warner-Lambert's turnaround period, was able to report that return on equity had increased from nine to 32 percent from 1979 to 1986, as sales shrunk through divestments and profits held fairly steady. Investing in research and development, and luring industry talent from competing companies, Williams hoped to develop and increase sales of high-margin prescription drugs, such as Lopid, a cholesterol-reducing drug that received positive publicity in the late 1980s. However, a trend among consumers toward treatment without medication, as well as swelling support for reform of the health care industry—and the attendant possibility of price controls—caused uncertainty among ethical drug producers. Business was also threatened by a late 1980s recession and discounting in the consumer goods segment.

In anticipation of these potentially adverse market forces, a new chairperson and CEO, Melvin R. Goodes, announced yet another reorganization of Warner-Lambert late in 1991. The plan called for a 2,700-person layoff, reorganization of the global management scheme, and consolidation of operations into two groups: pharmaceuticals and consumer products. Goodes also began to concentrate the company's marketing efforts on three primary geographic markets: North America, Europe, and Japan. The company invested $1.3 billion in advertising and promotion and $473 million in research and development, apparently banking on its consumer goods, which still constituted 60 percent of annual sales in 1992.

That year, Warner-Lambert became the fourth company to enter the competitive and controversial market for transdermal nicotine patches. Its prescription smoking cessation device, branded Nicotrol, was strongly promoted through direct consumer advertising, and the product enjoyed early success. However, sales quickly declined in 1993; Warner-Lambert's late entry into the segment, chronic product shortages, a lower than expected success rate, side effects, and especially reports that some users had suffered heart attacks, all led to declines in sales.

In 1993, the company became the first to win approval from the FDA for a drug that retarded the progression of Alzheimer's disease. Warner-Lambert also formed joint ventures with Glaxo Holdings plc and Wellcome plc to orchestrate the movement of the companies' drugs from prescription to over-the-counter and generic markets.

Although still known for reporting some of the industry's lowest profit margins, Warner-Lambert enjoyed steadily increasing sales and profits from 1988 through 1992. Revenue grew from $3.91 billion to $5.6 billion, and profits nearly doubled from $340 million to $644 million during that period. While the consumer goods segment held out relatively low profits, it enjoyed strong international expansion in the late 1980s and early 1990s, helping Warner-Lambert offset some of the losses associated with its ethical drugs.

Principal Subsidiaries: Adams S. A.; American Chicle Co.; Chicle Adams, S. A.; Euronett, Inc.; Family Products Corp.; Keystone Cemurgic Corp.; Parke, Davis & Co.; Tabor Corp.; Warner-Chilcott Inc.

Further Reading:

Baum, Laurie, ''A Powerful Tonic for Warner-Lambert,'' *Business Week,* November 30, 1987, pp. 44, 146.

Lubove, Seth, ''Failure Focuses the Mind,'' *Forbes,* November 8, 1993, pp. 76–78.

Starr, Cynthia, ''First-Ever Alzheimer's Drug Brings Some Hope to Millions,'' *Drug Topics,* October 11, 1993, pp. 16–18.

Weber, Joseph, ''Curing Warner-Lambert—Before It Gets Sick,'' *Business Week,* December 9, 1991, pp. 91, 94.

—updated by April Dougal Gasbarre

Whitman Corporation

3501 Algonquin Road
Rolling Meadows, Illinois 60008
U.S.A.
(708) 818-5000
Fax: (708) 818-5045

Public Company
Incorporated: 1962 as Illinois Central Industries, Inc.
Employees: 14,868
Operating Revenues: $2.5 billion
Stock Exchanges: New York
SICs: 2086 Bottled & Canned Soft Drinks; 3585
   Refrigeration and Heating Equipment; 3714 Motor Vehicle
   Parts & Accessories

Whitman Corporation, known until 1988 as IC Industries, is a Chicago-based firm that owns and operates the largest independent Pepsi bottler company, the largest franchise for car services, and one of the leading manufacturers of refrigerators in the world, along with several other manufacturing divisions. Pepsi General, with factories located in the Midwest and Southeast portions of the United States, provides Whitman with approximately 40 percent of its revenues. Midas repair shops, with over 2,500 outlets worldwide, and Hussmann refrigerators, with operations in Canada, Mexico, Britain, and licensees in the Far East, provide approximately 20 percent and 30 percent respectively of the parent company's revenues.

Whitman has a company history dating back to 1851, when a group of European bankers decided to take advantage of the growing railroad business in America. Initially, the railroad, named the Illinois Central, was operated only inside Illinois, but just after the U.S. Civil War the company began a vigorous expansion plan, incorporating more than 200 railroads into its system. By 1867 the railroad had crossed the Mississippi into Iowa, eventually stretching southward through Kentucky, Tennessee, Arkansas, Alabama, Mississippi, and on to New Orleans. Additional Illinois Central lines ran to South Dakota, Minnesota, Wisconsin, Indiana, Missouri, and Nebraska. For more than a hundred years the Illinois Central Railroad hauled freight and passengers up and down the Mississippi Valley and throughout the northern portion of the Midwest.

On August 31, 1962, the railroad was incorporated as Illinois Central Industries, Inc. And under William Johnson's leadership the company had a new goal—diversification. The Johnson blueprint called for the building of a consumer and commercial products conglomerate by using company cash and stock to buy other businesses, and company tax credits to shelter their earnings. With the single-mindedness typical of its president, the company began methodically to work toward that end.

The first dramatic step was taken in 1968 when the company ventured into the nonrail business, purchasing the Abex Corporation. Formerly known as American Brake Shoe and Foundry, the company produced brakes, wheels and couplings for railroad cars, brake linings for cars and trucks, hydraulic systems for airplanes and ships, and specialized metal castings for industrial uses such as sugar mills and locomotives.

Sixteen years after this initial acquisition, Johnson bought the Pneumo Corporation, a Boston-based aerospace, food, and drug company, for $593 million. The Pneumo purchase was viewed as a means of increasing overall revenue. The subsidiary also provided income from its military contracts, and gave credence to Johnson's theory of growth through acquisition. Over a year later he orchestrated the merger of Abex and Pneumo, forming the Pneumo Abex Corporation.

In 1970 Illinois Central Industries diversified into the real estate business by becoming a major partner in the Illinois Center. The Center is a complex of office buildings, hotels, and condominiums that sprawls across 83 acres of lakefront property in downtown Chicago. In another real estate transaction, the company sold land it owned in New Orleans so that the city could build its athletic stadium, called the Superdome, on the site. Illinois Central Industries maintained ownership of 11 adjoining acres for future developments that included the Hyatt Regency hotel. The company has also developed an array of industrial parks in or near Fort Lauderdale, Memphis, and New Orleans.

This diversification toward real estate came at a time of increasing debate over what role the traditional railroad business should play in the evolving structure of the company. The faltering railway operations, on the one hand, were aided by a merger with the Gulf, Mobile, and Ohio Railroad, which was a combination of several railroads including: the Gulf, Mobile, and Northern, the Mobile and Ohio, and the Chicago and Alton. The merger was formally completed on August 10, 1972, and the new line was named the Illinois Central Gulf Railroad by the parent company.

The sale of some of the company's prime property, on the other hand, indicated movement away from continuing the railroad business. Indeed, by the late 1970s Johnson vacillated back and forth, placing the railroad for sale on the market and then removing it. Eventually, the piecemeal sale of the line proved immensely profitable and solidified Johnson's reputation as an astute businessman.

When the railroad was first placed on the market, no serious purchaser stepped forward, mainly because Johnson had let the railroad deteriorate through lack of maintenance. Johnson then decided to dismantle the line and sell it part by part. This process was greatly aided by capital improvements and rail deregulation during the mid 1980s, and Johnson netted handsome profits for his company.

As Johnson's strategy of diversification unfolded, the company changed its name in 1975 to IC Industries, Inc. Three areas of business were identified as important and company acquisitions fell into these categories: consumer products, commercial products, and railroad activities. The holding company was structured around decentralized management and a growing list of subsidiaries that maintained primarily autonomous operations.

In the consumer products group, a 1978 acquisition brought in the Pet Company, the St. Louis, Missouri, firm that produces evaporated milk. Since then the company has expanded into a variety of food products, including Whitman Chocolates and Old El Paso, the best selling brand of Mexican foods in the United States. The enterprise has grown to 30 owned and eight leased manufacturing plants located in the United States and six foreign countries.

The Hussmann Corporation, a manufacturer of refrigeration equipment for food retailers and processors, composed an important branch of IC's commercial products group. In the early part of the 1980s Hussmann suffered a slump in sales and profits, but by 1984 the subsidiary regained its profitable standing and earned about $44 million before taxes. Later that same year, Hussmann acquired Riordan Holdings, Ltd., a London-based producer of food refrigeration equipment, which served to heighten Hussmann's overseas profile. There are 20 Hussmann-owned and ten leased manufacturing facilities in the United States, Mexico, the United Kingdom, and Canada, as well as three owned and 95 leased branch facilities in these same countries (excluding Mexico) that sell, install, and maintain Hussmann products.

The Pneumo Abex Corporation currently manufacturers products that fall into three basic components: aerospace, industrial, and fluid power products. There is stiff competition, particularly in the aerospace business, but IC regards the competition as a challenge to invest more of its dollars and technology in the field, enabling it to compete with larger firms such as Cleveland Pneumatic Company. Industrial products include braking materials for the automotive original equipment and replacement outlets, and safety equipment for recreational vehicles, trucks, and automobiles. Products are manufactured for use in mining, earthmoving, steel making, and food processing, to name a few. Canadian and U.S. railroads are markets for the iron and composition brake shoes, cast steel wheels, and custom-made track work manufactured by Pneumo Abex. Fluid power products include complete hydraulic systems that are used in construction and mobile equipment, industrial and marine machinery, materials-handling equipment, off-shore drilling and nuclear power plants. This division also manufactures products for aerospace and general aviation markets from 33 plants in the United States and 16 abroad.

When market analysts examine William Johnson's formula for corporate success, which entails pruning acquisitions of all but their most profitable divisions, they most often look to Pet, the largest subsidiary in Whitman's $1.8 billion consumer division. One year following the acquisition of Pet, its pre-tax profits almost tripled to an estimated $85 million in 1984, on a revenue increase of 33 percent. Part of Johnson's carefully crafted plan involves selling low-return operations. Over a six year period, 22 of Pet's units, with sales totalling $400 million, have been sold in order to funnel money into Pet's more profitable products.

Pepsi-Cola General Bottlers is the second largest franchise bottler of Pepsi-Cola beverages in the United States, claiming the greatest share of the soft-drink market in Chicago, Cincinnati, Kansas City, and Louisville. This branch of Whitman's consumer products group also handles other soft-drinks, including Dad's Root Beer, 7-Up, Dr. Pepper, Orange Crush, Canada Dry, and Hawaiian Punch. In 1984 Pepsi General garnered only minimal profits, partly because of heavily discounted prices and partly because both Pepsi-Cola and Coca-Cola introduced new products to the consumer. However, for the next two years Pepsi General's sales growth averaged seven percent, outstripping the industry's as a whole.

Another of Whitman's major consumer product holdings is Midas International, a company that makes and installs automotive exhaust systems, suspension systems, and braking systems through approximately 2,000 franchised and company-owned Midas shops in America, Canada, England, France, Australia, Belgium, Germany, Austria, Panama, and Mexico. Originally specializing in replacement mufflers, Midas has broadened its range to include repairing and replacing brakes and shock absorbers at about 95 percent of its outlets. The expansion of services accounts for the estimated nine percent profit growth shown during 1985 through 1986.

When Johnson retired in 1987, the new leadership was committed to continuing his strategy for the company. Under chairman Karl D. Bays, IC Industries changed its name to Whitman Corporation in 1988 to emphasize its focus on consumer goods and services. Part of this strategy included selling over 65 companies, such as the Pneumo Abex aerospace operation and spinning off the remnants of its Illinois Central Railroad holdings to shareholders. Management also decided to sell most of its real estate holdings. Yet during the same time, Bays went on an acquisition rampage and purchased nearly 100 new companies, including Orval Kent salad products and Van de Kamp's frozen seafood products. When Bays died in November of 1989, Whitman was well on its way toward a reorganization of its product lines.

Whitman's board of directors appointed James W. Cozad, an Amoco vice-chairman, to take Bays' place. Cozad was determined to transform Whitman into an even tighter organization, and immediately announced another restructuring of the company. His strategy was to encourage Whitman's growth by focusing on Pet Inc., Pepsi-Cola General Bottlers, and Midas International, while selling Hussmann and its manufacturing facilities for supermarket refrigerators. But sales for both Pet and Hussmann decreased substantially due to greater market competition, and Cozad was forced to take Hussmann off the market when no acceptable offer to purchase it was forthcoming.

Undismayed, Cozad embarked on a new reorganization strategy. He decided to concentrate on just three businesses, Pepsi-Cola bottlers, Midas International, and Hussmann refrigerators. As a result, Whitman spun off Pet Inc. to its shareholders and lost such well-known brands as Old El Paso, Progresso, and Whitman Chocolates. At the same time, the company eliminated a significant number of jobs in order to reduce its long-term debt of $1.9 billion.

When Whitman changed leadership in 1992, with Bruce Chelberg replacing Cozad, there was no disruption in the development of the company. Chelberg put all his energy into developing the three core businesses of Whitman: Hussmann upgraded its operations throughout its domestic and foreign facilities; Pepsi-Cola General Bottlers doubled production capacity at its Chicago plant, installed state-of-the-art canning equipment, and entered into a joint venture with Grayson Mountain Water to produce a new one-calorie beverage; and Midas International continued to expand its international car service network with new outlets in Mexico and Europe.

Under Chelberg's direction, all of Whitman's holdings have fared well. Pepsi-Cola's operating profit increasing by 18 percent in 1993, led by its core brands of Pepsi-Cola and Diet Pepsi. Midas operating profits for 1993 were up seven percent from the previous year, with sales steadily increasing in Mexico. Hussmann operating profits were down, but demand for supermarket refrigerators appeared to be on the rise in Britain, Mexico, and Canada. With its operations so successfully diversified, Whitman should remain profitable even if one or even two of its core businesses begin to exhibit problems.

Principal Subsidiaries: Mid-American Improvement Corp.; Hussmann Distributing Co., Inc.; IC Equities, Inc.; IC Leasing, Inc.; Illinois Center Corp.; Illinois Central Gulf Railroad Co.; La Salle Properties, Inc.; South Properties, Inc.; IC Products Co.; Bubble Up Co., Inc.; Dad's Root Beer Co.; IC Industries International; ICP Holding Corp.; BIH Foodservice, Inc.; Midas International Corp. The company also lists subsidiaries in the following countries: Australia, Austria, Bermuda, Canada, Denmark, France, Italy, Japan, Mexico, The Netherlands, Sweden, Switzerland, United Kingdom, Venezuela, and West Germany.

Further Reading:

Johnson, William B., *IC Industries,* New York: Newcomen Society, 1973.
Therrien, Lois, "Whitman Is Still Trying to Balance Its Diet," *Business Week,* September 3, 1990, 72–73.

—updated by Thomas Derdak

WordPerfect Corporation

1555 N. Technology Way
Orem, Utah 84057-2399
U.S.A.
(801) 225-5000
Fax: (801) 222-5077

Public Company
Incorporated: 1979 as Satellite Software International
Employees: 4,500
Sales: $705 million
SICs: 7372 Prepackaged Software

WordPerfect Corporation is the manufacturer of the world's all-time best selling, prepackaged word processing software. Along with its flagship WordPerfect word processing program, the company develops and markets software for a variety of computer operating systems. Its products serve three principal markets: business, work group, and consumer applications. The company is additionally recognized as the software industry leader in providing customer support for its products, which are offered in 28 languages and marketed throughout the world by more than 55 international affiliates serving nearly 120 countries.

WordPerfect traces its roots to a partnership which began in 1976 between Bruce Bastian, a Brigham Young University (BYU) graduate student and director of BYU's marching band, and BYU computer science professor Alan Ashton. The two collaborated in devising a software program which would display band formations in three-dimensional graphics. After Bastian received his master's degree in computer science the pair again joined forces to design a word processing system for the city of Orem's Data General Corp. minicomputer system in 1979. Bastian and Ashton kept the rights to the WordPerfect software they designed for Orem, deciding to market it through their own company.

With only one customer reference and a meager expense budget, Ashton and Bastian started Satellite Software International (SSI) in 1980. Relying largely on word-of-mouth advertising, SSI began to sell WordPerfect 1.0, which represented a significant departure from the Wang standard for word processing. The WordPerfect program was based on the idea that distracting computer functions should be kept off of the computer screen and that users should be able to simply start typing on a blank screen.

Bastian was responsible for overseeing program improvements while Ashton taught at BYU in the mornings and worked on program development and recruiting the best students from his classes during the afternoons. Bastian and Ashton hired W. E. "Pete" Peterson to serve as an office manager and organize the fledgling company's books. Peterson was given a tie-breaking 0.2 percent stake in SSI, while Bastian and Ashton each kept a 49.9 percent interest in the company. SSI's initial growth allowed the company to purchase its own development computer (it had been sharing time on the city's of Orem's machines) and conduct business on a broader scale. By the end of 1980, SSI had 16 employees. The following year, the company began international marketing of its word processing software.

The creation of the personal computer market, with the release of the IBM PC, set in motion the development of a number of competing word processing systems. In November 1982, SSI joined the competition with its first version of WordPerfect for an IBM-compatible MS-DOS system, which was released to a user base of about 600. The company's program featured a 30,000-word dictionary, newspaper-style columns, and proportional spacing, as well as automatic footnotes, a four-function math package, and a built-in print spooler. SSI's 1982 sales were a modest $1 million.

By 1983, MicroPro International's WordStar was the leading word processing system. To better compete, SSI enhanced its offerings. It released WordPerfect 3.0, which featured one and two keystroke commands, a keyboard overlay, an automatic insert mode, and the ability to have documents printed as they appeared on-screen. That same month the company also released Personal WordPerfect, designed for non-business use. At a cost of $195 (compared to $495 for the more comprehensive WordPerfect versions), the Personal WordPerfect package allowed for user-defined margins, page lengths, and spacing.

WordPerfect began gaining ground on WordStar during the mid 1980s after MicroPro introduced a version of its word processing program that significantly differed from its earlier WordStar program. SSI's updated WordPerfect versions only added to the features offered in previous programs, making it easy for users to adjust to the newer products. By the end of 1984, WordPerfect was the number three word-processing software, trailing only MultiMate, a Wang look-alike program, and the declining WordStar. That same year SSI began to introduce non-word-processing software and released its first major spreadsheet program, Math Plan 1.0.

In addition to new offerings, SSI took steps to broaden the market for WordPerfect. With its 4.1 version, released in 1985, SSI made WordPerfect available for IBM as well as Apricot, DEC Rainbow, Tandy 2000, TI professional, Victor 9000, and Zenith Z-100 computers. Later versions were modified for Apple computers. Industry journals gave positive reviews to the WordPerfect 4.0 and 4.1 versions, helping to propel SSI's status.

While SSI was introducing word processing programs for the burgeoning PC industry, the WordPerfect customer support network—established early on in SSI's operations—grew into the industry's best user support system and became a major selling point for WordPerfect software. WordPerfect's toll-free hotline not only served as a major drawing card for customers, but was also used by the company to gather new ideas for program features and detect bugs in software.

By 1986, WordPerfect was the nation's best selling word processing software. The program was used by more than 300 major corporations and captured nearly a third of the market for IBM-compatible word processing software. Company surveys at that time revealed that 60 percent of WordPerfect sales stemmed from word-of-mouth referrals rather than advertising. The success of WordPerfect propelled SSI into the position of the fifth largest independent personal computer software company. To take advantage of the name-recognition of its flagship software and clarify any misconceptions consumers might have about the company's product line, SSI changed its name to WordPerfect Corporation in April 1986. With WordPerfect's product line enjoying increasing popularity, the company's 1986 annual revenues mushroomed to $52 million.

In May 1987, the company released its WordPerfect Executive program. Designed primarily for laptop computers, the software included word processing, spreadsheet, calendar, and information management capabilities. While most leading software companies at the time designed programs only for IBM or Apple Macintosh machines unless commissioned by computer manufacturers, WordPerfect broke with tradition and became the first major word-processor serving Amiga and Atari and in the process quickly gained a monopoly for those machines and recouped its developmental investment.

WordPerfect also introduced several non-word processing programs in 1987, including Repeat Performance, designed to increase the speed of programs and cursor movement, and PlanPerfect, an advanced and faster version of Math Plan. The company also released the updated WordPerfect Library 1.1, designed to work with other manufacturer's software by adding cut and paste options to other software programs and allowing users to append data to WordPerfect Library's clipboard, then access that data from other programs on a computer's menu.

In 1987, with WordPerfect's work force having grown to 350, including 100 technicians in customer support, Ashton left BYU to serve full-time as WordPerfect president. He soon began directing WordPerfect's international division, which was translating the company's software and manuals into 12 languages. WordPerfect closed its 1987 books with more than $100 million in sales.

To support growth into the 1990s, the company expanded its offerings, introducing DataPerfect, a relational database software program, DrawPerfect, its first presentation graphics package, and products compatible for Macintosh computers. As the company's products gained popularity, the company enjoyed rapid growth both domestically and internationally. WordPerfect's annual sales rose from $196 to more than $500 million between 1988 and 1990. At the same time, the number of WordPerfect's worldwide users rose from two to seven million and the company's work force expanded nearly fourfold from 1,110 to 4,000. By 1990, the company had grown into one of the world's largest PC software companies.

During the late 1980s, an initial shake out in the software word processing industry left WordPerfect with Microsoft Corp.'s ''Microsoft Word'' as its principal competitor, beginning an era of competitive jousting between the companies which featured price wars and a race to match and then better features of updated program versions. In early 1988, both companies released updated word processors.

With Microsoft's 1990 introduction of a program called Windows, millions of DOS-oriented PC owners began updating their computers with Windows, which provided a means of controlling word processing programs through the use of a mouse device pointed at visual prompts on a display screen, rather than through the use of memorized key commands. Sixteen months after Microsoft's Word for Windows was introduced and began making significant gains in the word processing market, WordPerfect began shipping its first version of WordPerfect for Windows. WordPerfect for Windows received less-than-enthusiastic reviews but nonetheless launched what would become an intense battle for leadership in the rapidly growing Windows segment of the word processing market. While WordPerfect entered 1992 claiming an 85 percent share of the MS-DOS market for word processing software, the company's delay in developing a product that would run on Microsoft's Windows cost it ground in that growing segment, where Microsoft controlled more than half the market and WordPerfect only a third.

With competition with Microsoft intensifying and WordPerfect's market dominance threatened, the company began a major transformation, signalled in March 1992 by the departure of Peterson, who had been actively managing WordPerfect as executive vice-president. Peterson sold his stake in WordPerfect back to Bastian and Ashton, and was replaced by a seven-member executive committee, including Bastian, Ashton, newly appointed Daniel W. Campbell, the company's first financial officer, and Adrian Rietveld, a co-founder of DELTAware (a WordPerfect 1987 acquisition) who became vice-president of sales and marketing.

In addition to the management shakeup, changes were evident on other fronts as the company began speeding up programming developments and spending increased sums on advertising, including the company's first national television ads. In addition, WordPerfect, largely an insular company built on a collegiate atmosphere of Mormon values, began forming partnerships with other firms and making acquisitions in order to expand its business beyond word processing, which accounted for 80 percent of its sales at the time.

In 1992, WordPerfect launched its WordPerfect Information Systems Environment (WISE) marketing strategy designed to promote multi-platform, multi-language, and multi-location software communication products. After teaming up with MagicSoft Inc., a software maker specializing in telecommunications programs designed for e-mail (electronic mail) and fax communications, the company released WordPerfect Works, an integrated software package which included word-processing, spreadsheet, communications, database, and graphics editor programs. The company also upgraded its DrawPerfect package and changed that program's name to WordPerfect Presentations, which offered paint tools and autotracing abilities as well as charting and text handling features. In December 1992, the company released an updated version of WordPerfect for Windows and early the following year was boasting that its Windows program had captured 51 percent of the Windows word-processing market in North America.

Despite the flurry of moves to make the company more aggressive, in 1992 annual revenues dipped from $622 to $579 million, with an increasing amount of sales coming from international markets. Figures from Dataquest Inc., a major independent software research firm, showed Microsoft's Word as the number one selling word-processor in 1992, with WordPerfect's share of the word-processing market having fallen from more than 70 percent in the late 1980s to 36 percent. WordPerfect disputed Dataquest's 1992 figures.

WordPerfect entered 1993 continuing to focus on product-expansion and competition with Microsoft, and early in the year released an updated version of WordPerfect for Windows, which was received with improved reviews and allowed WordPerfect to recoup some of the Windows market share. In 1993, in order to broaden its product base and enhance its cross-platform reputation, WordPerfect acquired Reference Software International, a developer of electronic reference works and software writing tools such as Grammatik, and SoftSolutions Technology Corporation, a prominent manufacturer of cross-platform and multi-lingual software.

After teaming up with Borland International Inc., a California-based software developer, in 1993 WordPerfect released its first "suite" or package of Windows programs which included WordPerfect's word-processor and Borland's spreadsheet. The suite was designed to compete with those being offered by Microsoft, which replied to the WordPerfect introduction in May 1993 with its newest suite, including a database program.

WordPerfect formed a consumer products division in 1993 to target the growing market for small business, educational, and entertainment software products brought on by the increased presence of computers in homes, small offices, and schools. Targeting the groupware market, in June 1993 the company released WordPerfect Office 4.0., an integrated software package which allowed PC users to share files, e-mail, work schedules, and databases, and carried the ability to work with DOS and Windows and integrate different operating systems into one network, a feature lacking in Microsoft's Windows for Workgroups products at the time.

WordPerfect released its WordPerfect 6.0 for DOS at about the same time Microsoft was releasing its updated word processor in 1993. Two months after WordPerfect delivered its upgrade, which was in the developmental stages for three years, the company released an extensive interim version of its namesake, WordPerfect 6.0a, which added numerous functions—including extensive editing capabilities, mouse support, and new tutorials—and addressed what was viewed by consumers as a host of shortcomings in the original upgrade.

At a time when both WordPerfect and Microsoft were in the midst of releasing versions of their flagship writing programs for Windows, WordPerfect filed a lawsuit seeking to stop Microsoft from advertising that it had "the most popular word processor in the world." WordPerfect argued that it deserved that title, based on the total number of WordPerfect programs sold. Microsoft, which had been claiming since June 1993 to have the "most popular" word-processor, responded to the suit by citing Dataquest Inc. figures which showed that Microsoft Word outsold WordPerfect in 1992; WordPerfect cited contradictory data showing it had a sales edge in both 1992 and the first quarter of 1993. Four days after the suit was filed the two software companies agreed in an out-of-court settlement that WordPerfect could use the terms "most popular" and "all-time best selling" while Microsoft would be allowed to call its Word program "best selling."

In January 1994, Ashton stepped down as president and chief executive of WordPerfect in a management restructuring program designed to pump young blood into the Utah firm which had grown into the world's fourth largest software firm and boasted more than 15 million users. Ashton joined Bastian as co-chairman while 39-year-old Rietveld was promoted from sales and marketing to succeed Ashton. Additionally, an office of the president, consisting of Rietveld, John C. Lewis, senior vice-president, and R. Duff Thompson, general counsel, was established.

In early 1994, WordPerfect launched its Main Street line of consumer products, including updates of Grammatik and a new Random House Webster's School and Office Dictionary. The company also announced the debut of a personal information manager software, WordPerfect InfoCentral 1.0, and plans to introduce home education products and entertainment products, including child-targeted software which featured sing-along and interactive cartoon programs.

WordPerfect moved into the mid 1990s facing heightening internal pressures to go public or merge with a publicly traded company so that the founders' families could realize some of the wealth created by the company and WordPerfect would be more attractive to new employees. In March 1994, WordPerfect signed a merger agreement with Novell, Inc., another Utah-based software firm specializing in computer networking. Under the terms of the agreement, which awaited regulatory approval before the end of 1994, WordPerfect would become a wholly owned subsidiary of Novell with WordPerfect's stock exchanged for 59 million shares of Novell common stock and options in a deal valued at $1.4 billion. Coinciding with the Novell-WordPerfect pact, Novell agreed to acquire Borland's spreadsheet business for approximately $145 million.

The merger, according to the *Wall Street Journal,* signalled the end of a time when small software companies could be viable competitors for the rich software business. For WordPerfect, the transaction was expected to help thrust the company's image out of the personal computing era and into a contemporary software arena increasingly focused on networking and connectivity. The deal was also expected to improve the financial position of both WordPerfect and Borland, which had been downsizing their work forces in recent years as a result of price wars with Microsoft. Additionally, the stock transfer was expected to place Bastian and Ashton among the wealthiest people in the United States, with each to net nearly $700 million in Novell shares.

Raymond Noorda, Novell's chief executive and chairman, remained chairman of what was to be an much-expanded Novell, while a new chief executive was expected to be announced in mid 1994. Rietveld was named to head up the WordPerfect business unit and also join the Novell office of the president. In a WordPerfect press release issued at the time of the agreement, Rietveld said that "customers will look back on the mid 1990s as marking a renaissance in the information systems industry. We are helping Novell create a software powerhouse to deliver stand-alone, software suites, groupware, and network applications that define new capabilities for information systems."

Further Reading:

Atchison, Sandra D., "The Land of Plenty—Of Software," *Business Week,* October 19, 1992, p. 84.

——, "WordPerfect: How Long Can it Lead the Band?" *Business Week,* August 11, 1986, p. 66A.

Bulkeley, William M., "Upstart WordPerfect Corp. Finds Niche: Word Processor Dents Position of 'Big Three'," *Wall Street Journal,* April 7, 1987, p. 6.

Fisher, Lawrence M., "WordPerfect Appoints a New Chief," *New York Times,* December 10, 1993, p. 24.

Impoco, Jim, "How Utah Created a Mountain of Jobs: A Pro-Business Climate Lures High-Tech Industry," *U.S. News & World Report,* February 22, 1993, pp. 43–44.

Rebello, Kathy, "The Glitch at WordPerfect," *Business Week,* May 17, 1993, pp. 90–91.

"Relearning Its Lines," *Economist,* June 26, 1993, pp. 73–74.

Rooney, Paula, "WP Duel Scars Smaller Companies," *PC Week,* June 22, 1992, p. 221.

Seymour, Jim, "Fast, Flexible, & Forward-looking," *PC Magazine,* February 29, 1988, pp. 92–104.

Strehlo, Christine, "What's so Special about WordPerfect," *Personal Computing,* March 1988, pp. 100–116.

"WordPerfect Corporation's Alan Ashton On: Taking Giant Steps," *Personal Computing,* March 1988, pp. 119–120.

Zachary, G. Pascal, "Novell to Buy WordPerfect, Lines of Borland," *Wall Street Journal,* March 22, 1994, pp. A3, A9.

——, "WordPerfect Ships Windows Version of Software, Heating Up Competition," *Wall Street Journal,* November 11, 1991, p. B3.

—Roger W. Rouland

WorldCorp, Inc.

13873 Park Center Road, Suite 490
Herndon, Virginia 22071
U.S.A.
(703) 834-9200
Fax: (703) 834-9412

Public Company
Incorporated: 1986
Employees: 640
Sales: $200.4 million
Stock Exchanges: New York Boston Pacific Philadelphia
SICs: 4522 Air Transportation, Nonscheduled; 7375
    Information Retrieval Services

WorldCorp, Inc. is an American holding company whose subsidiaries operate in two industries: air transportation and transaction processing. The oldest of the company's businesses is World Airways, a leading worldwide provider of passenger and cargo air transportation for commercial and governmental customers. Another major subsidiary, World Flight Crew Services, works in the same general field, contracting out flight crews to foreign airlines. WorldCorp's transaction processing businesses include US Order, Inc., of which WorldCorp owns 51 percent, and WorldGames, a wholly owned subsidiary. US Order develops and markets automated ordering systems for residential and commercial use; WorldGames is the sole licensee of US Order's patented technology for applications in the gaming industry.

Although WorldCorp was created and incorporated in 1986, its primary subsidiary, World Airways, had its start decades earlier. Edward J. Daly, known as a boxer, a gambler, and an "adventurer," founded World Airways in 1948. With $50,000 in poker winnings, Daly bought two surplus C-46 Army planes and began passenger service from Teterboro, New Jersey, to the Caribbean. He soon established a base in southern California and expanded the company's service to transcontinental flights of both passengers and cargo. As major airlines strengthened their hold on the air transportation business with their scheduled service, successful airlines offering nonscheduled service dwindled. World Airways became known as one of the few prosperous "non-scheds" of its time.

The U.S. entry into the Korean War offered World Airways an opportunity to increase its business with military contracts. The charter contributed to the rapid air lift in the early 1950s by

moving materials and troops. With the end of the war in 1954, World Airways transferred its military experience to the commercial civilian air transport market. By that time, Daly had purchased two DC-4s, thereby doubling his fleet and tripling his payload capacity. Despite the end of the war, World's relationship with the U.S. military solidified. The DC-4's extended range and pressurized cabins helped World win a "Call" contract from the Military Transport Service, which extended World's flying operations to distant locations, including Guam, Casablanca, Morocco, and Frankfurt, Germany. Soon World was providing daily flights to such Far East countries as Japan, Manila, and Formosa (Taiwan).

In 1957, Daly added the bigger and more powerful DC-6 to his fleet. The new planes had interiors that could be quickly converted from a passenger configuration to a cargo configuration. This flexibility enabled World to proportion its fleet according to the current market needs, an ability uncommon in the charter industry. Unfettered by a fleet of single-purpose planes, World rode out the cycles of the airline industry, simply converting its planes to passenger or cargo configurations as needed. Soon, World Airways boasted operations that justified its name: it had become the world's largest charter airline serving the government and the airline industry.

In the 1960s, World Airways began a long history of leading the charter industry in its acquisition of new types of aircraft. The company purchased the first three convertible B707-320Cs ever made, allowing it to introduce its first charter jet service in 1962. The planes reduced flight times and offered more safety and comfort features. World kept pace with jet technology by adding the B727-100Qs to its fleet in 1966, the first charter airline to do so. The company again upgraded its fleet a short time later with the DC-8-63CFs, which were also convertible. In 1973, World Airways became the first charter airline to purchase wide-body aircraft when it acquired the first three B747-200Cs manufactured by Boeing. Daly moved the company headquarters to Oakland, California in 1973. The new World Air Center the company had opened there covered seven acres and could house four 747s or six DC-8-63s in its hangar. The facility was intended to service and maintain both the company's fleet and third-party aircraft.

World Airways' role in the Vietnam War would earn it a place in history. In the late 1960s and early 1970s, World pilots faced enemy fire to transport troops, food, and supplies into Vietnam and Cambodia. It was the company's airlifts of refugee children out of Southeast Asia, however, that garnered the public's attention. The famous "Baby Lift," which transported Vietnamese orphans from Saigon to the United States in 1975, was conducted by Edward Daly himself. Defying even the U.S. Department of State, Daly arranged the "Last Flight from Da Nang," a mission into Da Nang Airport, under siege by North Vietnamese and Viet Cong troops. World Airways crews evacuated numerous Vietnamese civilians in that airlift.

World's business was not consumed by the war, however. The company began offering customized development services to new airlines in the 1970s. The Republic of Mali contracted with World to operate scheduled service from 1971 to 1978. Yemen Airways, the flag carrier of Yemen, leased three 727-100 aircraft from World and arranged for the company to provide support service in the areas of flight crews, cabin crews, maintenance, and in-flight services from 1976 to 1979. The company again updated its fleet by acquiring new DC-10-30CFs in 1979 and 1980. Throughout the 1970s and 1980s, World aircraft set distance and speed records, and the company was recognized for its high maintenance standards.

In 1973, World Airways contracted with national carriers in Indonesia, Algeria, and Niger to transport Muslims to Saudi Arabia for the Hadj pilgrimage. For decades, World provided transportation for pilgrims to the Islamic Holy Land, in what had become an annual commitment to various national airlines. As of 1994, World continued this tradition with its contracts with Malaysia Airlines and Garuda Indonesia.

Daly's purchase of jumbo aircraft in 1973 was among the early indications that World hoped to compete with the major airlines on their own scheduled-flight turf. Daly lobbied for years for airline deregulation; when it came in 1978 he increased his efforts to get World scheduled routes. The next year the Civil Aeronautics Board granted World permission to provide scheduled transcontinental service. Using a new fleet of DC-10s, World began flying four scheduled coast-to-coast flights a day. The service began on April 12, with $99.99 one-way fares. Daly had risked a great deal; the purchase of the new DC-10s had increased the company's long-term debt from $83 million in 1977 to $294 million in 1978, almost triple its $109 million in shareholders' equity. However, with one-way fares $135 lower than the standard economy fare other carriers were offering, Daly felt sure World could easily compete. World's first days providing the service were aided by the 58-day strike that United Airlines, the transcontinental leader, was battling.

World's honeymoon lasted less than a month, however. United's strike ended and the airline resumed service with fares that matched World's. A price war ensued, with most major lines meeting the low fares. Another blow to World came when DC-10s were grounded indefinitely following an American Airline crash that killed 275 people. Although the extensive safety checks affected other airlines, none were as dependent upon the DC-10 as World. World survived what turned out to be a six-week grounding only to suffer a four-and-a-half-month strike soon after. Despite these setbacks, World achieved a 77 percent load factor by 1981, although the company's debt and low-fare strategy left no room for profit. Losses mounted and, early in 1982, World laid off 800 workers and demanded wage and productivity concessions from the remaining 1,700.

World abandoned scheduled service in 1986, after six years of consecutive losses. With this huge cut in operations, World laid off 1,500 of its 2,600 employees. Daly did not witness the end of World's challenge to the major airlines; he had died in 1984. The string of chief executives that followed Daly had fared no better than he had with scheduled service. The price wars World had initiated and the company's hefty long-term debt left it constantly struggling for capital. That lack of resources prevented World from scheduling flights frequently enough to attract business travelers, the primary customers of the major airlines. In addition, World had chosen important routes—between the coasts and to Europe and Hawaii—that the larger carriers were not willing to share.

WorldCorp, Inc. was created in 1986 as a holding company for World Airways, and T. Coleman Andrews III, the fifth chief executive since Daly, was brought on to refocus the airline on its traditional commercial and military charters. A $62 million loan from Drexel Burnham and an agreement from United Airlines and Pan Am to honor World's remaining tickets gave the company the breathing room to recover from its brush with bankruptcy. Although the U.S. charter industry had been hurt by the proliferation of discount fares that followed airline deregulation, World had a strong history of military contracts to fall back on. In addition, its service to foreign airlines, such as its yearly charters for the Muslim pilgrims, had remained strong.

Within a year, World Airways was once again profitable. It had had a loss in 1986 of $28 million on revenues of $106 million; in 1987 it turned a profit of $7 million on revenues of $144 million. Two-thirds of World's revenues came from transporting personnel for the military. A year after taking over World Airways, Andrews arranged for the company to buy Key Airlines, a Nevada-based military and charter airline he had chaired before joining World. The $18 million deal indicated, as Andrews told *Business Week,* that World had "moved beyond the question of survival."

For the next five years, World Airways maintained its profitability, a distinct achievement not only because of the company's seven previous years of losses, but also because of the general downturn in the air transportation industry. World's 1990–92 net income of around $100 million compared very favorably with the losses incurred by the major airlines, which ranged from United's $600 million loss to Continental's over $1.5 billion loss. In addition, during the 1980s, World's stock price more than tripled.

World's convertible passenger/cargo aircraft helped the company adapt to sudden changes in the market during the late 1980s and early 1990s. "The Gulf War was the best example of our flexibility," World Airways president Charles Pollard told *Aviation Week and Space Technology.* "From the start we were flying troops on aircraft configured for passenger; we then converted to the all-freighter configuration and flew the sustainment mission to the end of the war, and we went back to passenger layout to fly troops back home."

Although military contracts accounted for a significant portion of World's business after it dropped its scheduled service, the company also developed several other important markets. Wet lease services, leasing aircraft and crews to other carriers, increased to include not only contracts with Malaysian Airlines and Garuda Indonesia for the Hadj pilgrimage, but also the major foreign carriers Virgin Atlantic, British Airways, and Qantas. Moreover, passenger flights for tour operators were expected to account for 18 percent of the company's total revenue in 1994. World also cultivated cargo business in Asia and with domestic shippers United Parcel Services and Burlington Air Express. In 1992, the company sold Key Airlines for $8 million, a move WorldCorp chairman Andrews admitted should have been taken earlier, when it became apparent that the airline would be unprofitable for World to run.

World led the charter industry again with its acquisition of seven MD-11s: four passenger aircraft, two convertible passenger/cargo aircraft, and one freighter. Compared to the company's DC-10s, the MD-11s provided 37 percent more cargo capacity yet burned 15 percent less fuel per hour. The company planned to phase out its DC-10s over the next several years.

In the mid 1990s, World prepared for a shift away from its core military and wet lease business. With the withdrawal of U.S. troops from Europe and defense spending cuts, the military's transportation needs were likely to decline. World also saw a decreased need for wet leases as other carriers built up surpluses of aircraft. The company's general plan was to lower the amount of ad hoc flying it performed by winning more long-term operating contracts and increasing the seasonal services it performed for tour operators, foreign passenger airlines, and express/shipping companies. In an effort to increase its market access in Asia, where the company already derived nearly 40 percent of its business, World sold 24.9 percent of its stock to Malaysian Helicopter Services in 1993 for $27.4 million in cash.

Part of World's new strategy was a return to regularly scheduled service. If successful, it would provide steady year round business that would balance the erratic financial results of World's contract business. World has carefully selected the routes it has requested, hoping to avoid the intense competition it aroused by entering the coast-to-coast market in the late 1970s. In 1994, the company asked the U.S. Transportation Department for three of the six frequencies to South Africa that had been awarded to USAfrica Airways, a start-up airline that had been unable to begin service due to a lack of financing. Charles Pollard, president of World Airways, explained to *Aviation Week and Space Technology* the company's reentry into a field where the company had failed before: "[Scheduled service to Johannesburg] is a defensible niche market that provides very high utilization of aircraft and crews, it offers moderate to high yields, and it has traffic rights that are not readily duplicated by other carriers." The company also sought three weekly frequencies to Tel Aviv from the Israeli Civil Aviation Administration, having already gotten approval from the U.S. Transportation Department and the State Department.

In the early 1990s, WorldCorp expanded its business outside the air transport industry by acquiring 46 percent of the preferred stock of US Order, a transaction processing company. US Order developed the ScanFone, a screen-based telephone system that facilitates the purchase of goods and services from the home, including home grocery shopping and delivery, electronic bill payment, and mail order catalog shopping. The company has developed business alliances with Michigan Bell, Ameritech, and Bell Atlantic. With their cooperation, US Order introduced the ScanFone system in the Detroit area in 1992 and planned to start service in the Washington, D.C., area in 1993. With 10,000 ScanFones in consumers' households as of early 1993, US Order was the clear leader in this nascent market.

As military contracts dwindled and the wet lease market shrank, WorldCorp's profitability depended on World Airway's ability to cultivate business in its other markets and to enter new ones. Its steady profits during the general industry recession in the early 1990s bodes well for its success in the future. WorldCorp's efforts to diversify into transaction processing may help stabilize World Airway's revenues from the difficult air transport industry.

Principal Subsidiaries: World Airways, Inc.; WorldCorp Leasing, Inc.; WorldCorp Leasing II, Inc.; WorldCorp Services, Inc.; World Airways Cargo, Inc.; WorldGames; World Flight Crew Services, Inc.; US Order, Inc. (51%).

Further Reading:

Armbruster, William, "World Airways Seeks Rebirth through Niche Service," *Journal of Commerce,* February 10, 1994, p. 1.
Banks, Howard, "Chartered Wings," *Forbes,* June 13, 1988, p. 124.
"Brave New World," *Air Cargo News International,* November 26, 1993.
"How Two Airlines Lost Their Way," *Business Week,* April 19, 1982, pp. 116–18.
Lenorowitz, Jeffrey M., "World Reshapes Services to Meet New Market Trends," *Aviation Week & Space Technology,* August 23, 1993, p. 44.
Levine, Jonathan B., "World Airways Beats a Timely Retreat," *Business Week,* September 15, 1986, p. 52.
"The Prodigy Who Came to World's Rescue," *Business Week,* April 27, 1987, p. 58.
"World Airways: When an Upstart Airline Owns Mostly DC-10s," *Business Week,* June 25, 1979, pp. 110–11.
"World Revises Fare Structure, Blames Losses on Competition," *Aviation Week & Space Technology,* February 16, 1981, p. 33.

—Susan Windisch Brown

Zenith Data Systems, Inc.

2150 East Lake Cook Road
Buffalo Grove, Illinois 60089
U.S.A.
(708) 808-5000
Fax: (708) 399-3898

Wholly Owned Subsidiary of Groupe Bull (France)
Incorporated: 1979
Employees: 2,100
Sales: $1 billion
SICs: 3571 Electronic Computers

Zenith Data Systems, Inc. (ZDS), a wholly owned subsidiary of the French corporation Groupe Bull, is a global leader in the manufacture of microcomputers, specifically desktop and notebook computers, servers, and related peripherals. According to a company statement, "ZDS has one of the broadest product offerings in the industry." The company's major customers include businesses, schools, and government agencies.

Although ZDS's headquarters are located in Buffalo Grove, Illinois (northwest of Chicago), the company maintains facilities in other locations including St. Joseph, Michigan, Santa Clara, California, Billerica, Massachusetts, and Europe. The St. Joseph site, with 900 employees, houses ZDS's manufacturing facility for North American desktop PCs and the company's primary research and development program. ZDS's circuit boards are supplied by another Bull facility, located in Massachusetts. Notebook and subnotebook products are manufactured in accordance with ZDS specifications by outside suppliers.

ZDS was founded in 1979 when Zenith Electronics Corporation, a leader in the North American electronics industry, purchased the Heath Company, a manufacturer of personal computers and do-it-yourself electronics equipment. Following the acquisition, Zenith Electronics created Zenith Data Systems. Until 1992, a vestige of the organization's roots remained in the name of its Heath/Zenith Computer chain of retail outlets. In March 1992, however, the stores were closed.

ZDS initially prospered by selling personal computers (PCs) on college campuses. In 1984, after a failed attempt to convince college bookstores to carry its products, ZDS turned to fraternity houses and succeeded in penetrating the college market. Early years at ZDS were marked by technological innovation.

For example, the company was the first to introduce a battery-operable portable PC with a backlit display.

By 1988, ZDS was the nation's number one laptop PC seller, with an estimated 23 percent share of the market. ZDS's reputation as a leading computer supplier was further bolstered when the company won contracts to sell computers to the U.S. Air Force and the Internal Revenue Service. According to one report, ZDS's revenues totaled $1.4 billion in 1988.

The company's fortunes soon shifted, however. One product introduced in 1989, a small notebook PC with a 2-inch floppy disk drive, failed to gain acceptance, and the company lost a major military contract to Unisys Corp. In an effort to increase sales of its desktop models, ZDS initiated a policy requiring its laptop dealers to sell its desktop models as well. *Business Week* estimated that 1,000 dealers, including ComputerLand Corp., stopped selling ZDS products rather than stock the unpopular desktop PCs.

Zenith Electronics Corporation, preparing to sell ZDS, cut research and development expenditures. The move left the company without new product offerings. Peter Burrows, writing for *Electronic Business,* noted that "products not at the cutting edge quickly lose their appeal, especially since most newer generation models are being priced competitively with their clunkier forerunners." As a result, ZDS saw its sales plummet and its inventories rendered obsolete.

In December 1989, Compagnie des Machines Bull (also known as Groupe Bull or Bull) purchased ZDS for $511 million. Groupe Bull, headquartered in Paris, France, was 75 percent owned by the State of France. Other shareholders included France Telecom (17 percent), NEC Corp. (4.4 percent), and International Business Machines Corp. (2.1 percent).

In January 1991, ZDS appointed Enrico Pesatori as CEO. Pesatori was given the responsibility of turning the company around and restoring its status. Under Pesatori's leadership, ZDS launched a new line of laptops and abandoned the requirement that dealers sell desktop models in order to carry laptops. Pesatori also focused research projects narrowly in order to provide more money for the most promising areas.

A new advertising campaign, with a budget 50 percent larger than previous campaigns, focused on business users. The company also continued expanding its distribution channels and reestablished a relationship with ComputerLand. Sales soon began to recover. According to an industry report, ZDS shipped an estimated 194,000 units in 1990 (down from 445,000 in 1988). In 1991, 228,000 units were shipped. Research and development investments were also increased; expenditures in 1991 were up 25 percent over 1990 and up another 20 percent in 1992.

One project was to redesign the company's portable and desktop PCs and monitors. The new design featured lines intended to produce a quality product image. The resulting Z-Series was released in June 1992. When initially introduced, the Z-Series notebooks were the lightest laptops available with color display technology and the first ones to offer built-in networking capability. The Z-Lite, a subnotebook, weighed in at only 3.9 pounds.

Although the Z-Series received industrial design awards, some reviewers complained. Gary McWilliams, writing for *Business Week*, suggested that ZDS had placed an emphasis on "style over function." McWilliams noted, "Critics say the design fails basic laptop ergonomics—for example, by using latches that require two hands to open."

Other good news for ZDS was also mixed with unfavorable criticism. The company's Z-NOTE was named among the 40 "Best Products of 1992" by *PC Magazine*. In another article, however, *PC Magazine* criticized ZDS for scoring lower than average in a reader survey measuring overall PC reliability and satisfaction with repair service and technical support.

ZDS also continued losing retail market share. The company's 3.4 percent in July 1991 fell to 1.0 percent in July 1992. ZDS officials claimed the sales decline was indicative of shifting consumer buying habits and a new preference for superstore outlets, a market in which the company had little presence. Total sales for 1992 were estimated at $900 million. European sales accounted for 55 percent of the total; 40 percent of the total sales were attributed to notebook models.

To help bolster U.S. sales, ZDS reorganized its field sales force in 1992. Company representatives began working directly with corporate accounts rather than exclusively with resellers. In another attempt to enhance distribution, one million copies of a 32-page "Z-Direct" catalog were mailed offering desktop, server, and notebook products via a toll-free phone number. The catalog also featured peripheral equipment from other manufacturers and software products produced by Microsoft Corp., Novell Inc., and Lotus Development Corp.

ZDS officials hoped that the direct sales effort would increase brand recognition and reach customers who were not served by other marketing channels. A company representative quoted in the *Wall Street Journal* stated that although ZDS did not expect a dramatic increase in sales to result from its direct mail efforts, the company hoped to "grow our business across the channels." Industry watchers questioned, however, whether the objective would be achieved. Some noted that other mail order firms, involved in steep price cutting, were experiencing dwindling margins. One critic expressed the opinion that the move would place ZDS in the position of competing with itself.

ZDS began 1993 with another change in leadership. Jacques Noels, former president of Nokia Consumer Electronics, replaced Pesatori as CEO. Noels expected to focus on bringing new products to the marketplace and faced the continuing challenge of improving the company's relationship with its dealers. In addition, Noels sought to recapture a U.S. government contract, termed Desktop IV, involving the sale of more than 300,000 PCs. ZDS had provided computers to the U.S. government under the Desktop I contract in effect from 1983 to 1986 and Desktop II from 1986 to 1989. Although the Desktop IV contract was initially awarded to a competitor, after judicial review, ZDS received the contract valued at approximately $724 million. By 1994, ZDS reported having installed a total of more than 700,000 PC's for the U.S. military and civilian agencies.

Products introduced in 1993 included the Z-NOTEPAD, a pen-capable version of Z-NOTE (a notebook PC) and Z-LITE 425L,

an extension of the ZDS subnotebook line. The company also unveiled its Z-STAR 433VL series. The Z-STAR series, comprised of three models, was a 486-based notebook PC featuring a 33 MHz 486SLC microprocessor. One of the key advantages of the 486SLC microprocessor was its ability to conserve power. Although battery life for notebook computers varied during actual usage depending on attached peripherals and power management features, the monochrome Z-STAR model was able to provide up to three hours of computing ability using a removable nickel cadmium battery pack. The Z-STAR notebooks also featured a "J-Mouse" key. A "J-Mouse" used the "J" key to function as a built in mouse for controlling cursor movement when light, continued pressure was applied. When used in conjunction with other keys, the "J-Mouse" was able to provide all the functions of a three-button mouse.

ZDS also unveiled a new series of desktop PCs in 1993, the Z-SELECT 100 line. Z-SELECT 100 desktop PCs featured pre-installed network software for Novell NetWare, Banyan VINES, and Microsoft LAN Manager. With this feature, by taking the computer out of the box and making a simple menu selection, a user was able to operate on a network without figuring out how to load and configure the system. David O'Connor, executive vice president of ZDS Worldwide Product Group, stated in a company press release "Z-SELECT 100 is destined to become a market leader in cost-effective, high performance desktop computing." Prices for the network-ready Z-Select models began at $999 for a system that included a 25MHz Intel 486SX microprocessor, 4MB of RAM, and a 170MB hard drive. Another feature of the Z-SELECT 100 line was its power management capability. Users were able to define the time period of inactivity after which the system would enter a rest mode without losing data. Full operation was resumed automatically upon engaging the mouse or keyboard or in response to input from a modem, network, or other device. According to a company statement, in the rest mode, Z-SELECT 100 products used only 60 watts, less power than the average light bulb.

In another 1993 move, ZDS's parent company, Groupe Bull, acquired a 19.9 percent interest in Packard-Bell. Packard-Bell, headquartered in Chatsworth, California, held a 37 percent share of the discount PC market and was the fourth largest PC seller in the United States (behind Apple, IBM, and Compaq Computer). Only five percent of Packard-Bell's sales were for notebooks, compared with an industry average of almost 20 percent. Under the terms of the acquisition, ZDS agreed to provide private-label versions of its notebook and subnotebook PCs to Packard-Bell. The two companies also agreed to work together in the design and manufacture of future desktop PCs.

By the end of 1993, ZDS reported an overall increase in worldwide revenues of 30 percent. North America revenues were up 53 percent, and European revenues were up 22 percent. The number of units shipped was also up (89 percent in the U.S. and 62 percent worldwide). ZDS products were being delivered to the marketplace by seven major distributors (BSM Computers, Inc., Gates/FA, Ingram Micro, Merisel, Microage, ROBEC, and Tech Data), and the company had sales outlets in more than 30 countries.

For ZDS, 1994 opened with the announcement of a new PC product line: the Z-STOR Personal Server. Z-STOR was designed to make networking simple and affordable. The line was developed by the Desktop Workgroup Computing Initiative, a joint effort conducted by ZDS and Novell, Inc. Novell was a leading developer of network services designed to facilitate the sharing of information resources within local area networks, wide area networks, and inter-networked information systems. Z-STOR products were designed to connect desktop or notebook PCs, or remote office locations, with a central facility in order to access sharable information. The Z-STOR line, with some models priced under $1,000, provided "plug-and-play" convenience because all the necessary software and network connections were pre-installed and pre-configured. Z-STOR, called the most innovative networking solution, won the "Highlight '94" award at CeBIT, the world's largest computer exhibition (held in Hanover, Germany).

Other product lines launched in early 1994 included an extension of the Z-STATION desktop system, called Z-STATION 500, and a new addition to its notebook family, the Z-NOTEFLEX. Z-STATION 500 PCs featured improved video capability, better power management, and greater system performance (achieved via higher data transfer rates, a wider data path, and increased expandability). They were designed for use by interconnected workgroups, irrespective of their location. The Z-NOTEBOOK was a modular notebook computer featuring interchangeable video displays, user-removable hard disk drives (allowing users to secure sensitive data or upgrade to a higher storage capacity without the use of tools), and a floppy drive that could be removed to accommodate an optional second battery pack.

Battery life was an important issue in notebook computing technology. To provide its customers with longer run-times, ZDS entered into an agreement with AER Energy Resources Inc. in 1994 to develop a product using AER's patented, rechargeable zinc-air battery. Although battery life depended on many variables such as power requirements, computer configuration, and user work habits, the zinc-air battery had the ability to operate for an estimated 10 to 20 hours without recharging.

During the first quarter of 1994, ZDS reported significant revenue increases in both its North American and European markets. A comparison of the first quarters of 1993 and 1994 showed an increase of 132 percent in North America and an increase of 42 percent in Europe. Combined, the figures yielded a 73 percent increase in comparative first quarter revenues. According to a company statement, ZDS's annual sales revenues of about $1 billion accounted for approximately 40 percent of its parent company's total hardware revenues. ZDS revenues were split approximately evenly between North American and European markets and also between desktop and notebook products.

Further Reading:

Boudette, Neal, "Departure of CEO Clouds ZDS' Future," *PC Week,* January 18, 1993; "Zenith Strives to Reclaim Lost PC Turf," *PC Week,* April 13, 1992;

"Zenith To Mount Aggressive Direct-Market Push," *PC Week,* August 17, 1992.

Burrows, Peter, "Power-Packed Portables are Storming PC Markets," *Electronic Business,* January 22, 1990.

Desposito, Joseph, "Zenith Data Systems," *PC Magazine,* May 26, 1992.

Hayes, Thomas C., "Zenith Data and Packard Bell in Deal for New PC's," *New York Times,* June 23, 1993.

McWilliams, Gary, "Zenith Data, Act II: Enter New Chief, Swinging," *Business Week,* May 27, 1991; "Zenith Data: Good Looks May Not Be Good Enough," *Business Week,* September 27, 1993.

Pepper, Jon, "ZDS Pins Big Hopes on Small Computers," *Marketing Computers,* July 1991.

Pope, Kyle, "Zenith Data Plans To Begin Selling Computers by Mail," *Wall Street Journal,* August 11, 1992.

Vlasic, Bill, "Zenith Data Closes Retail Chain," *Detroit News,* April 1, 1992.

"Zenith Data Systems and AER Energy Sign Letter of Intent to Develop Long Run-Time Battery Option for Portable Computers," *PR Newswire,* March 24, 1994.

—Karen Bellenir

INDEX TO COMPANIES AND PERSONS _____

Listings are arranged in alphabetical order under the company name; thus Eli Lilly & Company will be found under the letter E. Definite articles (The) and forms of incorporation that precede the name (A.B. and N.V.) are ignored for alphabetical purposes. Company names appearing in bold type have historical essays on the page numbers appearing in bold. Updates to entries that appeared in earlier volumes are signified by (upd.). The index is cumulative with volume numbers printed in bold type.

American Oil Pipe Line Co., **IV** 370

American Olean Tile Co., **III** 424

American Optical Co., **I** 711–12; **III** 607; **7** 436

American Overseas Holdings, **III** 350

American Paging, **9** 494–96

American Petrofina, Inc., **IV** 498; **7** 179–80

American Photographic Group, **III** 475; **7** 161

American Physicians Service Group, Inc., **6** 45

American Platinum Works, **IV** 78

American Postage Meter Co., **III** 156

American Potash and Chemical Corp., **IV** 95, 446

American Power & Light Co., **6** 545, 596–97

American Premier Underwriters, Inc., 10 71–74

American President Companies Ltd., III 512; **6 353–55**

American President Domestic Company, **6** 354

American President Lines Ltd., **6** 353–54

American Protective Mutual Insurance Co. Against Burglary, **III** 230

American Publishing Co., **IV** 597

American Pure Oil Co., **IV** 497

American Radiator & Standard Sanitary Corp., **III** 663–64

American Radiator Co., **III** 663–64

American Railway Express Co., **II** 382, 397; **10** 61

American Railway Publishing Co., **IV** 634

American Re Corporation, 10 75–77

American Re-Insurance Co., **III** 182

American Record Corp., **II** 132

American Ref-Fuel, **V** 751

American Refrigeration Products S.A, **7** 429

American Republic Assurance Co., **III** 332

American Research and Development Corp., **II** 85; **III** 132; **6** 233

American Residential Holding Corporation, **8** 30–31

American Residential Mortgage Corporation, 8 30–31

American Resorts Group, **III** 103

American River Transportation Co., **I** 421

American Robot Corp., **III** 461

American Rolling Mill Co., **IV** 28; **8** 176–77

American Royalty Trust Co., **IV** 84; **7** 188

American RX Pharmacy, **III** 73

American Safety Equipment Corp., **IV** 136

American Safety Razor Co., **III** 27–29

American Sales Book Co., Ltd., **IV** 644

American Satellite Co., **6** 279

American Savings & Loan, **10** 117

American Savings Bank, **9** 276

American Sealants Company. *See* Loctite Corporation.

American Seating Co., **I** 447

American Seaway Foods, Inc, **9** 451

American Sheet Steel Co., **IV** 572; **7** 549

American Smelters Securities Co., **IV** 32

American Smelting and Refining Co., **IV** 31–33

American Standard Inc., III 437, **663–65**

American States Insurance Co., **III** 276

American Steamship Company, **6** 394–95

American Steel & Wire Co., **I** 355; **IV** 572; **7** 549

American Steel Foundries, **7** 29–30

American Steel Hoop Co., **IV** 572; **7** 549

American Stock Exchange, **10** 416–17

American Stores Company, II 604–06

American Technical Services Company. *See* American Building Maintenance Industries, Inc.

American Telephone and Telegraph Company, I 462; **II** 13, 54, 61, 66, 80, 88, 120, 252, 403, 430–31, 448; **III** 99, 110–11, 130, 145, 149, 160, 162, 167, 246, 282; **IV** 95, 287; **V 259–64,** 265–68, 269, 272–75, 302–04, 308–12, 318–19, 326–30, 334–36, 341–342, 344–346; **6** 267, 299, 306–07, 326–27, 338–40; **7** 88, 118–19, 146, 288, 333; **8** 310–11; **9** 32, 43, 106–07, 138, 320, 321, 344, 478–80, 495, 514; **10** 19, 58, 87, 97, 175, 202–03, 277–78, 286, 431, 433, 455–57

American Telephone and Telegraph Technologies Inc., **V** 339

American Television and Communications Corp., **I** 534–35; **II** 161; **IV** 596, 675; **7** 528–30

American Textile Co., **III** 571

American Tin Plate Co., **IV** 572; **7** 549

American Title Insurance, **III** 242

American Tobacco Co., **I** 12–14, 28, 37, 425; **V** 395–97, 399, 408–09, 417–18, 600

American Tool & Machinery, **III** 420

American Totalisator Corporation, **10** 319–20

American Tourister, Inc., **10** 350

American Tractor Corporation, **10** 379

American Trading and Production Corporation, **7** 101

American Transport Lines, **6** 384

American Trust and Savings Bank, **II** 261

American Trust Co., **II** 336, 382

American Ultramar Ltd., **IV** 567

American Viscose Corp. *See* Avisco.

American Water Works & Electric Company, **V** 543–44

American Water Works Company, 6 443–45

American Woolen, **I** 529

American Yearbook Company, **7** 255

American-Marietta Corp., **I** 68, 405

American-Palestine Trading Corp., **II** 205–06

American-South African Investment Co. Ltd., **IV** 79

American-Strevell Inc., **II** 625

America's Favorite Chicken Company, Inc., 7 26–28

Amerifirst Federal Savings, **10** 340

Amerimark Inc., **II** 682

Amerisystems, **8** 328

Ameritech, V 265–68; **6** 248; **7** 118; **10** 431

Ameritech Development, **V** 265–68

Ameritech Information Systems, **V** 265, 268

Ameritech Mobile Communications, Inc., **V** 265–68

Ameritech Publishing Inc., **V** 265–68

Ameritrust Corporation, **9** 476

Amerman, John W., **7** 306

Amerotron, **I** 529

Amersil Co., **IV** 78

Ames, C.B., **7** 409

Ames, Charles W., **7** 580

Ames Department Stores, Inc., V 197–98; **9 20–22**; **10** 497

Ames, Jack, **8** 268

Ames, Oakes, **V** 529

Ames, Oliver, **V** 529

Ames Worsted Textile Company, **9** 20

Amesh, Salem Mohammed, **IV** 453

AMETEK, Inc., 9 23–25

N.V. Amev, III 199–202

AMEV Australia, **III** 200

AMEV Finance, **III** 200

AMEV Financial Group, **III** 200

AMEV General Insurance, **III** 200

AMEV Holdings, **III** 201

AMEV Inc., **III** 200

AMEV International, **III** 199, 201

AMEV Levensverzekeringen, **III** 200–01

AMEV Life Assurance, **III** 200

AMEV Maatschappij voor belegging in aandelen NV, **III** 201

AMEV Nederland, **III** 199, 201

AMEV Schadeverzekering, **III** 201

AMEV South East Asia, **III** 200–01

AMEV Venture Management, **III** 200

AMEV Verzekeringen, **III** 200

Amey Roadstone Corp., **III** 503

Amey Roadstone Corporation, America, **7** 209

Amfac Inc., I 417–18, 566; **IV** 703; **10** 42

Amfas, **III** 310

Amgen, Inc., I 266; **8 216–17**; **10 78–81**

Amherst Coal Co., **IV** 410; **7** 309

Amiga Corporation, **7** 96

Aminoil, Inc., **IV** 523. *See also* American Independent Oil Co.

AMISA, **IV** 136

Amitron S.A., **10** 113

AMK Corporation, **II** 595; **7** 85

Ammentorp, Kjeld, **III** 737–38

Ammo-Phos, **I** 300; **8** 24

L'Ammoniac Sarro-Lorrain S.a.r.l., **IV** 197

Amoco Canada, **II** 376; **IV** 371

Amoco Chemicals Corp., **I** 202; **IV** 370–71

Amoco Corporation, I 516; **IV 368–71**, 412, 424–25, 453, 525; **7** 107, 443; **10** 83–84

Amoco Fabrics & Fibers Co., **IV** 371

Amoco International Oil Co., **IV** 370–71

Amoco Iran Oil Co., **IV** 371

Amoco Performance Products, **III** 611

Amory, Jean-Pierre, **IV** 499

Amos, Bill, **III** 187–88; **10** 28–29

Amos, Daniel P., **III** 188–89; **10** 29–30

Amos, John B., **III** 187–89; **10** 28–30

Amos, Paul S., **III** 187–89; **10** 30

Amos, Shelby, **III** 187; **10** 28

Amoseas, **IV** 453–54

Amoskeag Company, 6 356; **8 32–33**; **9** 213–14, 217

AMP, Inc., II 7–8

AMP Special Industries, **II** 7

AMPAL. *See* American-Palestine Trading Corp.

AMPCO Auto Parks, Inc. *See* American Building Maintenance Industries, Inc.

AMPEP, **III** 625

Ampex Corp., **III** 549; **6** 272

Ampol Exploration Ltd., **III** 729

Ampol Ltd., **III** 729

Ampol Petroleum Ltd., **III** 729

AMR Corp., **I** 90–91; **6** 76; **8** 315

AMR Information Services, **9** 95

AMRE, **III** 211

Aoi, Joichi, **I** 535
Aoi, Tadao, **V** 127–28
Aoki Corporation, **9** 547, 549
AON Corporation, **III 203–05**
Aon Reinsurance Agency, **III** 205
AON Risk Services, **III** 205
AP. *See* Associated Press.
AP&L. *See* American Power & Light Co.
AP-Dow Jones, **10** 277
AP-Dow Jones/Telerate Company, **10** 277
APAC, Inc., **IV** 374
Apache Corp., **10 102–04**
Apache Petroleum Company, **10** 103
Apex Financial Corp., **8** 10
Apex Smelting Co., **IV** 18
Apita, **V** 210
APL. *See* American President Lines Ltd.
APL Associates, **6** 353
APL Corporation, **9** 346
APL Information Services, Ltd., **6** 354
APL Land Transport Services Inc., **6** 354
APM Ltd., **IV** 248–49
Apogee Enterprises, Inc., **8 34–36**
Apollo Computer, **III** 143; **6** 238; **9** 471
Apollo Technologies, **I** 332
Apotekarnes Droghandel A.B., **I** 664–65
Appel, Daniel F., **III** 313
Appel, Uranus J. (Bob), **III** 73
Appell, Louis J., **8** 509
Appell, Louis J., Jr., **8** 509–10
Apple Computer, Inc., **I** 6, 62, 103, 107,
124; **III** 114, **115–16**, 121, 125, 149,
172; **6 218–20 (upd.)**, 222, 225, 231,
244, 248, 254–58, 260, 289; **8** 138; **9**
166, 170–71, 368, 464; **10** 22–23, 34,
57, 233, 235, 404, 458–59, 518–19
Apple Container Corp., **III** 536
Apple Europe, **6** 219
Apple Pacific, **6** 219
Apple Products, **6** 219
Apple USA, **6** 219
Appleton & Cox, **III** 242
Appleton Papers, **I** 426
Appleton Wire Works Corp., **8** 13
Appliance Buyers Credit Corp., **III** 653
Les Applications du Roulement, **III** 623
Applied Bioscience International, Inc., **10
105–07**
Applied Color Systems, **III** 424
Applied Communications, Inc., **6** 280
Applied Data Research, Inc., **6** 225
Applied Digital Data Systems Inc., **II** 83; **9**
514
Applied Engineering Services, Inc. *See* The
AES Corporation.
Applied Komatsu Technology, Inc., **10** 109
Applied Learning International, **IV** 680
Applied Materials, Inc., **10 108–09**
Applied Power, Inc., **9 26–28**
Applied Solar Energy, **8** 26
Approvisionnement Atlantique, **II** 652
Appryl, **I** 303
Apps, Frederick L., **III** 274
APS. *See* Arizona Public Service
Company.
Apura GmbH, **IV** 325
APUTCO, **6** 383
Aqua Glass, **III** 570
Aqua Pure Water Co., **III** 21
Aqua-Chem, Inc., **I** 234; **10** 227
Aquarius Group, **6** 207
Aquila, **IV** 486
Aquila Energy Corp., **6** 593
Aquino, Corazon, **6** 106–07

Aquitaine. *See* Société Nationale des
Petroles d'Aquitaine.
AR-TIK Systems, Inc., **10** 372
ARA Holding Co., **II** 608
ARA Services, **II 607–08**
Arab Contractors, **III** 753
Arab Japanese Insurance Co., **III** 296
Arab Petroleum Pipeline Co., **IV** 412
Arabian American Oil Co., **I** 570; **IV** 386,
429, 464–65, 512, 536–39, 552, 553,
559; **7** 172, 352. *See also* Saudi Arabian
Oil Co.
Arabian Gulf Oil Co., **IV** 454
Arabian Oil Co., **IV** 451
Arai, Akira, **IV** 656
Arakawa, Masashi, **7** 220–21
Araki, Yoshiro, **II** 293
Aral, **IV** 487
Aramco. *See* Arabian American Oil Co.
and Saudi Arabian Oil Company.
de Araoz, Daniel, **6** 95
Araskog, Rand Vincent, **I** 462, 464
Aratsu Sekiyu, **IV** 554
ARBED Finance S.A., **IV** 26
ARBED S.A., **IV 24–27**, 53
ARBED-Felten & Guilleaume Tréfileries
Réunies, **IV** 26
Arbitron Corp., **III** 128; **10** 255, 359
Arbor Living Centers Inc., **6** 478
Arbuckle, Ernest C., **II** 382
Arbuckle, Fatty, **II** 154
Arbuthnot & Co., **III** 522
Arby's, **II** 614; **8** 536–37
ARC Ltd., **III** 501
ARC Materials Corp., **III** 688
Arcadian Marine Service, Inc., **6** 530
Arcata National Corp., **9** 305
Arcelik, **I** 478
Arch Mineral Corporation, **IV** 374; **7
32–34**
Archbold, John D., **IV** 428, 488; **7** 171
Archer Daniels Midland Chemicals Co., **IV**
373
Archer Drug, **III** 10
Archer, George A., **I** 419
Archer, James, **6** 558
Archer, Shreve M., Jr., **I** 420
Archer-Daniels Linseed Co., **I** 419
Archer-Daniels-Midland Co., **I 419–21**; **7
432–33**; **8** 53
Archers Gilles & Co., **II** 187
Archibald, Nolan D., **III** 437
ARCO. *See* Atlantic Richfield Company.
ARCO Alaska, **IV** 376
ARCO Chemical Company, **IV 376–77**,
456–57; **10 110–11**
ARCO Coal Co., **IV** 376
Arco Electronics, **9** 323
ARCO International, **IV** 376
ARCO Oil and Gas, **IV** 376; **8** 261
ARCO Products Co., **IV** 376–77, 456
Arco Societa Per L'Industria Elettrotecnica,
II 82
ARCO Solar, **IV** 376–77
ARCO Transportation, **IV** 376
Arctic, **III** 479
ARD. *See* American Research &
Development.
Ardal og Sunndal Verk AS, **10** 439
Ardbo, Martin, **9** 381
Ardell, William, **7** 488
Arden, Elizabeth, **8** 166–68
Ardent Computer Corp., **III** 553
Ardic, Furuzan, **IV** 563

Ardrey, Alex H., **II** 230
Areal Technologies, **III** 715
Areces Rodriguez, Ramón, **V** 51–53
Arend, Francis, **III** 419
Argbeit-Gemeinschaft Lurgi und
Ruhrchemie, **IV** 534
Argo Communications Corporation, **6** 300
Argonaut, **I** 523–24; **10** 520–22
Argos, **I** 426
Argus, **IV** 22, 611
Argus Chemical Co., **I** 405
Argus Corp., **IV** 272
Argus Energy, **7** 538
Argyll Foods, **II** 609
Argyll Group PLC, **I**, 241; **II 609–10**,
656
Arison, Micky, **6** 367–68
Arison, Ted, **6** 367–68
Arizona Copper Co., **IV** 177
Arizona Edison Co., **6** 545
Arizona Public Service Company, **6**
545–47
Ark Securities Co., **II** 233
Arkady Co., **I** 421
Arkansas Breeders, **II** 585
Arkansas Chemicals Inc., **I** 341
Arkansas Louisiana Gas Company. *See*
Arkla, Inc.
Arkansas Power & Light, **V** 618
Arkay Computer, **6** 224
ARKE, **II** 164
Arkla, Inc., **V 550–51**
Arkwright, Preston, **V** 446–47
Arledge, Roone, **II** 130
Arlesey Lime and Portland Cement Co.,
III 669
Arlington Corporation, **6** 295
Arlington Motor Holdings, **II** 587
Armacost, Samuel, **II** 228
Armani, Georgio, **8** 129
Armaturindistri, **III** 569
Armco Financial Corp., **IV** 29
Armco Financial Services Corp., **IV** 28–29
Armco Inc., **III** 259, 721; **IV 28–30**, 125,
171; **10** 448
Armco Steel Corp., **IV** 28–29
Armco-Boothe Corp., **IV** 29
Armin Corp., **III** 645
Armin Poly Film Corp., **III** 645
Armitage Shanks, **III** 671
Armour & Company, **8** 144
Armour Dial, **I** 14
Armour family, **IV** 372
Armour Food Co., **I** 449–50, 452; **II** 494,
518
Armour, J. Ogden, **6** 510–11
Armour Pharmaceutical Co., **III** 56
Armour-Dial, **8** 144
Armsby, George, **7** 131
Armsby, J.K., **7** 131
Armstrong Advertising Co., **I** 36
Armstrong Air Conditioning Inc., **8**
320–22
Armstrong Autoparts, **III** 495
Armstrong, Brother & Co., Inc., **III** 422
Armstrong, Charles Dickey, **III** 422–23
Armstrong Communications, **IV** 640
Armstrong Cork Co., **III** 422–23
Armstrong, F. Wallis, **I** 36
Armstrong, Neil, **II** 89
Armstrong Nurseries, **I** 272
Armstrong Rees Ederer Inc., **IV** 290
Armstrong, Thomas Morton, **III** 422

Brazos Gas Compressing, **7** 345
Breakstone Bros., Inc., **II** 533
Breakthrough Software, **10** 507
Bredel Exploitatie B.V., **8** 546
Bredell Paint Co., **III** 745
Bredero's Bouwbedrijf of Utrecht, **IV** 707–08, 724
Breech, Ernest R., **I** 141–42, 166–67
Breed, Richard E., **V** 546
Breedband NV, **IV** 133
Breen, John G., **III** 745
Brega Petroleum Marketing Co., **IV** 453, 455
Brégou, Christian, **IV** 615
Breguet Aviation, **I** 44
Breguet, Louis, **I** 45
Breitenburger Cementfabrik, **III** 701
Breitschwerdt, Werner, **I** 151
Breitweiser, Stanley, **IV** 392
Bremner Biscuit Co., **II** 562
Brenda Mines Ltd., **7** 399
Brengel, Fred L., **III** 535
Brennan, Bernard, **V** 148
Brennan, Edward, **V** 182
Brennan, Patrick, **8** 125
Brenner, Joseph D., **II** 8
Brenninkmeyer, August, **V** 23
Brenninkmeyer, Clemens, **V** 23
Brenntag AG, 8 68–69, 496
Brenntag Eurochem GmbH, **8** 69
Brentano's, **7** 286
Breslube Enterprises, **8** 464
Bressler, Richard M., **10** 190
Brestle, Daniel J., **9** 204
Breton, Louis, **IV** 617–18
Brett, Bruce Y., **7** 286
Brett, George Edward, **7** 285
Brett, George Platt, **7** 285
Brett, George Platt, Jr., **7** 285
Brett, Herbert, **III** 697
Brewer, Gene, **IV** 264
Brewster, J. Christopher, **7** 375
Brewster Lines, **6** 410
Breyer Ice Cream Co., **II** 533
Brezhnev, Leonid, **I** 313
BRI Bar Review Institute, Inc., **IV** 623
Brian Mills, **V** 118
Bricker, William H., **IV** 409–10; **7** 309
Brickwood Breweries, **I** 294
Bridge Oil Ltd., **I** 438
Bridge Technology, Inc., **10** 395
Bridgeman Creameries, **II** 536
Bridgeport Brass, **I** 377
Bridges, Harry, **IV** 541
Bridgestone (U.S.A.), Inc., **V** 235
Bridgestone Corporation, V 234–35
Bridgestone Cycle Co., Ltd., **V** 235
Bridgestone/Firestone, Inc., **V** 235
Bridgestone Liquefied Gas, **IV** 364
Bridgestone Ltd., **V** 234
Bridgestone Sports Co., Ltd., **V** 235
Bridgestone Tire Co., Ltd., **V** 234
Bridgeway Plan for Health, **6** 186
Bridgman, Thomas, **10** 127
Brier Hill, **IV** 114
Briggs & Stratton Corporation, III 597; **8 70–73**
Briggs, Alky, **II** 247
Briggs, Asa, **I** 216
Briggs, Guy, **7** 462
Briggs, Roger, **I** 441
Briggs, Stephen F., **III** 597–98
Briggs, Stephen Foster, **8** 70–71
Briggs-Shaffner Division, **8** 476

Brigham, Dwight S., **9** 304
Bright, Charles D., **I** 80
Brighton Federal Savings and Loan Assoc., **II** 420
Brill, Ronald, **V** 75
Brill, Sol, **II** 169
Brimsdown Lead Co., **III** 680
Brin, Arthur, **I** 314
Brin, Leon Quentin, **I** 314
Brin's Oxygen Co., **I** 314
Brinckman, Donald W., **8** 462–64
Brinco Ltd., **II** 211
Brink's Home Security, Inc., **IV** 182
Brink's, Inc., **IV** 180–82
Brinker International, Inc., 10 176–78
Brinker, Norman E., **10** 176–78
Brinsfield, Shirley D., **10** 262–63
BRIntec, **III** 434
Brinton Carpets, **III** 423
Brisbane Gas Co., **III** 673
Bristol Aeroplane, **I** 50, 197; **10** 261
Bristol, Henry, **III** 17; **9** 88
Bristol Laboratories, **III** 17
Bristol, Lee, **III** 17; **9** 88
Bristol PLC, **IV** 83
Bristol, William, Jr., **III** 17; **9** 88
Bristol, William McLaren, **III** 17; **9** 88
Bristol-BTR, **I** 429
Bristol-Myers Co., **I** 26, 30, 37, 301, 696, 700, 703; **III** 17–19, 36, 67; **IV** 272; **6** 27; **7** 255; **8** 282–83
Bristol-Myers Squibb Company, III 17–19; **8** 210; **9 88–91 (upd.)**; **10** 70
Bristol-Siddeley Ltd., **I** 50
Britannia Airways, **8** 525–26
Britannica Software, **7** 168
Britches of Georgetowne, **10** 215–16
British & Commonwealth Shipping Company, **10** 277
British Aerospace plc, I 42, 46, **50–53**, 55, 74, 83, 132, 532; **III** 458, 507; **V** 339; **7** 9, 11, 458–59; **8** 315; **9** 499
British Aircraft Corp., **I** 50–51
British Airways Ltd., **IV** 658
British Airways plc, I 34, 83, **92–95**, 109; **IV** 658; **6** 60, 78–79, 118, 132
British Aluminium, Ltd., **II** 422; **IV** 15
British American Cosmetics, **I** 427
British American Insurance Co., **III** 350
British American Nickel, **IV** 110
British American Tobacco Co. See BAT Industries plc.
British and Dominion Film Corp., **II** 157
British and Foreign Marine, **III** 350
British and French Bank, **II** 232–33
British Bank of North America, **II** 210
British Bank of the Middle East, **II** 298
British Borneo Timber Co., **III** 699
British Broadcasting Corporation, III 163; **IV** 651; **7 52–55**
British Caledonian Airways, **I** 94–95; **6** 79
British Can Co., **I** 604
British Celanese Ltd., **I** 317
British Cellulose and Chemical Manufacturing Co., **I** 317
British Chrome, **III** 699
British Coal Corporation, IV 38–40
British Columbia Forest Products Ltd., **IV** 279
British Columbia Packers, **II** 631–32
British Columbia Resources Investment Corp., **IV** 308
British Columbia Telephone Company, IV 308; **6 309–11**

British Columbia Telephone Company, Limited. See British Columbia Telephone Company.
British Commonwealth Insurance, **III** 273
British Commonwealth Pacific Airways, **6** 110
British Continental Airlines, **I** 92
British Credit Trust, **10** 443
British Dyestuffs Corp., **I** 351
British Dynamite Co., **I** 351
British Engine, **III** 350
British European Airways, **I** 93, 466
British Executive, **I** 50
British Fuels, **III** 735
British Gas plc, II 260; **V 559–63**; **6** 478–79
British General, **III** 234
British Goodrich Tyre Co., **I** 428
British Home Stores, **II** 658
British Hovercraft Corp., **I** 120
British India and Queensland Agency Co. Ltd., **III** 522
British India Steam Navigation Co., **III** 521–22
British Industrial Solvents Ltd., **IV** 70
British Industry, **III** 335
British Insulated and Helsby Cables Ltd., **III** 433–34
British Insulated Cables, **III** 433
British Insulated Callender's Cables Ltd., **III** 433–34
British Insulated Wire Co., **III** 433
British Isles Transport Co. Ltd., **II** 564
British Land Company, **10** 6
British Leyland, **I** 175, 186; **III** 516, 523
British Linen Bank, **10** 336
British Marine Air Navigation, **I** 92
British Metal Corp., **IV** 140, 164
British Motor Corporation, **III** 555; **7** 459
British Motor Holdings, **7** 459
British National Films Ltd., **II** 157
British National Oil Corp., **IV** 40
British Newfoundland Corporation, **6** 502
British Nuclear Fuels PLC, I 573; **6 451–54**
British Overseas Airways Corp., **I** 51, 93, 120–21; **III** 522; **6** 78–79, 100, 110, 112, 117
British Oxygen Co. See BOC Group.
British Petroleum Company Ltd., **7** 141
British Petroleum Company PLC, I 241, 303; **II** 449, 563; **IV** 61, 280, 363–64, **378–80**, 381–82, 412–13, 450–54, 456, 466, 472, 486, 497–99, 505, 515, 524–25, 531–32, 557; **6** 304; **7 56–59 (upd.)**, 140, 332–33, 516, 559; **9** 490, 519
British Plasterboard, **III** 734
British Portland Cement Manufacturers, **III** 669–70
British Printing and Communications Corp., **IV** 623–24, 642; **7** 312
British Printing Corp., **IV** 641–42; **7** 311–12
British Prudential Assurance Co., **III** 335
British Rail, **III** 509; **V** 421–24; **10** 122
British Railways, **6** 413
British Railways Board, V 421–24
British Road Services, **6** 413
British Royal Insurance Co., Ltd., **III** 242
British Satellite Broadcasting, **10** 170
British Shoe Corporation, **V** 178
British South Africa Co., **IV** 23, 94
British South American Airways, **I** 93

DeForest, Lee, **III** 534
Deft Software, Inc., **10** 505
DEG. *See* Deutsche Edison Gesellschaft.
Degener, Carl, **II** 163
Degener, Herbert, **II** 164
Degolia, E.B., **9** 548
DeGolyer, Everette, **IV** 365
DeGroat, C.H., **10** 328
Degussa AG. *See* Degussa Group.
Degussa Carbon Black Corp., **IV** 71
Degussa Corp., **IV** 71
Degussa Group, **I** 303; **IV** 69–72, 118
Degussa s.a., **IV** 71
Deihl, Richard H., **II** 182; **10** 343
Deikel, Ted, **9** 218–19, 360
Deinhard, **I** 281
Dejouany, Guy, **V** 633–34
DeKalb AgResearch Inc., **9** 411
Dekker, Nicholas, **III** 241–42
Dekker, Wisse, **II** 80
Del Monte Corporation, **II** 595; **7** 130–32
del Valle Inclan, Miguel Angel, **V** 415
Del-Rey Petroleum, **I** 526
Delagrange, **I** 635
Delahye Ripault, **II** 356
Delaney, Don, **6** 79
Delaware Charter Guarantee & Trust Co., **III** 330
Delaware Lackawanna & Western, **I** 584
Delaware Management Holdings, **III** 386
Delaware North Companies Incorporated, **7** 133–36
Delbard, **I** 272
Delbrück, Adalbert, **I** 410
Delchamps, **II** 638
Delco, **6** 265
Delco Electronics, **II** 32–35; **III** 151
Deledda, Grazia, **IV** 585
Delestrade, René, **III** 393
Delfont, Bernard, **I** 532
Delhaize Freres & Cie, "Le Lion," **II** 626
Delhi Gas Pipeline Corporation, **7** 551
Delhi International Oil Corp., **III** 687
Dell Computer Corp., **9** 165–66; **10** 309, 459
Dell, Michael, **9** 165
della Vida, Samuel, **III** 206
Dellwood Elevator Co., **I** 419
Delmar Chemicals Ltd., **II** 484
Delmar Paper Box Co., **IV** 333
Delmarva Properties, Inc., **8** 103
Delmonico Foods Inc., **II** 511
Delmonico International, **II** 101
Deloitte & Touche, **9** 167–69, 423
Deloitte, Haskins, & Sells. *See* Deloitte & Touche.
Deloitte Touche Tohmatsu International, **9** 167–68
Deloitte, William Welch, **9** 167
DeLong Engineering Co., **III** 558
DeLong-McDermott, **III** 558
Deloraine, Maurice, **I** 464
DeLorean Motors Company, **10** 117
Delorme, Jean, **I** 358
Delorme, Paul, **I** 357
Delort, Jean-Jacques, **V** 10
Delphax, **IV** 252
Delprat, **IV** 58
Delprat, Guillaume, **IV** 44–45
Delta Air Corporation. *See* Delta Air Lines, Inc.

Delta Air Lines Inc., **I** 29, 91, 97, **99–100**, 102, 106, 120, 132; **6** 61, **81–83 (upd.)**, 117, 131–32, 383
Delta Air Service. *See* Delta Air Lines, Inc.
Delta Apparel, Inc., **8** 141–43
Delta Communications, **IV** 610
Delta Faucet Co., **III** 568–69
Delta Lloyd, **III** 235
Delta Manufacturing, **II** 85
Delta Mills Marketing Company, **8** 141, 143
Delta Motors, **III** 580
Delta Savings Assoc. of Texas, **IV** 343
Delta Steamship Lines, **9** 425–26
Delta Woodside Industries, Inc., **8** 141–43
DeLuxe Check Printers, Inc., **7** 137
Deluxe Corporation, **7** 137–39
DeLuxe Laboratories, **IV** 652
Delvag Luftürsicherungs A.G., **I** 111
DelZotto, Angelo, **9** 512
DelZotto, Elvio, **9** 512–13
DelZotto, Leo, **9** 512
Demag AG, **II** 22; **III** 566; **IV** 206
DeMille, Cecil B., **II** 154–55
Deminex, **IV** 413, 424
Deming Company, **8** 135
Deming, W. Edward, **8** 383
Deming, William Edwards, **III** 61, 545, 548; **IV** 162
Demka, **IV** 132–33
Demonque, Marcel, **III** 703–04
Dempsey & Siders Agency, **III** 190
Dempsey, Jerry E., **V** 753
Den Fujita, **9** 74
Den, Kenjiro, **I** 183
Den norske Creditbank, **II** 366
Den Norske Stats Oljeselskap AS, **IV** 405–07, 486
Den-Tal-Ez, **I** 702
Denain-Nord-Est-Longwy, **IV** 227
Denault Ltd., **II** 651
Denenberg, Herbert, **III** 326
Deneuve, Catherine, **10** 69
Denison Corp., **III** 628
Denison, Merrill, **I** 275
Denius, Homer, **II** 37–38
Denki Seikosho, **IV** 62
Denney-Reyburn, **8** 360
Dennison, Aaron, **IV** 251
Dennison and Co., **IV** 251
Dennison, Andrew, **IV** 251
Dennison Carter, **IV** 252
Dennison, Charles, **IV** 251
Dennison, Eliphalet Whorf (E.W.), **IV** 251–52
Dennison, Henry B., **IV** 251
Dennison, Henry Sturgis, **IV** 251–52
Dennison Manufacturing Co., **IV** 251–52, 254
Dennison National, **IV** 252
Denny, Arthur, **9** 539
Denny, Charles, **10** 18–20
Denny's, **II** 680; **III** 103
Denny's Japan, **V** 88–89
Denshi Media Services, **IV** 680
Dent & Co., **II** 296
Dent, Hawthorne K., **III** 352–53
Dental Houses/Dentsply, **10** 272
The Dentists' Supply Co. *See* Dentsply International Inc.
Dentsply International Inc., **10** 270–72
Dentsu Inc., **I** 9–11, 36, 38; **9** 30
Dentsu, Ltd., **6** 29

Denver Chemical Company, **8** 84
Denver Consolidated Electric Company. *See* Public Service Company of Colorado.
Denver Gas & Electric Company, **IV** 391; **6** 558
Denver Gas & Electric Light Company. *See* Public Service Company of Colorado.
Denver Gas Company. *See* Public Service Company of Colorado.
Department Stores International, **I** 426
Depew, Chauncey M., **10** 72
Deposito and Administratie Bank, **II** 185
Depositors National Bank of Durham, **II** 336
Depuy Inc., **10** 156–57
Der Anker, **III** 177
Deramus, William N., **6** 400
Deramus, William N., III, **6** 400–01
Derby Commerical Bank, **II** 318
Derbyshire Stone and William Briggs, **III** 752
Dercksen, Gerrit Jan, **III** 308
Derr, Kenneth, **IV** 387
Deruluft, **6** 57
Derwent Publications, **8** 526
Des Moines Electric Light Company, **6** 504
Des Voeux, William (Sir), **IV** 699
DESA Industries, **8** 545
DesBarres, John P., **V** 740
Desert Partners, **III** 763
Design Craft Ltd., **IV** 640
DeSimone, L.D., **8** 371
Desmarais Frères, **IV** 557, 559
DeSoto, Inc., **8** 553
Desoutter, **III** 427
Despret, Maurice, **II** 202
Destray, Ellen, **10** 383
Det Danske Luftartselskab, **I** 119
Det Norske Luftartselskab, **I** 119
Deterding, Henri, **IV** 379, 530–31
Detra, Ralph W., **III** 643
Detroit Aircraft Corp., **I** 64
Detroit Automobile Co., **I** 164
Detroit Chemical Coatings, **8** 553
Detroit City and Gas Company. *See* MCN Corporation.
Detroit City Gas Company. *See* MCN Corporation.
Detroit Copper Co., **IV** 176
Detroit Copper Mining Co., **IV** 177
Detroit Diesel Allison. *See* Detroit Diesel Corporation.
Detroit Diesel Corporation, **V** 494–95; **9** 18; **10** 273–75
Detroit Edison Company, **I** 164; **V** 592–95; **7** 377–78
Detroit Fire & Marine Insurance Co., **III** 191
Detroit Gaslight Company. *See* MCN Corporation.
Detroit Gear and Machine Co., **III** 439
Detroit Radiator Co., **III** 663
Detroit Red Wings, **7** 278–79
Detroit Steel Products Co. Inc., **IV** 136
Detroit Toledo & Ironton Railroad, **I** 165
Detroit Vapor Stove Co., **III** 439
Detroit-Graphite Company, **8** 553
Detrola, **II** 60
Deupree, Richard R., **III** 52; **8** 432
Deutsch Erdol A.G., **IV** 552
Deutsch, Felix, **I** 410
Deutsch Shea & Evans Inc., **I** 15

Larkin, Frederick, Jr., **II** 349
Laroche, Guy, **8** 129
Laroche Navarron, **I** 703
Larousse Group, **IV** 615
Larousse, Pierre, **IV** 614
Larousse-Nathan, **IV** 614–15
Larroque, Louis, **I** 519; **IV** 215
Larrowe Milling Co., **II** 501; **10** 322
Larsen & Toubro, **IV** 484
Larsen Company, **7** 128
Larsen, Ralph S., **III** 37; **8** 283
Larsen, Roy E., **IV** 674; **7** 527
Larson, Elwin S., **6** 455–57
Larson, Gary, **III** 13; **6** 386
Larson, Gustav, **I** 209; **7** 565–66
Larson Lumber Co., **IV** 306
Larwin Group, **III** 231
Lasala, Joseph, **II** 316
LaSalle National Bank, **II** 184
LaSalles & Koch Co., **8** 443
Lasell, Chester, **II** 432
Oy Läskelä Ab, **IV** 300
Lasker, Albert, **I** 12–13, 25, 36
Lasky, David, **10** 263
Lasky, Jesse, **II** 154
Lasky's, **II** 141
Lasmo, **IV** 455, 499
Lasser, J.K., **IV** 671
Lassila, Jaakko, **IV** 349
Latécoère, Pierre, **V** 471
Lathière, Bernard, **I** 41
Latrobe, Ferdinand C., **III** 395
Latrobe Steel Company, **8** 529–31
Lattès, Jean-Claude, **IV** 617, 619
Latzer, John, **7** 428–29
Latzer, Louis, **7** 428–29
Latzer, Robert, **7** 429
Laubach, Gerald, **I** 663; **9** 404
Lauder, Estée, **9** 201–02, 290
Lauder, Evelyn, **9** 202, 204
Lauder, Joseph, **9** 201–03
Lauder, Leonard, **9** 201–04
Lauder, Ronald, **9** 202–04
Lauder, William, **9** 204
Lauer, John N., **V** 233
Laughlin, James, **II** 342
Lauman, J.F., **II** 681
Laura Scudder's, **7** 429
Lauren, Ralph, **III** 55; **8** 130–31, 408
Laurentien Hotel Co., **III** 99
Laurenzo, Vince, **III** 652
Lauson Engine Company, **8** 515
Lautenberg, Frank, **8** 117–18
Lautenberg, Frank R., **9** 48
de Laval, Carl Gustaf Patrik, **7** 235
de Laval, Gustaf, **II** 1; **III** 417–19
Laval, Gustaf de. *See* de Laval, Gustaf.
Lavanchy, Henri-Ferdinand, **6** 9
Laventhol, David, **IV** 678
Lavin, Leonard H., **8** 15–17
Lavine, Larry, **10** 176
LaVoisier, Antoine, **I** 328
Law Life Assurance Society, **III** 372
Lawn Boy, **7** 535–36
Lawn Boy Inc., **8** 72
Lawrence, Harding, **I** 96–97
Lawrence, John, **III** 472
Lawrence Manufacturing Co., **III** 526
Lawrence, T.E., **I** 194
Lawrence Warehouse Co., **II** 397–98; **10** 62
Lawrenceburg Gas Company, **6** 466
Lawrenceburg Gas Transmission Corporation, **6** 466

The Lawson Co., **7** 113
Lawson, Dominic, **III** 503
Lawson Milk, **II** 572
Lawson-Johnston, Peter, **9** 363
Lawyers Cooperative, **8** 528
Lawyers Cooperative Publishing Company, **8** 527
Lawyers Trust Co., **II** 230
Laxalt, Paul, **III** 188
Lay, Beirne, **I** 486
Lay, Herman, **I** 278; **III** 136; **10** 452
Layton, F.D., **III** 229
Layton, Joseph E., **8** 515
Lazard Bros. & Co., **IV** 658–59
Lazard Frères, **II** 268, 402, 422; **IV** 23, 79, 659; **7** 287, 446; **10** 399
Lazard Freres and Company, **6** 356
Lazarus, Charles, **V** 203–06
Lazarus, Fred, **V** 26–27
Lazarus, Fred, Jr., **9** 209–10
Lazarus, Hyman (Judge), **IV** 581–82
Lazarus, Ralph, **V** 26; **9** 210–11
Lazarus, Wilhelm, **III** 206
Lazell, H.G. Leslie, **III** 65–66
Lazenby, Robert S., **9** 177
LBS Communications, **6** 28
LDDS Communications, Inc., **7** 336
LDDS-Metro Communications, Inc., 8 310–12
LDX NET, Inc., **IV** 576
Le Brun and Sons, **III** 291
Le Buffet System-Gastronomie, **V** 74
Le Courviour S.A., **10** 351
Lea & Perrins, **II** 475
Lea County Gas Co., **6** 580
Lea, R.W., **III** 707; **7** 292
Lead Industries Group Ltd., **III** 681; **IV** 108
Leadership Housing Inc., **IV** 136
Leaf River Forest Products Inc., **IV** 282, 300; **9** 261
Leahy, Patrick, **III** 188
Leaman, June, **9** 202
Leamington Priors & Warwickshire Banking Co., **II** 318
Lear Inc., **II** 61; **8** 49, 51
Lear, John, **I** 662; **9** 403
Lear Romec Corp., **8** 135
Lear Siegler Inc., I 481–83; III 581
Lear Siegler Seating Corp., **III** 581
Lear, William Powell, **8** 313–16
Lear-Siegler Inc., **8** 313
Learjet Inc., 8 313–16; 9 242
Learned, Stanley, **IV** 522
Leasco Data Processing Equipment Corp., **III** 342–44; **IV** 641–42; **7** 311
Lease International SA, **6** 358
Leaseway Transportation, **V** 494
Leatherdale, Douglas W., **III** 357
Leavey, W.M., **IV** 708
Leblanc, Nicolas, **I** 394
Leca, Dominique, **III** 393
Lecerf, Olivier, **III** 704–05
Lechmere Inc., 10 391–93
Leclerc, Edouard, **10** 204
Ledder, Edward J., **I** 619–20
Ledebur, Adolf, **IV** 156
Lederle Laboratories, **I** 300–02, 657, 684
Lederle Labs, **8** 24–25
Ledoux, Fréderic, **IV** 107
Lee Apparel Company, Inc., 8 317–19
Lee, Archie, **I** 233; **10** 226
Lee Brands, **II** 500
Lee, Byung-Chull, **I** 515–16

Lee Company, **V** 390–92
Lee, Frank A., **6** 145–46
Lee, George, **9** 105–06
Lee Hecht Harrison, **6** 10
Lee, Henry David, **8** 317–18
Lee, Kun-Hee, **I** 516
Lee, Kyung Hoon, **III** 458
Lee, Quo Wei, **IV** 717
Lee, Sung Won, **III** 749
Lee Telephone Company, **6** 313
Lee, W. S., **V** 601
Lee, Wallace L., **6** 447–48
Lee Way Motor Freight, **I** 278
Lee, William S., **V** 601–02
Leeds & County Bank, **II** 318
Leeds & Northrup Co., **III** 644–45
Leeman, Hermann, **I** 671–72
Lees, David, **III** 495
Lefaucheux, Pierre, **I** 189
LeFauve, Richard G., **7** 462
Lefebre, Pierre, **I** 188
Lefébure, Charles, **I** 395
Lefebvre, Andre, **7** 36
Lefebvre, Gordon, **II** 15
Lefeldt, **III** 417, 418
Lefeldt, Wilhelm, **III** 417
Lefevre, Jacques, **III** 705
Lefrak Organization, **8** 357
Legal & General Assurance Society, **III** 272–73
Legal & General Group plc, III 272–73; IV 705, 712
Legal & General Life Assurance Society, **III** 272
Legal & General Netherlands, **III** 273
Legault and Masse, **II** 664
Legent Corporation, 10 394–96
Leggett & Platt, **9** 93
Leggett, Will, **V** 12
Lehigh Railroad, **III** 258
Lehman Bros., **I** 78, 125, 484; **II** 259, 448; **6** 199; **10** 63
Lehman Bros. Kuhn Loeb, **II** 192, 398, 450–51; **10** 62
Lehman, Clarence, **7** 592
Lehman, Fred, Jr., **9** 411
Lehman, John, **I** 59, 62, 527
Lehman, Robert, **I** 89
Lehmer Company, **6** 312. *See also* McGraw Electric Company.
Lehmkuhl, Joakim, **7** 531
Lehn & Fink, **I** 699
Lehnkering AG, **IV** 140
Lehr, Lewis, **I** 500; **8** 371
Lehrman Bros., **III** 419
Lehrman, Jacob, **II** 633–34
Lehrman, Samuel, **II** 633
Lehtinen, William, **IV** 276–77
Leigh, Claude Moss, **IV** 710–11
Leigh, Vivien, **II** 148, 175
Leigh-Pemberton, Robin, **II** 334
Leighton, Charles M., **10** 215
Leinenkugel, **I** 253
Leipsner, Steven, **7** 472–73
Leisen, Mitchell, **II** 155
Leisenring, E.B., **7** 582
Leisenring, Edward B., Jr., (Ted), **7** 583–84
Leisure Lodges, **III** 76
Leitz, **III** 583–84
Leland, Glenn, **8** 517
Leland, Henry, **I** 171; **10** 325
Leland, Marc, **9** 112
Lemaire, Raymond, **10** 482

Nippon Funtai Kogyo Co., **III** 714
Nippon Gakki Co., Ltd., **III** 656–58
Nippon Ginko, **III** 408
Nippon Glass Fiber Co., **III** 714
Nippon Gyomo Sengu Co. Ltd., **IV** 555
Nippon Hatsujo Kabushikikaisha. *See* NHK Spring Co., Ltd.
Nippon Helicopter & Aeroplane Transport Co., Ltd., **6** 70
Nippon Hoso Kyokai. *See* Japan Broadcasting Corporation.
Nippon Idou Tsushin, **7** 119–20
Nippon International Container Services, **8** 278
Nippon Interrent, **10** 419–20
Nippon K.K. *See* Nippon Kokan K.K.
Nippon Kairiku Insurance Co., **III** 384
Nippon Kakoh Seishi, **IV** 293
Nippon Kangyo Bank, **II** 273–74
Nippon Kangyo Kakumara Securities, **II** 274
Nippon Kogaku K.K., **III** 583–84
Nippon Kogyo Co. Ltd. *See* Nippon Mining Co. Ltd.
Nippon Kokan, **8** 449
Nippon Kokan K.K., **IV** 161–63, 184, 212
Nippon Life Insurance Company, **II** 374, 451; **III** 273, 288, **318–20**; **IV** 727; **9** 469
Nippon Life Lifesaving Society, **III** 318
Nippon Light Metal Company, Ltd., **IV** 153–55
Nippon Machinery Trading, **I** 507
Nippon Meat Packers, Inc., **II** 550–51
Nippon Menka Kaisha, **IV** 150–51
Nippon Merck-Banyu, **I** 651
Nippon Mining Co., Ltd., **III** 759; **IV** 475–77
Nippon Motorola Manufacturing Co., **II** 62
Nippon New Zealand Trading Co. Ltd., **IV** 327
Nippon Oil Company, Limited, **IV** 434, 475–76, **478–79**, 554
Nippon Onkyo, **II** 118
Nippon Pelnox Corp., **III** 715
Nippon Petrochemicals Co., Ltd., **IV** 479
Nippon Petroleum Gas Co., Ltd., **IV** 479
Nippon Petroleum Refining Co., Ltd., **IV** 479
Nippon Polaroid Kabushiki Kaisha, **III** 608; **7** 437
Nippon Pulp Industries, **IV** 321
Nippon Rayon, **V** 387
Nippon Safety Glass, **III** 715
Nippon Sangyo Co., Ltd., **IV** 475
Nippon Sanso, **I** 359
Nippon Seiko Goshi Gaisha, **III** 589
Nippon Seiko K.K., **III** 589–90, 595
Nippon Sekiyu Co. *See* Nippon Oil Company, Limited.
Nippon Sheet Glass Company, Limited, **III 714–16**
Nippon Shinpan Company, Ltd., **II** 436–37, 442; **8** 118
Nippon Shinyo Hanbai Co., **II** 436
Nippon Silica Kogyo Co., **III** 715
Nippon Soda, **II** 301
Nippon Sogo Bank, **II** 371
Nippon Soken, **III** 592
Nippon Steel Chemical Co., **10** 439
Nippon Steel Corporation, **I** 466, 493–94, 509; **II** 300, 391; **IV** 116, 130, **156–58**, 184, 212, 228, 298; **6** 274

Nippon Suisan Kaisha, Limited, **II 552–53**
Nippon Tar, **I** 363
Nippon Telegraph and Telephone Corporation, **II** 51, 62; **III** 139–40; **V 305–07**; **7** 118–20; **10** 119
Nippon Telegraph and Telephone Public Corporation, **V** 305–06
Nippon Television, **7** 249; **9** 29
Nippon Tire Co., Ltd., **V** 234
Nippon Trust Bank, **II** 405
Nippon Typewriter, **II** 459
Nippon Victor (Europe) GmbH, **II** 119
Nippon Wiper Blade Co., Ltd., **III** 592
Nippon Yusen Kabushiki Kaisha, **V 481–83**
Nippon Yusen Kaisha, **IV** 713; **6** 398
Nippondenso (Deutschland) GmbH, **III** 593
Nippondenso (Europe) B.V., **III** 592
Nippondenso (Italia), **III** 594
Nippondenso (Malaysia) SDN./BHD., **III** 593
Nippondenso (U.K.) Ltd., **III** 593
Nippondenso Canada, **III** 592
Nippondenso Co., Ltd., **III 591–94**, 637–38
Nippondenso Finance (Holland) B.V., **III** 593
Nippondenso Manufacturing U.S.A., **III** 593
Nippondenso of Los Angeles, **III** 592
Nippondenso Sales, Inc., **III** 592
Nippondenso Taiwan Co., **III** 593
Nippondenso Tool and Die (Thailand) Co., Ltd., **III** 593
NIPSCO Development Company, **6** 533
NIPSCO Industries, Inc., **6 532–33**
Nirenberg, Charles, **7** 113–14
Nirenberg, Jan, **7** 114
Nishi, Itsuki, **IV** 297
Nishi Taiyo Gyogyo Tosei K.K., **II** 578
Nishikawa, Choju, **V** 209
Nishikawa, Toshio, **V** 209–10
Nishikawa, Yoshio, **V** 210
Nishikawaya Chain Co., Ltd., **V** 209
Nishikawaya Co., Ltd., **V** 209
Nishimbo Industries Inc., **IV** 442
Nishimura, Ryousuke, **III** 548
Nishio, Tetsuo, **8** 279
Nishiyama, Yataro, **IV** 124–25
Nishizono Ironworks, **III** 595
Nissan Construction, **V** 154
Nissan Diesel, **7** 219
Nissan Motor Acceptance Corp., **III** 485
Nissan Motor Company Ltd., **I** 9, **183–84**, 207, 494; **II** 118, 292–93, 391; **III** 517, 536, 579, 591, 742, 750; **IV** 63; **7** 111, 120; **9** 243, 340–42; **10** 353
Nissan Motor Corp. USA, **I** 10, 183
Nisshin Badische Co., **II** 554
Nisshin Chemical Industries, **I** 397
Nisshin Chemicals Co., **II** 554
Nisshin Ferrite Co., Ltd., **IV** 160
Nisshin Flour Milling Company, Ltd., **II 554**
Nisshin Foods Co., **II** 554
Nisshin Pharaceutical Co., **II** 554
Nisshin Seifun do Brasil, **II** 554
Nisshin Steel Co., Ltd., **I** 432; **IV** 130, **159–60**
Nisshin Steel Corporation, **7** 588
Nisshin Stockfarming Center Co., **II** 554
Nissho Co., **I** 509–10
Nissho Iwai Corp., **8** 392

Nissho Iwai K.K., **I** 432, **509–11**; **IV** 160, 383; **V** 373; **6** 386
Nissho Kosan Co., **III** 715
Nissho-Iwai American Corporation, **8** 75
Nissui. *See* Nippon Suisan Kaisha.
Nitratos de Portugal, **IV** 505
Nitro Nobel, **9** 380
Nitroglycerin Ltd., **9** 380
Nittetsu Curtainwall Corp., **III** 758
Nittetsu Sash Sales Corp., **III** 758
Nitto Warehousing Co., **I** 507
Nittoku Metal Industries, Ltd., **III** 635
Nittsu. *See* Nippon Express Co., Ltd.
Niwa, Masaharu, **III** 710–11; **7** 302–03
Niwa, Yasujiro, **II** 66–67
Nixdorf Computer AG, **I** 193; **II** 279; **III** 109, **154–55**
Nixdorf, Heinz, **III** 154–55
Nixon, Richard M., **I** 20, 29, 76, 97, 136, 184, 277, 313, 420, 493, 500; **II** 152; **III** 137, 142, 505; **IV** 36, 366, 522, 596, 689; **10** 368
NKK Corporation, **IV** 74, **161–63**, 212–13; **V** 152
NL Industries, Inc., **III** 681; **10 434–36**
NLM City-Hopper, **I** 109
NLM Dutch Airlines, **I** 108
NLT Corp., **II** 122; **III** 194; **10** 66
NMH Stahlwerke GmbH, **IV** 128
NMT. *See* Nordic Mobile Telephone.
No-Leak-O Piston Ring Company, **10** 492
Nobel, Alfred Bernhard, **I** 351; **III** 693; **9** 380
Nobel Industries AB, **9 380–82**
Nobel Industries Ltd., **I** 351
Nobel-Bozel, **I** 669
Nobel-Hoechst Chimie, **I** 669
Noble, Daniel, **II** 60
Noble, Donald E., **III** 613–14
Noble, Edward, **II** 89, 129
Noble, L.C., **II** 507
Noble, Sherb, **10** 371
Noblitt, Niles, **10** 156, 158
Noblitt, Quintin G., **8** 37–38
Noblitt-Sparks Industries, Inc., **8** 37–38
Noell, **IV** 201
Noels, Jacques, **10** 564
Nogano, Shigeo, **IV** 158
Nogawa, Shoji, **III** 546
Noguchi, Isamu, **8** 255
Nogues, Maurice, **V** 471
Noha, Edward J., **III** 231–32
Nokia Consumer Electronics, **IV** 296
Nokia Corporation, **II 69–71**; **IV** 296
Nokia Data, **6** 242
Nokia Smurfit Ltd., **IV** 296
Nollen, Gerard, **III** 329
Noma family, **IV** 633
Noma, Hasashi, **IV** 632
Noma, Koremichi, **IV** 633
Noma, Sae, **IV** 632
Noma, Sawako, **IV** 631, 633
Noma, Seiji, **IV** 631–33
Noma, Shoichi, **IV** 632–33
Nomura and Co., **II** 438
Nomura Bank, **II** 276
Nomura Europe GmbH, **II** 440
Nomura Europe N.V., **II** 440
Nomura International (Hong Kong), **II** 440
Nomura Investment Trust Management Co., **II** 440
Nomura Investment Trust Sales Co., **II** 440
Nomura Real Estate Development Co., Ltd., **II** 439

Schwan, Marvin, **7** 468–69
Schwan, Paul, **7** 468–69
**Schwan's Sales Enterprises, Inc., 7
468–70**
Schwartz, Bernard, **8** 338–39; **9** 323–24
Schwartz, Fredric N., **III** 17; **9** 88
Schwartz, Robert, **III** 293–94
Schweber, Seymour, **9** 55
Schwed, Peter, **IV** 672
Schweiz Allgemeine, **III** 377
Schweiz Allgemeine Direkt Versicherung
AG, **III** 377
Schweiz Allgemeine Versicherungs-Aktien-
Gesellschaft, **III** 377
Schweiz Transport-Vericherungs-
Gesellschaft, **III** 410
Schweizer Rück Holding AG, **III** 377
Schweizer, Samuel, **II** 369
Schweizerische Bankgesellschaft AG, **II**
379; **V** 104
Schweizerische Kreditanstalt, **III** 375, 410;
6 489
Schweizerische Lebensversicherungs-und
Rentenanstalt, **III** 375
Schweizerische Nordostbahn, **6** 424
**Schweizerische Post-, Telefon- und
Telegrafen-Betriebe, V 321–24**
Schweizerische Ruckversicherungs-
Gesellschaft. *See* Swiss Reinsurance
Company.
Schweizerische Unfallversicherungs-
Actiengesellschaft in Winterthur, **III** 402
Schweizerische Unionbank, **II** 368
Schweizerischer Bankverein, **II** 368
Schwemm, John B., **IV** 661
Schwenk, Otto G., **III** 467
Schweppe, Jacob, **II** 476
Schweppe, Paul & Gosse, **II** 476
Schweppes France, **II** 477
Schweppes Ltd., **I** 220, 288; **II** 476
Schweppes South Africa, **II** 477
Schweppes USA, **II** 477
Schwettmann, Fred, **10** 464
Schwitzer, **II** 420
SCI. *See* Service Corporation International.
SCI Manufacturing, Inc., **9** 464
SCI Systems, Inc., 9 463–64
SCI Technology, Inc., **9** 464
Scientific Communications, Inc., **10** 97
Scientific Data Systems, **II** 44; **III** 172; **6**
289; **10** 365
Scientific Games, Inc., **III** 431
Scientific-Atlanta, Inc., 6 335–37
Scifres, Robert, **10** 422
SciMed Life Systems, **III** 18–19
Scioto Bank, **9** 475
SCM Corp., **I** 29; **III** 502; **IV** 330; **7** 208;
8 223–24
Scobie, John C., **9** 423
Scohier, Pierre, **V** 65
Scor SA, **III** 394
Scot Bowyers, **II** 587
Scotia Securities, **II** 223
Scotiabank. *See* The Bank of Nova Scotia.
Scotsman Industries, **II** 420
Scott & Fetzer Co., **III** 214
Scott, Arthur Hoyt, **IV** 329
Scott, B.A., **III** 228
Scott, Bernard, **III** 556
Scott, C. Dennis, **10** 186–87
Scott, Clarence R., **IV** 329
Scott Communications, Inc., **10** 97
Scott, E. Irvin, **IV** 329
Scott, Foresman, **IV** 675

Scott, George E., **7** 30
Scott Graphics, **IV** 289; **8** 483
Scott, J.D., **7** 412
Scott, J.L., **7** 20
Scott, Joe, **I** 157
Scott, Jonathan L., **II** 602, 605–06, 637
Scott, Lary, **V** 434; **6** 390
Scott Lithgow, **III** 516; **7** 232
Scott, Mike, **III** 115; **6** 218
Scott Paper Company, III 749; **IV** 258,
289–90, 311, 325, 327, **329–31**; **8** 483
Scott, Peter, **6** 15–16
Scott, W.C., **III** 599
Scott, Wallie, **6** 142
Scott, Walter, **7** 165
Scott, Walter Jr., **8** 424
Scott Worldwide, Inc., **IV** 331
Scott-McDuff, **II** 107
Scottish Aviation, **I** 50
Scottish Electric, **6** 453
Scottish General Fire Assurance Corp., **III**
256
Scottish Land Development, **III** 501; **7** 207
Scottish Malt Distillers, **I** 240
Scottish Union Co., **III** 358
Scotts Stores, **I** 289
Scovill Mfg., **IV** 11
Scranton Corrugated Box Company, Inc., **8**
102
Scranton Plastics Laminating Corporation,
8 359
Screen Gems, **II** 135–36
SCREG, **I** 563
Scribbans-Kemp Ltd., **II** 594
Scriha & Deyhle, **10** 196
Scripps and Sweeney Co., **7** 157
Scripps, Charles E., **IV** 608
Scripps, E.W. *See* Scripps, Edward Willis.
Scripps, Edward Willis (E.W.), **IV** 606–09;
7 157–58
Scripps, Ellen, **IV** 606
Scripps, George, **IV** 606
Scripps, George Henry, **7** 157
Scripps Howard Broadcasting Company, **7**
158–59
Scripps Howard Inc., **7** 64
Scripps Howard League, **7** 158
Scripps Howard Productions, **IV** 609
Scripps, James, **IV** 606–07
Scripps, James Edmund, **7** 157
Scripps, James G., **7** 158
Scripps, John P., **IV** 609
Scripps News Assoc., **IV** 607
Scripps, Robert Paine, **IV** 607–08
Scripps, Robert Paine, Jr., **IV** 608
Scripps-Howard Broadcasting Co., **IV** 608
Scripps-Howard, Inc., **IV** 609, 628
Scripps-Howard Radio, Inc., **IV** 607
Scripps-McRae League, **7** 157
Scripps-McRae Press Assoc., **IV** 607
Scudder, Horace Elisha, **10** 355
Scudder, Stevens & Clark, **II** 448
Sculley, John, **III** 116; **6** 219–20
Scully, Vincent, **IV** 209
Scurlock Oil Co., **IV** 374
SDC Coatings, **III** 715
SDGE. *See* San Diego Gas & Electric
Company.
SDK Parks, **IV** 724
Sea Diamonds Ltd., **IV** 66; **7** 123
Sea Far of Norway, **II** 484
Sea Insurance Co. Ltd., **III** 220
Sea Life Centre aquariums, **10** 439
Sea Ray, **III** 444

Sea World, Inc., **IV** 623–24
Sea-Alaska Products, **II** 494
Sea-Land Service Inc., **I** 476; **9** 510–11
Seaboard Fire and Marine Insurance Co.,
III 242
Seaboard Life Insurance Co., **III** 193
Seaboard Lumber Sales, **IV** 307
Seaboard Oil Co., **IV** 552
Seaboard Surety Co., **III** 357
Seabourn Cruise Lines, **6** 368
Seabury & Smith, **III** 283
Seabury, Charles Ward, **III** 283
Seacoast Products, **III** 502
Seafirst. *See* Seattle First National Bank,
Inc.
SeaFirst Corp., **II** 228
Seagal, Martin A., **7** 310
Seagate Technology, Inc., 6 230–31; **8**
466–68; **9** 57; **10** 257, 403–04, 459
Seagram Company Ltd., I 26, 240, 244,
284–86, 329, 403; **II** 456, 468; **IV** 401;
7 155
Seagram, Joseph Emm, **I** 284
Seagrove, Gordon, **I** 711; **10** 550
Sealand Petroleum Co., **IV** 400
Sealectro, **III** 434
**Sealed Power Corporation, I 199–200;
10** 492–94
Sealed Power Technologies, **10** 492, 494
Seaman, Barrett, **I** 145
Seamless Rubber Co., **III** 613
Seaquist Manufacturing Corporation, **9**
413–14
Searle & Co. *See* G.D. Searle & Co.
Searle, Daniel, **I** 686–88
Searle, Gideon D., **I** 686
Searle, John G., **I** 686
Searle, William L., **I** 686
Searls, Fred, **7** 385
Sears, John, **V** 177
Sears plc, V 177–79
Sears, Richard W., **V** 180
Sears, Roebuck & Co., I 26, 146, 516,
556; **II** 18, 60, 134, 331, 411, 414; **III**
259, 265, 340, 536, 598, 653–55; **V**
180–83; **6** 12–13; **7** 166, 479; **8** 224,
287–89; **9** 44, 65–66 156, 210, 213,
219, 235–36, 430–31, 538; **10** 10,
50–52, 199, 236–37, 288, 304–05,
490–91
Sears, William, **V** 177
Season-all Industries, **III** 735
SEAT. *See* Sociedad Española de
Automoviles de Turismo.
Seaton, W. Bruce, **6** 354–55
Seattle Electric Company, **6** 565
Seattle Electric Light Company, **6** 565
**Seattle First National Bank Inc., 8
469–71**
Seaview Oil Co., **IV** 393
Seaway Express, **9** 510
Seaway Food Town, Inc., **9** 452
Seawell, William, **I** 116
SEB-Fastigheter A.B., **II** 352
Sebart, Carl, **IV** 203
SECA, **IV** 401
de Secada, C. Alexander G., **I** 550
Secchia, Peter F., **10** 539–40
SECDO, **III** 618
SECO Industries, **III** 614
Second Bank of the United States, **II** 213;
9 369
Second National Bank, **II** 254
Second National Bank of Bucyrus, **9** 474

Seyama, Seigoro, **IV** 726
Seybold, **6** 602
Seybold, L. F., **6** 602
Seybold Machine Co., **II** 37
Seydoux, Jérôme, **6** 373–75
Seydoux, René, **III** 617
Seymour, Dan, **I** 20
Seymour International Press Distributor Ltd., **IV** 619
Seymour, Lester, **I** 89; **6** 75
Seymour Press, **IV** 619
SGC. *See* Supermarkets General Corporation.
SGS, **II** 117
Shabazian, Michael R., **6** 243–44
Shad, John, **II** 409
Shafer, Thomas, **7** 463
Shaffer Clarke, **II** 594
Shaffer, Richard A., **6** 244
Shaftesbury (seventh Earl of), **IV** 118
Shagari, Alhaji Shehu, **IV** 473
Shah, Eddy, **IV** 652
Shah of Iran. *See* Muhammad Reza Shah Pahlevi (Shah of Iran).
Shakespeare, William, **III** 15; **IV** 671
Shalit, Gene, **I** 344
Shamrock Advisors, Inc., **8** 305
Shamrock Capital L.P., **7** 81–82
Shamrock Holdings, **III** 609; **7** 438; **9** 75
Shamrock Oil & Gas Co., **I** 403–04; **IV** 409; **7** 308
Shanghai Hotels Co., **IV** 717
Shanks, Carroll M., **III** 338–39
Shannahan, John N., **6** 532, 555
Shapiro, Irving, **I** 329–30; **8** 152
Shapiro, Moses, **10** 319–20
Sharbaugh, H. Robert, **I** 631; **IV** 550
Sharbaugh, Robert, **7** 414
Shared Financial Systems, Inc., **10** 501
Shared Systems Corporation, **10** 501
Shared Use Network Systems, Inc., **8** 311
Sharer, Kevin W., **10** 80
Sharon Steel Corp., **I** 497; **7** 360–61; **8** 536
Sharon Tank Car Corporation, **6** 394
Sharp and Dohme Inc., **I** 650
Sharp, Bill, **7** 217
Sharp Corporation, **I** 476; **II** 95–96; **III** 14, 428, 455, 480; **6** 217, 231
Sharp, Henry, **I** 314
Sharp, Isadore, **9** 237–38
Sharp, Richard, **9** 122
Sharp, Sir Eric, **6** 320
Sharp-Hughes Tool Co., **III** 428
The Sharper Image Corporation, **10** 486–88
Sharples Co., **I** 383
Sharples Separator Co., **III** 418–20
Shasta, **II** 571–73
Shattuck, Frank C., **III** 440
Shattuck, Robert, **III** 440
Shaub, Harold A., **II** 480; **7** 67
Shaver, Clarence H., **III** 763
Shaw, Alexander, **V** 491
Shaw, Bud, **9** 465
Shaw, George, **II** 37
Shaw, H.A., **8** 241
Shaw, Harry A., III, **7** 226
Shaw Industries, **9** 465–67
Shaw, J.C., **9** 465
Shaw, John S., **6** 577
Shaw, Neil, **II** 582
Shaw, R. Nelson, **V** 140
Shaw, Robert, **9** 465–66

Shaw's Supermarkets, **II** 658–59
Shawinigan Water and Power Company, **6** 501–02
Shawmut National Bank, **II** 207
Shea, James, Jr., **III** 506
Shea, John, **10** 491
Shea's Winnipeg Brewery Ltd., **I** 268
Shearson Hammill & Co., **II** 445, 450
Shearson Hayden Stone, **II** 450
Shearson Lehman Bros., **I** 202; **II** 478; **III** 319; **8** 118
Shearson Lehman Brothers Holdings Inc., **II** 398–99, 450; **9** 468–70 (upd.); **10** 62–63
Shearson Lehman Hutton, **II** 399, 451; **III** 119; **10** 59, 63
Shearson Lehman Hutton Holdings Inc., **II** 450–52; **9** 125
Shearson Loeb Rhoades Inc., **II** 398; **10** 62
Shedd's Food Products Company, **9** 318
Shedden, William Ian H., **I** 647
Sheehy, Patrick, **I** 426–27
Sheepbridge Engineering, **III** 495
Sheets, Harold, **IV** 558
Sheffield Banking Co., **II** 333
Sheffield, Bill, **7** 559
Sheffield Motor Co., **I** 158; **10** 292
Sheffield Twist Drill & Steel Co., **III** 624
Sheib, Simon, **9** 55–56
Sheinberg, Sidney, **6** 162–63
Sheinberg, Sidney J., **II** 144
Shelby Insurance Company, **10** 44–45
Shelby Steel Tube Co., **IV** 572; **7** 550
Sheldon, Clifford, **IV** 666
Shell. *See* Shell Transport and Trading Company p.l.c. *and* Shell Oil Company.
Shell Australia Ltd., **III** 728
Shell BV, **IV** 518
Shell Chemical Co., **IV** 410, 481, 531–32, 540
Shell Chemical Corporation, **8** 415
Shell Co.-Qatar, **IV** 524
Shell Co. of California, **IV** 540
Shell Co. of Portugal, **IV** 504
Shell Coal International, **IV** 532
Shell Development Co., **IV** 540
Shell Mining Co., **IV** 541
Shell Nederland BV, **V** 658–59
Shell of Colombia, **IV** 417
Shell Oil Company, **I** 20, 26, 569; **III** 559; **IV** 392, 400, 531, 540–41; **6** 382, 457; **8** 261–62
Shell Petroleum Corp., **IV** 540
Shell Pipe Line Corp., **IV** 540
Shell Sekiyu, **IV** 542–43
Shell Transport and Trading Company p.l.c., **I** 605; **II** 436, 459; **III** 522, 735; **IV** 363, 378–79, 381–82, 403, 412, 423, 425, 429, 440, 454, 466, 470, 472, 474, 484–86, 491, 505, 508, 530–32, 564. *See also* Royal Dutch Petroleum Company *and* Royal Dutch/Shell.
Shell Union Oil Corp., **IV** 531, 540
Shell Western E & P, **7** 323
Shell Winning, **IV** 413–14
Shell-BP Petroleum Development Co. of Nigeria Ltd., **IV** 472
Shell-Mex, **IV** 531
Sheller Manufacturing Corp., **I** 201
Sheller-Globe Corporation, **I** 201–02
Sheller-Ryobi Corp., **I** 202
Shelley, R. Gene, **II** 87
Shenley Laboratories, **I** 699

Shenstone, Naomi Ann. *See* Donnelley, Naomi Shenstone.
Shepard, Alan, **I** 79
Shepard, Horace, **I** 539–40
Shepard Warner Elevator Co., **III** 467
Shepard's Citations, Inc., **IV** 636–37
Shepherd, Mark, Jr., **II** 113–14
Shepherd, William C., **10** 47–48
Shepler Equipment Co., **9** 512
Sheppard, Allen, **I** 249
Sheppard, Dick, **IV** 711
Sheppard, John R., **10** 270
Shepperd, A.J., **I** 715
Sheraton Corp. of America, **I** 463–64, 487; **III** 98–99
Sheridan Bakery, **II** 633
Sheridan Catheter & Instrument Corp., **III** 443
Sherix Chemical, **I** 682
Sherman, Clifton W., **IV** 73
Sherman, Frank A., **IV** 73
Sherman, George M., **7** 117
Sherman, Harry W., **II** 507
Sherman, Nate H., **10** 414
Sherman, William Tecumseh, **6** 446
Sherrill, Colonel, **II** 644
Sherritt Gordon Mines, **7** 386–87
Sherwell, Chris, **IV** 250
Sherwin, E. D., **V** 712
Sherwin, Henry, **III** 744
Sherwin-Williams Company, **III** 744–46; **8** 222, 224
Sherwood, J. D., **6** 595
Sherwood Medical Group, **I** 624; **III** 443–44; **10** 70
Shetterly, Robert B., **III** 20–21
SHI Resort Development Co., **III** 635
ShianFu Optical Fiber, **III** 491
Shibaura Engineering Works, **I** 533
Shibusawa, Eiichi, **I** 265, 502–03, 506; **II** 273; **III** 383; **IV** 320
Shield, Lansing P., **7** 202
Shields & Co., **9** 118
Shields, Paul V., **9** 118–19
Shiely, Vincent R., **8** 71
Shiff, Richard, **9** 83–84
Shiflett, G. S. (Sam), **10** 448
Shijo, Takafusa, **III** 405
Shiki, Moriya, **II** 59
Shikoku Coca-Cola Bottling Co., **IV** 297
Shikoku Drinks Co., **IV** 297
Shikoku Electric Power Company, Inc., **V** 718–20
Shikoku Information & Telecommunications Network, **V** 719
Shikoku Machinery Co., **III** 634
Shimada family, **I** 506
Shimada, Mitsuhiro, **I** 63
Shimizu, Norihiku, **III** 552
Shimizu, Tsutomu, **V** 487
Shimkin, Leon, **IV** 671–72
Shimomura, Hikoemon, **V** 41
Shimomura, Shotaro, **V** 41
Shimotsuke Electric Railway Company, **6** 431
Shimura Kako, **IV** 63
Shin Nippon Machine Manufacturing, **III** 634
Shin-Nihon Glass Co., **I** 221
Shinano Bank, **II** 291
Shindo, Sadakazu, **II** 58–59
Shinji, Ichiro, **II** 119
Shinko Electric Co., Ltd., **IV** 129

Todd, Alan (Col.), **III** 350
Todd Company, **7** 138
Todd, Harry, **9** 460
Todd Shipbuilding Corp., **IV** 121
Todorovich Agency, **III** 204
Toei, **9** 29–30
Toeplitz, Giuseppe, **I** 368
Tofas, **I** 479–80
Toggenburger Bank, **II** 378
Togo, Yukiyasu, **I** 205
Toho Chemical Co., **I** 363
Toho Oil Co., **IV** 403
Tohoku Alps, **II** 5
Tohoku Pulp Co., **IV** 297
Tohuku Electric Power Company, Inc.,
    V 724, 732
Tojo Railway Company, **6** 430
Tojura, Sotaro, **III** 406
Tokai Aircraft Co., Ltd., **III** 415
Tokai Bank, Ltd., II 373–74
Tokai Bank of California, **II** 374
Tokai Bank of Canada, **II** 374
Tokai Paper Industries, **IV** 679
Tokai Trust Co. of New York, **II** 374
Tokan Kogyo, **I** 615
Tokio Marine and Fire Insurance Co.,
    Ltd., II 323; **III** 248, 289, 295, **383–86**
Tokio Marine Insurance Co., **III** 383–84
Tokiwa, Fumikatsu, **III** 38
Tokugawa family, **IV** 214
Tokugawa, Nariaki (Lord), **III** 532
Tokumasu, Sumao, **III** 368
Tokushima Ham Co., **II** 550
Tokushima Meat Processing Factory, **II**
    550
Tokushu Seiko, Ltd., **IV** 63
Tokuyama Soda, **I** 509
Tokuyama Teppan Kabushikigaisha, **IV**
    159
Tokyo Broadcasting, **7** 249; **9** 29
Tokyo Car Manufacturing Co., **I** 105
Tokyo Confectionery Co., **II** 538
Tokyo Corporation, **V** 199
Tokyo Dairy Industry, **II** 538
Tokyo Denki Kogaku Kogyo, **II** 109
Tokyo Dento Company, **6** 430
Tokyo Disneyland, **IV** 715; **6** 123, 176
Tokyo Electric Co., **I** 533
Tokyo Electric Express Railway Co., **IV**
    728
Tokyo Electric Light Co., **IV** 153
Tokyo Electric Power Company, IV 167,
    518; **V** 729–33
Tokyo Express Highway Co., Ltd., **IV**
    713–14
Tokyo Express Railway Company, **V** 510,
    526
Tokyo Fire Insurance Co. Ltd., **III** 405–06,
    408
Tokyo Food Products, **I** 507
Tokyo Fuhansen Co., **I** 502, 506
Tokyo Gas and Electric Industrial
    Company, **9** 293
Tokyo Gas Co., Ltd., IV 518; **V** 734–36
Tokyo Ishikawajima Shipbuilding and
    Engineering Company, **9** 293
Tokyo Ishikawajima Shipyard Co., Ltd.,
    III 532
Tokyo Maritime Insurance Co., **III** 288
Tokyo Motors, **9** 293
Tokyo Sanyo Electric, **II** 91–92
Tokyo Shibaura Electric Co., **I** 507, 533
Tokyo Steel Works Co., Ltd., **IV** 63
Tokyo Tanker Co., Ltd., **IV** 479

Tokyo Telecommunications Engineering
    Corp. *See* Tokyo Tsushin Kogyo K.K.
Tokyo Trust & Banking Co., **II** 328
Tokyo Tsushin Kogyo K.K., **II** 101, 103
Tokyo Yokohama Electric Railways Co.,
    Ltd., **V** 199
Tokyu Companies, **V** 199
Tokyu Construction Industry, **IV** 728
Tokyu Corporation, IV 728; **V** 199,
    526–28
Tokyu Department Store Co., Ltd., V
    199–202
Tokyu Electric Power Company, **V** 736
Tokyu Gravel Co., **IV** 728
Tokyu Kyuko Elwctric Railway Coompany
    Ltd., **V** 526
Tokyu Land Corporation, IV 728–29
Tokyu Railway Company, **V** 461
Tokyu Real Estate Co., Ltd., **IV** 728
Toledo Edison Company. *See* Centerior
    Energy Corporation.
Toledo Scale Corp., **9** 441
Toledo Seed & Oil Co., **I** 419
Tom Bowling Lamp Works, **III** 554
Tom Huston Peanut Co., **II** 502; **10** 323
Tom Piper Ltd., **I** 437
Tomakomai Paper Co., Ltd., **IV** 321
Tombs, Francis, **I** 82
Tombs, Lord, **7** 456
Tomei Fire and Marine Insurance Co., **III**
    384–85
Tomen Corporation, IV 224–25
Tomen Electronics Corp., **IV** 225
Tomen Information Systems Corp., **IV** 225
Tomen Transportgerate, **III** 638
Tomioka, Hiroshi, **III** 548–49
Tomlee Tool Company, **7** 535
Tomlinson, Alexander, **II** 403
Tomlinson, Allan J., **IV** 410
Tomlinson, Roy E., **II** 543
Tomoe Trading Co., **III** 595
Tompkins, Doug, **8** 169–70
Tompkins, Susie, **8** 169–71
Tomyo, Kubo, **III** 578; **7** 348
Tonami Transportation Company, **6** 346
Tonen Corporation, IV 554–56
Tonen Energy International Corp., **IV** 555
Tonen Sekiyukagaku Co. Ltd., **IV** 555
Tonen System Plaza Inc., **IV** 556
Tonen Tanker Co. Ltd., **IV** 555
Tong Yang Group, **III** 304
Toni Co., **III** 28; **9** 413
Tonti, Lorenzo, **III** 291
Toohey, **10** 170
Tooker, Sterling, **III** 389
Toot, Jr., Joseph F., **8** 531
Tootal Group, **V** 356–57
Top Man, **V** 21
Top Shop, **V** 21
Top Value Enterprises, **II** 645
Top Value Stamp Co., **II** 644; **6** 364
Topaloglu, Ihsan (Dr.), **IV** 562
Topol, Sidney, **6** 335–36
Toppan Containers, **IV** 679
Toppan Interamerica, **IV** 680
Toppan Moore Co., Ltd., **IV** 645, 679–80
Toppan Moore Learning, **IV** 680
Toppan Moore Systems, **IV** 680
Toppan Printing Co., Ltd., IV 598–99,
    679–81
Toppan Printronics U.S.A., **IV** 681
Toppan Shoji, **IV** 679
Toppan Technical Design Center, **IV** 680
Toppan West, **IV** 680

Topy Industries, Limited, **8** 506–07
Toray Industries, Inc., V 380, **383**
Torbensen Gear & Axle Co., **I** 154
Torchmark Corporation, III 194; **9**
    506–08; **10** 66
Torise Ham Co., **II** 550
Tormey, John L., **V** 502
Tornator Osakeyhtiö, **IV** 275–76
Törnudd, G., **IV** 275
Toro Assicurazioni, **III** 347
The Toro Company, III 600; **7** 534–36
Toro Manufacturing Company, **7** 534
Toronto and Scarborough Electric Railway,
    9 461
Toronto Electric Light Company, **9** 461
Toronto-Dominion Bank, II 319, **375–77,**
    456
Torpshammars, **IV** 338
Torres, Phillip, **9** 78
Torrey Canyon Oil, **IV** 569
Torrington Co., **III** 526, 589–90
Torstar Corp., **IV** 672; **7** 488–89
Tory, John A., **8** 525
Tosa Electric Railway Co., **II** 458
Tosaki, Shinobu, **IV** 125
Tosco Corporation, 7 537–39
Toshiba Corporation, I 221, 507–08,
    533–35; II 5, 56, 59, 62, 68, 73, 99,
    102, 118, 122, 326, 440; **III** 298, 461,
    533, 604; **6** 101, 231, 244, 287; **7** 529; **9**
    7, 181; **10** 518–19
Toshimitsu, Tsurumatasu, **V** 487
Toshin Kaihatsu Ltd., **V** 195
Toshin Paper Co., Ltd., **IV** 285
Tostem. *See* Toyo Sash Co., Ltd.
Tostem Cera Co., **III** 757
Tostem Thai Co., Ltd., **III** 758
Total. *See* Total Compagnie Française des
    Pétroles S.A.
Total CFD, **IV** 560
Total CFP. *See* Total Compagnie Française
    des Pétroles S.A.
Total Chimie, **IV** 560
Total Compagnie Française des Pétroles, **7**
    481, 483–84
Total Compagnie Française des Pétroles
    S.A., I 303; **III** 673; **IV** 425, 498, 515,
    525, 544, 547, **557–61; V** 628
Total Compagnie Minière, **IV** 560
Total Global Sourcing, Inc., **10** 498
Total-Austria, **IV** 486
TOTE, **9** 509–11
Totem Ocean Trailer Express, Inc. *See*
    TOTE.
Totem Resources Corporation, 9 509–11
Totino's Finer Foods, **II** 556
Toto Bank, **II** 326
Toto, Ltd., III 755–56
Totsu I., **I** 493
Touborg, Jens, **8** 514
Toucey, Isaac, **III** 236
Touche Remnant Holdings Ltd., **II** 356
Touche Ross, **10** 529. *See also* Deloitte &
    Touche.
Touchstone Films, **II** 172–74; **6** 174–76
Tour d'Argent, **II** 518
Tourang Limited, **7** 253
Touristik Union International GmbH.
    and Company K.G., II 163–65
Touron y Cia, **III** 419
Touropa, **II** 163–64
Toval Japon, **IV** 680
Tow, Andrew, **10** 210
Tow, Claire, **10** 210

Trek, **IV** 90, 92
Trek Beleggings, **IV** 93
Trelleborg A.B., **III** 625; **IV** 166
Tremletts Ltd., **IV** 294
Trent Tube, **I** 435
Trenton Foods, **II** 488
Tresco, **8** 514
Tresnowski, Bernard, **10** 160
Trethowal China Clay Co., **III** 690
Treves, Emilio, **IV** 585
Trevor-Roper, Hugh (Lord Dacre), **IV** 651–52; **7** 391
de Trey, August, **10** 271
de Trey, Caesar, **10** 271
Treybig, James G., **6** 278–79
Tri-City Federal Savings and Loan Association, **10** 92
Tri-City Utilities Company, **6** 514
Tri-County National Bank, **9** 474
Tri-Miller Packing Company, **7** 524
Tri-Star Pictures, **I** 234; **II** 134, 136–37; **6** 158; **10** 227
Tri-State Improvement Company, **6** 465–66
Tri-State Refining Co., **IV** 372
Triangle Auto Springs Co., **IV** 136
Triangle Industries, **I** 602, 607–08, 614; **II** 480–81
Triangle Portfolio Associates, **II** 317
Triangle Publications, **IV** 652; **7** 391
Triangle Refineries, **IV** 446
Triarc Companies, Inc. (formerly DWG Corporation), 8 535–37
Triathlon Leasing, **II** 457
Tribune Company, III 329; **IV 682–84;** **10** 56
Tribune Entertainment Co., **IV** 684
Trical Resources, **IV** 84
Tricity Cookers, **I** 531–32
Trico Industries, **I** 186
Tridel Enterprises Inc., 9 512–13
Trident Seafoods, **II** 494
Trifari, Krussman & Fishel, Inc., **9** 157
Trigano, Gilbert, **6** 206–08
Trigen Energy Corp., **6** 512
Trilan Developments Ltd., **9** 512
Trilon Bancorp, **II** 456–57
Trilon Capital Markets, **II** 457
Trilon Financial Corporation, II 456–57; **IV** 721; **9** 391
TriMas Corp., **III** 571
Trinidad Oil Co., **IV** 95, 552
Trinidad-Tesoro Petroleum Company Limited, **7** 516, 518
Trinity Industries, Incorporated, 7 540–41
Trinkaus und Burkhardt, **II** 319
TRINOVA Corporation, III 640–42, 731
Trintex, **6** 158
Triology Corp., **III** 110
Tripcovich, Diodato, **III** 208
Tripcovich, Mario, **III** 208
Triplex, **6** 279
Triplex (Northern) Ltd., **III** 725
Tripp, Frank, **IV** 612; **7** 190
Trippe, Juan, **I** 67, 89–90, 96, 99, 112, 115–16; **6** 81, 103; **9** 231, 417
Trippe Manufacturing Co., **10** 474
Triquet Paper Co., **IV** 282; **9** 261
Triton Bioscience, **III** 53
Triton Group Ltd., **I** 447
Triton Oil, **IV** 519
Tritton, John Henton, **II** 235

Triumph-Adler, **I** 485; **III** 145
Trivest Insurance Network, **II** 457
Trizec Corporation Ltd., 9 84–85; **10** 529–32
Trojan, **III** 674
Trona Corp., **IV** 95
Tropical Oil Co., **IV** 415–16
Tropical Shipping & Construction Ltd., **6** 531
Tropical Shipping, Inc., **6** 529
Tropicana Products, **II** 468, 525
Tropsch, Hans, **IV** 534
Trotsky, Leon, **IV** 671
Trotter, Billy, **II** 613
Trotter, Jimmy, **II** 613
Trotter, Ronald (Sir), **IV** 278–79
Troughton, Charles, **V** 212
Troy Metal Products. *See* KitchenAid.
Troyfel Ltd., **III** 699
TRT Communications, **6** 327
Trudeau, Pierre Elliott, **IV** 494
True Form, **V** 177
True Value Hardware Stores, **V** 37–38
Trueller, Harry, **I** 543
Trugg-Hansa Holding AB, **III** 264
Truitt Bros., **10** 382
Trujillo, Bernardo, **10** 205
Truman Dunham Co., **III** 744
Truman Hanburg, **I** 247
Truman, Harry S, **I** 71, 90, 507; **IV** 114–15, 237, 522, 573, 621, 689; **7** 550; **8** 313
Trumball Asphalt, **III** 721
Trümmer-Verwertungs-Gesellschaft, **IV** 140
Trump, Donald, **III** 92, 431; **6** 201, 211; **9** 125, 426–27
Trunkline Gas Company, **6** 544
Trunkline LNG Co., **IV** 425
Trust House Forte, **I** 215
Trust Houses Group, **III** 104–05
Trustcorp, Inc., **9** 475–76
Trustees, Executors and Agency Co. Ltd., **II** 189
Trusthouse Forte PLC, III 104–06
TRW Inc., I 539–41; II 33; **6** 25; **8** 416; **9** 18, 359; **10** 293
Tryart Pty. Limited, **7** 253
Trygger, Ernst, **III** 419
Tsai, Gerald, **I** 614; **II** 412
Tsai, Gerald, Jr., **III** 231
Tsai, Gerry, **8** 194
Tsai Management & Research Corp., **III** 230–31
Tse, K.K., **III** 195
TSO. *See* Teacher's Service Organization, Inc.
TSO Financial Corp., **II** 420; **8** 10
Tsuang Hine Co., **III** 582
Tsuchida, Terumichi, **III** 289
Tsuganuma, Toshihiko, **III** 715
Tsuji, Gentaro, **III** 639
Tsuji, Haruo, **II** 96
Tsukumo Shokai, **I** 502; **III** 712
Tsumeb Corp., **IV** 17–18
Tsurumi Steelmaking and Shipbuilding Co., **IV** 162
Tsurumi, Yoshi, **I** 455
Tsurusaki Pulp Co., Ltd., **IV** 285
Tsutsumi, Seiji, **V** 184, 187–88
Tsutsumi, Yasujiro, **V** 184, 510–11
Tsutsumi, Yoshiaki, **V** 187, 511
Tsutsunaka Plastic, **8** 359
Tsutsunaka Plastic Industry Co., **III** 714

Tsuzuki, Mikihiko, **V** 537
TTK. *See* Tokyo Tsushin Kogyo K.K.
TTX Company, 6 436–37
Tube Investments, **II** 422; **IV** 15
Tuborg, **9** 99
Tuborgs Fabrikker, **9** 99
Tuchbreiter, Roy, **III** 229–30
Tucher, Hans Christof Freiherr von, **II** 242
Tuck, Samuel, **8** 552
Tucker, Joe, **III** 651
Tuckey, James, **IV** 712
Tuckis, Robert, **7** 431
TUCO, Inc., **8** 78
Tucson Electric Power Company, V 713; **6 588–91**
Tucson Gas, Electric Light & Power Company. *See* Tuscon Electric Power Company.
Tucson Resources Inc., **6** 590
TUI. *See* Touristik Union International GmbH. and Company K.G.
Tuke, Anthony Favill, **II** 236; **IV** 192
Tuke, Anthony William, **II** 236
Tuke, Mary, **II** 568
Tuke, William, **II** 568
Tuke, William Favill, **II** 236
Tulagin, Vsevolod, **I** 338
Tullis, Richard, **II** 37–38
Tullis, Robert H., **III** 263
Tumpeer, David, **I** 404–05
Tumpeer, Julius, **I** 404–05
Tunhems Industri A.B., **I** 387
Tuohy, Walter J., **V** 439
Tupper, Earl, **III** 610
Tupperware, **I** 29; **II** 534; **III** 610–12
Tupperware Home Parties, **III** 610
Turbay, Julio Cesar, **IV** 417
Turbinbolaget, **III** 419
Turk, Seymour, **IV** 672
Turkish Engineering, Consultancy and Contracting Corp., **IV** 563
Turkish Petro Chemical Corp., **IV** 563
Turkish Petroleum Co. *See* Türkiye Petrolleri Anonim Ortakliği.
Turkish-Petroleum International Co., **IV** 563–64
Türkiye Garanti Bankasi, **I** 479
Türkiye Petrolleri Anonim Ortakliği, IV 464, 557–58, **562–64; 7** 352
N.V. Turkse Shell, **IV** 563
Turley, K. L., **6** 546
Turley, Stewart, **9** 186–87
Turmel, Antoine, **II** 651–52
Turnbull, **III** 468
Turnbull, George, **7** 232
Turnbull, George (Sir), **III** 516, 523
Turner Advertising Co., **II** 166
Turner Broadcasting System, Inc., II 134, 149, 161 **166–68; IV** 676; **6** **171–73 (upd.); 7** 64, 99, 306, 529
Turner, Cedric, **6** 110
Turner Communications Corp., **II** 166
The Turner Corporation, 8 538–40
Turner, Frank, **7** 456
Turner, Fred, **II** 646–47; **7** 318–19
Turner, Henry C., **8** 538–39
Turner, Henry Gyles, **II** 388
Turner, Jim, **7** 494
Turner, Mark, **IV** 191–92
Turner, Michael, **II** 298
Turner Pictures, **II** 167
Turner Program Services, **II** 166
Turner Publishing, **II** 167

INDEX TO INDUSTRIES

Index to Industries

McDonald's Corporation, II; 7 (upd.)
Meijer Incorporated, 7
Nash Finch Company, 8
National Convenience Stores Incorporated, 7
The Oshawa Group Limited, II
P&C Foods Inc., 8
Pizza Hut Inc., 7
Provigo Inc., II
Publix Supermarkets Inc., 7
Richfood Holdings, Inc., 7
Riser Foods, Inc., 9
Safeway Stores Incorporated, II
Service America Corp., 7
Shoney's, Inc., 7
Smith's Food & Drug Centers, Inc., 8
The Southland Corporation, II; 7 (upd.)
Spartan Stores Inc., 8
Steinberg Incorporated, II
The Stop & Shop Companies, Inc., II
Super Valu Stores, Inc., II
Supermarkets General Holdings Corporation, II
Sysco Corporation, II
Taco Bell, 7
Tesco PLC, II
TW Services, Inc., II
Village Super Market, Inc., 7
The Vons Companies, Incorporated, 7
Wegmans Food Markets, Inc., 9
Wendy's International, Inc., 8
Wetterau Incorporated, II
Winn-Dixie Stores, Inc., II

HEALTH & PERSONAL CARE PRODUCTS

Alberto-Culver Company, 8
Alco Health Services Corporation, III
Allergan, Inc., 10
Amway Corporation, III
Avon Products Inc., III
Bausch & Lomb Inc., 7
Bindley Western Industries, Inc., 9
Block Drug Company, Inc.
Bristol-Myers Squibb Company, III; 9 (upd.)
C.R. Bard Inc., 9
Carter-Wallace, Inc., 8
Chesebrough-Pond's USA, Inc., 8
The Clorox Company, III
Colgate-Palmolive Company, III
Cosmair, Inc., 8
Dentsply International Inc., 10
Elizabeth Arden Co., 8
Estée Lauder Inc., 9
The Gillette Company, III
Helene Curtis Industries, Inc., 8
Henkel KGaA, III
Johnson & Johnson, III; 8 (upd.)
Kao Corporation, III
Kimberly-Clark Corporation, III
Kyowa Hakko Kogyo Co., Ltd., III
L'Oreal, III; 8 (upd.)
Lever Brothers Company, 9
Lion Corporation, III
Mary Kay Corporation, 9
Medco Containment Services Inc., 9
Medtronic, Inc., 8
The Procter & Gamble Company, III; 8 (upd.)
Revlon Group Inc., III
S. C. Johnson & Son, Inc., III
Shionogi & Co., Ltd., III
Shiseido Company, Limited, III
SmithKline Beecham PLC, III
Tambrands Inc., 8
United States Surgical Corporation, 10

Wella Group, III

HEALTH CARE SERVICES

American Medical International, Inc., III
Applied Bioscience International, Inc., 10
Beverly Enterprises, Inc., III
Caremark International Inc., 10
Continental Medical Systems, Inc., 10
Extendicare Health Services, Inc., 6
FHP International Corporation, 6
Hospital Corporation of America, III
Humana Inc., III
Jenny Craig, Inc., 10
Manor Care, Inc., 6
Maxicare Health Plans, Inc., III
Mayo Foundation, 9
National Medical Enterprises, Inc., III
U.S. Healthcare, Inc., 6
United HealthCare Corporation, 9
Universal Health Services, Inc., 6

HOTELS

Caesars World, Inc. , 6
Circus Circus Enterprises, Inc., 6
Club Méditerranée SA, 6
Four Seasons Hotels Inc., 9
Helmsley Enterprises, Inc., 9
Hilton Hotels Corporation, III
Holiday Inns, Inc., III
Hyatt Corporation, III
ITT Sheraton Corporation, III
Marriott Corporation, III
Mirage Resorts, Inc., 6
Promus Companies, Inc., 9
Ritz-Carlton Hotel Company, 9
Trusthouse Forte PLC, III
Westin Hotel Co., 9

INFORMATION TECHNOLOGY

Adobe Systems Incorporated, 10
Advanced Micro Devices, Inc., 6
Aldus Corporation, 10
Amdahl Corporation, III
America Online, Inc., 10
Amstrad PLC, III
Analytic Sciences Corporation, 10
Apple Computer, Inc., III; 6 (upd.)
ASK Group, Inc., 9
AST Research Inc., 9
Automatic Data Processing, Inc., III; 9 (upd.)
Battelle Memorial Institute, Inc., 10
Bell and Howell Company, 9
Booz Allen & Hamilton Inc., 10
Borland International, Inc., 9
Canon Inc., III
CHIPS and Technologies, Inc., 9
Commodore International Ltd., 7
Compagnie des Machines Bull S. A., III
Compaq Computer Corporation, III; 6 (upd.)
CompuCom Systems, Inc., 10
CompuServe Incorporated, 10
Computer Associates International, Inc., 6
Computer Sciences Corporation, 6
Computervision Corporation, 10
Compuware Corporation, 10
Conner Peripherals, Inc., 6
Control Data Corporation, III
Control Data Systems, Inc., 10
Corporate Software Inc., 9
Cray Research, Inc., III
Data General Corporation, 8
Dell Computer Corp., 9
Digital Equipment Corporation, III; 6 (upd.)

Egghead Inc., 9
Electronic Arts Inc., 10
Electronic Data Systems Corporation, III
FlightSafety International, Inc., 9
Fujitsu Limited, III
Gateway 2000, Inc., 10
Hewlett-Packard Company, III; 6 (upd.)
ICL plc, 6
Information Resources, Inc., 10
Informix Corp., 10
Ing. C. Olivetti & C., S.p.a., III
Intelligent Electronics, Inc., 6
Intergraph Corporation, 6
International Business Machines Corporation, III; 6 (upd.)
Legent Corporation, 10
Lotus Development Corporation, 6
Maxtor Corporation, 10
Mead Data Central, Inc., 10
Microsoft Corporation, 6
National Semiconductor Corporation, 6
NCR Corporation, III; 6 (upd.)
Nextel Communications, Inc., 10
Nixdorf Computer AG, III
Novell, Inc., 6
Oracle Systems Corporation, 6
Pitney Bowes Inc., III
Quantum Corporation, 10
Ricoh Company, Ltd., III
SAS Institute Inc., 10
Seagate Technology, Inc., 8
STC PLC, III
Storage Technology Corporation, 6
Stratus Computer, Inc., 10
Sun Microsystems, Inc., 7
Sybase, Inc., 10
Symantec Corporation, 10
System Software Associates, Inc., 10
Tandem Computers, Inc., 6
Unisys Corporation, III; 6 (upd.)
Wang Laboratories, Inc., III; 6 (upd.)
WordPerfect Corporation, 10
Xerox Corporation, III; 6 (upd.)

INSURANCE

AEGON N.V., III
Aetna Life and Casualty Company, III
AFLAC Inc., 10 (upd.)
Alexander & Alexander Services Inc., 10
Alleghany Corporation, 10
Allianz AG Holding, III
The Allstate Corporation, 10
American Family Corporation, III
American Financial Corporation, III
American General Corporation, III; 10 (upd.)
American International Group, Inc., III
American National Insurance Company, 8
American Premier Underwriters, Inc., 10
American Re Corporation, 10
N.V. AMEV, III
Aon Corporation, III
Assicurazioni Generali SpA, III
Axa, III
Berkshire Hathaway Inc., III
Blue Cross and Blue Shield Association, 10
Capital Holding Corporation, III
The Chubb Corporation, III
CIGNA Corporation, III
CNA Financial Corporation, III
Commercial Union PLC, III
Connecticut Mutual Life Insurance Company, III
Conseco Inc., 10
The Continental Corporation, III
Empire Blue Cross and Blue Shield, III

LEGAL SERVICES

MANUFACTURING

Service Corporation International, 6

PETROLEUM

Abu Dhabi National Oil Company, IV
Amerada Hess Corporation, IV
Amoco Corporation, IV
Anadarko Petroleum Corporation, 10
Apache Corp., 10
Ashland Oil, Inc., IV
Atlantic Richfield Company, IV
British Petroleum Company PLC, IV; 7
    (upd.)
Burlington Resources Inc., 10
Burmah Castrol plc, IV
Chevron Corporation, IV
Chiles Offshore Corporation, 9
Chinese Petroleum Corporation, IV
CITGO Petroleum Corporation, IV
The Coastal Corporation, IV
Compañia Española de Petróleos S.A., IV
Conoco Inc., IV
Cosmo Oil Co., Ltd., IV
Crown Central Petroleum Corporation, 7
Den Norske Stats Oljeselskap AS, IV
Deutsche BP Aktiengesellschaft, 7
Diamond Shamrock, Inc., IV
Egyptian General Petroluem Corporation,
    IV
Empresa Colombiana de Petróleos, IV
Ente Nazionale Idrocarburi, IV
Entreprise Nationale Sonatrach, IV
Exxon Corporation, IV; 7 (upd.)
FINA, Inc., 7
General Sekiyu K.K., IV
Global Marine Inc., 9
Hunt Oil Company, 7
Idemitsu Kosan K.K., IV
Imperial Oil Limited, IV
Indian Oil Corporation Ltd., IV
Kanematsu Corporation, IV
Kerr-McGee Corporation, IV
Koch Industries, Inc., IV
Kuwait Petroleum Corporation, IV
Libyan National Oil Corporation, IV
The Louisiana Land and Exploration
    Company, 7
Lyondell Petrochemical Company, IV
MAPCO Inc., IV
Maxus Energy Corporation, 7
Mitchell Energy and Development
    Corporation, 7
Mitsubishi Oil Co., Ltd., IV
Mobil Corporation, IV; 7 (upd.)
Murphy Oil Corporation, 7
Nabors Industries, Inc., 9
National Iranian Oil Company, IV
Neste Oy, IV
Nigerian National Petroleum Corporation,
    IV
Nippon Mining Co. Ltd., IV
Nippon Oil Company, Limited, IV
Occidental Petroleum Corporation, IV
Oil and Natural Gas Commission, IV
ÖMV Aktiengesellschaft, IV
Oryx Energy Company, 7
Pennzoil Company, IV
PERTAMINA, IV
Petro-Canada Limited, IV
Petrofina, IV
Petróleo Brasileiro S.A., IV
Petróleos de Portugal S.A., IV
Petróleos de Venezuela S.A., IV
Petróleos del Ecuador, IV
Petróleos Mexicanos, IV
Petroleum Development Oman LLC, IV
Petronas, IV
Phillips Petroleum Company, IV

Qatar General Petroleum Corporation, IV
Quaker State Corporation, 7
Repsol S.A., IV
Royal Dutch Petroleum Company/ The
    ''Shell'' Transport and Trading Company
    p.l.c., IV
Sasol Limited, IV
Saudi Arabian Oil Company, IV
Shell Oil Company, IV
Showa Shell Sekiyu K.K., IV
Société Nationale Elf Aquitaine, IV; 7
    (upd.)
Sun Company, Inc., IV
Talisman Energy, 9
Tesoro Petroleum Corporation, 7
Texaco Inc., IV
Tonen Corporation, IV
Tosco Corporation, 7
Total Compagnie Française des Pétroles
    S.A., IV
Türkiye Petrolleri Anonim Ortakliği, IV
Ultramar PLC, IV
Union Texas Petroleum Holdings, Inc., 9
Unocal Corporation, IV
USX Corporation, IV; 7 (upd.)
Valero Energy Corporation, 7
The Williams Companies, Inc., IV
YPF Sociedad Anonima, IV

PUBLISHING & PRINTING

A.H. Belo Corporation, 10
Advance Publications Inc., IV
Affiliated Publications, Inc., 7
American Greetings Corporation, 7
Arnoldo Mondadori Editore S.p.A., IV
Axel Springer Verlag A.G., IV
Bauer Publishing Group, 7
Bertelsmann A.G., IV
Central Newspapers, Inc., 10
Commerce Clearing House, Inc., 7
Cox Enterprises, Inc., IV
Dai Nippon Printing Co., Ltd., IV
De La Rue PLC, 10
Deluxe Corporation, 7
Dow Jones & Company, Inc., IV
The Dun & Bradstreet Corporation, IV
The E.W. Scripps Company, IV; 7 (upd.)
Elsevier N.V., IV
Encyclopedia Britannica, Inc., 7
Enquirer/Star Group, Inc., 10
Gannett Co., Inc., IV; 7 (upd.)
Groupe de la Cite, IV
Hachette, IV
Hallmark Cards, Inc., IV
Harcourt Brace Jovanovich, Inc., IV
Havas, SA, 10
The Hearst Corporation, IV
Her Majesty's Stationery Office, 7
Houghton Mifflin Company, 10
International Data Group, 7
IPC Magazines Limited, 7
John Fairfax Holdings Limited, 7
Knight-Ridder, Inc., IV
Kodansha Ltd., IV
Maclean Hunter Limited, IV
Macmillan, Inc., 7
Marvel Entertainment Group, Inc., 10
Maxwell Communication Corporation plc,
    IV; 7 (upd.)
McGraw-Hill, Inc., IV
Mirror Group Newspapers plc, 7
Moore Corporation Limited, IV
National Geographic Society, 9
The New York Times Company, IV
News Corporation Limited, IV; 7 (upd.)
Nihon Keizai Shimbun, Inc., IV
Pearson plc, IV

R.L. Polk & Co., 10
R.R. Donnelley & Sons Company, IV; 9
    (upd.)
The Reader's Digest Association, Inc., IV
Reed International P.L.C., IV
Reuters Holdings PLC, IV
Scholastic Corporation, 10
Simon & Schuster Inc., IV
Southam Inc., 7
The Thomson Corporation, 8
The Times Mirror Company, IV
Toppan Printing Co., Ltd., IV
Tribune Company, IV
United Newspapers plc, IV
Valassis Communications, Inc., 8
The Washington Post Company, IV
West Publishing Co., 7

REAL ESTATE

Bramalea Ltd., 9
Cheung Kong (Holdings) Limited, IV
The Edward J. DeBartolo Corporation, 8
The Haminerson Property Investment and
    Development Corporation plc, IV
Hongkong Land Holdings Limited, IV
JMB Realty Corporation, IV
Kaufman and Broad Home Corporation, 8
The Koll Company, 8
Land Securities PLC, IV
Lend Lease Corporation Limited, IV
Lincoln Property Company, 8
Melvin Simon and Associates, Inc., 8
MEPC plc, IV
Mitsubishi Estate Company, Limited, IV
Mitsui Real Estate Development Co., Ltd.,
    IV
New World Development Company Ltd.,
    IV
Olympia & York Developments Ltd., IV; 9
    (upd.)
Perini Corporation, 8
Slough Estates PLC, IV
Sumitomo Realty & Development Co.,
    Ltd., IV
Tokyu Land Corporation, IV
Trammell Crow Company, 8
Tridel Enterprises Inc., 9
Trizec Corporation Ltd., 10

RETAIL & WHOLESALE

ABC Appliance, Inc., 10
Ames Department Stores, Inc., 9
Au Printemps S.A., V
AutoZone, Inc., 9
Babbage's, Inc., 10
Barnes & Noble, Inc., 10
Belk Stores Services, Inc., V
Bergen Brunswig Corporation, V
Best Buy Co., Inc., 9
The Bombay Company, Inc., 10
The Boots Company PLC, V
Burlington Coat Factory Warehouse
    Corporation, 10
The Burton Group plc, V
C&A Brenninkmeyer KG, V
Campeau Corporation, V
Carrefour SA, 10
Carter Hawley Hale Stores, Inc., V
Circuit City Stores, Inc., 9
CML Group, 10
Coles Myer Ltd., V
Comdisco, Inc., 9
CompUSA, Inc., 10
Costco Wholesale Corporation, V
Cotter & Company, V
County Seat Stores Inc., 9
Crate and Barrel, 9

WASTE SERVICES

NOTES ON CONTRIBUTORS _____

Notes on Contributors

BELLENIR, Karen. Free-lance writer and editor whose essays and journalism have appeared in the *Detroit Free Press, Studies in American Fiction,* and other publications.

BELSITO, Elaine. Free-lance writer and editor. Assistant managing editor, *Archives of Physical Medicine and Rehabilitation,* 1988-90.

BERNATEK, Bradley T. Free-lance writer.

BILAS, Wendy Johnson. Free-lance writer; MBA in marketing, Wake Forest University; director of marketing for the Charlotte Symphony Orchestra.

BOYER, Dean. Newspaper reporter and free-lance writer in the Seattle area.

BROWN, Susan Windisch. Free-lance writer and editor.

COHEN, Kerstan. Free-lance writer and French translator; editor for *Letter-Ex* poetry review.

COLLINS, C. L. Free-lance writer and researcher.

COVELL, Jeffrey L. Free-lance writer and corporate history contractor.

DERDAK, Thomas. Free-lance writer, poet, and instructor of philosophy at Loyola University.

DUBLANC, Robin. Free-lance writer and copyeditor in Yorkshire, England.

FELDMAN, Heidi. Free-lance writer and arts consultant.

GASBARRE, April Dougal. Archivist and free-lance writer specializing in business and social history in Cleveland, Ohio.

GOPNIK, Hilary. Free-lance writer.

GRANT, Tina. Free-lance writer and editor.

HEDDEN, Heather Behn. Business periodical abstractor and indexer, Information Access Company. Senior staff writer, *Middle East Times* Cairo bureau, 1991–92.

JACOBSON, Robert R. Free-lance writer and musician.

JAMES, Marinell. San Francisco–based writer and editor specializing in business and health-care topics.

KEELEY, Carol I. Free-lance writer and researcher; columnist for *Neon;* researcher for *Ford Times* and *Discovery.* Contributor to *Oxford Poetry,* 1987, and *Voices International,* 1989.

KERNS, Jennifer. Free-lance writer and editor in Paris.

MCMANUS, Donald Cameron. Free-lance writer.

MOTE, Dave. President of information retrieval company Performance Database.

PEDERSON, Jay P. Free-lance writer and editor.

PENDERGAST, Sara. Free-lance writer and copyeditor.

PENDERGAST, Tom. Free-lance writer and graduate student in American studies at Purdue University.

RICE, David B. Displaced New Yorker who writes and trains for marathons in Chapel Hill, North Carolina.

ROTA, Marina L. Free-lance writer and Italian translator in Washington, D.C.

ROULAND, Roger. Free-lance writer whose essays and journalism have appeared in the *International Fiction Review,* Chicago *Tribune,* and Chicago *Sun-Times.*

ROURKE, Elizabeth. Free-lance writer.

SCHNEIDER, Bob. CPA, MBA, and NYSE supervisory analyst. Schneider is also a free-lance writer and Japanese translator.

SIMLEY, John. Corporate issues analyst and former research editor for *International Directory of Company Histories.*

SUN, Douglas. Assistant professor of English at California State University at Los Angeles.

TAYLOR-BABCOCK, Susan. Free-lance writer.

TROESTER, Maura. Free-lance writer based in Chicago.

VLESSING, Etan. Free-lance writer and editor. Former editor of Insight; news editor, *Financial Weekly.*

WOLF, Gillian. Free-lance writer.

WOODWARD, Angela. Free-lance writer.